THE

Works

OF

THOMAS CHALMERS, D. D.

MINISTER OF THE TRON CHURCH, GLASGOW.

COMPLETE IN ONE VOLUME.

Philadelphia:

A. TOWAR, 19 ST. JAMES-ST.   HOGAN & THOMPSON, 139½ MARKET-ST.

SOLD ALSO BY D. M. HOGAN, *Pittsburg*; P. HAVEN, *New York*;
PIERCE & PARKER, *Boston*; D. WOODRUFF, *Tuscaloosa*, (*Ala.*)
STEREOTYPED BY L. JOHNSON.

1833.

CONTENTS.

EVIDENCES OF CHRISTIANITY.

CHAPTER I.—On the Principles of Historical Evidence, and their Application to the Question of the Truth of Christianity. Page 9
CHAP. II.—On the Authenticity of the different Books of the New Testament. 16
CHAP. III.—On the internal Marks of Truth and Honesty to be found in the New Testament. 21
CHAP. IV.—On the Testimony of the Original Witnesses to the Truth of the Gospel Narrative. 27
CHAP. V.—On the Testimony of Subsequent Witnesses. 30
CHAP. VI.—Remarks on the Argument from Prophecy. 42
CHAP. VII.—Remarks on the Scepticism of Geologists. 45
CHAP. VIII.—On the Internal Evidence, and the Objections of Deistical Infidels. 48
CHAP. IX.—On the Way of Proposing the Argument to Atheistical Infidels. 56
CHAP. X.—On the Supreme Authority of Revelation. 58

DISCOURSES ON THE CHRISTIAN REVELATION, VIEWED IN CONNEXION WITH THE MODERN ASTRONOMY.

DISCOURSE I.—A Sketch of the Modern Astronomy. 68
"When I consider thy heavens, the work of thy fingers, the moon and the stars, which thou hast ordained; What is man, that thou art mindful of him? and the son of man, that thou visitest him?"—*Psalm* viii. 3, 4.
DISC. II.—The Modesty of True Science. 75
"And if any man think that he knoweth any thing, he knoweth nothing yet as he ought to know."—1 *Cor.* viii. 2.
DISC. III.—On the Extent of the Divine Condescension. 83
"Who is like unto the Lord our God, who dwelleth on high; Who humbleth himself to behold the things that are in heaven, and in the earth!"—*Psalm* cxiii. 5, 6.
DISC. IV.—On the Knowledge of Man's Moral History in the Distant Places of Creation. 89
"Which things the angels desire to look into.—1 *Peter* i. 12.
DISC. V.—On the Sympathy that is felt for Man in the Distant Places of Creation. 96
"I say unto you, that likewise joy shall be in heaven over one sinner that repenteth, more than over ninety and nine just persons which need no repentance."—*Luke* xv. 7.
DISC. VI.—On the Contest for an Ascendency over Man, among the Higher Orders of Intelligence. 102
"And having spoiled principalities and powers, he made a show of them openly, triumphing over them in it."—*Col.* ii. 15.
DISC. VII.—On the slender Influence of mere Taste and Sensibility in Matters of Religion. 107
"And lo! thou art unto them as a very lovely song of one that hath a pleasant voice, and can play well on an instrument; for they hear thy words, but they do them not."—*Ezekiel* xxxiii. 32.
Appendix. 116

SERMONS ON THE DEPRAVITY OF HUMAN NATURE.

SERMON I.—The Necessity of the Spirit to give Effect to the Preaching of the Gospel. 122
"And my speech, and my preaching, was not with enticing words of man's wisdom, but in demonstration of the Spirit and of power; that your faith should not stand in the wisdom of men, but in the power of God."—1 *Cor.* ii. 4, 5.
SERM. II.—The mysterious Aspect of the Gospel to the Men of the World. 130
"Then said I, Ah, Lord God! they say of me, Doth he not speak parables?"—*Ezek.* xx. 49.
SERM. III.—The Preparation necessary for Understanding the Mysteries of the Gospel. 136
"He answered and said unto them, Because it is given unto you to know the mysteries of the kingdom of heaven, but to them it is not given. For whosoever hath, to him shall be given, and he shall have more abundance; but whosoever hath not, from him shall be taken away even that he hath."—*Matth.* xiii. 11, 12.
SERM. IV.—An Estimate of the Morality that is without Godliness. 142
"If I wash myself with snow water, and make my hands never so clean; yet shalt thou plunge me in the ditch, and mine own clothes shall abhor me. For he is not a man, as I am, that I should answer him, and we should come together in judgment. Neither is there any day's-man betwixt us, that might lay his hand upon us both."—*Job* ix. 30—33.
SERM. V.—The Judgment of Men, compared with the Judgment of God. 147
"With me it is a very small thing that I should be judged of you, or of man's judgment;—he that judgeth me is the Lord."—1 *Cor.* iv. 3, 4.
SERM. VI.—The Necessity of a Mediator between God and Man. 154
"Neither is there any day's-man betwixt us, that might lay his hand upon us both."—*Job* ix. 33.
SERM. VII.—The Folly of Men measuring themselves by themselves. 158
"For we dare not make ourselves of the number, or compare ourselves with some that commend themselves: but they, measuring themselves by themselves, and comparing themselves among themselves, are not wise."—2 *Cor.* x. 12.
SERM. VIII.—Christ the Wisdom of God. 165
"Christ the Wisdom of God."—1 *Cor.* i. 24.
SERM. IX.—The Principles of Love to God. 171
"Keep yourselves in the love of God."—*Jude* 21.
SERM. X.—Gratitude, not a Sordid Affection. 176
"We love him, because he first loved us."—1 *John* iv 19.

SERM. XI.—The Affection of Moral Esteem towards God. 185
"One thing have I desired of the Lord, that will I seek after; that I may dwell in the house of the Lord all the days of my life, to behold the beauty of the Lord, and to inquire in his temple."—*Psalm* xxvii. 4.

SERM. XII.—The Emptiness of Natural Virtue. 192
"But I know you, that ye have not the love of God in you."—*John* v. 42.

SERM. XIII.—The natural Enmity of the Mind against God. 201
"The carnal mind is enmity against God."—*Rom.* viii. 7.

SERM. XIV.—The Power of the Gospel to dissolve the Enmity of the human Heart against God. 206
"Having slain the enmity thereby."—*Ephes.* ii. 16.

SERM. XV.—The Evils of false Security. 211
"They have healed also the hurt of the daughter of my people slightly, saying, Peace, peace; when there is no peace."—*Jer.* vi. 14.

SERM. XVI.—The Union of Truth and Mercy in the Gospel. 217
"Mercy and truth are met together; righteousness and peace have kissed each other."—*Psalm* lxxxv. 10.

SERM. XVII.—The purifying Influence of the Christian Faith. 222
"Sanctified by faith."—*Acts* xxvi. 18.

DISCOURSES ON THE APPLICATION OF CHRISTIANITY TO THE COMMERCIAL AND ORDINARY AFFAIRS OF LIFE.

DISCOURSE I.—On the mercantile Virtues which may exist without the Influence of Christianity. 229
"Finally, brethren, whatsoever things are true, whatsoever things are honest, whatsoever things are just, whatsoever things are pure, whatsoever things are lovely, whatsoever things are of good report; if there be any virtue, and if there be any praise, think on these things."—*Phil.* iv. 8.

DISC. II.—The Influence of Christianity in aiding and augmenting the mercantile Virtues. 235
"For he that in these things serveth Christ is acceptable to God, and approved of men."—*Rom.* xiv. 18.

DISC. III.—The Power of Selfishness in promoting the Honesties of mercantile Intercourse. 241
"And if you do good to them which do good to you, what thank have ye? for sinners also do even the same."—*Luke* vi. 33.

DISC. IV.—The Guilt of Dishonesty not to be estimated by the Gain of it. 249
"He that is faithful in that which is least, is faithful also in much; and he that is unjust in the least, is unjust also in much."—*Luke* xvi. 10.

DISC. V.—On the great Christian Law of Reciprocity between Man and Man. 257
"Therefore all things whatsoever ye would that men should do to you, do ye even so to them; for this is the law and the prophets."—*Matth.* vii. 12.

DISC. VI.—On the Dissipation of large Cities. 264
"Let no man deceive you with vain words; for because of these things cometh the wrath of God upon the children of disobedience."—*Eph.* v. 6.

DISC. VII.—On the vitiating Influence of the higher upon the lower Orders of Society. 271
"Then said he unto the disciples, It is impossible but that offences will come: but woe unto him through whom they come! It were better for him that a millstone were hanged about his neck, and he cast into the sea, than that he should offend one of these little ones."—*Luke* xvii. 1, 2.

DISC. VIII.—On the Love of Money. 279
"If I have made gold my hope, or have said to the fine gold, Thou art my confidence; If I rejoiced because my wealth was great, and because mine hand had gotten much; If I beheld the sun when it shined, or the moon walking in brightness; and my heart hath been secretly enticed, or my mouth hath kissed my hand; this also were an iniquity to be punished by the judge; for I should have denied the God that is above."—*Job* xxxi. 24—28.

SERMONS PREACHED IN ST. JOHN'S CHURCH, GLASGOW.

SERMON I.—The Constancy of God in His Works an Argument for the Faithfulness of God in His Word. 371
"For ever, O Lord, thy word is settled in heaven. Thy faithfulness is unto all generations: thou hast established the earth, and it abideth. They continue this day according to thy ordinances: for all are thy servants."—*Psalm* cxix. 89, 90, 91.

SERM. II.—The expulsive Power of a new Affection. 381
"Love not the world, neither the things that are in the world. If any man love the world, the love of the Father is not in him."—1 *John* ii. 15.

SERM. III.—The sure Warrant of a Believer's Hope. 388
"For if, when we were enemies, we were reconciled to God by the death of his Son, much more, being reconciled, we shall be saved by his life."—*Romans* v. 10.

SERM. IV.—The Restlessness of human Ambition. 395
"How say ye to my soul, Flee as a bird to your mountain?—O that I had the wings of a dove, that I may fly away, and be at rest."—*Psalm* xi. 1, and lv. 6.

SERM. V.—The transitory Nature of visible Things. 399
"The things that are seen are temporal."—2 *Cor.* iv. 18.

SERM. VI.—On the Universality of spiritual Blindness. 404
"Stay yourselves, and wonder, cry ye out, and cry: they are drunken, but not with wine; they stagger, but not with strong drink. For the Lord hath poured out upon you the spirit of deep sleep, and hath closed your eyes; the prophets and your rulers, the seers hath he covered. And the vision of all is become unto you as the words of a book that is sealed, which men deliver to one that is learned, saying, Read this, I pray thee: and he saith, I cannot; for it is sealed. And the book is delivered to him that is not learned, saying, Read this, I pray thee: and he saith, I am not learned."—*Isaiah* xxix. 9—12.

SERM. VII.—On the new Heavens and the new Earth. 411
"Nevertheless we, according to his promise look for new heavens and a new earth wherein dwelleth righteousness."—2 *Peter* iii. 13.

SERM. VIII.—The Nature of the Kingdom of God. 417

"For the kingdom of God is not in word, but in power."—1 *Cor.* iv. 20.

SERM. IX.—On the Reasonableness of Faith. 423
"But before faith came, we were kept under the law, shut up unto the faith which should afterwards be revealed."—*Gal.* iii. 23.

SERM. X. On the Christian Sabbath. 429
"And he said unto them, The Sabbath was made for man, and not man for the Sabbath."—*Mark* ii. 27.

SERM. XI.—On the Doctrine of Predestination. 435
"And now I exhort you to be of good cheer: for there shall be no loss of any man's life among you, but of the ship. Paul said to the centurion and to the soldiers, Except these abide in the ship, ye cannot be saved."—*Acts* xxvii. 22, 31.

SERM. XII.—On the Nature of the Sin against the Holy Ghost. 442
"Wherefore I say unto you, All manner of sin and blasphemy shall be forgiven unto men; but the blasphemy against the Holy Ghost shall not be forgiven unto men. And whosoever speaketh a word against the Son of man, it shall be forgiven him: but whosoever speaketh against the Holy Ghost, it shall not be forgiven him, neither in this world, neither in the world to come."—*Matth.* xii. 31, 32.

SERM. XIII.—On the Advantages of Christian Knowledge to the Lower Orders of Society. 450
"Better is a poor and a wise child than an old and foolish King, who will no more be admonished."—*Eccl.* iv. 13.

SERM. XIV.—On the Duty and the Means of Christianizing our Home Population. 455
"And he said unto them, Go ye into all the world, and preach the Gospel to every creature."—*Mark* xvi. 15.

SERM. XV.—On the Distinction between Knowledge and Consideration. 460
"The ox knoweth his owner, and the ass his master's crib: but Israel doth not know, my people doth not consider."—*Isaiah* i. 3.

OCCASIONAL SERMONS, &c.

A SERMON before the Society for Relief of the destitute Sick. 286
"Blessed is he that considereth the poor; the Lord will deliver him in time of trouble."—*Psalm* xli. 1.

SERMON.—Thoughts on universal Peace. 295
"Nation shall not lift up sword against nation, neither shall they learn war any more."—*Isaiah* xi. 4.

The Duty of giving an immediate Diligence to the Business of the Christian Life.—An Address to the inhabitants of the Parish of Kilmany. 304

The Influence of Bible Societies on the temporal Necessities of the Poor. 320

SERMON.—A Sermon preached before the Society in Scotland for propagating Christian Knowledge. 331
"And Nathaniel said unto him, Can there any good thing come out of Nazareth? Philip saith unto him, come and see."—*John* i. 46.

SERMON.—A Sermon delivered on the Day of the Funeral of the Princess Charlotte of Wales. 339
"For when thy judgments are in the earth, the inhabitants of the world will learn righteousness."—*Isaiah* xxvi. 9.

SERMON.—The Doctrine of Christian Charity applied to the Case of Religious Differences. 350
"And why beholdest thou the mote that is in thy brother's eye, but considerest not the beam that is in thine own eye?—Or how wilt thou say to thy brother, Let me pull out the mote out of thine eye; and behold a beam is in thine own eye? Thou hypocrite! first cast out the beam out of thine own eye, and then shalt thou see clearly to cast out the mote out of thy brother's eye."—*Matth.* vii 3, 4, 5.

A SERMON on Cruelty to Animals. 361
"A righteous man regardeth the life of his beast."—*Prov.* xii. 10.

ADVERTISEMENT.

The contents of the first part of this volume form the substance of the article CHRISTIANITY, in the EDINBURGH ENCYCLOPÆDIA. Its appearance is due to the liberality of the Proprietors of that Work—nor did the Author conceive the purpose of presenting it to the world in another shape, till he was permitted and advised by them to republish it in a separate form. It is chiefly confined to the exposition of the historical argument for the truth of Christianity; and the aim of the Author is fulfilled if he has succeeded in proving the external testimony to be so sufficient, as to leave Infidelity without excuse, even though the remaining important branches of the Christian defence had been less strong and satisfactory than they are. "The works that I do in my Father's name, they bear witness of me." "And if I had not done the works among them which none other man did, they had not had sin."

The Author is far from asserting the study of the historical evidence to be the only channel to a faith in the truth of Christianity. How could he, in the face of the obvious fact, that there are thousands and thousands of Christians, who bear the most undeniable marks of the truth having come home to their understanding "in demonstration of the Spirit and of power?" They have an evidence within themselves, which the world knoweth not, even the promised manifestations of the Saviour. This evidence is a "sign to them that believe;" but the Bible speaks also of a "sign to them which believe not;" and should it be effectual in reclaiming any of these from their infidelity, a mighty object is gained by the exhibition of it. Should it not be effectual, it will be to them "a savour of death unto death;" and this is one of the very effects ascribed to the proclamation of Christian truth in the first ages. If, even in the face of that kind of evidence, which they have a relish and respect for, they still hold out against the reception of the Gospel, this must aggravate the weight of the threatening which lies upon them; "How shall they escape, if they neglect so great a salvation?"

It will be a great satisfaction to the writer of the following pages, if any shall rise from the perusal of them with a stronger determination than before to take his Christianity exclusively from his Bible. It is not enough to entitle a man to the name of a Christian, that he professes to believe the Bible to be a genuine communication from God. To be the disciple of any book, he must do something more than satisfy himself that its contents are true—he must read the book—he must obtain a knowledge of the contents. And how many are there in the world, who do not call the truth of the Bible message in question, while they suffer i to lie beside them unopened, unread, and unattended to!

EVIDENCES OF CHRISTIANITY.

CHAPTER I.

On the Principles of Historical Evidence, and their Application to the Question of the Truth of Christianity.

WERE a verbal communication to come to us from a person at a distance, there are two ways in which we might try to satisfy ourselves, that this was a true communication, and that there was no imposition in the affair. We might either sit in examination upon the substance of the message; and then from what we knew of the person from whom it professed to come, judge whether it was probable that such a message would be sent by him; or we may sit in examination upon the credibility of the messengers.

It is evident, that in carrying on the first examination, we might be subject to very great uncertainty. The professed author of the communication in question may live at such a distance from us, that we may never have it in our power to verify his message by any personal conversation with him. We may be so far ignorant of his character and designs, as to be unqualified to judge of the kind of communication that should proceed from him. To estimate aright the probable authenticity of the message from what we know of its author, would require an acquaintance with his plans, and views, and circumstances, of which we may not be in possession. We may bring the greatest degree of sagacity to this investigation; but then the highest sagacity is of no avail, when there is an unsufficiency of data. Our ingenuity may be unbounded; but then we may want the materials. The principle which we assume may be untrue in itself, and therefore may be fallacious in its application.

Thus, we may derive very little light from our first argument. But there is still a second in reserve,—the credibility of the messengers. We may be no judges of the kind of communication which is natural, or likely to proceed from a person with whom we are but imperfectly acquainted; but we may be very competent judges of the degree of faith that is to be reposed in the bearers of that communication. We may know and appreciate the natural signs of veracity. There is a tone, and a manner characteristic of honesty, which may be both intelligible and convincing. There may be a concurrence of several messengers. There may be their substantial agreement. There may be the total want of any thing like concert or collusion among them. There may be their determined and unanimous perseverance, in spite of all the incredulity and all the opposition which they meet with. The subject of the communication may be most unpalatable to us; and we may be so unreasonable, as to wreak our unpleasant feeling upon the bearers of it. In this way, they may not only have no earthly interest to deceive us, but have the strongest inducement possible to abstain from insisting upon that message which they were charged to deliver. Last of all, as the conclusive seal of their authenticity, they may all agree in giving us a watchword, which we previously knew could be given by none but their master; and which none but his messengers could ever obtain the possession of. In this way, unfruitful as all our efforts may have been upon the first subject of examination, we may derive from the second the most decisive evidence, that the message in question is a real message, and was actually transmitted to us by its professed author.

Now, this consideration applies in all its parts to a message from God. The argument for the truth of this message resolves itself into the same two topics of examination. We may sit in judgment upon the subject of the message; or we may sit in judgment upon the credibility of its bearers.

The first forms a great part of that argument for the truth of the Christian religion, which comes under the head of its *internal evidences*. The substance of the message is neither more nor less, than that particular scheme of the divine economy which is revealed to us in the New Testatament; and the point of inquiry is, whether this scheme be consistent with that knowledge of God and his attributes which we are previously in possession of?

It appears to many, that no effectual argument can be founded upon this consideration, because they do not count themselves enough acquainted with the designs or character of the being from whom the message professes to have come. Were the author of the message some distant and unknown individual of our own species, we would scarcely be entitled to found an argument upon any comparison of ours, betwixt the import of the message and the character of the individual, even though we had our general experience of human nature to help us in the speculation. Now, of the invisible God, we have no experience whatever. We are still further removed from all direct and personal observation of him or of his counsels. Whether we think of the eternity of his government, or the mighty range of its influence over the wide departments of nature and providence, he stands at such a distance from us, as to make the management of his empire a subject inaccessible to all our faculties.

It is evident, however, that this does not apply to the second topic of examination. The bearers of the message were beings like ourselves; and we can apply our safe and certain experience of man to their conduct and testimony. We may know too little of God, to found any argument upon the coincidence which we conceive to exist between the subject of the message and our previous conceptions of its author. But we may know enough of man to pronounce upon the credibility of the messengers. Had they the manner and physiognomy of honest men? Was their testimony resisted, and did they persevere in it? Had they any interest in fabricating the message; or did they suffer in consequence of this perseverance? Did they suffer to such a degree, as to constitute a satisfying pledge of their integrity? Was there more than one messenger, and did they agree as to the substance of that communication which they made to the world? Did they exhibit any special mark of their office as the messengers of God; such a mark as none but God could give, and none but his approved messengers could obtain the possession of? Was this mark the power of working miracles; and were these miracles so obviously addressed to the senses, as to leave no suspicion of deceit behind them? These are questions which we feel our competency to take up, and to decide upon. They lie within the legitimate boundaries of human observation; and upon the solution of these do we rest the question of the truth of the Christian religion.

This, then, is the state of the question with those to whom the message was originally addressed. They had personal access to the messengers; and the evidences of their veracity lay before them. They were the eye and ear-witnesses of those facts which occurred at the commencement of the Christian religion, and upon which its credibility rests. What met their observation must have been enough to satisfy them; but we live at the distance of nearly 2000 years, and is there enough to satisfy us? Those facts, which constitute the evidence for Christianity, might have been credible and convincing to them, if they really saw them; but is there any way by which they can be rendered credible and convincing to us, who only read of them? What is the expedient by which the knowledge and belief of the men of other times can be transmitted to posterity? Can we distinguish between a corrupt and a faithful transmission? Have we evidence before us, by which we can ascertain what was the belief of those to whom the message was first communicated? And can the belief which existed in their minds be derived to ours, by our sitting in judgment upon the reasons which produced it?

The surest way in which the belief and knowledge of the men of former ages can be transmitted to their descendants, is through the medium of written testimony; and it is fortunate for us, that the records of the Christian religion are not the only historical documents which have come down to us. A great variety of information has come down to us in this way; and a great part of that information is as firmly believed, and as confidently proceeded upon, as if the thing narrated had happened within the limits of our eye-sight. No man doubts the invasion of Britain by Julius Cæsar; and no man doubts, therefore, that a conviction of the truth of past events may be fairly produced in the mind by the instrumentality of a written memorial. This is the kind of evidence which is chiefly appealed to for the truth of ancient history; and it is counted satisfying evidence for all that part of it, which is received and depended upon.

In laying before the reader, then, the evidence for the truth of Christianity, we do not call his mind to any singular or unprecedented exercises of its faculties. We call him to pronounce upon the credibility of written documents, which profess to have been published at a certain age, and by certain authors. The inquiry involves in it no principle which is not appealed to every day in questions of ordinary criticism. To sit in judgment on the credibility of a written document, is a frequent and familiar exercise of the understanding with literary men. It is fortunate for the human mind, when so interesting a question as its religious faith can be placed under the tribunal of such evidence as it is competent to pronounce upon. It was fortunate for those to whom Christianity (a professed communication from heaven) was first addressed, that they could decide upon the genuineness of the communication by such familiar and every-day principles, as the marks of truth or falsehood in the human bearers of that communication. And it is fortunate for us that when, after that communication has assumed the form of a historical document, we can pronounce upon the degree of credit which should be attached to it, by the very same exercise of mind which we so confidently engage in, when sitting in examination upon the other historical documents that have come down to us from antiquity.

If two historical documents possess equal degrees of evidence, they should produce equal degrees of conviction. But if the object of the one be to establish some fact connected with our religious faith, while the object of the other is to establish some fact, about which we feel no other interest than that general curiosity which is gratified by the solution of any question in literature, this difference in the object produces a difference of effect in the feelings and tendencies of the mind. It is impossible for the mind, while it inquires into the evidence of a Christian document, to abstain from all reference to the important conclusion of the inquiry. And this will necessarily mingle its influence with the arguments which engage its attention. It may be of importance to attend to the peculiar feelings which are thus given to the investigation, and in how far they have affected the impression of the Christian argument.

We know it to be the opinion of some, that in this way an undue advantage has been given to that argument. Instead of a pure question of truth, it has been made a question of sentiment; and the wishes of the heart have mingled with the exercises of the understanding. There is a class of men who may feel disposed to overrate its evidences, because they are anxious to give every support and stability to a system, which they conceive to be most intimately connected with the dearest hopes and wishes of humanity; because their imagination is carried away by the sublimity of its doctrines, or their heart engaged by that amiable morality which is so much calculated to improve and adorn the face of society.

Now we are ready to admit, that as the object of the inquiry is not the character, but the truth of Christianity, the philosopher should be careful to protect his mind from the delusion of its charms. He should separate the exercises of the understanding from the tendencies of the fancy or of the heart. He should be prepared to follow the light of evidence, though it may lead him to conclusions the most painful and melancholy. He should train his mind to all the hardihood of abstract and unfeeling intelligence. He should give up every thing to the supremacy of argument, and be able to renounce, without a sigh, all the tenderest possessions of infancy, the moment that truth demands of him the sacrifice. Let it be remembered, however, that while one species of prejudice operates in favour of Christianity, another prejudice operates against it. There is a class of men who are repelled from the investigation of its evidences, because in their minds Christianity is allied with the weakness of superstition; and they feel that they are descending when they bring down their attention to a subject which engrosses so much respect and admiration from the vulgar.

It appears to us, that the peculiar feeling which the sacredness of the subject gives to the inquirer, is, upon the whole, unfavourable to the impression of the Christian argument. Had the subject not been sacred, and had the same testimony been given to the facts that are connected with it, we are satisfied that the history of Jesus in the New Testament would have been looked upon as the best supported by evidence of any history that has come down to us. It would assist us in appreciating the evidence for the truth of the gospel history, if we could conceive for a moment, that Jesus, instead of being the founder of a new religion, had been merely the founder of a new school of philosophy, and that the different histories which have come down to us had merely represented him as an extraordinary person, who had rendered himself illustrious among his countrymen by the wisdom of his sayings, and the beneficence of his actions. We venture to say, that had this been the case, a tenth part of the testimony which has actually been given, would have been enough to satisfy us. Had it been a question of mere erudition, where neither a predilection in favour of a religion, nor an antipathy against it, could have impressed a bias in any one direction, the testimony, both in weight and in quantity, would have been looked upon as quite unexampled in the whole compass of ancient literature.

To form a fair estimate of the strength and decisiveness of the Christian argument, we should, if possible, divest ourselves of all reference to religion, and view the truth of the gospel history, purely as a question of erudition. If at the outset of the investigation we have a prejudice against the Christian religion, the effect is obvious; and without any refinement of explanation, we see at once how such a prejudice must dispose us to annex suspicion and distrust to the testimony of the Christian writers. But even when the prejudice is on the side of Christianity, the effect is unfavourable on a mind that is at all scrupulous about the rectitude of its opinions. In these circumstances, the mind gets suspicious of itself. It feels a predilection, and becomes apprehensive lest this predilection may have disposed it to cherish a particular conclusion, independently of the evidences by which it is supported. Were it a mere speculative question, in which the interests of man, and the attachments of his heart had no share, he would feel greater confidence in the result of his investigation. But it is difficult to separate the moral impressions of piety, and it is no less difficult to calculate their precise influence on the exercises of the understanding. In the complex sentiment of attachment and conviction, which he annexes to the Christian religion, he finds it difficult to say, how much is due to the tendencies of the heart, and how much is due to the pure and unmingled influence of argument. His very anxiety for the truth, disposes him to overrate the circumstances which give a bias to his understanding, and through the whole process of the inquiry, he feels a suspicion and an embarrassment, which he would not have felt, had it been a question of ordinary erudition.

The same suspicion which he attaches to himself, he will be ready to attach to all whom he conceives to be in similar circumstances. Now, every author who writes in defence of Christianity, is supposed to be a Christian; and this, in spite of every argument to the contrary, has the actual effect of weakening the impression of his testimony. This suspicion effects, in a more remarkable degree, the testimony of the first writers on the side of Christianity. In opposition to it, you have no doubt, to allege the circumstances under which the testimony was given; the tone of sincerity which runs through the performance of the author; the concurrence of other testimonies; the persecutions which were sustained in adhering to them, and which can be accounted for on no other principle, than the power of conscience and conviction; and the utter impossibility of imposing a false testimony on the world, had they even been disposed to do it. Still there is a lurking suspicion, which often survives this strength of all argument, and which it is difficult to get rid of, even after it has been demonstrated to be completely unreasonable. He is a Christian. He is one of the party. Am I an infidel? I persist in distrusting the testimony. Am I a Christian? I rejoice in the strength of it; but this very joy becomes matter of suspicion to a scrupulous inquirer. He feels something more than the concurrence of his belief in the testimony of the writer. He catches the infection of his piety and his moral sentiments. In addition to the acquiescence of the understanding, there is a *con amore* feeling both in himself, and in his author, which he had rather been without, because he finds it difficult to compute the precise amount of its influence; and the consideration of this restrains him from that clear and decided conclusion, which he would infallibly have landed in, had it been purely a secular investigation.

There is something in the very sacredness of the subject, which intimidates the understanding, and restrains it from making the same firm and confident application of its faculties, which it would have felt itself perfectly warranted to do, had it been a question of ordinary history. Had the apostles been the disciples of some eminent philosopher, and the fathers of the church, their immediate successors in the office of presiding over the discipline and instruction of the numerous schools which they had established, this would have given a secular complexion to the argument, which we think would have been more satisfying to the mind, and have impressed upon it a closer and more familiar conviction of the history in question. We should have immediately brought it into comparison with the history of other philosophers, and could not have failed to recognize, that, in minuteness of information, in weight and quantity of evidence, in the concurrence of numerous and independent testimonies, and in the total absence of every circumstance that should dispose us to annex suspicion to the account which lay before us, it far surpassed any thing that had come down to us from antiquity. It so happens, however, that, instead of being the history of a philosopher, it is the history of a prophet. The veneration we annex to the sacredness of such a character, mingles with our belief in the truth of his history. From a question of simple truth, it becomes a question in which the heart is interested; and the subject from that moment assumes a certain holiness and mystery, which veil the strength of the argument, and takes off from that familiar and intimate conviction which we annex to the far less authenticated histories of profane authors.

It may be further observed, that every part of the Christian argument has been made to undergo a most severe scrutiny. The same degree of evidence which in questions of ordinary history commands the easy and universal acquiescence of every inquirer, has, in the subject before us, been taken most thoroughly to pieces, and pursued, both by friends and enemies, into all its ramifications. The effect of this is unquestionable. The genuineness and authenticity of the profane historian, are admitted upon much inferior evidence to what we can adduce for the different pieces which make up the New Testament. And why? Because the evidence has been hitherto thought sufficient, and the genuineness and authenticity have never been questioned. Not so with the Gospel history. Though its evidence is precisely the same in kind, and vastly superior in degree to the evidence for the history of the profane writer, its evidence has been questioned, and the very circumstance of its being questioned has annexed a suspicion to it. At all points of the question, there has been a struggle and a controversy. Every ignorant objection, and every rash and petulant observation, has been taken up and commented upon by the defenders of Christianity. There has at last been so much said about it, that a general feeling of insecurity is apt to accompany the whole investigation. There has been so much fighting, that Christianity now is looked upon as debatable ground. Other books, where the evidence is much inferior, but which have had the advantage of never being questioned, are received as of established authority. It is striking to observe the perfect confidence with which an infidel will quote a passage from an ancient historian. He perhaps does not overrate the credit due to him. But present him with a tabellated and comparative view of all the evidences that can be adduced for the gospel of Matthew, and any profane historian, which he chooses to fix upon, and let each distinct evidence be discussed upon no other principle than the ordinary and approved principles of criticism, we assure him that the sacred history would far outweigh the profane in the number and value of its testimonies.

In illustration of the above remarks, we can refer to the experience of those who have attended to this examination. We ask them to recollect the satisfaction which they felt, when they came to those parts of the examination, where the argument assumes a secular complexion. Let us take the testimony of Tacitus for an example. He asserts the execution of our Saviour in the reign of Tiberius, and under the procuratorship of Pilate; the temporary check, which this gave to his religion; its revival, and the progress it had made, not only over Judea, but to the city of Rome. Now all this is att sted in the Annals of Tacitus. But it is also attested in a far more direct and circumstantial manner in the annals of another author, in a book entitled the *History of the Acts of the Apostles by the Evangelist Luke*. Both of these performances carry on the very face of them the appearance of unsuspicious and well-authenticated documents. But there are several circumstances, in which the testimony of Luke possesses a decided advantage over the testimony of Tacitus. He was the companion of these very apostles. He was an eye witness to many of the events recorded by him. He had the advantage over the Roman historian in time and in place, and in personal knowledge of many of the circumstances in his history. The genuineness of his publication, too, and the time of its appearance, are far better established, and by precisely that kind of argument which is held decisive in every other question of erudition. Besides all this, we have the testimony of at least five of the Christian fathers, all of whom had the same, or a greater, advantage in point of time than Tacitus, and who had a much nearer and readier access to original sources of information. Now, how comes it that the testimony of Tacitus, a distant and later historian, should yield such delight and satisfaction to the inquirer, while all the antecedent testimony (which, by every principle of approved criticism, is much stronger than the other) should produce an impression that is comparatively languid and ineffectual? It is owing, in a great measure, to the principle to which we have already alluded. There is a sacredness annexed to the subject, so long as it is under the pen of fathers and evangelists, and this very sacredness takes away from the freedom and confidence of the argument. The moment that it is taken up by a profane author, the spell which held the understanding in some degree of restraint is dissipated. We now tread on the more familiar ground of ordinary history; and the evidence for the truth of the Gospel appears more assimilated to that evidence, which brings home to our conviction the particulars of the Greek and Roman story.

To say that Tacitus was upon this subject a disinterested historian, is not enough to explain the preference which you give to his testimony. There is no subject in which the triumph of the Christian argument is more conspicuous, than the moral qualifications which give credit to the testimony of its witnesses. We have every possible evidence, that there could be neither mistake nor falsehood in their testimony: a much greater quantity of evidence, indeed, than can actually be produced to establish the credibility of any other historian. Now all we ask is, that where an exception to the veracity of any historian is removed, you restore him to that degree of credit and influence which he ought to have possessed, had no such exception been made. In no case has an exception to the credibility of an author been more triumphantly removed, than in the case of the early Christian writers; and yet, as a proof that there really exists some such delusion as we have been labouring to demonstrate, though our eyes are perfectly open to the integrity of the Christian witnesses, there is still a disposition to give the preference to the secular historian. When Tacitus is placed by the side of the evangelist Luke, even after the decisive argument, which establishes the credit of the latter historian has convinced the understanding, there remains a tendency in the mind to annex a confidence to the account of the Roman writer, which is altogether disproportioned to the relative merits of his testimony.

Let us suppose, for the sake of farther illustration, that Tacitus had included some more particulars in his testimony, and that, in addition to the execution of our Saviour, he had asserted, in round and unqualified terms, that this said Christus had risen from the dead, and was seen alive by some hundreds of his acquaintances. Even this would not have silenced altogether the cavils of enemies, but it would have reclaimed many an infidel; been exulted in by many a sincere Christian; and made to occupy a foremost place in many a book upon the evidences of our religion. Are we to forget all the while, that we are in actual possession of much stronger testimony? that we have the concurrence of eight or ten contemporary authors, most of whom had actually seen Christ after the great event of his resurrection? that the veracity of these authors, and the genuineness of their respective publications, are established on grounds much stronger than have ever been alleged in behalf of Tacitus, or any ancient author? Whence this unaccountable preference of Tacitus? Upon every received principle of criticism, we are bound to annex greater confidence to the testimony of the apostles. It is vain to recur to the imputation of its being an interested testimony. This the apologists for Christianity undertake to disprove, and actually have disproved it, and that by a much greater quantity of evidence than would be held perfectly decisive in a question of common history. If after this there should remain any lurking sentiment of diffidence or suspicion, it is entirely resolvable into some such principle as I have already alluded to. It is to be treated as a mere feeling,—a delusion which should not be admitted to have any influence on the convictions of the understanding.

The principle which we have been attempting to expose, is found, in fact, to run through every part of the argument, and to accompany the inquirer through all the branches of the investigation. The authenticity of the different books of the New Testament forms a very important inquiry, wherein the object of the Christian Apologist is to prove, that they were really written by their professed authors. In proof of this, there is an uninterrupted series of testimony from the days of the apostles; and it was not to be expected, that a point so isoteric to the Christian society could have attracted the attention of profane authors, till the religion of Jesus, by its progress in the world, had rendered itself conspicuous. It is not then till about eighty years after the publication of the different pieces, that we meet with the testimony of Celsus, an avowed enemy to Christianity, and who asserts, upon the strength of its general notoriety, that the historical parts of the New Testament were written by the disciples of our Saviour. This is very decisive evidence. But how does it happen, that it should throw a clearer gleam of light and satisfaction over the mind of the inquirer, than he had yet experienced in the whole train of his investigation? Whence that disposition to underrate the antecedent testimony of the Christian writers? Talk not of theirs being an interested testimony; for, in point of fact, the same disposition operates, after reason is convinced that the suspicion is totally unfounded. What we contend for is, that this indifference to the testimony of the Christian writers implies a dereliction of principles, which apply with the utmost confidence to all similar inquiries.

The effects of this same principle are perfectly discernible in the writings of even our most judicious apologists. We offer no reflection against the assiduous Lardner, who, in his credibility of the Gospel history, presents us with a collection of testimonies which should make every Christian proud of his religion. In his evidence for the authenticity of the different pieces which make up the New Testament, he begins with the oldest of the fathers, some of whom were the intimate companions of the original writers. According to our view of the matter, he should have dated the commencement of his argument from a higher point, and begun with the testimonies of these original writers to one another. In the second Epistle of Peter, there is a distinct reference made to the writings of Paul; and in the Acts of the Apostles, there is a reference made to one of the four Gospels. Had Peter, instead of being an apostle, ranked only with the fathers of the church, and had his epistle not been admitted into the canon of scripture, this testimony of his would have had a place in the catalogue, and been counted peculiarly valuable, both for its precision and its antiquity. There is certainly nothing in the estimation he enjoyed, or in the circumstances of his epistle being bound up with the other books of the New Testament, which ought to impair the credit of his testimony. But in effect, his testimony does make a weaker impression on the mind, than a similar testimony from Barnabas, or Clement, or Polycarp. It certainly ought not to do it, and there is a delusion in the preference that is thus given to the latter writers. It is in fact, another example of the principle which we have been so often insisting upon. What profane authors are in reference to Christian authors at large, the fathers of the church are in reference to the original writers of the New Testament. In contradiction to every approved principle, we prefer the distant and later testimony, to the testimony of writers who carry as much evidence and legitimate authority along with them, and who only differ from others in being nearer the original source of information. We neglect and undervalue the evidence which the New Testament itself furnishes, and rest the whole of the argument upon the external and superinduced testimony of subsequent authors.

A great deal of all this is owing to the manner in which the defence of Christianity has been conducted by its friends and supporters. They have given too much into the suspicions of the opposite party. They have yielded their minds to the infection of their skepticism, and maintained, through the whole process, a caution and a delicacy which they often carry to a degree that is excessive; and by which, in fact, they have done injustice to their own arguments. Some of them begin with the testimony of Tacitus as a first principle, and pursue the investigation upwards, as if the evidence that we collect from the annals of the Roman historian were stronger than that of the Christian writers who flourished nearer the scene of the investigation, and whose credibility can be established on grounds which are altogether independent of his testimony. In this way, they come at last to the credibility of the New Testament writers, but by a lengthened and circuitous procedure. The reader feels as if the argument were diluted at every step in the process of derivation, and his faith in the Gospel history is much weaker than his faith in histories that are far less authenticated. Bring Tacitus and the New Testament to an immediate comparison, and subject them both to the touchstone of ordinary and received principles, and it will be found that the latter leaves the former out of sight in all the marks, and characters, and evidences of an authentic history. The truth of the Gospel stands on a much firmer and more independent footing, than many of its defenders would dare to give us any conception of. They want that boldness of argument which the merits of the question entitle them to assume. They ought to maintain a more decided front to their adversaries, and tell them, that, in the New Testament itself—in the concurrence of its numerous, and distant, and independent authors—in the uncontradicted authority which it has maintained from the earliest times of the church—in the total inability of the bitterest adversaries of our religion to impeach its credibility—in the genuine characters of honesty and fairness which it carries on the very face of it; that in these, and in every thing else, which can give validity to the written history of past times, there is a weight and a splendour of evidence, which the testimony of Tacitus cannot confirm, and which the absence of that testimony could not have diminished.

If it were necessary in a court of justice to ascertain the circumstances of a certain transaction which happened in a particular neighbourhood, the obvious expedient would be to examine the agents and eye-witnesses of that transaction. If six or eight concurred in giving the same testimony—if there was no appearance of collusion among them—if they had the manner and aspect of creditable men—above all, if this testimony were made public, and not a single individual, from the numerous spectators of the transaction alluded to, step forward to falsify it, then, we apprehend, the proof would be looked upon as complete. Other witnesses might be summoned from a distance to give in their testimony, not of what they saw, but of what they heard upon the subject; but their concurrence, though a happy enough circumstance, would never be looked upon as any material addition to the evidence already brought forward. Another court of justice might be held in a distant country, and years after the death of the original witnesses. It might have occasion to verify the same transaction, and for this purpose might call in the only evidence which it was capable of collecting—the testimony of men who lived after the transaction in question, and at a great distance from the place where it happened. There would be no hesitation, in ordinary cases, about the relative value of the two testimonies; and the record of the first court could be appealed to by posterity as by far the more valuable document, and far more decisive of the point in controversy. Now, what we complain of, is, that in the instance before us this principle is reversed. The report of hearsay witnesses is held in higher estimation than the report of the original agents and spectators. The most implicit credit is given to the testimony of the distant and later historians, and the testimony of the original witnesses is received with as much distrust as if they carried the marks of villany and imposture upon their foreheads. The genuineness of the first record can be established by a much greater weight and variety of evidence, than the genuineness of the second. Yet all the suspicion that we feel upon this subject annexes to the former; and the apostles and evangelists, with every evidence in their favour which it is in the power of testimony to furnish, are, in fact, degraded from the place which they ought to occupy among the accredited historians of past times.

The above observations may help to prepare the inquirer for forming a just and impartial estimate of the merits of the Christian testimony. His great object should be to guard against every bias of the understanding. The general idea is, that a predilection in favour of Christianity may lead him to overrate the argument. We believe that if every unfair tendency of the mind could be subjected to a rigorous computation, it would be found, that the combined operation of them all has the effect of impressing a bias in a contrary direction. All we wish for, is, that the arguments which are held decisive in other historical questions, should not be looked upon as nugatory when applied to the investigation of those facts which are connected with the truth and establishment of the Christian religion, that every prepossession should be swept away, and room left for the understanding, to expatiate without fear, and without incumbrance.

CHAPTER II.

On the Authenticity of the different Books of the New Testament.

THE argument for the truth of the different facts recorded in the gospel history, resolves itself into four parts. In the first, it shall be our object to prove, that the different pieces which make up the New Testament, were written by the authors whose names they bear, and the age which is commonly assigned to them. In the second, we shall exhibit the internal marks of truth and honesty, which may be gathered from the compositions themselves. In the third, we shall press upon the reader the known situation and history of the authors, as satisfying proofs of the veracity with which they delivered themselves. And, in the fourth, we shall lay before them the additional and subsequent testimonies, by which the narrative of the original writers is supported.

In every point of the investigation, we shall meet with examples of the principle which we have already alluded to. We have said, that if two distinct inquiries be set on foot, where the object of the one is to settle some point of sacred history, and the object of the other is to settle some point of profane history, the mind acquiesces in a much smaller quantity of evidence in the latter case than it does in the former. If this be right, (and to a certain degree it undoubtedly is,) then it is incumbent on the defender of Christianity to bring forward a greater quantity of evidence than would be deemed sufficient in a question of common literature, and to demand the acquiescence of his reader upon the strength of this superior evidence. If it be not right beyond a certain degree—and if there be a tendency in the mind to carry it beyond that degree, then this tendency is founded upon a delusion, and it is well that the reader should be apprised of its existence, that he may protect himself from its influence. The superior quantity of evidence which we can bring forward, will, in this case, all go to augment the positive effect upon his convictions; and he will rejoice to perceive that he is far safer in believing what has been handed down to him of the history of Jesus Christ, and the doctrine of his apostles, than in believing what he has never doubted—the history of Alexander, and the doctrine of Socrates. Could all the marks of veracity, and the list of subsequent testimonies, be exhibited to the eye of the reader in parallel columns, it would enable him, at one glance, to form a complete estimate. We shall have occasion to call his attention to this so often, that we may appear to many of our readers to have expatiated upon our introductory principle to a degree that is tiresome and unnecessary. We conceive, however, that it is the best and most perspicuous way of putting the argument.

I. The different pieces which make up the New Testament, were written by the authors whose names they bear, and at the time which is commonly assigned to them.

After the long slumber of the middle ages, the curiosity of the human mind was awakened, and felt its attention powerfully directed to those old writings, which have survived the waste of so many centuries. It were a curious speculation to ascertain the precise quantity of evidence which lay in the information of these old documents. And it may help us in our estimate, first to suppose, that in the researches of that period, there was only one composition found which professed to be a narrative of past times. A number of circumstances can be assigned, which might give a certain degree of probability to the information even of this solitary and unsupported document. There is, first, the general consideration, that the principle upon which a man feels himself induced to write a true history, is of more frequent and powerful operation, than the principle upon which a man feels himself induced to offer a false or a disguised representation of facts to the world. This affords a general probability on the side of the document in question being a true narrative; and there may be some particulars connected with the appearance of the performance itself, which might strengthen this probability. We may not be able to discover in the story itself any inducement which the man could have in publishing it, if it were mainly and substantially false.

We might see an expression of honesty, which it is in the power of written language, as well as of spoken language, to convey. We might see that there was nothing monstrous or improbable in the narrative itself. And, without enumerating every particular calculated to give it the impression of truth, we may, in the progress of our inquiries, have ascertained, that copies of this manuscript were to be found in many places, and in different parts of the world, proving, by the evidence of its diffusion, the general esteem in which it was held by the readers of past ages. This gives us the testimony of these readers to the value of the performance; and as we are supposing it is a history, and not a work of imagination, it could only be valued on the principle of the information which was laid before them being true. In this way a solitary document, transmitted to us from a remote antiquity, might gain credit in the world, though it had been lost sight of for many ages, and only brought to light by the revival of a literary spirit, which had lain dormant during a long period of history.

We can further suppose, that in the progress of these researches, another manuscript was discovered, having the same characters, and possessing the same separate and original marks of truth with the former. If they both touched upon the same period of history, and gave testimony to the same events, it is plain that a stronger evidence for the truth of these events would be afforded, than what it was in the power of either of the testimonies taken separately to supply. The separate circumstances which gave a distinct credibility to each of the testimonies are added together, and give also much higher credibility to those points of information upon which they deliver a common testimony. This is the case when the testimonies carry in them the appearance of being independent of one another. And even when the one is derived from the other, it still affords an accession to the evidence; because the author of the subsequent testimony gives us the distinct assertion, that he believed in the truth of the original testimony.

The evidence may be strengthened still farther, by the accession of a third manuscript, and a third testimony. All the separate circumstances which confer credibility upon any one document, even though it stands alone and unsupported by any other, combine themselves into a much stronger body of evidence, when we have obtained the concurrence of several. If, even in the case of a single narrative, a probability lies on the side of its being true, from the multitude and diffusion of copies, and from the air of truth and honesty discernible in the composition itself, the probability is heightened by the coincidence of several narratives, all of them possessing the same claims upon our belief. If it be improbable that one should be written for the purpose of imposing a falsehood upon the world, it is still more improbable that many should be written, all of them conspiring to the same perverse and unnatural object. No one can doubt, at least, that of the multitude of written testimonies which have come down to us, the true must greatly preponderate over the false; and that the deceitful principle, though it exists sometimes, could never operate to such an extent, as to carry any great or general imposition in the face of all the documents which are before us. The supposition must be extended much farther than we have yet carried it, before we reach the degree of evidence and of testimony, of which on many points of ancient history, we are at this moment in actual possession. Many documents have been collected, professing to be written at different times, and by men of different countries. In this way a great body of ancient literature has been formed, from which we can collect many points of evidence, too tedious to enumerate. Do we find the express concurrence of several authors to the same piece of history? Do we find, what is still more impressive, events formally announced in one narrative, not told over again, but implied and proceeded upon as true in another? Do we find the succession of history, through a series of ages, supported in a way that is natural and consistent? Do we find those compositions which profess a higher antiquity, appealed to by those which profess a lower? These, and a number of other points, which meet every scholar who betakes himself to the actual investigation, give a most warm and living character of reality to the history of past times. There is a perversity of mind which may resist all this. There is no end to the fancies of scepticism. We may plead in vain the number of written testimonies, their artless coincidence, and the perfect undesignedness of manner by which they often supply the circumstances that serve both to guide and satisfy the inquirer, and to throw light and support upon one another. The infidel will still have something behind which he can entrench himself; and his last supposition, monstrous and unnatural as it is, may be, that the whole of written history is a laborious fabrication, sustained for many ages, and concurred in by many individuals, with no other purpose than to enjoy the anticipated blunders of the men of future times, whom they had combined with so much dexterity to bewilder and lead astray.

If it were possible to summon up to the presence of the mind the whole mass of spoken testimony, it would be found, that what was false bore a very small proportion to what was true. For many obvious reasons, the proportion of the false to the true must be also small in written testimony. Yet instances of falsehood occur in both; and the actual ability to separate the false from the true in written history, proves that historical evidence has its principles and its probabilities to go upon. There may be the natural signs of dishonesty. There may be the wildness and improbability of the narrative. There may be a total want of agreement on the part of other documents. There may be the silence of every author for ages after the pretended date of the manuscript in question. There may be all these, in sufficient abundance, to convict the manuscript of forgery and falsehood. This has actually been done in several instances. The skill and discernment of the human mind upon the subject of historical evidence, have been improved by the exercise. The few cases in which sentence of condemnation has been given, are so many testimonies to the competency of the tribunal which has sat in judgment over them, and give a stability to their verdict, when any document is approved of. It is a peculiar subject, and the men who stand at a distance from it may multiply their suspicions and their skepticism at pleasure; but no intelligent man ever entered into the details, without feeling the most familiar and satisfying conviction of that credit and confidence which it is in the power of historical evidence to bestow.

Now, to apply this to the object of our present division, which is to ascertain the age of the document, and the person who is the author of it. These are points of information which may be collected from the performance itself. They may be found in the body of the composition, or they may be more formally announced in the title page—and every time that the book is referred to by its title, or the name of the author and age of the publication are announced in any other document that has come down to us, these points of information receive additional proof from the testimony of subsequent writers.

The New Testament is bound up in one volume, but we would be underrating its evidence if we regarded it only as one testimony, and that the truth of the facts recorded in it rested upon the testimony of one historian. It is not one publication, but a collection of several publications, which are ascribed to different authors and made their first apearance in different parts of the world. To fix the date of their appearance, it is necessary to institute a separate inquiry for each publication; and it is the unexcepted testimony of all subsequent writers, that two of the Gospels and several of the Epistles, were written by the immediate disciples of our Saviour, and published in their lifetime. Celsus, an enemy of the Christian faith, refers to the affairs of Jesus as written by his disciples. He never thinks of disputing the fact; and from the extracts which he makes for the purpose of criticism, there can be no doubt in the mind of the reader that it is one or other of the four Gospels to which he refers. The single testimony of Celsus may be considered as decisive of the fact, that the story of Jesus and of his life was actually written by his disciples. Celsus writes about a hundred years after the alleged time of the publication of this story; but that it was written by the companions of this Jesus, is a fact which he never thinks of disputing. He takes it upon the strength of its general notoriety, and the whole history of that period furnishes nothing that can attach any doubt or suspicion to this circumstance. Referring to a principle already taken notice of, had it been the history of a philosopher instead of a prophet, its authenticity would have been admitted without any formal testimony to that effect. It would have been admitted so to speak, upon the mere existence of the title-page, combined with this circumstance, that the whole course of history or tradition does not furnish us with a single fact, leading us to believe that the correctness of this title-page was ever questioned. It would have been admitted, not because it was asserted by subsequent writers, but because they made no assertion upon the subject, because they never thought of converting it into a matter of discussion, and because their occasional references to the book in question would be looked upon as carrying in them a tacit acknowledgement, that it was the very same book which it professed to be at the present day. The distinct assertion of Celsus that the pieces in question were written by the companions of Jesus, though even at the distance of a hundred years, is an argument in favour of their authenticity, which cannot be alleged for many of the most esteemed compositions of antiquity. It is the addition of a formal testimony to that kind of general evidence, which is founded upon the tacit or implied concurrence of subsequent writers, and which is held to be perfectly decisive in similar cases.

Had the pieces, which make up the New Testament, been the only documents of past times, the mere existence of a pretension to such an age, and to such an author, resting on their own information, would have been sustained as a certain degree of evidence, that the real age and the real author had been assigned to them. But we have the testimony of subsequent authors to the same effect; and it is to be remarked, that it is by far the most crowded, and the most closely sustained series of testimonies, of which we have any example in the whole field of ancient history. When we assigned the testimony of Celsus, it is not to be supposed that this is the very first which occurs after the days of the apostles. The blank of a hundred years betwixt the publication of the original story and the publication of Celsus, is filled up by antecedent testimonies, which, in all fairness, should be counted more decisive of the point in question. They are the testimonies of Christian writers, and, in as far as a nearer opportunity of obtaining correct information is concerned, they should be held more valuable than the testimony of Celsus. These references are of three kinds:—*First*, In some cases, their reference to the books of the New Testament is made in the form of an express quotation, and the author particularly named. *Secondly*, In other cases, the quotation is made without reference to the particular author, and ushered in by the general words, "*as it is written.*" And, *Thirdly*, There are innumerable allusions to the different parts of the New Testament, scattered over all the writings of the earlier fathers. In this last case there is no express citation; but we have the sentiment, the turn of expression, the very words of the New Testament, repeated so often, and by such a number of different writers, as to leave no doubt upon the mind that they were copied from one common original, which was at that period held in high reverence and estimation. In pursuing the train of references, we do not meet with a single chasm from the days of the original writers. Not to repeat what we have already made some allusion to, the testimonies of the original writers to one another, we proceed to assert, that some of the fathers whose writings have come down to us, were the companions of the apostles, and are even named in the books of the New Testament. St. Clement, bishop of Rome, is, with the concurrence of all ancient authors, the same whom Paul mentions in his epistle to the Philippians. In his epistle to the church of Corinth, which was written in the name of the whole church of Rome, he refers to the first epistle of Paul to the former church. "Take into your hands the epistle of the blessed Paul the apostle." He then makes a quotation, which is to be found in Paul's first epistle to the Corinthians. Could Clement have done this to the Corinthians themselves, had no such epistle been in existence? And is not this an undoubted testimony, not merely from the mouth of Clement, but on the part of the churches both of Rome and Corinth, to the authenticity of such an epistle? There are in this same epistle of Clement several quotations of the second kind, which confirm the existence of some other books of the New Testament; and a multitude of allusions or references of the third kind, to the writings of the evangelists, the Acts of the Apostles, and a great many of those epistles which have been admitted into the New Testament. We have similar testimonies from some more of the fathers, who lived and conversed with Jesus Christ. Besides many references of the second and third kind, we have also other instances of the same kind of testimony which Clement gave to St. Paul's first Epistle to the Corinthians, than which nothing can be conceived more indisputable. Ignatius, writing to the church of Ephesus, takes notice of St. Paul's epistle to that church; and Polycarp, an immediate disciple of the apostles, makes the same express reference to St. Paul's epistle to the Philippians in a letter addressed to the people. In carrying our attention down from the apostolical fathers, we follow an uninterrupted series of testimonies to the authenticity of the canonical scriptures. They get more numerous and circumstantial as we proceed—a thing to be expected from the progress of Christianity, and the greater multitude of writers, who came forward in its defence and illustration.

In pursuing the series of writers from the days of the apostles down to about 150 years after the publication of the pieces which make up the New Testament, we come to Tertullian, of whom Lardner says, " that there are perhaps more and longer quotations of the small volume of the New Testament in this one Christian author, than of all the works of Cicero, though of so uncommon excellence for thought and style, in the writers of all characters for several ages."

We feel ourselves exposed, in this part of our investigation, to the suspicion which adheres to every Christian testimony. We have already made some attempts to analyse that suspicion into its ingredients, and we conceive, that the circumstance of the Christians being an interested party, is only one, and not perhaps the principal of these ingredients. At all events, this may be the proper place for disposing of that one ingredient, and for offering a few general observations on the strength of the Christian testimony.

In estimating the value of any testimony, there are two distinct objects of consideration; the person who gives the testimony, and the people to whom the testimony is addressed. It is quite needless to enlarge on the resources which, in the present instance, we derive from both these considerations, and how much each of them contributes to the triumph and solidity of the Christian argument. In as far as the people who give the testimony are concerned, how could they be mistaken in their account of the New Testament, when some of them lived in the same age with the original writers, and were their intimate acquaintances, and when all of them had the benefit of an uncontrolled series of evidence, reaching down from the date of the earliest publications to their own times? Or, how can we suspect that they falsified, when there runs through their writings the same tone of plainness and sincerity, which is allowed to stamp the character of authenticity on other productions; and, above all, when, upon the strength even of heathen testimony, we conclude that many of them, by their sufferings and death, gave the highest evidence that man can give, of his speaking under the influence of a real and honest conviction? In as far as the people who received the testimony are concerned, to what other circumstances can we ascribe their concurrence, than to the truth of that testimony? In what way was it possible to deceive them upon a point of general notoriety? The books of the New Testament are referred to by the ancient fathers, as writings generally known and respected by the Christians of that period. If they were obscure writings, or had no existence at the time, how can we account for the credit and authority of those fathers who appealed to them, and had the effrontery to insult their fellow Christians by a falsehood so palpable, and so easily detected? Allow them to be capable of this treachery, we have still to explain, how the people came to be the dupes of so glaring an imposition; how they could be persuaded to give up every thing for a religion, whose teachers were so unprincipled as to deceive them, and so unwise as to commit themselves upon ground where it was impossible to elude discovery. Could Clement have dared to refer the peoof Corinth to an Epistle said to be received by themselves, and which had no existence? or could he have referred the Christians at large to writings which they never heard of. And it was not enough to maintain the semblance of truth with the people of their own party.

Where were the Jews all the time? and how was it possible to escape the correction of these keen and vigilant observers? We mistake the matter much, if we think that Christianity at that time was making its insidious way in silence and in secrecy, through a listless and unconcerned public. All history gives an opposite representation. The passions and curiosity of men were quite upon the alert. The popular enthusiasm had been excited on both sides of the question. It had drawn the attention of established authorities in different provinces of the empire, and the merits of the Christian cause had become a matter of frequent and formal discussion in courts of judicature. If, in these circumstances, the Christian writers had the hardihood to venture upon a falsehood, it would have been upon safer ground than what they actually adopted. They would never have hazarded to assert what was so open to contradiction, as the existence of books held in reverence among all the churches, and which nobody either in or out of these churches ever heard of. They would never have been so unwise as to commit in this way a cause, which had not a single circumstance to recommend it but its truth and its evidences.

The falsehood of the Christian testimony on this point, would carry along with it a concurrence of circumstances, each of which is the strangest and most unprecedented that ever was heard of. First, That men, who sustained in their writings all the characters of sincerity, and many of whom submitted to martyrdom, as the highest pledge of sincerity which can possibly be given, should have been capable of falsehood at all. Second, That this tendency to falsehood should have been exercised so unwisely as to appear in an assertion perfectly open to detection, and which could be so readily converted to the discredit of that religion, which it was the favourite ambition of their lives to promote and establish in the world Third, that this testimony could have gained the concurrence of the people to whom it was addressed, and that, with their eyes perfectly open to its falsehood, they should be ready to make the sacrifice of life, and of fortune in supporting it. Fourth, That this testimony should never have been contradicted by the Jews, and that they should have neglected so effectual an opportunity of disgracing a religion, the progress of which they contemplated with so much jealousy and alarm. Add to this, that it is not the testimony of one writer which we are making to pass through the ordeal of so many difficulties. It is the testimony of many writers, who lived at different times and in different countries, and who add the very singular circumstance of their entire agreement with one another, to the other circumstances equally unaccountable, which we have just now enumerated. The falsehood of their united testimony is not to be conceived. It is a supposition which we are warranted to condemn, upon the strength of any one of the above improbabilities taken separately. But the fair way of estimating their effect upon the argument, is to take them jointly, and in the language of the doctrine of chances, to take the product of all the improbabilities into one another. The argument which this product furnishes for the truth of the Christian testimony, has, in strength and conclusiveness, no parallel in the whole compass of ancient literature.

The testimony of Celsus is looked upon as peculiarly valuable, because it is disinterested. But if this consideration gives so much weight to the testimony of Celsus why should so much doubt and suspicio annex to the testimony of Christian writer several of whom, before his time, hav given a fuller and more express testimon to the authenticity of the Gospels? In th persecutions they sustained; in the obviou tone of sincerity and honesty which run through their writings; in their general agreement upon this subject; in the multitude of their followers, who never could have confided in men that ventured to commit themselves, by the assertion of what was obviously and notoriously false; in the check which the vigilance, both of Jews and Heathens, exercised over every Christian writer of that period,—in all these circumstances, they give every evidence of having delivered a fair and unpolluted testimony.

CHAPTER III.

On the internal Marks of Truth and Honesty to be found in the New Testament.

II. WE shall now look into the New Testament itself, and endeavour to lay before the reader the internal marks of truth and honesty, which are to be found in it.

Under this head, it may be right to insist upon the minute accuracy, which runs through all its allusions to the existing manners and circumstances of the times. To appreciate the force of this argument, it would be right to attend to the peculiar situation of Judea, at the time of our Saviour. It was then under the dominion of the Roman emperors, and comes frequently under the notice of the profane historians of that period. From this source we derive a great variety of information, as to the manner in which the emperors conducted the government of their different provinces; what degree of indulgence was allowed to the religious opinions of the people whom they held in subjection; in how far they were suffered to live under the administration of their own laws; the power which was vested in the presidents of provinces; and a number of other circumstances relative to the criminal and civil jurisprudence of that period. In this way, there is a great number of different points in which the historians of the New Testament can be brought into comparison with the secular historians of the age. The history of Christ and his apostles contains innumerable references to the state of public affairs. It is not the history of obscure and unnoticed individuals. They had attracted much of the public attention. They had been before the governors of the country. They had passed through the established forms of justice; and some of them underwent the trial and punishment of the times. It is easy to perceive, then, that the New Testament writers were led to allude to a number of these circumstances in the political history and constitution of the times, which came under the cognizance of ordinary historians. This was delicate ground for an inventor to tread upon; and particularly, if he lived at an age subsequent to the time of his history. He might in this case have fabricated a tale, by confining himself to the obscure and familiar incidents of private history; but it is only for a true and a contemporary historian to sustain a continued accuracy, through his minute and numerous allusions to the public policy and government of the times.

Within the period of the Gospel history, Judea experienced a good many vicissitudes in the state of its government. At one time it formed part of a kingdom under Herod the Great. At another, it formed part of a smaller government under Archelaus. It after this came under the direct administration of a Roman governor; which form was again interrupted for several years, by the elevation of Herod Agrippa to the sovereign power, as exercised by his grandfather; and it is at last left in the form of a province at the conclusion of the evangelical history. There were also frequent changes in the political state of the countries adjacent to Judea, and which are often alluded to in the New Testament. A caprice of the reigning emperor often gave rise to a new form of government, and a new distribution of territory. It will be readily conceived, how much these perpetual fluctuations in the state of public affairs, both in Judea and its neighbourhood, must add to the power and difficulty of that ordeal to which the Gospel history has been subjected.

On this part of the subject, there is no want of witnesses with whom to confront the writers of the New Testament. In addition to the Roman writers who have touched upon the affairs of Judea, we have the benefit of a Jewish historian, who has given us a professed history of his own country. From him, as was to be expected, we have a far greater quantity of copious and detailed narrative, relative to the internal affairs of Judea, to the manners of the people, and those particulars which are connected with their religious belief, and ecclesiastical constitution. With many, it will be supposed to add to the value of his testimony, that he was not a Christian; but that, on the other hand, we have every reason to believe him to have been a most zealous and determined enemy to the cause. It is really a most useful exercise, to pursue the harmony which subsists between the writers of the New Testament, and those Jewish and profane authors, with whom we bring them into comparison. Throughout the whole examination, our attention is confined to forms of justice; successions of governors in different provinces; manners, and political institutions. We are therefore apt to forget the sacredness of the subject; and we appeal to all, who have prosecuted this inquiry, if this circumstance is not favourable to their having a closer and more decided impression of the truth of the Gospel history. By instituting a comparison between the evangelists and contemporary authors, and restricting our attention to those points which come under the cognizance of ordinary history, we put the apostles and evangelists on the footing of ordinary historians; and it is for those, who have actually undergone the labour of this examination, to tell how much this circumstance adds to the impression of their authenticity. The mind gets emancipated from the peculiar delusion which attaches to the sacredness of the subject, and which has the undoubted effect of restraining the confidence of its inquiries. The argument assumes a secular complexion, and the writers of the New Testament are restored to that credit, with which the reader delivers himself up to any other historian, who has a much less weight and quantity of historical evidence in his favour.

We refer those readers who wish to prosecute this inquiry, to the first volume of Lardner's *Credibility of the Gospels.* We shall restrict ourselves to a few general observations on the nature and precise effect of the argument.

In the first place, the accuracy of the numerous allusions to the circumstances of that period, which the Gospel history embraces, forms a strong corroboration of that antiquity, which we have already assigned to its writers from external testimony. It amounts to a proof, that it is the production of authors who lived antecedent to the destruction of Jerusalem, and consequently about the time that is ascribed to them by all the external testimony which has already been insisted upon. It is that accuracy, which could only be maintained by a contemporary historian. It would be difficult, even for the author of some general speculation, not to betray his time by some occasional allusion to the ephemeral customs and institutions of the period in which he wrote. But the authors of the New Testament run a much greater risk. There are five different pieces of that collection which are purely historical, and where there is a continued reference to the characters, and politics, and passing events of the day. The destruction of Jerusalem swept away the whole fabric of Jewish polity; and it is not to be conceived, that the memory of a future generation could have retained that minute, that varied, that intimate acquaintance with the statistics of a nation no longer in existence, which is evinced in every page of the evangelical writers. We find, in point of fact, that both the Heathen and Christian writers of subsequent ages do often betray their ignorance of the particular customs which obtained in Judea during the time of our Saviour. And it must be esteemed a strong circumstance in favour of the antiquity of the New Testament, that on a subject, in which the chances of detection are so numerous, and where we can scarcely advance a single step in the narrative, without the possibility of betraying our time by some mistaken allusion, it stands distinguished from every later composition, in being able to bear the most minute and intimate comparison with the contemporary historians of that period.

The argument derives great additional strength, from viewing the New Testament, not as one single performance, but as a collection of several performances. It is the work of no less than eight different authors, who wrote without any appearance of concert, who published in different parts of the world, and whose writings possess every evidence, both internal and external, of being independent productions. Had only one author exhibited the same minute accuracy of allusion, it would have been esteemed a very strong evidence of his antiquity. But when we see so many authors exhibiting such a well-sustained and almost unexpected accuracy through the whole of their varied and distinct narratives, it seems difficult to avoid the conclusion, that they were either the eye-witnesses of their own history, or lived about the period of its accomplishment.

When different historians undertake the affairs of the same period, they either derive their information from one another, or proceed upon distinct and independent information of their own. Now, it is not difficult to distinguish the copyist from the original historian. There is something in the very style and manner of an original narrative, which announces its pretensions. It is not possible that any one event, or any series of events, should make such a similar impression upon two witnesses, as to dispose them to relate it in the same language, to describe it in the same order, to form the same estimate as to the circumstances which should be noticed as important, and those other circumstances which should be suppressed as immaterial. Each witness tells the thing in his own way, makes use of his own language, and brings forward circumstances which the other might omit altogether, as not essential to the purpose of his narrative. It is this agreement in the facts, with this variety in the manner of describing them, that never fails to impress upon the inquirer that additional conviction which arises from the concurrence of separate and independent testimonies. Now, this is precisely that kind of coincidence which subsists between the New Testament writers and Josephus, in their allusions to the peculiar customs and institutions of that age. Each party maintains the style of original and independent historians. The one often omits altogether, or makes only a slight and distant allusion to what occupies a prominent part in the composition of the other. There is not the slightest vestige of any thing like a studied coincidence between them. There is variety, but no opposition; and it says much for the authenticity of both histories, that the most scrupulous and attentive criticism can scarcely detect a single example of an apparent contradiction in the testimony of these different authors, which does not admit of a likely, or at least a plausible reconciliation.

When the difference between two historians is carried to the length of a contradiction, it enfeebles the credit of both their testimonies. When the agreement is carried to the length of a close and scrupulous resemblance in every particular, it destroys the credit of one of the parties as an independent historian. In the case before us, we neither perceive this difference, nor this agreement. Such are the variations, that, at first sight, the reader is alarmed with the appearance of very serious and embarrassing difficulties. And such is the actual coincidence, that the difficulties vanish when we apply to them the labours of a profound and intelligent criticism. Had it been the object of the Gospel writers to trick out a plausible imposition on the credulity of the world, they would have studied a closer resemblance to the existing authorities of that period; nor would they have laid themselves open to the superficial brilliancy of Voltaire, which dazzles every imagination, and reposed their vindication with the Lelands and Lardners of a distant posterity, whose sober erudition is so little attended to, and which so few know how to appreciate.

In the Gospels, we are told that Herod the Tetrarch of Galilee, married his brother Philip's wife. In Josephus we have the same story; only he gives a different name to Philip, and calls him Herod; and what adds to the difficulty, there was a Philip of that family, whom we know not to have been the first husband of Herodias. This is at first sight a little alarming. But, in the progress of our inquiries, we are given to understand from this same Josephus, that there were three Herods of the same family, and therefore no improbability in there being two Philips. We also know, from the histories of that period, that it was quite common for the same individual to have two names; and this is never more necessary, than when employed to distinguish brothers who have one name the same. The Herod who is called Philip, is just as likely a distinction, as Simon who is called Peter, or Saul who is called Paul. The name of the high priest, at the time of our Saviour's crucifixion, was Caiaphas, according to the evangelists. According to Josephus, the name of the high priest at that period was Joseph. This would have been precisely a difficulty of the same kind, had not Josephus happened to mention, that this Joseph was also called Caiaphas. Would it have been dealing fairly with the evangelists, we ask, to have made their credibility depend upon the accidental omission of another historian? Is it consistent with any acknowledged principle of sound criticism, to bring four writers so entirely under the tribunal of Josephus, each of whom stands as firmly supported by all the evidences which can give authority to a historian; and who have greatly the advantage of him in this, that they can add the argument of their concurrence to the argument of each separate and independent testimony? It so happens, however, in the present instance, that even Jewish writers, in their narrative of the same circumstance, give the name of Philip to the first husband of Herodias. We by no means conceive, that any foreign testimony was necessary for the vindication of the evangelists. Still, however, it must go far to dissipate every suspicion of artifice in the construction of their histories. It proves, that in the confidence with which they delivered themselves up to their own information, they neglected appearance, and felt themselves independent of it. This apparent difficulty, like many others of the same kind, lands us in a stronger confirmation of the honesty of the evangelists; and it is delightful to perceive, how truth receives a fuller accession to its splendour, from the attempts which are made to disgrace and to darken it.

On this branch of the argument, the impartial inquirer must be struck with the little indulgence which infidels, and even Christians, have given to the evangelical writers. In other cases, when we compare the narratives of contemporary historians, it is not expected, that all the circumstances alluded to by one will be taken notice of by the rest; and it often happens, that an event or a custom is admitted upon the faith of a single historian; and the silence of all other writers is not suffered to attach suspicion or discredit his testimony. It is an allowed principle, that a scrupulous resemblance between two histories is very far from necessary to their being held consistent with one another. And, what is more, it sometimes happens, that with contemporary historians there may be an apparent contradiction, and the credit of both parties remain as entire and unsuspicious as before. Posterity is in these cases disposed to make the most liberal allowances. Instead of calling it a contradiction, they often call it a difficulty. They are sensible, that in many instances, a seeming variety of statement has, upon a more extensive knowledge of ancient history, admitted of a perfect reconciliation. Instead, then, of referring the difficulty in question to the inaccuracy or bad faith of any of the parties, they with more justness and more modesty, refer it to their own ignorance, and to that obscurity which necessarily hangs over the history of every remote age. These principles are suffered to have great influence in every secular investigation; but so soon as, instead of a secular, it becomes a sacred investigation, every ordinary principle is abandoned, and the suspicion annexed to the teachers of religion is carried to the dereliction of all that candour and liberality, with which every other document of antiquity is judged of and appreciated. How does it happen, that the authority of Josephus should be acquiesced in as a first principle, while every step in the narrative of the evangelists must have foreign testimony to confirm and support it? How comes it that the silence of Josephus should be construed into an impeachment of the testimony of the evangelists, while it is never admitted for a single moment, that the silence of the evangelists can impart the slightest blemish to the testimony of Josephus? How comes it that the supposition of two Philips in one family should throw a damp of scepticism over the Gospel narrative, while the only circumstance which renders that supposition necessary is the single testimony of Josephus; in which very testimony, it is necessarily implied, that there are two Herods in the same family? How comes it, that the evangelists, with as much internal, and a vast deal more of external evidence in their favour, should be made to stand before Josephus, like so many prisoners at the bar of justice? In any other case, we are convinced that this would be looked upon as *rough handling*. But we are not sorry for it. It has given more triumph and confidence to the argument. And it is no small addition to our faith, that its first teachers have survived an examination, which, in point of rigour and severity, we believe to be quite unexampled in the annals of criticism.

It is always looked upon as a favourable presumption, when a story is told circumstantially. The art and the safety of an impostor, is to confine his narrative to generals, and not to commit himself by too minute a specification of time and place, and allusion to the manners or occurrences of the day. The more of circumstance that we introduce into a story, we multiply the chances of detection, if false; and therefore, where a great deal of circumstance is introduced, it proves, that the narrator feels the confidence of truth, and labours under no apprehension for the fate of his narrative. Even though we have it not in our power to verify the truth of a single circumstance, yet the mere property of a story being circumstantial is always felt to carry an evidence in its favour. It imparts a more familiar air of life and reality to the narrative. It is easy to believe, that the groundwork of a story may be a fabrication; but it requires a more refined species of imposture than we can well conceive, to construct a harmonious and well-sustained narrative, abounding in minute and circumstantial details which support one another, and where, with all our experience of real life, we can detect nothing misplaced, or inconsistent, or improbable.

To prosecute this argument in all its extent, it would be necessary to present the reader with a complete analysis or examination of the Gospel history. But the most superficial observer cannot fail to perceive, that it maintains, in a very high degree, the character of being a circumstantial narrative. When a miracle is recorded, we have generally the name of the town or neighbourhood where it happened; the names of the people concerned; the effect upon the hearts and convictions of the by-standers; the arguments and examinations it gave birth to; and all that minuteness of reference and description which impresses a strong character of reality upon the whole history. If we take along with us the time at which this history made its appearance, the argument becomes much stronger.— It does not merely carry a presumption in its favour, from being a circumstantial history:—it carries a proof in its favour, because these circumstances were completely within the reach and examination of those to whom it was addressed. Had the evangelists been false historians, they would not have committed themselves upon so many particulars. They would not have furnished the vigilant inquiries of that period with such an effectual instrument for bringing them into discredit with the people; nor foolishly supplied, in every page of their narrative, so many materials for a cross-examination, which would infallibly have disgraced them.

Now, we of this age can institute the same cross-examination. We can compare the evangelical writers with contemporary authors, and verify a number of circumstances in the history, and government, and peculiar economy of the Jewish people. We therefore have it in our power to institute a cross-examination upon the writers of the New Testament; and the freedom and frequency of their allusions to these circumstances supply us with ample materials for it. The fact, that they are borne out in their minute and incidental allusions by the testimony of other historians, gives a strong weight of what has been called circumstantial evidence in their favour. As a specimen of the argument, let us confine our observations to the history of our Saviour's trial, and execution, and burial. They brought him to Pontius Pilate. We know both from Tacitus and Josephus, that he was at that time governor of Judea. A sentence from him was necessary before they could proceed to the execution of Jesus; and we know that the power of life and death was usually vested in the Roman governor. Our Saviour was treated with derision; and this we know to have been a customary practice at that time, previous to the execution of criminals, and during the time of it. Pilate scourged Jesus before he gave him up to be crucified. We know from ancient authors, that this was a very usual practice among the Romans. The account of an excution generally run in this form:— he was stripped, whipped, and beheaded or executed. According to the evangelists, his accusation was written on the top of the cross; and we learn from Suetonius and others, that the crime of a person to be executed was affixed to the instrument of his punishment. According to the evangelist, this accusation was written in three different languages; and we know from Josephus, that it was quite common in Jerusalem to have all public advertisements written in this manner. According to the evangelists, Jesus had to bear his cross; and we know from other resources of information, that this was the constant practice of these times. According to the evangelists, the body of Jesus was given up to be buried at the request of friends. We know that, unless the criminal was infamous, this was the law, or the custom with all Roman governors.

These, and a few more particulars of the same kind, occur within the compass of a single page of the evangelical history. The circumstantial manner of the history affords a presumption in its favour, antecedent to all examination into the truth of the circumstances themselves. But it makes a strong addition to the evidence, when we find, that in all the subordinate parts of the main story, the evangelists maintain so great a consistency with the testimony of other authors, and with all we can collect from other sources of information, as to the manners and institutions of that period. It is difficult to conceive, in the first instance, how the inventor of a fabricated story would hazard such a number of circumstances, each of them supplying a point of comparison with other authors, and giving to the inquirer an additional chance of detecting the imposition. And it is still more difficult to believe, that truth should have been so artfully blended with falsehood in the composition of this narrative, particularly as we perceive nothing like a forced introduction of any one circumstance. There appears to be nothing out of place, nothing thrust in with the view of imparting an air of probability to the history. The circumstance upon which we bring the evangelists into comparison with profane authors, is often not intimated in a direct form, but in the form of a slight or distant allusion. There is not the most remote appearance of its being fetched or sought for. It is brought in accidentally, and flows in the most natural and undesigned manner out of the progress of the narrative.

The circumstance, that none of the Gospel writers are inconsistent with one another, falls better under a different branch of the argument. It is enough for our present purpose, that there is 1.0 single writer inconsistent with himself. It often happens, that falsehood carries its own refutation along with it; and that, through the artful disguises which are employed in the construction of a fabricated story, we can often detect a flaw or a contradiction, which condemns the authority of the whole narrative. Now, every single piece of the New Testament wants this mark or character of falsehood. The different parts are found to sustain, and harmonize, and flow out of each other. Each has at least the merit of being a consistent narrative. For any thing we see upon the face of it, it may be true, and a further hearing must be given before we can be justified in rejecting it as the tale of an impostor.

There is another mark of falsehood which each of the Gospel narratives appear to be exempted from. There is little or no parading about their own integrity. We can collect their pretensions to credit from the history itself, but we see no anxious display of these pretensions. We cannot fail to perceive the force of that argument which is derived from the publicity of the Christian miracles, and the very minute and scrupulous examination which they had to sustain from the rulers and official men of Judea. But this publicity, and these examinations, are simply recorded by the evangelists. There is no boastful reference to these circumstances, and no ostentatious display of the advantage which they give to the Christian argument. They bring their story forward in the shape of a direct and unencumbered narrative, and deliver themselves with that simplicity and unembarrassed confidence, which nothing but their consciousness of truth, and the perfect feeling of their own strength and consistency, can account for. They do not write, as if their object was to carry a point that was at all doubtful or suspicious. It is simply to transmit to the men of other times, and of other countries, a memorial of the events which led to the establishment of the Christian religion in the world. In the prosecution of their narrative, we challenge the most refined judge of the human character to point out a single symptom of diffidence in the truth of their own story, or of art to cloak this diffidence from the notice of the most severe and vigilant observers. The manner of the New Testament writers does not carry in it the slightest idea of its being an assumed manner. It is quite natural, quite unguarded, and free of all apprehension that their story is to meet with any discredit or contradiction from any of those numerous readers who had it fully in their power to verify or to expose it. We see no expedient made use of to obtain or to conciliate the acquiescence of their readers. They appear to feel as if they did not need it. They deliver what they have to say, in a round and unvarnished manner; nor is it in general accompanied with any of those strong asseverations by which an impostor so often attempts to practice upon the credulity of his victims.

In the simple narrative of the evangelists, they betray no feeling of wonder at the extraordinary nature of the events which they record, and no consciousness that what they are announcing is to excite any wonder among their readers. This appears to us to be a very strong circumstance. Had it been the newly broached tale of an impostor, he would, in all likelihood, have feigned astonishment himself, or at least have laid his account with the doubt and astonishment of those to whom it was addressed. When a person tells a wonderful story to a company who are totally unacquainted with it, he must be sensible, not merely of the surprise which is excited in the minds of the hearers, but of a corresponding sympathy in his own mind with the feelings of those who listen to him. He lays his account with the wonder, if not the incredulity, of his hearers; and this distinctly appears in the terms with which he delivers his story, and the manner in which he introduces it. It makes a wide difference, if, on the other hand, he tells the same story to a company, who have long been apprised of the chief circumstances, but who listen to him for the mere purpose of obtaining a more distinct and particular narrative. Now, in as far as we can collect from the manner of the evangelists, they stand in this last predicament. They do not write as if they were imposing a novelty upon their readers. In the language of Luke, they write for the sake of giving more distinct information; and that the readers *might know the certainty of those things, wherein they had been instructed.* In the prosecution of this task, they deliver themselves with the most familiar and unembarrassed simplicity. They do not appear to anticipate the surprise of their readers, or to be at all aware, that the marvellous nature of their story is to be any obstacle to its credit or reception in the neighbourhood. At the first performance of our Saviour's miracles, there was a strong and a widely spread sensation over the whole country. *His fame went abroad, and all people were amazed.* This is quite natural; and the circumstance of no surprise being either felt or anticipated by the evangelists, in the writing of their history, can best be accounted for by the truth of the history itself, that the experience of years had blunted the edge of novelty, and rendered miracles familiar, not only to them, but to all the people to whom they addressed themselves.

What appears to us a most striking internal evidence for the truth of the Gospel, is that perfect unity of mind and of purpose which is ascribed to our Saviour. Had he been an impostor, he could not have foreseen all the fluctuations of his history, and yet no expression of surprise is recorded to have escaped from him. No event appears to have caught him unprepared. We see no shifting of doctrine or sentiment, with a view to accommodate to new or unexpected circumstances. His parables and warnings to his disciples give sufficient intimation, that he laid his account with all those events which appeared to his unenlightened friends to be so untoward and so unpromising. In every explanation of his objects, we see the perfect consistency of a mind before whose prophetic eye all futurity lay open; and when the events of this futurity came round, he met them, not as chances that were unforeseen, but as certainties which he had provided for. This consistency of his views is supported through all the variations of his history, and it stands finally contrasted in the record of the evangelists, with the misconceptions, the surprises, the disappointments of his followers. The gradual progress of their minds from the splendid anticipations of earthly grandeur, to a full acquiescence in the doctrine of a crucified Saviour, throws a stronger light on the perfect unity of purpose and of conception which animated his, and which can only be accounted for by the inspiration that filled and enlightened it. It may have been possible enough to describe a well-sustained example of this contrast from an actual history before us. It is difficult, however, to conceive, how it could be sustained so well, and in a manner so apparently artless, by means of invention, and particularly when the inventors made their own errors and their own ignorance form part of the fabrication.

CHAPTER IV.

On the Testimony of the Original Witnesses to the Truth of the Gospel Narrative

III. THERE was nothing in the situation of the New Testament writers, which leads us to perceive that they had any possible inducement for publishing a falsehood.

We have not to allege the mere testimony of the Christian writers, for the danger to which the profession of Christianity exposed all its adherents at that period. We have the testimony of Tacitus to this effect. We have innumerable allusions, or express intimations, of the same circumstance in the Roman historians. The treatment and persecution of the Christians make a principle figure in the affairs of the empire; and there is no point better established in ancient history, than that the bare circumstance of being a Christian, brought many to the punishment of death, and exposed all to the danger of a suffering the most appalling and repulsive to the feelings of our nature.

It is not difficult to perceive, why the Roman government, in its treatment of Christians, departed from its usual principles of toleration. We know it to have been their uniform practice, to allow every indulgence to the religious belief of those different countries in which they established themselves. The truth is, that such an indulgence demanded of them no exertion of moderation or principle. It was quite consonant with the Spirit of Paganism. A different country worshipped different gods, but it was a general principle of Paganism, that each country had its gods, to which the inhabitants of that country owed their peculiar homage and veneration. In this way there was no interference between the different religions which prevailed in the world. It fell in with the policy of the Roman government to allow the fullest toleration to other religions, and it demanded no sacrifice of principle. It was even a dictate of principle with them to respect the gods of other countries; and the violation of a religion different from their own, seems to have been felt, not merely as a departure from policy or justice, but to be viewed with the same sentiment of horror which is annexed to blasphemy or sacrilege. So long as we were under Paganism, the truth of one religion did not involve in it the falsehood or rejection of another. In respecting the religion of another country, we did not abandon our own; nor did it follow, that the inhabitants of that other country annexed any contempt or discredit to the religion in which we had been educated. In this mutual reverence for the religion of each other, no principle was departed from, and no object of veneration abandoned. It did not involve in it the denial or relinquishment of our own gods, but only the addition of so many more gods to our catalogue.

In this respect, however, the Jews stood distinguished from every other people within the limits of the Roman empire. Their religious belief carried in it something more than attachment to their own system. It carried in it the contempt and detestation of every other. Yet, in spite of this circumstance, their religion was protected by the mild and equitable toleration of the Roman government. The truth is, that there was nothing in the habits or character of the Jews, which was calculated to give much disturbance to the establishments of other countries. Though they admitted converts from other nations, yet their spirit of proselytism was far from being of that active or adventurous kind, which could alarm the Roman government for the safety of any existing institutions. Their high and exclusive veneration for their own system gave an unsocial disdain to the Jewish character, which was not at all inviting to foreigners; but still, as it led to nothing mischievous in point of effect, it seems to have been overlooked by the Roman government as a piece of impotent vanity.

But the case was widely different with the Christian system. It did not confine itself to the denial or rejection of every other system. It was for imposing its own exclusive authority over the consciences of all, and for detaching as many as it could from their allegiance to the religion of their own country. It carried on its forehead all the offensive characters of a monopoly, and not merely excited resentment by the supposed arrogance of its pretensions, but from the rapidity and extent of its innovations, spread an alarm over the whole Roman empire for the security of all its establishments. Accordingly, at the commencement of its progress, so long as it was confined to Judea and the immediate neighbourhood, it seems to have been in perfect safety from the persecution of the Roman government. It was at first looked upon as a mere modification of Judaism, and that the first Christians differed from the rest of their countrymen only *in certain questions of their own superstition*. For a few years after the crucifixion of our Saviour, it seems to have excited no alarm on the part of the Roman emperors, who did not depart from their usual maxims of toleration, till they began to understand the magnitude of its pretensions, and the unlooked for success which attended them.

In the course of a very few years after its first promulgation, it drew upon it the hostility of the Roman government; and the fact is undoubted, that some of its first teachers, who announced themselves to be the companions of our Saviour, and the eye-witnesses of the remarkable events in his history, suffered martyrdom for their adherence to the religion which they taught.

The disposition of the Jews to the religion of Jesus was no less hostile; and it manifested itself at a still earlier stage of the business. The causes of this hostility are obvious to all who are in the slightest degree conversant with the history of those times. It is true, that the Jews did not at all times possess the power of life and death; nor was it competent for them to bring the Christians to execution by the exercise of legal authority. Still, however, their powers of mischief were considerable. Their wishes had always a certain controul over the measures of the Roman governor; and we know, that it was this controul which was the means of extorting from Pilate the unrighteous sentence by which the very first teacher of our religion was brought to a cruel and ignominious death. We also know, that under Herod Agrippa the power of life and death was vested in a Jewish sovereign, and that this power was actually exerted against the most distinguished Christians of that time. Add to this, that the Jews had, at all times, the power of inflicting the lesser punishments. They could whip, they could imprison. Besides all this, the Christians had to brave the frenzy of an enraged multitude; and some of them actually suffered martyrdom in the violence of the popular commotions.

Nothing is more evident than the utter disgrace which was annexed by the world at large to the profession of Christianity at that period. Tacitus calls it "*superstitio exitiabilis*," and accuses the Christians of enmity to mankind. By Epictetus and others, their heroism is termed obstinacy, and it was generally treated by the Roman governors as the infatuation of a miserable and despised people. There was none of that glory annexed to it which blazes around the martyrdom of a patriot or a philosopher. That constancy, which, in another case, would have made them illustrious, was held to be a contemptible folly, which only exposed them to the derision and insolence of the multitude. A name and a reputation in the world might sustain the dying moments of Socrates or Regulus; but what earthly principles can account for the intrepidity of those poor and miserable outcasts, who consigned themselves to a voluntary martyrdom in the cause of their religion?

Having premised these observations, we offer the following alternative to the mind of every candid inquirer. The first Christians either delivered a sincere testimony, or they imposed a story upon the world which they knew to be a fabrication.

The persecutions to which the first Christians voluntarily exposed themselves, compel us to adopt the first part of the alternative. It is not to be conceived, that a man would resign fortune, and character, and life, in the assertion of what he knew to be a falsehood. The first Christians must have believed their story to be true; and it only remains to prove, that if they believed it to be true, it must be true indeed.

A voluntary martyrdom must be looked upon as the highest possible evidence which it is in the power of man to give of his sincerity. The martyrdom of Socrates has never been questioned, as an undeniable proof of the sincere devotion of his mind to the principles of that philosophy for which he suffered. The death of Archbishop Cranmer will be allowed by all to be a decisive evidence of his sincere rejection of what he conceived to be the errors of Popery, and his thorough conviction in the truth of the opposite system. When the council of Geneva burnt Servetus, no one will question the sincerity of the latter's belief, however much he may question the truth of it. Now, in all these cases, the proof goes no farther than to establish the sincerity of the martyr's belief. It goes but a little way, indeed, in establishing the justness of it. This is a different question. A man may be mistaken, though he be sincere. His errors, if they are not seen to be such, will exercise all the influence and authority of truth over him. Martyrs have bled on the opposite sides of the question. It is impossible, then, to rest on this circumstance as an argument for the truth of either system; but the argument is always deemed incontrovertible, in as far as it goes to establish the sincerity of each of the parties, and that both died in the firm conviction of the doctrines which they professed.

Now, the martyrdom of the first Christians stands distinguished from all other examples by this circumstance, that it not merely proves the sincerity of the martyr's belief, but it also proves that what he believed was true. In other cases of martyrdom, the sufferer, when he lays down his life, gives his testimony to the truth of an opinion. In the case of the Christians, when they laid down their lives, they gave their testimony to the truth of a fact of which they affirmed themselves to be the eye and the ear witnesses. The sincerity of both testimonies is unquestionable; but it is only in the latter case that the truth of the testimony follows as a necessary consequence of its sincerity. An opinion comes under the cognizance of the understanding, ever liable, as we all know, to error and delusion. A fact comes under the cognizance of the senses, which have ever been esteemed as infallible, when they give their testimony to such plain, and obvious, and palpable appearances, as those which make up the evangelical story. We are still at liberty to question the philosophy of Socrates, or the orthodoxy of Cranmer and Servetus; but if we were told by a Christian teacher in the solemnity of his dying hour, and with the dreadful apparatus of martyrdom before him, that he saw Jesus after he had risen from the dead; that he conversed with him many days; that he put his hand into the print of his sides; and, in the ardour of his joyful conviction, exclaimed, "My Lord, and my God!" we should feel that there was no truth in the world, did this language and this testimony deceive us.

If Christianity be not true, then the first Christians must have been mistaken as to the subject of their testimony. This supposition is destroyed by the nature of the subject. It was not testimony to a doctrine which might deceive the understanding. It was something more than testimony to a dream, or a trance, or a midnight fancy, which might deceive the imagination. It was testimony to a multitude, and a succession of palpable facts, which could never have deceived the senses, and which preclude all possibility of mistake, even though it had been the testimony only of one individual. But when, in addition to this, we consider, that it is the testimony, not of one but of many individuals; that it is a story repeated in a variety of forms, but substantially the same; that it is the concurring testimony of different eye-witnesses, or the companions of eye-witnesses—we may, after this, take refuge in the idea of falsehood and collusion; but it is not to be admitted, that these eight different writers of the New Testament, could have all blundered the matter with such method, and such uniformity.

We know, that, in spite of the magnitude of their sufferings, there are infidels, who, driven from the first part of the alternative, have recurred to the second, and have affirmed, that the glory of establishing a new religion, induced the first Christians to assert, and to persist in asserting, what they knew to be a falsehood. But (though we should be anticipating the last branch of the argument) they forget, that we have the concurrence of two parties to the truth of Christianity, and that it is the conduct only of one of the parties, which can be accounted for by the supposition in question. The two parties are the teachers and the taught. The former may aspire to the glory of founding a new faith; but what glory did the latter propose to themselves from being the dupes of an imposition so ruinous to every earthly interest, and held in such low and disgraceful estimation by the world at large? Abandon the teachers of Christianity to every imputation which infidelity, on the rack for conjectures to give plausibility to its system, can desire, how shall we explain the concurrence of its disciples? There may be a glory in leading, but we see no glory in being led. If Christianity were false, and Paul had the effrontery to appeal to his five hundred living witnesses, whom he alleges to have seen Christ after his resurrection, the submissive acquiescence of his disciples remains a very inexplicable circumstance. The same Paul, in his epistles to the Corinthians, tells them that some of them had the gift of healing, and the power of working miracles; and that the signs of an apostle had been wrought among them in wonders and mighty deeds. A man aspiring to the glory of an accredited teacher, would never have committed himself on a subject, where his falsehood could have been so readily exposed. And in the veneration with which we know his epistles to have been preserved by the church of Corinth, we have not merely the testimony of their writer to the truth of the Christian miracles, but the testimony of a whole people, who had no interest in being deceived.

Had Christianity been false, the reputation of its first teachers lay at the mercy of every individual among the numerous proselytes which they had gained to their system. It may not be competent for an unlettered peasant to detect the absurdity of a doctrine; but he can at all times lift his testimony against a fact, said to have happened in his presence, and under the observation of his senses. Now it so happens, that in a number of the epistles, there are allusions to, or express intimations of, the miracles that had been wrought in the different churches to which these epistles are addressed. How comes it, if it be all a fabrication, that it was never exposed? We know, that some of the disciples were driven, by the terrors of persecuting violence, to resign their profession. How should it happen, that none of them ever attempted to vindicate their apostacy, by laying open the artifice and insincerity of their Christian teachers? We may be sure that such a testimony would have been highly acceptable to the existing authorities of that period. The Jews would have made the most of it; and the vigilant and discerning officers of the Roman government would not have failed to turn it to account. The mystery would have been exposed and laid open, and the curiosity of latter ages would have been satisfied as to the wonderful and unaccountable steps by which a religion could make such head in the world, though it rested its whole authority on facts, the falsehood of which was accessible to all who were at the trouble to inquire about them. But no! We hear of no such testimony from the apostates of that period. We read of some, who, agonized at the reflection of their treachery, returned to their first profession, and expiated, by martyrdom, the guilt which they felt they had incurred by their dereliction of the truth. This furnishes a strong example of the power of conviction, and when we join with it, that it is conviction in the integrity of those teachers who appealed to miracles which had been wrought among them, it appears to us a testimony in favour of our religion which is altogether irresistible.

CHAPTER V.

On the Testimony of Subsequent Witnesses.

IV. But this brings us to the last division of the argument, viz. that the leading facts in the history of the Gospel are corroborated by the testimony of others.

The evidence we have already brought forward for the antiquity of the New Testament, and the veneration in which it was held from the earliest ages of the church, is an implied testimony of all the Christians of that period to the truth of the Gospel history. By proving the authenticity of St. Paul's Epistles to the Corinthians, we not merely establish his testimony to the truth of the Christian miracles,—we establish the additional testimony of the whole church of Corinth, who would never have respected these Epistles, if Paul had ventured upon a falsehood so open to detection, as the assertion, that miracles were wrought among them, which not a single individual ever witnessed. By proving the authenticity of the New Testament at large, we secure, not merely that argument, which is founded on the testimony and concurrence of its different writers, but also the testimony of those immense multitudes, who, in distant countries, submitted to the New Testament as the rule of their faith. The testimony of the teachers, whether we take into consideration the subject of that testimony, or the circumstances under which it was delivered, is of itself a stronger argument for the truth of the Gospel history, than can be alleged for the truth of any other history, which has been transmitted down to us from ancient times. The concurrence of the taught carries along with it a host of additional testimonies, which gives an evidence to the evangelical story, that is altogether unexampled. On a point of ordinary history, the testimony of Tacitus is held decisive, because it is not contradicted. The history of the New Testament is not only not contradicted, but confirmed by the strongest possible expressions which men can give of their acquiescence in its truth; by thousands who were either agents or eye-witnesses of the transactions recorded, who could not be deceived, who had no interest, and no glory to gain by supporting a falsehood, and who, by their sufferings in the cause of what they professed to be their belief, gave the highest evidence that human nature can give of sincerity.

In this circumstance, it may be perceived how much the evidence for Christianity goes beyond all ordinary historical evidence. A profane historian relates a series of events which happen in a particular age; and we count it well, if it be his own age, and if the history which he gives us be the testimony of a contemporary author. Another historian succeeds him at the distance of years, and, by repeating the same story, gives the additional evidence of his testimony to its truth. A third historian perhaps goes over the same ground, and lends another confirmation to the history. And it is thus, by collecting all the lights which are thinly scattered over the tract of ages and of centuries, that we obtain all the evidence which can be got, and all the evidence that is generally wished for.

Now, there is room for a thousand presumptions, which, if admitted, would overturn the whole of this evidence. For any thing we know, the first historians may have had some interest in disguising the truth, or substituting in its place a falsehood, and a fabrication. True, it has not been contradicted, but they form a very small number of men, who feel strongly or particularly interested in a question of history. The literary and speculative men of that age may have perhaps been engaged in other pursuits, or their testimonies may have perished in the wreck of centuries. The second historian may have been so far removed in point of time from the events of his narratives, that he can furnish us, not with an independent, but with a derived testimony. He may have copied his account from the original historian, and the falsehood have come down to us in the shape of an authentic and well-attested history. Presumptions may be multiplied without end; yet in spite of them, there is a natural confidence in the veracity of man, which disposes us to as firm a belief in many of the facts of ancient history, as in the occurrences of the present day.

The history of the Gospel, however, stands distinguished from all other history by the uninterrupted nature of its testimony, which carries down its evidence, without a chasm, from its earliest promulgation to the present day. We do not speak of the superior weight and splendour of its evidences, at the first publication of that history, as being supported, not merely by the testimony of one, but by the concurrence of several independent witnesses. We do not speak of its subsequent writers, who follow one another in a far closer and more crowded train, than there is any other example of in the history or literature of the world. We speak of the strong though unwritten testimony of its numerous proselytes, who, in the very fact of their proselytism, give the strongest possible confirmation to the Gospel, and fill up every chasm in the recorded evidence of past times.

In the written testimonies for the truth of the Christian religion, Barnabas comes next in order to the first promulgators of the evangelical story. He was a contemporary of the apostles, and writes a very few years after the publication of the pieces which make up the New Testament. Clement follows, who was a fellow-labourer of Paul, and writes an epistle in the name of the church of Rome, to the church of Corinth. The written testimonies follow one another with a closeness and a rapidity of which there is no example; but what we insist on at present, is the unwritten and implied testimony of the people who composed these two churches. There can be no fact better established, than that these two churches were planted in the days of the apostles, and that the Epistles which were respectively addressed to them, were held in the utmost authority and veneration. There is no doubt, that the leading facts of the Gospel history were familiar to them; that it was in the power of many individuals amongst them to verify these facts, either by their own personal observation, or by an actual conversation with eye-witnesses; and that in particular, it was in the power of almost every individual in the church of Corinth, either to verify the miracles which St. Paul alludes to, in his epistle to that church, or to detect and expose the imposition, had there been no foundation for such an allusion. What do we see in all this, but the strongest possible testimony of a whole people to the truth of the Christian miracles? There is nothing like this in common history,—the formation of a society, which can only be explained by the history of the Gospel, and where the conduct of every individual furnishes a distinct pledge and evidence of its truth. And to have a full view of the argument, we must reflect, that it is not one, but many societies, scattered over the different countries of the world; that the principle upon which each society was formed, was the divine authority of Christ and his apostles, resting upon the recorded miracles of the New Testament; that these miracles were wrought with a publicity, and at a nearness of time, which rendered them accessible to the inquiries of all, for upwards of half a century; that nothing but the power of conviction could have induced the people of that age to embrace a religion so disgraced and so persecuted; that every temptation was held out for its disciples to abandon it; and that though some of them, overpowered by the terrors of punishment, were driven to apostacy, yet not one of them has left us a testimony which can impeach the miracles of Christianity, or the integrity of its first teachers.

It may be observed, that in pursuing the line of continuity from the days of the apostles, the written testimonies for the truth of the Christian miracles follow one another in closer succession, than we have any other example of in ancient history. But what gives such peculiar and unprecedented evidence to the history of the Gospel is, that in the concurrence of the multitudes who embraced it, and in the existence of those numerous churches and societies of men who espoused the profession of the Christian faith, we cannot but perceive, that every small interval of time between the written testimonies of authors is filled up by materials so strong and so firmly cemented, as to present us with an unbroken chain of evidence, carrying as much authority along with it, as if it had been a diurnal record, commencing from the days of the apostles, and authenticated through its whole progress by the testimony of thousands.

Every convert to the Christian faith in those days, gives one additional testimony to the truth of the Gospel history. Is he a Gentile? The sincerity of his testimony is approved by the persecutions, the sufferings, the danger, and often the certainty of martyrdom, which the profession of Christianity incurred. Is he a Jew? The sincerity of his testimony is approved by all these evidences, and in addition to them by this well known fact, that the faith and doctrine of Christianity were in the highest degree repugnant to the wishes and prejudices of that people. It ought never to be forgotten, that in as far as Jews are concerned

Christianity does not owe a single proselyte to its doctrines, but to the power and credit of its evidences, and that Judea was the chief theatre on which these evidences were exhibited. It cannot be too often repeated, that these evidences rest not upon arguments, but upon facts; and that the time, and the place, and the circumstances, rendered these facts accessible to the inquiries of all who chose to be at the trouble of this examination. And there can be no doubt that this trouble was taken, whether we reflect on the nature of the Christian faith, as being so offensive to the pride and bigotry of the Jewish people, or whether we reflect on the consequences of embracing it, which were derision, and hatred, and banishment, and death. We may be sure, that a step which involved in it such painful sacrifices, would not be entered into upon light and insufficient grounds. In the sacrifices they made, the Jewish converts gave every evidence of having delivered an honest testimony in favour of the Christian miracles; and when we reflect, that many of them must have been eye-witnesses, and all of them had it in their power to verify these miracles, by conversation and correspondence with by-standers, there can be no doubt, that it was not merely an honest, but a competent testimony. There is no fact better established, than that many thousands among the Jews believed in Jesus and his apostles; and we have therefore to allege their conversion, as a strong additional confirmation to the written testimony of the original historians.

One of the popular objections against the truth of the Christian miracles, is the general infidelity of the Jewish people. We are convinced, that at the moment of proposing this objection, an actual delusion exists in the mind of the infidel. In his conception, the Jews and the Christians stand opposed to each other. In the belief of the latter, he sees nothing but a party or an interested testimony, and in the unbelief of the former, he sees a whole people persevering in their ancient faith, and resisting the new faith on the ground of its insufficient evidences. He forgets all the while, that the testimony of a great many of these Christians, is in fact the testimony of Jews. He only attends to them in their present capacity. He contemplates them in the light of Christians, and annexes to them all that suspicion and incredulity which are generally annexed to the testimony of an interested party. He is aware of what they are at present, Christians and defenders of Christianity; but he has lost sight of their original situation, and is totally unmindful of this circumstance, that in their transition from Judaism to Christianity, they have given him the very evidence he is in quest of. Had another thousand of these Jews renounced the faith of their ancestors, and embraced the religion of Jesus, they would have been equivalent to a thousand additional testimonies in favour of Christianity, and testimonies too of the strongest and most unsuspicious kind, that can well be imagined. But this evidence would make no impression on the mind of an infidel, and the strength of it is disguised, even from the eyes of the Christian. These thousand, in the moment of their conversion, lose the appellation of Jews, and merge into the name and distinction of Christians. The Jews, though diminished in number, retain the national appellation; and the obstinacy with which they persevere in the belief of their ancestors, is still looked upon as the adverse testimony of an entire people. So long as one of that people continues a Jew, his testimony is looked upon as a serious impediment in the way of Christian evidences. But the moment he becomes a Christian, his motives are contemplated with distrust. He is one of the obnoxious and suspected party. The mind carries a reference only to what he is, and not to what he has been. It overlooks the change of sentiment, and forgets, that, in the renunciation of old habits, and old prejudices, in defiance to sufferings and disgrace, in attachment to a religion so repugnant to the pride and bigotry of their nation, and above all, in submission to a system of doctrines which rested its authority on the miracles of their own time, and their own remembrance, every Jewish convert gives the most decisive testimony which man can give for the truth and divinity of our religion.

But why, then, says the infidel, did they not all believe? Had the miracles of the Gospel been true, we do not see how human nature could have held out against an evidence so striking and so extraordinary; nor can we at all enter into the obstinacy of that belief which is ascribed to the majority of the Jewish people, and which led them to shut their eyes against a testimony that no man of common sense could have resisted.

Many Christian writers have attempted to resolve this difficulty, and to prove that the infidelity of the Jews, in spite of the miracles which they saw, is perfectly consistent with the known principles of human nature. For this purpose, they have enlarged, with much force and plausibility, on the strength and inveteracy of the Jewish prejudices—on the bewildering influence of religious bigotry upon the understanding of men—on the woeful disappointment which Christianity offered to the pride and interest of the nation—on the selfishness of the priesthood—and on the facility with which they might turn a blind and fanatical multitude, who had been trained, by their earliest habits, to follow and to revere them

In the Gospel history itself, we have a very consistent account at least of the Jewish opposition to the claims of our Saviour. We see the deeply wounded pride of a nation, that felt itself disgraced by the loss of its independence. We see the arrogance of its peculiar and exclusive claims to the favour of the Almighty. We see the anticipation of a great prince, who was to deliver them from the power and subjection of their enemies. We see their insolent contempt for the people of other countries, and the foulest scorn that they should be admitted to an equality with themselves in the honours and benefits of a revelation from heaven. We may easily conceive, how much the doctrine of Christ and his apostles was calculated to gall, and irritate, and disappoint them; how it must have mortified their national vanity; how it must have alarmed the jealousy of an artful and interested priesthood; and how it must have scandalized the great body of the people, by the liberality with which it addressed itself to all men, and to all nations, and raised to an elevation with themselves, those whom the firmest habits and prejudices of their country had led them to contemplate under all the disgrace and ignominy of outcasts.

Accordingly, we know, in fact, that bitterness, and resentment, and wounded pride, lay at the bottom of a great deal of the opposition, which Christianity experienced from the Jewish people. In the New Testament history itself, we see repeated examples of their outrageous violence; and this is confirmed by the testimony of many other writers. In the history of the martyrdom of Polycarp, it is stated, that the Gentiles and Jews inhabiting Smyrna, in a furious rage, and with a loud voice, cried out, "This is the teacher of Asia, the father of the Christians, the destroyer of our gods, who teaches all men not to sacrifice, nor to worship them!" They collected wood, and the dried branches of trees for his pile; and it is added, "the Jews also, according to custom, assisting with the greatest forwardness." It is needless to multiply testimonies to a point so generally understood; as, that it was not conviction alone, which lay at the bottom of their opposition to the Christians; that a great deal of passion entered into it; and that their numerous acts of hostility against the worshippers of Jesus, carry in them all the marks of fury and resentment.

Now we know that the power of passion will often carry it very far over the power of conviction. We know that the strength of conviction is not in proportion to the quantity of evidence *presented*, but to the quantity of evidence *attended* to, and perceived, in consequence of that attention. We also know, that attention is, in a great measure, a voluntary act; and that it is often in the power of the mind, both to turn away its attention from what would land it in any painful or humiliating conclusion, and to deliver itself up exclusively to those arguments which flatter its taste and its prejudices. All this lies within the range of familiar and every-day experience. We all know how much it insures the success of an argument, when it gets a *favourable* hearing. In by far the greater number of instances, the parties in a litigation are not merely each *attached* to their own side of the question; but each *confident and believing* that theirs is the side on which justice lies. In those contests of opinion, which take place every day between man and man, and particularly if passion and interest have any share in the controversy, it is evident to the slightest observation, that though it might have been selfishness, in the first instance, which gave a peculiar direction to the understanding, yet each of the parties often comes, at last, to entertain a sincere conviction in the truth of his own argument. It is not that truth is not one and immutable. The whole difference lies in the observers; each of them viewing the object through the medium of his own prejudices, or cherishing those peculiar habits of attention and understanding, to which taste or inclination had disposed him.

In addition to all this, we know, that though the evidence for a particular truth be so glaring, that it forces itself upon the understanding, and all the sophistry of passion and interest cannot withstand it; yet if this truth be of a very painful and humiliating kind, the obstinacy of man will often dispose him to resist its influence, and, in the bitterness of his malignant feelings, to carry a hostility against it, and that too in proportion to the weight of the argument which may be brought forward in its favour.

Now, if we take into account the inveteracy of the Jewish prejudices, and reflect how unpalatable and how mortifying to their pride must have been the doctrine of a crucified Saviour; we believe that their conduct, in reference to Christianity and its miraculous evidences, presents us with nothing anomalous or inexplicable, and that it will appear a possible and a likely thing to every understanding, that has been much cultivated in the experience of human affairs, in the nature of mind, and in the science of its character and phenomena.

There is a difficulty, however, in the way of this investigation. From the nature of the case, it bears no resemblance to any thing else, that has either been recorded in history, or has come within the range of our own personal observation. There is no other example of a people called upon to renounce the darling faith and principles of their country, and that upon the authority of miracles exhibited before them. All the experience we have about the operation of prejudice, and the perverseness of the human temper and understanding, cannot afford a complete solution of the question. In many respects, it is a case *sui generis*, and the only creditable information which we can obtain to enlighten us in this inquiry, is through the medium of that very testimony upon which the difficulty in question has thrown the suspicion that we want to get rid of.

Let us give all the weight to this argument of which it is susceptible, and the following is the precise degree in which it affects the merits of the controversy. When the religion of Jesus was promulgated in Judea, its first teachers appealed to miracles wrought by themselves in the face of day, as the evidence of their being commissioned by God. Many adopted the new religion upon this appeal, and many rejected it. An argument in favour of Christianity is derived from the conduct of the first. An objection against Christianity is derived from the conduct of the second. Now, allowing that we are not in possession of experience enough for estimating, in *absolute terms*, the strength of the objection, we propose the following as a solid and unexceptionable principle, upon which to estimate a comparison between the strength of the objection and the strength of the argument. We are sure that the first would not have embraced Christianity had its miracles been false; but we are not sure beforehand, whether the second would have rejected this religion on the supposition of the miracles being true. If experience does not enlighten us as to how far the exhibition of a real miracle would be effectual in inducing men to renounce their old and favourite opinions, we can infer nothing decisive from the conduct of those who still kept by the Jewish religion. This conduct was a matter of uncertainty, and any argument which many be extracted from it cannot be depended upon. But the case is widely different with that party of their nation who were converted from Judaism to Christianity. We know that the alleged miracles of Christianity were perfectly open to examination. We are sure, from our experience of human nature, that in a question so interesting, this examination would be given. We know, from the very nature of the miraculous facts, so remote from every thing like what would be attempted by jugglery, or pretended to by enthusiasm, that, if this examination were given, it would fix the truth or falsehood of the miracles. The truth of these miracles, then, for any thing we know, may be consistent with the the conduct of the Jewish party; but the falsehood of these miracles, from all that we do know of human nature, is not consistent with the conduct of the Christian party. Granting that we are not sure whether a miracle would force the Jewish nation to renounce their opinions, all that we can say of the conduct of the Jewish party is, that we are not able to explain it. But there is one thing that we are sure of. We are sure, that if the pretensions of Christianity be false, it never could have forced any part of the Jewish nation to renounce their opinions, with its alleged miracles, so open to detection, and its doctrines so offensive to every individual. The conduct of the Christian party, then, is not only what we are able to explain, but we can say with certainty, that it admits of no other explanation than the truth of that hypothesis which we contend for. We may not know in how far an attachment to existing opinions will prevail over an argument which is felt to be true.; but we are sure, that this attachment will never give way to an argument which is perceived to be false; and particularly when danger, and hatred, and persecution, are the consequences of embracing it. The argument for Christianity, from the conduct of the first proselytes, rests upon the firm ground of experience. The objection against it, from the conduct of the unbelieving Jews, has no experience whatever to rest upon.

The conduct of the Jews may be considered as a solitary fact in the history of the world, not from its being an exception to the general principles of human nature, but from its being an exhibition of human nature in singular circumstances. We have no exprerience to guide us in our opinion as to the probability of his conduct; and nothing, therefore, that can impeach a testimony which all experience in human affairs leads us to repose in as unquestionable. But after this testimony is admitted, we may submit to be enlightened by it; and in the history which it gives us of the unbelieving Jews, it furnishes a curious fact as to the power of prejudice upon the human mind, and a valuable accession to what we before knew of the principles of our nature. It lays before us an exhibition of the human mind in a situation altogether unexampled, and furnishes us with the result of a singular experiment, if we may so call it, in the history of the species. We offer it as an interesting fact to the moral and intellectual philosopher, that a previous attachment may sway the mind even against the impression of a miracle; and those who believe not in the historical evidence which established the authority of Christ and of the apostles, would not believe even though one rose from the dead.

We are inclined to think, that the argument has come down to us in the best possible form, and that it would have been enfeebled by that very circumstance, which the infidel demands as essential to its validity. Suppose for a moment that we could give him what he wants, that all the priests and people of Judea were so borne down by the resistless evidence of miracles, as by one universal consent to become the disciples of the new religion. What interpretation might have been given to this unanimous movement in favour of Christianity? A very unfavourable one, we apprehend, to the authenticity of its evidences. Will the infidel say, that he has a higher respect for the credibility of those miracles which ushered in the dispensation of Moses, because they were exhibited in the face of a whole people, and gained their unexcepted submission to the laws and the ritual of Judaism? This new revolution would have received the same explanation. We would have heard of its being sanctioned by their prophecies, of its being agreeable to their prejudices, of its being supported by the countenance and encouragement of their priesthood, and that the jugglery of its miracles imposed upon all, because all were willing to be deceived by them. The actual form in which the history has come down, presents us with an argument free of all these exceptions. We, in the first instance, behold a number of proselytes, whose testimony to the facts of Christianity is approved of by what they lost and suffered in the maintenance of their faith; and we, in the second instance, behold a number of enemies, eager, vigilant, and exasperated at the progress of the new religion, who have not questioned the authenticity of our histories, and whose silence, as to the public and widely talked of miracles of Christ and his apostles, we have a right to interpret into the most triumphant of all testimonies.

The same process of reasoning is applicable to the case of the Gentiles. Many adopted the new religion, and many rejected it. We may not be sure, if we can give an adequate explanation of the conduct of the latter on the supposition that the evidences are true; but we are perfectly sure, that we can give no adequate explanation of the conduct of the former, on the supposition that the evidences are false. For any thing we know, it is possible that the one party may have adhered to their former prejudices, in opposition to all the force and urgency of argument, which even an authentic miracle carries along with it. But we know that it is not possible that the other party should renounce these prejudices, and that too in the face of danger and persecution, unless the miracles had been authentic. So great is the difference between the strength of the argument and the strength of the objection, that we count it fortunate for the merits of the cause, that the conversions to Christianity were partial. We, in this way, secure all the support which is derived from the inexplicable fact of the silence of its enemies, inexplicable on every supposition, but the undeniable evidence and certainty of the miracles. Had the Roman empire made a unanimous movement to the new religion, and all the authorities of the state lent their concurrence to it, there would have been a suspicion annexed to the whole history of the Gospel, which cannot at present apply to it; and from the collision of the opposite parties, the truth has come down to us in a far more unquestionable form than if no such collision had been excited.

The silence of Heathen and Jewish writers of that period, about the miracles of Christianity, has been much insisted upon by the enemies of our religion; and has even excited something like a painful suspicion in the breasts of those who are attached to its cause. Certain it is, that no ancient facts have come down to us, supported by a greater quantity of historical evidence, and better accompanied with all the circumstances which can confer credibility on that evidence. When we demand the testimony of Tacitus to the Christian miracles, we forget all the while that we can allege a multitude of much more decisive testimonies; no less than eight contemporary authors, and a train of succeeding writers, who follow one another with a closeness and a rapidity, of which there is no example in any other department of ancient history. We forget that the authenticity of these different writers, and their pretensions to credit, are founded on considerations, perfectly the same in kind, though much stronger in degree, than what have been employed to establish the testimony of the most esteemed historians of former ages. For the history of the Gospel, we behold a series of testimonies, more continuous, and more firmly sustained, than there is any other example of in the whole compass of erudition. And to refuse this evidence, is a proof that in this investigation there is an aptitude in the human mind to abandon all ordinary principles, and to be carried away by the delusions which we have already insisted on.

But let us try the effect of that testimony which our antagonists demand. Tacitus has actually attested the existence of Jesus Christ; the reality of such a personage; his public execution under the administration of Pontius Pilate; the temporary check which this gave to the progress of his religion; its revival a short time after his death; its progress over the land of Judea, and to Rome itself, the metropolis of the empire;—all this we have in a Roman historian; and, in opposition to all established reasoning upon these subjects, it is by some more firmly confided in upon his testimony, than upon the numerous and concurring testimonies of nearer and contemporary writers. But be this as it may, let us suppose that Tacitus had thrown one particular more into his testimony, and that his sentence had run thus; "They had their denomination from Christus, who, in the reign of Tiberius, was put to death as a criminal by the procurator, Pontius Pilate, *and who rose from the dead on the third day after his execution, and ascended into heaven.*" Does it not strike every body, that however true the last piece of information may be, and however well established by its proper historians, this is not the place where we can expect to find it? If Tacitus did not believe the resurrection of our Saviour, (which is probably the case, as he never, in all likelihood, paid any attention to the evidence of a faith which he was led to regard, from the outset, as a pernicious superstition, and a mere modification of Judaism,) it is not to be supposed that such an assertion could ever have been made by him. If Tacitus did believe the resurrection of our Saviour, he gives us an example of what appears not to have been uncommon in these ages—he gives us an example of a man adhering to that system which interest and education recommended, in opposition to the evidence of a miracle which he admitted to be true. Still, even on this supposition, it is the most unlikely thing in the world, that he would have admitted the fact of our Saviour's resurrection into his history. It is most improbable, that a testimony of this kind would have been given, even though the resurrection of Jesus Christ be admitted; and, therefore, the want of this testimony carries in it no argument that the resurrection is a falsehood. If, however, in opposition to all probability, this testimony had been given, it would have been appealed to as a most striking confirmation of the main fact of the evangelical history. It would have figured away in all our elementary treatises, and been referred to as a master argument in every exposition of the evidences of Christianity. Infidels would have been challenged to believe in it on the strength of their own favourite evidence, the evidence of a classical historian; and must have been at a loss how to dispose of this fact, when they saw an unbiassed heathen giving his round and unqualified testimony in its favour.

Let us now carry the supposition a step farther. Let us conceive that Tacitus not only believed the fact, and gave his testimony to it, but that he believed it so far as to become a Christian. Is his testimony to be refused, because he gives this evidence of its sincerity? Tacitus asserting the fact, and remaining a heathen, is not so strong an argument for the truth of our Saviour's resurrection, as Tacitus asserting the fact and becoming a Christian in consequence of it. Yet the moment that this transition is made—a transition by which, in point of fact, his testimony becomes stronger—in point of impression it becomes less; and, by a delusion, common to the infidel and the believer, the argument is held to be weakened by the very circumstance which imparts greater force to it. The elegant and accomplished scholar becomes a believer. The truth, the novelty, the importance of this new subject, withdraw him from every other pursuit. He shares in the common enthusiasm of the cause, and gives all his talents and eloquence to the support of it. Instead of the Roman historian, Tacitus comes down to posterity in the shape of a Christian father, and the high authority of his name is lost in a crowd of similar testimonies.

A direct testimony to the miracles of the New Testament from the mouth of a heathen, is not to be expected. We cannot satisfy this demand of the infidel; but we can give him a host of much stronger testimonies than he is in quest of—the testimonies of those men who were heathens, and who embraced a hazardous and a disgraceful profession, under a deep conviction of those facts to which they gave their testimony. "O, but you now land us in the testimony of Christians!" This is very true; but it is the very fact of their being Christians in which the strength of the argument lies: and in each of the numerous fathers of the Christian church, we see a stronger testimony than the required testimony of the heathen Tacitus. We see men who, if they had not been Christians, would have risen to as high an eminence as Tacitus in the literature of the times; and whose direct testimonies to the gospel history would, in that case, have been most impressive, even to the mind of an infidel. And are these testimonies to be less impressive, because they were preceded by conviction, and sealed by martyrdom?

Yet though, from the nature of the case, no direct testimony to the Christian miracles from a heathen can be looked for, there are heathen testimonies which form an important accession to the Christian argument. Such are the testimonies to the state of Judea; the testimonies to those numerous particulars in government and customs, which are so often alluded to in the New Testament, and give it the air of an authentic history; and above all, the testimonies to the sufferings of the primitive Christians, from which we learn, through a channel clear of every suspicion, that Christianity, a religion of facts, was the object of persecution at a time, when eye-witnesses taught and eye-witnesses must have bled for it.

The silence of Jewish and heathen writers, when the true interpretation is given to it, is all on the side of the Christian argument. Even though the miracles of the Gospel had been believed to be true, it is most unlikely that the enemies of the Christian religion would have given their testimony to them; and the absence of this testimony is no impeachment therefore upon the reality of these miracles. But if the miracles of the Gospel had been believed to be false, it is most likely that this falsehood would have been asserted by the Jews and heathens of that period; and the circumstance of no such assertion having been given, is a strong argument for the reality of these miracles. Their silence in not asserting the miracles, is perfectly consistent with their truth; but their silence in not denying them, is not at all consistent with their falsehood. The entire silence of Josephus upon the subject of Christianity, though he wrote after the destruction of Jerusalem, and gives us the history of that period in which Christ and his apostles lived, is certainly a very striking circumstance. The sudden progress of Christianity at that time, and the fame of its miracles, (if not the miracles themselves,) form an important part of the Jewish history. How came Josephus to abstain from every particular respecting it? Will you reverse every principle of criticism, and make the silence of Josephus carry it over the positive testimony of the many historical documents which have come down to us? If you refuse every Christian testimony upon the subject, you will not refuse the testimony of Tacitus, who asserts, that this religion spread over Judea, and reached the city of Rome, and was looked upon as an evil of such importance, that it became the object of an authorised persecution by the Roman government; and all this several years before the destruction of Jerusalem, and before Josephus composed his history. Whatever opinion may be formed as to the *truth* of Christianity, certain it is, that its *progress* constituted an object of sufficient magnitude, to compel the attention of any historian who undertook the affairs of that period. How then shall we account for the scrupulous and determined exclusion of it from the history of Josephus? Had its miracles been false, this Jewish historian would gladly have exposed them. But its miracles were true, and silence was the only refuge of an antagonist, and his wisest policy.

But though we gather no direct testimony from Josephus, yet his history furnishes us with many satisfying additions to the Christian argument. In the details of policy and manners, he coincides in the main with the writers of the New Testament; and these coincidences are so numerous, and have so undesigned an appearance, as to impress on every person, who is at the trouble of making the comparison, the truth of the evangelical story.

If we are to look for direct testimonies to the miracles of the New Testament, we must look to that quarter, where alone it would be reasonable to expect them,—to the writings of the Christian fathers, men who were not Jews or heathens at the moment of recording their testimony; but who had been Jews or heathens, and who, in their transition to the ultimate state of Christians, give a stronger evidence of integrity, than if they had believed these miracles, and persisted in a cowardly adherence to the safest profession.

We do not undertake to satisfy every demand of the infidel. We think we do enough, if we prove that the thing demanded is most unlikely, even though the miracles should be true; and therefore that the want of it carries no argument against the truth of the miracles. But we do still more than this, if we prove that the testimonies which we actually possess are much stronger than the testimonies he is in quest of. And who can doubt this, when he reflects, that the true way of putting the case between the testimony of the Christian father, which we do have, and the testimony of Tacitus, which we do not have, is that the latter would be an assertion not followed up by that conduct, which would have been the best evidence of its sincerity; whereas the former is an assertion substantiated by the whole life, and by the decisive fact of the old profession having been renounced, and the new profession entered into,—a change where disgrace, and danger, and martyrdom were the consequences?

Let us, therefore, enter into an examination of these testimonies.

This subject has been in part anticipated, when we treated of the authenticity of the books of the New Testament. We have quotations and references to those books from five apostolic fathers, the companions of the original writers. We have their testimonies sustained and extended by their immediate successors; and as we pursued the crowded series of testimonies downwards, they become so numerous, and so explicit, as to leave no doubt on the mind of the inquirers, that the different books of the New Testament are the publications of the authors whose names they bear; and were received by the Christian world, as books of authority, from the first period of their appearance.

Now, every sentence in a Christian father, expressive of respect for a book in the New Testament, is also expressive of his faith in its contents. It is equivalent to his testimony for the miracles recorded in it. In the language of the law, it is an act by which he homologates the record, and superinduces his own testimony to that of the original writers. It would be vain to attempt speaking of all these testimonies. It cost the assiduous Lardner many years to collect them. They are exhibited in his Credibility of the New Testament; and in the multitude of them, we see a power and a variety of evidence for the Christian miracles, which is quite unequalled in the whole compass of ancient history.

But, in addition to these testimonies in the gross, for the truth of the evangelical history, have we no distinct testimonies to the individual facts which compose it? We have no doubt of the fact, that Barnabas was acquainted with the Gospel by Matthew, and that he subscribed to all the information contained in that history. This is a most valuable testimony from a contemporary writer; and a testimony which embraces all the miracles narrated by the evangelist. But, in addition to this, we should like if Barnabas, upon his own personal conviction, could assert the reality of any of these miracles. It would be multiplying the original testimonies; for he was a companion and a fellow-labourer of the apostles. We should have been delighted, if, in the course of our researches into the literature of past times, we had met with an authentic record, written by one of the five hundred, that are said to have seen our Saviour after his resurrection, and adding his own narrative of this event to the narratives that have already come down to us. Now, is any thing of this kind to be met with in ecclesiastical antiquity? How much of this kind of evidence are we in actual possession of? and if we have not enough to satisfy our keen appetite for evidence on a question of such magnitude, how is the want of it to be accounted for?

Let it be observed, then, that of the twenty-seven books which make up the New Testament, five are narrative or historical, viz. the four Gospels, and the Acts of the Apostles, which relate to the life and miracles of our Saviour, and the progress of his religion through the world, for a good many years after his ascension into heaven. All the rest, with the exception of the Revelation of St. John, are doctrinal or admonitory; and their main object is to explain the principles of the new religion, or to impress its duties upon the numerous proselytes who had even at that early period been gained over to the profession of Christianity.

Besides what we have in the New Testament, no other professed narrative of the miracles of Christianity has come down to us, bearing the marks of an authentic composition by any apostle, or any contemporary of the apostles. Now, to those, who regret this circumstance, we beg leave to submit the following observations. Suppose that one other narrative of the life and miracles of our Saviour had been composed, and, to give all the value to this additional testimony of which it is susceptible, let us suppose it to be the work of an apostle. By this last circumstance, we secure to its uttermost extent the advantage of an original testimony, the testimony of another eye-witness, and constant companion of our Saviour. Now, we ask, what would have been the fate of this performance? It would have been incorporated into the New Testament along with the other gospels. It may have been the Gospel according to Philip. It may have been the Gospel according to Bartholomew. At all events, the whole amount of the advantage would have been the substitution of five Gospels instead of four, and this addition, the want of which is so much complained of, would scarcely have been felt by the Christian, or acknowledged by the infidel, to strengthen the evidence of which we are already in possession.

But to vary the supposition, let us suppose that the narrative wanted, instead of being the work of an apostle, had been the work of some other contemporary, who writes upon his own original knowledge of the subject, but was not so closely associated with Christ, or his immediate disciples, as to have his history admitted into the canonical scriptures. Had this history been preserved, it would have been transmitted to us in a separate state; it would have stood out from among that collection of writings, which passes under the general name of the New Testament, and the additional evidence thus afforded, would have come down in the form most satisfactory to those with whom we are maintaining our present argument. Yet though, in point of form, the testimony might be more satisfactory; in point of fact it would be less so. It is the testimony of a less competent witness,—a witness who, in the judgment of his contemporaries, wanted those accomplishments which entitled him to a place in the New Testament. There must be some delusion operating upon the understanding, if we think that a circumstance, which renders an historian less accredited in the eyes of his own age, should render him more accredited in the eyes of posterity. Had Mark been kept out of the New Testament, he would have come down to us in that form, which would have made his testimony more impressive to a superficial inquirer; yet there would be no good reason for keeping him out, but precisely that reason which should render his testimony less impressive. We do not complain of this anxiety for more evidence, and as much of it as possible; but it is right to be told, that the evidence we have is of far more value than the evidence demanded, and that, in the concurrence of four canonical narratives, we see a far more effectual argument for the miracles of the New Testament, than in any number of those separate and extraneous narratives, the want of which is so much felt, and so much complained of.

That the New Testament is not one, but a collection of many testimonies, is what has been often said, and often acquiesced in. Yet even after the argument is formally acceded to, its impression is unfelt; and on this subject there is a great and an obstinate delusion, which not only confirms the infidel in his disregard to Christianity, but even veils the strength of the evidence from its warmest admirers.

There is a difference between a mere narrative and a work of speculation or morality. The latter subjects embrace a wider range, admit a greater variety of illustration, and are quite endless in their application to the new cases that occur in the everchanging history of human affairs. The subject of a narrative again admits of being exhausted. It is limited by the number of actual events. True, you may expatiate upon the character or importance of these events, but, in so doing, you drop the office of a pure historian, for that of the politician, or the moralist, or the divine. The evangelists give us a very chaste and perfect example of the pure narrative. They never appear in their own persons, or arrest the progress of the history for a single moment, by interposing their own wisdom, or their own piety. A gospel is a bare relation of what has been said or done; and it is evident that, after a few good compositions of this kind, any future attempts would be superfluous and uncalled for.

But, in point of fact, these attempts were made. It is to be supposed, that, after the singular events of our Saviour's history, the curiosity of the public would be awakened and there would be a demand for written accounts of such wonderful transactions. These written accounts were accordingly brought forward. Even in the interval of time between the ascension of our Saviour, and the publication of the earliest Gospel, such written histories seem to have been frequent. "Many," says St. Luke, (and in this he is supported by the testimony of subsequent writers,) "have taken in hand to set forth in order a declaration of these things." Now what has been the fate of all these performances? Such as might have been anticipated. They fell into disuse and oblivion. There is no evil design ascribed to the authors of them. They may have been written with perfect integrity, and been useful for a short time, and within a limited circle; but, as was natural, they all gave way to the superior authority, and more complete information, of our present narratives. The demand of the christian world was withdrawn from the less esteemed, to the more esteemed histories of our Saviour. The former ceased to be read, and copies of them would be no longer transcribed or multiplied. We cannot find the testimony we are in quest of, not because it was never given, but because the early Christians, who were the most competent judges of that testimony, did not think it worthy of being transmitted to us.

But, though the number of narratives be necessarily limited by the nature of the subject, there is no such limitation upon works of a moral, didactic, or explanatory kind. Many such pieces have come down to us, both from the apostles themselves, and from the earlier fathers of the church. Now, though the object of these compositions is not to deliver any narrative of the Christian miracles, they may perhaps give us some occasional intimation of them. They may proceed upon their reality. We may gather either from incidental passages, or from the general scope of the performance, that the miracles of Christ and his apostles were recognised, and the divinity of our religion acknowledged, as founded upon these miracles.

The first piece of the kind with which we meet besides the writings of the New Testament, is an epistle ascribed to Barnabas, and, at all events, the production of a man who lived in the days of the apostles. It consists of an exhortation to constancy in the Christian profession, a dissuasive from Judaism, and other moral instructions. We shall only give a quotation of a single clause from this work. "And he (i. e. our Saviour) making great signs and prodigies to the people of the Jews, they neither believed nor loved him."

The next piece in the succession of Christian writers, is the undoubted epistle of Clement, the bishop of Rome, to the church of Corinth, and who, by the concurrent voice of all antiquity, is the same Clement who is mentioned in the epistle to the Philippians, as the fellow-labourer of Paul. It is written in the name of the church of Rome, and the object of it is to compose certain dissensions which had arisen in the church of Corinth. It was out of his way to enter into any thing like a formal narrative of the miraculous facts which are to be found in the evangelical history. The subject of his epistle did not lead him to this; and besides the number and authority of the narratives already published, rendered an attempt of this kind altogether superfluous. Still, however, though a miracle may not be formally announced, it may be brought in incidentally, or it may be proceeded upon, or assumed as the basis of an argument. We give one or two examples of this. In one part of his epistle, he illustrates the doctrine of our resurrection from the dead, by the change and progression of natural appearances, and he ushers in this illustration with the following sentence: "Let us consider, my beloved, how the Lord shows us our future resurrection perpetually, of which he made the Lord Jesus Christ the first fruits, by raising him from the dead." This incidental way of bringing in the fact of our Lord's resurrection, appears to us the strongest possible form in which the testimony of Clement could have come down to us. It is brought forward in the most confident and unembarrassed manner. He does not stop to confirm this fact by any strong asseveration, nor does he carry, in his manner of announcing it, the most remote suspicion of its being resisted by the incredulity of those to whom he is addressing himself. It wears the air of an acknowledged truth, a thing understood and acquiesced in by all parties in this correspondence. The direct narrative of the evangelists give us their original testimony to the miracles of the Gospel. The artless and indirect allusions of the apostolic fathers, give us not merely their faith in this testimony, but the faith of the whole societies to which they write. They let us see, not merely that such a testimony was given, but that such a testimony was generally believed, and that too at a time when the facts in question lay within the memory of living witnesses.

In another part, speaking of the apostles, Clement says, that "receiving the commandments, and being filled with full certainty by the resurrection of Jesus Christ, and confirmed by the word of God, with the assurance of the Holy Spirit, they went out announcing the advent of the kingdom of God."

It was no object in those days for a Christian writer to come over the miracles of the New Testament, with the view of lending his formal and explicit testimony to them. This testimony had already been completed to the satisfaction of the whole Christian world. If much additional testimony has not been given, it is because it was not called for. But we ought to see, that every Christian writer, in the fact of his being a Christian, in his expressed reverence for the books of the New Testament, and in his numerous allusions to the leading points of the Gospel history, has given as satisfying evidence to the truth of the Christian miracles, as if he had left behind him a copious and distinct narrative.

Of all the miracles of the Gospel, it was to be supposed, that the resurrection of our Saviour would be oftenest appealed to; not as an evidence of his being a teacher,— for that was a point so settled in the mind of every Christian, that a written exposition of the argument was no longer necessary,—but as a motive to constancy in the Christian profession, and as the great pillar of hope in our own immortality. We accordingly meet with the most free and confident allusions to this fact in the early fathers. We meet with five intimations of this fact in the undoubted epistle of Polycarp to the Philippians: a father who had been educated by the apostles, and conversed with many who had seen Christ.

It is quite unnecessary to exhibit passages from the epistles of Ignatius to the same effect, or to pursue the examination downwards through the series of written testimonies. It is enough to announce it as a general fact, that, in the very first age of the Christian church, the teachers of this religion proceeded as confidently upon the reality of Christ's miracles and resurrection in their addresses to the people, as the teachers of the present day: Or, in other words, that they were as little afraid of being resisted by the incredulity of the people, at a time when the evidence of the facts was accessible to all, and habit and prejudice were against them, as we are of being resisted by the incredulity of an unlettered multitude, who listen to us with all the veneration of a hereditary faith.

There are five apostolic fathers, and a series of Christian writers who follow after them in rapid succession. To give an idea to those who are not conversant in the study of ecclesiastical antiquities, how well sustained the chain of testimony is from the first age of Christianity, we shall give a passage from a letter of Irenæus, preserved by Eusebius. We have no less than nine compositions from different authors, which fill up the interval between him and Polycarp; and yet this is the way in which he speaks, in his old age, of the venerable Polycarp, in a letter to Florinus. "I saw you, when I was very young, in the Lower Asia with Polycarp. For I better remember the affairs of that time than those which have lately happened; the things which we learn in our childhood growing up in the soul, and uniting themselves to it. Insomuch, that I can tell the place in which the blessed Polycarp sat and taught, and his going out, and coming in, and the manner of his life, and the form of his person, and his discourses to the people; and how he related his conversation with John, and others who had seen the Lord; and how he related their sayings, and what he had heard from them concerning the Lord, both concerning his miracles and his doctrines, as he had received them from the eye-witnesses of the Word of Life: all which Polycarp related agreeably to the Scriptures. These things I then, through the mercy of

God towards me, diligently heard and attended to, recording them not on paper, but upon my heart."

Now is the time to exhibit to full advantage the argument which the different epistles of the New Testament afford. They are, in fact, so many distinct and additional testimonies. If the testimonies drawn from the writings of the Christian fathers are calculated to make any impression, then the testimonies of these epistles, where there is no delusion, and no prejudice in the mind of the inquirer, must make a greater impression. They are more ancient, and were held to be of greater authority by competent judges. They were held sufficient by the men of those days who were nearer to the sources of evidence; and they ought, therefore, to be held sufficient by us. The early persecuted Christians had too great an interest in the grounds of their faith, to make a light and superficial examination. We may safely commit the decision to them; and the decision they have made, is, that the authors of the different epistles in the New Testament, were worthier of their confidence, as witnesses of the truth, than the authors of those compositions which were left out of the collection, and maintain, in our eye, the form of a separate testimony. By what unaccountable tendency is it, that we feel disposed to reverse this decision, and to repose more faith in the testimony of subsequent and less esteemed writers? Is there any thing in the confidence given to Peter and Paul by their contemporaries, which renders them unworthy of ours? or, is the testimony of their writings less valuable and less impressive, because the Christians of old have received them as the best vouchers of their faith?

It gives us a far more satisfying impression than ever of the truth of our religion, when, in addition to several distinct and independent narratives of its history, we meet with a number of contemporaneous productions addressed to different societies, and all proceeding upon the truth of that history, as an agreed and unquestionable point among the different parties in the correspondence. Had that history been a fabrication, in what manner, we ask, would it have been followed up by the subsequent compositions of those numerous agents in the work of deception? How comes it, that they have betrayed no symptom of that insecurity which it would have been so natural to feel in their circumstances? Through the whole of these epistles, we see nothing like the awkward or embarrassed air of impostors. We see no anxiety, either to mend or to confirm the history that had already been given. We see no contest which they might have been called upon to maintain with the incredulity of their converts, as to the miracles of the Gospel. We see the most intrepid remonstrance against errors of conduct, or discipline, or doctrine. This savours strongly of upright and independent teachers; but is it not a most striking circumstance, that among the severe reckonings which St. Paul had with some of his churches, he was never once called upon to school their doubts, or their suspicions, as to the reality of the Christian miracles? This is a point universally acquiesced in; and, from the general strain of these epistles, we collect, not merely the testimony of their authors, but the unsuspected testimony of all to whom they addressed themselves.

And let it never be forgotten, that the Christians, who compose these churches, were in every way well qualified to be arbiters in this question. They had the first authorities within their reach. The five hundred who, Paul says to them, had seen our Saviour after his resurrection, could be sought after; and, if not to be found, Paul would have had his assertion to answer for. In some cases, they were the first authorities themselves, and had therefore no confirmation to go in search of. He appeals to the miracles which had been wrought among them, and in this way he commits the question to their own experience. He asserts this to the Galatians; and at the very time, too, that he is delivering against them a most severe and irritating invective. He intimates the same thing repeatedly to the Corinthians; and after he had put his honesty to so severe a trial, does he betray any insecurity as to his character and reputation among them? So far from this, that in arguing the general doctrine of the resurrection from the dead, as the most effectual method of securing assent to it, he rests the main part of the argument upon their confidence in his fidelity as a witness. "But if there be no resurrection from the dead, then is Christ not risen.—Yea, and we are found false witnesses of God, because we have testified of God, that he raised up Christ, whom he raised not up, if so be that the dead rise not." Where, we ask, would have been the mighty charm of this argument, if Paul's fidelity had been questioned; and how shall we account for the free and intrepid manner in which he advances it, if the miracles which he refers to, as wrought among them, had been nullities of his own invention?

For the truth of the Gospel history, we can appeal to one strong and unbroken series of testimonies from the day of the apostles. But the great strength of the evidence lies in that effulgence of testimony, which enlightens this history at its commencement—in the number of its original witnesses—in the distinct and independent records which they left behind them, and in the undoubted faith they bore among the numerous societies which they instituted. The concurrence of the apostolic fathers, and their immediate successors, forms a very strong and a very satisfying argument; but let it be further remembered, that out of the materials which compose, if we may be allowed the expression, the original charter of our faith, we can select a stronger body of evidence than it is possible to form out of the whole mass of subsequent testimonies.

CHAPTER VI.

Remarks on the Argument from Prophecy.

VI. PROPHECY is another species of evidence to which Christianity professes an abundant claim, and which can be established on evidence altogether distinct from the testimony of its supporters. The prediction of what is future may not be delivered in terms so clear and intelligible as the history of what is past; and yet, in its actual fulfilment, it may leave no doubt on the mind of the inquirer that it was a prediction, and that the event in question was in the contemplation of him who uttered it. It may be easy to dispose of one isolated prophecy, by ascribing it to accident; but when we observe a number of these prophecies, delivered in different ages, and all bearing an application to the same events, or the same individual, it is difficult to resist the impression that they were actuated by a knowledge superior to human.

The obscurity of the prophetical language has been often complained of; but it is not so often attended to, that if the prophecy which foretels an event were as clear as the narrative which describes it, it would in many cases annihilate the argument. Were the history of any individual foretold in terms as explicit as it is in the power of narrative to make them, it might be competent for any usurper to set himself forward, and in as far as it depended upon his own agency, he might realize that history. He has no more to do than to take his lesson from the prophecy before him; but could it be said that fulfilment like this carried in it the evidence of any thing divine or miraculous? If the prophecy of a Prince and a Saviour, in the Old Testament, were different from what they are, and delivered in the precise and intelligible terms of an actual history; then every accomplishment which could be brought about by the agency of those who understood the prophecy, and were anxious for its verification, is lost to the argument. It would be instantly said that the agents in the transaction took their clue from the prophecy before them. It is the way, in fact, in which infidels have attempted to evade the argument as it actually stands. In the New Testament, an event is sometimes said to happen, that *it might be* *fulfilled* what was spoken by some of the old prophets. If every event which enters into the Gospel had been under the controul of agents merely human, and friends to Christianity, then we might have had reason to pronounce the whole history to be one continued process of artful and designed accommodation to the Old Testament prophecies. But the truth is, that many of the events pointed at in the Old Testament, so far from being brought about by the agency of Christians, were brought about in opposition to their most anxious wishes. Some of them were brought about by the agency of their most decided enemies; and some of them, such as the dissolution of the Jewish state, and the dispersion of its people among all countries, were quite beyond the controul of the apostles and their followers, and were effected by the intervention of a neutral party, which at the time took no interest in the question, and which was a stranger to the prophecy, though the unconscious instrument of its fulfilment.

Lord Bolingbroke has carried the objection so far, that he asserts Jesus Christ to have brought about his own death, by a series of wilful and preconcerted measures, merely to give the disciples who came after him the triumph of an appeal to the old prophecies. This is ridiculous enough; but it serves to show with what facility an infidel might have evaded the whole argument, had these prophecies been free of all that obscurity which is now so loudly complained of.

The best form, for the purposes of argument, in which a prophecy can be delivered, is to be so obscure, as to leave the event, or rather its main circumstances, unintelligible before the fulfilment, and so clear as to be intelligible after it. It is easy to conceive that this may be an attainable object; and it is saying much for the argument as it stands, that the happiest illustrations of this clearness on the one hand, and this obscurity on the other, are to be gathered from the actual prophecies of the Old Testament.

It is not, however, by this part of the argument, that we expect to reclaim the enemy of our religion from his infidelity; not that the examination would not satisfy him, but that the examination will not be given. What a violence it would be offering to all his antipathies, were we to land him, at the outset of our discussions, among the chapters of Daniel or Isaiah! He has too inveterate a contempt for the Bible. He nauseates the whole subject too strongly to be prevailed upon to accompany us to such an exercise. On such a subject as this, there is no contract, no approximation between us; and we therefore leave him with the assertion, (an assertion which he has no title to pronounce upon, till after he has finished the very examination in which we are most anxious to engage him,) that in the numerous prophecies of the Old Testament, there is such a multitude of allusions to the events of the New, as will give a strong impression to the mind of every inquirer, that the whole forms one magnificent series of communications between the visible and the invisible world; a great plan over which the unseen God presides in wisdom, and which, beginning with the first ages of the world, is still receiving new developements from every great step in the history of the species.

It is impossible to give a complete exposition of this argument without an actual reference to the prophecies themselves; and this we at present abstain from. But it can be conceived, that a prophecy, when first announced, may be so obscure, as to be unintelligible in many of its circumstances; and yet may so far explain itself by its accomplishment, as to carry along with it the most decisive evidence of its being a prophecy. And the argument may be so far strengthened by the number, and distance, and independence, of the different prophecies, all bearing an application to the same individual and the same history, as to leave no doubt on the mind of the observer, that the events in question were in the actual contemplation of those who uttered the prediction. If the terms of the prophecy were not comprehended, it at least takes off the suspicion of the event being brought about by the controul or agency of men who were interested in the accomplishment. If the prophecies of the Old Testament are just invested in such a degree of obscurity, as is enough to disguise many of the leading circumstances from those who lived before the fulfilment, —while they derive from the event an explanation satisfying to all who live after it, then, we say, the argument for the divinity of the whole is stronger, than if no such obscurity had existed. In the history of the New Testament, we see a natural and consistent account of the delusion respecting the Messiah, in which this obscurity has left the Jewish people; of the strong prejudices, even of the first disciples; of the manner in which these prejudices were dissipated, only by the accomplishment; and of their final conviction in the import of these prophecies being at last so strong, that it often forms their main argument for the divinity of that new religion which they were commissioned to publish to the world. Now, assuming, what we still persist in asserting, and ask to be tried upon, that an actual comparison of the prophecies in the Old Testament, with their alleged fulfilment in the New, will leave a conviction behind it, that there is a real correspondence between them; we see, in the great events of the new dispensation brought about by the blind instrumentality of prejudice and opposition, far more unambiguous characters of the finger of God, than if every thing had happened with the full concurrence and anticipation of the different actors in this history.

There is another essential part of the argument, which is much strengthened by this obscurity. It is necessary to fix the date of the prophecies, or to establish, at least, that the time of their publication was antecedent to the events to which they refer. Now, had these prophecies been delivered in terms so explicit, as to force the concurrence of the whole Jewish nation, the argument for their antiquity, would not have come down in a form as satisfying, as that in which it is actually exhibited. The testimony of the Jews, to the date of their sacred writings, would have been refused as an interested testimony. Whereas, to evade the argument as it stands, we must admit a principle, which, in no question of ordinary criticism, would be suffered for a single moment to influence your understanding. We must conceive, that two parties, at the very time that they were influenced by the strongest mutual hostility, combined to support a fabrication; that they have not violated this combination; that the numerous writers on both sides of the question have not suffered the slightest hint of this mysterious compact to escape them; and that, though the Jews are galled incessantly by the triumphant tone of the Christian appeals to their own prophecies, they have never been tempted to let out a secret, which would have brought the argument of the Christians into disgrace, and shown the world how falsehood and forgery mingled with their pretensions.

In the rivalry which, from the very commencement of our religion, has always obtained between Jews and Christians, in the mutual animosities of Christian sects, in the vast multiplication of copies of the Scriptures, in the distant and independent societies which were scattered over so many countries, we see the most satisfying pledge, both for the integrity of the sacred writings, and for the date which all parties agree in ascribing to them. We hear of the many securities which have been provided in the various forms of registrations, and duplicates, and depositories; but neither the wisdom, nor the interest of men ever provided more effectual checks against forgery and corruption, than we have in the instance before us. And the argument, in particular, for the antecedence of the prophecies to the events in the New Testament, is so well established by the concurrence of the two rival parties, that we do not see, how it is in the power of additional testimony to strengthen it.

But neither is it true, that the prophecies are delivered in terms so obscure, as to require a painful examination, before we can obtain a full perception of the argument. Those prophecies which relate to the fate of particular cities, such as Nineveh, and Tyre, and Babylon; those which relate to the issue of particular wars, in which the kings of Israel and Judah were engaged; and some of those which relate to the future history of the adjoining countries, are not so much veiled by symbolical language, as to elude the understanding, even of the most negligent observers. It is true, that in these instances, both the prophecy and the fulfilment appear to us in the light of a distant antiquity. They have accomplished their end. They kept alive the faith and worship of successive generations. They multiplied the evidences of the true religion, and account for a phenomenon in ancient history that is otherwise inexplicable, the existence and preservation of one solitary monument of pure theism in the midst of a corrupt and idolatrous world.

But to descend a little farther. We gather from the state of opinions at the time of our Saviour so many testimonies to the clearness of the old prophecies. The time and the place of our Saviour's appearance in the world, and the triumphant progress, if not the nature of his kingdom, were perfectly understood by the priests and chief men of Judea. We have it from the testimony of profane authors, that there was, at that time, a general expectation of a prince and a prophet all over the East. The destruction of Jerusalem was another example of the fulfilment of a clear prophecy; and this, added to other predictions uttered by our Saviour, and which received their accomplishment in the first generation of the Christian church, would have its use in sustaining the faith of the disciples amidst the perplexities of that anxious and distressing period.

We can even come down to the present day, and point to the accomplishment of clear prophecies in the actual history of the world. The present state of Egypt, and the present state of the Jews, are the examples which we fix upon. The one is an actual fulfilment of a clear prophecy; the other is also an actual fulfilment, and forms in itself the likeliest preparation for another accomplishment that is yet to come. Nor do we conceive, that these clear and literal fulfilments exhaust the whole of the argument from prophecy. They only form one part of the argument, but a part so obvious and irresistible, as should invite every lover of truth to the examination of the remainder. They should secure such a degree of respect for the subject, as to engage the attention, and awaken even in the mind of the most rapid and superficial observer, a suspicion that there may be something in it. They should soften that contempt which repels so many from investigating the argument at all; or at all events, they render that contempt inexcusable.

The whole history of the Jews is calculated to allure the curiosity, and had it not been leagued with the defence and illustration of our faith, would have drawn the attention of many a philosopher, as the most singular exhibition of human nature that ever was recorded in the annals of the world. The most satisfying cause of this phenomenon is to be looked for in the history which describes its origin and progress; and by denying the truth of that history, you abandon the only explanation which can be given of this wonderful people. It is quite in vain to talk of the immutability of Eastern habits, as exemplified in the nations of Asia. What other people ever survived the same annihilating processes? We do not talk of conquest, where the whole amount of the effect is in general a change of dynasty or of government; but where the language, the habits, the denomination, and above all, the geographical position, still remain to keep up the identity of the people. But in the history of the Jews, we see a strong indestructible principle, which maintained them in a separate form of existence amid changes that no other nation ever survived. We confine ourselves to the overthrow of their nation in the first century of our epoch, and appeal to the disinterested testimonies of Tacitus and Josephus, if ever the cruelty of war devised a process of more terrible energy for the utter extirpation of a name, and a remembrance from the world. They have been dispersed among all countries. They have no common tie of locality or government to keep them together. All the ordinary principles of assimilation, which make law, and religion, and manners, so much a matter of geography, are in their instance suspended. Even the smallest particles of this broken mass have resisted an affinity of almost universal operation, and remain undiluted by the strong and overwhelming admixture of foreign ingredients. And in exception to every thing which history has recorded of the revolutions of the species, we see in this wonderful race a vigorous principle of identity, which has remained in undiminished force for nearly two thousand years, and still pervades every shred and fragment of their widely scattered population. Now if the infidel insists upon it, we shall not rest on this as an argument. We can afford to give it up: for in the abundance of our resources, we feel independent of it. We shall say that it is enough, if it can reclaim him from his levity, and compel his attention to the other evidences which we have to offer him.

All we ask of him is to allow, that the undeniable singularity which is before his eyes, gives him a sanction at least, to examine the other singularities to which we make pretensions. If he goes back to the past history of the Jews, he will see in their wars the same unexampled preservation of their name and their nation. He will see them surviving the process of an actual transportation into another country. In short, he will see them to be unlike all other people in what observation offers, and authentic history records of them; and the only concession that we demand of him from all this, is, that their pretensions to be unlike other people in their extraordinary revelations from heaven, is at least possible, and deserves to be inquired into.

It may not be out of place to expose a species of injustice, which has often been done to the Christian argument. The defence of Christianity consists of several distinct arguments, which have sometimes been multiplied beyond what is necessary, and even sometimes beyond what is tenable. In addition to the main evidence which lies in the testimony given to the miracles of the Gospel, there is the evidence of prophecy; there is the evidence of collateral testimony; there is the internal evidence. The argument under each of these heads, is often made to undergo a farther subdivision; and it is not to be wondered at, that in the multitude of observations, the defence of Christianity may often be made to rest upon ground, which, to say the least of it, is precarious or vulnerable. Now the injustice which we complain of is, that when the friends of our religion are dislodged from some feeble outwork, raised by an unskilful officer in the cause, its enemies raise the cry of a decisive victory. But, for our own part, we could see her driven from all her defences, and surrender them without a sigh, so long as the phalanx of her historical evidence remains impenetrable. Behind this unscaled barrier, we could entrench ourselves, and eye the light skirmishing before us with no other sentiment than of regret, that our friends should, by the eagerness of their misplaced zeal, have given our enemy the appearance of a triumph. We offer no opinion as to the two-fold interpretation of prophecy; but though it were refuted by argument, and disgraced by ridicule, all that portion of evidence which lies in the numerous examples of literal and unambiguous fulfilment remains unaffected by it. Many there are who deny the inspiration of the Song of Solomon. But in what possible way does this affect the records of the evangelical history? Just as much as it affects the lives of Plutarch, or the Annals of Tacitus. There are a thousand subjects on which infidels may idly push the triumph, and Christians be as idly galled by the severity, or even the truth of their observations. We point to the historical evidence of the New Testament, and ask them to dispose of it. It is there, that we call them to the onset; for there lies the main strength of the Christian argument. It is true, that in the evidence of prophecy, we see a rising barrier, which, in the progress of centuries, may receive from time to time a new accumulation to the materials which form it. In this way, the evidence of prophecy may come, in time, to surpass the evidence of miracles. The restoration of the Jews will be the fulfilment of a clear prophecy, and form a proud and animating period in the history of our religion. "Now if the fall of them be the riches of the world, and the diminishing of them the riches of the Gentiles, how much more their fulness."

CHAPTER VII.

Remarks on the Scepticism of Geologists.

VII. The late speculations in geology form another example of a distant and unconnected circumstance, being suffered to cast an unmerited disgrace over the whole of the argument. They give a higher antiquity to the world than most of those who read the Bible had any conception of. Admit this antiquity, and in what possible way does it touch upon the historical evidence of the New Testament? The credibility of the Gospel miracles stands upon its own appropriate foundation, the recorded testimony of numerous and unexceptionable witnesses. The only way in which we can overthrow that credibility is by attacking the testimony, or disproving the authenticity of the record. Every other science is tried upon its own peculiar evidence; and all we contend for is, that the same justice be done to theology. When a mathematician offers to apply his reasoning to the phenomena of mind, the votaries of moral science resent it as an invasion, and make their appeal to the evidence of consciousness. When an amateur of botany, upon some vague analogies, offers his confident affirmations as to the structure and parts of the human body, there would be an instantaneous appeal to the knife and demonstrations of the anatomist. Should a mineralogist, upon the exhibition of an ingenious or well-supported theory, pronounce upon the history of our Saviour and his miracles; we would call it another example of an arbitrary and unphilosophical extension of principles beyond the field of their legitimate application. We would appeal to the kind and the quantity of testimony upon which that history is supported. We would suffer ourselves to be delighted by the brilliancy, or even convinced by the evidence of his speculations; but we would feel that the history of those facts, which form the ground-work of our faith, is as little affected by them, as the history of any storm, or battle, or warrior, which has come down to us in the most genuine and approved records of past ages.

But whatever be the external evidence of testimony, or however strong may be its visible characters of truth and honesty, is not the falsehood or the contradiction which we may detect in the subject of that testimony sufficient to discredit it? Had we been original spectators of our Saviour's miracles, we must have had as strong a conviction of their reality, as it is in the power of testimony to give us. Had we been the eyewitnesses of his character and history, and caught from actual observation the impression of his worth, the internal proofs that no jugglery or falsehood could have been intended, would have been certainly as strong as the internal proofs which are now exhibited to us, and which consist in the simplicity of the narrative, and that tone of perfect honesty which pervades, in a manner so distinct and intelligible, every composition of the apostles. Yet, with all these advantages, if Jesus Christ had asserted as a truth, what we confidently knew to be a falsehood; had he for example, upon the strength of his prophetical endowments, pronounced upon the secret of a person's age, and told us that he was thirty, when we knew him to be forty, would not this have made us stumble at all his pretensions, and, in spite of every other argument and appearance, would we not have withdrawn our confidence from him as a teacher from God? This we allow would have been a most serious dilemma. It would have been that state of neutrality which admits of nothing positive or satisfying on either side of the question; or rather, what is still more distressing, which gives me the most positive and satisfactory appearances on both sides. We could not abandon the truth of the miracles, because we saw them. Could we give them up, we should determine on a positive rejection, and our minds would find repose in absolute infidelity. But as the case stands it is scepticism. There is nothing like it in any other department of inquiry. We can appeal to no actual example; but a student of natural science may be made to understand the puzzle, when we ask him, how he would act, if the experiment, which he conducts under the most perfect sameness of circumstances, were to land him in opposite results? He would vary and repeat his experiments. He would try to detect the inconsistency, and would rejoice, if he at last found that the difficulty lay in the errors of his own observation, and not in the inexplicable nature of the subject. All this he would do in anxious and repeated endeavours, before he inferred that nature persevered in no law, and that that constancy, which is the foundation of all science, was perpetually broke in upon by the most capricious and unlooked for appearances, before he would abandon himself to scepticism, and pronounce philosophy to be an impossible attainment.

It is our part to imitate this example. If Jesus Christ has, on the one hand, performed miracles, and sustained in the whole tenor of his history the character of a prophet, and, on the other hand, asserted to be true what we undeniably know to be a falsehood, this is a dilemma which we are called upon to resolve by every principle, that can urge the human mind in the pursuit of liberal inquiry. It is not enough to say, that the phenomena in question do not fall within the dominion of philosophy; and we therefore leave them as a fair exercise an amusement to commentators. The mathematician may say, and has said the same thing of the moralist, yet there are moralists in the world who will prosecute their speculations in spite of him; and what is more, there are men who take a wider survey than either, who rise above these professional prejudices, and will allow that, in each department of inquiry, the subjects which offer are entitled to a candid and respectful consideration. The naturalist may pronounce the same rapid judgment upon the difficulties of the theologian; yet there ever will be theologians who feel a peculiar interest in their subject; and we trust that there ever will be men, with a higher grasp of mind than either the mere theologian, or the mere naturalist, who are ready to acknowledge the claims of truth in every quarter,—who are superior to that narrow contempt, which has made such an unhappy and malignant separation among the different orders of scientific men,—who will examine the evidences of the Gospel history, and, if they are found to be sufficient, will view the miracles of our Saviour with the same liberal and philosophic curiosity with which they would contemplate any grand phenomenon in the moral history of the species. If there really appears, on the face of this investigation, to be such a difficulty as the one in question, a philosopher of the order we are now describing will make many an anxious effort to extricate himself; he will not soon acquiesce in a scepticism, of which there is no other example in the wide field of human speculation; he will either make out the insufficiency of the historical evidence, or prove that the falsehood ascribed to Jesus Christ has no existence. He will try to dispose of one of the terms of the alleged contradiction, before he can prevail upon himself to admit both, and deliver his mind to a state of uncertainty most painful to those who respect truth in all her departments.

We offer the above observations, not so much for the purpose of doing away a difficulty which we conscientiously believe to have no existence, as for the purpose of exposing the rapid, careless, and unphilosophical procedure of some enemies to the Christian argument. They, in the first instance, take up the rapid assumption, that Jesus Christ has, either through himself, or his immediate disciples, made an assertion as to the antiquity of the globe, which, upon the faith of their geological speculations, they know to be a falsehood. After having fastened this strain upon the subject of the testimony, they by one summary act of the understanding, lay aside all the external evidence for the miracles and general character of our Saviour. They will not wait to be told, that this evidence is a distinct subject of examination; and that, if actually attended to, it will be found much stronger than the evidence of any other fact or history which has come down to us in the written memorials of past ages. If this evidence is to be rejected it must be rejected on its own proper grounds; but if all positive testimony, and all sound reasoning upon human affairs, go to establish it, then the existence of such proof is a phenomenon which remains to be accounted for, and must ever stand in the way of positive infidelity. Until we dispose of it, we can carry our opposition to the claims of our religion no farther than to the length of an ambiguous and midway scepticism. By adopting a decisive infidelity, we reject a testimony, which, of all others, has come down to us in the most perfect and unsuspicious form. We lock up a source of evidence, which is often repaired to in other questions of science and history. We cut off the authority of principles, which, if once exploded, will not terminate in the solitary mischief of darkening and destroying our theology, but will shed a baleful uncertainty over many of the most interesting speculations on which the human mind can expatiate.

Even admitting, then, this single objection in the subject of our Saviour's testimony, the whole length to which we can legitimately carry the objection is scepticism, or that dilemma of the mind into which it is thrown by two contradictory appearances. This is the unavoidable result of admitting both terms in the alleged contradiction. Upon the strength of all the reasoning which has hitherto occupied us, we challenge the infidel to dispose of the one term, which lies in the strength of the historical evidence. But in different ways, we may dispose of the other which lies in the alleged falsehood of our Saviour's testimony. We may deny the truth of the geological speculation; nor is it necessary to be an accomplished geologist, that we may be warranted to deny it. We appeal to the speculations of the geologists themselves. They neutralize one another, and leave us in possession of free ground for the informations of the Old Testament. Our imaginations have been much regaled by the brilliancy of their speculations, but they are so opposite to each other, that we now cease to be impressed by their evidence. But there are other ways of disposing of the supposed falsehood of our Saviour's testimony. Does he really assert what has been called the Mosaical antiquity of the world? It is true that he gives his distinct testimony to the divine legation of Moses; but does Moses ever say, that when God created the heavens and the earth, he did more at the time alluded to than transform them out of previously existing materials? Or does he ever say, that there was not an interval of many ages between the first act of creation, described in the first verse of the book of Genesis, and said to have been performed at the beginning; and those more detailed operations, the account of which commences at the second verse, and which are described to us as having been performed in so many days? Or, finally, does he ever make us to understand, that the genealogies of man went any farther than to fix the antiquity of the species, and, of consequence, that they left the antiquity of the globe a free subject for the speculations of philosophers?—We do not pledge ourselves for the truth of one or all of these suppositions. Nor is it necessary that we should. It is enough that any of them is infinitely more rational than the rejection of Christianity in the face of its historical evidence. This historical evidence remains in all the obstinacy of experimental and well-attested facts; and as there are so many ways of expunging the other term in the alleged contradiction, we appeal to every enlightened reader, if it is at all candid or philosophical to suffer it to stand.

CHAPTER VIII.

On the Internal Evidence, and the Objections of Deistical Infidels.

THERE is another species of evidence for Christianity, which we have not yet noticed,—what is commonly called the internal evidence, consisting of those proofs that Christianity is a dispensation from heaven, which are founded upon the nature of its doctrines, and the character of the dispensation itself. The term "internal evidence" may be made, indeed, to take up more than this. We may take up the New Testament as a human composition, and without any reference to its subsequent history, or to the direct and external testimonies by which it is supported. We may collect from the performance itself such marks of truth and honesty, as entitle us to conclude, that the human agents employed in the construction of this book were men of veracity and principle. This argument has already been resorted to, and a very substantial argument it is. It is of frequent application in questions of general criticism; and upon its authority alone many of the writers of past times have been admitted into credit, and many have been condemned as unworthy of it. The numerous and correct allusions to the customs and institutions, and other statistics of the age in which the pieces of the New Testament profess to have been written, give evidence of their antiquity. The artless and undesigned way in which these allusions are interwoven with the whole history, impresses upon us the perfect simplicity of the authors, and the total absence of every wish or intention to palm an imposture upon the world. And there is such a thing too as a general air of authenticity, which, however difficult to resolve into particulars, gives a very close and powerful impression of truth to the narrative. There is nothing fanciful in this species of internal evidence. It carries in it all the certainty of experience, and experience too upon a familiar and well-known subject,—the characters of honesty in the written testimony of our fellow men. We are often called upon in private and every-day life to exercise our judgment upon the spoken testimony of others, and we both feel and understand the powerful evidence which lies in the tone, the manner, the circumstantiality, the number, the agreement of the witnesses, and the consistency of all the particulars with what we already know from other sources of information. Now it is undeniable, that all those marks which give evidence and credibility to spoken testimony, may also exist to a very impressive degree in written testimony; and the argument founded upon them, so far from being fanciful or illegitimate, has the sanction of a principle which no philosopher will refuse; the experience of the human mind on a subject on which it is much exercised, and which lies completely within the range of its observation.

We cannot say so much, however, for the other species of internal evidence, that which is founded upon the reasonableness of the doctrines, or the agreement which is conceived to subsist between the nature of the Christian religion and the character of the Supreme Being. We have experience of man, but we have no experience of God. We can reason upon the procedure of man in given circumstances, because this is an accessible subject, and comes under the cognizance of observation; but we cannot reason on the procedure of the Almighty in given circumstances. This is an inaccessible subject and comes not within the limits of direct and personal observation. The one, like the scale, and compass, and measurements of Sir Isaac Newton, will lead you on safe and firm footing to the true economy of the heavens; the other, like the ether and whirlpools, and unfounded imaginations of Des Cartes, will not only lead you to misconceive that economy, but to maintain a stubborn opposition to the only competent evidence that can be offered upon the subject.

We feel that in thus disclaiming all support from what is commonly understood by the internal evidence, we do not follow the general example of those who have written on the Deistical controversy. Take up Leland's performance, and it will be found that one half of his discussion is expended upon the reasonableness of the doctrines, and in asserting the validity of the argument which is founded upon that reasonableness. It would save a vast deal of controversy, if it could be proved that all this is superfluous and uncalled for; that upon the authority of the proofs already insisted on, the New Testament must be received as a revelation from heaven; and that, instead of sitting in judgment over it, nothing remains on our part but an act of unreserved submission to all the doctrine and information which it offers to us. It is conceived, that in this way the general argument might be made to assume a more powerful and impressive aspect; and the defence of Christianity be more accommodated to the spirit and philosophy of the times.

Since the spirit of Lord Bacon's philosophy began to be rightly understood, the science of external nature has advanced with a rapidity unexampled in the history of all former ages. The great axiom of his philosophy is so simple in its nature, and so undeniable in its evidence, that it is astonishing how philosophers were so late in acknowledging it, or in being directed by its authority. It is more than two thousand years since the phenomena of external nature were objects of liberal curiosity to speculative and intelligent men. Yet two centuries have scarcely elapsed since the true path of investigation has been rightly pursued, and steadily persevered in; since the evidence of experience has been received as paramount to every other evidence, or, in other words, since philosophers have agreed that the only way to learn the magnitude of an object is to measure it, the only way to learn its tangible properties is to touch it, and the only way to learn its visible properties is to look at it.

Nothing can be more safe or more infallible than the procedure of the inductive philosophy as applied to the phenomena of external nature. It is the eye, or the ear-witness of every thing which it records. It is at liberty to classify appearances, but then in the work of classifying, it must be directed only by observation. It may group phenomena according to their resemblances. It may express these resemblances in words, and announce them to the world in the form of general laws. Yet such is the hardihood of the inductive philosophy, that though a single well-attested fact should overturn a whole system, that fact must be admitted. A single experiment is often made to cut short the finest process of generalization, however painful and humiliating the sacrifice; and though a theory, the most simple and magnificent that ever charmed the eye of an enthusiast, was on the eve of emerging from it.

In submitting, then, to the rules of the inductive philosophy, we do not deny that certain sacrifices must be made, and some of the most urgent propensities of the mind put under severe restraint and regulation. The human mind feels restless and dissatisfied under the anxieties of ignorance. It longs for the repose of conviction; and to gain this repose, it will often rather precipitate its conclusions, than wait for the tardy lights of observation and experiment. There is such a thing, too, as the love of simplicity and system—a prejudice of the understanding, which disposes it to include all the phenomena of nature under a few sweeping generalities—an indolence, which loves to repose on the beauties of a theory, rather than encounter the fatiguing detail of its evidences—a painful reluctance to the admission of facts, which, however true, break in upon the majestic simplicity that we would fain ascribe to the laws and operations of the universe.

Now, it is the glory of Lord Bacon's philosophy, to have achieved a victory over all these delusions; to have disciplined the minds of its votaries into an entire submission to evidence; to have trained them up in a kind of steady coldness to all the splendour and magnificence of theory, and taught them to follow, with unfaultering step, wherever the sure though humble path of experiment may lead them.

To justify the cautious procedure of the inductive philosophy, nothing more is necessary than to take a view of the actual powers and circumstances of humanity; of the entire ignorance of man when he comes into the world, and of the steps by which that ignorance is enlightened; of the numerous errors into which he is misled the moment he ceases to observe, and begins to presume or to excogitate; of the actual history of science; its miserable progress, so long as categories and principles retained their ascendency in the schools; and the splendour and rapidity of its triumphs, so soon as man understood that he was nothing more than the disciple of Nature, and must take his lesson as Nature offers it to him.

What is true of the science of external nature, holds equally true of the science and phenomena of mind. On this subject, too, the presumptuous ambition of man carried him far from the sober path of experimental inquiry. He conceived that his business was not to observe, but to speculate; to construct systems rather than consult his own experience and the experience of others; to collect the materials of his theory, not from the history of observed facts, but from a set of assumed and excogitated principles. Now the same observations apply to this department of inquiry. We must admit to be true, not what we presume, but what we find to be so. We must restrain the enterprises of fancy. A law of the human mind must be only a series of well-authenticated facts, reduced to one general description, or grouped together under some general points of resemblance. The business of the moral as well as of the natural philosopher is not to assert what he excogitates, but to record what he observes; not to amuse himself with the speculations of fancy, but to describe phenomena as he sees or as he feels them. This is the business of the moral as well as of the natural inquirer. We must extend the application of Lord Bacon's principles to moral and metaphysical subjects. It was long before this application was recognized, or acted upon by philosophers. Many of the continental speculations are still infected with the presumptuous *a priori* spirit of the old schools; though the writings of Reid and Stewart have contributed much to chase away this spirit from the metaphysics of our own country, and to bring the science of mind, as well as matter, under the entire dominion of the inductive philosophy.

These general observations we conceive to be a most direct and applicable introduction to that part of the subject which is before us. In discussing the evidence of Christianity, all that we ask of our reader is to bring along with him the same sober and inductive spirit, that is now deemed so necessary in the prosecution of the other sciences; to abandon every system of theology, that is not supported by evidence, however much it may gratify his taste, or regale his imagination, and to admit any system of theology, that is supported by evidence, however repugnant to his feelings or his prejudices; to make conviction, in fact, paramount to inclination, or to fancy; and to maintain, through the whole process of the investigation, that strength and intrepidity of character, which will follow wherever the light of argument may conduct him, though it should land him in conclusions the most nauseous and unpalatable.

We have no time to enter into causes; but the fact is undeniable. Many philosophers of the present day are disposed to nauseate every thing connected with theology. They associate something low and ignoble with the prosecution of it. They regard it, as not a fit subject for liberal inquiry. They turn away from it with disgust, as one of the humblest departments of literary exertion. We do not say that they reject its evidences, but they evade the investigation of them. They feel no conviction; not because they have established the fallacy of a single argument, but because they entertain a general dislike at the subject, and will not attend to it. They love to expatiate in the more kindred fields of science or elegant literature; and while the most respectful caution, and humility, and steadiness, are seen to preside over every department of moral and physical investigation, theology is the only subject that is suffered to remain the victim of prejudice, and of a contempt the most unjust, and the most unphilosophical.

We do not speak of this feeling as an impiety; we speak of it as an offence against the principles of just speculation. We do not speak of it as it allures the heart from the influence of religion; we speak of it as it allures the understanding from the influence of evidence and truth. In a word, we are not preaching against it; we reason against it. We contend that it is a transgression against the rules of the inductive philosophy. All that we want is, the application of Lord Bacon's principles to the investigation before us; and as the influence of prejudice and disgust is banished from every other department of inquiry, we conceive it fair that it should be banished from theology also, and that our subject should have the common advantage of a hearing,—where no partiality of the heart or fancy is admitted, and no other influence acknowledged than the influence of evidence over the convictions of the understanding.

Let us therefore endeavour to evince the success and felicity with which Lord Bacon's principles may be applied to the investigation before us.

According to Bacon, man is ignorant of every thing antecedent to observation; and there is not a single department of inquiry, in which he does not err the moment that he abandons it. It is true that the greater part of every individual's knowledge is derived immediately from testimony; but it is only from testimony that brings home to his conviction the observation of others. Still it is observation which lies at the bottom of his knowledge. Still it is man taking his lesson from the actual condition of the thing which he contemplates; a condition that is altogether independent of his will, and which no speculation of his can modify or destroy. There is an obstinacy in the processes of nature, which he cannot controul. He must follow it. The construction of a system should not be a creative, but an imitative process, which admits nothing but what evidence assures us to be true, and is founded only on the lessons of experience. It is not by the exercise of a sublime and speculative ingenuity that man arrives at truth. It is by letting himself down to the drudgery of observation. It is by descending to the sober work of seeing, and feeling, and experimenting. Wherever, in short, he has not had the benefit of his own observation, or the observation of others brought home to his conviction by credible testimony, there he is ignorant.

This is found to hold true, even in those sciences where the objects of inquiry are the most familiar and the most accessible. Before the right method of philosophising was acted upon, how grossly did philosophers misinterpret the phenomena of external nature, when a steady perseverance in the path of observation could have led them to infallible certainty! How misled in their conception of every thing around them, when, instead of making use of their senses, they delivered themselves up to the exercises of a solitary abstraction, and thought to explain every thing by the fantastic play of unmeaning terms, and imaginary principles! And, when at last set on the right path of discovery, how totally different were the results of actual observation, from those systems which antiquity had rendered venerable, and the authority of great names had recommended to the acquiescence of many centuries! This proves that even in the most familiar subjects, man knows every thing by observation, and is ignorant of every thing without it; and that he cannot advance a single footstep in the acquirement of truth, till he bid adieu to the delusions of theory, and sternly refuse indulgence to its fondest anticipations.

Thus, there is both a humility and a hardihood in the philosophical temper. They are the same in principle, though different in display. The first is founded on a sense of ignorance, and disposes the mind of the philosopher to pay the most respectful attention to every thing that is offered in the shape of evidence. The second consists in a determined purpose to reject and to sacrifice every thing that offers to oppose the influence of evidence, or to set itself up against its legitimate and well-established conclusions. In the ethereal whirlpools of Des Cartes, we see a transgression against the humility of the philosophical character. It is the presumption of knowledge on a subject, where the total want of observation should have confined him to the modesty of ignorance. In the Newtonian system of the world, we see both humility and hardihood. Sir Isaac commences his investigation with all the modesty of a respectful inquirer. His is the docility of a scholar, who is sensible that he has all to learn. He takes his lesson as experience offers it to him, and yields a passive obedience to the authority of this great schoolmaster. It is in his obstinate adherence to the truth which his master has given him, that the hardihood of the philosophical character begins to appear. We see him announce, with entire confidence, both the fact and its legitimate consequences. We see him not deterred by the singularity of his conclusions, and quite unmindful of that host of antipathies which the reigning taste and philosophy of the times mustered up to oppose him. We see him resisting the influence of every authority, but the authority of experience. We see that the beauty of the old system had no power to charm him from that process of investigation by which he destroyed it. We see him sitting upon its merits with the severity of a judge, unmoved by all those graces of simplicity and magnificence which the sublime genius of its inventor had thrown around it.

We look upon these two constituents of the philosophical temper, as forming the best preparation for finally terminating in the decided Christian. In appreciating the pretensions of Christianity, there is a call both upon the humility and the hardihood of every inquirer; the humility which feels its own ignorance, and submits without reserve to whatever comes before it in the shape of authentic and well-established evidence; and the hardihood, which sacrifices every taste and every prejudice at the shrine of conviction, which defies the scorn of a pretended philosophy, which is not ashamed of a profession that some conceive to be degraded by the homage of the superstitious vulgar, which can bring down its mind to the homeliness of the Gospel, and renounce, without a sigh, all that is elegant, and splendid, and fascinating, in the speculations of moralists. In attending to the complexion of the Christian argument, we are widely mistaken, if it is not precisely that kind of argument which will be most readily admitted by those whose minds have been trained to the soundest habits of philosophical investigation; and if that spirit of cautious and sober-minded inquiry to which modern science stands indebted for all her triumphs, is not the very identical spirit which leads us to "cast down all our lofty imaginations, and to bring every thought into the captivity of the obedience of Christ."

On entering into any department of inquiry, the best preparation is that docility of mind which is founded on a sense of our total ignorance of the subject: and nothing is looked upon as more unphilosophical than the temerity of that *a priori* spirit, which disposes many to presume before they investigate. But if we admit the total ignorance of man antecedent to observation, even in those sciences where the objects of inquiry are the nearest and the most familiar, we will be more ready to admit his total ignorance of those subjects which are more remote and more inaccessible. If caution and modesty be esteemed so philosophical, even when employed in that little field of investigation which comes within the range of our senses; why should they not be esteemed philosophical when employed on a subject so vast, so awful, so remote from direct and personal observation, as the government of God? There can be nothing so completely above us, and beyond us, as the plans of the Infinite Mind, which extend to all time, and embrace all worlds. There is no subject to which the cautious and humble spirit of Lord Bacon's philosophy is more applicable; nor can we conceive a more glaring rebellion against the authority of his maxims, than for the beings of a day to sit in judgment upon the Eternal, and apply their paltry experience to the counsels of his high and unfathomable wisdom. We do not speak of it as impious; we speak of it as unphilosophical. We are not bringing the decrees of the orthodox to bear against it; we are bringing the principles of our modern and enlightened schools. We are applying the very same principles to a system of theism, that we would do to a system of geology. Both may regale the fancy with the grandeur of their contemplations; both may receive embellishment from the genius and imagination of their inventors; both may carry us along with the powers of a captivating eloquence. But all this is not enough to satisfy the severe and scrupulous spirit of the modern philosophy. Give us facts. Give us appearances. Show us how, from the experience of a life or a century, you can draw a legitimate conclusion so boundless in its extent, and by which you propose to fix down both the processes of a remote antiquity, and the endless progressions either of nature or of providence in future ages. Are there any historical documents? Any memorials of the experience of past times? On a question of such magnitude, we would esteem the recorded observations of some remote age to be peculiarly valuable, and worth all the ingenuity and eloquence which a philosopher could bestow on the limited experience of one or two generations. A process of geology may take millions of years before it reaches its accomplishment. It is impossible that we can collect the law or the character of this process from the experience of a single century, which does not furnish us one single step in this vast and immeasurable progression. We look as far as we can into a distant antiquity, and take hold with avidity of any authentic document, by which we can ascertain a single fact to guide and to enlighten us in this interesting speculation. The same caution is necessary in the subject before us. The administration of the Supreme Being is coeval with the first purposes of his uncreated mind, and it points to eternity. The life of man is but a point in that progress, to which we see no end, and can assign no beginning. We are not able to collect the law or the character of this administration from an experience so momentary. We therefore cast an eye on the history of past times. We examine every document which comes before us. We compare all the moral phenomena which can be collected from the narratives of antiquity. We seize with avidity every record of the manifestations of Providence, every fact which can enlighten the ways of God to man; and we would esteem it a deviation from the right spirit and temper of philosophical investigation, were we to suffer the crude or fanciful speculations of our own limited experience to take a precedency over the authentic informations of history.

But this is not all. Our experience is not only limited in point of time; it is also limited in point of extent. To assign the character of the divine administration from the little that offers itself to the notice of our own personal experience, would be far more absurd than to infer the history and character of the kingdom from the history and character of our own family. Vain is the attempt to convey in language what the most powerful imagination sinks under; how small the globe, and "all which it inherits," is in the immensity of creation! How humble a corner in the immeasurable fields of nature and of providence! If the whole visible creation were to be swept away, we think of the dark and awful solitude which it would leave behind it in the unpeopled regions of space. But to a mind that could take in the whole, and throw a wide survey over the innumerable worlds which roll beyond the ken of the human eye, there would be no blank, and the universe of God would appear a scene as goodly and majestic as ever. Now it is the administration of this God that we sit in judgment upon; the counsels of Him, whose wisdom and energy are of a kind so inexplicable; whom no magnitude can overpower, whom no littleness can escape, whom no variety can bewilder; who gives vegetation to every blade of grass, and moves every particle of blood which circulates through the veins of the minutest animal; and all this by the same omnipotent arm that is abroad upon the universe, and presides in high authority over the destiny of all worlds.

It is impossible not to mingle the moral impressions of piety with such a contemplation. But suppose these impressions to be excluded, that the whole may be reduced to a matter of abstract and unfeeling intelligence. The question under consideration is, How far the experience of man can lead him to any certain conclusions, as to the character of the divine administration; if it does lead him to some certain conclusions, then in the spirit of the Baconian philosophy, he will apply these conclusions to the information derived from other sources; and they will of course affect, or destroy, or confirm the credibility of that information. If, on the other hand, it appears that experience gives no light, no direction on the subject, then, in the very same spirit, he will submit his mind as a blank surface to all the positive information which comes to it from any other quarter. We take our lesson as it comes to us, provided we are satisfied beforehand, that it comes from a source which is authentic. We set up no presumptions of our own against the authority of the unquestionable evidence that we have met with, and reject all the suggestions which our defective experience can furnish, as the follies of a rash and fanciful speculation.

Now, let it be observed, that the great strength of the Christian argument lies in the historical evidence for the truth of the Gospel narrative. In discussing the light of this evidence, we walk by the light of experience. We assign the degree of weight that is due to the testimony of the first Christians upon the observed principles of human nature. We do not step beyond the cautious procedure of Lord Bacon's philosophy. We keep within the safe and certain limits of experimental truth. We believe the testimony of the apostles, because, from what we know of the human character, it is impossible that men in their circumstances could have persevered as they did in the assertion of a falsehood; it is impossible that they could have imposed this falsehood upon such a multitude of followers; it is impossible that they could have escaped detection, surrounded as they were by a host of enemies, so eager and so determined in their resentments. On this kind of argument we are quite at home. There is no theory, no assumption. We feel every inch of the ground we are treading upon. The degree of credit that should be annexed to the testimony of the apostles, is altogether a question of experience. Every principle which we apply towards the decision of this question is founded upon materials which lie before us, and are every day within the reach of observation. Our belief in the testimony of the apostles, is founded upon our experience of human nature and human affairs. In the whole process of the inquiry, we never wander from that sure, though humble path, which has been pointed out to us by the great master of philosophising. We never cast off the authority of those maxims which have been found in every other department of knowledge to be sound and infallible. We never suffer assumption to take the precedency of observation, or abandon that safe and certain mode of investigation, which is the only one suited to the real mediocrity of our powers.

It appears to us, that the disciples of the infidel philosophy have reversed this process. They take a loftier flight. You seldom find them upon the ground of the historical evidence. It is not in general, upon the weight, or the nature of human testimony, that they venture to pronounce on the credibility of the Christian revelation. It is on the character of that revelation itself. It is on what they conceive to be the absurdity of its doctrines. It is because they see something in the nature or dispensation of Christianity, which they think disparaging to the attributes of God, and not agreeable to that line of proceeding which the Almighty should observe in the government of his creatures. Rousseau expresses his astonishment at the strength of the historical testimony; so strong, that the inventor of the narrative appeared to him to be more miraculous than the hero. But the absurdities of this said revelation are sufficient in his mind to bear down the whole weight of its direct and external evidences. There was something in the doctrines of the New Testament repulsive to the taste and the imagination, and perhaps even to the convictions of this interesting enthusiast. He could not reconcile them with his pre-established conceptions of the divine character and mode of operation. To submit to these doctrines, he behoved to surrender that theism, which the powers of his ardent mind had wrought up into a most beautiful and delicious speculation. Such a sacrifice was not to be made. It was too painful. It would have taken away from him, what every mind of genius and sensibility esteems to be the highest of all luxuries. It would destroy a system, which had all that is fair and magnificent to recommend it, and mar the gracefulness of that fine intellectual picture, on which this wonderful man had bestowed all the embellishments of feeling, and fancy, and eloquence.

In as far, then, as we can judge of the conduct of man in given circumstances, we would pass a favourable sentence upon the testimony of the apostles. But, says the Deist, I judge of the conduct of God; and what the apostles tell me of him is so opposite to that judgment, that I discredit their testimony. The question at issue between us is, shall we admit the testimony of the apostles, upon the application of principles founded on observation, and as certain as is our experience of human affairs? Or, shall we reject that testimony upon the application of principles that are altogether beyond the range of observation, and as doubtful and imperfect in their nature, as is our experience of the counsels of heaven? In the first argument there is no assumption. We are competent to judge of the behaviour of man in given circumstances. This is a subject completely accessible to observation. The second argument is founded upon assumption entirely. We are not competent to judge of the conduct of the Almighty in given circumstances. Here we are precluded, by the nature of the subject, from the benefit of observation. There is no antecedent experience to guide or to enlighten us. It is not right, for man to assume what is right, or proper, or natural for the Almighty to do. It is not in the mere spirit of piety that we say so; it is in the spirit of the soundest experimental philosophy. The argument of the Christian is precisely what the maxims of Lord Bacon would dispose us to acquiesce in. The argument of the infidel is precisely that argument which the same maxims would dispose us to reject; and when put by the side of the Christian argument, it appears as crude and as unphilosophical as do the ingenious speculations of the schoolmen, when set in opposition to the rigour, and evidence, and precision, which reign in every department of modern science.

The application of Lord Bacon's philosophy to the study of external nature was a happy epoch in the history of physical science. It is not long since this application has been extended to the study of moral and intellectual phenomena. All that we contend for is, that our subject should have the benefit of the same application; and we count it hard while, in every other department of inquiry, a respect for truth is found sufficient to repress the appetite for system-building, that theology, the loftiest and most inaccessible of all the sciences, should still remain infected with a spirit so exploded, and so unphilosophical; and that the fancy, and theory, and unsupported speculation, so current among the Deists and demi-infidels of the day, should be held paramount to the authority of facts, which have come down to us with a weight of evidence and testimony, that is quite unexampled in the history of ancient times.

What is science, but a record of observed phenomena, grouped together according to certain points of resemblance, which have been suggested by an actual attention to the phenomena themselves? We never think of questioning the existence of the phenomena, after we have demonstrated the genuineness and authenticity of the record. After this is demonstrated, the singular or unexpected nature of the phenomena is not suffered to weaken their credibility,—a credibility which can only be destroyed by the authority of our own personal observation, or some other record possessed of equal or superior pretensions. But in none of the inductive sciences is it in the power of a student to verify every thing by his own personal observation. He must put up with the observations of others, brought home to the convictions of his own mind by creditable testimony. In the science of geology, this is eminently the case. In a science of such extent, our principles must be in part founded upon the observations of others, transmitted to us from a distant country. And in a science, the processes of which are so lengthened in point of time, our principles should also in part be founded on the observations of others, transmitted to us from a remote antiquity. Any observations of our own are so limited, both in point of space and of time, that we never think of opposing their authority to the evidence which is laid before us. Our whole attention is directed to the validity of the record; and the moment that this validity is established, we hold it incumbent upon us to submit our minds to the entire and unmodified impression of the testimony contained in it. Now, all that we ask is, that the same process of investigation be observed in theology, which is held to be so sound and so legitimate in other sciences. In a science of such extent, as to embrace the wide domain of moral and intelligent nature, we feel the littleness of that range to which our own personal observations are confined. We shall be glad, not merely of the information transmitted to us from a distant country, but of the authentic information transmitted to us by any other order of beings, in some distant and unknown part of the creation. In a science, too, which has for its object the lengthened processes of the divine administration, we should like, if any record of past times could enable us to extend our observations beyond the limits of our own ephemeral experience; and if there are any events of a former age possessed of such a peculiar and decisive character, as would help us to some satisfactory conclusion in this greatest and most interesting of the sciences.

On a subject so much above us and beyond us, we would never think of opposing any preconceptions to the evidence of history. We would maintain the humility of the inductive spirit. We would cast about for facts, and events and appearances. We would offer our minds as a blank surface to every thing that came to them, supported by unexceptionable evidence. It is not upon the nature of the facts themselves, that we would pronounce upon their credibility, but upon the nature of that testimony by which they were supported. Our whole attention would be directed to the authority of the record. After this was established, we would surrender our whole understanding to its contents. We would school down every antipathy within us, and disown it as a childish affection, unworthy of a philosopher who professes to follow truth through all the disgusts and discouragements which surround it. There are men of splendid reputation in our enlightened circles, who never attended to this speculation, and who annex to the Gospel of Christ nothing else than ideas of superstition and vulgarity. In braving their contempt, we would feel ourselves in the best element for the display and exercise of the philosophical temper. We would rejoice in the omnipotence of truth, and anticipate, in triumph, the victory which it must accomplish over the pride of science, and the fastidiousness of literature. It would not be the enthusiasm of a visionary which would support us, but the inward working of the very same principle which sustained Galileo, when he adhered to the result of his experiments, and Newton, when he opposed his measurements and observations to the tide of prejudice he had to encounter from the prevailing taste and philosophy of the times.

We conceive that inattention to the above principles has led many of the most popular and respected writers in the Deistical controversy to introduce a great deal of discussion that is foreign to the merits of the question altogether; and in this way the attention is often turned away from the point in which the main strength of the argument lies. An infidel, for example, objects against one of the peculiar doctrines of Christianity. To repel the objection, the Christian conceives it necessary to vindicate the reasonableness of that doctrine, and to show how consistent it is with all those antecedent conceptions which we derived from the light of natural religion. All this we count superfluous. It is imposing an unnecessary task upon ourselves. Enough for us to have established the authority of the Christian revelation upon the ground of its historical evidence. All that remains is to submit our minds to the fair interpretation of Scripture. Yes; but how do you dispose of the objection drawn from the light of natural religion? In precisely the same way that we would dispose of an objection drawn from some speculative system, against the truth of any physical fact that has been well established by observation or testimony. We would disown the system, and oppose the obstinacy of the fact to all the elegance and ingenuity of the speculation.

We are sensible that this is not enough to satisfy a numerous class of very sincere and well disposed Christians. There are many of this description, who, antecedent to the study of the Christian revelation altogether, repose a very strong confidence in the light of natural religion, and think that upon the mere strength of its evidence, they can often pronounce with a considerable degree of assurance on the character of the divine administration. To such as these, something more is necessary than the external evidences on which Christianity rests. You must reconcile the doctrines of Christianity with those previous conceptions which the light of nature has given them; and a great deal of elaborate argument is often expended in bringing about this accommodation. It is, of course, a work of greater difficulty, to convince this description of people, though in point of fact, this difficulty has been overcome, in a way the most masterly and decisive, by one of the soundest and most philosophical of our theologians.

To another description of Christians, this attempt to reconcile the doctrines of Christianity with the light of natural religion is superfluous. Give them historical evidence for the truth of Christianity, and all that natural religion may have taught them will fly like so many visionary phantoms before the light of its overbearing authority. With them the argument is reduced to a narrower compass. Is the testimony of the apostles and first Christians sufficient to establish the credibility of the facts which are recorded in the New Testament? The question is made to rest exclusively on the character of this testimony, and the circumstances attending it; and no antecedent theology of their own is suffered to mingle with the investigation. If the historical evidence of Christianity is found to be conclusive, they conceive the investigation to be at an end; and that nothing remains on their part, but an act of unconditional submission to all its doctrines.

Though it might be proper, in the present state of opinion, to accommodate to both these cases, yet we profess ourselves to belong to the latter description of Christians. We hold by the total insufficiency of natural religion to pronounce upon the intrinsic merits of any revelation, and think that the authority of every revelation rests exclusively upon its external evidences, and upon such marks of honesty in the composition itself as would apply to any human performance. We rest this opinion, not upon any fanatical impression of the ignorance of man, or how sinful it is for a weak and guilty mortal to pronounce upon the counsels of heaven, and the laws of the divine administration. We disown this presumption, not merely because it is sinful, but because we conceive it to be unphilosophical, and precisely analogous to that theorising *a priori* spirit, which the wisdom of Bacon has banished from all the schools of philosophy.

For the satisfaction of the first class, we refer them to that argument which has been prosecuted with so much abilhy and success by Bishop Butler, in his Analogy of Natural and Revealed Religion. It is not so much the object of this author to found any positive argument on the accordancy which subsists between the process of the divine administration in nature, and the processes ascribed to God by revelation, as to repel the argument founded upon their supposed discordancy. To one of the second class, the argument of Bishop Butler is not called for; but as to one of the first class, we can conceive nothing more calculated to quiet his difficulties. He believes a God, and he must therefore believe the character and existence of God to be reconcileable with all that he observes in the events and phenomena around him. He questions the claims of the New Testament to be a revelation from heaven, because he conceives, that it ascribes a plan and an economy to the Supreme Being, which are unworthy of his character. We offer no positive solution of this difficulty. We profess ourselves to be too little acquainted with the character of God; and that in this little corner of his works, we see not far enough to offer any decision on the merits of a government, which embraces worlds, and reaches eternity. We think we do enough, if we give a sufficiency of external proof for the New Testament being a true and authentic message from heaven; and that therefore nothing remains for us, but to attend and to submit to it. But the argument of Bishop Butler enables us to do still more than this. It enables us to say, that the very thing objected against in Christianity exists in nature; and that therefore the same God who is the author of nature, may be the author of Christianity. We do not say that any positive evidence can be founded upon this analogy. But in as far as it goes to repel the objection, it is triumphant. A man has no right to retain his theism, if he rejects Christianity upon difficulties to which natural religion is equally liable. If Christianity tells us, that the guilt of a father has brought sufferings and vice upon his posterity, it is what we see exemplified in a thousand instances among the families around us. If it tells us, that the innocent have suffered for the guilty, it is nothing more than what all history and all observation have made perfectly familial to us. If it tells us of one portion of the human race being distinguished by the sovereign will of the Almighty for superior knowledge, or superior privileges, it only adds one inequality more to the many inequalities which we perceive every day in the gifts of nature, of fortune, and of providence. In short, without entering into all the details of that argument, which Butler has brought forward in a way so masterly and decisive, there is not a single impeachment which can be offered against the God of Christianity, that may not, if consistently proceeded upon, be offered against the God of Nature itself; if the one be unworthy of God, the other is equally so; and if in spite of these difficulties, you still retain the conviction, that there is a God of Nature, it is not fair or rational to suffer them to outweigh all that positive evidence and testimony, which have been adduced for proving that the same God is the God of Christianity also.

CHAPTER IX.

On the Way of Proposing the Argument to Atheistical Infidels.

If Christianity be still resisted, it appears to us that the only consistent refuge is Atheism. The very same peculiarities in the dispensation of the Gospel, which lead the infidel to reject it as unworthy of God, go to prove, that nature is unworthy of him, and land us in the melancholy confusion, that whatever theory can be afforded as to the mysterious origin and existence of the things which be, they are not under the dominion of a supreme and intelligent mind. Nor do we look upon Atheism as a more hopeless species of infidelity than Deism, unless in so far as it proves a more stubborn disposition of the heart to resist every religious conviction. Viewed purely as an intellectual subject, we look upon the mind of an Atheist, as in a better state of preparation for the proofs of Christianity than the mind of the Deist. The one is a blank surface, on which evidence may make a fair impression, and where the finger of history may inscribe its credible and well-attested information. The other is occupied with pre-conceptions. It will not take what history offers to it. It puts itself into the same unphilosophical posture, in which the mind of a prejudiced Cartesian opposed its theory of the heavens to the demonstration and measurment of Newton. The theory of the Deist upon a subject where truth is still more inaccessible, and speculation still more presumptuous, sets him to resist the only safe and competent evidence that can be appealed to. What was originally the evidence of observation, and is now transformed into the evidence of testimony, comes down to us in a series of historical documents, the closest and most consistent that all antiquity can furnish. It is the unfortunate theory which forms the grand obstacle to the admission of the Christian miracles, and which leads the Deist to an exhibition of himself so unphilosophical, as that of trampling on the soundest laws of evidence, by bringing an historical fact under the tribunal of a theoretical principle. The Deistical speculation of Rousseau, by which he neutralized the testimony of the first Christians, is as complete a transgression against the temper and principles of true science, as a category of Aristotle when employed to overrule an experiment in chemistry. But however this be, it is evident that Rousseau would have given a readier reception to the Gospel history, had his mind not been pre-occupied with the speculation; and the negative state of Atheism would have been more favourable to the admission of those facts which are connected with the origin and establishment of our religion in the world.

This suggests the way in which the evidence for Christianity should be carried home to the mind of an Atheist. He sees nothing in the phenomena around him, that can warrant him to believe in the existence of a living and intelligent principle, which gave birth and movement to all things. He does not say that he would refuse credit to the existence of God upon sufficient evidence, but he says that there are not such appearances of design in nature, as to supply him with that evidence. He does not deny the existence of God to be a possible truth; but he affirms, that while there is nothing before him but the consciousness of what passes within, and the observation of what passes without, it remains an assertion destitute of proof, and can have no more effect upon his conviction than any other nonentity of the imagination. There is a mighty difference between *not proven* and *disproven*. We see nothing in the argument of the Athiest which goes farther than to establish the former sentence upon the question of God's existence. It is altogether an argument *ab ignorantia;* and the same ignorance which restrains them from asserting in positive terms that God exists, equally restrains them from asserting in positive terms that God does not exist. The assertion may be offered, that, in some distant regions of the creation, there are tracts of space which, instead of being occupied like the tracts around us with suns and planetary systems, teem only with animated beings, who, without being supported like us on the firm surface of a world, have the power of spontaneous movements in free spaces. We cannot say that the assertion is not true, but we can say that it is not proven. It carries in it no positive character either of truth or falsehood, and may therefore be admitted on appropriate and satisfying evidence. But till that evidence comes, the mind is in a state entirely neutral; and such we conceive to be the neutral state of the Atheist, as to what he holds to be the unproved assertion of the existence of God.

To the neutral mind of the Atheist, then, unfurnished as it is with any previous conception, we offer the historical evidence of Christianity. We do not ask him to presume the existence of God. We ask him to examine the miracles of the New Testament merely as recorded events, and to admit no other principle into the investigation, than those which are held to be satisfying and decisive, on any other subject of written testimony. The sweeping principle upon which Rosseau, filled with his own assumptions, condemned the historical evidence for the truth of the Gospel narrative, can have no influence on the blank and unoccupied mind of an Atheist. He has no presumptions upon the subject; for to his eyes the phenomena of nature sit so loose and unconnected with that intelligent Being, to whom they have been referred as their origin, that he does not feel himself entitled, from the phenomena, to ascribe any existence, any character, any attributes, or any method of administration to such a Being. He is therefore in the best possible condition for submitting his understanding to the entire impression of the historical evidence. Those difficulties which perplex the Deist, who cannot recognize in the God of the New Testament the same features and the same principles in which they have invested the God of Nature, are no difficulties to him. He has no God of nature to confront with that real though invisible power which lay at the bottom of those astonishing miracles, on which history has stamped her most authentic characters. Though the power which presided there should be an arbitrary, an unjust, or a malignant being, all this may startle a Deist, but it will not prevent a consistent Atheist from acquiescing in any legitimate inference, to which the miracles of the Gospel, viewed in the simple light of historical facts, may chance to carry him. He cannot bring his antecedent information into play upon this question. He professes to have no antecedent information on the subject; and this sense of his entire ignorance, which lies at the bottom of his Atheism, would expunge from his mind all that is theoretical, and make it the passive recipient of every thing which observation offers to its notice, or which credible testimony has brought down to it of the history of past ages.

What then, we ask, does the Atheist make of the miracles of the New Testament? If he questions their truth, he must do it upon grounds that are purely historical; he is precluded from every other ground by the very principle on which he has rested his Atheism; and we therefore, upon the strength of that testimony which has been already exhibited, press the admission of these miracles as facts. If there be nothing then, in the ordinary phenomena of nature, to infer a God, do these extraordinary phenomena supply him with no argument? Does a voice from heaven make no impression upon him? And we have the best evidence which history can furnish, that such a voice was uttered; "This is my beloved Son in whom I am well pleased." We have the evidence of a fact for the existence of that very Being from whom the voice proceeded, and the evidence of a thousand facts, for a power superior to nature; because, on the impulse of a volition, it counteracted her laws and processes, it allayed the wind, it gave sight to the blind, health to the diseased, and, at the utterance of a voice, it gave life to the dead. The ostensible agent in all these wonderful proceedings gave not only credentials of his power, but he gave such credentials of his honesty, as dispose our understanding to receive his explanation of them. We do not avail ourselves of any other principle than what an Atheist will acknowledge. He understands as well as we do, the natural signs of veracity which lie in the tone, the manner, the countenance, the high moral expression of worth and benevolence, and, above all, in that firm and undaunted constancy, which neither contempt, nor poverty, nor death, could shift from any of its positions. All these claims upon our belief, were accumulated to an unexampled degree in the person of Jesus of Nazareth; and when we couple with them his undoubted miracles, and the manner in which his own personal appearance was followed up by a host of witnesses, who, after a catastrophe which would have proved a death-blow to any cause of imposture, offered themselves to the eye of the public, with the same powers, the same evidence, and the same testimony, it seems impossible to resist his account of the invisible principle, which gave birth and movement to the whole of this wonderful transaction. Whatever Atheism we may have founded on the common phenomena around us, here is a new phenomena which demands our attention,—the testimony of a man who in addition to evidences of honesty more varied and more satisfying than were ever offered by a brother of the species, had a voice from the clouds, and the power of working miracles, to vouch for him. We do not think the account which this man gives of himself can be viewed either with indifference or distrust, and the account is most satisfying. "I proceeded forth, and came from God."—"He whom God hath sent speaketh the words of God."—"Even as the Father said unto me, so I speak." He hath elsewhere said that God was his Father. The existence of God is here laid before us, by an evidence altogether distinct from the natural argument of the schools; and it may therefore be admitted in spite of the deficiency of that argument. From the same pure and unquestionable source we gather our information of his attributes. "God is true."—"God is a spirit." He is omnipotent, "for with God all things are possible." He is intelligent, "for he knoweth what things we have need of." He sees all things, and he directs all things, "for the very hairs of our head are numbered," and "a sparrow falleth not to the ground without his permission."

The evidences of the Christian religion are suited to every species of infidelity. We do not ask the Atheist to furnish himself with any previous conception. We ask him to come as he is; and upon the strength of his own favourite principle, viewing it as a pure intellectual question, and abstracting from the more unmanageable tendencies of the heart and temper, we conceive his understanding to be in a high state of preparation, for taking in Christianity in a far purer and more scriptural form, than can be expected from those whose minds are tainted and pre-occupied with their former speculations.

CHAPTER X.

On the Supreme Authority of Revelation.

If the New Testament be a message from God, it behoves us to make an entire and unconditional surrender of our minds, to all the duty and to all the information which it sets before us.

There is, perhaps, nothing more thoroughly beyond the cognizance of the human faculties, than the truths of religion, and the ways of that mighty and invisible Being who is the object of it; and yet nothing, we will venture to say, has been made the subject of more hardy and adventurous speculation. We make no allusion at present to Deists, who reject the authority of the New Testament, because the plan and the dispensation of the Almighty which is recorded there, is different from that plan and that dispensation which they have chosen to ascribe to him. We speak of Christians, who profess to admit the authority of this record, but who have tainted the purity of their profession by not acting upon its exclusive authority; who have mingled their own thoughts and their own fancy with its information; who, instead of repairing in every question, and in every difficulty, to the principle of "What readest thou," have abridged the sovereignty of this principle, by appealing to others, of which we undertake to make out the incompetency; who, in addition to the word of God, talk also of the reason of the thing, or the standard of orthodoxy; and have in fact brought down the Bible from the high place which belongs to it, as the only tribunal to which the appeal should be made, or from which the decision should be looked for.

But it is not merely among partizans or the advocates of a system, that we meet with this indifference to the authority of what is written. It lies at the bottom of a great deal of that looseness, both in practice and speculation, which we meet with every day in society, and which we often hear expressed in familiar conversation. Whence that list of maxims which are so indolently conceived, but which, at the same time, are so faithfully proceeded upon? "We have all our passions and infirmities; but we have honest hearts, and that will make up for them. Men are not all cast in the same mould. God will not call us to task too rigidly for our foibles; at least this is our opinion, and God can never be so unmerciful, or so unjust, as to bring us to a severe and unforgiving tribunal for the mistakes of the understanding." Now it is not licentiousness in general, which we are speaking against. It is against that sanction which it appears to derive from the self-formed maxims of him who is guilty of it. It is against the principle, that either an error of doctrine, or an indulgence of passion, is to be exempted from condemnation, because it has an opinion of the mind to give it countenance and authority. What we complain of is, that a man no sooner sets himself forward and says, "this is my sentiment," than he conceives that all culpability is taken away from the error, either of practice or speculation, into which he has fallen. The carelessness with which the opinion has been formed, is of no account in the estimate. It is the mere existence of the opinion, which is pleaded in vindication; and under the authority of *our maxim, and our mode of thinking*, every man conceives himself to have a right to his own way and his own peculiarity.

Now this might be all very fair, were there no Bible and no revelation in existence. But it is not fair, that all this looseness, and all this variety, should be still floating in the world, in the face of an authoritative communication from God himself. Had no messsage come to us from the Fountain-head of truth, it were natural enough for every individual mind to betake itself to its own speculation. But a message has come to us, bearing on its forehead every character of authenticity; and is it right now, that the question of our faith, or of our duty, should be committed to the capricious variations of this man's taste, or of that man's fancy? Our maxim, and our sentiment! God has put an authorative stop to all this. He has spoken, and the right or the liberty of speculation no longer remains to us. The question now is, not "What thinkest thou?" In the days of Pagan antiquity, no other question could be put; and to the wretched delusions and idolatries of that period let us see what kind of answer the human mind is capable of making, when left to its own guidance, and its own authority. But we call ourselves Christians, and profess to receive the Bible as the directory of our faith; and the only question in which we are concerned, is, " What is written in the law? how readest thou?"

But there is a way of escaping from this conclusion. No man calling himself a Christian, will ever disown in words the authority of the Bible. Whatever be counted the genuine interpretation, it must be submitted to. But in the act of coming to this interpretation, it will be observed, there is room for the unwarrantable principles which we are attempting to expose. The business of a scripture critic is to give a fair representation of the sense of all its passages as they exist in the original. Now, this is a process which requires some investigation, and it is during the time that this process is carrying on, that the tendencies and antecedent opinions of the mind are suffered to mislead the inquirer from the true principles of the business in which he is employed. The mind and meaning of the author, who is translated, is purely a question of language, and should be decided upon no other principles than those of grammar or philology. Now, what we complain of is, that while this principle is recognized and acted upon in every other composition which has come down to us from antiquity, it has been most glaringly departed from in the case of the Bible; that the meaning of its author, instead of being made singly and entirely a question of grammar, has been made a question of metaphysics, or a question of sentiment; that instead of the argument resorted to being, "such must be the rendering from the structure of the language, and the import and significancy of its phrases," it has been, "such must be the rendering from the analogy of the faith, the reason of the thing, the character of the Divine mind, and the wisdom of all his dispensations." And whether this argument be formally insisted upon or not, we have still to complain, that in reality it has a most decided influence on the understanding of many a Christian; and in this way, the creed which exists in his mind, instead of being a fair transcript of the New Testament, is the result of a compromise which has been made between its authoritative decisions and the speculations of his own fancy.

What is the reason why there is so much more unanimity among critics and grammarians about the sense of any ancient author, than about the sense of the New Testament? Because the one is made purely a question of criticism: the other has been complicated with the uncertain fancies of a daring and presumptuous theology. Could we only dismiss these fancies, sit down like a school-boy to his task, and look upon the study of divinity as a mere work of translation, then we would expect the same unanimity among Christians that we meet with among scholars and literati, about the system of Epicurus or the philosophy of Aristotle. But here lies the distinction between the two cases. When we make out, by a critical examination of the Greek of Aristotle, that such was his meaning, and such his philosophy, the result carries no authority with it, and our mind retains the congenial liberty of its own speculations. But if we make out by a critical examination of the Greek of St. Paul, that such is the theology of the New Testament, we are bound to submit to this theology; and our minds must surrender every opinion, however dear to it. It is quite in vain to talk of the mysteriousness of the subject, as being the cause of the want of unanimity among Christians. It may be mysterious, in reference to our former conceptions. It may be mysterious in the utter impossibility of reconciling it with our own assumed fancies and self-formed principles. It may be mysterious in the difficulty which we feel in comprehending the manner of the doctrine, when we ought to be satisfied with the authoritative revelation which has been made to us of its existence and its truth. But if we could only abandon all our former conceptions, if we felt that our business was to submit to the oracles of God, and that we are not called upon to effect a reconciliation between a revealed doctrine of the Bible, and an assumed or excogitated principle of our own;—then we are satisfied, that we would find the language of the Testament to have as much clear, and precise, and didactic simplicity, as the language of any sage or philosopher that has come down to us.

Could we only get it reduced to a mere question of language, we should look, at no distant period, for the establishment of a pure and unanimous Christianity in the world. But, no. While the mind and the meaning of any philosopher is collected from his words, and these words tried, as to their import and significancy, upon the appropriate principles of criticism, the mind and the meaning of the Spirit of God is not collected upon the same pure and competent principles of investigation. In order to know the mind of the Spirit, the communications of the Spirit, and the expression of these communications in written language, should be consulted. These are the only data upon which the inquiry should be instituted. But, no. Instead of learning the designs and character of the Almighty from his own mouth, we sit in judgment upon them, and make our conjecture of what they should be, take the precedency of his revelation of what they are. We do him the same injustice that we do to an acquaintance, whose proceedings and whose intentions we venture to pronounce upon, while we refuse him a hearing, or turn away from the letter in which he explains himself. No wonder, then, at the want of unanimity among Christians, so long as the question of " What thinkest thou ?" is made the principle of their creed, and, for the safe guidance of criticism, they have committed themselves to the endless caprices of the human intellect. Let the principle of "what thinkest thou" be exploded, and that of "what readest thou" be substituted in its place. Let us take our lesson as the Almighty places it before us, and, instead of being the judge of his conduct, be satisfied with the safer and humbler office of being the interpreter of his language.

Now this principle is not exclusively applicable to the learned. The great bulk of Christians have no access to the Bible in its original languages; but they have access to the common translation, and they may be satisfied by the concurrent testimony of the learned among the different sectaries of this country, that the translation is a good one. We do not confine the principle to critics and translators; we press it upon all. We call upon them not to form their divinity by independent thinking, but to receive it by obedient reading; to take the words as they stand, and submit to the plain English of the Scriptures which lie before them. It is the office of a translator to give a faithful representation of the original. Now that this faithful representation has been given, it is our part to peruse it with care, and to take a fair and a faithful impression of it. It is our part to purify our understanding of all its previous conceptions. We must bring a free and unoccupied mind to the exercise. It must not be the pride or the obstinacy of self-formed opinions, or the haughty independence of him who thinks he has reached the manhood of his understanding. We must bring with us the docility of a child, if we want to gain the kingdom of heaven. It must not be a partial, but an entire and unexcepted obedience. There must be no garbling of that which is entire, no darkening of that which is luminous, no softening down of that which is authoritative or severe. The Bible will allow of no compromise. It professes to be the directory of our faith, and claims a total ascendency over the souls and the understandings of men. It will enter into no composition with us, or our natural principles. It challenges the whole mind as its due, and it appeals to the truth of heaven for the high authority of its sanctions. "Whosoever addeth to, or taketh from, the words of this book, is accursed," is the absolute language in which it delivers itself. This brings us to its terms. There is no way of escaping after this. We must bring every thought into the captivity of its obedience, and as closely as ever lawyer stuck to his document or his extract, must we abide by the rule and the doctrine which this authentic memorial of God sets before us.

Now we hazard the assertion, that with a number of professing Christians, there is not this unexcepted submission of the understanding to the authority of the Bible; and that the authority of the Bible is often modified, and in some cases superseded by the authority of other principles. One of these principles is the reason of the thing. We do not know if this principle would be at all felt or appealed to by the earliest Christians. It may perhaps by the disputations or the philosophising among converted Jews and Greeks, but not certainly by those of whom Paul said, that "not many wise men after the flesh, not many mighty, not many noble, were called." They turned from dumb idols to serve the living and the true God. There was nothing in their antecedent theology which they could have any respect for: nothing which they could confront, or bring into competition with the doctrines of the New Testament. In those days, the truth as it is in Jesus came to the mind of its disciples, recommended by its novelty, by its grandeur, by the power and recency of its evidences, and above all by its vast and evident superiority over the fooleries of a degrading Paganism. It does not occur to us, that men in these circumstances would ever think of sitting in judgment over the mysteries of that sublime faith which had charmed them into an abandonment of their earlier religion. It rather strikes us, that they would receive them passively; that, like scholars who had all to learn, they would take their lesson as they found it; that the information of their teachers would be enough for them; and that the restless tendency of the human mind to speculation, would for a time find ample enjoyment in the rich and splendid discoveries, which broke like a flood of light upon the world. But we are in different circumstances. To us, these discoveries, rich and splendid as they are, have lost the freshness of novelty. The sun of righteousness, like the sun of the firmament, has become familiarized to us by possession. In a few ages, the human mind deserted its guidance, and rambled as much as ever in quest of new speculations. It is true, that they took a juster and loftier flight since the days of Heathenism. But it was only because they walked in the light of revelation. They borrowed of the New Testament without acknowledgment, and took its beauties and its truths to deck their own wretched fancies and self-constituted systems. In the process of time, the delusion multiplied and extended. Schools were formed, and the ways of the Divinity were as confidently theorized upon, as the processes of chemistry, or the economy of the heavens. Universities were endowed, and natural theology took its place in the circle of the sciences. Folios were written, and the respected luminaries of a former age poured their *a priori* and their *a posteriori* demonstrations on the world. Taste, and sentiment, and imagination, grew apace; and every raw untutored principle which poetry could clothe in prettiness, or over which the hand of genius could throw the graces of sensibility and elegance, was erected into a principle of the divine government, and made to preside over the counsels of the Deity. In the mean time, the Bible which ought to supersede all, was itself superseded. It was quite in vain to say that it was the only authentic record of an actual embassy which God had sent into the world. It was quite in vain to plead its testimonies, its miracles, and the unquestionable fulfilment of its prophecies. These mighty claims must lie over, and be suspended, till we have settled —what? the reasonableness of its doctrines. We must bring the theology of God's ambassador to the bar of our self-formed theology. The Bible, instead of being admitted as the directory of our faith upon its external evidences, must be tried upon the merits of the work itself; and if our verdict be favorable, it must be brought in, not as a help to our ignorance, but as a corollary to our demonstrations. But is this ever done? Yes! by Dr. Samuel Clarke, and a whole host of followers and admirers. Their first step in the process of theological study, is to furnish their minds with the principles of natural theology. Christianity, before its external proofs are looked at or listened to, must be brought under the tribunal of these principles. All the difficulties which attach to the reason of the thing, or the fitness of the doctrines, must be formally discussed, and satisfactorily got over. A voice was heard from heaven, saying of Jesus Christ, "This is my beloved Son, hear ye him." The men of Galilee saw him ascend from the dead to the heaven which he now occupies. The men of Galilee gave their testimony; and it is a testimony which stood the fiery trial of persecution in a former age, and of sophistry in this. And yet, instead of hearing Jesus Christ as disciples, they sit in authority over him as judges. Instead of forming their divinity after the Bible, they try the Bible by their antecedent divinity; and this book, with all its mighty train of evidences, must drivel in their anti-chambers, till they have pronounced sentence of admission, when they have got its doctrines to agree with their own airy and unsubstantial speculations.

We do not condemn the exercise of reason in matters of theology. It is the part of reason to form its conclusions, when it has data and evidences before it. But it is equally the part of reason to abstain from its conclusions, when these evidences are wanting. Reason can judge of the external evidences for Christianity, because it can discern the merits of human testimony: and it can perceive the truth or the falsehood of such obvious credentials as the performance of a miracle, or the fulfilment of a prophecy. But reason is not entitled to sit in judgment over those internal evidences, which many a presumptuous theologian has attempted to derive from the reason of the thing, or from the agreement of the doctrine with the fancied character and attributes of the Deity. One of the most useful exercises of reason, is to ascertain its limits, and to keep within them; to abandon the fields of conjecture, and to restrain itself within that safe and certain barrier which forms the boundary of human experience. However humiliating you may conceive it, it is this which lies at the bottom of Lord Bacon's philosophy, and it is to this that modern science is indebted for all her solidity, and all her triumphs. Why does philosophy flourish in our days? Because her votaries have learned to abandon their own creative speculations, and to submit to evidence, let her conclusions be as painful and as unpalatable as they will. Now all that we want, is to carry the same lesson and the same principle into theology. Our business is not to guess, but to learn. After we have established Christianity to be an authentic message from God upon those historical grounds on which the reason and experience of man entitle him to form his conclusions,—nothing remains for us, but an unconditional surrender of the mind to the subject of the message. We have a right to sit in judgment over the credentials of heaven's ambassador, but we have no right to sit in judgment over the information he gives us. We have no right either to refuse or to modify that information, till we have accommodated it to our previous conceptions.

It is very true that if the truths which he delivered lay within the field of human observation, he brings himself under the tribunal of our antecedent knowledge. Were he to tell us, that the bodies of the planetary system moved in orbits which are purely circular, we would oppose to him the observations and measurements of astronomy. Were he to tell us, that in winter the sun never shone, and that in summer no cloud ever darkened the brilliancy of his career, we would oppose to him the certain remembrances, both of ourselves and of our whole neighbourhood. Were he to tell us, that we were perfect men, because we were free from passion, and loved our neighbours as ourselves, we should oppose to him the history of our own lives, and the deeply-seated consciousness of our own infirmities. On all these subjects, we can confront him; but when he brings truth from a quarter which no human eye ever explored; when he tells us the mind of the Deity, and brings before us the counsels of that invisible Being, whose arm is abroad upon all worlds, and whose views reach to eternity, he is beyond the ken of eye or of telescope, and we must submit to him. We have no more right to sit in judgment over his information, than we have to sit in judgment over the information of any other visitor, who lights upon our planet, from some distant and unknown part of the universe, and tells us what worlds roll in those remote tracts which are beyond the limits of our astronomy, and how the Divinity peoples them with wonders. Any previous conceptions of ours are of no more value than the fooleries of an infant; and should we offer to resist or to modify upon the strength of these conceptions, we would be as unsound and as unphilosophical as ever schoolman was with his categories, or Cartesian with his whirlpools of ether.

Let us go back to the first Christians of the Gentile world. They turned from dumb idols to serve the living and the true God. They made a simple and entire transition from a state as bad, if not worse, than that of entire ignorance, to the Christianity of the New Testament. Their previous conceptions instead of helping them, behoved to be utterly abandoned; nor was there that intermediate step which so many of us think to be necessary, and which we dignify with the name of the rational theology of nature. In those days this rational theology was unheard of; nor have we the slightest reason to believe that they were initiated into its doctrines, before they were looked upon as fit to be taught the peculiarities of the Gospel. They were translated at once from the absurdities of Paganism to that Christianity which has come down to us in the records of the evangelical history, and the epistles which their teachers addressed to them. They saw the miracles; they acquiesced in them, as satisfying credentials of an inspired teacher; they took the whole of their religion from his mouth; their faith came by hearing, and hearing by the words of a divine messenger. This was their process, and it ought to be ours. We do not see the miracles, but we see their reality through the medium of that clear and unsuspicious testimony which has been handed down to us. We should admit them as the credentials of an embassy from God. We should take the whole of our religion from the records of this embassy; and, renouncing the idolatry of our own self-formed conceptions, we should repair to that word which was spoken to them that heard it, and transmitted to us by the instrumentality of written language. The question with them was, What hearest thou? The question with us is, What readest thou? They had their idols, and they turned away from them. We have our fancies, and we contend, that, in the face of an authoritative revelation from heaven it is as glaring idolatry in us to adhere to them, as it would be were they spread out upon canvass, or chiselled into material form by the hands of a statuary.

In the popular religions of antiquity, we see scarcely the vestige of a resemblance to that academical theism which is delivered in our schools, and figures away in the speculations of our moralists. The process of conversion among the first Christians was a very simple one. It consisted of an utter abandonment of their heathenism, and an entire submission to those new truths which came to them through the revelation of the Gospel, and through it only. It was the pure theology of Christ and of his apostles. That theology which struts in fancied demonstration from a professor's chair, formed no part of it. They listened as if they had all to learn: we listen as if it was our office to judge, and to give the message of God its due place and subordination among the principles which we had previously established. Now these principles were utterly unknown at the first publication of Christianity. The Galatians, and Corinthians, and Thessalonians, and Philippians, had no conception of them. And yet, will any man say, that either Paul himself, or those who lived under his immediate tuition, had not enough to make them accomplished Christians, or that they fell short of our enlightened selves, in the wisdom which prepares for eternity, because they wanted our rational theology as a stepping-stone to that knowledge which came, in pure and immediate revelation, from the Son of God? The Gospel was enough for them, and it should be enough for us also. Every natural or assumed principle, which offers to abridge its supremacy, or even so much as to share with it in authority and direction, should be instantly discarded. Every opinion in religion should be reduced to the question of, What readest thou? and the Bible be acquiesced in, and submitted to, as the alone directory of our faith, where we can get the whole will of God for the salvation of man.

But is not this an enlightened age? and, since the days of the Gospel, has not the wisdom of two thousand years accumulated upon the present generation? has not science been enriched by discovery? and is not theology one of the sciences? Are the men of this advanced period to be restrained from the high exercise of their powers? and, because the men of a remote and barbarous antiquity lisped and drivelled in the infancy of their acquirements, is that any reason why we should be restricted like so many school-boys to the lesson that is set before us? It is all true that this is a very enlightened age; but on what field has it acquired so flattering a distinction? On the field of experiment. The human mind owes all its progress to the confinement of its efforts within the safe and certain limits of observation, and to the severe restraint which it has imposed upon its speculative tendencies. Go beyond these limits, and the human mind has not advanced a single inch by its own independent exercises. All the philosophy which has been reared by the labour of successive ages, is the philosophy of facts reduced to general laws, or brought under a general description from observed points of resemblance. A proud and wonderful fabric we do allow; but we throw away the very instrument by which it was built, the moment that we cease to observe, and begin to theorise and excogitate. Tell us a single discovery which has thrown a particle of light on the details of the divine administration. Tell us a single truth in the whole field of experimental science, which can bring us to the moral government of the Almighty by any other road than his own revelation.

Astronomy has taken millions of suns and of systems within its ample domain; but the ways of God to man stand at a distance as inaccessible as ever; nor has it shed so much as a glimmering over the counsels of that mighty and invisible Being, who sits in high authority over all worlds. The boasted discoveries of modern science are all confined to that field, within which the senses of man can expatiate. The moment we go beyond this field, they cease to be discoveries, and are the mere speculations of the fancy. The discoveries of modern science have, in fact, imparted a new energy to the sentiment in question. They all serve to exalt the Deity, but they do not contribute a single iota to the explanation of his purposes. They make him greater, but they do not make him more comprehensible. He is more shrouded in mystery than ever. It is not himself whom we see, it is his workmanship; and every new addition to its grandeur or to its variety, which philosophy opens to our contemplation, throws our understanding at a greater distance than before, from the mind and conception of the sublime Architect. Instead of the God of a single world, we now see him presiding in all the majesty of his high attributes, over a mighty range of innumerable systems. To our little eye he is wrapt in more awful mysteriousness, and every new glimpse which astronomy gives us of the universe, magnifies to the apprehension of our mind, that impassable barrier which stands between the counsels of its Sovereign, and those fugitive beings who strut their evanescent hour in the humblest of its mansions. If this invisible Being would only break that mysterious silence in which he has wrapt himself, we feel that a single word from his mouth, would be worth a world of darkling speculations. Every new triumph which the mind of man achieves in the field of discovery, binds us more firmly to our Bible; and by the very proportion in which philosophy multiplies the wonders of God, do we prize that book, on which the evidence of history has stamped the character of his authentic communication.

The course of the moon in the heavens has exercised astronomers for a long series of ages, and now that they are able to assign all the irregularities of its period, it may be counted one of the most signal triumphs of the modern philosophy.

The question lay within the limits of the field of observation. It was accessible to measurement, and, upon the sure principles of calculation, men of science have brought forward the confident solution of a problem, the most difficult and trying that ever was submitted to the human intellect. But let it never be forgotten, that those very maxims of philosophy which guided them so surely and so triumphantly within the field of observation, also restrained them from stepping beyond it; and though none were more confident than they, whenever they had evidence and experiment to enlighten them, yet none were more scrupulous in abstaining to pronounce upon any subject, where evidence and experiment were wanting. Let us suppose that one of their number, flushed with the triumph of success, passed on from the work of calculating the periods of the moon, to theorise upon its chemical constitution. The former question lies within the field of observation, the other is most thoroughly beyond it; and there is not a man, whose mind is disciplined to the rigour and sobriety of modern science, that would not look upon the theory with the same contempt, as if it were the dream of a poet, or the amusement of a schoolboy. We have heard much of the moon, and of the volcanoes which blaze upon its surface. Let us have incontestible evidence, that a falling stone proceeds from the eruption of one of those volcanoes, and the chemistry of the moon will receive more illustration from the analysis of that stone, than from all the speculations of all the theorists. It brings the question in part within the limits observation. It now becomes a fair subject for the exercise of the true philosophy. The eye can now see, and the hand can now handle it; and the information furnished by the laborious drudgery of experimental men, will be received as a truer document, than the theory of any philosopher, however ingenious, or however splendid.

At the hazard of being counted fanciful, we bring forward the above as a competent illustration of the principle which we are attempting to establish. We do all homage to modern science, nor do we dispute the loftiness of its pretensions. But we maintain, that however brilliant its career in those tracks of philosophy, where it has the light of observation to conduct it, the philosophy of all that lies without the field of observation is as obscure and inaccesible as ever. We maintain, that to pass from the motions of the moon to an unauthorised speculation upon the chemistry of its materials, is a presumption disowned by philosophy. We ought to feel, that it would be a still more glaring transgression of all her maxims, to pass from the brightest discovery in her catalogue, to the ways of that mysterious Being, whom no eye hath seen, and whose mind is capacious as infinity. The splendour and the magnitude of what we do know, can never authorise us to pronounce upon what we do not know; nor can we conceive a transition more violent or more unwarrantable, than to pass from the truths of natural sience to a speculation on the details of God's administration, or on the economy of his moral government. We hear much of revelations from heaven. Let any one of these bear the evidence of an actual communication from God himself, and all the reasonings of all theologians must vanish, and give place to the substance of this communication. Instead of theorising upon the nature and properties of that divine light which irradiates the throne of God, and exists at so immeasurable a distance from our faculties, let us point our eyes to that emanation, which has actually come down to us. Instead of theorising upon the counsels of the divine mind, let us go to that volume which lighted upon our world nearly two thousand years ago, and which bears the most authentic evidence, that it is the depository of part of these counsels. Let us apply the proper instrument to this examination. Let us never conceive it to be a work of speculation or fancy. It is a pure work of grammatical analysis. It is an unmixed question of language. The commentator who opens this book with the one hand, and carries his system in the other, has nothing to do with it. We admit of no other instrument than the vocabulary and the lexicon. The man whom we look to is the scripture critic, who can appeal to his authorities for the import and significancy of phrases, and whatever be the strict result of his patience and profound philology, we submit to it. We call upon every enlightened disciple of Lord Bacon to approve the steps of this process, and to acknowledge, that the same habits of philosophising to which science is indebted for all her elevation in these latter days, will lead us to cast down all our lofty imaginations, and bring into captivity every thought to the obedience of Christ.

But something more remains to be done. The mind may have discernment enough to acquiesce in the speculative justness of a principle; but it may not have vigour or consistency enough to put it into execution. Lord Bacon pointed out the method of true philosophising; yet, in practice, he abandoned it, and his own physical investigations may be ranked among the most effectual specimens of that rash and unfounded theorising, which his own principles have banished from the schools of philosophy. Sir Isaac Newton completed in his own person the character of the true philosopher. He not only saw the general principle, but he obeyed it. He both betook himself to the drudgery of observation, and he endured the pain which every mind must suffer in the act of renouncing its old habits of conception. We call upon our readers to have manhood and philosophy enough to make a similar sacrifice. It is not enough that the Bible be acknowledged as the only authentic source of information respecting the details of that moral economy, which the Supreme Being has instituted for the government of the intelligent beings who occupy this globe. Its authenticity must be something more than acknowledged. It must be felt, and, in act and obedience, submitted to. Let us put them to the test. "Verily I say unto you," says our Saviour, "unless a man shall be born again, he shall not enter into the kingdom of God." "By grace ye are saved through faith, and that not of yourselves, it is the gift of God." "Justified freely by his grace through the redemption that is in Christ Jesus, whom God has set forth to be a propitiation through faith in his blood." We need not multiply quotations; but if there be any repugnance to the obvious truths which we have announced to the reader in the language of the Bible, his mind is not yet tutored to the philosophy of the subject. It may be in the way, but the final result is not yet arrived at. It is still a slave to the elegance or the plausibility of its old speculations; and though it admits the principle, that every previous opinion must give way to the supreme authority of an actual communication from God, it wants consistency and hardihood to carry the principle into accomplishment.

DISCOURSES

ON

THE CHRISTIAN REVELATION,

VIEWED IN CONNEXION WITH

THE MODERN ASTRONOMY.

PREFACE.

THE astronomical objection against the truth of the Gospel does not occupy a very prominent place in any of our Treatises of Infidelity. It is often, however, met with in conversation—and we have known it to be the cause of serious perplexity and alarm in minds anxious for the solid establishment of their religious faith.

There is an imposing splendour in the science of astronomy; and it is not to be wondered at, if the light it throws, or appears to throw, over other tracks of speculation than those which are properly its own, should at times dazzle and mislead an inquirer. On this account we think it were a service to what we deem a true and a righteous cause, could we succeed in dissipating this illusion; and in stripping Infidelity of those pretensions to enlargement, and to a certain air of philosophical greatness, by which it has often become so destructively alluring to the young, and the ardent, and the ambitious.

In my first Discourse, I have attempted a sketch of the Modern Astronomy—nor have I wished to throw any disguise over that comparative littleness which belongs to our planet, and which gives to the argument of Freethinkers all its plausibility.

This argument involves in it an assertion and an inference. The assertion is, that Christianity is a religion which professes to be designed for the single benefit of our world; and the inference is, that God cannot be the author of this religion, for he would not lavish on so insignificant a field, such peculiar and such distinguishing attentions as are ascribed to him in the Old and New Testament.

Christianity makes no such profession. That it is designed for the single benefit of our world, is altogether a presumption of the Infidel himself—and feeling that this is not the only example of temerity which can be charged on the enemies of our faith, I have allotted my second Discourse to the attempt of demonstrating the utter repugnance of such a spirit with the cautious and enlightened philosophy of modern times.

In the course of this Sermon I have offered a tribute of acknowledgment to the theology of Sir Isaac Newton; and in such terms, as if not farther explained, may be liable to misconstruction. The grand circumstance of applause in the character of this great man, is, that unseduced by all the magnificence of his own discoveries, he had a solidity of mind which could resist their fascination, and keep him in steady attachment to that book whose general evidences stamped upon it the impress of a real communication from heaven. This was the sole attribute of his theology which I had in my eye when I presumed to eulogize it.

I do not think, that, amid the distraction and the engrossment of his other pursuits, he has at all times succeeded in his interpretation of the book; else he would never, in my apprehension, have abetted the leading doctrine of a sect, or a system, which has now nearly dwindled away from public observation.

In my third Discourse I am silent as to the assertion and attempt to combat the inference that is founded on it. I insist, that upon all the analogies of nature and of providence, we can lay no limit on the condescension of God, or on the multiplicity of his regards even to the very humblest departments of creation; and that it is not for us, who see the evidences of divine wisdom and care spread in such exhaustless profusion around, to say, that the Deity would not lavish all the wealth of his wondrous attributes on the salvation even of our solitary species.

At this point of the argument I trust that the intelligent reader may be enabled to perceive in the adversaries of the gospel, a twofold dereliction from the maxims of the Baconian philosophy; that, in the first instance, the assertion which forms the groundwork of their argument, is gratuitously fetched out of an unknown region where they are utterly abandoned by the light of experience; and that, in the second instance, the inference they urge from it, is in the face of manifold and undeniable truths, all lying within the safe and accessible field of human observation.

In my subsequent Discourses, I proceed to the informations of the record. The infidel objection, drawn from astronomy, may be considered as by this time disposed of; and if we have succeeded in clearing it away, so as to deliver the Christian testimony from all discredit upon this ground, then may we submit, on the strength of other evidences, to be guided by its information. We shall thus learn, that Christianity has a far more extensive bearing on the other orders of creation than the infidel is disposed to allow; and whether he will own the authority of this information or not, he will at least be forced to admit, that the subject matter of the Bible itself is not chargeable with that objection which he has attempted to fasten upon it.

Thus, had my only object been the refutation of the Infidel argument, I might have spared the last Discourses of the Volume altogether. But the tracts of Scriptural information to which they directed me, I considered as worthy of prosecution on their own account—and I do think, that much may be gathered from these less observed portions of the field of revelation, to cheer, and to elevate, and to guide the believer.

But, in the management of such a discussion as this, though for a great degree of this effect it would require to be conducted in a far higher style than I am able to sustain, the taste of the human mind may be regaled, and its understanding put into a state of the most agreeable exercise. Now, this is quite distinct from the conscience being made to feel the force of a personal application; nor could I either bring this argument to its close in the pulpit, or offer it to the general notice of the world, without adverting, in the last Discourse, to a delusion which, I fear, is carrying forward thousands, and tens of thousands to an undone eternity.

I have closed the volume with an Appendix of Scriptural authorities. I found that I could not easily interweave them in the texture of the Work, and have, therefore, thought fit to present them in a separate form. I look for a twofold benefit from this exhibition—first, on those more general readers, who are ignorant of the Scriptures, and of the riches and variety which abound in them—and, secondly, on those narrow and intolerant professors, who take an alarm at the very sound and semblance of philosophy, and feel as if there was an utter irreconcileable antipathy between its lessons on the one hand, and the soundness and piety of the Bible on the other. It were well, I conceive, for our cause, that the latter could become a little more indulgent on this subject; that they gave up a portion of those ancient and hereditary prepossessions, which go so far to cramp and to enthral them; that they would suffer theology to take that wide range of argument and of illustration which belongs to her; and that less, sensitively jealous of any desecration being brought upon the Sabbath, or the pulpit, they would suffer her freely to announce all those truths, which either serve to protect Christianity from the contempt of science, or to protect the teachers of Christianity from those invasions which are practised both on the sacredness of the office, and on the solitudes of its devotional and intellectual labours.

I shall only add, for the information of readers at a distance, that these Discourses were chiefly delivered on the occasion of the week-day sermon that is preached in rotation by the Ministers of Glasgow.

DISCOURSE I.

A Sketch of the Modern Astronomy.

"When I consider thy heavens, the work of thy fingers, the moon and the stars, which thou hast ordained; What is man, that thou art mindful of him? and the son of man, that thou visitest him."

Psalm viii. 3, 4.

In the reasonings of the Apostle Paul, we cannot fail to observe how studiously he accommodates his arguments to the pursuits, or principles, or prejudices of the people whom he was addressing. He often made a favourite opinion of their own the starting point of his explanation; and educing a dexterous but irresistible train of argument from some principle upon which each of the parties had a common understanding, did he force them out of all their opposition, by a weapon of their own choosing—nor did he scruple to avail himself of a Jewish peculiarity, or a heathen superstition, or a quotation from Greek poetry, by which he might gain the attention of those whom he labored to convince, and by the skilful application of which he might "shut them up unto the faith."

Now, when Paul was thus addressing one class of an assembly or congregation, another class might, for the time, have been shut out of all direct benefit and application from his arguments. When he wrote an Epistle to a mixed assembly of Christianised Jews and Gentiles, he had often to direct such a process of argument to the former, as the latter would neither require nor comprehend. Now, what should have been the conduct of the Gentiles at the reading of that part of the Epistle which bore almost an exclusive reference to the Jews? Should it be impatience at the hearing of something for which they had no relish or understanding? Should it be a fretful disappointment, because every thing that was said, was not said for their edification? Should it be angry discontent with the Apostle, because, leaving them in the dark, he had brought forward nothing for them, through the whole extent of so many successive chapters? Some of them may have felt in this way; but surely it would have been vastly more Christian to have sat with meek and unfeigned patience, and to have rejoiced that the great Apostle had undertaken the management of those obstinate prejudices which kept back so many human beings from the participation of the Gospel. And should Paul have had reason to rejoice, that, by the success of his arguments, he had reconciled one or any number of Jews to Christianity, then it was the part of these Gentiles, though receiving no direct or personal benefit from the arguments, to have blessed God, and rejoiced along with him.

Conceive that Paul were at this moment alive, and zealously engaged in the work of pressing the Christian religion on the acceptance of the various classes of society. Should he not still have acted on the principle of being all things to all men? Should he not have accommodated his discussion to the prevailing taste, and literature, and philosophy of the times? Should he not have closed with the people, whom he was addressing, on some favourite principle of their own; and, in the prosecution of this principle, might he not have got completely beyond the comprehension of a numerous class of zealous, humble, and devoted Christians? Now, the question is not, how these would conduct themselves in such circumstances? but how should they do it? Would it be right in them to sit with impatience, because the argument of the apostles contained in it nothing in the way of comfort or edification to themselves? Should not the benevolence of the Gospel give a different direction to their feelings? And, instead of that narrow, exclusive, and monopolizing spirit, which I fear is too characteristic of the more declared professors of the truth as it is in Jesus, ought they not to be patient, and to rejoice; when to philosophers, and to men of literary accomplishment, and to those who have the direction of the public taste among the upper walks of society, such arguments are addressed as may bring home to their acceptance also, "the words of this life?" It is under the impulse of these considerations, that I have, with some hesitation, prevailed upon my self to attempt an argument which I think fitted to soften and subdue those prejudices which lie at the bottom of what may be called the infidelity of natural science; if possible to bring over to the humility of the Gospel, those who expatiate with delight on the wonders and sublimities of creation; and to convince them that a loftier wisdom still than that even of their high and honourable acquirements, is the wisdom of him who is resolved to know nothing but Jesus Christ, and him crucified.

It is truly a most Christian exercise to extract a sentiment of piety from the works and the appearances of nature. It has the authority of the Sacred Writers upon its side, and even our Saviour himself gives it the weight and the solemnity of his example. "Behold the lilies of the field; they toil not, neither do they spin, yet your heavenly Father careth for them." He expatiates on the beauty of a single flower, and draws from it the delightful argument of confidence in God. He gives us to see that taste may be combined with piety, and that the same heart may be occupied with all that is serious in the contemplations of religion, and be at the same time alive to the charms and the loveliness of nature.

The Psalmist takes a still loftier flight. He leaves the world, and lifts his imagination to that mighty expanse which spreads above it and around it. He wings his way through space, and wanders in thought over its immeasurable regions. Instead of a dark and unpeopled solitude, he sees it crowded with splendour, and filled with the energy of the Divine presence. Creation rises in its immensity before him, and the world, with all which it inherits, shrinks into littleness at a contemplation so vast and so overpowering. He wonders that he is not overlooked amid the grandeur and the variety which are on every side of him, and passing upward from the majesty of nature to the majesty of nature's Architect, he exclaims, "What is man that thou art mindful of him, or the son of man that thou shouldest deign to visit him?"

It is not for us to say, whether inspiration revealed to the Psalmist the wonders of the modern astronomy. But even though he mind be a perfect stranger to the science of these enlightened times, the heavens present a great and an elevating spectacle; an immense concave reposing upon the circular boundary of the world, and the innumerable lights which are suspended from on high, moving with solemn regularity along its surface. It seems to have been at night that the piety of the Psalmist was awakened by this contemplation, when the moon and the stars were visible, and not when the sun had risen in his strength, and thrown a splendour around him, which bore down and eclipsed all the lesser glories of the firmament. And there is much in the scenery of a nocturnal sky, to lift the soul to pious contemplation. That moon, and these stars, what are they? They are detached from the world, and they lift you above it. You feel withdrawn from the earth, and rise in lofty abstraction above this little theatre of human passions and human anxieties. The mind abandons itself to reverie, and is transferred, in the ecstacy of its thoughts, to distant and unexplored regions. It sees nature in the simplicity of her great elements, and it sees the God of nature invested with the high attributes of wisdom and majesty.

But what can these lights be? The curiosity of the human mind is insatiable, and the mechanism of these wonderful heavens has, in all ages, been its subject and its employment. It has been reserved for these latter times, to resolve this great and interesting question. The sublimest powers of philosophy have been called to the exercise, and astronomy may now be looked upon as the most certain and best established of the sciences.

We all know that every visible object appears less in magnitude as it recedes from the eye. The lofty vessel as it retires from the coast, shrinks into littleness, and at last appears in the form of a small speck on the verge of the horizon. The eagle with its expanded wings, is a noble object; but when it takes its flight into the upper regions of the air, it becomes less to the eye, and is seen like a dark spot upon the vault of heaven. The same is true of all magnitude. The heavenly bodies appear small to the eye of an inhabitant of this earth, only from the immensity of their distance. When we talk of hundreds of millions of miles, it is not to be listened to as incredible. For remember that we are talking of those bodies which are scattered over the immensity of space, and that space knows no termination. The conception is great and difficult, but the truth is unquestionable. By a process of measurement which it is unnecessary at present to explain, we have ascertained first the distance, and then the magnitude of some of those bodies which roll in the firmament; that the sun, which presents itself to the eye under so diminutive a form, is really a globe, exceeding, by many thousands of times, the dimensions of the earth which we inhabit; that the moon itself has the magnitude of a world; and that even a few of those stars, which appear like so many lucid points to the unassisted eye of the observer, expand into large circles upon the application of the telescope, and are some of them much larger than the ball which we tread upon, and to which we proudly apply the denomination of the universe.

Now, what is the fair and obvious presumption? The world in which we live, is a round ball of a determined magnitude, and occupies its own place in the firmament. But when we explore the unlimited tracts of that space, which is every where around us, we meet with other balls of equal or superior magnitude, and from which our earth would either be invisible, or appear as small as any of those twinkling stars which are seen on the canopy of heaven. Why then suppose that this little spot, little at least in the immensity which surrounds it, should be the exclusive abode of life and of intelligence? What reason to think that those mightier globes which roll in other parts of creation, and which we have discovered to be worlds in magnitude, are not also worlds in use and in dignity? Why should we think that the great Architect of nature, supreme in wisdom as he is in power, would call these stately mansions into existence, and leave them unoccupied? When we cast our eye over the broad sea, and look at the country on the other side, we see nothing but the blue land stretching obscurely over the distant horizon. We are too far away to perceive the richness of its scenery, or to hear the sound of its population. Why not extend this principle to the still more distant parts of the universe? What though, from this remote point of observation, we can see nothing but the naked roundness of yon planetary orbs? Are we therefore to say, that they are so many vast and unpeopled solitudes; that desolation reigns in every part of the universe but ours; that the whole energy of the divine attributes is expended on one insignificant corner of these mighty works; and that to this earth alone belongs the bloom of vegetation, or the blessedness of life, or the dignity of rational and immortal existence?

But this is not all. We have something more than the mere magnitude of the planets to allege, in favour of the idea that they are inhabited. We know that this earth turns round upon itself; and we observe that all those celestial bodies, which are accessible to such an observation, have the same movement. We know that the earth performs a yearly revolution round the sun; and we can detect in all the planets which compose our system, a revolution of the same kind, and under the same circumstances. They have the same succession of day and night. They have the same agreeable vicissitude of the seasons. To them, light and darkness succeed each other; and the gaiety of summer is followed by the dreariness of winter. To each of them the heavens present as varied and magnificent a spectacle; and this earth the encompassing of which would require the labour of years from one of its puny inhabitants, is but one of the lesser lights which sparkle in their firmament. To them, as well as to us, has God divided the light from the darkness, and he has called the light day, and the darkness he has called night. He has said let there be lights in the firmament of their heaven, to divide the day from the night: and let them be for signs, and for seasons, and for days, and for years; and let them be for lights in the firmament of heaven, to give light upon their earth; and it was so. And God has also made to them great lights. To all of them he has given the sun to rule the day; and to many of them has he given moons to rule the night. To them he has made the stars also. And God has set them in the firmament of heaven, to give light unto their earth; and to rule over the day, and over the night, and to divide the light from the darkness; and God has seen that it was good.

In all these greater arrangements of divine wisdom, we can see that God has done the same things for the accommodation of the planets that he has done for the earth which we inhabit. And shall we say, that the resemblance stops here, because we are not in a situation to observe it? Shall we say, that this scene of magnificence has been called into being, merely for the amusement of a few astronomers? Shall we measure the counsels of heaven by the narrow importance of the human faculties? or conceive, that silence and solitude reign throughout the mighty empire of nature, that the greater part of creation is an empty parade; and that not a worshipper of the Divinity is to be found through the wide extent of yon vast and immeasurable regions?

It lends a delightful confirmation to the argument, when, from the growing perfection of our instruments, we can discover a new point of resemblance between our earth and the other bodies of the planetary system. It is now ascertained, not merely that all of them have their day and night, and that all of them have their vicissitudes of seasons, and that some of them have their moons to rule their night and alleviate the darkness of it. We can see of one, that its surface rises into inequalities, that it swells into mountains and stretches into valleys; of another, that it is surrounded by an atmosphere which may support th respiration of animals; of a third, that clouds are formed and suspended over it, which may minister to it all the bloom and luxuriance of vegetation; and of a fourth, that a white colour spreads over its northern regions, as its winter advances, and that on the approach of summer this whiteness is dissipated—giving room to suppose, that the element of water abounds in it, that it rises by evaporation into its atmosphere, that it freezes upon the application of cold, that it is precipitated in the form of snow, that it covers the ground with a

A SKETCH OF THE MODERN ASTRONOMY.

fleecy mantle, which melts away from the heat of a more vertical sun; and that other worlds bear a resemblance to our own, in the same yearly round of beneficent and interesting changes.

Who shall assign a limit to the discoveries of future ages? Who can prescribe to science her boundaries, or restrain the active and insatiable curiosity of man within the circle of his present acquirements? We may guess with plausibility what we cannot anticipate with confidence. The day may yet be coming, when our instruments of observation shall be inconceivably more powerful. They may ascertain still more decisive points of resemblance. They may resolve the same question by the evidence of sense which is now so abundantly convincing by the evidence of analogy. They may lay open to us the unquestionable vestiges of art, and industry, and intelligence. We may see summer throwing its green mantle over these mighty tracts, and we may see them left naked and colourless after the flush of vegetation has disappeared. In the progress of years, or of centuries, we may trace the hand of cultivation spreading a new aspect over some portion of a planetary surface. Perhaps some large city, the metropolis of a mighty empire, may expand into a visible spot by the powers of some future telescope. Perhaps the glass of some observer, in a distant age, may enable him to construct a map of another world, and to lay down the surface of it in all its minute and topical varieties. But there is no end of conjecture, and to the men of other times we leave the full assurance of what we can assert with the highest probability, that yon planetary orbs are so many worlds, that they teem with life, and that the mighty Being who presides in high authority over this scene of grandeur and astonishment, has there planted worshippers of his glory.

Did the discoveries of science stop here, we have enough to justify the exclamation of the Psalmist, "What is man that thou art mindful of him, or the son of man that thou shouldest deign to visit him?" They widen the empire of creation far beyond the limits which were formerly assigned to it. They give us to see that yon sun, throned in the centre of his planetary system, gives light, and warmth, and the vicissitude of seasons, to an extent of surface several hundreds of times greater than that of the earth which we inhabit. They lay open to us a number of worlds, rolling in their respective circles around this vast luminary—and prove, that the ball which we tread upon, with all its mighty burden of oceans and continents, instead of being distinguished from the others, is among the least of them; and, from some of the more distant planets, would not occupy a more visible point in the concave of their firmament. They let us know, that though this mighty earth, with all its myriads of people, were to sink into annihilation, there are some worlds where an event so awful to us would be unnoticed and unknown, and others where it would be nothing more than the disappearance of a little star which had ceased from its twinkling. We should feel a sentiment of modesty at this just but humiliating representation. We should learn not to look on our earth as the universe of God, but one paltry and insignificant portion of it; that it is only one of the many mansions which the supreme Being has created for the accommodation of his worshippers, and only one of the many worlds rolling in that flood of light which the sun pours around him to the outer limits of the planetary system.

But is there nothing beyond these limits? The planetary system has its boundary, but space has none; and if we wing our fancy there, do we only travel through dark and unoccupied regions? There are only five, or at most six, of the planetary orbs visible to the naked eye. What, then, is that multitude of other lights which sparkle in our firmament, and fill the whole concave of heaven with innumerable splendours? The planets are all attached to the sun; and, in circling around him, they do homage to that influence which binds them to perpetual attendance on this great luminary. But the other stars do not own his dominion. They do not circle around him. To all common observation, they remain immoveable; and each, like the independent sovereign of his own territory, appears to occupy the same inflexible position in the regions of immensity. What can we make of them? Shall we take our adventurous flight to explore these dark and untravelled dominions? What mean these innumerable fires lighted up in distant parts of the universe? Are they only made to shed a feeble glimmering over this little spot in the kingdom of nature? or do they serve a purpose worthier of themselves, to light up other worlds, and give animation to other systems?

The first thing which strikes a scientific observer of the fixed stars, is their immeasurable distance. If the whole planetary system were lighted up into a globe of fire, it would exceed, by many millions of times, the magnitude of this world, and yet only appear a small lucid point from the nearest of them. If a body were projected from the sun with the velocity of a cannon-ball, it would take hundreds of thousands of years before it described that mighty interval which separates the nearest of the fixed stars from our sun and from our system. If this earth, which moves at more than the inconceivable velocity of a million and a half miles a day, were to be hurried from its orbit, and to take the same rapid flight over this immense tract, it would not have arrived at the termination of its journey, after taking all the time which has elapsed since the creation of the world. These are great numbers, and great calculations, and the mind feels its own impotency in attempting to grasp them. We can state them in words. We can exhibit them in figures. We can demonstrate them by the powers of a most rigid and infallible geometry. But no human fancy can summon up a lively or an adequate conception—can roam in its ideal flight over this immeasureable largeness—can take in this mighty space in all its grandeur, and in all its immensity—can sweep the outer boundaries of such a creation—or lift itself up to the majesty of that great and invisible arm, on which all is suspended.

But what can those stars be which are seated so far beyond the limits of our planetary system? They must be masses of immense magnitude, or they could not be seen at the distance of place which they occupy. The light which they give must proceed from themselves, for the feeble reflection of light from some other quarter, would not carry through such mighty tracts to the eye of an observer. A body may be visible in two ways. It may be visible from its own light, as the flame of a candle, or the brightness of a fire, or the brilliancy of yonder glorious sun, which lightens all below, and is the lamp of the world. Or it may be visible from the light which falls upon it, as the body which receives its light from the taper that falls upon it—or the whole assemblage of objects on the surface of the earth, which appear only when the light of day rests upon them—or the moon, which, in that part of it which is towards the sun, gives out a silvery whiteness to the eye of the observer, while the other part forms a black and invisible space in the firmament—or as the planets, which shine only because the sun shines upon them, and which, each of them, present the appearance of a dark spot on the side that is turned away from it. Now apply this question to the fixed stars. Are they luminous of themselves, or do they derive their light from the sun, like the bodies of our planetary system? Think of their immense distance, and the solution of this question becomes evident. The sun, like any other body, must dwindle into a less apparent magnitude as you retire from it. At the prodigious distance even of the very nearest of the fixed stars, it must have shrunk into a small indivisible point. In short, it must have become a star itself, and could shed no more light than a single individual of those glimmering myriads, the whole assemblage of which cannot dissipate, and can scarcely alleviate the midnight darkness of our world. These stars are visible to us, not because the sun shines upon them, but because they shine of themselves, because they are so many luminous bodies scattered over the tracts of immensity; in a word, because they are so many suns each throned in the centre of his own dominions, and pouring a flood of light over his own portion of these unlimitable regions.

At such an immense distance for observation, it is not to be supposed, that we can collect many points of resemblance between the fixed stars, and the solar star which forms the centre of our planetary system. There is one point of resemblance, however, which has not escaped the penetration of our astronomers. We know that our sun turns round upon himself, in a regular period of time. We also know, that there are dark spots scattered over his surface, which, though invisible to the naked eye, are perfectly noticeable by our instruments. If these spots existed in greater quantity upon one side than upon another, it would have the general effect of making that side darker, and the revolution of the sun must, in such a case, give us a brighter and a fainter side, by regular alternations. Now, there are some of the fixed stars which present this appearance. They present us with periodical variations of light. From the splendour of a star of the first or second magnitude, they fade away into some of the inferior magnitudes—and one, by becoming invisible might give reason to apprehend that we had lost him altogether—but we can still recognize him by the telescope, till at length he re-appears in his own place, and, after a regular lapse of so many days and hours, recovers his original brightness. Now, the fair inference from this is, that the fixed stars, as they resemble our sun in being so many luminous masses of immense magnitude, they resemble him in this also, that each of them turns round upon his own axis; so that if any of them should have an inequality in the brightness of their sides, this revolution is rendered evident, by the regular variations in the degree of light which it undergoes.

Shall we say, then, of these vast luminaries, that they were created in vain? Were they called into existence for no other purpose than to throw a tide of useless splendour over the solitudes of immensity? Our sun is only one of these luminaries, and we know that he has worlds in his train. Why should we strip the rest of this princely attendance? Why may not each of them be the centre of his own system, and give light to his own worlds? It is true that we see them not, but could the eye of man take its flight into those distant regions, it should lose sight of our little world, before it reached the outer limits of our system—the greater planets should disappear in their turn—be fore it had described a small portion of that abyss which separates us from the fixed stars, the sun should decline into a little spot, and all its splendid retinue of worlds be lost in the obscurity of distance—he should, at last, shrink into a small indivisible atom, and all that could be seen of this magnificent system, should be reduced to the glimmering of a little star. Why resist any longer the grand and interesting conclusion? Each of these stars may be the token of a system as vast and as splendid as the one which we inhabit. Worlds roll in these distant regions; and these worlds must be the mansions of life and intelligence. In yon gilded canopy of heaven we see the broad aspect of the universe, where each shining point presents us with a sun, and each sun with a system of worlds—where the Divinity reigns in all the grandeur of his attributes—where he peoples immensity with his wonders; and travels in the greatness of his strength through the dominions of one vast and unlimited monarchy.

The contemplation has no limits. If we ask the number of suns and of systems, the unassisted eye of man can take in a thousand, and the best telescope which the genius of man has constructed can take in eighty millions. Fancy may take its flight far beyond the ken of eye or of telescope. Shall we have the boldness to say, that there is nothing there—that the wonders of the Almighty are at an end—that the creative energy of God has sunk into repose, because the imagination is enfeebled by the magnitude of its efforts?

There are two points of interesting speculation, both of which serve to magnify our conceptions of the universe. If a body be struck in the direction of its centre, it obtains a progressive motion, but without any movement of revolution being at the same time impressed upon it. But, again, should the stroke not be in the direction of the centre—should the line which joins the point of percussion to the centre, make an angle with that line in which the impulse was communicated, then the body is both made to go forward in space, also to wheel upon its axis. Thus, each of our planets may have had their compound motion communicated to it by one single impulse; and, on the other hand, if ever the rotatory motion be communicated by one blow, then the progressive motion must go along with it. In order to have the first motion without the second, there must be a twofold force applied to the body in opposite directions. It must be set agoing in the same way as a spinning-top, so as to revolve about an axis, and to keep unchanged its situation in space.

But at this stage of the argument, the matter only remains a conjectural point of speculation. The sun may have had his rotation impressed upon him by a spinning impulse; or, this movement may be coeval with his being, and he may have derived both from an immediate fiat of the Creator. But there is an actually observed phenomenon of the heavens which advances the conjecture into a probability. In the course of age, the stars in one quarter of the celestial sphere are apparently receding from each other; and in the opposite quarter, they are apparently drawing nearer to each other. If the sun be approaching the former and receding from the latter, this phenomenon admits of an easy explanation, and we are furnished with a magnificent step in the scale of the Creator's workmanship. In the same manner as the planets, with their satellites, revolve round the sun, may the sun, with all its tributaries, be moving in common with other stars, around some distant centre, from which there emanates an influence to bind and to subordinate them all. Our sun may, therefore, be only one member of a higher family—taking his part, along with millions of others, in some loftier system of mechanism, by which they are all subjected to one law, and to one arrangement—describing the sweep of such an orbit in space, and completing the mighty revolution in such a period of time, as to reduce our planetary seasons and our planetary movements, to a very humble and fractionary rank in the scale of a higher astronomy. There is room for all this in immensity; and there is even argument for all this in the records of actual observation; and, from the whole of this speculation, do we gather a new emphasis to the lesson, how minute is the place, and how secondary is the importance of our world, amid the glories of such a surrounding magnificence!

Another very interesting tract of speculation, has been opened up to us by the more recent observations of astronomy, the discovery of the *nebulæ*. We allow that it is but a dim and indistinct light which this discovery has thrown upon the structure of the universe; but still it has spread before the eye of the mind a field of very wide and lofty contemplation. Before this the universe might appear to have been composed of an indefinite number of suns, about equidistant from each other, and each encompassed by such a planetary attendance as takes place in our own system. But, it now appears instead of lying uniformly and in a state of equidistance from each other, they are arranged into distinct clusters—that, in the same manner as the distance of the nearest fixed stars, marks the separation of the solar systems, so the distance of two contiguous clusters may be so inconceivably superior to the reciprocal distance of those fixed stars which belong to the same cluster, as to mark an equally distinct separation of the clusters, and to constitute each of them an individual member of some higher and more extended arrangement. This carries us upwards through another ascending step in the scale of magnificence, and there leaves us wildering in the uncertainty, whether even here the wonderful progression is ended; and at all events fixes the assured conclusion in our minds, that, to an eye which could spread itself over the whole, the mansion which accommodates our species might be so very small as to lie wrapped in microscopical concealment; and, in reference to the only Being who possesses this universal eye, well might we say, "What is man that thou art mindful of him, or the son of man that thou shouldest deign to visit him?"

And, after all, though it be a mighty and difficult conception, yet who can question it? What is seen may be nothing to what is unseen; for what is seen is limited by the range of our instruments. What is unseen has no limit; and, though all which the eye of man can take in, or his fancy can grasp at, were swept away, there might still remain as ample a field, over which the Divinity may expatiate, and which he may have peopled with innumerable worlds. If the whole visible creation were to disappear, it would leave a solitude behind it—but to the infinite Mind, that can take in the whole system of nature, this solitude might be nothing, a small unoccupied point in that immensity which surrounds it, and which he may have filled with the wonders of his omnipotence. Though this earth were to be burned up, though the trumpet of its dissolution were sounded, though yon sky were to pass away as a scroll, and every visible glory, which the finger of Divinity has inscribed on it, were to be put out for ever—an event so awful, to us and to every world in our vicinity, by which so many suns would be extinguished, and so many varied scenes of life and of population would rush into forgetfulness—what is it in the high scale of the Almighty's workmanship? a mere shred, which, though scattered into nothing, would leave the universe of God one entire scene of greatness and of majesty. Though this earth, and these heavens, were to disappear, there are other worlds, which roll afar; the light of other suns shines upon them; and the sky which mantles them, is garnished with other stars. Is it presumption to say, that the moral world extends to these distant and unknown regions? that they are occupied with people? that the charities of home and of neighbourhood flourish there? that the praises of God are there lifted up, and his goodness rejoiced in? that piety has its temples and its offerings? and the richness of the divine attributes is there felt and admired by intelligent worshippers?

And what is this world in the immensity which teems with them—and what are they who occupy it? The universe at large would suffer as little, in its splendour and variety, by the destruction of our planet, as the verdure and sublime magnitude of a forest would suffer by the fall of a single leaf. The leaf quivers on the branch which supports it. It lies at the mercy of the slightest accident. A breath of wind tears it from its stem, and it lights on the stream of water which passes underneath. In a moment of time, the life which we know, by the microscope, it teems with, is extinguished; and, an occurrence, so insignificant in the eye of man, and on the scale of his observation, carries in it, to the myriads which people this little leaf, an event as terrible and as decisive as the destruction of a world. Now, on the grand scale of the universe, we, the occupiers of this ball, which performs its little round among the suns and the systems that astronomy has unfolded—we may feel the same littleness and the same insecurity. We differ from the leaf only in this circumstance, that it would require the operation of greater elements to destroy us. But these elements exist. The fire which rages within, may lift its devouring energy to the surface of our planet, and transform it into one wide and wasting volcano. The sudden formation of elastic matter in the bowels of the earth—and it lies within the agency of known substances to accomplish this—may explode it into fragments. The exhalation of noxious air from below, may impart a virulence to the air that is around us; it may affect the delicate proportion of its ingredients; and the whole of animated nature may wither and die under the malignity of a tainted atmosphere. A blazing comet may cross this fated planet in its orbit, and realize all the terrors which superstition has conceived of it. We cannot anticipate with precision the consequences of an event which every astronomer must know to be within the limits of chance and probability. It may hurry our globe towards the sun—or drag it to the outer regions of the planetary system: or give it a new axis of revolution—and the effect which I shall simply announce, without explaining it, would be to change the place of the ocean, and bring another mighty flood upon our islands and continents. These are changes which may happen in a single instant of time, and against which nothing known in the present system of things provides us with any security. They might not annihilate the earth, but they would unpeople it; and we who tread its surface with such firm and assured footsteps, are at the mercy of devouring elements, which, if let loose upon us by the hand of the Almighty, would spread solitude, and silence, and death over the dominions of the world.

Now it is this littleness, and this insecurity which make the protection of the Almighty so dear to us, and bring, with such emphasis, to every pious bosom, the holy lessons of humility and gratitude. The God who sitteth above, and presides in high authority over all worlds, is mindful of man; and, though at this moment his energy is felt in the remotest provinces of creation, we may feel the same security in his providence, as if we were the objects of his undivided care. It is not for us to bring our minds up to this mysterious agency. But, such is the incomprehensible fact, that the same Being, whose eye is abroad over the whole universe, gives vegetation to every blade of grass, and motion to every particle of blood which circulates through the veins of the minutest animal; that, though his mind takes into its comprehensive grasp, immensity and all its wonders, I am as much known to him as if I were the single object of his attention; that he marks all my thoughts; that he gives birth to every feeling and every movement within me; and that, with an exercise of power which I can neither describe nor comprehend, the same God who sits in the highest heaven and reigns over the glories of the firmament, is at my right hand, to give me every breath which I draw, and every comfort which I enjoy.

But this very reflection has been appropriated to the use of infidelity, and the very language of the text has been made to bear an application of hostility to the faith. "What is man, that God should be mindful of him, or the son of man, that he should deign to visit him?" Is it likely, says the Infidel, that God would send his eternal Son to die for the puny occupiers of so insignificant a province in the mighty field of his creation? Are we the befitting objects of so great and so signal an interposition? Does not the largeness of that field which astronomy lays open to the view of modern science, throw a suspicion over the truth of the gospel history; and how shall we reconcile the greatness of that wonderful movement which was made in heaven for the redemption of fallen man, with the comparative meanness and obscurity of our species?

This is a popular argument against Christianity, not much dwelt upon in books, but, we believe, a good deal insinuated in conversation, and having no small influence on the amateurs of a superficial philosophy. At all events, it is right that every such argument should be met, and manfully confronted; nor do we know a more discreditable surrender of our religion, than to act as if she had any thing to fear from the ingenuity of her most accomplished adversaries. The author of the following treatise engages in his present undertaking, under the full impression that a something may be found with which to combat Infidelity in all its forms: that the truth of God and of his message, admits of a noble and decisive manifestation, through every mist which the pride, or the prejudice, or the sophistry of man may throw around it; and elevated as the wisdom of him may be, who has ascended the heights of science, and poured the light of demonstration over the most wondrous of nature's mysteries, that even out of his own principles, it may be proved how much more elevated is the wisdom of him who sits with the docility of a little child, to his Bible, and casts down to its authority all his lofty imaginations.

DISCOURSE II.

The Modesty of True Science.

"And if any man think that he knoweth any thing, he knoweth nothing yet as he ought to know."
1 *Corinthians* vii. 2.

There is much profound and important wisdom in that proverb of Solomon, where it is said, that the heart knoweth its own bitterness. It forms part of a truth still more comprehensive, that every man knoweth his own peculiar feelings, and difficulties, and trials, far better than he can get any of his neighbours to perceive them. It is natural to us all, that we should desire to engross, to the uttermost, the sympathy of others with what is most painful to the sensibilities of our own bosom, and with what is most aggravating in the hardships of our own situation. But, labour it as we may, we cannot, with every power of expression make an adequate conveyance, as it were, of all our sensations, and of all our circumstances, into another understanding. There is a something in the intimacy of a man's own experience, which he cannot make to pass entire into the heart and mind even of the most familiar companion—and thus it is, that he is so often defeated in his attempts to obtain a full and a cordial possession of his sympathy. He is mortified, and he wonders at the obtuseness of the people around him—and how he cannot get them to enter into the justness of his complainings—nor to feel the point upon which turn the truth and the reason of his remonstrances—nor to give their interested attention to the case of his peculiarities and of his wrongs—nor to kindle, in generous resentment along with him, when he starts the topic of his indignation. He does not reflect, all the while that, with every human being he addresses, there is an inner man, which forms a theatre of passions, and of interests, as busy, as crowded, and as fitted as his own to engross the anxious and the exercised feelings of a heart, which can alone understand its own bitterness, and lay a correct estimate on the burden of its own visitations. Every man we meet, carries about with him, in the unperceived solitude of his bosom, a little world of his own—and we are just as blind, and as insensible, and as dull, both of perception and of sympathy about his engrossing objects, as he is about ours; and, did we suffer this observation to have all its weight upon us, it might serve to make us more candid, and more considerate of others. It might serve to abate the monopolizing selfishness of our nature. It might serve to soften down all the malignity which comes out of those envious contemplations that we are so apt to cast on the fancied ease and prosperity which are around us. It might serve to reconcile every man to his own lot, and dispose him to bear, with thankfulness, his own burden; and sure I am, if this train of sentiment were prosecuted with firmness, and calmness, and impartiality, it would lead to the conclusion, that each profession in life has its own peculiar pains, and its own besetting inconveniences; that, from the very bottom of society, up to the golden pinnacle which blazons upon its summit, there is much in the shape of care and of suffering to be found—that, throughout all the conceiveable varieties of human condition, there are trials, which can neither be adequately told on the one side, nor fully understood on the other—that the ways of God to man are as equal in this, as in every department of his administration—and that, go to whatever quarter of human experience we may, we shall find how he has provided enough to exercise the patience, and to accomplish the purposes of a wise and a salutary discipline upon all his children.

I have brought forward this observation, that it may prepare the way for a second. There are perhaps no two sets of human beings, who comprehend less the movements, and enter less into the cares and concerns of each other, than the wide and busy public on the one hand; and, on the other, those men of close and studious retirement, whom the world never hears of, save when, from their thoughtful solitude, there issues forth some splendid discovery, to set the world on a gaze of admiration. Then will the brilliancy of a superior genius draw every eye towards it—and the homage paid to intellectual superiority, will place its idol on a loftier eminence than all wealth or than all titles can bestow—and the name of the successful philosopher will circulate, in his own age, over the whole extent of civilized society, and be borne down to posterity in the characters of ever-during remembrance—and thus it is, that, when we look back on the days of Newton, we annex a kind of mysterious greatness to him, who, by the pure force of his understanding, rose to such a gigantic elevation above the level of ordinary men—and the kings and warriors of other days sink into insignificance around him; and he, at this moment, stands forth to the public eye, in a prouder array of glory than circles the memory of all the men of former generations—and, while all the vulgar grandeur of other days is now mouldering in forgetfulness, the achievements of our great astronomer are still fresh in the veneration of his countrymen, and they carry him forward on the stream of time, with a reputation ever gathering, and the triumphs of a distinction that will never die.

Now, the point that I want to impress upon you is, that the same public, who are so dazzled and overborne by the lustre of all this superiority, are utterly in the dark as to what that is which confers its chief merit on the philosophy of Newton. They see the result of his labours, but they know not how to appreciate the difficulty or the extent of them. They look on the stately edifice he has reared, but they know not what he had to do in settling the foundation which gives to it all its stability—nor are they aware what painful encounters he had to make, both with the natural predilections of his own heart, and with the prejudices of others, when employed on the work of laying together its unperishing materials. They have never heard of the controversies which this man, of peaceful, unambitious modesty, had to sustain, with all that was proud and all that was intolerant in the philosophy of the age. They have never, in thought, entered that closet which was the scene of his patient and profound exercises—nor have they gone along with him, as he gave his silent hours to the labours of the midnight oil, and plied that unwearied task, to which the charm of lofty contemplation had allured him—nor have they accompanied him through all the workings of that wonderful mind, from which, as from the recesses of a laboratory, there came forth such gleams and processes of thought as shed an effulgency over the whole amplitude of nature. All this, the public have not done; for of this the great majority, even of the reading and cultivated public, are utterly incapable; and therefore is it, that they need to be told what that is, in which the main distinction of his philosophy lies; that when labouring in other fields of investigation, they may know how to borrow from his safe example, and how to profit by that superior wisdom which marked the whole conduct of his understanding.

Let it be understood, then, that they are the positive discoveries of Newton, which, in the eye of a superficial public, confer upon him all his reputation. He discovered the mechanism of the planetary system. He discovered the composition of light. He discovered the cause of those alternate movements which take place on the waters of the ocean. These form his actual and his visible achievements. These are what the world look at as the monuments of his greatness. These are doctrines by which he has enriched the field of philosophy; and thus it is that the whole of his merit is supposed to lie in having had the sagacity to perceive, and the vigour to lay hold of the proofs, which conferred upon these doctrines all the establishment of a most rigid and conclusive demonstration.

But, while he gets all his credit, and all his admiration for those articles of science which he has added to the creed of philosophers, he deserves as much credit and admiration for those articles which he kept out of his creed, as for those which he introduced into it. It was the property of his mind, that it kept a tenacious hold of every one position which had proof to substantiate it—but it forms a property equally characteristic, and which, in fact, gives its leading peculiarity to the whole spirit and style of his investigations, that he put a most determined exclusion on every one position that was destitute of such proof. He would not admit the astronomical theories of those who went before him, because they had no proof. He would not give in to their notions about the planets wheeling their rounds in whirlpools of ether—for he did not see this ether—he had no proof of its existence—and, besides, even supposing it to exist, it would not have impressed, on the heavenly bodies, such movements as met his observation. He would not submit his judgment to the reigning systems of the day—for, though they had authority to recommend them, they had no proof: and thus it is, that he evinced the strength and the soundness of his philosophy, as much by his decisions upon those doctrines of science which he rejected, as by his demonstration of those doctrines of science, which he was the first to propose, and which now stand out to the eye of posterity as the only monuments to the force and superiority of his understanding.

He wanted no other recommendation for any one article of science, than the recommendation of evidence—and, with this recommendation, he opened to it the chamber of his mind, though authority scowled upon it, and taste was disgusted by it, and fashion was ashamed of it, and all the beauteous speculation of former days was cruelly broken up by this new announcement of the better philosophy, and scattered like the fragments of an aerial vision, over which the past generations of the world had been slumbering their profound and their pleasing reverie. But, on the other hand, should the article of science want the recommendation of evidence, he shut against it all the avenues of his understanding—aye, and though all antiquity lent their suffrages to it, and all eloquence had thrown around it the most attractive brilliancy, and all habit had incorporated it with every system of every seminary in Europe, and all fancy had arrayed it in graces of the most tempting solicitation; yet was the steady and inflexible mind of Newton proof against this whole weight of authority and allurement, and, casting his cold and unwelcome look at the specious plausibility, he rebuked it from his presence. The strength of his philosophy lay as much in refusing admittance to that which wanted evidence, as in giving a place and an occupancy to that which possessed it. In that march of intellect, which led him onwards through the rich and magnificent field of his discoveries, he pondered every step; and, while he advanced with a firm and assured movement, wherever the light of evidence carried him, he never suffered any glare of imagination or prejudice to seduce him from his path.

Sure I am, that, in the prosecution of his wonderful career, he found himself on a way beset with temptation upon every side of him. It was not merely that he had the reigning taste and philosophy of the times to contend with; but, he expatiated on a lofty region, where, in all the giddiness of success, he might have met with much to solicit his fancy, and tempt him to some devious speculation. Had he been like the majority of other men, he would have broken free from the fetters of a sober and chastised understanding, and, giving wing to his imagination, had done what philosophers have done after him—been carried away by some meteor of their own forming, or found their amusement in some of their own intellectual pictures, or palmed some loose and confident plausibilities of their own upon the world. But Newton stood true to his principle, that he would take up with nothing which wanted evidence, and he kept by his demonstrations, and his measurements, and his proofs; and, if it be true that he who ruleth his own spirit is greater than he who taketh a city, there was won, in the solitude of his chamber, many a repeated victory over himself, which should give a brighter lustre to his name than all the conquests he has made on the field of discovery, or than all the splendour of his positive achievements.

I trust you understand, how, though it be one of the maxims of the true philosophy, never to shrink from a doctrine which has evidence on its side, it is another maxim, equally essential to it, never to harbour any doctrine when this evidence is wanting. Take these two maxims along with you, and you will be at no loss to explain the peculiarity, which, more than any other, goes both to characterise and to ennoble the philosophy of Newton. What I allude to is, the precious combination of its strength and of its modesty. On the one hand, what greater evidence of strength than the fulfilment of that mighty enterprise, by which the heavens have been made its own, and the mechanism of unnumbered worlds has been brought within the grasp of the human understanding? Now, it was by walking in the light of a sound and competent evidence, that all this was accomplished. It was by the patient, the strenuous, the unfaltering application of the legitimate instruments of discovery. It was by touching that which was tangible, and looking to that which was visible, and computing that which was measureable, and in one word, by making a right and a reasonable use of all that proof which the field of nature around us has brought within the limit of sensible observation. This is the arena on which the modern philosophy has won all her victories, and fulfilled all her wondrous achievements, and reared all her proud and enduring monuments, and gathered all her magnificent trophies to that power of intellect with which the hand of a bounteous heaven has so richly gifted the constitution of our species.

But, on the other hand, go beyond the limits of sensible observation, and, from that moment, the genuine disciples of this enlightened school cast all their confidence and all their intrepidity away from them. Keep them on the firm ground of experiment, and none more bold and more decisive in their announcements of all that they have evidence for—but, off this ground, none more humble, or more cautious of any thing like positive announcements, than they. They choose neither to know, nor to believe, nor to assert, where evidence is wanting; and they will sit, with all the patience of a scholar to his task, till they have found it. They are utter strangers to that haughty confidence with which some philosophers of the day sport the plausibilities of unauthorised speculation, and by which, unmindful of the limit that separates the region of sense from the region of conjecture, they make their blind and their impetuous inroads into a province which does not belong to them. There is no one object to which the exercised mind of a true Newtonian disciple is more familiarized than this limit, and it serves as a boundary by which he shapes, and bounds, and regulates, all the enterprises of his philosophy. All the space which lies within this limit, he cultivates to the uttermost, and it is by such successive labours, that every year which rolls over the world, is witnessing some new contribution to experimental science, and adding to the solidity and aggrandizement of this wonderful fabric. But, if true to their own principle, then, in reference to the forbidden ground which lies without this limit, those very men, who, on the field of warranted exertion, evinced all the hardihood and vigour of a full grown understanding, show, on every subject where the light of evidence is withheld from them, all the modesty of children. They give you positive opinion only when they have indisputable proof—but, when they have no such proof, then they have no such opinion. The single principle of their respect to truth, secures their homage for every one position, where the evidence of truth is present, and, at the same time, begets an entire diffidence about every one position, from which this evidence is disjoined. And thus you may understand, how the first man in the accomplishments of philosophy, which the world ever saw, sat at the book of nature in the humble attitude of its interpreter and its pupil—how all the docility of conscious ignorance threw a sweet and softening lustre around the radiance even of his most splendid discoveries—and, while the flippancy of a few superficial acquirements is enough to place a philosopher of the day on the pedestal of his fancied elevation, and to vest him with an assumed lordship over the whole domain of natural and revealed knowledge; I cannot forbear to do honour to the unpretending greatness of Newton, than whom I know not if there ever lighted on the face of our world, one in the character of whose admirable genius so much force and so much humility were more attractively blended.

I now propose to carry you forward, by a few simple illustrations, to the argument of this day. All the sublime truths of th modern astronomy lie within the field of actual observation, and have the firm evidence to rest upon of all that information which is conveyed to us by the avenue of the senses. Sir Isaac Newton never went beyond this field, without a reverential impression upon his mind, of the precariousness of the ground on which he was standing. On this ground, he never ventured a positive affirmation—but, resigning the lofty tone of demonstration, and putting on the modesty of conscious ignorance, he brought forward all he had to say in the humble form of a doubt, or a conjecture, or a question. But, what he had not confidence to do, other philosophers have done after him—and they have winged their audacious way into forbidden regions—and they have crossed that circle by which the field of observation is enclosed—and there have they debated and dogmatized with all the pride of a most intolerant assurance.

Now, though the case be imaginary, let us conceive, for the sake of illustration, that one of these philosophers made so extravagant a departure from the sobriety of experimental science, as to pass from the astronomy of the different planets, and to attempt the natural history of their animal and vegetable kingdoms. He might get hold of some vague and general analogies, to throw an air of plausibility around his speculation. He might pass from the botany of the different regions of the globe that we inhabit, and make his loose and confident application to each of the other planets, according to its distance from the sun, and the inclination of its axis to the plane of its annual revolution; and out of some such slender materials, he may work up an amusing philosophical romance, full of ingenuity, and having, withal, the colour of truth and of consistency spread over it.

I can conceive how a superficial public might be delighted by the eloquence of such a composition, and even be impressed by its arguments; but were I asked, which is the man of all the ages and countries in the world, who would have the least respect for this treatise upon the plants which grow on the surface of Jupiter, I should be at no loss to answer the question. I should say, that it would be he who had computed the motions of Jupiter—that it would be he who had measured the bulk and the density of Jupiter—that it would be he who had estimated the periods of Jupiter—that it would be he whose observant eye and patiently calculating mind, had traced the satellites of Jupiter through all the rounds of their mazy circulation, and unravelled the intricacy of all their movements. He would see at once that the subject lay at a hopeless distance beyond the field of legitimate observation. It would be quite enough for him, that it was beyond the range of his telescope. On this ground, and on this ground only, would he reject it as one of the puniest imbecilities of childhood. As to any character of truth or of importance, it would have no more effect on such a mind as that of Newton, than any illusion of poetry; and from the eminence of his intellectual throne, would he cast a penetrating glance at the whole speculation, and bid its gaudy insignificance away from him.

But let us pass onward to another case, which, though as imaginary as the former, may still serve the purpose of illustration.

This same adventurous philosopher may be conceived to shift his speculation from the plants of another world to the character of its inhabitants. He may avail himself of some slender correspondencies between the heat of the sun and the moral temperament of the people it shines upon. He may work up a theory, which carries on the front of it some of the characters of plausibility: but surely it does not require the philosophy of Newton to demonstrate the folly of such an enterprise. There is not a man of plain understanding, who does not perceive that this said ambitious inquirer has got without his reach—that he has stepped beyond the field of experience, and is now expatiating on the field of imagination—that he has ventured on a dark unknown, where the wisest of all philosophy, is the philosophy of silence, and a profession of ignorance is the best evidence of a solid understanding; that if he thinks he knows any thing on such a subject as this, he knoweth nothing yet as he ought to know. He knows not what Newton knew, and what he kept a steady eye upon throughout the whole march of his sublime investigations. He knows not the limit of his own faculties. He has overleaped the barrier which hems in all the possibilities of human attainment. He has wantonly flung himself off from the safe and firm field of observation, and got on that undiscoverable ground, where, by every step he takes, he widens his distance from the true philosophy, and by every affirmation he utters, he rebels against the authority of all its maxims.

I can conceive it the feeling of every one of you, that I have hitherto indulged in a vain expense of argument, and it is most natural for you to put the question, "What is the precise point of convergence to which I am directing all the light of this abundant and seemingly superfluous illustration?"

In the astronomical objection which infidelity has proposed against the truth of the Christian revelation, there is first an assertion, and then an argument. The assertion is, that Christianity is set up for the exclusive benefit of our minute and solitary world. The argument is, that God would not lavish such a quantity of attention on so insignificant a field. Even though the assertion were admitted, I should have a quarrel with the argument. But the futility of the objection is not laid open in all its extent, unless we expose the utter want of all essential evidence even for the truth of the assertion. How do infidels know that Christianity is set up for the single benefit of this earth and its inhabitants? How are they able to tell us, that if you go to other planets, the person and the religion of Jesus, are there unknown to them? We challenge them to the proof of this said positive announcement of theirs. We see in this objection the same rash and gratuitous procedure, which was so apparent in the two cases that we have already advanced for the purpose of illustration. We see in it the same glaring transgression on the spirit and the maxims of that very philosophy which they profess to idolize. They have made their argument against us, out of an assertion which has positively no feet to rest upon—an assertion which they have no means whatever of verifying—an assertion, the truth or the falsehood of which can only be gathered out of some supernatural message; for it lies completely beyond the range of human observation. It is willingly admitted, that by an attempt at the botany of other worlds, the true method of philosophising is trampled on; for this is a subject that lies beyond the range of actual observation, and every performance upon it must be made up of assertions without proofs. It is also willingly admitted, that an attempt at the civil and political history of their people, would be an equally extravagant departure from the spirit of the true philosophy; for this also lies beyond the field of actual observation; and all that could possibly be mustered up on such a subject as this, would still be assertions without proofs. Now, the theology of these planets, is, in every way, as inaccessible a subject as their politics or their natural history; and therefore it is, that the objection, grounded on the confident assumption of those infidel astronomers, who assert Christianity, to be the religion of this one world, or that the religion of these other worlds is not our very Christianity, can have no influence on a mind that has derived its habits of thinking from the pure and rigorous school of Newton; for the whole of this assertion is just as glaringly destitute, as in the two former instances, of proof.

The man who could embark in an enterprise so foolish and so fanciful, as to theorise it on the details of the botany of another world, or to theorise it on the natural and moral history of its people, is just making as outrageous a departure from all sense, and science, and all sobriety, when he presumes to speculate, or to assert on the details or the methods of God's administration among its rational and accountable inhabitants. He wings his fancy to as hazardous a region, and vainly strives a penetrating vision through the mantle of as deep an obscurity. All the elements of such a speculation are hidden from him. For any thing he can tell, sin has found its way into these other worlds. For any thing he can tell, their people have banished themselves from communion with God. For any thing he can tell, many a visit has been made to each of them, on the subject of our common Christianity, by commissioned messengers from the throne of the Eternal. For any thing he can tell, the redemption proclaimed to us is not one solitary instance, or not the whole of that redemption which is by the Son of God—but only our part in a plan of mercy, equal in magnificence to all that astronomy has brought within the range of human contemplation. For any thing he can tell, the moral pestilence, which walks abroad over the face of our world, may have spread its desolation over all the planets of all the systems, which the telescope has made known to us. For any thing he can tell, some mighty redemption has been devised in heaven, to meet this disaster in the whole extent and malignity of its visitations. For any thing he can tell, the wonder working God, who has strewed the field of immensity with so many worlds, and spread the shelter of his omnipotence over them, may have sent a message of love to each, and re-assured the hearts of its despairing people by some overpowering manifestation of tenderness. For any thing he can tell, angels from paradise may have sped to every planet their delegated way, and sung, from each azure canopy, a joyful annunciation, and said, "Peace be to this residence, and good will to all its families, and glory to Him in the highest, who, from the eminency of his throne, has issued an act of grace so magnificent, as to carry the tidings of life and of acceptance to the unnumbered orbs of a sinful creation." For any thing he can tell, the Eternal Son, of whom it is said, that by him the worlds were created, may have had the government of many sinful worlds laid upon his shoulders; and by the power of his mysterious word, have awoke them all from that spiritual death, to which they had sunk in lethargy as profound as the slumbers of nonexistence. For any thing he can tell, the one Spirit who moved on the face of the waters, and whose presiding influence it was, that hushed the wild war of nature's elements, and made a beauteous system emerge out of its disjointed materials, may now be working with the fragments of another chaos; and educing order, and obedience, and harmony, out of the wrecks of a moral rebellion, which reaches through all these spheres, and spreads disorder to the uttermost limits of our astronomy.

But, here I stop—nor shall I attempt to grope my dark and fatiguing way, by another inch, among such sublime and mysterious secrecies. It is not I who am offering to lift this curtain. It is not I who am pitching my adventurous flight to the secret things which belong to God, away from the things that are revealed, and which belong to me and to my children. It is the champion of that very infidelity which I am now combating. It is he who props his unchristian argument, by presumptions fetched out of those untravelled obscurities which lie on the other side of a barrier that I pronounce to be impassable. It is he who transgresses the limits which Newton forbore to enter; because, with a justness which reigns throughout all his inquiries, he saw the limit of his own understanding, nor would he venture himself beyond it. It is he who has borrowed from the philosophy of this wondrous man, a few dazzling conceptions, which have only served to bewilder him—while, an utter stranger to the spirit of this philosophy, he has carried a daring and an ignorant speculation far beyond the boundary of its prescribed and allowable enterprises. It is he who has mustered against the truths of the Gospel, resting, as it does, on the evidence within the reach of his faculties, an objection, for the truth of which he has no evidence whatever. It is he who puts away from him a doctrine, for which he has the substantial and the familiar proof of human testimony; and substitutes in its place a doctrine for which he can get no other support than from a reverie of his own imagination. It is he who turns aside from all that safe and certain argument, that is supplied by the history of this world, of which he knows something; and who loses himself in the work of theorising about other worlds, of the moral and theological history of which he positively knows nothing. Upon him, and not upon us, lies the folly of launching his impetuous way beyond the province of observation—of letting his fancy afloat among the unknown of distant and mysterious regions; and by an act of daring, as impious as it is unphilosophical, of trying to unwrap that shroud, which, till drawn aside by the hand of a messenger from heaven, will ever veil, from human eye, the purposes of the Eternal.

If you have gone along with me in the preceding observations, you will perceive how they are calculated to disarm of all its point and all its energy, that flippancy of Voltaire; when, in the examples he gives of the dotage of the human understanding, he tells us of Bacon having believed in witchcraft, and Sir Isaac Newton having written a Commentary on the Book of Revelation. The former instance we shall not undertake to vindicate; but in the latter instance, we perceive what this brilliant and spacious, but withal superficial, apostle of infidelity, either did not see, or refused to acknowledge. We see in this intellectual labour of our great philosopher, the working of the very same principles which carried him through the profoundest and the most successful of his investigations; and how he kept most sacredly and most consistently by those very maxims, the authority of which he, even in the full vigor and manhood of his faculties, ever recognized. We see in the theology of Newton, the very spirit and principle which gave all its stability, and all its sureness, to the philosophy of Newton. We see the same tenacious adherence to every one doctrine, that had such valid proof to uphold it, as could be gathered from the field of human experience; and we see the same firm resistance of every one argument, that had nothing to recommend it, but such plausibilities as could easily be devised by the genius of man, when he expatiated abroad on those fields of creation, which the eye never witnessed, and from which no messenger ever came to us with any credible information. Now, it was on the former of these two principles that Newton clung so determinedly to his Bible, as the record of an actual annunciation from God to the inhabitants of this world. When he turned his attention to this book, he came to it with a mind tutored to the philosophy of facts—and, when he looked at its credentials, he saw the stamp and the impress of this philosophy on every one of them. He saw the fact of Christ being a messenger from heaven, in the audible language by which it was conveyed from heaven's canopy to human ears. He saw the fact of his being an approved ambassador of God, in those miracles which carried their own resistless evidence along with them to human eyes. He saw the truth of this whole history brought home to his own conviction, by a sound and substantial vehicle of human testimony. He saw the reality of that supernatural light, which inspired the prophecies he himself illustrated, by such an agreement with the events of a various and distant futurity as could be taken cognizance of by human observation. He saw the wisdom of God pervading the whole substance of the written message, in such manifold adaptations to the circumstances of man, and to the whole secrecy of his thoughts, and his affections, and his spiritual wants, and his moral sensibilities, as even in the mind of an ordinary and unlettered peasant, can be attested by human consciousness. These formed the solid materials of the basis on which our experimental philosopher stood; and there was nothing in the whole compass of his own astronomy to dazzle him away from it; and he was too well aware of the limit between what he knew and what he did not know, to be seduced from the ground he had taken, by any of those brilliancies which have since led so many of his humbler successors into the track of infidelity. He had measured the distances of these planets. He had calculated their periods. He had estimated their figures, and their bulk, and their densities, and he had subordinated the whole intricacy of their movements to the simple and sublime agency of one commanding principle. But he had too much of the ballast of a substantial understanding about him, to be thrown afloat by all this success among the plausibilities of wanton and unauthorized speculation. He knew the boundary which hemmed him. He knew that he had not thrown one particle of light on the moral or religious history of these planetary regions. He had not ascertained what visits of communication they received from the God who upholds them. But he knew that the fact of a real visit made to this planet, had such evidence to rest upon, that it was not to be disposted by any aerial imagination. And when I look at the steady and unmoved Christianity of this wonderful man; so far from seeing any symptom of dotage and imbecility, or any forgetfulness of those principles on which the fabric of his philosophy is reared; do I see that in sitting down to the work of a Bible Commentator, he hath given us their most beautiful and most consistent exemplification.

I did not anticipate such a length of time, and of illustration, in this stage of my argument. But I will not regret it, if I have familiarised the minds of any of my readers to the reigning principle of this Discourse. We are strongly disposed to think, that it is a principle which might be made to apply to every argument of every unbeliever —and so to serve not merely as an antidote against the infidelity of astronomers, but to serve as an antidote against all infidelity. We are well aware of the diversity of complexion which infidelity puts on. It looks one thing in the man of science and of liberal accomplishment. It looks another thing in the refined voluptuary. It looks still another thing in the common-place railer against the artifices of priestly domination. It looks another thing in the dark and unsettled spirit of him, whose every reflection is tinctured with gall, and who casts his envious and malignant scowl at all that stands associated with the established order of society. It looks another thing in the prosperous man of business, who has neither time nor patience for the details of the christian evidence—but who, amid the hurry of his other occupations, has gathered as many of the lighter petulances of the infidel writers, and caught from the perusal of them, as contemptuous a tone towards the religion of the New Testament, as to set him at large from all the decencies of religious observation, and to give him the disdain of an elevated complacency over all the follies of what he counts a vulgar superstition.

And, lastly, for infidelity has now got down among us to the humblest walks of life; may it occasionally be seen lowering on the forehead of the resolute and hardy artificer, who can lift his menacing voice against the priesthood, and, looking on the Bible as a jugglery of theirs, can bid stout defiance to all its denunciations. Now, under all these varieties, we think that there might be detected the one and universal principle which we have attempted to expose. The something, whatever it is, which has dispossessed all these people of their Christianity, exists in their minds, in the shape of a position, which they hold to be true, but which, by no legitimate evidence, they have ever realized—and a position which lodges within them as a wilful fancy or presumption of their own, but which could not stand the touchstone of that wise and solid principle, in virtue of which, the followers of Newton give to observation the precedence over theory. It is a principle altogether worthy of being laboured—as, if carried round in faithful and consistent application, among these numerous varieties, it is able to break up all the existing infidelity of the world.

But there is one other most important conclusion to which it carries us. It carries us, with all the docility of children, to the Bible; and puts us down into the attitude of an unreserved surrender of thought and understanding, to its authoritative information. Without the testimony of an authentic messenger from heaven, I know nothing of heaven's counsels. I never heard of any moral telescope that can bring to my observation the doings or the deliberations which are taking place in the sanctuary of the Eternal. I may put into the registers of my belief, all that comes home to me through the senses of the outer man, or by the consciousness of the inner man. But neither the one nor the other can tell me of the purposes of God; can tell me of the transactions or the designs of his sublime monarchy; can tell me of the goings forth of Him who is from everlasting unto everlasting; can tell me of the march and the movements of that great administration which embraces all worlds, and takes into its wide and comprehensive survey the mighty roll of innumerable ages. It is true that my fancy may break its impetuous way into this lofty and inaccessible field; and through the devices of my heart, which are many, the visions of an ever-shifting theology may take their alternate sway over me; but the counsel of the Lord, it shall stand. And I repeat it, that if true to the leading principle of that philosophy, which has poured such a flood of light over the mysteries of nature, we shall dismiss every self-formed conception of our own, and wait in all the humility of conscious ignorance, till the Lord himself shall break his silence, and make his counsel known, by an act of communication. And now that a professed communication is before me, and that it has all the solidity of the experimental evidence on its side, and nothing but the reveries of a daring speculation to oppose it, what is the consistent, what is the rational, what is the philosophical use that should be made of this document, but to set me down like a schoolboy, to the work of turning its pages, and conning its lessons, and submitting the every exercise of my judgment to its information and its testimony? We know that there is a superficial philosophy, which casts the glare of a most seducing brilliancy around it; and spurns the Bible, with all the doctrine, and all the piety of the Bible, away from it; and has infused the spirit of Antichrist into many of the literary establishments of the age; but it is not the solid, the profound, the cautious spirit of that philosophy, which has done so much to ennoble the modern period of our world; for the more that this spirit is cultivated and understood, the more will it be found in alliance with that spirit, in virtue of which all that exalteth itself against the knowledge of God, is humbled, and all lofty imaginations are cast down, and every thought of the heart is brought into the captivity of the obedience of Christ.

DISCOURSE III.

On the Extent of the Divine Condescension.

"Who is like unto the Lord our God, who dwelleth on high? Who humbleth himself to behold the things that are in heaven, and in the earth?"—*Psalm* cxiii. 5, 6.

IN our last discourse we attempted to expose the total want of evidence for the assertion of the infidel astronomer—and this, reduces the whole of our remaining controversy with him to the business of arguing against a mere possibility. Still, however, the answer is not so complete as it might be, till the soundness of the argument be attended to, as well as the credibility of the assertion—or, in other words, let us admit the assertion, and take a view of the reasoning which has been constructed upon it.

We have already attempted to lay before you the wonderful extent of that space, teeming with unnumbered worlds, which modern science has brought within the circle of its discoveries. We even ventured to expatiate on those tracts of infinity, which lie on the other side of all that eye or that telescope hath made known to us—to shoot afar into those ulterior regions which are beyond the limits of our astronomy—to impress you with the rashness of the imagination, that the creative energy of God had sunk exhausted by the magnitude of its efforts, at that very line, through which the art of man, lavished as it has been on the work of perfecting the instruments of vision, has not yet been able to penetrate: and upon all this we hazarded the assertion, that though all these visible heavens were to rush into annihilation, and the besom of the Almighty's wrath were to sweep from the face of the universe, those millions, and millions more of suns and of systems, which lie within the grasp of our actual observation —that this event, which, to our eye, would leave so wide, and so dismal a solitude behind it, might be nothing in the eye of Him who could take in the whole, but the disappearance of a little speck from that field of created things, which the hand of his omnipotence had thrown around him.

But to press home the sentiment of the text, it is not necessary to stretch the imagination beyond the limit of our actual discoveries. It is enough to strike our minds with the insignificance of this world, and of all who inhabit it, to bring it into measurement with that mighty assemblage of worlds, which lie open to the eye of man, aided as it has been by the inventions of his genius. When we told you of the eighty millions of suns, each occupying his own independent territory in space, and dispensing his own influences over a cluster of tributary worlds; this world could not fail to sink into littleness in the eye of him who looked to all the magnitude and variety which are around it. We gave you but a feeble image of our comparative insignificance, when we said that the glories of an extended forest would suffer no more from the fall of a single leaf, than the glories of this extended universe would suffer, though the globe we tread, "and all that it inherits, should dissolve." And when we lift our conceptions to Him who has peopled immensity with all these wonders—who sits enthroned on the magnificence of his own works, and by one sublime idea can embrace the whole extent of that boundless amplitude, which he has filled with the trophies of his divinity: we cannot but resign our whole heart to the Psalmist's exclamation of "What is man, that thou art mindful of him, or the son of man, that thou shouldest deign to visit him!"

Now mark the use to which all this has been turned by the genius of infidelity. Such a humble portion of the universe as ours, could never have been the object of such high and distinguishing attentions as Christianity has assigned to it. God would not have manifested himself in the flesh for the salvation of so paltry a world. The monarch of a whole continent, would never move from his capital, and lay aside the splendour of royalty, and subject himself for months, or for years, to perils, and poverty, and persecution; and take up his abode in some small islet of his dominions, which, though swallowed by an earthquake, could not be missed amid the glories of so wide an empire; and all this to regain the lost affections of a few families upon its surface. And neither would the eternal Son of God—he who is revealed to us as having made all worlds, and as holding an empire, amid the splendours of which the globe that we inherit, is shaded insignificance; neither would he strip himself of the glory he had with the Father before the world was, and light on this lower scene, for the purpose imputed to him in the New Testament. Impossible, that the concerns of this puny ball, which floats its little round among an infinity of larger worlds, should be of such mighty account in the plans of the Eternal, or should have given birth in heaven to so wonderful a movement, as the Son of God putting on the form of our degraded species, and sojourning among us, and sharing in all our infirmities, and crowning the whole scene of humiliation by the disgrace and the agonies of a cruel martyrdom.

This has been started as a difficulty in the way of the Christian Revelation; and it is the boast of many of our philosophical infidels, that by the light of modern discovery, the light of the New Testament is eclipsed and overborne; and the mischief is not confined to philosophers, for the argument has got into other hands, and the popular illustrations that are now given to the sublimest truths of science, have widely disseminated all the deism that has been grafted upon it; and the high tone of a decided contempt for the Gospel, is now associated with the flippancy of superficial acquirements: and, while the venerable Newton, whose genius threw open those mighty fields of contemplation, found a fit exercise for his powers in the interpretation of the Bible, there are thousands and tens of thousands, who, though walking in the light which he holds out to them, are seduced by a complacency which he never felt, and inflated by a pride which never entered into his pious and philosophical bosom, and whose only notice of the Bible, is to depreciate, and to deride, and to disown it.

Before entering into what we conceive to be the right answer to this objection, let us previously observe, that it goes to strip the Deity of an attribute which forms a wonderful addition to the glories of his incomprehensible character. It is indeed a mighty evidence of the strength of his arm, that so many millions of worlds are suspended on it; but it would surely make the high attribute of his power more illustrious, if while it expatiated at large among the suns and the systems of astronomy, it could, at the very same instant, be impressing a movement and a direction on all the minuter wheels of that machinery, which is working incessantly around us. It forms a noble demonstration of his wisdom, that he gives unremitting operation to those laws which uphold the stability of this great universe; but it would go to heighten that wisdom inconceivably, if while equal to the magnificent task of maintaining the order and harmony of the spheres, it was lavishing its inexhaustible resources on the beauties, and varieties, and arrangements, of every one scene, however humble, of every one field, however narrow, of the creation he had formed. It is a cheering evidence of the delight he takes in communicating happiness, that the whole of immensity should be so strewed with the habitations of life and of intelligence; but it would surely bring home the evidence, with a nearer and more affecting impression, to every bosom, did we know, that at the very time his benignant regard took in the mighty circle of created beings, there was not a single family overlooked by him, and that every individual in every corner of his dominions, was as effectually seen to, as if the object of an exclusive and undivided care. It is our imperfection, that we cannot give our attention to more than one object at one and the same instant of time; but surely it would elevate our every idea of the perfections of God, did we know, that while his comprehensive mind could grasp the whole amplitude of nature, to the very outermost of its boundaries, he had an attentive eye fastened on the very humblest of its objects, and pondered every thought of my heart, and noticed every footstep of my goings, and treasured up in his remembrance every turn and every movement of my history.

And, lastly, to apply this train of sentiment to the matter before us; let us suppose that one among the countless myriads of worlds, should be visited by a moral pestilence, which spread through all its people, and brought them under the doom of a law, whose sanctions were unrelenting and immutable; it were no disparagement to God, should he, by an act of righteous indignation, sweep this offence away from the universe which it deformed—nor should we wonder, though, among the multitude of other worlds from which the ear of the Almighty was regaled with the songs of praise, and the incense of a pure adoration ascended to his throne, he should leave the strayed and solitary world to perish in the guilt of its rebellion. But, tell me, oh! tell me, would it not throw the softening of a most exquisite tenderness over the character of God, should we see him putting forth his every expedient to reclaim to himself those children who had wandered away from him—and, few as they were when compared with the host of his obedient worshippers, would it not just impart to his attribute of compassion the infinity of the Godhead, that, rather than lose the single world which had turned to its own way, he should send the messengers of peace to woo and to welcome it back again; and, if justice demanded so mighty a sacrifice, and the law behoved to be so magnified and made honourable, tell me whether it would not throw a moral sublime over the goodness of the Deity, should he lay upon his own Son the burden of its atonement, that he might again smile upon the world, and hold out the sceptre of invitation to all its families?

We avow it, therefore, that this infidel argument goes to expunge a perfection from the character of God. The more we know of the extent of nature, should not we have the loftier conception of him who sits in high authority over the concerns of so wide a universe? But, is it not adding to the bright catalogue of his other attributes, to say, that, while magnitude does not overpower him, minuteness cannot escape him, and variety cannot bewilder him; and that, at the very time while the mind of the Deity is abroad over the whole vastness of creation, there is not one particle of matter, there is not one individual principle of rational or of animal existence, there is not one single world in that expanse which teems with them, that his eye does not discern as constantly, and his hand does not guide as unerringly, and his spirit does not watch and care for as vigilantly, as if it formed the one and exclusive object of his attention.

The thing is inconceivable to us, whose minds are so easily distracted by a number of objects; and this is the secret principle of the whole infidelity I am now alluding to. To bring God to the level of our own comprehension, we would clothe him in the impotency of a man. We would transfer to his wonderful mind all the imperfection of our own faculties. When we are taught by astronomy, that he has millions of worlds to look after, and thus add in one direction to the glories of his character; we take away from them in another, by saying, that each of these worlds must be looked after imperfectly. The use that we make of a discovery, which should hasten our every conception of God, and humble us into the sentiment, that a Being of such mysterious elevation is to us unfathomable, is to sit in judgment over him, aye, and to pronounce such a judgment as degrades him, and keeps him down to the standard of our own paltry imagination! We are introduced by modern science to a multitude of other suns and of other systems; and the perverse interpretation we put upon the fact, that God *can* diffuse the benefits of his power and of his goodness over such a variety of worlds, is, that he *cannot*, or will not, bestow so much goodness on one of those worlds, as a professed revelation from Heaven has announced to us. While we enlarge the provinces of his empire, we tarnish all the glory of this enlargement, by saying, he has so much to care for, that the care of every one province must be less complete, and less vigilant, and less effectual, than it would otherwise have been. By the discoveries of modern science, we multiply the places of the creation; but along with this, we would impair the attribute of his eye being in every place to behold the evil and the good; and thus, while we magnify one of his perfections, we do it at the expense of another; and to bring him within the grasp of our feeble capacity, would deface one of the glories of that character, which it is our part to adore, as higher than all thought, and as greater than all comprehension.

The objection we are discussing, I shall state again in a single sentence. Since astronomy has unfolded to us such a number of worlds, it is not likely that God would pay so much attention to this one world, and set up such wonderful provisions for its benefit, as are announced to us in the Christian Revelation. This objection will have received its answer, if we can meet it by the following position:—that God, in addition to the bare faculty of dwelling on a multiplicity of objects at one and the same time, has this faculty in such wonderful perfection that he can attend as fully and provide as richly, and manifest all his attributes as illustriously, on every one of these objects, as if the rest had no existence, and no place whatever in his government or in his thoughts. For the evidence of this position, we appeal, in the first place, to the personal history of each individual among you. Only grant us, that God never loses sight of any one thing he has created, and that no created thing can continue either to be or to act independently of him; and then, even upon the face of this world, humble as it is on the great scale of astronomy, how widely diversified and how multiplied into many thousand distinct exercises, is the attention of God! His eye is upon every hour of my existence. His spirit is intimately present with every thought of my heart. His inspiration gives birth to every purpose within me. His hand impresses a direction on every footstep of my goings. Every breath I inhale, is drawn by an energy which God deals out to me. This body, which, upon the slightest derangement, would become the prey of death, or of woful suffering, is now at ease, because he at this moment is warding off from me a thousand dangers, and upholding the thousand movements of its complex and delicate machinery. His presiding influence keeps by me through the whole current of my restless and ever changing history. When I walk by the way side, he is along with me. When I enter into company, amid all my forgetfulness of him, he never forgets me. In the silent watches of the night, when my eyelids have closed, and my spirit has sunk into unconsciousness, the observant eye of him who never slumbers, is upon me. I cannot fly from his presence. Go where I will, he tends me, and watches me, and cares for me; and the same being who is now at work in the remotest domains of Nature and of Providence, is also at my right hand to eke out to me every moment of my being, and to uphold me in the exercise of all my feelings, and of all my faculties.

Now, what God is doing with me, he is doing with every distinct individual of this world's population. The intimacy of his presence, and attention, and care, reaches to one and to all of them. With a mind unburdened by the vastness of all its other concerns, he can prosecute, without distraction, the government and guardianship of every one son and daughter of the species.— And is it for us, in the face of all this experience, ungratefully to draw a limit around the perfections of God?—to aver, that the multitude of other worlds has withdrawn any portion of his benevolence from the one we occupy?—or that he, whose eye is upon every separate family of the earth, would not lavish all the riches of his unsearchable attributes on some high plan of pardon and immortality, in behalf of its countless generations?

But, secondly, were the mind of God so fatigued, and so occupied with the care of other worlds, as the objection presumes him to be, should we not see some traces of neglect, or of carelessness, in his management of ours? Should we not behold, in many a field of observation, the evidence of its master being overcrowded with the variety of his other engagements? A man oppressed by a multitude of business, would simplify and reduce the work of any new concern that was devolved upon him. Now, point out a single mark of God being thus oppressed. Astronomy has laid open to us so many realms of creation, which were before unheard of, that the world we inhabit shrinks into one remote and solitary province of his wide monarchy. Tell me, then, if, in any one field of this province, which man has access to, you witness a single indication of God sparing himself—of God reduced to languor by the weight of his other employments—of God sinking under the burden of that vast superintendence which lies upon him—of God being exhausted, as one of ourselves would be, by any number of concerns, however great, by any variety of them, however manifold? and do you not perceive, in that mighty profusion of wisdom and of goodness, which is scattered every where around us, that the thoughts of this unsearchable Being are not as our thoughts, nor his ways as our ways?

My time does not suffer me to dwell on this topic, because, before I conclude, I must hasten to another illustration. But when I look abroad on the wondrous scene that is immediately before me—and see, that in every direction it is a scene of the most various and unwearied activity—and expatiate on all the beauties of that garniture by which it is adorned, and on all the prints of design and of benevolence which abound in it—and think, that the same God, who holds the universe, with its every system, in the hollow of his hand, pencils every flower, and gives nourishment to every blade of grass—and actuates the movements of every living thing—and is not disabled, by the weight of his other cares, from enriching the humble department of nature I occupy, with charms and accommodations, of the most unbounded variety—then, surely, if a message, bearing every mark of authenticity, should profess to come to me from God, and inform me of his mighty doings for the happiness of our species, it is not for me, in the face of all this evidence, to reject it as a tale of imposture, because astronomers have told me that he has so many other worlds and other orders of beings to attend to—and, when I think that it were a deposition of him from his supremacy over the creatures he has formed, should a single sparrow fall to the ground without his appointment, then let science and sophistry try to cheat me of my comfort as they may—I will not let go the anchor of my confidence in God —I will not be afraid, for I am of more value than many sparrows.

But thirdly, it was the telescope, that by piercing the obscurity which lies between us and distant worlds, put infidelity in possession of the argument, against which we are now contending. But, about the time of its invention, another instrument was formed, which laid open a scene no less wonderful, and rewarded the inquisitive spirit of man with a discovery, which served to neutralize the whole of this argument. This was the microscope. The one led me to see a system in every star. The other leads me to see a world in every atom. The one taught me, that this mighty globe, with the whole burden of its people, and of its countries, is but a grain of sand on the high field of immensity. The other teaches me, that every grain of sand may harbour within it the tribes and the families of a busy population. The one told me of the insignificance of the world I tread upon. The other redeems it from all its insignificance; for it tells me that in the leaves of every forest, and in the flowers of every garden, and in the waters of every rivulet, there are worlds teeming with life, and numberless as are the glories of the firmament. The one has suggested to me, that beyond and above all that is visible to man, there may lie fields of creation which sweep immeasurably along, and carry the impress of the Almighty's hand to the remotest scenes of the universe. The other suggests to me, that within and beneath all that minuteness which the aided eye of man has been able to explore, there may be a region of invisibles; and that could we draw aside the mysterious curtain which shrouds it from our senses, we might there see a theatre of as many wonders as astronomy has unfolded, a universe within the compass of a point so small, as to elude all the powers of the microscope, but where the wonder working God finds room for the exercise of all his attributes, where he can raise another mechanism of worlds, and fill and animate them all with the evidences of his glory.

Now, mark how all this may be made to meet the argument of our infidel astronomers. By the telescope they have discovered, that no magnitude, however vast, is beyond the grasp of the Divinity. But by the microscope we have also discovered, that no minuteness, however shrunk from the notice of the human eye, is beneath the condescension of his regard. Every addition to the powers of the one instrument, extends the limit of his visible dominions. But, by every addition to the powers of the other instrument, we see each part of them more crowded than before, with the wonders of his unwearying hand. The one is constantly widening the circle of his territory. The other is as constantly filling up its separate portions, with all that is rich, and various, and exquisite. In a word, by the one I am told that the Almighty is now at work in regions more distant than geometry has ever measured, and among worlds more manifold than numbers have ever reached. But, by the other, I am also told, that, with a mind to comprehend the whole, in the vast compass of its generality, he has also a mind to concentrate a close and a separate attention on each and on all of its particulars; and that the same God, who sends forth an upholding influence among the orbs and the movements of astronomy, can fill the recesses of every single atom with the intimacy of his presence, and travel, in all the greatness of his unimpaired attributes, upon every one spot and corner of the universe he has formed.

They, therefore, who think that God will not put forth such a power, and such a goodness, and such a condescension, in behalf of this world, as are ascribed to him in the New Testament, because he has so many other worlds to attend to, think of him as a man. They confine their view to the informations of the telescope, and forget altogether the informations of the other instrument. They only find room in their minds for his one attribute of a large and general superintendence, and keep out of their remembrance, the equally impressive proofs we have for his other attribute of a minute and multiplied attention to all that diversity of operations, where it is he that worketh all in all. And then I think, that as one of the instruments of philosophy has heightened our every impression of the first of these attributes, so another instrument has no less heightened our impression of the second of them—then I can no longer resist the conclusion, that it would be a transgression of sound argument, as well as a daring of impiety, to draw a limit around the doings of this unsearchable God—and, should a professed revelation from heaven, tell me of an act of condescension, in behalf of some separate world, so wonderful that angels desired to look into it, and the Eternal Son had to move from his seat of glory to carry it into accomplishment, all I ask is the evidence of such a revelation; for, let it tell me as much as it may of God letting himself down for the benefit of one single province of his dominions, this is no more than what I see lying scattered, in numberless examples, before me; and running through the whole line of my recollections; and meeting me in every walk of observation to which I can betake myself; and, now that the microscope has unveiled the wonders of another region, I see strewed around me, with a profusion which baffles my every attempt to comprehend it, the evidence that there is no one portion of the universe of God too minute for his notice, nor too humble for the visitations of his care.

As the end of all these illustrations, let me bestow a single paragraph on what I conceive to be the precise state of this argument.

It is a wonderful thing that God should be so unincumbered by the concerns of a whole universe, that he can give a constant attention to every moment of every individual in this world's population. But, wonderful as it is, you do not hesitate to admit it as true, on the evidence of your own recollections. It is a wonderful thing that he whose eye is at every instant on so many worlds, should have peopled the world we inhabit with all the traces of the varied design and benevolence which abound in it. But, great as the wonder is, you do not allow so much as the shadow of improbability to darken it, for its reality is what you actually witness, and you never think of questioning the evidence of observation. It is wonderful, it is passing wonderful, that the same God, whose presence is diffused through immensity, and who spreads the ample canopy of his administration over all its dwelling-places, should, with an energy as fresh and as unexpended as if he had only begun the work of creation, turn him to the neighbourhood around us, and lavish on its every handbreadth, all the exuberance of his goodness, and crowd it with the many thousand varieties of conscious existence. But, be the wonder incomprehensible as it may, you do not suffer in your mind the burden of a single doubt to lie upon it because you do not question the report of the miscroscope. You do not refuse its information, nor turn away from it as an incompetent channel of evidence. But to bring it still nearer to the point at issue, there are many who never looked through a microscope; but who rest an implicit faith in all its revelations; and upon what evidence, I would ask? Upon the evidence of testimony—upon the credit they give to the authors of the books they have read, and the belief they put in the record of their observations. Now, at this point I make my stand. It is wonderful that God should be so interested in the redemption of a single world, as to send forth his well-beloved Son upon the errand, and he, to accomplish it, should, mighty to save, put forth all his strength, and travail in the greatness of it. But such wonders as these have already multiplied upon you; and when evidence is given of their truth, you have resigned your every judgment of the unsearchable God, and rested in the faith of them. I demand, in the name of sound and consistent philosophy, that you do the same in the matter before us—and take it up as a question of evidence—and examine that medium of testimony through which the miracles and informations of the Gospel have come to your door—and go not to admit as argument here, what would not be admitted as argument in any of the analogies of nature and observation—and take along with you in this field of inquiry, a lesson which you should have learned upon other fields—even the depth of the riches both of the wisdom and the knowledge of God, that his judgments are unsearchable, and his ways are past finding out.

I do not enter at all into the positive evidence for the truth of the Christian Revelation, my single aim at present being to dispose of one of the objections which is conceived to stand in the way of it. Let me suppose then that this is done to the satisfaction of a philosophical inquirer, and that the evidence is sustained, and that the same mind that is familiarised to all the sublimities of natural science, and has been in the habit of contemplating God in association with all the magnificence which is around him, shall be brought to submit its thoughts to the captivity of the doctrine of Christ. Oh! with what veneration, and gratitude, and wonder, should he look on the descent of him into this lower world, who made all these things, and without whom was not any thing made that was made. What a grandeur does it throw over every step in the redemption of a fallen world, to think of its being done by him who unrobed him of the glories of so wide a monarchy, and came to this humblest of its provinces, in the disguise of a servant, and took upon him the form of our degraded species, and let himself down to sorrows and to sufferings, and to death, for us. In this love of an expiring Saviour to those for whom in agony he poured out his soul, there is a height, and a depth, and a length, and a breadth, more than I can comprehend; and let me never, never from this moment neglect so great a salvation, or lose my hold of an atonement, made sure by him who cried, that it was finished, and brought in an everlasting righteousness. It was not the visit of an empty parade that he made to us. It was for the accomplishment of some substantial purpose; and, if that purpose is announced, and stated to consist in his dying the just for the unjust, that he might bring us unto God, let us never doubt of our acceptance in that way of communication with our Father in heaven, which he hath opened and made known to us. In taking to that way, let us follow his every direction with that humility which a sense of all this wonderful condescension is fitted to inspire. Let us forsake all that he bids us forsake. Let us do all that he bids us do. Let us give ourselves up to his guidance with the docility of children, overpowered by a kindness that we never merited, and a love that is unequalled by all the perverseness and all the ingratitude of our stubborn nature—for what shall we render unto him for such mysterious benefits—to him who has thus been mindful of us—to him who thus has deigned to visit us?

But the whole of this argument is not yet exhausted. We have scarcely entered on the defence that is commonly made against the plea which infidelity rests on the wonderful extent of the universe of

God, and the insignificancy of our assigned position of it. The way in which we have attempted to dispose of this plea, is by insisting on the evidence that is every where around us, of God combining with the largeness of a vast and mighty superintendence, which reaches the outskirts of creation, and spreads over all its amplitudes—the faculty of bestowing as much attention, and exercising as complete and manifold a wisdom, and lavishing as profuse and inexhaustible a goodness on each of its humblest departments, as if it formed the whole extent of his territory.

In the whole of this argument we have looked upon the earth as isolated from the rest of the universe altogether. But according to the way in which the astronomical objection is commonly met, the earth is not viewed as in a state of detachment from the other worlds, and the other orders of being which God has called into existence. It is looked upon as the member of a more extended system. It is associated with the magnificence of a moral empire, as wide as the kingdom of nature. It is not merely asserted, what in our last Discourse has been already done, that for any thing we can know by reason, the plan of redemption may have its influences and its bearings on those creatures of God who people other regions, and occupy other fields in the immensity of his dominions; that to argue, therefore, on this plan being instituted for the single benefit of the world we live in, and of the species to which we belong, is a mere presumption of the infidel himself; and that the objection he rears on it, must fall to the ground, when the vanity of the presumption is exposed. The Christian apologist thinks he can go further than this—that he cannot merely expose the utter baselessness of the infidel assertion, but that he has positive ground for erecting an opposite and a confronting assertion in its place—and that after having neutralised their position, by showing the entire absence of all observation in its behalf, he can pass on to the distinct affirmative testimony of the Bible.

We do think that this lays open a very interesting track, not of wild and fanciful, but of most legitimate and sober-minded speculation. And anxious as we are to put every thing that bears upon the Christian argument into all its lights; and fearless as we feel for the result of a most thorough sifting of it; and thinking as we do think it, the foulest scorn that any pigmy philosopher of the day should mince his ambiguous scepticism to a set of giddy and ignorant admirers, or that a half-learned or superficial public should associate with the christian priesthood, the blindness and the bigotry of a sinking cause—with these feelings, we are not disposed to blink a single question that may be started on the subject of the Christian evidences. There is not one of its parts or bearings which needs the shelter of a disguise thrown over it. Let the priests of another faith ply their prudential expedients, and look so wise and so wary in the execution of them. But Christianity stands in a higher and a firmer attitude. The defensive armour of a shrinking or timid policy does not suit her. Hers is the naked majesty of truth; and with all the grandeur of age, but with none of its infirmities, has she come down to us, and gathered new strength from the battles she has won in the many controversies of many generations. With such a religion as this there is nothing to hide. All should be above boards. And the broadest light of day should be made fully and freely to circulate throughout all the secrecies. But secrets she has none. To her belong the frankness and the simplicity of conscious greatness; and whether she grapple it with the pride of philosophy, or stand in fronted opposition to the prejudices of the multitude, she does it upon her own strength, and spurns all the props and all the auxiliaries of superstition away from her.

DISCOURSE IV.

On the Knowledge of Man's Moral History in the Distant Places of Creation.

"Which things the angels desire to look into."—1 *Peter* i. 12.

THERE is a limit, across which man cannot carry any one of his perceptions, and from the ulterior of which he cannot gather a single observation to guide or to inform him. While he keeps by the objects which are near, he can get the knowledge of them conveyed to his mind through the ministry of several of the senses. He can feel a substance that is within reach of his hand. He can smell a flower that is presented to him. He can taste the food that is before him. He can hear a sound of certain pitch and intensity; and, so much does this sense of hearing widen his intercourse with external nature, that, from the distance of miles, it can bring him in an occasional intimation.

But of all the tracks of conveyance which God has been pleased to open up between the mind of man, and the theatre by which he is surrounded, there is none by which he so multiplies his acquaintance with the rich and the varied creation on every side of him, as by the organ of the eye. It is this which gives to him his loftiest command over the scenery of nature. It is this by which so broad a range of observation is submitted to him. It is this which enables him, by the act of a single moment, to send an exploring look over the surface of an ample territory, to crowd his mind with the whole assembly of its objects, and to fill his vision with those countless hues which diversify and adorn it. It is this which carries him abroad over all that is sublime in the immensity of distance; which sets him as it were on an elevated platform, from whence he may cast a surveying glance over the arena of innumerable worlds; which spreads before him so mighty a province of contemplation, that the earth he inhabits, only appears to furnish him with the pedestal on which he may stand, and from which he may descry the wonders of all that magnificence which the Divinity has poured so abundantly around him. It is by the narrow outlet of the eye, that the mind of man takes its excursive flight over those golden tracks, where, in all the exhaustlessness of creative wealth, lie scattered the suns, and the systems of astronomy. But oh! how good a thing it is, and how becoming well, for the philosopher to be humble even amid the proudest march of human discovery, and the sublimest triumphs of the human understanding, when he thinks of that unscaled barrier, beyond which no power, either of eye or of telescope, shall ever carry him: when he thinks that on the other side of it, there is a height, and a depth, and a length, and a breadth, to which the whole of this concave and visible firmament dwindles into the insignificancy of an atom—and above all, how ready should he be to cast his every lofty imagination away from him, when he thinks of the God, who, on the simple foundation of his word, has reared the whole of this stately architecture, and, by the force of his preserving hand, continues to uphold it; aye, and should the word again come out from him, that this earth shall pass away, and a portion of the heavens which are around it, shall again fall back into the annihilation from which he at first summoned them, what an impressive rebuke does it bring on the swelling vanity of science, to think that the whole field of its most ambitious enterprises may be swept away altogether, and there remain before the eye of him who sitteth on the throne, an untravelled immensity, which he hath filled with innumerable splendours, and over the whole face of which he hath inscribed the evidence of his high attributes, in all their might, and in all their manifestations.

But man has a great deal more to keep him humble of his understanding, than a mere sense of that boundary which skirts and terminates the material field of his contemplations. He ought also to feel how within that boundary, the vast majority of things is mysterious and unknown to him; that even in the inner chamber of his own consciousness, where so much lies hidden from the observation of others, there is also, to himself, a little world of incomprehensibles; that if stepping beyond the limits of this familiar home, he look no further than to the members of his family, there is much in the cast and the colour of every mind that is above his powers of divination; that in proportion as he recedes from the centre of his own personal experience, there is a cloud of ignorance and secrecy, which spreads, and thickens, and throws a deep and impenetrable veil over the intricacies of every one department of human contemplation; that of all around him his knowledge is naked and superficial, and confined to a few of those more conspicuous lineaments which strike upon his senses; that the whole face both of nature and of society, presents him with questions which he cannot unriddle, and tells him how beneath the surface of all that the eye can rest upon, there lies the profoundness of a most unsearchable latency; aye, and should he in some lofty enterprise of thought, leave this world, and shoot afar into those tracks of speculation which astronomy has opened—should he, baffled by the mysteries which beset his every footstep upon earth attempt an ambitious flight towards the mysteries of heaven—let him go, but let the justness of a pious and philosophical modesty go along with him; let him forget not, that from the moment his mind has taken its ascending way for a few little miles above the world he treads upon, his every sense abandons him but one—that number, and motion, and magnitude, and figure, make up all the barrenness of its elementary informations—that these orbs have sent him scarce another message, than told by their feeble glimmering upon his eye, the simple fact of their existence—that he sees not the landscape of other worlds—that he knows not the moral system of any one of them—nor athwart the long and trackless vacancy which lies between, does there fall upon his listening ear, the hum of their mighty populations.

But the knowledge which he cannot fetch up himself from the obscurity of this wondrous but untravelled scene, by the exercise of any one of his own senses, might be fetched to him by the testimony of a competent messenger. Conceive a native of one of these planetary mansions to light upon our world, and all we should require, would be, to be satisfied of his credentials, that we may tack our faith to every point of information he had to offer us. With the solitary exception of what we have been enabled to gather by the instruments of astronomy, there is not one of his communications about the place he came from, on which we possess any means at all of confronting him; and, therefore, could he only appear before us invested with the characters of truth, we should never think of any thing else than taking up the whole matter of his testimony just as he brought it to us.

It were well had a sound philosophy schooled its professing disciples to the same kind of acquiescence in another message, which has actually come to the world; and has told us of matters still more remote from every power of unaided observation; and has been sent from a more sublime and mysterious distance, even from that God of whom it is said, that "clouds and darkness are the habitation of his throne;" and treating of a theme so lofty and so inaccessible, as the counsels of that Eternal Spirit, "whose goings forth are of old, even from everlasting," challenges of man that he should submit his every thought to the authority of this high communication. O! had the philosophers of the day known as well as their great Master, how to draw the vigorous land-mark which verges the field of legitimate discovery, they should have seen when it is that philosophy becomes vain, and science is falsely so called; and how it is, that when philosophy is true to her principles, she shuts up her faithful votary to the Bible, and makes him willing to count all but loss, for the knowledge of Jesus Christ, and of him crucified.

But let it be well observed, that the object of this message is not to convey information to us about the state of these planetary regions. This is not the matter with which it is fraught. It is a message from the throne of God to this rebellious province of his dominions; and the purpose of it is, to reveal the fearful extent of our guilt and of our danger, and to lay before us the overtures of reconciliation. Were a similar message sent from the metropolis of a mighty empire, to one of its remote and revolutionary districts, we should not look to it for much information about the state or economy of the intermediate provinces. This were a departure from the topic on hand—though still there may chance to be some incidental allusions to the extent and resources of the whole monarchy, to the existence of a similar spirit of rebellion in other quarters of the or to the general principle of loyalty which it was pervaded. Some casual of this kind may be inserted in a proclamation, or they may not—

and it is with this precise feeling of ambiguity that we open the record of that embassy which has been sent us from heaven, to see if we can gather any thing there, about other places of the creation, to meet the objections of the infidel astronomer. But, while we pursue this object, let us have a care not to push the speculation beyond the limits of the written testimony; let us keep a just and a steady eye on the actual boundary of our knowledge, that, throughout every distinct step of our argument, we might preserve that chaste and unambitious spirit, which characterizes the philosophy of him who explored these distant heavens, and, by the force of his genius, unravelled the secret of that wondrous mechanism which upholds them.

The informations of the Bible upon this subject, are of two sorts—that from which we confidently gather the fact, that the history of the redemption of our species is known in other and distant places of the creation—and that, from which we indistinctly guess at the fact, that the redemption itself may stretch beyond the limits of the world we occupy.

And, here it may shortly be adverted to, that, though we know little or nothing of the moral and theological economy of the other planets, we are not to infer, that the beings who occupy these widely extended regions, even though not higher than we in the scale of understanding, know little of ours. Our first parents, ere they committed that act by which they brought themselves and their posterity into the need of redemption, had frequent and familiar intercourse with God. He walked with them in the garden of paradise; and there did angels hold their habitual converse; and, should the same unblotted innocence which charmed and attracted these superior beings to the haunts of Eden, be perpetuated in every planet but our own, then might each of them be the scene of high and heavenly communications, an open way for the messengers of God be kept up with them all, and their inhabitants be admitted to a share in the themes and contemplations of angels, and have their spirit exercised on those things, of which we are told that the angels desired to look into them; and thus, as we talk of the public mind of a city, or the public mind of an empire—by the well-frequented avenues of a free and ready circulation, a public mind might be formed throughout the whole extent of God's sinless and intelligent creation—and, just as we often read of the eyes of all Europe being turned to the one spot where some affair of eventful importance is going on, there might be the eyes of a whole universe turned to the one world, where rebellion against the Majesty of heaven had planted its standard; and for the re-admission of which within the circle of his fellowship, God, whose justice was inflexible, but whose mercy he had, by some plan of mysterious wisdom, made to rejoice over it, was putting forth all the might, and travelling in all the greatness of the attributes which belong to him.

But, for the full understanding of this argument, it must be remarked, that, while in our exiled habitation, where all is darkness and rebellion, and enmity, the creature engrosses every heart, and our affections, when they shift at all, only wander from one fleeting vanity to another, it is not so in the habitations of the unfallen. There, every desire and every movement is subordinated to God. He is seen in all that formed, and in all that is spread around them—and, amid the fulness of that delight with which they expatiate over the good and the fair of this wondrous universe, the animating charm which pervades their every contemplation, is that they behold, on each visible thing, the impress of the mind that conceived, and of the hand that made and that upholds it. Here, God is banished from the thoughts of every natural man, and by a firm and constantly maintained act of usurpation, do the things of sense and of time wield an entire ascendancy. There God is all in all. They walk in his light. They rejoice in the beatitudes of his presence. The veil is from off their eyes, and they see the character of a presiding Divinity in every scene, and in every event to which the Divinity has given birth. It is this which stamps a glory and an importance on the whole field of their contemplations; and when they see a new evolution in the history of created things, the reason they bend towards it so attentive an eye, is, that it speaks to their understanding some new evolution in the purposes of God; some new manifestation of his high attributes—some new and interesting step in the history of his sublime administration.

Now, we ought to be aware how it takes off, not from the intrinsic weight, but from the actual impression of our argument, that this devotedness to God which reigns in other places of the creation, this interest in him as the constant and essential principle of all enjoyment; this concern in the untaintedness of his glory; this delight in the survey of his perfections and his doings, are what the men of our corrupt and darkened world cannot sympathize with.

But however little we may enter into it, the Bible tells us by many intimations, that among those creatures who have not fallen from their allegiance, nor departed from the living God, God is their all—that love to him sits enthroned in their hearts, and fills them with all the ecstacy of an overwhelming affection—that a sense of grandeur never so elevates their souls, as when they look at the might and majesty of the Eternal—that no field of clou ess transparency so enchants them by the blissfulness of its visions, as when at the shrine of infinite and unspotted holiness, they bend themselves in raptured adoration—that no beauty so fascinates and attracts them, as does that moral beauty which throws a softening lustre over the awfulness of the Godhead—in a word, that the image of his character is ever present to their contemplations, and the unceasing joy of their sinless existence lies in the knowledge and the admiration of the Deity.

Let us put forth an effort, and keep a steady hold of this consideration; for the deadness of our earthly imaginations makes an effort necessary; and we shall perceive, that though the world we live in were the alone theatre of redemption, there is a something in the redemption itself that is fitted to draw the eye of an arrested universe towards it. Surely, surely, where delight in God is the constant enjoyment, and the earnest intelligent contemplation of God is the constant exercise, there is nothing in the whole compass of nature or of history, that can so set his adoring myriads upon the gaze, as some new and wondrous evolution of the character of God. Now this is found in the plan of our redemption; nor, do I see how in any transaction between the great Father of existence, and the children who have sprung from him, the moral attributes of the Deity could, if I may so express myself, be put to so severe and so delicate a test. It is true, that the great matters of sin and of salvation fall without impression, on the heavy ears of a listless and alienated world. But they who, to use the language of the Bible, are light in the Lord, look otherwise at these things. They see sin in all its malignity, and salvation in all its mysterious greatness. Aye, and it would put them on the stretch of all their faculties, when they saw rebellion lifting up its standard against the Majesty of heaven, and the truth and the justice of God embarked on the threatenings he had uttered against all the doers of iniquity, and the honours of that august throne, which has the firm pillars of immutability to rest upon, linked with the fulfilment of the law that had come out from it; and when nothing else was looked for, but that God, by putting forth the power of his wrath, should accomplish his every denunciation, and vindicate the inflexibility of his government, and by one sweeping deed of vengeance, assert in the sight of all his creatures, the sovereignty which belongeth to him—Oh! with what desire must they have pondered on his ways, when amid the urgency of all these demands which looked so high and so indispensable, they saw the unfoldings of the attribute of mercy—and how the supreme Lawgiver was bending upon his guilty creatures an eye of tenderness—and how in his profound and unsearchable wisdom, he was devising for them some plan of restoration—and how the eternal Son had to move from his dwelling-place in heaven, to carry it forward through all the difficulties by which it was encompassed—and how, after, by the virtue of his mysterious sacrifice, he had magnified the glory of every other perfection, he made mercy rejoice over them all, and threw open a way by which we sinful and polluted wanderers might, with the whole lustre of the Divine character untarnished, be re-admitted into fellowship with God, and be again brought back within the circle of his loyal and affectionate family.

Now, the essential character of such a transaction, viewed as a manifestation of God, does not hang upon the number of worlds, over which this sin and this salvation may have extended. We know that over this one world such an economy of wisdom and of mercy is instituted—and, even should this be the only world that is embraced by it, the moral display of the Godhead is mainly and substantially the same, as if it reached throughout the whole of that habitable extent which the science of astronomy has made known to us. By the disobedience of this one world, the law was trampled on; and, in the business of making truth and mercy to meet, and have a harmonious accomplishment on the men of this world, the dignity of God was put to the same trial; the justice of God appeared to lay the same immoveable barrier; the wisdom of God had to clear a way through the same difficulties; the forgiveness of God had to find the same mysterious conveyance to the sinners of a solitary world, as to the sinners of half a universe. The extent of the field upon which this question was decided, has no more influence on the question itself, than the figure or the dimensions of that field of combat, on which some great political question was fought, has on the importance or on the moral principles of the controversy that gave rise to it. This objection about the narrowness of the theatre, carries along with it all the grossness of materialism. To the eye of spiritual and intelligent beings, it is nothing. In their view, the redemption of a sinful world derives its chief interest from the display it gives of the mind and purposes of the Deity—and, should that world be but a single speck in the immensity of the works of God, the only way in which this affects their estimate of him, is to magnify his loving kindness—who rather than lose one solitary world of the myriads he has formed, would lavish all the riches of his beneficence and of his wisdom on the recovery of its guilty population.

Now, though it must be admitted that the Bible does not speak clearly or decisively as to the proper effect of redemption being extended to other worlds; it speaks most clearly and most decisively about the knowledge of it being disseminated among other orders of created intelligence than our own. But if the contemplation of God be their supreme enjoyment, then the very circumstance of our redemption being known to them, may invest it, even though it be but the redemption of one solitary world, with an importance as wide as the universe itself. It may spread among the hosts of immensity a new illustration of the character of Him who is all their praise, and looking toward whom every energy within them is moved to the exercise of a deep and delighted admiration. The scene of the transaction may be narrow in point of material extent; while in the transaction itself there may be such a moral dignity, as to blazon the perfections of the Godhead over the face of creation; and from the manifested glory of the Eternal, to send forth a tide of ecstacy, and of high gratulation, throughout the whole extent of his dependent provinces.

I will not, in proof of the position, that the history of our redemption is known in other and distant places of creation, and is matter of deep interest and feeling among other orders of created intelligence—I will not put down all the quotations which might be assembled together upon this argument. It is an impressive circumstance, than when Moses and Elias made a visit to our Saviour on the mount of transfiguration, and appeared in glory from heaven, the topic they brought along with them, and with which they were fraught, was the decease he was going to accomplish at Jerusalem. And however insipid the things of our salvation may be to an earthly understanding; we are made to know, that in the sufferings of Christ, and the glory which should follow, there is matter to attract the notice of celestial spirits, for these are the very things, says the Bible, which angels desire to look into. And however listlessly we, the dull and grovelling children of an exiled family, may feel about the perfections of the Godhead, and the display of those perfections in the economy of the Gospel, it is intimated to us in the book of God's message, that the creation has its districts and its provinces; and we accordingly read of thrones, and dominions, and principalities, and powers; and whether these terms denote the separate regions of government, or the beings who, by a commission granted from the sanctuary of heaven, sit in delegated authority over them—even in their eyes the mystery of Christ stands arrayed in all the splendour of unsearchable riches; for we are told that this mystery was revealed for the very intent, that unto the principalities and powers in heavenly places, might be made known by the church, the manifold wisdom of God. And while we, whose prospect reaches not beyond the narrow limits of the corner we occupy, look on the dealings of God in the world, as carrying in them all the insignificancy of a provincial transaction; God himself, whose eye reaches to places which our eye hath not seen, nor our ear heard of, neither hath it entered into the imagination of our heart to conceive, stamps a universality on the whole matter of the Christian salvation, by such revelations as the following: That he is to gather together in one all things in Christ, both which are in heaven, and which are in earth, even in him—and that at the name of Jesus every knee should bow, of things in heaven, and things in earth, and things under the earth—and that by him God reconciled all things unto himself, whether they be things in earth, or things in heaven.

We will not say in how far some of these passages extend the proper effect of that redemption which is by Christ Jesus, to other quarters of the universe of God; but they at least go to establish a widely disseminated knowledge of this transaction among the other orders of created intelligence. And they give us a distant glimpse of something more extended. They present a faint opening, through which may be seen some few traces of a wider and a nobler dispensation. They bring before us a dim transparency, on the other side of which the images of an obscure magnificence dazzle indistinctly upon the eye; and tell us that in the economy of redemption, there is a grandeur commensurate to all that is known of the other works and purposes of the Eternal. They offer us no details; and man, who ought not to attempt a wisdom above that which is written, should never put forth his hand to the drapery of that impenetrable curtain which God in his mysterious wisdom has spread over those ways, of which it is but a very small portion that we know of them. But certain it is, that we know as much of them from the Bible; and the infidel, with all the pride of his boasted astronomy, knows so little of them, from any power of observation, that the baseless argument of his, on which we have dwelt so long, is overborne in the light of all that positive evidence which God has poured around the record of his own testimony, and even in the light of its more obscure and casual intimations.

The minute and variegated details of the way in which this wondrous economy is extended, God has chosen to withhold from us; but he has oftener than once made to us a broad and a general announcement of its dignity. He does not tell us whether the fountain opened in the house of Judah, for sin and for uncleanness, send forth its healing streams to other worlds than our own. He does not tell us the extent of the atonement. But he tells us that the atonement itself, known as it is among the myriads of the celestial, forms the high song of eternity; that the Lamb who was slain, is surrounded by the acclamations of one wide and universal empire; that the might of his wondrous achievements, spreads a tide of gratulation over the multitudes who are about his throne; and that there never ceases to ascend from the worshippers of him who washed us from our sins in his blood, a voice loud as from numbers without number, sweet as from blessed voices uttering joy, when heaven rings jubilee, and loud hosannas fill the eternal regions.

"And I beheld, and I heard the voice of many angels round about the throne, and the number of them was ten thousand times ten thousand, and thousands of thousands; saying with a loud voice, Worthy is the Lamb that was slain, to receive power, and riches, and wisdom, and strength, and glory, and honour, and blessing. And every creature which is in heaven, and on earth, and under the earth, and such as are in the sea, and all that are in them, heard I saying, Blessing, and honour, and glory, and power, be unto him that sitteth on the throne, and unto the Lamb, forever and ever."

A king might have the whole of his reign crowded with the enterprises of glory: and by the might of his arms, and the wisdom of his counsels might win the first reputation among the potentates of the world; and be idolized throughout all his provinces, for the wealth and the security that he had spread around them—and still it is conceivable, that by the act of a single day in behalf of a single family; by some soothing visitation of tenderness to a poor and solitary cottage; by some deed of compassion, which conferred enlargement and relief on one despairing sufferer; by some graceful movement of sensibility at a tale of wretchedness; by some noble effort of self-denial, in virtue of which he subdued his every purpose of revenge, and spread the mantle of a generous oblivion over the fault of the man who has insulted and aggrieved him; above all, by an exercise of pardon so skilfully administered, as that instead of bringing him down to a state of defencelessness against the provocation of future injuries, it threw a deeper sacredness over him, and stamped a more inviolable dignity than ever on his person and character:—why, my brethren, on the strength of one such performance, done in a single hour, and reaching no further in its immediate effects than to one house, or to one individual, it is a most possible thing, that the highest monarch upon earth might draw such a lustre around him as would eclipse the renown of all his public achievements—and that such a display of magnanimity, or of worth, beaming from the secrecy of his familiar moments, might waken a more cordial veneration in every bosom, than all the splendour of his conspicuous history—aye, and that it might pass down to posterity, as a more enduring monument of greatness, and raise him further by its moral elevation above the level of ordinary praise; and when he passes in review before the men of distant ages, may this deed of modest, gentle, unobtrusive virtue, be at all times appealed to, as the most sublime and touching memorial of his name.

In like manner did the King eternal, immortal, and invisible, surrounded as he is with the splendours of a wide and everlasting monarchy, turn him to our humble habitation; and the foot-steps of God manifest in the flesh, have been on the narrow spot of ground we occupy; and small though our mansion be, amid the orbs and the systems of immensity, hither hath the King of glory bent his mysterious way, and entered the tabernacle of men, and in the disguise of a servant did he sojourn for years under the roof which canopies our obscure and solitary world. Yes, it is but a twinkling atom in the peopled infinity of worlds that are around it—but look to the moral grandeur of the transaction, and not to the material extent of the field upon which it was executed—and from the retirement of our dwelling-place, there may issue forth such a display of the Godhead, as will circulate the glories of his name among all his worshippers. Here sin entered. Here was the kind and universal beneficence of a Father, repaid by the ingratitude of a whole family. Here the law of God was dishonoured, and that too in the face of its proclaimed and unalterable sanctions. Here the mighty contest of the attributes was ended—and when justice put forth its demands, and truth called for the fulfilment of its warnings, and the immutability of God would not recede by a single iota, from any one of its positions, and all the severities he had ever uttered against the children of iniquity, seemed to gather into one cloud of threatening vengeance on the tenement that held us—did the visit of the only-begotten Son chase away all these obstacles to the triumph of mercy—and humble as the tenement may be, deeply shaded in the obscurity of insignificance as it is, among the statelier mansions which are on every side of it—yet will the recal of its exiled family never be forgotten—and the illustration that has been given here of the mingled grace and majesty of God, will never lose its place among the themes and the acclamations of eternity.

And here it may be remarked, that as the earthly king who throws a moral aggrandizement around him, by the act of a single day, finds, that after its performance, he may have the space of many years for gathering to himself the triumphs of an extended reign—so the king who sits on high, and with whom one day is as a thousand years, and a thousand years as one day, will find, that after the period of that special administration is ended, by which this strayed world is again brought back within the limits of his favoured creation, there is room enough along the mighty track of eternity, for accumulating upon himself a glory as wide and as universal as is the extent of his dominions. You will allow the most illustrious of this world's potentates, to give some hour of his private history to a deed of cottage or domestic tenderness; and every time you think of the interesting story, you will feel how sweetly and how gracefully the remembrance of it blends itself with the fame of his public achievements. But still you think that there would not have been room enough for these achievements of his, had much of his time been spent, either among the habitations of the poor, or in the retirement of his own family; and you conceive, that it is because a single day bears so small a proportion to the time of his whole history, that he has been able to combine an interesting display of private worth, with all that brilliancy of exhibition, which has brought him down to posterity in the character of an august and a mighty sovereign.

Now apply this to the matter before us. Had the history of our redemption been confined within the limits of a single day, the argument that infidelity has drawn from the multitude of other worlds, would never have been offered. It is true, that ours is but an insignificant portion of the territory of God—but if the attentions by which he has signalized it, had only taken up a single day, this would never have occurred to us as forming any sensible withdrawment of the mind of the Deity from the concerns of his vast and universal government. It is the time which the plan of our salvation requires, that startles all those on whom this argument has any impression. It is the time taken up about this paltry world, which they feel to be out of proportion to the number of other worlds, and to the immensity of the surrounding creation. Now, to meet this impression, I do not insist at present on what I have already brought forward, that God, whose ways are not as our ways, can have his eye at the same instant on every place, and can divide and diversify his attention into any number of distinct exercises. What I have now to remark, is, that the infidel who urges the astronomical objection to the truth of Christianity, is only looking with half an eye to the principle on which it rests. Carry out the principle, and the objection vanishes. He looks abroad on the immensity of space, and tells us how impossible it is, that this narrow corner of it can be so distinguished by the attentions of the Deity. Why does he not also look abroad on the magnificence of eternity; and perceive how the whole period of these peculiar attentions, how the whole time which elapses between the fall of man and the consummation of the scheme of his recovery, is but the twinkling of a moment to the mighty roll of innumerable ages? The whole interval between the time of Jesus Christ's leaving his Father's abode, to sojourn among us, to that time when he shall have put all his enemies under his feet, and delivered up the kingdom to God, even his Father, that God may be all in all; the whole of this interval bears as small a proportion to the whole of the Almighty's reign, as this solitary world does to the universe around it, and an infinitely smaller proportion than any time, however short, which an earthly monarch spends on some enterprise of private benevolence, does to the whole walk of his public and recorded history.

Why, then, does not the man, who can shoot his conceptions so sublimely abroad over the field of an immensity that knows no limits—why does he not also shoot them forward through the vista of a succession, that ever flows without stop and without termination? He has burst across the confines of this world's habitation in space, and out of the field which lies on the other side of it, has he gathered an argument against the truth of revelation. I feel that I have nothing to do but to burst across the confines of this world's history in time, and out of the futurity which lies beyond it, can I gather that which will blow the argument to pieces, or stamp upon it all the narrowness of a partial and mistaken calculation. The day is coming, when the whole of this wondrous history shall be looked back upon by the eye of the remembrance, and be regarded as one incident in the extended annals of creation, and with all the illustration and all the glory it has thrown on the character of the Deity, will it be seen as a single step in the evolution of his designs; and long as the time may appear, from the first act of our redemption to its final accomplishment, and close and exclusive as we may think the attentions of God upon it, it will be found that it has left him room enough for all his concerns, and that on the high scale of eternity, it is but one of those passing and ephemeral transactions, which crowd the history of a never-ending administration.

DISCOURSE V.

On the Sympathy that is felt for Man in the Distant Places of Creation.

"I say unto you, that likewise joy shall be in heaven over one sinner that repenteth, more than over ninety and nine just persons which need no repentance."—*Luke* xv. 7

I HAVE already attempted at full length to establish the position, that the infidel argument of astronomers goes to expunge a natural perfection from the character of God, even that wondrous property of his, by which he, at the same instant of time, can bend a close and a careful attention on a countless diversity of objects, and diffuse the intimacy of his power and of his presence, from the greatest to the minutest and most insignificant of them all. I also adverted shortly to this other circumstance, that it went to impair a moral attribute of the Deity. It goes to impair the benevolence of his nature. It is saying much for the benevolence of God, to say, that a single world, or a single system, is not enough for it—that it must have the spread of a mightier region, on which it may pour forth a tide of exuberancy throughout all its provinces—that as far as our vision can carry us, it has strewed immensity with the floating receptacles of life, and has stretched over each of them the garniture of such a sky as mantles our own habitation—and that even from distances which are far beyond the reach of human eye, the songs of gratitude and praise may now be arising to the one God, who sits surrounded by the regards of his one great and universal family.

Now, it is saying much for the benevolence of God, to say that it sends forth these wide and distant emanations over the surface of a territory so ample, that the world we inhabit, lying imbedded as it does amidst so much surrounding greatness, shrinks into a point that to the universal eye might appear to be almost imperceptible. But does it not add to the power and to the perfection of this universal eye, that at the very moment it is taking a comprehensive survey of the vast, it can fasten a steady and undistracted attention on each minute and separate portion of it; that at the very moment it is looking at all worlds, it can look most pointedly and most intelligently to each of them: that at the very moment it sweeps the field of immensity, it can settle all the earnestness of its regards upon every distinct hand-breadth of that field; that at the very moment at which it embraces the totality of existence, it can send a most thorough and penetrating inspection into each of its details, and into every one of its endless diversities? You cannot fail to perceive how much this adds to the power of the all-seeing eye. Tell me, then, if it do not add as much perfection to the benevolence of God, that while it is expatiating over the vast field of created things, there is not one portion of the field overlooked by it; that while it scatters blessings over the whole of an infinite range, it causes them to descend in a shower of plenty on every separate habitation: that while his arm is underneath and round about all worlds, he enters within the precincts of every one of them, and gives a care and a tenderness to each individual of their teeming population. Oh! does not the God, who is said to be love, shed over this attribute of his its finest illustration, when, while he sits in the highest heaven, and pours out his fulness on the whole subordinate domain of nature and of providence, he bows a pitying regard on the very humblest of his children, and sends his reviving Spirit into every heart, and cheers by his presence every home, and provides for the wants of every family, and watches every sick-bed, and listens to the complaints of every sufferer; and while by his wondrous mind the weight of universal government is borne, oh! is it not more wondrous and more excellent still, that he feels for every sorrow, and has an ear open to every prayer?

"It doth not yet appear what we shall be," says the apostle John, "but we know that when he shall appear, we shall be like him, for we shall see him as he is." It is the present lot of the angels, that they behold the face of our Father in heaven, and it would seem as if the effect of this was to form and to perpetuate in them the moral likeness of himself, and that they reflect back upon him his own image, and that thus a diffused resemblance to the Godhead is kept up among all those adoring worshippers who live in the near and rejoicing contemplation of the Godhead. Mark then how that peculiar and endearing feature in the goodness of the Deity, which we have just now adverted to—mark how beauteously it is reflected downwards upon us in the revealed attitude of angels. From the high eminences of heaven, are they bending a wakeful regard over the men of this sinful world; and the repentance of every one of them spreads a joy and a high gratulation throughout all its dwelling places. Put this trait of the angelic character into contrast with the dark and lowering spirit of an infidel. He is told of the multitude of other worlds, and he feels a kindling magnificence in the conception, and he is seduced by an elevation which he cannot carry, and from this airy summit does he look down on the insignificance of the world we occupy, and pronounces it to be unworthy of those visits and of those attentions which we read of in the New Testament. He is unable to wing his way upward along the scale, either of moral or of natural perfection; and when the wonderful extent of the field is made known to him, over which the wealth of the Divinity is lavished—there he stops, and wilders, and altogether misses this essential perception, that the power and perfection of the Divinity are not more displayed by the mere magnitude of the field, than they are by that minute and exquisite filling up, which leaves not its smallest portions neglected; but which imprints the fulness of the Godhead upon every one of them; and proves, by every flower of the pathless desert, as well as by every orb of immensity, how this unsearchable being can care for all, and provide for all; and, throned in mystery too high for us, can, throughout every instant of time, keep his attentive eye on every separate thing that he has formed, and by an act of his thoughtful and presiding intelligence, can constantly embrace all.

But God, compassed about as he is with light inaccessible, and full of glory, lies so hidden from the ken and conception of all our faculties, that the spirit of man sinks exhausted by its attempts to comprehend him. Could the image of the Supreme be placed direct before the eye of the mind, that flood of splendour, which is ever issuing from him on all who have the privilege of beholding, would not only dazzle, but overpower us. And therefore it is, that I bid you look to the reflection of that image, and thus to take a view of its mitigated glories, and to gather the lineaments of the Godhead in the face of those righteous angels, who have never thrown away from them the resemblance in which they were created; and, unable as you are to support the grace and the majesty of that countenance, before which the sons and the prophets of other days fell, and became as dead men, let us, before we bring this argument to a close, borrow one lesson of Him who sitteth on the throne, from the aspect and the revealed doings of those who are surrounding it.

The infidel, then, as he widens the field of his contemplations would suffer its every separate object to die away into forgetfulness: these angels, expatiating as they do over the range of a loftier universality, are represented as all awake to the history of each of its distinct and subordinate provinces. The infidel, with his mind afloat among suns and among systems, can find no place in his already occupied regards, for that humble planet which lodges and accommodates our species; the angels, standing on a loftier summit, and with a mightier prospect of creation before them, are yet represented as looking down on this single world, and attentively marking the every feeling and the every demand of all its families. The infidel, by sinking us down to an unnoticeable minuteness, would lose sight of our dwelling-place altogether, and spread a darkening shroud of oblivion over all the concerns and all the interests of men; but the angels will not so abandon us; and undazzled by the whole surpassing grandeur of that scenery which is around them, are they revealed as directing all the fulness of their regard to this our habitation, and casting a longing and benignant eye on ourselves and on our children. The infidel will tell us of those worlds which roll afar, and the number of which outstrips the arithmetic of the human understanding—and then with the hardness of an unfeeling calculation, will he consign the one we occupy, with all its guilty generations, to despair.

But he who counts the number of the stars, is set forth to us as looking at every inhabitant among the millions of our species, and by the word of the Gospel beckoning to him with the hand of invitation, and on the very first step of his return, as moving towards him with all the eagerness of the prodigal's father, to receive him back again into that presence from which he had wandered. And as to this world, in favour of which the scowling infidel will not permit one solitary movement, all heaven is represented as in a stir about its restoration; and there cannot a single son or a single daughter be recalled from sin unto righteousness, without an acclamation of joy among the hosts of paradise. Aye, and I can say it of the humblest and the unworthiest of you all, that the eye of angels is upon him, and that his repentance would at this moment, send forth a wave of delighted sensibility throughout the mighty throng of their innumerable legions.

Now, the single question I have to ask, is, On which of the two sides of this contrast do we see most of the impress of heaven? Which of the two would be most glorifying to God? Which of them carries upon it the most of that evidence which lies in its having a celestial character? For if it be the side of the infidel, then must all our hopes expire with the ratifying of that fatal sentence, by which the world is doomed, through its insignificancy, to perpetual exclusion from the attentions of the Godhead. I have long been knocking at the door of your understanding, and have tried to find an admittance to it for many an argument. I now make my appeal to the sensibilities of your heart; and tell me, to whom does the moral feeling within it yield its readiest testimony—to the infidel, who would make this world of ours vanish away into abandonment—or to those angels, who ring throughout all their mansions the hosannas of joy, over every one individual of its repentant population?

And here I cannot omit to take advantage of that opening with which our Saviour has furnished us, by the parables of this chapter, and admits us into a familiar view of that principle on which the inhabitants of heaven are so awake to the deliverance and the restoration of our species. To illustrate the difference in the reach of knowledge and of affection, between a man and an angel, let us think of the difference of reach between one man and another. You may often witness a man, who feels neither tenderness nor care beyond the precincts of his own family; but who, on the strength of those instinctive fondnesses which nature has implanted in his bosom, may earn the character of an amiable father, or a kind husband, or a bright example of all that is soft and endearing in the relations of domestic society. Now, conceive him, in addition to all this, to carry his affections abroad, without, at the same time, any abatement of their intensity towards the objects which are at home—that stepping across the limits of the house he occupies, he takes an interest in the families which are near him—that he lends his services to the town or the district wherein he is placed, and gives up a portion of his time to the thoughtful labours of a humane and public-spirited citizen. By this enlargement in the sphere of his attention he has extended his reach; and, provided he has not done so at the expense of that regard which is due to his family—a thing which, cramped and confined as we are, we are very apt, in the exercise of our humble faculties, to do—I put it to you, whether, by extending the reach of his views and his affections, he has not extended his worth and his moral respectability along with it?

But I can conceive a still further enlargement. I can figure to myself a man, whose wakeful sympathy overflows the field of his own immediate neighbourhood—to whom the name of country comes with all the omnipotence of a charm upon his heart, and with all the urgency of a most righteous and resistless claim upon his services— who never hears the name of Britain sounded in his ears, but it stirs up all his enthusiasm in behalf of the worth and the welfare of its people—who gives himself up, with all the devotedness of a passion, to the best and purest objects of patriotism —and who, spurning away from him the vulgarities of party ambition, separates his life and his labours to the fine pursuit of augmenting the science, or the virtue, or the substantial prosperity of his nation. Oh! could such a man retain all the tenderness, and fulfil all the duties which home and which neighbourhood require of him, and at the same time expatiate, in the might of his untired faculties, on so wide a field of benevolent contemplation—would not this extension of reach place him still higher than before, on the scale both of moral and intellectual gradation, and give him a still brighter and more enduring name in the records of human excellence?

And lastly, I can conceive a still loftier flight of humanity—a man, the aspiring of whose heart for the good of man, knows no limitations—whose longings, and whose conceptions on this subject, overleap all the barriers of geography—who, looking on himself as a brother of the species, links every spare energy which belongs to him with the cause of its melioration—who can embrace within the grasp of his ample desires the whole family of mankind—and who, in obedience to a heaven-born movement of principle within him, separates himself to some big and busy enterprise, which is to tell on the moral destinies of the world. Oh! could such a man mix up the softenings of private virtue with the habit of so sublime a comprehension—if, amid those magnificent darings of thought and of performance, the mildness of his benignant eye could still continue to cheer the retreat of his family, and to spend the charm and the sacredness of piety among all its members—could he even mingle himself, in all the gentleness of a soothed and a smiling heart, with the playfulness of his children—and also find strength to shed the blessings of his presence and his counsel over the vicinity around him;—oh! would not the combination of so much grace with so much loftiness, only serve the more to aggrandize him? Would not the one ingredient of a character so rare, go to illustrate and to magnify the other? And would not you pronounce him to be the fairest specimen of our nature, who could so call out all your tenderness, while he challenged and compelled all your veneration?

Nor can I proceed, at this point of my argument, without adverting to the way in which this last and this largest style of benevolence is exemplified in our own country—where the spirit of the Gospel has given to many of its enlightened disciples the impulse of such a philanthropy, as carries abroad their wishes and their endeavours to the very outskirts of human population—a philanthropy, of which, if you asked the extent or the boundary of its field, we should answer, in the language of inspiration, that the field is the world—philanthropy, which overlooks all the distinctions of cast and of colour, and spreads its ample regards over the whole brotherhood of the species—a philanthropy, which attaches itself to man in the general; to man throughout all his varieties: to man as the partaker of one common nature, and who, in whatever clime or latitude you may meet with him, is found to breathe the same sympathies, and to possess the same high capabilities both of bliss and improvement.

It is true that upon this subject, there is often a loose and unsettled magnificence of thought, which is fruitful of nothing but empty speculation. But the men to whom I allude have not imagined the enterprise in the form of a thing unknown. They have given it a local habitation. They have bodied it forth in deed and in accomplishment. They have turned the dream into a reality. In them, the power of a lofty generalization meets with its happiest attemperament in the principle and perseverance, and all the chastening and subduing virtues of the New Testament. And, were I in search of that fine union of grace and of greatness, which I have now been insisting on, and in virtue of which the enlightened Christian can at once find room in his bosom for the concerns of universal humanity and for the play of kindliness towards every individual he meets with—I could no where more readily expect to find it, than with the worthies of our own land—the Howard of a former generation, who paced it over Europe in quest of the unseen wretchedness which abounds in it; or in such men of our present generation as Wilberforce, who lifted his unwearied voice against the biggest outrage ever practised on our nature, till he wrought its extermination; and Clarkson, who plied his assiduous task at rearing the materials of its impressive history, and at length carried, for this righteous cause, the mind of Parliament; and Carey, from whose hand the generations of the East are now receiving the elements of their moral renovation, and, in fine, those holy and devoted men, who count not their lives dear unto them; but, going forth every year from the island of our habitation, carry the message of heaven over the face of the world; and in the front of severest obloquy are now labouring in remotest lands; and are reclaiming another and another portion from the wastes of dark and fallen humanity; and are widening the domains of gospel light and gospel principle among them; and are spreading a moral beauty around the every spot on which they pitch their lowly tabernacle; and are at length compelling even the eye and the testimony of gainsayers, by the success of their noble enterprise; and are forcing the exclamation of delighted surprise from the charmed and arrested traveller, as he looks at the softening tints which they are now spreading over the wilderness, and as he hears the sound of the chapel bell, and as in those haunts where, at the distance of half a generation, savages would have scowled upon his path, he regales himself with the hum of missionary schools, and the lovely spectacle of peaceful and christian villages.

Such, then, is the benevolence, at once so gentle and so lofty, of those men, who, sanctified by the faith that is in Jesus, have had their hearts visited from heaven by a beam of warmth and of sacredness.—What then, I should like to know, is the benevolence of the place from whence such an influence cometh? How wide is the compass of this virtue there, and how exquisite is the feeling of its tenderness, and how pure and how fervent are its aspirings among those unfallen beings who have no darkness and no encumbering weight of corruption to strive against? Angels have a mightier reach of contemplation. Angels can look upon this world, and all which it inherits, as the part of a larger family. Angels were in the full exercise of their powers even at the first infancy of our species, and shared in the gratulations of that period, when at the birth of humanity all intelligent nature felt a gladdening impulse, and the morning stars sang together for joy. They loved us even with that love which a family on earth bears to a younger sister; and the very childhood of our tinier faculties did only serve the more to endear us to them; and though born at a later hour in the history of creation, did they regard us as heirs of the same destiny with themselves, to rise along with them in the scale of moral elevation, to bow at the same footstool, and to partake in those high dispensations of a parent's kindness and a parent's care, which are ever emanating from the throne of the Eternal on all the members of a duteous and affectionate family. Take the reach of an angel's mind, but, at the same time take the seraphic fervour of an angel's benevolence along with it; how from the eminence on which he stands he may have an eye upon many worlds, and a remembrance upon the origin and the successive concerns of every one of them; how he may feel the full force of a most affecting relationship with the inhabitants of each, as the offspring of one common Father; and though it be both the effect and the evidence of our depravity, that we cannot sympathise with these pure and generous ardours of a celestial spirit; how it may consist with the lofty comprehension, and the everbreathing love of an angel, that he can both shoot his benevolence abroad over a mighty expanse of planets and of systems, and lavish a flood of tenderness on each individual of their teeming population.

Keep all this in view, and you cannot fail to perceive how the principle, so finely and so copiously illustrated in this chapter may be brought to meet the infidelity we have thus long been employed in combating. It was nature, and the experience of every bosom will affirm it—it was nature in the shepherd to leave the ninety and nine of his flock forgotten and alone in the wilderness, and betaking himself to the mountains, to give all his labour and all his concern to the pursuit of one solitary wanderer. It was nature; and we are told in the passage before us, that it is such a portion of nature as belongs not merely to men but to angels; when the woman, with her mind in a state of listlessness as to the nine pieces of silver that were in secure custody, turned the whole force of her anxiety to the one piece which she had lost, and for which she had to light a candle, and to sweep the house, and to search diligently until she found it. It was nature in her to rejoice more over that piece, than over all the rest of them, and to tell it abroad among friends and neighbours, that they might rejoice along with her—aye, and sadly effaced as humanity is, in all her original lineaments, this is a part of our nature, the very movements of which are experienced in heaven, "where there is more joy over one sinner that repenteth, than over ninety and nine just persons who need no repentance." For any thing I know, the very planet that rolls in the immensity around me may be a land of righteousness; and be a member of the household of God; and have her secure dwelling-place within that ample limit, which embraces his great and universal family. But I know at least of one wanderer; and how wofully she has strayed from peace and from purity; and how in 'dreary alienation from him who made her, she has bewildered herself among those many devious tracts, which have carried her afar from the path of immortality; and how sadly tarnished all those beauties and felicities are, which promised, on that morning of her existence when God looked on her, and saw that all was very good—which promised so richly to bless and to adorn her; and how in the eye of the whole unfallen creation, she has renounced all this goodliness, and is fast departing away from them into guilt, and wretchedness, and shame. Oh! if there be any truth in this chapter, and any sweet or touching nature in the principle which runs throughout all its parables, let us cease to wonder, though they who surround the throne of love should be looking so intently toward us—or though in the way by which they have singled us out, all the other orbs of space should, for one short season, on the scale of eternity, appear to be forgotten—or though for every step of her recovery, and for every individual who is rendered back again to the fold from which he was separated, another and another message of triumph should be made to circulate among the hosts of paradise—or though lost as we are, and sunk in depravity as we are, all the sympathies of heaven should now be awake on the enterprise of him who has travailed, in the greatness of his strength, to seek and to save us.

And here I cannot but remark how fine a harmony there is between the law of sympathetic nature in heaven, and the most touching exhibitions of it on the face of our world. When one of a numerous household droops under the power of disease, is not that the one to whom all the tenderness is turned, and who, in a manner, monopolizes the inquiries of his neighbourhood, and the care of his family? When the sighing of the midnight storms sends a dismal foreboding into the mother's heart, to whom of all her offspring, I would ask, are her thoughts and her anxieties then wandering? Is it not to her sailor boy whom her fancy has placed amid the rude and angry surges of the ocean? Does not this, the hour of his apprehended danger, concentrate upon him the whole force of her wakeful meditations? And does not he engross, for a season, her every sensibility, and her every prayer? We sometimes hear of shipwrecked passengers thrown upon a barbarous shore; and seized upon by its prowling inhabitants; and hurried away through the tracks of a dreary and unknown wilderness; and sold into captivity; and loaded with the fetters of irrecoverable bondage; and who, stripped of every other liberty but the liberty of thought, feel even this to be another ingredient of wretchedness, for what can they think of but home; and as all its kind and tender imagery comes upon their remembrance, how can they think of it but in the bitterness of despair? Oh tell me, when the fame of all this disaster reaches his family, who is the member of it to whom is directed the full tide of its griefs and of its sympathies? Who is it that, for weeks and for months, usurps their every feeling, and calls out their largest sacrifices, and sets them to the busiest expedients for getting him back again? Who is it that makes them forgetful of themselves and of all around them; and tell me if you can assign a limit to the pains, and the exertions, and the surrenders which afflicted parents and weeping sisters would make to seek and to save him.

Now conceive, as we are warranted to do by the parables of this chapter, the principle of all these earthly exhibitions to be in full operation around the throne of God. Conceive the universe to be one secure and rejoicing family, and that this alienated world is the only strayed, or only captive member belonging to it; and we shall cease to wonder, that from the first period of the captivity of our species, down to the consummation of their history in time, there should be such a movement in heaven; or that angels should so often have sped their commissioned way on the errand of our recovery; or that the Son of God should have bowed himself down to the burden of our mysterious atonement; or that the Spirit of God should now, by the busy variety of his all-powerful influences, be carrying forward that dispensation of grace which is to make us meet for re-admittance into the mansions of the celestial. Only think of love as the reigning principle there; of love, as sending forth its energies and aspirations to the quarter where its object is most in danger of being for ever lost to it; of love, as called forth by this single circumstance to its uttermost exertion, and the most exquisite feeling of its tenderness; and then shall we come to a distinct and a familiar explanation of this whole mystery: Nor shall we resist by our incredulity the gospel message any longer, though it tells us that throughout the whole of this world's history, long in our eyes, but only a little month in the high periods of immortality, so much of the vigilance, and so much of the earnestness of heaven, should have been expended on the recovery of its guilty population.

There is another touching trait of nature, which goes finely to heighten this principle, and still more forcibly to demonstrate its application to our present argument. So long as the dying child of David was alive, he was kept on the stretch of anxiety and of suffering with regard to it. When it expired, he arose and comforted himself. This narrative of King David is in harmony with all that we experience of our own movements and our own sensibilities. It is the power of uncertainty which gives them so active and so interesting a play in our bosoms; and which heightens all our regards to a tenfold pitch of feeling and exercise; and which fixes down our watchfulness upon our infant's dying bed; and which keeps us so painfully alive to every turn and to every symptom in the progress of its malady; and which draws out all our affections for it to a degree of intensity that is quite unutterable; and which urges us on to ply our every effort and our every expedient, till hope withdraw its lingering beam, or till death shut the eyes of our beloved in the slumber of its long and its last repose.

I know not who of you have your names written in the book of life—nor can I tell if this be known to the angels which are in heaven. While in the land of living men, you are under the power and application of a remedy, which if taken as the gospel prescribes, will renovate the soul, and altogether prepare it for the bloom and the vigour of immortality. Wonder not then that with this principle of uncertainty in such full operation, ministers should feel for you; or angels should feel for you; or all the sensibilities of heaven should be awake upon the symptoms of your grace and reformation; or the eyes of those who stand upon the high eminences of the celestial world, should be so earnestly fixed on the every footstep and new evolution of your moral history. Such a consideration as this should do something more than silence the infidel objection. It should give a practical effect to the calls of repentance. How will it go to aggravate the whole guilt of our impenitency, should we stand out against the power and the tenderness ot these manifold applications—the voice of a beseeching God upon us—the word of salvation at our very door—the free offer of strength and of acceptance sounded in our hearing—the spirit in readiness with his agency to meet our every desire and our every inquiry—angels beckoning us to their company—and the very first movements of our awakened conscience drawing upon us all their regard, and all their earnestness!

DISCOURSE VI.

On the Contest for an Ascendency over Man, among the Higher Orders of Intelligence.

"And having spoiled principalities and powers, he made a show of them openly, triumphing over them in it."—*Colossians* ii. 15.

Though these astronomical Discourses be now drawing to a close, it is not because I feel that much more might not be said on the subject of them, both in the way of argument and of illustration. The whole of the infidel difficulty proceeds upon the assumption, that the exclusive bearing of Christianity is upon the people of our earth; that this solitary planet is in no way implicated with the concerns of a wider dispensation; that the revelation we have of the dealings of God, in this district of his empire, does not suit and subordinate itself to a system of moral administration, as extended as in the whole of his monarchy. Or, in other words, because infidels have not access to the whole truth, will they refuse a part of it however well attested or well accredited it may be; because a mantle of deep obscurity rests on the government of God, when taken in all its eternity and all its entireness, will they shut their eyes against that allowance of light which has been made to pass downwards upon our world from time to time, through so many partial unfoldings; and till they are made to know the share which other planets have in these communications of mercy, will they turn them away from the actual message which has come to their own door, and will neither examine its credentials, nor be alarmed by its warnings, nor be won by the tenderness of its invitations.

On that day when the secrets of all hearts shall be revealed, there will be found such a wilful duplicity and darkening of the mind in the whole of this proceeding, as shall bring down upon it the burden of a righteous condemnation. But, even now, does it lie open to the rebuke of philosophy, when the soundness and the consistency of her principles are brought faithfully to bear upon it. Were the characters of modern science rightly understood, it would be seen, that the very thing which gave such strength and sureness to all her conclusions, was that humility of spirit which belonged to her. She promulgates all that is positively known; but she maintains the strictest silence and modesty about all that is unknown. She thankfully accepts of evidence wherever it can be found; nor does she spurn away from her the very humblest contribution of such doctrine as can be witnessed by human observation, or can be attested by human veracity. But with all this she can hold out most sternly against that power of eloquence and fancy, which often throws so bewitching a charm over the plausibilities of ingenious speculation. Truth is the alone idol of her reverence; and did she at all times keep by her attachments, nor throw them away when theology submitted to her cognizance its demonstrations and its claims, we should not despair of witnessing as great a revolution in those prevailing habitudes of thought which obtain throughout our literary establishments, on the subject of Christianity, as that which has actually taken place in the philosophy of external nature. This is the first field on which have been successfully practised the experimental lessons of Bacon; and they who are conversant with these matters, know how great and how general a uniformity of doctrine now prevails in the sciences of astronomy, and mechanics, and chemistry, and almost all the other departments in the history and philosophy of matter. But this uniformity stands strikingly contrasted with the diversity of our moral systems, with the restless fluctuations both of language and of sentiment which are taking place in the philosophy of mind, with the palpable fact that every new course of instruction upon this subject, has some new articles, or some new explanations to peculiarize it: and all this is to be attributed, not to the progress of the science, not to a growing, but to an alternating movement; not to its perpetual additions, but to its perpetual vibrations.

I mean not to assert the futility of moral science, or to deny her importance, or to insist on the utter hopelessness of her advancement. The Baconian method will not probably push forward her discoveries with such a rapidity, or to such an extent, as many of her sanguine disciples have anticipated. But if the spirit and the maxims of this philosophy were at all times proceeded upon, it would certainly check that rashness and variety of excogitation, in virtue of which it may almost be said, that every new course presents us with a new system, and that every new teacher has some singularity or other to characterize him. She may be able to make out an exact transcript of the phenomena of mind, and in so doing, she yields a most important contribution to the stock of human acquirements. But when she attempts to grope her darkling way through the counsels of the Deity, and the futurities of his administration; when, without one passing acknowledgment to the embassy which professes to have come from Him, or to the facts and to the testimonies by which it has so illustriously been vindicated, she launches forth her own speculations on the character of God, and the destiny of man; when, though this be a subject on which neither the recollections of history, nor the ephemeral experience of any single life, can furnish one observation to enlighten her, she will nevertheless utter her own plausibilities, not merely with a contemptuous neglect of the Bible, but in direct opposition to it; then it is high time to remind her of the difference between the reverie of him who has not seen God, and the well-accredited declaration of Him who was in the beginning with God, and was God; and to tell her that this so far from being the argument of an ignoble fanaticism, is in harmony with the very argument upon which the science of experiment has been reared, and by which it has been at length delivered from the influence of theory, and purified of all its vain and visionary splendours.

In my last Discourses, I have attempted to collect from the records of God's actual communication to the world, such traces of relationship between other orders of being and the great family of mankind, as serve to prove that Christianity is not so paltry and provincial a system as infidelity presumes it to be. And as I said before, I have not exhausted all that may legitimately be derived upon this subject from the informations of Scripture. I have adverted, it is true, to the knowledge of our moral history, which obtains throughout other provinces of the intelligent creation. I have asserted the universal importance which this may confer on the transactions even of one planet, in as much as it may spread an honourable display of the Godhead among all the mansions of infinity. I have attempted to expatiate on the argument, that an event little in itself, may be so pregnant with character, as to furnish all the worshippers of heaven with a theme of praise for eternity. I have stated that nothing is of magnitude in their eyes, but that which serves to endear to them the Father of their spirits, or to shed a lustre over the glory of his incomprehensible attributes—and that thus, from the redemption even of our solitary species, there may go forth such an exhibition of the Deity, as shall bear the triumphs of his name to the very outskirts of the universe.

I have further adverted to another distinct scriptural intimation, that the state of fallen man was not only matter of knowledge to other orders of creation, but was also matter of deep regret and affectionate sympathy; that, agreeably to such laws of sympathy as are most familiar even to human observation, the very wretchedness of our condition was fitted to concentrate upon us the feelings, and the attentions, and the services, of the celestial—to single us out for a time to the gaze of their most earnest and unceasing contemplation—to draw forth all that was kind and all that was tender within them—and just in proportion to the need and to the helplessness of us miserable exiles from the family of God, to multiply upon us the regards, and call out in our behalf the fond and eager exertions of those who had never wandered away from Him. This appears from the Bible to be the style of that benevolence which glows and which circulates around the throne of heaven. It is the very benevolence which emanates from the throne itself, and the attentions of which have for so many thousand years signalized the inhabitants of our world. This may look a long period for so paltry a world. But how have infidels come to their conception that our world is so paltry? By looking abroad over the countless systems of immensity But why then have they missed the conception, that the time of those peculiar visitations, which they look upon as so disproportionate to the magnitude of this earth, is just as evanescent as the earth itself is insignificant? Why look they not abroad on the countless generations of eternity;

and thus come back to the conclusion, that after all, the redemption of our species is but an ephemeral doing in the history of intelligent nature; that it leaves the Author of it room for all the accomplishments of a wise and equal administration; and not to mention, that even during the progress of it, it withdraws not a single thought or a single energy of his from other fields of creation; that there remains time enough to him for carrying round the visitations of as striking and as peculiar a tenderness, over the whole extent of his great and universal monarchy?

It might serve still further to incorporate the concerns of our planet with the general history of moral and intelligent beings, to state, not merely the knowledge which they take of us, and not merely the compassionate anxiety which they feel for us; but to state the importance derived to our world from its being the actual theatre of a keen and ambitious contest among the upper orders of creation. You know that how, for the possession of a very small and insulated territory, the mightiest empires of the world would have put forth all their resources; and on some field of mustering competition have monarchs met, and embarked for victory, all the pride of a country's talent, and all the flower and strength of a country's population. The solitary island, around which so many fleets are hovering, and on the shores of which so many armed men are descending, as to an arena of hostility, may well wonder at its own unlooked for estimation. But other principles are animating the battle, and the glory of nations is at stake; and a much higher result is in the contemplation of each party, than the gain of so humble an acquirement as the primary object of the war; and honour, dearer to many a bosom than existence, is now the interest on which so much blood and so much treasure is expended; and the stirring spirit of emulation has now got hold of the combatants; and thus, amid all the insignificancy, which attaches to the material origin of the contest, do both the eagerness and the extent of it, receive from the constitution of our nature, their most full and adequate explanation.

Now, if this be also the principle of higher natures, if, on the one hand God be jealous of his honour, and on the other, there be proud and exalted spirits, who scowl defiance at him and at his monarchy;—if, on the side of heaven, there be an angelic host rallying around the standard of loyalty, who flee with alacrity at the bidding of the Almighty, who are devoted to his glory, and feel a rejoicing interest in the evolution of his counsels; and if, on the side of hell, there be a sullen front of resistance, a hate and malice inextinguishable, an unequalled daring of revenge to baffle the wisdom of the Eternal, and to arrest the hand, and to defeat the purposes of Omnipotence;—then let the material prize of victory be insignificant as it may, it is the victory in itself, which upholds the impulse of this keen and stimulated rivalry. If, by the sagacity of one infernal mind, a single planet has been seduced from its allegiance, and been brought under the ascendency of him, who is called in Scripture, "the god of this world," and if the errand on which our Redeemer came, was to destroy the works of the devil—then let this planet have all the littleness which astronomy has assigned to it—call it what it is, one of the smaller islets which float on the ocean of vacancy, it has become the theatre of such a competition, as may have all the desires and all the energies of a divided universe embarked upon it. It involves in it other objects than the single recovery of our species. It decides higher questions. It stands linked with the supremacy of God, and will at length demonstrate the way in which he inflicts chastisement and overthrow upon all his enemies. I know not if our rebellious world be the only strong-hold which Satan is possessed of, or if it be but the single post of an extended warfare, that is now going on between the powers of light and of darkness. But be it the one or the other, the parties are in array, and the spirit of the contest is in full energy, and the honour of mighty combatants is at stake; and let us therefore cease to wonder that our humble residence has been made the theatre of so busy an operation, or that the ambition of loftier natures has here put forth all its desire and all its strenuousness.

This unfolds to us another of those high and extensive bearings, which the moral history of our globe may have on the system of God's universal administration. Were an enemy to touch the shore of this high-minded country, and to occupy so much as one of the humblest villages, and there to seduce the natives from their loyalty, and to sit down along with them in entrenched defiance to all the threats, and to all the preparations of an insulted empire—oh! how would the cry of wounded pride resound throughout all the ranks and varieties of our mighty population; and this very movement of indignancy would reach the king upon his throne; and circulate among those who stood in all the grandeur of chieftainship around him; and be heard to thrill in the eloquence of Parliament; and spread so resistless an appeal to a nation's honour, or a nation's patriotism, that the trumpet of war would summon to its call all the spirit and all the willing energies of our kingdom; and rather than sit down in patient endurance under the burning disgrace of such a violation, would the whole of its strength and resources be embarked upon the contest; and never, never would we let down our exertions and our sacrifices, till either our deluded countrymen were reclaimed, or till the whole of this offence were by one righteous act of vengeance, swept away altogether from the face of the territory it deformed.

The Bible is always most full and most explanatory on those points of revelation to which men are personally interested. But it does at times offer a dim transparency, through which may be caught a partial view of such designs and of such enterprises as are now-afloat among the upper orders of intelligence. It tells us of a mighty struggle that is now going on for a moral ascendency over the hearts of this world's population. It tells us that our race were seduced from their allegiance to God, by the plotting sagacity of one who stands pre-eminent against him, among the hosts of a very wide and extended rebellion. It tells us of the Captain of Salvation, who undertook to spoil him of this triumph, and throughout the whole of that magnificent train of prophecy which points to him, does it describe the work he had to do as a conflict, in which strength was to be put forth, and painful suffering to be endured, and fury to be poured upon enemies, and principalities to be dethroned, and all those toils, and dangers, and difficulties to be borne, which strewed the path of perseverance that was to carry him to victory.

But it is a contest of skill, as well as of strength and of influence. There is the earnest competition of angelic faculties embarked on this struggle for ascendency. And while in the Bible there is recorded, (faintly and partially, we admit,) the deep and insidious policy that is practised on the one side; we are also told, that on the plan of our world's restoration, there are lavished all the riches of an unsearchable wisdom upon the other. It would appear, that for the accomplishment of his purpose, the great enemy of God and of man plied his every calculation; and brought all the devices of his deep and settled malignity to bear upon our species; and thought that could he involve us in sin, every attribute of the Divinity stood staked to the banishment of our race from beyond the limits of the empire of righteousness; and thus did he practise his invasions on the moral territory of the unfallen; and glorying in his success, did he fancy and feel that he had achieved a permanent separation between the God who sitteth in heaven, and one at least of the planetary mansions which he had reared.

The errand of the Saviour was to restore this sinful world, and have its people readmitted within the circle of heaven's pure and righteous family. But in the government of heaven, as well as in the government of earth, there are certain principles which cannot be compromised; and certain maxims of administration which must never be departed from; and a certain character of majesty and of truth, on which the taint even of the slightest violation can never be permitted; and a certain authority which must be upheld by the immutability of all its sanctions, and the unerring fulfilment of all its wise and righteous proclamations. All this was in the mind of the archangel, and a gleam of malignant joy shot athwart him as he conceived his project for hemming our unfortunate species within the bound of an irrecoverable dilemma; and as surely as sin and holiness could not enter into fellowship, so surely did he think, that if man were seduced to disobedience, would the truth, and the justice, and the immutability of God, lay their insurmountable barriers on the path of his future acceptance.

It was only in that plan of recovery of which Jesus Christ was the author and the finisher, that the great adversary of our species met with a wisdom which overmatched him. It is true, that he reared, in the guilt to which he seduced us, a mighty obstacle in the way of this lofty undertaking. But when the grand expedient was announced, and the blood of that atonement, by which sinners are brought nigh, was willingly offered to be shed for us, and the eternal Son, to carry this mystery into accomplishment, assumed our nature—then was the prince of that mighty rebellion, in which the fate and the history of our world are so deeply implicated, in visible alarm for the safety of all his acquisitions:—nor can the record of this wondrous history carry forward its narrative, without furnishing some transient glimpses of a sublime and a superior warfare, in which, for the prize of a spiritual dominion over our species, we may dimly perceive the contest of loftiest talent, and all the designs of heaven in behalf of man, met at every point of their evolution, by the counter-workings of a rival strength and a rival sagacity.

We there read of a struggle which the Captain of our salvation had to sustain, when the lustre of the Godhead lay obscured, and the strength of its omnipotence was mysteriously weighed down under the infirmities of our nature—how Satan singled him out, and dared him to the combat of the wilderness—how all his wiles and all his influences were resisted—how he left our Saviour in all the triumphs of unsubdued loyalty—how the progress of this mighty achievement is marked by the every character of a conflict—how many of the Gospel miracles were so many direct infringements on the power and empire of a great spiritual rebellion—how in one precious season of gladness among the few which brightened the dark career of our Saviour's humiliation, he rejoiced in spirit, and gave as the cause of it to his disciples, that "he saw Satan fall like lightning from heaven"—how the momentary advantages that were gotten over him, are ascribed to the agency of this infernal being, who entered the heart of Judas, and tempted the disciple to betray his Master and his Friend. I know that I am treading on the confines of mystery. I cannot tell what the battle that he fought. I cannot compute the terror or the strength of his enemies. I cannot say, for I have not been told, how it was that they stood in marshalled and hideous array against him:—nor can I measure how great the firm daring of his soul, when he tasted that cup in all its bitterness, which he prayed might pass away from him; when with the feeling that he was forsaken by his God, he trod the winepress alone; when he entered single-handed upon that dreary period of agony, and insult, and death, in which from the garden to the cross, he had to bear the burden of a world's atonement. I cannot speak in my own language, but I can say in the language of the Bible, of the days and the nights of this great enterprise, that it was the season of the travail of his soul; that it was the hour and the power of darkness; that the work of redemption was a work accompanied by the effort, and the violence, and the fury of a combat; by all the arduousness of a battle in its progress, and all the glories of a victory in its termination; and after he called out that it was finished, after he was loosed from the prison-house of the grave, after he had ascended up on high, he is said to have made captivity captive: and to have spoiled principalities and powers; and to have seen his pleasure upon his enemies; and to have made a show of them openly.

I will not affect a wisdom above that which is written, by fancying such details of this warfare as the Bible has not laid before me. But surely it is no more than being wise up to that which is written, to assert, that in achieving the redemption of our world, a warfare had to be accomplished; that upon this subject there was among the higher provinces of creation, the keen and the animated conflict of opposing interests; that the result of it involved something grander and more affecting, than even the fate of this world's population; that it decided a question of rivalship between the righteous and everlasting Monarch of universal being, and the prince of a great and widely extended rebellion, of which I neither know how vast is the magnitude, nor how important and diversified are the bearings; and thus do we gather from this consideration, another distinct argument, helping us to explain, why on the salvation of our solitary species so much attention appears to have been concentred, and so much energy appears to have been expended.

But it would appear from the records of inspiration, that the contest is not yet ended; that on the one hand the Spirit of God is employed in making for the truths of Christianity, a way into the human heart, with all the power of an effectual demonstration; that on the other there is a spirit now abroad, which worketh in the children of disobedience; that on the one hand, the Holy Ghost is calling men out of darkness into the marvellous light of the Gospel; and that on the other hand, he who is styled the god of this world, is blinding their hearts, lest the light of the glorious gospel of Christ should enter into them; that they who are under the dominion of the one, are said to have overcome, because greater is he that is in them than he that is in the world; and that they who are under the dominion of the other, are said to be the children of the devil, and to be under his snare, and to be taken captive by him at his will. How these respective powers do operate, is one question. The fact of their operation, is another. We abstain from the former. We attach ourselves to the latter, and gather from it, that the prince of darkness still walketh abroad among us; that he is still working his insidious policy, if not with the vigorous inspiration of hope, at least with the frantic energies of despair; that while the overtures of reconciliation are made to circulate through the world, he is plying all his devices to deafen and to extinguish the impression of them; or, in other words, while a process of invitation and of argument has emanated from heaven, for reclaiming men to their loyalty—the process is resisted at all its points, by one who is putting forth his every expedient, and wielding a mysterious ascendency, to seduce and to enthral them.

To an infidel ear, all this carries the sound of something wild and visionary along with it; but though only known through the medium of revelation, after it is known, who can fail to recognize its harmony with the great lineaments of human experience? Who has not felt the workings of a rivalry within him, between the power of conscience and the power of temptation? Who does not remember those seasons of retirement, when the calculations of eternity had gotten a momentary command over the heart; and time, with all its interests and all its vexations, had dwindled into insignificancy before them? And who does not remember, how upon his actual engagement with the objects of time, they resumed a control, as great and as omnipotent, as if all the importance of eternity adhered to them—how they emitted from them such an impression upon his feelings, as to fix and to fascinate the whole man into a subserviency to their influence—how in spite of every lesson of their worthlessness, brought home to him at every turn by the rapidity of the seasons, and the vicissitudes of life, and the ever-moving progress of his own earthly career, and the visible ravages of death among his acquaintances around him, and the desolations of his family, and the constant breaking up of his system of friendships, and the affecting spectacle of all that lives and is in motion, withering and hastening to the grave; —oh! how comes it that in the face of all this experience, the whole elevation of purpose, conceived in the hour of his better understanding, should be dissipated and forgotten? Whence the might, and whence the mystery of that spell, which so binds and so infatuates us to the world? What prompts us so to embark the whole strength of our eagerness and of our desires in pursuit of interests which we know a few little years will bring to utter annihilation? Who is it that imparts to them all the charm and all the colour of an unfailing durability? Who is it that throws such an air of stability over these earthly tabernacles, as makes them look to the fascinated eye of man like resting places for eternity? Who is it that so pictures out the objects of sense, and so magnifies the range of their future enjoyment, and so dazzles the fond and deceived imagination, that in looking onward through our earthly career, it appears like the vista, or the perspective of innumerable ages? He who is called the god of this world. He who can dress the idleness of its waking dreams in the garb of reality. He who can pour a seducing brilliancy over the panorama of its fleeting pleasures and its vain anticipations. He who can turn it into an instrument of deceitfulness; and make it wield such an absolute ascendency over all the affections, that man, become the poor slave of its idolatries, and its charms, puts the authority of conscience, and the warnings of the Word of God, and the offered instigations of the Spirit of God, and all the lessons of calculation, and the wisdom even of his own sound and sober experience, away from him.

But this wondrous contest will come to a close. Some will return to their loyalty, and others will keep by their rebellion; and, in the day of the winding up of the drama of this world's history, there will be made manifest to the myriads of the various orders of creation, both the mercy and vindicated majesty of the Eternal. Oh! on that day how vain will this presumption of the Infidel astronomer appear, when the affairs of men come to be examined in the presence of an innumerable company; and beings of loftiest nature are seen to crowd around the judgment-seat; and the Saviour shall appear in our sky, with a celestial retinue, who have come with him from afar to witness all his doings, and to take a deep and solemn interest in all his dispensations; and the destiny of our species, whom the Infidel would thus detach, in solitary insignificance, from the universe altogether, shall be found to merge and to mingle with higher destinies—the good to spend their eternity with angels—the bad to spend their eternity with angels—the former to be readmitted into the universal family of God's obedient worshippers—the latter to share in the everlasting pain and ignominy of the defeated hosts of the rebellious—the people of this planet to be implicated, throughout the whole train of their never-ending history, with the higher ranks, and the more extended tribes of intelligence; and thus it is that the special administration we now live under, shall be seen to harmonize in its bearings, and to accord in its magnificence, with all that extent of nature and of her territories, which modern science has unfolded.

DISCOURSE VII.

On the slender Influence of mere Taste and Sensibility in Matters of Religion.

"And lo, thou art unto them as a very lovely song of one who hath a pleasant voice, and can play well on an instrument; for they hear thy words, but they do them not."—*Ezekiel* xxxiii. 32.

You easily understand how a taste for music is one thing, and a real submission to the influence of religion is another;—how the ear may be regaled by the melody of sound, and the heart may utterly refuse the proper impression of the sense that is conveyed by it; how the sons and daughters of the world may, with their every affection devoted to its perishable vanities, inhale all the delights of enthusiasm, as they sit in crowded assemblage around the deep and solemn oratorio;—aye, and whether it be the humility of penitential feeling, or the rapture of grateful acknowledgment, or the sublime of a contemplative piety, or the aspiration of pure and of holy purposes, which breathes throughout the words of the performance, and gives to it all the spirit and all the expression by which it is pervaded; it is a very possible thing, that the moral, and the rational, and the active man, may have given no entrance into his bosom for any of these sentiments; and yet so overpowered may he be by the charm of the vocal conveyance through which they are addressed to him, that he may be made to feel with such an emotion, and to weep with such a tenderness, and to kindle with such a transport, and to glow with such an elevation, as may one and all carry upon them the semblance of sacredness.

But might not this semblance deceive him? Have you never heard any tell, and with complacency too, how powerfully his devotion was awakened by an act of attendance on the oratorio—how his heart, melted and subdued by the influence of harmony, did homage to all the religion of which it was the vehicle—how he was so moved and overborne, that he had to shed the tears of contrition, and to be agitated by the terrors of judgment, and to receive an awe upon his spirit of the greatness and the majesty of God—and that wrought up to the lofty pitch of eternity, he could look down upon the world, and by the glance of one commanding survey, pronounce upon the littleness and the vanity of all its concerns? Oh! it is very, very possible that all this might thrill upon the ears of the man, and circulate a succession of solemn and affecting images around his fancy—and yet that essential principle of his nature, upon which the practical influence of Christianity turns, might have met with no reaching and no subduing efficacy whatever to arouse it. He leaves the exhibition, as dead in trespasses and sins as he came to it. Conscience has not awakened upon him. Repentance has not turned him. Faith has not made any positive lodgement within him of her great and her constraining realities. He speeds him back to his business and to his family, and there he plays off the old man in all the entireness of his uncrucified temper, and of his obstinate worldliness, and of all those earthly and unsanctified affections, which are found to cleave to him with as great tenacity as ever. He is really and experimentally the very same man as before—and all those sensibilities which seemed to bear upon them so much of the air and unction of heaven, are found to go into dissipation, and be forgotten with the loveliness of the song.

Amid all that illusion which such momentary visitations of seriousness and of sentiment throw around the character of man, let us never lose sight of the test, that "by their fruits ye shall know them." It is not coming up to this test, that you hear and are delighted. It is that you hear and do. This is the ground upon which the reality of your religion is discriminated now; and on the day of reckoning, this is the ground upon which your religion will be judged then; and that award is to be passed upon you, which will fix and perpetuate your destiny for ever. You have a taste for music. This no more implies the hold and the ascendency of religion over you, than that you have a taste for beautiful scenery, or a taste for painting, or even a taste for the sensualities of epicurism. But music may be made to express the glow and the movement of devotional feeling; and it is saying nothing to say that the heart of him who listens with a raptured ear, is through the whole time of the performance, in harmony with such a movement? Why, it is saying nothing to the purpose. Music may lift the inspiring note of patriotism; and the inspiration may be felt; and it may thrill over the recesses of the soul, to the mustering up of all its energies; and it may sustain to the last cadence of the song, the firm nerve and purpose of intrepidity; and all this may be realized upon him, who in the day of battle, and upon actual collision with the dangers of it, turns out to be a coward. And music may lull the feelings into unison with piety; and stir up the inner man to lofty determinations; and so engage for a time his affections, that, as if weaned from the dust, they promise an immediate entrance on some great and elevated career, which may carry him through his pilgrimage superior to all the sordid and grovelling enticements that abound in it. But he turns him to the world, and all this glow abandons him; and the words which he hath heard, he doeth them not; and in the hour of temptation he turns out to be a deserter from the law of allegiance; and the test I have now specified looks hard upon him, and discriminates him amid all the parading insignificance of his fine but fugitive emotions, to be the subject both of present guilt and of future vengeance.

The faithful application of this test would put to flight a host of other delusions. It may be carried round among all those phenomena of human character, where there is the exhibition of something associated with religion, but which is not religion itself. An exquisite relish for music is no test of the influence of Christianity. Neither are many other of the exquisite sensibilities of our nature. When a kind mother closes the eyes of her expiring babe, she is thrown into a flood of sensibility, and soothing to her heart are the sympathy and the prayers of an attending minister. When a gathering neighbourhood assemble to the funeral of an acquaintance, one pervading sense of regret and tenderness sits on the face of the company; and the deep silence, broken only by the solemn utterance of the man of God, carries a kind of pleasing religiousness along with it. The sacredness of the hallowed day, and the decencies of its observation, may engage the affections of him who loves to walk in the footsteps of his father; and every recurring Sabbath may bring to his bosom, the charm of its regularity and its quietness. Religion has its accomplishments; and in these, there may be something to soothe, and to fascinate, even in the absence of the appropriate influences of religion. The deep and tender impression of a family bereavement, is not religion. The love of established decencies, is not religion. The charm of all that sentimentalism which is associated with many of its solemn and affecting services, is not religion. They form the distinct folds of its accustomed drapery; but they do not, any or all of them put together, make up the substance of the thing itself. A mother's tenderness may flow most gracefully over the tomb of her departed little one; and she may talk the while of that heaven whither its spirit has ascended. The man whom death had widowed of his friend, may abandon himself to the movements of that grief, which for a time will claim an ascendency over him; and, among the multitude of his other reveries, may love to hear of the eternity, where sorrow and separation are alike unknown. He who has been trained, from his infant days, to remember the Sabbath, may love the holiness of its aspect; and associate himself with all its observances; and take a delighted share in the mechanism of its forms. But, let not these think, because the tastes and the sensibilities which engross them, may be blended with religion, that they indicate either its strength or its existence within them. I recur to the test. I press its imperious exactions upon you. I call for fruit, and demand the permanency of a religious influence on the habits and the history. Oh! how many who take a flattering unction to their souls, when they think of their amiable feelings, and their becoming observations, with whom this severe touch-stone would, like the head of Medusa, put to flight all their complacency. The afflictive dispensation is forgotten—and he on whom it was laid, is practically as indifferent to God and to eternity as before. The Sabbath services come to a close; and they are followed by the same routine of week-day worldliness as before. In neither the one case nor the other, do we see more of the radical influence of Christianity than in the sublime and melting influence of sacred music upon the soul; and all this tide of emotion is found to die away from the bosom, like the pathos or like the loveliness of a song.

The instances may be multiplied without number. A man may have a taste for eloquence, and eloquence the most touching or sublime may lift her pleading voice on the side of religion. A man may love to have his understanding stimulated by the ingenuities, or the resistless urgencies of an argument; and argument the most profound and the most overbearing, may put forth all the might of a constraining vehemence in behalf of religion. A man may feel the rejoicings of a conscious elevation, when some ideal scene of magnificence is laid before him; and where are these scenes so readily to be met with, as when led to expatiate in thought over the track of eternity, or to survey the wonders of creation, or to look to the magnitude of these great and universal interests which lie within the compass of religion? A man may have his attention riveted and regaled by that power of imitative description, which brings all the recollections of his own experience before him; which presents him with a faithful analysis of his own heart; which embodies in language such intimacies of observation and of feeling, as have often passed before his eyes, or played within his bosom, but had never been so truly or so ably pictured to the view of his remembrance. Now, all this may be done in the work of pressing the duties of religion; in the work of instancing the application of religion; in the work of pointing those allusions to life and to manners, which manifest the truth to the conscience, and plant such a conviction of sin, as forms the very basis of a sinner's religion. Now, in all these cases, I see other principles brought into action, and which may be in a state of most lively and vigorous movement, and be yet in a state of entire separation from the principle of religion. I will make bold to say, on the strength of these illustrations, that as much delight may emanate from the pulpit, on an arrested audience beneath it, as ever emanated from the boards of a theatre—aye, and with as total a disjunction of mind too, in the one case as in the other, from the essence or the habit of religion. I recur to the test. I make my appeal to experience; and I put it to you all, whether your finding upon the subject do not agree with my saying about it, that a man may weep, and admire, and have many of his faculties put upon the stretch of their most intense gratification—his judgment established, and his fancy enlivened, and his feelings overpowered, and his hearing charmed, as by the accents of heavenly persuasion, and all within him feasted by the rich and varied luxuries of an intellectual banquet!—Oh! it is cruel to frown unmannerly in the midst of so much satisfaction. But I must not forget that truth has her authority, as well as her sternness; and she forces me to affirm, that after all this has been felt and gone through, there might not be one principle which lies at the turning point of conversion, that has experienced a single movement—not one of its purposes be conceived—not one of its doings be accomplished—not one step of that repentance, which, if we have not, we perish, so much as entered upon—not one announcement of that faith, by which we are saved, admitted into a real and actual possession by the inner man. He has had his hour's entertainment, and willingly does he award this homage to the performer, that he hath a pleasant voice, and can play well on an instrument—but, in another hour, it fleets away from his remembrance, and goes all to nothing, like the loveliness of a song.

Now, in bringing these Astronomical Discourses to a close, I feel it my duty to advert to this exhibition of character in man. The sublime and interesting topic which has engaged us, however feebly it may have been handled; however inadequately it may have been put in all its worth, and in all its magnitude before you; however short the representation of the speaker or the conception of the hearers may have been of that richness, and that greatness, and that loftiness, which belong to it; possesses in itself a charm to fix the attention, to regale the imagination, and to subdue the whole man into a delighted reverence; and, in a word, to beget such a solemnity of thought, and of emotion, as may occupy and enlarge the soul for hours together, as may waft it away from the grossness of ordinary life, and raise it to a kind of elevated calm above all its vulgarities and all its vexations.

Now, tell me whether the whole of this effect upon the feelings, may not be formed without the presence of religion. Tell me whether there might not be such a constitution of mind, that it may both want altogether that principle in virtue of which the doctrines of Christianity are admitted into the belief, and the duties of Christianity are admitted into a government over the practice—and yet, at the very same time, it may have the faculty of looking abroad over some scene of magnificence, and of being wrought up to ecstacy with the sense of all those glories among which it is expatiating. I want you to see clearly the distinction between these two attributes of the human character. They are, in truth, as different the one from the other, as a taste for the grand and the graceful of scenery differs from the appetite of hunger; and the one may both exist and have a most intense operation within the bosom of that very individual, who entirely disowns, and is entirely disgusted with the other. What! must a man be converted, ere from the most elevated peak of some Alpine wilderness, he becomes capable of feeling the force and the majesty of those great lineaments which the hand of nature has thrown around him, in the varied forms of precipice, and mountain, and the wave of mighty forests, and the rush of sounding waterfalls, and distant glimpses of human territory, and pinnacles of everlasting snow, and the sweep of that circling horizon, which folds in its ample embrace the whole of this noble amphitheatre? Tell me whether, without the aid of Christianity, or without a particle of reverence for the only name given under heaven whereby men can be saved, a man may not kindle at such a perspective as this, into all the raptures, and into all the movements of a poetic elevation; and be able to render into the language of poetry, the whole of that sublime and beauteous imagery which adorns it; aye, and as if he were treading on the confines of a sanctuary which he has not entered, may he not mix up with the power and the enchantment of his description, such allusions to the presiding genius of the scene: or to the still but animating spirit of the solitude; or to the speaking silence of some mysterious character which reigns throughout the landscape; or, in fine, to that eternal Spirit, who sits behind the elements he has formed, and combines them into all the varieties of a wide and a wondrous creation; might not all this be said and sung with an emphasis so moving, as to spread the colouring of piety over the pages of him who performs thus well upon his instrument; and yet, the performer himself have a conscience unmoved by a single warning of God's actual communication, and the judgment unconvinced, and the fears unawakened, and the life unreformed by it?

Now what is true of a scene on earth, is also true of that wider and more elevated scene which stretches over the immensity around it, into a dark and a distant unknown. Who does not feel an aggrandisement of thought and of faculty, when he looks abroad over the amplitudes of creation—when placed on a telescopic eminence, his aided eye can find a pathway to innumerable worlds—when that wondrous field, over which there had hung for many ages the mantle of so deep an obscurity, is laid open to him, and instead of a dreary and unpeopled solitude, he can see over the whole face of it such an extended garniture of rich and goodly habitations! Even the Atheist, who tells us that the universe is self-existent and indestructible—even he, who instead of seeing the traces of a manifold wisdom in its manifold varieties, sees nothing in them all but the exquisite structures and the lofty dimensions of materialism—even he, who would despoil creation of its God, cannot look upon its golden suns, and their accompanying systems, without the solemn impression of a magnificence that fixes and overpowers him. Now, conceive such a belief of God as you all profess, to dawn upon his understanding. Let him become as one of yourselves—and so be put into the condition of rising from the sublime of matter to the sublime of mind. Let him now learn to subordinate the whole of this mechanism to the design and authority of a great presiding intelligence; and re-assembling all the members of the universe, however distant, into one family, let him mingle with his former conceptions of the grandeur which belonged to it, the conception of that eternal Spirit who sits enthroned on the immensity of his own wonders, and embraces all that he has made, within the ample scope of one great administration. Then will the images and the impressions of sublimity come in upon him from a new quarter. Then will another avenue be opened, through which a sense of grandeur may find its way into his soul, and have a mightier influence than ever to fill, and to elevate and to expand it. Then will be established a new and a noble association, by the aid of which all that he formerly looked upon as fair becomes more lovely; and all that he formerly looked upon as great, becomes more magnificent. But will you believe me, that even with this accession to his mind of ideas gathered from the contemplation of the Divinity; even with that pleasurable glow which steals over his imagination, when he now thinks him of the majesty of God; even with as much of what you would call piety, as I fear is enough to soothe and to satisfy many of yourselves, and which stirs and kindles within you when you hear the goings forth of the Supreme set before you in the terms of a lofty representation; even with all this, I say there may be as wide a distance from the habit and the character of godliness, as if God was still atheistically disowned by him. Take the conduct of his life and the currency of his affections; and you may see as little upon them of the stamp of loyalty to God, or of reverence for any one of his authenticated proclamations, as you may see in him who offers his poetic incense to the genii, or weeps enraptured over the visions of a beauteous mythology. The sublime of Deity has wrought up his soul to a pitch of conscious and pleasing elevation—and yet this no more argues the will of Deity to have a practical authority over him, than does that tone of elevation which is caught by looking at the sublime of a naked materialism. The one and the other have their little hour of ascendency over him; and when he turns him to the rude and ordinary world, both vanish alike from his sensibilities as does the loveliness of a song.

To kindle and be elevated by a sense of the majesty of God, is one thing. It is totally another thing to feel a movement of obedience to the will of God, under the impression of his rightful authority over all the creatures whom he has formed. A man may have an imagination all alive to the former; while the latter never prompts him to one act of obedience; never leads him to compare his life with the requirements of the Lawgiver; never carries him from such a scrutiny as this, to the conviction of sin; never whispers such an accusation to the ear of his conscience, as causes him to mourn, and to be in heaviness for the guilt of his hourly and habitual rebellion; never shuts him up to the conclusion of the need of a Saviour; never humbles him to acquiescence in the doctrine of that revelation, which comes to his door with such a host of evidence, as even his own philosophy cannot bid away; never extorts a single believing prayer in the name of Christ, or points a single look, either of trust or of reverence, to his atonement; never stirs any effective movement of conversion; never sends an aspiring energy into his bosom after the aids of that Spirit, who alone can waken him out of his lethargies, and by the anointing which remaineth, can rivet and substantiate in his practice, those goodly emotions which have hitherto plied him with the deceitfulness of their momentary visits, and then capriciously abandoned him.

The mere majesty of God's power and greatness, when offered to your notice, lays hold of one of the faculties within you. The holiness of God, with his righteous claim of legislation, lays hold of another of these faculties. The difference between them is so great, that the one may be engrossed and interested to the full, while the other remains untouched, and in a state of entire dormancy. Now, it is no matter what it be that ministers delight to the former of these two faculties: If the latter be not arrested and put on its proper exercise, you are making no approximation whatever to the right habit and character of religion. There are a thousand ways in which we may contrive to regale your taste for that which is beauteous and majestic. It may find its gratification•in the loveliness of a vale, or in the freer and bolder outlines of an upland situation, or in the terrors of a storm, or in the sublime contemplations of astronomy, or in the magnificent idea of a God who sends forth the wakefulness of his omniscient eye, and the vigour of his upholding hand, throughout all the realms of nature and of providence. The mere taste of the human mind may get its ample enjoyment in each and in all of these objects, or in a vivid representation of them; nor does it make any material difference, whether this representation be addressed to you from the stanzas of a poem, or from the recitations of a theatre, or finally from the discourses and the demonstrations of a pulpit. And thus it is, that still on the impulse of the one principle only, people may come in gathering multitudes to the house of God; and share with eagerness in all the glow and bustle of a crowded attendance; and have their every eye directed to the speaker; and feel a responding movement in their bosom to his many appeals and his many arguments; and carry a solemn and overpowering impression of all the services away with them; and yet throughout the whole of this seemly exhibition, not one effectual knock may have been given at the door of conscience. The other principle may be as profoundly asleep, as if hushed into the insensibility of death. There is a spirit of deep slumber, it would appear, which the music of no description, even though attuned to a theme so lofty as the greatness and majesty of the Godhead, can ever charm away. Oh! it may have been a piece of parading insignificance altogether—the minister playing on his favourite instrument, and the people dissipating away their time on the charm and idle luxury of a theatrical emotion.

The religion of taste, is one thing. The religion of conscience, is another. I recur to the test. What is the plain and practical doing which ought to issue from the whole of our argument? If one lesson come more clearly or more authoritatively out of it than another, it is the supremacy of the Bible. If fitted to impress one movement rather than another, it is that movement of a docility, in virtue of which, man, with the feeling that he has all to learn, places himself in the attitude of a little child, before the book of the unsearchable God, who has deigned to break his silence, and to transmit, even to our age of the world, a faithful record of his own communication. What progress then are you making in this movement? Are you, or are you not, like newborn babes, desiring the sincere milk of the word, that you may grow thereby? How are you coming on in the work of casting down your lofty imaginations? With the modesty of true science, which is here at one with the humblest and most penitentiary feeling which Christianity can awaken, are you bending an eye of earnestness on the Bible, and appropriating its informations, and moulding your every conviction to its doctrines and its testimonies? How long, I beseech you, has this been your habitual exercise? By this time do you feel the darkness and the insufficiency of nature? Have you found your way to the need of an atonement? Have you learned the might and the efficacy which are given to the principle of faith? Have you longed with all your energies to realize it? Have you broken loose from the obvious misdoings of your former history? Are you convinced of your total deficiency from the spiritual obedience of the affections? Have you read of the Holy Ghost, by whom renewed in the whole desire and character of your mind, you are led to run with alacrity in the way of the commandments? Have you turned to its practical use, the important truth, that he has given to the believing prayers of all, who really want to be relieved from the power both of secret and of visible iniquity? I demand something more than the homage you have rendered to the pleasantness of the voice that has been sounding in your hearing. What I have now to urge upon you, is the bidding of the voice, to read, and to reform and to pray, and, in a word, to make your consistent step from the elevations of philosophy, to all those exercises, whether of doing or of believing, which mark the conduct of the earnest, and the devoted, and the subdued, and the aspiring Christian.

This brings under our view a most deeply interesting exhibition of human nature, which may often be witnessed among the cultivated orders of society. When a teacher of Christianity addresses himself to that principle of justice within us, in virtue of which we feel the authority of God to be a prerogative which righteously belongs to him, he is then speaking the appropriate language of religion, and is advancing its naked and appropriate claim over the obedience of mankind. He is then urging that pertinent and powerful consideration, upon which alone he can ever hope to obtain the ascendency of a practical influence over the purposes and the conduct of human beings. It is only by insisting on the moral claim of God to a right of government over his creatures, that he can carry their loyal subordination to the will of God. Let him keep by this single argument, and urge it upon the conscience, and then, without any of the other accompaniments of what is called christian oratory, he may bring convincingly home upon his hearers all the varieties of christian doctrine. He may establish within their minds the dominion of all that is essential in the faith of the New Testament. He may, by carrying out this principle of God's authority into all its applications, convince them of sin. He may lead them to compare the loftiness and spirituality of his law, with the habitual obstinacy of their own worldly affections. He may awaken them to the need of a Saviour. He may urge them to a faithful and submissive perusal of God's own communication. He may thence press upon them the truth and the immutability of their Sovereign. He may work in their hearts an impression of this emphatic saying, that God is not to be mocked—that his law must be upheld in all the significancy of its proclamations—and that either his severities must be discharged upon the guilty, or in some other way an adequate provision be found for its outraged dignity, and its violated sanctions. Thus may he lead them to flee for refuge to the blood of the atonement. And he may further urge upon his hearers, how, such is the enormity of sin, that it is not enough to have found an expiation for it; how its power and its existence must be eradicated from the hearts of all, who are to spend their eternity in the mansions of the celestial; how, for this purpose, an expedient is made known to us in the New Testament; how a process must be described upon earth, to which there is given the appropriate name of sanctification; how, at the very commencement of every true course of discipleship, this process is entered upon with a purpose in the mind of forsaking all; how nothing short of a single devotedness to the will of God, will ever carry us forward through the successive stages of this holy and elevated career; how, to help the infirmities of our nature, the Spirit is ever in readiness to be given to those who ask it; and that thus the life of every Christian becomes a life of entire dedication to Him who died for us—a life of prayer, and vigilance, and close dependance on the grace of God; and, as the infallible result of the plain but powerful and peculiar teaching of the Bible, a life of vigorous unwearied activity in the doing of all the commandments.

Now, this I would call the essential business of Christianity. This is the truth as it is in Jesus, in its naked and unassociated simplicity. In the work of urging it, nothing more might have been done, than to present certain views, which may come with as great clearness, and freshness, and take as full possession of the mind of a peasant as of the mind of a philosopher. There is a sense of God, and of the rightful allegiance that is due to him. There are plain and practical appeals to the conscience. There is a comparison of the state of the heart, with the requirements of a law which proposes to take the heart under its obedience. There is the inward discernment of its coldness about God; of its unconcern about the matters of duty and of eternity; of its devotion to the forbidden objects of sense; of its constant tendency to nourish within its own receptacles, the very element and principle of rebellion, and in virtue of this, to send forth the stream of an hourly and accumulating disobedience over those doings of the outer man, which make up his visible history in the world. There is such an earnest and overpowering impression of all this, as will fix a man down to the single object of deliverance; as will make him awake only to those realities which have a significant and substantial bearing on the case that engrosses him; as will teach him to nauseate all the impertinences of tasteful and ambitious description; as will attach him to the truth in its simplicity; as will fasten his every regard upon the Bible, where, if he persevere in the work of honest inquiry, he will soon be made to perceive the accordancy between its statements, and all those movements of fear, or guilt, or deeply-felt necessity, or conscious darkness, stupidity, and unconcern about the matters of salvation, which pass within his own bosom; in a word, as will endear him to that plainness of speech, by which his own experience is set evidently before him, and that plain phraseology of scripture, which is best fitted to bring home to him the doctrine of redemption, in all the truth, and in all the preciousness of its applications.

Now, the whole of this work may be going on, and that too in the wisest and most effectual manner, without so much as one particle of incense being offered to any of the subordinate principles of the human constitution. There may be no fascinations of style. There may be no magnificence of description. There may be no poignancy of acute and irresistible argument. There may be a rivetted attention on the part of those whom the Spirit of God hath awakened to seriousness about the plain and affecting realities of conversion. Their conscience may be stricken, and their appetite be excited for an actual settlement of mind on those points about which they feel restless and unconfirmed. Such as these are vastly too much engrossed with the exigencies of their condition, to be repelled by the homeliness of unadorned truth. And thus it is, that while the loveliness of the song has done so little in helping on the influences of the gospel, our men of simplicity and prayer have done so much for it. With a deep and earnest impression of the truth themselves, they have made manifest that truth to the consciences of others. Missionaries have gone forth with no other preparation than the simple Word of the Testimony—and thousands have owned its power, by being both the hearers of the word and the doers of it also. They have given us the experiment in a state of unmingled simplicity; and we learn, from the success of their noble example, that without any one human expedient to charm the ear, the heart may, by the naked instrumentality of the Word of God, urged with plainness on those who feel its deceit and its worthlessness, be charmed to an entire acquiescence in the revealed way of God, and have impressed upon it the genuine stamp and character of godliness.

Could the sense of what is due to God, be effectually stirred up within the human bosom, it would lead to a practical carrying of all the lessons of Christianity. Now, to awaken this moral sense, there are certain simple relations between the creature and the

Creator, which must be clearly apprehended, and manifested with power unto the conscience. We believe, that however much philosophers may talk about the comparative ease of forming those conceptions which are simple, they will, if in good earnest after a right footing with God, soon discover in their own minds, all that darkness and incapacity about spiritual things, which are so broadly announced to us in the New Testament. And, oh! it is a deeply interesting spectacle, to behold a man, who can take a masterly and commanding survey over the field of some human speculation, who can clear his discriminated way through all the turns and ingenuities of some human argument, who by the march of a mighty and resistless demonstration, can scale with assured footstep the sublimities of science, and from his firm stand on the eminence he has won, can descry some wondrous range of natural or intellectual truth spread out in subordination before him;—and yet this very man may, in reference to the moral and authoritative claims of the Godhead, be in a state of utter apathy and blindness! All his attempts, either at the spiritual discernment, or the practical impression of this doctrine, may be arrested and baffled by the weight of some great inexplicable impotency. A man of homely talents, and still homelier education, may see what he cannot see, and feel what he cannot feel; and wise and prudent as he is, there may lie the barrier of an obstinate and impenetrable concealment, between his accomplished mind, and those things which are revealed unto babes.

But while his mind is thus utterly devoid of what may be called the main or elemental principle of theology, he may have a far quicker apprehension, and have his taste and his feelings much more powerfully interested, than the simple Christian who is beside him, by what may be called the circumstantials of theology. He can throw a wider and more rapid glance over the magnitudes of creation. He can be more delicately alive to the beauties and the sublimities which abound in it. He can, when the idea of a presiding God is suggested to him, have a more kindling sense of his natural majesty, and be able, both in imagination and in words, to surround the throne of the Divinity by the blazonry of more great, and splendid, and elevating images. And yet, with all those powers of conception which he does possess, he may not possess that on which practical Christianity hinges. The moral relation between him and God, may neither be effectively perceived, nor faithfully proceeded on. Conscience may be in a state of the most entire dormancy, and the man be regaling himself with the magnificence of God, while he neither loves God, nor believes God, nor obeys God.

And here I cannot but remark, how much effect and simplicity go together in the annals of Moravianism. The men of this truly interesting denomination, address themselves exclusively to that principle of our nature on which the proper influence of Christianity turns. Or, in other words, they take up the subject of the gospel message, that message devised by him who knew what was in man, and who, therefore, knew how to make the right and the suitable application to man.—They urge the plain Word of the Testimony; and they pray for a blessing from on high; and that thick impalpable veil, by which the god of this world blinds the hearts of men who believe not, lest the light of the glorious gospel of Christ should enter into them—that veil, which no power of philosophy can draw aside, gives way to the demonstration of the Spirit; and thus it is, that a clear perception of scriptural truth, and all the freshness and permanency of its moral influences, are to be met with among men who have just emerged from the rudest and the grossest barbarity.—Oh! when one looks at the number and the greatness of their achievements; when he thinks of the change they have made on materials so coarse and so unpromising; when he eyes the villages they have formed; and around the whole of that engaging perspective by which they have chequered and relieved the grim solitude of the desert, he witnesses the love, and listens to the piety of reclaiming savages;—who would not long to be in possession of the charm by which they have wrought this wondrous transformation—who would not willingly exchange for it all the parade of human eloquence, and all the confidence of human argument —and for the wisdom of winning souls, who is there that would not rejoice to throw the loveliness of the song, and all the insignificance of its passing fascination away from him?

And yet it is right that every cavil against Christianity should be met, and every argument for it be exhibited, and all the grace and sublimities of its doctrine be held out to their merited admiration. And if it be true, as it certainly is, that throughout the whole of this process, a man may be carried rejoicingly along from the mere indulgence of his taste, and the mere play and exercise of his understanding; while conscience is untouched, and the supremacy of moral claims upon the heart and the conduct is practically disowned by him— it is further right that this should be adverted to; and that such a melancholy unhingement in the constitution of man should be fully laid open, and that he should be driven out of the seductive complacency which he is so apt to cherish, merely because he delights in the loveliness of the song and that he should be urged with the imperiousness of a demand which still remains unsatisfied, to turn him from the corrupt indifference of nature, and to become personally a religious man; and that he should be assured how all the gratification he felt in listening to the word which respected the kingdom of God, will be of no avail, unless that kingdom come to himself in power—that it will only go to heighten the perversity of his character—that it will not extenuate his real and practical ungodliness, but will serve most fearfully to aggravate the condemnation of it.

With a religion so argumentable as ours, it may be easy to gather out of it a feast for the human understanding. With a religion so magnificent as ours, it may be easy to gather out of it a feast for the human imagination. But with a religion so humbling, and so strict, and so spiritual, it is not easy to mortify the pride; or to quell the strong enmity of nature; or to arrest the currency of the affections; or to turn the constitutional habits; or to pour a new complexion over the moral history; or to stem the domineering influence of things seen and things sensible; or to invest faith with a practical supremacy; or to give its objects such a vivacity of influence as shall overpower the near and the hourly impressions, that are ever emanating upon man from a seducing world. It is here that man feels himself treading upon the limit of his helplessness. It is here that he sees where the strength of nature ends; and the power of grace must either be put forth, or leave him to grope his darkling way, without one inch of progress towards the life and the substance of Christianity. It is here that a barrier rises on the contemplation of the inquirer—the barrier of separation between the carnal and the spiritual, and on which he may idly waste the every energy which belongs to him, in the enterprise of surmounting it. It is here, that after having walked the round of nature's acquisitions, and lavished upon the truth of all his ingenuities, and surveyed it in its every palpable character of grace and majesty; he will still feel himself on a level with the simplest and most untutored of the species. He needs the power of a living manifestation. He needs the anointing which remaineth. He needs that which fixes and perpetuates a stable revolution upon the character, and in virtue of which he may be advanced from the state of one who hears, and is delighted, to the state of one who hears, and is a doer. Oh! how strikingly is the experience even of vigorous and accomplished nature at one on this point with the announcements of revelation, that to work this change, there must be the putting forth of a peculiar agency; and that it is an agency, which,

withheld from the exercise of loftiest talent, is often brought down on an impressed audience, through the humblest of all instrumentality, with the demonstration of the Spirit and with power.

Think it not enough, that you carry in your bosom an expanded sense of the magnificence of creation. But pray for a subduing sense of the authority of the Creator. Think it not enough, that with the justness of a philosophical discernment, you have traced that boundary which hems in all the possibilities of human attainment, and have found that all beyond it is a dark and fathomless unknown. But let this modesty of science be carried, as in consistency it ought, to the question of revelation, and let all the antipathies of nature be schooled to acquiescence in the authentic testimonies of the Bible. Think it not enough that you have looked with sensibility and wonder at the representation of God throned in immensity, yet combining with the vastness of his entire superintendence, a most thorough inspection into all the minute and countless diversities of existence. Think of your own heart as one of these diversities; and that he ponders all its tendencies; and has an eye upon all its movements; and marks all its waywardness; and, God of judgment as he is, records its every secret, and its every sin, in the book of his remembrance. Think it not enough, that you have been led to associate a grandeur with the salvation of the New Testament; when made to understand that it draws upon it the regards of an arrested universe. How is it arresting your own mind? What has been the earnestness of your personal regards towards it? And tell me, if all its faith, and all its repentance, and all its holiness are not disowned by you? Think it not enough, that you have felt a sentimental charm when angels were pictured to your fancy as beckoning you to their mansions, and anxiously looking to the every symptom of your grace and reformation. Oh! be constrained by the power of all this tenderness, and yield yourselves up in a practical obedience to the call of the Lord God merciful and gracious. Think it not enough that you have shared for a moment in the deep and busy interest of that arduous conflict which is now going on for a moral ascendency over the species. Remember the conflict is for each of you individually; and let this alarm you into a watchfulness against the power of every temptation, and a cleaving dependence upon him through whom alone you will be more than conquerors. Above all, forget not that while you only hear and are delighted, you are still under nature's powerlessness, and nature's condemnation—and that the foundation is not laid, the mighty and essential change is not accomplished, the transition from death unto life is not undergone, the saving faith is not formed, nor the passage taken from darkness to the marvellous light of the gospel, till you are both hearers of the word and doers also. "For if any be a hearer of the word and not a doer, he is like unto a man beholding his natural face in a glass: for he beholdeth himself, and goeth his way, and straightway forgetteth what manner of man he was."

APPENDIX.

The writer of these Discourses has drawn up the following compilation of passages from Scripture, as serving to illustrate or to confirm the leading arguments which have been employed in each separate division of his subject.

DISCOURSE I.

In the beginning God created the heaven and the earth. Gen. i. 1.

Thus the heavens and the earth were finished, and all the host of them. Gen. ii. 1.

Behold the heaven, and the heaven of heavens, is the Lord's thy God, the earth also, with all that therein is. Deut. x. 14.

There is none like unto the God of Jeshurun, who rideth upon the heaven in thy help, and in his excellency on the sky. Deut. xxxiii. 26.

And Hezekiah prayed before the Lord, and said, O Lord God of Israel, which dwellest between the cherubims, thou art the God, even thou alone, of all the kingdoms of the earth; thou hast made heaven and earth. 2 Kings xix. 15.

For all the gods of the people are idols; but the Lord made the heavens. 1 Chronicles xvi. 26.

Thou, even thou, art Lord alone; thou hast made heaven, the heaven of heavens, with all their host, the earth and all things that are therein, the seas and all that is therein; and thou preservest them all; and the host of heaven worship thee. Nehemiah ix. 6.

Which alone spreadeth out the heavens, and treadeth upon the waves of the sea; which maketh Arcturus, Orion, and Pleiades, and the chambers of the south. Job ix. 8, 9.

He stretcheth out the north over the empty place, and hangeth the earth upon nothing. Job xxvi. 7.

By his spirit he hath garnished the heavens. Job xxvi. 13.

The heavens declare the glory of God; and the firmament showeth his handy-work. Psalm xix. 1.

By the word of the Lord were the heavens made; and all the host of them by the breath of his mouth. Psalm xxxiii. 6.

Of old hast thou laid the foundation of the earth; and the heavens are the work of thy hands. Psalm cii. 25.

Who coverest thyself with light as with a garment; who stretchest out the heavens like a curtain. Psalm civ. 2.

He appointed the moon for seasons; the sun knoweth his going down. Psalm civ. 19.

You are blessed of the Lord which made heaven and earth. The heaven, even the heavens, are the Lord's, but the earth hath he given to the children of men. Psalm cxv. 15, 16.

My help cometh from the Lord, which made heaven and earth. Psalm cxxi. 2.

Our help is in the name of the Lord, who made heaven and earth. Psalm cxxiv. 8.

The Lord that made heaven and earth, bless thee out of Zion. Psalm cxxxiv. 3.

Which made heaven and earth, the sea, and all that therein is. Psalm cxlvi. 6.

The Lord by wisdom hath founded the earth; by understanding hath he established the heavens. Prov. iii. 19.

Who hath measured the waters in the hollow of his hand, and meted out heaven with the span, and comprehended the dust of the earth in a measure, and weighed the mountains in a scale, and the hills in a balance. Isa. xl. 12.

It is he that sitteth upon the circle of the earth, and the inhabitants thereof are as grasshoppers; that stretcheth out the heaven as a curtain, and spreadeth them out as a tent to dwell in. Isa. xl. 22.

Thus saith God the Lord, he that created the heavens, and stretched them out; he that spread forth the earth, and that which cometh out of it; he that giveth breath unto the people upon it, and spirit to them that walk therein. Isa. xlii. 5.

Thus saith the Lord, thy Redeemer, and he that formed thee from the womb, I am the Lord that maketh all things; that stretcheth forth the heavens alone; that spreadeth abroad the earth by myself. Isa. xliv. 24.

I have made the earth, and created man upon it; I, even my hands, have stretched out the heavens, and all their host have I commanded. Isa. xlv. 12.

For thus saith the Lord that created the heavens, God himself that formed the earth and made it, he hath established it, he created it not in vain, he formed it to be inhabited. Isa. xlv. 18.

Mine hand also hath laid the foundation of the earth, and my right hand hath spanned the heavens; when I call unto them, they stand up together. Isa. xlviii. 13.

He hath made the earth by his power, he hath established the world by his wisdom, and hath stretched out the heavens by his discretion. Jer. x. 12.

Ah Lord God! behold, thou hast made the heaven and the earth by thy great power and stretched out arm, and there is nothing too hard for thee. Jer. xxxii. 17.

He hath made the earth by his power, he hath established the world by his wisdom, and hath stretched out the heaven by his understanding. Jer. li. 15.

It is he that buildeth his stories in the heaven, and hath founded his troop in the earth; he that calleth for the waters of the sea, and poureth them out upon the face of the earth, The Lord is his name. Amos ix. 6.

We also are men of like passions with you, and preach unto you, that ye should turn from these vanities unto the living God, which made heaven, and earth, and the sea, and all things that are therein. Acts xiv. 15.

Hath in these last days spoken unto us by his Son, whom he hath appointed heir of all things, by whom also he made the worlds. Heb. i. 2.

Thou, Lord, in the beginning hast laid the foundation of the earth; and the heavens are the work of thine hands. Heb. i. 10.

Through faith, we understand that the worlds were framed by the word of God. Heb. xi. 3.

DISCOURSE II.

THE secret things belong unto the Lord our God, but those things which are revealed belong unto us and to our children for ever, that we may do all the words of this law. Deut. xxix. 29.

I would seek unto God, and unto God would I commit my cause; Which doeth great things and unsearchable; marvellous things without number. Job v. 8, 9.

Which doeth great things past finding out; yea, and wonders without number. Job ix. 10.

Canst thou by searching find out God? Canst thou find out the Almighty unto perfection? Job xi. 7.

Hast thou heard the secret of God? and dost thou restrain wisdom to thyself? Job xv. 8.

Lo, these are parts of his ways; but how little a portion is heard of him? but the thunder of his power who can understand? Job xxvi. 14.

Behold, God is great, and we know him not; neither can the number of his years be searched out. Job xxxvi. 26.

God thundereth marvellously with his voice; great things doeth he, which we cannot comprehend. Job xxxvii. 5.

Touching the Almighty, we cannot find him out; he is excellent in power, and in judgment, and in plenty of justice. Job xxxvii. 23.

Thy way is in the sea, and thy path in the great waters, and thy footsteps are not known. Psalm lxxvii. 19.

Great is the Lord, and greatly to be praised; and his greatness is unsearchable. Psalm cxlv. 3.

For my thoughts are not your thoughts, neither are your ways my ways, saith the Lord. For as the heavens are higher than the earth, so are my ways higher than your ways, and my thoughts than your thoughts. Isa. lv. 8, 9.

Verily I say unto you, except ye be converted, and become as little children, ye shall not enter into the kingdom of heaven. Matt. xviii. 3.

Verily I say unto you, whosoever shall not receive the kingdom of God, as a little child, shall in no wise enter therein. Luke xviii. 17.

O the depth of the riches, both of the wisdom and knowledge of God! how unsearchable are his judgments, and his ways past finding out! For who hath known the mind of the Lord? Or who hath been his counsellor? Rom. xi. 33. 24.

Let no man deceive himself. If any man among you seemeth to be wise in this world, let him become a fool, that he may be wise. 1 Cor. iii. 18.

For if a man thinketh himself to be something, when he is nothing, he deceiveth himself. Gal. vi. 3.

Beware lest any man spoil you through philosophy and vain deceit, after the tradition of men, after the rudiments of the world, and not after Christ. Col. ii. 8.

O Timothy, keep that which is committed to thy trust, avoiding profane and vain babblings, and oppositions of science falsely so called. 1 Tim. vi. 20.

DISCOURSE III.

BUT will God indeed dwell on the earth? Behold the heaven, and the heaven of heavens, cannot contain thee; how much less this house that I have builded? Yet have thou respect unto the prayer of thy servant, and to his supplication, O Lord my God, to hearken unto the cry and to the prayer which thy servant prayeth before thee to-day. That thine eyes may be open towards this house night and day, even towards the place of which thou hast said, My name shall be there; that thou mayest hearken unto the prayer which thy servant shall make towards this place. 1 Kings viii. 27, 28, 29.

For he looketh to the ends of the earth, and seeth under the whole heaven. Job xxviii. 24.

For his eyes are upon the ways of man, and he seeth all his goings. Job xxxiv. 21.

Though the Lord be high, yet hath he respect unto the lowly. Psalm cxxxviii. 6.

O Lord, thou hast searched me and known me. Thou knowest my down-sitting and mine uprising: thou understandest my thoughts afar off. Thou compasseth my path and my lying down, and art acquainted with all my ways. For there is not a word in my tongue, but lo, O Lord! thou knowest it altogether. Thou hast beset me behind and before, and laid thine hand upon me. Such knowledge is too wonderful for me; it is high I cannot attain unto it. Whither shall I go from thy Spirit, or whither shall I flee from thy presence? Psalm cxxxix. 1—7.

How precious also are thy thoughts unto me, O God! how great is the sum of them! If I should count them, they are more in number than the sand: when I awake I am still with thee. Psalms cxxxix. 17, 18.

The eyes of the Lord are in every place, beholding the evil and the good. Prov. xv. 3.

Can any hide himself in secret places that I shall not see him? saith the Lord: do not I fill heaven and earth? saith the Lord. Jer. xxiii. 24.

Behold the fowls of the air; for they sow not, neither do they reap, nor gather into barns; yet your heavenly Father feedeth them. Are ye not much better than they? And why take ye thought for raiment? Consider the lilies of the field how they grow? they toil not, neither do they spin; And yet I say unto you, that even Solomon, in all his glory, was not arrayed like one of these. Wherefore if God so clothe the grass of the field, which to-day is, and to-morrow is cast into the oven, shall he not much more clothe you, O ye of little of faith? Matt. vi. 26, 28, 29, 30.

Neither is there any creature that is not manifest in his sight; but all things are naked and opened unto the eyes of him with whom we have to do. Heb. iv. 13.

DISCOURSE IV.

AND he dreamed, and behold a ladder set up on the earth, and the top of it reached to heaven; and behold the angels of God ascending and descending on it. Gen. xxviii. 12.

For a thousand years in thy sight, are but as yesterday when it is past, and as a watch in the night. Psalm xc. 4.

Lift up your eyes to the heavens, and look upon the earth beneath: for the heavens shall vanish away like smoke, and the earth shall wax old like a garment, and they that dwell therein shall die in like manner; but my salvation shall be for ever, and my righteousness shall not be abolished. Isa. li. 6.

For the son of man shall come in the glory of his Father with his angels; and then he shall reward every man according to his works. Matt. xvi. 27.

When the Son of Man shall come in his glory, and all the holy angels with him, then shall he sit upon the throne of his glory. Matt. xxv. 31.

Also, I say unto you, Whosoever shall confess me before men, him shall the Son of Man also confess before the angels of God. But he that denieth me before men, shall be denied before the angels of God. Luke xii. 8, 9.

And he saith unto him, Verily, verily, I say unto you, hereafter ye shall see heaven open, and the angels of God ascending and descending upon the Son of Man. John i. 51.

We are made a spectacle to the world, and to angels, and to men. 1 Cor. v. 9.

Wherefore God also hath highly exalted him, and given him a name which is above every name. That at the name of Jesus every knee should bow, of things in heaven and things in earth, and things under the earth; and that every tongue should confess that Jesus Christ is Lord, to the glory of God the Father. Phil. ii. 9, 10, 11.

When the Lord Jesus shall be revealed from heaven with his mighty angels. 2 Thess. i. 7.

And without controversy great is the mystery of godliness; God was manifest in the flesh, justified in the Spirit, seen of angels, preached unto the Gentiles, believed on in the world, received up into glory. 1 Tim. iii. 16.

I charge thee before God, and the Lord Jesus Christ, and the elect angels, that thou observe these things. 1 Tim. v. 21.

And again, when he bringeth in the first-begotten into the world, he saith, And let all the angels of God worship him. Heb. i. 6.

But ye are come unto Mount Zion, and unto the city of the living God, the heavenly Jerusalem, and to an innumerable company of angels, To the general assembly and church of the first born, which are written in heaven, and to God the the Judge of all, and to the spirits of just men made perfect, and to Jesus, the mediator of the new covenant. Hebrews xii. 22, 23, 24.

But, beloved, be not ignorant of this one thing, that one day is with the Lord as a thousand years, and a thousand years as one day. The Lord is not slack concerning his promise, as some men count slackness; but is long-suffering to us-ward, not willing that any should perish, but that all should come to repentance. But the day of the Lord will come as a thief in the night; in the which the heavens shall pass away with a great noise, and the elements shall melt with fervent heat, the earth also and the works that are therein, shall be burnt up. 2 Peter iii. 8, 9, 10.

And the angel which I saw stand upon the sea and upon the earth, lifted up his hand to heaven, And sware by him that liveth for ever and ever, who created heaven and the things that therein are, and the earth and the things that therein are, and the sea and the things which are therein, that there should be time no longer. Rev. x. 5, 6.

And the third angel followed them, saying with a loud voice, if any man worship the beast and his image, and receive his mark in his forehead or in his hand, The same shall drink of the wine of the wrath of God, which is poured out without mixture into the cup of his indignation; and he shall be tormented with fire and brimstone in the presence of the holy angels, and in the presence of the Lamb. Rev. xiv. 9, 10.

And I saw a great white throne, and him that sat on it, from whose face the earth and the heaven fled away, and there was found no place for them. Rev. xx. 11.

DISCOURSE V.

AND Nathan departed unto his house; and the Lord struck the child that Uriah's wife bare unto David, and it was very sick. David, therefore, besought God for the child: and David fasted and went in and lay all night upon the earth. And the elders of his house arose, and went to him, to raise him up from the earth; but he would not, neither did he eat bread with them. And it came to pass on the seventh day, that the child died. And the servants of David feared to tell him that the child was dead; for they said, Behold, while the child was yet alive, we spake unto him, and he would not hearken unto our voice, how will he then vex himself, if we tell him that the child is dead? But when David saw that his servants whispered, David perceived that the child was dead; therefore David said unto his servants, Is the child dead? And they said he is dead. Then David arose from the earth and washed, and anointed himself, and changed his apparel, and came into the house of the Lord, and worshipped: then he came to his own house; and, when he required, they set bread before him, and he did eat. Then said his servants unto him, What thing is that thou hast done? Thou didst fast and weep for the child while it was alive: but when the child was dead, thou didst rise and eat bread. And he said, while the child was yet alive, I fasted and wept; for I said who can tell whether God will be gracious to me, that the child may live? But now he is dead, wherefore should I fast? Can I bring him back again? I shall go to him, but he shall not return to me. 2 Sam. xii. 15—23.

The angel of the Lord encampeth round about them that fear him, and delivereth them. Psalm xxxiv. 7.

For he shall give his angels charge over thee, to keep thee in all thy ways. Psalm xci. 2.

And he shall send his angels with a great sound of a trumpet; and they shall gather together his elect from the four winds, from the one end of heaven to the other. Matt. xxiv. 31.

Likewise I say unto you, There is joy in the presence of the angels of God over one sinner that repenteth. Luke xv. 10.

Are they not all ministering spirits, sent forth to minister for them who shall be heirs of salvation. Heb. i. 14.

DISCOURSE VI.

THEN was Jesus led up of the Spirit into the wilderness, to be tempted of the devil. Matt. iv. 1.

The enemy that sowed them is the devil; the

harvest is the end of the world; and the reapers are the angels. The Son of Man shall send forth his angels, and they shall gather out of his kingdom all things that offend, and them which do iniquity. Matt. xiii. 39, 41.

Then shall he say also unto them on the left hand, Depart from me, ye cursed, into everlasting fire prepared for the devil and his angels. Matt. xxv. 41.

And in the synagogue there was a man which had a spirit of an unclean devil, and cried out with a loud voice, saying, Let us alone; what have we to do with thee, thou Jesus of Nazareth; art thou come to destroy us? I know thee who thou art: the Holy One of God. Luke iv. 33, 34.

Those by the way-side are they that hear; then cometh the devil and taketh away the word out of their hearts, lest they should believe and be saved. Luke viii. 12.

But he knowing their thoughts, said unto them, Every kingdom divided against itself is brought to desolation; and a house divided against a house, falleth. If Satan also be divided against himself, how shall his kingdom stand? because ye say that I cast out devils through Beelzebub. Luke xi. 17, 18.

Ye are of your father the devil, and the lusts of your father ye will do; he was a murderer from the beginning, and abode not in the truth, because there is no truth in him. When he speaketh a lie, he speaketh of his own: for he is a liar, and the father of it. John viii. 44.

And supper being ended, (the devil having now put into the heart of Judas Iscariot, Simon's son to betray him.) John xiii. 2.

But Peter said, Ananias, why hath Satan filled thine heart to lie to the Holy Ghost, and to keep back part of the price of the land? Acts v. 3.

To open their eyes, and to turn them from darkness to light, and from the power of Satan unto God, that they may receive forgiveness of sins, and an inheritance among them which are sanctified by faith that is in me. Acts xxvi. 18.

And the God of peace shall bruise Satan under your feet shortly. The grace of our Lord Jesus Christ be with you. Amen. Rom. xvi. 20.

Lest Satan should get an advantage of us; for we are not ignorant of his devices. 2 Cor. ii. 11.

In whom the God of this world hath blinded the minds of them which believe not, lest the light of the glorious gospel of Christ, who is the image of God, should shine unto them. 2 Cor. iv. 4.

Wherein in time past ye walked according to the course of this world, according to the prince of the power of the air, the spirit that now worketh in the children of disobedience. Eph. ii. 2.

Put on the whole armour of God, that ye may be able to stand against the wiles of the devil. For we wrestle not against flesh and blood, but against principalities, against powers, against the rulers of the darkness of this world, against spiritual wickedness in high places. Eph. vi. 11, 12.

For some are already turned aside after Satan. 1 Timothy v. 15.

Forasmuch then as the children are partakers of flesh and blood, so also himself likewise took part of the same; that through death he might destroy him that had the power of death, that is the devil. Heb. ii. 14.

Submit yourselves therefore to God. Resist the devil, and he will flee from you. James iv. 1.

Be sober, be vigilant; because your adversary the devil, as a roaring lion, walketh about, seeking whom he may devour; whom resist steadfast in the faith, knowing that the same afflictions are accomplished in your brethren that are in the world. 1 Peter v. 8, 9.

He that committeth sin is of the devil; for the devil sinneth from the beginning. For this purpose the Son of God was manifested, that he might destroy the works of the devil.

In this the children of God are manifest and the children of the devil; whosoever doeth not righteousness is not of God, neither he that loveth not his brother. 1 John iii. 8, 10.

Ye are of God, little children, and have overcome them; because greater is he that is in you, than he that is in the world. 1 John iv. 4.

And the angels which kept not their first estate, but left their own habitation, he hath reserved in everlasting chains, under darkness, unto the judgment of the great day. Jude 6.

He that overcometh, the same shall be clothed in white raiment; and I will not blot out his name out of the book of life, but I will confess his name before my Father, and before his angels. Rev. iii. 5.

And there was war in heaven; Michael and his angels fought against the dragon; and the dragon fought and his angels, And prevailed not; neither was their place found any more in heaven. And the great dragon was cast out, that old serpent, called the Devil, and Satan, which deceiveth the whole world; he was cast out into the earth, and his angels were cast out with him. Therefore rejoice, ye heavens, and ye that dwell in them. Wo to the inhabiters of the earth and of the sea! for the devil is come down unto you, having great wrath, because he knoweth that he hath but a short time. Rev. xii. 7, 8, 9, 12.

And he laid hold on the dragon, that old serpent, which is the Devil, and Satan, and bound him a thousand years. And when the thousand years are expired, Satan shall be loosed out of his prison. And the devil that deceived them was cast into a lake of fire and brimstone, where the beast and the false prophet are, and shall be tormented day and night, for ever and ever. Rev. xx. 2, 7, 10.

DISCOURSE VII.

Therefore, whosoever heareth these sayings of mine, and doeth them, I will liken him to a wise man, which built his house upon a rock: And the rain descended, and the floods came, and the winds blew, and beat upon that house; and it fell not; for it was founded upon a rock. And every one that heareth these sayings of mine, and doeth them not, shall be likened unto a foolish man, which built his house upon the sand: And the rain descended, and the floods came, and the winds blew, and beat upon that house; and it fell; and great was the fall of it. Matt. vii. 24—27.

At that time, Jesus answered and said, I thank thee, O Father! Lord of heaven and earth, because thou hast hid these things from the wise and prudent, and hast revealed them unto babes. Matt. xi. 25.

Then shall ye begin to say, we have eaten and drank in thy presence, and thou hast taught in our streets. But he shall say, I tell you, I know you not whence ye are; depart from me all ye workers of iniquity. Luke xiii. 26, 27.

For not the hearers of the law are just before God, but the doers of the law shall be justified. Rom. ii. 13.

And I, brethren, when I came to you, came not

with excellency of speech or of wisdom, declaring unto you the testimony of God. For I determined not to know any thing among you, save Jesus Christ and him crucified. And my speech and my preaching was not with enticing words of man's wisdom, but in demonstration of the Spirit and of power. That your faith should not stand in the wisdom of men, but in the power of God. Now we have received not the spirit of the world, but the Spirit which is of God; that we might know the things that are freely given to us of God. Which things also we speak, not in the words which man's wisdom teacheth, but which the Holy Ghost teacheth; comparing spiritual things with spiritual. But the natural man receiveth not the things of the Spirit of God; for they are foolishness unto him; neither can he know them, because they are spiritually discerned. 1 Cor. ii. 1, 2, 4, 5, 12, 13, 14.

For the wisdom of this world is foolishness with God. 1 Cor. iii. 19.

For the kingdom of God is not in word, but in power. 1 Cor. iv. 20.

Forasmuch as ye are manifestly declared to be the epistle of Christ ministered by us, written not with ink, but with the Spirit of the living God; not in tables of stone, but in fleshly tables of the heart. Not that we are sufficient of ourselves to think any thing as of ourselves; but our sufficiency is of God: who also hath made us able ministers of the New Testament; not of the letter, but of the spirit; for the letter killeth, but the spirit giveth life. 2 Cor. iii. 3, 5, 6.

That the God of our Lord Jesus Christ, the Father of glory, may give unto you the spirit of wisdom and revelation in the knowledge of him; The eyes of your understanding being enlightened; that ye may know what is the hope of his calling, and what the riches of the glory of his inheritance in the saints. And what is the exceeding greatness of his power to us-ward who believe, according to the working of his mighty power. Eph. i. 17, 18, 19.

And you hath he quickened, who were dead in trespasses and sins. For we are his workmanship, created in Christ Jesus unto good works. Eph. ii. 1, 10.

For our gospel came not unto you in word only, but also in power, and in the Holy Ghost, and in much assurance. 1 Thes. i. 5.

Of his own will begat he us with the word of truth, that we should be a kind of first-fruits of his creatures.

But be ye doers of the word, and not hearers only, deceiving yourselves. For if any be a hearer of the word, and not a doer, he is like unto a man beholding his natural face in a glass. For he beholdeth himself, and goeth his way, and straightway forgetteth what manner of man he was. But whoso looketh into the perfect law of liberty, and continueth therein, he being not a forgetful hearer, but a doer of the work, this man shall be blessed in his deed. James i. 18, 22—25.

But ye are a chosen generation, a royal priesthood, an holy nation, a peculiar people, that ye should show forth the praises of him who has called you out of darkness into his marvellous light. 1 Peter ii. 9.

But ye have an unction from the Holy One, and ye know all things.

But the anointing which ye have received of him abideth in you; and ye need not that any man teach you; but as the same anointing teacheth you of all things, and is truth, and is no lie, and even as it hath taught you, ye shall abide in him. 1 John ii. 20, 27.

SERMONS

ON THE

DEPRAVITY OF HUMAN NATURE.

PREFACE.

The doctrine which is most urgently, and most frequently insisted on in the following volume, is that of the depravity of human nature; and it were certainly cruel to expose the unworthiness of man for the single object of disturbing him. But the cruelty is turned into kindness, when, along with the knowledge of the disease, there is offered an adequate and all-powerful remedy. It is impossible to have a true perception of our own character, in the sight of God, without feeling our need of acquittal; and in opposition to every obstacle, which the justice of God seems to hold out to it, this want is provided for in the Gospel. And it is equally impossible, to have a true perception of the character of God, as being utterly repugnant to sin, without feeling the need of amendment; and in opposition to every obstacle, which the impotency of man holds out to it, this want is also provided for in the Gospel. There we behold the amplest securities for the peace of the guilty. But there do we also behold securities equally ample for their progress, and their perfection in holiness. Insomuch, that in every genuine disciple of the New Testament, we not only see one who, delivered from the burden of his fears, rejoices in hope of a coming glory—but we see one who, set free from the bondage of corruption, and animated by a new love and a new desire, is honest in the purposes, and strenuous in the efforts, and abundant in the works of obedience. He feels the instigations of sin, and in this respect he differs from an angel. But he follows not the instigations of sin, and in this respect he differs from a natural or unconverted man. He may experience the motions of the flesh—but he walks not after the flesh. So that in him we may view the picture of a man, struggling with effect against his earth-born propensities, and yet hateful to himself for the very existence of them—holier than any of the people around him, and yet humbler than them all—realizing, from time to time, a positive increase to the grace and excellency of his character, and yet becoming more tenderly conscious every day of its remaining deformities—gradually expanding in attainment as well as in desire, towards the light and the liberty of heaven, and yet groaning under a yoke from which death alone will fully emancipate him.

When time and space have restrained an author of sermons from entering on what may be called the ethics of Christianity,—it is the more incumbent on him to avouch of the doctrine of the gospel, that while it provides directly for the peace of a sinner, it provides no less directly and efficiently for the purity of his practice—that faith in this doctrine never terminates in itself, but is a mean to holiness as an end—and that he who truly accepts of Christ, as the alone foundation of his meritorious acceptance before God, is stimulated, by the circumstances of his new condition, to breathe holy purposes, and to abound in holy performances. He is created anew unto good works. He is made the workmanship of God in Christ Jesus.

The anxious enforcement of one great lesson on the part of a writer, generally proceeds from the desire to effect a full and adequate conveyance, into the mind of another, of some truth which has filled his own mind, by a sense of its importance; and, in offering this volume to the public, the author is far from being insensible to the literary defects that from this cause may be charged upon it. He knows, in particular, that throughout these discourses there is a frequent recurrence of the same idea, though generally expressed in different language, and with some new speciality, either in its bearing or in its illustration. And he further knows, that the habit of expatiating on one topic may be indulged to such a length, as to satiate the reader, and that, to a degree, far beyond the limits of his forbearance.

And yet, if a writer be conscious that, to gain a reception for his favorite doctrine, he must combat with certain elements of opposition, in the taste, or the pride, or the indolence, of those whom he is addressing, this will only serve to make him the more importunate, and so to betray him still farther into the fault of redundancy. If the lesson he is urging be of an intellectual character, he will labour to bring it home, as nearly as possible, to the understanding. If it be a moral lesson, he will labour to bring it home, as nearly as possible, to the heart. It is difficult, and it were hard to say in how far it would be right, to restrain this propensity in the pulpit, where the high matters of salvation are addressed to a multitude of individuals, who bring before the minister every possible variety of taste and of capacity; and it it no less difficult, when the compositions of the pulpit are transferred to the press, to detach from them a peculiarity by which their whole texture may be pervaded, and thus to free them from what may be counted by many to be the blemish of a very great and characteristic deformity.

There is, however, a difference between such truths as are merely of a speculative nature, and such as are allied with practice and moral feeling; and much ought to be conceded to this difference. With the former, all repetition may often be superfluous; with the latter, it may just be by earnest repetition, that their influence comes to be thoroughly established over the mind of an inquirer. And, if so much as one individual be gained over in this way to the cause of righteousness, he is untrue to the spirit and to the obligations of his office, who would not, for the sake of this one, willingly hazard all the rewards, and all the honours of literary estimation.

And, if there be one truth which, more than another, should be habitually presented to the notice, and proposed to the conviction of fallen creatures, it is the humbling truth of their own depravity. This is a truth which may be recognized and read in every exhibition of unrenewed nature; but it often lurks under a specious disguise, and it is surely of the utmost practical importance to unveil and elicit a principle, which, when admitted into the heart, may be considered as the great basis of a sinner's religion.

SERMON I.

The Necessity of the Spirit to give Effect to the Preaching of the Gospel.

"And my speech, and my preaching, was not with enticing words of man's wisdom, but in demonstration of the Spirit and of power: that your faith should not stand in the wisdom of man but in the power of God."—1 *Corinthians*, ii. 4, 5.

PAUL, in his second epistle to the Corinthians has expressed himself to the same effect as in the text, in the following words: "Not that we are sufficient of ourselves to think any thing as of ourselves; but our sufficiency is of God; who also hath made us able ministers of the New Testament; not of the letter, but of the Spirit."

In both these passages, the Apostle points to a speciality in the work of a Christian teacher,—a something essential to its success, and, which is not essential to the proficiency of scholars in the ordinary branches of education,—an influence that is beyond the reach of human power and human wisdom; and to obtain which, immediate recourse must be had, in the way of prayer and dependence, to the power of God. Without attempting a full exposition of these different verses, we shall, first, endeavour to direct your attention to that part of the work of a Christian teacher, which it has in common with any other kind of education; and, secondly, offer a few remarks on the speciality that is adverted to in the text.

I. And here it must be admitted, that even in the ordinary branches of human learning, the success of the teacher, on the one hand, and the proficiency of the scholars on the other, are still dependent on the will of God. It is true, that in this case, we are not so ready to feel our dependence. God is apt to be overlooked in all those cases where he acts with uniformity. Wherever we see, what we call, the operation of a law of nature, we are apt to shut our eyes against the operation of his hand, and faith in the constancy of this law, is sure to beget, in the mind, a sentiment of independence on the power and will of the Deity. Now, in the matters of human education, God acts with uniformity. Let there be zeal and ability on the part of the teacher, and an ordinary degree of aptitude on the part of the taught,—and the result of their vigorous and well sustained co-operation may in general be counted upon. Let the parent, who witnesses his son's capacity, and his generous ambition for improvement, send him to a well qualified instructor, and he will be filled with the hopeful sentiment of his future eminence, without any reference to God whatever,—without so much as ever thinking of his purpose or of his agency in the matter, or its once occurring to him to make the proficiency of his son the subject of prayer. This is the way in which nature, by the constancy of her operations, is made to usurp the place of God: and it goes far to spread, and to establish the delusion, when we attend to the obvious fact, that a man of the most splendid genius may be destitute of piety; that he may fill the office of an instructor with the greatest talent and success, and yet be without reverence for God, and practically disown him; and that thousands of our youth may issue every year warm from the schools of Philosophy, stored with all her lessons, and adorned with all her accomplishments, and yet be utter strangers to the power of godliness, and be filled with an utter distaste and antipathy for its name. All this helps on the practical conviction, that common education is a business, with which prayer and the exercise of dependence on God, have no concern. It is true that a Christian parent will see through the vanity of this delusion. Instructed to make his requests known unto God in all things, he will not depose him from the supremacy of his power and of his government over this one thing,—he will commit to God the progress of his son in every one branch of education he may put him to,—and, knowing that the talent of every teacher, and the continuance of his zeal, and his powers of communication, and his faculty of interesting the attention of his pupils,—that all these are the gifts of God, and may be withdrawn by him at pleasure,—he will not suffer the regular march and movement of what is visible or created to cast him out of his dependence on the Creator. He will see that every one element which enters into the business of education, and conspires to the result of an accomplished and a well-informed scholar, is in the hand of the Deity, and he will pray for the continuation of these elements,—and while science is raising her wondrous monuments, and drawing the admiration of the world after her,—it remains to be seen, on the day of the revelation of hidden things, whether the prayers of the humble and derided Christian, for a blessing on those to whom he has confided the object of his tenderness, have not sustained the vigour and brilliancy of those very talents on which the world is lavishing the idolatry of her praise.

Let us now conceive the very ablest of these teachers, to bring all his powers and all his accomplishments, to bear on the subject of Christianity. Has he skill in the languages? The very same process by which he gets at the meaning of any ancient author, carries him to a fair and faithful rendering of the scriptures of the Old and New Testament. Has he a mind enlightened and exercised on questions of erudition? The very same principles which qualify him to decide on the genuineness of any old publication, enable him to demonstrate the genuineness of the Bible, and how fully sustained it is on the evidence of history. Has he that sagacity and comprehension of talent, by which he can seize on the leading principles which run through the writings of some eminent philosopher? This very exercise may be gone through on the writings of Inspiration; and the man, who, with the works of Aristotle before him can present the world with the best system or summary of his principles, might transfer these very powers to the works of the Apostles and Evangelists, and present the world with a just and interesting survey of the doctrines of our faith. And thus it is, that the man who might stand the highest of his fellows in the field of ordinary scholarship, might turn his entire mind to the field of Christianity; and, by the very same kind of talent, which would have made him the most eminent of all the philosophers, he might come to be counted the most eminent of all the theologians; and he who could have reared to his fame some monument of literary genius might now, by the labours of his midnigh oil, rear some beauteous and consistent fabric of orthodoxy, strengthened, in all its parts, by one unbroken chain of reasoning, and recommended throughout by the powers of a persuasive and captivating eloquence.

So much for the talents which a Christian teacher may employ, in common with other teachers, and even though they did make up all the qualifications necessary for his office, there would still be a call, as we said before, for the exercise of dependence upon God. Well do we know, that both he and his hearers would be apt to put their faith in the uniformity of nature; and forgetting that it is the inspiration of the Almighty which giveth and preserveth the understanding of all his creatures, might be tempted to repose that confidence in man, which displaces God from the sovereignty that belongs to him. But what we wish to prepare you for, by the preceding observations, is, that you may understand the altogether peculiar call, that there is for dependence on God in the case of a Christian teacher. We have made a short enumeration of those talents which a teacher of Christianity might possess, in common with other teachers; but it is for the purpose of proving that he might possess them all, and heightened to such a degree, if you will, as would have made him illustrious on any other field, and yet be utterly destitute of powers for acquiring himself, or of experience for teaching others, that knowledge of God and of Jesus Christ which is life everlasting.

With the many brilliant and imposing things which he may have, there is one thing which he may not have, and the want of that one thing may form an invincible barrier to his usefulness in the vineyard of Christ. If, conscious that he wants it, he seeks to obtain from God the sufficiency which is not in himself, then he is in a likely way of being put in possession of that power, which alone is mighty to the pulling down of strong holds. But if he, on the one hand, proudly conceiving the sufficiency to be in himself, enters with aspiring confidence into the field of argument, and think that he is to carry all before him, by a series of invincible demonstration; or, if his people, on the other hand, ever ready to be set in motion by the idle impulse of novelty, or to be seduced by the glare of human accomplishments, come in trooping multitudes around him, and hang on the eloquence of his lips, or the wisdom of his able and profound understanding, a more unchristian attitude cannot be conceived, nor shall we venture to compute the weekly accumulation of guilt which may come upon the parties, when such a business as this is going on. How little must the presence of God be felt in that place where the high functions of the pulpit are degraded into a stipulated exchange of entertainment on the one side, and of admiration on the other; and surely it were a sight to make angels weep when a weak and vapouring mortal, surrounded by his fellow sinners, and hastening to the grave and the judgment along with them, finds it a dearer object to his bosom, to regale his hearers by the exhibition of himself, than to do in plain earnest the work of his Master, and urge on the business of repentance and of faith by the impressive simplicities of the Gospel.

II. This brings us to the second head of discourse, under which we shall attempt to give you a clear view of what that is which constitutes a speciality in the work of a Christian teacher. And to carry you at once by a few plain instances to the matter we are aiming to impress upon you, let us suppose a man to take up his Bible, and with the same powers of attention and understanding which enable him to comprehend the subject of any other book, there is much in this book also which he will be able to perceive and to talk of intelligently. Thus, for example, he may come, by the mere exercise of his ordinary powers, to understand that it is the Holy Spirit which taketh of the things of Christ and showeth them to the mind of man. But is not his understanding of this truth, as it is put down in the plain language of the New Testament, a very different thing from the Holy Spirit actually taking of these things and showing them unto him? Again, he will be able to say, and to annex a plain meaning to what he says, that man is rescued from his natural darkness about the things of God, by God who created the light out of darkness shining in his heart, and giving him the light of the knowledge of his glory in the face of Jesus Christ. But is not his saying this, and understanding this, by taking up these words in the same obvious way in which any man of plain and honest understanding would do, a very different thing from God actually putting forth his creative energy upon him, and actually shining upon his heart, and giving him that light and that knowledge which are expressed in the passage here alluded to? Again, by the very same exercise wherewith he renders the sentence of an old author into his own language, and perceives the meaning of that sentence, will he annex a meaning to the following sentence of the Bible—" the natural man receiveth not the things of the Spirit of God, for they are foolishness unto him; neither can he know them, because they are spiritually discerned." By the mere dint of that shrewdness and sagacity with which nature has endowed him, he will perceive a meaning here which you will readily acknowledge could not be perceived by a man in a state of idiotism. In the case of the idiot, there is a complete barrier against his ever acquiring that conception of the meaning of this passage, which is quite competent to a man of a strong and accomplished understanding. For the sake of illustration, we may conceive this poor outcast from the common light of humanity, in some unaccountable fit of attention, listening to the sound of these words, and making some strenuous but abortive attempts to arrive at the same comprehension of them with a man whose reason is entire. But he cannot shake off the fetters which the hand of nature has laid upon his understanding, and he goes back again to the dimness and delirium of his unhappy situation; and his mind locks itself up in the prison-hold of its confined and darkened faculties; and if, in his mysterious state of existence, he formed any conception whatever of the words now uttered in your hearing, we may rest assured that it stands distinguished by a wide and impassable chasm, from the conception of him, who has all the common powers and perceptions of the species.

Now, we would ask what kind of conception is that which a man of entire faculties may form? Only grant us the undeniable truth, that he may understand how he cannot discern the things of the Spirit, unless the Spirit reveal them to him; and yet with this understanding, he may not be one of those in behalf of whom the Spirit hath actually interposed with his peculiar office of revelation; and then you bring into view another barrier, no less insurmountable than that which fixes an immutable distinction between the conceptions of an idiot and of a man of sense,—even that wonderful barrier which separates the natural from the spiritual man. You can conceive him struggling with every power which nature has given him to work his way through this barrier. You can conceive him vainly attempting, by some energies of his own, to force an entrance into that field of light where every object of faith has the bright colouring of reality thrown over it,—where he can command a clear view of the things of eternity,—where spiritual truth comes home with effect upon his every feeling and his every conviction,—where he can expatiate at freedom over a scene of manifestation, which the world knoweth not,—and breathe such a peace, and such a joy, and such a holiness, and such a superiority to time, and such a devotedness of all his affections to the things which are above, as no man of the highest natural wisdom can ever reach with all his attention to the Bible, and all the efforts of his sagacity, however painful, to unravel, and to compare and to comprehend its passages. And it is indeed a deeply interesting object to see a man of powerful understanding thus visited with an earnest desire after the light of the gospel, and toiling at the entrance with all the energies which belong to him,—pressing into the service all the resources of argument and philosophy,—mustering to the high enterprise his attention, and his conception, and his reason, and his imagination, and the whole host of his other faculties, on which science has conferred her imposing names, and laid before us in such a pompous catalogue, as might tempt us to believe, that man, by one mighty grasp of his creative mind, can make all truth his own, and range at pleasure over the wide variety of her dominions. How natural to think that the same powers and habits of investigation which carried him to so respectable a height in the natural sciences will enable him to clear his way through all the darkness of theology. It is well that he is seeking,—for if he persevere and be in earnest, he will obtain an interest in the promise, and will at length find;—but not till he find, in the progress of those inquiries on which he entered with so much alacrity, and prosecuted with so much confidence, that there is a barrier between him and the spiritual discernment of his Bible, which all the powers of philosophy cannot scale,—not till he find, that he must cast down his lofty imaginations, and put the pride of all his powers and his pretensions away from him,—not till he find, that, divested of those fancies which deluded his heart into a feeling of its own sufficiency, he must become like a little child, or one of those babes to whom God reveals the things which he hides from the wise and from the prudent,—not till he find, that the attitude of self-dependence must be broken down, and he be brought to acknowledge that the light he is aspiring after, is not created by himself, but must be made to shine upon him at the pleasure of another,—not in short, till, humbled by the mortifying experience that many a simple cottager who reads his Bible and loves his Saviour has got before him, he puts himself on a level with the most illiterate of them all, and prays that light and truth may beam on his darkened understanding from the sanctuary of God.

We read of the letter, and we read also of the spirit, of the New Testament. It would require a volume, rather than a single paragraph of a single sermon, to draw the line between the one and the other. But you will readily acknowledge that there are many things of this book which a man, though untaught by the Spirit of God, may be made to know. One of the simplest instances is, he may learn the number of chapters in every book, and the number of verses in every chapter. But is this all? No,—for by the natural exercise of his memory he may be able to master all its historical information. And is this all? No, for by the natural exercise of his judgment he may compare scripture with scripture,— he may learn what its doctrines are,—he may demonstrate the orthodoxy of every one article in our national confession,—he may rank among the ablest and most judicious of the commentators,—he may read, and with understanding, too, many a ponderous volume,—he may store himself with the learning of many generations,—he may be familiar with all the systems, and have mingled with all the controversies,—and yet, with a mind supporting as it does the burden of the erudition of whole libraries, he may have gotten to himself no other wisdom than the wisdom of the letter of the New Testament. The man's creed, with all its arranged and its well weighed articles, may be no better than the dry bones in the vision of Ezekiel, put together into a skeleton, and fastened with sinews, and covered with flesh and skin, and exhibiting to the eye of the spectators, the aspect, and the lineaments of a man, but without breath, and remaining so, till the Spirit of God breathed into it, and it lived. And it is in truth a sight of wonder, to behold a man who has carried his knowledge of scripture as far as the wisdom of man can carry it,—to see him blest with all the light which nature can give, but labouring under all the darkness which no power of nature can dispel,—to see this man of many accomplishments, who can bring his every power of demonstration to bear upon the Bible, carrying in his bosom a heart uncheered by any one of its consolations, unmoved by the influence of any one of its truths, unshaken out of any one attachment to the world, and an utter stranger to those high resolves, and the power of those great and animating prospects, which shed a glory over the daily walk of a believer, and give to every one of his doings the high character of a candidate for eternity.

We are quite aware of the doubts which this is calculated to excite in the mind of the hearer,—nor is it possible within the compass of an hour to stop and satisfy them all; or to come to a timely conclusion, without leaving a number of unresolved questions behind us.

There is one, however, which we cannot pass without observation. Does not this doctrine of a revelation of the Spirit, it may be asked, additional to the revelation of the word, open a door to the most unbridled variety? May it not give a sanction to any conceptions of any visionary pretenders, and clothe in all the authority of inspiration a set of doctrines not to be found within the compass of the written record? Does it not set aside the usefulness of the Bible, and break in upon the unity and consistency of revealed truth, by letting loose upon the world a succession of fancies, as endless and as variable as are the caprices of the human imagination? All very true, did we ever pretend that the office of the Spirit was to reveal any thing additional to the information, whether in the way of doctrine or of duty, which the Bible sets before us. But his office, as defined by the Bible itself, is not to make known to us any truths which are not contained in the Bible; but to make clear to our understandings the truths which are contained in it. He opens our understandings to understand the Scriptures. The word of God is called the sword of the Spirit. It is the instrument by which the Spirit worketh. He does not tell us any thing that is out of the record; but all that is within it he sends home, with clearness and effect, upon the mind. He does not make us wise above that which is written but he makes us wise, up to that which is written. When a telescope is directed to some distant landscape, it enables us to see what we could not otherwise have seen but it does not enable us to see any thing which has not a real existence in the prospect before us. It does not present to the eye any delusive imagery,—neither is that a fanciful and fictitious scene which it throws open to our contemplation. The natural eye saw nothing but blue land stretching along the distant horizon. By the aid of the glass, there bursts upon it a charming variety of fields, and woods, and spires, and villages. Yet who would say that the glass added one feature to this assemblage? It discovers nothing to us which is not there nor, out of that portion of the book of nature which we are employed in contemplating, does it bring into view a single character which is not really and previously inscribed upon it. And so of the Spirit He does not add a single truth, or a single character, to the book of revelation. He enables the spiritual man to see what the natural man cannot see; but the spectacle which he lays open is uniform and immutable. It is the word of God which is ever the same;—and he, whom the Spirit of God has enabled to look to the Bible with a clear and affecting discernment, sees no phantom passing before him; but amid all the visionary extravagance with which he is charged can, for every one article of his faith, and every one duty of his practice, make his triumphant appeal to the law and to the testimony.

We trust that this may be made clear by one example. We have not to travel out of the record for the purpose of having this truth made known to us,—that God is every where present. It meets the observation of the natural man in his reading of the Bible; and he understands, or thinks he understands, the terms in which it is delivered; and he can speak of it with consistency; and he ranks it with the other attributes of God; and he gives it an avowed and formal admission among the articles of his creed; and yet, with all this parade of light and knowledge, he, upon the subject of the all-seeing and ever-present Deity labours under all the obstinacy of an habitual blindness. Carry him abroad, and you will find that the light which beams upon his senses, from the object of sight, completely overpowers that light which ought to beam upon his spirit, from this object of faith. He may occasionally think of as he does of other things; but for every one practical purpose the thought abar dons him, as soon as he goes into the next company or takes a part in the next worldly concern, which, in the course of his business, comes round to him. It completely disappears as an element of conduct, and he talks, and thinks, and reasons just as he would have done, had his mind, in reference to God, been in a state of entire darkness. If any thing like a right conception of the matter ever exist in his heart, the din and the day light of the world drive it all away from him. Now, to rectify this case, it is surely not necessary, that the Spirit add any thing to the truth of God's omnipresence, as it is put down in the written record. It will be enough, that he gives to the mind upon which he operates, a steady and enduring impression of this truth. Now, this is one part of his office, and accordingly it is said of the unction of the Spirit, that it is an unction which remaineth. Neither is it necessary that the light, which he communicates, should consist in any vision which he gives to the eye, or in any bright impression upon the fancy, of any one thing not to be found within the pages of the Bible. It will be enough if he give a clear and vigorous apprehension of the truth, just as it is written, to the understanding. Though the Spirit should do no more than give vivacity and effect to the truth of the constancy of God's presence, just as it stands in the written record—this will be quite enough to make the man who is under its influence carry a habitual sense of God about with him, think of him in the shop and in the market-place, walk with him all the day long, and feel the same moral restraint upon his doings, as if some visible superior, whose virtues he revered, and whose approbation he longed after, haunted his every footstep, and kept an attentive eye fastened upon the whole course of his history. The natural man may have sense, and he may have sagacity, and a readiness withal to admit the constancy of God's presence, as an undeniable doctrine of the Bible. But to the power of this truth he is dead; and it is only to the power of this world's interests and pleasures that he is alive. The spiritual man is the reverse of all this, and that without carrying his conceptions a single hair breadth beyond the communications of the written message. He makes no pretensions to wisdom by one jot or one tittle beyond the testimony of Scripture, and yet, after all, he lives under a revelation to which the other is a stranger. It does not carry him by a single footstep without the field of the written revelation, but it throws a radiance over every object within it. It furnishes him with a constant light which enables him to withstand the domineering influence of sight and of sense. He dies unto the world, he lives unto God,—and the reason is, that there rests upon him a peculiar manifestation, by which the truth is made visible to the eye of his mind, and a peculiar energy, by which it comes home upon his conscience. And if you come to inquire into the cause of this speciality, it is the language of the Bible, confirmed, as we believe it to be, by the soundest experience, that every power which nature has conferred upon man, exalted to its highest measure, and called forth to its most strenuous exercise is not able to accomplish it,— that it is due to a power above nature, and beyond it; that it is due to what the Apostle calls the demonstration of the Spirit,—a demonstration withheld from the self-sufficient exertions of man, and given to his believing prayers.

And here we are reminded of an instructive passage in the life of one of our earliest and most eminent reformers. When the light of divine truth broke in upon his heart, it was so new and so delightful to one formerly darkened by the errors of popery,— he saw such a power and such an evidence along with it,—he was so ravished by its beauties, and so carried along by its resistless arguments, that he felt as if he had nothing to do, but to brandish those mighty weapons, that he might gain all hearts and carry every thing before him. But he did not calculate on the stubborn resistance of corrupt human nature, to him and to his reasonings. He preached and he argued, and he put forth all his powers of eloquence amongst them. But mortified that so many hearts remained hardened, that so many hearers resisted him, that the doors of so many hearts were kept shut in spite of all loud and repeated warnings, that so many souls remained unsubdued, and dead in trespasses and sins, he was heard to exclaim that old Adam was too strong for young Melancthon.

There is the malignity of the fall which adheres to us. There is a power of corruption and of blindness along with it, which it is beyond the compass of human means to overthrow. There is a dark and settled depravity in the human character, which maintains its gloomy and obstinate resistance to all our warnings and all our arguments. There is a spirit working in the children of disobedience which no power of human eloquence can lay. There is a covering of thick darkness upon the face of all people, a mighty influence abroad upon the world, with which the Prince of the power of the air keeps his thousands and his tens of thousands under him. The minister who enters into this field of conflict may have zeal, and talents, and eloquence. His heart may be smitten with the love of the truth, and his mind be fully fraught with its arguments. Thus armed, he may come forth among his people, flushed with the mighty enterprise of turning souls from the dominion of Satan unto God. In all the hope of victory he may discharge the weapons of his warfare among them. Week after week, he may reason with them out of the Scriptures. Sabbath after Sabbath he may declaim, he may demonstrate, he may put forth every expedient, he may at one time set in array before them the terrors of the law, at another he may try to win them by the free offer of the Gospel; and, in the proud confidence of success, he may think that nothing can withstand him, and that the heart of every hearer must give way before the ardour of his zeal and the power of his invincible arguments. Yes; they may admire him, and they may follow him, but the question we have to ask is, will they be converted by him? They may even go so far as to allow that it is all very true he says. He may be their favourite preacher, and when he opens his exhortations upon them, there may be a deep and a solemn attention in every countenance. But how is the heart coming on all the while? How do those people live, and what evidence are they giving of being born again under the power of his ministry? It is not enough to be told of those momentary convictions which flash from the pulpit, and carry a thrilling influence along with them through the hearts of listening admirers. Have these hearers of the word, become the doers of the word? Have they sunk down into the character of humble, and sanctified, and penitent, and pains-taking Christians? Where, where is the fruit? And while the preaching of Christ is all their joy, has the will of Christ become all their directions? Alas, he may look around him, and at the end of the year, after all the tumults of a sounding popularity, he may find the great bulk of them just where they were,—as listless and unconcerned about the things of eternity,—as obstinately alienated from God,—as firmly devoted to selfish and transitory interests,—as exclusively set upon the farm, and the money, and the merchandize,—and, with the covering of many external decencies, to make them as fair and plausible as their neighbours around them, proving by a heart given, with the whole tide of its affections, to the vanities of the world, that they have their full share of the wickedness which abounds in it. After all his sermons, and all his loud and passionate addresses, he finds that the power of darkness still keeps its ground among them. He is grieved to learn that all he has said, has had no more effect, than the foolish and the feeble lispings of infancy. He is overwhelmed by a sense of his own helplessness, and the lesson is a wholesome one. It makes him feel that the sufficiency is not in him, but in God; it makes him understand that another power must be brought to bear upon the mass of resistance which is before him; and let the man of confident and aspiring genius, who thought he was to assail the dark seats of human corruption, and to carry them by storm, let him be reduced in mortified and dependent humbleness to the expedient of the Apostle, let him crave the intercessions of his people, and throw himself upon their prayers.

Let us now bring the whole matter to a practical conclusion. For the acquirement of a saving and spiritual knowledge of the gospel, you are on the one hand, to put forth all your ordinary powers, in the very same way that you do for the acquirement of knowledge in any of the ordinary branches of human learning. But in the act of doing so, you, on the other hand, are to proceed on a profound impression of the utter fruitlessness of all your endeavours, unless God meet them by the manifestations of his Spirit. In other words, you are to read your Bible, and to bring your faculties of attention, and understanding, and memory, to the exercise, just as strenuously as if these and these alone could conduct you to the light after which you are aspiring. But you are at the same time to pray as earnestly for this object, as if God accomplished it without your exertions at all, instead of accomplishing it in the way he actually does, by your exertions. It is when your eyes are turned toward the book of God's testimony, and not when your eyes are turned away from it, that he fulfils upon you the petition of the Psalmist,—" Lord, do thou open mine eyes, that I may behold the wondrous things contained in thy law." You are not to exercise your faculties in searching after truth without prayer, else God will withhold from you his illuminating influences. And you are not to pray for truth, without exercising your faculties, else God will reject your prayers, as the mockery of a hypocrite. But you are to do both, and this is in harmony with the whole style of a Christian's obedience, who is as strenuous in doing as if his doings were to accomplish all, and as fervent in prayer, as if without the inspiring energy of God, all his doings were vanity and feebleness. And the great Apostle may be quoted as the best example of this observation.

There never existed a man more active than Paul, in the work of the Christian ministry. How great the weight and the variety of his labours! What preaching, what travelling, what writing of letters, what daily struggling with difficulties, what constant exercise of thought in watching over the Churches, what a world of perplexity in his dealings with men, and in the hard dealings of men with him; and were they friends, or were they enemies, how his mind behooved to be ever on the alert, in counsel ling the one and warding off the hostility of the other. Look to all that is visible in the life of this Apostle, and you see nothing but bustle, and enterprise, and variety. You see a man intent on the furtherance of some great object, and in the prosecution of it, as ever diligent, and as ever doing, as if the whole burden of it lay upon himself, or as if it were reserved for the strength of his solitary arm to accomplish it. To this object he consecrated every moment of his time, and even when he set him down to the work of a tent-maker, for the sake of vindicating the purity of his intentions, and holding forth an example of honest independence to the poorer brethren; even here, you just see another display of the one principle which possessed his whole heart, and gave such a character of wondrous activity to all the days of his earthly pilgrimage. There are some, who are so far misled by a kind of perverse theology which they have adopted, as to hesitate about the lawfulness of being diligent and doing in the use of means. While they are slumbering over their speculation, and proving how honestly they put faith in it by doing nothing, let us be guided by the example of the pains-taking and industrious Paul, and remember, that never since the days of this Apostle, who calls upon us to be followers of him, even as he was of Christ,—never were the labours of human exertion more faithfully rendered,—never were the workings of a human instrument put forth with greater energy.

But it forms a still more striking part of the example of Paul, that while he did as much toward the extension of the Christian faith, as if the whole success of the cause depended upon his doing,—he prayed as much, and as fervently for this object, as if all his doings were of no consequence. A fine testimony to the supremacy of God, from the man, who, in labours was more abundant than any that ever come after him, that he counted all as nothing, unless God would interfere to put his blessings upon all, and to give his efficacy to all! He who looked so busy, and whose hand was so constantly engaged, in the work that was before him, looked for all his success to that help which cometh from the sanctuary of God. There was his eye directed. Thence alone did he expect a blessing upon his endeavours. He wrought, and that with diligence too, because God bade him; but he also prayed, and that with equal diligence, because God had revealed to him, that plant as he may, and water as he may, God alone giveth the increase. He did homage to the will of God, by the labours of the ever-working minister,—and he did homage to the power of God, by the devotions of the ever-praying minister. He did not say, what signifies my working, for God alone can work with effect? This is very true, but God chooses to work by instruments,—and Paul, by the question, "Lord, what wilt thou have me to do?" expressed his readiness to be an instrument in his hand. Neither did he say, what signifies my praying, for I have got a work here to do, and it is enough that I be diligent in the performance of it. No—for the power of God must be acknowledged, and a sense of his power must mingle with all our performances; and therefore it is that the Apostle kept both working and praying, and with him they formed two distinct emanations of the same principle; and while there are many who make these Christian graces to neutralize each other, the judicious and the clear-sighted Paul, who had received the spirit of a sound mind, could give his unembarrassed vigour to both these exercises, and combine, in his own example, the utmost diligence in doing, with the utmost dependence on him who can alone give to that doing all its fruit and all its efficacy.

The union of these two graces has at times been finely exemplified in the latter, and uninspired ages of the Christian Church; and the case of the missionary Elliot is the first, and the most impressive that occurs to us. His labours, like those of the great Apostle, were directed to the extension of the vineyard of Christ,—and he was among the very first who put forth his hand to the breaking up the American wilderness. For this purpose did he set himself down to the acquirement of a harsh and barbarous language; and he became qualified to confer with savages; and he grappled for years with their untractable humours; and he collected these wanderers into villages; and while other reformers have ennobled their names by the formation of a new set of public laws, did he take upon him the far more arduous task of creating for his untamed Indians, a new set of domestic habits; and such was the power of his influence that he carried his christianizing system into the very bosom of their families; and he spread art, and learning, and civilization amongst them; and to his visible labours among his people he added the labours of the closet; and he translated the whole Bible into their tongue; and he set up a regular provision for the education of their children; and lest the spectator who saw his fourteen towns risen as by enchantment in the desert, and peopled by the rudest of his tribes, should ask in vain for the mighty power by which such wondrous things had been brought to pass,—this venerable priest left his testimony behind him; and neither overlooking the agency of God, nor the agency of man as the instrument of God, he tells us in the one memorable sentence written by himself at the end of his Indian grammar, that "prayers and pains through faith in Christ Jesus can do any thing."

The last inference we shall draw from this topic, is the duty and importance of prayer among Christians, for the success of the ministry of the Gospel. Paul had a high sense of the efficacy of prayer. Not according to that refined view of it, which, making all its influence to consist in its improving and moralizing effect upon the mind, fritters down to nothing the plain import and significancy of this ordinance. With him it was a matter of asking and of receiving. And just as when in pursuit of some earthly benefit which is at the giving of another, you think yourselves surer of your object the more you multiply the number of askers and the number of applications—in this very way did he, if we may be allowed the expression, contrive to strengthen and extend his interest in the court of heaven. He craved the intercession of his people. There were many believers formed under his ministry, and each of these could bring the prayer of faith to bear upon the counsels of God, and bring down a larger portion of strength and of fitness to rest on the Apostle for making more believers. It was a kind of creative or accumulating process. After he had travelled in birth with his new converts till Christ was formed in them—this was the use he put them to. It is an expedient which harmonizes with the methods of Providence and the will of God, who orders intercessions, and on the very principle too, that he willeth all men to be saved, and to come to the knowledge of the truth. The intercession of christians, who are already formed, is the leaven which is to leaven the whole earth with Christianity. It is one of the destined instruments in the hand of God for hastening the glory of the latter days. Take the world at large, and the doctrine of intercession, as an engine of mighty power, is derided as one of the reveries of fanaticism. This is a subject on which the men of the world are in a deep slumber; but there are watchmen who never hold their peace day nor night, and to them God addresses these remarkable words, "Ye that make mention of the Lord, keep not silence, and give him no rest, till he establish, and till he make Jerusalem a praise in the earth."

SERMON II.

The mysterious Aspect of the Gospel to the Men of the World.

"Then said I, Ah, Lord God! they say of me, Doth he not speak parables?"—*Ezekiel* xx. 49.

IN parables, the lesson that is meant to be conveyed is to a certain degree shaded in obscurity. They are associated by the Psalmist with dark sayings—"I will open my mouth in a parable, I will utter dark sayings of old." We read in the New Testament of a parable leaving all the effect of an unexplained mystery upon the understanding of the general audience to which it was addressed; and the explanation of the parable given to a special few was to them the clearing up of a mystery. "It is given unto you to know the mysteries of the kingdom of heaven; but to them it is not given!"

The prophets of old were often commissioned to address their countrymen under the guise of symbolical language. This threw a veil over the meaning of their communications; and though it was a veil of such transparency as could be seen through by those who looked earnestly and attentively, and with a humble desire to be taught in the will of God,—yet there was dimness enough to intercept all the moral, and all the significancy, from the minds of those who wanted principle to be in earnest; or who wanted patience for the exercise of attention; or who wanted such a concern about God, as either to care very much for his will, or to feel that any thing which respected him was worth the trouble of a very serious investigation.

They who wanted this concern and this principle, from them was taken away even that which they had. God at length ceased from his messages, and the Spirit of God ceased from his warnings. They who had the preparation of all this docility, to them more was given. Their honest desire after knowledge, was rewarded by the acquirement of it. They continued to look, and to enquire, and at length they were illuminated; and thus was fulfilled the saying of the Saviour, that "whosoever hath, to him shall be given, and he shall have more abundantly,—but whosoever hath not, from him shall be taken away even that he hath."

It is not difficult to conceive how the obscure intimations of Ezekiel would be taken by the careless and ungodly men of his generation. It is likely that even from the naked denunciations of vengeance they would have turned contemptuously away.

And it is still more likely that they would refuse the impression of them, when offered to their notice, under a figurative disguise. It is not at all to be supposed that they would put forth any activity of mind in quest of that which they nauseated, and of that which, if ever they had found, they would have found to be utterly revolting to all their habits of impiety. They are the very last men we should expect to meet with at the work of a pains-taking search after the interpretation of these parables. Nay, they would gladly fasten upon the obscurity of them both as a circumstance of reproach against the prophet, and as an apology for their own indifference. And thus it is, that to be a teacher of parables might at length become a scoff and a by-word; and the prophet seems to have felt the force of it as an opprobrious designation, seems to be looking forward to the mixture of disdain and impatience with which he would be listened to, when God charged him with an allegorical communication to his countrymen, and he answered, "Ah, Lord God! they say of me, Doth he not speak parables?"

Now the question we have to put is—Is there no similar plea of resistance ever preferred against the faithful messengers of God in the present day? It is true, that in our time there is no such thing as a man coming amongst you, charged with the utterance of a direct and personal inspiration. But it is the business of every minister truly to expound the record of inspiration; and is it not very possible that in so doing he may be reproached, not for preaching parabolically, but for preaching mysteriously? Have you never heard of a sermon being called mystical; and what shall we think of it, if, in point of fact, this imputation falls most readily and most abundantly on the sermon that is most pervaded by the spirit, and most overrun with the phraseology of the New Testament? In that composition there are certain terms which recur incessantly, and which would therefore appear to represent certain very leading and prominent ideas. Now, whether are these ideas clearly and promptly suggested to your mind, by the utterance of terms? What are the general character and effect which in your eye is imparted to a sermon, when, throughout the whole of it, the words of the apostolic vocabulary are ever and anon obtruded upon your hearing—and the whole stress of the argument is made to lie on such matters as sanctification; and the atonement; and the blood of the everlasting covenant; and the indwelling of the Holy Ghost, who takes up his habitation in the soul of the believer; and salvation by grace; and the spirit of adoption poured forth on the heart, and filling it with all the peace and joy of a confident reconciliation; and the exercise of fellowship with the Father, and the Son; and the process of growing up unto Christ; and the habit of receiving out of his fulness, and of beholding with open face his glory, so as to be changed into the same image, from glory to glory, even as by the spirit of the Lord. We are not at present asking, if you feel the disgust with which unsubdued nature ever listens to these representations, or in what degree they are offensive to your taste, and painfully uncongenial with the whole style and habit of your literature. But we ask, if such terms and such phrases as have now been specified, do not spread before the eye of your mind an aspect of exceeding dimness over the preacher's demonstration? Does he not appear to you as if he wrapped himself up in the obscurity of a technical language, which you are utterly at a loss to comprehend? When the sermon in question is put by the side of some lesson of obvious morality, or some exposition of those principles which are recognized and acted upon in ordinary life, does it not look to you as if it was shrouded from common observation altogether; and that ere you could be initiated into the mystery of such language and of such doctrine, you would need to describe a mighty and still untrodden interval from all your present habits of conception? And yet, what if it be indeed the very language and the very doctrine of the New Testament?—if all the jargon that is charged on the interpretation of the word be the actual word itself?—and if the preacher be faithfully conveying the message of the Bible, at the very time that the hearer is shielding himself from the impression of it by the saying, that he preacheth mysteries?

But to keep the two parties at a still more hopeless distance from each other,—the message of such a preacher, incomprehensible as many of its terms and many of its particulars may be, evidently bears a something upon it that is fitted to alarm the fears, and utterly to thwart the strongest tendencies of nature. Let him be just a faithful expounder of the Gospel of Jesus Christ, and let the blindness of the natural man be what it may, still there is scarcely a hearer who can fail to perceive, that, anterior to the reception of this Gospel, the preacher looks upon him as the enemy of God,—and strongly points at such a controversy between him and his maker, as can only be made up through an appointed Mediator—and requires of him such a faith as will transform his character, and as will shift the whole currency of his affections and desires—and affirms the necessity of such a regeneration, as that all old things shall be done away, and all things shall become new;—and lets him know, that to be a Christian indeed he must die unto sense, he must be crucified unto the world, and, renouncing its charms and its predilections, must learn to have his conversation in heaven, and to choose God as the strength of his heart and his portion for evermore. All this flashes plainly and significantly enough, through that veil of mysticism which appears to overspread the general doctrine of the preacher; and imparts a forbidding character to it in the eyes of those to whom we are alluding; and they will be glad of any pretence to shun a painful and a revolting contemplation; and they will complain of him on the very ground on which the Jews of old complained of Ezekiel, as a dealer in parables—and while much of their antipathy is founded upon his being so strict and so spiritual, and so unaccommodating to the general tone of society, one of the charges which will be most frequently and most loudly preferred against him, is, that he is so very mysterious.

In the prosecution of the following discourse, we shall endeavour in the first place to state shortly the ground on which the religion of the New Testament looks so mysterious a thing to the men of the world, and then conclude with a short practical remonstrance upon this subject.

I. There are certain experiences of human life so oft repeated, and so familiar to all our recollections, that when we perceive, or think we perceive, an analogy between them and the matters of religion, then religion does not appear to us to be mysterious. There is not a more familiar exhibition in society than that of a servant who performs his allotted work, and who obtains his stipulated reward—and we are all servants, and one is our master, even God.

There is nothing more common than that a son should acquit himself to the satisfaction of his parents,—and we are all the children of an universal parent, whom it is our part to please in all things. Even when that son falls under displeasure, and is either visited with compunction or made to receive the chastisement of his disobedience, there is nothing more common than to witness the relentings of an earthly father, and the readiness with which forgiveness is awarded on the repentance and sorrow of the offender,—and we, in like manner, liable to err from the pure law of heaven, have surely a kind and indulgent Father to deal with. And, lastly, there is nothing more common than that the loyalty of a zealous and patriotic subject should be rewarded by the patronage, or at least by the protection of the civil magistrate,—and that an act of transgression against the laws should be visited by an act of vengeance on the part of him who is a terror to evil-doers, while a praise to such as do well. And thus it is, too, that we are under a lawgiver in heaven who is able both to save and to destroy.

Now so long as the work of religious instruction can be upheld by such analogies as these,—so long as the relations of civil or of domestic society can be employed to illustrate the relation between God and the creatures whom he has formed,—so long as the recollections of daily experience can thus be applied to the method of the divine administration,—a vein of perspicuity will appear to run through the clear and rational exposition of him who has put all the mist and all the technicals of an obscure theology away from him. All his lessons will run in an easy and direct train. Nor do we see how it is possible to be bewildered amongst such explanations, as are suggested by the most ordinary doings and concerns of human society;—and did the preacher only confine himself to such doctrine, as that God rewards the upright, and punishes the rebellious, and upon the impulse of that compassion which belongs to him, takes again the penitent into acceptance, and in the great day of remuneration, will give unto every man according to his works,—did he only confine himself to truths so palpable, and build upon it applications so obvious, as just to urge us to the performance of duty by the promised reward, and deter us from the infraction of it by the severities of the threatened punishment, and call us to reformation by affectionately pleading with us the mercies of God, and warn us with all his force and all his fidelity, that should we persist in obstinate impenitence we shall be cut off from happiness for ever,—there might be something to terrify,—but there would at least be nothing to darken or to perplex us in these interpretations—nothing that would not meet common intelligence, and be helped forward by all the analogies of common observation,—and should this therefore prove the great burden of the preacher's demonstration, we should be the last to reproach him, as a dealer in parables, or as a dealer in mysteries.

To attach us the more to this rational style of preaching, we cannot but perceive that it obtains a kind of experimental countenance from the actual distinctions of character which are realized in the peopled world around us. Can any thing be more evident than that there is a line of separation between the sensual and the temperate, between the selfish and the disinterested, between the sordid and the honourable; or if you require a distinction more strictly religious, between the profane and the decent keeper of all the ordinances? Do not the former do, what, in the matter of it, is contrary to the law of God, and the latter do, what, in the matter of it, is agreeable to that law? Here then at once we witness the two grand divisions of human society, in a state of real and visible exemplification

—and what more is necessary than just to employ the most direct and intelligible motives of conduct, for persuading men to withdraw from one of these divisions, and pass over to the other of them? Surely it is just as we occupy the higher and the lower places in the scale of character, that we shall be found on the right and on the left hand of the judge on the day of reckoning: And what more obvious way, then, of preparing a people for eternity—than just to point our urgency to the one object of prevailing upon men to cross the line of separation, to cease from the iniquities which abound on the one side of it, and to put on the reformations which are practised on the other side of it? For this purpose, what else is to be done than plainly to tell the whole amount of the interest and obligation which lies on the side of virtue, and as plainly to tell of the ruin and the degradation both of character and of prospect which lie on the side of vice—to press the accomplishments of a good life on the one hand, and to denounce the falsehoods and the dishonesties, and the profligacies of a bad life on the other,—in a word, to make our hearers the good subjects of God, much in the same way, as you would propose to make them the good servants of their master or the good subjects of their government; and thus by the simple and direct enforcements of duty, to shun all the difficulties of a scholastic theology, and to keep clear of all its mysteriousness.

It is needless to say how much this process is reversed by many a teacher of Christianity. It is true that they hold out most prominently the need of some great transition—but it is a transition most mysteriously different from the act of crossing that line of separation, to which we have just been adverting. Without referring at all in fact to any such line, do they come forth from the very outset with one sweeping denunciation of worthlessness and guilt, which they carry round among all the varieties of character, and by which they affirm every individual of the human race, to be an undone sinner in the sight of God. Instead of bidding him look to other sinners less deformed by blemishes, and more .ch in moral accomplishments, than himself, and then attempt to recover his distance from the divine favour by the imitation of them, they bid him think of the awful amount of debt and of deficiency that lies between the lawgiver in heaven, and a whole world guilty before him. They speak of a depravity so entire, and of an alienation from God, so deep, and so universal, as positively to obliterate that line of separation which is supposed to mark off those, who, upon the degree of their obedience, are rightful claimants to the honours of eternity, from those, who, upon the degree of their disobedience, are wretched outcasts of condemnation. They reduce the men of all casts and of all characters, to the same footing of worthlessness in the sight of God; and speak of the evil of the human heart in such terms, as will sound to many a mysterious exaggeration, and, like the hearers of Ezekiel, will these not be able to comprehend the argument of the preacher, when he tells them, though in the very language of the Bible, that they are the heirs of wrath; that none of them is righteous, no not one; that all flesh have corrupted their ways, and have fallen short of the glory of God; that the world at large is a lost and a fallen world, and that the natural inheritance of all who live in it, is the inheritance of a temporal death, and a ruined eternity.

When the preacher goes on in this strain, those hearers whom the spirit has not convinced of sin will be utterly at a loss to understand him,—nor are we to wonder, if he seem to speak to them in a parable, when he speaks of the disease,—that all the darkness of a parable should still seem to hang over his demonstrations, when as a faithful expounder of the revealed will and counsel of God, he proceeds to tell them of the remedy. For God hath not only made known the fearful magnitude of his reckoning against us, but he has prescribed, and with that authority which only belongs to him, the way of its settlement; and that he has told us all the works and all the efforts of unrenewed nature are of no avail in gaining us acceptance, and that he has laid the burden of our atonement on him who alone was able to bear it; and he not only invites, but he commands, and he beseeches us to enter into peace and pardon on the footing of that expiation which Christ hath made, and of that righteousness which Christ hath wrought out for us; and he further declares, that we have come into the world with such a moral constitution, as will not merely need to be repaired, but as will need to be changed or made over again, ere we be meet for the inheritance of the saints; and still for this object does he point our eyes to the great Mediator who has undertaken, not merely for the forgiveness, but who has undertaken for the sanctification of all who put their trust in him; and he announces that out of his fulness there ever come forth supplies of strength for the new obedience of new creatures in Jesus Christ our Lord. Now, it is when the preacher is unfolding this scheme of salvation,—it is when he is practically applying it to the conscience and the conduct of his hearers,—it is when the terms of grace, and faith, and sanctification, are pressed into frequent employment for the work of these very peculiar explanations,—it is when, instead of illustrating his subject by those analogies of common life which might have done for men of an untainted nature, but which will not do for the men of this corrupt world, he faithfully unfolds that economy of redemption which God hath actually set up for the recovery of our degenerate species,—it is then, that to a hearer still in darkness, the whole argument sounds as strangely and as obscurely, as if it were conveyed to him in an unknown language,—it is then, that the repulsion of his nature to the truth as it is in Jesus, finds a willing excuse in the utter mysteriousness of its articles, and its terms; and gladly does he put away from him the unwelcome message, with the remark, that he who delivers it, is a speaker of parables, and there is no comprehending him.

It will readily occur as an observation upon all that has been delivered, that by the great majority of hearers, this imputation of mysteriousness is never preferred,—that in fact, they are most habituated to this style of preaching,—and that they recognise the very thing which they value most, and are best acquainted with, when they hear a sermon replete with the doctrine, and abounding in the terms, and uttered in the cadence of orthodoxy. Of this we are perfectly aware. The point to carry with the great bulk of hearers is, not to conquer their disgust at the form of sound words, but to conquer their resistance to the power of them; to alarm them by the consideration, that the influence of the lesson is altogether a distinct matter from the pleasantness of the song,—that their ready and delighted acquiescence in the preaching of the faith, may consist with a total want of obedience to the faith,—and that with all the love they bear to the phraseology of the gospel, and all their preference for its ministers, and all their attendance upon its sacraments, the kingdom of God, however much it may have come to them in word, may not at all have come to them in power. This is a distinct error from the one we have been combating,—a weed which grows abundantly in another quarter of the field altogether,—a perverseness of mind, more deceitful than the other, and perhaps still more unmanageable, and against which the faithful minister has to set himself amongst that numerous class of professors, who like to hear of the faith, but never apply a single practical test to the question, Am I in the faith? who like to hear of regeneration, but never put the question, Am I really regenerated? who like to hear that without Christ they can do nothing, but may be enabled to do all things through him strengthening them, but never enter into the important personal inquiry, Is he really strengthening me, and am I, by my actual victory over the world, and my actual progress in the accomplishments of personal Christianity, bearing evidence upon myself that I have a real part and interest in these things?

There can be no doubt as to the existence of such a class,—and under another text, there could be no difficulty in finding out a spiritual application, by which to reach and to reprove them. But the matter suggested by the present text is, that if a minister of the present day should preach as the Apostles did before him,—if the great theme of his ministrations be Jesus Christ, and him crucified,—if the doctrine of the sermon be a faithful transcript of the doctrine of the New Testament,—there is one class, we have every warrant for believing, from whom the word will not return unto him void,—and there is another class who will be the willing hearers, but not the obedient doers of the word: but there is still a third class, made up of men of cultivated literature, and men of polished and respectable society, and men of a firm secular intelligence in all the ordinary matters of business, who, at the same time, possessing no sympathies whatever with the true spirit and design of Christianity, are exceedingly shut up, in all the avenues both of their heart and understanding, against the peculiar teaching of the gospel. Like the hearers of Ezekiel, they feel an impression of mysteriousness. There is a certain want of adjustment between the truth as it is in Jesus, and the prevailing style of their conceptions. All their views of human life, and all the lessons they may have gathered from the school of civil or classical morality, and all their preferences for what they count the clearness and the rationality of legal preaching, and all the predilections they have gotten in its favour, from the most familiar analogies in human society,—all these, coupled with their utter blindness to the magnitude of that guilt which they have incurred under the judgment of a spiritual law, enter as so many elements of dislike in their hearts, towards the whole tone and character of the peculiar doctrines of Christianity. And they go to envelope the subject in such a shroud of mysticism to their eyes, that many of the preachers of the gospel are, by them, resisted on the same plea with the prophet of old, to whom his contemptuous countrymen meant to attach the ridicule and the ignominy of a proverb, when they said,—he is a dealer in parables.

We mistake the matter, if we think that the offence of the cross has yet ceased from the land. We mistake it, if we think that the persecution of contempt, a species of persecution more appalling to some minds than even direct and personal violence, is not still the appointed trial of all who would live godly, and of all who would expound zealously and honestly the doctrine of

Christ Jesus our Lord. We utterly mistake it, if we think that Christianity is not even to this very hour the same very peculiar thing that it was in the days of the Apostles,—that it does not as much signalize and separate us from a world lying in wickedness,—that the reproach cast upon Paul, that he was mad, because he was an intrepid follower of Christ, is not still ready to be preferred against every faithful teacher, and every consistent disciple of the faith,—and that, under the terms of methodism, and fanaticism, and mysticism, there is not ready to be discharged upon them from the thousand batteries of a hostile and unbelieving world, as abundant a shower of invective and contumely as in the first ages.

II. Now, if there be any hearers present who feel that we have spoken to them, when we spoke of the resistance which is held out against peculiar Christianity, on the ground of that mysteriousness in which it appears to be concealed from all ordinary discernment,—we should like to take our leave of them at present with two observations. We ask them, in the first place, if they have ever, to the satisfaction of their own minds, disproved the Bible,—and if not, we ask them how they can sit at ease, should all the mysteriousness which they charge upon Evangelical truth, and by which they would attempt to justify their contempt for it, be found to attach to the very language, and to the very doctrine of God's own communication? What if it be indeed the truth of God? What if it be the very language of the offended lawgiver? What if they be the only overtures of reconciliation, upon the acceptance of which a sinner can come nigh unto him? Now he actually does say that no man cometh unto the Father but by the Son,—and that his is the only name given under heaven whereby men can be saved,—and that he will be magnified only in the appointed Mediator,—and that Christ is all in all,—and that there is no other foundation on which man can lay, and that he who believeth on him shall not be confounded.

He further speaks of our personal preparation for heaven—and here, too, may his utterance sound mysteriously in your hearing, as he tells that without holiness no man can see God,—and that we are without strength while we are without the Spirit to make us holy—and that unless a man be born again he shall not enter into the kingdom of God,—and that he should wrestle in prayer for the washing of regeneration —and that he should watch for the Holy Ghost with all perseverance,—and that he should aspire at being perfect through Christ strengthening him—and that he should, under the operation of those great provisions which are set up in the New Testament for creating us anew unto good works, conform himself unto that doctrine of grace by which he is brought to deny ungodliness and worldly lusts, and to live soberly, righteously, and godly in the present evil world. We again ask them, if all this be offensive to their taste, and utterly revolting to their habits and inclinations, and if they turn with disgust from the bitterness of such an application, and can behold no strength to constrain them in any such arguments, and no eloquence to admire in them. With what discernment truly is your case taken up in this very Bible, whose phraseology and whose doctrine are so unpalatable to you, when it tells us of the preaching of the cross being foolishness,—but remember that it says it is foolishness to those who perish : when it tells of the natural man not receiving of the things of the Spirit,—but remember that it says, if ye have not the Spirit of God, ye are none of his ; when it tells of the gospel being hid,—but hid to them who are lost : "In whom the God of this world hath blinded the minds of those which believe not, lest the light of the glorious gospel of Christ, who is the image of God, should shine unto them."

Secondly, let us assure the men, who at this moment bid the stoutest defiance to the message of the gospel—the men whose natural taste appears to offer an invincible barrier against the reception of its truths, the men who, upon the plea of mysteriousness, or the plea of fanaticism, or the plea of excessive and unintelligible peculiarity, are most ready to repudiate the whole style and doctrine of the New Testament,—let us assure them that the time may yet come, when they shall render to this very gospel the most striking of all acknowledgments, even by sending to the door of its most faithful ministers, and humbly craving from them their explanations and their prayers. It indeed offers an affecting contrast to all the glory of earthly prospects, and to all the vigour of confident and rejoicing health, and to all the activity and enterprize of business, when the man who made the world his theatre, and felt his mountain to stand strong on the fleeting foundation of its enjoyments and its concerns,—when he comes to be bowed down with infirmity, or receives from the trouble within, the solemn intimation that death is now looking to him in good earnest: When such a man takes him to the bed of sickness, and he knows it to be a sickness unto death,—when, under all the weight of breathlessness and pain, he listens to the man of God, as he points the way that leadeth to eternity,—what, I would ask, is the kind of gospel that is most fitted to charm the sense of guilt and the anticipations of vengeance away from him? Sure we are, that we never in these affecting circumstances—through which you have all to pass—we never saw the man who could maintain a stability, and a hope, from the sense of his own righteousness; but who, if leaning on the righteousness of Christ, could mix a peace and an elevation with his severest agonies. We never saw the expiring mortal who could look with an undaunted eye on God as his lawgiver; but often has all its languor been lighted up with joy at the name of Christ as his Saviour. We never saw the dying acquaintance, who upon the retrospect of his virtues and of his doings, could prop the tranquillity of his spirit on the expectation of a legal reward. O no! this is not the element which sustains the tranquillity of deathbeds. It is the hope of forgiveness. It is a believing sense of the efficacy of the atonement. It is the prayer of faith, offered up in the name of him who is the captain of all our salvation. It is a dependence on that power which can alone impart a meetness for the inheritance of the saints, and present the spirit holy, and unreproveable, and unblamable, in the sight of God,

Now, what we have to urge is, that if these be the topics, which, on the last half hour of your life, are the only ones that will possess, in your judgment, any value or substantial importance, why put them away from you now? You will recur to them then; and for what? that you may get the forgiveness of your sins. But there is a something else you must get, ere you can obtain an entrance into peace or glory. You must get the renovation of that nature, which is so deeply tainted at this moment with the guilt of ingratitude and forgetfulness towards God. This must be gone through ere you die; and say if a change so mighty should be wantonly postponed to the hour of dying?—when all your refusals of the gospel have hardened and darkened the mind against it; when a demonstration of the Spirit then, is surely not to be counted on, as the return that you will experience for resisting all his intimations now; when the effects of the alienation of a whole life, both in extinguishing the light of your conscience, and in riveting your distaste for holiness, will be accumulated into such a barrier in the way of your return to God, as stamps upon death-bed conversions, a grievous unlikelihood, and should give an imperious force to the call of "To-day,"—" while it is called to-day, harden not your hearts, seeing that now is your accepted time, and now is your day of salvation."

SERMON III.

The Preparation necessary for Understanding the Mysteries of the Gospel.

"He answered and said unto them, Because it is given unto you to know the mysteries of the kingdom of heaven, but to them it is not given. For whosoever hath, to him shall be given, and he shall have more abundance; but whosoever hath not, from him shall be taken even that he hath."—*Matthew* xiii. 11, 12.

It is of importance to mark the principle of distribution on which it is given to some to know the mysteries of the kingdom of heaven, and it is not given to others. Both may at the outset be equally destitute of a clear understanding of these mysteries. But the former may have what the latter have not. With the former there may be a desire for explanation; with the latter there may be no such desire. The former may, in the earnest prosecution of this desire, be praying earnestly, and reading diligently, and striving laboriously, to do all that they know to be the will of God. With the latter, there may be neither the habit of prayer, nor the habit of inquiry, nor the habit of obedience. To the one class will be given what they have not. From the other class what they have shall be taken away. We have already attempted to excite in the latter class a respectful attention to the truths of the gospel, and shall now confine ourselves chiefly to the object of encouraging and directing those who feel the mysteriousness of these truths, and long for light to arise in the midst of it;—shall address ourselves to those who have an honest anxiety after that truth, which is unto us salvation, but find the way to it beset with many doubts and many perplexities,—to those who are impressed with a general conviction on the side of Scripture, but in whose eyes a darkness impenetrable still broods over its pages,—to those who are haunted by a sense of the imperious necessity of religion, and at the same time cannot escape from the impression, that if it is any where to be found, it is to be found within the records of the Old and New Testament, but from whose heart in the reading of these records the veil still remains untaken away.

In the further prosecution of this discourse, let us attempt, in the first place, to explain what it is that we ought to have, in order to attain an understanding of the mysteries of the gospel; and, in the second place, how it is that in many cases these mysteries are evolved upon the mind in a clear and convincing manifestation.

I. First, then, we ought to have an honest desire after light; and if we have this desire, it will not remain unproductive. There is a connexion repeatedly announced to us in Scripture between desire upon this subject, and its accomplishment. He that willeth to do the will of God shall know of my doctrine. He who hungereth and thirsteth shall be filled. He who lacketh wisdom and is desirous of obtaining it, let him vent his desire in prayer,—and if it be the prayer of confidence in God, his desire shall be given him. There are thousands to whom the Bible is a sealed book, and who are satisfied that it should remain so, who share in the impetuous contempt of the Pharisees against a doctrine to which they are altogether blind, who have no understanding of the matter, and no wish that it should be otherwise,—and unto them it will not be given to know the mysteries of the kingdom of heaven. They have not, and from them therefore shall be taken away even that which they have. There are others, again, who have an ardent and unquenchable thirst after the mysteries of the gospel; who, like the prophet in the apocalypse, weep much because the book is not opened to them; who complain of darkness, like the Apostles of old when they expostulated with their Teacher he spoke in parables, and, like them, who go to him with their requests for an explanation. These shall find that what they cannot do for themselves, the Lion of the tribe of Judah will do for them. He will prevail to open the book, and to loose the seals thereof. There is something they already have, even an honest wish to be illuminated, and to this more will be given. They are awake to the disirableness, they are awake to the necessity of a revelation, which they have not yet gotten,—and to them belongs the promise of, Awake, O sinner, and Christ shall give thee light.

Secondly, We ought to have a habit of prayer conjoined with a habit of inquiry; and to this more will be given. We have already adverted to the circumstance, that it is in the Bible, and not out of the Bible, where this light is to be met with. It is by the Spirit of God, shining upon the word of God, that his truth is reflected with clearness upon the soul. It is by his operation that the characters of this book are made to stand as visibly out to the eye of the understanding, as they do to the eye of the body; and therefore it is evident that it is not in the act of looking away from the written revelation, but in the act of looking towards it, that the wished-for illumination will at length come into the mind of an inquirer. If your present condition then be that of a darkness as helpless and as unattainable as can possibly be imagined, there still remains an obvious and practicable direction which you can be doing with in the mean time. You can persevere in the exercise of reading your Bible. There you are at the place of meeting etween the Spirit of God and your own spirit. You may have to wait, as if at the pool of Siloam; but the many calls of the Bible to wait upon God, to wait upon him with patience, to wait and to be of good courage, all prove that this waiting is a frequent and a familiar part of that process by which a sinner finds his way out of darkness into the marvellous light of the gospel.

And we have also adverted already, though in a very general way, to the difference in point of result between the active inquiries of a man who looks forward to the acquisition of saving truth as the natural and necessary termination of his inquiries, and of a man who mingles with every personal attempt after this object, the exercise of prayer, and a reverential sense of his dependence on God. The latter is just as active, and just as inquisitive as the former. The difference between them does not lie in the one putting forth diligence without a feeling of dependence, and the other feeling dependence, without a putting forth of diligence. He who is in the right path towards the attainment of light, combines both these properties.

It is through the avenues of a desirous heart and of an exercised understanding, and of sustained attention, and of faculties in quest of truth, and labouring after the possession of it, that God sends into the mind his promised manifestations. All this exercise on the one hand, without such an acknowledgement of him as leads to prayer, will be productive of nothing in the way of spiritual discernment. And prayer, without this exercise, is the mere form and mockery of an acknowledgement. He who calls upon us to hearken diligently, when he addresses us by a living voice, does in effect call upon us to read and to ponder diligently when he addresses us by a written message. To ask truth of God, while we neglect to do for this object what he bids us, is in fact not to recognize God, but to insult him. It is to hold out the appearance of presenting ourselves before him, while we are not doing it at the place of meeting, which he has assigned for us. It is to address an imaginary Being, whom we have invested with a character of our own conception, and not the Being who bids us search his Scriptures, and incline unto his testimonies, and stir ourselves up that we may lay hold of him. Such prayer is utterance, and nothing more. It wants all the substantial characters of prayer. It may amount to the seeking of those who shall not be able to enter the strait gate. It falls short of the striving of those who take the kingdom of heaven by force, and of whom that kingdom suffereth violence.

He who without prayer looks confidently forward to success as the fruit of his own investigations, is not walking humbly with God. If he were humble he would pray. But whether is he the more humble, who joins with a habit of prayer all those accompanying circumstances which God hath prescribed, or he who, in neglect of these circumstances, ventures himself into his presence in the language of supplication? There may be the show of humility in confiding the whole cause of our spiritual and saving illumination to the habit of praying for it to God. But if God himself tells us, that we must read, and seek, and meditate, then it is no longer humility to keep by the solitary exercise of praying. It is, in fact, keeping pertinaciously by our own way, heedless of his will and his way altogether. It is approaching God in the pride of our own understanding. It is detaching from the whole work of seeing after him some of those component parts which he himself hath recommended. In the very act of making prayer stand singly out as alone instrument of success, we are in fact drawing the life and the spirit out of prayer itself; and causing it to wither into a thing of no power and no significancy in the sight of God. It is not the prayer of acknowledgement, unless it comes from him who acknowledges the will of God in other things as well as in prayer. It is not the prayer of submission unless it comes from the heart of a man who manifests a principle of submission in all things.

Thirdly, We ought to do all that we know to be God's will; and to this habit of humble earnest desirous reformation, more will be given.

We trust that what has been said will prepare you for the reception of another advice besides that of reading or praying for the attainment of that manifestation which you are in quest of,—and that is, doing. There is an alarm raised in many a heart at the very suggestion of doing for an inquirer, lest he should be misled as to the ground of his justification; lest among the multitude or the activity of his works, he should miss the truth, that a man is accepted, not through the works of the law, but by faith in Jesus Christ; lest by every one performance of duty, he should just be adding another stone to the fabric of a delusive confidence, and presumptuously try to force his own way to heaven, without the recognition of the gospel or any of its peculiarities. Now, doing stands precisely in the same relation to prayer that reading does. Without the one or the other it is the prayer either of presumption or hypocrisy. If he both read and pray, it is far more likely that he will be brought unto the condition of a man being justified through faith in Christ, than that he will rest his hopes before God in the mere exercise of reading. If he both do and pray, it is far more likely that he will come to be established in the righteousness of Christ, as the foundation of all his trust, than that he will rest upon his own righteousness. For a man to give up sin at the outset, is just to do what God wills him at the outset. For a man at the commencement of his inquiries, to be strenuous in the relinquishment of all that he knows to be evil, is just to enter on the path of approach towards Christ, in the very way that Christ desires him. He who cometh unto me must forsake all. For a man to put forth an immediate hand to the doing of the commandments, while he is groping his way towards a firm basis on which he might rear his security before God, is not to deviate or diverge from the Saviour. He may do it with an eye of most intense earnestness towards the Saviour,—and while the artificial interpreter of Christ's doctrine holds him to be wrong, Christ himself may recognize him to be one of those who keep his sayings, and to whom therefore he stands pledged to manifest himself. The man in fact by strenuously doing, is just the more significantly and the more energetically praying. He is adding one ingredient to the business of seeking, without which the other ingredient would be in God's sight an abomination. He is struggling against all regard to iniquity in his heart, seeing that if he have this regard God will not hear him. To say, that it is dangerous to tell a man in these circumstances to do, lest he rest in his doings, and fall short of the Saviour, is to say, that it would be dangerous to place a man on the road to his wished-for home, lest, when he has got upon the road, he should stand still and be satisfied. The more, in fact, that the man's conscience is exercised and enlightened (and what more fitted than wilful sin to deafen the voice of conscience altogether?) the less will it let him alone, and the more will it urge him onward to that righteousness which is the only one commensurate to God's law, and in which alone the holy and inflexible God can look upon him with complacency. Let him humbly betake himself, then, to the prescribed path of reading, and prayer, and obvious reformation,—and let us see if there do not evolve upon his mind, in the prosecution of it, the worthlessness of all that man can do for his meritorious acceptance with the Lawgiver—and the deep ungodliness of character which adheres to him—and the suitableness of Christ's atonement to all his felt necessities, and all his moral aspirations—and the need in which he stands of a regenerating influence, to make him a a spiritual subject of God. Let us see whether, though the light which he at length receives be marvellous, the way is not plain which leads to it; and whether though nature be compassed about with a darkness which no power of nature can dissipate,—there is not a clear and obvious procedure, by the steps of which the most alienated of her children may be carried onwards to all the manifestation of the kingdom of grace, and to the discernment of all its mysteries.

Though to the natural eye, then, the doctrine of Christ be not plain, the way is plain by which we arrive at it. Though, ere we see the things of Christ, the Spirit must take of them and show them unto us,—yet this Spirit deals out such admonitions to all, that, if we follow them, he will not cease to enlarge, and to extend his teaching, till we have obtained a saving illumination. He is given to those who obey him. He abandons those who resist him. When conscience tells us to read, and to pray, and to reform, it is he who is prompting this faculty. It is he who is sending through this organ, the whispers of his own voice to the ear of the inner man. If we go along with the movement, he will follow it up by other movements. He will visit him who is the willing subject of his first influences by higher demonstrations. He will carry forward his own work in the heart of that man, who, while acting upon the suggestions of his own moral sense, is in fact acting in conformity to the warnings of this kind and faithful monitor. So that the Holy Spirit will connect his very first impulses on the mind of that inquirer, who, under the reign of earnestness, has set himself to read his Bible, and to knock with importunity at the door of heaven, and to forsake the evil of his ways, and to turn him to the practice of all that he knows to be right,—the Spirit will connect these incipient measures of a seeker after Zion, with the acquirement of wisdom and revelation in the knowledge of Christ.

Let it not be said, then, that because the doctrine of Christ is shrouded in mystery to the general eye of the world, it is such a mystery as renders it inaccessible to the men of the world. Even to them does the trumpet of invitation blow a certain sound. They may not yet see the arcana of the temple, but they may see the road which leads to the temple. If they are never to obtain admission there, it is not because they cannot, but because they will not, come to it. "Ye will not come to me," says the Saviour, "that ye might have life," Reading, and prayer, and reformation, these are all obvious things; and it is the neglect of these obvious things which involves them in the guilt and the ruin of those who neglect the great salvation. This salvation is to be found of those who seek after it. The knowledge of God and of Jesus Christ, which is life everlasting, is a knowledge open and acquirable to all. And, on the day of judgment, there will not be found a single instance of a man condemned because of unbelief, who sought to the uttermost of his opportunities; and evinced the earnestness of his desire after peace with God, by doing all that he might have done, and by being all that he might have been.

Be assured, then, that it will be for want of seeking, if you do not find. It will be for want of learning, if you are not taught. It will be for want of obedience to the movements of your own conscience, if the Holy Ghost, who prompts and who stimulates the conscience to all its movements, be not poured upon you, in one large and convincing manifestation. It may still be the day of small things with you—a day despised by the accomplished adepts of a systematic and articled theology. But God will not despise it. He will not leave your longings for ever unsatisfied. He will not keep you standing always at the threshold of vain desires and abortive endeavours, That faith, which is the gift of God, you have already attained, in a degree, if you have obtained a general conviction of the importance and the reality of the whole matter. He will increase that faith. Act up to the light that you have gotten, by reading earnestly, and praying importunately, and striving laboriously,—and to you more will be given. You will at length obtain a clear and satisfying impression of the things of God, and the things of salvation. Christ will be recognised in all his power and in all his preciousness. You will know what it is to be established upon him. The natural legality of your hearts will give way to the pure doctrine of acceptance with God, through faith in the blood of a crucified Saviour. The sanctifying influence of such a faith will not merely be talked of in word, but be experienced in power; and you will evince that you are God's workmanship in Christ Jesus, by your abounding in all those fruits of righteousness which are through him, to the praise and glory of the Father.

II. We shall now attempt to explain, how it is that the mysteries of the gospel are, in many cases, evolved upon the mind in a clear and convincing manifestation.

And here let it be distinctly understood, that the way in many cases may be very far from the way in all cases. The experience of converts is exceedingly various,—nor do we know a more frequent, and at the same time a more groundless cause of anxiety, than that by which the mind of an inquirer is often harassed, when he attempts to realize the very process by which another has been called out of darkness to the marvellous light of the gospel.

Referring, then, to those grounds of mysteriousness which we have already specified in a former discourse,—God may so manifest himself to the mind of an inquirer, as to convince him, that all those analogies of common life which are taken from the relation of a servant to his master, or of a son to his father, or of a subject to his sovereign, utterly fail in the case of man, as he is by nature, in relation to his God. A servant may discharge all his obligations; a son may acquit himself of all his duties, or may, with his occasional failures, and his occasional chastisements, still keep his place in the instinctive affection of his parents; and a subject may persevere in unseduced loyalty to the earthly government under which he lives. But the glaring and the demonstrable fact with regard to man, viewed as a creature, is, that the habit of his heart is one continued habit of dislike and resistance to the Creator who gave him birth.

The earthly master may have all those services rendered to which he has a right, and so be satisfied. The earthly father may have all the devotedness, and all the attachment from his family, which he can desire, and so be satisfied. The earthly sovereign may have all that allegiance from a loyal subject, who pays his taxes, and never transgresses his laws, which he expects or cares for, and so be satisfied. But go upward from them to the God who made us,—to the God who keeps us,—to the God in whom we live, and move, and have our being,—to the God whose care and whose presence are ever surrounding us, who, from morning to night, and from night to morning, watches over us, and tends us while we sleep, and guides us in our waking moments, and follows us to the business of the world, and brings us back in safety to our homes, and never for a single instant of time withdraws from us the superintendence of an eye that never slumbers, and of a hand that is never weary. Now, all we require is a fair estimate of the claims of such a God. Does he ask too much, when he asks the affections of a heart that receives its every beat, and its every movement, from the impulse of his power? Does he ask too much, when he asks the devotedness of a life, which owes its every hour and its every moment to him, whose right hand preserves us continually? Has he no right to complain, when he knocks at the door of our hearts, and trying to possess himself of the love and the confidence of his own creatures, he finds that all their thoughts, and all their pursuits, and all likings, are utterly away from him? Is there no truth, and no justice in the charge which he prefers against us,—when, surrounded as we are by the gifts of nature and of providence, all of which are his, the giver is meanwhile forgotten, and, amid the enjoyments of his bounty, we live without him in the world. If it indeed be true, that it is his sun which lights us on our path, and his earth on which we tread so firmly, and his air which circulates a freshness around our dwellings, and his rain which produces all the luxuriance that is spread around us, and drops upon every field the smiling promise of abundance for all the wants of his dependent children,—if all this be true, can it at the same time be right, that this all-providing God should have so little a place in our remembrance? that the whole man should be otherwise engaged than with a sense of him, and the habitual exercise of acknowledgment to him? that in fact the full play of his regards should be expended on the things which are formed, and through the whole system of his conduct and his affairs, there should be so utter a neglect of him who formed them? Surely if this be the true description of man, and the character of his heart in reference to God, then it is a case of too peculiar a nature to be illustrated by any of the analogies of human society. It must be taken up on its own grounds; and should the injured and offended Lawgiver offer to make it the subject of any communication, it is our part humbly to listen and implicitly to follow it.

And here it is granted, that amongst the men who are utter strangers to this communication, you meet with the better and the worse; and that there is an obvious line of distinction which marks off the base and the worthless amongst them, from those of them who are the valuable and the accomplished members of society. And yet do we aver that one may step over that line and not be nearer than he was to God,—that, between the men on either side of it, and Him who created them, there lies an untrodden gulf of separation,—that, with all the justice which rules their transactions, and all the honour which animates their bosoms, and all the compassion which warms their hearts, and streams forth either in tears of pity, or in acts of kindness, upon the miserable,—with all these virtues which they do have, and which serve both to bless and to adorn the condition of humanity, there is one virtue, which, prior to the reception and the influence of the gospel of Christ, they most assuredly do not have,—they are utterly devoid of godliness. They have no desire, and no inclination towards God. There may be the dread of him, and the occasional remembrance of him; but there is no affection for him.

This is the charge which we carry round amongst all the sons and daughters of Adam, who have not submitted themselves

DEPRAVITY OF HUMAN NATURE.

to the only name that is given under heaven whereby men can be saved. We are not denying that the persons of some of them are dignified by the more respectable attributes of character; and that, from the persons of others of them, there are beauteously reflected the more amiable and endearing attributes of character. But we affirm, that with all these random varieties of moral exhibition which are to be found— the principle of loyalty to God has lost the hold of a presiding influence over all the children of our degraded and undone nature. We ask you to collect all the scattered remnants of what is great, and of what is graceful in accomplishments that may have survived the fall of our first parents; and we pronounce, of the whole assemblage, that they go not to alleviate, by one iota, the burden of that controversy which lies between God and their posterity, —that throughout all the ranks and diversities of character which prevail in the world, there is one pervading affection of enmity to him; that the man of talents forgets that he has nothing which he did not receive, and so, courting by some lofty enterprize of mind, the gaze of this world's admiration, he renounces his God, and makes an idol of his fame,—that the man of ambition feels not how subordinate he is to the might and the majesty of his Creator, but turning away all his reverence from him, falls down to the idol of power,— that the man of avarice withdraws all his trust from the living God, and, embarking all his desire in the pursuit of riches, and all his security in the possession of them, he makes an idol of wealth,—that, descending from these to the average and the every-day members of our world's population, we see each walking after the counsel of his own heart, and in the sight of his own eyes, with every wish directed to the objects of time, and every hope bounded by its anticipations: and, amid all the love they bear to their families, and all the diligence they give to their business, and all the homage of praise and attachment they obtain from their friends, are they so surrounded by the influences of what is seen and what is sensible, that the invisible God is scarcely ever thought of, and his character not at all dwelt on with delight, and his will never admitted to an habitual and a practical ascendency over their conduct, so as to make it true of all, and of every one of us, that there is none who understandeth, and none who seeketh after God.

Now, if a man do not see this case made out against himself in all its enormity, he will feel that the man who talks of it, and who proposes the gospel application to it, talketh mysteriously. If the Spirit have not convinced him of sin, and he have not learned to submit his character to the lofty standard of a law which offers to subordinate to the will of God, not merely the whole habit of his outward history, but also the whole habit of his inward affections, both the disease and the remedy are alike unknown to him. His character may be fair and respectable in the eyes of men; but it will not carry upon it one feature of that spirituality and holiness, and relish for those exercises that have God for their immediate object, which assimilate men to angels, and make them meet for the joys of eternity. His morality will be the morality of life, and his virtues will be the virtues of the world; and all the mystery of a parable, or of a dark saying will appear to hang over the terms and the explanations of that gospel, against the light of which, the god of this world blindeth the minds of those who believe not.

Let us therefore reflect that the principle on which the peculiarities of the gospel look so mysterious, is just the feeling which nature has of its own sufficiency; and, that you may renounce this delusive feeling altogether, we ask you to think, how totally destitute you are of that whic God chiefly requires of you. He requires your heart, and we venture to say of every man amongst you, who has heretofore lived in neglect of the great salvation, that his heart, with all its objects and affections, is away from God,—that it is not a sense of obligation to him which forms the habitual and the presiding influence of its movements,—that therefore every day and every hour of your history in the world, accumulates upon you the guilt of a disobedience of a far deeper and more offensive character than even the disobedience of your more notorious and external violations. There is ever with you, lying folded in the recesses of your bosom, and pervading the whole system both of your desires and your doings, that which gives to sin all its turpitude, and all its moral hideousness in the sight of God. There is a rooted preference of the creature to the Creator. There is a full desire after the gift, and a listless ingratitude towards the giver. There is an utter devotedness, in one shape or other, to the world that is to be burnt up,—and an utter forgetfulness, amid all your forms, and all your decencies, of him who endureth for ever. There is that universal attribute of the carnal mind—enmity against God; and we affirm that, with this distaste in your hearts towards him, you, on every principle of a spiritual and intelligent morality, are as chargeable with rebellion against your Maker, as if some apostate angel had been your champion, and you warred with God, under the waving standards of defiance. It was to clear away the guilt of this monstrous iniquity that Christ died. It was to make it possible for God, with his truth unviolated, and his holiness untarnished, and all the high attributes of his eternal and unchangeable nature unimpaired, to hold out forgiveness to the world,—that propitiation was made through the blood of his own son, even that God might be just, while the justifier of them who believe in Jesus. It is to make it possible for man to love the Being whom nature taught him to hate and to fear, that God now lifts, from his mercy-seat, a voice of the most beseeching tenderness, and smiles upon the world as God in Christ, reconciling the world unto himself, and not imputing unto them their trespasses. It was utterly to shift the moral constitution of our minds,—an achievement beyond any power of humanity,—that the Saviour, after he died and rose again, obtained the promise of the Father, even that Spirit, through whom alone the fixed and radical disease of nature can be done away. And thus, by the ministration of the baptism of the Holy Ghost, does he undertake not only to improve but to change us,—not only to repair but to re-make us,—not only to amend our evil works, but to create us anew unto good works, that we may be the workmanship of God in Christ Jesus our Lord. These are the leading and essential peculiarities of the New Testament. This is the truth of Christ; though to the general mind of the world it is the truth of Christ in a mystery. These are the parables which the commissioned messengers of grace are to deal out to the sinful children of Adam,—and dark as they may appear, or disgusting as they may sound in the ears of those who think that they are rich, and have need of nothing, they are the very articles upon which hope is made to beam on the heart of a converted sinner,—and peace is restored to him,—and acceptance with God is secured by the terms of an unalterable covenant,—and the only effective instruments of a vital and substantial reformation are provided; so that he who before was dead in trespasses and sins is quickened together with Christ, and made alive unto God, and renewed again after his image, and enabled to make constant progress in all the graces of a holy and spiritual obedience.

SERMON IV.

An Estimate of the Morality that is without Godliness.

"If I wash myself with snow water, and make my hands never so clean: Yet shalt thou plunge me in the ditch, and mine own clothes shall abhor me. For he is not a man, as I am, that I should answer him, and we should come together in judgment. Neither is there any day's-man betwixt us, that might lay his hand upon us both."—*Job* ix. 30—33.

To the people of every Christian country the doctrine of a Mediator between God and man is familiarized by long possession; though to many of them it be nothing more than the familiarity of a name recognized as a well-known sound by the ear, without sending one fruitful or substantial thought into the understanding. For, let it be observed, that the listless acquiescence of the mind in a doctrine, to the statement or to the explanation of which it has been long habituated, is a very different thing from the actual hold which the mind takes of the doctrine,—insomuch that it is very possible for a man to be a lover of orthodoxy, and to sit with complacency under its ministers, and to be revolted by the heresies of those who would either darken or deny any of its articles,—and, in a word, to be most tenacious in his preference for that form of words to which he has been accustomed; while to the meaning of the words themselves, the whole man is in a state of entire dormancy; and delighted though he really be by the utterance of the truth, exhibits not in his person, or in his history, one evidence of that practical ascendency which Christian truth is sure to exert over the heart and the habits of every genuine believer.

In the midst of all that dimness, and all this indolence about the realities of salvation, it is refreshing to view the workings of a mind that is in earnest; and of a mind too, which, instead of being mechanically carried forward in the track of a prescribed or authoritative orthodoxy, is prompted to all its aspirations by a deep feeling of guilt, and of necessity. Such we conceive to hav been the mind of Job, to whom the doctrine of a Redeemer had not been explicitly unfolded, but who seems at times to have been favoured with a prophetic glimpse of him through the light of a dim and distant futurity. The state of his body, covered as it was with disease, makes him an object of sympathy. But there is a still deeper and more attractive sympathy excited by the state of his soul, labouring under the visitation of a hand that was too heavy for him; called out to combat with God, and struggling to maintain it; at one time, tempted to measure the justice of his cause with the righteousness of Heaven's dispensations; at another, closing his complaint with the murmurs of a despairing acquiescence; and at length brought, through all the varieties of an exercised and agitated spirit, to submit himself to God, and to repent in dust and in ashes.

There is a darkness in the book of Job. He, at one time, under the soreness of his calamity, gives way to impatience; and, at another, he seems to recall the hasty utterance of his more distempered moments. He, in one place, fills his mouth with arguments; and, in another, he appears willing to surrender them all, and to decline the unequal struggle of man contending with his Maker. He is evidently oppressed throughout by a feeling of want, without the full understanding of an adequate or an appropriate remedy. Now, it does give a higher sense of the value of this remedy, when we are made to witness the unsatisfied longings of one who lived in a dark and early period of the world,—when we hear him telling, as he does in these verses, where the soreness lies, and obscurely guessing at the ministration that is suited to it,—nor do we know a single passage of the Bible which carries home with greater effect the necessity of a Mediator, than that where Job, on his restless bed, is set before us, wearying himself in the hopeless task of arguing with God, and calling for some day's-man betwixt them who might lay his hand upon them both.

The afflictions which were heaped upon Job made him doubt his acceptance with his Maker. This was the great burden of his complaint, and the recovery of this acceptance was the theme of many a fruitless and fatiguing speculation. We have one of these speculations in the verses which are now submitted to you; and as they are four in number, so there is such a distinction in the subjects of them, that the passage naturally resolves itself into four separate topics of illustration. In the 30th verse, we have an expedient proposed by Job, for the pupose of obtaining the acceptance which he longed after: "If I wash myself with snow water, and make my hands never so clean." In the 31st verse, we have the inefficacy of this expedient; "Yet shalt thou plunge me in the ditch, and mine own clothes shall abhor me.". In the 32d verse, he gives the reason of this inefficacy; "For he is not man, as I am, that I should answer him, and we should come together in judgment." And in the 33d verse, he intimates to us the right expedient, under the form of complaining that he himself has not the benefit of it: "Neither is there any day's-man betwixt us, that might lay his hand upon us both."

I. It is not to be wondered at, that even a mistaken efficacy should be ascribed to snow water, in the country of Job's residence, where snow, if ever it fell at all, must have fallen rarely, at very extraordinary seasons, and in the more elevated parts of his neighbourhood. This rarity, added to its unsullied whiteness, might have given currency to an idea of its efficacy as a purifier, beyond what actually belonged to it. Certain it is, too, that snow water, like water deposited from the atmosphere, in any other form, does not possess that hardness which is often to be met with in spring water. But however this be, and whether the popular notion of the purifying virtues of snow water, taken up by Job, be well founded or not, we have here an expedient suggested for making the hands clean, and the man pure and acceptable in the sight of God,—a method proposed within the reach of man, and which man can perform, for making himself an object of complacency to his Maker; a method, too, which is quite effectual for beautifying all that meets the discernment of the outward eye, and which is here set before us as connected with the object of gaining the eye of that high and heavenly Witness, with whom we have to do. This is what we understand to be represented by washing with snow water. It comprehends all that man can do for washing himself, and for making himself clean in the sight of God. Job complains of the fruitlessness of this expedient, and perhaps mingles with his complaints the reproaches of a spirit that was not yet subdued to entire acquiescence in the righteousness of God. Let us try to examine this matter, and, if possible, ascertain whether man is able, on the utmost stretch of his powers and of his performances, to make himself an object of approbation to his Judge.

Without entering into the metaphysical controversy about the extent or the freedom of human agency, let it be observed, that there is a plain and a popular understanding on the subject of what man can do and of what he cannot do. We wish to proceed on this understanding for the present, and to illustrate it by a few examples. Should it be asked, if a man can keep his hands from stealing, it would be the unhesitating answer of almost every one that he can do it,—and if he can keep his tongue from lying, that he can do it,—and if he can constrain his feet to carry him every Sabbath to the house of God, that he can do this also,—and if he can tithe his income, or even reducing himself to the necessaries of life, make over the mighty sacrifice of all the remainder to the poor, that it is certainly possible for him to do it,—and if he can keep a guard upon his lips, so that not one whisper of malignity shall escape from them, that he can also prescribe this task to himself, and is able to perform it,—and if he can read much of his Bible, and utter many prayers in private, that he can do it, —and if he can assemble his family on the morning and the evening of every day, and go through the worship of God along with them, that all this he can do,—that all this lies within the compass of human agency.

Let any one man do, then, what all men think it possible for him to do, and he will wear upon his person the visible exhibition of much to recommend him to the favourable judgment of his fellows. He will be guilty of no one transgression against the peace and order of society. He will be correct, and regular, and completely inoffensive. He will contribute many a deed of positive beneficence to the welfare of those around him; and may even, on the strength of his many decencies, and many observations, hold out an aspect of religiousness to the general eye of the world. There will be a wide and most palpable distinction of character between him, and those who, at large from the principle of self-control, resign themselves to the impulse of every present temptation; and are either intemperate, or dishonest, or negligent of ordinances, just as habit, or the urgency of their feelings and their circumstances, may happen to have obtained the ascendancy over them. Those do not what they might, and what, in common estimation, they can do; and it is just because the man has put forth all his strenuousness to the task of accomplishing all that he is able for, that he looks so much more seemly than those who are beside him, and holds out a far more engaging display of what is moral and praiseworthy to all his acquaintances.

II. I will not be able to convince you how superficial the reformation of all these doings is, without passing on to the 31st verse, and proving, that in the pure eye of God the man who has made the most copious application in his power of snow-water to the visible conduct, may still be an object of abhorrence; and that if God enter into judgment with him, he will make him appear as one plunged in the ditch, his righteousness as filthy rags, and himself as an unclean thing. There are a thousand things which, in popular and understood language, man can do. It is quite the general sentiment, that he can abstain from stealing, and lying, and calumny,—that he can give of his substance to the poor, and attend church, and pray, and read his Bible, and keep up the worship of God in his family. But, as an instance of distinction between what he can do, and what he cannot do, let us make the undoubted assertion, that he can eat wormwood, and just put the question, if he can also relish wormwood. That is a different affair. I may command the performance; but have no such command over my organs of sense, as to command a liking, or a taste for the performance. The illustration is homely; but it is enough for our purpose, if it be effective. I may accomplish the doing of what God bids; but have no pleasure in God himself. The forcible constraining of the hand, may make out many a visible act of obedience, but the relish of the heart may refuse to go along with it. The outer man may be all in a bustle about the commandments of God, while to the inner man God is an offence and a weariness. His neighbours may look at him, and all that their eye can reach may be as clean as snow-water can make it. But the eye of God reaches a great deal farther. He is the discerner of the thoughts and intents of the heart, and he may see the foulness of spiritual idolatry in every one of its receptacles. The poor man has no more conquered his rebellious affections, than he has conquered his distaste for wormwood. He may fear God; he may listen to God; and, in outward deed, may obey God. But, he does not, and he will not, love God; and while he drags a heavy load of tasks, and duties, and observances after him, he lives in the hourly violation of the first and greatest of the commandments.

Would any parent among you count it enough that you obtained a service like this from one of your children? Would you be satisfied with the obedience of his hand, while you knew that the affections of his heart were totally away from you? Let every one requirement, issued from the chair of parental authority, be most rigidly and punctually done by him, would not the sullenness of his alienated countenance turn the whole of it into bitterness? It is the heart of his son which the parent longs after; and the lurking distaste and disaffection which rankle there, can never, never be made up by such an obedience, as the yoked and the tortured negro is compelled to yield to the whip of the overseer. The service may be done; but all that can minister satisfaction in the principle of the service, may be withheld from it; and though the very last item of the bidden performance is rendered, this will neither mend the deformity of the unnatural child, nor soothe the feelings of the afflicted and the mortified father.

God is the Father of spirits; and the willing subjection of the spirit is that which he requires of us. "My son, give me thy heart;" and if the heart be withheld, God says of all our visible performances, "To what purpose is the multitude of your sacrifices unto me?" The heart is his requirement; and full, indeed, is the title which he prefers to it. He put life into us; and it is he who hath drawn a circle of enjoyments, and friendships, and interests around us. Every thing that we take delight in, is ministered to us out of his hand. He plies us every moment with his kindness; and when at length the gift stole the heart of man away from the Giver, so that he became a lover of his own pleasure, rather than a lover of God, even then would he not leave us to perish in the guilt of our rebellion. Man made himself an alien, but God was not willing to abandon him; and, rather than lose him for ever, did he devise a way of access by which to woo, and to welcome him back again. The way of our recovery is indeed a way that his heart was set upon; and to prove it, he sent his own eternal Son into the world, who unrobed him of all his glories and made himself of no reputation. He had to travel in the greatness of his strength, that he might unbar the gates of acceptance to a guilty world; and now that, in full harmony with the truth and the justice of God, sinners may draw nigh through the blood of the atonement, what is the wonderful length to which the condescension of God carries him? Why, he actually beseeches us to be reconciled; and, with a tone more tender than the affection of an earthly father ever prompted, does he call upon us to turn, and to turn, for why should we die? if, after all this, the antipathy of nature to God still cleave to us; if, under the power of this antipathy, the service we yield be the cold and unwilling service of constraint; if, with many of the visible outworks of obedience, there be also the strugglings of a reluctant heart to take away from this obedience all its cheerfulness, is not God defrauded of his offering? Does there not rest on the moral aspect of our character, in reference to him, all the odiousness of unnatural children? Let our outer doings be what they may, does there not adhere to us the turpitude of having deeply revolted against that Being whose kindness has never abandoned us? And, though pure in the eye of our fellows, and our hands be clean as with snow-water, is there nothing in our hearts against which a spiritual law may denounce its severities, and, the giver of that law may lift a voice of righteous expostulation? "Hear ye now what the Lord saith: Arise, contend thou before the mountains, and let the hills hear thy voice. Hear ye, O mountains, the Lord's controversy, and ye strong foundations of the earth: for the Lord hath a controversy with his people, and he will plead with Israel. O my people, what have I done unto thee, and wherein have I wearied thee? testify against me."

It is not easy to lay open the utter nakedness of the natural heart in reference to God; or to convince the possessor of it, that, under the guise of his many plausibilities, there may lurk that which gives to sin all its hideousness.

The mere man of ordinances cannot acquiesce in what he reckons to be the exaggerations of orthodoxy upon this subject; nor can he at all conceive how it is possible that, with so much of the semblance of godliness about him, there should, at the same time, be within him the very opposite of godliness. It is, indeed, a difficult task to carry upon this point the conviction of him who positively loves the Sabbath, and to whom the chime of its morning bells brings the delightful associations of peace and of sacredness,—who has his hours of prayer, at which he gathers his family around him, and his hours of attendance on that house where the man of God deals out his weekly lessons to the assembled congregation. It may be in vain to tell him, that God in fact is a weariness to his heart, when it is attested to him by his own consciousness; that when the preacher is before him, and the people are around him, and the professed object of their coming together is to join in the exercise of devotion, and to grow in the knowledge of God, he finds in fact that all is pleasantness, that his eye is not merely filled with the public exhibition, and his ear regaled by the impressiveness of a human voice, but that the interest of his heart is completely kept up by the succession and variety of the exercises. It may be in vain to tell him, that this religion of taste or this religion of habit, or this religion of inheritance, may utterly consist with the deep and the determined worldliness of all his affections,—that he whom he thinks to be the God of his Sabbath is not the God of his week; but that, throughout all the successive days of it, he is going astray after the idols of vanity, and living without God in the world. This is demonstration enough of all his forms, and all his observations, being a mere surface display, without a living principle of piety. But perhaps it may serve more effectually to convince him of it, should we ask him, how his godliness thrives in the closet, and what are the workings of his heart, in the abstract and solitary hour of intercourse with the unseen Father. In church, there may be much to interest him, and to keep him alive. But when alone, and deserted by all the accompaniments of a solemn assembly, we should like to know with what vivacity he enters on the one business of meditating on God, and holding converse with God. Is the sense of the all-seeing and ever-present Deity enough for him; and does love to God brighten and sustain the moments of solitary prayer? The mind may have enough to interest it in church; but does the secret exercise of fellowship with the Father bring no distaste, and no weariness along with it? Is it any thing more than the homage of a formal presentation? And when the business of devotion is thus unpeopled of all its externals, and of all its accessaries; when thus reduced to a naked exercise of spirit, can you appeal to the longings, and the affections of that spirit, as the essential proof of your godliness? And do you never, on occasions like this, discover that which is in your hearts, and detect their enmity to him who formed them? Do you afford no ground for the complaint which he uttered of old, when he said, "Have I been a wilderness unto Israel, and a land of darkness?" and do you not perceive that with this direction of your feelings and your desires away from the living God, though you be outwardly clean, as by the operation of snow water, he may plunge you in the ditch, and make your own clothes to abhor you.

We shall conclude this part of our subject with two observations.

First. The efforts of nature may, in point of inadequacy, be compared to the application of snow water. Yet there is a practical mischief here, in which the zeal of controversy, bent on its one point, and its one principle, may unconsciously involve us. We are not, in pursuit of any argument whatever, to lose sight of efforts. We are not to deny them the place, and the importance which the Bible plainly assigns to them; nor are we to forbear insisting upon their performance by men, previous to conversion, and in the very act of conversion, and in every period of the progress, however far advanced it may be, of the new creature in Jesus Christ our Lord. We speak just now of men, previous to conversion, and we call to your remembrance the example of John the Baptist. The injudicious way in which the doings of men have been spoken of, has had practically this effect on many an inquirer. Since doing is of so little consequence, let us even abstain from it. Now the forerunner of Christ spake a very different language. He unceasingly called upon the people to do; and this was the very preaching which the divine wisdom appointed as a preparation for the Saviour. "He that hath two coats, let him impart to him that hath none; and he that hath meat, let him do likewise."—"Exact no more than that which is appointed."—"Do violence to no man; neither accuse any falsely, and be content with your wages." Was not John, then, it may be said, a mere superficial reformer? Had he stopped short at this, he would have been no better. His teaching could have done no more than is done by the mere application of snow water. But he did not stop here. He told the people that there was a preacher and a preaching to come after him, in comparison of which he and his sermons were nothing. He pointed the eye and the expectation of his hearers full upon one that was greater than himself; and, while he baptized with water unto repentance, and called upon the people to frame their doings, he told them of one mightier than he, who was to baptize with the Holy Ghost and with fire.

And, Secondly, That you may be convinced of the utter necessity of such a baptism; let us affirm the inadequacy of all the fairest virtues and accomplishments of nature. God has, for the well-being of society, provided man with certain feelings and constitutional principles of action, which lead him to a conduct beneficial to those around him; to which conduct he may be carried by the impulse of these principles, with as little reference to the will of God, as a mother, among the inferior animals, when constrained by the sweet and powerful influences of natural affection, to guard the safety, and provide for the nourishment of her young. Take account of these principles as they exist in the bosom of man, and you there find compassion for the unfortunate; the shame of detection in any thing mean, or disgraceful; the desire of standing well in the opinion of his fellows; the kindlier charities, which shed a mild and a quiet lustre over the walks of domestic life; and those wider principles of patriotism and public usefulness which, combined with an appetite for distinction, will raise a few of the more illustrious of our race to some high and splendid career of beneficence. Now, these are the principles which, scattered in various proportions among the individuals of human kind, gave rise to the varied hues of character among them. Some possess them in no sensible degree; and they are pointed at with abhorrence, as the most monstrous and deformed of the species. Others have an average share of them; and they take their station amongst the common-place characters of society. And others go beyond the average; and are singled out from amongst their fellows, as the kind, the amiable, the sweet-tempered, the upright, whose hearts swell with honourable feeling, or whose pulse beats high in the pride of integrity.

Now, conceive for a moment, that the belief of a God were to be altogether expunged from the world. We have no doubt that society would suffer most painfully in its temporal interests by such an event. But the machine of society might still be kept up; and on the face of it you might still meet with the same gradations of character, and the same varied distribution of praise, among the individuals who compose it. Suppose it possible, that the world could be broken off from the system of God's administration altogether; and that he were to consign it, with all its present accommodations, and all its natural principles, to some far and solitary place, beyond the limits of his economy—we should still find ourselves in the midst of a moral variety of character; and man, sitting in judgment over it, would say of some, that they are good, and of others, that they are evil. Even in this desolate region of atheism, the eye of the sentimentalist might expatiate among beauous and interesting spectacles,—amiable mothers shedding their graceful tears over the tomb of departed infancy; high-toned integrity maintaining itself unsullied amid the allurements of corruption; benevolence plying its labours of usefulness; and patriotism earning its proud reward, in the testimony of an approving people. Here, then, you have compassion, and natural affection, and justice, and public spirit—but would it not be a glaring perversion of language to say, that there was godliness in a world, where there was no feeling and no conviction about God.

In the midst of this busy scene, let God reveal himself, not to eradicate these principles of action—but giving his sanction to whatsoever things are just, and lovely, and honourable, and of good report, to make himself known, at the same time as the Creator and Upholder of all things, and as the Being with whom all his rational offspring had to do. Is this solemn announcement from the voice of the Eternal to make no difference upon them? Are those principles which might flourish and be sustained on a soil of atheism, to be counted enough even after the wonderful truth of a living and a reigning God has burst upon the world? You are just;—right, indispensably right. You say you have asserted no more than your own. But this property is not your own. He gave it to you, and he may call upon you to give to him an account of your stewardship. You are compassionate;—right also. But what if he set up the measure of the sanctuary upon your compassion? and, instead of a desultory instinct, excited to feeling by a moving picture of sensibility, and limited in effect to a humble fraction of your expenditure, he call upon you to love your neighbour as yourself, and to maintain this principle at the expense of self-denial, and in the midst of manifold provocations? You love your children;—still indispensably right. But what if he should say, and he has actually said it, that you may know how to give good gifts unto your children, and still be evil? and that if you love father, or mother, or wife, or children, more than him, you are not worthy of him? The lustre of your accomplishments dazzles the eye of your neighbourhood, and you bask with a delighted heart in the sunshine of glory. But what if he should say, that his glory, and not your own, should be the constant aim of your doings? and that if you love the praise of men more than the praise of God, you stand, in the pure and spiritual records of heaven, convicted of idolatry? You love the things of the world; and the men of the world, coming together in judgment upon you, take no offence at it. But God takes offence at it. He says,— and is he not right in saying?—that if the gift withdraw the affections from the Giver, there is something wrong; that the love of these things is opposite to the love of the Father; and that, unless you withdraw your affections from a world that perisheth, you will perish along with it. Surely if these, and such like principles, may consist with the atheism of a world where God is unthought of and unknown,—you stand convicted of a still deeper and more determined atheism, who under the revelation of a God challenging the honour that is due unto his name, are satisfied with your holding in society, and live without him in the world.

SERMON V.

The Judgment of Men, compared with the Judgment of God.

"With me it is a very small thing that I should be judged of you, or of man's judgment—he that judgeth me is the Lord."—1 *Corinthians* iv. 3, 4.

III. When two parties meet together on the business of adjusting their respective claims, or when, in the language of our text, they come together in judgment, the principles on which they proceed must depend on the relation in which they stand to each other: and we know not a more fatal or a more deep laid delusion, than that by which the principles, applicable to the case of a man entering into judgment with his fellow-men, are transferred to the far different case of man's entering into judgment with his God. Job seems to have been aware of this difference, and at times to have been humbled by it. In reference to man, he stood on triumphant ground, and often spoke of it in a style of boastful vindication. No one could impeach his justice. No one could question his generosity. And he made his confident appeal to the remembrance of those around him, when he says of himself, that he delivered the poor that cried, and the fatherless, and him that had none to help him; that the blessing of him that was ready to perish came upon him, and he caused the widow's heart to sing for joy; that he put on righteousness, and it clothed him, and his judgment was as a robe and a diadem; that he was eyes to the blind, and feet was he to the lame; that he was a father to the poor, and the cause that he knew not, he searched out. On these grounds did he challenge the judgment of man, and actually obtained it. For we are told, because he did all this, that when the ear heard him, then it blessed him, and when the eye saw him, it gave witness unto him.

There is not a more frequent exercise of mind in society, than that by which the members of it form and declare their judgment of each other—and the work of thus deciding is a work which they all share in, and on which, perhaps, there is not a day of their lives wherein they are not called upon to expend some measure of attention and understanding—and we know not if there be a single topic that more readily engages the conversation of human beings—and often do we utter our own testimony, and hear the testimony of others to the virtues and vices of the absent—and out of all this has arisen a standard of estimation—and it is such a standard as many may actually reach, and some have actually exceeded—and thus it is, that it appears to require a very extended scale of reputation to take in all the varieties of human character—and while the lower extremity of it is occupied by the dishonest, and the perfidious, and the glaringly selfish, who are outcasts from general respect; on the higher extremity of it, do we behold men, to whom are awarded, by the universal voice, all the honours of a proud and unsullied excellence—and their walk in the world is dignified by the reverence of many salutations—and as we hear of their truth and their uprightness, and their princely liberalities, and of a heart alive to every impulse of sympathy, and of a manner sweetened by all the delicacies of genuine kindness;—who does not see that, in this assemblage of moral graces and accomplishments, there is enough to satisfy man, and to carry the admiration of man? and can we wonder if, while we gaze on so fine a specimen of our nature, we should not merely pronounce upon him an honourable sentence at the tribunal of human judgment, but we should conceive of him that he looks as bright and faultless in the eye of God, and that he is in every way meet for his presence and his friendship in eternity.

Now, if there be any truth in the distinction of our text; if a man may have the judgment of his fellows, and yet be utterly unfit for contending in judgment with God;

if there be any emphasis in the consideration, that he is God, and not man; or any delusion in conceiving of him, that he is altogether like unto ourselves,—may not all that ready circulation of praise, and of acknowledgement, which obtains in society, carry a most ruinous, and a most bewitching influence along with it? Is it not possible that on the applause of man there may be reared a most treacherous self-complacency? Might not we build a confidence before God, on this sandy foundation? Think you not, that it is just this ill-supported confidence which shuts out from many a heart the humiliating doctrine of the gospel? Is there no such imagination as that because we are so well able to stand our ground before the judgment of the world, we shall be equally well able to stand our ground before the judgment-seat of the great day? Are there not many who, upon this very principle, count themselves rich and to have need of nothing? And have you never met with men of character, and estimation in society, who, surrounded by the gratulations of their neighbourhood, find the debasing views of humanity, which are set before us in the New Testament, to be beyond their comprehension; who are utterly in the dark, as to the truth and the justness of such representations, and with whom the voice of God is therefore deafened by the voice and the testimony of men? They see not themselves in that character of vileness and of guilt which he ascribes to them. They are blind to the principle of the text, that he is not a man; and that they may not be able to answer him, though they may be able to meet the every reproach, and to hold out the lofty vindication against every charge, which any one of their fellows may prefer. And thus it is, that many live in the habitual neglect of a salvation which they cannot see that they require; and spend their days in an insidious security, from which nothing but the voice of the last messenger, or the call of the last trumpet, shall awaken them.

To do away this delusion, we shall advert to two leading points of distinction between the judgment of men and that of God. There is a distinction founded upon the claims which God has a right to prefer against us, when compared with the claims which our fellow-men have a right to prefer against us;—and there is a distinction founded upon that clearer and more elevated sense which God has of that holiness without which no man shall see his face, of that moral worth without which we are utterly unfit for the society of heaven.

The people around me have no right to complain, if I give to every man his own; or, in other words, if I am true to all my promises, and faithful to all my bargains; and if what I claim as justice to myself, I most scrupulously render to others, when

DEPRAVITY OF HUMAN NATURE.

they are in like circumstances with myself. Now, let me do all this, and I earn amongst my fellows the character of a man of honour and of equity. Did I live with such a character in an unfallen world, these virtues would not at all signalize me, though the opposite vices would mark me out for universal surprise and indignation. But it so happens that I live in a world full of corruption, where deceit and dishonesty are common;—where, though the higher degrees of them are spoken of with abhorrence, the lower degrees of them are looked at with a very general connivance;—where the inflexibility of a truth that knows not one art of concealment, and the delicacy of an honour that was never tainted, would greatly signalize me;—and thus it is, that though I went not beyond the strict requirements of integrity, yet by my nice and unvarying fulfilment of them, should I rise above the ordinary level of human reputation, and be rewarded by the most flattering distinctions of human applause.

But again, I may in fact give to others more than their own; and in so doing I may earn the credit of other virtues. I may gather an additional lustre around my character, and collect from those around me the tribute of a still louder and more rapturous approbation. I may have a heart constitutionally framed to the feeling and the exercise of compassion. I may scatter on every side of me the treasures of beneficence. I may have an eye for pity, and a hand open as day for melting charity. I may lay aside a large proportion of my wealth to the service of others,—and what with a bosom open to every impulse of pity, and with an eye ever lighted up by the smile of courteousness, and with a ready ear to all that is offered in the shape of complaint or supplication, I may not go beyond the demands of others, but I may go greatly beyond all that they have a right to demand, and if I signalize myself by rendering faithfully to every man his due, —still more shall I signalize myself by a kindness that is never weary, by a liberality that never is exhausted.

Now, we need not offer to assign the precise degree to which a man must carry the exercise of these gratuitous virtues, ere he can obtain for them the good will, and the good opinion of society. We need not say by how small a fraction of his income, he may thus purchase the homage of his acquaintances,—at how easy a rate he may send away one person delighted by his affability; or another by the hospitality of his reception; or a third by the rendering of a personal service; or a fourth by the direct conveyance of a present,—or, finally, for what expense he may surround himself by the gratitude of many poor, and the blessings and the prayers of many cottages.

We cannot bring forward any rigid computation of this matter. But we appeal to the experience of your own history, and to your observation of others, if a man might not, without any painful, or any sensible surrender of enjoyment at all, stand out to the eye of others in a blaze of moral reputation—if the substantial citizen might not, on the convivialities of friendship, be indulging his own taste, and at the very time be securing from his pleased and satisfied guests, the attestations of their cordiality—if the man of business might not be nobly generous to his friends in adversity, and at the same time be running one unvaried career of accumulation—if the man of society might not be charming every acquaintance by the truth and the tenderness of his expressions, and at the same time, instead of impairing, be heightening his share of that felicity, which the Author of our being has annexed to human intercourse—if a thousand little acts of accommodation from one neighbour to another, might not swell the tide of praise and of popularity, and yet, as ample a remainder of pleasurable feeling be left to each as before. And even when the sacrifice is more painful, and the generosity more romantic, and man can appeal to some mighty reduction of wealth as the measure of his beneficence to others, might it not be said of him, if the life be more than meat, and the body than raiment, that still there is left to him more than he can possibly surrender? that, though he strip himself of all his goods to feed the poor, there remains to him that, without which all is nothingness,—that a breathing and a conscious man, he still treads on the face of our world, and bears his part in that universe of life, where the unfailing compassion of God still continues to uphold him,—that instead of lying wrapt in the insensibility of an eternal grave, he has all the images of a waking existence around him, and all the glories of immortality before him,—that instead of being withered to a thing of nought, and gone to that dark and hidden land, where all is silence and deep annihilation, a thousand avenues of enjoyment are still open to him, and the promise of a daily provision is still made sure, and he is free to all the common blessings of nature, and he is freer still to all the consolations, and to all the privileges of the gospel.

Thus it appears that after I have fulfilled all the claims of men, and men are satisfied,—that after having gone, in the exercise of liberality, beyond these claims, and men are filled with delight and admiration, —that after, on the footing of equal and independent rights, I have come into judgment with my fellows, and they have awarded to me the tribute of their most honourable testimony, the footing on which

I stand with God still remains to be attended to, and his claims still remain to be adjusted,—and the mighty account still lies uncancelled between the creature and the Creator,—between the man who, in reference to his neighbours, can say, I give every one his own, and out of my own I expatiate in acts of tenderness and generosity amongst them, and the God who can say, You have nothing that you did not receive, and all you ever gave is out of the ability which I have conferred upon you, and this wealth is not your own, but his who bestowed it, and who now calls upon you to render an account of your stewardship,—between the man who has purchased, by a fraction of his property, the good will of his acquaintances, and the God who asserts his right to have every fraction of it turned into an expression of gratitude, and devoted to his glory,—between the man who holds up his head in society, because his justice, and the ministrations of his liberality, have distinguished him, and the God who demands the returns of duty and of acknowledgement, for giving him the fund of these ministrations, and for giving what no money can purchase,—for putting the principle of life into his bosom,—for furnishing him with all his senses, and, through these inlets of communication, giving him a part, and a property, in all that is around him,—for sustaining him in all the elements of his being, and conferring upon him all his capacities, and all his joys.

Now, what we wish you to feel is, that the judgment of men may be upon your side, and the judgment of God be most righteously against you—that while from the one nothing is heard but admiration and gratitude, from the other, there may be such a charge of sinfulness, as, when set in order before your eye, will convince you, that he by whom you consist, is defrauded of all his offerings,—that, while all the common honesties and humanities of social life, are acquitted to the entire satisfaction of others, and to the entire purity of your own reputation in the world, your whole heart and conduct may be utterly pervaded by the habit of ungodliness,—that, while not one claim which your neighbours can prefer, is not met most readily, and discharged most honourably, the great claims of the Creator, over those whom he has formed, may lie altogether unheeded; and he, your constant benefactor, be not loved,—and he, your constant preserver, be not depended on,—and he, your most legitimate sovereign, be not obeyed,—and he, the unseen Spirit, who pervades all, and upholds all, be neither worshipped in spirit and in truth, nor vested with the hold of a rightful supremacy over your rebellious affections.

God is not man; nor can we measure what is due to him, by what is due to our fellows in society. He made us, and he upholds us, and at his will the life which is in us, will, like the expiring vapour, pass away; and the tabernacle of the body, that curious frame-work which man thinks he can move at his own pleasure, when it is only in God that he moves, as well as lives, and has his being, will, when abandoned by its spirit, mix with the dust out of which it was formed, and enter again into the unconscious glebe from which it was taken. It was, indeed, a wondrous preferment for unshapen clay to be wrought into so fine an organic structure, but not more wondrous surely than that the soul which animates it should have been created out of nothing; and what shall we say, if the compound being so originated, and so sustained, and depending on the will of another for every moment of his continuance, is found to spurn the thought of God, in distaste and disaffection away from him? When the spirit returns to him who sitteth on the throne; when the question is put, Amid all the multitude of your doings in the world, what have you done unto me? When the rightful ascendency of his claims over every movement of the creature is made manifest by him who judgeth righteously; when the high but just pretensions of all things being done to his glory; of the entire heart being consecrated in every one of its regards to his person and character; of the whole man being set apart to his service, and every compromise being done away, between the world on the one hand, and that Being on the other, who is jealous of his honour:—when these high pretensions are set up and brought into comparison with the character and the conduct of any one of us, and it be inquired in how far we have rendered unto God the ever-breathing gratitude that is due to him, and that obedience which we should feel at all times to be our task and our obligation; how shall we fare in that great day of examination, if it be found that this has not been the tendency of our nature at all? and when he who is not a man shall thus enter into judgment with us, how shall we be able to stand?

Amid all the praise we give and receiv from each other, we may have no claims to that substantial praise which cometh from God only. Men may be satisfied, but it followeth not that God is satisfied. Under a ruinous delusion upon this subject, we may fancy ourselves to be rich, and have need of nothing, while, in fact, we are naked, and destitute, and blind, and miserable. And thus it is, that there is a morality of this world, which stands in direct opposition to the humbling representations of the Gospel; which cannot comprehend what it means by the utter worthlessness and depravity of our nature; which passionately repels this statement, and that too on its own consciousness of attainments superior to those of the sordid, and the profligate, and the dishonourable; and is fortified in its resistance to the truth as it is in Jesus, by the flattering testimonials which it gathers to its respectability and its worth from the various quarters of human society.

A just sense of the extent of claim which God has upon his own creatures, would lay open this hiding-place of security: would lead us to see, that to do some things for our neighbours, is not the same with doing all things for our Maker; that a natural principle of honesty to man, is altogether distinct from a principle of entire devotedness to God; that the tithe which we bestow upon others is not an equivalent for a total dedication unto God of ourselves, and of all which belongs to us; that we may present those around us with many an offering of kindness, and not present our bodies a living sacrifice to God, which is our reasonable service; that we may earn a cheap and easy credit for such virtues as will satisfy the world, and be utter strangers to the self-denial, and the spirituality, and the mortification of every earthly desire, and the affection for the things that are above;—all of which graces enter as essential ingredients into the sanctification of the gospel.

But this leads us to the second point of distinction between the judgment of man and that of God,—even his clearer and more elevated sense of that holiness without which no man shall see his face, and of that moral worth without which we are utterly unfit for the society of heaven.

Man's sense of the right and the wrong may be clear and intelligent enough, in so far as that part of character is concerned which renders us fit for the society of earth. Those virtues, without which a community could not be held together, are both urgently demanded by that community, and highly appreciated by it. The morality of our earthly life, is a morality which is in direct subservience to our earthly accommodation; and seeing that equity, and humanity, and civility, are in such visible and immediate connexion with all the security, and all the enjoyment which they spread around them, it is not to be wondered at, that they should throw over the character of him by whom they are exhibited, the lustre of a grateful and a superior estimation. And thus it is, that even without any very nice or exquisite refinement of these virtues, many an ordinary character will pass;—and should that character be deformed by the levities, or even by the profligacies of intemperance, he who sustains it may still bear his part among the good men of society,—and keep away from it all that malignity, and all that dishonesty, which have a disturbing effect on the enjoyments of others, and these others will still retain their kindliness for the good-humoured convivialist,—and he will be suffered to retain his own taste, and his own peculiarities; and, though it may be true, that chastity, and self-control, and the severer virtues of personal discipline and restraint, would in fact give a far more happy and healthful tone to society than at present it possesses, yet this influence is not so conspicuous, and heedless men do not look so far: and therefore it is, that in spite of his many outward and positive transgressions of the divine law, many an individual can be referred to, who, with his average share of the integrities and the sensibilities of social life, has stamped upon him the currency of a very fair every-day character, who moves among his fellows without disgrace, and meets with acceptance throughout the general run of this world's companies.

If such a measure of indulgence be extended to the very glaring iniquities of the outer man, let us not wonder though the errors of the heart, the moral diseases of the spirit, the disorganization of the inner man, with its turbulent passions, and its worldly affections, and its utter deadness to the consideration of an overruling God, should find a very general indulgence among our brethren of the species. Bring a man to sit in judgment over the depravities of our common nature, and unless these depravities are obviously pointed against the temporal good of society, what can we expect, but that he will connive at the infirmities of which he feels himself to be so large and so habitual a partaker? What can we expect but that his moral sense, clouded as it is against the discernment of his own exceeding turpitude, will also perceive but dimly, and feel but obtusely, a similar turpitude in the character of others? What else can we look for, than that the man who fires so promptly on the reception of an injury, will tolerate in his fellow all the vindictive propensities?—or, that the man who feels not in his bosom a single movement of principle or of tenderness towards God, will tolerate in another an equally entire habit of ungodliness?—or, that the man who surrenders himself to the temptations of voluptuousness, will perceive no enormity of character at all in the unrestrained dissipations of an acquaintance?—and, in a word, when I see a man whose rights I have never invaded, who has no complaint of personal wrong or provocation to allege against me, and who shares equally with myself in nature's blindness and nature's propensities, I will not be afraid of entering into judgment with him;—nor shall I stand in awe of any penetrating glance from his eye, of any indignant remonstrance from his offended sense of what is righteous, though there be made bare to his inspection all my devotedness to the world, and all my proud disdain at the insolence of others, and all my anger at the sufferings of injustice, and all my indifference to the God who formed me, and all those secrecies of an unholy and an unheavenly character, which are to be brought out into full manifestation on the great day of the winding up of this world's history.

It is a very capital delusion that God is like unto man,—" Thou thoughtest that I was altogether such a one as thyself; but I will reprove thee, and set thy sins in order before thine eyes. Now consider this, ye that forget God, lest I tear you in pieces, and there be none to deliver."

Man and man may come together in judgment, and retire from each other in mutual complacency. But when man and God thus come together, there is another principle, and another standard of examination. There is a claim of justice on the part of the Creator, totally distinct from any claim which a fellow-creature can prefer,—and while the one will tolerate all that is consistent with the economy and the interest of the society upon earth, the other can tolerate nothing that is inconsistent with the economy and the character of the society in heaven. God made us for eternity. He designed us to be the members of a family which never separates, and over which he himself presides in the visible glory of all that worth, and of all that moral excellence, which belong to him. He formed us at first after his own likeness; and ere we can be re-admitted into that paradise from which we have been exiled, we must be created anew in the image of God. These spirits must be made perfect, and every taint of selfishness and impurity be done away from them. Heaven is the place into which nothing that is unclean or unholy can enter; and we are not preparing for our inheritance there, unless there be gathering upon us here, the lineaments of a celestial character. Now, a man may be accomplished in the moralities of civil and of social life, without so much as the semblance of such a character resting upon him. He may have no share whatsoever in the tastes, or in the enjoyments, or in the affections of paradise. There might not be a single trace of the mark of the Lamb of God upon his forehead. He who ponders so intelligently the secrets of the heart, may be able to discover there no vestige of any love for himself,—no sensibility at all to what is amiable or to what is great in the character of the Godhead,—no desire whatever after his glory,—no such feeling towards him who is to tabernacle with men, as will qualify him to bear a joyful part in the songs, and the praises of that city which has foundations. Surrounded as he is by the perishable admiration of his fellows, he is altogether out of affection, and out of acquaintance, with that Being with whom he has to do; and it will be found, on the great day of the doings, and the deliberations of the judgment-seat, that as he had no relish for God in time, so is he utterly unfit for his presence, or for his friendship in eternity.

It is said of God, that he created man after his own image, and it was upon losing this image that he was cast out of paradise: and ere he can be again admitted, the image that has been lost must again be formed on him. The grand qualification for the society of heaven is, that each of its members be like unto God. In the selfish and sensual society of earth, there is many a feature of resemblance to the Godhead that is most readily dispensed with; and many as individual here obtains applause and toleration among his fellows, though there is not one attribute of the saintly character belonging to him. Let him only fulfil the stipulations of integrity, and smile benignity upon his friends, and render the alacrity of willing and valuable services to those who have never offended him, and on the strength of such performances as these, may he rise to a conspicuous place in the scale of this world's reputation. But what would have been the sad event to us, had these been the only performances which went to illustrate the character of the Godhead,—had he been a God of whom we could say no more, than that he possessed the one attribute of an unrelenting justice, or even that he went beyond this attribute, in the exercise of kindness to those who loved him, and in acts of beneficence to those who had never offended him? Do we not owe our place and our prospect to the love of God for his enemies? Is it not from the riches of his forbearance and long-suffering, that we draw all our enjoyments in time, and all our hopes for eternity? Is it not because, though grieved with sinners every day, he still waits to be gracious; that he holds out to us, his heedless and wayward children, the beseeching voice of reconciliation; and puts on such an aspect of tenderness to those who have not ceased from their birth to vex his Holy Spirit, and to thwart him every hour by the perverseness of their disobedience? This is the godlike attribute on which all the privileges of our fallen race are suspended; and yet against the intimation of which, nature, when urged by the provocations of injustice, rises in such a tumult of strong and impetuous resistance. It is through the putting forth of this attribute, that any redeemed sinners are to be found among the other society of heaven; but into which no member shall be admitted out of this corrupt world, till there be stamped and realized on his own person, that feature of the divinity to which he owes a distinction so exalted. And tell us, ye men who are so jealous of right and of honour, who take sudden fire at every insult, and suffer the slightest imagination of another's contempt, or another's unfairness, to chase from your bosom every feeling of complacency;—ye men whom every fancied affront puts into such a turbulence of emotion, and in whom every fancied infringement stirs up the quick and the resentful appetite for justice—how will you stand the rigorous application of that test by which the forgiven of God are ascertained, even that the spirit of forgiveness is in them, and by which it will be pronounced whether you are indeed the children of the highest, and perfect as your Father in heaven is perfect?

But we must hasten to a close, and will, therefore, barely suggest some other matters of self-examination. We ask you, to think of the facility with which you might obtain the approbation of men, without being at all like unto God in the holiness of his character. We ask you to think of the delight which he takes in the contemplation of what is pure, and moral, and righteous. We ask you to think how one great object of his creation, was to diffuse over the face of it a multiplied resemblance of himself,—and that, therefore, however fit you may be for sustaining your part in the alienated community of this world, you are most assuredly unfit for the great and the general assembly of the spirits of just men made perfect,—if unlike unto God who is in the midst of them, you have no congenial delight with the Father of all, in the contemplation of spiritual excellence. Now, are you not blind to the glories and the perfections of that Being who realizes this excellence to a degree that is infinite? Does not the creature fill up all your avenues of enjoyment, while the Creator is forgotten? In reference to God, is there not an utter dulness and insensibility of all your regards to him? If thus blind to the perception of that supreme virtue and loveliness which reside in the Godhead, are you not, in fact, and by nature an outcast from the Godhead? And an outcast will you ever remain, until your character be brought under some mighty revolutionizing influence which is able to shift the currency of your desires, and to over-rule nature with all her obstinate habits, and all her fond and favourite predilections.

These are topics of great weight and great pregnancy; but we leave them to your own thoughts, and only ask you at present to look at the vivid illustration of them that may be gathered out of the history of Job. In reference to his fellows, he could make a triumphant appeal to the honour and the humanity which adorned him,—he could speak of the splendid career of beneficence that he had run,—and in the recollection of the plaudits that had surrounded him, he could boldly challenge the inspection of all his neighbours, and of all his enemies, on the whole tract of his visible history in the world. He protested his innocence before them, and even so long as he had only heard of God by the hearing of the ear did he address him in the language of justification. But when God at length revealed himself,—when the worth and the majesty of the Eternal stood before him in visible array,—when the actual presence of his Maker brought the claims of his Maker to bear impressively upon his conscience, it was not merely the presence of the power of God which overawed him; it was the presence of the righteousness of God which convinced him,—and when, from the bright assemblage of all that was pure, and holy, and graceful in the aspect of the Divinity, he turned the eye of contemplation downward upon himself,—O it is instructive to be told, how the vaunting patriarch shrunk into all the depths of self-abasement at so striking a manifestation; and how he said, "I have heard of thee by the hearing of the ear, but now mine eye seeth thee; wherefore I abhor myself, and repent in dust and in ashes."

It is indeed a small matter to be judged of man's judgment. He who judges us is God. From this judgment there is no escape, and no hiding place. The testimony of our fellows will as little avail us in the day of judgment, as the help of our fellows will avail us in the hour of death.

We may as well think of seeking a refuge in the applause of men, from the condemnation of God, as we may think of seeking a refuge in the power or the skill of men, from the mandate of God, that our breath shall depart from us. And, have you never thought, when called to the chamber of the dying man,—when you saw the warning of death upon his countenance, and how its symptoms gathered and grew, and got the ascendency over all the ministrations of human care and of human tenderness,—when it every day became more visible, that the patient was drawing to his close, and that nothing in the whole compass of art or any of its resources, could stay the advances of the sure and the last malady, —have you never thought, on seeing the bed of the sufferer surrounded by other comforters than those of the Patriarch,—when, from morning to night, and from night to morning, the watchful family sat at his couch, and guarded his broken slumbers, and interpreted all his signals, and tried to hide from his observation the tears which attested him to be the kindest of parents,—when the sad anticipation spread its gloomy stillness over the household, and even set forth an air of seriousness and concern upon the men of other families,—when you have witnessed the despair of friends, who could only turn them to cry at the spectacle of his last agonies, and had seen how little it was that weeping children and inquiring neighbours could do for him,—when you have contrasted the unrelenting necessity of the grave, with the feebleness of every surrounding endeavour toward it, has the thought never entered within you, How powerless is the desire of man!—how sure and how resistless is the decree of God!

And on the day of the second death, will it be found, that it is not the imagination of man, but the sentence of God that shall stand. When the sound of the last trumpet awakens us from the grave, and the ensigns of the last day are seen on the canopy of heaven, and the tremor of the dissolving elements is felt upon the earth, and the Son of God with his mighty angels are placed around the judgment-seat, and the men of all ages and of all nations are standing before it, and waiting the high decree of eternity,—then will it be found, that as no power of man can save his fellow from going down to the grave of mortality, so no testimony of man can save his fellow from going down to the pit of condemnation. Each on that day will mourn apart. Each of those on the left hand, engrossed by his own separate contemplation, and overwhelmed by the dark and the louring futurity of his own existence, will not have a thought or a sympathy to spare for those who are around him. Each of those on the right hand will see and acquiesce in the righteousness of God, and be made to acknowledge, that those things which are highly esteemed among men are in his sight an abomination. When the judge and his attendants shall come on the high errand of this world's destinies, they will come from God,—and the pure principle they shall bring along with them from the sanctuary of heaven, will be the entire subordination of the thing formed to him who formed it. In that praise which upon earthly feelings the creatures offer one to another, we behold no recognition of this principle whatever; and therefore it is, that it is so very different from the praise which cometh from God only. And should any one of these creatures be made on that great day of manifestation, to see his nakedness,—should the question, what have you done unto me? leave him speechless; should at length, convicted of his utter rebelliousness against God, he try to find among the companions of his pilgrimage, some attestation to the kindness that beamed from him upon his fellow mortals in the world,—they will not be able to hide him from the coming wrath. In the face of all the tenderness they ever bore him, the severity of an unreconciled lawgiver must have upon him its resistless operation. They may all bear witness to the honour and the generosity of his doings among men, but there is not one of them who can justify him before God. Nor among all those who now yield him a ready testimony on earth will he find a day's-man betwixt him and his Creator, who can lay his hand upon them both.

SERMON VI.

The Necessity of a Mediator between God and Man.

"Neither is there any day's-man betwixt us, that might lay his hands upon us both."—*Job* ix. 33.

IV. THE feeling of Job, at the time of his uttering the complaint which is recorded in the verses before us, might not have been altogether free of a reproachful spirit towards those friends who had refused to advocate his cause, and who had even added bitterness to his distress by their most painful and unwelcome arguments. And well may it be our feeling, and that too without the presence of any such ingredient along with it—that there is not a man upon earth who can execute the office of a day's-man betwixt us and God,—that taking the common sense of this term, there is none who can act as an umpire between us the children of ungodliness, and the Lawgiver, whom we have so deeply offended; or taking up the term that occurs in the Septuagint version of the Bible, that amongst all our brethren of the species, not an individual is to be found who, standing in the place of a mediator, can lay his hand upon us both. It is, indeed, very possible, that all this may carry the understanding, and at the same time have all the inefficiency of a cold and general speculation. But should the Spirit, whose office it is to convince us of sin, lend the power of his demonstration to the argument,—should he divide asunder our thoughts, and enable us to see that, with the goodly semblance of what is fair and estimable in the sight of man, all within us is defection from the principle of loyalty to God—that while we yield a duty as the members of society, the duty that lies upon us, as the creatures of the Supreme Being, is, in respect of the spirit of allegiance which gives it all its value, fallen away from, by every one of us,—should this conviction cleave to us like an arrow sticking fast, and work its legitimate influence, in causing us to feel all the worthlessness of our characters, and all the need and danger of our circumstances,—then would the urgency of the case be felt as well as understood by us, —nor should we be long of pressing the inquiry of where is the day's-man betwixt us that might lay his hand upon us both!

And, in fact, by putting the Mediator away from you,—by reckoning on a state of safety and acceptance without him, what is the ground upon which, in reference to God, you actually put yourselves? We speak not at present of the danger of persisting in such an attitude of independence, of its being one of those refuges of treachery in which the good man of the world is often to be found,—of its being a state wherein peace, when there is no peace, lulls him by its flatteries unto a deceitful repose. We are not at present saying how ruinous it is to rest a security upon an imposing exterior, when in fact the heart is not right in the sight of God, and while the reproving eye of him, who judgeth not as man judgeth, is upon him, or how poisonous is the unction that comes upon the soul from those praises which upon the mere exhibition of the social virtues, are rung and circulated through society. But, in addition to the danger, let us insist upon the guilt of thus casting the offered Mediator away from us. It implies in the most direct possible way, a sentiment of the sufficiency of our own righteousness. It is expressly saying of our obedience, that it is good enough for God. It is presumptuously thinking that what pleases the world may please the Maker of it, even though he himself has declared it to be a world lying in wickedness. There is an aggravation you will perceive in all this which goes beyond the simple infraction of the commandment. It is, after the infraction of it, challenging for some remainder or for some semblance of conformity, the reward and approbation of the God whose law we have dishonoured. It is, after we have braved the attribute of the Almighty's justice, by incurring its condemnation, making an attempt upon the attribute itself, by bringing it down to the standard of a polluted obedience. It is, after insulting the throne of God's righteousness, embarking in the still deadlier enterprize of demolishing all the stabilities which guard it; and spoiling it of that truth which has pronounced a curse on the children of iniquity,—of that holiness which cannot dwell with evil,—of that unchangeableness which will admit of no compromise with sinners that can violate the honours of the Godhead, or weaken the authority of his government over the universe that he has formed. It is laying those paltry accomplishments which give you a place of distinction among your fellows, before that God of whose throne justice and judgment are the habitation, and calling upon him to connive at all that you want, and to look with complacency on all that you possess. It is to bring to the bar of judgment the poor and the starving samples of virtue which are current enough in a world broken loose from its communion with God, and to defy the inspection upon them of God's eternal Son, and of the angels he brings along with him to witness the righteousness of his decisions. Sin has indeed been the ruin of our nature—but this refusal of the Saviour of sinners lands them in a perdition still deeper and more irrecoverable. It is blindness to the enormity of sin. It is equivalent to a formally announced sentiment on your part that your performances, sinful as they are, and polluted as they are, are good enough for heaven. It is just saying of the offered Saviour that you do not see the use of him. It is a provoking contempt of mercy; and causing the measure of ordinary guilt to overflow, by heaping the additional blasphemy upon it, of calling upon God to honour it by his rewards, and to look to it with the complacency of his approbation.

We cannot, then, we cannot draw near unto God, by a direct or independent approach to him. And who in these circumstances, is fit to be the day's-man betwixt you? There is not a fellow-mortal from Adam downward, who has not sins of his own to answer for. There is not one of them who has not the sentence of guilt inscribed upon his own forehead, and who is not arrested by the same unscaled barrier which keeps you at an inaccessible distance from God. There is not one of them whose entrance into the holiest of all would not inflict on it as great a profanation, as if any of you were to present yourselves before him, who dwelleth there, without a Mediator. There lieth a great gulf between God and the whole of this alienated world; and after looking round amongst all the men of all its generations, we may say, in the language of the text, that there is not a day's-man betwixt us who can lay his hand upon us both.

What we aim at as the effect of all these observations, is, that you should feel your only security to be in the revealed and the offered mediator; that you should seek to him as your only effectual hiding-place; and who alone, in the whole range of universal being, is able to lay his hand upon you, and shield you from the justice of the Almighty, and to lay his hand upon God, and stay the fury of the avenger. By him the deep atonement has been rendered.

By him the mystery has been accomplished, which angels desired to look into. By him such a sacrifice for sin has been offered, as that, in the acceptance of the sinner, every attribute of the Divinity is exalted; and the throne of the Majesty in the heavens, though turned into a throne of grace, is still upheld in all its firmness, and in all its glory. Through the unchangeable priesthood of Christ, the vilest of sinners may draw nigh, and receive of that mercy which has met with truth, and of that peace which is in close alliance with righteousness; and without one perfection of the Godhead being surrendered by this act of forgiveness, all are made to receive a higher and more wondrous manifestation; for though he will by no means clear the guilty, yet there is no place for vengeance, when all their guilt is cleared away by the blood of the everlasting covenant; and though he executeth justice upon the earth, yet he can be just while the justifier of them who believe in Jesus.

The work of our redemption is every where spoken of as an achievement of strength—as done by the putting forth of mighty energies—as the work of one who, travelling in his own unaided greatness, had to tread the wine-press alone; and who, when of the people there was none to help him, did by his own arm bring unto him salvation. To move aside the obstacle which beset the path of acceptance; to reinstate the guilty into favour with the offended and unchangeable Lawgiver: to avert from them the execution of that sentence to which there were staked the truth and justice of the Divinity; to work out a pardon for the disobedient, and at the same time to uphold in all their strength the pillars of that throne which they had insulted; to intercept the defied penalties of the law, and at the same time magnify it, and to make it honourable; thus to bend, as it were, the holy and everlasting attributes of God, and in doing so, to pour over them the lustre of a high and awful vindication,—this was an enterprise of such height, and depth, and length, as no created being could fulfil, and which called forth the might and the counsel of him who is the power of God, and the wisdom of God.

When no man could redeem his neighbour from the grave,—God himself found out a ransom. When not one of the beings whom he had formed could offer an adequate expiation,—did the Lord of hosts awaken the sword of vengeance against his fellow. When there was no messenger among the angels who surrounded his throne, that could both proclaim and purchase peace for a guilty world,—did God manifest in the flesh descend in shrouded majesty amongst our earthly tabernacles, and pour out his soul unto the death for us, and purchase the church by his own blood, and bursting away from the grave which could not hold him, ascend to the throne of his appointed mediatorship; and now he, the first and the last, who was dead and is alive, and maketh intercession for transgressors, is able to save to the uttermost all who come unto God through him; and standing in the breach between a holy God and the sinners who have offended him, does he make reconciliation, and lay his hand upon them both.

But it is not enough that the Mediator be appointed by God,—he must be accepted by man. And to incite our acceptance does he hold forth every kind and constraining argument. He casts abroad, over the whole face of the world, one wide and universal assurance of welcome. "Whosoever cometh unto me shall not be cast out." "Come unto me all ye who labour and are heavy laden, and I will give you rest." "Where sin hath abounded, grace hath much more abounded." "Whatsoever ye ask in my name ye shall receive." The path of access to Christ is open and free of every obstacle, which kept fearful and guilty man at an impracticable distance from the jealous and unpacified Lawgiver. He hath put aside the obstacle, and now stands in its place. Let us only go in the way of the Gospel, and we shall find nothing between us and God but the author and finisher of the Gospel,—who, on the one hand, beckons to him the approach of man with every token of truth and of tenderness; and, on the other hand, advocates our cause with God, and fills his mouth with arguments, and pleads that very atonement which was devised in love by the Father, and with the incense of which he was well pleased, and claims, as the fruit of the travail of his soul, all who put their trust in him; and thus, laying his hand upon God, turns him altogether from the fierceness of his indignation.

But Jesus Christ is something more than the agent of our justification,—he is the agent of our sanctification also. Standing between us and God, he receives from him of that Spirit which is called the promise of the Father, and he pours it forth in free and generous dispensation on those who believe in him. Without this spirit there may, in a few of the goodlier specimens of our race, be within us the play of what is kindly in constitutional feeling, and without us the exhibition of what is seemly in a constitutional virtue; and man, thus standing over us in judgment, may pass his verdict of approbation; and all that is visible in our doings may be pure as by the operation of snow water. But the utter irreligiousness of our nature will remain as entire and as obstinate as ever. The alienation of our desires from God will persist with unsubdued vigour in our bosoms; and sin, in the very essence of its elementary principle, will still lord it over the inner man with all the power of its original ascendency,—till the deep, and the searching, and the pervading influence of the love of God be shed abroad in our hearts by the Holy Ghost. This is the work of the great Mediator. This is the might and the mystery of that regeneration, without which we shall never see the kingdom of God. This is the office of Him to whom all power is committed, both in heaven and in earth,—who reigning in heaven, and uniting its mercy with its righteousness, causes them to flow upon earth in one stream of celestial influence; and reigning on earth, and working mightily in the hearts of its people, makes them meet for the society of heaven,—thereby completing the wonderful work of our redemption, by which, on the one hand he brings the eye of a holy God to look approvingly on the sinner, and on the other hand, makes the sinner fit for the fellowship, and altogether prepared for the enjoyment of God.

Such are the great elements of a sinner's religion. But if you turn from the prescribed use of them, the wrath of God abideth on you. If you kiss not the Son while he is in the way, you provoke his anger, and when once it begins to burn, they only are blessed who have put their trust in him. If, on the fancied sufficiency of a righteousness that is without godliness, you neglect the great salvation, you will not escape the severities of that day, when the Being with whom you have to do shall enter with you into judgment; and it is only by fleeing to the Mediator, as you would from a coming storm, that peace is made between you and God, and that, sanctified by the faith which is in Jesus, you are made to abound in such fruits of righteousness, as shall be to praise and glory at the last and the solemn reckoning.

Before we conclude, we shall just advert to another sense, in which the Mediator between God and man may be affirmed to have laid his hand upon them bo h:—He fills up that mysterious interval which lies between every corporeal being, and the God who is a spirit and is invisible.

No man hath seen God at any time,—and the power which is unseen is terrible. Fancy trembles before its own picture, and superstition throws its darkest imagery over it. The voice of the thunder is awful, but not so awful as the conception of that angry being who sits in mysterious concealment, and gives it all its energy. In these sketches of the imagination, fear is sure to predominate. We gather an impression of Nature's God, from those scenes where Nature threatens, and looks dreadful. We speak not of the theology of the schools, and the empty parade of its demonstrations. We speak of the theology of actual feeling,—that theology which is sure to derive its lessons from the quarter whence the human heart derives its strongest sensations,—and we refer both to your own feelings, and to the history of this world's opinions, if God is more felt or more present to your imaginations in the peacefulness of spring, or the loveliness of a summer landscape, than when winter with its mighty elements sweeps the forest of its leaves,—when the rushing of the storm is heard upon our windows, and man flees to cover himself from the desolation that walketh over the surface of the world.

If nature and her elements be dreadful, how dreadful that mysterious and unseen Being, who sits behind the elements he has formed, and gives birth and movement to all things! It is the mystery in which he is shrouded,—it is that dark and unknown region of spirits, where he reigns in glory, and stands revealed to the immediate view of his worshippers,—it is the inexplicable manner of his being so far removed from that province of sense, within which the understanding of man can expatiate,—it is its total unlikeness to all that nature can furnish to the eye of the body, or to the conception of the mind, which animates it,—it is all this which throws the Being who formed us at a distance so inaccessible,—which throws an impenetrable mantle over his way, and gives us the idea of some dark and untrodden interval betwixt the glory of God, and all that is visible and created.

Now, Jesus Christ has lifted up this mysterious veil, or rather he has entered within it. He is now at the right hand of God; and though the brightness of his Father's glory, and the express image of his person, he appeared to us in the palpable characters of a man; and those high attributes of truth, and justice, and mercy, which could not be felt or understood, as they existed in the abstract and invisible Deity, are brought down to our conceptions in a manner the most familiar and impressive, by having been made, through Jesus Christ, to flow in utterance from human lips, and to beam in expressive physiognomy from a human countenance.

So long as I had nothing before me but the unseen spirit of God, my mind wandered in uncertainty, my busy fancy was free to expatiate, and its images filled my heart with disquietude and terror. But in the life, and person, and history of Jesus Christ, the attributes of the Deity are brought down to the observation of the senses; and I can no longer mistake them, when in the Son, who is the express image of his Father, I see them carried home to my understanding by the evidence and expression of human organs,—when I see the kindness of the Father, in the tears which fell from his Son at the tomb of Lazarus,—when I see his justice blended with his mercy, in the exclamation, "O Jerusalem, Jerusalem," by Jesus Christ; uttered with a tone more tender than the sympathy of human bosom ever prompted, while he bewailed the sentence of its desolation,—and in the look of energy and significance which he threw upon Peter, I feel the judgment of God himself, flashing conviction upon my conscience, and calling me to repent while his wrath is suspended, and he still waiteth to be gracious.

And it was not a temporary character which he assumed. The human kindness, and the human expression which makes it intelligible to us, remained with him till his latest hour. They survived his resurrection, and he has carried them along with him to the mysterious place which he now occupies. How do I know all this? I know it from his history; I hear it in the parting words to his mother from the cross; I see it in his unaltered form when he rose triumphant from the grave; I perceive it in his tenderness for the scruples of the unbelieving Thomas; and I am given to understand, that as his body retained the impression of his own sufferings, so his mind retains a sympathy for ours, as warm, and gracious, and endearing, as ever. We have a Priest on high, who is touched with a fellow feeling of our infirmities. My soul, unable to support itself in its aerial flight among the spirits of the invisible, now reposes on Christ, who stands revealed to my conceptions in the figure, the countenance, the heart, the sympathies of a man. He has entered within that veil which hung over the glories of the Eternal; and the mysterious inaccessible throne of God is divested of all its terrors, when I think that a friend who bears the form of the species, and knows its infirmities, is there to plead for me.

SERMON VII.

The Folly of Men measuring themselves by themselves.

"For we dare not make ourselves of the number, or compare ourselves with some that commend themselves; but they, measuring themselves by themselves, and comparing themselves among themselves, are not wise."—2 *Corinthians*, x. 12.

St. Paul addressed these words to the members of a Christian congregation; and were we to confine their application to those people of the present day, who in circumstances, bear the nearest resemblance to them, we would, in the present discourse, have chiefly to do with the more serious and declared professors of the Gospel. Nor should we be long at a loss for a very observable peculiarity amongst them, against which to point the admonition of the Apostle. For, in truth there is a great disposition with the members of the religious world, to look away from the unalterable standard of God's will, and to form a standard of authority out of the existing attainments of those whom they conceive to be in the faith. We know nothing that has contributed more than this to reduce the tone of practical Christianity. We know not a more insidious security, than that which steals over the mind of him who when he looks to another of eminent name for godliness, or orthodoxy, and perceives in him a certain degree of conformity to the world, or a certain measure of infirmity of temper, or a certain abandonment of himself to the natural enjoyments of luxury, or of idle gossiping, or of commenting with malignant pleasure on the faults and failings of the absent, thinks, that upon such an example, it is safe for him to allow in himself an equal extent of indulgence; and to go the same lengths of laxity or transgression; and thus, instead of measuring himself by the perfect law of the Almighty, and making conformity to it the object of his strenuous aspirings,—does he measure himself and compare himself with his fellow-mortals,—and pitches his ambition to no greater height than the accidental level which obtains amongst the members of his own religious brotherhood, and finds a quiet repose in the mediocrity of their actual accomplishments, and of their current and conventional observations.

There is much in this consideration to alarm many of those who within the pale of a select and peculiar circle, look upon themselves as firmly seated in an enclosure of safety. They may be recognized by the society around them as one of us; and they may keep the even pace of acquirement along with them; and they may wear all those marks of distinction which separate them from the general and unprofessing public; and, in respect of Church, and of sacrament, and of family observances, and of exclusive preference for each other conversation, and of meetings for prayer and the other exercises of Christian fellowship, they may stand most decidedly o from the world, and most decidedly in with those of their own cast and their own denomination;—and yet, in fact, there may be individuals, even of such a body as this, who instead of looking upwards to the Being with whom they have to do, are looking no further than to the testimony and example of those who are immediately around them; who count it enough that they are highly esteemed among men; who feel no earnestness, and put forth no strength in the pursuit of a lofty sanctification; who are not living as in the sight of God, and are not in the habit of bringing their conduct into measurement with the principles of that great day, when God's righteousness shall be vindicated in the eyes of all his creatures; who, satisfied, in short, with the countenance of the people of their own communion, come under the charge of my text, that measuring themselves by themselves and comparing themselves among themselves, they are not wise.

Now, though this habit of measuring ourselves by ourselves, and comparing ourselves among ourselves, be charged by the Apostle, in the text, against the professors of a strict and peculiar Christianity; it is a habit so universally exemplified in the world, and ministers such a deep and fatal security to the men of all characters who live in it, and establishes in their hearts so firm a principle of resistance against the humbling doctrines of the New Testament, that we trust we shall be excused if we leave out, for a time, the consideration of those who are within the limits of the Church, and dwell on the operation of this habit among those who are without these limits; and going beyond that territory of observation to which the words now read would appear to restrict us, we shall attend to the effects of that principle in human nature which are there adverted to, in as far as it serves to fortify the human mind against an entire reception of the truths and the overtures of the Gospel.

It may be remarked, by way of illustration, that the habit condemned in the text is an abundant cause of that vanity which is founded on a sense of our importance. If, instead of measuring ourselves by our companions and equals in society, we brought ourselves into measurement with our superiors, it might go far to humble and chastise our vanity. The rustic conqueror on some arena of strength or of dexterity, stands proudly elevated among his fellow-rustics who are around him. Place him beside the returned warrior, who can tell of the hazards, and the achievements, and the desperations of the great battle in which he had shared the renown and the danger; and he will stand convicted of the humility of his own performances. The man who is most keen, and, at the same time, most skilful in the busy politics of his corporation, triumphs in the consciousness of that sagacity by which he has baffled and overpowered the devices of his many antagonists. But take him to the high theatre of Parliament, and bring him into fellowship with the man who has there won the mighty game of superiority, and he will feel abashed at the insignificance of his own tamer and homelier pretensions. The richest individual of the district struts throughout his neighbourhood in all the glories of a provincial eminence. Carry him to the metropolis of the empire, and he hides his diminished head under the brilliancy of rank far loftier than his own, and equipage more splendid than that by which he gathers from his surrounding tributaries, the homage of a respectful admiration. The principle of all this vanity was seen by the discerning eye of the Apostle. It is put down for our instruction in the text before us. And if we, instead of looking to our superiority above the level of our immediate acquaintanceship, pointed an eye of habitual observation to our inferiority beneath the level of those in society who are more dignified and more accomplished than ourselves,—such a habit as this might shed a graceful humility over our characters, and save us from the pangs and the delusions of a vanity which was not made for man.

And let it not be said of those, who, in the more exalted walks of life, can look to few or to none above them, that they can derive no benefit from the principle of my text, because they are placed beyond the reach of its application. It is true of him who is on the very pinnacle of human society, that standing sublimely there, he can cast a downward eye on all the ranks and varieties of the world. But, though in the act of looking beneath him to men, he may gather no salutary lesson of humility—the lesson should come as forcibly upon him as upon any of his fellow mortals, in the act of looking above him to God. Instead of comparing himself with the men of this world, let him leave the world and expatiate in thought over the tracts of immensity,—let him survey the mighty apparatus of worlds scattered in such profusion over its distant regions; let him bring the whole field of the triumphs of his ambition into measurement with the magnificence that is above him, and around him,—above all, let him rise through the ascending series of angels, and principalities, and powers, to the throne of the august Monarch on whom all is suspended,—and then will the lofty imagination of his heart be cast down, and all vanity die within him.

Now, if all this be obviously true of that vanity which is founded on a sense of our importance, might it not be as true of that complacency which is founded on a sense of our worth. Should it not lead us to suspect the ground of this complacency, and to fear lest a similar delusion be misleading us into a false estimate of our own righteousness? When we feel a sufficiency in the act of measuring ourselves by ourselves, and comparing ourselves among ourselves, is it not the average virtue of those around us that is the standard of measurement? Do we not at the time, form our estimate of human worth upon the character of man as it actually is, instead of forming it upon the high standard of that pure and exalted law which tells us what the character ought to be? Is it not thus that many are lulled into security, because they are as good or better than their neighbours? This may do for earth, but the question we want to press is, will it do for heaven? It may carry us through life with a fair and equal character in society, and even when we come to die, it may gain us an epitaph upon our tombstones. But after death cometh the judgment; and in that awful day judgment is laid to the line and righteousness to the plummet, every refuge of lies will be swept away, and every hiding-place of security be laid open.

Under the influence of this delusion, thousands and tens of thousands are posting their infatuated way to a ruined and undone eternity. The good man of society lives on the applause and cordiality of his neighbours. He compares himself with his fellow-men, and their testimony to the graces of his amiable, and upright, and honourable character, falls like the music of paradise upon his ears. And it were also the earnest of paradise, if these his flatterers and admirers in time were to be his judges in the day of reckoning. But, alas! they will only be his fellow-prisoners at the bar. The eternal Son of God will preside over the solemnities of that day. He will take the judgment upon himself, and he will conduct it on his own lofty standard of examination, and not on the maxims or the habits of a world lying in wickedness. O ye deluded men! who carry your heads so high, and look so safe and so satisfied amid the smooth and equal measurements of society,—do you ever think how you are to stand the admeasurement of Christ and of his angels? and think you that the fleeting applause of mortals, sinful as yourselves, will carry an authority over the mind of your judge, or prescribe to him that solemn award which is to fix you for eternity?

In the prosecution of the following discourse, let us first attempt to expose the folly of measuring ourselves by ourselves, and comparing ourselves amongst ourselves; and then point out the wisdom opposite to this folly, which is recommended in the gospel.

I. The folly of measuring ourselves by ourselves is a lesson which admits of many illustrations. The habit is so universal. It is so strikingly exemplified, even among the most acknowledged outcasts from all that is worthy, and all that is respectable in general estimation. There is not a congregated mass of human beings, associated in one common pursuit, or brought together by one common accident, among whom there is not established either some tacit or proclaimed morality, to the observance of which, or to the violation of which, there is awarded admiration or disgrace, by the voice of the society that is formed by them. You cannot bring two or more human beings to act in concert without some conventional principle of right and wrong arising out of it, which either must be practically held in regard, or the concert is dissipated. And yet it may be altogether a concert of iniquity. It may be a concert of villany and injustice against the larger interests of human society. It may be a banded conspiracy against the peace and the property of the commonwealth; and there may not be a member belonging to it who does not carry the stamp of outlawry upon his person, and who is not liable, and rightly liable, to the penalties of an outraged government, against which he is bidding, by the whole habit of his life, a daily and systematic defiance. And yet even among such a class of the species as this, an enlightened observer of our nature will not fail to perceive a standard of morality, both recognized and acted upon by all its individuals, and in reference to which morality, there actually stirs in many a bosom amongst them a very warm and enthusiastic feeling of obligation,—and some will you find, who, by their devoted adherence to its maxims, earn among their companions all the distinctions of honour and of virtue,—and others who, by falling away from the principles of the compact, become the victims of a deep and general execration. And thus may the very same thing be perceived with them, that we see in the more general society of mankind—a scale of character, and, corresponding to it, a scale of respectability, along which the members of the most wicked and worthless association upon earth may be ranged according to the gradation of such virtues as are there held in demand, and in reverence; and thus there will be a feeling of complacency, and a distribution of applause, and a conscious superiority of moral and personal attainment, and all this grounded on the habit of measuring themselves by themselves, and comparing themselves amongst themselves.

The first case of such an exhibition which we offer to your notice, comes so aptly in for the purpose of illustration, that homely and familiar as it is, we cannot resist the introduction of it We allude to the case of smugglers. These men, in as far at least as it respects one tie of allegiance, may be considered as completely broken loose from the government of their country. They have formed themselves into a plot against the interests of the public revenue, and it may be generally said of them, that they have no feeling whatever of the criminality of their undertaking. On this point there is utterly wanting the sympathy of any common principle between the administrators of the law and the transgressors of the law,—and yet it would be altogether untrue to nature and to experience to say of the latter, that they are entire strangers to the feeling of every moral obligation. They have a very strong sense of obligation to each other. There are virtues amongst them which serve to signalize certain members, and vices amongst them which doom to infamy certain other members of their own association. In reference to the duties which they owe to government, they may be dead to every impression of them. But in reference to those duties, on the punctual fulfilment of which depends the success, or even the continuance, of their system of operations, they may be most keenly and sensitively alive. They may speak of the informer who has abandoned them, with all the intensity of moral hatred and contempt; and of the man, again, who never once swerved from his fidelity; of the man, who, with all the notable dexterity of his evasions from the vigilance that was sent forth to track and to discover him, was ever known to be open as day amongst the members of his own brotherhood; of the man, who, with the unprincipledness of a most skilful and systematic falsehood, in reference to the agents and pursuers of the law, was the most trusty, and the most incorruptible, in reference to his fellows of the trade; of the man who stands highest amongst them in all the virtues of pledged and sworn companionship;—why, of such a man will these roving mountaineers speak in terms of honest and heartfelt veneration; and nothing more is necessary, in order to throw a kind of chivalric splendour over him, than just to be told, along with his inflexible devotedness to the cause, of his hardy adventures, and his hair-breadth miracles of escape, and his inexhaustible resources, and of the rapidity of his ever-suiting and ever-shifting contrivances, and of his noble and unquelled spirit of daring, and of the art and activity by which he has eluded his opponents, and of the unfaltering courage by which he has resisted them. We doubt not, that even in the history of this ignominious traffic, there do occur such deeds and characters of unrecorded heroism; and still the men who carry it on, measuring themselves by themselves, may never think of the ignominy. They will enjoy the praise they have one of another, and care not for the distant blame that is cast upon them by the public voice. They will carry in their bosoms the swelling consciousness of worth, and be regaled by the home testimony of those who are about them; and all this at the very time when, to the general community, they offer a spectacle of odiousness; all this at the very time, when the power and the justice of an incensed government are moving forth upon them.

But another case, still more picturesque, and, what is far better, still more subservient to the establishment of the lesson of our text, may be taken from another set of adventurers, hardier, and more ferocious, and more unprincipled than the former. We allude to the men of rapine; and who, rather than that their schemes of rapine should be frustrated, have so far overcome all the scruples and all the sensibilities of nature, that they have become men of blood. They live as commoners upon the world; and, at large from those restraints, whether of feeling or of principle, which hold in security together the vast majority of this world's families, they are looked at by general society with a revolting sense of terror and of odiousness. And yet, among these monsters of the cavern, and practised as they are in all the atrocities of the highway, will you find a virtue of their own, and a high-toned morality of their own. Living as they do, in a state of emancipation from the law universal, still there is among them a law isoterical, in doing homage to which, the hearts of these banditti actually glow with the movements of honourable principle; and the path of their conduct is actually made to square with the conformities of right and honourable practice. Extraordinary as you may think it, the very habit of my text is in full operation among these very men, who have wandered so far from all that is deemed righteous in society; and disowning, as they do, our standard of principle altogether, they have a standard among themselves, on which they can adjust a scale of moral estimation, and apply it in every exercise of judgment on the character of each individual who belongs to them. In reference to every deviation that is made by them from the general standard of right, there is an entire obliteration of all their sensibilities,—and this is not the ground on which they ever think either of reproaching themselves, or of casting any imputation of disgrace on their companions. But, in reference to their own particular standard of right, they are all awake to the enormity of every act of transgression against it,—and thus it is, that measuring themselves by themselves, and comparing themselves amongst themselves, there is just with them as varied a distribution of praise and of obloquy as is to be met with on the face of any regular and well-ordered commonwealth. And who, we would ask, is the man among all these prowling outcasts of nature, on whom the law of his country would inflict the most unrelenting vengeance? He who is most signalized by the moralities of his order,—he who has gained by fidelity, and courage, and disinterested honour, the chieftainship of confidence and affection amongst them,—he, the foremost of all the desperadoes, on whose character perhaps the romance of generosity and truth is strangely blended with the stern barbarities of his calling,—and who, the most admired among the members of his own brotherhood, is, at the same time, the surest to bring down upon his person all the rigours and all the severities of the judgment-seat.

Let us now follow with the eye of our observation, a number of these transgressors into another scene. Let us go into the place of their confinement; and, in this receptacle of many criminals, with all their varied hues of guilt and of depravity, we shall perceive the habit of my text in full and striking exemplification. The murderer stands lower in the scale of character than the thief. The first is worse than the second—and you have only to reverse the terms of the comparison, that you may be enabled to see how the second is better than the first. Thus, even in this repository of human worthlessness, we meet with gradations of character; with the worse and the better and the best; with an ascending and a descending scale, which runs in continuity, from the one who stands upon its pinnacle, to the one who is the deepest and most determined in wickedness amongst them. It is utter ignorance of our nature to conceive that this moral gradation is not fully and frequently in the minds of the criminals themselves,—that there is not, even here, the habit of each measuring himself with his fellow-prisoners around him, and of some soothed by the consciousness of a more untainted character, and rejoicing over it with a feeling of secret elevation. They, in truth, know themselves to be the best of their kind,—and this knowledge brings a complacency along with it,—and, even in this mass of profligacy, there swells and kindles the pride of superior attainments. But there is at least one delusion from which one and all of them stand exempted. The very best of them, however much he may be regaled by the inward sense of his advantage over others, knows, that in reference to the law, he is not on a footing of merit, but on a footing of criminality,—knows, that though he will be the most gently dealt with, and that on him the lightest penalty will fall, yet still he stands to his judge and to his country, in the relation of a condemned malefactor—feels, how preposterous it were, if, on the plea of being the most innocent of the whole assemblage, he was to claim, not merely exemption from punishment, but the reward of some high and honourable distinction at the hands of the magistrate. He is fully aware of the gap that lies between him and the administrators of justice,—is sensible, that though he deserves to be beaten with fewer stripes than others, yet still, that, in the eye of the law, he deserves to be beaten; and that he stands at as hopeless a distance, as the most depraved of his fellows, from a sentence of complete justification.

Let us, last of all, go along with these malefactors to the scene of their banishment. Let us view them as the members of a separated community; and we shall widely mistake it, if we think, that in this settlement of New South Wales, there is not the same shading of moral variety, there is not the same gradation of character, there is not the same scale of reputation, there is not the same distribution of respect, there is not the same pride of loftier principle, and debasement of more shameful and abandoned profligacy, there is not the same triumph of conscious superiority on the one hand, and the same crouching sense of unworthiness on the other, which you find in the more decent, and virtuous, and orderly society of Europe.

Within the limits of this colony there exists a tribunal of public opinion, from which praise and popularity, and reproach, are awarded in various proportions among all the inhabitants. And without the limits of this colony there exists another tribunal of public opinion, by the voice of which an unexpected stigma of exclusion and disgrace is cast upon every one of them. Insomuch, that the same individual may by a nearer judgment, be extolled as the best and the most distinguished of all who are around him,—and by a more distant judgment, he may have all the ignominy of an outcast laid upon his person and his character. He may, at one and the same time, be regaled by the applause of one society, and held in rightful execration by another society. In the former, he may have the deference of a positive regard rendered to him for his virtues,—while, from the latter, he is justly exiled by the hateful contamination of his vices. And in him do we behold the instructive picture of a man, who, at the bar of his own neighbourhood, stands the highest in moral estimation,—while, at a higher bar, he has had a mark of foulest ignominy stamped upon him.

We want not to shock the pride or the delicacy of your feelings. But on a question so high as that of your eternity, we want to extricate you from the power of every vain and bewildering delusion. We want to urge upon you the lesson of Scripture, that this world differs from a prison-house, only in its being a more spacious receptacle of sinners,—and that there is not a wider distance, in point of habit and of judgment, between a society of convicts, and the general community of mankind, than there is between the whole community of our species, and the society of that paradise, from which, under the apostacy of our fallen nature, we have been doomed to live in dreary alienation. We refuse not to the men of our world the possession of many high and honourable virtues; but let us not forget, that amongst the marauders of the highway, we hear, too, of inflexible faith, and devoted friendship, and splendid generosity. We deny not, that there exists among our species, as much truth and as much honesty, as serve to keep society together: but a measure of the very same principle is necessary, in order to perpetuate and to accomplish the end of the most unrighteous combinations. We deny not, that there flourishes on the face of our earth a moral diversity of hue and of character, and that there are the better and the best who have signalized themselves above the level of its general population; but so it is in the malefactor's dungeon; and as there, so here, may a positive sentence of condemnation be the lot of the most exalted individual. We deny not, there are many in every neighbourhood, to whose character, and whose worth, the cordial tribute of admiration is awarded; but the very same thing may be witnessed amongst the outcasts of every civilized territory,—and what they are, in reference to the country from which they have been exiled, we may be, in reference to the whole of God's unfallen creation. In the sight of men we may be highly esteemed,—and we may be an abomination in the sight of angels. We may receive homage from our immediate neighbours for all the virtues of our relationship with them,—while our relationship with God may be utterly dissolved, and its appropriate virtues may neither be recognized nor acted on. There may emanate from our persons a certain beauteousness of moral colouring on those who are around us,—but when seen through the universal morality of God's extended and all-pervading government, we may look as hateful as the outcasts of felony,—and living, as we do, in a rebellious province, that has broken loose from the community of God's loyal and obedient worshippers, we may, at one and the same time, be surrounded by the cordialities of an approving fellowship, and be frowned upon by the supreme judicatory of the universe. At one and the same time, we may be regaled by the incense of this world's praise, and be the objects of Heaven's most righteous execration.

But is this the real place, it may be asked, that our world occupies in the moral universe of God? The answer to this question may be obtained either out of the historical informations of Scripture, or out of a survey that may be made of the actual character of man, and a comparison that may be instituted between this character and the divine law. We can conceive nothing more uniform and more decisive than the testimony of the Bible, when it tells us that however fair some may be in the eyes of men, yet that all are guilty before God; that in his eyes none are righteous, no not one: that he, who is of purer eyes than to behold iniquity, finds out iniquity in every one of us; that there is none who understandeth, and none who seeketh after God; that however much we may compare ourselves amongst ourselves, and found a complacency upon the exercise, yet that we have altogether gone out of the way; that however distinctly we may retain, even in the midst of this great moral rebellion, our relative superiorities over each other, there is a wide and a general departure of the species from God; that one and all of us have deeply revolted against him: that the taint of a most inveterate spiritual disease has overspread all the individuals of all the families upon earth; insomuch, that the heart of man is deceitful above all things and desperately wicked, and the imaginations of his thoughts are only evil, and that continually.

The fall of Adam is represented, in the Bible, as that terribly decisive event, on which took place this deep and fatal unhingement of the moral constitution of our species. From this period the malady has descended, and the whole history of our world gives evidence to its state of banishment from the joys and the communications of paradise. Before the entrance of sin did God and man walk in sweet companionship together, and saw each other face to face in the security of a garden. A little further down in the history, we meet with another of God's recorded manifestations. We read of his descent in thunder upon mount Sinai. O what a change from the free and fearless intercourse of Eden! God, though surrounded by a people whom he had himself selected, here sits, if we may use the expression, on a throne of awful and distant ceremony; and the lifting of his mighty voice scattered dismay among the thousands of Israel. When he looked now on the children of men, he looked on them with an altered countenance. The days were, when they talked together in the lovely scenes of paradise as one talketh with a friend. But, on the top of Sinai, he wraps himself in storms, and orders to set bounds about the mount, lest the people should draw near, and God should break forth upon them.

But we have an evidence to our state of banishment from God, which is nearer home. We have it in our own hearts. The habitual attitude of the inner man is not an attitude of subordination to God. The feeling of allegiance to him is practically and almost constantly away from us. All that can give value to our obedience, in the sight of an enlightened Spirit who looks to motive, and sentiment, and principle, has constitutionally no place, and no residence in our characters. We are engrossed by other anxieties than anxiety to do the will, and to promote the honour, of him who formed us. We are animated by other affections altogether, than love to him, whose right hand preserves us continually. That Being by whom we are so fearfully and wonderfully made; whose upholding presence it is that keeps us in life, and in movement, and in the exercise of all our faculties; who has placed us on the theatre of all our enjoyments, and claims over his own creatures the ascendency of a most rightful authority;—that surely is the Being with whom we have to do. And yet, when we take account of our thoughts and of our doings, how little of God is there? In the random play and exhibition of such feelings as instinctively belong to us, we may gather around us the admiration of our fellows,— and so it is in a colony of exiled criminals. But as much wanting there, as is the homage of loyalty to the government of their native land; so much wanting here, is the homage of any deference or inward regard, to the government of Heaven. And yet this is the very principle of all that obedience which Heaven can look upon. If it be true that obedience is rewardable by God, but that which has respect unto God, then this must be the essential point on which hinges the difference between a rebel, and a loyal subject to the supreme Lawgiver. The requirement we live under is to do all things to his glory; and this is the measure of principle and of performance that will be set over you,—and tell us, ye men of civil and relative propriety, who, by exemplifying in the eye of your fellows such virtue, as may be exemplified by the outcasts of banishment, have shed around your persons the tiny lustre of this world's moralities; tell us how you will be able to stand such a severe and righteous application? The measure by which we compare ourselves with ourselves, is not the measure of the sanctuary. When the judge comes to take account of us, he will come fraught with the maxims of a celestial jurisprudence, and his question will be, not, what have you done at the shrine of popularity,—not, what have you done to sustain a character amongst men,—not what have you done at the mere impulse of sensibilities however amiable, or of native principles however upright, and elevated, and manly,—but what have you done unto me? how much of God, and of God's will, was there in the principle of your doings? This is the heavenly measure, and it will set aside all your earthly measures and comparisons. It will sweep away all these refuges of lies. The man whose accomplishments of character, however lively, were all social, and worldly, and relative, will hang his head in confusion when the utter wickedness of his pretensions is thus laid open,—when the God who gave him every breath, endowed him with every faculty, enquires after his share of reverence and acknowledgment,—when he tells him from the judgment-seat, I was the Being with whom you had to do, and yet in the vast multiplicity of your doings, I was seldom or never thought of,—when he convicts him of habitual forgetfulness of God, and setting aside all the paltry measurements which men apply in their estimates of one another, he brings the high standard of Heaven's law, and Heaven's allegiance to bear upon them.

It must be quite palpable to any man who has seen much of life, and still more if he has travelled extensively, and witnessed the varied complexions of morality that obtain in distant societies,—it must be quite obvious to such a man, how readily the moral feeling, in each of them, accommodates itself to the general state of practice and observation,—that the practices of one country, for which there is a most complacent toleration, would be shuddered at as so many atrocities in another country,—that in every given neighbourhood, the sense of right and of wrong, becomes just as fine or as obtuse as to square with its average purity, and its average humanity, and its average uprightness,—that what would revolt the public feeling of a retired parish in Scotland as gross licentiousness or outrageous cruelty, might attach no disgrace whatever to a residenter in some colonial settlement, —that, nevertheless, in the more corrupt and degraded of the two communites, there is a scale of differences, a range of character, along which are placed the comparative stations of the disreputable, and the passible, and the respectable, and the superexcellent; and yet it is a very possible thing, that if a man in the last of these stations were to import all his habits and all his profligacies into his native land, superexcellent as he may be abroad, at home he would be banished from the general association of virtuous and well-ordered families. Now, all we ask of you is, to transfer this consideration to the matter before us,—to think how possible a thing it is, that the moral principle of the world at large, may have sunk to a peaceable and approving acquiescence, in the existing practice of the world at large,—that the security which is inspired by the habit of measuring ourselves by ourselves, and comparing ourselves amongst ourselves, may therefore be a delusion altogether,—that the very best member of society upon earth, may be utterly unfit for the society of heaven,—that the morality which is current here, may depend upon totally another set of principles from the morality which is held to be indispensable there;—and when we gather these principles from the book of God's revelation,—when we are told that the law of the two great commandments is, to love the Lord our God with all our strength, and heart, and mind, and to bear the same love to our neighbour that we do to ourselves,—the argument advances from a conjecture to a certainty, that every inhabitant of earth when brought to the bar of Heaven's judicature, is altogether wanting; and that unless some great moral renovation take effect upon him, he can never be admitted within the limits of the empire of righteousness.

SERMON VIII.

Christ the Wisdom of God.

"Christ the Wisdom of God."—1 *Corinthians* i. 24.

We cannot but remark of the Bible, how uniformly and how decisively it announces itself in all its descriptions of the state and character of man,—how, without offering to palliate the matter, it brings before us the totality of our alienation, how it represents us to be altogether broken off from our allegiance to God,—and how it fears not, in the face of those undoubted diversities of character which exist in the world, to assert of the whole world, that it is guilty before him. And if we would only seize on what may be called the elementary principle of guilt,—if we would only take it along with us, that guilt, in reference to God, must consist in the defection of our regard and our reverence from him,—if we would only open our eyes to the undoubted fact, that there may be such an utter defection, and yet there may be many an amiable, and many a graceful exhibition, both of feeling and of conduct, in reference to those who are around us,—then should we recognize, in the statements of the Bible, a vigorous, discerning, and intelligent view of human nature,—an unfaltering announcement of what that nature essentially is, under all the plausibilities which serve to disguise it,—and such an insight, in fact, into the secrecies of our inner man, as if carried home by that Spirit, whose office it is to apply the word with power into the conscience, is enough, of itself, to stamp upon this book, the evidence of the Divinity which inspired it.

But it is easier far to put an end to the resistance of the understanding, than to alarm the fears, or to make the heart soft and tender, under a sense of its guiltiness, or to prompt the inquiry,—if all those securities, within the entrenchment of which I want to take my quiet and complacent repose, are thus driven in, where in the whole compass of nature or revelation can any effectual security be found? It may be easy to find our way amongst all the complexional varieties of our nature, to its radical and pervading ungodliness; and thus to carry the acquiescence of the judgment in some extended demonstration about the utter sinfulness of the species. But it is not so easy to point this demonstration towards the bosom of any individual,—to gather it up, as it were, from its state of diffusion over the whole field of humanity, and send it with all its energies concentered to a single heart, in the form of a sharp, and humbling, and terrifying conviction,—to make it enter the conscience of some one listener, like an arrow sticking fast,—or, when the appalling picture of a whole world lying in wickedness, is thus presented to the understanding of a general audience, to make each of that audience mourn apart over his own wickedness; just as when, on the day of judgment, though all that is visible be shaking, and dissolving, and giving way, each despairing eye-witness shall mourn apart over the recollection of his own guilt, over the prospect of his own rueful and undone eternity. And yet, if this be not done, nothing is done. The lesson of the text has come to you in word only and not in power. To look to the truth in its generality, is one thing; to look to your own separate concern in it, is another. What we want is that each of you shall turn his eye homewards; that each shall purify his own heart from the influence of a delusion which we pronounce to be ruinous; that each shall beware of leaning a satisfaction, or a triumph, on the comparison of himself with corrupt and exiled men, whom sin has degraded into outcasts from the presence of

God, and the joys of paradise; that each of you shall look to the measure of God's law, so that when the commandment comes upon you, in the sense of its exceeding broadness, a sense of your sin, and of your death in sin, may come along with it. "Without the commandment I was alive," says the Apostle; "but when the commandment came, sin revived, and I died." Be assured, that if the utterance of such truth in your hearing, impress no personal earnestness, and lead to no personal measures, and be followed up by no personal movements, then to you it is as a sounding brass and as a tinkling cymbal. The preacher has been beating the air. That great Agent, whose revealed office it is to convince of sin, has refused to go along with him. Another influence altogether, than that which is salutary and saving, has been sent into your bosom; and the glow of the truth universal has deafened or intercepted the application of the truth personal, and of the truth particular.

This leads us to the second thing proposed in our last discourse, under which we shall attempt to explain the wisdom opposite to that folly of measuring ourselves by ourselves, and comparing ourselves among ourselves, which we have already attempted to expose.

The first step is to give up all satisfaction with yourselves, on the bare ground, that your conduct comes up to the measure of human character, and human reputation around you. This consideration may be of importance to your place in society; but, as to your place in the favour of God, it is utterly insignificant. The moral differences which obtain in a community of exiles, are all quite consistent with the entire obliteration amongst them, of the allegiance that is due to the government of their native land. And the moral differences which obtain in the world, may, in every way, be as consistent with the fact, that one and all of us, in our state of nature, are alienated from God by wicked works. And, in like manner, as convicts may be all alive to a sense of their reciprocal obligations, while dead, in feeling and in principle, to the supreme obligation under which they lie to the sovereign,—so may we, in reference to our fellow-men, have a sense of rectitude, and honour, and compassion, while, in reference to God, we may labour under the entire extinction of every moral sensibility,—so that the virtues which signalize us, may, in the language of some of our old divines, be neither more nor less than splendid sins. With the possession of these virtues, we may not merely be incurring every day the guilt of trespassing and sinning against our Maker in heaven; but devoid as we are of all apprehension of the enormity of this, we may strikingly realize the assertion of the Bible, that we are *dead* in trespasses and sins. And we pass our time in all the tranquillity of death. We say peace, when there is no peace. Though in a state of disruption from God, we live as securely and as inconsiderately as if there were no question and no controversy betwixt us. About this whole matter, there is within us a spirit of heaviness and of deep slumber. We lie fast asleep on the brink of an unprovided eternity,—and, if possible to awaken you, let us urge you to compare, not your own conduct with that of acquaintances and neighbours, but to compare your own finding of the ungodliness that is in your heart with the doctrine of God's word about it,—to bring down the loftiness of your spirit to its humbling declarations—to receive it as a faithful saying, that man is lost by nature, and that unless there be some mighty transition, in his history, from a state of nature to a state of salvation, the wrath of God abideth on him.

The next inquiry comes to be, What is this transition? Tell me the step I should take, and I will take it. It is not enough, then, that you exalt upon your own person the degree of those virtues, by which you have obtained a credit and a distinction among men. It is not enough, that you throw a brighter and a lovelier hue over your social accomplishments. It is not enough, that you multiply the offerings of your charity, or observe a more rigid compliance, than heretofore, with all the requisitions of justice. All this you may do, and yet the great point, on which your controversy with God essentially hinges, may not be so much as entered upon. All this you may do, and yet obtain no nearer approximation to Him who sitteth on the throne, than the outlaws of an offended government for their fidelities to each other. To the eye of man you may be fairer than before, and in civil estimation be greatly more righteous than before,—and yet, with the unquelled spirit of impiety within you, and as habitual an indifference as ever to all the subordinating claims of the divine will over your heart and your conduct, you may stand at as wide a distance from God as before. And besides, how are we to dispose of the whole guilt of your past iniquities? Whether, is it the malefactor or the Lawgiver who is to arbitrate this question? God may remit our sins, but it is for him to proclaim this. God may pass them over; but it is for him to issue the deed of amnesty. God may have found out a way whereby, in consistency with his own character, and with the stability of his august government, he may take sinners into reconciliation; but it is for him both to devise and to publish this way; —and we must just do what convicts do, when they obtain a mitigation or a cancelment of the legal sentence under which they lie,—we must passively accept of it, on the terms of the deed,—we must look to the warrant as issued by the sovereign, and take the boon or fulfil the conditions, just as it is there presented to us. The question is between us and God; and in the adjustment of this question, we must look singly to the expression of his will, and feel that it is with him, and with his authority, that we have exclusively to do. In one word, we must wait his own revelation, and learn from his own mouth how it is that he would have us to come nigh unto him.

Let us go then to the record. "No man cometh unto the Father but through the Son." "There is no other name given under heaven, but the name of Jesus, whereby we can be saved." "Without the shedding of blood there is no remission of sin;" and "God hath set forth Christ to be a propitiation through faith in his blood." "He was once offered to bear the sins of many,"—and "became sin for us, though he knew no sin, that we might be made the righteousness of God in him." "God is in Christ reconciling the world unto himself, and not imputing unto them their trespasses." "Justified by faith, we have peace with God through Jesus Christ our Lord;"—" and we become the children of God, through the faith that is in Christ Jesus." We are "reconciled to God by the death of his Son,"—" and by his obedience are many made righteous,"—and "where sin abounded, grace did much more abound." These verses sound foolishness to many; but the cross of Christ is foolishness to those that perish. They appear to them invested with all the mysteriousness of a dark and hidden saying; but if this Gospel be hid, it is hid to them which are lost. They have eyes that they cannot see the wondrous things contained in this book of God's communication; but they have minds which believe not, because they are blinded by the god of this world, lest the light of the glorious Gospel of Christ, who is the image of God, should shine into them.

And here we cannot but insist on the utter hopelessness of their circumstances, who hear these overtures of reconciliation, but will not listen to them. Theirs is just the case of rebels turning their back on a deed of grace and of amnesty. We are quite confident in stating it to the stubborn experience of human nature, that all who reject Christ, as he is offered in the Gospel, persist in that radical ungodliness of character on which the condemnation of our world mainly and essentially rests. And as they thus refuse to build their security on the foundation of his merits,—what, we would ask, is the other foundation on which they build it? If ever they think seriously of the matter, or feel any concern about a foundation on which they might rest their confidence before God, they conceive it to lie in such feelings, and such humanities, and such honesties, as make them even with the world, or as elevate them to a certain degree above the level of the world's population. These are the materials of the foundation on which they build. It is upon the possession of virtues which in truth have not God for their object, that they propose to support in the presence of God the attitude of fearlessness. It is upon the testimony of fellow rebels that they brave the judgment of the Being who has pronounced of them all, that they have deeply revolted against him. And all this in the face of God's high prerogative, to make and to publish his own overtures. All this in contempt of that Mediator whom he has appointed. All this in resistance to the authentic deed of grace and of forgiveness, which has been sent to our world, and from which we gather the full assurance of God's willingness to be reconciled; but, at the same time, are expressly bound down to that particular way in which he has chosen to dispense reconciliation. Who does not see, that, in these circumstances, the guilt of sin is fearfully aggravated on the part of sinners, by their rejection of the Gospel? Who does not see, that thus to refuse the grant of everlasting life in the terms of the grant, is just to set an irretrievable seal upon their own condemnation? Who does not see, that, in the act of declining to take the shelter which is held out to them, they vainly imagine, that God will let down his approbation to such performances as are utterly devoid of any spirit of devout or dutiful allegiance to the Lawgiver? This is, in fact, a deliberate p sting of themselves, and that more firmly and more obstinately than ever, on the ground of their rebellion—and let us no longer wonder, then, at the terms of that alternative of which we read so often in the Bible. We there read, that if we believe, we shall be saved; but we also read, that if we believe not, we shall be damned. We are there told of the great salvation; but how shall we escape if we neglect it? We are there invited to lay hold of the Gospel, as the savour of life unto life: but, if we refuse the invitation, it shall be to us the savour of death unto death. The gospel is there freely proclaimed to us, for our acceptance; but if we will not obey the Gospel, we shall be punished with everlasting destruction from the presence of the Saviour's power. We are asked to kiss the Son while he is in the way; but if we do not, the alternative is that he will be angry, and that his wrath will burn against us. He is revealed to us a sure rock, on which if we lean we shall not be confounded; but if we shift our dependence away from it, it will fall upon us and grind us to powder.

And this alternative, so far from a matter to be wondered at, appears resolvable into a principle that might be easily comprehended. God is the party sinned against: and if he have the will to be reconciled, it is surely for him to prescribe the way of it: and this he has actually done in the revelation of the New Testament: and whether he give a reason for the way or not, certain it is, that in order to give it accomplishment, he sent his eternal Son into our world; and this descent was accompanied with such circumstances of humiliation, and conflict, and deep suffering, that heaven looked on with astonishment, and earth was bidden to rejoice, because of her great salvation. It is enough for us to know that God lavished on this plan the riches of a wisdom that is unsearchable; that, in the hearing of sinful men, he has proclaimed its importance and its efficacy; that every Gospel messenger felt himself charged with tidings pregnant of joy, and of mighty deliverance to the world. And we ask you just to conceive, in these circumstances, what effect it should have on the mind of the insulted Sovereign, if the world, instead of responding, with grateful and delighted welcome, to the message, shall either nauseate its terms, or, feeling in them no significancy, shall turn with indifference away from it? Are we at all to wonder if the King, very wroth with the men of such a world shall at length send his armies to destroy it? Do you think it likely that the same God, who after we had broken his commandment, was willing to pass by our transgressions, will be equally willing to pass them by after we have thus despised the proclamation of his mercy; after his forbearance and his long-suffering have been resisted; and that scheme of pardon, with the weight and the magnitude of which angels appear to labour in amazement, is received by the very men for whom it was devised, as a thing of no estimation? Surely, if there had been justice in the simple and immediate punishment of sin—this justice will be discharged in still brighter manifestation on him, who, in the face of such an embassy, holds out in his determination to brave it. And, if it be a righteous thing in God to avenge every violation of his law, how clearly and how irresistibly righteous will it appear, when, on the great day of his wrath, he taketh vengeance on those who have added to the violation of his law, the rejection of the Gospel!

But what is more than this—God hath condescended to make known to us a reason, for that peculiar way of reconciliation, which he hath set before us. It is, that he might be just while the justifier of those who believe in Jesus. In the dispensation of his mercy, he had to provide for the dignity of his throne. He had to guard the stability of his truth and of his righteousness. He had to pour the lustre of a high and awful vindication, over the attributes of a nature that is holy and unchangeable. He had to make peace on earth and good will to men meet, and be at one with glory to God in the highest; and for this purpose did the eternal Son pour out his soul an offering for sin, and by his obedience unto death, bring in an everlasting righteousness. It is through the channel of this great expiation that the guilt of every believer is washed away; and it is through the imputed merits of him with whom the Father was well pleased, that every believer is admitted to the rewards of a perfect obedience. Conceive any man of this world to reject the offers of reward and forgiveness in this way, and to look for them in another. Conceive him to challenge the direct approbation of his Judge, on the measure of his own worth, and his own performances, and to put away from him that righteousness of Christ, in the measure of which there is no short coming. Is he not, by this attitude, holding out against God, and that too, on a question in which the justice of God stands committed against him? Is not the poor sinner of a day entering into a fearful controversy, with all the plans, and all the perfections of the Eternal? Might not you conceive every attribute of the Divinity, gathering into a frown of deeper indignation against the daringness of him, who thus demands the favour of the Almighty on some plea of his own, and resolutely declines it on that only plea, under which the acceptance of the sinner can be in harmony with the glories of God's holy and inviolable character? Surely, if we have fallen short of the obedience of his law, and so short as to have renounced altogether that godliness which imparts to obedience its spiritual and substantial quality,—then do we aggravate the enormity of our sin, by building our hope before God on a foundation of sin? To sin is to defy God: but the very presumption that he will smile complacency upon it, involves in it another, and a still more deliberate attack upon his government; and all its sanctions, and all its severities, are let loose upon us in greater force and abundance than before, if we either rest upon our own virtue, or mix up this polluted ingredient with the righteousness of Christ, and refuse our single, entire, and undivided reliance on him who alone has magnified the law and made it honourable.

But such, if we may be allowed the expression, is the constitution of the Gospel of Jesus Christ, that, in proportion to the terror which it holds out to those who neglect it, is the security that it provides to all who flee for refuge to the hope which is set before them. Paul understood this well, when, though he profited over many of his equals in his own nation,—when, though had he measured himself by them, he might have gathered from the comparison a feeling of proud superiority,—when, though in all that was counted righteous among his fellows, he signalized himself in general estimation,—yet he willingly renounced a dependence upon all, that he might win Christ, and be found in him, not having his own righteousness, which was of the law, but that righteousness which is through the faith of Christ, even the righteousness which is of God by faith. He felt the force of the alternative, between the former and the latter righteousness. He knew that the one admitted of no measurement with the other; and that whatever appearance of worth it had in the eyes of men, when brought to their relative and earthly standard, it was reduced to nothing, and worse than nothing, when brought to the standard of Heaven's holy and unalterable law. Jesus Christ has in our nature fulfilled this law; and it is in the righteousness which he thus wrought, that we are invited to stand before God. You do not then take in a full impression of Gospel security, if you only believe that God is merciful, and has forgiven you. You are called farther to believe, that God is righteous, and has justified you. You have a warrant to put on the righteousness of Christ as a robe and a diadem, and to go to the throne of grace with the petition of Look upon me in the face of him who hath fulfilled all righteousness. You are furnished with such a measure of righteousness as God can accept, without letting down a single attribute which belongs to him. The truth, and the justice, and the holiness, which stand in such threatening array against the sinner who is out of Christ, now form into a shield and a hiding-place around him. And while he who trusts in the general mercy of God does so at the expense of his whole character, he who trusts in the mercy of God, which hath appeared unto all men through the Saviour, offers in that act of confidence an homage to every perfection of the Divinity, and has every perfection of the Divinity upon his side. And thus it is, that under the economy of redemption, we now read, not merely of God being merciful, but of God being just and faithful in forgiving our sins, and in cleansing us from all our unrighteousness.

Thus much for what may be called the *judicial righteousness* with which every believer is invested by having the merits of Christ imputed to him through faith. But this faith is something more than a name. It takes up a positive residence in the mind as a principle. It has locality and operation there, and has either no existence at all, or by its purifying and reforming influence on the holder of it, does it invest him also with a personal righteousness.

Now, to apply the conception of our text to this personal righteousness, the first thing we would say of it is, that it admits of no measurement whatever with the social worth, or the moral virtue, or any other of the personal accomplishments of character which may belong to those who have not the faith of the Gospel. Faith accepts of the offered reconciliation, and moves away from the alienated heart those suspicions, and aversions, and fears, which kept man asunder from his God. We would not say, then, of the personal righteousness of a believer, that it consisted in a higher degree of that virtue which may exist in a lower degree with him who is not a believer. It consists in the dawn, and the progress, and the perfecting of a virtue, which, before he was a believer, had no existence whatever. It consists in the possession of a character of which, previous to his acceptance of Christ, he had not the smallest feature of reality; though to the external eye, there may have been some features of resemblance. The principle of Christian sanctification, which, if we were to express it by another name, we would call devotedness to God, is no more to be found in the unbelieving world, than the principle of an allegiance to their rightful sovereign, is to be found among the outcasts of banishment. It is not by any stretching out of the measure of your former virtues, then, that you can attain this principle. There needs to be originated within you a new virtue altogether. It is not by the fostering of that which is old,—it is by the creation of something new, that a man comes to have the personal righteousness of a disciple of the New Testament. It is by giving existence to that which formerly had no existence. And let us no longer wonder, then, at the magnitude of the terms which are employed in the Bible, to denote the change, the personal change, which in point of character, and affection, and principle, takes place on all who become meet for the inheritance of the saints. It is there called life from the dead, and a new birth, and a total renovation,—all old things are said to be done away, and all things to become new. With many it is a wonder how a change of such totality and of such magnitude, should be accounted as indispensable to the good and creditable man of society, as the sunken profligate. But if the one and the other are both dead to a sense of their Lawgiver in heaven,—then both need to be made alive unto him. With both there must be the power and the reality of a spiritual resurrection. And after this great transition has been made, it will be found that the virtues of the new state, and those of the old state, cannot be brought to any common standard of measurement at all. The one distances the other by a wide and impassable interval. There is all the difference in point of principle between a man of the world and a new creature in Christ, that there is between him who has the Spirit of God, and him who has it not,—and all the difference in point of performance, that there is between him who is without Christ, and can therefore do nothing, and him who can do all things through Christ strengthening him. There is a new principle now, which formerly had no operation, even that of godliness,—and a new influence now, even that of the Holy Ghost, given to the prayers of the believer;—and under these provisions will he attain a splendour and an energy of character, with which, the better and the best of this world can no more be brought into comparison, than earth will compare with heaven, or the passions and the frivolities of time, with the pure ambition and the lofty principles of eternity.

And let it not be said, that the transformation of which we are now speaking, instead of being thus entire and universal, consists only with a good man of the world in the addition of one virtue, to his previous stock of many virtues. We admit that he had justice before, and humanity before, and courteousness before, and that the godliness which he had not before, is only one virtue. But the station which it asserts, among the other virtues, is a station of supreme authority. It no sooner takes its place among them, than it animates them all, and subordinates them all. It sends forth among them a new and pervading quality, which makes them essentially different from what they were before. I may take daily exercise from a regard to my health, and by so doing I may deserve the character of a man of prudence; or I may take daily exercise apart from this consideration altogether, and because it is the accidental wish of my parents that I should do so; and thus may I deserve the character of a man of filial piety. The external habit is the same; but under the one principle, the moral character of this habit is totally and essentially different from what it is under the other principle. Yet the difference here, is, most assuredly, not greater than is the difference between the justice of a good man of society, and the justice of a Christian disciple. In the former case, it is done unto others, or done unto himself. In the latter case, it is done unto God. The frame-work of his outer doings is animated by another spirit altogether. There is the breath of another life in it. The inscription of Holiness to God stands engraven on the action of the believer; and if this character of holiness be utterly effaced from the corresponding action of the good man of society, then, surely, in character, in worth, in spiritual and intelligent estimation, there is the utmost possible diversity between the two actions. So that, should the most upright and amiable man upon earth embrace the Gospel faith, and become the subject of the Gospel regeneration,—it is true of him, too, that all old things are done away, and that all things have become new.

Thus it is, that while none of the Christian virtues can be made to come into measurement with any of what may be called the constitutional virtues, in respect of their principle, because the principle of the one set differs from that of the other set, in kind as well as in degree, yet there are certain corresponding virtues in each of the classes, which might be brought together into measurement, in respect of visible and external performance. And it is a high point of obligation with every disciple of the faith, so to sustain his part in this competition, as to shew forth the honour of Christianity; to prove by his own personal history in the world, how much the morality of grace outstrips the morality of nature; to evince the superior lustre and steadiness of the one, when compared with the frail, and fluctuating, and desultory character of the other; and to make it clear to the eye of experience, that it is only under the peculiar government of the doctrine of Christ, that all which is amiable in human worth, becomes most lovely, and all which is justly held in human admiration, becomes most great, and lofty, and venerable. The Bible tells us to provide things honest in the sight of men, as well as of God. It tells us, that upon the person of every Christian, the features of excellence should stand so legibly engraven, that, as a living epistle, he might be seen and read of all men. It is true, there is much in the character of a genuine believer which the world cannot see, and cannot sympathize with. There is the rapture of faith, when in lively exercise. There is the ecstacy of devotion. There is a calm and settled serenity amid all the vicissitudes of life. There is the habit of having no confidence in the flesh, and of rejoicing in the Lord Jesus. There is a holding fast of our hope in the promises of the Gospel. There is a cherishing of the Spirit of adoption. There is the work of a believing fellowship with the Father and with the Son. There is a movement of affection towards the things which are above. There is a building up of ourselves on our most holy faith. There is a praying in the Holy Ghost. There is a watching for his influence with all perseverance. In a word, there is all which the Christian knows to be real, and which the world hates, and denounces as visionary, in the secret, but sublime and substantial processes of experimental religion.

But, on the other hand, there is also much in the doings of an altogether Christian of that palpable virtue which forces itself upon general observation; and he is most grievously untrue to his master's cause, if he do not, on this ground, so outrun the world, as to force from the men of it, an approving testimony. The eye of the world cannot enter within the spiritual recesses of his heart; but let him ever remember that it is fastened, and that too with keen and scrutinizing jealousy, on the path of his visible history. It will offer no homage to the mere sanctity of his complexion; nor, unless there be shed over it the expression of what is mild in domestic, or honourable in public virtue, will it ever look upon him in any other light, than as an object of the most unmingled disgust. And therefore it is, that he must enter on the field of ostensible accomplishment, and there bear away the palm of superiority, and be the most eminent of his fellows in all those recognized virtues, that can bless or embellish the condition of society; the most untainted in honour, and the most disinterested in justice, and the most alert in beneficence, and the most unwearied in all these graces, under every discouragement and every provocation.

We have now only time to say, that we shall not regret the length of this discourse, or even the recurrence of some of its arguments, if any hearer amongst you, not in the faith, be led by it, to withdraw his confidence from the mere accomplishments of nature,—and if any believer amongst you be led by it not to despise these accomplishments, but to put them on, and to animate them all with the spirit of religiousness,—if any hearer amongst you, beginning to perceive his own nothingness in the sight of God, be prompted to inquire, Wherewithal shall I appear before him? and not to rest from the inquiry, till he flee from his hiding-place, to that everlasting righteousness which the Saviour hath brought in: and if any believer amongst you, rightly dividing the word of truth, shall act on the principle, that though nothing but the doctrine of Christ crucified, can avail him for acceptance with God, yet he is bound to adorn this doctrine in all things. And knowing that one may acquiesce in the whole of such a demonstration, without carrying it personally home, we leave off with the single remark, that every conviction not prosecuted, every movement of conscience not followed up, every ray of light or of truth not turned to individual application, will aggravate the reckoning of the great day,— and that in proportion to the degree of urgency which has been brought to bear upon you, and been resisted, will be the weight and the justness of your final condemnation.

SERMON IX.

The Principle of Love to God.

"Keep yourselves in the love of God."—*Jude* 21.

It is not easy to give the definition of a term, which is currently and immediately understood without one. But, should not this ready understanding of the term supersede the definition of it, what can we tell of love in the way of explanation, but by a substitution of terms, not more simple and more intelligible than itself? Can this affection of the soul be made clearer to you by words, than it is already clear to you by your own consciousness? Are we to attempt the elucidation of a term, which, without any feeling of darkness or of mystery, you make familiar use of every day? You say with the utmost promptitude, and you have just as ready an apprehension of the meaning of what you say, that I love this man, and bear a still higher regard to another, but have my chief and my best liking directed to a third. We will not attempt to go in search of a more luminous or expressive term, for this simple affection, than the one that is commonly employed. But it is a different thing to throw light upon the workings of this affection,—to point your attention to the objects on which it rests, and finds a complacent gratification,— and to assign the circumstances, which are either favourable or unfavourable to its excitement. All this may call forth an exercise of discrimination. But instead of dwelling any more on the significancy of the term love, which is the term of my text, let us forthwith take it unto use, and be confident that, in itself, it carries no ambiguity along with it.

The term love, indeed, admits of a real and intelligible application to inanimate objects. There is a beauty in sights, and a beauty in sounds, and I may bear a positive love to the mute and unconscious individuals in which this beauty hath taken up its residence. I may love a flower, or a murmuring stream, or a sunny bank, or a humble cottage peeping forth from its concealment,—or in fine, a whole landscape may teem with such varied graces, that I may say of it, this is the scene I most love to behold, this is the prospect over which my eye and my imagination most fondly expatiate.

The term love admits of an equally real,

and equally intelligible application to our fellow-men. They, too, are the frequent and familiar objects of this affection, and they often are so, because they possess certain accomplishments of person and of character, by which it is excited. I love the man whose every glance speaks an effusive cordiality towards those who are around him. I love the man whose heart and whose hand are ever open to the representations of distress. I love the man who possesses such a softness of nature, that the imploring look of a brother in want, or of a brother in pain, disarms him of all his selfishness, and draws him out to some large and willing surrender of generosity. I love the man who carries on his aspect, not merely the expression of worth, but of worth maintained in the exercise of all its graces, under every variety of temptation and discouragement; who, in the midst of calumny, can act the warm and enlightened philanthropist; who, when beset with many provocations, can weather them all in calm and settled endurance; who can be kind even to the unthankful and the evil; and who, if he possess the awful virtues of truth and of justice, only heightens our attachment the more, that he possesses goodness, and tenderness, and benignity along with them.

Now, we would have you to advert to one capital distinction between the former and the latter class of objects. The inanimate reflect no love upon us back again. They do not single out any one of their admirers, and, by an act of preference, either minister to his selfish appetite for esteem, or minister to his selfish appetite for enjoyment, by affording to him a larger share than to others, of their presence, and of all the delights which their presence inspires. They remain motionless in their places, without will and without sensibility; and the homage they receive, is from the disinterested affection which men bear to their loveliness. They are loved, and that purely, because they are lovely. There is no mixture of selfishness in the affection that is offered to them. They do not put on a sweeter smile to one man than to another; but all the features of that beauty in which they are arrayed, stand inflexibly the same to every beholder; and he, without any conscious mingling whatever of self-love, in the emotion with which he gazes at the charms of some external scenery, is actuated by a love towards it, which rests and which terminates on the objects that he is employed in contemplating.

But this is not always the case when our fellow men are objects of this affection. I should love cordiality, and benevolence, and compassion for their own sakes; but let your own experience tell how far more sweetly and more intensely the love is felt, when this cordiality is turned, in one stream of kindliness, towards myself; when the eye of friendship has singled out me, and looks at me with a peculiar graciousness; when the man of tenderness has pointed his way to the abode of my suffering family, and there shed in secrecy over them his liberalities, and his tears; when he has forgiven me the debt that I was unable to discharge; and when, oppressed as I am, by the consciousness of having injured or reviled him, he has nobly forgotten or overlooked the whole provocation, and persists in a regard that knows no abatement, in a well-doing that is never weary

There is an element, then, in the love I bear to a fellow man, which does not exist in the love I bear to an inanimate object; and which may serve, perhaps, to darken the character of the affection I feel towards the former. We most readily concede it, that the love of another, on account of the virtues which adorn him, changes its moral character altogether, if it be a love to him, solely on account of the benefit which I derive from the exercise of these virtues. I should love compassion on its own account, as well as on the account that it is I who have been the object of it. I should love justice on its own account, as well as on the account that my grievances have been redressed by the dispensation of it. On looking at goodness, I should feel an affection resting on this object, and finding there its full and its terminating gratification; and that, though I had never stood in the way of any one of its beneficent operations.

How is it, then, that the special direction of a moral virtue in another, towards the object of my personal benefit, operates in enhancing both the sensation which it imparts to my heart, and the estimate which I form of it? What is the peculiar quality communicated to my admiration of another's friendship, and another's goodness, by the circumstance of myself being the individual towards whom that friendship is cherished, and in favour of whom, that goodness puts itself forth into active exertion? At the sight of a benevolent man, there arises in my bosom an instantaneous homage of regard and of reverence;—but should that homage take a pointed direction towards myself,—should it realize its fruits on the comfort, and the security of my own person,—should it be employed in gladdening my home, and spreading enjoyment over my family, oppressed with want and pining in sickness, there is, you will allow, by these circumstances, a heightening of the love and the admiration that I formerly rendered him. And, we should like to know what is the precise character of the addition that has thus been given to my regard for the virtue of benevolence. We should like to know, if it be altogether a pure and a praise-worthy accession that has thus come upon the sentiment with which I now look at my benefactor,—or, if, by contracting any taint of selfishness, it has lost the high rank that formerly belonged to it, as a disinterested affection, towards the goodness which beautifies and adorns his character.

There is one way, however, in which this special direction of a moral virtue towards my particular interest, may increase my affection for it, and without changing the moral character of my affection. It gives me a nearer view of the virtue in question. It is true, that the virtue may just be as lovely when exercised in behalf of my neighbour, as when exercised in behalf of myself. But, in the former case, I am not an eye-witness to the display and the evolution of its loveliness. I am a limited being, who cannot take in so full and so distinct an impression of the character of what is distant, as of the character of what is immediately beside me. It is true, that all the circumstances may be reported. But you know very well, that a much livelier representation is obtained of any object, by the seeing of it, than by the hearing of it. To be told of kindness, does not bring this attribute of character so forcibly, or so clearly home to my observation, as to receive a visit from kindness, and to take it by the hand, and to see its benignant mien, and to hear its gentle and complacent voice, and to witness the solicitude of its inquiries, and to behold its tender and honest anxiety for my interest, and to share daily and weekly in the liberalities which it has bestowed upon me. When all this goes on around my own person, and within the limits of my own dwelling-place, it is very true that self is gratified, and that this circumstance may give rise to sensations, which are altogether distinct from the love I bear to moral worth, or to moral excellence. But this does not hinder, that along with these sensations, a disinterested love for the moral virtue of which I have been the object, may, at the same time, have its room and its residence within my bosom. I may love goodness more than ever, on its own account, since it has taken its specific way to my habitation, and that, just because I have obtained a nearer acquaintance with it. I may love it better, because I know it better. My affection for it may have become more intense, and more devoted than before, because its beauty is now more fully unfolded to the eye of my observation than before. And thus, while we admit that the goodness of which I am the object, originates within me certain feelings different in kind from that which is excited by goodness in the general, yet it may heighten the degree of this latter feeling also. It may kindle or augment the love I bear to moral virtue in itself; or, in other words, it may enhance my affection for worth, without any change whatever in the moral character of that affection.

Now, before we proceed to consider those peculiar emotions which are excited within me, by being the individual, in whose favour certain virtues are exercised, and which emotions are, all of them, different in kind from the affection that I bear for these virtues,—let us farther observe, that the term love, when applied to sentient beings considered as the object of it, may denote an affection, different in the principle of its excitement, from any that we have been yet considering. My love to another may lie in the liking I have for the moral qualities which belong to him; and this, by way of distinctness, may be called the love of moral esteem or approbation. Or, my love to another may consist in the desire I have for his happiness; and this may be called the love of kindness. These two are often allied to each other in fact, but there is a real difference in their nature. The love of kindness which I bear to my infant child may have no reference to its moral qualities whatever. This love finds its terminating gratification in obtaining, for the object of it, exemption from pain, or in ministering to its enjoyments. It is very true, that the sight of what is odious or revolting in the character of another, tends, in point of fact, to dissipate all the love of kindness I may have ever borne to him. But it does not always do so, and one instance of this proves a real distinction, in point of nature, between the love of kindness, and the love of moral esteem. And the highest and most affecting instance which can be given of this distinction, is in the love wherewith God hath loved the world; is in that kindness towards us, through Christ Jesus, which he hath made known to men in the Gospel; is in that longing regard to his fallen creatures, whereby he was not willing that any should perish, but rather that all should live. There was the love of kindness standing out, in marked and separate display, from the love of moral esteem; for, alas! in the degraded race of mankind, there was not one quality which could call forth such an affection in the breast of the Godhead. It was, when we were hateful to him in character, that in person and in interest we were the objects of his most unbounded tenderness. It was, when we were enemies by wicked works, that God looked on with pity, and stretched forth, to his guilty children, the arms of offered reconciliation. It was when we had wandered far in the paths of worthlessness and alienation, that he devised a message of love, and sent his Son into our world, to seek and to save us.

And this, by the way, may serve to illustrate the kind of love which we are required to bear to our enemies. We are required to love them, in the same way in which God loves his enemies. A conscientious man will feel oppressed by the difficulty of such a precept, if he try to put it into obedience, by loving those who have offended, with the same feeling of complacency with which he loves those who have befriended him. But the truth is, that the love of moral esteem often enters, as a principal ingredient, into the love of complacency; and we are not required, by our imitation of the Godhead, to entertain any such affection for the depraved and the worthless. It is enough, that we cherish towards them in our hearts the love of kindness; and this will be felt a far more practicable achievement, than to force up the love of complacency into a bosom, revolted by the aspect of treachery, or dishonesty, or unprincipled selfishness. There is no possible motive to excite the latter affection. There may be a thousand to excite the former: and we have only to look to the unhappy man in all his prospects, and in all his relations; we have only to pity his delusions, and to view him as the hapless victim of a sad and ruinous infatuation; we have only to carry our eye onwards to the agonies of that death, which will shortly lay hold of him, and to compute the horrors of that eternity, which, if not recovered from the error of his way, he is about to enter; we have only, in a word, to put forth an exercise of faith in certain near and impending realities, the evidence of which is altogether resistless, in order to summon up such motives, and such considerations, as may cause the compassion of our nature to predominate over the resentment of our nature: and as will assure to a believer the victory over such urgencies of his constitution as, to the unrenewed heart, are utterly unconquerable.

But to resume our argument, let it be observed that the kindness of God is one of the loveliest, and most estimable of the attributes which belong to him. It is a bright feature in that assemblage of excellencies, which enter into the character of the Godhead: and, as such, independently altogether of this kindness being exercised upon me, I should offer to it the homage of my moral approbation. But, should I be the special and the signalized object of his kindness, there is another sentiment towards God, beside the love of moral esteem, that ought to be formed within me by that circumstance, and which, in the business of reasoning, should be kept apart from it. There is the love of gratitude. These often go together, and may be felt simultaneously, towards the one being we are employed in contemplating. But they are just as distinct, each from the other, as is the love of moral esteem from the love of kindness. We trust that we have already convinced you, that God feels towards us, his inferiors, the love of kindness, when he cannot, from the nature of the object, feel for us the slightest degree of the love of moral esteem. In the same manner may we feel, we are not saying towards God, but towards an earthly benefactor, the love of gratitude, when, from the nature of the object we are employed in contemplating, there is much to impair within us the love of moral esteem, or to extinguish it altogether. Is it not most natural to say of the man, who has been personally benevolent to myself, and who has, at the same time, disgraced himself, by his vices, that, bad as he is, he has been at all times remarkably kind to me, and felt many a movement of friendship towards my person, and done many a deed of important service to my family, and that I, at least, owe him a gratitude for all this,—that I, at least, should be longer than others, of dismissing from my bosom the last remainder of cordiality towards him,—that if, infamy and poverty have followed, in the career of his wickedness, and he have become an outcast from the attentions of other men, it is not for me to spurn him instantly from my door,—or, in the face of my particular recollections, to look unpitying and unmoved, at the wretchedness into which he has fallen.

It is the more necessary, to distinguish the love of gratitude from the love of moral esteem, that each of these affections may be excited simultaneously within me, by one act or by one exhibition of himself, on the part of the Deity. Let me be made to understand, that God has passed by my transgression, and generously admitted me into the privileges and the rewards of obedience,—I see in this a tenderness, and a mercy, and a love, for his creatures, which, if blended at the same time with all that is high and honourable in the more august attributes of his nature, have the effect of presenting him to my mind, and of drawing out my heart in moral regard to him, as a most amiable and estimable object of contemplation. But besides this, there is a peculiar love of gratitude, excited by the consideration that I am the object of this benignity,—that I am one of the creatures to whom he has directed this peculiar regard,—that he has singled out me, and conceived a gracious purpose towards me, and in the execution of this purpose is lavishing upon my person, the blessings of a father's care, and a father's tenderness. Both the love of moral esteem, and the love of gratitude, may thus be in contemporaneous operation within me; and it will be seen to accomplish a practical, as well as a metaphysical purpose, to keep the one apart from the other, in the view of the mind, when love towards God is the topic of speculation which engages it.

But, farther, let it be understood, that the

love of gratitude differs from the love of moral esteem, not merely in the cause which immediately originates it, but also in the object, in which it finds its rest and its gratification. It is the kindness of another being to myself, which originates within me the 'ove of gratitude towards him; and it is the view of what is morally estimable in this being, that originates within me all the love of moral esteem, that I entertain for him. There is a real distinction of cause between these two affections, and there is also between them a real distinction of object. The love of moral esteem finds its complacent gratification, in the act of dwelling contemplatively on that Being, by whom it is excited; just as a tasteful enthusiast inhales delight from the act of gazing on the charms of some external scenery. The pleasure he receives, emanates directly upon his mind, from the forms of beauty and of loveliness, which are around him. And if, instead of a taste for the beauties of nature, there exists within him, a taste for the beauties of holiness, then will he love the Being, who presents to the eye of his contemplation the fullest assemblage of them, and his taste will find its complacent gratification in dwelling upon him, whether as an object of thought, or as an object of perception. "One thing have I desired," says the Psalmist, "that I may dwell in the house of the Lord all the days of my life, to behold the beauty of the Lord, and to inquire in his temple." Now, the love of gratitude is distinct from this in its object. It is excited by the love of kindness; and the feeling which is thus excited, is just a feeling of kindness back again. It is kindness begetting kindness. The language of this affection is, "What shall I render unto the Lord for all his benefits?" He has done what is pleasing and gratifying to me. What shall I do to please, and to gratify him? The love of gratitude seeks for answers to this question, and finds its delight in acting upon them, and whether the answer be,—this is the will of God, even your sanctification,—or, with the sacrifices of liberality God is well pleased,—or, obedience to parents is well pleasing in his sight,—these all point out so many lines of conduct, to which the impulse of the love of gratitude would carry us, and attest this to be the love of God,—that ye keep his commandments.

And, indeed, when the same Being combines, in his own person, that which ought to excite the love of moral esteem, with that which ought to excite the love of gratitude,—the two ingredients, enter with a mingled but harmonious concurrence, into the exercise of one compound affection. It is true, that the more appropriate offering of the former is the offering of praise,— just as when one looks to the beauties of nature, he breaks out into a rapturous acknowledgment of them; and so it may be, when one looks to the venerable, and the lovely in the character of God. The more appropriate offering of the latter, is the offering of thanksgiving, or of such services as are fitted to please, and to gratify a benefactor. But still it may be observed, how each of these simple affections tends to express itself, by the very act which more characteristically marks the workings of the other; or, how the more appropriate offering of the first of them, may be prompted under the impulse, and movement of the second of them, and conversely. For, if I love God because of his perfections, what principle can more powerfully or more directly lead to the imitation of them?— which is the very service that he requires, and the very offering that he is most pleased with. And, if I love God because of his goodness to me, what is more fitted to prompt my every exertion, in the way of spreading the honours of his character and of his name among my fellows,— and, for this purpose, to magnify in their hearing the glories and the attributes of his nature? It is thus that the voice of praise and the voice of gratitude may enter into one song of adoration; and that whilst the Psalmist, at one time, gives thanks to God at the remembrance of his holiness, he, at another, pours forth praise at the remembrance of his mercies.

To have the love of gratitude towards God, it is essential that we know and believe his love of kindness towards us. To have the love of moral esteem towards him, it is essential that the loveliness of his character be in the eye of the mind: or, in other words, that the mind keep itself in steady and believing contemplation of the excellencies which belong to him. The view that we have of God, is just as much in the order of precedency to the affection that we entertain for him, as any two successive steps can be, in any of the processes of our mental constitution. To obtain the introduction of love into the heart, there must, as a preparatory circumstance, be the introduction of knowledge into the understanding; or, as we can never be said to know what we do not believe—ere we have love, we must have faith; and, accordingly, in the passage from which our text is extracted, do we perceive the one pointed to, as the instrument for the production of the other. "Keep yourselves in the love of God, building yourselves up on your most holy faith."

And here, it ought to be remarked, that a man may experience a mental process, and yet have no taste or no understanding for the explanation of it. The simple truths of the Gospel, may enter with acceptance into the mind of a peasant, and there work all the proper influences on his heart and character, which the Bible ascribes to them: and yet he may be utterly incapable of tracing that series of inward movements, by which he is carried onward from a belief in the truth, to all those moral and affectionate regards, which mark a genuine disciple of the truth. He may be the actual subject of these movements, though altogether unable to follow or to analyze them. This is not peculiar to the judgments or the feelings of Christianity. In the matters of ordinary life, a man may judge sagaciously, and feel correctly while ardently;—and experience, in right and natural order, the play of his various faculties, without having it at all in his power, either to frame or to follow a true theory of his faculties. It is well, that the simple preaching of the Gospel has its right practical operation on men, who make no attempt whatever, to comprehend the metaphysics of the operation. But, if ever metaphysics be employed to darken the freeness of the Gospel offer, or to dethrone faith from the supremacy which belongs to it, or to forbid the approaches of those whom God has not forbidden; then must it be met upon its own ground, and the real character of our beneficent religion be asserted, amid the attempts of those who have in any way obscured or injured it by their illustrations.

SERMON X.

Gratitude, not a sordid Affection.

"We love him, because he first loved us."—1 John iv. 19.

Some theologians have exacted from an inquirer, at the very outset of his conversion, that he should carry in his heart what they call the disinterested love of God. They have set him on the most painful efforts to acquire this affection,—and that too, before he was in circumstances in which it was at all possible to entertain it. They have led him to view with suspicion the love of gratitude, as having in it a taint of selfishness. They are for having him to love God, and that on the single ground that he is lovely, without any reference to his own comfort, or even to his own safety. Strange demand which they make on a sentient being, that even amidst the fears and the images of destruction, he should find room in his heart for the love of complacency! and equally strange demand to make on a sinful being, that ere he admit such a sense of reconciliation into his bosom, as will instantly call forth a grateful regard to him who has conferred it, he must view God with a disinterested affection; that from the deep and helpless abyss of his depravity, he must find, unaided, his ascending way to the purest and the sublimest emotion of moral nature; that ere he is delivered from fear he must love, even though it be said of love, that it casteth out fear; and that ere he is placed on the vantage ground of the peace of the Gospel, he must realize on his character, one of the most exalted of its perfections.

The effect of all this on many an anxious seeker after rest, has been most discouraging. With the stigma that has been affixed to the love of gratitude, they have been positively apprehensive of the inroads of this affection, and have studiously averted the eye of their contemplation from the objects which are fitted to inspire it. In other words, they have hesitated to entertain the free offers of salvation, and misinterpreted all the tokens of an embassy, which has proclaimed peace on earth and good will to men. They think that all which they can possibly gather, in the way of affection, from such a contemplation, is the love of gratitude; and that gratitude is selfishness; and that selfishness is not a gracious affection; and that ere they be surely and soundly converted, the love they bear to God must be of a totally disinterested character; and thus through another medium than that of a free and gratuitous dispensation of kindness, do they strive, by a misunderstood gospel, or without the gospel altogether, to reach a peace and a preparation which we fear, in their way of it, is to sinners utterly unattainable.

In the progress of this discourse let us endeavour, in the first place, to rescue the love of gratitude from the imputations which have been preferred against it,—and secondly, to assign to the love of kindness manifested to the world in the gospel, and to the faith by which that love is made to arise in the heart, the place and the pre-eminence which belong to them.

I. The proper object of the love of gratitude, is the being who has exercised towards me the love of kindness; and this is more correct than to say, that the proper object of this affection is the being who has conferred benefits upon me. I can conceive another to load me with benefactions, and at the same time, to evince that kindness towards me was not the principle which impelled him. It may be done reluctantly at the bidding of another, or it may be done to serve some interested purpose, or it may be done to parade his generosity before the eye of the public. If it be not done from a real principle of kindness to myself, I may take his gifts, and I may find enjoyment in the use of them; but I feel no gratitude towards the dispenser of them. Unless I see his kindness in them, I will not be grateful. It is true, that, in point of fact, gratitude often springs from the rendering of a benefit; but, lest we should confound things which are different, let it be well observed, that this is only when the benefit serves as the indication of a kind purpose, or of a kind affection, on the part of him who hath granted it. And this may be proved, not merely by showing, that there may be no gratitude where there is a benefit, but also by showing, that there may be gratitude where there is no material benefit whatever. Just let the naked principle of kindness discover itself, and though it have neither the power, nor the opportunity of coming forth with the dispensation of any service, it is striking to observe, how, upon the bare existence of this affection being known, it is met by a grateful feeling, on the part of him to whom it is directed; and what mighty augmentations may be given in this way, to the stock of enjoyment, and that, by the mere reciprocation of kindness begetting kindness. For, to send the expression of this kindness into another's bosom, it is not always necessary to do it on the vehicle of positive donation. It may be conveyed by a look of benevolence; and thus it is, that by the mere feeling of cordiality, a tide of happiness may be made to circulate throughout all the individuals of an assembled company. Or it may be done by a very slight and passing attention, and thus it is, that the cheap services of courteousness, may spread such a charm over the face of a neighbourhood. Or it may be done by the very poorest member of human society; and thus it is, that the ready and sincere homage of attachment from such a man, may beam a truer felicity upon me, and call forth a livelier gratitude to him who has conferred it, than some splendid act of patronage on the part of a superior. Or it may be done by a Christian visiter in some of the humblest of our city lanes, who, without one penny to bestow on the children of want, may spread among them the simple conviction of her good will, and call down upon her person the voice of thankfulness and of blessing from all their habitations. And thus it is, that by good will creating good will, a pure and gladdening influence will at length go abroad over the face of our world, and mankind will be made to know the might and the mystery of that tie which is to bind them together into one family, and they will rejoice in the power of that secret charm which so heightens and so multiplies the pleasure of all the members of it; and, when transported from earth to heaven, they will still feel, that while it is to the benefits which God hath conferred that they owe the possession and all the privileges of existence; it is to a sense of the love which prompted these benefits, that they will owe the ecstatic charm of their immortality. It is the beaming kindness of God upon them, that will put their souls into the liveliest transports of gratitude and joy; and it is the reciprocation of this kindness on the part of those, who, while they have fellowship with the Father, and with the Son, have fellowship also with one another, that will cause the joy of heaven to be full.

The distinction which we are now adverting to, is something more, than a mere shadowy refinement of speculation. It may be realized on the most trodden and ordinary path of human experience, and is, in fact, one of the most familiar exhibitions of genuine and unsophisticated nature in those ranks of society where refinement is unknown. Let one man go over any given district of the city fully fraught with the *materiel* of benevolence; let him be the agent of some munificent subscription, and with nothing in his heart but just such affections, and such jealousies, and such thoughtful anxieties, about a right and equitable division, as belong to the general spirit of his office; let him leave some substantial deposit with each of the families; and then compute, if he can, the quantity of gratitude which he carries away with him. It were a most unkind reflection on the lower orders, and not more unkind than untrue, to deny that there will be the mingling of some gratitude, along with the clamour, and the envy, and the discontent, which are ever sure to follow in the train of such a ministration. It is not to discredit the poor, that we introduce our present observation; but to bring out, if possible, into broad and luminous exhibition, one of the finest sensibilities which adorns them. It is to let you know the high cast of character of which they are capable; and how the glow of pleasure which arises in their bosoms, when the eye of simple affection beams upon their persons, or upon their habitations, may not have one single taint of sordidness to debase it. And to prove this, just let another man go over the same district, and in the train of the former visitation; conceive him unbacked by any public institution, to have nothing in his hand that might not be absorbed by the needs of a single family, but that, utterly destitute as he is of the *materiel*, he has a heart charged and overflowing with the whole *morale* of benevolence. Just let him go forth among the people, without one other recommendation than an honest and undissembled good will to them; and let this good will manifest its existence, in any one of the thousand ways, by which it may be authenticated; and whether it be by the cordiality of his manners, or by his sympathy with their griefs, or by the nameless attentions and offices of civility, or by the higher aim of that kindness which points to the welfare of their immortality, and evinces its reality by its ready and unwearied services among the young, or the sick, or the dying; just let them be satisfied of the one fact, that he is their friend, and that all their joys and all their sorrows are his own; he may be struggling with hardships and necessities as the poorest of them all; but poor as they are, they know what is in his heart, and well do they know how to value it; and from the voice of welcome, which meets him in the very humblest of their tenements; and from the smile of that heartfelt enjoyment, which his presence is ever sure to awaken, and from the influence of graciousness which he carries along with him into every house, and by which he lights up an honest emotion of thankfulness in the bosom of every family, may we gather the existence of a power, which worth alone, and without the accompaniment of wealth, can bestow; a power to sweeten and subdue, and tranquillize, which no money can purchase, which no patronage can create.

It will be readily acknowledged by all, that the most precious object in the management of a town, is to establish the reign of happiness and contentment among those who live in it. And it is interesting to mark the operations of those, who, without adverting to the principle that I now insist upon, think that all is to be achieved by the beggarly elements which enter into the arithmetic of ordinary business; who rear their goodly scheme upon the basis of sums and computations; and think that by an overwhelming discharge of the *materiel* of benevolence, they will reach an accomplishment which the *morale* of benevolence alone is equal to. We are sure that it is not to mortify our men of grave, and official, and calculating experience, that we tell them, how, with all their strength, and all their sagacity, they have only given their money for that which is not meat, and their labour for that which satisfieth not. It is to illustrate a principle of our common nature, so obvious, that to be recognized, it needs only to be spoken of. And it were well, if in so doing their thoughts could be led to the instrumentality of this principle, as the only way, in which they can redeem the failures of their by-gone experience; if they could be convinced, that the agents of a zealous and affectionate Christianity can alone do what all the influence of municipal weight and municipal wisdom cannot do; if they could be taught what the ministrations are, by which a pure and a responding gratitude, may be made to circulate throughout all our dwelling-places; if, in a word, while they profess to serve the poor, they could be led to respect the poor, to do homage to that fineness of moral temperament which belongs to them, and which hitherto seems to have escaped, altogether, the eye of civil or political superintendence; and they may rest assured, that let them give as much in the shape of munificence as they will, if they add not the love to the liberality of the Gospel, they will never soften one feature of unkindness, or chase away one exasperated feeling, from the hearts of a neglected population.

But, beside the degree of purity in which this principle may exist among the most destitute of our species, it is also of importance to mark the degree of strength, in which it actually exists among the most depraved of our species. And, on this subject, do we think that the venerable Howard has bequeathed to us a most striking and valuable observation. You know the history of this man's enterprises; how his doings, and his observations, were among the veriest outcasts of humanity,—how he descended into prison houses, and there made himself familiar with all that could most revolt or terrify, in the exhibition of our fallen nature; how, for this purpose, he made the tour of Europe; but instead of walking in the footsteps of other travellers, he toiled his painful and persevering way through these receptacles of worthlessness; —and, sound experimentalist as he was, did he treasure up the phenomena of our nature, throughout all the stages of misfortune, or depravity. We may well conceive the scenes of moral desolation that would often meet his eye; and that, as he looked to the hard, and dauntless, and defying aspect of criminality before him, he would sicken in despair of ever finding one remnant of a purer and better principle, by which he might lay hold of these unhappy men, and convert them into the willing and the consenting agents of their own amelioration. And yet such a principle he found, and found it, as he tells us, after years of intercourse, as the fruit of his greater experience, and his longer observation; and gives, as the result of it, that convicts, and that among the most desperate of them all, are not ungovernable, and that there is a way of managing even them, and that the way is, without relaxing, in one iota, from the steadiness of a calm and resolute discipline, to treat them with tenderness, and to show them that you have humanity; and thus a principle, of itself so beautiful, that to expatiate upon it, gives in the eyes of some, an air of fantastic declamation to our argument, is actually deponed to, by an aged and most sagacious observer. It is the very principle of our text; and it would appear that it keeps a lingering hold of our nature, even in the last and lowest degree of human wickedness; and that when abandoned by every other principle, this may still be detected,—that even among the most hackneyed and most hardened of malefactors there is still about them a softer part which will give way to the demonstrations of tenderness: that this one ingredient of a better character is still found to survive the dissipation of all the others,—that, fallen as a brother may be, from the moralities which at one time adorned him, the manifested good-will of his fellow-man still carries a charm and an influence along with it; and that, therefore, there lies in this, an operation which, as no poverty can vitiate, so no depr vity can extinguish.*

Now, this is the very principle which is brought into action, in the dealings of God with a whole world of malefactors. It looks as if he confided the whole cause of our recovery to the influence of a demonstration of good will. It is truly interesting to mark, what, in the devisings of his unsearchable wisdom, is the character which he has made to stand most visibly out, in the great scheme and history of our redemption: and surely if there be one feature of prominency more visible than another, it is the love of kindness. There appears to be no other possible way, by which a responding affection can be deposited in the heart of man. Certain it is, that the law of love cannot be carried to its ascendency over us by storm. Authority cannot command it. Strength cannot implant it. Terror cannot charm it into existence. The threatenings of vengeance may stifle, or they may repel, but they never can woo this delicate principle of our nature, into a warm and confiding attachment. The human heart remains shut, in all its receptacles, against the force of these various applications; and God, who knew what was in man, seems to have known, that in his dark and guilty bosom, there was but one solitary hold that he had over him; and that to reach it, he must just put on a look of graciousness, and tell us that he has no pleasure in our death, and manifest towards us the longings of a bereaved parent, and even humble himself to a suppliant in the cause of our return, and send a Gospel of peace into the world, and bid his messengers to bear throughout all its habitations, the tidings of his good-will to the children of men. This is the topic of his most anxious and repeated demonstration. This manifested good will of God to his creatures, is the band of love, and the cord of a man, by which he draws them. It is

---

* The operation of the same principle has, of late, been strikingly exemplified by Mrs. Fry, and her coadjutors, in the prison at Newgate.

true, that from the inaccessible throne of his glory, we see no direct emanation of his tenderness upon us, from this face of the King who is invisible. But, as if to make up for this, he sent his Son into the world, and declared him to be God manifest in the flesh, and let us see, in his tears, and in his sympathies, and in all the recorded traits of his kindness, and gentleness, and love, what a God we have to deal with. It is true, that even in love to us, he did not let down one attribute of truth or of majesty which belonged to him. But, in love to us, he hath laid upon his own Son the burden of their vindication;—and now, that every obstacle is done away; now, that the barrier which lay across the path of acceptance, is levelled by the power of him who travailed in the greatness of his strength for us; now, that the blood of atonement has been shed, and that the justice of God has been magnified, and that our iniquities have been placed on the great Sacrifice, and so borne away that there is no more mention of them: now, that with his dignity entire, and his holiness untainted, the door of heaven may be opened, and sinners be called upon to enter in,—is the voice of a friendly and beseeching God, lifted up without reserve, in the hearing of us all;—his love of kindness is published abroad among men;—and this one mighty principle of attraction is brought to bear upon a nature, that might have remained sullen and unmoved under every other application.

And, as God, in the measure of restoring a degenerate world unto himself, hath set in operation the very same principle as that which we have attempted to illustrate,—so the operation hath produced the very same result that we have ascribed to it. As soon as his love of kindness is believed, so soon does the love of gratitude spring up in the heart of the believer. As soon as man gives up his fear and his suspicion of God, and discerns him to be his friend, so soon does he render him the homage of a willing and affectionate loyalty. There is not a man who can say, I have known and believed the love which God hath to us, who cannot say also, I have loved God because he first loved me. There has not, we will venture to affirm, been a single example in the whole history of the church, of a man who had a real faith in the overtures of peace and of tenderness which are proposed by the Gospel, and who did not, at the same time, exemplify this attribute of the Christian faith, that it worketh by love.

It is thus that the faith, which recognizes God, as God in Christ reconciling the world unto himself, lies at the turning point of conversion. In this way, and in this way alone, is there an inlet of communication open to the heart of man, for that principle of love to God, which gives all its power and all its character to the new obedience of the gospel. So soon as a man really knows the truth, and no man can be said to know what he does not believe, will this truth enthrone a new affection in his bosom, which will set him free from the dominion of all such affections as are earthly and rebellious. The whole style and spirit of his obedience are transformed. The man now walks with the vigour, and the confidence, and the enlargement, of one who is set at liberty. It looks a mysterious revolution in the general eye of the world. But the fact is, that from the moment a sinner closes with the overtures of the gospel, from that moment a new era is established in the history of his mind altogether. As soon as he sees what he never saw before, so soon does he feel what he never felt before. Without the faith of the gospel he may serve God in the spirit of bondage: he may be driven, by the terrors of his law, into many outward and reluctant conformities; he may even, without the influence of these terrors, maintain a thousand decencies of tastes, and custom, and established observation. But he is still an utter stranger to the first and the greatest commandment. There may be the homage of many a visible movement with the body, while, in the whole bent and disposition of the soul there is nothing but aversion, and distance, and enmity. Even the word of the gospel may be addressed, Sabbath after Sabbath, and that too, to hearers who offer no positive resistance to it,—but coming to them only in word, they remain as motionless and unimpressed as ever, and with an utter dormancy in their hearts as to any responding movement of gratitude. The heart, in fact, remains unapproachable in every other way, but by the gospel coming to it, not in word only, but in power, and in the Holy Ghost, and in much assurance. Then is it, that the love of God is shed abroad in our hearts; and that the gospel approves itself to be his power, and his wisdom, to the sanctification of all who believe in it.

Now, the theologians to whom we allude, have set up obstacles in the way of such a process. They hold a language about the disinterested love of God, and demand this at the very outset of a man's conversion, in such a way, as may retard his entrance upon a life of faith,—as may have prolonged the darkness of many an inquirer, and have kept him in a state of despair, whom a right understanding of the gospel would have relieved of all his doubts, and all his perplexities. They seem to look on the love of gratitude, as having in it a taint of selfishness. They say that to love a being, because he is my benefactor, is little better than to love the benefit which he has conferred upon me; and that this, instead of any evidence of a state of grace, is the mere effect of an appetite which belongs essentially and universally to the animal state of nature. They appear to have missed the distinction, between the love that is felt towards the benefit itself, and the love of gratitude that is felt towards the author of it; though certainly there are here two objects of affection altogether distinct from each other.

My liking for the gift is a different phase of mind from my liking for the giver. In the one exercise, I am looking to a different object, and my thoughts have a different employment, from what they have in the other. Had I an affection for the gift, without an affection for the giver, then might I evince an unmixed selfishness of character. But I may have both; and my affection for the giver may be purely in obedience to that law of reciprocity, whereby if another likes me, I am disposed by that circumstance, and by that alone, to like him back again. The gift may serve merely the purpose of an indication. It is the medium through which I perceive the love that another bears me. But it is possible for me to perceive this through another medium, and, in this case, the rising gratitude of my bosom might look a purer and more disinterested emotion. But the truth is, that it retains the very same character, though a gift has been the occasion of its excitement,—and, therefore, it ought not to have been so assimilated to the principle of selfishness. It ought not to have been so discouraged, and made the object of suspicion, at that moment of its evolution, when the returning sinner looks by faith to the truths and the promises of the gospel, and sees in them the tenderness of an inviting God. It ought not to have been so stigmatized, as a mere portion of his unrenewed nature; for, in truth, it will heighten and grow upon him, with every step in the advancement of his moral renovation. It will be one of the gracefullest of his accomplishments in this world; and so far from being extinguished in the next, along with the baser and more selfish affections of our constitution, it will pour an animating spirit into many a song of ecstacy, to him who loved us, and washed us from our sins in his own blood. The law of love begetting love, will obtain in eternity. Like the law of reciprocal attraction in the material world, it will cement the immutable and everlasting order of that moral system, which is to emerge with the new heavens and the new earth, wherein dwelleth righteousness. The love which emanates from the throne of God, upon his surrounding family, will call back a voice of blessing, and thanksgiving, and glory, from all the members of it. And the love which his children bear to each other, will, in like manner, be reflected and multiplied. All that is wrong in selfishness will be there unknown. But gratitude, so far from being counted an unseemly companion for paradise, will be one chief ingredient in the fulness of its joy; one of the purest and most exquisite of those pleasures which are for evermore.

The first consideration, then, upon which we would elevate gratitude to the rank of a virtue, is, that in its object, it is altogether distinct from selfishness. It is enough, indeed, to dissolve the imagination of any kindred character between selfishness and gratitude, that the man without selfishness, seems to the eye of a beholder, as standing on a lofty eminence of virtue. The man without gratitude, is held, by all, to be a monster of deformity. Give me a man who seizes with ravenous appropriation all that I have to bestow,—and who hoards it, or feeds upon it, or, in any way rejoices over it, without one grateful movement of his heart towards me,—and you lay before me a character, not merely unlike, but diametrically opposite, to the character of him who obtains the very same gift, and, perhaps, derives from the use of it, an equal, or a greater degree of enjoyment, to the sensitive part of his nature,—but who, in addition to all this, has thought, and affection, and the higher principles of his nature, excited by the consideration of the giver; and looks to the manifested love that appears in this act of generosity; and is touched with love back again; and, under the influence of this responding affection, conceives the kindest wishes, and pours out the warmest prayers, for the interest of his benefactor, and shows him all the symptoms of friendship, and surrounds him with all its services.

The second consideration upon which we would elevate gratitude to the rank of a pure virtue, has already been glanced at. Were it not a virtue, it would have no place in heaven. Did it only appertain to the unrenewed part of our nature, it would find no admittance among the saints in paradise. But one of the songs of the redeemed, is a song of gratitude.

And, thirdly, by looking more closely to this affection, both in its origin and in its exercises, we shall perceive in it, more clearly, all the characteristics of virtue.

Let it be remarked, then, that an affection may simply exist, and yet be no evidence of any virtue, or of any moral worth in the holder of it. I may look on a beautiful prospect, and be drawn out to an involuntary sentiment of admiration. Or, I may look on my infant child, and without one effort of volition, feel a parental tenderness towards it. Or, I may be present at a scene of distress, and without choosing or willing to be so, I may be moved to the softest compassion. And, in this way, I may have a character made up of many affections, some of which are tasteful, some of which are most amiable in themselves, and some of which are most useful to society and yet none of which may possess the smallest portion of the essential character of virtue. They may be brought into exercise without any working of a sense of duty whatever. One of those we have specified—the instinctive affection of parents for their young, is exemplified in all its strength, and in all its tenderness, by the inferior animals. And, therefore, if we want to know what that is which constitutes the character of virtue, or moral worth, in a human being, we must look to something else, than to the mere existence of certain affections, however valuable they may prove to others, or whatever gracefulness they may shed over the complexion of him who possesses them.

Now, it would be raising a collateral into a main topic, were we to enter upon a full explanation of the matter that has now been suggested. And we shall, therefore, briefly remark, that to give the character of virtue to any grace of the inner man, the will, acting under a sense of duty, must, in some way or other, have been concerned in the establishment, or in the continuance of it; and that to give the same character of virtue to a deed of the outer man, the will must also be concerned. A deed is only virtuous in as far as it is voluntary; and it is only in proportion to the share which the will has in the performance of it, and the will impelling us to do, what we are persuaded ought to be done, that there can be awarded, to the deed in question, any character of moral estimation.

This will explain what the circumstances are, under which the gratitude of a human being may at one time be an instinct, and at another time a virtue. I may enter the house of an individual who is an utter stranger to the habit of acting under a sense of duty; who is just as much the creature of mere impulse, as the animals beneath him; and who, therefore, though some of these impulses are more characteristic of his condition as a man, and most subservient to the good of his fellows, may be considered as possessing no virtue whatever, in the strict and proper sense of the term. But he has the property of being affected by external causes. And I, by some ministration of friendship, may flash upon his mind such an overpowering conviction of the good will that I bear him, as to affect him with a sense of gratitude even unto tears. The moral obligation of gratitude may not be present to his mind at all. But the emotion of gratitude comes into his heart unbidden, and finds its vent in acknowledgments, and blessings, on the person of his benefactor. We would say, of such a person, that he possesses a happier original constitution than another, who, in the same circumstances, would not be so powerfully or so tenderly affected. And yet he may have hitherto evinced nothing more than the workings of a mere instinct, which springs spontaneously within him, and gives its own impulse to his words and his performances, without a sense of duty having any share in the matter, or without the will prompting the individual by any such consideration, as, let me do this thing because I ought to do it.

Let us now conceive the moral sense to be admitted to its share of influence over this proceeding. Let it be consulted on the question of what ought to be felt, and what ought to be done, by one being, when another evinces the love of kindness towards him. A mere instinct may, in point of fact, draw out a return of love and of service back again. But it is the province of the moral sense to pronounce on the point of obligation, and we speak its universal suggestion, when we say, that the love of gratitude ought to be felt, and the services of gratitude ought to be rendered.

Now, to make this decision of the moral sense practically effectual, and, indeed, to make the moral sense have any thing to do with this question at all, the feeling of gratitude must, in some way or other, be dependent either for its existence, or its growth, or its continuance, upon the will; and the same will must also have a command over the services of gratitude. The moral sense, in fact, never interposes with any dictate, or with any declaration about the feelings, or the conduct of man, unless in so far as the will of man has an influence, and a power of regulation over them. It never makes the rate of the circulation of the blood a question of duty, because this is altogether an involuntary movement. And it never would have offered any authoritative intimation, about the way in which gratitude ought to be felt, or ought to be expressed, unless the will had had some kind of presiding sovereignty over both the degree and the workings of this affection.

The first way, then, in which the will may have to do with the love of gratitude, is by the putting forth of a desire for the possession of it. It may long to realize this moral accomplishment. It may hunger and thirst after this branch of righteousness. Even though it has not any such power under its command as would enable it to fulfil such a volition, the volition itself has, upon it, the stamp and the character of virtue. The man who habitually wills to have in his heart a love of gratitude towards God, is a man at least of holy desires, if not of holy attainments. And, when we consider that a way has actually been established, in which the desire may be followed up by the attainment,—when we read of the promise given to those who seek after God,— when we learn the assurance that he will grant the heart's desire of those who will stir themselves up to lay hold of him,—when we think that prayer is the natural expression of desire for an object which man cannot reach, but which God is both able and willing to confer upon him,—then do we see how the very existence of the love of gratitude may have had its pure and holy commencement, in such a habitude of the will as has the essential character of virtue engraven upon it. "Keep yourselves," says the Apostle, "in the love of God, by praying in the Holy Ghost."

But, again, there are certain doings of the mind, over which the will has a control, and by which the affection of gratitude may either be brought into being, or be sustained in lively and persevering exercise. At the bidding of the will, I can think of one topic, rather than of another. I can transfer my mind to any given object of contemplation. I can keep that object steadily in view, and make an effort to do so, when placed in such circumstances as might lead me to distraction or forgetfulness. And it is in this way that moral praise or moral responsibility, may be attached to the love of gratitude. Ere the heart can be moved by this affection to another, there must be in the mind a certain appropriate object, that is fitted to call it, and to keep it in existence,—and that object is the love of kindness which the other bears me. I may endeavour, and I may succeed in the endeavour, to hold this love of kindness in daily and perpetual remembrance. If the will have to do with the exercises of thought and memory, then the will may be responsible for the gratitude that would spring in my bosom, did I only think of the love of God, and that would continue with me in the shape of an habitual affection, did I only keep that love in habitual remembrance. It is thus that the forgetfulness of God is chargeable with criminality,—and it will appear a righteous thing in the day of judgment, when they, who are thus forgetful of him, shall be turned into hell. It is this which arms, with such a moral and condemnatory force, the expostulation he holds with Israel, "that Israel doth not know, that my people do not consider." It is because we like not to retain God in our knowledge, that our minds become reprobate;—and, on the other hand, it is by a continuous effort of my will, towards the thought of him, that I forget not his benefits. It is by the strenuousness of a voluntary act, that I connect the idea of an unseen benefactor, with all the blessings of my present lot, and all the anticipations of my futurity. It is by a combat with the most urgent propensities of nature, that I am ever looking beyond this surrounding materialism, and setting God and his love before me all the day long

There is no virtue, it is allowed, without voluntary exertion; but this is the very character which runs throughout the whole work and exercise of faith. To keep himself in the love of God is a habit, with the maintenance of which the will of man has most essentially to do, because it is at his will that he keeps himself in the thought of God's love towards him. To bid away from me such intrusions of sense, and of time, as would shut God out of my recollections; to keep alive the impression of him in the midst of bustle, and company, and worldly avocations; to recall the thought of him and of his kindness, under crosses, and vexations, and annoyances; to be still, and know that he is God, even when beset with temptations to impatience and discontent; never to lose sight of him as merciful and gracious; and above all, never to let go my hold of that great Propitiation, by which in every time of trouble, I have the privilege of access with confidence to my reconciled Father; these are all so many acts of faith, but they are just such acts as the will bears a share, and a sovereignty, in the performance of. And, as they are the very acts which go to aliment and to sustain the love of gratitude within me, it may be seen, how an affection which, in the first instance, may spring involuntarily, and be therefore regarded as a mere instinct of nature, or as bearing upon it a complexion of selfishness, may, in another view, have upon it a complexion of deepest sacredness, and be rendered unto God in the shape of a duteous and devoted offering from a voluntary agent, and be, in fact, the laborious result of a most difficult, and persevering, and pains-taking habit of obedience.

And if this be true of the mere sense of gratitude, it is still more obviously true of the services of gratitude. "What shall I render unto the Lord for all his benefits?" is the genuine language of this affection. It seeks to make a gratifying return of service, and that, under the feeling that it ought to do so. Or, in other words, do we behold that it is the will of man, prompted by a sense of duty, which leads him on to the obedience of gratitude, and that the whole of this obedience is pervaded by the essential character of virtue. This is the love of God, that ye keep his commandments. This is the most gratifying return unto him, that ye do those things which are pleasing in his sight. And thus it is, that the love of gratitude may be vindicated in its character of moral worth, from its first commencement in the heart to its ultimate effect on the walk and conversation. It is originally distinct from selfishness in its object; and it derives a virtuousness at its very outset, from the aspirations of a soul bent on the acquirement of it, because bent on being what it ought to be; and it is sustained, both in life and in exercise, by such habits of thought as are of voluntary cultivation; and it nobly sustains an aspect of moral righteousness onwards to the final result of its operation on the character, by setting him who is under its power, on a career of obedience to God, and introducing him to an arduous contest of principle, with all the influences of sense and of the world.

If, to render an affection virtuous, the will acting under a sense of duty, should be concerned either in producing or in perpetuating it; then the love of moral esteem coming into the heart, as an involuntary sensation, may, in certain circumstances, have as little of the character of virtue as the love of gratitude. In this respect, both these affections are upon a footing with each other; and the first ought not to have been exalted at the expense of the second. That either be upheld within us in our present state, there must, in fact, be the putting forth of the same voluntary control over the thoughts and contemplations of the understanding; the same active exercise of faith; the same laborious resistance to all those urgencies of sense which would expel from the mind the idea of an unseen and spiritual object; the same remembrance of God sustained by effort, and prayer, and meditation.

II. We now feel ourselves in a condition to speak of the Gospel, in its free and gratuitous character; to propose its blessings as a gift; to hold out the pardon, and the strength, and all the other privileges which it proclaims to believers, as so many articles for their immediate acceptance; to make it known to men that they are not to delay their compliance with the overtures of mercy, till the disinterested love of God arises in their hearts; but that they have a warrant for entering even now, into instant reconciliation with God. Nor are we to dread the approach of any moral contamination, though when, after their eyes are opened to the marvellous spectacle of a pleading, and offering, and beseeching God, holding out eternal life unto the guilty, through the propitiation which his own Son hath made for them, they should, from that moment, open their whole soul, to the influences of gratitude, and love the God who thus hath first loved them.

We conclude then with remarking, that the whole of this argument gives us another view of the importance of faith. We do not say all for it that we ought, when we say that by faith we are justified in the sight of God. By faith also our hearts are purified. It is in fact the primary and the presiding principle of regeneration. It brings the heart into contact with that influence by which the love of gratitude is awakened. The love of God to us, if it is not believed, will exert no more power over our affections than if it were a nonentity. They are the preachers of faith, then, who alone deal out to their hearers, the elementary and pervading spirit of the Christian morality. And the men who have been stigmatized as the enemies of good works, are the very men who are most sedulously employed in depositing within you, that good seed which has its fruit unto holiness. We are far from asserting, that the agency of grace is not concerned, in every step of that process, by which a sinner is conducted from the outset of his conversion to the state of being perfect, and complete in the whole will of God. But there is a harmony between the processes of grace and of nature; and in the same manner, as in human society, the actual conviction of a neighbour's good-will to me, takes the precedency in point of order of any returning movement of gratitude on my part; so, in the great concerns of our fellowship with God, my belief that he loves me, is an event prior and preparatory to the event of my loving him. So that the primary obstacle to the love of God is not the want of human gratitude, but the want of human faith.

The reason why man is not excited to the love of God by the revelation of God's love to him, is just because he does not believe that revelation. This is the barrier which lies between the guilty and their offended Lawgiver. It is not the ingratitude of man, but the incredulity of man, that needs, in the first instance, to be overcome. It is the sullenness, and the hardness, and the obstinacy of unbelief which stands as a gate of iron, between him and his enlargement. Could the kindness of God, in Christ Jesus, be seen by him, the softening of a kindness back again, would be felt by him. And let us cease to wonder, then, at the preachers of the gospel, when they lay upon belief all the stress of a fundamental operation;—when they lavish so much of their strength on the establishment of a principle, which is not only initial, but indispensable; when they try so strenuously to charm that into existence, without which all the elements of a spiritual obedience are in a state of dormancy or of death;—when they labour at the only practicable way by which the heart of a sinner can be touched, and attracted towards God;—when they try so repeatedly to hold and to fasten him by that link which God himself hath put into their hands—and bring the mighty principle to bear upon their hearers, which any one of us may exemplify upon the poorest, and by which both HOWARD and FRY have tried with success, to soften and to reclaim the most worthless of mankind.

This also suggests a practical direction to Christians, for keeping themselves in the love of God. They must keep themselves in the habit, and in the exercise of faith. They must hold fast that conviction in their minds, the presence of which is indispensable to the keeping of that affection in their hearts. This is one of the methods recommended by the Apostle Jude, when he tells his disciples to build themselves up on their most holy faith. This direction to you is both intelligible and practicable. Keep in view the truths which you have learned. Cherish that belief of them which you already possess. Recall them to your thoughts, and, in general, they will not come alone, but they will come accompanied by their own power, and their own evidence. You may as well think of maintaining a steadfast attachment to your friend, after you have expunged from your memory all the demonstrations of kindness he ever bestowed upon you, as think of keeping your heart in the love of God, after the thoughts and contemplations of the gospel have fled from it. It is just by holding these fast, and by building yourself up on their firm certainty, that you preserve this affection. Any man, versant in the matters of experimental religion, knows well what it is when a blight and a barrenness come over the mind, and when, under the power of such a visitation, it loses all sensibility towards God. There is at that time a hiding of his countenance, and you lose your hold of the manifestation of that love wherewith God loved the world, even when he sent his only begotten Son into it, that we might live through him. You will recover a right frame, when you recover your hold of this consideration. If you want to recall the strayed affection to your heart—recall to your mind the departed object of contemplation. If you want to reinstate the principle of love in your bosom—reinstate faith, and it will work by love. It is got at through the medium of believing, and trusting;—nor do we know a more summary, and, at the same time, a more likely direction for living a life of holy and heavenly affection, than that you should live a life of faith.

SERMON XI.

The Affection of Moral Esteem towards God.

"One thing have I desired of the Lord, that will I seek after; that I may dwell in the house of the Lord all the days of my life, to behold the beauty of the Lord, and to inquire in his temple."—*Psalm* xxvii. 4.

In our last discourse we adverted to the effect of a certain theological speculation about love, in darkening the freeness of the gospel, and intercepting the direct influence of its overtures and its calls on the mind of an inquirer. Ere we can conceive the love of gratitude towards another, we must see in him the love of kindness towards us; and thus, by those who have failed to distinguish between a love of the benefit, and a love of the benefactor, has the virtue of gratitude been resolved into the love of ourselves. And they have thought that there must surely be a purer affection than this, to mark the outset of the great transition from sin unto righteousness; and the one they have specified is the disinterested love of God. They have given to this last affection a place so early, as to distract the attention of an inquirer from that which is primary. The invitation of "come and buy without money, and without price," is not heard by the sinner along with the exaction of loving God for himself,—of loving him on account of his excellences,—of loving him because he is lovely. Let us, therefore, try to ascertain whether even this love of moral esteem is not subordinate to the faith of the gospel; and whether it follows, that because this affection forms so indispensable a part of godliness, faith should, on that account, be deposed from the place of antecedency which belongs to it.

And here let it be most readily and most abundantly conceded, that we are not perfect and complete in the whole of God's will, till the love of moral esteem be in us, as well as the love of gratitude,—till that principle, of which, by nature, we are utterly destitute, be made to arise in our hearts, and to have there a thorough establishment, and operation,—till we love God, not merely on account of his love to our persons, but on account of the glory, and the residing excellence, which meet the eye of the spiritual beholder, upon his own character. We are not preparing for heaven,—we shall be utterly incapable of sharing in the noblest of its enjoyments,—we shall not feel ourselves surrounded by an element of congeniality in paradise,—there will be no happiness for us, even in the neighbourhood of the throne of God, and with the moral lustre of the Godhead made visible to our eyes, if we are strangers to the emotion of loving God for himself,—if additional altogether, to the consideration that God is looking with complacency upon me, I do not feel touched and attracted by the beauties of his character, when I look with the eye of contemplation towards him. I am without the most essential of all moral accomplishments in myself, if I am without the esteem of moral accomplishments in another; and if my heart be of such a constitution that nothing in the character of God can draw my admiration, or my regard, to him—then, though admitted within the portals of the city which hath foundations, and removed from the torments of hell, I am utterly unfit for the joys and the exercises of heaven. I may spend an eternity of exemption from pain, but without one rapture of positive felicity to brighten it. Heaven, in fact, would be a wilderness to my heart; and, in the midst of its acclaiming throng would I droop, and be in heaviness under a sense of perpetual dissolution.

And let this convince us of the mighty transition that must be described by the men of this world, ere they are meet for the other world of the spirits of just men made perfect. It is not speaking of this transition, in terms too great and too lofty, to say, that they must be born again, and made new creatures, and called out of darkness into a light that is marvellous. The truth is, that out of the pale of vital Christianity, there is not to be found among all the varieties of taste, and appetite, and sentimental admiration, any love for God as he is,—any relish for the holiness of his character,—any echoing testimony, in the bosom of alienated man, to what is graceful, or to what is venerable in the character of the Deity. He may be feelingly alive to the beauties of what is seen, and what is sensible. The scenery of external nature may charm him. The sublimities of a surrounding materialism may kindle and dilate him with images of grandeur. Even the moralities of a fellow-creature may engage him; and these, with the works of genius, may fascinate him into an idolatrous veneration of human power, or of human virtue. But while he thus luxuriates and delights himself with the forms of derived excellence, there is no sensibility in his heart towards God. He rather prefers to keep by the things that are made, and, surrounded by them, to bury himself into a forgetfulness of his Maker. He is most in his element, when in feeling, or in employment, he is most at a distance from God. There is a coldness, or a hatred, or a terror, which mixes up with all his contemplations of the Deity; and gives to his mind a kind of sensitive recoil from the very thought of him. He would like to live always in the world, and be content with such felicity as it can give, and cares not, could he only get what his heart is set upon here, and be permitted to enjoy it for ever, though he had no sight of God, and no fellowship with him through eternity. The event to which, of all others, he looks forward with the most revolting sense of aversion and dismay, is that event which is to bring him into a nearer contact with God,—which is to dissolve his present close relationship with the creature, and to conduct his disembodied spirit into the immediate presence of the Creator. There is nothing in death, in grim, odious, terrific death, that he less desires, or is more afraid of, than a nearer manifestation of the Deity. The world, in truth, the warm and the well known world, is his home; and the men who live in it, and are as regardless of the Divinity as himself, form the whole of his companionship. Were it not for the fear of hell, he would shrink from heaven as a dull and melancholy exile. All its songs of glory to him who sitteth on the throne, would be to his heart a burden and a weariness;—and thus it is, that the foundation of every natural man has its place in that perishable earth, from which death will soon carry him away, and which the fiery indignation of God will at length burn up; and as to the being who endureth for ever, and with whom alone he has to do, he sees in him no form nor comeliness, nor no beauty that he should desire him.

Now, is not this due to the darkness of nature, as well as to the depravity of nature? There is in our diseased constitution, a spiritual blindness to the excellences of the Godhead, as well as a spiritual disrelish for them. The truth is, that these two elements go together in the sad progress of human degeneracy. Man liked not to retain God in his knowledge, and God gave him over to a reprobate mind; and again, man walking in vanity, and an enemy to God by wicked works, had his understanding darkened, and was visited with ignorance, and blindness of heart. We do not apprehend God, and therefore it is that we must be renewed in the knowledge of him, ere we can be formed again to the love of him. The natural man can no more admire the Deity through the obscurities in which he is shrouded, than he can admire a landscape which he never saw, and which at the time of his approach to it, is wrapped in the gloom of midnight. He can no more, with every effort to stir up his faculties to lay hold of him, catch an endearing view of the Deity, than his eye can by straining, penetrate its way through a darkened firmament, to the features of that material loveliness which lies before him, and around him. It must be lighted up to him, ere he can love it, or enjoy it, and tell us what the degree of his affection for the scenery would be, if instead of being lighted up by the peaceful approach of a summer morn, it were to blaze into sudden visibility, with all its cultivation and cottages, by the fires of a bursting volcano. Tell us, if all the glory and gracefulness of the landscape which had thus started into view, would charm the beholder for a moment, from the terrors of his coming destruction? Tell us, if it is possible for a sentient being to admit another thought in such circumstances as these, than the thought of his own preservation. O would not the sentiment of fear about himself, cast out every sentiment of love for all that he now saw, and were he only safe could look upon with ecstacy?—and let the beauty be as exquisite as it may, would not all the power and pleasure of its enchantments fly away from his bosom, were it only seen through the glowing fervency of elements that threatened to destroy him?

Let us now conceive, that through that thick spiritual darkness by which every child of nature is encompassed, there was forced upon him a view of the countenance of the Deity,—that the perfections of God were made visible,—and that the character on which the angels of paradise gaze with delight, because they there behold all the lineaments of moral grandeur, and moral loveliness, were placed before the eye of his mind, in bright and convincing manifestation. It is very true, that on what he would be thus made to see, all that is fair and magnificent are assembled,—that whatever of greatness, or whatever of beauty can be found in creation, is but a faint and shadowy transcript of that original substantial excellence, which resides in the conceptions of him who is the fountain of being,—that all the pleasing of goodness, and all the venerable of worth, and all the sovereign command of moral dignity meet and are realised on the person of God,—that through the whole range of universal existence there cannot be devised a single feature of excellence which does not serve to enrich the character of him who sustains all things, and who originated all things. No wonder that the pure eye of an angel takes in such fulness of pleasure from a contemplation so ravishing. But let all this burst upon the eye of a sinner, and let the truth and the righteousness of God out of Christ stand before it in visible array, along with the other glories of character which belong to him. The love of moral esteem, you may say, ought to arise in his bosom;—but it cannot. The affection is in such circumstances impossible. The man is in terror. And he can no more look with complacency upon his God, than he can delight himself with the fair forms of a landscape, opened to his view by the flashes of an impending volcano. He cannot draw an emotion so sweet and delightful as love, from the view of that countenance on which he beholds a purpose of vengeance against himself, as one of the children of iniquity. The fear which hath torment casteth out this affection altogether. There is positively no room for it within the bosom of a sentient being, along with the dread and the alarm by which he is agitated. It is this which explains the recoil of his sinful nature from the thought of God. The sense of guilt comes into his heart, and the terrors and the agitations of guilt come along with it. It is because he sees the justice of God frowning upon him, and the truth of God pledged to the execution of its threatenings against him, and the holiness of God which cannot look upon him without abhorrence, and all the sacred attributes of a nature that is jealous, and unchangeable, leagued against him for his everlasting destruction. He cannot love the Being, with the very idea of whom there is mixed up a sense of danger, and a dread of condemnation, and all the images of a wretched eternity. We cannot love God, so long as we look upon him as an enemy armed to destroy us. Ere we love him, we must be made to feel the security, and the enlargement of one who knows himself to be safe. Let him take his rod away from me, and let not his fear terrify me,—and then may I love him and not fear him; but it is not so with me.

But let him who commanded the light to shine out of darkness, shine in our hearts to give us the light of the knowledge of his own glory, in the face of Jesus Christ,—let us only look upon him as God in Christ reconciling the world unto himself, and not imputing unto them their trespasses,—let him without expunging the characters of truth and majesty, from that one aspect of perfect excellence which belongs to him,—let him in his own unsearchable wisdom devise a way by which he can both bring them out in the eye of sinners with brighter illustration, and make these sinners feel that they are safe;—let him lift off from the men of this guilty world, the burden of his violated law, and cause it to be borne by another who can magnify that law, and make it honourable,—let him publish a full release from all its penalties, but in such a way, as that the truth which proclaimed them, and the justice which should execute them, shall remain untainted under the dispensation of mercy,—let him instead of awaking the sword of vengeance against us, awake it against a sufferer of such worth and such dignity, that his blood shall be the atonement of a world, and by pouring out his soul unto death, he shall make the pardon of the transgressor meet, and be at one with the everlasting righteousness of God,—in a word, instead of the character of God being lighted up to the eye of the sinner, by the fire of his own indignation, let it through the demonstration of the Spirit be illustrated, and shone upon, by the mild, but peaceful light of the Sun of righteousness, and then may the sinner look in peace and safety on the manifested character of the Godhead. Delivered from the burden of his fears, he may now open his whole heart to the influences of affection. And that love of moral esteem, which before the entrance of the faith of the gospel, the sense of condemnation was sure to scare away, is now free to take its place beside the love of gratitude, and to arise along with it in the offering of one spiritual sacrifice to a reconciled Father.

Thus, then, it would appear, that the love of moral esteem is in every way as much posterior, and subordinate to faith, as is the love of gratitude. That we may be able to love God, either according to the one or the other of its modifications, we must *first* know that God loved us. We cannot harbour this affection in any one shape whatever, so long as there is the suspicion, and the dread of a yet unsettled controversy between us and God. Peace with our offended Lawgiver, is not the fruit of our love, but of our faith;—and faith, if it be a reality, and not a semblance, worketh by love. We have peace with God through Jesus Christ our Lord. And we love much when we know, and believe, that our sins are forgiven us.

God did not wait for any returning affection on the part of a guilty world, ere he felt an affection for it himself. At that period when he so loved the world, as to send his only begotten Son into it,—did it exhibit the spectacle of an immense prisonhouse of depravity. Among the men of it, there was friendship one for another, but there was one unalleviated character of enmity against God. Measuring themselves by themselves, there was often a high mutual esteem for such accomplishments as were in demand for the good of society;—but that which is highly esteemed among men, is in God's sight an abomination; and when brought to the measure of that universal righteous which forms the standard and rule of Heaven's government, was it found that our species had through all its generations broken off from their allegiance, and stood at as wide a distance from the obedient, and unfallen creation, as does a colony of convicts, from the country which has cast them out of its borders. And it was at such a time, when the world liked not to retain God in their knowledge,—when all flesh had corrupted their ways,—when there was none seeking after God,—when there was not the thought, or the wish, of a movement to him back again, that he looked with pity on our fallen race, and in the fulness of time, sent his Son into the world to seek and to save us.

And the same is true of every individual to whom the overtures of reconciliation are proposed. God does not wait for any change of affection in our heart, ere we accept of pardon at his hands. But he asks one and all of us now to accept of pardon, and to submit our heart and character to the influences of that grace which he is ready to bestow upon us. In the gospel he proclaims a pardon ready made for you,—a deed of amnesty which he is even now stretching out for your acceptance, a preventing offer of mercy, of which, if you believe the reality, you will feel that he is your friend, and in which feeling you will not be disappointed. He does not expect from you the love of gratitude, till you have known and believed the great things that he hath done for you. But he expects from you the offering of an homage to his truth. He does not expect from you the love of moral esteem, till, released from the terror of having him for your enemy, you may contemplate with all the tranquil calmness of conscious safety, the glories and the graces of his manifested character. But he expects from you faith in his declaration, that he is not your enemy,—that he has no pleasure in your death,—that in Christ he is beseeching you to be reconciled,—and stretching out to you the arms of invitation.

The first matter on hand, then, between God and sinners, in the work of making reconciliation, is, that they believe in him. It is, that the tidings of great joy shall fall upon them with credit and acceptance. It is, that they count the sayings of the word of this life to be faithful sayings. It is, that they put faith in the record which God hath given of his Son, which if they do, they will believe that God hath given them eternal life, and that this life is in his Son.

There is a certain speculation about the disinterested love of God, which has served to darken and to embarrass this process. It has cast an unmerited stigma on the love of gratitude. But its worst effect, by far, is, that it has impeded the freeness of the overtures of the gospel. It has perplexed the outset of many an inquirer. It has made him search in his own mind for the evidences of an affection which he never can meet with, till he embraces the offers, and relies upon the promises of the New Testament. It has deposed faith from that post of presiding supremacy which belongs to it, and shifted from its place that great principle on which both the love of gratitude and the love of moral esteem are suspended.

Let us cease to wonder, then, why faith occupies so much the station of a preliminary in the New Testament. It is the great starting point, as it were, of Christian discipleship. Grant but this principle, and love, with all the vigour, and all the alacrity which it gives to obedience, will emerge from its operation. There is no other way, in fact, of charming love into existence; and the gratitude which devotes me to the service of a reconciled God, and the love of his character, which makes me meet for the enjoyment of him in heaven, can only arise in my bosom after I have believed.

Let this consideration shut you up unto the faith. Let it exalt in your estimation, the mighty importance of a principle, without which there can neither be any sanctification here, nor any salvation hereafter. Think it not enough that you import it into your mind as a bare existence. Know what it is to put it into habitual exercise, to dwell upon the truths which it embraces, and to submit, in feeling and practice, to their genuine operation. This is the only way in which you can ever live a life of faith on the Son of God,—or live by the power of a world to come,—or keep yourselves in the love of God, seeing that it is only when you know and believe that God first loved you, that you can be made to love him.

In the progress of these observations, a few thoughts have occurred, which we trust may be deemed of sufficient importance to be brought forward,—and which we bring forward now, as supplementary to the whole argument.

It will have been remarked, that we do not consider man as altogether incapable of the love of moral esteem towards any being whatever. There are certain virtues of character which do call forth the admiration and the tenderness, even of our diseased nature, when they reside somewhere else than in the person of the Deity. Let our depravity be what it may, it were in the face of all observation to affirm, that man does not love the truth rather than falsehood, and compassion rather than cruelty, in a fellow-man,—and the interesting question comes to be, how is it that these qualities appear to lose all the force which naturally belongs to them, of attracting our regard, so as to awaken no such sentiment towards God, though they be exemplified by him, in a degree that is infinite?

It will help us, in part, to resolve this question, if we conceive of our man of moral virtues, that his very truth, and justice, and compassion, lead him, in the defence of wronged or calumniated innocence, to turn the whole force of his indignation on the head of an oppressor; and then think of the feeling which will arise, of consequence, in the heart of the latter. It will be a feeling of hatred and antipathy. And yet we do not see far into the secrecies of the human constitution, if we do not perceive, that, in perfect consistency with this feeling of personal dislike to the man of virtue, who is hostile to him, there may exist, even in his vitiated soul, the love of moral esteem towards virtue residing in some other quarter, or exemplified by some other individual. Instead of this virtue being realized on the person of one who is an enemy to myself, let it be offered by description to my notice, in the person of one who lives in a distant country, or who lived in a distant age, and let the thought of my particular adversary be not offensively suggested to my mind by such a contemplation,—and I, with all those depravities which have provoked the resentment of my upright neighbour against me, and have called forth in my heart a corresponding hatred towards him, will offer the homage of my regard and reverence towards the picture of moral excellence, that is thus set before me. This may look an anomalous exhibition of our nature; but it certainly is not more so, than the well-known fact of a slave proprietor, at one time wreaking his caprice and his cruelty on the living men who are around him, and at another weeping, in all the softness of pathetic emotion, over the distresses of a fictitious narrative. Distress in one quarter may move our pity. Distress in another may be inflicted by our own hand, to glut our vindictive propensities. Worth in the person of one who is indifferent, and still more of one who is friendly, may call forth our warm and honest acknowledgments. Worth in the person of another, the very principles of whose character have moved him to irritate our pride, or to wound our selfishness, may turn him into the object of our most passionate, determined, and unrelenting hostility.

And thus it is, that I may have a natural taste for several of the virtues which enter into the Godhead, and at the same time, may have a hatred towards the person of the Godhead.—This natural taste may be regarded by some, as a predisposing element in my heart towards the love of God; but so long as I view him armed in righteousness to destroy me, will this as effectually repress the embryo affection, as if still it were fast slumbering in the depths of nonentity. It is willingly admitted, that there are certain partial sketches of the character of the Deity, which, if offered to our notice, in a state of separation from his anger against us, the children of disobedience, would kindle in our bosoms a feeling of tasteful admiration. But the dread, or the suspicion of his anger absorbs this feeling altogether; and however much we may bear the semblance of love for his character, when we look to certain traits of it in a detached and broken exhibition,—yet this is perfectly consistent with the fact, that the natural mind hates the person of the Deity,—that the natural mind is enmity against God. And this ought to convince us, that even though there should be predisposing elements of love to him for his worth, it is still indispensable, in order to change our hatred into affection, that we should look upon God as having ceased from his anger, or that we should see him arrayed in all the tenderness of offered and inviting friendship. There is a spell by which these elements are fastened, and which can never be done away, till God woo me to friendship and confidence, by an exhibition of good-will.

Faith in the cross of Christ, is the primary step of this approximation. To call for a disinterested affection towards God, from one who looks upon God as an adversary, and that even though there should be in his bosom the undeveloped seeds of regard to the worth or character of the Supreme, is to make a demand on a sentient being, which, by his very constitution, he is unable to meet or to satisfy. And is not this demand still more preposterous, when it comes from a quarter where the depravity of man is held to be so entire, that not one latent or predisposing element towards the love of God is ascribed to him? Is it not a still vainer expectation to think, in such hopeless circumstances as these, that ere man seizes the gift of redemption, he shall import into his character the grace of a pure and spiritual affection; that with the terror of his bosom yet unpacified, and the countenance of God upon him as unrelenting as ever, there shall arise, in the midst of all this agitation, a love to that Being, the very thought of whom brings a sense of insecurity along with it; or that a guilty creature, who, even if he had in a state of dormancy within him the principles of moral regard to the Divinity, could not, under the burden of wrath still unappeased, charm these principles out of the state of their inaction,—that he, even were he utterly destitute of these principles should be able, under this burden, to charm them out of the state of non-existence?

And this, by the way, may serve to show the whole amount of that tasteful sentimentalism, in virtue of which, a transient but treacherous and hollow regard towards the Divinity, may be detected in the hearts of those who nauseate the whole spirit and contents of the Gospel. They admit into their contemplation only as much of the character of God, as may serve to make out a tender or an engaging exhibition of him. They may leave entire the groundwork of his natural attributes; but, in every survey they take of the moral complexion of the Godhead, they refuse to look to all his moral attributes put together, and only fasten their regard upon one of them, even the attribute of indulgence. They cannot endure the view of his whole character; and should this view ever intrude itself, it puts to flight all the pathos and elegance of mere natural piety. Truth, as directed against themselves; holiness, as refusing to dwell in peaceful or approving fellowship with themselves; justice, as committed to a sentence of severe and inflexible retribution upon themselves,—all these are out of their contemplation at that moment, when the votaries of a poetical theism feel towards their imagined deity an evanescent glow of affection or reverence. But truth and conscience are ever meddling with this enjoyment; and piety resting on so frail and partial a foundation, never can attain an habitual ascendency over the character; and what at the best is fictitious, does not, and ought not, to have more than a rare and little hour of emotion given to it; and this may explain how it is, that with the very same individual, there may be both an occasional recurrence of devotional feeling, and a life of rooted and practical ungodliness. An illusory representation of God will no more draw away our affections from the world, or engage us in the solid and experimental business of obedience to its Maker, than the flippancy of a novel will practically influence the habits of nature, or of society. And thus it is, that the religion which is apart from Christianity, falls as far short of true religion, as the humanity we have just quoted, falls short of true humanity.

But to return. We have already said, that even though there did exist in the heart of man a native regard to certain ingredients of worth in the character of the Divinity, a previous exhibition of good will is still essential, that the person of the Divinity may be endeared to him. And the argument for such a priority becomes much stronger, when it is made out, on a farther attention to this matter, that there is, in fact, no such native or predisposing regard. For, though it be true, that there are certain moral virtues, which, when realized upon man, draw towards them the love and the reverence even of our depraved nature, and which, when heightened into perfection upon God, should therefore, it might be conceived, obtain from nature, if placed in favourable circumstances, the homage of a love still more tender, and of a reverence still more profound;—yet there is one great and comprehensive quality by which all the moral attributes of the Godhead are pervaded, and for which we can detect no native and no kindred principle of attachment whatever, in the constitution of our species. We allude to the holiness of the Godhead. Were we asked to define this holiness, we should feel that we were not giving to the term its full significancy, by saying, that it merely consisted in the absolute perfection of all the moral virtues of the Divinity. It is a term which, in the appropriate force of it, denotes contrast or separation. It was for this reason assigned to the vessels of the temple, and just because they were set apart from common use. To have made them common, would have been to make them unclean, or unholy. To have turned them to any ordinary or household purposes, would have been to inflict upon them such a touch of profanation, that their holiness would have departed from them. Had there been a full and perfect sense of God in every house, and in every heart,—had the presence of the Divinity been equally felt by his creatures at all times, and in all places,—had the will of the Divinity held as presiding an influence over the every-day doings, as over the services of the solemn and extraordinary occasion,—then there might have been no temple, and no ritual observation, and, of consequence, no room for such an application of the term holiness. A thing is not consecrated by being set apart from that which is equally pure and sacred with itself; and did there obtain an equal and universal purity throughout the whole system of nature, there could be no need for separation. In these circumstances, there would have been no contrast, and, therefore, no demand for such a term as that of holiness.

This may serve to illustrate the force and import of the term, as applied to the character of God. It does not signify the moral perfection of his character, taken absolutely. It signifies this perfection in relation to its opposite. When we look to the holiness of the divine character, we look to it in its aspect of lofty separation from all that can either taint or debase it. We look to its irreconcilable variance with sin. We look to the inaccessible height at which it stands above all the possible acquirements of created nature, insomuch, that he who possesses it, charges even his angels with folly: and when created nature is not only imperfect, but sinful, when we look to the recoil of the Divinity from all contact, and from all approximation, we think of the purer eyes than can behold iniquity, and of the presence so sacred, that evil cannot dwell with it. We think of that sanctuary into which there cannot enter any thing that defileth, or that maketh a lie,—a sanctuary guarded by all the jealousies of the Divine nature, and so repugnant to the approach of pollution, that if it offer to draw nigh, the fire of a consuming indignation will either check, or will destroy it.

Now, were the whole severity of this attribute directed against the violations of social kindness, and social equity, we would admit that there was a ready coalescence with it in the principles of our natural constitution. But when it searches into the character of the most urgent affections of nature, and there detects the very essence of sinfulness;—when it sits in judgment over the preference given by every child of Adam to the creature, rather than the Creator, and who holds this in righteous abomination;—when it looks through a society of human beings, and pronounces, in spite of all the justice by which its interests are guarded, and of all the humanity by which its ills are softened, or done away, that, wholly given over to the enjoyment of the world, it is wholly immersed in the guilt of an idolatry, by which the jealousies of the supreme and spiritual God are provoked to the uttermost; —when holiness is thus seen, not merely in its antipathy to crime, which is occasional and rare, but in its antipathy to an affection, the rooted obstinacy of which, and the engrossing power of which, are universal,— then so far from the coalescence of approving nature, do we behold the revolt of pained and irritated nature. It no more follows, because man loathes the cruelty or the injustice of his fellow-man, that he therefore carries in his heart a predisposing element of regard for the essential character of God, than it follows, because a man would sicken with disgust at the atrocities of a prison-house, that he therefore feels his element and his joy to be in the humble piety of a conventicle. A high-minded and an honourable merchant finds room in his bosom for the love both of truth and of the world. Yet the one is an attribute of God, while the love of the other is opposite to the love of God. "If any man love the world," says an apostle, "the love of the Father is not in him." He may like the transcript of truth, and of many other virtues on the face of the creature, but he likes not the Creator. He can gaze, and that even with rapture on the partial and imperfect sketches of the unfinished copy, but he shrinks from the view of the entire original. He can hold the intercourse of wistful thoughts, and fervent aspiration, the absent object of his earthly regard, but he has neither taste nor capacity for communion with his Father in heaven. "Holy, holy, holy, Lord God Almighty," is the anthem of the celestial, but theirs is a delight which he cannot share in. And as surely as his body would need to be transformed, ere it could cease to have pain amid the agonies of hell,—so surely would his mind need to be transformed, ere it ceased to feel a confinement, and an irksomeness amid the halleluiahs of paradise.

Even though man, then, had in his heart a nascent affection for the character of God, this would be restrained from passing onwards to an affection for his person, by a sense of guilt, and the consequent dread of God as an enemy. Nor could the love of God be inserted in his bosom, till by faith in the expiation of the gospel, that which letteth was taken out of the way. But still more, if, in conformity to our present argument, there be no such nascent affection for the Divine character, is it hopeless to attempt the establishment of love antecedently to belief, or that attachment should take possession of the heart, ere fear takes its departure away from it. Even if by the working of some power unknown in the human constitution, or by some effort, the success of which has never yet, in a single instance, been experienced, there could be made to arise in the soul, the love of holiness, previous to the act of trusting in the offered Saviour,—a terror at God, which, in the absence of this trust, is the instinctive and universal feeling of nature, would just as effectually repress the love of holiness, as it does the love of truth, or of compassion, or of justice, from carrying us onwards to a regard for the person of the Godhead. To put the love of God's character into a heart not yet brought into enlargement by the faith of the gospel, would just be to put it into a prison-hold, and there to chain it down to a fruitlessness and inactivity, where it would be wholly unproductive of love to God himself. Confidence must take the precedency of this love, even in a bosom already furnished with the preparatory elements of affection; and how much more essential then is it, that it should take the precedency in a bosom, where these elements are altogether wanting? Faith is thus more strongly evinced to be a thing of prior and indispensable necessity. Without it, even the seed of any precious affection for the Godhead, stifled in embryo, would not blow into luxuriance. And if our nature be such a wilderness that no seed is there,—if the thing wanted be the germination of a new principle, and not the developement of an old,—if it be by a creative and not by a mere fostering process, that we are transformed into a meetness for heaven,—if the agency that is made to bear upon the human soul, must have a power to regenerate as well as to repair,—and if the promise of this agency be given only to those who believe, then let us no more linger, or be bewildered, in that abyss of helplessness from which faith alone can extricate the inquirer,—let us no longer arrest the eye of confidence from that demonstration of good will, which is held out to the most widely alienated of sinners,—but hasten to place ourselves, even now, on that foundation of trust, where alone we are made the workmanship of God in Christ Jesus, and the love of God is shed abroad in our hearts by the Holy Ghost.

"Destroy this temple," says the Saviour, "and I will raise it up again in three days."

It is there alone that we can behold the beauty of the lord and be safe. This place of greatest security, is also the place of chiefest glory. It is when admitted into this greater and more perfect tabernacle, that we can look on majesty without terror, and on holiness without an overwhelming sense of condemnation. The sinner encircled in mercy looks in tranquil contemplation on all that is awful and venerable in the character of the Godhead,—and never do truth, and righteousness, and purity, appear in loftier exhibition before him, than, when withheld from his own person, he sees the whole burden of their avenging laid upon the head of the great Sacrifice.

"One thing have I desired of the Lord," says the Psalmist, "that I may dwell in the courts of the Lord, all the days of my life, to behold the beauty of the Lord, and to enquire in his temple." It is not till we are within the portals of the place of refuge that this desire can obtain its fulfilment. Selfishness may have originated the movement which took us there. The fear of the coming wrath may have lent celerity to our footsteps. A joyful sense of deliverance may have been felt, ere the glories of the divine character were seen in bright and convincing manifestation. The love of gratitude may have kindled within us,—and, with the Psalmist, we may have to seek, and to inquire, and to have daily exercise and meditation, ere the love of moral esteem has attained the place of ascendency which belongs to it. Nevertheless, the chief end of man is to glorify God, and to enjoy him for ever. This is the real destination of every individual who is redeemed from among men. This should be the main object of all his prayers, and all his preparations. It is this which fits him for the company of heaven; and unless there be a growing taste for God, in the glories of his excellency,—for God, in the beauties of his holiness,—there is no ripening, and no perfecting, for the mansions of immortality. Though you have to combat, then, with the sluggishness of sense, and with the real aversion of nature to every spiritual exercise, you must attempt, and stenuously cultivate the habit of communion with God. And as no man knoweth the Father save the Son reveal him, and as it is by the Spirit that Christ gives light to those who believe in him;—for the attainment of this great moral and spiritual accomplishment, do what the Apostle directs you, when he says, "Keep yourselves in the love of God, by praying in the Holy Ghost." Your first endeavours may be feeble, and fatiguing, and fruitless. But God will not despise the day of small things,—nor will the light of his countenance be always withheld from those who aspire after it,—nor will the soul that thirsts after God, be left for ever unsatisfied,—and the life and peace of being spiritually minded, will come in rich experience to his feelings,—and the whole habit of his tastes and enjoyments, will be in a diametric opposition to that of the children of the world, —God being the habitation to which he resorts continually,—God being the strength of his heart, and his portion for evermore.

SERMON XII.

The Emptiness of Natural Virtue.

"But I know you, that ye have not the love of God in you."—*John* v. 24.

WHEN it is said, in a former verse of the gospel, that Jesus knew what was in man, we feel, that it is a tribute of acknowledgment, rendered to his superior insight into the secrecies of our constitution. It was not the mere faculty of perceiving what lay before him, that was ascribed to him by the Evangelist. It was the faculty of perceiving what lay disguised under a semblance, that would have imposed on the understanding of other men. It was the faculty of detecting. It was a discerning of the spirit, and that not through the transparency of such unequivocal symptoms, as brought its character clearly home to the view of the observer. But it was a discerning of the spirit, as it lay wrapt in what, to an ordinary spectator, was a thick and impenetrable hiding place. It was a discovery then of the real posture and habitude of the soul. It was a searching of it out, through all the recesses of duplicity, winding and counter winding in such a way as to elude altogether the eye of common acquaintanceship. It was the assigning to it of one attribute, at the time when it wore the guise of another attribute,—of utter antipathy to the nature and design of his mission, at the very time that multitudes were drawn around him by the fame of his miracles,—of utter indifference about God, at the very time that they zealously asserted the sanctity of his sabbaths, and resented as blasphemous whatever they felt to be an usurpation of the greatness which belonged to him only.

It was in the exercise of this faculty, that

Jesus came forward with the utterance of our text. The Jews, by whom he was surrounded, had charged him with the guilt of profanation, and sought even to avenge it by his death, because he had healed a man on the sabbath day. And their desire of vengeance was still more inflamed, by what they understood to be an assertion, on his part, of equality with God. And yet, under all this appearance, and even with all this reality of a zeal about God, did he who knew what was in man pronounce of these his enemies, that the love of God was not in them. I know you says he,—as if at this instant he had put forth a stretch of penetration, in order to find his way through all the sounds of godliness which he heard, and through all the symptoms of godliness which he saw,—I know that there does not exist within you that principle, which links to God, the whole of God's obedient creation,—I know that you do not love him, and that, therefore, you are utterly in want of that affection, which lies at the root of all real, and of all acceptable godliness.

It is mortifying to the man who possesses many accomplishments of character, to be told, that the greatest and most essential accomplishment of a moral being, is that of which he has no share,—that the principle on which we expatiated in our last discourses does not, in any of its varieties, belong to him,—that, wanting it, he wants not merely obedience to the first and the greatest commandment, which is the love of God, but he wants what may be called the impregnating quality of all acceptable obedience whatever,—the spirit which ought to animate the performance of every other commandment, and without which the most laborious conformity to the law of Heaven, may do no more than impress upon his person the cold and lifeless image of loyalty, while in his mind there is not one of its essential attributes.

We know not a more useful exercise than that of carrying round this conviction amongst all the classes and conditions of humanity. In the days of our Saviour, the pride of the Pharisees stood opposed to such a demonstration; and in our own days, too, there are certain pretensions of worth, and of excellence, which must be disposted, ere we can hope to obtain admittance for the humiliating doctrine of the gospel. For this gospel, it must be observed, proceeds upon the basis, not of a partial, but of an entire and universal depravity among the men of the world. It assimilates all the varieties of the human character into one common condition of guilt, and need, and helplessness. It presumes the existence of such a moral disease in every son and daughter of Adam, as renders the application of the same moral remedy indispensable to them all. The formalists of Judea did not like to be thus grouped with publicans and harlots, under one description of sinfulness. Nor do men of taste, and feeling, and graceful morality, in our present day, readily understand how they should require the same kind of treatment, in the work of preparing them for immortality, with the most glaringly profligate and unrighteous of their neighbourhood. They look to the ostensible marks of distinction between themselves and others;—and what wider distinction, they think, can possibly be assigned, than that which obtains between the upright or the kind-hearted, on the one hand, and the ungenerous or dishonest, on the other? Now, what we propose, in the following discourse, is to lead them to look a little farther,—and then they will see at least one point of similarity between these two classes, the want of one common ingredient with both, and which attaches to each of them a great moral defect, that can only be repaired by one and the same application.

It is well when we can find out an accordancy between the actual exhibition of human nature on the field of experience, and the representation that is given of this nature on the field of revelation. Now, the Bible every where groups the individuals of our species, into two general and distinct classes, and assigns to each of them its appropriate designation. It tells us of the vessels of wrath, and of the vessels of mercy; of the travellers on a narrow path, and on a broad way; of the children of this world, and the children of light; and, lastly, of men who are carnally minded, and men who are spiritually minded. It employs these terms in a meaning so extensive, that by each couplet of them it embraces all individuals. There is no separate number of persons, forming of themselves a neutral class, and standing without the limits of the two others. And were it possible to conceive, that human nature, as it exists at present in the world, were laid in a map before us, you would see no intermediate ground between the two classes which are thus contrasted in the Bible,—but these thrown into two distinct regions, with one clear and vigorous line of demarcation between them.

We often read of this line, and we often read of the transition from the one to the other side of it. But there is no trace of any middle department to be met with in the New Testament. The alternative has only two terms, and ours must be the one or the other of them. And as surely as a day is coming, when all the men of our assembled world shall be found on the right or on the left hand of the throne of judgment—so surely do the carnal and the spiritual regions of human nature, stand apart from each other; and all the men who are now living on the surface of the world, are to be found on the right, or on the wrong side, of the line of demarcation.

We cannot conceive, then, a question of mightier interest, than the situation of this line,—a line which takes its own steady and unfaltering way through the thousand varieties of character that exist in the world; and which reduces them all to two great, and awfully important divisions. It marks off one part of the species from the other. We are quite aware that the terms which are employed to characterize the two sets are extremely unfashionable; and, what is more, are painfully offensive to many a mind, whose taste, and whose habits, have not yet been brought under the overpowering controul of God's own message expressed in God's own language. They are such terms as would be rejected with a positive sensation of disgust by many a moralist, and would be thought by many more, to impart the blemish of a most hideous deformity, to his eloquent and philosophical pages. It is curious here to observe how much the Maker of the human mind, and the mere observer of the human mind, differ in their views and representations of the same object. But when told, on the highest of all authority, that to be carnally minded is death, and to be spiritually minded is life and peace, we are compelled to acknowledge with a feeling of earnestness, greater than mere curiosity can inspire, that the application of these terms, is a question of all others the most deeply affecting to the fears and the wishes of humanity.

In the prosecution of this question, let me attempt to bring a succession of characters before you, most of which must have met your own distinct and familiar observation; and of which, while exceedingly various in their complexion, we hope to succeed in convincing you, that the love of God, at least, is not in them. If this can be made out against them, it may be considered as experimentally fixing to which of the two great divisions of humanity they belong. All who love God, may have boldness when they think of the day of judgment, because, like unto God, who himself is love, they will be pronounced meet for the enjoyment, and the fellowship of him through eternity. And they who want this affection, when they die shall be turned into hell. They shall be found to possess that carnal mind which is enmity against God. So that upon the single point of whether they possess this love or not, hinges the question which I have just now started,—a question surely which it were better for every man to decide at the bar of conscience now, ere it comes under the review of that dread tribunal which is to award to him his everlasting habitation.

I. Let us first offer to your notice, a man living in the grossness of animal indulgence,—a man, the field of whose enjoyments is altogether sensual,—and who, therefore, in addition to the charge he brings down upon himself, of directly violating the law of God, is regarded by the admirers of what is tasteful and refined in the human character, as a loathsome object of contemplation. There is something more here than mere wickedness of character to excite the regret or detestation of the godly. There is sordidness of character to excite the disgust of the elegant. And let us just add one feature more to this portrait of deformity. Let us suppose the man in question to have so abandoned himself to the impulses of selfishness, that no feeling and no principle whatever, restrains him from yielding to its temptations,—that to obtain the gratification he is in quest of, he can violate all the decencies, and bid away from him all the tendernesses of our common humanity,—that he has the hardihood to set the terrors of the civil law at defiance,—and that, for the money which ministers to every earthly appetite, he can even go so far, as to steel his heart against the atrocity of a murder. When we have thus set before you, the picture of one feasting on the prey of his inhuman robberies, we have surely brought our description as far down in the scale of character, as it can well be carried. And we have done so, on purpose that you may be at no loss to assign the place which belongs to him. It were a monstrous supposition altogether, that either the love of gratitude, or the love of moral esteem for the Deity, were to be found in the bosom of such a man. He, then, of all others, is not spiritual but carnal; nor do we anticipate a single dissenting voice when we say, that whatever be the doubts and the delusions which may prevail about men of another aspect, the man whose habits and pursuits have now been sketched to you, stands on the wrong side of the line of demarcation.

We are far from saying, that a man of such a character as this is of frequent occurrence in society. We merely set him up as a kind of starting-post, for the future train of our argument. It is a mighty advantage, in every discussion, to have a clear and undisputed outset,—and we trust, that, if thus far we have kept cordially by the side of each other, we shall not cast out by the way, in the progress of our remaining observations.

II. Let us now proceed, then, to detach one offensive feature from the character of him, whom we have thus set before you, as a compound of many abominations. Let us leave entire all his dishonesty, and all his devotedness to the pleasures of sense, but soften and transform his heart to such a degree, that he would recoil from the perpetration of a murder. This is a different portrait from the one which we formerly exhibited. There is in it an instinctive horror at an act of violence, which did not belong to the other;—and the question we have now to put, is, Has the man who owns this improved representation, become, on this single difference, a spiritual man? We answer this question by another. Is the difference that we have now assigned to him, due to the love of God, or to such a principle of loyal subjection to his authority, as this love is sure to engender? You will not call him spiritual from the mere existence of a feeling which would rise spontaneously in his heart, even though the Father of spirits were never thought of. We appeal to your own consciousness of what passes within you, if the heart do not experience the movement of many a constitutional feeling, altogether unaccompanied by any reference of the mind, to the love, or to the character, or even to the existence of God. Are you not quite sensible, that though the idea of a God lay in a state of dormancy for hours and for days together, many of the relentings of nature would, in the meanwhile, remain with you? For the preservation and the order of society, God has been kind enough to implant in the bosom of man, many a natural predilection, and many a natural horror,—of which he feels the operation, and the people of his neighbourhood enjoy the advantage, at the very time that one. and all of them, unmindful of God, are walking in the counsel of their own hearts, and after the sight of their own eyes. He has done the same thing to the inferior animals. He has endowed them with a principle of attachment to their offspring, in virtue of which, they, generally speaking, would recoil from the murder of their young with as determined an abhorrence, as you would do from the murder of a fellow-creature. You would not surely say of the irrational instinct, that because amiable, or useful, or pleasing to contemplate, there is any thing spiritual in the impulse it communicates. Then do not offer a violence both to Scripture and philosophy, by confounding, in the mind of man, principles which are distinct from each other. Do not say, that he is spiritual, merely because he is moving in obedience to his constitutional tendencies. Do not say, that he is not carnal, while all that he has done, or abstained from doing, may be done or abstained from, though he lived without God in the world. And go not to infer, while the pleasures of sense are the idols of his every affection, that because he would shudder to purchase them, at the expence of another's blood, he, on that single account, may be looked on as a spiritual man, and as standing on the right side of the line of demarcation.

III. All this may be looked upon, as too indisputable for argument. And yet it is the very principle which, if carried to its fair extent, and brought faithfully home to the conscience, would serve to convince of ungodliness, the vast majority of this world's generations. If a natural recoil from murder, may be experienced by the bosom, in which there exists no love to God,—why may not this natural recoil be carried still farther, and yet the love of God be just as absent from the bosom as before? There are other dishonesties, of a far less outrageous character, than that by which you would commit an act of depredation; and other cruelties far less enormous, than that by which you would imbrue your hand in another's blood,—which still the generality of men would revolt from constitutionally, and that, too, without the movement of any affection for their God, or even so much as any thought of him. We have only to conceive the softening of a further transformation, to take place on the man with whom we set out at the beginning of our argument; and he may thus become, like the man we read of in the parable, who took comfort to himself in the security, that he had goods laid up for many years, and at the same time is not charged either with violence or dishonesty in the acquirement of them. He is charged with nothing but a devoted attachment to wealth, and to the pleasures which that wealth can purchase. And yet, what an awful reckoning did he come under! He seems to have been just such a man as we can be at no loss to meet with every day in the range of our familiar acquaintances,—enjoying themselves in easy and comfortable abundance; but at an obvious and unquestionable distance from any thing that can be called atrocity of character. There is not one of them, perhaps, who would not recoil from an act of barbarity; and who would not be moved with honest indignation, at the tale of perfidy, or of violence. They live in a placid course of luxury, and good humour; and we are far from charging them with any thing which the world calls monstrous,—when we say, that the Father of spirits is unminded, and unregarded by them, and that the good things of the world are their gods. If it be a vain superfluity of argument to prove, that a man may not be spiritual, and yet be endowed with such a degree of natural tenderness, as to recoil from the perpetration of a murder,—then it is equally indisputable, that a man may not be spiritual, though endowed with such a degree of natural tenderness, as to recoil from many lesser acts of cruelty, or injustice. In other words, he may be a very fair every-day character; and if it be so sure a principle, that a man may not be a murderer, and yet be carnal, then let one and all of you look well to your own security; for it is the very principle which might be employed, to shake the thousands and tens of thousands of ordinary men, out of the security in which they have entrenched themselves.

IV. But to proceed in this work of transformation. Let us now conceive a still more exquisite softening of affection and tenderness, to be thrown over the whole of our imaginary character. We thus make another step, and another departure, from the original specimen. By the first step, the mind is made to feel a kind of revolting, at the atrocity of a murder; and the character ceases to be monstrous. By the second, the mind is made to share in all the common antipathies of our nature, to what is cruel and unfeeling; and it is thus wrought up to the average of character which obtains in society. By the third step the mind is endowed with the warmer and more delicate sympathies of our nature, and thus rises to a more exalted place in the scale of character. It becomes positively amiable. You look to him, who owns all these graceful sensibilities, even as the Saviour looked unto the young man of the gospels, and, like the Saviour, you love him. Who can, in fact, refrain from doing homage to such a lovely exhibition of all that is soothing in humanity; and whether he be employed in mingling his tears, and his charities, with the unfortunate, or in shedding a gentle lustre over the retirement of his own family, even orthodoxy herself, stern and unrelenting as she is conceived to be, cannot find it in her heart to frown upon him. But, feeling is one thing, and truth is another; and when the question is put, Do all these sensibilities, heightened and adorned as they are, on the upper walks of society, constitute a spiritual man?—it is not by a sigh, or an aspiration of tenderness, that we are to answer it. We are put on a cool exercise of the understanding, and we cannot close it against the fact, that all these feelings may exist apart from the love of God, and apart from the religious principle,—that the idea of a God may be expunged from the heart of man, and yet that heart be still the seat of the same constitutional impulses as ever,—that in reference to the realities of the unseen and spiritual world, the mind may be an entire blank, and there, at the same time, be room in it for the play of kindly and benevolent emotions. We commit these truths to your own experience, and if carried faithfully to the conscience, they may chase away another of the delusions which encompass it. There is no fear of me, for I have a feeling heart, is a plea which they put a decisive end to. This feeling heart, if unaccompanied by any sense of God, is no better evidence of a spiritual man, than is the circulation of the blood. We are far from refusing it the homage of our tenderness. We feel a love to it, but we will not make a lie about it. We can make no more of it, than Scripture and experience enable us to do. And, if it be true, that a man's heart may be the habitual seat of kind affections, while an affection for God is habitually away from it, if it be true that no man can be destitute of this affection, and at the same time be a spiritual man,—if it be true, that he who is not spiritual, is carnal, and that the carnally-minded cannot inherit the kingdom of God;—then the necessity lies upon us: he is still in the region and shadow of death; and if he refuse the arguments and invitations of the gospel, calling him over to another region than that which he now occupies, he must just be numbered among those more beauteous wrecks of our fallen nature, which are destined to perish and be forgotten.

V. But let us go still farther. Let us suppose the heart to be furnished, not merely with the finest sensibilities of our nature, but with its most upright and honourable principles. Let us conceive a man whose pulse beats high with the pride of integrity; whose every word carries security along with it; whose faithfulness in the walks of business has stood the test of many fluctuations; who, amid all the varieties of his fortune, has nobly sustained the glories of an untainted character; and whom we see by the salutations of the market-place, to be acknowledged and revered by all, as the most respectable of the citizens. Now, which of the two great regions of human character shall we make him to occupy? This question depends upon another. May all this manly elevation of soul, and of sentiment, stand disunited in the same heart, with the influence of the authority of God, or with that love of God which is the keeping of his commandments? The discerning eye of Hume saw that it could; and he tells us that natural honesty of temper is a better security for the faithfulness of a man's doings, than all the authority of religious principle over him. We deny the assertion; but the distinction between the two principles on which it proceeds, is indisputable. There is a principle of honour, apart in the human mind altogether, from any reference to the realities of a spiritual world. It varies in the intensity of its operation, with different individuals. It has the chance of being more entire, when kept aloof from the temptations of poverty: and therefore it is, that we more frequently meet with it in the upper and middling classes of life. And we can conceive it so strong in its original influence, or so grateful to the possessor from the elevating consciousness which goes along with it, or so nourished by the voice of an applauding world, as to throw all the glories of a romantic chivalry over the character of him, with whom God is as much unthought of, as he is unseen. We are far from refusing our admiration. But we are saying, that the Being who brought this noble specimen of our nature into existence; who fitted his heart for all its high and generous emotions; who threw a theatre around him for the display and exercise of his fine moral accomplishments; who furnished each of his admirers with a heart to appreciate his worth, and a voice to pour into his ear the flattering expression of it;—the Being whose hand upholds and perpetuates the whole of this illustrious exhibition, may all the while be forgotten, and unnoticed as a thing of no consequence. We are merely saying, that the man whose heart is occupied with a sentiment of honour, and is at the same time unoccupied with a sense of Him, who is the first and greatest of spiritual beings, is not a spiritual man. But, if not spiritual, we are told in the Bible, that there are only two terms in the alternative, and he must be carnal: and the God whom he has disregarded in time, will find, that in the praises and enjoyments of time, he has gotten all his reward, and that he owes him no recompense in eternity.

We appeal to the state of the public mind some years ago, on the subject of Africa, as a living exemplification of the whole argument. " Love thy neighbour as thyself," says the Bible; and this precept, coming with all the force of its religious influence upon the hearts of men, who carry their respects to the will of a spiritual and unseen God, have urged them on, and with noble effect, to the abolition of the deadliest mischief that was ever let loose upon the species. And whether we look to the Quakers, who originated the cause, or to him who pioneered the cause, or to him who plead the cause, or to him who has impregnated with such a moral charm, the atmosphere of his country, that no human creature can breathe of its air without taking in the generous inspiration of liberty along with it,—we cannot fail to observe, that one and all of them speak the language, and evince the tastes, and are not ashamed to own their most entire and decided preference for the objects of spiritual men. There is an evident sense of religious duty, which gives the tone of Christianity, and throws the aspect of sacredness over the whole of their doings; and the unbaffled perseverance of the many years they had to struggle with difficulties, and to spend in the weariness of ever recurring disappointments, bears striking proof to the unquenchable energy of the Christian principle within them. But who can deny the large and important contributions which came in upon the cause from other quarters? We hold it quite consistent with the truth of human nature, to aver, that in this enlightened country, other principles may have lent their aid to the cause, and, apart from Christianity altogether, may have sent a commanding influence into the hearts of some of its ablest and most efficient supporters. There is nothing in the presence of Christian principle to quell the impassioned fervour of our desires after right objects; but the absence of Christian principle does not necessarily extinguish this fervour. When we look back to the animating ferment of the British public, on the subject of Africa, we will ever contend, that a feeling of obligation to a spiritual being, was the ingredient which set it a going, and which kept it a going. But who can deny the existence, and the powerful operation of other ingredients? An instinctive horror at cruelty, is a separate and independent attribute of the heart, and sufficient of itself to inspire the deepest tones of that eloquence which sounded in parliament, and issued from the press, and spread an infection over all the provinces of the empire, and mustered around the cause, thousands and tens of thousands of our rallying population, and gave such an energy to the public voice, that all the resisting jealousies and interests of the country were completely overborne;—and hence the interesting spectacle, of carnal and spiritual men lending their respective energies to the accomplishment of one object, and securing, by their success, a higher name for Britain in the world, than all the wisdom of her counsels, and all the pride of her victories can ever achieve for her.

Were it our only aim to carry the acquiescence of the understanding, there might be a danger in affirming, and urging, and illustrating to excess, the position, that we want to establish among you;—and it were, perhaps, better, to limit ourselves to one simple delivery of the argument. But our aim is, if possible, to affect the conscience, and to accomplish this object, not with one, but with many individuals. And when it is reflected, that one developement of the principle may come home more forcibly to some man's experience than another, we must beg to be excused for one recurrence more to a topic, so pregnant of consequence to your everlasting interests. There is a sadly meagre and frivolous conception of human sinfulness, that is prevalent amongst you,—and it goes to foster this delusion, that when we look abroad on the face of society, we must be struck with the diversity of character which obtains among the individuals who compose it. Some there are, who, in the estimation of the world, are execrable for their crimes, but others, who, in the same estimation are illustrious for their virtues. In that general mass of corruption, to which we would reduce our unfortunate species, is there, it may be asked, no solitary example of what is pure, and honourable, and lovely? Do we never meet with the charity which melts at suffering; with the honesty which disdains, and is proudly superior to falsehood; with the active beneficence which gives to others its time and its labour; with the modesty which shrinks from notice, and gives all its sweetness to retirement; with the gentleness which breathes peace to all, and throws a beautiful lustre over the walks of domestic society? If we find these virtues to be sometimes exhibited, is not this an argument against the doctrine of such an entire, and unmitigated depravity, as we have been contending for? Will it not serve to redeem humanity from that sweeping, indiscriminate charge of corruption, which is so often advanced against it, in all the pride and intolerance of orthodoxy? What better evidence can be given of our love to God, than our adherence to his law? And are not the virtues which we have just now specified, part of that law? Are not they the very virtues which his authority requires of us, and which imparts such a charm to the morality of the New Testament?

Now, it carries us at once to the bottom of this delusion, to observe, that though the religious principle can never exist, without the amiable and virtuous conduct of the New Testament; yet, that conduct may, in some measure, be maintained, without the religious principle. A man may be led to precisely the same conduct, on the impulse of many different principles. He may be gentle, because it is a prescription of the divine law:—or, he may be gentle, because he is naturally of a peaceful, or indolent constitution;—or, he may be gentle, because he sees it to be an amiable gracefulness, with which he wishes to adorn his own character;—or, he may be gentle, because it is the ready way of perpetuating the friendship of those around him;—or, he may be gentle, because taught to observe it, as a part of courtly and fashionable deportment,—and what was implanted by education, may come, in time, to be confirmed, by habit and experience. Now, it is only under the first of these principles, that there is any religion in gentleness. The other principles may produce all the outward appearance of this virtue, and much even of its inward complacency, and yet be as distinct from the religious principle, as they are distinct from one another. To infer the strength of the religious principle, from the taste of the human mind for what is graceful and lovely in character, would just be as preposterous, as to infer it from the admiration of a fine picture, or a cultivated landscape. They are not to be confounded. They occupy a different place, even in the classifications of philosophy. We do not deny, that the admiration of what is fine in character, is a principle of a higher order, than a taste for the sensualities of the epicure. But they, one and all of them, stand at a wide distance from the religious principle: and whether it be taste, or temper, or the love of popularity, or the high impulse of honourable feeling, or even the love of truth, and a natural principle of integrity,—the virtues in question may be so unconnected with religion, as to flourish in the world, and be rewarded by its admiration, even though God were expunged from the belief, and immortality from the prospects, of the species.

The virtues, then, to which the enemies of our doctrine make such a confident appeal, may have no force whatever in the argument,—because, properly speaking, they may not be exemplifications of the religious principle. If you do what is virtuous, because God tells you so, then, and then only, do you give us a fair example of the authority of religion over your practice. But, if you do it merely because it is lovely, because it is honourable, or because it is a fine moral accomplishment,—we will not refuse the testimony of our admiration, but we cannot submit to such an error, either of conception, or of language, as to allow that there is any religion in all this. These qualities have our utmost friendship; and we give the most substantial evidence of this, when, instead of leaving them to their own solitary claims upon the human heart, we call in the aid of religion, and support them by its authority: "Whatsoever things are pure, or lovely, or honest, or of good report; if there be any virtue, if there be any praise, think of these things." But we will not admit, that the mere circumstance of their being lovely, supersedes the authority of religion; nor can we endure such an injustice to the Author of all that is graceful, both in nature and morality, as that the native charms of virtue should usurp, in our admiration, the place of God—of him who gave to virtue all its charms, and formed the heart of man to love and to admire them.

Be not deceived, then, into a rejection of that doctrine which forms the great basis of a sinner's religion, by the specimens of moral excellence which are to be met with in society; or by the praise which your own virtues extort from an applauding neighbourhood. Virtue may exist, and in such a degree too, as to constitute it a lovely object in the eyes of the world, but if there be in it no reference of the mind to the will of God, there is no religion in it.

Such virtue as this has its reward in its natural consequences, in the admiration of others, or in the delights of conscious satisfaction. But we cannot see why God will reward it in the capacity of your master, when his service was not the principle of it, and you were therefore not acting at all the part of a servant to him,—nor do we see how he can reward it in the capacity of your judge, when, in the whole process of virtuous feeling, and virtuous sentiment, and virtuous conduct, you carried in your heart no reference whatever, for a single moment, to him as your lawgiver. We do not deny that there are many such examples of virtue in the world; but then we insist upon it, that they cannot be put down to the account of religion. They often may, and actually do, exist in a state of entire separation from the religious principle; and in that case, they go no farther than to prove that your taste is unvitiated, that your temper is amiable, that your social dispositions promote the peace and welfare of society; and they will be rewarded with its approbation. Now, it is well that you act your part as a member of society; and religion, by making this one of its injunctions, gives us the very best security, that wherever its influence prevails, it will be done in the most perfect manner. But the point we labour to impress is, that a man may be what we all understand by a good member of society, without the authority of God, as his legislator, being either recognized or acted upon. We do not say that his error lies in being a good member of society. This, though only a circumstance at present, is a very fortunate one. The error lies in his having discarded the authority of God, or rather, in his never having admitted the influence of that authority over his heart, or his practice. We want to guard him against the delusion, that the principle which he has, can ever be accepted as a substitute for the principle he has not,—or, that the very highest sense of duty, which his situation as a member of society, impresses upon his feelings, will ever be received as an atonement for wanting that sense of duty to God, which he ought to feel in the far more exalted capacity of his servant, and candidate for his approbation. We stand on the high ground, that he is the subject of the Almighty,—nor shall we shrink from declaring the whole extent of the principle. Let his path in society be ever so illustrious, by the virtues which adorn it; let every word, and every performance, be as honourable as a proud sense of integrity can make it; let the salutations of the market-place mark him out as the most respectable of the citizens; and the gratitude of a thousand families sing the praises of his beneficence to the world: If the actor in this splendid exhibition, carry in his mind no reference to the authority of God, we do not hesitate to pronounce him unworthy,—nor shall all the execrations of generous, but mistaken principle, deter us from putting forth our hand to strip him of his honours. What! is the world to gaze in admiration on this fine spectacle of virtue; and are we to be told that the Being, who gave such faculties to one of his children, and provides the theatre for their exercise,—that the Being, who called this moral scene into existence, and gave it all its beauties,—that he is to be forgotten, and neglected as of no consequence? Shall we give a deceitful lustre to the virtues of him who is unmindful of his God,—and with all the grandeur of eternity before us, can we turn to admire those short-lived exertions, which only shed a fleeting brilliancy over a paltry and perishable scene? It is true, that he who is counted faithful in little will also be counted faithful in much; and when God is the principle of his fidelity, the very humblest wishes of benevolence will be rewarded. But its most splendid exertions without this principle, have no inheritance in heaven. Human praise, and human eloquence, may acknowledge it; but the Discerner of the heart never will. The heart may be the seat of every amiable feeling, and every claim which comes to it in the shape of human misery may find a welcome; but if the love of God be not there, it is not right with God,—and he who owns it, will die in his sins: he is in a state of impenitency.

Having thus disposed of those virtues which exist in a state of independence on the religious principle, we must be forced to recur to the doctrine of human depravity, in all its original aggravation. Man is corrupt, and the estrangement of his heart from God, is the decisive evidence of it. Every day of his life the first commandment of the law is trampled on,—and it is that commandment on which the authority of the whole is suspended. His best exertions are unsound in their very principle; and as the love of God reigns not within him, all that has usurped the name of virtue, and deceived us by its semblance, must be a mockery and a delusion.

We shall conclude with three observations: First, there is nothing more justly fitted to revolt the best feelings of the human heart against orthodoxy, than when any thing is said to its defence, which tends to mar the credit or the lustre of a moral accomplishment so lovely as benevolence. Let it be observed, then, that substantial benevolence is rarely, if ever, to be found apart from piety,—and that piety is but the hypocrisy of a name, when benevolence, in all the unweariedness of its well doing, does not go along with it. Benevolence may make some brilliant exhibitions of herself without the instigation of the religious principle. But in these cases you seldom have the touchstone of a painful sacrifice,—and you never have a spiritual aim, after the good of our imperishable nature. It is easy to indulge a constitutional feeling. It is easy to make a pecuniary surrender. It is easy to move gently along, amid the visits and the attentions of kindness, when every eye smiles welcome, and the soft whispers of gratitude minister their pleasing reward, and flatter you into the delusion that you are an angel of mercy. But give us the benevolence of him, who can ply his faithful task in the face of every discouragement,—who can labour in scenes where there is no brilliancy whatever to reward him,—whose kindness is that sturdy and abiding principle which can weather all the murmurs of ingratitude, and all the provocations of dishonesty,—who can find his way through poverty's putrid lanes, and depravity's most nauseous and disgusting receptacles,—who can maintain the uniform and placid temper, within the secrecy of his own home, and amid the irksome annoyances of his own family,—who can endure hardships as a good soldier of Christ Jesus,—whose humanity acts with as much vigour amid the reproach, and the calumny, and the contradiction of sinners, as when soothed and softened by the poetic accompaniment of weeping orphans and interesting cottages,—and, above all, who labours to convert sinners, to subdue their resistance of the gospel, and to spiritualize them into a meetness for the inheritance of the saints. We maintain, that no such benevolence, realizing all these features, exists, without a deeply seated principle of piety lying at the bottom of it. Walk from Dan to Beersheba, and, away from christianity, and beyond the circle of its influences, there is positively no such benevolence to be found. The patience, the meekness, the difficulties of such a benevolence, cannot be sustained without the influence of a heavenly principle,—and when all that decks the theatre of this world is withdrawn, what else is there but the magnificence of eternity, to pour a glory over its path, and to minister encouragement in the midst of labours unnoticed by human eye, and unrewarded by human testimony? Even the most splendid enterprizes of benevolence, which the world ever witnessed, can be traced to the operation of what the world laughs at, as a quakerish and methodistical piety. And we appeal to the abolition of the slave trade, and the still nobler abolition of vice and ignorance, which is now accomplishing amongst the uncivilized countries of the earth, for the proof, that in good will to men, as well as glory to God, they are the men of piety who bear away the palm of superiority and of triumph.

But, Secondly, If all Scripture and all observation, are on the side of our text, should not this be turned by each of us into a personal concern? Should it not be taken up, and pursued, as a topic in which we all have a deep individual interest? Should it not have a more permanent hold of us, than a mere amusing general speculation? Are not prudence, and anticipation, and a sense of danger, all linked with the conclusion we have attempted to press upon you? In one word, if there be such a thing as a moral government on the part of God,—if there be such a thing as the authority of a high and divine legislature,—if there be such a thing as a throne in heaven, and a judge sitting on that throne,—should not the question, What shall I do to be saved? come with all its big and deeply felt significancy into the heart and conscience of every one of us? We know that there is a very loose and general security upon this subject,—that the question, if it ever be suggested at all, is disposed of in an easy, indolent, and superficial way, by some such presumption, as that God is merciful, and that should be enough to pacify us. But why recur to any presumption, for the purpose of bringing the question to a settlement, when, upon this very topic, we are favoured with an authoritative message from God,—when an actual embassy has come from him, and that on the express errand of reconciliation?—when the records of this embassy have been collected into a volume, within the reach of all who will stretch forth their hand to it;—when the obvious expedient of consulting this record is before us? And surely, if what God says of himself, is of higher signification than what we think him to be, and if he tell us not merely that he is merciful, but that there is a particular way in which he chooses to be so;—nothing remains for us but submissively to learn that way, and obediently to go along with it. But he actually tells us, that there is no other name given under heaven, whereby man can be saved, but the name of Jesus. He tells, that it is only in Christ, that he has reconciled the world unto himself. He tells us, that our alone redemption is in him whom God hath set forth to be a propitiation through faith in his blood,—that he might be just, while the justifier of him who believeth in Jesus;—and surely, we must either give up the certainty of the record, or count these to be faithful sayings, and worthy of all acceptation.

Lastly, The question may occur, after having established the fact of human corruption, and recommended a simple acquiescence in the Saviour for forgiveness, What becomes of the corruption after this? Must we just be doing with it as an obstinate peculiarity of our nature, bearing down all our powers of resistance, and making every struggle with it hopeless and unavailing? For the answer to this question, we commit you, as before, to the record. He who is in Christ Jesus is a new creature. Sin has no longer dominion over him. That very want which constituted the main violence of the disease, is made up to him. He wanted the love of God; and this love is shed abroad in his heart by the Holy Ghost. He wanted the love of his neighbour; but God enters into a covenant with him, by which he puts this law in his heart, and writes it in his mind. The spirit is given to them who ask it in faith, and the habitual prayer, of, Support me in the performance of this duty,—or, Carry me in safety through this trial of my heart and of my principles,—is heard with acceptance, and answered with power. The power of Christ is made to rest on those who look to him; and they will find to be their experience what Paul found to be his,—they will be able to do all things through Christ strengthening them. Now, the question we have to put is,—Tell us, if all this sound strange, and mysterious, and foreign to the general style of your conceptions? Then be alarmed for your safety. The things you thus profess to be strange to you, are not the peculiar notions of one man, or the still more peculiar phraseology of another. They are the very notions and the very phraseology of the Bible,—and you, by your antipathy or disregard to them, bring yourselves under precisely the same reckoning with God, that you do with a distant acquaintance, whom you insult by returning his letter unopened, or despise, by suffering it to lie beside you unread and unattended to. In this indelible word of God, you will meet with the free offer of forgiveness for the past, and a provision laid before you, by which all who make use of it, are carried forward to amendment, and progressive virtue for the future. They are open to all, and at the taking of all; but in proportion to the frankness, and freeness, and universality of the offer, will be the severity of that awful threatening to them who despise it. How shall they escape, if they neglect so great a salvation?

SERMON XIII.

The natural Enmity of the Mind against God.

"The carnal mind is enmity against God."—*Romans* viii. 7.

We should be blinding ourselves against the light of experience, did we deny of many of our acquaintances, that they have either brought into the world, or have acquired, by a natural process of education, such a gentleness of temper, such a docility, such a taste for the amiable and the kind, such an honourable sense of integrity, such a feeling sympathy for the wants, and misfortunes of others, that it would not be easy, and what is more, we may venture to say, from the example of our Saviour, who, when he looked to the young man, loved him; that it would positively not be right, to withhold from them our admiration and our tenderness. Still it were a violation of all scriptural propriety in language, to say of them that they were not carnal, or not carnally minded. All, by the very signification of the term, are carnal, whose minds either retain their original constitution, or have undergone no other transforming process than a mere process of natural education. Some minds are in these circumstances, more agreeable to look upon than others, just as some faces are more agreeable than others, to the eye. Each mind has its own peculiar character, just as each face has its own set of features, and its own complexion. But as all the varieties in the latter, from exquisite beauty to most revolting deformity, do not exclude from any, the one and universal attribute of decay,—so neither may all the constitutional varieties in the former, from the most sordid to the most naturally upright and amiable, exclude the possession of some one and universal attribute; and it may be the very attribute assigned to nature in the text—even hostility against God.

Let us first offer some remarks on the affirmation of the text, that the carnal mind is enmity against God,—and then shortly consider how it is that the gospel of Jesus Christ suits its applications to this great moral disease.

I. It appears a very presumptuous attempt, on the part of a human interpreter, when the object which he proposes, and which he erects into a separate head of discussion, is to prove the assertion of the text. Should not the very circumstance of its being the assertion of the text, be proof enough for you? On what better foundation can your belief be laid than on the testimony of God? and when we come to understand the meaning of the thing testified, is not the bare fact of God being the witness of it, sufficient ground for its credibility to rest upon? Shall man's reasoning carry a greater authority along with it than God's declaration? Is your faith to depend on the success or the failure of his argument? Whether he succeed in establishing the truth of the assertion or not, upon independent reasonings of his own,—remember that by reading it out in his text, he has already come forward with an argument more conclusive than any which his ingenuity can devise. And yet, how often do your convictions lie suspended on the ability of the preacher, and on the soundness of his demonstrations? You refuse to believe truth, plainly set before you in the Bible, because the minister has failed in making out his point. Now, the truth of the point in question may have already received its decisive settlement, from the text delivered in your hearing. We may try, and take our own way of bringing the truth of your enmity against God, close and home upon your consciences. But, if there be truth in all the sayings of the Bible, enough has been already said to undermine the security of your fancied attainments. It is said, that in our nature there is a rooted and an embodied character of hostility to our Maker. This should make the wisest and most sufficient among you feel that you are poor indeed,—and let other expedients, to press home the melancholy truth fail, or be effectual as they may, this is surely enough to convince and to alarm you.

But, though we cannot add to the truth of God, there is such a thing as what the Apostle calls making that truth manifest to your consciences. Your own observation may attest the very same truth, which God announces to you in his word. And if it be a truth, respecting the state of your own heart, this agreement between what God says you are, and what you find yourselves to be, is often most powerfully instrumental in reclaiming men to the acknowledgment of the truth, and bringing their heart under its influence. This is the very argument which compelled the faith of the woman of Samaria. "Come and see the man which told me all the things that ever I did; is not this the Christ?" It is the very argument by which many an unbeliever was convinced in the Apostle's days. The secrets of his heart were made manifest, and so falling down on his face, he worshipped God, and reported that God was in them, of a truth. We cannot make the assertion in the text stronger than God has made it already; but we may be able to guide your observations to that which is the subject of it—even to your own mind. We may lead you to attend more closely, and to view more distinctly, the state of your minds, than you have ever yet done. If your finding of the matter shall agree with God's saying about it, it may make the truth of the text tell with energy upon your consciences;—and it were well for one and all of us, that we obtained a more overwhelming sense of our necessities than we have ever yet gotten; that we saw ourselves in those true colours of deformity which really belong to us; that the inveteracy of our disease as sinners were more known and more felt by us; that we could lift up the mantle of delusion, which the accomplishments of nature throw over the carnal mind, and by which they spread a most bewildering gloss over all the rebelliousness and ingratitude of the inner man. Could we but make you feel your need and your helplessness as sinners,—could we chase away from you the pride and the security of your fancied attainments ; could we lead you to mourn and be in heaviness, under a sense of your alienations and idolatries, and risings of hatred against the God who created and who sustains you;—then might we look for the overtures of the gospel being more thankfully listened to, more cordially embraced, more rejoiced in as the alone suitable remedy to the wants and the soreness of your fallen nature,—then might we look for the attitude of self-dependence being broken down, and for all trust, and all glorying, being transferred from ourselves, and laid upon Jesus Christ, and him crucified.

It is no proof of love to God that we do many things, and that too with the willing consent of the mind, the performance of which is agreeable to his law. If the same thing might be done upon either of two principles, then the doing of it may only prove the existence of one of these principles, while the other has no presence or operation in the mind whatever. I do not steal, and the reason of it may be either that I love God, and so keep his commandments, or it may be that I have honourable feelings, and would spurn at the disgracefulness of such an action. This is only one example, but the bare statement of it serves for a thousand more. It lets us in at once to the decisive fact that there are many principles of action applauded, and held in reverence, and most useful to society, and withal urging us to the performance of what, in the matter of it, is agreeable to the law of God, which may have a practical ascendency over a man whose heart is alienated from the love of God. Propose the question to yourself, Would not I do this good thing, or abstain from this evil thing, though God had no will in this matter? If you would, then, put not down what is altogether due to other principles to the principle of love to God, or a desire of pleasing him. The principle upon which you have acted may be respectable, and honourable, and amiable. We are not disputing all this. We are only saying, that it is not the love of God; and should we hear any one of you assert, that I have nothing to reproach myself with, and that I give every body their own, and that I possess a fair character in society, and have done nothing to forfeit it, and that I have my share of generosity, and honour, and tenderness, and civility, our only reply is, that this may be very true. You may have a very large share of these and of other estimable principles, but along with the possession of these many things, you may lack one thing, and that one thing may be the love of God. An enlightened discerner of the heart may look into you, and say, with our Saviour in the text, "I know you that you have not the love of God in you."

It is no test whatever of your love to God, that you tolerate him, when he calls upon you to do the things which your natural principles incline you to do, and which you would have done at any rate. But when he claims that place in your affections which you give to many of the objects of the world,—when he puts in for that share of your heart which you give to wealth, or pleasure, or reputation among men,—then is not God a weariness? and does not the inner man feel impatience and dislike at these grievous exactions; and when the will of God thwarts the natural current of your tastes and employments, is not God, at the moment of urging that will, with all the natural authority which belongs to him, a positive offence to you?

How would you like the visit of a man whose presence broke up some arrangement that you had set your heart upon; or marred the enjoyment of some favourite scheme that you were going to put into execution? Would not you hate the visit? and if it were often repeated,—if the disappointments you received from this cause were frequent and perpetual,—if you saw a systematic design of thwarting you by these galling and numerous interruptions, would not you also cordially hate the visitor, and give the most substantial evidence of your hatred, too, by shunning him, or shutting him out? Now, is not God just such a visitor? O how many favourite schemes of enjoyment would the thought of him, and of his will, if faithfully admitted to the inner chambers of the mind, put to flight! How many fond calculations be given up about the world, the love of which is opposite to the love of the Father. How many trifling amusements behooved to be painfully surrendered, if a sense of God's will were to tell upon the conscience with all the energy that is due to it. How many darling habits abandoned, if the whole man were brought under the dominion of this imperious visitor,—how many affections torn away from the objects on which they are now fastened, if his presence were at all times attended to, and he was regarded with that affection which he at all times demands of us!

This may explain a fact, which we fear must come near to the conscience of many a respectable man, and that is, the recoil which he has often experienced, as if from some object of severe and unconquerable aversion, when the preacher urges upon his thoughts some scriptural representation either of the will or the character of God. Or take this fact in another way, and in which it presents itself, if not more strikingly, at least more habitually; and that is, the undeniable circumstance of God being shut out of his thoughts for the great majority of his time, and him feeling the same kind of ease at the exclusion, as when he shuts the door on the most unwelcome of his visitors. The reason is, that the inner man, busied with other objects, would positively be offended at the intrusion of the thought of God. It is because, to admit him, with all his high claims and spiritual requirements into your mind, would be to disturb you in the enjoyment of objects which are better loved and more sought after than he. It is because your heart is occupied with idols that God is shut out of it. It is because your heart is after another treasure. It is because your heart is set upon other things. Whether it be wealth, or amusement, or distinction, or the ease and the pleasures of life, we pretend not to know; but there is a something which is your god, to the exclusion of the great God of heaven and earth. The Being who is upholding you all the time, and in virtue of whose preserving hand, you live, and think, and enjoy, is all the while unminded and unregarded by you. You look upon him as an interruption. It is of no consequence to the argument what the occupation of your heart be, if it is such an occupation as excludes God from it. It may be what the world calls a vicious occupation,—the pursuits of a dishonest, or the debaucheries of a profligate life,—and, in this case, the world has no objection to stigmatize you with enmity against God. Or it may be what the world calls an innocent occupation—amusement to make you happy, work to earn a subsistence, business to establish a liberal provision for your families. But your heart may be so given to it that God is robbed of his portion of your heart altogether. Or it may be what the world calls an honourable occupation,—the pursuit of eminence in the walks of science or of patriotism; and still there may be an exclusion, or a hatred of the God who puts in for all things being done to his glory. Or it may be what the world calls an elegant occupation,—even that of a mind enamoured with the tastefulness of literature; but it may be so cru-

moured with this, that the God who created your mind, and all the tastes which are within it, and all the objects which are without it, and which minister to its most exquisite gratification,—this God, we say, may be turned away from with a feeling of the most nauseous antipathy, and you may give the most substantial evidence of your hatred to him, by ridding your thoughts of him altogether. Or, lastly, it may be what the world calls a virtuous occupation, even that of a mind bustling with the full play of its energies, among enterprises of charity and plans of public good. Yet even here, wonderful as you may think it, there may be a total exclusion and forgetfulness of God; and, while the mind is filled and gratified with a rejoicing sense of its activity and its usefulness, it may be merely delighting itself with a constitutional gratification,—and God the author of that constitution, be never thought of,—or if thought of according to the holiness of his attributes, and the nature of that friendship, opposite to the friendship of the world, which he demands of us, and the kind of employment which forms the reward and the happiness of his saints in eternity, even the praise and the contemplation of himself,—if thought of, we say, according to this his real character, and these the real requirements that he lays upon us,—even the man to whom the world yields the homage of virtue may think of his God with feelings of offensiveness and disgust.

There is nothing monstrous in all this, to the men of our world, seeing that they have each a share in that deep and lurking ungodliness, which has both so vitiated our nature, and so blinded all who inherit this nature, against a sense of its enormity. But only conceive how it must be thought of, and how the contemplation of it must be felt, among those who can look on character with a spiritual and intelligent estimation. How must the pure eye of an angel be moved at such a spectacle of worthlessness,—and surely, in the records of heaven, this great moral peculiarity of our outcast race must stand engraven as that, which of all others, has the character of guilt most nakedly and most essentially belonging to it. That the bosom of a thing formed should feel cold or indifferent to him who formed it,—that not a thought or an image should be so unwelcome to man as that of his Maker, that the creature should thus turn round on its Creator, and eye disgust upon him,—that its every breath should be envenomed with hatred against him who inspired it,—or, if it be not hatred, but only unconcern, or disinclination, that even this should be the real disposition of a fashioned and sustained being, towards the hand of his Preserver,—there is a a perversity here which time may palliate for a season, but which, under a universal reign of justice, must at length be brought out to its adequate condemnation. And on that day, when the earth is to be burnt up, and all its flatteries shall have subsided, will it be seen of many a heart that rejoiced in the applause and friendship of this world, that, alienated from the love of God, it was indeed in the gall of bitterness, and in the bond of iniquity.

Nor does it palliate the representation which we have now given, that a God, in the fancied array of poetic loveliness—that a God of mere natural perfection, and without one other moral attribute than the single attribute of indulgence—that a God, divested of all which can make him repulsive to sinners, and, for this purpose, shorn of all those glories, which truth and authority, and holiness, throw around his character—that such a God should be idolized at times by many a sentimentalist. It would form no deduction from our enmity against the true God, that we gave an occasional hour to the worship of a graven image, made with our own hands—and it is just of as little significancy to the argument, that we feel an occasional glow of affection or of reverence, towards a fictitious being of our own imagination. If there be truth in the Bible, it is there where God has made an authentic exhibition of his nature, —and if God in Christ be an offence to you —if you dislike this way of approach—if you shrink from the contemplation of that Being, who bids you sanctify him in your hearts, and who claims such a preference in your regard, as shall dispossess your affections for all that is earthly—if you have no relish for the intercourse of prayer, and of spiritual communion with such a God— if your memory neither love to recal him, nor your fancy to dwell upon him, nor he be the being with whom you greatly delight yourself, the habitation to which you resort continually,—then be assured, that amid the painted insignificancy of all your other accomplishments, your heart is not right with God; and he who is the Father of your existence, and of all that gladdens it, may still be to you a loathing and an abomination.

Neither does it palliate the representation which we have now offered, that we do many things with the direct object of doing that which is pleasing to God. It is true, there cannot be love where there is no desire to please; but it is as true, that there may be a desire to please where there is no love. Why, I may both hate and fear the man, whom I may find it very convenient to please; and to secure whose favour, I may practice a thousand arts of accommodation and compliance. I may comply by action—but instead of complying with my will, I may abominate the necessity which constrains me. I may be subject to his pleasure in my person, and in my performances—but you would not say, while hatred rankled within me, that I was subject to him with my mind. A sovereign may overrule the humours of a rebellious province, by the presence of his resistless military—but you would not say that there was any loyalty in this forced subordination. He may compel the bondage of their actual services —but you would not say, that it was in this part of his dominions, where the principle of subjection to him existed in the minds of the people. We have already affirmed, that though our will went along with a number of performances, which in the matter of them were agreeable to God's law—this was far from an unfailing indication of love to God; for there may be a thousand other constitutional principles, the residence and operation of which in the heart may give rise to these performances, while there was an utter distaste, and hostility on our part to God. They may be done, not because God wills the doing, but because the doing falls in with our humour, or our interest, or our vanity, or our instinctive gratification. But now we are prepared to go farther, and say, that they may be done, because God wills the doing, and yet there may be an utter want of subjection in the mind, to the law of God. The terror of his power may constrain you to many acts of obedience, even as the call, "Flee from the coming wrath," told on the disciples of John the Baptist. But obedience may be rendered to all the requirements of this prophet. Thieves and swearers, and sabbath-breakers, may, under the fear of the coming vengeance, give up their respective enormities, and yet their minds be altogether carnal, and utterly destitute of subjection to the law of God. There may be the obedience of the hand while there is the gall of bitterness in the heart, at the necessity which constrains it. It may not be the consenting of the mind, to the law of him whom you delight to please and to honour. Now, this is the service for which it is the aim of Christianity to prepare you. It is by putting that law, which was graven on tables of stone, upon the tables of your heart, that it enables you to yield that obedience which is acceptable to God. He is grieved at the reluctancy of your services. No performances can satisfy him, while your heart remains in shut and shielded alienation against him. What he wants, is to gain the friendship and the confidence of his creatures; and he feels all the concern of a wounded and mortified father when he knocks at the door of your heart and finds its affections to be away from him. He condescends to plead the matter, and with the tenderness of a disappointed father, does he say, "Wherein have I wearied you, O children of Israel, testify against me?" You may fear him; you may heap sacrifices upon his altar: you may bring the outer man to something like a slavish obedience, at his bidding, but till your heart be subdued, by that great process, which all who are his spiritual subjects must undergo, you are carnal, and you do not love him. Your obedience is like a body without a soul. The very principle which gives it all its value, is wanting. It is this, which turns the whole to bitterness. It is this, which, with all the bustling activity of your services, keeps you dead in trespasses and sins. It is this which mars every religious performance, and imparts the character of rebelliousness to every one item, in the list of your plausible and ostentatious duties. There is not one of them which is not accompanied with an act of disobedience, and that too, to the first and greatest commandment, by which we are called upon to love the Lord with all our heart, strength, and soul. Though the hand should be subject,—though the mouth should be subject,—though all the organs of the outer man should be subject; yet it availeth nothing, if the will of the mind is not subject. I could sell all my goods to feed the poor. I could compel my hand to sign an order to that effect,—and I could keep my hand from reversing that order till it was executed. But all this I may do says Paul, and yet have nothing, because I have not charity. It is not the act of well-doing to your neighbour, but a principle of love to your neighbour, on which God stamps the testimony of his approbation. In like manner, it is not the act of well-doing to God, but the principle of love to God, which he values;—and if this be withheld from him, you are carnal; and with all your painful and multiplied attempts at obedience, your mind is not subject to the law of God.

We shall conclude, at present, with two short reflections.

First, If any of you are convinced of the justness of the representations which we have now given, you will perceive that your guilt in the sight of God, may be of a far deeper and more alarming kind, than men are generally aware of. And such a view of the matter may be quite intolerable to him who nauseates the peculiarities of the gospel,—to him who has a contempt for the foolishness of that preaching, of which the great burden is Jesus Christ, and him crucified,—to him, in a word, whom the true description of our moral disease, must terrify or offend,—seeing that he carries a distaste in his heart toward the alone remedy, by which the disease can be met and extirpated.

But secondly, There is another class of people, whom such a view of the actual state of human nature ought to tranquillize.

by bringing their minds out of perplexity, into a state of firm and confident decision. There are often in a congregation, a set of hearers not yet shut up into the faith, but approaching towards it,—with a growing taste for the Christianity of the New Testament, but without a full and a final acquiescence in it,—with an opening and an enlarging sense of the importance of the gospel, but still halting between two opinions respecting it; who, in particular, are not sure where their sole dependence for salvation should be placed, whether singly upon their own performances, or singly upon the righteousness of Christ, or jointly upon both. Now, we trust that the lesson of our text may have the effect with some, of bringing this unsettled account more speedily to its termination. You may have hitherto, perhaps, been under the impression, that the condition of man was not just so bad as to require a Saviour, who must undertake the whole of his cure, and bring about the whole of his salvation. You have attempted to share with the Saviour in the matter of your redemption. Instead of looking upon it with the eye of the Apostle, as being all of grace, or all of works, you have in some way or other, attempted a compromise between them; and this has the undoubted effect of keeping you at a distance from Christ. You have not felt your entire need of him, and therefore you have not leaned in close and constant dependence upon him. But let the torch of a spiritual law be lifted over your characters, and through the guise of its external decencies reveal to you the mountain of iniquity within; let the deformity of the heart be made known, and you become sensible of the fruitlessness of every endeavour, so long as the consent of a willing cordiality is withheld from the person and authority of God; let the utter powerlessness of all your doings, be contrasted with the perversity of your stubborn and unmanageable desires, and the case is seen in all its helplessness;—you become desperate of salvation in one way, and you are led to look for it in another way. The question, whether salvation is of grace or of works, receives its most decisive settlement;—when thus driven away from one term of the alternative, you are compelled, as your only resource, to the other term. You feel that nothing else will do for your acceptance with God, but your acceptance of the offered Saviour. You stand at the foot of the cross,—you make an absolute surrender of yourself to the terms of the gospel.

And we know not a more blissful or a more memorable event, in the history of the human soul, than, when convinced that there is no other righteousness than in the merits, and no other sanctification than in the grace of the Saviour, it henceforth glories only in his cross; and now, that every other expedient of reformation has been tried, and failed of its accomplishment, it takes to the remaining one of crying mightily to God and pressing, at a throne of grace, the supplication of the Psalmist, "Create a clean heart, and renew a right spirit within me.'

One thing is certain; you are welcome at this moment, to lay hold of the righteousness of God, in Christ Jesus; you are welcome, at this moment, to the use of his prevailing name, in your prayers to the Father you are welcome, at this moment, to the plea of his meritorious obedience, and of his atoning death: and you are welcome, at this moment, to the promise of the Spirit, given unto all who believe, whereby the enmity of their carnal minds will be done away,—God will no longer be regarded with antipathy and disgust,—he will appear in the face of Jesus Christ as a reconciled father,—he will pour upon you the spirit of adoption,—you will walk before him without fear,—and those bonds being loosed, wherewith you were formerly held, you will yield to him the willing obedience of those whose hearts are enlarged, and who run, with delight, in the way of his commandments.

SERMON XIV.

The Power of the Gospel to dissolve the Enmity of the human Heart against God.

"Having slain the enmity thereby."—*Ephesians* ii. 16.

II. WE shall now consider how it is that the gospel of Jesus Christ suits its application to this great moral disease.

The necessity of some singular expedient for restoring the love of God to the alienated heart of man, will appear from the utter impossibility of bringing this about by any direct application of authority whatever. For, do you think that the delivery of the law of love, in his hearing, as a positive and indispensable enactment coming forth from the legislature of heaven will do it? You may as well pass a law, making it imperative upon him to delight in pain, and to feel comfort on a bed of torture. Or, do you think, that you will ever give a practical establishment to the law of love, by surrounding it with accumulated penalties? This may irritate, or it may terrify,—but for the purpose of begetting any thing like attachment, one may as well think of lashing another into tender regard for him. Or, do you think, that the terrors of the coming vengeance will ever incline a human being to love the God who threatens him? Powerful as these terrors are, in persuading man to turn from the evil of his ways,—they most assuredly do not form the artillery by which the heart of man can be carried. They draw not forth a single affection, but the affection of fear. They never can charm the human bosom into a feeling of attachment to God. And it goes to prove the necessity of some singular expedient, for restoring man to fellowship with his Maker; that the only obedience on which this fellowship can be perpetuated, is an obedience which no threatenings can force,—to which no warnings of displeasure can reclaim,—which all the solemn proclamations of law and justice cannot carry,—and all the terrors and severities of a sovereignty resting on power, as its only foundation, can never subdue. The utterance of the words, Thou shalt love the Lord thy God, or perish everlastingly, can no more open the shut and alienated heart of man, than it can open a gate of iron. Multiply these arguments of terror as you may,—arm them with tenfold energy, and make them to fall in thunder on the sinner's ears,—tell him of the God of judgment, and manifest to him the frown of his angry countenance,—lay before him the grim aspect of his impending death, and spread a deeper mantle of despair over the vast field of that eternity which is on the other side of it;—you may disquiet him, and right that he should be so,—you may prevail on him to give up many evil doings; and right that the whole urgency of the coming wrath should be employed to make him give them up immediately,—you may set him a trembling at the power of God, and better this than spending his guilty career, in thoughtlessness and unconcern, about the great Lawgiver;—but where, in the midst of all this, shall we find obedience to the very first and greatest commandment of the law? Has this obedience been yet so much as entered on? Has love to God so much as reached the infancy of its existence in that heart which is now beginning to be agitated by its terrors? Amid all the bitterness of remorse, and all the fearful looking for of judgment, and all the restless anxieties of conscious guilt, and anticipated vengeance, tell us, if a single particle of tenderness towards God has any place in this restless and despairing bosom? Tell us, if it act as an element at all, in this wild war of turbulence and disorder? Or, has it yet begun to dawn upon the mind, and spread its salutary and composing charm over that dark scene of conflict, under which many a sinner has to sustain the burden of the wearisome nights that are appointed to him? You may seek for love to God throughout all the chambers of his heart, and seek in vain. The man may be acting such reformations as he is driven to, and may be clothing himself in such visible decencies, as he feels himself compelled to put on, and may be labouring away at the drudgery of such observances as he thinks will give him relief from the corrosions of that undying worm, which never ceases to goad him with its reproaches; but as to the love of God, there is as grim and determined an exclusion of this principle as ever,—that avenue to his heart has never been unlocked, through which it might be made to find its way,—every former argument, so far from having dissolved the barrier, has only served to rivet and to make it more unmoveable. And the difficulty still lies upon us,—how are we to deposit in the heart of man, the only right principle of obedience to God,—and to lead him onward in the single way of a pure, and spiritual, and substantial repentance?

This, then, is a case of difficulty, and, in the Bible, God is said to have lavished all the riches of his unsearchable wisdom on the business of managing it. No wonder that to his angels it appeared a mystery, and that they desired to look into it. It appears a matter of direct and obvious facility to intimidate man,—and to bring his body into a forced subordination to all the requirements. But the great matter was, how to attach man,—how to work in him a liking to God, and a relish for his character;—or, in other words, how to communicate to human obedience, that principle, without which it is no obedience at all,—to make him serve God because he loved him; and to run in the way of all his commandments, because this was the thing in which he greatly delighted himself. To lay upon us the demand of satisfaction for his violated law, could not do it. To press home the claims of justice upon any sense of authority within us, could not do it. To bring forward, in threatening array, the terrors of his judgment, and of his power against us, could not do it. To unveil the glories of that throne where he sitteth in equity, and manifest to his guilty creatures the awful inflexibilities of his truth and righteousness, could not do it. To look out from the cloud of vengeance, and trouble our darkened souls as he did those of the Egyptians of old, with the aspect of a menacing Deity, could not do it. To spread the field of an undone eternity before us, and tell us of those dreary abodes where each criminal hath his bed in hell, and the centuries of despair which pass over him are not counted, because there no seasons roll, and the unhappy victims of the tribulation, and the wrath, and the anguish, know, that for the mighty burden of the sufferings which weigh upon them, there is no end, and no mitigation; this prospect, appalling as it is, and coming home upon the belief with all the characters of the most immutable certainty, could not do it. The affections of the inner man remain as unmoved as ever, under the successive and repeated influence of all these dreadful applications. There is not one of them, which, instead of conciliating, does not stir up a principle of resistance; and, subject any human creature to the treatment of them all, and to nothing else, and he may tremble at God, and shrink at the contemplation of God, and feel an overpowering awe at the thought of God, when that thought visits him;— but we maintain, that not one particle of influence has been sent into his heart, to make him love God. Under such applications as these, we can conceive the creature, gathering a new energy from despair, and mustering up a stouter defiance than ever to the God who threatens him. Strange contest between the thing formed and him who formed it;—but we see it exhibited among the determined votaries of wickedness in life; and it is the very contest which gives its moral aspect to hell throughout all eternity. There God reigns in vindictive majesty, and there every heart of every outcast, sheathed in impenetrable hardness, mutters its blasphemies against him. O hideous and revolting spectacle! and how awful to think that the unreclaimed sons of profligacy, who pour along our streets, and throng our markets, and form the fearful majority in almost every chamber of business, and in every workshop of industry, are thither speeding their infatuated way! What a wretched field of contemplation is around us, when we see on every side of it the mutual encouragement,—the everplying allurements,—the tacit, though effectual and well understood, combination, sustaining, over the whole face of this alienated world, a firm and systematic rebellion against God! We are not offering an exaggerated picture when we say, that within reach of the walk of a single hour, there are thousands, and thousands more, who have cast away from them the authority of God; and who have been nerved by all his threatenings into a more determined attitude of wickedness; and who glory in their unprincipled dissipations; and who, without one sigh at the moving spectacle of ruined innocence, will, in the hearing of companions younger than themselves, scatter their pestilential levities around them, and care not though the hope of parents, and the yet unvitiated delicacy of youth, shall wither and expire under the contagion of their ruffian example; and will patronize every step of that progress which leads from one depravity to another, till their ill fated proselyte, made as much the child of hell as themselves, shall share in that common ruin which, in the great day of the revelation of the righteous judgment of God, will come forth from the storehouse of his wrath, in one mighty torrent, on the heads of all who boast of their iniquity. We have now touched on the limits of a subject of which half its horrors are untold; but through which, the minister of the counsels of heaven must clear his intrepid way, in spite of all its painfulness. We will not pursue it at present, but neither will we count the digression out of place, should a single parent among you be led, from what we have now uttered, to be jealous over his children with a godly jealousy, and not to suffer those, for whose eternity he is so deeply responsible, to take their random direction through society, just where the prospects of business, and of worldly advantage, may chance to carry them; to calculate on the possibilities of moral corruption, as well as on the possibilities of lucrative employment; to look well to exposures and acquaintances, and hours of social entertainment, as well as to the common-place object of a situation in the world. And when you talk of a good line for your children, just think a little more of the line that leadeth to eternity, and have a care lest you be the instrument of putting them on such a path of danger, that it shall only be the very rarest miracle of grace that your helpless young can be kept from falling, or be renewed again into repentance.

But the difficulty in question still remains unresolved. How then is this regeneration to be wrought, if no threatenings can work it,—if no terrors of judgment can soften the heart into that love of God, which forms the chief feature of repentance,—if all the direct applications of law and of righteous authority, and of its tremendous and immutable sanctions, so far from attaching man in tenderness to his God, have only the effect of impressing a violent recoil upon all his affections, and, by the hardening influence of despair, of stirring up in his bosom a more violent antipathy than ever? Will the high and solemn proclamations of a menacing Deity not do it? This is not the way in which the heart of man can be carried. He is so constituted, that the law of love can never, never be established within him by the engine of terror; and here is the barrier to this regeneration on the part of man. But if a threat of justice cannot do it, will an act of forgiveness do it? This again is not the way in which God can admit the guilty to acceptance. He is so constituted, that his truth cannot be trampled upon, and his government cannot be despoiled of its authority, and its sanctions cannot, with impunity, be defied, and every solemn utterance of the Deity cannot but find its accomplishment, in such a way as may vindicate his glory, and make the whole creation he has formed stand in awe of its Almighty Sovereign. And here is another barrier on the part of God; and that economy of redemption, in which a dead and undiscerning world see no skilfulness to admire, and no feature of graciousness to allure, was so planned, in the upper counsels of heaven, that it maketh known, to principalities and powers, the manifold wisdom of Him who devised it. The men of this infidel generation, whose every faculty is so bedimmed by the grossness of sense, that they cannot lay hold of the realities of faith, and cannot appreciate them,—to them the barriers we have now insisted on, which lie in the way of man taking God into his love, and of God taking man into his acceptance, may appear to be so many faint and shadowy considerations, of which they feel not the significancy; but, to the pure and intellectual eye of angels, they are substantial obstacles, and One Mighty to save had to travail in the greatness of his strength, in order to move them away. The Son of God descended from heaven, and he took upon him the nature of man, and he suffered in his stead, and he consented that the whole burden of offended justice should fall upon him, and he bore in his own body on the tree, the weight of all those accomplishments by which his Father behooved to be glorified, and after having magnified the law, and made it honourable, by pouring out his soul unto the death for us, he went up on high, and by an arm of everlasting strength, levelled that wall of partition which lay across the path of acceptance; and thus it is, that the barrier on the part of God is done away, and he, with untarnished glory, can dispense forgiveness over the whole extent of a guilty creation, because he can be just, while he is the justifier of them who believe in Jesus.

And if the barrier, on the part of God, is thus moved aside, why not the barrier on the part of man? Does not the wisdom of redemption show itself here also? Does it not embrace some skilful contrivance, by which it penetrates those mounds that beset the human heart, and ward the entrance of the principle of love away from it, and which all the direct applications of terror and authority, have only the effect of fixing more immoveably upon their basis? Yes it does,—for it changes the aspect of the Deity towards man; and were man only to have faith in the announcements of the gospel, so as to see God with the eye of his mind under this new aspect,—love to God would spring up in his heart, as the unfailing consequence. Let man see God as he sets himself forth in this wonderful revelation, and let him believe the reality of what he sees; and he cannot but love the Being he is employed in contemplating. Without this gospel, he may see him to be a God of justice; but he cannot do this without seeing the frown of severity directed against himself, a wretched offender: With this gospel, he sees the full burden of violated justice borne away from him; and God stands before him unrobed of all his severities, and tenderly inviting him to draw near through that blood of atonement which was shed, the just for the unjust, to bring the sinner unto God. Without this gospel, he may see the truth of God; but he sees it pledged to the fulfilment of the most awful threatenings against him: With this gospel, he sees the full weight of all these accomplishments resting on the head of the great sacrifice; and God's truth is now fully embarked on the most cheering assurances of pardon, on the most liberal invitations of good will, on the most exceeding great and precious promises. Without this gospel, he may see the government of God leaning on the pillars of that immutability which upholds it; but this very immutability is to him the sentence of despair; and how can he love that face, on which are stamped the characters of a stern and vindictive majesty? With this gospel, the face of God stands legibly revealed to him in other characters. That law which, resting on the solemn authority of its firm and unalterable requirements, demanded a fulfilment, up to the last jot and tittle of it, has been magnified, and has been made honourable, by one illustrious sufferer, who put forth the greatness of his strength, in that dark hour of the travail of his soul, when he bore the burden of all its penalties. That wrath which should have been discharged on the guilty millions he died for, was all concentred upon him, who took upon himself the chastisement of our peace, and on that day of mysterious agony, drank, to the very dregs, the cup of our expiation. And God, who planned the whole work of this wonderful redemption, —God, who in love to a guilty world sent his Son amongst us to accomplish it,— God, who rather than lose his alienated creatures, as he could not strip his eternal throne of a single attribute that supported it, awoke the sword of vengeance against his fellow, that on him the truth and the justice of the Deity might receive their most illustrious vindication,—God, who, out of Christ, sits surrounded with all the darkness of unapproachable majesty, is now God in Christ, reconciling the world unto himself, and not imputing unto them their trespasses; his tender mercy is now free to rejoice amid all the glory of his other bright and untarnished perfections, and he pours the expression of his tenderness, with an unsparing hand, over the whole extent of his sinful creation—and he lets himself down to the language of a beseeching supplicant, praying that each and every one of us might be reconciled unto him— and, putting on a winning countenance of invitation to the guiltiest of us all, he tells us, that if we only come to him through the appointed mediator, he will blot out, as with a thick cloud, our transgressions,— and that, as if carried away to a land that was not inhabited, he will make no more mention of them.

And thus it is, that the goodness of God destroyeth the enmity of the human heart. When every other argument fails, this, if perceived by the eye of faith, finds its powerful and persuasive way through every barrier of resistance. Try to approach the heart of man by the instruments of terror and of authority, and it will disdainfully repel you. There is not one of you skilled in the management of human nature, who does not perceive, that, though this may be a way of working on the other principles of our constitution,— of working on the fears of man, or on his sense of interest,—this is not the way of gaining by a single hair-breadth on the attachments of his heart. Such a way may force, or it may terrify, but it never, never can endear; and after all the threatening array of such an influence as this, is brought to bear upon man, there is not one particle of service it can extort from him, but what is all rendered in the spirit of a painful and reluctant bondage. Now, this is not the service which prepares for heaven. This is not the service which assimilates men to angels. This is not the obedience of those glorified spirits, whose every affection harmonizes with their every performance; and the very essence of whose piety consists of delight in God, and the love they bear to him. To bring up man to such an obedience as this, his heart behooved to be approached in a peculiar way; and no such way is to be found, but within the limits of the Christian revelation. There alone you see God, without injury to his other attributes, plying the heart of man with the irresistible argument of kindness. There alone do you see the great Lord of heaven and of earth, setting himself forth to the most worthless and the most wandering of his children,—putting forth his own hand to the work of healing the breach which sin had made between them,—telling him that his word could not be set aside, and his threatenings could not be mocked, and his justice could not be defied and trampled on, and that it was not possible for his perfections to receive the slightest taint in the eyes of the creation he had thrown around him; but that all this was provided for, and not a single creature within the compass of the universe he had formed, could now say, that forgiveness to man was degrading to the authority of God, and that by the very act of atonement, which poured a glory over all the high attributes of his character, his mercy might now burst forth without limit, and without controul, upon a guilty world, and the broad flag of invitation be unfurled in the sight of all its families.

Let the sinner, then, look to God through the medium of such a revelation; and the sight which meets him there, may well tame the obstinacy of that heart which had wrapped itself up in impenetrable hardness against the force of every other consideration. Now that the storm of the Almighty's wrath has been discharged upon him who bore the burden of the world's atonement, he has turned his throne of glory into a throne of grace, and cleared away from the pavilion of his residence, all the darkness which encompassed it. The God who dwelleth there, is God in Christ; and the voice he sends from it, to this dark and rebellious province of his mighty empire, is a voice of the most beseeching tenderness. Good will to men is the announcement with which his messengers come fraught to a guilty world; and, since the moment in which it burst upon mortal ears from the peaceful canopy of heaven, may the ministers of salvation take it up, and go round with it among all the tribes and individuals of the species. Such is the real aspect of God towards you. He cannot bear that his alienated children should be finally and everlastingly away from him. He feels for you all the longing of a parent bereaved of his offspring. To woo you back again unto himself, he scatters among you the largest and the most liberal assurances, and with a tone of imploring tenderness, does he say to one and all of you, "Turn ye, turn ye, why will you die?" He has no pleasure in your death. He does not wish to glorify himself by the destruction of any one of you. "Look to me all ye ends of the earth, and be saved," is the wide and the generous announcement, by which he would recal, from the very outermost limits of his sinful creation, the most worthless and polluted of those who have wandered away from him. Now give us a man who perceives, with the eye of his mind, the reality of all this, and you give us a man in possession of the principle of faith. Give us a man in possession of this faith; and his heart, shielded, as it were, against the terrors of a menacing Deity, is softened and subdued, and resigns its every affection at the moving spectacle of a beseeching Deity; and thus it is that faith manifests the attribute which the Bible assigns to it, of working by love. Give us a man in possession of this love; and animated as he is, with the living principle of that obedience, where the willing and delighted consent of the inner man goes along with the performance of the outer man, his love manifests the attribute which the Bible assigns to it, when it says, "This is the love of God, that ye keep his commandments." And thus it is, amid the fruitlessness of every other expedient, when power threatened to crush the heart which it could not soften,—when authority lifted its voice, and laid on man an enactment of love which it could not carry,—when terror shot its arrows, and they dropped ineffectual from that citadel of the human affections, which stood proof against the impression of every one of them,—when wrath mustered up its appalling severities, and filled that bosom with despair which it could not fill with the warmth of a confiding attachment,—then the kindness of an inviting God was brought to bear on the heart of man, and got an opening through all its mysterious avenues. Goodness did what the nakedness of power could not do. It found its way through all the intricacies of the human constitution, and there, depositing the right principle of repentance, did it establish the alone effectual security for the right purposes, and the right fruits of repentance.

SERMON XV.

The Evils of false Security.

"They have healed also the hurt of the daughter of my people slightly, saying Peace, Peace; when there is no peace."—*Jeremiah* vi. 14.

WE must all have remarked, on what a slight and passing consideration people will dispose of a question which relates to the interest of their eternity; and how strikingly this stands contrasted with the very deep, and earnest, and long sustained attention, which they bestow on a question which relates to their interest, or their fortune, in this world. Ere they embark, for example, on an enterprise of trade, they will look at all the sides, and all the possibilities of the speculation; and every power of thought within them, will be put to its busiest exercise, and they will enter upon it with much fearfulness, and they will feel an anxious concern in every step, and every new evolution of such an undertaking. Compare this with the very loose and summary way in which they make up their minds about the chance of happiness in another world. See at how easy a rate they will be satisfied with some maxim of security, the utterance of which serves as a bar against all further prosecution of the subject. Behold the use they make of some hastily assumed principle in religion,—not for the purpose of fastening their minds upon it, but for the purpose, in fact, of hurrying their minds away from it. For it must be observed of the people to whom we allude, that, in spite of all their thoughtlessness about the affairs of the soul, they are not altogether without some opinion on the matter; and in which opinion there generally is comprised all the theology of which they are possessed. Without some such opinion, even the most regardless of men might feel themselves in a state of restlessness; and therefore it is, however seldom they are visited with any thought about eternity, and however gently this thought touches them, and however quickly it passes away, to be replaced by some of the more urgent vanities and interests of time, yet, with most men, there is something like an actual making up of their minds, on this awfully important subject. There is a settlement they have come to about it, which, generally speaking, serves them to the end of their days;—and on the strength of which, there are many who can hush within them every alarm of conscience, and repel from without them, the whole force of a preacher's demonstration, and all that power of disquietude which lies in his faithful and impressive warnings.

We speak in reference to a very numerous set of individuals, among the upper and middling classes of society. There is a class of what may be called slender and sentimental religionists, who do profess a reverence for the matter, and maintain many of its outward decencies, and are visited with occasional thoughts, and occasional feelings of tenderness about death, and duty, and eternity, and would be shocked at the utterance of an infidel opinion; and with all these symptoms of a religious inclination about them, have their minds very comfortably made up, and altogether free from any apprehension, either of present wrath or of coming vengeance. Now, on examining the ground of their tranquillity, we are at a loss to detect a single ingredient of that peace and joy in believing, which we read of among the Christians of the New Testament. It is not that Christ is set forth a propitiation for their sins,—it is not that they stagger not at the promise of God, because of unbelief,—it is not that the love of him is shed abroad in their hearts, by the Holy Ghost,—it is not that they carry along with them any consciousness whatever, of a growing conformity to the image of the Saviour,—it is not that their calling and their election are made sure to them, by the successful diligence with which they are cultivating the various accomplishments of the Christian character;—there is not one of these ingredients, will we venture to say, which enters into the satisfaction that many feel with their own prospects, and into the complacency they have in their own attainments, and into their opinion, that God is looking to them with indulgence and friendship. With most of them, there is not only an ignorance, but a positive disgust, about these things. They associate with them the charges of methodism, and mysticism, and fanaticism: and meanwhile cherish in their own hearts a kind of impregnable confidence, resting entirely on some other foundation.

We believe the real cause of their tranquillity to be, just that eternity is not seen nearly enough, or urgently enough, to disturb them. It stands so far away on the back ground of their contemplation, that they are almost entirely taken up with the intervening objects. Any glimpse they have of the futurity which lies on the other side of time, is so faint, and so occasional, that its concerns never come to them with the urgency of a matter on hand. It is not so much because they think in a particular way on this topic, that they feel themselves to be at peace. It is rather because they think so little of it. Still, however, they do have a transient and occasional thought, and it is all on the side of tranquillity; and could this thought be exposed as a minister of deceitful complacency to the heart, it may have the effect of working in it a salutary alarm, and of making the possessor of it see the nakedness of his condition, and of undermining every other trust but a trust in the offered salvation of the gospel, and of unsettling the blind and easy confidence of his former days, and of prompting him with the question, "What shall I do to be saved?" and of leading him to try this question by the light of revelation, and to prosecute it to a scriptural conclusion, till he came to the answer of, "Believe in the Lord Jesus Christ, and thou shalt be saved."

What is the way, then, in which they do actually make up their minds upon this subject? There is, in the first place, a pretty general admission, that we are sinners, though along with this, there is a disposition to palliate the enormity of sin, and to gloss it over with the gentle epithet of an infirmity. It is readily allowed, then, that we have our infirmities; and then to make all right, and secure, and comfortable, the sentiment with which they bring the matter round again, is, that though we have our infirmities, God is a merciful God, and he will overlook them. This vague, and general, and indistinct apprehension of the attribute of mercy is the anchor of their hope; not a very sure and steadfast one, certainly, but just as sure and as steadfast, as, in their peaceful state of unconcern, they have any demand for. A vessel in smooth water needs not be very strongly fastened in her moorings; and really any convictions of sin they have, agitate them so gently, that a very slender principle indeed, uttered occasionally by the mouth, and with no distinct or perceptible hold upon the heart, is enough to quiet and subdue all that is troublesome within them. A slight hurt needs but a slight remedy, and however virulent the disease may be, yet if the patient be but gently alarmed, a gentle application is enough to pacify him in the mean time. Now, a tasteful and a tender sentiment about the goodness of God, is just such an application. He will not be severe upon our weaknesses; he will not cast a glance of stern and unrelenting indignation upon us. It is true, that there is to be met with, among the vilest dregs and refuse of society, a degree of profligacy for which it would really be too much to expect forgiveness. The use of hell is for the punishment of such gross and enormous wickedness as this. But the people who are so very depraved, and so very shocking, stand far beneath the place which we occupy in the scale of character. We, with our many amiable, and good, and neighbourlike points and accomplishments, are fair and befitting subjects for the kindness of God. When we err, we shall betake ourselves to a trust in that indulgence, which gives to our religion the aspect of so much cheerfulness; and we will school down all that is disquieting, by a sentiment of confidence in that mercy which is soothing to our hearts, and which we delight to hear expatiated upon in terms of tastefulness, by the orators of a genteel and cultivated piety.

Under this loose system of confidence, then, by which the peace of so many a sinner is upheld, it is the general mercy of God on which he rests. I shall, therefore, in the first place, endeavour to prove the vanity of such a confidence; and, in the second place, the evils of it.

I. There is one obvious respect, in which this mercy that is so slenderly spoken of, and so vaguely trusted in, is not in unison with truth; and that is, it is not the mercy which has been made the subject of an actual offer from God to man, in the true message that he has been pleased to deliver to the world. In this message, God makes a free offer of his mercy, no doubt; but he offers it on a particular footing, and on that footing only, will he have it to be received. Along with the revelation he makes of his attribute of mercy, he bids us look to the particular way in which he chooses that attribute to be put forth. The man who steps forward to relieve you of your debts, by an act of gratuitous kindness, may surely reserve the privilege of doing it in his own way; and whether it be by a present in goods, or by a present in money, or by an order upon a third person, or by the appointment of one whom he makes the agent of his beneficence, and whom he asks you to correspond with and to draw upon, it would surely be most preposterous in you to quarrel with his generosity, because it would have been more to your taste, had it come to you through a different channel of conveyance. He has a fair right of insisting upon his own way of it; and if you will not acquiesce in this way, and he leaves you under your burden, you have nothing to complain of. You might have liked it better had he authorized you to draw upon himself, rather than on the agent he has fixed upon. But no; he has his reasons, and he persists in his own way of it, and you must either go along with this way, or throw yourself out of the benefit of his generosity altogether. It is conceivable that, in spite of all this, you may be so very perverse as to draw upon himself, instead of drawing upon the authorized agent. Well, the effect is, just that your draft is dishonoured, and your debt still lies upon you; and, by your wilful resistance to the plan of relief laid down, are left to remain under the full weight of your embarrassments.

And so of God. He may, and he actually has stepped forward, to relieve us from that debt of sin under which we lie. But he has taken his own way of it. He has not left us to dictate the matter to him,—but he himself has found out a ransom. He offers us eternal life; but he tells us where this is to be found, even in his Son, and he bids us look unto him, and be saved; and he says, that he who hath the Son hath life, and that he who believeth not the Son, the wrath of God abideth on him. To restrain, as it were, our immediate approaches to himself, he reveals an agent, a Mediator between God and man,—and he lets us know, that no one cometh unto the Father, but by him. He makes a free offer of salvation,—but it is in and through Jesus Christ, to whom the whole revealed word of God directs our eye, as the prime agent in the recovery of a guilty world. To say that we have our infirmities, but God is merciful, is like drawing direct upon God himself. But God tells us that he will not be so drawn upon. He chooses, and has he not the right of choosing, to bestow all his favours upon a guilty world, in and through his Son Christ Jesus? If you choose to object to this way, you must just abide by the consequences. The offer is made. God sets himself forward as merciful. But he lets you know, at the same time, the particular way in which he chooses to be so. This way may be an offence to you. You would, perhaps, have liked better, had there been no Christ, no preaching of his cross, nothing said about his cleansing and peace-speaking blood,—in a word, nothing of all that which forms the burden of methodistical sermons, and which, if met with in the New Testament at all, is only to be found in what you may think its dark and mystical passages. It would have been more congenial to your taste, perhaps, had you been left to the undisturbed enjoyment of your own soothing and elegant conceptions,—could you just have gone direct to God himself, whom the eye of your imagination had stripped of all tremendous severity against sin, of all the pure and holy jealousies of his nature, of all that is majestic in the high attributes of truth and righteousness. A God singly possessed of tenderness, in virtue of which, he would smile connivance at all our infirmities, and bend an indulgent eye over the waywardness of a heart devoted with all its affections to the vanities and pleasures of time,—this would be a God highly suited to the taste and convenience of a guilty world. But, alas! there is no such God. To trust in the mercy of such a Being as this, is to lean on a nonentity of your own imagination. It is to be led astray, by a fancy picture of your own forming. There is no other God to whom you can repair for mercy, but God in Christ, reconciling the world unto himself, and not imputing unto them their trespasses. And if you resist the preaching of Christ as foolishness,—if you will not recognize him, but persist in your hoping, and your trusting, on the general ground that God is merciful, you are just wrapping yourselves up in a delusive confidence, and pleasing yourselves with your own imagination; and the only real offer that ever was, or ever will be made to sinful man, you are putting away from you. The mercy upon which you rest, is in disunion with truth. It is a spark of your own kindling, and if you continue to walk in it, it will lead you into a path of darkness, and bewilder you to your final undoing.

II. The evils of such a confidence as we have been attempting to expose, are mainly reducible to two, which we shall consider in order.

First, this delusive confidence casts an

aspersion on the character of God. It would inflict a mutilation upon that character. It is confidence in such a mercy as would dethrone the lawgiver, and establish the anarchy of a wild misrule, over his fallen and dishonoured attributes. We may lightly take up with the conception that God is all tenderness, and nothing else, and thus try to accommodate the character of the Eternal, to the standard of our own convenience and our own wishes. We, instead of looking to the immutability of the Godhead, and taking our fixed and permanent lesson from such a contemplation, may fancy of the Godhead, that he is ever assuming a new shape, and a new character, according to the frail and fluctuating caprices of human opinion. Instead of God making man according to his pleasure, man would form God in the mould of his own imagination. He forgets that, in the whole range of existence, he can only meet with one object who is inflexibly and everlastingly the same, and that is God,—that he may sooner think of causing the everlasting hills to recede from their basis, than of causing an infringement on the nature of the unalterable Deity, or on the designs and maxims which support the method of his administration,—that to assume a character for him in our own mind, instead of learning what the character is from himself, is in fact to make the foolish thought of the creature, paramount to the eternal and immutable constitution of the Creator.

Let us therefore give up our own conceptions, and look steadily to that light in which God hath actually put himself forth to us. He has dealt out a variety of communications respecting his own ever-during character and attributes, to the children of men; and he tells us, that he is a God of truth, and that he is jealous of his honour, and that he will not be mocked, and that heaven and earth shall pass away, ere any of his words pass away. Let us just attend to some of these words. He who continues not in the whole book of this law, is accursed. The whole world is guilty before God. He will by no means clear the guilty. Without shedding of blood, there is no remission. These are the words of God. He has put them into a record. Every one of us may read them, and compare the sayings of God, with the doings of God, and if they do not correspond, the one with the other, we may charge him with falsehood in the face of his insulting enemies, and lift the voice of mockery against him, and feel the triumph which rebels feel, when they witness the timidity of a feeble monarch, who does not, or dares not, carry his threats into accomplishment. And is it possible, that the throne of the eternal God can rest on a basis so tottering,— or that, if ever he shall descend to the manifestation of mercy, he will not give the manifestation of his truth and his righteousness along with it?

Now, those who, without any reference to Christ, find their way to comfort on the strength of their own general confidence in God's mercy, make no account whatever of his truth, or his righteousness. What becomes of the threatenings of God? What becomes of the immutability of his purposes? What becomes of the unfailing truth of all his communications? What becomes of the solemnity of his warnings? and how is it possible to be at all impressed by them,— if they are ever and anon done away by a weak and capricious system of connivance? What becomes of the wide and everlasting distinctions, between obedience and sin? What becomes of the holiness of the Deity? What becomes of reverence for his name, among the wide circle of angels, and archangels, and seraphim, and cherubim, who have all heard his awful proclamations against the children of iniquity,—if they see that any one of them may, by a mere act of confidence in his mercy, turn all that has been uttered against them into an unmeaning parade? Where, in a word, are all those sanctions and securities which can alone make the government of the Deity, to be a government at all? These are all questions which the people to whom we allude, never think of entertaining; nor do they feel the slightest concern about them · and they count it quite enough, if they can just work themselves up into such a tolerable feeling of security, as that they shall not be disturbed in the quiet enjoyment of the good things of this life, which form all in fact that their hearts long after, and which if only permitted to retain in peace, they positively care not for the glory of God, or how shall it be kept inviolate. This is not their affair. The engrossing desire of their bosoms, is just a selfish desire after their own ease: and the strange preparation for that heaven, the unceasing song of which is, Holy and righteous are thy judgments, O thou king of Saints, is such a habit of confidence, as lays prostrate all the majesty of these high and unchangeable perfections.

And yet if you examine these people closely, you will obtain their consent to the position, that there is a law, and that the human race are bound to obedience, and that the authority of the law is supported by sanctions, and that the truth, and justice, and dignity of the Supreme Being, are involved in these sanctions being enforced and executed. They do not refuse the tenet that man is an accountable subject, and that God is a judge and a lawgiver. All that we ask of them, then, is, to examine the account which this subject has to render, and they will find, in characters too glaring to be resisted, that, with the purest and most perfect individual amongst us, it is a wretched account of guilt and of deficiency. That law, which is held to be in full authority and operation over us, has been most unquestionably violated. Now, what is to be made of this? Is the subject to rebel, and disobey every hour, and the king, by a perpetual act of indulgence, to efface every character of truth and dignity from his government? Do this and you depose the legislator from his throne. You reduce the sanction of his law to a name and a mockery. You bring down the high economy of heaven, to the standard of human convenience. You pull the fabric of God's moral government to pieces; and unsubstantiate all the solemnity of his proclaimed sayings,—all the lofty annunciations of the law, and of the prophets,—all that is told of the mighty apparatus of the day of judgment, all that revelation points to, or conscience can suggest, of a living and a reigning God, who will not let himself down to be affronted, or trampled upon, by the creatures whom he has formed.

They who, in profession, admit the truth of God, and yet take comfort from his mercy, without looking to him who bare in his own person, the accomplishment of all the threatenings, do in fact turn that truth into a lie. They, who, in profession, admit the justice of God, and yet trust in the remission of their sins, without any distinct acknowledgement of him on whom God has laid the burden of their condemnation, do in fact prove, that in their mouths justice is nothing but an unmeaning articulation. They who, in profession, admit the authority of those great and unchanging principles, which preside over the whole of God's moral administration, and yet assign to him such a loose and easy connivance at iniquity, as by a mere act of tenderness, to recal the every denunciation that he had uttered against it, do in fact put forth a sacrilegious hand, to the pillars of that immutability, by which the government of creation is upheld and perpetuated. Let them rest assured, that there is no way of reconciliation, but such a way as shields all the holy, and pure, and inflexible attributes of the Divinity, from degradation and contempt.

Out of that hiding-place which is made known in the gospel, all that is just, and severe, and inflexible in the perfections of God, stands in threatening array against every son and daughter of the species. And if they will not look to God as he sets himself forth to us in the New Testament,—if they refuse to look unto him as God in Christ, reconciling the world unto himself, and not imputing unto them their trespasses,—if they set aside all that is said about the blood of the everlasting covenant, and the new and living way of access, and the manner in which the mediatorship of Christ hath repaired all the indignities of sin, and shed a glory over the truth and justice of the lawgiver,—if they will still persist in looking to him through another channel than that of his own revelation; he will persist in looking to them with the aspect of a stern and unappeased enemy. He will not let down the honours of his inflexible character, for the sake of those who refuse his way of salvation. He will not fall in with the delusions of those who profess to revere this character, and then shake the whole burden of conscious guilt and infirmity away from them by the presumption, that in some way or other, the mercy of God will interpose to defend them from the vengeance of his more severe and unrelenting perfections. The one and the only way, in which he dispenses mercy, is through the atonement of Christ,—and if your confidence be laid in any other quarter, he will put that confidence to shame. He will not accept the prayers of those, who can thus make free with the unchangeable attributes which belong to him. He will not descend with such to any intercourse of affection whatever. He will not own the approaches, nor will he deal out any boon from the storehouse of his grace, to those who profess a general confidence in his mercy—when, instead of a mercy which guards, and dignifies, and keeps entire the whole glory and character of God, it is a mercy which belies his word, which invades his other perfections, which spoils the divine image of its grandeur, which breaks up the whole fabric of his moral government, and would make the throne of heaven the seat of an unmeaning pageant, the throne of an insulted and degraded sovereign.

The religion of nature,—or the religion of unaided demonstration,—or the religion of our most fashionable and philosophical schools, leaves this question totally undisposed of;—and at the same time, till the question be resolved, all the hopes of the human soul are in a state of the most fearful uncertainty. This religion makes God the subject of its demonstrations, and it draws out a list of attributes, and it makes the justice of God to be one of these attributes, and the placability of God to be another of them, and it admits that it is in virtue of the former perfection of his nature, that he makes condemnation and punishment to rest on the head of those who violate his law, and that it is in virtue of the latter perfection that he looks connivance, and extends pardon to such violations.

Now, the question which the disciples of this religion have never settled, is, how to strike the compromise between these attributes. They cannot dissipate the cloud of mystery, which hangs over the line of demarcation that is between them. They cannot tell in how far the justice of God will insist on its exactions and its claims, or what the extent of that disobedience is, over which the placability of God will spread the shelter of a generous forgiveness. There is a dilemma here, out of which they cannot unwarp themselves,—a question to which they can give no other answer, than the expressive answer of their silence,—and it is such a silence, as leaves our every apprehension unquelled, and the whole burden of our unappeased doubts and difficulties as insupportable as before. What we demand is, that they shall lay down the steady and unalterable position of that limit, at which the justice of God, and the placability of God, cease their respective encroachments on each other. If they cannot tell this, they can tell nothing that is of any consequence, either to the purpose of comfort, or of direction. The sinner wishes to know on which side of this unknown and undetermined limit, his degree of sinfulness is placed. He wishes to know whether his offences are such as come under the operation of justice, or of mercy,—whether the one attribute will exact from him the penalty, or the other will smile on him connivance. It is in vain to say, that if he repent and turn from them, mercy will claim him as her own, and recover him from the dominion of justice, and spread over all his sins the mantle of an everlasting oblivion. This may still be saying nothing,—for the work of repentance is a work, which, though he should be always trying, he always falls in; and in spite of his every exertion, there is a sin and a shortness in all his services. And when he casts his eye along the scale of character, he sees the better and the worse on each side of him; and the difficulty still recurs, how far down in the scale does mercy extend, or how far up on this scale does justice carry its fiery sentence of condemnation. And thus it is, that he feels no fixed security, which he can lay hold of,—no solid ground on which he can lay the trust of his acceptance with God. And this religion, which has left the whole problem of the attributes undetermined, which can furnish the sinner with no light, by which he may be made to perceive how justice can be displayed, but at the expense of mercy, or how mercy can be displayed, but by breaking in upon the entireness of justice; this hollow, baseless, unsupported system, which, by mangling and deforming the whole aspect of the Deity, has virtually left man without God,—has also, by the faint and twilight obscurity, or rather by the midnight darkness in which it has involved the question about the point of sinfulness, at which the one attribute begins the exercise of its rigour, and the other ceases its indulgence, not only left man without God, but also left him without any solid hope in the world.

But, Secondly, the confidence we have been attempting to expose, is hostile to the cause of practical righteousness in the world.

For what is the real and experimental effect of the obscurity in question on the practice of mankind? The question about our interest with God, is felt to be unresolvable; and, under this feeling, no genuine attempt is made to resolve it. Man eases himself of the difficulty by putting it away from him; and, as he cannot find the point of gradation in the scale of character, on the one side of which, there lies acceptance with God, and on the other side of it, condemnation,—he just upholds himself in tranquillity at any one point, throughout every one variety of this gradation.

Let the question only be put, How far down, in the scale of character, may this loose system of confidence be carried? and where is the limit between those sins, to which forgiveness may be looked for, and those sins from which it is withheld? and you will seldom find the man who gives an answer against himself. The world, in fact, is so much the home and the resting-place of every natural man, that you will not get him so to press, and so to prosecute the question, as to come to any conclusion, that is at all likely to alarm him. He will not barter his present peace, for a concern that looks so distant to him as that of his eternity. The question touches but lightly on his feelings, and an answer conceived lightly, and given lightly, will be enough to pacify him. Go to the man, whose decent and unexceptionable proprieties make him the admiration of all his acquaintances, and even he will allow that he has his infirmities; but he can smother all his apprehensions, and regale his fancy with the smile of an indulgent God. Take, now, a descending step in the scale of character; and do you think there is not to be met with there, the very same process of conscious infirmity on the one hand, and of vague, general, and bewildering confidence on the other? Will the people of the lower station not do the very same thing with the people above them?—Compare themselves with themselves, and find equals to keep them in countenance, and share in the average respect that circulates around them, and take comfort in the review of their very fair and neighbourlike accomplishments, and with the allowance of being just such sinners as they are in the daily habit of associating with, get all their remorse, and all their gloomy anticipations disposed of, by throwing the whole burden of them, in a loose and general way, on the indulgence of God?

And where, in the name of truth and of righteousness, will this stop? We can answer that question. It will not stop at all.

It will describe the whole range of human character; and we challenge you to put your finger on that point where it is to terminate, or to find out the place where a barrier is to be raised against the progress of this mischievous security. It will go downwards and downwards, till it come to the very verge of the malefactor's dungeon. Nay, it will enter there; and we doubt not, that an enlightened discerner may witness, even in this receptacle of outcasts, the operation of the very sentiment which gives such peace and such buoyancy to him whose moral accomplishments throw around him the lustre of a superior estimation. But this lustre will not impose on the eye of God. The Discerner of the heart sees that one and all of us are alienated from him, and strangers to the obligation of his high and spiritual acquirements. He declares the name of Christ to be the only one given under heaven, whereby men can be saved; and after this, every act of confidence, disowning his name, is an expression of the most insulting impiety. On the system of general confidence, every man is left to sin just as much as he likes, and to take comfort just as much as his powers of delusion can administer to him. At this rate, the government of God is unhinged,—the whole earth is broken loose from the system of his administration,—he is deposed from his supremacy altogether,—peace, when there is no peace, spreads its deadly poison over the face of society,—and one sentiment, of deep and fatal tranquillity about the things of God, takes up its firm residence in a world, which, from one end to the other of it, sends up the cry of rebellion against him.

This is a sore evil. The want of a fixed and clearly perceptible line between the justice and placability of the divine nature, not only buries in utter darkness the question of our acceptance with God; but, by throwing every thing loose and undetermined, it opens up the range of a most lawless and uncontrolled impunity for the disobedience of man, up from its gentler deviations, and down to its most profligate and daring excesses. If there be no intelligible line to separate the exercise of the justice of God from the exercise of his placability, every individual will fix this line for himself; and he will make these two attributes to be yea and nay, or fast and loose with each other; and he will stretch out the placability, and he will press upon the justice, just as much as to accommodate the standard of his religious principles to the state of his religious practice; and he will make every thing to square with his own existing taste, and wishes, and convenience; and his mind will soon work its own way to a system of religious opinions which gives him no disturbance; and the spirit of a deep slumber will lay hold of his deluded conscience; and thus, from the want of a settled line,—from the vague, ambiguous, and indefinite way in which this matter is taken up, and brought to a very loose and general conclusion,—or, in other words, from that very way in which natural religion, whether among deists, or our more slender professors of Christianity, leaves the whole question, about the limit of the attributes, unentered upon,—will every man take comfort in the imagined tenderness of God, just as much as he stands in need of it, and experiment on the patience of God just as far as his natural desires may carry him,—so that when we look to the men of the world, as they pass smoothly onward, from the cradle to the grave, do we see each of them in a state of profound security as to his interest with God; each of them solacing himself with his own conception about the slenderness of his guilt, and the kindness of an indulgent Deity; each of them in a state of false and fancied peace with Heaven, while every affection of the inner man, and many of the doings of the outer man, bear upon them the stamp of rebellion against Heaven's law; each of them walking without uneasiness, and without terror, while, at the same time, each and all of them do in fact walk in the counsel of their own hearts, and after the sight of their own eyes.

SERMON XVI.

The Union of Truth and Mercy in the Gospel.

"Mercy and truth are met together: righteousness and peace have kissed each other."—Psalm lxxxv. 10.

It was not by a simple deed of amnesty, that man was invited to return and be at peace with God. It was by a deed of exaction. It was not by nullifying the sanctions of the law, that man was offered a free and a full discharge from the penalties he had incurred by breaking it. It was by executing these sanctions on another, who voluntarily took them upon himself, and who, in so doing, magnified the law, and made it honourable. To redeem us from the curse of the law, Christ became a curse for us. It was not by God lifting off our iniquities from our persons, and scattering them away into a region of forgetfulness, without one demonstration of his abhorrence, and without the fulfilment of his threatenings against them; but lifting them off from us, he laid them on another, who bare, in his own person, the punishment that we should have borne. God laid upon his own Son the iniquities of us all. The guilt of our sins is not done away by a mere act of forgiveness. It is washed away by the blood of the Lamb. God set him forth a propitiation. He was smitten for our transgressions. He gave himself for us an offering and a sacrifice to God. The system of the gospel no more expunges the attribute of mercy from the character of the Godhead, than it expunges the attributes of truth and righteousness. But all the mercy which it offers and proclaims to a guilty world, is the mercy which flows upon it through the channel of that Mediatorship, by which his truth and his justice have been asserted and vindicated; and, while it reveals to us the openness of this channel, it also reveals to us that every other which the heart of man may conceive, is shut, and intercepted, and utterly impassable. There is none other name given under heaven, whereby man can be saved, but the name of him who poured out his soul unto the death for us. Without the shedding of his blood, there could have been no remission. And he who hath not the Son, hath the wrath of God abiding on him.

It is due to our want of moral sensibility, that sin looks so light and so trivial in our estimation. We have no adequate feeling of its malignity, of its exceeding sinfulness. And, liable as we are to think of God, that he is altogether like unto ourselves, do we think that he may cancel our guilt as easily from the book of his condemnation, by an act of forgiveness, as we cancel it from our own memory, by an act of forgetfulness. But God takes his own way, and most steadfastly asserts, throughout the whole process of our recovery, the prerogatives of his own truth, and his own righteousness. He so loved the world, as to send his Son to it, not to condemn, but to save. But he will not save us in such a way as to confirm our light estimation of sin, or to let down the worth and dignity of his own character. The method of our salvation is not left to the random caprices of human thought, and human fancy. It is a method devised for us by unsearchable wisdom, and made known to us by fixed and unalterable truth, and prescribed to us by a supreme authority, which has debarred every other method; and though we may behold no one feature, either of greatness or of beauty to admire in it—yet do angels admire it; and to accomplish it, did the Son of God move from the residence of his glory, and all heaven appears to have laboured with the magnitude and the mystery of the great undertaking; and along the whole tract of revelation, from the first age of the world, do we behold the notices of the coming atonement; and while man sits at his ease, and can see nothing to move him either to gratitude or to wonder, in the evolution of that mighty scheme, by which mercy and truth have been made to meet together, and righteousness and peace to kiss each other,—it is striking to mark the place and the prominency which are given to it, in the councils of the Eternal. And it might serve to put us right, and to rebuke the levities which are so currently afloat in this dead and darkened world, did we only look at the stress that is laid on this great work, throughout the whole of its preparation and its performance,—and how, to bring it to its accomplishment, the Father had to send the Son into the world, and to throw a veil over his glory,—and to put the cup of our chastisement into his hand,—and to bid the sword of righteous vengeance awake against his fellow,—and, that he might clear a way of access to a guilty world, had to do it through the blood of an everlasting covenant,—and to lay the full burden of our atonement on the head of the innocent sufferer,—and to endure the spectacle of his bitterness, and his agonies, and his tears, till he cried out that it was finished, and so bowed himself and gave up the ghost.

Man is blind to the necessity, but God sees it. The prayer of Christ in his agony was, that the cup, if possible, might be removed from him. But it was not possible. He could have called twelve legions of angels, and they would have eagerly flown to rescue their beloved Lord from the hands of his persecutors. But he knew that the Scripture must be fulfilled, and they looked on in silent forbearance. It behooved him to undergo all this. And there was a need, and a propriety, why he should suffer all these things, ere he entered into his glory.

We shall offer three distinct remarks on this method of our redemption, in order to prove that it fulfils the whole assertion of our text, that it has made mercy and truth to meet together, and righteousness and peace to kiss each other.

First, it maintains the entireness and glory of all the attributes of the Godhead. Secondly, it provides a solid foundation for the peace of every sinner who concurs in it. And, thirdly, it strengthens all the securities for the cause of practical righteousness among men.

I. In darkness, as we are, about the glory and character of the Supreme Being, it would offer a violence even to our habitual conceptions of him, to admit of any limit, or any deduction from the excellencies of his nature. We should even think it a lessening of the Deity, were the extent of his perfections such, as that we should be able to grasp them within the comprehension of our understandings. The property of chiefest admiration to his creatures is, that they know but a part, and are not aware how small a part that is, to what is unknown; and never is their obeisance more lowly, than when, under the sense of a greatness that is undefined and unsearchable, they feel themselves baffled by the infinitude of the Creator. It is not his power, as attested by all that exists within the limits of actual discovery; but his power, as conceived to form and uphold a universe, whose outskirts are unknown.—It is not his wisdom, as exhibited in what has been seen by human eye; but his wisdom, as pervading the unnumbered secresies of mechanism, which no eye can penetrate. It is not his knowledge, as displayed in the greater and prophetic outlines of the history of this world; but his knowledge, as embracing all the mazes of creation, and all the mighty periods of eternity.—It is not his antiquity, as prior to all that is visible, and as reaching far above and beyond the remote infancy of nature; but his antiquity, as retiring upwards from the loftiest ascent of our imaginations, and lost in the viewless depth of an existence, that was from everlasting.—These are what serve to throne the Deity in grandeur inaccessible. It is the thought of what eye hath not seen, and ear hath not heard, neither hath it entered into the heart of man to conceive, that places him on such a height of mystery before us. And should we ever be able to overtake, in thought, the dimensions of any attribute that belongs to him,—and far more should we ever be able to outstrip, in fancy, a single feature of that character which is realised by the living and reigning God,—should defect or impotency attach to him who dwelleth in the light which no man can approach unto, would we feel as if all our most rooted and accustomed conceptions of the Godhead had sustained an overthrow, would we feel as if the sanctuary of him who is the King eternal and invisible had suffered violence.

And this is just as true of the moral as of the natural attributes of the Godhead. When we think of his truth, it is a truth which, if heaven and earth stand committed to the fulfilment of its minutest article, heaven and earth must, for its vindication, pass away. When we think of his holiness, it is such that, if sin offer to draw nigh, a devouring fire goeth forth to burn up and to destroy it. When we think of his law, it is a law which must be made honourable, even though, by the enforcement of its sanctions, it shall sweep into an abyss of misery all the generations of the rebellious. And yet this God, just, and righteous, and true, is a God of love, and of compassion, infinite. He is slow to anger, and of great mercy. He does not afflict willingly; and as a father rejoices over his children, does he long to rejoice in tenderness over us all; and out of the store-house of a grace that is inexhaustible, does he deal out the offers of pardon and reconciliation to every one of us. Even in some way or other does the love of God for his creatures find its way through the barrier of their sinfulness; and he who is of purer eyes than to behold iniquity,—he who hath spoken the word, and shall he not perform it,—he of whose law it has been said, that not one jot or one tittle of it, shall pass away, till all be fulfilled,—he holds out the overtures of friendship to the children of disobedience, and invites the guiltiest among them to the light of his countenance, in time, and to the enjoyment of his glory and presence, in eternity.

There is no one device separate from the gospel, by which the glory of any one of these attributes can be exalted, but by the surrender or the limitation of another attribute. It is in the gospel alone that we perceive how each of them may be heightened to infinity, and yet each of them reflect a lustre on the rest. When Christ died, justice was magnified. When he bore the burden of our torment, the truth of God received its vindication. When the sins of the world brought him to the cross, the lesson taught by this impressive spectacle was, holiness unto the Lord. All the severer perfections of the Godhead, were, in fact, more powerfully illustrated by the deep and solemn propitiation that was made for sin, than they could have been by the direct punishment of sin itself.—Yet all redounding to the triumph of his mercy.—For mercy, in the exercise of a simple and spontaneous tenderness, does not make so high an exhibition, as mercy forcing its way through restraints and difficulties,—as mercy accomplishing its purposes by a plan of unsearchable wisdom,—as mercy surrendering what was most dear for the attainment of its object,—as the mercy of God, not simply loving the world, but so loving it as to send his only beloved Son, and to lay upon him the iniquities of us all,—as mercy, thus surmounting a barrier which, to created eye, appeared immoveable, and which both pours a glory on the other excellencies of the Godhead, and rejoices over them.

It is the gospel of Jesus Christ, which has poured the light of day into all the intricacies of this contemplation. We there see no compromise, and no surrender, of the attributes to each other. We see no mutual encroachment on their respective provinces,—no letting down of that entire and absolute perfection which belongs to every part in the character of the Godhead. The justice of God has not been invaded; for by him, who poured out his soul unto the death for us, has the whole weight of this aggrieved and offended attribute been borne; and from that cross of agony, where he cried out that it was finished, does the divine Justice send forth a brighter and a nobler radiance of vindicated majesty, than if the minister of vengeance had gone forth and wreaked the whole sentence of condemnation on every son and daughter of the species. And as the justice of God has suffered no encroachment, so, such is the admirable skilfulness of this expedient, that the mercy of God is restrained by no limitation. It is arrested in its offers by no questions about the shades, and the degrees, and the varieties of sinfulness. It stops at no point in the descending scale of human depravity. The blood of Christ cleansing from all sin, has spread such a field for its invitations, that in the full confidence of a warranted and universal commission, may the messengers of grace walk over the face of the world, and lay the free gift of acceptance at the door of every individual, and of every family. Such is the height, and depth, and breadth, and length, of the mercy of God in Christ Jesus; and yet it is a mercy so exercised, as to keep the whole council and character of God unbroken,—and a mercy, from the display of which, there beams a brighter radiance than ever from each lineament in the image of the Godhead.

Now if the glory of God be so involved in this way of redemption, what shall we think of the disparagement, that is rendered to him, and to all his attributes, by the man who, without respect to the work and the righteousness of Christ, seeks to be justified by his own righteousness? It is quite possible for man to toil and to waste his strength on the object of his salvation, and yet, by all he can make out, may be only widening his laborious deviation from the path which leads to it. Do his uttermost to establish a righteousness of his own, and what is the whole fruit of his exertion?—the mere semblance of righteousness, without the infusion of its essential quality,—labour without love,—the drudgery of the hand, without the desire and devotedness of the heart, as its inspiring principle. If the man be dissatisfied, as he certainly ought to be, then a sense of unexpiated guilt will ever and anon intrude itself upon his fears; and a resistless conviction of the insufficiency of all his performances will never cease to haunt and to paralyze him. In these circumstances, there may be the conformity of the letter extorted from him, in the spirit of bondage; but the animating soul is not there, which turns obedience into a service of delight and a service of affection. In Heaven's account, such obedience as this is but the mockery of a lifeless skeleton; and, even as a skeleton, it is both wanting in its parts, and unshapely in its proportions. It is an obedience defective, even in the tale and measure of its external duties. But what pervades the whole of it by the element of worthlessness is, that, destitute of love to God, it is utterly destitute of a celestial character, and can never prepare an inhabitant of this world for the joys or the services of the great celestial family.

And, on the other hand, if the man be satisfied, this very circumstance gives to the righteousness that he would establish for himself, the character of an insult upon God, instead of a reverential offering. It is a righteousness accompanied with a certain measure of confident feeling, that it is good enough for the acceptance of the Lawgiver. There is in it the audacity of a claim and a challenge upon his approbation. Short as it is, in respect of outward performance, and tainted within by the very spirit of earthliness, it is brought like a lame and diseased victim in sacrifice, and laid upon the altar before him. It is an evil and a bitter thing to sin against God; but it is a still more direct outrage upon his attributes, to expect that he will look on sinfulness with complacency. It is an open defiance to the law, to trample upon its requirements; but it were a still deadlier overthrow of its authority, to reverse its sanctions, and make it turn its threatenings into rewards. The sinner who disobeys and trembles, renders at least the homage of his fears to the truth and power of the Eternal. But the sinner who makes a righteousness of his infirmities; and puts a gloss upon his disobedience, and brings the accursed thing to the gate of the sanctuary, and bids the piercing eye of Omniscience look upon it, and be satisfied,—tell us whether the fire which cometh forth will burn up the offering, that it may rise in sweetly smelling savour to him who sitteth on the throne; or will it seize on the presumptuous offerer, who could thus dare the inspection, and thrust his unprepared footstep within the precincts of unspotted holiness?

And how must it go to aggravate the offence of such an approach, when it is made in the face of another righteousness which God himself hath provided, and in which alone he hath proclaimed that it is safe for a sinner to draw nigh. When the alternative is fairly proposed, to come on the merit of your own obedience and tried by it, or to come on the merit of the obedience of

Christ, and receive in your own person the reward which he hath purchased for you,—only think of the aspect it must bear in the eye of Heaven, when the offer of the perfect righteousness is contemptuously set aside, and the sinner chooses to appear in his own character before the presence of the Eternal. When the imputation of vanity and uselessness is thus fastened on all that the Son hath done, and on all that the Father hath devised for the redemption of the guilty,—when that righteousness, to accomplish which, Christ had to travail in the greatness of his strength, is thus held to be nothing, by creatures whose every thought, and every performance, have the stain of corruption in them—when that doctrine of his death, on which, in the book of God's counsel, is made to turn the deliverance of our world, is counted to be foolishness,—when the sinner thus persists in obtruding his own virtue on the notice of the Lawgiver, and refuses to put on, as a covering of defence, the virtue of his Saviour,—we have only to contrast the lean, shrivelled, paltry dimensions of the one, with the faultless, and sustained, and Godlike perfection of the other, to perceive how desperate is the folly, and how unescapable is the doom of him who hath neglected the great salvation.

It is thus that the refusal of Christ, as our righteousness, stamps a deeper and a more atrocious character of rebellion on the guilty than before,—and it is thus that the word of his mouth, like a two-edged sword, performs one function on him who accepts, and an opposite function on him who despises it. If the gospel be not the savour of life unto life, it will be the savour of death unto death. If it be not a rock of confidence, it will be a rock of offence, and it will fall upon him who resists it, and grind him into powder. If we kiss not the Son, in the day of our peace, the day of his wrath is coming, and who shall be able to stand when his anger is kindled but a little? We have already offended God by the sinfulness of our practice,—we may yet offend him still more by the haughtiness of our pretensions. The evil of our best works constitutes them an abomination in his sight; but nothing remains to avert the hostility of his truth and his holiness against us, if by those works we seek to be justified. It will indeed be the sealing up of our iniquity, if our obedience, impregnated as it is with the very spirit of that iniquity, shall be set up in rivalship to the obedience of his only and well beloved Son,—if, by viewing the defect of our righteousness, as a thing of indifference, and the fulness of his, as a thing of no value, we shall heap insult upon transgression,—and if, after the provocation of a broken law, we shall maintain the boastful attitude of him who hath won the merit and the reward of victory, and in this attitude add the farther provocation of a slighted and rejected gospel.

II. We shall conclude, for the present, these brief and imperfect remarks, by adverting to the solidity of that foundation of peace, which the gospel scheme of mercy provides for every sinner who concurs in it. It is altogether worthy of observation, how, under this exquisite contrivance, the very elements of disquietude in a sinner's bosom, are turned into the elements of comfort and confidence in the mind of a believer. It is the unswerving truth of God, which haunts the former by the thought of the certainty of his coming vengeance. But this very truth, committed to the fulfilment of all those promises, which are yea and amen in Christ Jesus, sustains the latter by the thought of the certainty of his coming salvation. It is justice, unbending justice, which sets such a seal on the condemnation of the disobedient, that every sinner who is out of Christ, feels it to be irrevocable. In Christ, this attribute, instead of a terror, becomes a security; for it is just in God to justify him who believes in Jesus. It is the sense of God's violated authority which fills the heart of an awakened sinner with the fear that he is undone. But this authority under the gospel proclamation, is leagued on the side of comfort, and not of fear; for this is the commandment of God, that we believe in the name of the Lord Jesus Christ, as he has given us commandment. It is not by an act of mercy, triumphing over the other attributes, that pardon is extended to the sinful; for, under the economy of the gospel, these attributes are all engaged on the side of mercy; and God is not only merciful, but he is faithful and just in forgiving the sins of those who accept of Christ, as he is offered to them in the gospel. Those very perfections, then, which fix and necessitate the doom of the rebellious, form into a canopy of defence around the head of the believer. The guarantees of a sinner's punishment now become the guarantees of promise; and while, like the flaming sword at the gate of paradise, they turn every way, and shut him out of every access to the Deity but one,—let him take to that one, and they instantly become to him the sureties and the safe-guard of that hiding-place into which he has entered.

The foundation, then, of a believer's peace, is, in every way, as sure and as solid as is the foundation of a sinner's fears. The very truth which makes the one tremble, because staked to the execution of an unfulfilled threat, ministers to the other the strongest consolation. It is impossible for God to lie, says an awakened sinner, and this thought pursues him with the agony of an arrow sticking fast. It is impossible for God to lie, says a believer; and as he hath not only said but sworn, there are two immutable things by which to anchor the confidence of him who hath fled for refuge to the hope set before him. He staggers not at the promises of God, because of unbelief. He holds himself steadfast, by simply counting him to be faithful who hath promised. It is through that very faith, by being strong in which he gives glory to God, that he gains peace to his own heart; and the justice which beams a terror on all who stand without, utterly passes by the shielded head of him who hath turned to the strong hold, and taken a place under the shadow of his wings, who hath satisfied the justice of God, and taken upon himself the burden of its fullest vindication.

SERMON XVII.

The purifying Influence of the Christian Faith.

"Sanctified by faith."—*Acts* xxvi. 18.

III. It is a matter of direct and obvious understanding, how the law, by its promises and its threatenings, should exert an influence over human conduct. We seem to walk in a plain path, when we pass onwards from the enforcements of the law, to the effect of them on the fears, and the hopes, and the purposes of man. Do this, and you shall live; and do the opposite of this, and you shall forfeit life, form two clear and distinct processes, in the conceiving of which, there is no difficulty whatever. The motive and the movement both stand intelligibly out to the discernment of common sense; nor in the application of such argument as this, to the design of operating on the character or life of a human being, is there any mystery to embarrass, any hidden step, which, by baffling our every attempt to seize upon it, leaves us in a state of helpless perplexity.

The same is not true of the gospel, or of the manner in which it operates on the springs of human action. It is not so readily seen how its privileges can be appropriated by faith, and at the same time its precepts can retain their practical authority over the conduct of a believer. There is an alarm, and an honest alarm, on the part of many, lest a proclamation of free grace unto the world, should undermine all our securities for the cause of righteousness in the world. They look with jealousy upon the freeness. They fear lest a deed so ample and unconditional, of forgiveness for the past, should give rise, in the heart of a sinner, to a secure opinion of its impunity for the future. What they dread is, that to proclaim such a freeness of pardon on the part of God, would be to proclaim a corresponding freeness of practice on the part of man. They are able to comprehend how the law, by its direct enforcements, should operate in keeping men from sin; but they are not able to comprehend how, when not under the law, but under grace, there should continue the same motives to abstain from sin, as those intelligible ones which the law furnishes, or even other motives of more powerful operation. We are quite sure that there is something here which needs to be made plain to the understandings of a very numerous class of inquirers,—a knot of difficulty which needs to be untied,—a hidden step in the process of explanation, on which they may firmly pass from what is known to what is unknown. There are not two terms in the whole compass of human language, which stand more frequently and more familiarly contrasted with each other, than those of faith and good works; and this, not merely on the question of our acceptance before God, but also on the question of the personal character and acquirements of a true disciple of Christ. It is positively not seen, how the possession of the one should at all stimulate to the performance of the other,—how the peace of the gospel should reside in the same heart, from which there emanates, on the life of a believer, the practice of the gospel,—how a righteousness that is without the deeds of the law, should stand connected, in the actual history of him who obtains it, with a zealous, and diligent, and every-day doing of these deeds.

There is much in all this to puzzle the man who is experimentally a stranger to the truth as it is in Jesus. Nor does it at all serve to extricate or to enlighten him, when he is made to perceive, that, in point of fact, those men who most cordially assent to the doctrine of salvation being all of grace and not of works, are most assiduous in so walking, and in so working, and in so painstaking, as if salvation were all of works, and not of grace. The fact is quite obvious and unquestionable. But the principle on which it rests, remains a mystery to the general eye of the world. They marvel, but they go no farther. They see that thus it is, but they see not how it is; and they put it down among those inexplicable oddities which do at times occur, both in the moral and natural kingdom of the creation.

But in all our attempts to dissipate this obscurity, it is well to advert to the total difference between him who has the faith, and him who has it not. The one has the materials of the argument under his eye, and within the grasp of his handling. The other may be able to recognize in the argument, a logical and consistent process; but he is at a loss about the simple conceptions, which form the materials of the argument. He is like a man who can perform all the manipulations of an algebraical process, while he feels not the force or the significancy of the symbols. His habits of ratiocination enable him to perceive, that there is a connexion between the ideas in the argument. But the ideas themselves are not manifest to him. It is not in the power of reasoning to supply this want. Reasoning cannot create the primary materials of the argument. It only cements them together. And here it is, that you are met by the impotency of human demonstration,—and are reduced to the attitude of knocking at a door which you cannot open,—and feel your need of an enlightening spirit,—and are made to perceive, that it is only on the threshold of Christianity, where you can hold the intercourse of a common sympathy and understanding with the world,—and that to be admitted to the mysteries of the kingdom of heaven, you must pass into a region of manifestation, where the world cannot follow, but where it will cast the imputation of madness and of mysticism after you.

Without attempting to define faith, as to the nature of it, which could not be done but with other words more simple than itself, let us look to the objects of faith, and see whether there do not emanate from them, a sanctifying influence on the heart of every real believer.

First, then, the whole object of faith, is the matter of the testimony of God in Scripture. So that though faith be a single principle, and is designated in language by a single term,—yet this by no means precludes it from being such a principle, as comes into contact, and is conversant, with a very great variety of objects. In this respect it may bear a resemblance to sight, or hearing, or any other of the senses, by which man holds communication with the external things that are near him, and around him. The same eye which, when open, looks to a friend, and can, from that very look, afford entrance into the heart for an emotion of tenderness, will also behold other visible things, and take in an appropriate influence from each of them,—will behold the prospect of beauty that is before it, and thence obtain gratification to the taste,—or will behold the sportive felicity of animals, and thence obtain gratification to the benevolence,—or will behold the precipice beneath, and thence obtain a warning of danger, or a direction of safety,—or may behold a thousand different objects, and obtain a thousand different feelings and different intimations.

Now the same of faith. It has been called the eye of the mind. But whether this be a well conceived image or not, it certainly affords an inlet to the mind for a great variety of communications. The Apostle calls faith the evidence of things not seen,—not of one such thing, but of very many such things. The man who possesses faith, can be no more intellectually blind to one of these things, and at the same time knowing and believing as to another of them, than the man who possesses sight can, with his eye open, perceive one external object, and have no perception of another, which stands as nearly and as conspicuously before him. The man who is destitute of sight, will never know what it is to feel the charm of visible scenery. But grant him sight; and he will not only be made alive to this charm, but to a multitude of other influences, all emanating from the various objects of visible nature, through the eye upon the mind, and against which his blindness had before opposed a hopeless and invincible barrier. And the man who is destitute of faith, will never know what it is to feel the charm of the peace-speaking blood of Christ. But grant him faith; and he will not only be made alive to this charm, but to a multitude of other influences, all emanating from the various truths of revelation, through this intellectual organ, on the heart of him who was at one time blind, but has now been made to see. This will help, in some measure, to clear up the perplexity to which we have just now adverted. They who are under its darkening influence, conceive of the faith which worketh peace, that it has only to do with one doctrine, and that that one doctrine relates to Christ, as a peace-offering for sin. Now, it is very true, that it has to do with this one doctrine; but it has also to do with other doctrines, all equally presented before it in the very same record, and the view of all which is equally to be had, from the very same quarter of contemplation. In other words, the very same opening of the mental eye, through which the peace of the gospel finds entrance into the bosom of a faithful man, affords an entrance for the righteousness of the gospel along with it. The truth that Christ died for the sins of the world, will cast upon his mind its appropriate influence. But so also will the truth that Christ is to judge the world, and the truth that unless ye repent ye shall perish, and the truth that they who have a right to the tree of life, are they who keep the commandments, and the truth that an unrighteous man shall not inherit the kingdom of God. If a man see not every one object that is placed within the sphere of his natural vision, he sees none of them, and his whole body is full of darkness. If a man believe the Bible to be the word of God, he will read it; but if he read it, and believe not every one truth that lies within the grasp of his understanding, he believes none of them, and is in darkness, and knoweth not whither he is going.

If I open the door of my mind to the word of God, I as effectually make it the repository of various truths, as, if I open the door of my chamber, and take in the Bible, I make this chamber the repository of the book, and of every chapter, and of every verse, that is contained in it. I thus bring my mind into contact with every one influence, that every one truth is fitted to exercise over it. If there be nothing in these truths contradictory to each other, (and if there be, let this set aside, as it ought, the authority of the whole communication,) then the mind acts a right and consistent part in believing each of them, and in submitting itself to the influence of each of them. And thus it is, that believing the propitiation which is through the blood of Christ, for the remission of sins that are past, I may feel through him the peace of reconciliation with the Father; and believing that he who cometh unto Christ for forgiveness must forsake all, I may also feel the necessity which lies upon me of departing from all iniquity; and believing that in myself there is no strength for the accomplishment of such a task, I may look around for other expedients, than such as can be devised by my own natural wisdom, or carried into effect by my own natural energies; and believing that, in the hand of Christ there are gifts for the rebellious, and that one of these gifts is the Holy Spirit to strengthen his disciples, I may look to him for my sanctification, even as I look unto him for my redemption: and believing that the gift is truly promised as an answer to prayer, I may mingle a habit of prayer, with a habit of watchfulness and of endeavour. And thus may I go abroad over the whole territory of divine truth, and turn to its legitimate account every separate portion of it, and be in all a trusting, and a working, and a praying, and a rejoicing, and a trembling disciple,—and that, not because I have given myself up to the guidance of clashing and contradictory principles,— but because, with a faith commensurate to the testimony of God, I give myself over in my whole mind, and whole person, to the authority of a whole Bible.

But secondly, let us take what some may think a more restricted view of the object of faith, and suppose it to be Jesus Christ in his person and in his character. It is a summary, but at the same time a most true and substantial affirmation, that we are saved by faith in Christ. And yet this very affirmation, true as it is, may have been so misunderstood as to darken the minds of many, into the very misconception that we are attempting to expose. I could not be said to have faith in an acquaintance, if I believed not all that he told me. Nor have I faith in Christ, if I believe not every item of that communication of which he is the author, either by himself or by his messengers. So that faith in Christ, so far from excluding any of the truths of the Bible, comprehends our assent to them all. But we are willing to admit, that the phrase is calculated to fasten our attention more particularly on such truth as relates, in a more immediate manner, to the person and the doings of the Saviour. Take it in this sense, and you will find, that though eminently and directly fitted to work peace in the heart of a believer, it is just as directly and powerfully on the side of his practical righteousness. When I think of Christ, and think of him as one who has poured out his soul unto the death for me, I feel a confidence in drawing near unto God. When employed in this contemplation, I look to him as a crucified Saviour. But without keeping mine eye for a single moment from off his person,—without another exercise of mind, than that by which I look unto Jesus, simply and entirely, as he is set forth unto me,—I also behold him at one time as an exalted Saviour, and at another time as a commanding Saviour, and at another time as a strengthening Saviour. In other words, by the mere work of faith in Christ, I bring my heart into contact with all those motives, and all those elements of influence, which give rise to the new obedience of the gospel. When the veil betwixt me and the Saviour is withdrawn,—when God shines in my heart with the light of the knowledge of his own glory in the face of his Son,—when the Spirit taketh of the things of Christ, and showeth them unto me, and I am asked which of the things it is that is most fitted to arrest a convicted sinner, in the midst of his cries and prayers for deliverance,—I would say, that it was Christ lifted up on the cross of his offences, and pouring out the blood of that mighty expiation, by which the guilt of them all is washed away. This is the rock on which he will build all his hopes of acceptance before God. He will look unto Christ and be at peace. But this is not the only attitude in which Christ is revealed to him. He will look to Christ as an example. He will look to him as a teacher. He will look to him in all the capacities which are attached to the person, or identified with the doings of the Saviour. He will look to him, asserting his right of authority and disposal over those whom he has purchased unto himself. He will, by the eye of faith, see that rebuking glance which our Saviour cast over the misconduct of his disciples,—and which, when Peter saw, by the eye of sight, he was so moved by the spectacle, that he went out and wept bitterly. That meekness and gentleness of Christ, in the name of which, Paul besought his disciples to walk no more after the flesh, will be present in its influence on those who, though they see him not, yet believe him, and have their conceptions filled and satisfied with his likeness. They will behold him to be an exalted Prince, as well as an exalted Saviour, and they will count it a faithful saying, that he came to sanctify as well as redeem,—and they will look upwards to his present might as a commander, as well as forwards to his future majesty as a judge,— and they will be thoroughly persuaded, that to persevere in sin, is altogether to thwart the great aim of the enterprize of our redemption,—and they will understand as Paul did, who affirmed, with expostulations and tears, that the enemies of righteousness are also the enemies of the cross;—and thus, from Christ, in all his various attitudes, will a moralizing power descend on the hearts of those who really believe in him,— and as surely as any man possesses the faith that is in Christ Jesus, so surely will he be sanctified by that faith.

And, thirdly, let us confine our attention still farther, to one particular article of our faith. Paul was determined to know nothing, save Jesus Christ, and him crucified. Now, conceive faith to attach itself to the latter clause of this verse, and that Christ crucified, for the time being, is the single object of its contemplation. There is still no such thing as a true faith, attaching itself to this one object exclusively; and though at one time it may be the sole contemplation which engrosses it, at other times it may have other contemplations. If, in fact, it shut out those other contemplations, which are furnished by the subject-matter of the testimony of God, it may be proved now, and it will be proved in the day of reckoning, to be no faith at all. But just as it has been said, that the mind can only think of one thing at a time, so faith may be employed, for a time, in looking only towards one object; and as we said before, let Christ crucified be conceived to be that one object. From what has been said already, it will be seen, that this one exercise of faith will not counteract the legitimate effect of the other exercises. But we should like to compute the influence of this one exercise on the heart and life of a believer. In the case of an Antinomian, the doctrine of the atonement may furnish a pretext and a pacification to his conscience, under a wilful habit of perseverance in iniquity. But, if this partial faith of his be not a real faith, then we are not responsible for his conduct, nor ought he to be at all quoted as an exception against that alliance, for which we are contending, between the faith of the gospel and the cause of practical righteousness. Only grant the faith to be real, and as there is no one doctrine of the Bible, out of which it may not gather a purifying influence to the heart, so out of this doctrine of the atonement, will such a purifying influence descend most abundantly on the heart of every genuine believer.

For, it first takes away a wall of partition, which, in the case of every man who has not received this doctrine, lies across the path of his obedience at the very commencement. So long as I think that it is quite impossible for me so to run as to obtain, I will not move a single footstep. Under the burden of a hopeless controversy between me and God, I feel as it were weighed down to the inactivity of despair. I live without hope; and so long as I do so, I live without God in the world. And besides, he, while the object of my terror, is also the object of my aversion. The helpless necessity under which I labour, so long as the question of my guilt remains unsettled is to dread the Being whom I am commanded to love. I may occasionally cast a feeble regard towards that distant and inaccessible Lawgiver: But so long as I view him shrouded in the darkness of frowning majesty, I can place in him no trust, and I can bear towards him no filial tenderness. I may occasionally consult the requirements of his law: But when I look to the uncancelled sentence that is against me, I can never tread, with hopeful or assured footsteps, on the career of obedience. But let me look unto Christ lifted up for our offences, and see the hand-writing of ordinances that was against us, and which was contrary unto us, nailed to his cross, and there blotted out and taken out of the way; and then I see the barrier in question levelled with the ground. I now behold the way of repentance cleared of the obstructions, by which it was aforetime rendered utterly impassable. This is the will of God —even your sanctification, may be sounded a thousand times in the ear of an unbeliever, and leave him as immoveable as it found him; because, while under a sense of unexpiated guilt, he sees a mighty parapet before him, which he cannot scale. But if the same words be sounded in the ears of a believer, they will put him into motion. For to him the parapet is opened up, and the rough way is made smooth, and the mountain and the hill are brought low, and the valley of separation is filled, and he is made to see the salvation of God. The path of obedience is made level before him, and he enters it with the inspiration of a new and invigorating principle; and that love to God, which the consciousness of guilt will ever keep at a distance from the heart, now takes up the room of this terrifying, and paralysing, and alienating sentiment; and the reception of this doctrine of atonement is just as much the turning point of a new character, as it is the turning point of a new hope; and it is the very point, in the history of every human soul, at which the alacrity of gospel obedience takes its commencement, as well as the cheerfulness of gospel anticipations. Till this doctrine be believed, there is no attempt at obedience at all; or else, it is such an obedience as is totally unanimated by the life and the love of real godliness. And it is not till this doctrine has taken possession of the mind, that any man can take up the language of the Psalmist, and say, "Lord, I am thy servant, I am thy servant, thou hast loosed my bonds."

Conceive, then, a believer with the career of obedience thus opened up and made hopeful to him,—conceive him with the necessity of obedience made just as authentically known to him as are the tidings of his deliverance from guilt,—conceive a man who, by the act of rendering homage to the truth of God, rests a confidence in the death of Christ for pardon, and who also, by the very same act, subscribes to the sayings of Christ about repentance, and the new walk of the new creature,—and then let me ask you to think of the securities which encompass his mind, and protect it from the delusion that we have already alluded to. We have said that the peace which is felt in a vague apprehension of God's mercy, and which makes no account of his truth, or of his justice, has the effect of making him who entertains it altogether stationary, in point of acquirement. With the semblance of good that he has about him, he will meet the sterner attributes of the Deity. For his defect of real good, he will draw on the indulgent attributes of the Deity. He will make the character of God, suit itself to his own character, so that any stimulus to advance or to perfect it, shall be practically done away. And thus it is, that along the whole range of human accomplishment, you may observe an unvaried state of repose,—the repose, in fact, of death,—for the repose of man who brought to the estimate of a spiritual law, will be found, to use the significant language of the Bible, dead in trespasses and sins,—sinning at one time without remorse, trusting at another time without foundation.

Now the gospel scheme of mercy is clear of this abuse altogether. It comes forth upon the sinner with an antidote against this security, just as strong and as prominent as is its antidote against despair. In-somuch that the state of the believer, in respect of motive and of practical influence, is the very reverse of what we have now adverted to. In the act of becoming a believer, he awakens from the deep and universal lethargy of nature. With his new hope commences his new life. He ceases to be stationary,—and what is more, he never ceases to be progressive. He does not satisfy himself with barely moving onwards to a higher point in the scale of human attainment, and then sitting down with the sentiment that it is enough. He never counts it enough. The practical attitude of the believer is that of one who is ever looking forwards. The practical movement of the believer is that of one who is ever pressing forwards. He could not, without a surrender of those essential principles which make him what he is, tarry at any one point in the gradation of moral excellence. It is not more inseparable from him to be ever doing well, than it is inseparable from him to be ever aspiring to do better. So that the paltry question about the degrees and the comparisons of virtue, he entertains not for a moment; and, with all the aids and expedients of the gospel for helping his advancement, does he strenuously prosecute the work of conforming to the precept of the gospel,—to be growing in grace, to be perfecting himself in holiness.

It has been a much controverted question, how far this process of continual advancement will carry a believer in this world. Some affirm it will carry him to the point of absolute perfection. Others more cautiously satisfy themselves by the remark, that whether perfection be ever our attainment or not, it ought always to be our aim. And one thing seems to be certain,—that there is no such perfection in this world, as might bring along with it the repose of victory.

Paul counted all that was behind as nothing, and he pressed onwards. And it is the experience of every Christian, who makes a real business of his sanctification, that there is a struggle between nature and grace, even unto the end. There is no discharge from this warfare, while we are in the body. To the last hour of life there will be the presence of a carnal nature to humble him, and to make him vigilant; and, with every true Christian, there will be the ascendency of grace, so as that this nature shall not have the dominion over him. The corruption of the old man will be effectually resisted; but not, we fear, till the materialism of our actual frames be resolved into dust, will this corruption be destroyed. The flesh lusting against the spirit, and the spirit against the flesh, is the short but compendious description of the state of every believer in the world;—and could the evil and adverse principle be eradicated, as well as overborne,—could a living man bid the sinful propensity, with all its workings and all its inclinations, conclusively away from him,—could the authority of the new creature obtain such unrivalled sway over the whole machinery of the affections and the doings, that resistance was no longer felt, and the battle was brought to its termination,—if it were possible, we say, for a disciple, on this side of the grave, to attain the eminency of a condition so glorious, then we know not of what use to him would be either a death or a resurrection, or why he might not bear his earthly tabernacle to heaven, and set him down by direct translation amongst the company of the celestial. But no! There hangs about the person of the most pure and perfect Christian upon earth, some mysterious necessity of dying. That body, styled with such emphasis a vile body, by the Apostle, must be pulverized and made over again. And not till that which is sown in corruption shall be raised in incorruption,—not till that which is sown in weakness shall be raised in power, —not till that which is sown a natural body shall be raised a spiritual body,—not till the soul of man occupy another tenement, and the body which now holds him be made to undergo some unknown but glorious transformation, will he know what it is to walk at perfect liberty, and, with the full play of his then emancipated powers, to expatiate without frailty, and without a flaw, in the service of his God.

We know that the impression which many have of the disciples of the gospel is, that their great and perpetual aim is, that they may be justified,—that the change of state which they are ever aspiring after, is a change in their forensic state, and not in their personal,—that if they can only attain delivery from wrath, they will be satisfied,—and that the only use they make of Christ, is, through his means, to obtain an erasure of the sentence of their condemnation. Now, though this, undoubtedly, be one great design of the gospel, it is not the design in which it terminates. It may, in fact, be only considered as a preparation for an ulterior accomplishment altogether. Christ came to redeem us from all iniquity, and to purify us unto himself a peculiar people, zealous of good works. It were selfishness under the guise of sacredness, to sit down, in placid contentment, with the single privilege of justification. It is only the introduction to higher privileges.

But not till we submit to the righteousness of Christ, as the alone meritorious plea of our acceptance, shall we become personally righteous ourselves,—not till we see the blended love and holiness of the Godhead, in our propitiation, shall we know how to combine a confidence in his mercy, with a reverence for his character, —not till we look to that great transaction, by which the purity of the divine nature is vindicated, and yet the sinner is delivered from the coming vengeance, shall we be freed from the dominion of sin, or be led to admire and to imitate the great Pattern of excellence. The renewing Spirit, indeed, is withheld from all those who withhold their consent from the doctrine of Christ, and of him crucified. Paul was determined to know nothing else; and it is in this knowledge, and in this alone, that we are renewed after the image of him who created us.

Now the God of peace, that brought again from the dead our Lord Jesus, that great Shepherd of the sheep, through the blood of the everlasting covenant, make you perfect in every good work to do his will, working in you that which is well-pleasing in his sight, through Jesus Christ, to whom be glory for ever and ever. Amen.

DISCOURSES

ON THE

APPLICATION OF CHRISTIANITY

TO THE

COMMERCIAL AND ORDINARY AFFAIRS OF LIFE.

PREFACE.

The following Discourses can be regarded in no other light, than as the fragment of a subject far too extensive to be overtaken within a compass so narrow. There has only a partial survey been taken of the morality of the actions that are current among people engaged in merchandise: and with regard to the morality of the affections which stir in their hearts, and give a feverish and diseased activity to the pursuits of worldly ambition, this has scarcely been touched upon, save in a very general way in the concluding discourse.

And yet, in the estimation of every cultivated Christian, this second branch of the subject should be by far the most interesting,—as it relates to that spiritual discipline by which the love of the world is overcome; and by which all that oppressive anxiety is kept in check, which the reverses and uncertainties of business are so apt to inject into the bosom; and by which the appetite that urges him who hasteth to be rich is effectually restrained—so as to make it possible for a man to give his hand to the duties of his secular occupation, and, at the same time, to maintain that sacredness of heart which becomes every fleeting traveller through a scene, all whose pleasures and whose prospects are so soon to pass away.

Should this part of the subject be resumed at some future opportunity, there are two questions of casuistry connected with it, which will demand no small degree of consideration. The first relates to the degree in which an affection for present things, and present interests ought to be indulged. And the second is, whether, on the supposition that a desire after the good things of the present life were reduced down to the standard of the gospel, there would remain a sufficient impulse in the world for upholding its commerce, at the rate which would secure the greatest amount of comfort and subsistence to its families.

Without offering any demonstration, at present, upon this matter, we simply state it as our opinion, that, though the whole business of the world were in the hands of men thoroughly Christianised, and who, rating wealth according to its real dimensions on the high scale of eternity, were chastened out of all their idolatrous regards to it—yet would trade, in these circumstances, be carried to the extreme limit of its being really productive or desirable. An affection for riches, beyond what Christianity prescribes, is not essential to any extension of commerce that is at all valuable or legitimate; and in opposition to the maxim, that the spirit of enterprise is the soul of commercial prosperity, do we hold, that it is the excess of this spirit beyond the moderation of the New Testament, which, pressing on the natural boundaries of trade, is sure, at length, to visit every country where it operates, with the recoil of all those calamities, which in the shape of beggared capitalists, and unemployed operatives, and dreary intervals of bankruptcy and alarm, are observed to follow a season of overdone speculation.

DISCOURSE I.

On the mercantile Virtues which may exist without the Influence of Christianity.

"Finally, brethren, whatsoever things are true, whatsoever things are honest, whatsoever things are just, whatsoever things are pure, whatsoever things are lovely, whatsoever things are of good report; if there be any virtue, if there be any praise, think on these things."—*Philippians* iv. 8.

The Apostle, in these verses, makes use of certain terms, without ever once proposing to advance any definition of their meaning. He presumes on a common understanding of this, between himself and the people whom he is addressing. He presumes that they know what is signified by Truth, and Justice, and Loveliness, and the other moral qualities which are included in the enumeration of our text. They, in fact, had words to express them, for many ages antecedent to the coming of Christianity into the world. Now, the very existence of the words proves, that, before the gospel was taught, the realities which they express must have existed also. These good and respectable attributes of character must have been occasionally exemplified by men, prior to the religion of the New Testament. The virtuous and the praiseworthy must, ere the commencement of the new dispensation, have been met with in society —for the Apostle does not take them up in this passage, as if they were unknown and unheard of novelties—but such objects of general recognition, as could be understood on the bare mention of them, without warning and without explanation.

But more than this. These virtues must not only have been exemplified by men, previous to the entrance of the gospel amongst them—seeing that the terms, expressive of the virtues, were perfectly understood—but men must have known how to love and to admire them. How is it that we apply the epithet lovely to any moral qualification, but only in as far as that qualification does in fact draw towards it a sentiment of love? How is it that another qualification is said to be of good report, but in as far as it has received from men an applauding or an honourable testimony? The Apostle does not bid his readers have respect to such things as are lovely, and then, for the purpose of saving them from error, enumerate what the things are which he conceives to possess this qualification. He commits the matter, with perfect confidence, to their own sense and their own apprehension. He bids them bear a respect to whatsoever things are lovely— nor does he seem at all suspicious that, by so doing, he leaves them in any darkness or uncertainty about the precise import of the advice which he is delivering. He therefore recognizes the competency of men to estimate the lovely and the honourable of character. He appeals to a tribunal in their own breasts, and evidently supposes, that, antecedently to the light of the Christian revelation, there lay scattered among the species certain principles of feeling and of action, in virtue of which, they both occasionally exhibited what was just and true, and of good report, and also could render to such an exhibition, the homage of their regard and of their reverence. At present we shall postpone the direct enforcement of these virtues upon the observation of Christians, and shall confine our thoughts of them to the object of estimating their precise importance and character, when they are realised by those who are not Christians.

While we assert with zeal every doctrine of Christianity, let us not forget that there is a zeal without discrimination; and that, to bring such a spirit to the defence of our faith, or of any one of its peculiarities, is not to vindicate the cause, but to discredit it. Now, there is a way of maintaining the utter depravity of our nature, and of doing it in such a style of sweeping and of vehement asseveration, as to render it not merely obnoxious to the taste, but obnoxious to the understanding. On this subject there is often a roundness and a temerity of announcement, which any intelligent man, looking at the phenomena of human character with his own eyes, cannot go along with; and thus it is, that there are injudicious defenders of orthodoxy, who have mustered against it not merely a positive dislike, but a positive strength of observation and argument. Let the nature of man be a ruin, as it certainly is, it is obvious to the most common discernment, that it does not offer one unvaried and unalleviated mass of deformity. There are certain phases, and certain exhibitions of this nature, which are more lovely than others— certain traits of character, not due to the operation of Christianity at all, and yet calling forth our admiration and our tenderness—certain varieties of moral complexion, far more fair and more engaging than certain other varieties; and to prove that the gospel may have had no share in the formation of them, they in fact stood out to the notice and respect of the world before the gospel was ever heard of. The classic page of antiquity sparkles with repeated exemplifications of what is bright and beautiful in the character of man; nor do all its descriptions of external nature waken up such an enthusiasm of pleasure, as when it bears testimony to some graceful or elevated doing out of the history of the species. And whether it be the kindliness of maternal affection, or the unweariedness of filial piety, or the constancy of tried and unalterable friendship, or the earnestness of devoted patriotism, or the rigour of unbending fidelity, or any other of the recorded virtues which shed a glory over the remembrance of Greece and of Rome—we fully concede it to the admiring scholar, that they one and all of them were sometimes exemplified in those days of Heathenism; and that, out of the materials of a period, crowded as it was with moral abominations, there may also be gathered things which are pure, and lovely, and true, and just, and honest, and of good report.

What do we mean, then, it may be asked, by the universal depravity of man? How shall we reconcile the admission now made, with the unqualified and authoritative language of the Bible, when it tells us of the totality and the magnitude of human corruption? Wherein lies that desperate wickedness, which is every where ascribed to all the men of all the families that be on the face of the earth? And how can such a tribute of acknowledgment be awarded to the sages and the patriots of antiquity, who yet, as the partakers of our fallen nature, must be outcasts from the favour of God, and have the character of evil stamped upon the imaginations of the thoughts of their hearts continually?

In reply to these questions, let us speak to your own experimental recollections on a subject in which you are aided, both by the consciousness of what passes within you, and by your observation of the characters of others. Might not a sense of honour elevate that heart which is totally unfurnished with a sense of God? Might not an impulse of compassionate feeling be sent into that bosom which is never once visited by a movement of duteous loyalty towards the Lawgiver in heaven? Might not occasions of intercourse with the beings around us, develope whatever there is in our nature of generosity, and friendship, and integrity, and patriotism; and yet the unseen Being, who placed us in this theatre, be neither loved, nor obeyed, nor listened to? Amid the manifold varieties of human character, and the number of constitutional principles which enter into its composition, might there not be an individual in whom the constitutional virtues so blaze forth and have the ascendency, as to give a general effect of gracefulness to the whole of this moral exhibition; and yet, may not that individual be as unmindful of his God, as if the principles of his constitution had been mixed up in such a different proportion, as to make him an odious and a revolting spectacle? In a word, might not Sensibility shed forth its tears, and Friendship perform its services, and Liberality impart of its treasure, and Patriotism earn the gratitude of its country, and Honour maintain itself entire and untainted, and all the softenings of what is amiable, and all the glories of what is chivalrous and manly gather into one bright effulgency of moral accomplishment on the person of him who never, for a single day of his life, subordinates one habit, or one affection, to the will of the Almighty; who is just as careless and as unconcerned about God, as if the native tendencies of his constitution had compounded him into a monster of deformity; and who just as effectually realizes this attribute of rebellion against his Maker, as the most loathsome and profligate of the species, that he walks in the counsel of his own heart, and after the sight of his own eyes?

The same constitutional variety may be seen on the lower fields of creation. You there witness the gentleness of one animal, the affectionate fidelity of another, the cruel and unrelenting ferocity of a third; and you never question the propriety of the language, when some of these instinctive tendencies are better reported of than others; or when it is said of the former of them, that they are the more fine, and amiable, and endearing. But it does not once occur to you, that, even in the very best of these exhibitions, there is any sense of God, or that the great master-principle of his authority is at all concerned in it. Transfer this contemplation back again to our species; and under the same complexional difference of the more and the less lovely, or the more and the less hateful, you will perceive the same utter insensibility to the consideration of a God, or the same utter inefficiency on the part of his law to subdue human habits and human inclinations. It is true, that there is one distinction between the two cases; but it all goes to aggravate the guilt and the ingratitude of man. He has an understanding which the inferior animals have not—and yet, with this understanding, does he refuse practically to acknowledge God. He has a conscience, which they have not—and yet, though it whisper in the ear of his inner man the claims of an unseen legislator, does he lull away his time in the slumbers of indifference, and live without him in the world.

Or go to the people of another planet, over whom the hold of allegiance to their maker is unbroken—in whose hearts the Supreme sits enthroned, and throughout the whole of whose history there runs the perpetual and the unfailing habit of subordination to his law. It is conceivable, that with them too, there may be varieties of temper and of natural inclination, and yet all of them be under the effective control of one great and imperious principle; that in subjection to the will of God, every kind and every honourable disposition is cherished to the uttermost; and that in subjection to the same will, every tendency to anger, and malignity, and revenge, is repressed at the first moment of its threatened operation; and that in this way, there will be the fostering of a constant encouragement given to the one set of instincts, and the struggling of a constant opposition made against the other. Now, only conceive this great bond of allegiance to be dissolved; the mighty and subordinating principle, which wont to wield an ascendency over every movement and every affection, to be loosened and done away; and then would this loyal, obedient world, become what ours is, independent of Christianity. Every constitutional desire would run out, in the unchecked spontaneity of its own movements. The law of heaven would furnish no counteraction to the impulses and tendencies of nature. And tell us, in these circumstances, when the restraint of religion was thus lifted off, and all the passions let out to take their own tumultuous and independent career—tell us, if though amid the uproar of the licentious and vindictive propensities, there did gleam forth at times some of the finer and the lovelier sympathies of nature—tell us, if this would at all affect the state of that world as a state of enmity against God; where his will was reduced to an element of utter insignificancy; where the voice of their rightful master fell powerless on the consciences of a listless and alienated family; where humour, and interest, and propensity—at one time selfish, and at another social—took their alternate sway over those hearts from which there was excluded all effectual sense of an overruling God. If he be unheeded and disowned by the creatures whom he has formed, can it be said to alleviate the deformity of their rebellion, that they, at times, experience the impulse of some amiable feeling which he hath implanted, or at times hold out some beauteousness of aspect which he hath shed over them? Shall the value of the multitude of the gifts release them from their loyalty to the giver; and when nature puts herself into the attitude of indifference or hostility against him, now is it that the graces and the accomplishments of nature can be plead in mitigation of her antipathy to him, who invested nature with all her graces, and upholds her in the display of all her accomplishments?

The way, then, to assert the depravity of man, is to fasten on the radical element of depravity, and to show how deeply it lies incorporated with his moral constitution. It is not by an utterance of rash and sweeping totality to refuse him the possession of what is kind in sympathy, or of what is dignified in principle—for this were in the face of all observation. It is to charge him direct with his utter disloyalty to God. It is to convict him of treason against the majesty of heaven. It is to press home upon him the impiety of not caring about God. It is to tell him, that the hourly and habitual language of his heart is, I will not have the Being who made me to rule over me. It is to go to the man of honour, and, while we frankly award it to him that his pulse beats high in the pride of integrity—it is to tell him, that he who keeps it in living play, and who sustains the loftiness of its movements, and who, in one moment of time, could arrest it for ever, is not in all his thoughts. It is to go to the man of soft and gentle emotions, and while we gaze in tenderness upon him—it is to read to him, out of his own character, how the exquisite mechanism of feeling may be in full operation, while he who framed it is forgotten; while he who poured into his constitution the milk of human kindness, may never be adverted to with one single sentiment of veneration, or on one single purpose of obedience; while he who gave him his gentler nature, who clothed him in all its adornments, and in virtue of whose appointment it is, that, instead of an odious and a revolting monster, he is the much loved child of sensibility, may be utterly disowned by him. In a word, it is to go around among all that Humanity has to offer in the shape of fair and amiable, and engaging, and to prove how deeply Humanity has revolted against that Being who has done so much to beautify and to exalt her. It is to prove that the carnal mind, under all its varied complexions of harshness, or of delicacy, is enmity against God. It is to prove that let nature be as rich as she may in moral accomplishments, and let the most favoured of her sons realize upon his own person the finest and the fullest assemblage of them—should he, at the moment of leaving this theatre of display, and bursting loose from the framework of mortality, stand in the presence of his judge, and have the question put to him, What hast thou done unto me? This man of constitutional virtue, with all the salutations he got upon earth, and all the reverence that he has left behind him, may, naked and defenceless, before him who sitteth on the throne, be left without a plea and without an argument.

God's controversy with our species, is not, that the glow of honour or of humanity is never felt among them. It is, that none of them understandeth, and none of them seeketh after God. It is, that he is deposed from his rightful ascendency. It is that he, who in fact inserted in the human bosom every one principle that can embellish the individual possessor, or maintain the order of society, is banished altogether from the circle of his habitual contemplations. It is, that man taketh his way in life as much at random, as if there was no presiding Divinity at all; and that, whether he at one time grovel in the depths of sensuality, or at another kindle with some generous movement of sympathy or of patriotism, he is at both times alike unmindful of him to whom he owes his continuance and his birth. It is, that he moves his every footstep at his own will; and has utterly discarded, from its supremacy over him, the will of that invisible Master who compasses all his goings, and never ceases to pursue him by the claims of a resistless and legitimate authority. It is this which is the essential or the constituting principle of rebellion against God. This it is which has exiled the planet we live in beyond the limits of his favoured creation—and whether it be shrouded in the turpitude of licentiousness or cruelty, or occasionally brightened with the gleam of the kindly and the honourable virtues, it is thus that it is seen as afar off, by Him who sitteth on the throne, and looketh on our strayed world, as athwart a wide and dreary gulf of separation.

And when, prompted by love towards his alienated children, he devised a way of recalling them—when, willing to pass over all the ingratitude he had gotten from their hands, he reared a pathway of return, and proclaimed a pardon and a welcome to all who should walk upon it—when through the offered Mediator, who magnified his broken law, and upheld, by his mysterious sacrifice, the dignity of that government, which the children of Adam had disowned, he invited all to come and be saved—should this message be brought to the door of the most honourable man upon earth, and he turn in contempt and hostility away from it, has not that man posted himself more firmly than ever on the ground of rebellion? Though an unsullied integrity should rest upon all his transactions, and the homage of confidence and respect be awarded to him from every quarter of society, has not this man, by slighting the overtures of reconciliation, just plunged himself the deeper in the guilt of a wilful and determined ungodliness? Has not the creature exalted itself above the Creator; and in the pride of those accomplishments, which never would have invested his person had not they come to him from above, has he not, in the act of resisting the gospel, aggravated the provocation of his whole previous defiance to the author of it?

Thus much for all that is amiable, and for all that is manly in the accomplishments of nature, disjoined from the faith of Christianity. They take up a separate residence in the human character from the principle of godliness. Anterior to this religion, they go not to alleviate the guilt of our departure from the living God; and subsequently to this religion, they may blazon the character of him who stands out against it; but on the principles of a most clear and intelligent equity, they never can shield him from the condemnation and the curse of those who have neglected the great salvation.

The doctrine of the New Testament will bear to be confronted with all that can be met or noticed on the face of human society. And we speak most confidently to the experience of many who now hear us, when we say, that often, in the course of their manifold transactions, have they met the man, whom the bribery of no advantage whatever could seduce into the slightest deviation from the path of integrity—the man, who felt his nature within him put into a state of the most painful indignancy, at every thing that bore upon it the character of a sneaking or dishonourable artifice—the man, who positively could not be at rest under the consciousness that he had ever betrayed, even to his own heart, the remotest symptom of such an inclination—and whom, therefore, the unaided law of justice and of truth has placed on a high and deserved eminence in the walks of honourable merchandize.

Let us not withhold from this character the tribute of its most rightful admiration; but let us further ask, if, with all that he thus possessed of native feeling and constitutional integrity, you have never observed in any such individual an utter emptiness of religion; and that God is not in all his thoughts; and that, when he does what happens to be at one with the will of the Lawgiver, it is not because he is impelled to it by a sense of its being the will of the Lawgiver, but because he is impelled to it by the working of his own instinctive sensibilities; and that, however fortunate, or however estimable these sensibilities are, they still consist with the habit of a mind that is in a state of total indifference about God? Have you never read in your own character, or observed in the character of others, that the claims of the Divinity may be entirely forgotten by the very man to whom society around him yield, and rightly yield, the homage of an unsullied and honourable reputation; that this man may have all his foundations in the world; that every security on which he rests, and every enjoyment upon which his heart is set, lieth on this side of death; that a sense of the coming day on which God is to enter into judgment with him, is to every purpose of practical ascendency, as good as expunged altogether from his bosom; that he is far in desire, and far in enjoyment, and far in habitual contemplation, away from that God who is not far from any one of us; that his extending credit and his brightening prosperity, and his magnificent retreat from business, with all the splendour of its accommodations—that these are the futurities at which he terminates; and that he goes not in thought beyond them to that eternity, which in the flight of a few little years, will absorb all, and annihilate all? In a word, have you never observed the man, who, with all that was right in mercantile principle, and all that was open and unimpeachable in the habit of his mercantile transactions, lived in a state of utter estrangement from the concerns of immortality? who, in reference to God, persisted, from one year to another, in the spirit of a deep slumber? who, in reference to the man that tries to awaken him out of his lethargy, recoils, with the most sensitive dislike, from the faithfulness of his ministrations? who, in reference to the Book which tells him of his nakedness and his guilt, never consults it with one practical aim, and never tries to penetrate beyond that aspect of mysteriousness which it holds out to an undiscerning world? who attends not church, or attends it with all the lifelessness of a form? who reads not his Bible, or reads it in the discharge of a self-prescribed and unfruitful task? who prays not, or prays with the mockery of an unmeaning observation? and, in one word, who while surrounded by all those testimonies which give to man a place of moral distinction among his fellows, is living in utter carelessness about God, and about all the avenues which lead to him?

Now, attend for a moment to what that is which the man has, and to what that is which he has not. He has an attribute of character which is in itself pure, and lovely, and honourable, and of good report. He has a natural principle of integrity; and under its impulse he may be carried forward to such fine exhibitions of himself, as are worthy of all admiration. It is very noble, when the simple utterance of his word carries as much security along with it as if he had accompanied that utterance by the signatures, and the securities, and the legal obligations which are required of other men. It might tempt one to be proud of his species when he looks at the faith that is put in him by a distant correspondent, who, without one other hold of him than his honour, consigns to him the wealth of a whole flotilla, and sleeps in the confidence that it is safe. It is indeed an animating thought, amid the gloom of this world's depravity, when we behold the credit which one man puts in another, though separated by oceans and by continents; when he fixes the anchor of a sure and steady dependence on the reported honesty of one whom he never saw; when, with all his fears for the treachery of the varied elements, through which his property has to pass, he knows, that should it only arrive at the door of its destined agent, all his fears and all his suspicions may be at an end. We know nothing finer than such an act of homage from one human being to another, when perhaps the diameter of the globe is between them; nor do we think that either the renown of her victories, or the wisdom of her councils, so signalizes the country in which we live, as does the honourable dealing of her merchants; that all the glories of British policy, and British valour, are far eclipsed by the moral splendour which British faith has thrown over the name and the character of our nation; nor has she gathered so proud a distinction from all the tributaries of her power, as she has done from the awarded confidence of those men of all tribes, and colours, and languages, who look to our agency for the most faithful of all management, and to our keeping for the most unviolable of all custody.

There is no denying, then, the very extended prevalence of a principle of integrity in the commercial world; and he who has such a principle within him, has that to which all the epithets of our text may rightly be appropriated. But it is just as impossible to deny, that, with this thing which he has, there may be another thing which he has not. He may not have one duteous feeling of reverence which points upward to God. He may not have one wish, or one anticipation, which points forward to eternity. He may not have any sense of dependence on the Being who sustains him; and who gave him his very principle of honour, as part of that interior furniture which he has put into his bosom; and who surrounded him with the theatre on which he has come forward with the finest and most illustrious displays of it; and who set the whole machinery of his sentiment and action agoing; and can, by a single word of his power, bid it cease from the variety, and cease from the gracefulness of its movements. In other words, he is a man of integrity, and yet he is a man of ungodliness.

He is a man born for the confidence and the admiration of his fellows, and yet a man whom his Maker can charge with utter defection from all the principles of a spiritual obedience. He is a man whose virtues have blazoned his own character in time, and have upheld the interests of society, and yet a man who has not, by one movement of principle, brought himself nearer to the kingdom of heaven, than the most profligate of the species. The condemnation, that he is an alien from God, rests upon him in all the weight of its unmitigated severity. The threat, that they who forget God shall be turned into hell, will, on the great day of its fell and sweeping operation, involve him among the wretched outcasts of eternity. That God from whom, while in the world, he withheld every due offering of gratitude, and remembrance, and universal subordination of habit and of desire, will show him to his face, how, under the delusive garb of such sympathies as drew upon him the love of his acquaintances, and of such integrities as drew upon him their respect and their confidence, he was in fact a determined rebel against the authority of heaven; that not one commandment of the law, in the true extent of its interpretation, was ever fulfilled by him; that the pervading principle of obedience to this law, which is love to God, never had its ascendency over him; that the beseeching voice of the Lawgiver, so offended and so insulted—but who, nevertheless, devised in love a way of reconciliation for the guilty,—never had the effect of recalling him; that, in fact, he neither had a wish for the friendship of God, nor cherished the hope of enjoying him, and that therefore, as he lived without hope, so he lived without God in the world; finding all his desire, and all his sufficiency, to be somewhere else, than in that favour which is better than life, and so, in addition to the curse of having continued not in all the words of the book of God's law to do them, entailing upon himself the mighty aggravation of having neglected all the offers of his gospel.

We say, then, of this natural virtue, what our Saviour said of the virtue of the Pharisees, many of whom were not extortioners, as other men—that, verily, it hath its reward. When disjoined from a sense of God, it is of no religious estimation whatever; nor will it lead to any religious blessing, either in time or in eternity. It has, however, its enjoyments annexed to it, just as a fine taste has its enjoyments annexed to it; and in these it is abundantly rewarded. It is exempted from that painfulness of inward feeling which nature has annexed to every act of departure from honesty. It is sustained by a conscious sense of rectitude and elevation. It is gratified by the homage of society; the members of which are ever ready to award the tribute of acknowledgment to those virtues that support the interests of society. And finally, it may be said, that prosperity, with some occasional variations, is the general accompaniment of that credit, which every man of undeviating justice is sure to draw around him. But what reward will you tell us is due to him on the great day of the manifestation of God's righteousness, when, in fact, he has done nothing unto God? What recompence can be awarded to him out of those books which are then to be opened, and in which he stands recorded as a man overcharged with the guilt of spiritual idolatry? How shall God grant unto him the reward of a servant, when the service of God was not the principle of his doings in the world; and when neither the justice he rendered to others, nor the sensibility that he felt for them, bore the slightest character of an offering to his Maker?

But wherever the religious principle has taken possession of the mind, it animates these virtues with a new spirit; and when so animated, all such things as are pure, and lovely, and just, and true, and honest, and of good report, have a religious importance and character belonging to them. The text forms part of an epistle addressed to all the saints in Christ Jesus, which were at Philippi; and the lesson of the text is matter of direct and authoritative enforcement on all who are saints in Christ Jesus at the present day. Christianity, with the weight of its positive sanctions on the side of what is amiable and honourable in human virtue, causes such an influence to rest on the character of its genuine disciples, that, on the ground both of inflexible justice and ever-breathing charity, they are ever sure to leave the vast majority of the world behind them. Simplicity and godly sincerity form essential ingredients of that peculiarity by which they stand signalized in the midst of an ungodly generation. The true friends of the gospel, tremblingly alive to the honour of their master's cause, blush for the disgrace that has been brought on it by men who keep its sabbaths, and yield an ostentatious homage to its doctrines and its sacraments. They utterly disclaim all fellowship with that vile association of cant and of duplicity, which has sometimes been exemplified, to the triumph of the enemies of religion; and they both feel the solemn truth, and act on the authority of the saying, that neither thieves, nor liars, nor extortioners, nor unrighteous persons, have any part in the kingdom of Christ and of God.

DISCOURSE II.

The Influence of Christianity in aiding and augmenting the mercantile Virtues.

"For he that in these things serveth Christ is acceptable to God, and approved of men."—*Romans* xiv. 18.

We have already asserted the natural existence of such principles in the heart of man, as lead him to many graceful and to many honourable exhibitions of character. We have further asserted, that this formed no deduction whatever from that article of orthodoxy which affirms the utter depravity of our nature; that the essence of this depravity lies in man having broken loose from the authority of God, and delivered himself wholly up to the guidance of his own inclinations; that though some of these inclinations are in themselves amiable features of human character, and point in their effects to what is most useful to human society, yet devoid as they all are of any reference to the will and to the rightful sovereignty of the Supreme Being, they could not avert, or even so much as alleviate that charge of ungodliness, which may be fully carried round amongst all the sons and daughters of the species; that they furnish not the materials of any valid or satisfactory answer to the question, "What hast thou done unto God?" and that whether they are the desires of a native rectitude, or the desires of an instinctive benevolence, they go not to purge away the guilt of having no love, and no care for the Being who formed and who sustains them.

But what is more. If the virtues and accomplishments of nature are at all to be admitted into the controversy between God and man, instead of forming any abatement upon the enormity of our guilt, they stamp upon it the reproach of a still deeper and more determined ingratitude. Let us conceive it possible, for a moment, that the beautiful personifications of scripture were all realized; that the trees of the forest clapped their hands unto God, and that the isles were glad at his presence; that the little hills shouted on every side, and that the vallies covered over with corn sent forth their notes of rejoicing; that the sun and the moon praised him, and the stars of light joined in the solemn adoration; that the voice of glory to God was heard from every mountain and from every water-fall; and that all nature, animated throughout by the consciousness of a pervading and presiding Deity, burst into one loud and universal song of gratulation. Would not a strain of greater loftiness be heard to ascend from those regions where the all-working God had left the traces of his own immensity, than from the tamer and the humbler scenery of an ordinary landscape? Would not you look for a gladder acclamation from the fertile field, than from the arid waste, where no character of grandeur made up for the barrenness that was around you? Would not the goodly tree, compassed about with the glories of its summer foliage, lift up an anthem of louder gratitude than the lowly shrub that grew beneath it? Would not the flower, from whose leaves every hue of loveliness was reflected, send forth a sweeter rapture than the russet weed, which never drew the eye of any admiring passenger? And in a word, wherever you saw the towering eminences of nature, or the garniture of her more rich and beauteous adornments, would it not be there that you looked for the deepest tones of devotion, or there for the tenderest and most exquisite of its melodies?

There is both the sublime of character, and the beauteous of character exemplified upon man. We have the one in that high sense of honour which no interest and no terror can seduce from any of its obligations. We have the other in that kindliness of feeling, which one look, or one sigh of imploring distress can touch into liveliest sympathy. Only grant that we have nothing either in the constitution of our spirits, or in the structure of our bodies, which we did not receive; and that mind, with all its varieties, is as much the product of a creating hand, as matter in all its modifications; and then, on the face of human society, do we witness all the gradations of a moral scenery, which may be directly referred to the operation of him who worketh all in all. It is our belief, that, as to any effectual sense of God, there is as deep a slumber throughout the whole of this world's living and rational generations, as there is throughout all the diversities of its mute and unconscious materialism; and that to make our alienated spirits again alive unto the Father of them, calls for as distinct and as miraculous an exertion of the Divinity, as would need to be put forth in the act of turning stones into the children of Abraham. Conceive this to be done then—and that a quickening and a realizing sense of the Deity pervaded all the men of our species—and that each knew how to refer his own endowments, with an adequate expression of gratitude to the unseen author of them—from whom we ask of all these various individuals, would you look for the halleluiahs of devoutest ecstacy?

Would it not be from him whom God had arrayed in the splendour of nature's brightest accomplishments? Would it not be from him, with whose constitutional feelings the movements of honour and benevolence were in fullest harmony? Would it not be from him whom his Maker had cast into the happiest mould, and attempered into sweetest unison with all that was kind, and generous, and lovely, and ennobled by the loftiest emotions, and raised above his fellows into the finest spectacle of all that was graceful and all that was manly? Surely, if the possession of these moralities be just another theme of acknowledgment to the Lord of the spirits of all flesh, then, if the acknowledgment be withheld, and these moralities have taken up their residence in the bosom of him who is utterly devoid of piety, they go to aggravate the reproach of his ingratitude; and to prove, that of all the men upon earth who are far from God, he stands at the widest distance, he remains proof against the weightiest claims, and he, of the dead in trespasses and sins, is the most profoundly asleep to the call of religion, and to the supremacy of its righteous obligations.

It is by argument such as this, that we would attempt to convince of sin, those who have a righteousness that is without godliness; and to prove, that, with the possession of such things as are pure, and lovely, and honest, and of good report, they in fact can only be admitted to reconciliation with God, on the same footing with the most worthless and profligate of the species; and to demonstrate, that they are in the very same state of need and of nakedness, and are therefore children of wrath, even as others; that it is only through faith in the preaching of the gospel of our Lord Jesus Christ that they can be saved; and that unless brought down from the delusive eminency of their own conscious attainments, they take their forgiveness through the blood of the Redeemer, and their sanctification through the spirit which is at his giving, they shall obtain no part in that inheritance which is incorruptible and undefiled, and which fadeth not away.

But the gospel of Jesus Christ does something more than hold out a refuge to the guilty. It takes all those who accept of its overtures under its supreme and exclusive direction. It keeps by them in the way of counsel and exhortation, and constant superintendence. The grace which it reveals, is a grace which not merely saves all men, but which teaches all men. He who is the proposed Saviour, also claims to be the alone master of those who put their trust in him. His cognizance extends itself over the whole line of their history; and there is not an affection of their heart, or a deed of their visible conduct, over which he does not assert the right of an authority that is above all control, and that refuses all rival ship.

Now, we want to point your attention to a distinction which obtains between one set and another set of his requirements. By the former, we are enjoined to practise certain virtues, which separately from his injunction altogether, are in great demand, and in great reverence, amongst the members of society—such as compassion, and generosity, and justice, and truth; which, independently of the religious sanction they obtain from the law of the Saviour, are in themselves so lovely, and so honourable, and of such good report, that they are ever sure to carry general applause along with them, and thus to combine both the characteristics of our text—that he who in these things serveth Christ, is both acceptable to God, and approved of men.

But there is another set of requirements, where the will of God, instead of being seconded by the applause of men, is utterly at variance with it. There are some who can admire the generous sacrifices that are made to truth or to friendship, but who, without one opposing scruple, abandon themselves to all the excesses of riot and festivity, and are therefore the last to admire the puritanic sobriety of him whom they cannot tempt to put his chastity or his temperance away from him; though the same God, who bids us lie not one to another, also bids us keep the body under subjection, and to abstain from fleshly lusts which war against the soul. Again, there are some in whose eye an unvitiated delicacy looks a beautiful and an interesting spectacle, and an undeviating self-control looks a manly and respectable accomplishment; but who have no taste in themselves, and no admiration in others, for the more direct exercises of religion; and who positively hate the strict and unbending preciseness of those who join in every ordinance, and on every returning night celebrate the praises of God in their family; and that, though the heavenly Lawgiver, who tells us to live righteously and soberly, tells us also to live godly in the present evil world. And lastly, there are some who have not merely a toleration, but a liking for all the decencies of an established observation; but who, with the homage they pay to sabbaths and to sacraments, nauseate the Christian principle in the supreme and regenerating vitality of its influences; who, under a general religiousness of aspect, are still in fact the children of the world—and therefore hate the children of light in all that is peculiar and essentially characteristic of that high designation; who understand not what is meant by having our conversation in heaven; and utter strangers to the separated walk, and the spiritual exercises, and the humble devotedness, and the consecrated affections, of the new creature in Jesus Christ, shrink from them altogether as from the extravagancies of a fanaticism in which they have no share, and with which they can have no sympathy—and all this, though the same scripture which prescribes the exercises of household and of public religion, lays claim to an undivided authority over all the desires and affections of the soul; and will admit of no compromise between God and the world; and insist upon an utter deadness to the one, and a most vehement sensibility to the other; and elevates the standard of loyalty to the Father of our Spirits, to the lofty pitch of loving him with all our strength, and of doing all things to his glory.

Let these examples serve to impress a real and experimental distinction which obtains between two sets of virtues; between those which possess the single ingredient of being approved by God, while they want the ingredient of being also acceptable unto men—and those which possess both these ingredients, and to the observance of which, therefore, we may be carried by a regard to the will of God, without any reference to the opinion of men—or by a regard to the opinion of men, without any reference to the will of God. Among the first class of virtues we would assign a foremost place to all those inward and spiritual graces which enter into the obedience of the affections—highly approved of God, but not at all acceptable to the general taste, or carrying along with them the general congeniality of the world. And then, though they do not possess the ingredient of God's approbation in a way so separate and unmixed, we would say that abstinence from profane language, and attendance upon church, and a strict keeping of the sabbath, and the exercises of family worship, and the more rigid decrees of sobriety, and a fearful avoidance of every encroachment on temperance or chastity, rank more appropriately with the first than with the second class of virtues; for though there be many in society who have no religion, and yet to whom several of these virtues are acceptable, yet you will allow, that they do not convey such a universal popularity along with them, as certain other virtues which belong indisputably to the second class. These are the virtues which have a more obvious and immediate bearing on the interest of society—such as the truth which is punctual to all its engagements, and the honour which never disappoints the confidence it has inspired, and the compassion which cannot look unmoved at any of the symptoms of human wretchedness, and the generosity which scatters unsparingly around it. These are virtues which God has enjoined, and in behalf of which man lifts the testimony of a loud and ready admiration—virtues in which there is a meeting and a combining of both the properties of our text; so that he who in these things serveth Christ, is both approved of God, and acceptable unto men.

Let a steady hold be kept of this distinction, and it will be found capable of being turned to very useful application, both to the object of illustrating principle, and to the important object of detecting character. For this purpose, let us carry the distinction along with us, and make it subservient to the establishment of two or three successive observations.

First. A man may possess, to a considerable extent, the second class of virtues, and not possess so much as one iota of the religious principle; and that among other reasons, because a man may feel a value for one of the attributes which belongs to this class of virtues, and have no value whatever for the other attribute. If justice be both approved by God, and acceptable to men, he may on the latter property alone, be induced to the strictest maintenance of this virtue—and that without suffering its former property to have any practical influence whatever on any of his habits, or any of his determinations, and the same with every other virtue belonging to this second class. As residing in his character, there may not be the ingredient of godliness in any one of them. He may be well reported on account of them by men; but with God he may lie under as fearful a severity of reckoning, as if he wanted them altogether. Surely, it does not go to alleviate the withdrawment of your homage from God, that you have such an homage to the opinion of men, as influences you to do things, to the doing of which the law of God is not able to influence you. It cannot be said to palliate the revolting of your inclinations from the Creator, that you have transferred them all to the creature; and given an ascendency to the voice of human reputation, which you have refused to the voice and authority of your Lawgiver in heaven. Your want of subordination to him, is surely not made up by the respectful subordination that you render to the taste or the judgment of society. And in addition to this, we would have you to remember, that though other constitutional principles, besides a regard to the opinion of others, helped to form the virtues of the second class upon your character; though compassion and generosity, and truth, would have broken out into full and flourishing display upon you, and that, just because you had a native sensibility, or a native love of rectitude; yet, if the first ingredient be wanting, if a regard to the approbation of God have no share in the production of the moral accomplishment—then all the morality you can pretend to, is of as little religious estimation, and is as utterly disconnected with the rewards of religion, as all the elegance of taste you can pretend to, or all the raptured love of music you can pretend to, or all the vigour and dexterity of bodily exercise you can pretend to. All these, in reference to the great question of immortality, profit but little; and it is godliness alone that is profitable unto all things. It is upon this consideration that we would have you to open your eyes to the nakedness of your condition in the sight of God; to look to the full weight of the charge that he may prefer against you; to estimate the fearful extent of the deficiency under which you labour; to resist the delusive whispering of peace, when there is no peace; and to understand, that the wrath of God abideth on every child of nature, however rich he may be in the virtues and accomplishments of nature.

But again. This view of the distinction between the two sets of virtues, will serve to explain how it is, that, in the act of turning unto God, the one class of them appears to gather more copiously, and more conspicuously, upon the front of a renewed character, than the other class; how it is that the former wear a more unequivocal aspect of religiousness than the latter; how it is, that an air of gravity, and decency, and seriousness, looks to be more in alliance with sanctity, than the air either of open integrity, or of smiling benevolence; how it is, that the most ostensible change in the habit of a converted profligate, is that change in virtue of which he withdraws himself from the companions of his licentiousness; and that to renounce the dissipations of his former life stands far more frequently, or, at least, far more visibly, associated with the act of putting on Christianity, than to renounce the dishonesties of his former life. It is true, that, by the law of the gospel he is laid as strictly under the authority of the commandment to live righteously, as of the commandment to live soberly. But there is a compound character in those virtues which are merely social; and the presence of the one ingredient serves to throw into the shade, or to disguise altogether, the presence of the other ingredient. There is a greater number of irreligious men, who are at the same time just in their dealings, than there is of irreligious men, who are at the same time pure and temperate in their habits; and therefore it is that justice, even the most scrupulous, is not so specifical, and of course not so satisfying a mark of religion, as is a sobriety that is rigid and unviolable. And all this helps to explain how it is, that when a man comes under the power of religion, to abandon the levities of his past conduct is an event which stands far more noticeably out upon him, at this stage of his history, than to abandon the iniquities of his past conduct; that the most characteristic transformation which takes place at such a time, is a transformation from thoughtlessness, and from licentious gaiety, and from the festive indulgencies of those with whom he is wont to run to all those excesses of riot, of which the Apostle says, that they which do these things shall not inherit the kingdom of God; for even then, and in the very midst of all his impiety, he may have been kindhearted, and there might be no room upon his person for a visible transformation from inhumanity of character; even then, he may have been honourable, and there might be as little room for a visible transformation from fraudulency of character.

Thirdly. Nothing is more obvious than the antipathy that is felt by a certain class of religionists against the preaching of good works; and the antipathy is assuredly well and warrantably grounded, when it is such a preaching as goes to reduce the importance, or to infringe upon the simplicity, of the great doctrine of justification by faith, but along with this, may there not be remarked the toleration with which they will listen to a discourse upon one set of good works, and the evident coldness and dislike with which they listen to a discourse on another set of them; how a pointed remonstrance against Sabbath breaking sounds in their ears as if more in character from the pulpit, than a pointed remonstrance against the commission of theft, or the speaking of evil; how an eulogium on the observance of family worship, feels, in their taste, to be more impregnated with the spirit of sacredness, than an eulogium on the virtues of the shop, or of the market-place; and that while the one is approved of as having about it the solemn and the suitable characteristics of godliness, the other is stigmatized as a piece of barren, heartless, heathenish, and philosophic morality? Now, this antipathy to the preaching of the latter species of good works, has something peculiar in it. It is not enough to say, that it arises from a sensitive alarm about the stability of the doctrine of justification; for let it be observed, that this doctrine stands opposed to the merit not of one particular class of performances, but to the merit of all performances whatsoever. It is just as unscriptural a detraction from the great truth of salvation by faith, to rest our acceptance with God on the duties of prayer, or of rigid Sabbath keeping, or of strict and untainted sobriety, as to rest it on the punctual fulfilment of all your bargains, and on the extent of your manifold liberalities. It is not, then, a mere zeal about the great article of justification which lies at the bottom of that peculiar aversion that is felt towards a sermon on some social or humane accomplishment; and that is not felt towards a sermon on sobermindedness, or a sermon on the observation of the sacrament, or a sermon on any of those performances which bear a more direct and exclusive reference to God. We shall find the explanation of this phenomenon, which often presents itself in the religious world, in that distinction of which we have just required that it should be kept in steady hold, and followed into its various applications. The aversion in question is often, in fact, a well founded aversion, to a topic, which, though religious in the matter of it, may, from the way in which it is proposed, be altogether secular in the principle of it. It is resistance to what is deemed, and justly deemed, an act of usurpation on the part of certain virtues, which, when unanimated by a sentiment of godliness, are entitled to no place whatever in the ministrations of the gospel of Christ. It proceeds from a most enlightened fear, lest that should be held to make up the whole of religion, which is in fact utterly devoid of the spirit of religion; and from a true and tender apprehension, lest, on the possession of certain accomplishments, which secure a fleeting credit throughout the little hour of this world's history, deluded man should look forward to his eternity with hope, and upward to his God with complacency, while he carries not on his forehead one vestige of the character of heaven, one lineament of the aspect of godliness.

And lastly. The first class of virtues bear the character of religiousness more *strongly*, just because they bear that character more *singly*. The people who are without, might, no doubt, see in every real Christian the virtues of the second class also; but these virtues do not belong to them peculiarly and exclusively. For though it be true, that every religious man must be honest, the converse does not follow, that every honest man must be religious. And it is because the social accomplishments do not form the specific, that neither do they form the most prominent and distinguishing marks of Christianity. They may also be recognized as features in the character of men, who utterly repudiate the whole style and doctrine of the New Testament; and hence a very prevalent impression in society, that the faith of the gospel does not bear so powerfully and so directly on the relative virtues of human conduct. A few instances of hypocrisy amongst the more serious professors of our faith, serve to rivet the impression, and to give it perpetuity in the world. One single example, indeed, of sanctimonious duplicity will suffice, in the judgment of many, to cover the whole of vital and orthodox Christianity with disgrace. The report of it will be borne in triumph amongst the companies of the irreligious. The man who pays no homage to sabbaths or to sacraments, will be contrasted in the open, liberal, and manly style of all his transactions, with the low cunning of this drivelling methodistical pretender; and the loud laugh of a multitude of scorners, will give a force and a swell to this public outcry against the whole character of the sainthood.

Now, this delusion on the part of the unbelieving world is very natural, and ought not to excite our astonishment. We are not surprised, from the reasons already adverted to, that the truth, and the justice, and the humanity, and the moral loveliness, which do in fact belong to every new creature in Jesus Christ our Lord, should miss their observation; or, at least, fail to be recognized among the other more obvious characteristics into which believers have been translated by the faith of the gospel. But, on this very subject there is a tendency to delusion on the part of the disciples of the faith. They need to be reminded of the solemn and indispensable religiousness of the second class of virtues. They need to be told, that though these virtues do possess the one ingredient of being approved by men, and may, on this single account, be found to reside in the characters of those who live without God—yet, that they also possess the other ingredient of being acceptable unto God; and, on this latter account, should be made the subjects of their most strenuous cultivation. They must not lose sight of the one ingredient in the other; or stigmatize, as so many fruitless and insignificant moralities, those virtues which enter as component parts, into the service of Christ; so that he who in these things serveth Christ, is both acceptable to God, and approved by men. They must not expend all their warmth on the high and peculiar doctrine of the New Testament, while they offer a cold and reluctant admission to the practical duties of the New Testament. The Apostle has bound the one to the other by a tie of immediate connexion. Wherefore, lie not one to another, as ye have put off the old man and his deeds, and put on the new man, which is formed after the image of God, in righteousness and true holiness. Here the very obvious and popular accomplishment of truth is grafted on the very peculiar doctrine of regeneration: and you altogether mistake the kind of transforming influence which the faith of the gospel brings along with it, if you think that uprightness of character does not emerge at the same time with godliness of character; or that the virtues of society do not form upon the believer into as rich and varied an assemblage, as do the virtues of the sanctuary; or that, while he puts on those graces which are singly acceptable to God, he falls behind in any of those graces which are both acceptable to God, and approved of men.

Let, therefore, every pretender to Christianity vindicate this assertion by his own personal history in the world. Let him not lay his godliness aside, when he is done with the morning devotion of his family; but carry it abroad with him, and make it his companion and his guide through the whole business of the day; always bearing in his heart the sentiment, that thou God seest me; and remembering, that there is not one hour that can flow, or one occasion that can cast up, where his law is not present with some imperious exaction or other. It is false, that the principle of christian sanctification possesses no influence over the familiarities of civil and ordinary life. It is altogether false, that godliness is a virtue of such a lofty and monastic order, as to hold its dominion only over the solemnities of worship, or over the solitudes of prayer and spiritual contemplation. If it be substantially a grace within us at all, it will give a direction and a colour to the whole of our path in society. There is not one conceivable transaction, amongst all the manifold varieties of human employment, which it is not fitted to animate by its spirit. There is nothing that meets us too homely to be beyond the reach of obtaining, from its influence, the stamp of something celestial. It offers to take the whole man under its ascendency, and to subordinate all his movements; nor does it hold the place which rightfully belongs to it, till it be vested with a presiding authority over the entire system of human affairs. And therefore it is, that the preacher is not bringing down Christianity—he is only sending it abroad over the field of its legitimate operation, when he goes with it to your counting-houses, and there rebukes every selfish inclination that would carry you ever so little within the limits of fraudulency; when he enters into your chambers of agency, and there detects the character of falsehood, which lurks under all the plausibility of your multiplied and excessive charges; when he repairs to the crowded market-place, and pronounces of every bargain, over which truth, in all the strictness of quakerism, has not presided, that it is tainted with moral evil; when he looks into your shops, and, in listening to the contest of argument between him who magnifies his article, and him who pretends to undervalue it, he calls it the contest of avarice, broken loose from the restraints of integrity. He is not, by all this, vulgarizing religion, or giving it the hue and the character of earthliness. He is only asserting the might and the universality of its sole preeminence over man. And therefore it is, that if possible to solemnize his hearers to the practice of simplicity and godly sincerity in their dealings, he would try to make the odiousness of sin stand visibly out on every shade and modification of dishonesty; and to assure them that if there be a place in our world, where the subtle evasion, and the dexterous imposition, and the sly but gainful concealment, and the report which misleads an inquirer, and the gloss which tempts the unwary purchaser—are not only currently practised in the walks of merchandize, but, when not carried forward to the glare and the literality of falsehood, are beheld with general connivance; if there be a place where the sense of morality has thus fallen, and all the nicer delicacies of conscience are overborne in the keen and ambitious rivalry of men hasting to be rich, and wholly given over to the idolatrous service of the god of this world—then that is the place, the smoke of whose iniquity rises before Him who sitteth on the throne, in a tide of the deepest and most revolting abomination.

And here we have to complain of the public injustice that is done to Christianity, when one of its ostentatious professors has acted the hypocrite, and stands in disgraceful exposure before the eyes of the world. We advert to the readiness with which this is turned into a matter of general impeachment, against every appearance of seriousness; and how loud the exclamation is against the religion of all who signalize themselves; and that, if the aspect of godliness be so very decided as to become an aspect of peculiarity, then is this peculiarity converted into a ground of distrust and suspicion against the bearer of it. Now, it so happens, that in the midst of this world lying in wickedness, a man, to be a Christian at all, must signalize himself. Neither is he in a way of salvation, unless he be one of a very peculiar people; nor would we precipitately consign him to discredit, even though the peculiarity be so very glaring as to provoke the charge of methodism. But instead of making one man's hypocrisy act as a draw-back upon the reputation of a thousand, we submit, if it would not be a fairer and more philosophical procedure, just to betake one's-self to the method of induction—to make a walking survey over the town, and record an inventory of all the men in it who are so very far gone as to have the voice of psalms in their family; or as to attend the meetings of fellowship for prayer; or as scrupulously to abstain from all that is questionable in the amusements of the world; or as, by any other marked and visible symptom whatever, to stand out to general observation as the members of a saintly and separated society. We know, that even of such there are a few, who, if Paul were alive, would move him to weep for the reproach they bring upon his master. But we also know, that the blind and impetuous world exaggerates the few into the many; inverts the process of atonement altogether, by laying the sins of one man upon the multitude; looks at their general aspect of sanctity, and is so engrossed with this single expression of character, as to be insensible to the noble uprightness, and the tender humanity with which this sanctity is associated. And therefore it is, that we offer the assertion, and challenge all to its most thorough and searching investigation, that the Christianity of these people, which many think does nothing but cant, and profess, and run after ordinances, has augmented their honesties and their liberalities, and that, tenfold beyond the average character of society; that these are the men we oftenest meet with in the mansions of poverty—and who look with the most wakeful eye over all the sufferings and necessities of our species—and who open their hand most widely in behalf of the imploring and the friendless—and to whom, in spite of all their mockery, the men of the world are sure, in the negociations of business, to award the readiest confidence —and who sustain the most splendid part in all those great movements of philanthropy which bear on the general interests of mankind—and who, with their eye full upon eternity, scatter the most abundant blessings over the fleeting pilgrimage of time—and who, while they hold their conversation in heaven, do most enrich the earth we tread upon, with all those virtues which secure enjoyment to families, and uphold the order and prosperity of the commonwealth.

DISCOURSE III.

The Power of Selfishness in promoting the Honesties of mercantile Intercourse.

"And if you do good to them which do good to you, what thank have ye? for sinners also do even the same."—*Luke* vi. 33.

It is to be remarked of many of those duties, the performance of which confers the least distinction upon an individual, that they are at the same time the very duties, the violation of which would confer upon him the largest measure of obloquy and disgrace. Truth and justice do not serve to elevate a man so highly above the average morality of his species, as would generosity, or ardent friendship, or devoted and disinterested patriotism; the former are greatly more common than the latter; and, on that account, the presence of them is not so calculated to signalize the individual to whom they belong. But that is one account, also, why the absence of them would make him a more monstrous exception to the general run of character in society. And, accordingly, while it is true, that there are more men of integrity in the world, than there are men of very wide and liberal beneficence—it is also true, that one act of falsehood, or one act of dishonesty, would stamp a far more burning infamy on the name of a transgressor than any defect in those more heroic charities, and extraordinary virtues, of which humanity is capable.

So it is far more disgraceful not to be just to another, than not to be kind to him; and, at the same time, an act of kindness may be held in higher positive estimation than an act of justice. The one is my right —nor is there any call for the homage of a particular testimony when it is rendered. The other is additional to my right—the offering of a spontaneous good will which I had no title to exact; and which, therefore, when rendered to me, excites in my bosom the cordiality of a warmer acknowledgement. And yet, our Saviour, who knew what was in man, saw, that much of the apparent kindness of nature, was resolvable into the real selfishness of nature; that much of the good done unto others, was done in the hope that these others would do something again. And, we believe it would be found by an able analyst of the human character, that this was the secret but substantial principle of many of the civilities and hospitalities of ordinary intercourse—that if there were no expectation either of a return in kind, or of a return in gratitude, or of a return in popularity, many of the sweetening and cementing virtues of a neighbourhood would be practically done away—all serving to prove, that a multitude of virtues, which, in effect, promoted the comfort and the interest of others, were tainted in principle by a latent regard to one's own interest; and that thus being the fellowship of those who did good, either as a return for the good done unto them, or who did good in hope of such a return, it might be, in fact, what our Saviour characterizes in the text—the fellowship of sinners.

But if to do that which is unjust, is still

more disgraceful than not to do that which is kind, it would prove more strikingly than before, how deeply sin had tainted the moral constitution of our species—could it be shown, that the great practical restraint on the prevalence of this more disgraceful thing in society, is the tie of that common selfishness which actuates and characterizes all its members. It were a curious but important question, were it capable of being resolved—if men did not feel it their interest to be honest, how much of the actual doings of honesty would still be kept up in the world? It is our own opinion of the nature of man, that it has its honourable feelings, and its instinctive principles of rectitude, and its constitutional love of truth and of integrity; and that, on the basis of these, a certain portion of uprightness would remain amongst us, without the aid of any prudence, or any calculation whatever. All this we have fully conceded; and have already attempted to demonstrate, that, in spite of it, the character of man is thoroughly pervaded by the very essence of sinfulness; because, with all the native virtues which adorn it, there adheres to it that foulest of all spiritual deformities—unconcern about God, and even antipathy to God. It has been argued against the orthodox doctrine of the universality of human corruption, that even without the sphere of the operation of the gospel, there do occur so many engaging specimens of worth and benevolence in society. The reply is, that this may be no deduction from the doctrine whatever, but be even an aggravation of it —should the very men who exemplify so much of what is amiable, carry in their hearts an indifference to the will of that Being who thus hath formed, and thus hath embellished them. But it would be a heavy deduction indeed, not from the doctrine, but from its hostile and opposing argument, could it be shown, that the vast majority of all equitable dealing amongst men, is performed, not on the principle of honour at all, but on the principle of selfishness—that this is the soil upon which the honesty of the world mainly flourishes, and is sustained; that, were the connexion dissolved between justice to others and our own particular advantage, this would go very far to banish the observation of justice from the earth; that, generally speaking, men are honest, not because they are lovers of God, and not even because they are lovers of virtue, but because they are lovers of their ownselves—insomuch, that if it were possible to disjoin the good of self altogether from the habit of doing what was fair, as well as from the habit of doing what was kind to the people around us, this would not merely isolate the children of men from each other, in respect of the obligations of beneficence, but it would arm them into an undisguised hostility against each other, in respect to their rights. The mere disinterested principle would set up a feeble barrier, indeed, against a desolating tide of selfishness, now set loose from the consideration of its own advantage. The genuine depravity of the human heart would burst forth and show itself in its true characters; and the world in which we live be transformed into a scene of unblushing fraud, of open and lawless depredation.

And, perhaps, after all, the best way of arriving practically at the solution of this question would be, not by a formal induction of particular cases, but by committing the matter to the gross and general experience of those who are most conversant in the affairs of business.—There is a sort of undefinable impression you all have upon this subject, on the justness of which however, we are disposed to lay a very considerable stress—an impression gathered out of the mass of the recollections of a whole life—an impression founded on what you may have observed in the history of your own doings—a kind of tact that you have acquired as the fruit of your repeated intercourse with men, and of the manifold transactions that you have had with them, and of the number of times in which you have been personally implicated with the play of human passions, and human interests. It is our own conviction, that a well exercised merchant could cast a more intelligent glance at this question, than a well exercised metaphysician; and therefore do we submit its decision to those of you who have hazarded most largely, and most frequently, on the faith of agents, and customers, and distant correspondents. We know the fact of a very secure and well warranted confidence in the honesty of others, being widely prevalent amongst you: and that, were it not for this, all the interchanges of trade would be suspended; and that confidence is the very soul and life of commercial activity; and it is delightful to think, how thus a man can suffer all the wealth which belongs to him to depart from under his eye, and to traverse the mightiest oceans and continents of our world, and to pass into the custody of men whom he never saw. And it is a sublime homage, one should think, to the honourable and high-minded principles of our nature, that, under their guardianship, the adverse hemispheres of the globe should be bound together in safe and profitable merchandise; and that thus one should sleep with a bosom undisturbed by jealousy, in Britain, who has all, and more than all his property treasured in the warehouses of India—and that, just because there he knows there is vigilance to defend it, and activity to dispose of it, and truth to account for it, and all those trusty virtues which ennoble the character of man to shield it from injury, and send it back again in an increasing tide of opulence to his door.

There is no question, then, as to the fact of a very extended practical honesty, between man and man, in their intercourse with each other. The only question is, as to the reason of the fact. Why is it, that he whom you have trusted acquits himself of his trust with such correctness and fidelity? Whether is his mind in so doing, most set upon your interest or upon his own? Whether is it because he seeks your advantage in it, or because he finds it is his own advantage? Tell us to which of the two concerns he is most tremblingly alive—to your property, or to his own character? and whether, upon the last of these feelings, he may not be more forcibly impelled to equitable dealing than upon the first of them? We well know, that there is room enough in his bosom for both; but to determine how powerfully selfishness is blended with the punctualities and the integrities of business, let us ask those who can speak most soundly and experimentally on the subject, what would be the result, if the element of selfishness were so detached from the operations of trade, that there was no such thing as a man suffering in his prosperity, because he suffered in his good name; that there was no such thing as a desertion of custom and employment coming upon the back of a blasted credit, and a tainted reputation; in a word, if the only security we had of man was his principles, and that his interest flourished and augmented just as surely without his principles as with them? Tell us, if the hold we have of a man's own personal advantage were thus broken down, in how far the virtues of the mercantile world would survive it? Would not the world of trade sustain as violent a derangement on this mighty hold being cut asunder, as the world of nature would on the suspending of the law of gravitation? Would not the whole system, in fact, fall to pieces, and be dissolved? Would not men, when thus released from the magical chain of their own interest, which bound them together into a fair and seeming compact of principle, like dogs of rapine let loose upon their prey, overleap the barrier which formerly restrained them? Does not this prove, that selfishness, after all, is the grand principle on which the brotherhood of the human race is made to hang together; and that he who can make the wrath of man to praise him, has also, upon the selfishness of man, caused a most beauteous order of wide and useful intercourse to be suspended?

But let us here stop to observe, that, while there is much in this contemplation to magnify the wisdom of the Supreme Contriver, there is also much in it to humble man, and to convict him of the deceitfulness of that moral complacency with which he looks to his own character, and his own attainments. There is much in it to demonstrate, that his righteousness are as filthy rags; and that the idolatry of self, however hidden in its operation, may be detected in almost every one of them. God may combine the separate interests of every individual of the human race, and the strenuous prosecution of these interests by each of them, into a harmonious system of operation, for the good of one great and extended family. But if, on estimating the character of each individual member of that family, we shall find that the mainspring of his actions is the urgency of a selfish inclination; and that to this his very virtues are subordinate: and that even the honesties which mark his conduct are chiefly, though, perhaps, insensibly due to the selfishness which actuates and occupies his whole heart;—then, let the semblance be what it may, still the reality of the case accords with the most mortifying representations of the New Testament. The moralities of nature are but the moralities of a day, and will cease to be applauded when this world, the only theatre of their applause, is burnt up. They are but the blossoms of that rank efflorescence which is nourished on the soil of human corruption, and can never bring forth fruit unto immortality. The discerner of all secrets sees that they emanate from a principle which is at utter war with the charity that prepares for the enjoyments, and that glows in the bosoms of the celestial; and, therefore, though highly esteemed among men, they may be in His sight an abomination.

Let us, if possible, make this still clearer to your apprehension, by descending more minutely into particulars. There is not one member of the great mercantile family, with whom there does not obtain a reciprocal interest between himself and all those who compose the circle of his various correspondents. He does them good; but his eye is all the while open to the expectation of their doing him something again. They minister to him all the profits of his employment; but not unless he minister to them of his service, and attention, and fidelity. Insomuch, that if his credit abandon him, his prosperity will also abandon him. If he forfeit the confidence of others, he will also forfeit their custom along with it. So that, in perfect consistency with interest being the reigning idol of his soul, he may still be, in every way, as sensitive of encroachment upon his reputation, as he would be of encroachment upon his property; and be as vigilant, to the full, in guarding his name against the breath of calumny, or suspicion, as in guarding his estate against the inroads of a depredator. Now, this tie of reciprocity, which binds him into fellowship and good faith with society at large, will sometimes, in the mere course of business, and its unlooked-for fluctuations, draw one or two individuals into a still more special intimacy with himself. There may be a lucrative partnership, in which it is the pressing necessity of each individual, that all of them, for a time at least, stick closely and steadily together. Or there may be a thriving interchange of commodities struck out, where it is the mutual interest of all who are concerned, that each take his assigned part and adhere to it. Or there may be a promising arrangement devised, which it needs concert and understanding to effectuate; and, for which purpose, several may enter into a skilful and well-ordered combination.

We are neither saying that this is very general in the mercantile world, or that it is in the slightest degree unfair. But you must be sensible, that, amid the reelings and movements of the great trading society, the phenomenon sometimes offers itself of a groupe of individuals who have entered into some compact of mutual accommodation, and who, therefore, look as if they were isolated from the rest by the bond of some more strict and separate alliance. All we aim at, is to gather illustration to our principle, out of the way in which the members of this associated cluster conduct themselves to each other; how such a cordiality may pass between them, as one could suppose to be the cordiality of genuine friendship; how such an intercourse might be maintained among their families, as might look like the intercourse of unmingled affection; how such an exuberance of mutual hospitality might be poured forth as to recal those poetic days when avarice was unknown, and men lived in harmony together on the fruits of one common inheritance; and how nobly disdainful each member of the combination appeared to be of such little savings, as could be easily surrendered to the general good and adjustment of the whole concern. And all this, you will observe, so long as the concern prospered, and it was for the interest of each to abide by it; and the respective accounts current gladdened the heart of every individual by the exhibition of an abundant share of the common benefit to himself. But then, every such system of operations comes to an end. And what we ask is, if it be at all an unlikely evolution of our nature, that the selfishness which lay in wrapt concealment, during the progress of these transactions, should now come forward and put out to view its cloven foot, when they draw to their termination? And as the tie of reciprocity gets looser, is it not a very possible thing, that the murmurs of something like unfair or unhandsome conduct should get louder? And that a fellowship, hitherto carried forward in smiles, should break up in reproaches? And that the whole character of this fellowship should show itself more unequivocally as it comes nearer to its close? And that some of its members, as they are becoming disengaged from the bond of mutual interest, should also become disengaged from the bond of those mutual delicacies and proprieties, and even honesties, which had heretofore marked the whole of their intercourse?—Insomuch, that a matter in which all the parties looked so fair, and magnanimous, and liberal, might at length degenerate into a contest of keen appropriation, a scramble of downright and undisguised selfishness?

But though this may happen sometimes, we are far from saying that it will happen generally. It could not, in fact, without such an exposure of character, as might not merely bring a man down in the estimation of those from whom he is now withdrawing himself, but also in the estimation of that general public with whom he is still linked; and on whose opinion of him there still rests the dependence of a strong personal interest. To estimate precisely the whole influence of this consideration, or the degree in which honesty of character is resolvable into selfishness of character, it would be necessary to suppose, that the tie of reciprocity was dissolved, not merely between the individual and those with whom he had been more particularly and more intimately associated—but that the tie of reciprocity was dissolved between the individual and the whole of his former acquaintanceship in business.

Now, the situation which comes nearest to this, is that of a man on the eve of bankruptcy, and with no sure hope of so retrieving his circumstances as again to emerge into credit, and be restored to some employment of gain or of confidence. If he have either honourable or religious feelings, then character, as connected with principle, may still, in his eyes, be something; but character, as connected with prudence, or the calculations of interest, may now be nothing. In the dark hour of the desperation of his soul, he may feel, in fact, that he has nothing to lose; and let us now see how he will conduct himself, when thus released from that check of reputation which formerly held him. In these circumstances, if you have ever seen the man abandon himself to utter regardlessness of all the honesties which at one time adorned him, and doing such disgraceful things as he would have spurned at the very suggestion of, in the days of his prosperity; and, forgetful of his former name practising all possible shifts of duplicity to prolong the credit of a tottering establishment; and to keep himself afloat for a few months of torture and restlessness, weaving such a web of entanglement around his many friends and companions, as shall most surely implicate some of them in his fall; and, as the crisis approaches, plying his petty wiles how to survive the coming ruin, and to gather up of its fragments to his family. O! how much is there here to deplore; and who can be so ungenerous as to stalk in unrelenting triumph over the helplessness of so sad an overthrow! But if ever such an exhibition meet your eye, while we ask you not to withhold your pity from the unfortunate, we ask you also to read in it a lesson of worthless and sunken humanity; how even its very virtues are tinctured with corruption; and that the honour, and the truth, and the equity, with which man proudly thinks his nature to be embellished, are often reared on the basis of selfishness, and lie prostrate in the dust when that basis is cut away.

But other instances may be quoted, which go still more satisfactorily to prove the very extended influence of selfishness on the moral judgments of our species; and how readily the estimate, which a man forms on the question of right and wrong, accommodates itself to his own interest. There is a strong general reciprocity of advantage between the government of a country and all its inhabitants. The one party, in this relation, renders a revenue for the expenses of the state. The other party renders back again protection from injustice and violence. Were the means furnished by the former withheld, the benefit conferred by the latter would cease to be administered. So that, with the government, and the public at large, nothing can be more strict, and more indispensable, than the tie of reciprocity that is between them. But this is not felt, and therefore not acted upon by the separate individuals who compose that public. The reciprocity does not come home with a sufficiently pointed and personal application to each of them. Every man may calculate, that though he, on the strength of some dexterous evasions, were to keep back of the tribute that is due by him, the mischief that would recoil upon himself is divided with the rest of his countrymen; and the portion of it which comes to his door would be so very small, as to be altogether insensible. To all feeling he will just be as effectually sheltered, by the power and the justice of his country, whether he pay his taxes in full, or under the guise of some skilful concealment, pay them but partially; and therefore, to every practical effect, the tie of reciprocity, between him and his sovereign, is in a great measure dissolved. Now, what is the actual adjustment of the moral sense, and moral conduct, of the population, to this state of matters? It is quite palpable. Subterfuges, which in private business, would be held to be disgraceful, are not held to be so disgraceful in this department of a man's personal transactions. The cry of indignation, which would be lifted up against the falsehood or dishonesty of a man's dealings in his own neighbourhood, is mitigated or unheard, though, in his dealings with the state, there should be the very same relaxation of principle. On this subject, there is a convenience of popular feeling, which, if extended to the whole of human traffic, would banish all its securities from the world. Giving reason to believe, that much of the good done among men, is done on the expectation of a good that will be rendered back again; and that many of the virtues, by which the fellowship of human beings is regulated and sustained, still leave the imputation unredeemed, of its being a fellowship of sinners; and that both the practice of morality, and the demand for it, are measured by the operation of a self-love, which, so far from signalizing any man, or preparing him for eternity, he holds in common with the fiercest and most degenerate of his species; and that, apart from the consideration of his own interest, simplicity and godly sincerity are, to a great degree, unknown; insomuch, that though God has interposed with a law, of giving unto all their dues, and tribute to whom tribute is due—we may venture an affirmation of the vast majority of this tribute, that it is rendered for wrath's sake, and not for conscience's sake. Of so little effect is unsupported and solitary conscience to stem the tide of selfishness. And it is chiefly when honesty and truth go overbearingly along with this tide, that the voice of man is lifted up to acknowledge them, and his heart becomes feelingly alive to a sense of their obligations.

And let us here just ask, in what relation of criminality does he who uses a contraband article stand to him who deals in it? In precisely the same relation that a receiver of stolen goods stands to a thief or a depredator. There may be some who revolt at the idea of being so classified. But, if the habit we have just denounced can be fastened on men of rank and seemly reputation, let us just humble ourselves into the admission of how little the righteous practice of the world has the foundation of righteous principle to sustain it; how feeble are the securities of rectitude, had it nothing to uphold it but its own native charms, and native obligations; how society is held together, only because the grace of God can turn to account the worthless propensities of the individuals who compose it; and how, if the virtues of fidelity, and truth, and justice, had not the prop of selfishness to rest upon, they would, with the exception of a few scattered remnants, take their departure from the world, and leave it a prey to the anarchy of the human passions—to the wild misrule of all those depravities which agitate and deform our ruined nature.

The very same exhibition of our nature may be witnessed in almost every parish of our sister kingdom, where the people render a revenue to the minister of religion, and the minister renders back again a return, it is true—but not such a return, as, in the estimation of gross and ordinary selfishness, is at all deemed an equivalent for the sacrifice which has been made. In this instance, too, that law of reciprocity which reigns throughout the common transactions of merchandise, is altogether suspended; and the consequence is, that the law of right is trampled into ashes. A tide of public odium runs against the men who are outraged of their property, and a smile of general connivance rewards the successful dexterity of the men who invade it. That portion of the annual produce of our soil, which, on a foundation of legitimacy as firm as the property of the soil itself, is allotted to a set of national functionaries—and which, but for them, would all have gone, in the shape of increased revenue, to the indolent proprietor, is altogether thrown loose from the guardianship of that great principle of reciprocity, on which we strongly suspect that the honesties of this world are mainly supported. The national clergy of England may be considered as standing out of the pale of this guardianship; and the consequence is, that what is most rightfully and most sacredly theirs, is abandoned to the gambol of many thousand depredators; and in addition to a load of most unmerited obloquy, have they had to sustain all the heartburnings of known and felt injustice; and that intercourse between the teachers and the taught, which ought surely to be an intercourse of peace, and friendship, and righteousness, is turned into a contest between the natural avarice of the one party, and the natural resentments of the other. It is not that we wish our sister church were swept away, for we honestly think, that the overthrow of that establishment would be a severe blow to the Christianity of our land. It is not that we envy that great hierarchy the splendor of her endowments—for better a dinner of herbs, when surrounded by the love of parishioners, than a preferment of stalled dignity, and strife therewith. It is not either that we look upon her ministers as having at all disgraced themselves by their rapacity; for look to the amount of the encroachments that are made upon them, and you will see that they have carried their privileges with the most exemplary forbearance and moderation. But from these very encroachments do we infer how lawless a human being will become, when emancipated from the bond of his own interest; how much such a state of things must multiply the temptations to injustice over the face of the country; and how desirable, therefore, that it were put an end to—not by the abolition of that venerable church, but by a fair and liberal commutation of the revenues which support her—not by bringing any blight on the property of her ecclesiastics, but by the removal of a most devouring blight from the worth of her population—that every provocative to justice may be done away, and the frailty of human principle be no longer left to such a ruinous and such a withering exposure.

This instance we would not have mentioned, but for the sake of adding another experimental proof to the lesson of our text; and we now hasten onward to the lesson itself, with a few of its applications.

We trust you are convinced, from what has been said, that much of the actual honesty of the world is due to the selfishness of the world. And then you will surely admit, that in as far as this is the actuating principle, honesty descends from its place as a rewardable, or even as an amiable virtue, and sinks down into the character of a mere prudential virtue—which, so far from conferring any moral exaltation on him by whom it is exemplified, emanates out of a propensity that seems inseparable from the constitution of every sentient being—and by which man is, in one point, assimilated either to the most worthless of his own species, or to those inferior animals among whom worth is unattainable.

And let it not deafen the humbling impression of this argument, that you are not distinctly conscious of the operation of selfishness, as presiding at every step over the honesty of your daily and familiar transactions; and that the only inward checks against injustice, of which you are sensible, are the aversion of a generous indignancy towards it, and the positive discomfort you would incur by the reproaches of your own conscience. Selfishness, in fact, may have originated and alimented the whole of this virtue that belongs to you, and yet the mind incur the same discomfort by the violation of it, that it would do by the violation of any other of its established habits. And as to the generous indignancy of your feelings against all that is fraudulently and disgracefully wrong, let us never forget, that this may be the nurtured fruit of that common selfishness which links human beings with each other into a relationship of mutual dependence. This may be seen, in all its perfection, among the leagued and sworn banditti of the highway; who, while execrated by society at large for the compact of iniquity into which they have entered, can maintain the most heroic fidelity to the virtues of their own brotherhood—and be, in every way, as lofty and as chivalric with their points of honour, as we are with ours; and elevate as indignant a voice against the worthlessness of him who could betray the secret of their association, or break up any of the securities by which it was held together. And, in like manner, may we be the members of a wider combination, yet brought together by the tie of reciprocal interest; and all the virtues essential to the existence, or to the good of such a combination, may come to be idolized amongst us; and the breath of human applause may fan them into a lustre of splendid estimation; and yet the good man of society on earth be, in common with all his fellows, an utter outcast from the society of heaven—with his heart altogether bereft of that allegiance to God which forms the reigning principle of his unfallen creation—and in a state of entire destitution either as to that love of the Supreme Being, or as to that disinterested love of those around us, which form the graces and the virtues of eternity.

We have not affirmed that there is no such thing as a native and disinterested principle of honour among men. But we have affirmed, on a former occasion, that a sense of honour may be in the heart, and the sense of God be utterly away from it. And we affirm now, that much of the honest practice of the world is not due to honesty of principle at all, but takes its origin from a baser ingredient of our constitution altogether. How wide is the operation of selfishness on the one hand, and how limited is the operation of abstract principle on the other, it were difficult to determine; and such a labyrinth to man is his own heart, that he may be utterly unable, from his own consciousness, to answer this question. But amid all the difficulties of such an analysis to himself, we ask him to think of another who is unseen by us, but who is represented to us as seeing all things. We know not in what characters this heavenly witness can be more impressively set forth, than as pondering the heart, as weighing the secrets of the heart, as fastening an attentive and a judging eye on all the movements of it, as treasuring up the whole of man's outward and inward history in a book of remembrance; and as keeping it in reserve for that day when, it is said, that the secrets of all hearts shall be laid open; and God shall bring out every secret thing, whether it be good, or whether it be evil. Your consciousness may not distinctly inform you, in how far the integrity of your habits is due to the latent operation of selfishness, or to the more direct and obvious operation of honour. But your consciousness may, perhaps, inform you distinctly enough, how little a share the will of God has in the way of influence on any of your doings. Your own sense and memory of what passes within you, may charge you with the truth of this monstrous indictment—that you live without God in the world; that however you may be signalized among your fellows, by that worth of character which is held in highest value and demand amongst the individuals of a mercantile society, it is at least without the influence of a godly principle that you have reached the maturity of an established reputation; that either the proud emotions of rectitude which glow within your bosom are totally untinctured by a feeling of homage to the Deity—or that, without any such emotions, Self is the divinity you have all along worshipped, and your very virtues are so many offerings of reverence at her shrine. If such be, in fact, the nakedness of your spiritual condition, is it not high time, we ask, that you awaken out of this delusion, and shake the lying spirit of deep and heavy slumber away from you? Is it not high time, when eternity is so fast coming on, that you examine your accounts with God, and seek for a settlement with that Being who will so soon meet your disembodied spirits with the question of—what have you done unto me?—And if all the virtues which adorn you are but the subserviences of time, and of its accommodation—if either done altogether unto yourselves, or done without the recognition of God on the spontaneous instigation of your own feelings—is it not high time that you lean no longer to the securities on which you have rested, and that you seek for acceptance with your Maker on a more firm and unalterable foundation?

This, then, is the terminating object of all the experience that we have tried to set before you. We want to be a schoolmaster to bring you unto Christ. We want you to open your eyes to the accordancy which obtains between the theology of the New Testament and the actual state and history of man. Above all, we want you to turn your eyes inwardly upon yourselves, and there to behold a character without one trace or lineament of godliness—there to behold a heart set upon totally other things than those which constitute the portion and the reward of eternity—there to behold every principle of action resolvable into the idolatry of self, or, at least into something independent of the authority of God—there to behold how worthless in their substance are those virtues which look so imposing in their semblance and their display, and draw round them here a popularity and an applause which will all be dissipated into nothing, when hereafter they are brought up for examination to the judgment seat. We want you, when the revelation of the gospel charges you with the totality and magnitude of your corruption, that you acquiesce in that charge; and that you may perceive the trueness of it, under the disguise of all those hollow and unsubstantial accomplishments, with which nature may deck her own fallen and degenerate children. It is easy to be amused, and interested, and intellectually regaled by an analysis of the human character, and a survey of human society. But it is not so easy to reach the individual conscience with the lesson—we are undone. It is not so easy to strike the alarm into your hearts of the present guilt, and the future damnation. It is not so easy to send the pointed arrow of conviction into your bosoms, where it may keep by you and pursue you like an arrow sticking fast; or so to humble you into the conclusion, that in the sight of God, you are an accursed thing, as that you may seek unto him who became a curse for you, and as that the preaching of his Cross might cease to be foolishness.

Be assured, then, if you keep by the ground of being justified by your present works, you will perish: and though we may not have succeeded in convincing you of their worthlessness, be assured that a day is coming when such a flaw of deceitfulness, in the principle of them all, shall be laid open, as will demonstrate the equity of your entire and everlasting condemnation. To avert the fearfulness of that day is the message of the great atonement sounded in your ears—and the blood of Christ, cleansing from all sin, is offered to your acceptance; and if you turn away from it, you add to the guilt of a broken law the insult of a neglected gospel. But if you take the pardon of the gospel on the footing of the gospel, then, such is the efficacy of this great expedient, that it will reach an application of mercy farther than the eye of your own conscience ever reached; that it will redeem you from the guilt even of your most secret and unsuspected iniquities; and thoroughly wash you from a taint of sinfulness, more inveterate than, in the blindness of nature, you ever thought of, or ever conceived to belong to you.

But when a man becomes a believer, there are two great events which take place at this great turning point in his history. One of them takes place in heaven —even the expunging of his name from the book of condemnation. Another of them takes place on earth—even the application of such a sanctifying influence to his person, that all old things are done away with him, and all things become new with him. He is made the workmanship of God in Christ Jesus our Lord. He is not merely forgiven the sin of every one evil work of which he had aforetime been guilty, but he is created anew unto the corresponding good work. And therefore, if a Christian, will his honesty be purified from that taint of selfishness by which the general honesty of this world is so deeply and extensively pervaded. He will not do this good thing, that any good thing may be done unto him again. He will do it on a simple regard to its own native and independent rectitude. He will do it because it is honourable, and because God wills him so to adorn the doctrine of his Saviour. All his fair dealing, and all his friendship, will be fair dealing and friendship without interest. The principle that is in him will stand in no need of aid from any such auxiliary— but strong in its own unborrowed resources, will it impress a legible stamp of dignity and uprightness on the whole variety of his transactions in the world. All men find it their advantage, by the integrity of their dealings, to prolong the existence of some gainful fellowship into which they may have entered. But with him, the same unsullied integrity which kept this fellowship together, and sustained the progress of it, will abide with him through its last transactions, and dignify its full and final termination. Most men find, that, without the reverberation of any mischief on their own heads, they could reduce beneath the point of absolute justice, the charges of taxation. But he has a conscience both towards God, and towards man, which will not let him; and there is a rigid truth in all his returns, a pointed and precise accuracy in all his payments. When hemmed in with circumstances of difficulty, and evidently tottering to his fall, the demand of nature is, that he should ply his every artifice to secrete a provision for his family. But a Christian mind is incapable of artifice; and the voice of conscience within him will ever be louder than the voice of necessity; and he will be open as day with his creditors, nor put forth his hand to that which is rightfully theirs, any more than he would put forth his hand to the perpetration of a sacrilege; and though released altogether from that tie of interest which binds a man to equity with his fellows, yet the tie of principle will remain with him in all its strength. Nor will it ever be found that he, for the sake of subsistence, will enter into fraud, seeing that, as one of the children of light, he would not, to gain the whole world, lose his own soul.

DISCOURSE IV.

The Guilt of Dishonesty not to be estimated by the Gain of it.

"He that is faithful in that which is least, is faithful also in much; and he that is unjust in the least, is unjust also in much."—*Luke* xvi. 10.

It is the fine poetical conception of a late poetical countryman, whose fancy too often grovelled among the despicable of human character—but who, at the same time, was capable of exhibiting, either in pleasing or in proud array, both the tender and the noble of human character—when he says of the man who carried a native, unborrowed, self-sustained rectitude in his bosom, that "his eye, even turned on empty space, beamed keen with honour." It was affirmed, in the last discourse, that much of the honourable practice of the world rested on the substratum of selfishness; that society was held together in the exercise of its relative virtues, mainly, by the tie of reciprocal advantage; that a man's own interest bound him to all those average equities which obtained in the neighbourhood around him; and in which, if he proved himself to be glaringly deficient, he would be abandoned by the respect, and the confidence, and the good will of the people with whom he had to do. It is a melancholy thought, how little the semblance of virtue upon earth betokens the real and substantial presence of virtuous principle among men. But on the other hand, though it be a rare, there cannot be a more dignified attitude of the soul, than when of itself it kindles with a sense of justice, and the holy flame is fed, as it were, by its own energies; than when man moves onwards in an unchanging course of moral magnanimity, and disdains the aid of those inferior principles, by which gross and sordid humanity is kept from all the grosser violations; than when he rejoices in truth as his kindred and congenial element;—so, that though unpeopled of all its terrestrial accompaniments; though he saw no interest whatever to be associated with its fulfilment; though without one prospect either of fame or of emolument before him, would his eye, even when turned on emptiness itself, still retain the living lustre that had been lighted up in it, by a feeling of inward and independent reverence.

It has already been observed, and that fully and frequently enough, that a great part of the homage which is rendered to integrity in the world, is due to the operation of selfishness. And this substantially is the reason, why the principle of the text has so very slender a hold upon the human conscience. Man is ever prone to estimate the enormity of injustice, by the degree in which he suffers from it. He brings this moral question to the standard of his own interest. A master will bear with all the lesser liberties of his servants, so long as he feels them to be harmless; and it is not till he is awakened to the apprehension of personal injury, from the amount or frequency of the embezzlements, that his moral indignation is at all sensibly awakened. And thus it is, that the maxim of our great teacher of righteousness seems to be very much unfelt, or forgotten, in society. Unfaithfulness in that which is little, and unfaithfulness in that which is much, are very far from being regarded, as they were by him, under the same aspect of criminality. If there be no great hurt, it is felt that there is no great harm. The innocence of a dishonest freedom in respect of morality, is rated by its insignificance in respect of matter. The margin which separates the right from the wrong, is remorselessly trodden under foot, so long as each makes only a minute and gentle encroachment beyond the landmark of his neighbour's territory. On this subject there is a loose and popular estimate, which is not at one with the deliverance of the New Testament; a habit of petty invasion on the side of aggressors, which is scarcely felt by them to be at all iniquitous—and even on the part of those who are thus made free with, there is a habit of loose and careless toleration. There is, in fact, a negligence or a dormancy of principle among men, which causes this sort of injustice to be easily practised on the one side, and as easily put up with on the other; and, in a general slackness of observation, is this virtue, in its strictness and in its delicacy, completely overborne.

It is the taint of selfishness, then, which has so marred and corrupted the moral sensibility of our world; and the man, if such a man can be, whose "eye, even turned on empty space, beams keen with honour;" and whose homage, therefore, to the virtue of justice, is altogether freed from the mixture of unworthy and interested feelings, will long to render to her, in every instance, a faultless and a completed offering. Whatever his forbearance to others, he could not suffer the slightest blot of corruption upon any doings of his own. He cannot be satisfied with any thing short of the very last jot and tittle of the requirements of equity being fulfilled. He not merely shares in the revolt of the general world against such outrageous departures from the rule of right, as would carry in their train the ruin of acquaintances or the distress of families. Such is the delicacy of the principle within him, that he could not have peace under the consciousness even of the minutest and least discoverable violation. He looks fully and fearlessly at the whole account which justice has against him; and he cannot rest, so long as there is a single article unmet, or a single demand unsatisfied. If, in any transaction of his there was so much as a farthing of secret and injurious reservation on his side, this would be to him like an accursed thing, which marred the character of the whole proceeding, and spread over it such an aspect of evil, as to offend and to disturb him. He could not bear the whisperings of his own heart, if it told him, that, in so much as by one iota of defect, he had balanced the matter unfairly between himself and the unconscious individual with whom he deals. It would lie a burden upon his mind to hurt and to make him unhappy, till the opportunity of explanation had come round, and he had obtained ease to his conscience, by acquitting himself to the full of all his obligations. It is justice in the uprightness of her attitude: it is justice in the onwardness of her path; it is justice disdaining every advantage that would tempt her, by ever so little to the right or to the left; it is justice spurning the littleness of each paltry enticement away from her, and maintaining herself, without deviation, in a track so purely rectilinear, that even the most jealous and microscopic eye could not find in it the slightest aberration: this is the justice set forth by our great moral Teacher in the passage now submitted to you; and by which we are told, that this virtue refuses fellowship with every degree of iniquity that is perceptible; and that, were the very least act of unfaithfulness admitted, she would feel as if in her sanctity she had been violated, as if in her character she had sustained an overthrow.

In the further prosecution of this discourse, let us first attempt to elucidate the principle of our text, and then urge onward to its practical consequences—both as it respects our general relation to God, and as it respects the particular lesson of faithfulness that may be educed from it.

I. The great principle of the text is, that he who has sinned though to a small amount in respect of the fruit of his transgression—provided he has done so, by passing over a forbidden limit which was distinctly known to him, has in the act of doing so, incurred a full condemnation in respect of the principle of his transgression. In one word, that the gain of it may be small, while the guilt of it may be great; that the latter ought not to be measured by the former; but that he who is unfaithful in the least, shall be dealt with in respect of the offence he has given to God, in the same way as if he had been unfaithful in much.

The first reason, which we would assign in vindication of this is, that by a small act of injustice, the line which separates the right from the wrong is just as effectually broken over as by a great act of injustice. There is a tendency in gross and corporeal man to rate the criminality of injustice by the amount of its appropriations—to reduce it to a computation of weight and measure—to count the man who has gained a double sum by his dishonesty, to be doubly more dishonest than his neighbour—to make it an affair of product rather than of principle; and thus to weigh the morality of a character in the same arithmetical balance with number or with magnitude. Now, this is not the rule of calculation on which our Saviour has proceeded in the text. He speaks to the man who is only half an inch within the limit of forbidden ground, in the very same terms by which he addresses the man who has made the furthest and the largest incursions upon it. It is true, that he is only a little way upon the wrong side of the line of demarcation. But why is he upon it at all? It was in the act of crossing that line, and not in the act of going onwards after he had crossed it—it was then that the contest between right and wrong was entered upon, and then it was decided. That was the instant of time at which principle struck her surrender. The great pull which the man had to make, was in the act of overleaping the fence of separation; and after that was done, justice had no other barrier by which to obstruct his progress over the whole extent of the field which she had interdicted. There might be barriers of a different description. There might be still a revolting of humanity against the sufferings that would be inflicted by an act of larger fraud or depredation. There might be a dread of exposure, if the dishonesty should so swell, in point of amount, as to become more noticeable. There might, after the absolute limit between justice and injustice is broken, be another limit against the extending of a man's encroachments, in a terror of discovery, or in a sense of interest, or even in the relentings of a kindly or a compunctious feeling towards him who is the victim of injustice. But this is not the limit with which the question of a man's truth, or a man's honesty, has to do. These have already been given up. He may only be a little way within the margin of the unlawful territory, but still he is upon it; and the God who finds him there will reckon with him, and deal with him accordingly. Other principles and other considerations, may restrain his progress to the very heart of the territory, but justice is not one of them. This he deliberately flung away from him at that moment when he passed the line of circumvallation; and, though in the neighbourhood of that line, he may hover all his days at the petty work of picking and purloining such fragments as he meets with, though he may never venture himself to a place of more daring or distinguished atrocity, God sees of him, that, in respect of the principle of justice, at least, there is an utter unhingement. And thus it is that the Saviour, who knew what was in man, and who, therefore, knew all the springs of that moral machinery by which he is actuated, pronounces of him who was unfaithful in the least, that he was unfaithful also in much.

After the transition is accomplished, the progress will follow of course, just as opportunity invites, and just as circumstances make it safe and practicable. For it is not with justice as it is with generosity, and some of the other virtues. There is not the same graduation in the former as there is in the latter. The man who, other circumstances being equal, gives away a double sum in charity, may, with more propriety be reckoned doubly more generous than his neighbour; than the man who, with the same equality of circumstances, only ventures on half the extent of fraudulency, can be reckoned only one half as unjust as his neighbour. Each has broken a clear line of demarcation. Each has transgressed a distinct and visible limit which he knew to be forbidden. Each has knowingly forced a passage beyond his neighbour's land-mark—and that is the place where justice has laid the main force of her interdict. As it respects the *materiel* of injustice, the question revolves itself into a mere computation of quantity. As it respects the *morale* of injustice, the computation is upon other principles. It is upon the latter that our Saviour pronounces himself. And he gives us to understand, that a very humble degree of the former may indicate the latter in all its atrocity. He stands on the breach between the lawful and the unlawful; and he tells us, that the man who enters by a single footstep on the forbidden ground, immediately gathers upon his person the full hue and character of guiltiness. He admits no extenuation of the lesser acts of dishonesty. He does not make right pass into wrong, by a gradual melting of the one into the other. He does not thus obliterate the distinctions of morality. There is no shading off at the margin of guilt, but a clear and vigorous delineation. It is not by a gentle transition that a man steps over from honesty to dishonesty. There is between them a wall rising up into heaven; and the high authority of heaven must be stormed ere one inch of entrance can be made into the region of iniquity. The morality of the Saviour never leads him to gloss over the beginnings of crime. His object ever is, as in the text before us, to fortify the limit, to cast a rampart of exclusion around the whole territory of guilt, and to rear it before the eye of man in such characters of strength and sacredness, as should make them feel that it is impregnable.

The second reason, why he who is unfaithful in the least has incurred the condemnation of him who is unfaithful in much, is, that the littleness of the gain, so far from giving a littleness to the guilt, is in fact a circumstance of aggravation. There is just this difference. He who has committed injustice for the sake of a less advantage, has done it on the impulse of a less temptation. He has parted with his honesty at an inferior price; and this circumstance may go so to equalize the estimate, as to bring it very much to one with the deliverance, in the text, of our great Teacher of righteousness. The limitation between good and evil stood as distinctly before the notice of the small as of the great depredator; and he has just made as direct a contravention to the first reason, when he passed over upon the wrong side of it. And he may have made little of gain by the enterprise, but this does not allay the guilt of it. Nay, by the second reason, this may serve to aggravate the wrath of the Divinity against him. It proves how small the price is which he sets upon his eternity, and how cheaply he can bargain the favour of God away from him, and how low he rates the good of an inheritance with him, and for what a trifle he can dispose of all interest in his kingdom and in his promises. The very circumstance which gives to his character a milder transgression in the eyes of the world, makes it more odious in the judgment of the sanctuary. The more paltry it is in respect of profit, the more profane it may be in respect of principle. It likens him the more to profane Esau, who sold his birthright for a mess of pottage. And thus it is, indeed, most woful to think of such a senseless and alienated world; and how heedlessly the men of it are posting their infatuated way to destruction; and how, for as little gain as might serve them a day, they are contracting as much guilt as will ruin them for ever; and are profoundly asleep in the midst of such designs and such doings, as will form the valid materials of their entire and everlasting condemnation.

It is with argument such as this that we would try to strike conviction among a very numerous class of offenders in society —those who, in the various departments of trust, or service, or agency, are ever practising, in littles, at the work of secret appropriation—those whose hands are in a state of constant defilement, by the putting of them forth to that which they ought to touch not, and taste not, and handle not—those who silently number such pilferments as can pass unnoticed among the perquisites of their office; and who, by an excess in their charges, just so slight as to escape detection—or by a habit of purloining, just so restrained as to elude discovery, have both a conscience very much at ease in their own bosoms, and a credit very fair, and very entire, among their acquaintances around them. They grossly count upon the smallness of their transgression. But they are just going in a small way to hell. They would recoil with violent dislike from the act of a midnight depredator. It is just because terrors, and trials, and executions, have thrown around it the pomp and the circumstance of guilt. But at another bar, and on a day of more dreadful solemnity, their guilt will be made to stand out in its essential characters, and their condemnation will be pronounced from the lips of Him who judgeth righteously. They feel that they have incurred no outrageous forfeiture of character among men, and this instils a treacherous complacency into their own hearts. But the piercing eye of Him who looketh down from heaven is upon the reality of the question; and He who ponders the secrets of every bosom, can perceive, that the man who recoils only from such a degree of injustice as is notorious, may have no justice whatever in his character. He may have a sense of reputation. He may have the fear of detection and disgrace. He may feel a revolt in his constitution against the magnitude of a gross and glaring violation. He may even share in all the feelings and principles of that conventional kind of morality which obtains in his neighbourhood. But, of that principle which is surrendered by the least act of unfaithfulness, he has no share whatever. He perceives no overawing sacredness in that boundary which separates the right from the wrong. If he only keep decently near, it is a matter of indifference to him whether he be on this or on that side of it. He can be unfaithful in that which is least. There may be other principles, and other considerations to restrain him; but certain it is, that it is not now the principle of justice which restrains him from being unfaithful in much.—This is given up; and, through a blindness to the great and important principle of our text, this virtue may, in its essential character, be as good as banished from the world. All its protections may be utterly overthrown. The line of defence is effaced by which it ought to have been firmly and scrupulously guarded. The sign-posts of intimation, which ought to warn and to scare away, are planted along the barrier; and when, in defiance to them, the barrier is broken, man will not be checked by any sense of honesty, at least, from expatiating over the whole of the forbidden territory. And thus may we gather from the countless peccadilloes which are so current in the various departments of trade, and service, and agency—from the secret freedoms in which many do indulge, without one remonstrance from their own heart—from the petty inroads that are daily practised on the confines of justice, by which its line of demarcation is trodden under foot, and it has lost the moral distinctness, and the moral charm, that should have kept it unviolate—from the exceeding multitude of such offences as are frivolous in respect of the matter of them, but most fearfully important in respect of the principle in which they originate—from the woful amount of that unseen and unrecorded guilt which escapes the cognizance of the human law, but on the application of the touchstone in our text, may be made to stand out in characters of severest condemnation—from instances, too numerous to repeat, but certainly too obvious to be missed, even by the observation of charity, may we gather the frailty of human principle, and the virulence of that moral poison, which is now in such full circulation to taint and to adulterate the character of our species.

Before finishing this branch of our subject, we may observe, that it is with this, as with many other phenomena of the human character, that we are not long in contemplation upon it, without coming in sight of that great characteristic of fallen man, which meets and forces itself upon us in every view that we take of him—even the great moral disease of ungodliness. It is at the precise limit between the right and the wrong that the flaming sword of God's law is placed. It is there that "Thus saith the Lord" presents itself, in legible characters, to our view. It is there where the operation of his commandment begins; and not at any of those higher gradations, where a man's dishonesty first appals himself by the chance of its detection, or appals others by the mischief and insecurity which it brings upon social life. An extensive fraud upon the revenue, for example, unpopular as this branch of justice is, would bring a man down from his place of eminence and credit in mercantile society. That petty fraud which is associated with so many of those smaller payments, where a lie in the written acknowledgment is both given and accepted, as a way of escape from the legal imposition, circulates at large among the members of the great trading community. In the former, and in all the greater cases of injustice, there is a human restraint, and a human terror, in operation. There is disgrace and civil punishment, to scare away. There are all the sanctions of that conventional morality which is suspended on the fear of man, and the opinion of man; and which, without so much as the recognition of a God, would naturally point its armour against every outrage that could sensibly disturb the securities and the rights of human society. But so long as the disturbance is not sensible—so long as the injustice keeps within the limits of smallness and secrecy—so long as it is safe for the individual to practise it, and, borne along on the tide of general example and connivance, he has nothing to restrain him but that distinct and inflexible word of God, which proscribes all unfaithfulness, and admits of it in no degrees, and no modifications—then, let the almost universal sleep of conscience attest, how little of God there is in the virtue of this world; and how much the peace and the protection of society are owing to such moralities, as the mere selfishness of man would lead him to ordain, even in a community of atheists.

II. Let us now attempt to unfold a few of the practical consequences that may be drawn from the principle of the text, both in respect to our general relation with God, and in respect to the particular lesson of faithfulness which may be educed from it.

1. There cannot be a stronger possible illustration of our argument, than the very first act of retribution that occurred in the history of our species. "And God said unto Adam, Of the tree of the knowledge of good and evil, thou shalt not eat of it. For in the day thou eatest thereof, thou shalt surely die. But the woman took of the fruit thereof, and did eat, and gave also unto her husband with her, and he did eat."

What is it that invests the eating of a solitary apple with a grandeur so momentous? How came an action in itself so minute, to be the germ of such mighty consequences? How are we to understand that our first parents, by the doing of a single instant, not only brought death upon themselves, but shed this big and baleful disaster over all their posterity? We may not be able to answer all these questions, but we may at least learn, what a thing of danger it is, under the government of a holy and inflexible God, to tamper with the limits of obedience. By the eating of that apple, a clear requirement was broken, and a distinct transition was made from loyalty to rebellion, and an entrance was effected into the region of sin—and thus did this one act serve like the opening of a gate for a torrent of mighty mischief; and if the act itself was a trifle, it just went to aggravate its guilt—that, for such a trifle, the authority of God could be despised and trampled on. At all events, his attribute of truth stood committed to the fulfilment of the threatening; and the very insignificancy of the deed, which provoked the execution of it, gives a sublimer character to the certainty of the fulfilment. We know how much this trait, in the dealings of God with man, has been the jeer of infidelity. But in all this ridicule, there is truly nothing else than the grossness of materialism. Had Adam, instead of plucking one single apple from the forbidden tree, been armed with the power of a malignant spirit, and spread a wanton havoc over the face of paradise, and spoiled the garden of its loveliness, and been able to mar and to deform the whole of that terrestrial creation over which God had so recently rejoiced—the punishment he sustained would have looked to these arithmetical moralists, a more adequate return for the offence of which he had been guilty. They cannot see how the moral lesson rises in greatness, just in proportion to the humility of the material accompaniments—and how it wraps a sublimer glory around the holiness of the Godhead—and how from the transaction, such as it is, the conclusion cometh forth more nakedly, and, therefore, more impressively, that it is an evil and a bitter thing to sin against the Lawgiver. God said, "Let there be light, and it was light;" and it has ever been regarded as a sublime token of the Deity, that, from an utterance so simple, an accomplishment so quick and so magnificent should have followed. God said, "That he who eateth of the tree in the midst of the garden should die." It appears indeed, but a little thing, that one should put forth his hand to an apple and taste of it. But a saying of God was involved in the matter—and heaven and earth must pass away, ere a saying of his can pass away; and so the apple became decisive of the fate of a world; and, out of the very scantiness of the occasion, did there emerge a sublimer display of truth and of holiness. The beginning of the world was, indeed, the period of great manifestations of the Godhead; and they all seem to accord, in style and character, with each other; and in that very history, which has called forth the profane and unthinking levity of many a scorner, may we behold as much of the majesty of principle, as in the creation of light, we behold of the majesty of power.

But this history furnishes the materials of a contemplation still more practical. If, for this one offence, Adam and his posterity have been so visited—if so rigorously and so inflexibly precise be the spirit of God's administration—if, under the economy of heaven, sin, even in the very humblest of its exhibitions, be the object of an intolerance so jealous and so unrelenting—if the Deity be such as this transaction manifests him to be, disdainful of fellowship even with the very least iniquity, and dreadful in the certainty of all his accomplishments against it—if, for a single transgression, all the promise and all the felicity of paradise had to be broken up, and the wretched offenders had to be turned abroad upon a world, now changed by the curse into a wilderness, and their secure and lovely home of innocence behooved to be abandoned, and to keep them out, a flaming sword had to turn every way, and guard their reaccess to the bowers of immortality—if sin be so very hateful in the eye of unspotted holiness, that, on its very first act, and first appearance, the wonted communion between heaven and earth was interdicted—if that was the time at which God looked on our species with an altered countenance, and one deed of disobedience proved so terribly decisive of the fate and history of a world—what should each individual amongst us think of his own danger, whose life has been one continued habit of disobedience? If we be still in the hands of that God who laid so fell a condemnation on this one transgression, let us just think of our many transgressions, and that every hour we live multiplies the account of them; and that, however they may vanish from our own remembrance, they are still alive in the records of a judge whose eye and whose memory never fail him. Let us transfer the lesson we have gotten of heaven's jurisprudence from the case of our first parents to our own case. Let us compare our lives with the law of God, and we shall find that our sins are past reckoning. Let us take account of the habitual posture of our souls, as a posture of dislike for the things that are above, and we shall find that our thoughts and our desires are ever running in one current of sinfulness. Let us just make the computation how often we fail in the bidden charity, and the bidden godliness, and the bidden long suffering—all as clearly bidden as the duty that was laid on our first parents—and we shall find, that we are borne down under a mountain of iniquity; that, in the language of the Psalmist, our transgressions have gone over our heads, and, as a heavy burden, are too heavy for us; and if we be indeed under the government of Him who followed up the offence of the stolen apple by so dreadful a chastisement, then is wrath gone out unto the uttermost against every one of us. —There is something in the history of that apple which might be brought specially to bear on the case of those small sinners who practise in secret at the work of their petty depredations. But it also carries in it a great and a universal moral. It tells us that no sin is small. It serves a general purpose of conviction. It holds out a most alarming disclosure of the charge that is against us; and makes it manifest to the conscience of him who is awakened thereby, that, unless God himself point out a way of escape, we are indeed most hopelessly sunk in condemnation. And, seeing that such wrath went out from the sanctuary of this unchangeable God, on the one offence of our first parents, it irresistibly follows, that if we, manifold in guilt, take not ourselves to his appointed way of reconciliation—if we refuse the overtures of Him, who then so visited the one offence through which all are dead, but is now laying before us all that free gift, which is of many offences unto justification—in other words, if we will not enter into peace through the offered Mediator, how much greater must be the wrath that abideth on us?

Now, let the sinner have his conscience schooled by such a contemplation, and there will be no rest whatever for his soul till he find it in the Saviour. Let him only learn, from the dealings of God with the first Adam, what a God of holiness he himself has to deal with; and let him further learn, from the history of the second Adam, that to manifest himself as a God of love, another righteousness had to be brought in, in place of that from which man had fallen so utterly away. There was a faultless obedience rendered by Him, of whom it is said, that he fulfilled all righteousness. There was a magnifying of the law by one in human form, who up to the last jot and tittle of it, acquitted himself of all its obligations. There was a pure, and lofty, and undefiled path, trodden by a holy and harmless Being, who gave not up his work upon earth, till ere he left it, he could cry out, that it was finished; and so had wrought out for us a perfect righteousness. Now, it forms the most prominent annunciation of the New Testament, that the reward of this righteousness is offered unto all—so that there is not one of us who is not put by the gospel upon the alternative of being either tried by our own merits, or treated according to the merits of Him who became sin for us, though he knew no sin, that we might be made the righteousness of God in him. Let the sinner just look unto himself, and look unto the Saviour. Let him advert not to his one, but to his many offences; and that, too, in the sight of a God, who, but for one so slight and so insignificant in respect of the outward description, as the eating of a forbidden apple, threw off a world into banishment, and entailed a sentence of death upon all its generations. Let him learn from this, that for sin, even in its humblest degrees, there exists in the bosom of the Godhead no toleration; and how shall he dare, with the degree and the frequency of his own sin, to stand any longer on a ground, where, if he remain, the fierceness of a consuming fire is so sure to overtake him? The righteousness of Christ is without a flaw, and there he is invited to take shelter. Under the actual regimen, which God has established in our world, it is indeed his only security—his refuge from the tempest, and hiding place from the storm. The only beloved Son offers to spread his own unspotted garment as a protection over him; and, if he be rightly alive to the utter nakedness of his moral and spiritual condition he will indeed make no tarrying till he be found in Christ, and find that in him there is no condemnation.

Now, it is worthy of remark, that those principles, which shut a man up unto the faith, do not take flight and abandon him, after they have served this temporary purpose. They abide with him, and work their appropriate influence on his character, and serve as the germ of a new moral creation; and we can afterwards detect their operation in his heart and life; so, that if they were present at the formation of a saving belief, they are not less unfailingly present with every true Christian, throughout the whole of his future history, as the elements of a renovated conduct. If it was sensibility to the evil of sin which helped to wean the man from himself, and led him to his Saviour, this sensibility does not fall asleep in the bosom of an awakened sinner, after Christ has given him light—but it grows with the growth, and strengthens with the strength, of his Christianity. If, at the interesting period of his transition from nature to grace, he saw, even in the very least of his offences, a deadly provocation of the Lawgiver, he does not lose sight of this consideration in his future progress—nor does it barely remain with him, like one of the unproductive notions of an inert and unproductive theory. It gives rise to a fearful jealousy in his heart of the least appearance of evil; and, with every man who has undergone a genuine process of conversion, do we behold the scrupulous avoidance of sin, in its most slender, as well as in its more aggravated forms. If it was the perfection of the character of Christ, who felt that it became him to fulfil all righteousness, that offered him the first solid foundation on which he could lean—then, the same character, which first drew his eye for the purpose of confidence, still continues to draw his eye for the purpose of imitation. At the outset of faith, all the essential moralities of thought, and feeling, and conviction, are in play; nor is there any thing in the progress of a real faith which is calculated to throw them back again into the dormancy out of which they had arisen. They break out, in fact, into more full and flourishing display on every new creature, with every new step, and new evolution, in his mental history. All the principles of the gospel serve, as it were, to fan and to perpetuate his hostility against sin; and all the powers of the gospel enable him, more and more, to fulfil the desires of his heart, and to carry his purposes of hostility into execution. In the case of every genuine believer, who walks not after the flesh, but after the spirit, do we behold a fulfilling of the righteousness of the law—a strenuous avoidance of sin, in its slightest possible taint or modification—a strenuous performance of duty, up to the last jot and tittle of its exactions—so, that let the untrue professors of the faith do what they will in the way of antinomianism, and let the enemies of the faith say what they will about our antinomianism, the real spirit of the dispensation under which we live is such, that whosoever shall break one of the least of these commandments, and teach men so, is accounted the least—whosoever shall do and teach them is accounted the greatest.

2. Let us, therefore, urge the spirit and the practice of this lesson upon your observation. The place for the practice of it is the familiar and week-day scene. The principle for the spirit of it descends upon the heart, from the sublimest heights of the sanctuary of God. It is not vulgarizing Christianity to bring it down to the very humblest occupations of human life. It is, in fact, dignifying human life, by bringing it up to the level of Christianity.

It may look to some a degradation of the pulpit, when the household servant is told to make her firm stand against the temptation of open doors, and secret opportunities; or when the confidential agent is told to resist the slightest inclination to any unseen freedom with the property of his employers, or to any undiscoverable excess in the charges of his management; or when the receiver of a humble payment is told, that the tribute which is due on every written acknowledgment ought faithfully to be met, and not fictitiously to be evaded. This is not robbing religion of its sacredness, but spreading its sacredness over the face of society. It is evangelizing human life, by impregnating its minutest transactions with the spirit of the gospel. It is strengthening the wall of partition between sin and obedience. It is the teacher of righteousness taking his stand at the outpost of that territory which he is appointed to defend, and warning his hearers of the danger that lies in a single footstep of encroachment. It is letting them know, that it is in the act of stepping over the limit, that the sinner throws the gauntlet of his defiance against the authority of God. And though he may deceive himself with the imagination that his soul is safe, because the gain of his injustice is small, such is the God with whom he has to do, that, if it be gain to the value of a single apple, then, within the compass of so small an outward dimension, may as much guilt be enclosed as that which hath brought death into our world, and carried it down in a descending ruin upon all its generations.

It may appear a very little thing, when you are told to be honest in little matters; when the servant is told to keep her hand from every one article about which there is not an express or understood allowance on the part of her superiors; when the dealer is told to lop off the excesses of that minuter fraudulency, which is so currently practised in the humble walks of merchandise; when the workman is told to abstain from those petty reservations of the material of his work, for which he is said to have such snug and ample opportunity; and when, without pronouncing on the actual extent of these transgressions, all are told to be faithful in that which is least, else, if there be truth in our text, they incur the guilt of being unfaithful in much. It may be thought, that because such dishonesties as these are scarcely noticeable, they are therefore not worthy of notice. But it is just in the proportion of their being unnoticeable by the human eye, that it is religious to refrain from them. These are the cases in which it will be seen, whether the controul of the omniscience of God makes up for the controul of human observation—in which the sentiment, that thou God seest me, should carry a preponderance through all the secret places of a man's history—in which, when every earthly check of an earthly morality is withdrawn, it should be felt, that the eye of God is upon him, and that the judgment of God is in reserve for him. To him who is gifted with a true discernment of these matters, will it appear, that often, in proportion to the smallness of the doings, is the sacredness of that principle which causes them to be done with integrity; that honesty, in little transactions, bears upon it more of the aspect of holiness, than honesty in great ones; that the man of deepest sensibility to the obligations of the law, is he who feels the quickening of moral alarm at its slightest violations; that, in the morality of grains and of scruples, there may be a greater tenderness of conscience, and a more heaven-born sanctity, than in that larger morality which flashes broadly and observably upon the world;—and that thus, in the faithfulness of the household maid, or of the apprentice boy, there may be the presence of a truer principle than there is in the more conspicuous transactions of human business—what they do, being done, not with eye-service—what they do, being done unto the Lord.

And here we may remark, that nobleness of condition is not essential as a school for nobleness of character; nor does man require to be high in office, ere he can gather around his person the worth and the lustre of a high minded integrity. It is delightful to think, that humble life may be just as rich in moral grace, and moral grandeur, as the loftier places of society; that as true a dignity of principle may be earned by him who in homeliest drudgery, plies his conscientious task, as by him who stands entrusted with the fortunes of an empire; that the poorest menial in the land, who can lift a hand unsoiled by the pilferments that are within his reach, may have achieved a victory over temptation, to the full as honourable as the proudest patriot can boast, who has spurned the bribery of courts away from him. It is cheering to know, from the heavenly judge himself, that he who is faithful in the least, is faithful also in much; and that thus, among the labours of the field and of the work-shop, it is possible for the peasant to be as bright in honour as the peer, and have the chivalry of as much truth and virtue to adorn him.

And, as this lesson is not little in respect of principle, so neither is it little in respect of influence on the order and well-being of human society. He who is unjust in the least, is, in respect of guilt, unjust also in much. And to reverse this proposition, as it is done in the first clause of our text—he who is faithful in that which is least, is, in respect both of righteous principle and of actual observation, faithful also in much. Who is the man to whom I would most readily confide the whole of my property? He who would most disdain to put forth an injurious hand on a single farthing of it. Who is the man from whom I would have the least dread of any unrighteous encroachment? He, all the delicacies of whose principle are awakened, when he comes within sight of the limit which separates the region of justice from the region of injustice. Who is the man whom we shall never find among the greater degrees of iniquity? He who shrinks with sacred abhorrence from the lesser degrees of it. It is a true, though a homely maxim of economy, that if we take care of our small sums, our great sums will take care of themselves. And, to pass from our own things to the things of others, it is no less true, that if principle should lead us all to maintain the care of strictest honesty over our neighbour's pennies, then will his pounds lie secure from the grasp of injustice, behind the barrier of a moral impossibility. This lesson, if carried into effect among you, would so strengthen all the ramparts of security between man and man, as to make them utterly impassable; and therefore, while, in the matter of it, it may look, in one view, as one of the least of the commandments, it, in regard both of principle and effect, is, in another view of it, one of the greatest of the commandments. And we therefore conclude with assuring you, that nothing will spread the principle of this commandment to any great extent throughout the mass of society, but the principle of godliness. Nothing will secure the general observation of justice amongst us, in its punctuality and in its preciseness, but such a precise Christianity as many affirm to be puritanical. In other words, the virtues of society, to be kept in a healthful and prosperous condition, must be upheld by the virtues of the sanctuary. Human law may restrain many of the grosser violations. But without religion among the people, justice will never be in extensive operation as a moral principle. A vast proportion of the species will be as unjust as the vigilance and the severities of law allow them to be. A thousand petty dishonesties, which never will, and never can be brought within the cognizance of any of our courts of administration, will still continue to derange the business of human life, and to stir up all the heartburnings of suspicion and resentment among the members of human society. And it is, indeed, a triumphant reversion awaiting the Christianity of the New Testament, when it shall become manifest as day, that it is her doctrine alone, which, by its searching and sanctifying influence, can so moralize our world—as that each may sleep secure in the lap of his neighbour's integrity, and charm of confidence, between man and man, will at length be felt in the business of every town, and in the bosom of every family.

DISCOURSE V.

On the great Christian Law of Reciprocity between Man and Man.

"Therefore all things whatsoever ye would that men should do to you, do ye even so to them: for this is the law and the prophets."—*Matthew* vii. 12.

THERE are two great classes in human society, between whom there lie certain mutual claims and obligations, which are felt by some to be of very difficult adjustment. There are those who have requests of some kind or other to make; and there are those to whom the requests are made, and with whom there is lodged the power either to grant or to refuse them. Now, at first sight, it would appear, that the firm exercise of this power of refusal is the only barrier by which the latter class can be secured against the indefinite encroachments of the former; and that, if this were removed, all the safeguards of right and property would be removed along with it. The power of refusal, on the part of those who have the right of refusal, may be abolished by an act of violence, on the part of those who have it not; and then, when this happens in individual cases, we have the crimes of assault and robbery; and when it happens on a more extended scale, we have anarchy and insurrection in the land. Or the power of refusal may be taken away by an authoritative precept of religion; and then might it still be matter of apprehension, lest our only defence against the inroads of selfishness and injustice were as good as given up, and lest the peace and interest of families should be laid open to a most fearful exposure, by the enactments of a romantic and impracticable system. Whenever this is apprehended, the temptation is strongly felt, either to rid ourselves of the enactments altogether, or at least to bring them down in nearer accommodation to the feelings and the conveniences of men.

And Christianity, on the very first blush of it, appears to be precisely such a religion. It seems to take away all lawfulness of resistance from the possessor, and to invest the demander with such an extent of privilege, as would make the two classes of society, to which we have just now adverted, speedily change places. And this is the true secret of the many laborious deviations that have been attempted in this branch of morality, on the obvious meaning of the New Testament. This is the secret of those many qualifying clauses, by which its most luminous announcements have been beset, to the utter darkening of them. This it is which explains the many sad invasions that have been made on the most manifest and undeniable literalities of the law and of the testimony. And our present text, among others, has received its full share of mutilation, and of what may be called "dressing up," from the hands of commentators—it having wakened the very alarms of which we have just spoken, and called forth the very attempts to quiet and to subdue them. Surely, it has been said, we can never be required to do unto others what they have no right, and no reason, to expect from us. The demand must not be an extravagant one. It must lie within the limits of moderation. It must be such as, in the estimation of every justly thinking person, is counted fair in the circumstances of the case. The principle on which our Saviour, in the text, rests the obligation of doing any particular thing to others, is, that we wish others to do that thing unto us. But this is too much for an affrighted selfishness; and, for her own protection, she would put forth a defensive sophistry upon the subject; and in place of that distinctly announced principle, on which the Bible both directs and specifies what the things are which we should do unto others, does she substitute another principle entirely—which is, merely to do unto others such things as are fair, and right, and reasonable.

Now, there is one clause of this verse which would appear to lay a positive interdict on all these qualifications. How shall we dispose of a phrase, so sweeping and universal in its import, as that of "all things whatsoever?" We cannot think that such an expression as this was inserted for nothing, by him who has told us, that "cursed is every one who taketh away from the words of this book." There is no distinction laid down between things fair, and things unfair—between things reasonable, and things unreasonable. Both are comprehended in the "all things whatsoever." The signification is plain and absolute, that, let the thing be what it may, if you wish others to do that thing for you, it lies imperatively upon you to do the very same thing for them also.

But, at this rate, you may think that the whole system of human intercourse would go into unhingement. You may wish your next-door neighbour to present you with half his fortune. In this case, we know not how you are to escape from the conclusion, that you are bound to present him with the half of yours. Or you may wish a relative to burden himself with the expenses of all your family. It is then impossible to save you from the positive obligation, if you are equally able for it, of doing the same service to the family of another. Or you may wish to engross the whole time of an acquaintance in personal attendance upon yourself. Then, it is just your part to do the same extent of civility to another who may desire it. These are only a few specifications, out of the manifold varieties, whether of service or of donation, which are conceivable between one man and another; nor are we aware of any artifice of explanation by which they can possibly be detached from the "all things whatsoever" of the verse before us. These are the literalities which we are not at liberty to compromise —but are bound to urge, and that simply, according to the terms in which they have been conveyed to us by the great Teacher of righteousness. This may raise a sensitive dread in many a bosom. It may look like the opening of a floodgate, through which a torrent of human rapacity would be made to set in on the fair and measured domains of property, and by which all the fences of legality would be overthrown. It is some such fearful anticipation as this which causes casuistry to ply its wily expedients, and busily to devise its many limits, and its many exceptions, to the morality of the New Testament. And yet, we think it possible to demonstrate of our text, that no such modifying is requisite; and that, though admitted strictly and rigorously as the rule of our daily conduct, it would lead to no practical conclusions which are at all formidable.

For, what is the precise circumstance which lays the obligation of this precept upon you? There may be other places in the Bible where you are required to do things for the benefit of your neighbour, whether you would wish your neighbour to do these things for your benefit or not. But this is not the requirement here. There is none other thing laid upon you in this place, than that you should do that good action in behalf of another, which you would like that other to do in behalf of yourself. If you would not like him to do it for you, then there is nothing in the compass of this sentence now before you, that at all obligates you to do it for him. If you would not like your neighbour to make so romantic a surrender to your interest, as to offer you to the extent of half his fortune, then there is nothing in that part of the gospel code which now engages us, that renders it imperative upon you to make the same offer to your neighbour. If you would positively recoil, in all the reluctance of ingenuous delicacy, from the selfishness of laying on a relation the burden of the expenses of all your family, then this is not the good office that you would have him to do unto you; and this, therefore, is not the good office which the text prescribes you to do unto him. If you have such consideration for another's ease, and another's convenience, that you could not take the ungenerous advantage of so much of his time for your accommodation, there may be other verses in the Bible which point to a greater sacrifice, on your part, for the good of others, than you would like these others to make for yours; but, most assuredly, this is not the verse which imposes that sacrifice. If you would not that others should do these things on your account, then these things form no part of the "all things whatsoever" you would that men should do unto you; and, therefore, they form no part of the "all things whatsoever" that you are required, by this verse, to do unto them. The bare circumstance of your positively not wishing that any such services should be rendered unto you, exempts you, as far as the single authority of this precept is concerned, from the obligation of rendering these services to others. This is the limitation to the extent of those services which are called for in the text; and it is surely better, that every limitation to a commandment of God's, should be defined by God himself, than that it should be drawn from the assumptions of human fancy, or from the fears and the feelings of human convenience.

Let a man, in fact, give himself up to a strict and literal observance of the precept in this verse, and it will impress a two-fold direction upon him. It will not only guide him to certain performances of good in behalf of others, but it will guide him to the regulation of his own desires of good from them. For his desires of good from others are here set up as the measure of his performances of good to others. The more selfish and unbounded his desires are, the larger are those performances with the obligation of which he is burdened. Whatsoever he would that others should do unto him, he is bound to do unto them; and, therefore, the more he gives way to ungenerous and extravagant wishes of service from those who are around him, the heavier and more insupportable is the load of duty which he brings upon himself.—The commandment is quite imperative, and there is no escaping from it; and if he, by the excess of his selfishness, should render it impracticable, then the whole punishment due to the guilt of casting aside the authority of this commandment, follows in that train of punishment which is annexed to selfishness. There is one way of being relieved from such a burden. There is one way of reducing this verse to a moderate and practicable requirement; and that is, just to give up selfishness—just to stifle all ungenerous desires—just to moderate every wish of service or liberality from others, down to the standard of what is right and equitable; and then there may be other verses in the Bible by which we are called to be kind even to the evil and the unthankful. But, most assuredly, this verse lays upon us none other thing, than that we should do such services for others as are right and equitable.

The more extravagant, then, a man's wishes of accommodation from others are, the wider is the distance between him and the bidden performances of our text. The separation of him from his duty, increases at the rate of two bodies receding from each other by equal and contrary movements. The more selfish his desires of service are from others, the more feeble, on that very account, will be his desires of making any surrender of himself to them, and yet the greater is the amount of that surrender which is due. The poor man, in fact, is moving himself away from the rule; and the rule is just moving as fast away from the man. As he sinks, in the scale of selfishness, beneath the point of a fair and moderate expectation from others, does the rule rise, in the scale of duty, with its demands upon him; and thus there is rendering to him double for every unfair and ungenerous imposition that he would make on the kindness of those who are around him.

Now, there is one way, and a very effectual one, of getting these two ends to meet. Moderate your own desires of service from others, and you will moderate, in the same degree, all those duties of service to others which are measured by these desires. Have the delicacy to abstain from any wish of encroachment on the convenience or property of another. Have the high-mindedness to be indebted for your own support to the exertions of your own honourable industry, rather than the dastardly habit of preying on the simplicity of those around you. Have such a keen sense of equity, and such a fine tone of independent feeling, that you could not bear to be the cause of hardship or distress to a single human creature, if you could help it. Let the same spirit be in you, which the Apostle wanted to exemplify before the eye of his disciples, when he coveted no man's gold, or silver, or apparel; when he laboured not to be chargeable to any of them; but wrought with his own hands, rather than be burdensome. Let this mind be in you, which was also in the Apostle of the Gentiles; and, then, the text before us will not come near you with a single oppressive or impracticable requirement. There may be other passages, where you are called to go beyond the strict line of justice, or common humanity, in behalf of your suffering brethren. But this passage does not touch you with any such preceptive imposition: and you, by moderating your wishes from others down to what is fair and equitable, do, in fact, reduce the rule which binds you to act according to the measure of these wishes, down to a rule of precise and undeviating equity.

The operation is somewhat like that of a governor or fly, in mechanism. This is a very happy contrivance, by which all that is defective or excessive in the motion, is confined within the limits of equability; and every tendency, in particular, to any mischievous acceleration, is restrained. The impulse given by this verse to the conduct of man among his fellows, would seem, to a superficial observer, to carry him to all the excesses of a most ruinous and quixotic benevolence. But let him only look to the skilful adaptation of the fly. Just suppose the control of moderation and equity to be laid upon his own wishes, and there is not a single impulse given to his conduct beyond the rate of moderation and equity. You are not required here to do all things whatsoever in behalf of others, but to do all things whatsoever for them, that you would should be done unto yourself. This is the check by which the whole of the bidden movement is governed, and kept from running out into any hurtful excess. And such is the beautiful operation of that piece of moral mechanism that we are now employed in contemplating, that while it keeps down all the aspirations of selfishness, it does, in fact, restrain every extravagancy, and impress on its obedient subjects no other movement, than that of an even and inflexible justice.

This rule of our Saviour's, then, prescribes moderation to our desires of good from others, as well as generosity to our doings in behalf of others; and makes the first the measure of obligation to the second. It may thus be seen how easily, in a Christian society, the whole work of benevolence could be adjusted, so as to render it possible for the givers not only to meet, but also to overpass, the wishes and expectations of the receivers. The rich man may have a heavier obligation laid upon him by other precepts of the New-Testament; but, by this precept, he is not bound to do more for the poor man, than what he himself would wish, in like circumstances, to be done for him. And let the poor man, on the other hand, wish for no more than what a Christian ought to wish for; let him work and endure to the extent of nature's sufferance, rather than beg—and only beg, rather than that he should starve; and in such a state of principle among men, a tide of beneficence would so go forth upon all the vacant places in society, as that there should be no room to receive it. The duty of the rich, as connected with this administration, is of so direct and positive a character, as to obtrude itself at once on the notice of the Christian moralist. But the poor also have a duty in it—to which we feel ourselves directed by the train of argument which we have now been prosecuting—and a duty, too, we think, of far greater importance even than the other, to the best interests of mankind.

For, let us first contrast the rich man who is ungenerous in his doings, with the poor man who is ungenerous in his desires; and see from which of the two it is, that the cause of charity receives the deadlier infliction. There is, it must be admitted, an individual to be met with occasionally, who represents the former of these two characters; with every affection gravitating to itself, and to its sordid gratifications and interests; bent on his own pleasure, or his own avarice—and so engrossed with these, as to have no spare feeling at all for the brethren of his common nature; with a heart obstinately shut against that most powerful of applications, the look of genuine and imploring distress—and whose very countenance speaks a surly and determined exclusion on every call that proceeds from it; who in a tumult of perpetual alarm about new cases, and new tales of suffering, and new plans of philanthropy, has at length learned to resist and to resent every one of them; and, spurning the whole of this disturbance impatiently away, to maintain a firm defensive over the close system of his own selfish luxuries, and his own snug accommodations. Such a man keeps back, it must be allowed, from the cause of charity, what he ought to have rendered it in his own person. There is a diminution of the philanthropic fund up to the extent of what benevolence would have awarded out of his individual means, and individual opportunities. The good cause is a sufferer, not by any positive blow it has sustained, but the simple negation of one friendly and fostering hand, that else might have been stretched forth to aid and patronise it. There is only so much less of direct countenance and support than would otherwise have been; for, in this our age, we have no conception whatever of such an example being at all infectious. For a man to wallow in prosperity himself and be unmindful of the wretchedness that is around him, is an exhibition of altogether so ungainly a character, that it will far oftener provoke an observer to affront it by the contrast of his own generosity, than to render it the approving testimony of his imitation. So that all we have lost by the man who is ungenerous in his doings, is his own contribution to the cause of philanthropy. And it is a loss that can be borne. The cause of this world's beneficence can do abundantly without him. There is a ground that is yet unbroken, and there are resources which are still unexplored, that will yield a far more substantial produce to the good of humanity, than he, and thousands as wealthy as he, could render to it out of all their capabilities.

But there is a far wider mischief inflicted on the cause of charity, by the poor man who is ungenerous in his desires; by him, whom every act of kindness is sure to call out to the reaction of some new demand, or new expectation; by him, on whom the hand of a giver has the effect, not of appeasing his wants, but of inflaming his rapacity; by him who, trading among the sympathies of the credulous, can dexterously appropriate for himself a portion tenfold greater than what would have blest and brightened the aspect of many a deserving family. Him we denounce as the worst enemy of the poor. It is he whose ravenous gripe wrests from them a far more abundant benefaction, than is done by the most lordly and unfeeling proprietor in the land. He is the arch-oppressor of his brethren; and the amount of the robbery which he has practised upon them, is not to be estimated by the alms which he has monopolized, by the food, or the raiment, or the money, which he has diverted to himself, from the more modest sufferers around him, he has done what is infinitely worse than turning aside the stream of charity. He has closed its floodgates. He has chilled and alienated the hearts of the wealthy, by the gall of bitterness which he has infused into this whole ministration.

A few such harpies would suffice to exile a whole neighbourhood from the attentions of the benevolent, by the distrust and the jealousy wherewith they have poisoned their bosoms, and laid an arrest on all the sensibilities that else would have flowed from them. It is he who, ever on the watch and on the wing about some enterprize of imposture, makes it his business to work and to prey on the compassionate principles of our nature; it is he who, in effect, grinds the faces of the poor, and that, with deadlier severity than even is done by the great baronial tyrant, the battlements of whose castle seem to frown, in all the pride of aristocracy, on the territory that is before it. There is, at all times, a kindliness of feeling ready to stream forth, with a tenfold greater liberality than ever, on the humble orders of life; and it is he, and such as he, who have congealed it. He has raised a jaundiced medium between the rich and the poor, in virtue of which, the former eye the latter with suspicion; and there is not a man who wears the garb, and prefers the applications of poverty, that has not suffered from the worthless impostor who has gone before him. They are, in fact, the deceit, and the indolence, and the low sordidness of a few who have made outcasts of the many, and locked against them the feelings of the wealthy in a kind of iron imprisonment. The rich man who is ungenerous in his doings, keeps back one labourer from the field of charity. But a poor man who is ungenerous in his desires, can expel a thousand labourers in disgust away from it. He sheds a cruel and extended blight over the fair region of philanthropy; and many have abandoned it, who, but for him, would fondly have lingered thereupon; very many, who, but for the way in which their simplicity has been tried and trampled upon, would still have tasted the luxury of doing good unto the poor, and made it their delight, as well as their duty, to expend and expatiate among their habitations.

We say not this to exculpate the rich; for it is their part not to be weary in well-doing, but to prosecute the work and the labour of love under every discouragement. Neither do we say this to the disparagement of the poor; for the picture we have given is of the few out of the many; and the closer the acquaintance with humble life becomes, will it be the more seen of what a high pitch of generosity even the very poorest are capable. They, in truth, though perhaps they are not aware of it, can contribute more to the cause of charity, by the moderation of their desires, than the rich can by the generosity of their doings. They, without, it may be, one penny to bestow, might obtain a place in the record of heaven, as the most liberal benefactors of their species. There is nothing in the humble condition of life they occupy, which precludes them from all that is great or graceful in human charity. There is a way in which they may equal, and even outpeer, the wealthiest of the land, in that very virtue of which wealth alone has been conceived to have the exclusive inheritance. There is a pervading character in humanity which the varieties of rank do not obliterate; and as, in virtue of the common corruption, the poor man may be as effectually the rapacious despoiler of his brethren, as the man of opulence above him—so, there is a common excellence attainable by both; and through which, the poor man may, to the full, be as splendid in generosity as the rich, and yield a far more important contribution to the peace and comfort of society.

To make this plain—it is in virtue of a generous doing on the part of a rich man, when a sum of money is offered for the relief of want; and it is in virtue of a generous desire on the part of a poor man, when this money is refused; when, with the feeling, that his necessities do not just warrant him to be yet a burden upon others, he declines to touch the offered liberality; when, with a delicate recoil from the unlooked-for proposal, he still resolves to put it for the present away, and to find, if possible, for himself a little longer; when, standing on the very margin of dependence, he would yet like to struggle with the difficulties of his situation, and to maintain this severe but honourable conflict, till hard necessity should force him to surrender. Let the money which he has thus nobly shifted from himself take some new direction to another; and who, we ask, is the giver of it? The first and most obvious reply is, that it is he who owned it: but, it is still more emphatically true, that it is he who has declined it. It came originally out of the rich man's abundance: but it was the noble-hearted generosity of the poor man that handed it onwards to its final destination. He did not emanate the gift; but it is just as much that he has not absorbed it, but left it to find its full conveyance to some neighbour poorer than himself, to some family still more friendless and destitute than his own. It was given the first time out of an overflowing fulness. It is given the second time out of stinted and self-denying penury. In the world's eye, it is the proprietor who bestowed the charity. But, in heaven's eye, the poor man who waived it away from himself to another is the more illustrious philanthropist of the two. The one gave it out of his affluence. The other gave it out of the sweat of his brow. He rose up early, and sat up late, that he might have it to bestow on a poorer than himself; and without once stretching forth a giver's hand to the necessities of his brethren, still is it possible, that by him, and such as him, may the main burden of this world's benevolence be borne.

It need scarcely be remarked, that, without supposing the offer of any sum made to a poor man who is generous in his desires, he, by simply keeping himself back from the distributions of charity, fulfils all the high functions which we have now ascribed to him. He leaves the charitable fund untouched for all that distress which is more clamorous than his own; and we, therefore, look, not to the original givers of the money, but to those who line, as it were, the margin of pauperism, and yet firmly refuse to enter it—we look upon them as the pre-eminent benefactors of society, who narrow, as it were, by a wall of defence, the ground of human dependence, and are, in fact, the guides and the guardians of all that opulence can bestow.

Thus it is, that when Christianity becomes universal, the doings of the one party, and the desires of the other, will meet and overpass. The poor will wish for no more than the rich will be delighted to bestow; and the rule of our text, which every real Christian at present finds so practicable, will, when carried over the face of society, bind all the members of it into one consenting brotherhood. The duty of doing good to others will then coalesce with that counterpart duty which regulates our desires of good from them; and the work of benevolence will, at length, be prosecuted without that alloy of rapacity on the one hand, and distrust on the other, which serves so much to fester and disturb the whole of this ministration. To complete this adjustment, it is in every way as necessary to lay all the incumbent moralities on those who ask, as on those who confer; and never till the whole text, which comprehends the wishes of man as well as his actions, wield its entire authority over the species, will the disgusts and the prejudices, which form such a barrier between the ranks of human life, be effectually done away. It is not by the abolition of rank, but by assigning to each rank its duties, that peace, and friendship, and order, will at length be firmly established in our world. It is by the force of principle, and not by the force of some great political overthrow, that a consummation so delightful is to be attained. We have no conception whatever, that, even in millennial days, the diversities of wealth and station will at length be equalized. On looking forward to the time when kings shall be the nursing fathers, and queens the nursing mothers of our church, we think that we can behold the perspective of as varied a distribution of place and property as before. In the pilgrimage of life, there will still be the moving procession of the few charioted in splendour on the highway, and the many pacing by their side along the line of the same journey. There will, perhaps, be a somewhat more elevated footpath for the crowd—there will be an air of greater comfort and sufficiency amongst them; and the respectability of evident worth and goodness will sit upon the countenance of this general population. But, bating these, we look for no great change in the external aspect of society. It will only be a moral and a spiritual change. Kings will retain their sceptres, and nobles their coronets; but, as they float in magnificence along, will they look with benignant feeling on the humble wayfarers; and the honest salutations of regard and reverence will arise to them back again; and, should any weary passenger be ready to sink unfriended on his career, will he, at one time, be borne onwards by his fellows on the pathway, and, at another, will a shower of beneficence be made to descend from the crested equipage that overtakes him. It is Utopianism to think, that in the ages of our world which are yet to come, the outward distinctions of life will not all be upholden. But it is not Utopianism, it is Prophecy to aver, that the breath of a new spirit will go abroad over the great family of mankind—so, that while, to the end of time, there shall be the high and the low in every passing generation, will the charity of kindred feelings, and of a common understanding, create a fellowship between them on their way, till they reach that heaven where human love shall be perfected, and all human greatness is unknown.

In various places in the New Testament, do we see the checks of spirit and delicacy laid upon all extravagant desires. Our text, while it enjoins the performance of good to others, up to the full measure of your desires of good from them, equally enjoins the keeping down of these desires to the measure of your performances. If Christian dispensers had only to do with Christian recipients, the whole work of benevolence would be with ease and harmony carried on. All that was unavoidable—all that came from the hand of Providence—all that was laid upon our suffering brethren by the unlooked-for visitations of accident or disease—all that pain and misfortune, which necessarily attaches to the constitution of the species—all this the text most amply provides for; and all this a Christian society would be delighted to stretch forth their means for the purpose of alleviating or doing away.

We should not have dwelt so long upon this lesson, were it not for the essential Christian principle that is involved in it. The morality of the gospel is not more strenuous on the side of the duty of giving of this world's goods when it is needed, than it is against the desire of receiving when it is not needed. It is more blessed to give than to receive, and therefore less blessed to receive than to give. For the enforcement of this principle among the poorer brethren, did Paul give up a vast portion of his apostolical time and labour; and that he might be an ensample to the flock of working with his own hands, rather than be burdensome, did he set himself down to the occupation of a tent-maker. That lesson is surely worthy of engrossing one sermon of an uninspired teacher, for the sake of which an inspired Apostle of the Gentiles engrossed as much time as would have admitted the preparation and the delivery of many sermons. But there is no more striking indication of the whole spirit and character of the gospel in this matter, than the example of him who is the author of it—and of whom we read these affecting words, that he came into the world not to be ministered unto, but to minister. It is a righteous thing in him who has of this world's goods, to minister to the necessities of others; but it is a still higher attainment of righteousness in him who has nothing but the daily earnings of his daily work to depend upon, so to manage and to strive that he shall not need to be ministered unto. Christianity overlooks no part of human conduct; and by providing for this in particular, does it, in fact, overtake, and that with a precept of utmost importance, the habit and condition of a very extended class in human society. And never does the gospel so exhibit its adaptation to our species—and never does virtue stand in such characters of strength and sacredness before us—as when impregnated with the evangelical spirit and urged by evangelical motives, it takes its most direct sanction from the life and doings of the Saviour.

And he who feels as he ought, will bear with cheerfulness all that the Saviour prescribes, when he thinks how much it is for him that the Saviour has borne. We speak not of his poverty all the time that he lived upon earth. We speak not of those years when, a houseless wanderer in an unthankful world, he had not where to lay his head. We speak not of the meek and uncomplaining sufferance with which he met the many ills that oppressed the tenor of his mortal existence. But we speak of that awful burden which crushed and overwhelmed its termination. We speak of that season of the hour and the power of darkness, when it pleased the Lord to bruise him, and to make his soul an offering for sin. To estimate aright the endurance of him who himself bore our infirmities, would we ask of any individual to recollect some deep and awful period of abandonment in his own history—when that countenance which at one time beamed and brightened upon him, from above, was mantled in thickest darkness—when the iron of remorse entered into his soul—and, laid on a bed of torture, he was made to behold the evil of sin, and to taste of its bitterness. Let him look back, if he can, on this conflict of many agitations, and then figure the whole of this mental wretchedness to be borne off by the ministers of vengeance into hell, and stretched out unto eternity. And if, on the great day of expiation, a full atonement was rendered, and all that should have fallen upon us was placed upon the head of the sacrifice—let him hence compute the weight and the awfulness of those sorrows which were carried by him on whom the chastisement of our peace was laid, and who poured out his soul unto the death for us. If ever a sinner, under such a visitation, shall again emerge into peace and joy in believing—if he ever shall again find his way to that fountain which is opened in the house of Judah—if he shall recover once more that sunshine of the soul, which, on the days that are past, disclosed to him the beauties of holiness here, and the glories of heaven hereafter—if ever he shall hear with effect, in this world, that voice from the mercy-seat, which still proclaims a welcome to the chief of sinners, and beckons him afresh to reconciliation—O! how gladly then should he bear throughout the remainder of his days, the whole authority of the Lord who bought him; and bind forever to his own person that yoke of the Saviour which is easy, and that burden which is light.

DISCOURSE VI.

On the Dissipation of large Cities.

"Let no man deceive you with vain words; for because of these things cometh the wrath of God upon the children of disobedience."—*Ephesians* v. 6.

There is one obvious respect in which the standard of morality amongst men, differs from that pure and universal standard which God hath set up for the obedience of his subjects. Men will not demand very urgently of each other, that, which does not very nearly, or very immediately, affect their own personal and particular interest. To the violations of justice, or truth, or humanity, they will be abundantly sensitive, because these offer a most visible and quickly felt encroachment on this interest. And thus it is, that the social virtues, even without any direct sanction from God at all, will ever draw a certain portion of respect and reverence around them; and that a loud testimony of abhorrence may often be heard from the mouths of ungodly men, against all such vices as may be classed under the general designation of vices of dishonesty.

Now, the same thing does not hold true of another class of vices, which may be termed the vices of dissipation. These do not touch, in so visible or direct a manner, on the security of what man possesses, and of what man has the greatest value for. But man is a selfish being, and therefore it is, that the ingredient of selfishness gives a keenness to his estimation of the evil and of the enormity of the former vices, which is scarcely felt at all in any estimation he may form of the latter vices. It is very true, at the same time, that if one were to compute the whole amount of the mischief they bring upon society, it would be found that the profligacies of mere dissipation go very far to break up the peace, and enjoyment, and even the relative virtues of the world: and that, if these profligacies were reformed, it would work a mighty augmentation on the temporal good both of individuals and families. But the connexion between sobriety of character, and the happiness of the community, is not so apparent, because it is more remote than the connexion which obtains between integrity of character, and the happiness of the community; and man being not only a selfish, but a shortsighted being, it follows, that while the voice of execration may be distinctly heard against every instance of fraud or of injustice, instances of licentiousness may occur on every side of us, and be reported on the one hand with the utmost levity, and be listened to, on the other, with the most entire and complacent toleration.

Here, then, is a point, in which the general morality of the world is at utter and irreconcilable variance with the law of God. Here is a case, in which the voice that cometh forth from the tribunal of public opinion pronounces one thing, and the voice that cometh forth from the sanctuary of God pronounces another. When there is an agreement between these two voices, the principle on which obedience is rendered to their joint and concurring authority, may be altogether equivocal; and, with religious and irreligious men, you may observe an equal exhibition of all the equities, and all the civilities of life. But when there is a discrepancy between these two voices—or when the one attaches a criminality to certain habits of conduct, and is not at all seconded by the testimony of the other—then do we escape the confusion of mingled motives, and mingled authorities. The character of the two parties emerges out of the ambiguity which involved it. The law of God points, it must be allowed, as forcible an anathema against the man of dishonesty, as against the man of dissipation. But the chief burden of the world's anathema is laid on the head of the former; and therefore it is, that, on the latter ground, we meet with more discriminative tests of principle, and gather more satisfying materials for the question of—who is on the side of the Lord of hosts, and who is against him?

The passage we have now submitted to you, looks hard on the votaries of dissipation. It is like eternal truth, lifting up its own proclamation, and causing it to be heard amid the errors and the delusions of a thoughtless world. It is like the Deity himself, looking forth, as he did, from a cloud, on the Egyptians of old, and troubling the souls of those who are lovers of pleasure, more than lovers of God. It is like the voice of heaven, crying down the voice of human society, and sending forth a note of alarm amongst its giddy generations. It is like the unrolling of a portion of that book of higher jurisprudence, out of which we shall be judged on the day of our coming account, and setting before our eyes an enactment, which, if we disregard it, will turn that day into the day of our coming condemnation. The words of man are adverted to in this solemn proclamation of God, against all unlawful and all unhallowed enjoyments, and they are called words of vanity. He sets aside the authority of human opinion altogether; and, on an irrevocable record, has he stamped such an assertion of the authority that belongeth to himself only, as serves to the end of time for an enduring memorial of his will; and as commits the truth of the Lawgiver to the execution of a sentence of wrath against all whose souls are hardened by the deceitfulness of sin. There is, in fact, a peculiar deceitfulness in the matter before us; and, in this verse, are we warned against it—"Let no man deceive you with vain words; for, because of these things, the wrath of God cometh on the children of disobedience."

In the preceding verse, there is such an enumeration as serves to explain what the things are which are alluded to in the text; and it is such an enumeration, you should remark, as goes to fasten the whole terror, and the whole threat, of the coming vengeance—not on the man who combines in his own person all the characters of iniquity which are specified, but on the man who realizes any one of these characters. It is not, you will observe, the conjunction *and*, but the conjunction *or*, which is interposed between them. It is not as if we said, that the man who is dishonest, and licentious, and covetous, and unfeeling, shall not inherit the kingdom of God—but the man who is either dishonest, or licentious, or covetous, or unfeeling. On the single and exclusive possession of any one of these attributes, will God deal with you as with an enemy. The plea, that we are a little thoughtless, but we have a good heart, is conclusively cut asunder by this portion of the law and of the testimony. And in a corresponding passage, in the ninth verse of the sixth chapter of Paul's first epistle to the Corinthians, the same peculiarity is observed in the enumeration of those who shall be excluded from God's favour, and have the burden of God's wrath laid on them through eternity. It is not the man who combines all the deformities of character which are there specified, but the man who realizes any one of the separate deformities. Some of them are the vices of dishonesty, others of them are the vices of dissipation; and, as if aware of a deceitfulness from this cause, he, after telling us that the unrighteous shall not inherit the kingdom of God, bids us not be deceived—for that neither the licentious, nor the abominable, nor thieves, nor covetous, nor drunkards, nor revilers, nor extortioners, shall inherit the kingdom of God.

He who keepeth the whole law, but offendeth in one point, says the Apostle James, is guilty of all. The truth is, that his disobedience on this one point may be more decisive of the state of his loyalty to God, than his keeping all the rest. It may be the only point on which the character of his loyalty is really brought to the trial. All his conformities to the law of God might have been rendered, because they thwarted not his own inclination; and, therefore, would have been rendered though there had been no law at all. The single infraction may have taken place in the only case where there was a real competition between the will of the creature, and the will of the Creator; and the event proves to which of the two the right of superiority is awarded. Allegiance to God in truth is but one principle, and may be described by one short and summary expression: and one act of disobedience may involve in it such a total surrender of the principle, as goes to dethrone God altogether from the supremacy which belongs to him. So that the account between a creature and the Creator is not like an account made up of many items, where the expunging of one item would only make one small and fractional deduction from the whole sum of obedience. If you reserve but a single item from this account, and another makes a principle of completing and rendering up the whole of it, then your character varies from his not by a slight shade of difference, but stands contrasted with it in direct and diametric opposition. We perceive, that, while with him the will of God has the mastery over all his inclinations, with you there is, at least, one inclination which has the mastery over God; that while in his bosom there exists a single and subordinating principle of allegiance to the law, in yours there exists another principle, which, on the coming round of a fit opportunity, developes itself in an act of transgression; that, while with him God may be said to walk and to dwell in him, with you there is an evil visitant, who has taken up his abode in your heart, and lodges there either in a state of dormancy or of action, according to circumstances; that, while with him the purpose is honestly proceeded on, of doing nothing which God disapproves, with you there is a purpose not only different, but opposite, of doing something which he disapproves. On this single difference is suspended not a question of degree, but a question of kind. There are presented to us not two hues of the same colour, but two colours, just as broadly contrasted with each other as light and darkness. And such is the state of the alternative between a partial and an unreserved obedience, that while God imperatively claims the one as his due, he looks on the other as an expression of defiance against him, and against his sovereignty.

It is the very same in civil government. A man renders himself an outcast by one act of disobedience. He does not need to accumulate upon himself the guilt of all the higher atrocities in crime, ere he forfeits his life to the injured laws of his country. By the perpetration of any of them is the whole vengeance of the state brought to bear upon his person, and sentence of death is pronounced on a single murder, or forgery, or act of violent depredation.

And let us ask you just to reflect on the tone and spirit of that man towards his God, who would palliate, for example, the vices of dissipation to which he is addicted, by alleging his utter exemption from the vices of dishonesty, to which he is not addicted. Just think of the real disposition and character of his soul, who can say, "I will please God, but only when, in so doing, I also please myself; or I will do homage to his law, but just in those instances by which I honour the rights, and fulfil the expectations, of society; or I will be decided by his opinion of the right and the wrong, but just when the opinion of my neighbourhood lends its powerful and effective confirmation. But in other cases, when the matter is reduced to a bare question between man and God, when he is the single party I have to do with, when his will and his wrath are the only elements which enter into the deliberation, when judgment, and eternity, and the voice of him who speaketh from heaven are the only considerations at issue—then do I feel myself at greater liberty, and I shall take my own way, and walk in the counsel of mine own heart, and after the sight of my own eyes." O! be assured, that when all this is laid bare on the day of reckoning, and the discerner of the heart pronounces upon it, and such a sentence is to be given, as will make it manifest to the consciences of all assembled, that true and righteous are the judgments of God—there is many a creditable man who has passed through the world with the plaudits and the testimonies of all his fellows, and without one other flaw upon his reputation but the very slender one of certain harmless foibles, and certain good-humoured peculiarities, who when brought to the bar of account, will stand convicted there of having made a divinity of his own will, and spent his days in practical and habitual atheism.

And this argument is not at all affected by the actual state of sinfulness and infirmity into which we have fallen. It is true, even of saints on earth, that they commit sin. But to be overtaken in a fault is one thing; to commit that fault with the deliberate consent of the mind is another. There is in the bosom of every true Christian a strenuous principle of resistance to sin, and it belongs to the very essence of the principle that it is resistance to *all* sin. It admits of no voluntary indulgence to one sin more than to another. Such an indulgence would not only change the character of what may be called the elementary principle of regeneration, but would destroy it altogether. The man who has entered on a course of Christian discipleship, carries on an unsparing and universal war with all iniquity. He has chosen Christ for his alone master, and he struggles against the ascendency of every other. It is his sustained and habitual exertion in following after him to forsake all; so that if his performances were as complete as his endeavour, you would not merely see a conformity to some of the precepts, but a conformity to the whole law of God. At all events, the endeavour is an honest one, and so far successful, that sin has not the dominion; and sure we are, that, in such a state of things, the vices of dissipation can have no existence. These vices can be more effectually shunned, and more effectually surmounted, for example, than the infirmities of an unhappy temper. So that, if dissipation still attaches to the character, and appears in the conduct of any individual, we know not a more decisive evidence of the state of that individual as being one of the many who crowd the broad way that leadeth to destruction. We look no further to make out our estimate of his present condition as being that of a rebel, and of his future prospect as being that of spending an eternity in hell. There is no halting between two opinions in this matter. The man who enters a career of dissipation throws down the gauntlet of defiance to his God. The man who persists in this career keeps on the ground of hostility against him.

Let us now endeavour to trace the origin, the progress, and the effects of a life of dissipation.

First, then, it may be said of a very great number of young men, on their entrance into the business of the world, that they have not been enough fortified against its seducing influences by their previous education at home. Generally speaking, they come out from the habitation of their parents unarmed and unprepared for the contest which awaits them. If the spirit of this world's morality reign in their own family, then it cannot be, that their introduction into a more public scene of life will be very strictly guarded against those vices on which the world placidly smiles, or at least regards with silent toleration. They may have been told, in early boyhood, of the infamy of a lie. They may have had the virtues of punctuality, and of economy, and of regular attention to business, pressed upon their observation. They may have heard a uniform testimony on the side of good behaviour, up to the standard of such current moralities as obtain in their neighbourhood; and this, we are ready to admit, may include in it a testimony against all such excesses of dissipation as would unfit them for the prosecution of this world's interests.

But let us ask, whether there are not parents, who, after they have carried the work of discipline thus far, forbear to carry it any farther; who, while they would mourn over it as a family trial should any son of theirs fall a victim to excessive dissipation, yet are willing to tolerate the lesser degrees of it; who, instead of deciding the question on the alternative of his heaven or his hell, are satisfied with such a measure of sobriety as will save him from ruin and disgrace in this life; who, if they can can only secure this, have no great objection to the moderate share he may take in this world's conformities; who feel, that in this matter there is a necessity and a power of example against which it is vain to struggle, and which must be acquiesced in; who deceive themselves with the fancied impossibility of stopping the evil in question—and say, that business must be gone through; and that, in the prosecution of it, exposures must be made; and that, for the success of it, a certain degree of accommodation to others must be observed; and seeing that it is so mighty an object for one to widen the extent of his connexions, he must neither be very retired nor very peculiar—nor must his hours of companionship be too jealously watched or inquired into—nor must we take him too strictly to task about engagements, and acquaintances, and expenditure—nor must we forget, that while sobriety has its time and its season in one period of life, indulgence has its season in another; and we may fetch from the recollected follies of our own youth, a lesson of connivance for the present occasion; and altogether there is no help for it; and it appears to us, that absolutely and totally to secure him from ever entering upon scenes of dissipation, you must absolutely and totally withdraw him from the world, and surrender all his prospects of advancement, and give up the object of such a provision for our families as we feel to be a first and most important concern with us.

"Seek ye first the kingdom of God, and his righteousness," says the Bible, "and all other things shall be added unto you." This is the promise which the faith of a Christian parent will rest upon; and in the face of every hazard to the worldly interests of his offspring, will he bring them up in the strict nurture and admonition of the Lord; and he will loudly protest against iniquity, in all its degrees and in all its modifications; and while the power of discipline remains with him, will it ever be exerted on the side of pure, faultless, undeviating obedience; and he will tolerate no exception whatever; and he will brave all that looks formidable in singularity, and all that looks menacing in separation from the custom and countenance of the world; and feeling that his main concern is to secure for himself and for his family a place in the city which hath foundations, will he spurn all the maxims and all the plausibilities of a contagious neighbourhood away from him. He knows the price of his Christianity, and it is that he must break off conformity with the world—nor for any paltry advantage which it has to offer, will he compromise the eternity of his children. And let us tell the parents of another spirit and principle, that they are as good as incurring the guilt of a human sacrifice; that they are offering up their children at the shrine of an idol; that they are parties in provoking the wrath of God against them here; and on the day when that wrath is to be revealed, shall they hear not only the moanings of their despair but the outcries of their bitterest execration. On that day, the glance of reproach from their own neglected offspring will throw a deeper shade of wretchedness over the dark and boundless futurity that lies before them. And if, at the time when prophets rung the tidings of God's displeasure against the people of Israel it was denounced as the foulest of all their abominations that they caused their children to pass through the fire unto Moloch—know, ye parents, who in placing your children on some road to gainful employment, have placed them without a sigh in the midst of depravity, so near and so surrounding, that, without a miracle, they must perish, you have done an act of idolatry to the god of this world; you have commanded your household after you to worship him as the great divinity of their lives; and you have caused your children to make their approaches unto his presence—and, in so doing, to pass through the fire of such temptations as have destroyed them.

We do not wish to offer you an overcharged picture on this melancholy subject. What we now say is not applicable to all. Even in the most corrupt and crowded of our cities, parents are to be found, who nobly dare the surrender of every vain and flattering illusion, rather than surrender the Christianity of their children. And what is still more affecting, over the face of the country do we meet with such parents, who look on this world as a passage to another, and on all the members of their household as fellow-travellers to eternity along with them; and who, in the true spirit of believers, feel the salvation of their children to be, indeed, the burden of their best and dearest interest; and who, by prayer, and precept, and example, have strenuously laboured with their souls, from the earliest light of their understanding; and have taught them to tremble at the way of evil doers, and to have no fellowship with those who keep not the commandments of God—nor is there a day more sorrowful in the annals of this pious family, than when the course of time has brought them onwards to the departure of their eldest boy—and he must bid adieu to his native home, with all the peace, and all the simplicity which abound in it—and as he eyes in fancy the distant town whither he is going, does he shrink as from the thought of an unknown wilderness—and it is his firm purpose to keep aloof from the dangers and the profligacies which deform it—and, should sinners offer to entice him, not to consent, and never, never to forget the lessons of a father's vigilance, the tenderness of a mother's prayers.

Let us now, in the next place, pass from that state of things which obtains among the young at their outset into the world, and take a look of that state of things which obtains after they have got fairly introduced into it—when the children of the ungodly, and the children of the religious, meet on one common arena—when business associates them together in one chamber, and the omnipotence of custom lays it upon them all to meet together at periodic intervals, and join in the same parties, and the same entertainments—when the yearly importation of youths from the country falls in with that assimilating mass of corruption which has got so firm and so rooted an establishment in the town—when the frail and unsheltered delicacies of the timid boy have to stand a rude and a boisterous contest with the hardier depravity of those who have gone before him—when ridicule, and example, and the vain words of a delusive sophistry, which palliates in his hearing the enormity of vice, are all brought to bear upon his scruples, and to stifle the remorse he might feel when he casts his principle and his purity away from him—when, placed as he is in a land of strangers, he finds, that the tenure of acquaintanceship, with nearly all around him, is, that he render himself up in a conformity to their doings—when a voice, like the voice of protecting friendship, bids him to the feast; and a welcome, like the welcome of honest kindness, hails his accession to the society; and a spirit, like the spirit of exhilarating joy, animates the whole scene of hospitality before him; and hours of rapture roll successively away on the wings of merriment, jocularity, and song; and after the homage of many libations has been rendered to honour, and fellowship, and patriotism, impurity is at length proclaimed in full and open cry, as one presiding divinity, at the board of their social entertainment.

And now it remains to compute the general result of a process, which we assert of the vast majority of our young, on their way to manhood, that they have to undergo. The result is, that the vast majority are initiated into all the practices, and describe the full career of dissipation. Those who have imbibed from their fathers the spirit of this world's morality, are not sensibly arrested in this career, either by the opposition of their own friends, or by the voice of their own conscience. Those who have imbibed an opposite spirit, and have brought it into competition with an evil world, and have at length yielded, have done so, we may well suppose, with many a sigh, and many a struggle, and many a look of remembrance on those former years when they were taught to lisp the prayer of infancy, and were trained in a mansion of piety to a reverence for God, and for all his ways; and, even still, will a parent's parting advice haunt his memory, and a letter from the good old man revive the sensibilities which at one time guarded and adorned him; and, at times, will the transient gleam of remorse lighten up its agony within him; and when he contrasts the profaneness and depravity of his present companions, with the sacredness of all he ever heard or saw in his father's dwelling, it will almost feel as if conscience were again to resume her power, and the revisiting spirit of God to call him back again from the paths of wickedness; and on his restless bed will the images of guilt conspire to disturb him, and the terrors of punishment offer to scare him away; and many will be the dreary and dissatisfied intervals when he shall be forced to acknowledge that in bartering his soul for the pleasures of sin, he has bartered the peace and enjoyment of the world along with it. But, alas! the entanglements of companionship have got hold of him; and the inveteracy of habit tyrannizes over all his purposes; and the stated opportunity again comes round; and the loud laugh of his partners in guilt chases, for another season, all his despondency away from him, and the infatuation gathers upon him every month; and a hardening process goes on within his heart; and the deceitfulness of sin grows apace; and he at length becomes one of the sturdiest and most unrelenting of her votaries; and he, in his turn, strengthens the conspiracy that is formed against the morals of a new generation; and all the ingenuous delicacies of other days are obliterated; and he contracts a temperament of knowing, hackneyed, unfeeling depravity; and thus the mischief is transmitted from one year to another, and keeps up the guilty history of every place of crowded population.

And let us here speak one word to those seniors in depravity—those men who give to the corruption of acquaintances, who are younger than themselves, their countenance, their agency; and who can initiate them without a sigh in the mysteries of guilt, and care not though a parent's hope should wither and expire under the contagion of their ruffian example. It is only upon their own conversion that we can speak to them the pardon of the gospel. It is only if they themselves are washed, and sanctified, and justified, that we can warrant their personal deliverance from the wrath that is to come. But under all the concealment which rests on the futurities of God's administration, we know that there are degrees of suffering in hell—and that while some are beaten with few stripes, others are beaten with many. And surely, if they who turn many to righteousness shall shine as the stars for ever and ever, we may be well assured that they who patronize the cause of iniquity—they who can beckon others to that way which leadeth on to the chambers of death—they who can aid and witness, without a sigh, the extinction of youthful modesty—surely, it may well be said of such, that on them a darker frown will fall from the judgment-seat, and through eternity will they have to bear the pains of a fiercer indignation.

Having thus looked to the commencement of a course of dissipation, and to its progress, let us now, in the third place, look to its usual termination. We speak not at present of the coming death, and of the coming judgment, but of the change which takes place on many a votary of licentiousness, when he becomes what the world calls a reformed man; and puts on the decencies of a sober and domestic establishment; and bids adieu to the pursuits and the profligacies of youth, not because he has repented of them, but because he has outlived them. You all perceive how this may be done without one movement of the heart, or of the understanding, towards God —that it is done by many, though duty to him be not in all their thoughts—that the change, in this case, is not from the idol of pleasure unto God, but only from one idol to another—and that, after the whole of this boasted transformation, we may still behold the same body of sin and of death, and only a new complexion thrown over it. There may be the putting on of sobriety, but there is no putting on of godliness. It is a common and easy transition to pass from one kind of disobedience to another, but it is not so easy to give up that rebelliousness of the heart which lies at the root of all disobedience. It may be easy, after the wonted course of dissipation is ended, to hold out another aspect altogether in the eye of acquaintances; but it is not so easy to recover that shock, and that overthrow, which the religious principle sustains, when a man first enters the world, and surrenders himself to the power of its enticements. Such were some of you, says the Apostle, but ye are washed, and sanctified, and justified. Our reformed man knows not the meaning of such a process; and, most assuredly, has not at all realized it in the history of his own person. We will not say what new object he is running after. It may be wealth, or ambition, or philosophy; but it is nothing connected with the interest of his soul. It bears no reference whatever to the concerns of that great relationship which obtains between the creature and the Creator. The man has withdrawn, and perhaps for ever, from the scenes of dissipation, and has betaken himself to another way—but still it is his own way. It is not the will or the way of God that he is yet caring for. Such a man may bid adieu to profligacy in his own person. But he lifts up the light of his countenance on the profligacy of others. He gives it the whole weight and authority of his connivance. He wields, we will say it, such an instrumentality of seduction over the young, as, though not so alarming, is far more dangerous than the undisguised attempts of those who are the immediate agents of corruption. The formal and deliberate conspiracy of those who club together, at stated terms of companionship, may be all seen, and watched, and guarded against. But how shall we pursue this conspiracy into its other ramifications? How shall we be able to neutralize that insinuating poison which distils from the lips of grave and respectable citizens? How shall we be able to dissipate that gloss which is thrown by the smile of elders and superiors over the sins of forbidden indulgence? How can we disarm the bewitching sophistry which lies in all these evident tokens of complacency, on the part of advanced and reputable men? How is it possible to trace the progress of this sore evil, throughout all the business and intercourse of society? How can we stem the influence of evil communications, when the friend, and the patron, and the man who has cheered and signalized us by his polite invitations, turns his own family-table into a nursery of licentiousness? How can we but despair of ever witnessing on earth a pure and a holy generation, when even parents will utter their polluting levities in the hearing of their own children; and vice, and humour, and gaiety, are all indiscriminately blended into one conversation; and a loud laugh, from the initiated and the uninitiated in profligacy, is ever ready to flatter and to regale the man who can thus prostitute his powers of entertainment? O! for an arm of strength to demolish this firm and far spread compact of iniquity; and for the power of some such piercing and prophetic voice, as might convince our reformed men of the baleful influence they cast behind them on the morals of the succeeding generation.

We, at the same time, have our eye perfectly open to that great external improvement which has taken place, of late years, in the manners of society. There is not the same grossness of conversation. There is not the same impatience for the withdrawment of him, who, asked to grace the outset of an assembled party, is compelled, at a certain step in the process of conviviality, by the obligations of professional decency, to retire from it. There is not so frequent an exaction of this as one of the established proprieties of social or of fashionable life. And if such an exaction was ever laid by the omnipotence of custom on a minister of Christianity, it is such an exaction as ought never, never, to be complied with. It is not for him to lend the sanction of his presence to a meeting with which he could not sit to its final termination. It is not for him to stand associated, for a single hour, with an assemblage of men who begin with hypocrisy, and end with downright blackguardism. It is not for him to watch the progress of the coming ribaldry, and to hit the well selected moment when talk, and turbulence, and boisterous merriment, are on the eve of bursting forth upon the company, and carrying them forward to the full acme and uproar of their enjoyment. It is quite in vain to say, that he has only sanctified one part of such an entertainment. He has as good as given his connivance to the whole of it, and left behind him a discharge in full of all its abominations; and, therefore, be they who they may, whether they rank among the proudest aristocracy of our land, or are charioted in splendour along, as the wealthiest of the citizens, it is his part to keep as purely and indignantly aloof from such society as this, as he would from the vilest and most debasing associations of profligacy.

And now the important question comes to be put; what is the likeliest way of setting up a barrier against this desolating torrent of corruption, into which there enter so many elements of power and strength, that to the general eye, it looks altogether irresistible? It is easier to give a negative, than an affirmative answer to this question. And, therefore, it shall be our first remark, that the mischief never will be effectually combatted by any expedient separate from the growth and the transmission of personal Christianity throughout the land. If no addition be made to the stock of religious principle in a country, then the profligacy of a country will make its obstinate stand against all the mechanism of the most skilful, and plausible, and well looking contrivances. It must not be disguised from you, that it does not lie within the compass either of prisons or penitentiaries to work any sensible abatement on the wickedness of our existing generation. The operation must be of a preventive, rather than of a corrective tendency. It must be brought to bear upon boyhood; and be kept up through that whole period of random exposures through which has to run, on its way to an established condition in society; and a high tone of moral purity must be infused into the bosom of many individuals; and their agency will effect through the channels of family and social connexion, what never can be effected by any framework of artificial regulations, so long as the spirit and character of society remain what they are. In other words, the progress of reformation will never be sensibly carried forward beyond the progress of personal Christianity in the world; and, therefore, the question resolves itself into the likeliest method of adding to the number of Christian parents who may fortify the principles of their children at their first outset in life—of adding to the number of Christian young men, who might nobly dare to be singular, and to perform the angelic office of guardians and advisers to those who are younger than themselves— of adding to the number of Christians in middle and advanced life, who might, as far as in them lies, alter the general feeling and countenance of society; and blunt the force of that tacit but most seductive testimony, which has done so much to throw a palliative veil over the guilt of a life of dissipation.

Such a question cannot be entered upon, at present, in all its bearings, and in all its generality. And we must, therefore, simply satisfy ourselves with the object, that as we have attempted already to approach the indifference of parents, and to reproach the unfeeling depravity of those young men who scatter their pestilential levities around the whole circle of their companionship, we may now shortly attempt to lay upon the men of middle and advanced life, in general society, their share of responsibility for the morals of the rising generation. For the promotion of this great cause, it is not at all necessary to school them into any nice or exquisite contrivances. Could we only give them a desire towards it, and a sense of obligation, they would soon find their own way to the right exercise of their own influence in forwarding the interests of purity and virtue among the young. Could we only affect their consciences on this point, there would be almost no necessity whatever to guide or enlighten their understanding. Could we only get them to be Christians, and to carry their Christianity into their business, they would then feel themselves invested with a guardianship; and that time, and pains, and attention, ought to be given to the fulfilment of its concerns. It is quite in vain to ask, as if there was any mystery, or any helplessness about it, "What can they do?" For, is it not the fact, most palpably obvious, that much can be done even by the mere power of example? Or might not the master of any trading establishment send the pervading influence of his own principles among some, at least, of the servants and auxiliaries who belong to it? Or can he, in no degree whatever, so select those who are admitted, as to ward off much contamination from the branches of his employ? Or might not he so deal out his encouragement to the deserving, as to confirm them in all their purposes of sobriety? Or might not he interpose the shield of his countenance and his testimony between a struggling youth and the ridicule of his acquaintances? Or, by the friendly conversation of half an hour, might not he strengthen within him every principle of virtuous resistance? By these, and by a thousand other expedients, which will readily suggest themselves to him who has the good will, might not a healing water be sent forth through the most corrupted of all our establishments; and it be made safe for the unguarded young to officiate in its chambers; and it be made possible to enter upon the business of the world without entering on such a scene of temptation, as to render almost inevitable the vice of the world, and its impiety, and its final and everlasting condemnation? Would Christians only be open and intrepid, and carry their religion into their merchandize; and furnish us with a single hundred of such houses in this city, where the care and character of the master formed a guarantee for the sobriety of all his dependents, it would be like the clearing out of a piece of cultivated ground in the midst of a frightful wilderness; and parents would know whither they could repair with confidence for the settlement of their offspring; and we should behold, what is mightily to be desired, a line of broad and visible demarcation between the church and the world; and an interest so precious as the immortality of children, would no longer be left to the play of such fortuitous elements, as operated at random throughout the confused mass of a mingled and indiscriminate society. And thus, the pieties of a father's house might bear to be transplanted even into the scenes of ordinary business; and instead of withering, as they do at present, under a contagion which spreads in every direction, and fills up the whole face of the community, they might flourish in that moral region which was occupied by a peculiar people, and which they had reclaimed from a world that lieth in wickedness.

DISCOURSE VII.

On the vitiating Influence of the higher upon the lower Orders of Society.

"Then said he unto the disciples, It is impossible but that offences will come; but wo unto him through whom they come! It were better for him that a millstone were hanged about his neck, and he cast into the sea, than that he should offend one of these little ones."—*Luke* xvii. 1, 2.

To offend another, according to the common acceptation of the words, is to displease him.—Now, this is not its acceptation in the verse before us, nor in several other verses of the New Testament. It were coming nearer to the scriptural meaning of the term, had we, instead of offence and offending, adopted the terms, scandal and scandalizing. But the full signification of the phrase to offend another, is to cause him to fall from the faith and obedience of the gospel. It may be such a falling away as that a man recovers himself—like the disciples, who were all offended in Christ, and forsook him; and, after a season of separation, were at length re-established in their discipleship.—Or it may be such a falling away as that there is no recovery—like those in the gospel of John, who, offended by the sayings of our Saviour, went back, and walked no more with him. If you put such a stumbling block in the way of a neighbour, who is walking on a course of christian discipleship, as to make him fall, you offend him. It is in this sense that our Saviour uses the word, when he speaks of your own right hand, or your own right eye, offending you. They may do so, by giving you an occasion to fall.—And what is here translated offend, is, in the first epistle to the Corinthians, translated to make to offend; where Paul says, "If meat make my brother to offend, I will eat no more flesh while the world standeth, lest I make my brother to offend."

The little ones to whom our Saviour alludes, in this passage, he elsewhere more fully particularises, by telling us, that they are those who believe in him. There is no call here for entering into any controversy about the doctrine of perseverance. It is not necessary, either for the purpose of explaining, or of giving force to the practical lesson of the text now submitted to you. We happen to be as much satisfied with the doctrine, that he who hath a real faith in the gospel of Christ will never fall away, as we are satisfied with the truth of any identical proposition. If a professing disciple do, in fact, fall away, this is a phenomenon which might be traced to an essential defect of principle at the first; which proves, in fact, that he made the mistake of one principle for another; and that, while he thought he had the faith, it was not that very faith of the New Testament which is unto salvation. There might have been the semblance of a work of grace without its reality. Such a work, if genuinely begun, will be carried onwards even unto perfection. But this is a point on which it is not at all necessary, at present, to dogmatize. We are led, by the text, to expatiate on the guilt of that one man who has wrecked the interest of another man's eternity. Now, it may be very true, that if the second has actually entered within the strait gate, it is not in the power of the first, with all his artifices, and all his temptations, to draw him out again. But instead of having entered the gate, he may only be on the road that leads to it; and it is enough, amid the uncertainties which, in this life, hang over the question of—who are really believers, and who are not? that it is not known in which of these two conditions the little one is; and that, therefore, to seduce him from obedience to the will of Christ, may, in fact, be to arrest his progress towards Christ, and to draw him back unto the perdition of his soul. The whole guilt of the text may be realized by him who keeps back another from the church, where he might have heard, and heard with acceptance, that word of life which he has not yet accepted; or by him, whose influence or whose example detains, in the entanglement of any one sin, the acquaintance who is meditating an outset on the path of decided Christianity—seeing, that every such outset will land in disappointment those who, in the act of following after Christ, do not forsake all; or by him who tampers with the conscience of an apparently zealous and confirmed disciple, so as to seduce him into some habitual sin, either of neglect or of performance—seeing, that the individual who but for this seduction might have cleaved fully unto the Lord, and turned out a prosperous and decided Christian, has been led to put a good conscience away from him—and so, by making shipwreck of his faith, has proved to the world, that it was not the faith which could obtain the victory. It is true, that it is not possible to seduce the elect. But even this suggestion, perverse and unjust as it would be in its application, is not generally present to the mind of him who is guilty of the attempt to seduce, or of the act which carries a seducing influence along with it. The guilt with which he is chargeable, is that of an indifference to the spiritual and everlasting fate of others. He is wilfully the occasion of causing those who are the little ones, or, for any thing he knows, might have been the little ones of Christ, to fall; and it is against him that our Saviour, in the text, lifts not a cool, but an impassioned testimony. It is of him that he utters one of the most severe and solemn denunciations of the gospel.

If this text were thoroughly pursued into its manifold applications, it would be found to lay a weight of fearful responsibility upon us all. We are here called upon not to work out our own salvation, but to compute the reflex influence of all our works, and of all our ways, on the principles of others. And when one thinks of the mischief which this influence might spread around it, even from Christians of chiefest reputation: when one thinks of the readiness of man to take shelter in the example of an acknowledged superior; when one thinks that some inconsistency of ours might seduce another into such an imitation as overbears the reproaches of his own conscience, and as, by vitiating the singleness of his eye, makes the whole of his body, instead of being full of light, to be full of darkness; when one takes the lesson along with him into the various conditions of life he may be called by Providence to occupy, and thinks, that if, either as a parent surrounded by his family, or as a master by the members of his establishment, or as a citizen by the many observers of his neighbourhood around him, he shall either speak such words, or do such actions, or administer his affairs in such a way as is unworthy of his high and immortal destination, that then a taint of corruption is sure to descend from such an exhibition, upon the immortals who are on every side of him; when one thinks of himself as the source and the centre of a contagion which might bring a blight upon the graces and the prospects of other souls besides his own—surely this is enough to supply him with a reason why, in working out his own personal salvation, he should do it with fear, and with watchfulness, and with much trembling.

But we are now upon the ground of a higher and more delicate conscientiousness, than is generally to be met with. Whereas, our object, at present, is to expose certain of the grosser offences which abound in society, and which spread a most dangerous and ensnaring influence among the individuals who compose it. To this we have been insensibly led, by the topics of that discourse which we addressed to you on a former occasion; and when it fell in our way to animadvert on the magnitude of that man's guilt, who, either by his example, or his connivance, or his direct and formal tuition, can speed the entrance of the yet unpractised young on a career of dissipation. And whether he be a parent, who, trenched in this world's maxims, can, without a struggle, and without a sigh, leave his helpless offspring to take their random and unprotected way through this world's conformities; or whether he be one of those seniors in depravity, who can cheer on his more youthful companion to a surrender of all those scruples, and all those delicacies, which have hitherto adorned him; or whether he be a more aged citizen, who, having run the wonted course of intemperance, can cast an approving eye on the corruption throughout all its stages, and give a tenfold force to all its allurements, by setting up the authority of grave and reformed manhood upon its side; in each of these characters do we see an offence that is pregnant with deadliest mischief to the principles of the rising generation: and while we are told by our text, that, for such offences, there exists some deep and mysterious necessity—insomuch, that it is impossible but that offences must come—yet let us not forget to urge on every one sharer in this work of moral contamination, that never does the meek and gentle Saviour speak in terms more threatening or more reproachful, than when he speaks of the enormity of such misconduct. There cannot, in truth, be a grosser outrage committed on the order of God's administration, than that which he is in the habit of inflicting. There cannot, surely, be a directer act of rebellion, than that which multiplies the adherents of its own cause, and which swells the hosts of the rebellious. There cannot be made to rest a feller condemnation on the head of iniquity, than that which is sealed by the blood of its own victims, and its own proselytes. Nor should we wonder when that is said of such an agent for iniquity which is said of the betrayer of our Lord. It were better for him that he had not been born. It were better for him, now that he is born, could he be committed back again to deep annihilation. Rather than that he should offend one of these little ones, it were better for him that a millstone were hanged about his neck, and he were cast into the sea.

This is one case of such offences as are adverted to in the text. Another and still more specific is beginning, we understand, to be exemplified in our own city, though it has not attained to the height or to the frequency at which it occurs in a neighbouring metropolis. We allude to the doing of weekday business upon the Sabbath. We allude to that violence which is rudely offered to the feelings and the associations of sacredness, by those exactions that an ungodly master lays at times on his youthful dependents—when those hours which they wont to spend in church, they are called upon to spend in the counting-house—when that day, which ought to be a day of piety, is turned into a day of posting and of penmanship—when the rules of the decalogue are set aside, and utterly superseded by the rules of the great trading establishment; and every thing is made to give way to the hurrying emergency of orders, and clearances, and the demands of instant correspondence. Such is the magnitude of this stumbling-block, that many is the young man who has here fallen to rise no more—that, at this point of departure, he has so widened his distance from God, as never, in fact, to return to him—that, in this distressing contest between principle and necessity, the final blow has been given to his religious principles—that the master whom he serves, and under whom he earns his provision for time, has here wrested the whole interests of his eternity away from him—that, from this moment, there gathers upon his soul the complexion of a hardier and more determined impiety—and conscience once stifled now speaks to him with a feebler voice—and the world obtains a firmer lodgement in his heart—and, renouncing all his original tenderness about Sabbath, and Sabbath employments, he can now, with the thorough unconcern of a fixed and familiarised proselyte, keep equal pace by his fellows throughout every scene of profanation—and he who wont to tremble and recoil from the freedoms of irreligion with the sensibility of a little one, may soon become the most daringly rebellious of them all—and that Sabbath which he has now learned, at one time, to give to business, he at another, gives to unhallowed enjoyments—and it is turned into a day of visits and excursions, given up to pleasure, and enlivened by all the mirth and extravagance of holiday—and, when sacrament is proclaimed from the city pulpits, he, the apt, the well trained disciple of his corrupt and corrupting superior, is the readiest to plan the amusements of the coming opportunity, and among the very foremost in the ranks of emigration—and though he may look back, at times, to the Sabbath of his Father's pious house, yet the retrospect is always becoming dimmer, and at length it ceases to disturb him—and thus the alienation widens every year, till, wholly given over to impiety, he lives without God in the world.

And were we asked to state the dimensions of that iniquity which stalks regardlessly, and at large, over the ruin of youthful principles—were we asked to find a place in the catalogue of guilt for a crime, the atrocity of which is only equalled, we understand, by its frequency—were we called to characterise the man who, so far from attempting one counteracting influence against the profligacy of his dependents, issues, from the chair of authority on which he sits, a commandment, in the direct face of a commandment from God—the man who has chartered impiety in articles of agreement, and has vested himself with a property in that time which only belongs to the Lord of the Sabbath—were we asked to look to the man who could thus overbear the last remnants of remorse in a struggling and unpractised bosom, and glitter in all the ensigns of a prosperity that is reared on the violated consciences of those who are beneath him—O! were the question put, to whom shall we liken such a man? or what is the likeness to which we can compare him? we would say, that the guilt of him who trafficked on the highway, or trafficked on that outraged coast, from whose weeping families children were inseparably torn, was far outmeasured by the guilt which could thus frustrate a father's fondest prayers, and trample under foot the hopes and the preparations of eternity.

There is another way whereby in the employ of a careless and unprincipled master, it is impossible but that offences must come. You know just as well as we do, that there are chicaneries in business; and, so long as we forbear stating the precise extent of them, there is not an individual among you who has a title to construe the assertion into an affronting charge of criminality against himself. But you surely know as well as we, that the mercantile profession, conducted, as it often is, with the purest integrity, and laying no resistless necessity whatever for the surrender of principle on any of its members; and dignified by some of the noblest exhibitions of untainted honour, and devoted friendship, and magnificent generosity, that have ever been recorded of our nature;—you know as well as we, that it was utterly extravagant, and in the face of all observation, to affirm, that each, and every one of its numerous competitors, stood clearly and totally exempted from the sins of an undue selfishness. And, accordingly, there are certain commodious falsehoods occasionally practised in this department of human affairs. There are, for example, certain dexterous and gainful evasions, whereby the payers of tribute are enabled, at times, to make their escape from the eagle eye of the exactors of tribute. There are even certain contests of ingenuity between individual traders, where in the higgling of a very keen and anxious negociation, each of them is tempted in talking of offers and prices, and the reports of fluctuations in home and foreign markets, to say the things which are not. You must assuredly know, that these, and such as these, then, have introduced a certain quantity of what may be called shuffling, into the communications of the trading world—insomuch, that the simplicity of yea, yea, and nay, nay, is in some degree exploded; there is a kind of understood toleration established for certain modes of expression, which could not, we are much afraid, stand the rigid scrutiny of the great day; and there is an abatement of confidence between man and man, implying, we doubt, such a proportionate abatement of truth, as goes to extend most fearfully the condemnation that is due to all liars, who shall have their part in the lake that burneth with fire and brimstone. And who can compute the effect of all this on the young and yet unpractised observer? Who does not see, that it must go to reduce the tone of his principles; and to involve him in many a delicate struggle between the morality he has learned from his catechism, and the morality he sees in the counting-house; and to obliterate, in his mind, the distinctions between right and wrong; and, at length, to reconcile his conscience to a sin, which, like every other, deserves the wrath and the curse of God; and to make him tamper with a direct commandment, in such a way, as that falsehoods and frauds might be nothing more in his estimation, than the peccadilloes of an innocent compliance with the current practices and moralities of the world? Here then is a point, at which the way of those who conform to this world, diverges from the way of those peculiar people who are redeemed from all iniquity, and are thoroughly furnished unto all good works. Here is a grievous occasion to fall. Here is a competition between the service of God and the service of Mammon. Here is the exhibition of another offence, and the bringing forward of another temptation, to those who are entering on the business of the world, little adverted to, we fear, by those who live in utter carelessness of their own souls, and never spend a thought or a sigh about the immortality of others—but most distinctly singled out by the text as a crime of foremost magnitude in the eye of Him who judgeth righteously.

And before we quit the subject of such offences as take place in ordinary trade, let us just advert to one example of it—not so much for the frequency of its occurrence, as for the way that it stands connected in principle with a very general, and, we believe, a very mischievous offence, that takes place in domestic society. It is neither, you will observe, the avarice nor the selfishness of our nature, which forms the only obstruction in the way of one man dealing plainly with another. There is another obstruction, founded on a far more pleasing and amiable principle—even on that delicacy of feeling, in virtue of which, one man cannot bear to wound or to mortify another. It would require, for instance, a very rare, and, certainly, not a very enviable degree of hardihood, to tell another, without pain, that you did not think him worthy of being trusted. And yet, in the doings of merchandise, this is the very trial of delicacy which sometimes offers itself. The man with whom you stand committed to as great an extent as you count to be advisable, would like, perhaps, to try your confidence in him, and his own credit with you, a little farther; and he comes back upon you with a fresh order; and you secretly have no desire to link any more of your property with his speculation; and the difficulty is, how to get the application in question disposed of; and you feel that by far the pleasantest way, to all the parties concerned, would be, to make him believe that you refuse the application, not because you will not comply, but because you cannot—for that you have no more of the article he wants from you upon hand. And it would only be putting your own soul to hazard, did you personally, and by yourself, make this communication: but you select, perhaps, as the organ of it, some agent or underling of your establishment, who knows it to be false; and to avoid the soreness of a personal encounter with the man whom you are to disappoint, you devolve the whole business of this lying apology upon others; and thus do you continue to shift this oppressive burden away from you—or, in other words, to save your own delicacy, you count not, and you care not, about another's damnation.

Now, what we call upon you to mark, is the perfect identity of principle between this case of making a brother to offend, and another case which obtains, we have heard, to a very great extent, among the most genteel and opulent of our city families. In this case, you put a lie into the mouth of a dependent, and that, for the purpose of protecting your substance from such an application as might expose it to hazard or diminution. In the second case, you put a lie into the mouth of a dependent, and that, for the purpose of protecting your time from such an encroachment as you would not feel to be convenient or agreeable. And, in both cases, you are led to hold out this offence by a certain delicacy of temperament, in virtue of which, you can neither give a man plainly to understand, that you are not willing to trust him, nor can you give him to understand that you count his company to be an interruption. But, in both the one and the other example, look to the little account that is made of a brother's or of a sister's eternity; behold the guilty task that is thus unmercifully laid upon one who is shortly to appear before the judgment-seat of Christ; think of the entanglement which is thus made to beset the path of a creature who is unperishable. That, at the shrine of Mammon, such a bloody sacrifice should be rendered by some of his unrelenting votaries, is not to be wondered at; but that the shrine of elegance and fashion should be bathed in blood—that soft and sentimental ladyship should put forth her hand to such an enormity—that she who can sigh so gently, and shed her graceful tear over the sufferings of others, should thus be accessary to the second and more awful death of her own domestics—that one who looks the mildest and the loveliest of human beings, should exact obedience to a mandate which carries wrath, and tribulation, and anguish, in its train—O! how it should confirm every Christian in his defiance to the authority of fashion, and lead him to spurn at all its folly, and at all its worthlessness.

And it is quite in vain to say, that the servant whom you thus employ as the deputy of your falsehood, can possibly execute the commission without the conscience being at all tainted or defiled by it; that a simple cottage maid can so sophisticate the matter, as, without any violence to her original principles, to utter the language of what she assuredly knows to be a downright lie; that she, humble and untutored soul, can sustain no injury when thus made to tamper with the plain English of these realms; that she can at all satisfy herself, how, by the prescribed utterance of "not at home," she is not pronouncing such words as are substantially untrue, but merely using them in another and perfectly understood meaning—and which, according to their modern translation, denote, that the person of whom she is thus speaking, instead of being away from home, is secretly lurking in one of the most secure and intimate of its receptacles. You may try to darken and transform this piece of casuistry as you will; and work up your own minds into the peaceable conviction that it is all right, and as it should be. But be very certain, that where the moral sense of your domestic is not already overthrown, there is, at least one bosom within which you have raised a war of doubts and difficulties; and where, if the victory be on your side, it will be on the side of him who is the great enemy of righteousness. There is, at least, one person along the line of this conveyance of deceit, who condemneth herself in that which she alloweth; who, in the language of Paul, esteeming the practice to be unclean, to her will it be unclean; who will perform her task with the offence of her own conscience, and to whom, therefore, it will indeed be evil: who cannot render obedience in this matter to her earthly superior, but by an act, in which she does not stand clear and unconscious of guilt before God; and with whom, therefore, the sad consequence of what we can call nothing else than a barbarous combination against the principles and the prospects of the lower orders, is—that as she has not cleaved fully unto the Lord, and has not kept by the service of the one master, and has not forsaken all at His bidding, she cannot be the disciple of Christ.

The aphorism, that he who offendeth in

one point is guilty of all, tells us something more than of the way in which God adjudges condemnation to the disobedient. It also tells us of the way in which one individual act of sinfulness operates upon our moral nature. It is altogether an erroneous view of the commandments, to look upon them as so many observances to which we are bound by as many distinct and independent ties of obligation—insomuch, that the transgression of one of them may be brought about by the dissolution of one separate tie, and may leave all the others, with as entire a constraining influence and authority as before. The truth is, that the commandments ought rather to be looked upon as branching out from one great and general tie of obligation; and that there is no such thing as loosening the hold of one of them upon the conscience, but by the unfastening of that tie which binds them all upon the conscience. So that if one member in the system of practical righteousness be made to suffer, all the other members suffer along with it; and if one decision of the moral sense be thwarted, the organ of the moral sense is permanently impaired, and a leaven of iniquity infused into all its other decisions; and if one suggestion of this inward monitor be stifled, a general shock is given to his authority over the whole man; and if one of the least commandments of the law is left unfulfilled, the law itself is brought down from its rightful ascendency; and thus it is, that one act of disobedience may be the commencement and the token of a systematic and universal rebelliousness of the heart against God. It is this which gives such a wide-wasting malignity to each of the separate offences on which we have now expatiated. It is this which so multiplies the means and the possibilities of corruption in the world. It is thus that, at every one point in the intercourse of human society, there may be struck out a fountain of poisonous emanation on all who approach it; and think not, therefore, that under each of the examples we have given, we were only contending for the preservation of one single feature in the character of him who stands exposed to this world's offences. We felt it, in fact, to be a contest for his eternity; and that the case involved in it his general condition with God; and that he who leads the young into a course of dissipation—or that he who tampers with their impressions of sabbath sacredness—or that he who, either in the walks of business, or in the services of the family, makes them the agents of deceitfulness—or that he, in short, who tempts them to transgress in any one thing, has, in fact, poured such a pervading taint into their moral constitution, as to spoil or corrupt them in all things; and that thus, upon one solitary occasion, or by the exhibition of one particular offence, a mischief may be done equivalent to the total destruction of a human soul, or to the blotting out of its prospects for immortality.

And let us just ask a master or a mistress, who can thus make free with the moral principle of their servants in one instance, how they can look for pure or correct principle from them in other instances? What right have they to complain of unfaithfulness against themselves, who have deliberately seduced another into a habit of unfaithfulness against God? Are they so utterly unskilled in the mysteries of our nature, as not to perceive, that if a man gather hardihood enough to break the Sabbath in opposition to his own conscience, this very hardihood will avail him to the breaking of other obligations?—that he whom, for their advantage, they have so exercised, as to fill his conscience with offence towards his God, will not scruple, for his own advantage, so to exercise himself, as to fill his conscience with offence towards his master? —that the servant whom you have taught to lie, has gotten such rudiments of education at your hand, as that, without any further help, he can now teach himself to purloin?—and yet nothing more frequent than loud and angry complainings against the treachery of servants; as if, in the general wreck of their other principles, a principle of consideration for the good and interest of their employer—and who, at the same time, has been their seducer—was to survive in all its power, and all its sensibility. It is just such a retribution as was to be looked for. It is a recoil upon their own heads of the mischief which they themselves have originated. It is the temporal part of the punishment which they have to bear for the sin of our text, but not the whole of it; far the better for them that both person and property were cast into the sea, than that they should stand the reckoning of that day, when called to give an account of the souls that they have murdered, and the blood of so mighty a destruction is required at their hands.

The evil against which we have just protested, is an outrage of far greater enormity than tyrant or oppressor can inflict, in the prosecution of his worst designs against the political rights and liberties of the commonwealth. The very semblance of such designs will summon every patriot to his post of observation; and, from a thousand watchtowers of alarm, will the outcry of freedom in danger be heard throughout the land. But there is a conspiracy of a far more malignant influence upon the destinies of the species that is now going on; and which seems to call forth no indignant spirit, and to bring no generous exclamation along with it. Throughout all the recesses of private and domestic history, there is an ascendency of rank and station against which no stern republican is ever heard to lift his voice—though it be an ascendency so exercised, as to be of most noxious operation to the dearest hopes and best interests of humanity. There is a cruel combination of the great against the majesty of the people—we mean the majesty of the people's worth. There is a haughty unconcern about an inheritance, which, by an unalienable right, should be theirs—we mean their future and everlasting inheritance. There is a deadly invasion made on their rights—we mean their rights of conscience; and, in this our land of boasted privileges, are the low trampled upon by the high—we mean trampled into all the degradation of guilt and worthlessness. They are utterly bereft of that homage which ought to be rendered to the dignity of their immortal nature; and to minister to the avarice of an imperious master, or to spare the sickly delicacy of the fashionables in our land, are the truth and the piety of our population, and all the virtues of their eternity, most unfeelingly plucked away from them. It belongs to others to fight the battle of their privileges in time. But who that looks with a calculating eye on their duration that never ends, can repress an alarm of a higher order? It belongs to others generously to struggle for the place and the adjustment of the lower orders in the great vessel of the state. But, surely, the question of their place in eternity is of mightier concern than how they are to sit and be accommodated in that pathway vehicle which takes them to their everlasting habitations.

Christianity is, in one sense, the greatest of all levellers. It looks to the elements, and not to the circumstantials of humanity; and regarding as altogether superficial and temporary the distinctions of this fleeting pilgrimage, it fastens on those points of assimilation which liken the king upon the throne to the very humblest of his subject population. They are alike in the nakedness of their birth. They are alike in the sureness of their decay. They are alike in the agonies of their dissolution. And after the one is tombed in sepulchral magnificence, and the other is laid in his sod-wrapt grave, are they most fearfully alike in the corruption to which they moulder. But it is with the immortal nature of each that Christianity has to do; and, in both the one and the other, does it behold a nature alike forfeited by guilt, and alike capable of being restored by the grace of an offered salvation. And never do the pomp and the circumstance of externals appear more humiliating, than when, looking onwards to the day of resurrection, we behold the sovereign standing without his crown, and trembling, with the subject by his side, at the bar of heaven's majesty. There the master and the servant will be brought to their reckoning together; and when the one is tried upon the guilt and the malignant influence of his Sabbath companies—and is charged with the profane and careless habit of his household establishment—and is reminded how he kept both himself and his domestics from the solemn ordinance—and is made to perceive the fearful extent of the moral and spiritual mischief which he has wrought as the irreligious head of an irreligious family—and how, among other things he, under a system of fashionable hypocrisy, so tampered with another's principles as to defile his conscience, and to destroy him—O! how tremendously will the little brief authority in which he now plays his fantastic tricks, turn to his own condemnation; for, than thus abuse his authority, it were better for him that a millstone were hanged about his neck, and he were cast into the sea.

And how comes it, we ask, that any master is armed with a power so destructive over the immortals who are around him? God has given him no such power: The state has not given it to him. There is no law, either human or divine, by which he can enforce any order upon his servants to an act of falsehood, or to an act of impiety. Should any such act of authority be attempted on the part of the master, it should be followed up on the part of the servant by an act of disobedience. Should your master or mistress bid you say not at home, when you know that they are at home, it is your duty to refuse compliance with such an order: and if it be asked, how can this matter be adjusted after such a violent and alarming innovation on the laws of fashionable intercourse, we answer, just by the simple substitution of truth for falsehood—just by prescribing the utterance of, engaged, which is a fact, instead of the utterance of, not at home, which is a lie—just by holding the principles of your servant to be of higher account than the false delicacies of your acquaintance—just by a bold and vigorous recurrence to the simplicity of nature—just by determinedly doing what is right, though the example of a whole host were against you; and by giving impulse to the current of example, when it happens to be moving in a proper direction. And here we are happy to say that fashion has of late been making a capricious and accidental movement on the side of principle—and to be blunt, and open, and manly, is now on the fair way to be fashionable—and a temper of a homelier quality is beginning to infuse itself into the luxuriousness, and the effeminacy, and the palling and excessive complaisance of genteel society—and the staple of cultivated manners is improving in firmness, and frankness, and honesty, and may, at length, by the aid of a principle of Christian rectitude, be so interwoven with the cardinal virtues, as to present a different texture altogether from the soft and silken degeneracy of modern days.

And that we may not appear the champions of an insurrection against the authority of masters, let us further say, that while it is the duty of clerk or apprentice to refuse the doing of weekday work on the Sabbath, and while it is the duty of servants to refuse the utterance of a prescribed falsehood, and while it is the duty of every dependent, in the service of his master, to serve him only in the Lord—yet this very principle, tending as it may to a rare and occasional act of disobedience, is also the principle which renders every servant who adheres to it a perfect treasure of fidelity, and attachment, and general obedience. This is the way in which to obtain a credit for his refusal, and to stamp upon it a noble consistency. In this way he will, even to the mind of an ungodly master, make up for all his particularities: and should he be what, if a Christian, he will be; should he be, at all times, the most alert in service, and the most patient of provocation, and the most cordial in affection, and the most scrupulously honest in the charge and custody of all that is committed to him—then let the post of drudgery at which he toils be humble as it may, the contrast between the meanness of his office and the dignity of his character will only heighten the reverence that is due to principle, and make it more illustrious. His scruples may, at first, be the topics of displeasure, and afterwards the topics of occasional levity; but, in spite of himself, will his employer be at length constrained to look upon them with respectful toleration. The servant will be to the master a living epistle of Christ, and he may read there what he has not yet perceived in the letter of the New Testament. He may read, in the person of his own domestic, the power and the truth of Christianity. He may positively stand in awe of his own hired servant—and, regarding his bosom as a sanctuary of worth which it were monstrous to violate, will he feel, when tempted to offer one command of impiety, that he cannot, that he dare not.

And before we conclude, let us, if possible, try to rebuke the wealthy out of their unfeeling indifference to the souls of the poor, by the example of the Saviour. Let those who look on the immortality of the poor as beneath their concern, only look unto Christ—to him who, for the sake of the poorest of us all, became poor himself, that we, through his poverty, might be made rich. Let them think how the principle of all these offences which we have been attempting to expose, is in the direct face of that principle which prompted, at first, and which still presides over, the whole of the gospel dispensation. Let them learn a higher reverence for the eternity of those beneath them, by thinking of him who, to purchase an inheritance for the poor, and to provide them with the blessings of a preached gospel, unrobed him of all his greatness; and descended himself to the lot and labours of poverty; and toiled, to the beginning of his public ministry, at the work of a carpenter; and submitted to all the horrors of a death which was aggravated by the burden of a world's atonement, and made inconceivably severe by their being infused into it all the bitter of expiation. Think, O think, when some petty design of avarice or vanity would lead you to forget the imperishable souls of those who are beneath you, that you are setting yourselves in diametric opposition to that which lieth nearest to the heart of the Saviour; that you are countervailing the whole tendency of his redemption; that you are thwarting the very object of that enterprise for which all heaven is represented as in motion—and angels are with wonder looking on—and God the Father laid an appointment on the Son of his love—and he, the august personage in whom the magnificent train of prophecy, from the beginning of the world, has its theme and its fulfilment, at length came amongst us, in shrouded majesty, and was led to the cross, like a lamb for the slaughter, and bowed his head in agony, and gave up the ghost.

And here let us address one word more to the masters and mistresses of families. By adopting the reformations to which we have been urging you, you may do good to the cause of Christianity, and yet not advance, by a single hair-breadth, the Christianity of your own souls. It is not by this one reformation, or indeed, by any given number of reformations, that you are saved. It is by believing in Christ that men are saved. You may escape, it is sure, a higher degree of punishment, but you will not escape damnation. You may do good to the souls of your servants, by a rigid observance of the lesson of this day. But we seek the good of your own souls, also, and we pronounce upon them that they are in a state of death, till one great act be performed, and one act, too, which does not consist of any number of particular acts, or particular reformations. What shall I do to be saved? Believe in the Lord Jesus Christ, and thou shalt be saved. And he who believeth not, the wrath of God abideth on him. Do this, if you want to make the great and important transition for yourselves. Do this if you want your own name to be blotted out of the book of condemnation. If you seek to have your own persons justified before God, submit to the righteousness of God—even that righteousness which is through the faith of Christ, and is unto all and upon all who believe. This is the turning point of your acceptance with the Lawgiver. And at this step, also, in the history of your souls, will there be applied to you a power of motive, and will you be endowed with an obedient sensibility to the influence of motive, which will make it the turning point of a new heart and a new character. The particular reformation that we have now been urging will be one of a crowd of other reformations; and, in the spirit of him who pleased not himself, but gave up his life for others, will you forego all the desires of selfishness and vanity, and look not merely to your own things, but also to the things of others.

DISCOURSE VIII.

On the Love of Money.

"If I have made gold my hope, or have said to the fine gold, Thou art my confidence; If I rejoiced because my wealth was great, and because mine hand had gotten much: If I beheld the sun when it shined or the moon walking in brightness; and my heart hath been secretly enticed, or my mouth hath kissed my hand; this also were an iniquity to be punished by the judge; for I should have denied the God that is above."—*Job* xxxi. 24—28.

WHAT is worthy of remark in this passage is, that a certain affection only known among the votaries of Paganism, should be classed under the same character and have the same condemnation with an affection, not only known, but allowed, nay cherished into habitual supremacy, all over Christendom. How universal is it among those who are in pursuit of wealth, to make gold their hope, and among those who are in possession of wealth, to make fine gold their confidence? Yet we are here told that this is virtually as complete a renunciation of God as to practise some of the worst charms of idolatry. And it might perhaps serve to unsettle the vanity of those who, unsuspicious of the disease that is in their hearts, are wholy given over to this world, and wholly without alarm in their anticipations of another,—could we convince them that the most reigning and resistless desire by which they are actuated, stamps the same perversity on them, in the sight of God, as he sees to be in those who are worshippers of the sun in the firmament, or are offering incense to the moon, as the queen of heaven.

We recoil from an idolater, as from one who labours under a great moral derangement, in suffering his regards to be carried away from the true God to an idol. But, is it not just the same derangement, on the part of man, that he should love any created good, and in the enjoyment of it lose sight of the Creator—that he should delight himself with the use and the possession of a gift, and be unaffected by the circumstance of its having been put into his hands by a giver—that thoroughly absorbed with the present and the sensible gratification, there should be no room left for the movements of duty or regard to the Being who furnished him with the materials, and endowed him with the organs, of every gratification,—that he should thus lavish all his desires on the surrounding materialism, and fetch from it all his delights, while the thought of him who formed it is habitually absent from his heart—that in the play of those attractions that subsist between him and the various objects in the neighbourhood of his person, there should be the same want of reference to God, as there is in the play of those attractions which subsist between a piece of unconscious matter and the other matter that is around it— that all the influences which operate upon the human will should emanate from so many various points in the mechanism of what is formed, but that no practical or ascendant influence should come down upon it from the presiding and the preserving Deity? Why, if such be man, he could not be otherwise, though there were no Deity. The part he sustains in the world is the very same that it would have been had the world sprung into being of itself, or without an originating mind had maintained its being from eternity. He just puts forth the evolutions of his own nature, as one of the component individuals in a vast independent system of nature, made up of many parts and many individuals. In hungering for what is agreeable to his senses, or recoiling from what is bitter or unsuitable to them, he does so without thinking of God, or borrowing any impulse to his own will from any thing he knows or believes to be the will of God. Religion has just as little to do with those daily movements of his which are voluntary, as it has to do with the growth of his body, which is involuntary; or, as it has to do, in other words, with the progress and the phenomena of vegetation. With a mind that ought to know God, and a conscience that ought to award to him the supreme jurisdiction, he lives as effectually without him as if he had no mind and no conscience; and, bating a few transient visitations of thought, and a few regularities of outward and mechanical observation, do we behold man running, and willing, and preparing, and enjoying, just as if there was no other portion than the creature—just as if the world, and its visible elements, formed the all with which he had to do.

I wish to impress upon you the distinction that there is between the love of money, and the love of what money purchases. Either of these affections may equally displace God from the heart. But there is a malignity and an inveteracy of atheism in the former which does not belong to the latter, and in virtue of which it may be seen that the love of money is, indeed, the root of all evil.

When we indulge the love of that which is purchased by money, the materials of gratification and the organs of gratification are present with each other—just as in the enjoyments of the inferior animals, and just as in all the simple and immediate enjoyments of man; such as the tasting of food, or the smelling of a flower. There is an adaptation of the senses to certain external objects, and there is a pleasure arising out of that adaptation, and it is a pleasure which may be felt by man, along with a right and a full infusion of godliness. The primitive Christians, for example, ate their meat with gladness and singleness of heart, praising God. But, in the case of every unconverted man, the pleasure has no such accompaniment. He carries in his heart no recognition of that hand, by the opening of which it is, that the means and the materials of enjoyment are placed within his reach. The matter of the enjoyment is all with which he is conversant. The Author of the enjoyment is unheeded. The avidity with which he rushes onward to any of the direct gratifications of nature, bears a resemblance to the avidity with which one of the lower creation rushes to its food, or to its water, or to the open field, where it gambols in all the wantonness of freedom, and finds a high-breathed joy in the very strength and velocity of its movements. And the atheism of the former, who has a mind for the sense and knowledge of his Creator, is often as entire as the atheism of the latter, who has it not. Man, who ought to look to the primary cause of all his blessings, because he is capable of seeing thus far, is often as blind to God, in the midst of enjoyment, as the animal who is not capable of seeing him. He can trace the stream to its fountain; but still he drinks of the stream with as much greediness of pleasure, and as little recognition of its source, as the animal beneath him. In other words, his atheism, while tasting the bounties of Providence, is just as complete, as is the atheism of the inferior animals. But theirs proceeds from their incapacity of knowing God. His proceeds from his not liking to retain God in his knowledge. He may come under the power of godliness, if he would. But he chooses rather that the power of sensuality should lord it over him, and his whole man is engrossed with the objects of sensuality.

But a man differs from an animal in being something more than a sensitive being. He is also a reflective being. He has the power of thought, and inference, and anticipation, to signalize him above the beasts of the field, or of the forest; and yet will it be found, in the case of every natural man, that the exercise of those powers, so far from having carried him nearer, has only widened his departure from God, and given a more deliberate and wilful character to his atheism, than if he had been without them altogether.

In virtue of the powers of a mind which belong to him, he can carry his thoughts beyond the present desires and the present gratification. He can calculate on the visitations of future desire, and on the means of its gratification. He cannot only follow out the impulse of hunger that is now upon him; he can look onwards to the successive and recurring impulses of hunger which await him, and he can devise expedients for relieving it. Out of that great stream of supply, which comes direct from Heaven to earth, for the sustenance of all its living generations, he can draw off and appropriate a separate rill of conveyance, and direct it into a reservoir for himself. He can enlarge the capacity, or he can strengthen the embankments of this reservoir. By doing the one, he augments his proportion of this common tide of wealth which circulates through the world, and by doing the other, he augments his security for holding it in perpetual possession. The animal who drinks out of the stream thinks not whence it issues. But man thinks of the reservoir which yields to him his portion of it. And he looks no further. He thinks not that to fill it, there must be a great and original fountain, out of which there issueth a mighty flood of abundance for the purpose of distribution among all the tribes and families of the world. He stops short at the secondary and artificial fabric which he himself hath formed, and out of which, as from a spring, he draws his own peculiar enjoyments; and never thinks either of his own peculiar supply, fluctuating with the variations of the primary spring, or of connecting these variations with the will of the great but unseen director of all things. It is true, that if this main and originating fountain be, at any time, less copious in its emission, he will have less to draw from it to his own reservoir; and in that very proportion will his share of the bounties of Providence be reduced. But still it is to the well, or receptacle, of his own striking out that he looks, as his main security for the relief of nature's wants, and the abundant supply of nature's enjoyments. It is upon his own work that he depends in this matter, and not on the work or the will of him who is the author of nature; who giveth rain from heaven, and fruitful seasons, and filleth every heart with food and gladness. And thus it is, that the reason of man, and the retrospective power of man, still fail to carry him, by an ascending process to the First Cause. He stops at the instrumental cause, which, by his own wisdom and his own power, he has put into operation. In a word, the man's understanding is over-run with atheism, as well as his desires. The intellectual as well as the sensitive part of his constitution seems to be infected with it. When, like the instinctive and unreflecting animal, he engages in the act of direct enjoyment, he is like it, too, in its atheism. When he rises above the animal, and, in the exercise of his higher and larger faculties, he engages in the act of providing for enjoyment, he still carries his atheism along with him.

A sum of money is, in all its functions, equivalent to such a reservoir. Take one year with another, and the annual consumption of the world cannot exceed the annual produce which issues from the storehouse of him who is the great and the bountiful Provider of all its families. The money that is in any man's possession represents the share which he can appropriate to himself of this produce. If it be a large sum it is like a capacious reservoir on the bank of the river of abundance. If it be laid out on firm and stable securities, still it is like a firmly embanked reservoir. The man who toils to increase his money is like a man who toils to enlarge the capacity of his reservoir. The man who suspects a flaw in his securities, or who apprehends, in the report of failures and fluctuations, that his money is all to flow away from him, is like a man who apprehends a flaw in the embankments of his reservoir.

Meanwhile, in all the care that is thus expended, either on the money or on the magazine, the originating source, out of which there is imparted to the one all its real worth, or there is imparted to the other all its real fulness, is scarcely ever thought of. Let God turn the earth into a barren desert, and the money ceases to be convertible to any purpose of enjoyment; or let him lock up that magazine of great and general supply, out of which he showers abundance among our habitations, and all the subordinate magazines formed beside the wonted stream of liberality, would re main empty. But all this is forgotten by the vast majority of our unthoughtful and unreflecting species. The patience of God is still unexhausted; and the seasons still roll in kindly succession over the heads of an ungrateful generation; and that period, when the machinery of our present system shall stop and be taken to pieces has not yet arrived; and that Spirit, who will not always strive with the children of men, is still prolonging his experiment on the powers and perversities of our moral nature; and still suspending the edict of dissolution, by which this earth and these heavens are at length to pass away. So that the sun still shines upon us; and the clouds still drop upon us; and the earth still puts forth the bloom and the beauty of its luxuriance; and all the ministers of heaven's liberality still walk their annual round, and scatter plenty over the face of an alienated world; and the whole of nature continues as smiling in promise, and as sure in fulfilment, as in the days of our forefathers; and out of her large and universal granary is there, in every returning year, as rich a conveyance of aliment as before, to the populous family in whose behalf it is opened. But it is the business of many among that population, each to erect his own separate granary, and to replenish it out of the general store, and to feed himself and his dependants out of it. And he is right in so doing. But he is not right in looking to his own peculiar receptacle, as if it were the first and the emanating fountain of all his enjoyments. He is not right in thus idolising the work of his own hands—awarding no glory and no confidence to him in whose hands is the key of that great storehouse, out of which every lesser storehouse of man derives its fulness. He is not right, in labouring after the money which purchaseth all things, to avert the earnestness of his regard from the Being who provides all things. He is not right, in thus building his security on that which is subordinate, unheeding and unmindful of him who is supreme. It is not right, that silver, and gold, though unshaped into statuary, should still be doing, in this enlightened land, what the images of Paganism once did. It is not right, that they should thus supplant the deference which is owing to the God and the governor of all things—or that each man amongst us should in the secret homage of trust and satisfaction which he renders to his bills, and his deposits, and his deeds of property and possession, endow these various articles with the same moral ascendency over his heart, as the household gods of antiquity had over the idolaters of antiquity—

making them as effectually usurp the place of the Divinity, and dethrone the one Monarch of heaven and earth from that pre-eminence of trust and of affection that belongs to him.

He who makes a god of his pleasure, renders to this idol the homage of his senses. He who makes a god of his wealth, renders to this idol the homage of his mind; and he, therefore, of the two, is the more hopeless and determined idolater. The former is goaded on to his idolatry, by the power of appetite. The latter cultivates his with wilful and deliberate perseverance; consecrates his very highest powers to its service; embarks in it, not with the heat of passion, but with the coolness of steady and calculating principle; fully gives up his reason and his time, and all the faculties of his understanding, as well as all the desires of his heart, to the great object of a fortune in this world; makes the acquirement of gain the settled aim, and the prosecution of that aim the settled habit of his existence; sits the whole day long at the post of his ardent and unremitting devotions; and, as he labours at the desk of his counting-house, has his soul just as effectually seduced from the living God to an object distinct from him, and contrary to him, as if the ledger over which he was bending was a book of mystical characters, written in honour of some golden idol placed before him, and with a view to render this idol propitious to himself and to his family. Baal and Moloch were not more substantially the gods of rebellious Israel, than Mammon is the god of all his affections. To the fortune he has reared, or is rearing, for himself and his descendants, he ascribes all the power and all the independence of a divinity. With the wealth he has gotten by his own hands, does he feel himself as independent of God, as the Pagan does, who, happy in the fancied protection of an image made with his own hands, suffers no disturbance to his quiet, from any thought of the real but the unknown Deity. His confidence is in his treasure, and not in God. It is there that he places all his safety and all his sufficiency. It is not on the Supreme Being, conceived in the light of a real and a personal agent, that he places his dependence. It is on a mute and material statue of his own erection. It is wealth, which stands to him in the place of God—to which he awards the credit of all his enjoyments—which he looks to as the emanating fountain of all his present sufficiency—from which he gathers his fondest expectations of all the bright and fancied blessedness that is yet before him—on which he rests as the firmest and stablest foundation of all that the heart can wish or the eye can long after, both for himself and for his children. It matters not for him, that all his enjoyment comes from a primary fountain, and that his wealth is only an intermediate reservoir. It matters not to him, that, if God were to set a seal upon the upper storehouse in heaven, or to blast and to burn up all the fruitfulness of earth, he would reduce, to the worthlessness of dross, all the silver and the gold that abound in it. Still the gold and the silver are his gods. His own fountain is between him and the fountain of original supply. His wealth is between him and God. Its various lodging places, whether in the bank, or in the place of registration, or in the depository of wills and title deeds—these are the sanctuaries of his secret worship—these are the highplaces of his adoration; and never did the devout Israelite look with more intentness towards Mount Zion, and with his face towards Jerusalem, than he does to his wealth, as to the mountain and strong hold of his security. Nor could the Supreme be more effectually deposed from the homage of trust and gratitude than he actually is, though this wealth were recalled from its various investments; and turned into one mass of gold; and cast into a piece of molten statuary; and enshrined on a pedestal, around which all his household might assemble, and make it the object of their family devotions; and plied every hour of every day with all the fooleries of a senseless and degrading Paganism. It is thus, that God may keep up the charge of Idolatry against us, even after all its images have been overthrown. It is thus that dissuasives from idolatry are still addressed, in the New Testament, to the pupils of a new and better dispensation; that little children are warned against idols; and all of us are warned to flee from covetousness, which is idolatry.

To look no further than to fortune as the dispenser of all the enjoyments which money can purchase, is to make that fortune stand in the place of God. It is to make sense shut out faith, and to rob the King eternal and invisible of that supremacy, to which all the blessings of human existence, and all the varieties of human condition, ought, in every instance, and in every particular, to be referred. But, as we have already remarked, the love of money is one affection, and the love of what is purchased by money is another. It was at first, we have no doubt, loved for the sake of the good things which it enabled its possessor to acquire. But whether, as the result of associations in the mind, so rapid as to escape the notice of our own consciousness—or as the fruit of an infection running by the sympathy among all men busily engaged in the prosecution of wealth, as the supreme good of their being—certain it is, that money, originally pursued for the sake of other things, comes at length to be prized for its own sake. And, perhaps, there is no one circumstance which serves more to liken the love of money to the most irrational of the heathen idolatries, than that it at length passes into the love of money for itself; and acquires a most enduring power over the human affections, separately altogether from the power of purchase and of command which belongs to it, over the proper and original objects of human desire. The first thing which set man agoing in the pursuit of wealth, was that, through it, as an intervening medium, he found his way to other enjoyments; and it proves him, as we have observed, capable of a higher reach of anticipation than the beast of the field, or the fowls of the air, that he is thus able to calculate, and to foresee, and to build up a provision for the wants of futurity. But, mark how soon this boasted distinction of his faculties is overthrown, and how near to each other lie the dignity and the debasement of the human understanding. If it evinced a loftier mind in man than in the inferior animals, that he invented money, and by the acquisition of it can both secure abundance for himself, and transmit this abundance to the future generations of his family—what have we to offer, in vindication of this intellectual eminence, when we witness how soon it is, that the pursuit of wealth ceases to be rational? How, instead of being prosecuted as an instrument, either for the purchase of ease, or the purchase of enjoyment, both the ease and enjoyment of a whole life are rendered up as sacrifices at its shrine? How, from being sought after as a minister of gratification to the appetites of nature, it at length brings nature into bondage, and robs her of all her simple delights, and pours the infusion of wormwood into the currency of her feelings?—making that man sad who ought to be cheerful, and that man who ought to rejoice in his present abundance, filling him either with the cares of an ambition which never will be satisfied, or with the apprehensions of a distress which, in all its pictured and exaggerated evils, will never be realised. And it is wonderful, it is passing wonderful, that wealth, which derives all that is true and sterling in its worth from its subserviency to other advantages, should, apart from all thought about this subserviency, be made the object of such fervent and fatiguing devotion. Insomuch, that never did Indian devotee inflict upon himself a severer agony at the footstool of his Paganism, than those devotees of wealth who, for its acquirement as their ultimate object, will forego all the uses for which alone it is valuable—will give up all that is genuine or tranquil in the pleasures of life; and will pierce themselves through with many sorrows; and will undergo all the fiercer tortures of the mind; and, instead of employing what they have, to smooth their passage through the world, will, upon the hazardous sea of adventure, turn the whole of this passage into a storm—thus exalting wealth from a servant unto a lord, who in return for the homage that he obtains from his worshippers, exercises them, like Rehoboam his subjects of old, not with whips but with scorpions—with consuming anxiety, with never-sated desire, with brooding apprehension, and its frequent and ever-flitting spectres, and the endless jealousies of competition with men as intently devoted, and as emulous of a high place in the temple of their common idolatry, as themselves. And, without going to the higher exhibitions of this propensity, in all its rage and in all its restlessness, we have only to mark its workings on the walk of even and every-day citizenship; and there see, how, in the hearts even of its most commonplace votaries, wealth is followed after for its own sake; how, unassociated with all for which reason pronounces it to be of estimation, but, in virtue of some mysterious and undefinable charm, operating not on any principle of the judgment, but on the utter perversity of judgment, money has come to be of higher account than all that is purchased by money, and has attained a rank co-ordinate with that which our Saviour assigns to the life and to the body of man, in being reckoned more than meat and more than raiment. Thus making that which is subordinate to be primary, and that which is primary subordinate; transferring, by a kind of fascination, the affections away from wealth in use, to wealth in idle and unemployed possession—insomuch, that the most welcome intelligence you could give to the proprietor of many a snug deposit, in some place of secure and progressive accumulation, would be, that he should never require any part either of it or of its accumulation back again for the purpose of expenditure—and that, to the end of his life, every new year should witness another unimpaired addition to the bulk or the aggrandizement of his idol. And it would just heighten his enjoyment could he be told, with prophetic certainty, that this process of undisturbed augmentation would go on with his children's children, to the last age of the world; that the economy of each succeeding race of descendants would leave the sum with its interest untouched, and the place of its sanctuary unviolated; and, that through a series of indefinite generations, would the magnitude ever grow, and the lustre ever brighten, of that household god which he had erected for his own senseless adoration, and bequeathed as an object of as senseless adoration to his family.

We have the authority of that word which

has been pronounced a discerner of the thoughts and intents of the heart, that it cannot have two masters, or that there is not room in it for two great and ascendent affections. The engrossing power of one such affection is expressly affirmed of the love for Mammon, or the love for money thus named and characterised as an idol. Or, in other words, if the love of money be in the heart, the love of God is not there. If a man be trusting in uncertain riches, he is not trusting in the living God, who giveth us all things richly to enjoy. If his heart be set upon covetousness, it is set upon an object of idolatry. The true divinity is moved away from his place, and, worse than atheism, which would only leave it empty, has the love of wealth raised another divinity upon his throne. So that covetousness offers a more daring and positive aggression on the right and territory of the Godhead, than even infidelity. The latter would only desolate the sanctuary of heaven; the former would set up an abomination in the midst of it. It not only strips God of love and of confidence, which are his prerogatives, but it transfers them to another. And little does the man who is proud in honour, but, at the same time, proud and peering in ambition—little does he think, that, though acquitted in the eye of all his fellows, there still remains an atrocity of a deeper character than even that of atheism, with which he is chargeable. Let him just take an account of his mind, amid the labours of his merchandise, and he will find that the living God has no ascendency there; but that wealth, just as much as if personified into life, and agency, and power, wields over him all the ascendency of God. Where his treasure is, his heart is also; and, linking as he does his main hope with its increase, and his main fear with its fluctuations and its failures, he has effectually dethroned the Supreme from his heart, and deified an usurper in his room, as if fortune had been embodied into a goddess, and he were in the habit of repairing, with a crowd of other worshippers, to her temple. She, in fact, is the dispenser of that which he chiefly prizes in existence. A smile from her is worth all the promises of the Eternal, and her threatening frown more dreadful to the imagination than all his terrors.

And the disease is as near to universal as it is virulent. Wealth is the goddess whom all the world worshippeth. There is many a city in our empire, of which, with an eye of apostolical discernment, it may be seen that it is almost wholly given over to idolatry. If a man look no higher than to his money for his enjoyments, then money is his god. It is the god of his dependence, and the god upon whom his heart is staid. Or if, apart from other enjoyments, it by some magical power of its own, has gotten the ascendency, then still it is followed after as the supreme good; and there is an actual supplanting of the living God. He is robbed of the gratitude that we owe him for our daily sustenance; for, instead of receiving it as if it came direct out of his hand, we receive it as if it came from the hand of a secondary agent, to whom we ascribe all the stability and independence of God. This wealth, in fact, obscures to us the character of God, as the real though unseen Author of our various blessings; and as if by a material intervention does it hide from the perception of nature, the hand which feeds, and clothes, and maintains us in life, and in all the comforts and necessaries of life. It just has the effect of thickening still more that impalpable veil which lies between God and the eye of the senses. We lose all discernment of him as the giver of our comforts; and coming, as they appear to do, from that wealth which our fancies have raised into a living personification, does this idol stand before us, not as a deputy but as a substitute for that Being, with whom it is that we really have to do. All this goes both to widen and to fortify that disruption which has taken place between God and the world. It adds the power of one great master idol to the seducing influence of all the lesser idolatries. When the liking and the confidence of men are towards money, there is no direct intercourse, either by the one or the other of these affections towards God; and, in proportion as he sends forth his desires, and rests his security on the former, in that very proportion does he renounce God as his hope, and God as his dependence.

And to advert, for one moment, to the misery of this affection, as well as to its sinfulness. He, over whom it reigns, feels a worthlessness in his present wealth, after it is gotten; and when to this we add the restlessness of a yet unsated appetite, lording it over all his convictions, and panting for more; when, to the dullness of his actual satisfaction in all the riches that he has, we add his still unquenched, and, indeed, unquenchable desire for the riches that he has not; when we reflect that as, in the pursuit of wealth, he widens the circle of his operations, so he lengthens out the line of his open and hazardous exposure, and multiplies, along the extent of it, those vulnerable points from which another and another dart of anxiety may enter into his heart; when he feels himself as if floating on an ocean of contingency, on which, perhaps, he is only borne up by the breath of a credit that is fictitious, and which, liable to burst every moment, may leave him to sink under the weight of his overladen speculation; when suspended on the doubtful result of his bold and uncertain adventure, he dreads the tidings of disaster in every arrival, and lives in a continual agony of feeling, kept up by the crowd and turmoil of his manifold distractions, and so overspreading the whole compass of his thoughts, as to leave not one narrow space for the thought of eternity;—will any beholder just look to the mind of this unhappy man, thus tost and bewildered and thrown into a general unceasing frenzy, made out of many fears and many agitations, and not to say, that the bird of the air, which sends forth its unreflecting song, and lives on the fortuitous bounty of Providence, is not higher in the scale of enjoyment than he? And how much more, then, the quiet Christian beside him, who, in possession of food and raiment has that godliness with contentment which is great gain—who, with the peace of heaven in his heart, and the glories of heaven in his eye, has found out the true philosophy of existence; has sought a portion where alone a portion can be found, and, in bidding away from his mind the love of money, has bidden away all the cross and all the carefulness along with it.

Death will soon break up every swelling enterprise of ambition, and put upon it a most cruel and degrading mockery. And it is, indeed, an affecting sight, to behold the workings of this world's infatuation among so many of our fellow mortals nearing and nearing every day to eternity, and yet, instead of taking heed to that which is before them, mistaking their temporary vehicle for their abiding home—and spending all their time and all their thought upon its accommodations. It is all the doing of our great adversary, thus to invest the trifles of a day in such characters of greatness and durability; and it is, indeed, one of the most formidable of his wiles. And whatever may be the instrument of reclaiming men from this delusion, it certainly is not any argument either about the shortness of life, or the certainty and awfulness of its approaching termination. On this point man is capable of a stout-hearted resistance, even to ocular demonstration; nor do we know a more striking evidence of the bereavement which must have passed upon the human faculties, than to see how, in despite of arithmetic,—how, in despite of manifold experience,—how, in despite of all his gathering wrinkles, and all his growing infirmities,—how, in despite of the ever-lessening distance between him and his sepulchre, and of all the tokens of preparation for the onset of the last messenger, with which, in the shape of weakness, and breathlessness, and dimness of eyes, he is visited; will the feeble and asthmatic man still shake his silver locks in all the glee and transport of which he is capable, when he hears of his gainful adventures, and his new accumulations. Nor can we tell how near he must get to his grave, or how far on he must advance in the process of dying, ere gain cease to delight, and the idol of wealth cease to be dear to him. But when we see that the topic is trade and its profits, which lights up his faded eye with the glow of its chiefest ecstacy, we are as much satisfied that he leaves the world with all his treasure there, and all the desires of his heart there, as if acting what is told of the miser's death-bed, he made his bills and his parchments of security the companions of his bosom, and the last movements of his life were a fearful, tenacious, determined grasp, of what to him formed the all for which life was valuable.

A SERMON,

PREACHED IN ST. ANDREW'S CHURCH EDINBURGH,

BEFORE

THE SOCIETY

FOR

THE RELIEF OF THE DESTITUTE SICK,

APRIL 18, 1813.

"Blessed is he that considereth the poor; the Lord will deliver him in time of trouble."—Psalm xli. 1.

THERE is an evident want of congeniality between the wisdom of this world, and the wisdom of the Christian. The term "wisdom," carries my reverence along with it. It brings before me a grave and respectable character, whose rationality predominates over the inferior principles of his constitution, and to whom I willingly yield that peculiar homage which the enlightened, and the judicious, and the manly, are sure to exact from a surrounding neighbourhood. Now, so long as this wisdom has for its object some secular advantage, I yield it an unqualified reverence. It is a reverence which all understand, and all sympathize with. If, in private life, a man be wise in the management of his farm, or his fortune, or his family; or if, in public life, he have wisdom to steer an empire through all its difficulties, and to carry it to aggrandizement and renown—the respect which I feel for such wisdom as this, is most cordial and entire, and supported by the universal acknowledgment of all whom I call to attend to it.

Let me now suppose that this wisdom has changed its object—that the man whom I am representing to exemplify this respectable attribute, instead of being wise for time, is wise for eternity—that he labours by the faith and sanctification of the gospel for unperishable honours—that, instead of listening to him with admiration at his sagacity, as he talks of business, or politics, or agriculture, we are compelled to listen to him talking of the hope within the veil, and of Christ being the power of God, and the wisdom of God, unto salvation. What becomes of your respect for him now? Are there not some of you who are quite sensible that this respect is greatly impaired, since the wisdom of the man has taken so unaccountable a change in its object and in its direction? The truth is, that the greater part of the world feel no respect at all for a wisdom which they do not comprehend. They may love the innocence of a decidedly religious character, but they feel no sublime or commanding sentiment of veneration for its wisdom. All the truth of the Bible, and all the grandeur of eternity, will not redeem it from a certain degree of contempt. Terms which lower, undervalue, and degrade, suggest themselves to the mind; and strongly dispose it to throw a mean and disagreeable colouring over the man who, sitting loose to the objects of the world, has become altogether a Christian. It is needless to expatiate; but what I have seen myself, and what must have fallen under the observation of many whom I address, carry in them the testimony of experience to the assertion of the Apostle, "that the things of the Spirit of God are foolishness to the natural man, neither can he know them, for they are spiritually discerned."

Now, what I have said of the respectable attribute of wisdom, is applicable, with almost no variation, to another attribute of the human character, to which I would assign the gentler epithet of "lovely." The attribute to which I allude, is that of benevolence. This is the burden of every poet's song, and every eloquent and interesting enthusiast gives it his testimony. I speak not of the enthusiasm of methodists and devotees—I speak of that enthusiasm of fine sentiment which embellishes the pages of elegant literature, and is addressed to all her sighing and amiable votaries, in the various forms of novel, and poetry, and dramatic entertainment. You would think if any thing could bring the Christian at one with the world around him, it would be this; and that in the ardent benevolence which figures in novels, and sparkles in poetry, there would be an entire congeniality with the benevolence of the gospel. I venture to say, however, that there never existed a stronger repulsion between two contending sentiments, than between the benevolence of the Christian, and the benevolence which is the theme of elegant literature—that the one, with all its accompaniments of tears, and sensibilities, and interesting cottages, is neither felt nor understood by the Christian as such; and the other, with its work and labours of love—its *enduring hardness as a good soldier of Jesus Christ*, and its living not to itself, but to the will of Him who died for us, and who rose again, is not only not understood, but positively nauseated, by the poetical *amateur*.

But the contrast does not stop here. The benevolence of the gospel is not only at antipodes with the visionary sons and daughters of poetry, but it even varies in some of its most distinguishing features with the experimental benevolence of real and familiar life. The fantastic benevolence of poetry is now indeed pretty well exploded; and, in the more popular works of the age, there is a benevolence of a far truer and more substantial kind substituted in its place—the benevolence which you meet with among men of business and observation—the benevolence which bustles and finds employment among the most public and ordinary scenes, and which seeks for objects, not where the flower blows loveliest, and the stream, with its gentle murmurs, falls sweetest on the ear, but finds them in his every-day walks—goes in quest of them through the heart of the great city, and is not afraid to meet them in its most putrid lanes and loathsome receptacles.

Now, it must be acknowledged, that this benevolence is of a far more respectable kind than that poetic sensibility, which is of no use, because it admits of no application. Yet I am not afraid to say, that, respectable as it is, it does not come up to the benevolence of the Christian, and is at variance, in some of its most capital ingredients, with the morality of the gospel. It is well, and very well, as far as it goes; and that Christian is wanting to the will of his master who refuses to share and go along with it. The Christian will do all this, but he would like to do more; and it is at the precise point where he proposes to do more, that he finds himself abandoned by the co-operation and good wishes of those who had hitherto supported him. The Christian goes as far as the votary of this useful benevolence, but then he would like to go further, and this is the point at which he is mortified to find that his old coadjutors refuse to go along with him; and that instead of being strengthened by their assistance, he has their contempt and their ridicule; or, at all events, their total want of sympathy, to contend with.

The truth is, that the benevolence I allude to, with all its respectable air of business and good sense, is altogether a secular benevolence. Through all the extent of its operations, it carries in it no reference to the eternal duration of its object. Time, and the accommodations of time, form all its subject and all its exercise. It labours, and often with success, to provide for its object a warm and well-sheltered tenement, but it looks not beyond the few little years when the earthly house of this tabernacle shall be dissolved—when the soul shall be driven from its perishable tenement, and the only benevolence it will acknowledge or care for, will be the benevolence of those who have directed it to a building not made with hands, eternal in the heavens. This, then, is the point at which the benevolence of the gospel separates from that worldly benevolence, to which, as far as it goes, I offer my cheerful and unmingled testimony. The one minds earthly things, the other has its conversation in heaven. Even when the immediate object of both is the same, you will generally perceive an evident distinction in the principle. Individuals, for example, may co-operate, and will often meet in the same room, be members of the same society, and go hand in hand cordially together for the education of the poor. But the forming habits of virtuous industry, and good members of society, which are the sole consideration in the heart of the worldly philanthropist, are but mere accessions in the heart of the Christian. The main impulse of his benevolence lies in furnishing the poor with the means of enjoying that bread of life which came down from heaven, and in introducing them to the knowledge of those scriptures which are the power of God unto salvation to every one who believeth. Now, it is so far a blessing to the world that there is a co-operation in the immediate object. But what I contend for, is, that there is a total want of congeniality in the principle—that the moment you strip the institution of its temporal advantages, and make it repose on the naked grandeur of eternity, it is fallen from, or laughed at as one of the chimeras of fanaticism, and left to the despised efforts of those whom they esteem to be unaccountable people, who subscribe for missions, and squander their money on Bible societies. Strange effect, you would think, of eternity, to degrade the object with which it is connected! But so it is. The blaze of glory, which is thrown around the martyrdom of a patriot or a philosopher, is refused to the martyrdom of a Christian. When a statesman dies, who lifted his intrepid voice for the liberty of the species, we hear of nothing but of the shrines and the monuments of immortality. Put into his place one of those sturdy reformers, who, unmoved by councils and inquisitions, stood up for the religious liberties of the world; and it is no sooner done, than the full tide of congenial sympathy and admiration is at once arrested. We have all heard of the benevolent apostleship of Howard, and what Christian will be behind his fellows with his applauding testimony? But will they, on the other hand, share his enthusiasm when he tells them of the apostleship of Paul, who, in the sublimer sense of the term, accomplished the liberty of the captive, and brought them that sat in darkness out of the prison-house? Will they share in the holy benevolence of the apostle when he pours out his ardent effusions in behalf of his countrymen? They were at that time on the eve of the cruelest sufferings. The whole vengeance of the Roman power was mustering to bear upon them. The siege and destruction of their city form one of the most dreadful tragedies in the history of war. Yet Paul seems to have had another object in his eye. It was their souls and their eternity which engrossed him. Can you sympathise with him in this principle, or join in kindred benevolence with him, when he says, that "my heart's desire and prayer for Israel is that they might be saved?"

But to bring my list of examples to a close, the most remarkable of them all may be collected from the history of the present attempts which are now making to carry the knowledge of divine revelation into the Pagan and uncivilized countries of the world. Now, it may be my ignorance, but I am certainly not aware of the fact, that without a book of religious faith—without religion, in fact, being the errand and occasion, we have never been able in modern times so far to compel the attentions and to subdue the habits of savages, as to throw in among them the use and possession of a written language. Certain it is, however, at all events, that this very greatest step in the process of converting a wild man of the woods into a humanized member of society, has been accomplished by christian missionaries. They have put into the hands of barbarians this mighty instrument of a written language, and they have taught them how to use it.* They have formed an orthography for wandering and untutored savages. They have given a shape and a name to their barbarous articulations; and the children of men, who lived on the prey of the wilderness, are now forming in village schools to the arts and the decencies of cultivated life. Now, I am not involving you in the controversy whether civilization should precede Christianity, or Christianity should precede civilization. It is not to what has been said on the subject, but to what has been done, that we are pointing your attention. We appeal to the fact; and as an illustration of the principle we have been attempting to lay before you, we call upon you to mark the feelings, and the countenance, and the language, of the mere academic moralist, when you put into his hand the authentic and proper document where the fact is recorded—we mean a missionary report, or a missionary magazine. We know that there are men who have so much of the firm nerve and hardihood of philosophy about them, as not to be repelled from the truth in whatever shape, or from whatever quarter it comes to them. But there are others of a humbler cast who have transferred their homage from the omnipotence of truth, to the omnipotence of a name; who, because missionaries, while they are accomplishing the civilization, are labouring also for the eternity of savages, have lifted up the cry of fanaticism against them—who, because missionaries revere the word of God, and utter themselves in the language of the New Testament, nauseate every word that comes from them as overrun with the flavour and phraseology of methodism—who determined, in short, to abominate all that is missionary, and suffer the very sound of the epithet to fill their minds with an overwhelming association of repugnance, and prejudice, and disgust.

We would not have counted this so remarkable an example, had it not been that missionaries are accomplishing the very object on which the advocates for civilization love to expatiate. They are working for the temporal good far more effectually than any adventurer in the cause ever did before; but mark the want of congeniality between the benevolence of this world, and the benevolence of the Christian; they incur contempt, because they are working for the spiritual and eternal good also. Nor do the earthly blessings which they scatter so

---

* As, for instance, Mr. John Elliot, and the Moravian brethren among the Indians of New England and Pennsylvania; the Moravians of South America; Mr. Hans Egede, and the Moravians in Greenland; the latter in Labradore, among the Eskimaux; the missionaries of Otaheite, and other South Sea islands; and Mr. Brunton, under the patronage of the Society for Missions to Africa and the East, who reduced the language of the Susoos, a nation on the coast of Africa, to writing and grammatical form, and printed in it a spelling-book, vocabulary, catechism, and some tracts. Other instances besides might be given.

abundantly in their way, redeem from scorn the purer and the nobler principle which inspires them.

These observations seem to be an applicable introduction to the subject before us. I call your attention to *the way* in which the Bible enjoins us to take up the care of the poor. It does not say, in the text before us, Commiserate the poor; for, if it said no more than this, it would leave their necessities to be provided for by the random ebullitions of an impetuous and unreflecting sympathy. It provides them with a better security than the mere feeling of compassion—a feeling which, however useful for the purpose of excitement, must be controlled and regulated. Feeling is but a faint and fluctuating security. Fancy may mislead it. The sober realities of life may disgust it. Disappointment may extinguish it. Ingratitude may embitter it. Deceit, with its counterfeit representations, may allure it to the wrong object. At all events, Time is the little circle within which it in general expatiates. It needs the impression of sensible objects to sustain it; nor can it enter with zeal or with vivacity into the wants of the abstract and invisible soul. The Bible, then, instead of leaving the relief of the poor to the mere instinct of sympathy, makes it a subject for *consideration*—Blessed is he that *considereth* the poor—a grave and prosaic exercise I do allow, and which makes no figure in those high wrought descriptions, where the exquisite tale of benevolence is made up of all the sensibilities of tenderness on the one hand, and of all the ecstacies of gratitude on the other. The Bible rescues the cause from the mischief to which a heedless or unthinking sensibility would expose it. It brings it under the cognizance of a higher faculty—a faculty of steadier operation than to be weary in well-doing, and of sturdier endurance than to give it up in disgust. It calls you to *consider* the poor. It makes the virtue of relieving them a matter of computation as well as of sentiment; and in so doing, it puts you beyond the reach of the various delusions by which you are at one time led to prefer the indulgence of pity to the substantial interest of its object; at another, are led to retire chagrined and disappointed from the scene of duty, because you have not met with the gratitude or the honesty that you laid your account with; at another, are led to expend all your anxieties upon the accommodation of time, and to overlook eternity. It is the office of *consideration* to save you from all these fallacies. Under its tutorage, attention to the wants of the poor ripens into principle. I want, my brethren, to press its advantages upon you, for I can in no other way recommend the society whose claims I am appointed to lay before you, so effectually to your patronage. My time will only permit me to lay before you a few of their advantages, and I shall therefore confine myself to two leading particulars.

I. The man who considers the poor, instead of slumbering over the emotions of a useless sensibility, among those imaginary beings whom poetry and romance have laid before him in all the elegance of fictitious history, will bestow the labour and the attention of actual business among the poor of the real and the living world. Benevolence is the burden of every romantic tale, and of every poet's song. It is dressed out in all the fairy enchantments of imagery, and eloquence. All is beauty to the eye and music to the ear. Nothing seen but pictures of felicity, and nothing heard but the soft whispers of gratitude and affection. The reader is carried along by this soft and delightful representation of virtue. He accompanies his hero through all the fancied varieties of his history. He goes along with him to the cottage of poverty and disease, surrounded, as we may suppose, with all the charms of rural obscurity, and where the murmurs of an adjoining rivulet accord with the finer and more benevolent sensibilities of the mind. He enters this enchanting retirement, and meets with a picture of distress, adorned in all the elegance of fiction. Perhaps a father laid on a bed of languishing, and supported by the labours of a pious and affectionate family, where kindness breathes in every word, and anxiety sits upon every countenance—where the industry of his children struggles in vain to supply the cordials which his poverty denies him—where nature sinks every hour, and all feel a gloomy foreboding, which they strive to conceal, and tremble to express. The hero of romance enters, and the glance of his benevolent eye enlightens this darkest recess of misery. He turns him to the bed of languishing, tells the sick man that there is still hope, and smiles comfort on his despairing children. Day after day he repeats his kindness and his charity. They hail his approach as the footsteps of an angel of mercy. The father lives to bless his deliverer. The family reward his benevolence by the homage of an affectionate gratitude; and, in the piety of their evening prayer, offer up thanks to the God of heaven, for opening the hearts of the rich to kindly and beneficent attentions. The reader weeps with delight. The visions of paradise play before his fancy. His tears flow, and his heart dissolves in all the luxury of tenderness.

Now, we do not deny that the members of the Destitute Sick Society *may* at times have met with some such delightful scene to soothe and encourage them. But put the question to any of their visitors, and he will not fail to tell you, that if they had never moved but when they had something like this to excite and to gratify their hearts, they would seldom have moved at all; and their usefulness to the poor would have been reduced to a very humble fraction of what they have actually done for them. What is this but to say, that it is the business of a religious instructor to give you, not the elegant, but the true representation of benevolence—to represent it not so much as a luxurious indulgence to the finer sensibilities of the mind, but according to the sober declaration of Scripture, as a work and as a labour—as a business in which you must encounter vexation, opposition, and fatigue; where you are not always to meet with that elegance, which allures the fancy, or with that humble and retired adversity, which interests the more tender propensities of the heart; but as a business where reluctance must often be overcome by a sense of duty, and where, though oppressed at every step, by envy, disgust, and disappointment, you are bound to persevere, in obedience to the law of God, and the sober instigation of principle.

The benevolence of the gospel lies in actions. The benevolence of our fictitious writers, in a kind of high-wrought delicacy of feeling and sentiment. The one dissipates all its fervour in sighs and tears, and idle aspirations—the other reserves its strength for efforts and execution. The one regards it as a luxurious enjoyment for the heart—the other, as a work and business for the hand. The one sits in indolence, and broods, in visionary rapture, over its schemes of ideal philanthropy—the other steps abroad, and enlightens by its presence, the dark and pestilential hovels of disease. The one wastes away in empty ejaculation—the other gives time and trouble to the work of beneficence—gives education to the orphan—provides clothes for the naked, and lays food on the table of the hungry. The one is indolent and capricious, and often does mischief by the occasional overflowings of a whimsical and ill-directed charity—the other is vigilant and discerning, and takes care lest his distributions be injudicious, and the effort of benevolence be misapplied. The one is soothed with the luxury of feeling, and reclines in easy and indolent satisfaction—the other shakes off the deceitful languor of contemplation and solitude, and delights in a scene of activity.—Remember, that virtue, in general, is not to feel, but to do; not merely to conceive a purpose, but to carry that purpose into execution; not merely to be overpowered by the impression of a sentiment, but to practise what it loves, and to imitate what it admires.

To be benevolent in speculation, is often to be selfish in action and in reality. The vanity and the indolence of man delude him into a thousand inconsistencies. He professes to love the name and the semblance of virtue, but the labour of exertion and of self-denial terrifies him from attempting it. The emotions of kindness are delightful to his bosom, but then they are little better than a selfish indulgence—they terminate in his own enjoyment—they are a mere refinement of luxury. His eye melts over the picture of fictitious distress while not a tear is left for the actual starvation and misery with which he is surrounded. It is easy to indulge the imaginations of a visionary heart in going over a scene of fancied affliction, because here there is no sloth to overcome—no avaricious propensity to control—no offensive or disgusting circumstance to allay the unmingled impression of sympathy which a soft and elegant picture is calculated to awaken. It is not so easy to be benevolent in action and in reality, because here there is fatigue to undergo—there is time and money to give—there is the mortifying spectacle of vice, and folly, and ingratitude, to encounter. We like to give you the fair picture of love to man, because to throw over it false and fictitious embellishments, is injurious to its cause. These elevate the fancy by romantic visions which can never be realized. They embitter the heart by the most severe and mortifying disappointments, and often force us to retire in disgust from what heaven has intended to be the theatre of our discipline and preparation. Take the representation of the Bible. Benevolence is a work and a labour. It often calls for the severest efforts of vigilance and industry—a habit of action not to be acquired in the school of fine sentiment, but in the walks of business, in the dark and dismal receptacles of misery—in the hospitals of disease—in the putrid lanes of great cities, where poverty dwells in lank and ragged wretchedness, agonized with pain, faint with hunger, and shivering in a frail and unsheltered tenement.

You are not to conceive yourself a real lover of your species, and entitled to the praise or the reward of benevolence, because you weep over a fictitious representation of human misery. A man may weep in the indolence of a studious and contemplative retirement; he may breathe all the tender aspirations of humanity; but what avails all this warm and diffusive benevolence, if it is never exerted—if it never rise to execution—if it never carry him to the accomplishment of a single benevolent purpose—if it shrink from activity, and sicken at the pain of fatigue? It is easy, indeed, to come forward with the cant and hypocrisy of fine sentiment—to have a heart trained to the emotions of benevolence, while the hand refuses the labours of discharging its offices—to weep for amusement, and to have nothing to spare for human suffering but the tribute of an indolent and unmeaning sympathy. Many of you must be acquainted with that corruption of Christian doctrine, which has been termed Antinomianism. It professes the highest reverence for the Supreme Being, while it refuses obedience to the lessons of his authority. It professes the highest gratitude for the sufferings of Christ, while it refuses that course of life and action, which he demands of his followers. It professes to adore the tremendous Majesty of heaven, and to weep in shame and in sorrow over the sinfulness of degraded humanity, while every day it insults Heaven by the enormity of its misdeeds, and evinces the insincerity of its wilful perseverance in the practice of iniquity. This Antinomianism is generally condemned; and none reprobate it more than the votaries of fine sentiment—your men of taste and elegant literature—your epicures of feeling, who riot in all the luxury of theatrical emotion, and who, in their admiration of what is tender, and beautiful, and cultivated, have always turned with disgust from the doctrines of a sour and illiberal theology. We may say to such, as Nathan to David, "Thou art the man." Theirs is to all intents and purposes Antinomianism—and an Antinomianism of a far more dangerous and deceitful kind, than the Antinomianism of a spurious and pretended orthodoxy. In the Antinomianism of religion, there is nothing to fascinate or deceive you. It wears an air of repulsive bigotry, more fitted to awaken disgust than to gain the admiration of proselytes. There is a glaring deformity in its aspect, which alarms you at the very outset, and is an outrage to that natural morality which, dark and corrupted as it is, is still strong enough to lift its loud remonstrance against it. But in the Antinomianism of high wrought sentiment, there is a deception far more insinuating. It steals upon you under the semblance of virtue. It is supported by the delusive colouring of imagination and poetry. It has all the graces and embellishments of literature to recommend it. Vanity is soothed, and conscience lulls itself to repose in this dream of feeling and of indolence.

Let us dismiss these lying vanities, and regulate our lives by the truth and soberness of the New Testament. Benevolence is not in word and in tongue, but in deed and in truth. It is a business with men as they are, and with human life as drawn by the rough hand of experience. It is a duty which you must perform at the call of principle, though there be no voice of eloquence to give splendour to your exertions, and no music or poetry to lead your willing footsteps through the bowers of enchantment. It is not the impulse of high and ecstatic emotion. It is an exertion of principle. You must go to the poor man's cottage, though no verdure flourish around it, and no rivulet be nigh to delight you by the gentleness of its murmurs. If you look for the romantic simplicity of fiction you will be disappointed: but it is your duty to persevere, in spite of every discouragement. Benevolence is not merely a feeling, but a principle; not a dream of rapture for the fancy to indulge in, but a business for the hand to execute.

It must now be obvious to all of you, that it is not enough that you give money, and add your name to the contributors of charity—you must give it with judgment. You must give your time and your attention. You must descend to the trouble of examination. You must rise from the repose of contemplation, and make yourself acquainted with the objects of your benevolent exercises. Will he husband your charity with care, or will he squander it away in idleness and dissipation? Will he satisfy himself with the brutal luxury of the moment, and neglect the supply of his more substantial necessities, or suffer his children to be trained in ignorance and depravity? Will charity corrupt him by laziness? What is his peculiar necessity? Is it the want of health or the want of employment? Is it the pressure of a numerous family? Does he need medicine to administer to the diseases of his children? Does he need fuel or raiment to protect them from the inclemency of winter? Does he need money to satisfy the yearly demands of his landlord, or to purchase books, and to pay for the education of his offspring?

To give money is not to do all the work and labour of benevolence. You must go to the poor man's bed. You must lend your hand to the work of assistance. You must examine his accounts. You must try to recover those debts which are due to his family. You must try to recover those wages which are detained by the injustice or the rapacity of his master. You must employ your mediation with his superiors. You must represent to them the necessities of his situation. You must solicit their assistance, and awaken their feelings to the tale of his calamity. This is benevolence in its plain, and sober, and substantial reality, though eloquence may have withheld its imagery, and poetry may have denied its graces and its embellishments. This is true and unsophisticated goodness. It may be recorded in no earthly documents; but if done under the influence of christian principle—in a word, done unto Jesus, it is written in the book of heaven, and will give a new lustre to that crown to which his disciples look forward in time, and will wear through eternity.

You have all heard of the division of labour, and I wish you to understand, that the advantage of this principle may be felt as much in the operations of charity, as in the operations of trade and manufactures. The work of beneficence does not lie in the one act of giving money; there must be the act of attendance; there must be the act of inquiry; there must be the act of judicious application. But I can conceive that an individual may be so deficient in the varied experience and attention which a work so extensive demands, that he may retire in disgust and discouragement from the practice of charity altogether. The institution of a Society, such as this, saves this individual to the cause. It takes upon itself all the subsequent acts in the work and labour of love, and restricts his part to the mere act of giving money. It fills the middle space between the dispensers and the recipients of charity. The habits of many who now hear me, may disqualify them for the work of examination. They may have no time for it; they may live at a distance from the objects; they may neither know how to introduce, nor how to conduct themselves in the management of all the details; their want of practice and of experience may disable them for the work of repelling imposition; they should try to gain the necessary habits; it is right that every individual among us, should each, in his own sphere, consider the poor, and qualify themselves for a judicious and discriminating charity. But, in the mean time, the Society for the Relief of the Destitute Sick, is an instrument ready made to our hands. Avail yourselves of this instrument immediately, as, by the easiest part of the exercise of charity, which is to give money, you carry home to the poor all the benefits of its most difficult exercises. The experience which you want, the members of this laudable Society are in possession of. By the work and observation of years, a stock of practical wisdom is now accumulated among them. They have been long inured to all that is loathsome and discouraging in this good work, and they have nerve, and hardihood, and principle to front it. They are every way qualified to be the carriers of your bounty, for it is a path they have long travelled in. Give the money, and these conscientious men will soon bring it into contact with the right objects. They know the way through all the obscurities of this metropolis, and they they can bring the offerings of your charity to people whom you will never see, and into houses which you will never enter. It is not easy to conceive, far less to compute the extent of human misery; but these men can give you experience for it. They can show you their registers of the sick and of the dying; they are familiar with disease in all its varieties of faintness, and breathlessness, and pain.—

Sad union! they are called to witness it in conjunction with poverty; and well do they know that there is an eloquence in the imploring looks of these helpless poor, which no description can set before you. Oh! my brethren, figure to yourselves the calamity in all its soreness, and measure your bounty by the actual greatness of the claims, and not by the feebleness of their advocate.

I have trespassed upon your patience; but, at the hazard of carrying my address to a length that is unusual, I must still say more. Nor would I ever forgive myself if I neglected to set the eternity of the poor in all its importance before you. This is the second point of consideration to which I wish to direct you. The man who considers the poor will give his chief anxiety to the wants of their eternity. It must be evident to all of you that this anxiety is little felt. I do not appeal for the evidence of this to the selfish part of mankind—there we are not to expect it. I go to those who are really benevolent—who have a wish to make others happy, and who take trouble in so doing; and it is a striking observation, how little the salvation of these others is the object of that benevolence which makes them so amiable. It will be found that in and by far the greater number of instances, this principle is all consumed on the accommodations of time, and the necessities of the body. It is the meat which feeds them—the garment which covers them—the house which shelters them—the money which purchases all things; these, I say, are what form the chief topics of benevolent anxieties. Now, we do not mean to discourage this principle. We cannot afford it; there is too little of it; and it forms too refreshing an exception to that general selfishness which runs throughout the haunts of business and ambition, for us to say any thing against it. We are not cold-blooded enough to refuse our delighted concurrence to an exertion so amiable in its principle, and so pleasing in the warm and comfortable spectacle which it lays before us. The poor, it is true, ought never to forget, that it is to their own industry, and to the wisdom and economy of their own management, that they are to look for the elements of subsistence—that if idleness and prodigality shall lay hold of the mass of our population, no benevolence, however unbounded, can ever repair a mischief so irrecoverable—that if they will not labour for themselves, it is not in the power of the rich to create a sufficiency for them; and that though every heart were opened, and every purse emptied in the cause, it would absolutely go for nothing towards forming a well-fed, a well-lodged, or a well conditioned peasantry. Still, however, there are cases which no foresight could prevent, and no industry could provide for—where the blow falls heavy and unexpected on some devoted son or daughter of misfortune, and where, though thoughtlessness and folly may have had their share, benevolence, not very nice in its calculations, will feel the overpowering claim of actual, helpless, and imploring misery. Now, I again offer my cheerful testimony to such benevolence as this; I count it delightful to see it singling out its object; and sustaining it against the cruel pressure of age and of indigence; and when I enter a cottage where I see a warmer fire-side, or more substantial provision, than the visible means can account for, I say that the landscape, in all its summer glories, does not offer an object so gratifying, as when referred to the vicinity of the great man's house, and the people who live in it, and am told that I will find my explanation *there*. Kind and amiable people! your benevolence is most lovely in its display, but oh! it is perishable in its consequences. Does it never occur to you that in a few years this favourite will die—and that he will go to the place where neither cold nor hunger will reach him, but that a mighty interest remains, of which both of us may know the certainty, though neither you nor I can calculate the extent. Your benevolence is too short.—It does not shoot far enough a-head.—It is like regaling a child with a sweetmeat or a toy, and then abandoning the happy, unreflecting infant to exposure. You make the poor old man happy with your crumbs and your fragments, but he is an infant on the mighty range of infinite duration; and will you leave the soul, which has the infinity to go through, to its chance? How comes it that the grave should throw so impenetrable a shroud over the realities of eternity? How comes it that heaven, and hell, and judgment, should be treated as so many nonentities, and that there should be as little real and operative sympathy felt for the soul which lives forever, as for the body after it is dead, or for the dust into which it moulders? Eternity is longer than time; the arithmetic, my brethren, is all one side upon this question; and the wisdom which calculates, and guides itself by calculation, gives its weighty and respectable support to what may be called the benevolence of faith.

Now, if there be one employment more fitted than another to awaken this benevolence, it is the peculiar employment of that Society for which I am now pleading. I would have anticipated such benevolence from the situation they occupy, and the information before the public bears testimony to the fact. The truth is, that the diseases of he body may be looked upon as so many outlets through which the soul finds its way to eternity. Now, it is at these outlets that the members of this Society have stationed themselves. This is the interesting point of survey at which they stand, and from which they command a look of both worlds. They have placed themselves in the avenues which lead from time to eternity, and they have often to witness the awful transition of a soul hovering at the entrance—struggling its way through the valley of the shadow of death, and at last breaking loose from the confines of all that is visible. Do you think it likely that men with such spectacles before them, will withstand the sense of eternity? No, my brethren, they cannot, they have not. Eternity, I rejoice to announce to you, is not forgotten by them; and with their care for the diseases of the body, they are neither blind nor indifferent to the fact, that the soul is diseased also. We know it well. There is an indolent and superficial theology, which turns its eyes from the danger, and feels no pressing call for the application of the remedy—which reposes more in its own vague and self-assumed conceptions of the mercy of God, than in the firm and consistent representations of the New Testament—which overlooks the existence of disease altogether, and therefore feels no alarm, and exerts no urgency in the business—which, in the face of all the truths and all the severities that are uttered in the word of God, leaves the soul to its chance; or, in other words, by neglecting to administer every thing specific for the salvation of the soul, leaves it to perish.

We do not want to involve you in controversies; we only ask you to open the New Testament, and attend to the obvious meaning of a word which occurs frequently in its pages—we mean the word *saved*. The term surely implies, that the present state of the thing to be saved is a lost and an undone state. If a tree be in a healthful state from its infancy, you never apply the term saved to it, though you see its beautiful foliage, its flourishing blossoms, its abundant produce, and its progressive ascent through all the varieties incidental to a sound and a prosperous tree. But if it were diseased in its infancy, and ready to perish, and if it were restored by management and artificial applications, then you would say of this tree that it was *saved*; and the very term implies some previous state of uselessness and corruption. What, then, are we to make of the frequent occurrence of this term in the New Testament, as applied to a human being? If men come into this world pure and innocent, and have nothing more to do but to put forth the powers with which nature has endowed them, and so rise through the progressive stages of virtue and excellence, to the rewards of immortality, you would not say of these men that they were saved, when they were translated to these rewards. These rewards of man are the natural effects of his obedience, and the term *saved* is not at all applicable to such a supposition. But the God of the Bible says differently. If a man obtain heaven at all, it is by being saved. He is in a diseased state, and it is by the healing application of the blood of the Son of God, that he is restored from that state. The very title applied to him proves the same thing. He is called *our Saviour*. The deliverance which he effects is called our salvation. The men whom he doth deliver are called the *saved*. Doth not this imply some previous state of disease and helplessness? And from the frequent and incidental occurrence of this term, may we not gather an additional testimony to the truth of what is elsewhere more expressly revealed to us, that we are lost by nature, and that to obtain recovery, we must be found in Him who came to seek and to save that which was lost. He that believeth on the Son of God shall be saved, but he that believeth not, the wrath of God abideth on him.

We know that there are some who loathe this representation; but this is just another example of the substantial interests of the poor being sacrificed to mismanagement and delusion. It is to be hoped that there are many who have looked the disease fairly in the face, and are ready to reach forward the remedy adapted to relieve it. We should have no call to attend to the spiritual interests of men, if they could safely be left to themselves, and to the spontaneous operation of those powers with which it is supposed that nature has endowed them. But this is not the state of the case. We come into the world with the principles of sin and condemnation within us; and, in the congenial atmosphere of this world's example, these ripen fast for the execution of the sentence. During the period of this short but interesting passage to another world, the remedy is in the gospel held out to all, and the freedom and universality of its invitations, while it opens assured admission to all who will, must aggravate the weight and severity of the sentence to those who will not; and upon them the dreadful energy of that saying will be accomplished,—"How shall they escape if they neglect so great a salvation?"

We know part of your labours for the eternity of the poor. We know that you have brought the Bible into contact with many a soul. And we are sure that this is suiting the remedy to the disease; for the Bible contains those words which are the power of God through faith unto salvation, to every one who believes them.

To this established instrument for working faith in the heart, add the instrument of hearing. When you give the Bible, accompany the gift with the living energy of a human voice—let prayer, and advice, and explanation, be brought to act upon them; and let the warm and deeply felt earnestness of your hearts, discharge itself upon theirs in the impressive tones of sincerity, and friendship, and good will. This is going substantially to work. It is, if I may use the expression, bringing the right element to bear upon the case before you; and be assured, every treatment of a convinced and guilty mind is superficial and ruinous, which does not lead it to the Saviour, and bring before it his sacrifice and atonement, and the influences of that spirit bestowed through his obedience on all who believe on Him.

While in the full vigour of health we may count it enough to take up with something short of this. But—striking testimony to evangelical truth! go to the awful reality of a human soul on the eve of its departure from the body, and you will find that all those vapid sentimentalities which partake not of the substantial doctrine of the New Testament, are good for nothing. Hold up your face, my brethren, for the truth and simplicity of the Bible. Be not ashamed of its phraseology. It is the right instrument to handle in the great work of calling a human soul out of darkness into marvellous light. Stand firm and secure on the impregnable principle, that this is the word of God, and that all taste, and imagination, and science, must give way before its overbearing authority. Walk in the footsteps of your Saviour, in the twofold office of caring for the diseases of the body, and administering to the wants of the soul; and though you may fail in the former—though the patient may never arise and walk, yet, by the blessing of Heaven upon your fervent and effectual endeavours, the latter object may be gained—the soul may be lightened of all its anxieties, the whole burden of its diseases may be swept away—it may be of good cheer, because its sins are forgiven—and the right direction may be impressed upon it, which will carry it forward in progress to a happy eternity. Death may not be averted, but death may be disarmed. It may be stript of its terrors, and instead of a devouring enemy, it may be hailed as a messenger of triumph.

THOUGHTS ON UNIVERSAL PEACE.

A SERMON,

DELIVERED ON THURSDAY, JANUARY 18, 1816, THE DAY OF NATIONAL THANKSGIVING FOR THE RESTORATION OF PEACE.

" Nation shall not lift up sword against nation, neither shall they learn war any more."—*Isaiah* ii. 4.

THERE are a great many passages in Scripture which warrant the expectation that a time is coming, when an end shall be put to war—when its abominations and its cruelties shall be banished from the face of the earth—when those restless elements of ambition and jealousy which have so long kept the species in a state of unceasing commotion, and are ever and anon sending another and another wave over the field of this world's politics, shall at length be hushed into a placid and ever-during calm; and many and delightful are the images which the Bible employs, as guided by the light of prophecy, it carries us forward to those millennial days, when the reign of peace shall be established, and the wide charity of the gospel, which is confined by no limits, and owns no distinctions, shall embosom the whole human race within the ample grasp of one harmonious and universal family.

But before I proceed, let me attempt to do away a delusion which exists on the subject of prophecy. Its fulfilments are all certain, say many, and we have therefore nothing to do, but to wait for them in passive and indolent expectation. The truth of God stands in no dependence on human aid to vindicate the immutability of all his announcements; and the power of God stands in no need of the feeble exertions of man to hasten the accomplishment of any of his purposes. Let us therefore sit down quietly in the attitude of spectators—let us leave the Divinity to do his own work in his own way, and mark, by the progress of a history over which we have no control, the evolution of his designs, and the march of his wise and beneficent administration.

Now, it is very true, that the Divinity will do his own work in his own way, but if he choose to tell us that that way is not without the instrumentality of men, but by their instrumentality, might not this sitting down into the mere attitude of spectators, turn out to be a most perverse and disobedient conclusion? It is true, that his purpose will obtain its fulfilment, whether we shall offer or not to help it forward by our co-operation. But if the object is to be brought about, and if, in virtue of the same sovereignty by which he determined upon the object, he has also determined on the way which leads to it, and that that way shall be by the acting of human principle, and the putting forth of human exertion, then, let us keep back our co-operation as we may, God will raise up the hearts of others to that which we abstain from; and they, admitted into the high honour of being fellow-workers with God, may do homage to the truth of his prophecy, while we, perhaps, may unconsciously do dreadful homage to the truth of another warning, and another prophecy: "I work a work in your days which you shall not believe, though a man declare it unto you. Behold, ye despisers, and wonder and perish."

Now this is the very way in which prophecies have been actually fulfilled. The return of the people of Israel to their own land, was an event predicted by inspiration, and was brought about by the stirring up of the spirit of Cyrus, who felt himself charged with the duty of building a house to God at Jerusalem. The pouring out of the Spirit on the day of Pentecost was foretold by the Saviour ere he left the world, and was accomplished upon men who assembled themselves together at the place to which they were commanded to repair; and there they waited, and they prayed. The rapid propagation of Christianity in those days was known by the human agents of this propagation, to be made sure by the word of prophecy; but the way in which it was actually made sure, was by the strenuous exertions, the unexampled heroism, the holy devotedness and zeal of martyrs, and apostles, and evangelists. And even now, my brethren, while no professing Christian can deny that their faith is to be one day the faith of all countries; but while many of them idly sit and wait the time of God putting forth some mysterious and unheard of agency, to bring about the universal diffusion, there are men who have betaken themselves to the obvious expedient of going abroad among the nations, and teaching them; and though derided by an undeserving world, they seem to be the very men pointed out by the Bible, who are going to and fro increasing the knowledge of its doctrines, and who will be the honoured instruments of carrying into effect the most splendid of all its anticipations.

Now, the same holds true, I apprehend, of the prophecy in my text. The abolition of war will be the effect not of any sudden or resistless visitation from heaven on the character of men—not of any mystical influence working with all the omnipotence of a charm on the passive hearts of those who are the subjects of it—not of any blind or overruling fatality which will come upon the earth at some distant period of its history, and about which, we, of the present day, have nothing to do but to look silently on, without concern, and without co-operation. The prophecy of a peace as universal as the spread of the human race, and as enduring as the moon in the firmament, will meet its accomplishment, ay, and at that very time which is already fixed by Him who seeth the end of all things from the beginning thereof. But it will be brought about by the activity of men. It will be done by the philanthropy of thinking and intelligent Christians. The conversion of the Jews—the spread of the gospel light among the regions of idolatry—these are distinct subjects of prophecy, on which the faithful of the land are now acting, and to the fulfilment of which they are giving their zeal and their energy. I conceive the prophecy which relates to the final abolition of war will be taken up in the same manner, and the subject will be brought to the test of christian principle, and many will unite to spread a growing sense of its follies and its enormities, over the countries of the world—and the public will be enlightened, not by the factious and turbulent declamations of a party, but by the mild dissemination of gospel sentiment through the land—and the prophecy contained in this book will pass into effect and accomplishment, by no other influence than the influence of its ordinary lessons on the hearts and consciences of individuals—and the measure will first be carried in one country, not by the unhallowed violence of discontent, but by the control of general opinion, expressed on the part of a people, who, if Christian in their repugnance to war, will be equally Christian in all the loyalties, and subjections, and meek unresisting virtues of the New Testament—and the sacred fire of good-will to the children of men will spread itself through all climes, and through all latitudes—and thus by scriptural truth conveyed with power from one people to another, and taking its ample round among all the tribes and families of the earth, shall we arrive at the magnificent result of peace throughout all its provinces, and security in all its dwelling-places.

In the further prosecution of this discourse, I shall, first, expatiate a little on the evils of war.

In the second place, I shall direct your attention to the obstacles which stand in the way of its extinction, and which threaten to retard for a time the accomplishment of the prophecy I have now selected for your consideration.

And, in the third place, I shall endeavour to point out, what can only be done at present in a hurried and superficial manner, some of the expedients by which these obstacles may be done away.

I. I shall expatiate a little on the evils of war. The mere existence of the prophecy in my text, is a sentence of condemnation upon war, and stamps a criminality on its very forehead. So soon as Christianity shall gain a full ascendency in the world, from that moment war is to disappear. We have heard that there is something noble in the art of war; that there is something generous in the ardour of that fine chivalric spirit which kindles in the hour of alarm, and rushes with delight among the thickest scenes of danger and of enterprise;—that man is never more proudly arrayed, than when, elevated by a contempt for death, he puts on his intrepid front, and looks serene, while the arrows of destruction are flying on every side of him:—that expunge war, and you expunge some of the brightest names in the catalogue of human virtue, and demolish that theatre on which have been displayed some of the sublimest energies of the human character. It is thus that war has been invested with a most pernicious splendour, and men have offered to justify it as a blessing and an ornament to society, and attempts have been made to throw a kind of imposing morality around it; and one might almost be reconciled to the whole train of its calamities and its horrors, did he not believe his Bible, and learn from its information, that in the days of perfect righteousness, there will be no war;—that so soon as the character of man has had the last finish of Christian principle thrown over it, from that moment all the instruments of war will be thrown aside, and all its lessons will be forgotten: that therefore what are called the virtues of war, are no virtues at all, or that a better and a worthier scene will be provided for their exercise; but in short, that at the commencement of that blissful era, when the reign of heaven shall be established, war will take its departure from the world with all the other plagues and atrocities of the species.

But apart altogether from this testimony to the evil of war, let us just take a direct look of it, and see whether we can find its character engraved on the aspect it bears to the eye of an attentive observer. The stoutest heart of this assembly would recoil, were he who owns it, to behold the destruction of a single individual by some deed of violence. Were the man who at this moment stands before you in the full play and energy of health, to be in another moment laid by some deadly aim a lifeless corpse at your feet, there is not one of you who would not prove how strong are the relentings of nature at a spectacle so hideous as death. There are some of you who would be haunted for whole days by the image of horror you had witnessed—who would feel the weight of a most oppressive sensation upon your heart, which nothing but time could wear away—who would be so pursued by it as to be unfit for business or for enjoyment—who would think of it through the day, and it would spread a gloomy disquietude over your waking moments—who would dream of it at night, and it would turn that bed which you courted as a retreat from the torments of an ever-meddling memory, into a scene of restlessness.

But generally the death of violence is not instantaneous, and there is often a sad and dreary interval between its final consummation, and the infliction of the blow which causes it. The winged messenger of destruction has not found its direct avenue to that spot, where the principle of life is situated—and the soul, finding obstacles to its immediate egress, has to struggle it for hours, ere it can make its weary way through the winding avenues of that tenement, which has been torn open by a brother's hand. O! my brother, if there be something appalling in the suddenness of death, think not that when gradual in its advances, you will alleviate the horrors of this sickening contemplation, by viewing it in a milder form. O! tell me, if there be any relentings of pity in your bosom, how could you endure it, to behold the agonies of the dying man—as goaded by pain, he grasps the cold ground in convulsive energy, or faint with the loss of blood, his pulse ebbs low, and the gathering paleness spreads itself over his countenance; or wrapping himself round in despair, he can only mark by a few feeble quiverings, that life still lurks and lingers in his lacerated body; or lifting up a faded eye, he casts on you a look of imploring helplessness, for that succour which no sympathy can yield him. It may be painful to dwell on such a representation; but this is the way in which the cause of humanity is served. The eye of the sentimentalist turns away from its sufferings, and he passes by on the other side, lest he hear that pleading voice, which is armed with a tone of remonstrance so vigorous as to disturb him. He cannot bear thus to pause, in imagination, on the distressing picture of one individual, but multiply it ten thousand times; say, how much of all this distress has been heaped together upon a single field; give us the arithmetic of this accumulated wretchedness, and lay it before us with all the accuracy of an official computation—and strange to tell, not one sigh is lifted up among the crowd of eager listeners, as they stand on tiptoe, and catch every syllable of utterance, which is read to them out of the registers of death. O! say, what mystic spell is that, which so blinds us to the sufferings of our brethren; which deafens to our ear the voice of bleeding humanity, when it is aggravated by the shriek of dying thousands; which makes the very magnitude of the slaughter, throw a softening disguise over its cruelties, and its horrors; which causes us to eye with indifference, the field that is crowded with the most revolting abominations, and arrests that sigh, which each individual would singly have drawn from us, by the report of the many who have fallen, and breathed their last in agony along with them.

I am not saying that the burden of all this criminality rests upon the head of the immediate combatants. It lies somewhere; but who can deny that a soldier may be a Christian, and that from the bloody field on which his body is laid, his soul may wing its ascending way to the shores of a peaceful eternity? But when I think that the Christians, even of the great world, form but a very little flock, and that an army is not a propitious soil for the growth of christian principle—when I think on the character of one such army, that had been led on for years by a ruffian ambition, and been inured to scenes of barbarity, and had gathered a most ferocious hardihood of soul, from the many enterprises of violence to which an unprincipled commander had carried them—when I follow them to the field of battle, and further think, that on both sides of an exasperated contest—the gentleness of Christianity can have no place in almost any bosom; but that nearly every heart is lighted up with fury, and breathes a vindictive purpose against a brother of the species, I cannot but reckon it among the most fearful of the calamities of war—that while the work of death is thickening along its ranks, so many disembodied spirits should pass into the presence of Him who sitteth upon the throne, in such a posture, and with such a preparation.

I have no time, and assuredly as little taste, for expatiating on a topic so melancholy, nor can I afford at present, to set before you a vivid picture of the other miseries which war carries in its train—how it desolates every country through which it rolls, and spreads violation and alarm among its villages—how, at its approach, every home pours forth its trembling fugitives —how all the rights of property, and all the provisions of justice must give way before its devouring exactions—how, when Sabbath comes, no Sabbath charm comes along with it—and for the sound of the church bell, which wont to spread its music over some fine landscape of nature, and summon rustic worshippers to the house of prayer—nothing is heard but the deathful vollies of the battle, and the maddening outcry of infuriated men—how, as the fruit of victory, an unprincipled licentiousness, which no discipline can restrain, is suffered to walk at large among the people—and all that is pure, and reverend, and holy, in the virtue of families, is cruelly trampled on, and held in the bitterest derision.

Oh! my brethren, were we to pursue those details, which no pen ever attempts, and no chronicle perpetuates, we should be tempted to ask, what that is which civilization has done for the character of the species? It has thrown a few paltry embellishments over the surface of human affairs, and for the order of society, it has reared the defences of law around the rights and the property of the individuals who compose it. But let war, legalized as you may, and ushered into the field with all the parade of forms and manifestos—let this war only have its season, and be suffered to overleap these artificial defences, and you will soon see how much the security of the commonwealth is due to positive restrictions, and how little of it is due to a natural sense of justice among men. I know well, that the plausibilities of human character which abound in every modern and enlightened society, have been mustered up to oppose the doctrine of the Bible, on the woful depravity of our race. But out of the history of war, I can gather for this doctrine the evidence of experiment. It tells me, that man when left to himself, and let loose among his fellows, to walk after the counsel of his own heart, and in the sight of his own eyes, will soon discover how thin that tinsel is, which the boasted hand of civilization has thrown over him. And we have only to blow the trumpet of war, and proclaim to man the hour of his opportunity, that his character may show itself in its essential elements—and that we may see how many, in this our moral and enlightened day, would spring forward, as to a jubilee of delight, and prowl like the wild men of the woods, amidst scenes of rapacity, and cruelty, and violence.

II. But let me hasten away from this part of the subject, and in the second place, direct your attention to those obstacles which stand in the way of the extinction of war, and which threaten to retard, for a time, the accomplishment of the prophecy I have now selected for your consideration.

Is this the time, it may be asked, to complain of obstacles to the extinction of war, when peace has been given to the nations, and we are assembled to celebrate its triumphs? Is this day of high and solemn gratulation, to be turned to such forebodings as these? The whole of Europe is now at rest from the tempest which convulsed it—and a solemn treaty with all its adjustments, and all its guarantees, promises a firm perpetuity to the repose of the world. We have long fought for a happier order of things, and at length we have established it—and the hard-earned bequest, we hand down to posterity as a rich inheritance, won by the labours and the sufferings of the present generation. That gigantic ambition which stalked in triumph over the firmest and the oldest of our monarchies, is now laid—and can never again burst forth from the confinement of its prison-hold to waken a new uproar, and to send forth new troubles over the face of a desolated world.

Now, in reply to this, let it be observed, that every interval of repose is precious; every breathing time from the work of violence is to be rejoiced in by the friends of humanity; every agreement among the powers of the earth, by which a temporary respite can be gotten from the calamities of war, is so much reclaimed from the amount of those miseries that afflict the world, and of those crimes, the cry of which ascendeth unto heaven, and bringeth down the judgments of God on this dark and rebellious province of his creation. I trust, that on this day, gratitude to Him who alone can still the tumults of the people, will be the sentiment of every heart; and I trust, that none who now hear me, will refuse to evince his gratitude to the Author of the New Testament, by their obedience to one of the most distinct and undoubted of its lessons; I mean the lesson of a reverential and submissive loyalty. I cannot pass an impartial eye over this record of God's will, without perceiving the utter repugnance that there is between the spirit of Christianity, and the factious, turbulent, unquenchable, and ever-meddling spirit of political disaffection. I will not compromise, by the surrender of a single jot or tittle, the integrity of that preceptive code which my Saviour hath left behind him for the obedience of his disciples. I will not detach the very minutest of its features, from the fine picture of morality that Christ hath bequeathed, both by commandment and example, to adorn the nature he condescended to wear—and sure I am that the man who has drunk in the entire spirit of the gospel—who, reposing himself on the faith of its promised immortality, can maintain an elevated calm amid all the fluctuations of this world's interest—whose exclusive ambition is to be the unexcepted pupil of pure, and spiritual, and self-denying Christianity—sure I am that such a man will honour the king and all who are in authority—and be subject unto them for the sake of conscience—and render unto them all their dues—and not withhold a single fraction of the tribute they impose upon him—and be the best of subjects, just because he is the best of Christians—resisting none of the ordinances of God, and living a quiet and a peaceable life in all godliness and honesty.

But it gives me pleasure to advance a further testimony in behalf of that government with which it has pleased God, who appointeth to all men the bounds of their habitation, to bless that portion of the globe that we occupy. I count it such a government, that I not only owe it the loyalty of my principles—but I also owe it the loyalty of my affections. I could not lightly part with my devotion to that government which the other year opened the door to the Christianization of India—I shall never withhold the tribute of my reverence from that government which put an end to the atrocities of the Slave Trade—I shall never forget the triumph, which, in that proudest day of Britain's glory, the cause of humanity gained within the walls of our enlightened Parliament. Let my right hand forget her cunning, ere I forget that country of my birth, where, in defiance to all the clamours of mercantile alarm, every calculation of interest was given to the wind, and braving every hazard, she nobly resolved to shake off the whole burden of infamy, which lay upon her. I shall never forget, that how to complete the object in behalf of which she has so honourably led the way, she has walked the whole round of civilized society, and knocked at the door of every government in Europe, and lifted her imploring voice for injured Africa, and plead with the mightiest monarchs of the world, the cause of her outraged shores, and her distracted families. I can neither shut my heart nor my eyes to the fact, that at this moment she is stretching forth the protection of her naval arm, and shielding, to the uttermost of her vigour, that coast where an inhuman avarice is still plying its guilty devices, and aiming to perpetuate among an unoffending people, a trade of cruelty, with all the horrid train of its terrors and abominations. Were such a government as this to be swept from its base, either by the violence of foreign hostility, or by the hands of her own misled and infatuated children—I should never cease to deplore it as the deadliest interruption, which ever had been given to the interests of human virtue, and to the march of human improvement. O! how it should swell every heart, not with pride, but with gratitude, to think that the land of our fathers, with all the iniquities which abound in it, with all the profligacy which spreads along our streets, and all the profaneness that is heard among our companies—to think that this our land, overspread as it is with the appalling characters of guilt, is still the securest asylum of worth and liberty—that this is the land, from which the most copious emanations of Christianity are going forth to all the quarters of the world—that this is the land, which teems from one end to the other of it with the most splendid designs and enterprises for the good of the species—that this is the land, where public principle is most felt, and public objects are most prosecuted, and the fine impulse of a public spirit is most ready to carry its generous people beyond the limits of a selfish and contracted patriotism. Yes, and when the heart of the philanthropist is sinking within him at the gloomy spectacle of those crimes and atrocities, which still deform the history of man, I know not a single earthly expedient more fitted to brighten and sustain him, than to turn his eye to the country in which he lives—and there see the most enlightened government in the world acting as the organ of its most moral and intelligent population.

It is not against the government of my country, therefore, that I direct my observations—but against that nature of man, in the infirmities of which we all share, and the evil of which no government can extinguish. We have carried a new political arrangement, and we experience the result of it, a temporary calm—but we have not yet carried our way to the citadel of human passions. The elements of war are hushed for a season—but these elements are not destroyed. They still rankle in many an unsubdued heart—and I am too well taught by the history of the past, and the experience of its restless variations, not to believe that they will burst forth again in thunder over the face of society. No, my brethren, it will only be when diffused and vital Christianity comes upon the earth, that an enduring peace will come along with it. The prophecy of my text will obtain its fulfilment—but not till the fulfilment of the verses which go before it;—not till the influence of the gospel has found its way to the human bosom, and plucked out of it the elementary principles of war;—not till the law of love shall spread its melting and all-subduing efficacy, among the children of one common nature: not till ambition be dethroned from its mastery over the affections of the inner man; —not till the guilty splendours of war shall cease to captivate its admirers, and spread the blaze of a deceitful heroism over the wholesale butchery of the species;—not till national pride be humbled, and man shall learn, that if it be individually the duty of each of us in honour to prefer one another; then let these individuals combine as they may, and form societies as numerous and extensive as they may, and each of these be swelled out to the dimensions of an empire, still, that mutual condescension and forbearance remain the unalterable christian duties of these empires to each other; —not till man learn to revere his brother as man, whatever portion of the globe he occupies, and all the jealousies and preferences of a contracted patriotism be given to the wind;—not till war shall cease to be prosecuted as a trade, and the charm of all that interest which is linked with its continuance, shall cease to beguile men in the peaceful walks of merchandise, into a barbarous longing after war; not, in one word, till pride, and jealousy, and interest, and all that is opposite to the law of God and the charity of the gospel, shall be for ever eradicated from the character of those who possess an effectual control over the public and political movements of the species;— not till all this be brought about, and there is not another agent in the whole compass of nature that can bring it about but the gospel of Christ, carried home by the all-subduing power of the Spirit to the consciences of men;—then, and not till then, my brethren, will peace come to take up its perennial abode with us, and its blessed advent on earth be hailed by one shout of joyful acclamation throughout all its families; then, and not till then, will the sacred principle of good will to men circulate as free as the air of heaven among all countries—and the sun looking out from the firmament, will behold one fine aspect of harmony throughout the wide extent of a regenerated world.

It will only be in the last days, "when it shall come to pass, that the mountain of the Lord's house shall be established in the top of the mountains, and shall be exalted above the hills, and all nations shall flow into it: And many people shall go, and say, Come ye, and let us go up to the mountain of the Lord, to the house of the God of Jacob; and he will teach us of his ways, and we will walk in his paths: for out of Zion shall go forth the law, and the word of the Lord from Jerusalem; and he shall judge among the nations, and shall rebuke many people;" then and not till then, "they shall beat their swords into plough-shares, and their spears into pruning-hooks. Nation shall not lift up sword against nation, neither shall they learn war any more."

The above rapid sketch glances at the chief obstacles to the extinction of war, and in what remains of this discourse, I shall dwell a little more particularly on as many of them as my time will allow me, finding it impossible to exhaust so wide a topic, within the limits of the public services of one day.

The first great obstacle, then, to the extinction of war, is the way in which the heart of man is carried off from its barbarities and its horrors, by the splendour of its deceitful accompaniments. There is a feeling of the sublime in contemplating the shock of armies, just as there is in contemplating the devouring energy of a tempest, and this so elevates and engrosses the whole man, that his eye is blind to the tears of bereaved parents, and his ear is deaf to the piteous moan of the dying, and the shriek of their desolated families. There is a gracefulness in the picture of a youthful warrior burning for distinction on the field, and lured by this generous aspiration to the deepest of the animated throng, where, in the fell work of death, the opposing sons of valour struggle for a remembrance and a name; and this side of the picture is so much the exclusive object of our regard, as to disguise from our view the mangled carcases of the fallen, and the writhing agonies of the hundreds and the hundreds more who have been laid on the cold ground, where they are left to languish and to die. There no eye pities them. No sister is there to weep over them. There no gentle hand is present to ease the dying posture, or bind up the wounds, which, in the maddening fury of the combat, have been given and received by the children of one common father. There death spreads its pale ensigns over every countenance, and when night comes on, and darkness around them, how many a despairing wretch must take up with the bloody field as the untended bed of his last sufferings, without one friend to bear the message of tenderness to his distant home, without one companion to close his eyes.

I avow it. On every side of me I see causes at work which go to spread a most delusive colouring over war, and to remove its shocking barbarities to the back ground of our contemplations altogether. I see it in the history which tells me of the superb appearance of the troops, and the brilliancy of their successive charges. I see it in the poetry which lends the magic of its numbers to the narrative of blood, and transports its many admirers, as by its images, and its figures, and its nodding plumes of chivalry, it throws its treacherous embellishments over a scene of legalized slaughter. I see it in the music which represents the progress of the battle; and where, after being inspired by the trumpet-notes of preparation, the whole beauty and tenderness of a drawing-room are seen to bend over the sentimental entertainment; nor do I hear the utterance of a single sigh to interrupt the death-tones of the thickening contest, and the moans of the wounded men as they fade away upon the ear, and sink into lifeless silence. All, all goes to prove what strange and half-sighted creatures we are. Were it not so, war could never have been seen in any other aspect than that of unmingled hatefulness; and I can look to nothing but to the progress of christian sentiment upon earth, to arrest the strong current of its popular and prevailing partiality for war. Then only will an imperious sense of duty lay the check of severe principle, on all the subordinate tastes and faculties of our nature. Then will glory be reduced to its right estimate, and the wakeful benevolence of the gospel chasing away every spell, will be turned by the treachery of no delusion whatever, from its simple but sublime enterprises for the good of the species. Then the reign of truth and quietness will be ushered into the world, and war, cruel, atrocious, unrelenting war, will be stript of its many and its bewildering fascinations.

But again, another obstacle to the extinction of war, is a sentiment which seems to be universally gone into, that the rules and promises of the gospel which apply to a single individual, do not apply to a nation of individuals. Just think of the mighty effect it would have on the politics of the world, were this sentiment to be practically deposed from its wonted authority over the counsels and the doings of nations, in their transactions with each other. If forbearance be the virtue of an individual, forbearance is also the virtue of a nation. If it be incumbent on men in honour to prefer each other, it is incumbent on the very largest societies of men, through the constituted organ of their government to do the same. If it be the glory of a man to defer his anger, and to pass over a transgression, that nation mistakes its glory which is so feelingly alive to the slightest insult, and musters up its threats and its armaments upon the faintest shadow of a provocation. If it be the magnanimity of an injured man to abstain from vengeance, and if by so doing, he heaps coals of fire upon the head of his enemy, then that is the magnanimous nation, which, recoiling from violence and from blood, will do no more than send its christian embassy, and prefer its mild and impressive remonstrance; and that is the disgraced nation which will refuse the impressiveness of the moral appeal that has been made to it.—O! my brethren, there must be the breathing of a different spirit to circulate round the globe, ere its christianized nations resign the jealousies which now front them to each other in the scowling attitude of defiance; and much is to do with the people of every land, ere the prophesied influence of the gospel shall bring its virtuous, and its pacifying controul to bear with effect on the counsels and governments of the world.

I find that I must be drawing to a close, and that I must forbear entering into several topics on which I meant at one time to expatiate. I wished, in particular, to have laid it fully before you how the extinction of war, though it should withdraw one of those scenes on which man earns the glory of intrepidity; yet it would leave other, and better, and nobler scenes, for the display and the exercise of this respectable attribute. I wished also to explain to you, that however much I admired the general spirit of Quakerism, on the subject of war; yet that I was not prepared to go all the length of its principles, when that war was strictly defensive. It strikes me, that war is to be abolished by the abolition of its aggressive spirit among the different nations of the world. The text seems to tell me that this is the order of prophecy upon the subject; and that it is when nation shall cease to lift up its sword against nation; or, in other words, when one nation shall cease to move, for the purpose of attacking another, that military science will be no longer in demand, and that the people of the earth will learn the art of war no more. I should also have stated, that on this ground, I refrained from pronouncing on the justice or necessity of any one war in which this country has ever been involved. I have no doubt that many of those who supported our former wars, looked on several of them as wars for existence; but on this matter I carefully abstain from the utterance of a single sentiment; for in so doing, I should feel myself to be descending from the generalities of christian principle, and employing that pulpit as the vehicle of a questionable policy, which ought never to be prostituted either to the unworthy object of sending forth the incense of human flattery to any one administration, or of regaling the factious, and turbulent, and disloyal passions of any party. I should next, if I had time, offer such observations as were suggested by my own views of political science, on the multitude of vulnerable points by which this country is surrounded, in the shape of numerous and distant dependencies, and which, however much they may tend to foster the warlike politics of our government, are, in truth, so little worth the expense of a war, that should all of them be wrested away from us, they would leave the people of our empire as great, and as wealthy, and as competent to every purpose of home security as ever. Lastly, I might have whispered my inclination, for a little more of the Chinese policy being imported into Europe, not for the purpose of restraining a liberal intercourse between its different countries, but for the purpose of quieting in each its restless spirit of alarm, about every foreign movement in the politics and designs of other nations; because, sure I am, that were each great empire of the world to lay it down as the maxim of its most scrupulous observance, not to meddle till it was meddled with, each would feel in such a maxim both its safety and its triumph;—for such are the mighty resources of defensive war, that though the whole transportable force of Europe were to land upon our borders, the result of the experiment would be such, that it should never be repeated—the rallying population of Britain could sweep them all from the face of its territory, and a whole myriad of invaders would melt away under the power of such a government as ours, trenched behind the loyalty of her defenders, and strong, as she deserves to be, in the love and in the confidence of all her children.

I would not have touched on any of the lessons of political economy, did they not lead me, by a single step, to a christian lesson, which I count it my incumbent duty to press upon the attention of you all. Any sudden change in the state of the demand, must throw the commercial world into a temporary derangement. And whether the change be from war to peace, or from peace to war, this effect is sure to accompany it. Now for upwards of twenty years, the direction of our trade has been accommodated to a war system, and when this system is put an end to, I do not say what amount of the distress will light upon this neighbourhood, but we may be sure that all the alarm of falling markets, and ruined speculation, will spread an impressive gloom over many of the manufacturing districts of the land. Now, let my title to address you on other grounds, be as questionable as it may, I feel no hesitation whatever in announcing it, as your most imperative duty, that no outcry of impatience or discontent from you, shall embarrass the pacific policy of his majesty's government. They have conferred a great blessing on the country, in conferring on it peace, and it is your part resignedly to weather the languid or disasterous months which may come along with it. The interest of trade is an old argument that has been set up in resistance to the dearest and most substantial interests of humanity.

When Paul wanted to bring Christianity into Ephesus, he raised a storm of opposition around him, from a quarter which, I dare say, he was not counting on. There happened to be some shrine manufactories in that place, and as the success of the Apostle would infallibly have reduced the demand for that article, forth came the decisive argument of, Sirs, by this craft we have our wealth, and should this Paul turn away the people from the worship of gods made with hands, thereby much damage would accrue to our trade. Why, my brethren, if this argument is to be admitted, there is not one conceivable benefit that can be offered for the acceptance of the species. Would it not be well if all the men of reading in the country were to be diverted from the poison which lurks in many a mischievous publication—and should this blessed reformation be effected, are there none to be found who would feel that much damage had accrued to their trade? Would it not be well, if those wretched sons of pleasure, before whom if they repent not, there lieth all the dreariness of an unprovided eternity —would it not be well, that they were reclaimed from the maddening intoxication which speeds them on in the career of disobedience—and on this event, too, would there be none to complain that much damage had accrued to their trade? Is it not well, that the infamy of the slave trade has been swept from the page of British history? and yet do not many of you remember how long the measure lay suspended, and that about twenty annual flotillas, burdened with the load of human wretchedness, were wafted across the Atlantic, while Parliament was deafened and overborne by unceasing clamours about the much damage that would accrue to the trade? And now, is it not well that peace has once more been given to the nations? and are you to follow up this goodly train of examples, by a single whisper of discontent about the much damage that will accrue to your trade? No, my brethren, I will not let down a single inch of the christian requirement that lies upon you. Should a sweeping tide of bankruptcy set in upon the land, and reduce every individual who now hears me, to the very humblest condition in society, God stands pledged to give food and raiment to all who depend upon him;—and it is not fair to make others bleed, that you may roll in affluence;—it is not fair to desolate thousands of families, that yours may be upheld in luxury and splendour—and your best, and noblest, and kindest part is, to throw yourselves on the promises of God, and he will hide you and your little ones in the secret of his pavilion till these calamities be overpast.

III. I trust it is evident from all that has been said, how it is only by the extension of christian principle among the people of the earth, that the atrocities of war will at length be swept away from it; and that each of us in hastening the commencement of that blissful period, in his own sphere, is doing all that in him lies to bring his own heart, and the hearts of others, under the supreme influence, of this principle. It is public opinion, which in the long run governs the world; and while I look with confidence to a gradual revolution in the state of public opinion from the omnipotence of gospel truth working its silent, but effectual way, through the families of mankind—yet I will not deny that much may be done to accelerate the advent of perpetual and universal peace, by a distinct body of men embarking their every talent, and their every acquirement in the prosecution of this, as a distinct object. This was the way in which, a few years ago, the British public were gained over to the cause of Africa. This is the way in which some of the other prophecies of the Bible are at this moment hastening to their accomplishment; and it is this way, I apprehend, that the prophecy of my text may be indebted for its speedier fulfilment to the agency of men selecting this as the assigned field on which their philanthropy shall expatiate. Were each individual member of such a scheme to prosecute his own walk, and come forward with his own peculiar contribution, the fruit of the united labours of all would be one of the finest collections of christian eloquence, and of enlightened morals, and of sound political philosophy, that ever was presented to the world. I could not fasten on another cause more fitted to call forth such a variety of talent, and to rally around it so many of the generous and accomplished sons of humanity, and to give each of them a devotedness, and a power far beyond whatever could be sent into the hearts of enthusiasts, by the mere impulse of literary ambition.

Let one take up the question of war in its principle, and make the full weight of his moral severity rest upon it, and upon all its abominations. Let another take up the question of war in its consequences, and bring his every power of graphical description to the task of presenting an awakened public with an impressive detail of its cruelties and its horrors. Let another neutralize the poetry of war, and dismantle it of all those bewitching splendours, which the hand of misguided genius has thrown over it. Let another teach the world a truer, and more magnanimous path to national glory, than any country of the world has yet walked in. Let another tell with irresistible argument, how the christian ethics of a nation is at one with the christian ethics of its humblest individual. Let another bring all the resources of his political science to unfold the vast energies of defensive war, and show, that instead of that ceaseless jealousy and disquietude, which are ever keeping alive the flame of hostility among the nations, each may wait in prepared security, till the first footstep of an invader shall be the signal for mustering around the standard of its outraged rights, all the steel, and spirit, and patriotism of the country. Let another pour the light of modern speculation into the mysteries of trade and prove that not a single war has been undertaken for any of its objects, where the millions and the millions more which were lavished on the cause, have not all been cheated away from us by the phantom of an imaginary interest. This may look to many like the Utopianism of a romantic anticipation—but I shall never despair of the cause of truth addressed to a christian public, when the clear light of principle can be brought to every one of its positions, and when its practical and conclusive establishment forms one of the most distinct of Heaven's prophecies—" that men shall beat their swords into plough-shares, and their spears into pruning-hooks—and that nation shall not lift up sword against nation, neither shall they learn the art of war any more."

THE DUTY

OF

GIVING AN IMMEDIATE DILIGENCE TO THE BUSINESS OF THE CHRISTIAN LIFE.

BEING AN

ADDRESS

TO THE INHABITANTS OF THE PARISH OF KILMANY.

When one writes a letter to an intimate, and a much loved friend, he never thinks of the graces of the composition. He unbosoms himself in a style of perfect freeness and simplicity. He gives way to the kindly affections of his heart, and though there may be many touches of tenderness in his performance, it is not because he aims at touches of any kind, but because all the tenderness that is written, is the genuine and the artless transcript of all the tenderness that is felt. Now conceive for a moment, that he wrote his letter under the consciousness that it was to be broadly exhibited before the eye of the public, this would immediately operate as a heavy restraint upon him. A man would much rather pour the expression of his friendship into the private ear of him who was the object of it, than he would do it under the full stare of a numerous company. And I, my brethren, could my time have allowed it, would much rather have written my earnest and longing aspiration for the welfare of you all by a private letter to each individual, than by this general Address, which necessarily exposes to the wide theatre of the public all that I feel, and all that I utter on the subject of my affectionate regard for you.

It were better, then, for the exercise to which I have now set myself, that I shut out all idea of the public; and never, within the whole recollection of my life, was I less disposed to foster that idea. It may be observed, that the blow of some great and calamitous visitation brings a kind of insensibility along with it. I ought not to lament my withdrawment from you as a calamity, but it has had all the effect of a calamity upon me. I am removed from those objects which habitually interested my heart, and, for a time, it refuses to be interested in other objects. I am placed at a distance from that scene to which I was most alive, and I feel a deadness to every other scene. The people who are now around me, carry an unquestionable kindness in their bosoms, and vie with one another in the expression of it. I can easily perceive that there exists abundantly among them all the constituents of a highly interesting neighbourhood, and it may look cold and ungrateful in me that I am not interested. But it takes a time before the heart can attune itself to the varieties of a new situation. It is ever recurring to the more familiar scenes of other days. The present ministers no enjoyment, and in looking to the past the painful circumstance is, that while the fancy will not be kept from straying to that neighbourhood which exercises over it all the power of a much-loved home, the idea that it is home no longer comes with dread reality upon the mind, and turns the whole to bitterness.

With a heart thus occupied, I do not feel that the admission of the public into our conference will be any great restraint upon me. I shall speak to you as if they were not present, and I do not conceive that they can take a great interest in what I say, because I have no time for the full and explicit statement of principles. I have this advantage with you that I do not have with others, that with you I can afford to be less explicit. I presume upon your recollections of what I have, for some time, been in the habit of addressing to you, and flatter myself that you may enter into a train of observation which to others may appear dark, and abrupt, and unconnected. In penning this short Address, I follow the impulse of my regard for you. You will receive it with indulgence, as a memorial from one who loves you, who is ever with you in heart, though not in person; who classes among the dearest of his recollections, the tranquil enjoyments he has had in your neighbourhood; who carries upon his memory the faithful image of its fields and of its families; and whose prayers for you all is, that you may so grow in the fruits of our common faith, as to be made meet for that unfading inheritance where sorrow and separation are alike unknown.

Were I to sit down for the purpose of drawing out a list of all the actions which may be called sinful, it would be long before I could complete the enumeration. Nay, I can conceive, that by adding one peculiarity after another, the variety may be so lengthened out as to make the attempt impossible. Lying, and stealing, and breaking the Sabbath, and speaking evil one of another, these are all so many sinful actions; but circumstances may be conceived which make one kind of lying different fom another, and one kind of theft different from another, and one kind of evil speaking different from another, and in this way the number of sinful actions may be greatly swelled out; and should we attempt to take the amount, they may be like the host which no man could number, and every sinner, realizing one of these varieties, may wear his own peculiar complexion, and have a something about him, which marks him out, and signalizes him from all the other sinners by whom he is surrounded.

Yet, amid all this variety of visible aspect, there is one summary expression to which all sin may be reduced. There is one principle which, if it always existed in the heart, and were always acted upon in the life, would entirely destroy the existence of sin, and the very essence of sin lies in the want of this one principle. Sin is a want of conformity to the will of God; and were a desire to do the will of God at all times the overruling principle of the heart and conduct, there would be no sin. It is this want of homage to him and to his authority, which gives to sin its essential character. The evil things coming out of the heart, which is the residence of this evil principle, may be exceedingly various, and may impart a very different complexion to different individuals. This complexion may be more or less displeasing to the outward eye. The evil speaker may look to us more hateful than the voluptuary, the man of cruelty than the man of profaneness, the breaker of his word than the breaker of the Sabbath. I believe it will generally be found, that the sin which inflicts the more visible and immediate harm upon men, is, in the eye of men, the more hateful sin. There is a readiness to execrate falsehood, and calumny, and oppression; and along with this readiness there is an indulgence for the good-humoured failings of him who is the slave of luxury, and makes a god of his pleasure, and spends his days in all the thoughtlessness of one who walks in the counsel of his own heart, and in the sight of his own eyes, provided that his love of society leads him to share with others the enjoyment of all these gratifications, and his wealth enables him, and his moral honesty inclines him, to defray the expense of them.

Behold, then, one frequent source of delusion. He whose sins are less hateful to the world than those of others, wraps up himself in a kind of security. I wrong no man. I have a heart that can be moved by the impulses of compassion. I carry in my bosom a lively sentiment of indignation at the tale of perfidy or violence; and surely I may feel a satisfaction which others have no title to feel, who are guilty of that from which my nature recoils with a generous abhorrence. He forgets all the while, that sin, in its essential character, may have as full and firm a possession of his heart, as of the man's with whom he is comparing himself: that there may be an entire disownal and forgetfulness of God; that not one particle of reverence, or of acknowledgment, may be given to the Being with whom he has to do; that whatever he may be in the eye of his neighbour, in the eye of him who seeth not as man seeth, he is guilty; that, walking just as he would have done though there had been no divine government whatever, he is a rebel to that government; and that amid all the complacency of his own feelings, and all the applause and good liking of his acquaintances, he wears all the deformity of rebelliousness in the eye of every spiritual being, who looks at the state of his heart, and passes judgment upon him by those very principles which are to try him at the great day when the secrets of all hearts shall be laid open.

If this were kept in view, it would lead to a more enlightened estimate of the character of man, than man in the thoughtlessness and unconcern of his natural state ever forms. It would lead us to see, that under all the hues and varieties of character, diversified as they are by constitutional taste, and the power of circumstances, there lurks one deep and universal disease, and that is the disease of a mind labouring under alienation from God, and without any practical sense of what is due to him. You will all admit it to be true, that the heart of a man may be under the full operation of this deadly poison, while the man himself has a constitutional taste for the pleasures of social intercourse. You see nothing unlikely or impossible in this combination. Now I want you to go along with me, when I carry my assertion still further; and sure I am that experience bears me out when I say, that the heart of a man may be under the full operation of a dislike or indifference to God, while the man himself has a constitutional abhorrence at cruelty, a constitutional repugnance to fraud, a constitutional antipathy to what is uncourteous in manners, or harsh and unfeeling in conversation, a constitutional gentleness of character; or, to sum up the whole in one clause, a man may be free from many things which give him a moral hatefulness in the eye of others, and he may have many things which throw a moral loveliness around him, and the soul be under the entire dominion of that carelessness about God, which gives to sin its essential character. And upon him, even upon him, graceful and engaging as he may be by the lustre of his many accomplishments, the saying of the Bible does not fail of being realised, that "the heart of man is deceitful above all things, and desperately wicked; who can know it?"

And thus it is, that our great and ultimate aim in the reformation of a sinner, is the reformation of his heart. There may be many reformations short of this, and in which many are disposed to rest with deceitful complacency. I can conceive, that the man who formerly stole may steal no more, not because he is now sanctified, and feels the obligation of religious principle, but because he is now translated into better circumstances, and by the power of example, has contracted that tone of honourable feeling which exists among the upper classes of society. Here, then, is a reformation of the conduct, while the heart, in respect of that which constitutes its exceeding sinfulness, is no better than before. The old leaven of ungodliness may overspread its every desire, and its every affection; and while the outer man has been washed of one of its visible deformities, the inner man may still persist in its unmindfulness of God; and the pollution of this greatest and vilest of all moral turpitude, may adhere to it as obstinately as ever.

Now, it appears to me, that these views, true in themselves, and deserving to be carried along with us through every inch of our religious progress, have often been practically misapplied. I can conceive an inquirer under the influence of these views, to fall into such a process of reflection as the following: 'If the outer conduct be of no estimation in the sight of God, unless it stand connected with the actings of a holy principle in the heart, let us begin with the heart, and from the establishment of a holy principle there, purity of conduct will follow as an effect of course. Let us beware of laying an early stress upon the doings of the outer man, lest we and others should have our eye turned from the reformation of the inner man, as the main and almost the exclusive object of a Christian's ambition. Let us be fearful how we urge such and such visible reformations, either upon ourselves or those around us, lest they be made to stand in the place of that grand renewing process, by which the soul, dead in trespasses and sins, is made alive unto God. Let us labour to impress the necessity of this process, and seeing the utter inability of man to change his own heart, let us turn his eye from any exertions of his own, to that fulness which is in Christ Jesus, through whom alone he can obtain the forgiveness of all his sins, and such a measure of power resting upon him, as carries along with it all the purifying influences of a spiritual reformation. In the mean time, let us take care how we speak about good works. Let the very mention of them put us into the defensive attitude of coldness and suspicion; and instead of giving our earnestness or our energy to them, let us press upon ourselves and others the exercises of that faith, by which alone we are made the workmanship of God, and created unto such good works as he hath ordained that we should walk in them.'

Now, there is a great deal of truth throughout the whole of this train of sentiment; but truth contemplated under such an aspect, and turned to such a purpose, as has the effect of putting an inquirer into a practical attitude, which appears to me to be unscriptural and wrong. I would not have him keep his hand for a single moment from the doing of that which is obviously right. I would not have him to refrain from grappling immediately with every one sin which is within the reach of his exertions. I would not have him to incur the delay of one instant in ceasing to do that which is evil; and I conceive that it is not till this is begun that he will learn to do that which is well. It ought not to restrain the energy of his immediate doing, that he is told how doings are of no account, unless they are the doings of one who has gone through a previous regeneration. This ought not to keep him from doing. It should only lead him to combine with the prescribed doing, an earnest aspiring after a cleaner heart, and a better spirit than he yet finds himself to have. It is very true, that a man may do an outwardly good thing, and rest in what he has done. But it is as true, that a man may do the outwardly good thing he is bidden do, and, instead of resting, may look forward with diligent striving, and earnest, humble prayer, to some greater things than this. Now, this last my brethren, is the attitude I want to put you into. Let the thief give up his stealing at this moment. Let the drunkard give up his intemperance. Let the evil speaker give up his calumnies. Let the doer of all that is obviously wrong break off his sins, and turn him to the doing of all that is obviously right. Let no one thing, not even the speculations of orthodoxy,* be suffered to stand a barrier against your entrance into the field of immediate exertion. I raise the very first blow of my trumpet against the visible iniquities which I see to be in you, and if there be any one obviously right thing you have hitherto neglected, I will not consume one particle of time before I call upon you to do it.

It is quite in vain to say that all this is not called for, or that I am now spending my strength and your time in combating an error which has no practical existence. You must be quite familiarised with the melancholy spectacle of a zealous professor mourning over the sinfulness of his heart, and, at the same time putting forth his hand, without one sigh of remorse, to what is sinful in ordinary conduct. Have you never witnessed one, who could speak evil of his neighbour, and was at the same time trenching among what he thought the speculations of orthodoxy, and made the utter corruption of the soul of man one of these speculations? Is it not enough to say that he is a mere speculative Christian? for the very same thing may be detected in the practice of one who feels a real longing to be delivered from the power of that sin, which he grieves has such an entire dominion over him. And yet, strange to tell, there is many an obvious and every-day sin, which is not watched against, which is not struggled against, and the commission of which gives no uneasiness whatever. The man is, as it were, so much occupied with the sinfulness of his heart, that he neither feels nor attends to the sinfulness of his conduct. He wants to go methodically to work. He wants to begin at the beginning, and he forms his estimate of what the beginning is upon the arrangements of human speculations.

It sounds very plausibly, that as out of the heart are the issues of life, the work of an inquiring Christian must begin there; but the mischief I complain of is, that in the first prosecution of this work, months or years may be consumed ere the purified fountain send forth its streams, or the repentance he is aspiring after tell on the plain and palpable doings of his ordinary conduct. Hence, my brethren, the mortifying exhibition of great zeal, and much talk, and diligent canvassing and conversing about the abstract principles of the christian faith, combined with what is visible in the christian practice, being at a dead stand, and not one inch of sensible progress being made in any one thing which the eye can witness, or the hand can lay a tangible hold upon. The man is otherwise employed. He is busy with the first principles of the subject. He still goes on with his wonted peevishness within doors, and his wonted dishonesties without doors. He has not yet come to these matters. He is taken up with laying and labouring at the foundation. The heart is the great subject of his anxiety; and in the busy exercise of mourning, and confessing, and praying, and studying the right management of his heart, he may take up months or years before he come to the deformities of his outward and ordinary conduct. I will venture to go farther, my brethren, and assert, that if this be the track he is on, it will be a great chance if he ever come to them at all. To the end of his days he may be a talking, and inquiring, and speculating, and I doubt not, along with all this, a church-going and ordinance-loving Christian. But I am much afraid that he is, practically speaking, not in the way to the solid attainments of a Christian, whose light shines before men. All that meets the eye of daily observers, may have undergone no change whatever, and the life of the poor man may be nothing better than the dream of a delusive and bewildering speculation.

Now, it is very true that, agreeably to the remarks with which I prefaced this argument, the great and ultimate aim of all reformation is to reform the heart, and to bring it into such a state of principle and desire, that God may be glorified in soul and in spirit, as well as in body. This is the point that is ever to be sought after, and ever to be pressed forward to. Under a sense of his deficiencies from this point, a true Christian will read diligently, that he may learn the gospel method of arriving at it. He will pray diligently that the clean heart may be created, and the right spirit may be renewed within him. The earnestness of his attention to this matter will shut him up more and more into the faith of that perfect sacrifice, which his short-comings from a holy and heart-searching law will ever remind him of, as the firm and the only ground of his acceptance with God. The same honest reliance on the divine testimony, which leads him to close with the doctrine of the atonement, and to rejoice in it, will also lead him to close with the doctrine of sanctification, and diligently to aspire after it. Now, in the business of so aspiring after this object, it is not enough that he read diligently in the Word; it is not enough that he pray diligently for the Spirit. These are two ingredients in the business of seeking after his object, but they are not the only ones; and what I lament is, that a fear about the

---

* Sorry should I be, if a term expressive of right notions on the most interesting of all subjects, were used by me with a levity at all calculated to beget an indifference to the soundness of your religious opinion, or to divert your most earnest attention from those inquiries, which have for their object the true will, and the true way of God for the salvation of men.

entireness of his orthodoxy leads many a zealous inquirer to look coldly and askance at another ingredient in this business. He should not only read diligently, and pray diligently, but he should do diligently every one right thing that is within his reach, and that he finds himself to have strength for.

Any one author who talks of the insignificance of doings, in such a way as practically to restrain an inquirer from vigorously and immediately entering upon the performance of them, misleads that inquirer from the scriptural method, by which we are directed to a greater measure of light and of holiness than we are yet in possession of. He detaches one essential ingredient from the business of seeking. He may set the spirit of his reader a roaming over some field of airy speculation; but he works no such salutary effect upon his spirit, as evinces itself by any one visible or substantial reformation. I have often and often attempted to press this lesson upon you, my brethren; and I bear you testimony, that, while a resistance to practical preaching has been imputed to the zealous professors of orthodoxy, you listened with patience, and I trust not without fruit, when addressing you as if you had just begun to stir yourselves in the matter of your salvation, I ranked it among my preliminary instructions, that you should cease from the evil of your doings; that you should give up all that you know to be wrong in your ordinary conduct; that the thief should restrain himself from stealing, the liar from falsehood, the evil speaker from backbiting, the slothful labourer in the field from eye-service, the faithless housemaid in the family from all purloining and all idleness.

The subterfuges of hypocrisy are endless; and if it can find one in a system of theology, it will be as glad of it from that quarter as from any other. Some there are who deafen the impressions of all these direct and immediate admonitions, by saying, that before all these doings are insisted on, we must lay well and labour well at the foundation of faith in Christ, without whom we can do nothing. The truth, that without Christ we can do nothing, is unquestionable; but it would take many a paragraph to expose its want of application to the use that is thus made of it. But to cut short this plea of indolence for delaying the painful work of surrendering all that is vicious in conduct; let me put it to your common sense whether a thief would not, and could not give up stealing for a week, if he had the reward of a fortune waiting him at the end of it; whether, upon the same reward, an evil speaker could not, for the same time, impose a restraint upon his lips, and the slothful servant become a most pains-taking and diligent worker, and the liar maintain an undeviating truth throughout all his conversations. Each of these would find himself to have strength for these things, were the inducement of a certain temporal reward held out, or the dread of a certain temporal punishment were made to hang over him Now, for the temporal punishment, I substitute the call of, "Flee from the coming wrath." Let this call have the effect it should have, and the effect it actually does have, on many who are not warped by a misleading speculation, and it will make them stir up such strength as they possess, and give up, indeed, much of their actual misconduct. This effect it had in the days of John the Baptist. People, on his call, gave up their violence and their extortions, and the evil of many of their doings, and were thus put into what God in his wisdom counted a fit state of preparation for the Saviour. If there was any thing in the revelation of the Gospel calculated to supersede this call of, "Cease you from the evil of your doings," then I could understand the indifference, or the positive hostility of zealous pretenders to the work of addressing practical exhortation to inquirers at the very outset of their progress. But so far from being superseded by any thing that the Gospel lays before us, the Author, and the first preachers of the Gospel, just took up the lesson of John, and at the very commencement of their ministry did they urge it upon people to turn them from the evil of their doings. Repent and believe the Gospel, says our Saviour. Repent and turn unto God, and do works meet for repentance, says the apostle Paul. And there must be something wrong, my brethren, if you resist me urging it upon you, to give up at this moment, even though it should be the first moment of your concern about salvation, to give up all that is obviously wrong; to turn you to all that is obviously right; to grapple with every sin you can lay your hand upon; and if it be true, in point of experience and common sense, that many a misdeed may be put away from you on the allurement of some temporal reward; then if you have faith in the reality of eternal things, the hope of an escape from the coming wrath may and will tell immediately upon you, and we shall see among you a stir, and a diligence, and a doing, and a visible reformation.

It is a great matter to chase away all mysticism from the path by which a sinner is led unto God; and it is to be lamented that many a speculation of many a respected divine, has the effect of throwing a darkening cloud of perplexity over the very entrance of this path. I tell you a very plain thing, and, if it be true, it is surely of importance that you should know it, when I tell you, that if you are a servant, and are visited with a desire after salvation, then a faithful performance of your daily task is a step without which the object you aim at is unattainable. If you are a son, a more punctual fulfilment of your parent's bidding is another step. If you are a neighbour, a more civil and obliging deportment to those around you is another step. If you are a dealer, the adoption of a just weight and a just measure is another step. There are some who, afraid of your attempting to get acceptance with God by the merit of your own doings, would not venture to urge all this at the outset, lest they should lead you to rest on a delusive ground of confidence. They would try to get a perfect and a clear understanding of the right ground of acceptance established, *previous* to the use of any such urgency; and then, upon this principle being well laid within you, they might take the liberty of telling you your duty. Their fearfulness upon this point forms a very striking contrast to the free, and unembarrassed, and energetic manner, in which the Bible, both of the Old and New Testament, calls on every man who comes within the reach of a hearing, to cease from all sin, and turn him to all righteousness. In following its example, let us be fearless of all consequences. It may not suit the artificial processes of some of our systems, nor fall in with the order of their well-weighed and carefully arranged articles, to tell at the very outset of those obvious reformations which I am now pressing upon you. But sure I am, that an apostle would have felt no difficulty on the subject; nor whatever the visible sin which deformed you, or whatever the visible act of obedience in which you were deficient, would he have been restrained from giving his immediate energy to the work of calling on you to abstain from the one and to do the other.

The disciples of John could not have such a clear view of the ground of acceptance before God, as an enlightened disciple of the apostles. Yet the want of this clear view did not prevent them from being right subjects for John's preparatory instructions. And what were these instructions? Soldiers were called on to give up their violence, and publicans their exactions, and rich men the confinement of their own wealth to their own gratification; and will any man hesitate for a moment to decide whether those who turned away from the directions of the forerunner, or those who followed them, were in the likeliest state for receiving light and improvement from the subsequent teaching of the Saviour?

But there is one difference between them and us. The whole of Christ's teaching, as put down in the word of God, is already before us. Now what precise effect should this have upon the nature of an initiatory address to sinners? The right answer to this question will confirm, or it will demolish the whole of our preceding argument. The alone ground of acceptance, is the righteousness of Christ imputed to all who believe. This truth deserves to be taken up, and urged immediately in the hearing of all who are within the reach of the preacher's voice. Till this truth be received, there should be no rest to the sinner, there is no reconciliation with God, nor will he attain that consummation of holiness, without which there can be no meetness for the enjoyment of heaven. But some are readier to receive this truth than others. The reforming publicans and harlots of John were in a state of greater readiness to receive this truth, than either the Pharisees, or those publicans and harlots who, unmindful of John, still persisted in their iniquities. And who will be in greater readiness to receive this truth in the present day? Will it be the obstinate and determinate doers of all that is sinful, and that too in the face of a call, that they should do works meet for repentance? Or will it be those who, under the influence of this call, do what the disciples of John did before them, turn them from the evil of their manifest iniquities, and so give proof of their earnestness in the way of salvation? It is true that, along with such a call, we might now urge a truth which even John could not. But are we to suspend the call of doing works meet for repentance, till this truth be urged and established in the mind of the hearer? Surely, if God thought it wise to ply sinners with a call to turn them from the evil of their ways, *before* he fully revealed to them the evangelical ground of their acceptance, we may count it scriptural and safe to ply them with this call *at the same time* that we state to them the evangelical ground of their acceptance.

It is true, that the statement may not be comprehended all at once. It may be years before it is listened to by the careless, before it is rested in by the desponding, before the comfort of it is at all felt or appropriated by the doubting and melancholy inquirer. Now what I contend for is, that during this interval of time, these people may and ought to be urged with the call of departing from their iniquities. This very call was brought to bear on the disciples of John, before the ground of their acceptance was fully made known to them; and it might be brought to bear on sinners now, even though it should be before the ground of their acceptance be fully understood by them. The effect of this preparatory instruction in these days, was to fit John's disciples for the subsequent revelation of Christ and his apostles. It is true that we are in possession of that doctrine which they only had the prospect of. But it accords with experience, that this doctrine might be addressed without effect for years to men inquiring after salvation. The doctrine of justification by the righteousness of Christ, might be announced in all its force, and in all its simplicity, to men who hold out against it; and you would surely say of them, that the way of the Lord had not been prepared to their minds, nor his paths made straight. Now we read of such a preparation set agoing in behalf of men to whom this doctrine had not yet been revealed. Will this preparation be altogether ineffectual in behalf of men, by whom this doctrine is not yet understood? Surely it is quite evident, that in the days of John, men who, in obedience to his call, were struggling with their sins, were in a likelier way for receiving those larger measures of truth, which were afterward revealed, than they who, in the face of that call, were obstinately and presumptuously retaining them. Suffer us to avail ourselves of the same advantage now. You, my brethren, who, in obedience to the calls that have been sounded in your hearing, are struggling with your sins, are in a likelier way for receiving those larger measures of truth which are now revealed, than those of you who feel no earnestness, and are making no endeavours upon the subject. While, therefore, I announce to you, in the most distinct terms, that you will not be saved unless you are found in the righteousness of Christ, this will not restrain me at the very same time from doing what John did. You know how his disciples were prepared for the baptism of the Holy Ghost, who guides unto all truth; and while I do not think that any one point of time is too early for offering Christ to you, in all the benefits of his sacrifice, in all the imputed merits of his perfect righteousness, in all the privileges which he has proclaimed and purchased for believers; all I contend for is, that neither is there any point of time too early for letting you know, that all sin must be abandoned, for calling on you to enter into the work of struggling with all sin immediately, for warning you, that while you persist in those sinful actions which you might give up, and would give up, were a temporal inducement held out to you, I have no evidence of your receiving benefit from the word of salvation that I am sounding in your ears. There is surely room for telling sinners more than one thing, in the course of the very earliest lesson that is laid before them. It is an exclusive deference to the one point, and the one principle, and the bringing of every thing else into a forced subordination upon it, which has enfeebled many an attempt to turn sinners to Christ from their iniquities. I can surely tell a man, that unless he is walking in a particular line, he will not reach the object he is aiming at; and I can tell him at the same time, that neither will he reach it, unless he have his eyes open, and he look upon the object. On these two unquestionable truths, I bid him both walk and look at the same time, and at the same time he can do both. In the same manner I may tell a man, that unless he give up stealing he shall not reach heaven; and I may also tell him, that unless he accept, by faith, Christ as his alone Saviour, he shall not reach heaven. On these two truths I found two practical directions; and I must be convinced, that the doing of the one hinders the doing of the other, ere I desist from that which the first teachers of Christianity did before me,—proclaim Christ, and within the compass of the same breathing, call on men to do works meet for repentance.

In the order of time, the practical instructions of John went before the full announcement of the doctrines of salvation. I do not think, however, that this order is authoritative upon us; but far less do I think that our full possession of the doctrine of salvation confers any authority upon us for reversing the historical process of the New Testament. I bring all the truths which the teachers of these days addressed to the sinners among whom they labour, to bear immediately upon you sinners now. And while I call upon you to turn from the evil of your ways, I also warn you of the danger of putting away from you the offered Saviour, or refusing all your confidence in that name than which there is no other given under heaven whereby men can be saved.

If by faith be meant the embracing of one doctrine, then I can understand how some might be alarmed lest an outset so practical should depose faith from the precedency which belongs to it. But if by faith be meant a reliance upon the whole testimony of Scripture, then the precedency of faith is not at all broken in upon. If, on the call of "Flee from the coming wrath," I get you to struggle it with your more palpable iniquities, I see in that very struggle the operation of a faith in the divine testimony about the realities of an invisible world, and I have reason to bless God that he has wrought in you what I am sure no argument and no vehemence of mine could, without the power of his Spirit, ever have accomplished. Those of you who have thus evinced one exercise of faith, I look upon as more hopeful subjects for another exercise, than those of you who remain trenched in obstinacy and unconcern. And when I tell the former, that nothing will get them acceptance with God, but the mediation of Christ offered to all who come, it will be to them, and not to the latter, that I should look for an earnest desire after the offered Saviour. When I tell them that they affront God by not receiving the record which he gives of his Son, it will be to them and not to the others, that I shall look for a submissive and thankful acquiescence in the whole of his salvation; and thus passing with the docility of little children from one lesson of the Bible to another; these are the people who, working because God so bids them, will count that a man is not justified by the works of the law, because God so tells them; these are the people who, not offended by what Christ told them at the outset, that he who cometh unto him must forsake all, will evince their willingness to forsake all, by turning from their iniquities, and coming unto Christ; these are the people who, while they do what they may with their hands, will think that while their heart is not directed to the love of God, they have done nothing; and counting it a faithful saying, that without Christ they can do nothing, they will take to him as their sanctifier as well as their Saviour, and having received him as the Lord their righteousness, will ever repair to him and keep by him as the Lord their strength.

While I urge upon you the doing of every obviously right thing, you will not conceive of me that I want you to rest in this doing. I trust that my introductory paragraphs may convince you how much of this doing may be gone through, and yet the mighty object of the obedience of the willing heart might be unreashed and unaccomplished. Not to urge the doing, lest you should rest, would be to deviate from scriptural example. And again, to urge the doing, and leave you to rest, would be also to deviate from scriptural example. John the Baptist urged the doing of many things, and his faithful disciples set themselves to the performance of what he bade them do. They entered immediately on the field of active and diligent service. But did they stop short? No; out of the very preaching of their master did they obtain a caution against resting; and the same submissive deference to his authority, in virtue of which they were set a working, led them also, along with their working at the things which he set them to, to look forward to greater things than these. He told them expressly, that all his preaching was as nothing to the preaching of one who was to come after him. They were diligent with present things, but be assured that they combined with this diligence the attitude of looking forward to greater things. Is this the attitude of men who place their repose and their dependance upon the performances on hand? Was it not the attitude of men walking in the way revealed by a messenger from heaven, to the object which this messenger pointed out to them? I call on you to commence at this moment an immediate struggle with all sin, and an immediate striving after all righteousness; but I would not be completing even the lesson of John, and far less would I be bringing forward the counsel of God, as made known to us in his subsequent revelation, were I to say any thing which led you to stop short at those visible reformations, which formed the great burden of John's practical addresses to his countrymen; and therefore along with your doing, and most diligently doing all that is within your reach, I call on you to pray, and most fervently and faithfully to pray for that larger baptism of the Holy Ghost, by which your hearts may be cleansed from all their corruptions, and you be enabled to render unto God all the purity of a spiritual obedience.

I cannot expatiate within the limits of this short address on the texts both of the Old and New Testament, which serve to establish, that the right attitude of a returning sinner is what I have sometimes called in your hearing, the compound attitude of service and expectation. But I shall repeat a few of these texts, that they may suggest what you have been in the habit of hearing from me upon this subject. "And Samuel spake to all the house of Israel, saying, if ye do return unto the Lord with all your hearts, then put away the strange gods and Ashtaroth from among you, and prepare your hearts unto the Lord, and serve him only, and he will deliver you out of the hand of the Philistines. Then the children of Israel did put away Baalim and Ashtaroth, and served the Lord alone." "They will not frame their doings to turn unto the Lord." "Thus saith the Lord, keep ye judgment and do justice, for my salvation is near to come, and my righteousness to be revealed. Blessed is the man that doeth this, and the son of man that layeth hold on it, that keepeth the Sabbath from polluting it, and keepeth his hand from doing evil." "Deal thy bread to the hungry, and bring the poor that are cast out into thy house. When thou seest the naked, cover him, and hide not thyself from thine own flesh. Then shall thy light break forth as the morning, and thine health shall spring forth speedily, and thy righteousness shall go before thee; the glory of the Lord shall be thy rereward." "He that hath my commandments and keepeth them, he it is that loveth me, and he that loveth me shall be loved of my Father, and I will love him, and will manifest myself unto him." "For whosoever hath, to him shall be given, and he shall have more abundance; but whosoever hath not, from him shall be taken away even that he hath." "Whosoever, therefore, shall break one of these least commandments, and shall teach men so, he shall be called the least in the kingdom of heaven; but whosoever shall do and teach them, the same shall be called great in the kingdom of heaven."

"And we are witnesses of these things; and so is also the Holy Ghost, whom God hath given to them that obey him." "Trust in the Lord and do good."

But danger presses on us in every direction; and in the work of dividing the word of truth, many, and very many, are the obstacles which lie in the way of our doing it rightly. When a minister gives his strength to one particular lesson, it often carries in it the appearance of his neglecting all the rest, and throwing into the back ground other lessons of equal importance. It might require the ministrations of many years to do away this appearance. Sure I am, that I despair of doing it away within the limits of this short address to any but yourselves. You know all that I have urged upon the ground of your acceptance with God; upon the freeness of that offer which is by Christ Jesus; upon the honest invitations which every where abound in the Gospel, that all who will, may take hold of it; upon the necessity of being found by God not in your own righteousness, but in the righteousness which is of Christ; upon the helplessness of man, and how all the strugglings of his own unaided strength can never carry him to the length of a spiritual obedience; upon the darkness and enmity of his mind about the things of God, and how this can never be dissolved, till he who by nature stands afar off is brought near by the blood of the atonement, and he receives that repentance and that remission of sins, which Christ is exalted a Prince and a Saviour to dispense to all who believe in him. These are offers and doctrines which might be addressed, and ought to be addressed immediately to all. But the call I have been urging upon you through the whole of this pamphlet, of "Cease ye from your manifest transgressions," should be addressed along with them.

Now, here lies the difficulty with many a sincere lover of the truth as it is in Jesus. He feels a backwardness in urging this call, lest it should some how or other impair the freeness of the offer, or encroach upon the singleness of that which is stated to be our alone meritorious ground of acceptance before God. In reply to this, let it be well observed, that though the offer be at all times free, it is not at all times listened to; and though the only ground of acceptance be that righteousness of Christ which is unto all them and upon all them that believe, yet some are in likelier circumstances for being brought to this belief than others. There is one class of hearers who are in a greater state of readiness for being impressed by the Gospel than another,—and I fear that all the use has not been made of this principle, which Scripture and experience warrant us to do. Every attempt to work man into a readiness for receiving the offer has been discouraged,' as if it carried in it a reflection against the freeness of the offer itself. The obedient disciples of John were more prepared for the doctrines of grace, than the careless hearers of this prophet; but their obedience did not confer any claim of merit upon them, it only made them more disposed to receive the good tidings of that salvation which was altogether of grace. A despiser of ordinances is put into a likelier situation for receiving the free offer of the Gospel, by being prevailed upon to attend a church where this offer is urged upon his acceptance. His attendance does not impair the freeness of the offer. Yet where is the man so warped by a misleading speculation, as to deny that the doing of this previous to his union with Christ, and preparatory to that union, may be the very mean of the free offer being received. Again, it is the lesson both of experience and of the Bible, that the young are likelier subjects for religious instruction than the old. The free offer may and ought to be addressed to both these classes; but generally speaking, it is in point of fact more productive of good when addressed to the first class than the second. And we do not say that youth confers any meritorious title to salvation, nor do we make any reflection on the freeness of the offer, when we urge it upon the young, lest they should get old, and it have less chance of being laid before them with acceptance. We make no reflection upon the offer as to its character of freeness, but we proceed upon the obvious fact, that, free as it is, it is not so readily listened to or laid hold of by the second class of hearers as by the first. And, lastly, when addressing sinners now, all of them might and ought to be plied with the free offer of salvation at the very outset. But if it be true, that those of them who wilfully persist in their misdoings, which they could give up on the inducement of a temporal reward, will not, in point of fact, be so impressed by the offer, or be so disposed to accept of it, as those who (on the call of—" Flee from the coming wrath;") and on being told, that, unless they repent they shall perish; and on being made to know, what our Saviour made inquirers know at the very starting point of their progress as his disciples, that he who followeth after him must forsake all,) have begun to break off their sins, and to put the evil of their doings away from them: then we are not stripping the offer of its attribute of perfect freeness, but we are only doing what God in his wisdom did two thousand years ago; we are, under Him, preparing souls for the reception of this offer, when along with the business of proposing it, which we cannot do too early, we bring the urgency of an immediate call to bear on the children of iniquity, that they should cease to do evil, and learn to do well.

The publicans and harlots entered into the kingdom of God before the Pharisees, and yet the latter were free from the outward transgressions of the former. Now, the fear which restrains many from lifting the immediate call of—"Cease ye from your transgressions," is, lest it should put those who obey the call into the state of Pharisees; and there is a secret, though not avowed, impression in their minds, that it were better for their hearers to remain in the state of publicans and harlots, and in this state to have the offer of Christ and all his benefits set before them. But mark well, that it was not the publicans and harlots who persisted in their iniquities, but they who counted John to be a prophet, and in obedience to his call, were putting their iniquities away from them, who had the advantage of the Pharisees. None will surely say, that those of them who continued as they were, were put into a state of preparation for the Saviour by the preaching of John. Some will be afraid to say, that those of them who gave up their iniquities at the bidding of John, were put into a state of preparation, lest it should encourage a pharisaical confidence in our own doings. But mark the distinction between these and the Pharisees: The Pharisees might be as free as the reforming publicans and harlots, of those visible transgressions which characterized them; but on this they rested their confidence, and put the offered Saviour away from them. The publicans and harlots, so far from resting their confidence on the degree of reformation which they had accomplished, were prompted to this reformation by the hope of the coming Saviour. They connected with all their doings the expectation of greater things. They waited for the kingdom of God that was at hand; and the preaching of John, under the influence of which they had put away from them many of their misdeeds, could never lead them to stop short at this degree of amendment, when the very same John told them of one who was to come after him, in comparison of whom he and all his sermons were as nothing. The Saviour did come, and he said of those publicans and harlots who believed and repented at the preaching of John, that they entered the kingdom of heaven before the Pharisees. They had not earned that kingdom by their doings, but they were in a fitter and readier state for receiving the tidings of it. The gospel came to them on the footing of a free and unmerited offer; and on this footing it should be proposed to all. But it is not on this footing that it will be accepted by all. Not by men who, free from many glaring and visible iniquities, rest on the decency of their own character; —not by men who, deformed by these iniquities, still wilfully and obstinately persist in them; but by men who, earnest in their inquiries after salvation, and who, made to know, as they ought to be at the very outset of their inquiries, that it is a salvation from sin as well as from punishment, have given up the practice of their outward iniquities, as the first fruit and evidence of their earnestness.

Let me, therefore, in addition to the lesson I have already urged upon you, warn you against a pharisaical confidence in your own doings. While, on the one hand, I tell you that none are truly seeking who have not begun to do; I, on the other hand, tell you, that none have truly found who have not taken up with Christ as the end of the law for righteousness. Let Jesus Christ, the same to-day, yesterday, and for ever, be the end of your conversation. Never take rest till you have found it in him. You never will have a well-grounded comfort in your intercourse with God, till you have learned the way of going to the throne of his grace in fellowship with Christ as your appointed Mediator;—you never will rejoice in hope of the coming glory, till your peace be made with God through Jesus Christ our Lord; you never will be sure of pardon, till you rest in the forgiveness of your sins as coming to you through the redemption which is in his blood. And what is more, addressing you as a people who have received a practical impulse to the obedience of the commandments, never forget, that, while the reformation of your first and earliest stages in the christian life went no farther than to the amendment of your more obvious and visible deficiencies, this reformation, to be completed, must bring the soul and spirit, as well as the body, under a subserviency to the glory of God; and it never can be completed but by the shedding abroad of that spirit which is daily poured on the daily prayers of believers: and I call upon you always to look up to God through the channel of Christ's appointed mediatorship, that you may receive through this same channel a constant and ever increasing supply of the washing of regeneration and renewing of the Holy Ghost.

I call upon you to be up and doing; but I call upon you with the very same breath, not to rest satisfied with any dark, or confused notions about your way of acceptance with God; and let it be your earnest and never-ceasing object to be found in that way. While you have the commandments and keep them, look at the same time for the promised manifestations. To be indifferent whether you have a clear understanding of the righteousness of Christ, is the same as thinking it not worth your while to inquire into that which God thought it worth his while to give up his Son unto the death that he might accomplish. It is to affront God, by letting him speak while you refuse to listen or attend to him. Have a care, lest it be an insulting sentiment on your part, as to the worth of your polluted services, and that, sinful as they are, and defective as they are, they are good enough for God. Lean not on such a bruised reed; but let Christ, in all the perfection of that righteousness, which is unto all them and upon all them that believe, be the alone rock of your confidence. Your feet will never get on a sure place till they be established on that foundation than which there is no other; and to delay a single moment in your attempts to reach it, and to find rest upon it, after it is so broadly announced to you, is to incur the aggravated guilt of those who neglect the great salvation, and who make God a liar, by suspending their belief of that record which he hath given of his Son,—" And this is the record that God hath given us eternal life, and this life is in his Son."

Again I call upon you to be up and doing; and I call upon you to accept of Christ as your alone Saviour: but I call upon you, at the same time, to look to the whole extent of his salvation. "You hath he quickened, having forgiven you all trespasses." There is the forgiveness of all that has been dead, and sinful, and alienated within you: but there is also a quickening, and a reforming, and a putting within you a near and a lively sense of God, so as that you may henceforth serve him with newness of heart, and walk before him in all newness of life and of conversation. Your hearts will be enlarged, so as that you may run the way of all the commandments. O, how it puts to flight all pharisaical confidence in the present exercises of obedience, when one casts an enlightened eye over the whole extent of the Christian race, and thinks of the mighty extent of those attainments which were exemplified by the disciples of the New Testament! The service which I now yield, and is perhaps offered up in the spirit of bondage, must be offered up in the spirit of adoption. It must be the obedience of a child, who yields the willing homage of his affections to his reconciled father. It must be the obedience of the heart: and O how far is a slavish performance of the bidden task, from the consent of the inner man to the law of that God whom he delights to honour! This love to him, and delight in him, occupy the foremost place in the list of the bidden requirements. If I love the creature more than the Creator, I trample on the authority of the first and greatest of the commandments; and what an imposing exhibition of sobriety, and justice, and almsgiving, and religious decency, may be presented in the character and doings of him whose conversation is not in heaven, who minds earthly things, who loves his wealth more than God, who likes his ease and comfort on this side of time more than all his prospects on the other side of it, and who, therefore, though he may never have looked upon himself to be any thing else than a fair Christian, is looked upon by every spiritual being as a rebel to his God, with the principle of rebellion firmly seated in his most vital part, even in his heart, turned in coldness and alienation away from him.

But if God be looked upon by you as a Father with whom you are reconciled through the blood of sprinkling, it will not be so with you. Now, this is what he calls you to do. He gives you a warrant to choose him as your God. He offers himself to your acceptance, and beseeches all to whom the word of salvation is sent, to be reconciled to Him. It is indeed a wonderful change in the state of a heart, when, giving up its coldness and indifference to God, (and I call upon every careless and unawakened man to tell me, upon his honesty, whether this be not the actual state of his heart,) it surrenders itself to him with the warm and the willing tribute of all its affections. Now, there is not one power, within the compass of nature, that can bring about this change. It does not lie with man to give up the radical iniquity of an alienated heart; the Ethiopian may as soon change his skin, and the leopard his spots. But what cannot be done by him, is done to him, when he accepts of the Gospel. The promises of Christ are abundantly peformed upon all who trust in him. Through him is the dispensation of forgiveness, and with him is the dispensation of the all-powerful and all-subduing Spirit. While, then, with the very first mention of his name, I call on you to cease your hand from doing evil, surely there is nothing in the call that can lead you to stop at any one point of obedience, when I, at the same time, tell you of the mighty change that must be accomplished, ere you are meet for the inheritance of the saints. You must be made the workmanship of God; you must be born again; you must be made to feel your dependance on the power of the renewing Spirit; and that power must come down upon you, and keep by you, and by his ever-needed supplies must form the habitual answer to your habitual and believing prayers.

I have now got upon ground on which many will refuse to go along with me. I can get their testimony to the spectacle of a reforming people, putting the visible iniquities of stealing, and lying, and evil speaking, and drunkenness, away from them; but from the moment we come to the only principle which confers any value on these visible expressions, even the willing homage of the heart to God, and to his law in all its spirituality and extent; and from the moment that we come to the only expedient by which such a principle can ever obtain an establishment within us, (and we challenge them to attempt the establishment of this principle in any other way,) even the operation of that spirit which is given to those who accept of Christ as he is laid before us in the Gospel; then, and at that moment, are we looked upon as having entered within the borders of fanaticism; and, while they lavish their superficial admiration on the flowers of virtue, do they refuse the patience of their attention to the root from which they spring, or to the nourishment which maintains them.

And here I cannot but record the effect of an actual though undesigned experiment, which I prosecuted for upwards of twelve years among you. For the greater part of that time, I could expatiate on the meanness of dishonesty, on the villainy of falsehood, on the despicable arts of calumny,—in a word, upon all those deformities of character, which awaken the natural indignation of the human heart against the pests and the disturbers of human society. Now could I, upon the strength of these warm expostulations, have got the thief to give up his stealing, and the evil speaker his censoriousness, and the liar his deviations from truth, I should have felt all the repose of one who had gotten his ultimate object. It never occurred to me that all this might have been done, and yet every soul of every hearer have remained in full alienation from God; and that even could I have established in the bosom of one who stole, such a principle of abhorrence at the meanness of dishonesty, that he was prevailed upon to steal no more, he might still have retained a heart as completely unturned to God, and as totally unpossessed by a principle of love to Him, as before. In a word, though I might have made him a more upright and honourable man, I might have left him as destitute of the essence of religious principle as ever. But the interesting fact is, that during the whole of that period in which I made no attempt against the natural enmity of the mind to God, while I was inattentive to the way in which this enmity is dissolved, even by the free offer on the one hand, and the believing acceptance on the other, of the gospel salvation; while Christ, through whose blood the sinner, who by nature stands afar off, is brought near to the heavenly Lawgiver whom he has offended, was scarcely ever spoken of, or spoken of in such a way, as stripped him of all the importance of his character and his offices, even at this time I certainly did press the reformations of honour, and truth, and integrity among my people; but I never once heard of any such reformations having been effected among them. If there was any thing at all brought about in this way, it was more than ever I got any account of. I am not sensible, that all the vehemence with which I urged the virtues and the proprieties of social life, had the weight of a feather on the moral habits of my parishioners. And it was not till I got impressed by the utter alienation of the heart in all its desires and affections from God; it was not till reconciliation to Him became the distinct and the prominent object of my ministerial exertions; it was not till I took the scriptural way of laying the method of reconciliation before them; it was not till the free offer of forgiveness through the blood of Christ was urged upon their acceptance, and the Holy Spirit given through the channel of Christ's mediatorship to all who ask him, was set before them as the unceasing object of their dependance and their prayers; it was not, in one word, till the contemplations of my people were turned to these great and essential elements in the business of a soul providing for its interest with God and the concerns of its eternity, that I ever heard of any of those subordinate reformations which I aforetime made the earnest and the zealous, but I am afraid at the same time, the ultimate object of my earlier ministrations. Ye servants, whose scrupulous fidelity has now attracted the notice, and drawn forth in my hearing a delightful testimony from your masters, what mischief you would have done, had your zeal for doctrines and sacraments been accompanied by the sloth and the remissness, and what, in the prevailing tone of moral relaxation, is counted the allowable purloining of your earlier days! But a sense of your heavenly Master's eye has brought another influence to bear upon you; and while you are thus striving to adorn the doctrine of God your Saviour in all things, you may, poor as you are, reclaim the great ones of the land to the acknowledgment of the faith. You have at least taught me, that to preach Christ is the only effective way of preaching morality in all its branches; and out of your humble cottages have I gathered a lesson, which I pray God I may be enabled to carry with all its simplicity into a wider theatre, and to bring with all the power of its subduing efficacy upon the vices of a more crowded population.

And here it gives me pleasure to observe, that, earnest as I have been for a plain and practical outset, the very first obedience of John's disciples was connected with a belief in the announcement of a common Saviour. This principle was present with them, and had its influence on the earliest movements of their repentance. Faith in

Christ had at that time but an obscure dawning in their minds; but they did not wait for its full and its finished splendour, till they should begin the work of keeping the commandments. To this infant faith there corresponded a certain degree of obedience, and this obedience grew more enlightened, more spiritual, more allied with the purity of the heart, and the movements of the inner man, just as faith obtained its brighter and larger accessions in the course of the subsequent revelations. The disciple of John keeping himself free from extortion and adultery, was a very different man from the Pharisee, who was neither an extortioner nor an adulterer. The mind of the Pharisee rested on his present performances; the mind of the disciple was filled with the expectation of a higher Teacher, and he looked forward to him, and was in the attitude of readiness to listen and believe, and obey. Many of them were transferred from the forerunner to the Saviour, and they companied with him during his abode in the world, and were found with one accord in one place on the day of Pentecost, and shared in the influences of that Comforter, whom Christ promised to send down upon his disciples on earth, from the place to which he had ascended in heaven; and thus it is that the same men who started with the preaching of John at the work of putting their obvious and palpable transgressions away from them, were met afterwards at the distance of years living the life of faith in Christ, and growing in meetness for a spiritual inheritance, by growing in all the graces and accomplishments of a spiritual obedience. There was a faith in Christ, which presided over the very first steps of their practical career; but it is worthy of being remarked, that they did not wait in indolence till this faith should receive its further augmentations. Upon this faith, humble as it was at its commencement, their teacher exacted a corresponding obedience, and this obedience, so far from being suspended till what was lacking in their faith should be perfected, was the very path which conducted them to larger manifestations. Now, is not faith a growing principle at this hour? Is not the faith of an incipient Christian different in its strength, and in the largeness of its contemplations, from the faith of him who, by reason of use, has had his senses well exercised to discern both the good and the evil? I am willing to concede it, for it accords with all my experience on the subject, that some anticipation, however faint, of the benefit to be derived from an offered Saviour; some apprehension, however indistinct, of the mercy of God in Christ Jesus: some hope, inspired by the peculiar doctrines of the Gospel, and which nothing but the preaching of that Gospel in all its peculiarity will ever awaken in the mind,—that these are the principles which preside over the very first movements of a sinner, casting away from him his transgressions, and returning unto God.

But let us not throw any impediment in the way of these first movements. Let us have a practical outset. Let us not be afraid of giving an immediate character of exertion to the very infancy of a Christian's career. To wait in slavish adherence to system, till the principle of faith be deposited with all the tenacity of a settled assurance in the mind, or the brilliancy of a finished light be thrown around it, would be to act in the face of scriptural example. Let the gospel be preached in all its freeness at the very outset; but let us never forget, that to every varying degree of faith in the mind of the hearer there goes an obedience along with it; that to forsake the evil of his ways can never be pressed too early upon his observance; that this, and every subsequent degree of obedience, is the prescribed path to clearer manifestations;* and that, to attempt the establishment of a perfect faith by the single work of expounding the truth, is to strike out a spark of our own kindling—it is to do the thing in our own way—it is to throw aside the use of scriptural expedients, and to substitute the mere possession of a dogma, for that principle which, growing progressively within us, animates and sustains the whole course of a humble, and diligent, and assiduous, and painstaking Christian.

Whence the fact, that the deriders and the enemies of evangelical truth set themselves forward as the exclusive advocates of morality? It is because many of its friends have not ventured to show so bold and so immediate a front on this subject as they ought to have done. They are positively afraid of placing morality on the fore-ground of their speculations. They do not like it to be so prominently brought forward at the commencement of their instructions. They have it, ay, and in a purer and holier form than its more ostentatious advocates; but they have thrown a doctrinal barrier around it, which hides it from the general observation. Would it not be better to drag it from this concealment—to bring it out to more immediate view—to place it in large and visible characters on the very threshold of our subject; and if our Saviour told his countrymen, at the very outset of their discipleship, that they who followed after him must forsake all, is there any thing to prevent us from battling it at the very outset of our ministrations, with all that is glaringly and obviously wrong? Much should be done to chase away the very general delusion which

---

* John, xiv. 21. Acts, v. 32.

exists among the people of this country, that the preachers of faith are not the preachers of morality. If there be any thing in the arrangements of a favourite system which are at all calculated to foster this delusion, these arrangements should just be broke in upon. Obedience should be written upon every signal; and departure from all iniquity, should be made to float, in a bright and legible inscription, upon all our standards.

I call on you, my brethren, to abound in those good deeds, by which, if done in the body, Christ will be magnified in your bodies. I call on you for a prompt vindication of the truth as it is in Jesus, by your example and your lives. Let me hear of your being the most equitable masters, and the most faithful servants, and the most upright members of society, and the most watchful parents, and the most dutiful children. Never forget, that the object of the Saviour is to redeem you from all iniquity, and that every act of wilful indulgence, in any one species of iniquity, is a refusal to go along with him. Do maintain to the eye of by-standers the conspicuous front of a reforming, and conscientious, and ever-doing people. Meet the charge of those who are strangers to the power of the truth, by the noblest of all refutations—by the graces and accomplishments of a life given in faithful and entire dedication to the will of the Saviour. Let the remembrance of what he gave for you, ever stir you up to the sense of what you should give him back again; and while others talk of good works, in such a way as to depose Christ from his pre-eminence, do you perform these good works through Christ, by the power of his grace working in you mightily.

And think not that you have attained, or are already perfect. Have your eye ever directed to the perfect righteousness of Christ, as the only ground of your acceptance with God, and as the only example you should never cease to aspire after. Rest not in any one measure of attainment. Think not that you should stop short till you are righteous, even as he is glorious. Take unto you the whole armour of God, that you be fitted for the contest, and prove that you are indeed born again by the anointing which you have received, being an anointing which remaineth. May the very God of peace sanctify you wholly. May he shed abroad his love in your hearts. And may the Spirit which I call on you to pray for, in the faith of Him who is entrusted with the dispensation of it, impel you to all diligence, that you may be found of Him, at his coming, without spot, and blameless.

I shall conclude this very hurried and imperfect Address, with the last words of my last sermon to you.

"It is not enough that you receive Christ for the single object of forgiveness, or as a Priest who has wrought out an atonement for you; for Christ offers himself in more capacities than this one, and you do not receive him truly, unless you receive him just as he offers himself. Again it is not enough that you receive Christ only as a Priest and a Prophet; for all that he teaches will be to you a dead letter, unless you are qualified to understand and to obey it; and if you think that you are qualified by nature, you in fact, refuse his teaching, at the very time that you profess him to be your teacher, for 'he says, 'without me ye can do nothing.' You must receive him for strength, as well as for forgiveness and direction, or, in other words, you must submit to him as your King, not merely to rule over you by his law, but to rule in you by his Spirit. You must live in constant dependance on the influences of his grace, and if you do so, you never will stop short at any one point of obedience; but, knowing that the grace of God is all-powerful, you will suffer no difficulties to stop your progress; you will suffer no paltry limit of what unaided human nature can do, to bound your ambition after the glories of a purer and a better character than an earthly principle can accomplish; you will enter a career, of which you at this moment see not the end; you will try an ascent, of which the lofty eminence is hid in the darkness of futurity; the chilling sentiment, that no higher obedience is expected of me than what I can yield, will have no influence upon you; for the mighty stretch of attainment that you look forward to, is not what I can do, but what Christ can do in me; and, with the all-subduing instrument of his grace to help you through every difficulty, and to carry you in triumph over every opposition, you will press forward conquering and to conquer; and, while the world knoweth not the power of those great and animating hopes which sustain you, you will be making daily progress in a field of discipline and acquirement which they have never entered; and in patience and forgiveness, and gentleness and charity, and the love of God and the love of your neighbour, which is like unto the love of God, you will prove that a work of grace is going on in your hearts, even that work by which the image you lost at the fall is repaired and brought back again, the empire of sin within you is overthrown, the subjection of your hearts to what is visible and earthly is exchanged for the power of the unseen world over its every affection, and you be filled with such a faith, and such a love, and such a superiority to perishable things, as will shed a glory over the whole of your daily walk, and give to every one of your doings the high character of a candidate for eternity.

"Christ is offered to all of you for forgiveness. The man who takes him for this single object must be looking at him with an eye half shut upon the revelation he makes of himself. Look at him with an open and a steadfast eye, and then I will call you a true believer; and sure I am, that if you do so, you cannot avoid seeing him in the earnestness of his desire that you should give up all sin, and enter from this moment into all obedience. True, and most true, my brethren, that faith will save you; but it must be a whole faith in a whole Bible. True, and most true, that they who keep the commandments of Jesus shall enter into life; but you are not to shrink from any one of these commandments, or to say because they are so much above the power of humanity, that you must give up the task of attempting them. True, and most true, that he who trusteth to his obedience as a saviour, is shifting his confidence from the alone foundation it can rest upon. Christ is your Saviour; and when I call upon you to rejoice in that reconciliation which is through him, I call upon you not to leave him for a single moment, when you engage in the work of doing those things which if left undone, will exclude us from the kingdom of heaven. Take him along with you into all your services. Let the sentiment ever be upon you, that what I am now doing I may do in my own strength to the satisfaction of man, but I must have the power of Christ resting upon the performance, if I wish to do it in the way that is acceptable to God. Let this be your habitual sentiment, and then the supposed opposition between faith and works vanishes into nothing. The life of a believer is made up of good works; and faith is the animating and the power-working principle of every one of them. The spirit of Christ actuates and sustains the whole course of your obedience. You walk not away from him, but in the language of the text, you 'walk in him,' (Col. ii. 6.) and as there is not one of your doings in which he does not feel a concern, and prescribe a duty for you, so there is not one of them in which his grace is not in readiness to put the right principle into your heart, and to bring it out into your conduct, and to make your walk accord with your profession, so as to let the world see upon you without, the power and the efficacy of the sentiment within; and thus, while Christ has the whole merit of your forgiveness, he has the whole merit of your sanctification also, and the humble and deeply-felt consciousness of 'nevertheless not me, but the grace of God that is in me,' restores to Jesus Christ all the credit and all the glory which belong to him, by making him your only, and your perfect, and your entire, and your altogether Saviour.

"Choose him, then, my brethren, choose him as the Captain of your salvation. Let him enter into your hearts by faith, and let him dwell continually there. Cultivate a daily intercourse and a growing acquaintance with him. O, you are in safe company, indeed, when your fellowship is with him! The shield of his protecting mediatorship is ever between you and the justice of God; and out of his fullness there goeth a constant stream, to nourish, and to animate, and to strengthen every believer. Why should the shifting of human instruments so oppress and so discourage you, when he is your willing friend; when he is ever present, and is at all times in readiness; when he, the same to-day, yesterday, and for ever, is to be met with in every place; and while his disciples here, giving way to the power of sight, are sorrowful, and in great heaviness, because they are to move at a distance from one another, he, my brethren, he has his eye upon all neighbourhoods and all countries, and will at length gather his disciples into one eternal family. With such a Master, let us quit ourselves like men. With the magnificence of eternity before us, let time, with its fluctuations, dwindle into its own littleness. If God is pleased to spare me, I trust I shall often meet with you in person, even on this side of the grave; but if not, let us often meet in prayer at the mercy-seat of God. While we occupy different places on earth, let our mutual intercessions for each other go to one place in heaven. Let the Saviour put our supplications into one censer; and be assured, my brethren, that after the dear and the much-loved scenery of this peaceful vale has disappeared from my eye, the people who live in it shall retain a warm and an ever-during place in my memory;—and this mortal body must be stretched on the bed of death, ere the heart which now animates it can resign its exercise of longing after you, and praying for you, that you may so receive Christ Jesus, and so walk in him, and so hold fast the things you have gotten, and so prove that the labour I have had among you has not been in vain; that when the sound of the last trumpet awakens us, these eyes, which are now bathed in tears, may open upon a scene of eternal blessedness, and we, my brethren, whom the providence of God has withdrawn for a little while from one another, may on that day be found side by side at the right hand of the everlasting throne."

APPENDIX.

Since the present edition of this work was putting to press, I have seen a review of it by the Christian Instructor, and the following are the immediate observations which the perusal of this review has suggested.

I meant no attack on any body of clergy, and I have made no attack upon them. The people whom I addressed were the main object on which my attention rested; and any thing I have said in the style of animadversion, was chiefly, if not exclusively, with a reference to that perverseness which I think I have witnessed in the conceptions and habits of private Christians.

I have alluded, no doubt, to a method of treatment on the part of some of the teachers of Christianity, and which I believe to be both inefficient and unscriptural. But have I at all asserted the extent to which this method prevails? Have I ventured to fasten an imputation upon any marked or general body of Christian ministers? It was no object of mine to set forth or to signalize my own peculiarity in this matter; and if I rightly understand who the men are whom the reviewer has in his eye when he speaks of the evangelical clergy, then does he represent me as dealing out my censures against those whom I honestly believe to be the instrumental cause of nearly all the vital and substantial Christianity in the land.

Again, is it not possible for a man to have an awakened and tender sense of the sinfulness of one sin, and to have a very slender and inadequate sense of the sinfulness of another? Might not the first circumstance beget in his mind an honest and a general desire to be delivered from sin; and might not the second circumstance account for the fact, that with this mourning for sin in the gross, he should put forth his hand without scruple to the commission of what is actually sinful? I do not know a more familiar exhibition of this, than of a man who would be visited with remorse were he to walk in the fields on a Sabbath day at the time of divine service, and the very same man indulging without remorse his propensity to throw ridicule or discredit on an absent character. His actual remorse on the commission of all that he feels to be sinful, might lead a man to mourn over sin in the general; but surely this general direction of his can have no such necessary influence, as the reviewer contends for, in the way of leading him to renounce what he does not feel to be sinful. But this is what he should be made to feel; and it may be done in two ways—either in the didactic way, by a formal announcement that the deed in question is contrary to the law of God; or in the imperative way, by bidding him cease from the doing of it,—a way no less effective and scriptural than the former, and brought to bear in the New Testament upon men at the earliest conceivable stage of their progress from sin unto righteousness.

I share most cordially in opinion with the reviewer, that he might extend his observations greatly beyond the length of the original pamphlet, were he to say all that might be said on the topics brought forward in it. I believe that it would require the compass of an extended volume to meet every objection, and to turn the argument in every possible way. I did not anticipate all the notice that has been taken of this performance, and am fearful lest it should defeat the intended effect on the hearts of a plain people. With this feeling I close the discussion for the present; and my desire is, that in all I may afterwards say upon this subject, I may be preserved from that tone of controversy, which I feel to be hurtful to the practical influence of every truth it accompanies; and which, I fear, may have in so far infected my former communications, as to make it more fitted to arouse the speculative tendencies of the mind, and provoke to an intellectual warfare, than to tell on the conscience and on the doings of an earnest inquirer.

THE

INFLUENCE OF BIBLE SOCIETIES,

ON THE

TEMPORAL NECESSITIES OF THE POOR.

ARGUMENT.

1. The Objection stated. 2. The Radical Answer to it. 3. But the Objection is not true in point of fact. 4. A former act of charity does not exempt from the obligation of a new act, if it can be afforded. 5. Estimate of the encroachment made by the Bible Society upon the funds of the country. 6. A Subscriber to the Bible Society does not give less to the Poor on that account. 7. Evidence for the truth of this assertion. 8. And explanation of its principle. (1.) The ability for other acts of charity nearly as entire as before. 9. (2.) And the disposition greater. 10. Poverty is better kept under by a preventive, than by a positive treatment. 11. Exemplified in Scotland. 12. The Bible Society has a strong preventive operation. 13. And therefore promotes the secular interests of the Poor. 14. The argument carried down to the case of Penny Societies. 15. Difficulty in the exposition of the argument. 16. The effects of a charitable endowment in a parish pernicious to the Poor. 17. By inducing a dependance upon it. 18. And stripping them of their industrious habits. 19. The effects of a Bible Association are in an opposite direction to those of a charitable endowment. 20. And it stands completely free of all the objections to which a tax is liable. 21. A Bible Association gives dignity to the Poor. 22. And a delicate reluctance to pauperism. 23. The shame of pauperism is the best defence against it. 24. How a Bible Association augments this feeling. 25. By dignifying the Poor. 26. And adding to the influence of Bible Principles. 27. Exemplified in the humblest situation. 28. The progress of these Associations in the country. 29. Compared with other Associations for the relief of temporal necessities. 30. The more salutary influence of Bible Associations. 31. And how they counteract the pernicious influence of other charities. 32. It is best to confide the secular relief of the Poor to individual benevolence. 33. And a Bible Association both augments and enlightens this principle.

1. WITHOUT entering into the positive claims of the Bible Society upon the generosity of the public, I shall endeavour to do away an objection which meets us at the very outset of every attempt to raise a subscription, or to found an institution in its favour. The secular necessities of the poor are brought into competition with it, and every shilling given to the Bible Society is represented as an encroachment upon that fund which was before allocated to the relief of poverty.

2. Admitting the fact stated in the objection to be true, we have an answer in readiness for it. If the Bible Society accomplish its professed object, which is, to make those who were before ignorant of the Bible better acquainted with it, then the advantage given more than atones for the loss sustained. We stand upon the high ground, that eternity is longer than time, and the unfading enjoyments of the one a boon more valuable than the perishable enjoyments of the other. Money is sometimes expended for the idle purpose of amusing the poor by the gratuitous exhibition of a spectacle or show. It is a far wiser distribution of the money when it is transferred from this object to the higher and more useful objects of feeding those among them who are hungry, clothing those among them who are naked, and paying for medicine or attendance to those among them who are sick. We make bold to say, that if money for the purpose could be got from no other quarter, it would be a wiser distribution still to withdraw it from the objects last mentioned to the supreme object of paying for the knowledge of religion to those among them who are ignorant; and, at the hazard of being execrated by many, we do not hesitate to affirm, that it is better for the poor to be worse fed and worse clothed, than that they should be left ignorant of those Scriptures, which are able to make them wise unto salvation through the faith that is in Christ Jesus.

3. But the statement contained in the objection is not true. It seems to go upon the supposition, that the fund for relieving the temporal wants of the poor is the only fund which exists in the country; and that when any new object of benevolence is started, there is no other fund to which we can re-

pair for the requisite expenses. But there are other funds in the country. There is a prodigious fund for the maintenance of government, nor do we wish that fund to be encroached upon by a single farthing. There is a fund out of which the people of the land are provided in the necessaries of life: and before we incur the odium of trenching upon necessaries, let us first inquire, if there be no other fund in existence. Go, then, to all who are elevated above the class of mere labourers, and you will find in their possession a fund, out of which they are provided with what are commonly called the superfluities of life. We do not dispute their right to these superfluities, nor do we deny the quantity of pleasure which lies in the enjoyment of them. We only state the existence of such a fund, and that by a trifling act of self-denial on the part of those who possess it, we could obtain all that we are pleading for. It is a little hard, that the competition should be struck between the fund of the Bible Society and the fund for relieving the temporal wants of the poor, while the far larger and more transferable fund for superfluities is left out of consideration entirely, and suffered to remain an untouched and unimpaired quantity. In this way, the odium of hostility to the poor is fastened upon those who are labouring for their most substantial interests, while a set of men who neglect the immortality of the poor, and would leave their souls to perish, are suffered to sheer off with the credit of all the finer sympathies of our nature.

4. To whom much is given, of them much will be required. Whatever be your former liberalities in another direction, when a new and a likely direction of benevolence is pointed out, the question still comes back upon you, What have you to spare? If there be a remainder left, it is by the extent of this remainder that you will be judged; and it is not right to set the claims of the Bible Society against the secular necessities of the poor, while means so ample are left, that the true way of instituting the competition is to set these claims against some personal gratification which it is in your power to abandon. Have a care, lest with the language of philanthropy in your mouth, you shall be found guilty of the cruelest indifference to the true welfare of the species, and lest the Discerner of your heart shall perceive how it prefers some sordid indulgence of its own to the dearest interests of those around you.

5. But let me not put to hazard the prosperity of our cause, by resting it on a standard of charity far too elevated for the general practice of the times. Let us now drop our abstract reasoning upon the respective funds, and come to an actual specification of their quantities. The truth is, that the fund for the Bible Society is so very small, that it is not entitled to make its appearance in any abstract argument whatever, and were it not to do away even the shadow of an objection, we would have been ashamed to have thrown the argument into the language of general discussion. What shall we think of the objection when told, that the whole yearly revenue of the Bible Society, as derived from the contributions of those who support it, does not amount to a half-penny per month from each householder in Britain and Ireland? Can this be considered as a serious invasion upon any one fund allotted to other destinations, and shall the most splendid and promising enterprise that ever benevolence was engaged in, be arrested upon an objection so fanciful? We do not want to oppress any individual by the extravagance of our demands. It is not in great sums, but in the combination of littles, that our strength lies. It is the power of combination which resolves the mystery. Great has been the progress and activity of the Bible Society since its first institution. All we want is, that this rate of activity be kept up and extended. The above statement will convince the reader, that there is ample room for the extension. The whole fund for the secular wants of the poor may be left untouched, and as to the fund for luxuries, the revenue of the Bible Society may be augmented a hundred-fold before this fund is sensibly encroached upon. The veriest crumbs and sweepings of extravagance would suffice us; and it will be long, and very long, before any invasion of ours upon this fund shall give rise to any perceivable abridgement of luxury, or have the weight of a straw upon the general style and establishment of families.

6. But there is still another way of meeting the objection. Let us come immediately to a question upon the point of fact. Does a man, on becoming a subscriber to the Bible Society, give less to the secular wants of the poor than he did formerly? It is true, there is a difficulty in the way of obtaining an answer to this question. He who knows best what answer to give will be the last to proclaim it. In as far as the subscribers themselves are concerned, we must leave the answer to their own experience, and sure we are that that experience will not be against us. But it is not from this quarter that we can expect to obtain the wished for information. The benevolence of an individual does not stand out to the eye of the public. The knowledge of its operations is confined to the little neighbourhood within which it expatiates. It is often kept from the poor themselves, and then the information we are in quest of is shut up with the giver in the silent consciousness of his bosom, and with God in the book of his remembrance.

7. But much good has been done of late years by the combined exertions of individuals; and benevolence, when operating in this way, is necessarily exposed to public observation. Subscriptions have been started for almost every one object which benevolence can devise, and the published lists may furnish us with data for a partial solution of the proposed question. In point of fact, then, those who subscribe for a religious object, subscribe with the greatest readiness and liberality for the relief of human affliction, under all the various forms in which it pleads for sympathy. This is quite notorious. The human mind, by singling out the eternity of others as the main object of its benevolence, does not withdraw itself from the care of sustaining them on the way which leads to eternity. It exerts an act of preference, but not an act of exclusion. A friend of mine has been indebted to an active and beneficent patron, for a lucrative situation in a distant country, but he wants money to pay his travelling expenses. I commit every reader to his own experience of human nature, when I rest with him the assertion, that if real kindness lay at the bottom of this act of patronage, the patron himself is the likeliest quarter from which the assistance will come. The man who signalizes himself by his religious charities, is not the last but the first man to whom I would apply in behalf of the sick and the destitute. The two principles are not inconsistent. They give support and nourishment to each other, or rather they are exertions of the same principle. This will appear in full display on the day of judgment; and even in this dark and undiscerning world, enough of evidence is before us upon which the benevolence of the Christian stands nobly vindicated, and from which it may be shown, that, while its chief care is for the immortality of others, it casts a wide and a wakeful eye over all the necessities and sufferings of the species.

8. Nor have we far to look for the explanation. The two elements which combine to form an act of charity, are the ability and the disposition, and the question simply resolves itself into this, "In how far these elements will survive a donation to the Bible Society, so as to leave the other charities unimpaired by it?" It is certainly conceivable, that an individual may give every spare farthing of his income to this institution. In this case, there is a total extinction of the first element. But in point of fact, this is never done, or done so rarely as not to be admitted into any general argument. With by far the greater number of subscribers, the ability is not sensibly encroached upon. There is no visible retrenchment in the superfluities of life. A very slight and partial change in the direction of that fund, which is familiarly known by the name of *pocket-money*, can, generally speaking, provide for the whole amount of the donation in question. There are a thousand floating and incidental expenses, which can be given up without almost the feeling of a sacrifice, and the diversion of a few of them to the charity we are pleading for, leaves the ability of the giver to all sense as entire as before.

9. But the second element is subject to other laws, and the formal calculations of arithmetic do not apply to it. The disposition is not like the ability, a given quantity, which suffers an abstraction by every new exercise. The effect of a donation upon the purse of a giver, is not the same with the moral influence of that donation upon his heart. Yet the two are assimilated by our antagonists, and the pedantry of computation carries them to results which are in the face of all experience. It is not so easy to awaken the benevolent principle out of its sleep, as, when once awakened in behalf of one object, to excite and to interest it in behalf of another. When the bar of selfishness is broken down, and the floodgates of the heart are once opened, the stream of beneficence can be turned into a thousand directions. It is true, that there can be no beneficence without wealth, as there can be no stream without water. It is conceivable that the opening of the floodgates may give rise to no flow, as the opening of a poor man's heart to the distresses of those around him may give rise to no act of almsgiving. But we have already proved the abundance of wealth. [Sec. 8.] It is the selfishness of the inaccessible heart which forms the mighty barrier, and if this could be done away, a thousand fertilizing streams would issue from it. Now, this is what the Bible Society, in many instances, has accomplished. It has unlocked the avenue to many a heart, which was before inaccessible. It has come upon them with all the energy of a popular and prevailing impulse. It has created in them a new taste and a new principle. It has opened the fountain, and we are sure that, in every district of the land where a Bible Association exists, the general principle of benevolence is more active and more expanding than ever.

10. And after all, what is the best method of providing for the secular necessities of the poor? Is it by labouring to meet the necessity after it has occurred, or by labouring to establish a principle and a habit which would go far to prevent its existence? If you wish to get rid of a noxious stream, you may first try to intercept it by throwing across a barrier; but in this way, you only spread the pestilential water over a greater extent of ground, and when the basin is filled, a stream as copious as before is formed out of its overflow. The

most effectual method, were it possible to carry it into accomplishment, would be to dry up the source. The parallel in a great measure holds. If you wish to extinguish poverty, combat with it in its first elements. If you confine your beneficence to the relief of actual poverty, you do nothing. Dry up, if possible, the spring of poverty, for every attempt to intercept the running stream has totally failed. The education and the religious principle of Scotland have not annihilated pauperism, but they have restrained it to a degree that is almost incredible to our neighbours of the South. They keep down the mischief in its principle. They impart a sobriety and a right sentiment of independence to the character of our peasantry. They operate as a check upon profligacy and idleness. The maintenance of parish schools is a burden upon the landed property of Scotland, but it is a cheap defence against the poor rates, a burden far heavier, and which is aggravating perpetually. The writer of the paper knows of a parish in Fife, the average maintenance of whose poor is defrayed by twenty-four pounds sterling a year, and of a parish, of the same population, in Somersetshire, where the annual assessments come to thirteen hundred pounds sterling. The preventive regimen of the one country does more than the positive applications of the other. In England, they have suffered poverty to rise to all the virulence of a formed and obstinate disease. But they may as well think of arresting the destructive progress of a torrent by throwing across an embankment, as think that the mere positive administration of relief, will put a stop to the accumulating mischiefs of poverty.

11. The exemption of Scotland from the miseries of pauperism is due to the education which their people receive at schools, and to the Bible which their scholarship gives them access to. The man who subscribes to the divine authority of this simple saying, "If any would not work neither should he eat," possesses, in the good treasure of his own heart, a far more effectual security against the hardships of indigence, than the man who is trained, by the legal provisions of his country, to sit in slothful dependence upon the liberalities of those around him. It is easy to be eloquent in the praise of those liberalities, but the truth is, that they may be carried to the mischievous extent of forming a depraved and beggarly population. The hungry expectations of the poor will ever keep pace with the assessments of the wealthy, and their eye will be averted from the exertion of their own industry, as the only right source of comfort and independence. It is quite in vain to think, that positive relief will ever do away the wretchedness of poverty. Carry the relief beyond a certain limit, and you foster the diseased principle which gives birth to poverty. On this subject, the people of England feel themselves to be in a state of almost inextricable helplessness, and they are not without their fears of some mighty convulsion, which must come upon them with all the energy of a tempest, before this devouring mischief can be swept away from the face of their community.

12. If any thing can avert this calamity from England, it will be the education of their peasantry, and this is a cause to which the Bible Society is contributing its full share of influence. A zeal for the circulation of the Bible, is inseparable from a zeal for extending among the people the capacity of reading it; and it is not to be conceived, that the very same individual can be eager for the introduction of this volume into our cottages, and sit inactive under the galling reflection, that it is still a sealed book to many thousands of the occupiers. Accordingly we find, that the two concerns are keeping pace with one another. The Bible Society does not overstep the simplicity of its assigned object: but the members of that Society receive an impulse from the cause, which carries them to promote the education of the poor, either by their individual exertions, or by giving their support to the Society for Schools. The two Societies move in concert. Each contributes an essential element in the business of enlightening the people. The one furnishes the book of knowledge, and the other furnishes the key to it. This division of employment, as in every other instance, facilitates the work, and renders it more effective. But it does not hinder the same individual from giving his countenance to both; and sure I am, that the man whose feelings have been already warmed, and whose purse has been already drawn in behalf of the one, is a likelier subject for an application in behalf of the other, than he whose money is still untouched, but whose heart is untouched also.

13. It will be seen, then, that the Bible Society is not barely defensible, but may be plead for upon that very ground on which its enemies have raised their opposition to it. Its immediate object is neither to feed the hungry nor to clothe the naked, but in every country under the benefit of its exertions, there will be less hunger to feed, and less nakedness to clothe. It does not cure actual poverty, but it anticipates eventful poverty. It aims its decisive thrust at the heart and principle of the mischief, and instead of suffering it to form into the obstinacy of an inextirpable disease, it smothers and destroys it in the infancy of its first elements. The love which worketh no ill to his neighbour will not suffer the true Christian to live in idleness upon another's bounty; and he will do as Paul did before him, he will labour with his hands

rather than be burdensome. Could we reform the improvident habits of the people, and pour the healthful infusion of Scripture principle into their hearts, it would reduce the existing poverty of the land to a very humble fraction of its present extent. We make bold to say, that in ordinary times there is not one-tenth of the pauperism of England due to unavoidable misfortune. It has grown out of a vicious and impolitic system, and the millions which are raised every year have only served to nourish and extend it. Now, the Bible Society is a prime agent in the work of counteracting this disorder. Its mode of proceeding carries in it all the cheapness and all the superior efficacy of a preventive operation. With a revenue not equal to the poor-rates of many a county, it is doing more even for the secular interests of the poor than all the charities of England united; and while a palling and injudicious sympathy is pouring out its complaints against it, it is sowing the seeds of character and independence, and rearing for future days the spectacle of a thriving, substantial, and well-conditioned peasantry.

14. I have hitherto been supposing, that the rich only are the givers, but I now call on the poor to be sharers in this work of charity. It is true, that of these poor there are some who depend on charity for their subsistence, and these have no right to give what they receive from others. And there are some who have not arrived at this state of dependence, but are on the very verge of it. Let us keep back no part of the truth from them, "If any provide not for his own, and specially for those of his own house, he hath denied the faith, and is worse than an infidel." There are others again, and these I apprehend form by far the most numerous class of society, who can maintain themselves in humble, but honest independence, who can spare a little and not feel it, who can do what Paul advises,* lay aside their penny a week as God hath prospered them, who can share that blessedness which the Saviour spoke of when he said, It was more blessed to give than to receive; who, though they cannot equal their rich neighbours in the amount of their donation, can bestow their something, and can, at all events, carry in their bosom a heart as warm to the cause, and call down as precious a blessing from the God who witnesses it. The Bible Society is opposed on the ground of its diverting a portion of relief from the secular necessities of the poor, even when the rich only are called upon to support it. When the application for support is brought down to the poor themselves, and instead of the recipients, it is proposed to make them the dispensers of charity, we may lay our account with the opposition being still more clamorous.—We undertake to prove, that this opposition is founded on a fallacy, and that, by interesting the great mass of a parish in the Bible Society, and assembling them into a penny association for the support of it, you raise a defence against the extension of pauperism.

15. We feel a difficulty in this undertaking, not from any uncertainty which hangs over the principle, but from the difficulty of bringing forward a plain and popular exhibition of it. However familiar the principle may be to a student of political science, it carries in it an air of paradox to the multitude, and it were well if this air of paradox were the only obstacle to its reception. But to the children of poesy and fine sentiment, the principle in question carries in it an air of barbarity also, and all the rigour of a pure and impregnable argument has not been able to protect the conclusions of Malthus from their clamorous indignation. There is a kind of hurrying sensibility about them which allows neither time nor temper for listening to any calculation on the subject, and there is not a more striking vanity under the sun, than that the substantial interests of the poor have suffered less from the malignant and the unfeeling, than from those who give without wisdom, and who feel without consideration;

Blessed is he that *wisely* doth
The poor man's case *consider.*

16. Let me put the case of two parishes, in the one of which there is a known and public endowment, out of which an annual sum is furnished for the maintenance of the poor; and that in the other there is no such endowment. At the outset, the poor of the first parish may be kept in greater comfort than the poor of the second; but it is the lesson of all experience, that no annual sum, however great, will be able to keep them permanently in greater comfort. The certain effect of an established provision for the poor is a relaxation of their economical habits, and an increased number of improvident marriages. When their claim to a provision is known, that claim is always counted upon, and it were well, if to flatter their natural indolence, they did not carry the calculation beyond the actual benefit they can ever receive. But this is what they always do. When a public charity is known and counted upon, the relaxation of frugal and provident habits is carried to such an extent, as not only to absorb the whole produce of the charity, but to leave new wants unprovided for, and the effect of the benevolent institution is just to create a population more wretched and more clamorous than ever.

17. In the second parish, the economical habits of the people are kept unimpaired,

---

* 1 Corinthians xvi. 2.

and just because their economy is forced to take a higher aim, and to persevere in it. The aim of the first people is to provide for themselves a part of their maintenance: The aim of the second people is to provide for themselves their whole maintenance. We do not deny, that even among the latter we will meet with distress and poverty, just such distress and such poverty as are to be found in the average of Scottish parishes. This finds its alleviation in private benevolence. To alleviate poverty is all that can be done for it; to extinguish it, we fear is hopeless. Sure we are, that the known and regular provisions of England will never extinguish it, and that, in respect of the poor themselves, the second parish is under a better system than the first. The poor-rates are liable to many exceptions, but there is none of them more decisive with him who cares for the eternity of the poor, than the temptation they hold out to positive guilt, the guilt of not working with their own hands, and so becoming burdensome to others.*

18. Let us conceive a political change in the circumstances of the country, and that the public charity of the first parish fell among the ruin of other institutions. Then its malignant influence would be felt in all its extent; and it would be seen, that it, in fact, had impoverished those whom it professed to sustain, that it had stript them of a possession far more valuable than all it had ever given, that it had stripped them of industrious habits, and left those whom its influence never reached, wealthier in the resources of their own superior industry, than the artificial provisions of an unwise and meddling benevolence could ever make them.

19. The comparison between these two parishes paves the way for another comparison. Let me now put the case of a third parish, where a Bible Association is instituted, and where the simple regulation of a penny a week, throws it open to the bulk of the people. What effect has this upon their economical habits? It just throws them at a greater distance from the thriftlessness which prevails in the first parish, and leads them to strike a higher aim in the way of economy than the people of the second. The general aim of economy in humble life, is to keep even with the world; but it is known to every man at all familiar with that class of society, that the great majority may strike their aim a little higher, and in point of fact, have it in their power to redeem an annual sum from the mere squanderings of mismanagement and carelessness. The unwise provisions in the parish have had the effect of sinking the income of the poor below their habits of expenditure, and they are brought, permanently and irrecoverably brought into a state of pauperism. In the second parish, the income, generally speaking, is even with the habits of expenditure. In the third, the income is above the habits of expenditure, and above it by the annual sum contributed to the Bible Society. The circumstance of being members to such a Society, throws them at a greater distance from pauperism than if they had not been members of it.

20. The effect on the economical habits of the people would just be the same in whatever way the stated annual sum was obtained from them, even though a compulsory tax were the instrument of raising it.* This assimilation of our plan to a tax may give rise to a world of impetuous declamation, but let it ever be remembered, that the institution of a Bible Society gives you the whole benefit of such a tax without its odiousness. It brings up their economy to a higher pitch, but it does so, not in the way which they resist, but in the way which they choose. The single circumstance of its being a *voluntary* act, forms the defence and the answer to all the clamours of an affected sympathy. You take from the poor. No! they give. You take beyond their ability. Of this they are the best judges. You abridge their comforts. No! there is a comfort in the exercise of charity; there is a comfort in the act of lending a hand to a noble enterprise; there is a comfort in the contemplation of its progress; there is a comfort in rendering a service to a friend, and when that friend is the Saviour, and that service the circulation of the message he left behind him, it is a comfort which many of the poor are ambitious to share in. Leave them to judge of their comfort, and if in point of fact, they do give their penny a week to a Bible Society, it just speaks them to have more comfort in this way of spending it than in any other which occurs to them.

21. Perhaps it does not occur to those friends of the poor while they are sitting in judgment on their circumstances and feelings, how unjustly and how unworthily they think of them. They do not conceive how truth and benevolence can be at all objects to them, and suppose, that after they have got the meat to feed, the house to shelter, the raiment to cover them, there is nothing else that they will bestow a penny upon. They may not be able to express their feelings on a suspicion so ungenerous, but I shall do it for them; "We have souls as well as you, and precious to our hearts is the Saviour who died for them. It is true

---

* Acts xx. 35. 1 Tim. v. 8.

* I must here suppose the sum to be a stated one, and a feeling of security on the part of the people, that the tax shall not be subject to variation at the caprice of an arbitrary government.

we have our distresses, but these have bound us more firmly to our Bibles, and it is the desire of our hearts, that a gift so precious, should be sent to the poor of other countries. The word of God is our hope and our rejoicing; we desire that it may be theirs also, that the wandering savage may know it and be glad, and the poor negro, under the lash of his master, may be told of a Master in heaven who is full of pity, and full of kindness. Do you think that sympathy for such as these is your peculiar attribute? Know that our hearts are made of the same materials with your own, that we can feel as well as you, and out of the earnings of a hard and honest industry, we shall give an offering to the cause; nor shall we cease our exertions till the message of salvation be carried round the globe, and made known to the countless millions who live in guilt, and who die in darkness."

22. And here it is obvious that a superior habit of economy is not the only defence which the Bible Society raises against pauperism. The smallness of the sum contributed may give a littleness to this argument, but not, let it be remembered, without giving an equal littleness to the objection of those who declaim against the institution, on the ground of its oppressiveness to the poor contributors. The great defence which such a Society establishes against pauperism, is the superior tone of dignity and independence which it imparts to the character of him who supports it. He stands on the high ground of being a dispenser of charity; and before he can submit to become a recipient of charity, he must let himself farther down than a poor man in ordinary circumstances. To him the transition will be more violent, and the value of this principle will be acknowledged by all who perceive that it is reluctance on the part of the poor man to become a pauper, which forms the mighty barrier against the extension of pauperism. A man by becoming the member of a benevolent association, puts himself into the situation of a giver. He stands at a greater distance than before from the situation of a receiver. He has a wider interval to traverse before he can reach this point. He will feel it a greater degradation, and to save himself from it, he will put forth all his powers of frugality and exertion. The idea of restraining pauperism by external administrations, seems now to be generally abandoned. But could we thus enter into the hearts of the poor, we could get in at the root of the mischief, and by fixing there a habit of economy and independence, more would be done for them, than by all the liberalities of all the opulent.

23. In those districts of Scotland where poor-rates are unknown, the descending avenue which leads to pauperism is powerfully guarded by the stigma which attaches to it. Remove this stigma, and our cottages, now rich in the possession of contentment and industry, would resign their habits, and crowd into the avenue by thousands. The shame of descending, is the powerful stimulus which urges them to contest it manfully with the difficulties of their situation, and which bears them through in all the pride of honest independence. Talk of this to the people of the South, and it sounds in their ears like an Arcadian story. But there is not a clergyman among us who has not witnessed the operation of the principle in all its fineness, and in all its moral delicacy; and surely a testimony is due to those village heroes who so nobly struggle with the difficulties of pauperism, that they may shun and surmount its degradation.

24. A Bible Association gives additional vigour and buoyancy to this elevated principle. The trifle which it exacts from its contributor is in truth never missed by him, but it puts him in the high attitude of a giver, and every feeling which it inspires, is on the side of independence and delicacy. Go over each of these feelings separately, and you find that they are all fitted to fortify his dislike at the shame and dependence of pauperism. There is a consciousness of importance which unavoidably attaches to the share he has taken in the support and direction of a public charity. There is the expanding effect of the information which comes to him through the medium of the circulated reports, which lays before him the mighty progress of an institution reaching to all countries, and embracing in its ample grasp, the men of all latitudes and all languages, which deeply interests him in the object, and perpetuates his desire of promoting it. A man with his heart so occupied, and his attention so directed, is not capable of a voluntary descent to pauperism. He has in fact become a more cultivated and intellectual being than formerly. His mind gathers an enlargement from the wide and animating contemplations which are set before him, and we appeal to the reflection of every reader, if such a man will descend as readily to a dependence on the charity of others, as he whose mind is void of information, and whose feelings are void of dignity.

25. In such associations, the rich and the poor meet together. They share in one object, and are united by the sympathy of one feeling and of one interest. We have not to look far into human nature to be convinced of the happy and the harmonizing influence which this must have upon society, and how, in the glow of one common cordiality, all asperity and discontent must give way to the kindlier principles of our nature. The days have been, when the very name of an association carried terror and suspicion along with it.—In a Bible Asso-

ciation there is nothing which our rulers need to be afraid of, and that they may rest assured, that the moral influence of such institutions is all on the side of peace and loyalty. But to confine myself to the present argument. Who does not see that they exalt the general tone and character of our people, that they bring them nearer to the dignity of superior and cultivated life, and that therefore, though their direct aim is not to mitigate poverty, they go a certain way to dry up the most abundant of its sources.

26. Let me add, that the direct influence of the Bible principles is inseparable from a zeal for the circulation of the Bible. It is not to be conceived, that anxiety for sending it to others can exist, while there is no reverence for it among ourselves, and we appeal to those districts where such associations have been formed, if a more visible attention to the Bible, and a more serious impression of its authority, is not the consequence of them. Now, the lessons of this Bible are all on the side of industry. They tell us that it is more blessed to give than to receive, and that therefore, a man who, by his own voluntary idleness, is brought under the necessity of receiving, has disinherited himself of a blessing. The poor must have bread, but the Bible commands and exhorts, that wherever it is possible, that bread should be *their own*, and that all who are able should make it their own by working for it.* No precept can be devised which bears more directly on the source of pauperism. The minister who, in his faithful exposition of the Bible, urged this precept successfully upon his people, would do much to extinguish pauperism among them. It is true that he does not always urge successfully; but surely if success is to be more looked for in one quarter than in another, it is among the pious and intelligent peasantry whom he has assembled around him, whom he has formed into a little society for the circulation of the Bible, and whose feelings he has interested in this purest and worthiest of causes.

27. Nor is the operation of this principle confined to the actual contributor. We have no doubt that it has been beautifully exemplified even among those who, unable to give their penny a week, either stand on the very verge of pauperism, or have got within its limits. They are unable to give any thing of their own, but they may be able at the same time to forego the wonted allowance which they received from another, or a part of it. The refusals of the poor to take an offered charity, or the whole amount of the offer, are quite familiar to a Scottish clergyman; and the plea on which they set the refusal, that it would be taking from others who are even needier than they, entitles them, when honestly advanced, to all the praise of benevolence. A spirit of pious attachment to the Bible would prompt a refusal of the same kind. You have other and higher claims upon you; you have the spiritual necessities of the world to provide for, and that you may be the more able to make the provision, leave me to the frugality of my own management. In this way the principle descends, and carries its healthful influence into the very regions of pauperism. It is the only principle competent to its extirpation. The obvious expedient of a positive supply to meet the wants of existing poverty, has failed, and the poor-rates of England will ever be a standing testimony to the utter inefficiency of this expedient, which, instead of killing the disease, has rooted and confirmed it. Try the other expedient then. The remedy against the extension of pauperism does not lie in the liberalities of the rich. It lies in the hearts and habits of the poor. Plant in their bosoms a principle of independence. Give a higher tone of delicacy to their characters. Teach them to recoil from pauperism as a degradation. The degradation may, at times, be unavoidable; but the thing which gives such an alarming extent to the mischief, is the debasing influence of poor-rates, whereby, in the vast majority of instances, the degradation is voluntary. But if there be an exalting influence in Bible Associations to counteract this, if they foster a right spirit of importance; above all, if they secure a readier submission to the lessons of the volume which they are designed to circulate, who does not see, that, in proportion as they are multiplied and extended over the face of the country, they carry along with them the most effectual regimen for preventing the extension of poverty.

28. And here it may be asked, if it be at all likely that these Associations will extend to such a degree as to have a sensible influence upon the habits of the country? Nothing more likely. A single individual of influence in each parish, would make the system universal. In point of fact, it is making progress every month, and such is the wonderful spirit of exertion which is now abroad, that in a few years every little district of the land may become the seat of a Bible Society. We are now upon the dawn of very high anticipations, and the wholesome effect upon the habits and principles of the people at home, is not the least of them. That part of the controversy which relates to the direct merits of the Bible Society may be looked upon as already exhausted;* and could the objection, founded

---

* 2 Thessalonians iii. 12.

* See Dealtry's pamphlets. Letter from the late Dr. Murray, professor of Hebrew in the Uni-

on its interference with the relief of the poor, be annihilated, or still more, could it be converted into a positive argument in its behalf, we are not aware of a single remaining plea upon which a rational or benevolent man can refuse his concurrence to it.

29. And the plea of conceived injury to the poor deserves to be attended to. It wears an amiable complexion, and we believe, that in some instances, a real sympathy with their distresses, lies at the bottom of it. Let sympathy be guided by consideration. It is the part of a Christian to hail benevolence in all its forms; but when a plan is started for the relief of the destitute, is he to be the victim of a popular and sentimental indignation, because he ventures to take up the question whether the plan be really an effective one? We know that in various towns of Scotland you meet with two distinct Penny Societies, one a Bible Association, the other for the relief of the indigent. It is to be regretted that there should ever be any jealousy between them, but we believe, that agreeably to what we have already said, it will often be found that the one suggested the other, and that the supporters of the former, are the most zealous, and active, and useful friends of the latter. We cannot, however, suppress the fact, that there is now a growing apprehension lest the growth of the latter Societies should break down the delicacies of the lower orders, and pave the way for a permanent introduction of poor-rates. There is a pretty general impression, that the system may be carried too far, and the uncertainty as to the precise limit has given the feeling to many who have embarked with enthusiasm, that they are now engaged in a ticklish and questionable undertaking. I do not attempt either to confirm or to refute this impression, but I count it a piece of justice to the associations I am pleading for, to assert, that they stand completely free of every such exception. The Bible Society is making steady advances towards the attainment of its object, and the sure effect of multiplying its subscribers is to conduct it in a shorter time to the end of its labours. A Society for the relief of temporal necessities is grasping at an object that is completely unattainable, and the mischief is, that the more known, and the more extensive, and the more able it becomes, it is sure to be more counted on, and at last, to create more poverty than it provides for. The Bible Society aims at making every land a land of Bibles, and this aim it will accomplish after it has translated the Bible into all languages, and distributed a sample large enough to create a native and universal demand for them.* After the people of the world have acquired such a taste for the Bible, and such a sense of its value as to purchase it for themselves, the Society terminates its career, and instead of the corruptions and abuses which other charities scatter in their way, it leaves the poor to whom it gives, more enlightened, and the poor from whom it takes, more elevated than it found them.

30. 'Charity,' says Shakspeare, 'is twice blest. It blesses him who gives, and him who takes.' This is far from being universally true. There is a blessing annexed to the heart which deviseth liberal things. Perhaps the founder of the English poor-rates acquired this blessing, but the indolence and depravity which they have been the instruments of spreading over the face of the country, are incalculable. If we wish to see the assertion of the poet realised in its full extent, go to such a charity as we are now pleading for, where the very exercise of giving on the one hand, and the instruction received on the other, have the effect of narrowing the limits of pauperism, by creating a more virtuous and dignified population.

31. There is poverty to be met with in every land, and we are ready to admit, that a certain proportion of it is due to unavoidable misfortune. But it is no less true, that in those countries where there is a known and established provision for the necessities of the poor, the greater proportion of the poverty which exists in them is due to the debasing influence of a public charity on the habits of the people. The institution we are pleading for, counteracts this influence. It does not annihilate all poverty, but it tends to annihilate the greater part of it. It arrests the progress of the many who were making a voluntary descent to pauperism, and it leaves none to be provided for but the few who have honestly struggled against their distresses, and have struggled in vain.

32. And how shall they be provided for? You may erect a public institution. This, in fact, is the same with erecting a signal of invitation, and the voluntary and self-created poor will rush in, to the exclusion of those modest and unobtrusive poor who are the genuine objects of charity. This is the never failing mischief of a known and established provision,† and it has been sadly

---

versity of Edinburgh, to Dr. Charles Stuart. Steinkoff's Tour on the Continent. Edinburgh Review, vol. xix. p. 39; and above all, the reports and summaries of the institution itself, where you will meet with a cloud of testimonies from Moravians, Missionaries, Roman Catholics, the Literati of our chief European towns, and men of piety and public spirit in all quarters of the world.

* But this native demand never will be created without the exertion of Missionaries, and the above reasoning applies, in its most important parts, to Missionary Associations. *See Appendix.*

† We must here except all those institutions, the object of which is to provide for involuntary distress, such as hospitals, and dispensaries, and

exemplified in England. The only method of doing away the mischief is to confide the relief of the poor to individual benevolence. This draws no dependence along with it. It is not counted upon like a public and proclaimed charity. It brings the claims of the poor under the discriminating eye of a neighbour, who will make a difference between a case of genuine helplessness, and a case of idleness or misconduct. It turns the tide of benevolence into its true channel, and it will ever be found, that under its operation, the poverty of misfortune is better seen to, and the poverty of improvidence and guilt is more effectually prevented.

33. My concluding observation then is, that the extension of Bible Societies, while it counteracts, in various directions, the mischief of poor-rates, augments that principle of individual benevolence which is the best substitute for poor-rates. You add to the stock of individual benevolence, by adding to the number of benevolent individuals, and this is the genuine effect of a Bible Association. Or, you add to the stock of individual benevolence in a country, by adding to the intensity of the benevolent principle, and this is the undoubted tendency of a Bible Association.* And what is of mighty importance in this argument, a Bible Association not only awakens the benevolent principle, but it enlightens it. It establishes an intercourse between the various orders of society, and on no former occasion in the history of this country, have the rich and the poor come so often together upon a footing of good will. The kindly influence of this is incalculable. It brings the poor under the eye of their richer neighbours. The visits and inquiries connected with the objects of the Bible Society, bring them into contact with one another. The rich come to be more skilled in the wants and difficulties of the poor, and by entering their houses, and joining with them in conversation, they not only acquire a benevolence towards them, but they gather that knowledge which is so essential to guide and enlighten their benevolence.

APPENDIX.

It is evident, that the above reasoning applies, in its chief parts, to benevolent Associations, instituted for any other religious purpose. It is not necessary to restrict the argument to the case of Bible Associations. I should be sorry if the Bible Society were to engross the religious benevolence of the public, and if, in the multiplication of its auxiliaries over the face of the country, it were to occupy the whole ground, and leave no room for the great and important claims of other institutions.

Of this I conceive that there is little danger. The revenue of each of these Societies is founded upon voluntary contributions, and what is voluntary may be withdrawn or transferred to other objects. I may give both to a Bible and a Missionary Society, or if I can only afford to give to one, I may select either, according to my impression of their respective claims. In this way a vigilant and discerning public will suit its benevolence to the urgency of the case, and it is evident, that each institution can employ the same methods for obtaining patronage and support. Each can, and does bring forward a yearly statement of its claims and necessities. Each has the same access to the public through the medium of the pulpit or the press. Each can send its advocates over the face of the country, and every individual, forming his own estimate of their respective claims, will apportion his benevolence accordingly.

Now what is done by an individual, may be done by every such Association as I am now pleading for. Its members may sit in judgment on the various schemes of utility which are now in operation, and though originally formed as an auxiliary to the Bible Society, it may keep itself open to other calls, and occasionally give of its funds to Missionaries, or Moravians, or the Society for Gaelic Schools, or the African Institution, or to the Jewish, and Baptist, and Hibernian, and Lancasterian Societies.

In point of fact, the subordinate Associations of the country are tending towards this arrangement, and it is a highly beneficial arrangement. It carries in it a most salutary control over all these various institutions, each labouring to maintain itself in reputation with the public, and to secure the countenance of this great Patron. Indolence and corruption may lay hold of an endowed charity, but when the charity depends upon public favour, a few glaring examples of mismanagement would annihilate it.

During a few of the first years of the Bible Society, the members of other Societies were alarmed at the rapid extension of its popularity, and expressed their fears lest it should engross all the attention and benevolence of the religious public. But the reverse has happened, and a principle made use of in the body of this pamphlet may be well illustrated by the history of this matter. [Sec. 9.] The Bible Society has drawn a great yearly sum of money from the public, and the first impression was, that it would exhaust the fund for religious charities. But while it drew money from

---

asylums for the lunatic or the blind. A man may resign himself to idleness, and become wilfully poor, that he may eat of the public bread, but he will not become wilfully sick or maimed that he may receive medicines from a dispensary, or undergo an operation in a hospital.

* Sec. 9.

the hand, it sent a fresh and powerful excitement of Christian benevolence into the heart, and under the influence of this creative principle, the fund has extended to such a degree, as not only to meet the demands of the new Society, but to yield a more abundant revenue to the older Societies than ever. We believe that the excitement goes much farther than this, and that many a deed of ordinary charity could be traced to the impulse of the cause we are pleading for. We hazard the assertion, that many thousands of those who contribute to the Bible Society, find in themselves a greater readiness to every good work, since the period of their connexion with it, and that in the wholesome channel of individual benevolence, more hunger is fed, and more nakedness clothed throughout the land, than at any period anterior to the formation of our Religious Societies.

The alarm grounded upon the tendency of these Societies with their vast revenues, to impoverish the country, is ridiculous. If ever their total revenue shall amount to a sum which can make it worthy of consideration to an enlightened economist at all, it may be proved that it trenches upon no national interest whatever, that it leaves population and public revenue on precisely the same footing of extent and prosperity in which it found them, and that it interferes with no one object which patriot or politician needs to care for. In the mean time it may suffice to state, that the income of all the Bible and Missionary Societies in the island, would not do more than defray the annual maintenance of one ship of the line. When put by the side of the millions which are lavished without a sigh on the enterprises of war, it is nothing; and shall this veriest trifle be grudged to the advancement of a cause, which, when carried to its accomplishment, will put an end to war, and banish all its passions and atrocities from the world?

I should be sorry if Penny Associations were to bind themselves down to the support of the Bible Society. I should like to see them exercising a judgment over the numerous claims which are now before the public, and giving occasionally of their funds to other religious institutions. The effect of this very exercise would be to create a liberal and well-informed peasantry, to open a wider sphere to their contemplations, and to raise the standard not merely of piety but of general intelligence among them. The diminution of pauperism is only part of the general effect which the multiplication of these Societies will bring about in the country; and if my limits allowed me, I might expatiate on their certain influence in raising the tone and character of the British population.

A SERMON

PREACHED BEFORE THE SOCIETY IN SCOTLAND,

FOR

PROPAGATING CHRISTIAN KNOWLEDGE.

(INCORPORATED BY ROYAL CHARTER,)

AT THEIR ANNIVERSARY MEETING, IN THE HIGH CHURCH OF EDINBURGH, ON THURSDAY, JUNE 2, 1814.

"And Nathaniel said unto him, Can there any good thing come out of Nazareth? Philip saith unto him, Come and see."—*John* i. 46.

THE principle of association, however useful in the main, has a blinding and misleading effect in many instances. Give it a wide enough field of induction to work upon, and it will carry you to a right conclusion upon any one case or question that comes before you. But the evil is, that it often carries you forward with as much confidence upon a limited, as upon an enlarged field of experience, and the man of narrow views will, upon a few paltry individual recollections, be as obstinate in the assertion of his own maxim, and as boldly come forward with his own sweeping generality, as if the whole range of nature and observation had been submitted to him.

To aggravate the mischief, the opinion thus formed upon the specialities of his own limited experience, obtains a holding and a tenacity in his mind, which dispose him to resist all the future facts and instances that come before him. Thus it is that the opinion becomes a prejudice; and that no statement, however true, or however impressive, will be able to dislodge it. You may accumulate facts upon facts, but the opinion he has already formed, has acquired a certain right of pre-occupancy over him. It is the law of the mind which, like the similar law of society, often carries it over the original principles of justice, and it is this which gives so strong a positive influence to error, and makes its overflow so very slow and laborious an operation.

I know not the origin of the prejudice respecting the town of Nazareth; or what it was that gave rise to an aphorism of such sweeping universality, as that no good thing could come out of it. Perhaps in two, three, or more instances, individuals may have come out of it who threw a discredit over the place of their nativity by the profligacy of their actions. Hence an association between the very name of the town, and the villainy of its inhabitants. The association forms into an opinion. The opinion is embodied into a proverb, and is transmitted in the shape of a hereditary prejudice to future generations. It is likely enough, that many instances could have been appealed to, of people from the town of Nazareth, who gave evidence in their characters and lives against the prejudice in question. But it is not enough that evidence be offered by the one party. It must be attended to by the other. The disposition to resist it must be got over. The love of truth and justice must prevail over that indolence which likes to repose, without disturbance, in its present convictions; and over that malignity which, I fear, makes a dark and hostile impression of others, too congenial to many hearts. Certain it is, that when the strongest possible demonstration was offered in the person of him who was the finest example of the good and fair, it was found that the inveteracy of the prejudice could withstand it; and it is to be feared that with the question, "Can any good come out of Nazareth?" there were many in that day who shut their eyes and their affections against him.

Thus it was that the very name of a town fastened an association of prejudice upon all its inhabitants. But this is only one example out of the many. A sect may be thrown into discredit by a very few of its individual specimens, and the same association be fastened upon all its members. A society may be thrown into discredit by the failure of one or two of its undertakings, and this will be enough to entail suspicion and ridicule upon all its future operations.

A system may be thrown into discredit by the fanaticism and folly of some of its advocates, and it may be long before it emerges from the contempt of a precipitate and unthinking public, ever ready to follow the impulse of her former recollections; it may be long before it is reclaimed from obscurity by the eloquence of future defenders; and there may be the struggle and the perseverance of many years before the existing association, with all its train of obloquies, and disgusts, and prejudices, shall be overthrown.

A lover of truth is thus placed on the right field for the exercise of his principles. It is the field of his faith and of his patience, and in which he is called to a manly encounter with the enemies of his cause. He may have much to bear, and little but the mere force of principle to uphold him. But what a noble exhibition of mind, when this force is enough for it; when, though unsupported by the sympathy of other minds, it can rest on the truth and righteousness of its own principle; when it can select its object from among the thousand entanglements of error, and keep by it amidst all the clamours of hostility and contempt; when all the terrors of disgrace cannot alarm it; when all the levities of ridicule cannot shame it; when all the scowl of opposition cannot overwhelm it.

There are some very fine examples of such a contest, and of such a triumph, in the history of philosophy. In the progress of speculation, the doctrine of the *occult qualities* fell into disrepute, and every thing that could be associated with such a doctrine was disgraced and borne down by the authority of the reigning school. When Sir Isaac Newton's Theory of Gravitation was announced to the world, if it had not the persecution of violence, it had at least the persecution of contempt to struggle with. It had the sound of an occult principle, and it was charged with all the bigotry and mysticism of the schoolmen. This kept it for a time from the chairs and universities of Europe, and for years a kind of obscure and ignoble sectarianism was annexed to that name, which has been carried down on such a tide of glory to distant ages. Let us think of this, when philosophers bring their names and their authority to bear upon us, when they pour contempt on the truth which we love, and on the system which we defend; and as they fasten their epithets upon us, let us take comfort in thinking that we are under the very ordeal through which philosophy herself had to pass, before she achieved the most splendid of her victories.

Sure I am, that the philosophers of that age could not have a more impetuous contempt for the occult principle, which they conceived to lie in the doctrine of gravitation, that many of our present philosophers have for the equally occult principle which they conceive to lie in the all-subduing efficacy of the christian faith over every mind which embraces it. Each of these two doctrines is mighty in its pretensions. The one, asserts a principle to be now in operation, and which, reigning over the material world, gives harmony to all its movements. The other, asserts a principle which it wants to put into operation, to apply to all minds, to carry round the globe, and to visit with its influence all the accessible dominions of the moral world. Mighty anticipation! It promises to rectify all disorder, to extirpate all vice, to dry up the source of all those sins, and sufferings, and sorrows, which have spread such dismal and unseemly ravages over the face of society, to turn every soul from Satan unto God; or, in other words, to annihilate that disturbing force which has jarred the harmony of the moral world, and make all its parts tend obediently to the Deity as its centre and its origin.

But how can this principle be put into operation? How shall it be brought into contact with a soul at the distance of a thousand miles from the place in which we are now standing? I know no other conceivable way than sending a messenger in possession of the principle himself, and able to convey it into the mind of another by his powers of communication. The precept of "Go and preach the Gospel unto every creature," would obtain a very partial obedience indeed, if there was no actual moving of the preacher from one place or neighbourhood to another. Were he to stand still he might preach to some creatures; he might get a smaller or a larger number to assemble around him, and it is to be hoped from the stationary pulpits of a christian country the preaching of the word has been made to bear with efficacy on the souls of multitudes. But in reference to the vast majority of the world, that may still be said which was said by an apostle in the infant state of our religion, how shall they hear without a preacher, and how shall they preach except they be sent? It is the single circumstance of being sent, which forms the peculiarity so much contended for by one part of the British public, and so much resisted by the other. The preacher who is so sent is, in good Latin, termed a *Missionary;* and such is the magical power which lies in the very sound of this hateful and obnoxious term, that it is no sooner uttered than a thousand associations of dislike and prejudice start into existence. And yet you would think it very strange: the term itself is perfectly correct in point of etymology. Many of those who are so clamorous in their hostility against it, feel no contempt for the mere act of preaching, sit with all decency and apparent seriousness under it, and have a becoming respect for the character of a preacher. Convert the preacher into a Missionary, and all you have done is merely to graft upon the man's preaching the circumstance of locomotion. How comes it that the talent, and the eloquence, and the principle, which appeared so respectable in your eyes, so long as they stood still, lose all their respectability so soon as they begin to move? It is certainly conceivable, that the personal qualities which bear with salutary influence upon the human beings of one place, may pass unimpaired and have the same salutary influence upon the human beings of another. But this is a missionary process, and though unable to bring forward any substantial exception against the thing, they cannot get the better of the disgust excited by the term. They cannot release their understanding from the influence of its old associations, and these philosophers are repelled from truth, and frightened out of the way which leads to it, by the bugbear of a name.

The precept is, "Go and preach the gospel to every creature under heaven." The people I allude to have no particular quarrel with the *preach;* but they have a mortal antipathy to the *go*—and should even their own admired preacher offer to go himself, or help to send others, he becomes a missionary, or the advocate of a mission; and the question of my text is set up in resistance to the whole scheme, "Can any good thing come out of it?"

I never felt myself in more favourable circumstances for giving an answer to the question, than I do at this moment, surrounded as I am by the members of a Society, which has been labouring for upwards of a century in the field of missionary exertion. It need no longer be taken up or treated as a speculative question. The question of the text may, in reference to the subject now before us, be met immediately by the answer of the text, "Come and see." We call upon you to look to a set of actual performances, to examine the record of past doings, and like good philosophers as you are, to make the sober depositions of history carry it over the reveries of imagination and prejudice. We deal in proofs, not in promises; in practice, not in profession; in experience, and not in experiment. The Society whose cause I am now appointed to plead in your hearing, is to all intents and purposes a Missionary Society. It has a claim to all the honour, and must just submit to all the disgrace which such a title carries along with it. It has been in the habit for many years of hiring preachers and teachers, and may be convicted times without number, of the act of sending them to a distance. What the precise distance is I do not understand to be of any signification to the argument; but even though it should, I fear that in the article of distance, our Society has at times been as extravagant as many of her neighbours. Her labours have been met with in other quarters of the world. They have been found among the haunts of savages. They have dealt with men in the very infancy of social improvement, and their zeal for proselytism has far outstript that sober preparatory management, which is so much contended for. Why, they have carried the Gospel message into climes on which Europe had never impressed a single trace of her boasted civilization. They have tried the species in the first stages of its rudeness and ferocity, nor did they keep back the offer of the Saviour from their souls, till art and industry had performed a sufficient part, and were made to administer in fuller abundance to the wants of their bodies. This process, which has been so much insisted upon, they did not wait for. They preached and they prayed at the very outset, and they put into exercise all the weapons of their spiritual ministry. In a word, they have done all the fanatical and offensive things which have been charged upon other missionaries. If there be folly in such enterprises as these, our Society has the accumulated follies of a whole century upon her forehead. She is among the vilest of the vile, and the same overwhelming ridicule which has thrown the mantle of ignominy over other Societies, will lay all her honours and pretensions in the dust.

We are not afraid of linking the claims of our Society with the general merits of the Missionary cause. With this cause she stands or falls. When the spirit of Missionary enterprise is afloat in the country, she will not be neglected among the multiplicity of other objects. She will not suffer from the number or the activity of kindred Societies. They who conceive alarm upon this ground, have not calculated upon the productive powers of benevolence. They have not meditated deeply upon the operation of this principle, nor do they conceive how a general impulse given to the Missionary spirit, may work the two fold effect of multiplying the number of Societies, and of providing for each of them more abundantly than ever.

The fact is undeniable. In this corner of the empire there is an impetuous and overbearing contempt for every thing connected with the name of Missionary. The cause has been outraged by a thousand indecencies. Every thing like the coolness of the philosophical spirit has been banished from one side of the controversy, and all the epithets of disgrace, which a perverted ingenuity could devise, have been unsparingly lavished on the noblest benefactors of the species. We have reason to believe that this opposition is not so extensive, nor so virulent in England. It is due to certain provincial associations, and may be accounted for. It is most a Scottish peculiarity; and while, with our neighbours in the South, it is looked upon as a liberal and enlightened cause; as a branch of that very principle which abolished the Slave Trade of Africa; as one of the wisest, and likeliest experiments, which in this age of benevolent enterprise, is now making for the interests of the world; as a scheme ennobled by the patronage of royalty; supported by the contributions of opulence; sanctified by the prayers and the wishes of philanthropy; assisted by men of the first science, and the first scholarship; carrying into execution by as hardy adventurers as ever trod the desert in quest of novelty; and enriching grammar, geography, and natural knowledge, by the discoveries they are making every year, as to the statistics of all countries, and the peculiarities of all languages; while, I say, such are the dignified associations thrown around the Missionary cause in England; in this country I am sorry to say a very different set of collaterals is annexed to it. A great proportion of our nobility, gentry, and clergy, look upon it as a very low and drivelling concern; as a visionary enterprize, and that no good thing can come out of it; as a mere dreg of sectarianism, and which none but sectarians, or men who should have been sectarians, have any relish or respect for. The torrent of prejudice runs strongly against it, and the very name of Missionary excites the most nauseous antipathy in the hearts of many, who, in other departments, approve themselves to be able, and candid, and reflecting inquirers.

We have no doubt that in the course of years all this will pass away. But reason and experience are slow in their operation; and, in the mean time, we count it fair to neutralize, if possible, one prejudice by another; to school down a Scottish antipathy by a Scottish predilection, and to take shelter from the contempt that is now so wantonly pouring on the best of causes under the respected name of a Society, which has earned by the services of a hundred years, the fairest claims on the gratitude and veneration of all our countrymen. Come, and see the effect of her Missionary exertions. It is palpable and near at hand. It lies within the compass of many a summer tour; and tell me, ye children of fancy, who expatiate with a delighted eye over the wilds of our mountain scenery, if it be not a dearer and worthier exercise still, to contemplate the habits of her once ragged and wandering population. What would they have been at this moment, had schools, and Bibles, and Ministers, been kept back from them? and had the men of a century ago been deterred by the flippancies of the present age, from the work of planting chapels and seminaries in that neglected land? The ferocity of their ancestors would have come down unsoftened and unsubdued to the existing generation. The darkening spirit of hostility would still have lowered upon us from the North; and these plains, now so peaceful and so happy, would have lain open to the fury of merciless invaders. O, ye soft and sentimental travellers, who wander so securely over this romantic land, you are right to choose the season when the angry elements of nature are asleep. But what is it that has charmed to their long repose the more dreadful elements of human passion and human injustice? What is it that has quelled the boisterous spirit of her natives?—and while her torrents roar as fiercely, and her mountain brows look as grimly as ever, what is that which has thrown so softening an influence over the minds and manners of her living population?

I know not that there are several causes; but sure I am, that the civilizing influence of our Society has had an important share. If it be true that our country is indebted to her Schools and her Bibles for the most intelligent and virtuous peasantry in Europe, let it never be forgotten that the Schools in the establishment of our Society are nearly equal to one-third of all the parishes in Scotland; that these schools are chiefly to be met with in the Highland district; that they bear as great a proportion to the Highland population, as all our parochial seminaries do to all our population; or, in other words, had the local convenience for the attendance of scholars been as great as in other parts of the country, the apparatus set a going by our Society, for the education of the Highland peasantry, would have been as effective as the boasted provision of the legislature, for the whole of Scotland.*

---

* This want of local convenience for the attendance of scholars, is the chief difficulty which our Society has to struggle with. The number of scholars bears to the population the proportion stated in the text; but think of the broad surface of a thinly peopled country, intersected with deep bays, and crossed in every direction by the natural barriers of lakes and mountains. There are only two ways in which education can be carried over the face of a country so peculiarly formed. The first way is, by the multiplication of stationary points, from which learning may emanate among the children in distinct neighbourhoods. The second way is, by the operation of circulating schools, which describe at intervals the blank spaces that are placed beyond the reach of stationary schools. In the present situation of the Highlands, both of these methods are putting into operation; and both are entitled to the support and patronage of the public. But without wishing to withdraw a single farthing from the latter of these methods, we are

I pass over the attempts of our Society to introduce the knowledge of the arts and the habits of useful industry among them. I will deny that the former, if it could be put into operation, is the most effectual, for the full and the regular education of the Highlanders. A fixed school, operating at all seasons, will do more for its neighbourhood than can be done by a moveable apparatus set up only at intervals, and transferring itself at the end of a few months to other scenes, and to other neighbourhoods. Let us aim, therefore, at the multiplication of the fixed points; but a mighty sum will be necessary before such a system is completed; and in the mean time, let not the population of the intermediate spaces be abandoned. Let the cheapest and readiest expedient that offers for their education be adopted, and let the public hold forth a liberal hand to the society for circulating schools. But what is to hinder us to combine with this, the gradual extension of the system of fixed and regular education? The parochial schools furnish us with so many fixed points. The Society I am now pleading for, furnish us so many more. The very existence of the Gaelic Society, is a proof both of the extent and multiplicity of those intermediate spaces, over which they are operating with so much efficiency. Now the precise ground upon which we lay claim to the support of the public, is, that we want to scatter a few more stationary schools over these intermediate spaces—not to supersede the labours of the other Society; for the period of time at which this can be possibly accomplished, is still at an indefinite distance from us—but by narrowing the ground of their operation, to enable them to do more complete justice to the mighty remainder, on which they have every prospect of expatiating for years and generations to come; to make the task more commensurate to their means, and enable them to circulate, with greater frequency and effect, over those remoter tracts, which we have as yet no immediate prospect of reaching.

Who would not give all jealousy to the wind, when they see how beautifully situated the operations of these two distinct societies are to one another? Circulate, with all possible activity, among the interjacent spaces on the one hand, but do not give up the prospect of permanent establishments in these spaces on the other. The last is the province of our Society, and is advanced as our distinct claim upon the generosity of the public. We lay claim to this generosity; and what is more, we stand in need of it. It is not true that we do not teach the Gaelic to our Highland scholars. The instructions given to every Schoolmaster, and the reports of the committees of Presbyteries, upon the examination of scholars, form a distinct refutation to the impression which has got abroad upon this subject. Strange that this Society should be charged with a hostility to Gaelic education, to whose exertion and whose patronage the Highlands of Scotland are indebted for the existence of the Gaelic Bible. On the other hand, it is not true that our funds are so ample as to make us independent of any appeals that can be made to the generosity of the public. Our expenditure is at this moment pressing upon our resources. We have done much. There are hundreds of Schools regularly supported by us; but we appeal to the very existence of other Societies for the fact, that we have still much to do. We appeal to the press of applications for more Schools, and more Schoolmasters, and more salaries. These applications have not room for every thing. And to reclaim, if possible, the prejudices of those who I fear have little sympathy with the wants of the ever-during soul, I have been lingering all the while upon the inferior ground of temporal advantage. But I may detain you for hours upon this ground, and after all I have said about a more peaceful neighbourhood, and a more civilized peasantry, I may positively have said nothing upon the essential merits of the cause. I can conceive the wish of his present Majesty, that every one in his dominions may be able to read the Bible, to meet an echo in every bosom. But why? Because the very habit of reading implies a more intelligent people, and must stand associated in every mind with habits of order, and comfort, and decency. But separate these from the religious principle, and what are they? At the very best they are the virtues of a life; their office is to scatter a few fleeting joys over a short and uncertain pilgrimage, and to deck a temporary scene with blessings, which are to perish and be forgotten. No! In our attempts to carry into effect the principle of being all things to all men, let us never exalt that which is subordinate; let us never give up our reckoning upon eternity, or be ashamed to own it as our sentiment, that though schools were to multiply, though Missionaries were to labour, and all the decencies and accomplishments of social life were to follow in their train, the great object would still be unattained, so long as the things of the Holy Spirit were unrelished and undiscerned among them, and they wanted that knowledge of God and of Jesus Christ, which is life everlasting. This is the ground upon which every Christian will rest the vindication of every Missionary enterprise; and this is the ground upon which he may expect to be abandoned by the infidel, who laughs at piety; or the lukewarm believer, who dreads to be laughed at for the extravagance to which he carries it. The Christian is not for giving up the social virtues; but the open enemy and the cold friend of the gospel are for giving up piety; and while they garnish all that is right and amiable in humanity, with the unsubstantial praises of their eloquence, they pour contempt upon that very principle which forms our best security for the existence of virtue in the world. We say nothing that can degrade the social virtues in the estimation of men; but by making them part of religion, we exalt them above all that poet or moralist can do for them. We give them God for their object, and for their end the grandeur of eternity. No! It is not

come upon us every year, and the painful necessity we are under of refusing many of them, proves to a demonstration, that the want of pecuniary aid is the only limit to the usefulness of our exertions.

the Christian who is the enemy of social virtue; it is he who sighs in all the ecstacy of sentiment over it, at the very time that he is digging away its foundation, and wreaking on that piety which is its principle, the cruelty of his scorn.

It is very well in its place to urge the civilizing influence of a Missionary Society. But this is not the main object of such an institution. It is not the end. It is only the accompaniment. It is a never-failing collateral, and may be used as a lawful instrument in fighting the battles of the Missionary cause. It is right enough to contest it with our enemies at every one point of advantage; and for this purpose to descend, if necessary, to the very ground on which they have posted themselves. But, when so engaged, let us never forget the main elements of our business; for there is a danger, that when turning the eye of our antagonist to the lovely picture of peace, and industry and cultivation, raised by many a Christian Missionary, among the wilds of heathenism, we turn it away from the very marrow and substance of our undertaking; the great aim of which is to preach Christ to sinners, and to rear human souls to a beauteous and never-fading immortality.

The wish of our pious and patriotic king, that every man in his dominions might be able to read the Bible, has circulated through the land. It has been commented upon with eloquence; and we doubt not, that something like the glow of a virtuous sensibility has been awakened by it. But let us never forget that in the breasts of many, all this may be little better than a mere theatrical emotion. Give me the man who is in the daily habit of opening his Bible, who willingly puts himself into the attitude of a little child when he reads it, and casts an unshrinking eye over its information and its testimony. This is the way of giving effect and consistency to their boasted admiration of the royal sentiment. The mere admiration in itself indicates nothing. It may be as little connected with the sturdiness of principle as the finery of any poetical delusion. O! it is easy to combine a vague and general testimony to the Bible, with a disgusted feeling of antipathy to the methodism of its actual contents; and thousands can profess to make it their rallying point, who pour contempt upon its doctrines, and give the lie to the faithfulness of its sayings.

Let us put you to the trial. The Bible tells us, that "he who believeth not the Son shall not see life, but the wrath of God abideth on him." It calls upon us "to preach the gospel to every creature," that every creature may believe it; for he who so "believeth shall not perish, but have everlasting life." Such is the mighty difference between believing and not believing. It makes all the difference between hell and heaven. He who believeth, hath passed from death even unto life; and the errand of the Missionary is to carry these overtures to the men of all languages, and all countries; that he may prevail upon them to make this transition. Some reject his overtures, and to them the gospel is the savour of death unto death. Others embrace them, and to them the gospel is the savour of life unto life. Whatever be his reception, he counts it his duty and his business to preach the gospel; and if he get some to hear, and others to forbear, he just fares as the Apostles did before him. Now, my brethren, have we got among the substantial realities of the Missionary cause. We have carried you forward from the accessaries to the radical elements of the business; and if you, offended at the hardness of these sayings, feel as if now we had got within the confines of methodism; then know that this feeling arose in your minds at the very moment that we got within the four corners of the Bible; and your fancied admiration of this book, however exquisitely felt, or eloquently uttered, is nothing better than the wretched flummery of a sickly and deceitful imagination.

Our venerable Society has given the sanction of her example to the best and the dearest objects of Missionaries. Like others she has kept a wakeful eye over all that could contribute to the interests of the species. She has given encouragement to art and to industry, but she has never been diverted from the religion of a people as the chief aim of all her undertakings. To this end she has multiplied schools, and made the reading of the Scriptures the main acquirement of her scholars. The Bible is her school-book, and it is to her that the Highlands of Scotland owe the translation of the sacred record into their own tongue. She sends preachers as well as teachers among them. As she has made the reading of the word a practicable acquirement, so she has made the hearing of the word an accessible privilege. In short, she has set up what may be called a christian apparatus in many districts, which the Legislature of the country had left unprovided for. She is filling up the blanks which, among the scattered and extended parishes of the North, occur so frequently over the broad surface of a thinly peopled country. She has come in contact with those remoter groups and hamlets, which the influence of the Establishment did not reach. And she has multiplied her endowments at such a rate, that very many people have got christian instruction in its different branches as nearly, and as effectively to bear upon them, as in the more favoured districts of the land.

When a wealthy native of a Highland parish, penetrated with a feeling of the wants of his neighbours, erects a chapel, or endows a seminary among them, his benevolence is felt and acknowledged by all; and I am not aware of a single association which can disturb our moral estimate of such a proceeding, or restrain the fulness of that testimony which is due to it. But should an individual, at a distance from the parish in question, do the same thing; should he, with no natural claim upon him, and without the stimulus of any of those affections, which the mere circumstance of vicinity is fitted to inspire; should he, I say, merely upon a moving representation of their necessities, devote his wealth to the same cause; what influence ought this to have upon our estimate of his character? Why, in all fairness, it should just lead us to infer a stronger degree of the principle of philanthropy, a principle which in his case was unaided by any local influence whatever, and which urged him to exertion, and to sacrifice, in the face of an obstacle which the other had not to contend with —the obstacle of distance. Now, what one individual may be conceived to do for one parish, a number of individuals may do for a number of parishes. They may form into a society, and combine their energies and their means for the benefit of the whole country, and should that country lie at a distance, the only way in which it affects our estimate of their exertions, is by leading us to see in them a stronger principle of attachment to the species, and a more determined zeal for the object of their benevolence, in spite of the additional difficulties with which it is encumbered.

Now the principle does not stop here. In the instance before us, it has been carried from the metropolis of Scotland to the distance of her Northern extremities. But tell me, why it might not be carried round the globe. This very Society has carried it over the Atlantic, and the very apparatus which she has planted in the Highlands and islands of our country, she has set a going more than once in the wilds of America. The very discipline which she has applied to her own population, she has brought to bear on human beings in other quarters of the world. She has wrought with the same instruments upon the same materials, and as in sound philosophy it ought to have been expected, she has obtained the same result—a christian people rejoicing in the faith of Jesus, and ripening for heaven, by a daily progress upon earth in the graces and accomplishments of the gospel. I have yet to learn what that is which should make the same teaching, and the same Bible, applicable to one part of the species, and not applicable to another. I am not aware of a single principle in the philosophy of man, which points to such a distinction; nor do I know a single category in the science of human nature, which can assist me in drawing the landmark between those to whom Christianity may be given, and those who are unworthy or unfit for the participation of its blessings. I have been among illiterate peasantry, and I have marked how apt they were in their narrow field of observation, to cherish a kind of malignant contempt for the men of another shire, or another country. I have heard of barbarians, and of their insolent disdain for foreigners. I have read of Jews, and of their unsocial and excluding prejudices. But I always looked upon these as the jealousies of ignorance, which science and observation had the effect of doing away, and that the accomplished traveller, liberalized by frequent intercourse with the men of other countries, saw through the vanity of all these prejudices, and disowned them. What the man of liberal philosophy is in sentiment, the Missionary is in practice. He sees in every man a partaker of his own nature, and a brother of his own species. He contemplates the human mind in the generality of its great elements. He enters upon the wide field of benevolence, and disdains those geographical barriers, by which little men would shut out one half of the species from the kind offices of the other. His business is with man, and let his localities be what they may, enough for his large and noble heart, that he is bone of the same bone. To get at him, he will shun no danger, he will shrink from no privation, he will spare himself no fatigue, he will brave every element of heaven, he will hazard the extremities of every clime, he will cross seas, and work his persevering way through the briers and thickets of the wilderness. In perils of waters, in perils of robbers, in perils by the heathen, in weariness and painfulness, he seeks after him. The cast and the colour are nothing to the comprehensive eye of a Missionary. His is the broad principle of good will to the children of men. His doings are with the species, and overlooking all the accidents of climate, or of country, enough for him, if the individual he is in quest of be a man—a brother of the same nature—with a body which a few years will bring to the grave, and a spirit that returns to the God who gave it.

But this man of large and liberal principles is a Missionary; and this is enough to put to flight all admiration of him, and of his doings. I forbear to expatiate; but sure I am that certain philosophers of the day, and certain fanatics of the day, should be made to change places; if those only are the genuine philosophers who keep to the principles in spite of names, and those only the genuine fanatics who are ruled by names instead of principles.

The Society for propagating Christian knowledge in the Highlands and Islands of Scotland, has every claim upon a religious public; and I trust that those claims will not be forgotten among the multiplicity of laudable and important objects, which are now afloat in this age of benevolent enterprise. She has all the experience and respectability and tried usefulness of age; may she have none of the infirmities of age. May she have nothing either of the rust or the indolence of an establishment about her. Resting on the consciousness of her own righteous and strongly supported cause; may she look on the operations of other societies with complacency, and be jealous of none of them. She confers with them upon their common objects; she assists them with her experience, and when, struggling with difficulties, they make their appeal to the generosity of the christian world, she nobly leads the way, and imparts to them with liberal hand, out of her own revenue. She has conferred lasting obligations upon the Missionary cause. She spreads over it the shelter of her venerable name, and by the answer of "Come and see," to those who ask if any good thing can come out of it, she gives a practical refutation to the reasonings of all its adversaries. She redeems the best of causes from the unmerited contempt under which it labours, and she will be repaid. The religious public will not be backward to own the obligation. We are aware of the prevalence of the Missionary spirit, and of the many useful directions in which it is now operating. But we are not afraid of the public being carried away from us. We know that there is room for all, that there are funds for all; and our policy is not to repress, but to excite the Missionary spirit, and then there will be a heart for all.

A SERMON,

DELIVERED IN THE TRON CHURCH, GLASGOW, ON WEDNESDAY, NOV. 19, 1817.

THE DAY OF THE FUNERAL OF HER ROYAL HIGHNESS,

THE

PRINCESS CHARLOTTE OF WALES.

ADVERTISEMENT.

The following Sermon is the fruit of a very hurried and unlooked-for exertion—and never was there any publication brought forward under circumstances of greater reluctancy, and with a more honest feeling of unpreparedness, on the part of the author. The truth is, that he was at a great distance from home, when the urgency of the public demand for his personal appearance on the nineteenth of November, reached him, and that so late, that he had no other resource than to write for the pulpit during the intervals, and after the exhaustion of a very rapid and fatiguing journey. It is true that he might revise. But to revise such a composition, would be to re-make it; and he has chosen rather to bring it forward, and that as nearly as possible, in the literal terms of its delivery.

But, it may be asked, if so unfit for the public eye, why make it public? It may be thought by many, that the avowal is not a wise one. But wisdom ought never to be held in reverence separately from truth; and it would be disguising the real motive, were it concealed, that a very perverse misconception which has gone abroad respecting one passage of the Sermon, and which has found its way into many of the newspapers, is the real and impelling cause of the step that has been taken; and that, had it not been for the spread of such a misconception, there never would have been obtruded on the public, a performance written on a call of urgent necessity, and most assuredly without the slightest anticipation of authorship.

But, it may be said, does not such a measure as this bring the pulpit into a state of the most degrading subordination to the diurnal press, since there is not a single sermon which cannot be so reported, as, without the literality of direct falsehood, to convey through the whole country, all the injuries of a substantial misrepresentation; and if a minister should condescend publicly to notice every such random and ephemeral statement, he might thereby incessantly involve himself in the most helpless and harassing of all controversy?

Now, in opposition to this, let it be observed, that a person placed in this difficult and disagreeable predicament, may advert for once to such a provocation, and that for the express purpose, that he may never have to do it again. He may count it enough to make one decisive exposure of the injustice which can be done in this way to a public instructor, and then hold himself acquitted of every similar attempt in all time coming. He thereby raises a sort of abiding or monumenta' antidote, which may serve to neutralize the mischief of any future attack, or future insinuation. By this one act, though he may not silence the obloquies of the daily press, he has at least purchased for himself the privilege of standing unmoved by all the mistakes, or by all the malignities which may proceed from it.

Yet, it is no more than justice to a numerous and very important class of writers, to state it as our conviction of the great majority of them, that they feel the dignity and responsibility of their office, and hold it to be the highest point of professional honour, ever to maintain the most gentlemanly avoidance of all that is calculated to wound the feelings of an unoffending individual.

There is one temptation, however, to which the editors of this department of literature are peculiarly liable, which may be briefly adverted to, and the influence of which, may be observed to extend even to a higher class of journalists. There is an eagerness to transmute every thing into metal of their own peculiar currency—there is an extreme avidity to lay hold of every utterance, and to send it abroad, tinged with the colouring of their own party—there is a ravenous desire of approbation, extending itself to every possible occurrence, and to every one individual whom they would like to enlist under the banners of their own partisanship, which, for their own credit, they would be more careful to repress, did they perceive with sufficient force, and sufficient distinctness, that it makes them look more like desperadoes of a sinking cause, than the liberal and honest expounders of public politics and literature, which claim so respectable a portion of the intelligence of the country.

The writer of this sermon has only to add, that he does not know how a sorer imputation could have been devised against the heart and the principles of a clergyman, than that, on the tender and hallowed day of a nation's repose from all the sordidness and all the irritations of party, he should have made the pulpit a vehicle of invective against any administration; or that, after mingling his tears with those of his people, over the untimely death of one so dear to us, he should have found room for any thing else than those lessons of general Christianity, by which an unsparing reproof is ministered to impiety, in whatever quarter it may be found—even that impiety which wears the very same features, and offers itself in the very same aspect, under all administrations.

SERMON.

"For when thy judgments are in the earth, the inhabitants of the world will learn righteousness."
Isaiah xxvi. 9.

I AM sorry that I shall not be able to extend the application of this text beyond its more direct and immediate bearing on that event on which we are now met to mingle our regrets, and our sensibilities, and our prayers—that, occupied as we all are with the mournful circumstance that has bereft our country of one of its brightest anticipations, I shall not be able to clear my way to the accomplishment of what is, strictly speaking, the congregational object of an address from the pulpit, which ought, in every possible case, to be an address to the conscience—that, therefore, instead of the concerns of personal Christianity, which, under my present text, I might, if I had space for it, press home upon the attention of my hearers, I shall be under the necessity of restricting myself to that more partial application of the text which relates to the matters of public Christianity. It is upon this account, as well as upon others, that I rejoice in the present appointment, for the improvement of that sad and sudden visitation, which has so desolated the hearts and the hopes of a whole people. I therefore feel more freedom in coming forward with such remarks as, to the eyes of many, may wear a more public and even political complexion, than is altogether suited to the ministrations of the Sabbath. And yet I cannot but advert, and that in such terms of reproof as I think to be most truly applicable, to another set of men, whose taste for preaching is very much confined to these great and national occasions—who, habitually absent from church on the Sabbath, are yet observed, and that most prominently, to come together in eager and clustering attendance, on some interesting case of pathos or of politics—who in this way obtrude upon the general notice, their loyalty to an earthly sovereign, while, in reference to their Lord and Master, Jesus Christ, they scandalize all that is Christian in the general feeling, by their manifest contempt for him and for his ordinances—who look for the ready compliance of ministers, in all that can gratify their inclinations for pageantry, while for the real, effective, and only important business of ministers, they have just as little reverence as if it were all a matter of hollow and insignificant parade. It is right to share in the triumphs of successful, and to shed the tears of afflicted, patriotism. But it is also right to estimate according to its true character, the patriotism of those who are never known to offer one homage to Christianity, except when it is associated with the affairs of state, or with the wishes, and the commands, and the expectations of statesmen.

But the frivolous and altogether despicable taste of the men to whom I am alluding, must be entirely separated from such an occasion as the present. For, in truth, there never was an occasion of such magnitude, and at the same time of such peculiarity. There never was an occasion on which a matter of deep political interest was so blended and mixed up with matter of very deep and affecting tenderness. It does not wear the aspect of an affair of politics at all, but of an affair of the heart; and the novel exhibition is now offered, of all party-irritations merging into one common and overwhelming sensibility. Oh! how it tends to quiet the agitations of every earthly interest and earthly passion, when Death steps forward and demonstrates the littleness of them all—when he stamps a character of such affecting insignificance on all that we are contending for—when, as if to make known the greatness of his power in the sight of a whole country, he stalks in ghastly triumph over the might and the grandeur of its most august family, and singling out that member of it on whom the dearest hopes and the gayest visions of the people were suspended, he, by one fatal and resistless blow, sends abroad the fame of his victory and his strength, throughout the wide extent of an afflicted nation. He has indeed put a cruel and impressive mockery on all the glories of mortality. A few days ago, all looked so full of life, and promise, and security—when we read of the bustle of the great preparation—and were told of the skill and the talent that were pressed into the service—and heard of the goodly attendance of the most eminent in the nation—and how officers of state, and the titled dignitaries of the land, were charioted in splendour to the scene of expectation, as to the joys of an approaching holiday—yes, and we were told too, that the bells of the surrounding villages were all in readiness for the merry peal of gratulation, and that the expectant metropolis of our empire, on tiptoe for the announcement of her future monarch, had her winged couriers of despatch to speed the welcome message to the ears of her citizens, and that from her an embassy of gladness was to travel over all the provinces of the land; and the country, forgetful of all that she had suffered, was at length to offer the spectacle of one wide and rejoicing jubilee. O Death! thou hast indeed chosen the time and the victim, for demonstrating the grim ascendancy of thy power over all the hopes and fortunes o. our species!—Our blooming Princess, whom fancy had decked with the coronet of these realms, and under whose gentle sway all bade so fair for the good and the peace of our nation, has he placed upon her bier! And, as if to fill up the measure of his triumph, he has laid by her side, that babe, who, but for him, might have been the monarch of a future generation; and he has done that, which by no single achievement he could otherwise have accomplished—he has sent forth over the whole of our land, the gloom of such a bereavement as cannot be replaced by any living descendant of royalty—he has broken the direct succession of the monarchy of England—by one and the same disaster, has he wakened up the public anxieties of the country, and sent a pang as acute as that of the most woful domestic visitation, into the heart of each of its families.

In the prosecution of the following discourse, as I have already stated, I shall satisfy myself with a very limited application of the text. I shall, in the first place, offer a few remarks on that branch of the righteousness of practical Christianity, which consists in the duty that subjects owe to their governors. And in the second place, I shall attempt to improve the present great national disaster, to the object of impressing upon you, that, under all our difficulties and all our fears, it is the righteousness of the people alone which will exalt and perpetuate the nation; and that therefore, if this great interest be neglected, the country, instead of reaping improvement from the judgments of God, is in imminent danger of being utterly overwhelmed by them.

I. But here let me attempt the difficult task of rightly dividing the Word of truth—and premise this head of discourse, by admitting that I know nothing more hateful than the crouching spirit of servility. I know not a single class of men more unworthy of reverence, than the base and interested minions of a court. I know not a set of pretenders who more amply deserve to be held out to the chastisement of public scorn, than they who, under the guise of public principle, are only aiming at personal aggrandizement. This is one corruption. But let us not forget that there is another—even a spurious patriotism which would proscribe loyalty as one of the virtues altogether. Now, I cannot open my Bible, without learning that loyalty is one branch of the righteousness of practical Christianity.—I am not seeking to please men, but God, when I repeat his words in your hearing—that you should honour the King—that you should obey Magistrates—that you should meddle not with those who are given to change—that you should be subject to principalities and powers—that you should lead a quiet and peaceable life in all godliness and honesty. This, then, is a part of the righteousness which it is our business to teach, and sure I am that it is a part of righteousness which the judgment now dealt out to us, should, of all others, dispose you to learn. I know not a virtue more in harmony with the present feelings, and afflictions, and circumstances of the country, than that of a steadfast and determined loyalty. The time has been, when such an event as the one that we are now assembled to deplore, would have put every restless spirit into motion, and set a guilty ambition upon its murderous devices, and brought powerful pretenders with their opposing hosts of vassalage into the field, and enlisted towns and families under the rival banners of a most destructive fray of contention, and thus have broken up the whole peace and confidence of society. Let us bless God that these days of barbarism are now gone by. But the vessel of the state is still exposed to many agitations. The sea of politics is a sea of storms, on which the gale of human passions would make her founder, were it not for the guidance of human principle; and, therefore, the truest policy of a nation is to christianize her subjects, and to disseminate among them the influence of religion. The most skilful arrangement for rightly governing a state, is to scatter among the governed, not the terrors of power—not the threats of jealous and alarmed authority—not the demonstrations of sure and ready vengeance held forth by the rigour of an offended law. These may, at times, be imperiously called for. But a permanent security against the wild outbreakings of turbulence and disaster, is only to be attained by diffusing the lessons of the Gospel throughout the great mass of our population—even those lessons which are utterly and diametrically at antipodes with all that is criminal and wrong in the spirit of political disaffection. The only radical counteraction to this evil is to be found in the spirit of Christianity; and though animated by such a spirit, a man may put on the intrepidity of one of the old prophets, and denounce even in the ear of royalty the profligacies which may disgrace or deform it—though animated by such a spirit, he may lift his protesting voice in the face of an unchristian magistracy, and tell them of their errors—though animated by such a spirit, he, to avoid every appearance of evil, will neither stoop to the flattery of power, nor to the solicitations of patronage—and though all this may bear, to the superficial eye, a hard, and repulsive, and hostile aspect towards the established dignities of the land—yet forget not, that if a real and honest principle of Christianity lie at the root of this spirit, there exists within the bosom of such a man, a foundation of principle, on which all the lessons of Christianity will rise into visible and consistent exemplification. And it is he, and such as he, who will turn out to be the salvation of the country, when the hour of her threatened danger is approaching—and it is just in proportion as you spread and multiply such a character, that you raise within the bosom of the nation, the best security against all her fluctuations—and, as in every other department of human concerns, so will it be found, that, in this particular department, Christians are the salt of the earth, and Christianity the most copious and emanating fountain of all the guardian virtues of peace, and order, and patriotism.

The judgment under which we now labour, supplies, I think, one touching, and, to every good and christian mind, one powerful argument of loyalty. It is the distance of the prince from his people which feeds the political jealousy of the latter, and which, by removing the former to a height of inaccessible grandeur, places him, as it were, beyond the reach of their sympathies. Much of the political rancour, which festers, and agitates, and makes such a tremendous appearance of noise and of hostility in our land, is due to the aggravating power of distance. If two of the deadliest political antagonists in our country, who abuse, and vilify, and pour forth their stormy eloquence on each other, whether in parliament or from the press, were actually to come into such familiar and personal contact, as would infuse into their controversy the sweetening of mere acquaintanceship, this very circumstance would disarm and do away almost all their violence. The truth is, that when one man rails against another across the table of a legislative assembly, or when he works up his fermenting imagination, and pens his virulent sentences against another, in the retirement of a closet—he is fighting against a man at a distance—he is exhausting his strength against an enemy whom he does not know —he is swelling into indignation, and into all the movements of what he thinks right and generous principle, against a chimera of his own apprehension; and a similar reaction comes back upon him from the quarter that he has assailed, and thus the controversy thickens, and the delusion every day gets more impenetrable, and the distance is ever widening, and the breach is always becoming more hopeless and more irreparable; and all this between two men, who, if they had been in such accidental circumstances of juxta-position as could have let them a little more into one another's feelings, and to one another's sympathies, would at least have had all the asperities of their difference smoothed away by the mere softenings and kindlinesses of ordinary human intercourse.

Now let me apply this remark to the mutual state of sentiment which obtains between the different orders of the community. Among the rich, there is apt at times to rankle an injurious and unworthy impression of the poor—and just because these poor stand at a distance from them—just because they come not into contact with that which would draw them out into courteousness to their persons, and in benevolent attentions to their families. Among the poor, on the other hand, there is often a disdainful suspicion of the wealthy, as if they were actuated by a proud indifference to them and to their concerns, and, as if they were placed away from them at so distant and lofty an elevation as not to require the exercise of any of those cordialities, which are ever sure to spring in the bosom of man to man, when they come to know each other, and to have the actual sight of each other. But let any accident place an individual of the higher before the eyes of the lower order, on the ground of their common humanity—let the latter be made to see that the former are akin to themselves in all the sufferings and in all the sensibilities of our common inheritance—let, for example, the greatest chieftain of the territory die, and the report of his weeping children, or of his distracted widow, be sent through the neighbourhood—or let an infant of his family be in suffering, and the mothers of the humble vicinity be run to for counsel and assistance—or in any other way let the rich, instead of being viewed by their inferiors through the dim and distant medium of that fancied interval which separates the ranks of society, be seen as heirs of the same frailty, and as dependent on the same sympathies with themselves—and at that moment, all the floodgates of honest sympathy will be opened—and the lowest servants of the establishment will join in the cry of distress which has come upon their family—and the neighbouring cottagers, to share in their grief, have only to recognise them as the partakers of one nature, and to perceive an assimilation of feelings and of circumstances between them.

Let me further apply this to the sons and the daughters of royalty. The truth is, that they appear to the public eye as stalking on a platform so highly elevated above the general level of society, that it removes them, as it were, from all the ordinary sympathies of our nature. And though we read at times of their galas, and their birthdays, and their drawing-rooms, there is nothing in all this to attach us to their interests and their feelings, as the inhabitants of a familiar home—as the members of an affectionate family. Surrounded as they are with the glare of a splendid notoriety, we scarcely recognize them as men and as women, who can rejoice, and weep, and pine with disease, and taste the sufferings of mortality, and be oppressed with anguish, and love with tenderness, and experience in their bosoms the same movements of grief or of affection that we do ourselves. And thus it is, that they labour under a real and heavy disadvantage. There is not in their case, the counteraction of that kindly influence, to alleviate the weight or the malignity of prejudice, which men of a humbler station are ever sure to enjoy. In the case of a man whose name is hardly known beyond the limits of his personal acquaintance, the tale of calumny that is raised against him extends not far beyond these limits; and, therefore, wherever it is heard, it meets with a something to blunt and to soften it, in those very cordialities which the familiar exhibition of him as a brother of our common nature is fitted to awaken. But it is not so with those in the elevated walks of society. Their names are familiar where their persons are unknown; and whatever malignity may attach to the one, circulates abroad, and is spread far beyond the limits of their possible intercourse with human beings, and meets with no kindly counteraction from our acquaintance with the other. And this may explain how it is, that the same exalted personage may, at one and the same time, be suffering under a load of most unmerited obloquy from the wide and the general public, and be to all his familiar domestics an object of the most enthusiastic devotedness and regard.

Now, if through an accidental opening, the public should be favoured with a domestic exhibition—if, by some overpowering visitation of Providence upon an illustrious family, the members of it should come to be recognised as the partakers of one common humanity with ourselves—if, instead of beholding them in their gorgeousness as princes, we look to them in their natural evolution of their sensibilities as men—if the stately palace should be turned into a house of mourning—in one word, if death should do what he has already done, he has met the Princess of England in the prime and promise of her days, and as she was moving onward on her march to a hereditary throne, he has laid her at his feet. Ah! my brethren, when the imagination dwells on that bed where the remains of departed youth and departed infancy are lying—when, instead of crowns and canopies of grandeur, it looks to the forlorn husband, and the weeping father, and the human feelings which agitate their bosom, and the human tears which flow down their cheeks, and all such symptoms of deep affliction as bespeak the workings of suffering and dejected nature—what ought to be, and what actually is, the feeling of the country at so sad an exhibition? It is just the feeling of the domestics and the labourers at Claremont. All is soft and tender as womanhood. Nor is there a peasant in our land, who is not touched to the very heart when he thinks of the unhappy Stranger who is now spending his days in grief and nights in sleeplessness—as he mourns alone in his darkened chamber, and refuses to be comforted—as he turns in vain for rest to his troubled feelings, and cannot find it—as he gazes on the memorials of an affection that blessed the brightest, happiest, shortest year of his existence—as he looks back on the endearments of the bygone months, and the thought that they have for ever fleeted away from him, turns all to agony—as he looks forward on the blighted prospect of this world's pilgrimage, and feels that all which bound him to existence, is now torn irretrievably away from him! There is not a British heart that does not feel to this interesting visitor, all the force and all the tenderness of a most affecting relationship; and go where he may, will he ever be recognised and cherished as a much loved member of the British family.

It is in this way that through the avenue of a nation's tenderness, we can estimate the strength and the steadfastness of a nation's loyalty. On minor questions of the constitution we may storm and rave, and look at each other a little ferociously—and it was by some such appearance as this, that he, who in the days of his strength, was the foulest and most formidable of all our enemies, said of the country in which we live, that, torn by factions, it was going rapidly to dissolution. Yet these are but the skirmishings of a petty warfare—the movements of nature and of passion, in a land of freemen—the harmless contests of men pulling in opposite ways at some of the smaller ropes in the tackling of our great national vessel. But look to these men in the time of need and the hour of suffering—look to them now, when in one great and calamitous visitation, the feeling of every animosity is overborne—look to them now, when the darkness is gathering, and the boding cloud of disaster hangs over us, and some chilling fear of insecurity is beginning to circulate in whispers through the land—look to them now, when in the entombment of this sad and melancholy day, the hopes of more than half a century are to be interred—look to them now, when from one end of the country to the other, there is the mourning of a very great and sore lamentation, so that all who pass by, may say, this is a grievous mourning to the people of the land. Oh! is it possible that these can be other than honest tears, or that tears of pity can on such an emergency as the present, be other than tears of patriotism. Who does not see this principle sitting in visible expression on the general countenance of the nation—that the people are sound at heart, and that with this, as the mainsheet of our dependence, we may still, under the blessing of God, weather and surmount all the difficulties which threaten us.

II. I now proceed to the second head of discourse, under which I was to attempt such an improvement of this great national disaster, as might enforce the lesson, that under every fear and every difficulty, it is the righteousness of the people alone which will exalt and perpetuate a nation; and that, therefore, if this great interest be neglected, instead of learning any thing from the judgments of God, we are in imminent danger of being utterly overwhelmed by them.

Under my first head I restricted myself exclusively to the virtue of loyalty, which is one of the special, but I most willingly admit, nay, and most earnestly contend, is also one of the essential attributes of righteousness. But there is a point on which I profess myself to be altogether at an issue with a set of men, who composed, at one time, whatever they do now, a very numerous class of society. I mean those men, who, with all the ostentation, and all the intolerance of loyalty, evinced an utter indifference either to their own personal religion, or to the religion of the people who were around them—who were satisfied with the single object of keeping the neighbourhood in a state of political tranquillity—who, if they could only get the population to be quiet, cared not for the extent of profaneness or of profligacy that was among them—and who, while they thought to signalize themselves in the favour of their earthly king, by keeping down every turbulent or rebellious movement among his subjects, did, in fact, by their own conspicuous example lead them and cheer them on in their rebellion against the king of heaven—and, as far as the mischief could be wrought by the contagion of their personal influence, these men of loyalty did what in them lay, to spread a practical contempt for Christianity, and for all its ordinances, throughout the land.

Now, I would have such men to understand, if any such there be within the sphere of my voice, that it is not with their loyalty that I am quarrelling. I am only telling them, that this single attribute of righteousness will never obtain a steady footing in the hearts of the people, except on the ground of a general principle of righteousness. I am telling them how egregiously they are out of their own politics, in ever thinking that they can prop the virtue of loyalty in a nation, while they are busily employed, by the whole instrumentality of their example and of their doings, in sapping the very foundation upon which it is reared. I am telling them, that if they wish to see loyalty in perfection, and such loyalty, too, as requires not any scowling vigilance of theirs to uphold it, they must look to the most moral, and orderly, and christianized districts of the country. I am merely teaching them a lesson of which they seem to be ignorant, that if you loosen the hold of Christianity over the hearts of the population, you pull down from their ascendency all the virtues of Christianity, of which loyalty is one. Yes, and I will come yet a little closer, and take a look of that loyalty which exists in the shape of an isolated principle in their own bosoms. I should like to gauge the dimensions of this loyalty of theirs, in its state of disjunction from the general principle of Christianity. I wish to know the kind of loyalty which characterizes the pretenders to whom I am alluding—the men who have no value for preaching, but as it stands associated with the pageantry of state—the men who would reckon it the most grievous of all heresies, to be away from church on some yearly day of the king's appointment, but are seldom within its walls on the weekly day of God's appointment—the men who, if ministers were away from their post of loyalty, on an occasion like the present, would, without mercy, and without investigation, denounce them as suspicious characters; but who, when we are at the post of piety, dispensing the more solemn ordinances of Christianity, openly lead the way in that crowded and eager emigration which carries half the rank and opulence of the town away from us. What, oh! what is the length, and the breadth, and the height, and the depth of this vapouring, swaggering, high-sounded loyalty?—It is nothing better than the loyalty of political subalterns, in the low game of partisanship, or of whippers-in to an existing administration—it is not the loyalty which will avail us in the day of danger—it is not to them that we need to look, in the evil hour of a country's visitation;—but to those right-hearted, sound-thinking christian men, who, without one interest to serve, or one hope to forward, honour their king, because they fear their God.

Let me assure such a man, if such a man there is within the limits of this assembly—that, keen as his scent may be after political heresies, the deadliest of all such heresies lies at his own door—that there is not to be found, within the city of our habitation, a rottener member of the community than himself—that, withering as he does by his example the principle which lies at the root of all national prosperity, it is he, and such as he, who stands opposed to the best and he dearest objects of loyalty—and if ever that shall happen, which it is my most delightful confidence that God will avert from us and from our children's children to the latest posterity—if ever the wild frenzy of revolution shall run through the ranks of Britain's population, these are the men who will be the most deeply responsible for all its atrocities and for all its horrors.*

* I cannot but advert here to a delicate impediment which lies in the way of the faithful exercise of the ministerial functions, from the existence of two great political parties, which would monopolize between them, all the sentiments and all the services of the country. Is it not a very possible thing that the line of demarcation between these parties, may not coalesce, throughout all its extent, with the sacred and immutable line of distinction between right and wrong?—and ought not this latter line to stand out so clearly and so prominently to the eye of the christian minister, that in the act of dealing around him the reproofs and the lessons of Christianity, the former line should be away from his contemplation altogether? But it is thus that, with the most scrupulous avoidance both of the one and of the other species of partisan ship, he may, in the direct and conscientious discharge of the duties of his office, deliver himself in such a way as to give a kind of general and corporate offence to one political denomination; and what is still more grievous, as to be appropriated by the men of another denomination, with whom in their capacity as politicians he desires no fellowship whatever, and whose applauses of him in this capacity are in every way most odious and insufferable.

It appears to us that a christian minister cannot keep himself in the true path of consistency at all, without refusing to each of the parties all right of appropriation. Their line of demarcation is not his line. Their objects are not his objects. He asks no patronage from the one—he asks no favour from the other, except that they shall not claim kindred with him. He may suffer, at times, from the intolerance of the unworthy underlings of the former party: but never will his sensations of distaste, for the whole business of party politics, become so intense and so painful, as when the hosannas of the latter party threaten to rise around him.

We often hear from each, and more particularly from one of these parties, of the virtue and the dignity of independence. The only way, it appears to us, in which a man can sustain the true and complete character of independence, is to be independent of both. He who cares for neither of them is the only independent man; and to him only belongs the privilege of crossing and re-crossing their factious line of demarcation, just as he feels himself impelled by the high, paramount, and subordinating principles of the Christianity which he professes. In the exercise of this privilege, I here take the opportunity of saying, that if the chastisement of public scorn should fall on those who, under the disguise of public principle, have *found* personal aggrandisement for themselves, it should fall with equal severity on those who, under the same disguise, are *seeking* precisely the same object—that if there be some men in the country who care not for the extent of profaneness and profligacy that is among the people, provided they can only keep them *quiet*, there are also some men who care not for their profaneness or their profligacy, provided they can only keep them *unquiet*—who bear no other regard to the people than merely as an instrument of annoyance against an existing administration—who can shed their serpent tears over their distresses, and yet be inwardly grieved, should either

Having thus briefly adverted to one of the causes of impiety and consequent disloyalty, I shall proceed to offer a few remarks on the great object of teaching the people righteousness, not so much in a general and didactic manner, as in the way of brief, and, if possible, of memorable illustration—gathering my argument from the present event, and availing myself, at the same time, of such principles as have been advanced in the course of the preceding observations.

My next remark, then, on this subject, will be taken from a sentiment, of which I think you must all on the present occasion

---

a favourable season or reviving trade disappoint their boding speculation—who, in the face of undeniable common sense, can ascribe to political causes, such calamities as are altogether due to what is essential and uncontrollable in the circumstances of the country—and who, if on the strength of misrepresentation and artifice they could only succeed in effecting the great object of their own instalment into office, and dispossession of their antagonists, would prove themselves, then, to be as indifferent to the comfort, as they show themselves now to be utterly indifferent to the religion and the virtue of the country's population.

But turning away from the beggarly elements of such a competition as this, let us remark, that on the one hand, a religious administration will never take offence at a minister who renders a pertinent reproof to any set of men, even though they should happen to be their own agents or their own underlings; and that, on the other hand, a minister who is actuated by the true spirit of his office, will never so pervert or so prostitute his functions, as to descend to the humble arena of partisanship. He is the faithful steward of such things as are profitable for reproof, and for doctrine, and for correction, and for instruction in righteousness. His single object with the men who are within reach of his hearing, is, that they should come to the knowledge of the truth and be saved. In the fulfilment of this object, he is not the servant of any administration—though he certainly renders such a service to the state as will facilitate the work of governing to all administrations—as will bring a mighty train of civil and temporal blessings along with it—and in particular, as will diffuse over the whole sphere of his influence, a loyalty as steadfast as the friends of order, and as free from every taint of political severity, as the most genuine friends of freedom can desire.

There is only one case in which it is conceived that this partisanship of a christian minister is at all justifiable. Should the government of our country ever fall into the hands of an infidel or demi-infidel administration—should the men at the helm of affairs be the patrons of all that is unchristian in the sentiment and literature of the country—should they offer a violence to its religious establishments—and thus attempt what we honestly believe would reach a blow to the piety and the character of our population—then I trust that the language of partisanship will resound from many of the pulpits of the land—and that it will be turned in one stream of pointed invective against such a ministry as this—till, by the force of public opinion, it be swept away as an intolerable nuisance, from the face of our kingdom.

feel the force and the propriety. Would it not have been most desirable could the whole population of the city have been admitted to join in the solemn services of the day? Do you not think that they are precisely such services as would have spread a loyal and patriotic influence among them? Is it not experimentally the case, that, over the untimely grave of our fair Princess, the meanest of the people would have shed as warm and plentiful a tribute of honest sensibility as the most refined and delicate among us? And, I ask, is it not unfortunate, that, on the day of such an affecting. and, if I may so style it, such a national exercise, there should not have been twenty more churches, with twenty more ministers, to have contained the whole crowd of eager and interested listeners? A man of mere loyalty, without one other accomplishment, will, I am sure, participate in a regret so natural; but couple this regret with the principle, that the only way in which the loyalty of the people can effectually be maintained, is on the basis of Christianity, and then the regret in question embraces an object still more general—and well were it for us, if, amid the insecurity of families, and the various fluctuations of fortune and of arrangement that are taking place in the highest walks of society, the country were led, by the judgment with which it has now been visited, to deepen the foundation of all its order and of all its interests, in the moral education of its people. Then indeed the text would have its literal fulfilment. When the judgments of God are in the earth, the rulers of the world would lead the inhabitants thereof to learn righteousness.

In our own city, much in this respect remains to be accomplished; and I speak of the great mass of our city and suburb population, when I say, that through the week they lie open to every rude and random exposure—and when Sabbath comes, no solemn appeal to the conscience, no stirring recollections of the past, no urgent calls to resolve against the temptations of the future, come along with it. It is undeniable, that within the compass of a few square miles, the daily walk of the vast majority of our people is beset with a thousand contaminations; and whether it be on the way to the market, or on the way to the workshop, or on the way to the crowded manufactory, or on the way to any one resort of industry that you may choose to condescend upon, or on the way to the evening home, where the labours of a virtuous day should be closed by the holy thankfulness of a pious and affectionate family; be it in passing from one place to another; or be it amid all the throng of sedentary occupations: there is not one day of the six, and not one hour of one of these days, when frail and unsheltered man is not plied by the many allurements of a world lying in wickedness—when evil communications are not assailing him with their corruptions—when the full tide of example does not bear down upon his purposes, and threaten to sweep all his purity and all his principle away from him. And when the seventh day comes, where, I would ask, are the efficient securities that ought to be provided against all those inundations of profligacy which rage without control through the week, and spread such a desolating influence among the morals of the existing generation?—Oh! tell it not in Gath, publish it not in the streets of Askelon—this seventh day, on which it would require a whole army of labourers to give every energy which belongs to them, to the plenteous harvest of so mighty a population, witnesses more than one half of the people precluded from attending the house of God, and wandering every man after the counsel of his own heart, and in the sight of his own eyes—on this day, the ear of heaven is assailed with a more audacious cry of rebellion than on any other, and the open door of invitation plies with its welcome the hundreds and the thousands who have found their habitual way to the haunts of depravity. And is there no room, then, to wish for twenty more churches, and twenty more ministers—for men of zeal and of strength, who might go forth among these wanderers, and compel them to come in—for men of holy fervour, who might set the terrors of hell and the free offer of salvation before them—for men of affection, who might visit the sick, the dying, and the afflicted, and cause the irresistible influence of kindness to circulate at large among their families—for men, who, while they fastened their most intense aim on the great object of preparing sinners for eternity, would scatter along the path of their exertions all the blessings of order, and contentment, and sobriety, and at length make it manifest as day, that the righteousness of the people is the only effectual antidote to a country's ruin—the only path to a country's glory?

My next remark shall be founded on a principle to which I have already alluded—the desirableness of a more frequent intercourse between the higher and the lower orders of society; and what more likely to accomplish this, than a larger ecclesiastical accommodation?—not the scanty provision of the present day, by which the poor are excluded from the church altogether, but such a wide and generous system of accommodation, as that the rich and the poor might set in company together in the house of God. It is this christian fellowship, which more than any other tie, links so intimately together, the high and the low in country parishes. There is, however, another particular to which I would advert, and though I cannot do so without magnifying my office, yet I know not a single circumstance which so upholds the golden line of life among our agricultural population, as the manner in which the gap between the pinnacle of the community and its base is filled up by the week-day duties of the clergyman—by that man, of whom it has been well said, that he belongs to no rank, because he associates with all ranks—by that man, whose presence may dignify the palace, but whose peculiar glory it is to earry the influences of friendship and piety into cottages.

This is the age of moral experiment, and much has been devised in our day for promoting the virtue, and the improvement, and the economical habits of the lower orders of society. But in all these attempts to raise a barrier against the growing profligacy of our towns, one important element seems to have passed unheeded, and to have been altogether omitted in the calculation. In all the comparative estimates of the character of a town and the character of a country population, it has been little attended to, that the former are distinguished from the latter by the dreary, hopeless, and almost impassible distance at which they stand from their parish minister. Now, though it be at the hazard of again magnifying my office, I must avow, in the hearing of you all, that there is a moral charm in his personal attentions and his affectionate civilities, and the ever-recurring influence of his visits and his prayers, which, if restored to the people, would impart a new moral aspect, and eradicate much of the licentiousness and the dishonesty that abound in our cities. On this day of national calamity, if ever the subject should be adverted to from the pulpit, we may be allowed to express our riveted convictions on the close alliance that obtains between the political interests and the religious character of a country. And I am surely not out of place, when, on looking at the mighty mass of a city population, I state my apprehension, that if something be not done to bring this enormous physical strength under the control of christian and humanized principle, the day may yet come when it may lift against the authorities of the land its brawny vigour, and discharge upon them all the turbulence of its rude and volcanic energy.

Apart altogether from the essential character of the gospel, and keeping out of view the solemn representations of Christianity, by which we are told that each individual of these countless myriads carries an undying principle in his bosom, and that it is the duty of the minister to cherish it, and to watch over it, as one who must render, at the judgment-seat, an account of the charge which has been committed to him—apart from this consideration entirely, which I do not now insist upon, though I blush not to avow its paramount importance over all that can be alleged on the inferior ground of political expediency, yet, on that ground alone, I can gather argument enough for the mighty importance of such men, devoted to the labours of their own separate and peculiar employments—giving an unbewildered attention to the office of dealing with the hearts and principles of the thousands who are around them—coming forth from the preparations of an unbroken solitude, armed with all the omnipotence of Truth among their fellow citizens—and who, rich in the resources of a mind which meditates upon these things, and gives itself wholly to them, are able to suit their admonitions to all the varieties of human character, and to draw their copious and persuasive illustrations from every quarter of human experience. But I speak not merely of their Sabbath ministrations. Give to each a manageable extent of town within the compass of his personal exertions, and where he might be able to cultivate a ministerial influence among all its families—put it into his power to dignify the very humblest of its tenements by the courteousness of his soothing and benevolent attentions—let it be such a district of population as may not bear him down by the multiplicity of its demands; but where, without any feverish or distracting variety of labour, he may be able to familiarize himself to every house, and to know every individual, and to visit every spiritual patient, and to watch every death-bed, and to pour out the sympathies of a pious and affectionate bosom over every mourning and bereaved family. Bring every city of the land under such moral regimen as this, and another generation would not pass away, ere righteousness ran down all their streets like a mighty river. That sullen depravity of character, which the gibbet cannot scare away, and which sits so immoveable in the face of the most menacing severities, and in despite of the yearly recurrence of the most terrifying examples,—could not keep its ground against the mild, but restless application of an effective christian ministry. The very worst of men would be constrained to feel the power of such an application. Sunk as they are in ignorance, and inured as they have been from the first years of their neglected boyhood, to scenes of week-day profligacy and Sabbath profanation—these men, of whom it may be said, that all their moralities are extinct, and all their tenderness blunted—even they would feel the power of that reviving touch, which the mingled influence of kindness and piety on often impress on the souls of the most abandoned—even they would open the flood-gates of their hearts, and pour forth the tide of an honest welcome on the men who had come in all the cordiality of good will to themselves and to their families. And thus might a humanizing and an exalting influence be made to circulate through all their dwelling-places: and such a system as this, labouring as it must do at first, under all the discouragements of a heavy and unpromising outset, would gather, during every year of its perseverance, new triumphs and new testimonies to its power. All that is ruthless and irreclaimable, in the character of the present day, would in time be replaced by the softening virtues of a purer and a better generation. This I know to be the dream of many a philanthropist: and a dream as visionary as the very wildest among the fancies of Utopianism it ever will be, under any other expedient than the one I am now pointing to: and nothing, nothing within the whole compass of nature, or of experience, will ever bring it to its consummation, but the multiplied exertions of the men who carry in their hearts the doctrine, and who bear upon their persons the seal and commission of the New Testament. And, if it be true that towns are the great instruments of political revolution—if it be there that all the elements of disturbance are ever found in busiest fermentation—if we learn, from the history of the past, that they are the favourite and frequented rallying-places for all the brooding violence of the land—who does not see that the pleading earnestness of the christian minister is at one with the soundest maxims of political wisdom, when he urges upon the rulers and magistrates of the land, that this is indeed the cheap defence of a nation—this the vitality of all its strength and of all its greatness.

And it is with the most undissembled satisfaction that I advert to the first step of such a process, within the city of our habitation, as I have now been recommending. It may still be the day of small things; but it is such a day as ought not to be despised. The prospect of another church and another labourer in this interesting field, demands the most respectful acknowledgement of the christian public, to the men who preside over the administration of our affairs; and they, I am sure, will not feel it to be oppressive, if, met by the willing cordialities of a responding population, the demand should ring in their ears for another, and another, till, like the moving of the spirit on the face of the waters, which made beauty and order to emerge out of the rude materials of creation, the germ of moral renovation shall at length burst into all the efflorescence of moral accomplishment—and the voice of psalms shall again be heard in our families—and impurity and violence shall be banished from our streets—and then the erasure made, in these degenerate days, on the escutcheons of our city, again replaced in characters of gold, shall tell to every stranger, that Glasgow flourisheth through the preaching of the word.*

And though, under the mournful remembrance of our departed Princess, we cannot but feel, on this day of many tears, as if a volley of lightning from heaven had been shot at the pillar of our State, and struck away the loveliest ornament from its pinnacle, and shook the noble fabric to its base; yet still, if we strengthen its foundation in the principle and character of our people, it will stand secure on the deep and steady basis of a country's worth, which can never be overthrown. And thus an enduring memorial of our Princess will be embalmed in the hearts of the people, and good will emerge out of this dark and bitter dispensation, if, when the judgments of God are in the earth, the inhabitants of the world shall learn righteousness.

---

* The original motto of the City is, "Let Glasgow flourish through the preaching of the Word;" which, by the curtailment alluded to, has been reduced to the words, "Let Glasgow flourish."

THE

DOCTRINE OF CHRISTIAN CHARITY

APPLIED TO THE

CASE OF RELIGIOUS DIFFERENCES.

A SERMON,

PREACHED BEFORE THE AUXILIARY SOCIETY, GLASGOW, TO THE HIBERNIAN SOCIETY, FOR ESTABLISHING SCHOOLS, AND CIRCULATING THE HOLY SCRIPTURES IN IRELAND.

PREFACE.

If the question were put, what is Popery? an answer might be given by the enumeration of what are conceived to be its leading principles. Without at all inquiring whether the conception be a just one or not, there are many persons who would tell us, that the members of this denomination ascribe an infallibility to the Pope; and that they hold the doctrine of transubstantiation; and that they offer religious worship to departed saints, and render an external homage to images; and that they give such an importance to the ceremonial of extreme unction, as to conceive, that by the administration of it, all the guilt of the most worthless and unrenewed character is expiated and done away.—It is enough to mark our aversion to these positions and practices, that we say, that every one of them is unscriptural; and that, if this be a real portraiture of Popery, it is a religion which has no foundation in truth or in the Bible. But it is altogether a different question, in how far Popery, as thus defined, is actually realized by those men who wear the name and the profession of it. Whether this was ever the Popery of a past age, is a question of erudition, into which we propose not to enter. And whether this be the Popery of any people of the present age, is a question of observation, into which we propose not to enter. We confine ourselves to the object of looking into our own hearts, and of looking to those who are immediately around us, with the view of ascertaining whether the contamination and the substantial mischief of these alleged principles might not be detected on a nearer field of observation.

We are all aware that such an attempt as this is not enough to satisfy many Protestants, or to fill up the measure of their zeal against what they hold to be a most blasphemous and pestilential heresy. They would not merely demand the disavowal of a corrupt system—but they would like to see it attached with all its deformities in the form of a personal charge to the men of a certain prominent and visible denomination. Now, we do not see how the former demand can be more effectually met, than by the denunciation of this system, under whatever shape, or in whatever quarter of society, it may be found.—Nor do we conceive how a more honest and decisive seal of reprobation can be set upon it, than by the expression of a dislike so strong and so irreconcilable, as to be felt, even when it obtrudes upon our notice any of its features amongst the individuals of our own connexion, and offers itself to view under the screen of an ostensible Protestantism. As to the latter demand, we frankly confess that we are not historically enough acquainted with the present state of the Catholic mind, to be at all able to comply with it. But should any member of that persuasion come forward with his own explanations, and give such a mitigated view of the peculiarities of Catholics, as to leave the great evangelical doctrines of faith and repentance unimpaired by them, and state that an averment of the Bible has never, in his instance, been neutralized or practically stript of its authority, by an averment of Popes or of Councils;—on what principle of candour shall the recognition of a common Christianity be withheld from him? Is it not better to confine our animadversion to the principles of the system, and to let persons alone: and if these persons shall step forward with the affirmation that the system is imaginary, or that, at least, it has no actual residence with them, whether is it the more Christian exhibition on our part, that we exercise, in their behalf, the charity which believeth all things, or that we pertinaciously keep by a charge, the truth of which they solemnly disclaim?

SERMON.

"And why beholdest thou the mote that is in thy brother's eye, but considerest not the beam that is in thine own eye?—Or how wilt thou say to thy brother, Let me pull out the mote out of thine eye; and behold a beam is in thine own eye?—Thou hypocrite! first cast out the beam out of thine own eye, and then shalt thou see clearly to cast out the mote out of thy brother's eye."—*Matthew* vii. 3, 4, 5.

THE word beam suggests the idea of a rafter; and it looks very strange that a thing of such magnitude should be at all conceived to have its seat or fixture in the eye. To remove, by a single sentence, this misapprehension, I shall just say, that the word in the original signifies also a thorn, a something that the eye has room for, but at the same time much larger than a mote, and which must, therefore, have a more powerful effect in deranging the vision, and preventing a man from forming a right estimate of the object he is looking at. Take this along with you, and the three verses will run thus:—Why beholdest thou the mote that is in thy brother's eye, but considerest not the thorn that is in thine own eye? Or how wilt thou say to thy brother, Let me pull out the mote out of thine eye; and behold a thorn is in thine own eye? Thou hypocrite! first cast out the thorn out of thine own eye, and then shalt thou see clearly to cast out the mote out of thy brother's eye."

In my farther observations on this passage, I shall first introduce what I propose o make the main subject of my discourse, by a very short application of the leading principle of my text, to the case of those judgments that we are so ready to pronounce on each other in private life. And I shall, secondly, proceed to the main subject, viz. that more general kind of judgment which we are apt to pass on the men of a different persuasion, in matters of religion.

I. Every fault of conduct in the outer man, may be run up to some defect of principle in the inner man. It is this defect of principle, which gives the fault all its criminality. It is this alone, which makes it odious in the sight of God. It is upon this that the condemnation of the law rests; and on the day of judgment, when the secrets of all hearts shall be laid open, it will be the share that the heart had in the matter, which will form the great topic of examination, when the deeds done in the body pass under the review of the Son of God. For example, it is a fault to speak evil one of another; but the essence of the fault lies in the want of that charity which thinketh no ill. Had the heart been filled with this principle, no such bad thing as slander would have come out of it; but if the heart be not filled with this principle, and in its stead there be the operation of envy—or a desire to avenge yourselves of others, by getting the judgment of men to go against them—or a taste for the ludicrous, which rather than be ungratified, will expose the peculiarities of the absent to the mirth of a company—or the idle and thoughtless levity of gossiping, which cannot be checked by any consideration of the mischief that may be done by its indulgence; I say, if any or all of these, take up that room in the heart, which should have been filled with charity, and sent forth the fruits of it, then the stream will just be as the fountain, and out of the treasure of the evil heart, there will flow that evil practice of censoriousness, on which the gospel of Christ pronounces its severe and decisive condemnation.

But though all evil-speaking be referable to the want of a good, or to the existence of an evil principle in the heart, yet there is one style of evil-speaking different from another; and you can easily conceive how a man addicted to one way of it, may hate, and despise, and have a mortal antipathy, to another way of it. In this case, it is not the thing itself in its essential deformity that he condemns; it is some of the disgusting accompaniments of the thing; and while these excite his condemnation, and he views the man in whom they are realized, as every way worthy of being reprobated, he may not be aware, all the while, that in himself there exists an equal, and perhaps a much larger portion of that very principle, which he should be reprobated for. The forms of evil-speaking break out into manifold varieties. There is the soft insinuation. There is the resentful outcry. There is the manly and indignant disapproval. There is the invective of vulgar malignity. There is the poignancy of satirical remark. There is the giddiness of mere volatility, which trips so carelessly along, and spreads its entertaining levities over a gay and light-hearted party. These are all so many transgressions of one and the same duty; and you can easily conceive an enlightened Christian sitting in judgment over them all, and taking hold of the right principle upon which he would condemn them all; and which, if brought to bear with efficacy on the consciences of the different offenders, would not merely silence the passionate evil-speaker out of his outrageous exclamations, and restrain the malignant evil-speaker from his deliberate thrusts at the reputation of the absent; but would rebuke the humorous evil-speaker out of his fanciful and amusing sketches, and the gossiping evil-speaker out of his tiresome and never-ending narratives. Now you may further conceive, how a man who realizes upon his own character one of these varieties, might have a positive dislike to another of them; how the open and generous-hearted denouncer of what is wrong, may hate from his very soul the poison of a sly and secret insinuation; how he who delivers himself in the chastened and well-bred tone of a gentleman, may recoil from the violence of an unmannerly invective; how he who enjoys the ridiculous of character, may be hurt and offended at hearing of the criminal of character;—and thus each, with the thorn in his own eye, may advert with regret and disapprobation to the mote in his brother's eye.

Now, mark the two advantages which arise from every man bringing himself to a strict examination, that he may if possible find out the principle of that fault in his own mind, which he conceives to deform the doings and the character of another. His attention is carried away from the mere accompaniment of the fault to its actual and constituting essence. He pursues his search from the outward and accidental varieties, to the one principle which spreads the leaven of iniquity over them all. By looking into his own heart, he is made acquainted with the movements of this principle. When forced to disapprove of others, his disapprobation is not a mere matter of taste, or of education, but the entire and well-founded disapprobation of principle. He sees where the radical mischief of the whole business lies. He sees that if the principle of doing no ill were established within the heart, it would cut up by the root all evil-speaking in all its shapes and in all its modifications. His own diligent keeping of his own heart upon this subject would bring the matter into his frequent contemplation, and enable him to perceive where its essence and its malignity lay, and give him an enlightened judgment of it in all its effects and workings upon others; and thus, by the very progress of struggling against it, and watching against it, and praying against it, and the strength of divine grace prevailing against it, and at length succeeding in pulling the thorn out of his own eye, he would see clearly to cast out the mote out of his brother's eye.

But another mighty advantage of this self-examination is, that the more a man does examine the more does he discover the infirmities of his own character. That very infirmity against which, in another, he might have protested with all the force of a vehement indignation, he might find lurking in his own bosom, though under the disguise of a different form. Such a discovery as this will temper his indignation. It will humble him into the meekness of wisdom. It will soften him into charity. It will infuse a candour and a gentleness into all his judgments. The struggle he has had with himself to keep down the sin he sees in another, will train him to an indulgence he might never have felt, had he been altogether blind to the diseases of his own moral constitution. When he tries to reform a neighbour, the attempt will be marked by all the mildness of one who is deeply conscious of his own frailties, and fearful of the exposures which he himself may have to endure. And I leave it to your own experience of human nature to determine, whether he bids fairer for success who rebukes with the intolerant tone of a man who is unconscious of his own blemishes; or he who, with all the spirituality of a humble and exercised Christian, endeavours to restore him who is overtaken in a fault, with the spirit of meekness, "considering himself lest he also be tempted."

Now, the fault of evil-speaking is only one out of the many. The lesson of the text might be farther illustrated by other cases and other examples. I might specify the various forms of worldliness, and wilfulness, and fraud, and falsehood, and profanity, and show how the man who realizes these sins in one form might pass his condemnatory sentence on the man who realizes the very same sins in another form; and I might succeed in saying to the conviction of his conscience, even as Nathan said to David, "Thou art the man;" and might press home upon him the mighty task of self-examination, and set him from that to the task of diligent reform, that he might be enabled to see the fault of his neighbour more clearly, and rebuke it more gently, and winningly, and considerately. But my time restrains me from expatiating; and however great my reluctance at being withdrawn from the higher office of dealing with the hearts and the consciences of individuals, to any other office, which, however good in itself, bears a most minute and insignificant proportion to the former, yet I must not forget that I stand here as the advocate of a public Society;—and I therefore propose to throw the remainder of my discourse into such a train of observation as may bear upon its designs and its enterprises.

II. I now proceed, then, to the more general kind of judgment which we are apt to pass on men of a different persuasion in matters of religion.—There is something in the very circumstance of its being a different religion from our own, which, prior to all our acquaintance with its details, is calculated to repel and to alarm us. It is not the religion in which we have been educated. It is not the religion which furnishes us with our associations of sacredness. Nay, it is a religion, which, if admitted into our creed, would tear asunder all these associations. It would break up all the repose of our established habits. It would darken the whole field of our accustomed contemplations. It would put to flight all those visions of the mind which stood linked with the favour of God, and the blissful prospects of eternity. It would unsettle, and disturb, and agitate; and this, not merely because it threw a doubtfulness over the question of our personal security, but because it shocked our dearest feelings of tenderness for that which we had been trained to love, and of veneration for that which we had been trained to look at in the aspect of awful and imposing solemnity.

Add to all this, the circumstance of its being a religion with the intolerance of which our fathers had to struggle unto the death; a religion which lighted up the fires of persecution in other days; a religion, which at one time put on a face of terror, and bathed its hands in the blood of cruel martyrdom; a religion, by resistance to which, the men of a departed generation are embalmed in the memory of the present, among the worthies of our established faith. We have only to contemplate the influence of these things, when handed down by tradition, and written in the most popular histories of the land, and told round the evening fire to the children of every cottage family, who listen, in breathless wonderment, to the tale of midnight alarm, and kindle at the battle-cry lifted by the patriots of a former age, when they made their noble stand for the outraged rights of conscience and of liberty; we have only to think of these things, and we shall cease our amazement, that such a religion, even though its faults and its merits be equally unknown, should light up a passionate aversion in many a bosom, and have a recoiling sense of horror, and sacrilege, and blasphemy associated with its very name.

Now Popery is just such a religion; and I appeal to many present, if, though ignorant of almost all its doctrines and all its distinctions, there does not spring up a quickly felt antipathy in their bosoms even at the very mention of Popery. There can be no doubt, that for one or two generations, this feeling has been rapidly on the decline. But it still lurks, and operates, and spreads a very wide and sensible infusion over the great mass of our Scottish population. There is now a dormancy about it, and it does not break out into those rude and tumultuary surges, which at one time filled our streets with violence, and sent a firmament of jealousy and alarm over the whole face of our country. But we still meet with the traces of its existence. We feel it in our bosoms when we hear of any of the ceremonials of Popery; and I just ask you to think of those peculiar sensations which rise within you at the mention of the holy water, or the consecrated wafer, or the extreme unction of the Catholic ritual. There is still a sensation of repugnance, though it be dim, and in its painfulness it be rapidly departing away from us; and I think that, even at this hour, should a Popish Chapel send up its lofty minarets, and spread a rich and expanded magnificence before the public eye, though many look with unmingled delight on the grandeur of the ascending pile, yet there may still be detected a visible expression of jealousy and offence in the sidelong glance, and the inward and half-suppressed murmuring of the occasional passenger.

Now, is it not conceivable that such a traditional repugnance to Popery may exist in the very same mind, with a total ignorance of what those things are for which it merits our repugnance? May there not be a kind of sensitive recoil in the heart against this religion, while the understanding is entirely blind to those alone features which justify our dislike to it? May there not be all the violence of antipathy within us at Popery, and there be at the same time within us all the faults and all the errors of Popery? May not the thorn be in our own eye, while the mote in our neighbour's eye is calling forth all the severity of our indignation? While we are sitting in the chair of judgment, and dealing forth from the eminence of a superior discernment, our invectives against what we think to be sacrilegious in the creed and practice of others, may it not be possible to detect in ourselves the same perversion of principle, the same idolatrous resistance to truth and righteousness; and surely, it well becomes us in this case, while we are so ready to precipitate our invectives upon the head of by-standers, to pass a humbling examination upon ourselves, that we may come to a more enlightened estimate of that which is the object of our condemnation; and that when we condemn, we may do it with wisdom, and with the meekness of wisdom.

Let us therefore take a nearer look of Popery, and try to find out how much of Popery there is in the religion of Protestants.

But, let it be premised, that many of the disciples of this religion disclaim much of what we impute to them; that the Popery of a former age may not be a fair specimen of the Popery of the present; that, in point of fact, many of its professors have evinced all the spirit of devout and enlightened Christians; that in many districts of Popery, the Bible is in full and active circulation; and that thus, while the name and externals are retained, and waken up all our traditional repugnance against it, there may be, among thousands and tens of thousands of its nominal adherents, all the soul, and substance, and principle, and piety of a reformed faith. When I therefore enumerate the errors of Popery, I do not assert the extent to which they exist. I merely say that such errors are imputed to them; and instead of launching forth into severities against those who are thus charged, all I propose is, to direct you to the far more profitable and Christian employment of shaming ourselves out of these very errors, that we may know how to judge of others, and that we may do it with the tenderness of charity.

First, then, it is said of Papists, that they ascribe an infallibility to the Pope, so that if he were to say one thing and the Bible another, his authority would carry it over the authority of God. And, think you, my brethren, that there is no such Popery among you? Is there no taking of your religion upon trust from another, when you should draw it fresh and unsullied from the fountain-head of inspiration? You all have, or you ought to have Bibles; and how often is it repeated there, "Hearken diligently unto me?" Now, do you obey this requirement, by making the reading of your Bible a distinct and earnest exercise? Do you ever dare to bring your favourite minister to the tribunal of the word, or would you tremble at the presumption of such an attempt; so that the hearing of the word carries a greater authority over your mind than the reading of the word. Now this want of daring, this trembling at the very idea of a dissent from your minister, this indolent acquiescence in his doctrine, is just calling another man master; it is putting the authority of man over the authority of God; it is throwing yourself into a prostrate attitude at the footstool of human infallibility; it is not just kissing the toe of reverence, but it is the profounder degradation of the mind and of all its faculties; and without the name of Popery—that name which lights up so ready an antipathy in your bosoms, your soul may be infected with the substantial poison, and your conscience be weighed down by the oppressive shackles, of Popery. And all this, in the noonday effulgence of a protestant country, where the Bible, in your mother tongue, circulates among all your families—where it may be met with in almost every shelf, and is ever soliciting you to look to the wisdom that is inscribed upon its pages. O! how tenderly should we deal with the prejudices of a rude and uneducated people, who have no Bibles, and no art of reading among them, to unlock its treasures, when we think that, even in this our land, the voice of human authority carries so mighty an influence along with it, and veneration for the word of God is darkened and polluted by a blind veneration for its interpreters.

We tremble to read of the fulminations that have issued in other days from a conclave of cardinals.—Have we no conclaves, and no fulminations, and no orders of inquisition, in our own country? Is there no professing brotherhood, or no professing sisterhood, to deal their censorious invectives around them, upon the members of an excommunicated world? There is such a thing as a religious public. There is a "little flock," on the one hand, and a "world lying in wickedness," on the other. But have a care, ye who think yourselves of the favoured few, how you never transgress the mildness, and charity, and unostentatious virtues of the gospel; lest you hold out a distorted picture of Christianity in your neighbourhood, and impose that as religion on the fancy of the credulous, which stands at as wide a distance from the religion of the New Testament, as do the services of an exploded superstition, or the mummeries of an antiquated ritual.

But, again, it is said of Papists, that they hold the monstrous doctrine of transubstantiation. Now, a doctrine may be monstrous on two grounds. It may be monstrous on the ground of its absurdity, or it may be monstrous on the ground of its impiety. It must have a most practically mischievous effect on the conscience, should a communicant sit down at the table of the Lord; and think that the act of appointed remembrance is equivalent to a real sacrifice, and a real expiation; and leave the performance with a mind unburdened of all its past guilt, and resolved to incur fresh guilt to be wiped away by a fresh expiation. But in the sacrament of our own country, is there no crucifying of the Lord afresh? Is there none of that which gives the doctrine of transubstantiation all its malignant influence on the hearts and lives of its proselytes? Is there no mysterious virtue annexed to the elements of this ordinance? Instead of being repaired to for the purpose of recruiting our languid affections to the Saviour, and strengthening our faith, and arming us with a firmer resolution, and more vigorous purpose of obedience, does the conscience of no communicant solace itself by the mere performance of the outward act, and suffer him to go back with a more reposing security to the follies, and vices, and indulgences of the world? Then, my brethren, his erroneous view of the sacrament may not be clothed in a term so appalling to the hearts and the feelings of Protestants as transubstantiation, but to it belongs all the immorality of transubstantiation; and the thorn must be pulled out of his eye, ere he can see clearly to cast the mote out of his brother's eye.

But, thirdly, it is said, that Papists worship saints, and fall down to graven images. This is very, very bad. "Thou shalt worship the Lord thy God, and him only shalt thou serve." But let us take ourselves to task upon this charge also. Have we no consecrated names in the annals of reformation—no worthies who hold too commanding a place in the remembrance and affection of Protestants? Are there no departed theologians, whose works hold too domineering an ascendency over the faith and practice of Christians? Are there no laborious compilations of other days, which instead of interpreting the Bible, have given its truths a shape, and a form, and an arrangement, that confer upon them another impression, and impart to them another influence, from the pure and original record? We may not bend the knee in any sensible chamber of imagery, at the remembrance of favourite saints. But do we not bend the understanding before the volumes of favourite authors, and do a homage to those representations of the minds of the men of other days, which should be exclusively given to the representation of the mind of the Spirit, as put down in the book of the Spirit's revelation? It is right that each of us should give the contribution of his own talents, and his own learning, to this most interesting cause; but let the great drift of our argument be to prop the authority of the Bible, and to turn the eye of earnestness upon its pages; for if any work, instead of exalting the Bible, shall be made, by the misjudging reverence of others, to stand in its place, then we introduce a false worship into the heart of a reformed country, and lay prostrate the conscience of men, under the yoke of a spurious authority.

But, fourthly and lastly—for time does not permit such an enumeration as would exhaust all the leading peculiarities ascribed to this faith—it is stated, that by the form of a confession, in the last days of a sinner's life, and the ministration of extreme unction upon his death-bed, he may be sent securely to another world, with all the unrepented profligacy, and fraud, and wickedness of this world upon his forehead; that this is looked forward to, and counted upon by every Catholic—and sets him loose from all those anticipations which work upon the terror of other men—and throws open to him an unbridled career, through the whole of which, he may wanton in all the varieties of criminal indulgence—and at length, when death knocks at his door, if he just allow him time to send for his minister, and to hurry along with him through the steps of an adjusted ceremonial, the man's passage through that dark vale, which carries him out of the world, is strewed with the promises of delusion—that every painful remembrance of the past is stifled amid the splendours and the juggleries of an imposing ritual: and in place of conscience rising upon him, and charging him with the guilty track of disobedience he has run, and forcing him to flee, amid the agitations of his restless bed, to the blood of the great Atonement, and alarming him into an earnest cry for the clean heart and the right spirit, knowing that unless he be born again unto repentance, he shall perish—why, my brethren, instead of these salutary exercises, we are told, that a fictitious hope is made to pour its treacherous sunshine into the bosom of a deceived Catholic—that, when standing on the verge of eternity, he can cast a fearless eye over its dark and untravelled vastness—and that, for the terror of its coming wrath, his guilty and unrenewed soul is filled with all the radiance and all the elevation of its anticipated glories.

O! my brethren, it is piteous to think of such a preparation, but it is just such a preparation as meets the sad experience of us all. The man, whose every affection has clung to the world, till the last hour of his possibility to enjoy it; who never put forth an effort or a prayer to be delivered from the power of sin, till every faculty of its pleasures had expired; who, through the varied progress of his tastes and his desires, from amusement to dissipation, and from dissipation to business, had always a something in all the successive stages of his career, to take up his heart to the exclusion of him who formed it;—why, such a man, who never thought of pressing the lessons of the minister upon his conscience, while life was vigorous, and the full swing of its delights and occupations could be indulged in,—do we never find, even in the bosom of this reformed country, that while his body retains all its health, his spirit retains all its hardihood; and not till the arrival of that week, or that month, or that year, when the last messenger begins to alarm him, does he think of sending to the man of God, an humble supplicant for his attendant prayers. Ah! my brethren, do you not think, amid the tones, and the sympathies, and the tears, which an affectionate pastor pours out in the fervency of his soul, and mingles with all his petitions, and all his addresses to the dying man, that no flattering unction ever steals upon him, to lull his conscience, and smooth the agony of his departure? Then, my brethren, you mistake it, you sadly mistake it; and even here, where I lift my voice among a crowd of men, in the prime and unbroken vigour of their days,—if even the youngest and likeliest of you all, shall, trusting to some future repentance, cherish the purpose of sin another hour, and not resolve at this critical and important Now, to break it all off, by an act of firm abandonment, then be your abhorrence of Popery what it may, you are exemplifying the worst of its errors, and wrapping yourselves up in the cruelest and most inveterate of its delusions.

I have left myself very little time for the application of all this to the particular objects of our Society.—First, Let it correct the very gross and vulgar tendency we all have, to think that the kingdom of God cometh with observation. That kingdom has its seat within us, and consists in the reign of principle over the hidden and invisible mind. The mere deposition of the Pope from that throne where he sits surrounded with the splendour of temporalities,—the mere ascendency of Protestant princes, over the counsels and politics of the world,—the mere exclusion of Catholic subjects from our administrations and our Parliaments,—these things are all very observable, but they may all happen, without one inch of progress being made towards the establishment of that kingdom, which cometh not with observation. Why, my brethren, the supposition may be a very odd one, nor do I say that it is at all likely to be realized,—but for the sake of illustration, I will come forward with it. Conceive that the Spirit of God, accompanying the circulation of the word of God, were to introduce all its truths and all its lessons into the heart of every individual of the Catholic priesthood; and that the Pope himself, instead of being brought down in person from the secular eminence he occupies, were brought down in spirit, with all his lofty imaginations, to the captivity of the obedience of Christ,—then I am not prepared to assert, that under the influence of this great Christian episcopacy, a mighty advancement may not be made in building up the kingdom of God, and in throwing down the kingdom of Satan, throughout all the territories of Catholic Christendom. And yet, with all this, the name of Catholic may be retained,—the external and visible marks of distinction, may be as prominent as ever,—and with all those insignia about them, which keep up our passionate antipathy to this denomination, there might not be a single ingredient in the spirit of its members, to merit our rational antipathy. I beg you will just take all this as an attempt at the illustration of what I count a very important principle;—and, to make the illustration more complete, let me take up the case of a Protestant country, and put the supposition, that, with the name of a pure and spiritual religion, the majority of its inhabitants are utter strangers to its power; that an indifference to the matters of faith and of eternity, works all the effect of a deep and fatal infidelity on their consciences; that the world engrosses every heart, and the kingdom which is not of this world, is virtually disowned and held in derision among the various classes and characters of society; that the spirit of the New Testament is banished from our Parliaments, and banished from our Universities, and banished from the great bulk of our ecclesiastical establishments, and it is only to be met with among a few inconsiderable men, who are scouted by the general voice as the fanatics and visionaries of the day;—then, my brethren, I am not to be charmed out of truth, and of principle, by the mockery of a name. Call such a country reformed, as you may, it is full of the strong-hold of antichrist, from one end to the other of it; and there must be a revolution of sentiment there, as well as in the darkest regions of Popery, ere the "enemies of the Son of God be consumed by the breath of his mouth," or "Babylon the great be fallen."

Now, secondly, mark the influence of such a train of sentiment, on the spirit of those who are employed in spreading the light of reformation among a Catholic people. It will purify their aim, and give it a judicious direction, and chase away from their proceedings that offensive tone of arrogance which is calculated to irritate, and to beget a more determined obstinacy of prejudice than ever. Their great aim, to express it in one word, is to plant in the hearts of all men of all countries, the religion of the Bible. Their great direction will be toward the establishment of right principle; and in the prosecution of it, they will carefully avoid multiplying the points of irritation, by giving vent to their traditional repugnance against the less material forms of Popery. And the meek consciousness of that woful departure from vital Christianity, which has taken place even in the reformed countries of Christendom, will divest them of that repulsive superiority which, I fear, has gone far to defeat the success of many an attempt, upon many an enemy of the truth as it is in Jesus. "The whole amount of our message is to furnish you with the Bible, and to furnish you with the art of reading it. We think the lessons of this book well fitted to chase away the manifold errors which rankle in the bosom of our own country. You are the subjects of error as well as we; and we trust that you will find them useful, in enlightening the prejudices, and in aiding the frailties to which, as the children of one common humanity, we are all liable. Amongst us, there is a mighty deference to the authority of man: if this exists among you, here is a book which tells us to call no man master, and delivers us from the fallibility of human opinions. Amongst us there is a delusive confidence in the forms of godliness, with little of its power: here is a book, which tells us that holiness of life is the great end of all our ceremonies, and of all our sacraments. Amongst us there is a host of theologians, each wielding his separate authority over the creed and the conscience of his countrymen, and you, Catholics, have justly reproached us with our manifold and never-ending varieties; but here is a book, the influence of which is throwing all these differences into the back ground, and bringing forward those great and substantial points of agreement, which lead us to recognise the man of another creed to be essentially a Christian,—and we want to widen this circle of fellowship, that we may be permitted to live in the exercise of one faith and of one charity along with you. Amongst us the great bulk of men pass through life forgetful of eternity, and think, that by the sighs and the ministrations of their last days, they will earn all the blessedness of its ever-during rewards. But here is a book which tells us that we should seek first the kingdom of God; and will not let us off with any other repentance than repentance now; and tells us, what we trusts will light with greater energy on your consciences than it has ever done upon ours, that we should haste and make no delay to keep the commandments." O! my brethren, let us not despair that such arguments, urged by the mild charity which adorns the Bible, and followed up by its circulation, will at length tell on the firmest defences that bigotry ever raised around the conscience and the principles of men—and that, out of those jarring elements which threaten our empire with a wild war of turbulence and disorder, we shall, by the blessing of God, be enabled to cement all its members into one great and harmonious family.

I conclude with saying, that, mainly and substantially speaking, I conceive this to be the very spirit of the attempt that is now making by the Society I am now pleading for. It is not an offensive declaration of war against Popery. It is true that it may be looked upon virtually as a measure of hostility against the errors of Catholics, but no more than it is a measure of hostility against the errors of Protestants. The light of truth is fitted to chase away all error, and there is something in that Bible which the agents of our Society are now teaching so assiduously, that is not more humbling and more severe on the general spirit of Ireland, than it is on the general spirit of our own country. It is true, that some of the Catholics set their face against the establishment of our schools, but this resistance to education is not peculiar to them. It is to be met with in England. It is to be met with in our own boasted and beloved Scotland. It is to be met with even among the enlightened classes of British society—and shall we speak of it as if it fastened a peculiar stigma on that country, which we have left to languish in depression and ignorance for so many generations? But, this resistance on the part of Catholics is far from general. In one district the teachers of our schools are chiefly Roman Catholics; many of the school-houses are Catholic chapels; and the great majority of the scholars are children of Catholic parents, who have appeared not a little elated that their children have proved more expert in their scriptural quotations than their neighbours.—Call you not this an auspicious commencement? Is there no loosening of prejudice here? Do you not perceive that the firmest system of bigotry, ever erected over the minds of a prostrate population, must give way before the continued operation of such an expedient as this? There is no one device of human policy that has done so much for Ireland in a whole century, as is now doing by the progress of education, and the freer circulation of the gospel of light through the dark mass and interior of their peasantry. Let me crave the assistance of the public in this place to one of the most powerful instruments that has yet been set agoing for helping forward this animating cause. It is an instrument ready made to your hand. The Hibernian Society have already established 347 schools in our sister country, a number equal to one third of the parishes in Scotland; and they are dealing out education, a pure scriptural education, to 27,700 Irish children. It will be a disgrace to us if we do not signalize ourselves in such a business as this. We talk of the Irish as a wild and uncivilized people. It will be the indication of a very gross and uncivilized public at home, if we restrict our interchange with the men of the opposite shore, to the one interchange of merchandise.

Let the rudeness of the Irish be what it may, sure I am, that there is much in their constitutional character to encourage us in this enterprise. They have many good points and engaging properties about them. I speak not of that peculiar style of genius and of eloquence, which gives such fascination to the poets, the authors, the orators of Ireland. I speak of the great mass, and I do think that I perceive a something in the natural character of Ireland, which draws me more attractively to the love of its people, than any other picture of national manners ever has inspired. Even amid the wildest extravagance of that humour which sits so visibly and so universally on the countenance of the Irish population, I can see a heart and a social sympathy along with it. Amid all the wayward and ungovernable flights of that rare pleasantry which belongs to them, there is a something by which the bosom of an Irishman can be seriously and permanently affected, and which I think in judicious hands is convertible into the finest results on the ultimate character of that people. It strikes me, that, of all the men on the face of the earth, they would be the worst fitted to withstand the expression of honest, frank, liberal, and persevering kindness;—that if they saw there was no artful policy in the attentions by which you plied them, but that an upright and firmly sustained benevolence lay at the bottom of all your exertions for the best interest of their families; could they attain the conviction, that, amid all the contempt and all the resistance you experienced from their hands, there still existed in your bosoms an unquelled and an undissembled love for them and for their children;—could they see the working of this principle divested of every treacherous and suspicious symptom, and unwearied amid every discouragement in prosecuting the task of their substantial amelioration,—why, my brethren, let all this come to be seen, and in a few years I trust our devoted missionaries will bring it before them broad and undeniable as the light of day, and those hearts that are now shut against you in sullenness and disdain will be subdued into tenderness; the strong emotions of gratitude and nature will at length find their way through all the barriers of prejudice; and a people whom no penalties could turn, whom no terror of military violence could overcome, who kept on a scowling front of hostility that was not to be softened, while war spread its desolating cruelties over their unhappy land, —this very people will do homage to the omnipotence of charity, and when the mighty armour of Christian kindness is brought to bear upon them, it will be found to be irresistible.

APPENDIX.

Extracts from the Eleventh Annual Report of the Hibernian Society, for establishing Schools, and circulating the Holy Scriptures in Ireland. London, 1817.

THE Committee are persuaded, that among the numerous Institutions which the Divine power and goodness have raised up in this kingdom, the Hibernian Society, if duly considered, will stand very high in the scale of moral and religious importance; and they are happy to add, that the present Report will present to its worthy supporters, continued and additional instances of the practicability of its designs, and the success of its operations.

"In the good work of establishing Schools for the education of the children of the poor, in Ireland, the Committee had proceeded so far, at the time of holding the last General Meeting, as to report, that the number of Schools exceeded three hundred; and that the children and adults educated therein were upwards of nineteen thousand. They have now the pleasure to state, that, by the annual return which was made up to Christmas last, the number of Schools is 347; and the children and adults educated therein, are 27,776.

"Such is the endearing and interesting spectacle which the present state of the labours of the Society presents to its benevolent supporters. Every Parent, every Christian, and every Briton must rejoice in the accomplishment of so much good to Ireland, where it was so peculiarly needed; and it is of such a nature, and is in such a course of extension and increase, as to afford the most reasonable expectations of enlarged and permanent benefits to that part of the United Kingdom.

"The Committee are happy to state, that the regulation for the conduct of the Schools are in full operation, and that the Inspectors are active and circumspect. The progress of the children in learning to read, and in committing the Scriptures to memory, and the interest that even Catholic parents feel in having their little ones appear with credit at the inspections, are truly gratifying. The attention of the Masters, in general, to the import of the sacred word, is pleasingly on the increase: and among such as have had their own understandings enlightened and informed, there exists a spirit of emulation to have their pupils excel in giving suitable answers to questions relating to the meaning of the passages which they repeat.

"These instances evidently show the immediate and direct influence which the Schools produce on the minds of the parents of the children who are educated therein; and that an emanation of Scripture light, and a portion of religious interest of the most important and useful kind, are introduced into the humble cottages of the poor. These now have some 'light in their dwelling,' in the midst of surrounding darkness and superstition; which, however, begins to be penetrated with the beams of Divine truth, and to be impressed with that word which is 'quick and powerful, and a discerner of the thoughts and intents of the heart.' On this interesting subject, a most valuable correspondent of the Committee thus writes:—

"From the many applications I receive from individuals from different parts of the country for Bibles and Testaments, there is strong evidence to the spreading of religious inquiry among the mass of the people. Many of them come from places remote from any of the Schools; but I always find that anxiety for the Scriptures has been excited by converse with some who have been pupils therein, who have lived in the neighbourhood of the Schools, or have been in some other ways immediately or remotely connected with them.

"Could the moral and religious improvement of the human mind be as easily discovered as the agricultural improvement of a country, those numerous districts where the Schools have been for any time established, would be found to exhibit a striking contrast to those wherein they have not yet taken place. While these would be seen in all the nakedness of sterility, or fruitful only in the production of noxious weeds; in the other it would appear that in a great degree the fallow ground has been broken up, the good seed sown and in a state of vegetation, waiting for the early and latter rain; in many, the appearance of a healthful crop would gladden the eye, and in some, the fields would appear already white unto the harvest.

"The great increase in the number of the Schools; the amazing anxiety for the Scriptures which they have been the means of exciting in every district; the increasing demand for Evening Schools for the instruction of the adult population,—all pressingly call for such a supply of Bibles and Testaments as I am unable to meet. Were the wonders doing in this country by the instrumentality of the Hibernian Society fully known in England, and their importance rightly appreciated, no Society would be found deserving of greater support."

"The Committee continue to give the greatest encouragement to the instruction of adults in the vicinity of the Schools; and they receive the most pleasing accounts of the efficacy of the word of God in the enlightening of the minds of those who probably would never have had an opportunity of reading the Scriptures, or of hearing them read, had it not been for the free Schools which this Society has established, and for the numerous copies of the Divine word which it has industriously circulated. Indeed, the Visitors to the Schools perceive and acknowledge, that, *were it not for the labours of this Institution, it would be impossible for the Bible Societies to get the Scriptures into the hands of the Catholics,* the great mass of the population of Ireland.

"The formation of Irish classes in the Schools which are appropriate thereto, continues to be sedulously promoted. An additional allowance has been granted to the Masters for their Irish Testament classes; and this has powerfully operated to increase the demand for Irish Testaments, both in the day Schools, and also in those which are held in the evening, for teaching the adults.

"The Committee could adduce additional instances of approbation and support from some of the Catholic Clergy, both of the Society's Schools, and of its exertions to circulate the Scriptures; but the limits of this Report will not permit an enlargement on this pleasing and interesting subject. If, however, the views and object of this Institution have only commended themselves as yet to a small part of the Catholic body, the Committee are happy to state, that, in the Protestant community, the high importance of the Hibernian Society increasingly arrests public attention; that the demands for Schools in almost every district are more numerous than can be attended to, and that in every place respectable individuals come forward, unsolicited, to carry into execution the benevolent designs of the Society. And here it is very appropriate and grateful to observe, that to the Clergy of the Established Church who have afforded their patronage to the Schools, and have condescended to act as Visitors, the Society are under very great obligations; and particularly to an excellent Dignitary of that Church, who has always entered into the views of the Society with a liberal mind, has furthered them with continued assiduity, and has recently from the pulpit pleaded the cause of the Institution, and thereby added to its celebrity and support. This last service called for the official thanks of the Committee. They were transmitted by the treasurer, and the answer which has been received from this estimable personage is so characteristic of his piety and philanthropy, and so highly honourable to the Hibernian Society, that it would be unsuitable and injurious to withhold the following extract:—

"I have received your very kind letter, communicating the thanks of the Committee of the Hibernian Society of London, to me, for the sermon I preached in Sligo Church on their behalf; and for other services which the Committee are pleased kindly to notice, as rendered by me to the Schools under their patronage. Whatever little I have been enabled to do, I have felt that therein I have been doing the best service I could to this quarter of my *poor benighted* country. And I thank God, that I see the exertions which the Society has made already (and they have been great) so largely owned of him. I am persuaded, that nothing is calculated so much, under the Divine blessing, to dispel the gross darkness that has covered this land, for so many ages, as such a system of general scriptural education, as that adopted by your Society. And I have to acknowledge that the establishment of the Society's Schools in the vicinity of my ministerial duties, has proved the happy instrument of a great enlargement of utterance and usefulness to me; and never more did I experience this enlargement, than on the late occasion of my visiting Sligo, to advocate the cause of the Society. If I have done this with any degree of success, I desire to thank, and give glory to God. Surely you well deserve the cordial co-operation of the Irish public; and you call forth from Irish Christians, thanksgivings to God for the grace bestowed upon you."

It has been noticed that the number of children and adults taught in the Society's Schools has increased, in the course of the last year, from 19,000 to 27,000, and that requisitions for additional Schools are far more numerous than can be complied with. It will also be remembered, that at the time of holding the last Annual Meeting, the expenditure of the Society had exceeded its income upwards of 600*l.* In this conflict of an enlarged establishment and a deficient revenue, of encouraging prospects and limited means, the Committee have endeavoured to increase the funds of the Society, and to lessen the expense of its future operations. To obtain the first-mentioned benefit, they have transmitted a circular letter to Ministers generally, in town and country, describing the state of the Institution, as to its importance, its usefulness, and its necessities; urging them to interest themselves in procuring subscriptions and donations: and particularly and earnestly requesting them to incorporate it amongst those other excellent Societies, for the assistance of which Auxiliary Institutions have in so many places been established. These dispense their tributary streams with fertilizing and invigorating energies; and if in their course, they were permitted to visit and enrich the Hibernian Society, Ireland would greatly benefit by the diffusion, and would ardently bless her pious and liberal benefactors.— With regard to lessening the expense of future operations, the Committee have endeavoured to connect the formation of *new* Schools, with an Annual Subscription; and, in this way, it is to be hoped, that many of the resident noblemen and gentlemen in Ireland, will assist in carrying into effect the designs, and in relieving the funds, of the Hibernian Society.

It has been truly gratifying to the Committee, to state the considerable increase of the Society's Schools, and the evident utility and success of its operations; but it is with regret that they view the inadequacy of the funds to defray the necessary expenses of the Institution; and with anxiety that they contrast the openings of Providence which present themselves, for exertions of a very extensive nature—in the highest degree important, and promising the most happy results,—with the alarming deficiency of pecuniary means for following those providential leadings, with the energies and the hopes which they are so well calculated to inspire.

With respect to the progress which has already been made in fulfilling the purposes for which the Society was formed, it may be observed,—that its advances in extension of operations, and its success by its means and instruments, have proved in the highest degree pleasing and satisfactory. It was not till about the year 1809, that Schools were established in Ireland, under the patronage of the Hibernian Society; from which period to the present time, these establishments have so increased as to include upwards of 27,000 pupils. And when it is considered that the Schools have been formed, and the children collected therein, for the purpose of imparting the benefits of education to the lower classes of the people, who had neither the means nor the hopes of these benefits from any other quarter; and also of diffusing the blessings of pure Scriptural instruction among those to whom the policy and the power of their superiors forbid the introduction of these blessings; surely it must be acknowledged, that the designs and operations of the Society have been appropriate and efficient, for the removal of the greatest of evils, and for the production of the most essential and important good. In fact, the gradually increasing operations of the Society have greatly exceeded its progressive means of support; its designs have been truly laudable and excellent, its means and instruments well adapted to execute them, and the sphere of its labours admirably calculated to gratify British benevolence, and to reward Christian zeal. Under all these circumstances, it is a matter of surprise and regret, that the income of this Institution, arising from annual subscriptions, does not amount to 500*l.*; whilst its annual expenditure is upwards of 4,000*l.* The deficiency has, in part, been supplied by donations and collections, and also by assistance received from Auxiliary Societies; but the arrears at length amount to a sum (1,605*l.*) which must have become burdensome to the Treasurer, embarrassing to the Committee, and prejudicial to the interest of the Society.

To relieve it of this debt, is the anxious wish of its Committee, and must be the earnest desire of its Members. And when it is considered, as having arisen out of the actual prosperity of the cause, which the Society was established to promote, and from the enlarged and successful exertions which it has been enabled to prosecute, the Committee are persuaded that every Member of the Institution will feel it to be his duty and his pleasure, to unite with them, in immediate and earnest efforts, to replenish and increase its funds, in order that the Society may be relieved from the pressure of present obligations, and be capacitated to enter on a course of additional labours, and of extensive and hopeful exertions.

That the operations of this Society should be stationary whilst the most fair and promising prospects open for their exertions; that the benefits of education which it has conferred, and the blessings of Scriptural instruction, which it has imparted, should be circumscribed comparatively to a few, while hundreds of thousands are perishing for lack of knowledge, is a state of things, which must wound the feelings, and disappoint the hopes, of the supporters of the Institution.

That a work so truly important, that objects so highly benevolent, and that efforts so eminently successful, will be impeded or paralyzed for want of pecuniary support, the Committee cannot believe. For the appeal to Christian principles, feelings, and generosity, is made, in the present instance, to the religious public in Great Britain; whose noble liberality supports efforts of compassion and mercy, amongst the ignorant and the miserable, in the most distant parts of the world. And this liberality will surely not be withheld from the Hibernian Society, whose labours are directed to remove the afflicting spectacle of ignorance, superstition, immorality, and mental degradation, which the lower classes of the community in Ireland exhibit; to place our "brethren according to the flesh," our fellow subjects, on the same high ground of moral and national advantage on which we stand, and thus to promote their best interest, their highest happiness, and their eternal salvation.

CRUELTY TO ANIMALS:

A SERMON

PREACHED IN EDINBURGH, ON THE 5th OF MARCH, 1826.

"A righteous man regardeth the life of his beast."—*Prov.* xii. 10.

The word regard is of two-fold signification, and may either apply to the moral or to the intellectual part of our nature. In the one application, the intellectual, it is the regard of attention. In the other, the moral, it is the regard of sympathy, or kindness. We do not marvel at this common term having been applied to two different things; for, in truth, they are most intimately associated; and the faculty by which a transition is accomplished from the one to the other, may be considered as the intermediate link between the mind and the heart. It is the faculty by which certain objects become present to the mind; and then the emotions are awakened in the heart, which correspond to these objects. The two act and re-act upon each other. But as we must not dwell too long on generalities, we shall satisfy ourselves with stating, that as, on the one hand, if the heart be very alive to any peculiar set of emotions, this of itself is a predisposing cause why the mind should be very alert in singling out the peculiar objects which excite them; so, on the other hand, that the emotions be specifically felt, the objects must be specifically noticed: and thus it is, that the faculty of attention—a faculty at the bidding of the will, and for the exercise of which, therefore, man is responsible—is of such mighty and commanding influence upon the sensibilities of our nature; insomuch that, if the regard of attention could be fastened strongly and *singly* on the pain of a suffering creature as its object, we believe that no other emotion than the regard of sympathy or compassion would in any instance be awakened by it.

So much is this indeed the case—so sure is this alliance between the mind simply noticing the distress of a sentient creature, and the heart being sympathetically affected by it, that Nature seems to have limited and circumscribed our power of noticing, and just for the purpose of shielding us from the pain of too pungent, or too incessant a sympathy. And, accordingly, one of the exquisite adaptations in the mechanism of the human frame may be observed in the very imperfection of the human faculties. The most frequently adduced example of this is, the limited power of that organ which is the instrument of vision. The imagination is, that, did man look out upon Nature with microscopic eye, so that many of those wonders which now lie hid in deep obscurity should henceforth start into open revelation, and be hourly and habitually obtruded upon his gaze, then, with his present sensibilities exposed to the torture and the disturbance of a perpetual and most agonizing offence from all possible quarters of contemplation, he would be utterly incapacitated for the movements of familiar and ordinary life. Did he actually see, for example, in the beverage which he carried to his lips, that teeming multitude of sentient and susceptible creatures wherewith it is pervaded, or if it were alike palpable to his senses, that, by the crush of every footstep, he inflicted upon thousands the pangs of dissolution, then it is apprehended that, to man as he is, the world would be insupportable. For, beside the irritation of that sore and incessant disgust, from which the power of escaping was denied to him, there would be another, and a most intense suffering, in the constantly aggrieved tenderness of his nature. Or if by the operation of habit, all these sensibilities were blunted, and he could behold unmoved the ruin and the wretchedness that he strewed along his path, then he might attain to comfort in the midst of this surrounding annoyance; but what would become of character in the utter extinction of all the delicacies and the feelings which wont to adorn it? Such a change in his physical, could only be adjusted to his happiness, by a reverse and most melancholy change in the moral constitution of his nature. The fineness of his bodily perceptions would need to be compensated by a proportional hardness in the temperament of his soul. With his now finer sensations, there behooved to be duller and coarser sensibilities; and to assort that eye, whose retina had become tenfold more soft and susceptible than before, its owner must be furnished with a heart of tenfold rigidity, and a nervous system as impregnable as iron,—that he might walk forth in ease and in complacency, while the conscious destroyer of millions by his tread, or the conscious devourer of a whole living and suffering hecatomb with every morsel of the sustenance which upheld him.

But, for the purpose of a nice and delicate balance between the actual feelings and faculties of our nature, something more is necessary than the imperfection of our outward senses. The bluntness of man's visual organs serves, no doubt, as a screen of protection against both the nausea and the horror of those many spectacles, which would else have either distressed or deteriorated the sensibilities that belong to him. But then, by help of the microscope, this screen can be occasionally lifted up; and what the eye then saw, the memory might retain, and the imagination might dwell upon, and the associating faculty might both constantly and vividly suggest; and thus, even in the absence of every provocative from without, the heart might be subjected either to a perpetual agitation, or a perpetual annoyance, by the meddling importunity of certain powers and activities which are within. It is not, therefore, an adequate defence of our species, against a very sore and hurtful molestation, that there should be a certain physical incapacity in our senses. There must, furthermore, be a certain physical inertness in our reflective faculties. In virtue of the former it is, that so many painful or disgusting objects are kept out of sight. But it seems indispensable to our happy or even tolerable existence, that, in virtue of the latter, these objects, when out of sight, should be also out of mind. In the one way, they lose their power to offend as objects of outward observation. In the other way, their power to haunt and to harass, by means of inward reflection, is also taken away. For the first purpose, Nature has struck with a certain impotency the organs of our material framework. For the second, she has infused, as it were, an opiate into the recesses of our mental economy, and made it of sufficient strength and sedative virtue for the needful tranquillity of man, and for upholding that average enjoyment in the midst both of agony and of loathsomeness, which either senses more acute, or a spirit more wakeful, must have effectually dissipated. It is to some such provision too, we think, that much of the heart's purity, as well as much of its tenderness is owing; and it is well that the thoughts of the spirit should be kept, though even by the weight of its own lethargy, from too busy a converse with objects which are alike offensive or alike hazardous to both.

It is more properly with the second of these adaptations than the first, that our argument has to do—with the inertness of our reflective faculties, rather than with the incapacity of our senses. It is in behalf of animals, and not of animalculæ, that we are called upon to address you—not of that countless swarm, the agonies of whose destruction are shrouded from observation by the vail upon the sight; but of those creatures who move on the face of the open perspective before us, and not as the others in a region of invisibles, and yet whose dying agonies are shrouded almost as darkly and as densely from general observation, by the vail upon the mind. For you will perceive, that in reference to the latter vail, and by which it is that what is out of sight is also out of mind, its purpose is accomplished, whether the objects which are disguised by it be without the sphere of actual vision, or beneath the surface of possible vision. Now it is without the sphere of your actual, although not beneath the surface of your possible vision, where are transacted the dreadful mysteries of a slaughter-house, and more especially those lingering deaths which an animal has to undergo for the gratifications of a refined epicurism. It were surely most desirable that the duties, if they may be so called, of a most revolting trade, were all of them got over with the least possible expense of suffering; nor do we ever feel so painfully the impression of a lurking cannibalism in our nature, as when we think of the intense study which has been given to the connexion between modes of killing, and the flavour or delicacy of those viands which are served up to mild, and pacific, and gentle-looking creatures, who form the grace and the ornament of our polished society. One is almost tempted, after all, to look upon them as so many savages in disguise; and so, in truth, we should, but for the strength of that opiate whose power and whose property we have just endeavoured to explain; and in virtue of which, the guests of an entertainment are all the while most profoundly unconscious of the horrors of that preparatory scene which went before it. It is not, therefore, that there is hypocrisy in these smiles wherewith they look so benignly to each other. It is not that there is deceit in their words or their accents of tenderness. The truth is, that one shriek of agony, if heard from without, would cast most impressive gloom over this scene of conviviality; and the sight, but for a moment, of one wretched creature quivering towards death, would, with Gorgon spell, dissipate all the gaieties which enlivened it. But Nature, as it were, hath practised most subtle *reticence*, both on the senses and the spirit of her children; or rather, the Author of Nature hath, by the skill of his master hand, instituted the harmony of a most exquisite balance between the tenderness of the human feelings and the listlessness of the human faculties, so as that, in the mysterious economy under which we live, he may at once provide for the sustenance, and leave entire the moral sensibilities of our species.

But there is a still more wondrous limitation than this, wherewith he hath bounded and beset the faculties of the human spirit. You already understand how it is, that the sufferings of the lower animals may, when out of sight, be out of mind. But more than this, these sufferings may be in sight, and yet out of mind. This is strikingly exemplified in the sports of the field, in the midst of whose varied and animating bustle, that cruelty which all along is present to the senses, may not, for one moment, have been present to the thoughts. There sits a somewhat ancestral dignity and glory on this favourite pastime of joyous old England; when the gallant knighthood, and the hearty yeomen, and the amateurs or virtuosos of the chase, and the full assembled jockeyship of half a province, muster together in all the pride and pageantry of their great emprize—and the panorama of some noble landscape, lighted up with autumnal clearness from an unclouded heaven, pours fresh exhilaration into every blithe and choice spirit of the scene—and every adventurous heart is braced, and impatient for the hazards of the coming enterprise—and even the high-breathed coursers catch the general sympathy, and seem to fret in all the restiveness of their yet checked and irritated fire, till the echoing horn shall set them at liberty—even that horn which is the knell of death to some trembling victim, now brought forth of its lurking place to the delighted gaze, and borne down upon with the full and open cry of its ruthless pursuers. Be assured that, amid the whole glee and fervency of this tumultuous enjoyment, there might not, in one single bosom, be aught so fiendish as a principle of naked and abstract cruelty. The fear which gives its lightning speed to the unhappy animal; the thickening horrors which, in the progress of exhaustion, must gather upon its flight; its gradually sinking energies, and, at length, the terrible certainty of that destruction which is awaiting it; that piteous cry, which the ear can sometimes distinguish amid the deafening clamour of the blood-hounds, as they spring exultingly upon their prey; the dread massacre and dying agonies of a creature so miserably torn;—all this weight of suffering, we admit, is not once sympathized with; but it is just because the suffering itself is not once thought of. It touches not the sensibilities of the heart; but just because it is never present to the notice of the mind. We allow that the hardy followers in the wild romance of this occupation, we allow them to be reckless of pain; but this is not rejoicing in pain. Theirs is not the delight of savage, but the apathy of unreflecting creatures. They are wholly occupied with the chase itself, and its spirit-stirring accompaniments, nor bestow one moment's thought on the dread violence of that infliction upon sentient nature which marks its termination. It is the spirit of the competition, and it alone, which goads onward this hurrying career; and even he, who in at the death, is foremost in the triumph, although to him the death itself is in sight, the agony of its wretched sufferer is wholly out of mind.

We are inclined to carry this principle much farther. We are not even sure if, within the whole compass of humanity, fallen as it is, there be such a thing as delight in suffering, for its own sake. But, without hazarding a controversy on this, we hold it enough for every practical object, that much, and perhaps the whole of this world's cruelty, arises not from the enjoyment that is felt in consequence of others' pain, but from the enjoyment that is felt in spite of it. It is something else in the spectacle of agony which ministers pleasure than the agony itself; and many is the eye which glistens with transport at the fray of animals met together for their mutual destruction, and which might be brought to weep, if, apart from all the excitements of such a scene, the anguish of wounded or dying creatures were placed nakedly before it. Were it strictly analyzed, it would be found that the charm, neither of the ancient gladiatorships, nor of our modern prize-fights, lies in the torture which is thereby inflicted; for we should feel the very same charm, and look with the very same intentness, on some doubtful, yet strenuous collision, even among the inanimate elements of nature—as, when the water and the fire contended for mastery, and the inherent force of the one was met by a plying and a powerful engineery that gave impulse and direction to the other. It is even so, when the engineery of bones and of muscles comes into rivalship; and every spectator of the ring fastens on the spectacle with that identical engrossment which he feels in the hazards of some doubtful game, or in the desperate conflict and effervescence even of the altogether mute unconscious elements. To him it is little else than a problem in dynamics. There is a science connected with the fight, which has displaced the sensibilities that are connected with its expiring moans, its piteous and piercing out---

cruel lacerations. In all this, we admit the utter heedlessness of pain; but we are not sure if even yet there be aught so hellishly revolting as any positive gratification in the pain itself—or whether, even in the lowest walks of blackguardism in society, it do not also hold, that when sufferings even unto death are fully in sight, the pain of these sufferings is as fully out of mind.

But the term science, so strangely applied as it has been in the example now quoted, reminds us of another variety in this most afflicting detail. Even in the purely academic walk we read or hear of the most appalling cruelties; and the interest of that philosophy wherewith they have been associated, has been plead in mitigation of them. And just as the moral debasement incurred by an act of theft is somewhat redeemed, if done by one of Science's enamoured worshippers, when, overcome by the mere passion of connoisseurship, he puts forth his hand on some choice specimen of most tempting and irresistible peculiarity—even so has a like indulgence been extended to certain perpetrators of stoutest and most resolved cruelty; and that just because of the halo wherewith the glories of intellect and of proud discovery have enshrined them. And thus it is, that, bent on the scrutiny of nature's laws, there are some of our race who have hardihood enough to explore and elicit them at the expense of dreadest suffering—who can make some quaking, some quivering animal, the subject of their hapless experiment—who can institute a questionary process by which to draw out the secrets of its constitution, and, like inquisitors of old, extract every reply by an instrument of torture—who can probe their unfaltering way among the vitalities of a system which shrinks, and palpitates, and gives forth, at every movement of their steadfast hand, the pulsations of deepest agony; and all, perhaps, to ascertain and to classify the phenomena of sensation, or to measure the tenacity of animal life, by the power and exquisiteness of animal endurance. And still, it is not because of all this wretchedness, but in spite of it, that they pursue their barbarous occupation. Even here it is possible, that there is nought so absolutely Satanic as delight in those sufferings of which themselves are the inflicters. That law of emotion by which the sight of pain calls forth sympathy, may not be reversed into an opposite law, by which the sight of pain would call forth satisfaction or pleasure. The emotion is not reversed—it is only overborne, in the play of other emotions, called forth by other objects. He is intent on the science of those phenomena which he investigates, and bethinks not himself of the suffering which they involve to the unhappy animal. So far from the sympathies of his nature being reversed, or even annihilated, there is in most cases an effort, and of great strenuousness, to keep them down; and his heart is differently affected from that of other men, just because the regards of his mental eye are differently pointed from those of other men. The whole bent and engagement of his faculties are similar to those of another operator who is busied with the treatment of a piece of inanimate matter, and may almost be said to subject it to the torture, when he puts it in the intensely heated crucible, or applies to it the test, and the various searching operations of a laboratory. The one watches every change of hue in the substance upon which he operates, and waits for the response which is given forth by a spark, or an effervescence, or an explosion; and the other, precisely similar to him, watches every change of aspect in the suffering or dying creature that is before him, and marks every symptom of its exhaustion, or sorer distress, every throb of renewed anguish, every cry, and every look of that pain which it can feel, though not articulate; marks and considers these in no other light than as the exponents of its variously affected physiology. But still, could merely the same interesting phenomena have been evolved without pain, he would like it better. Only he will not be repelled from the study of them by pain. Even he would have had more comfort in the study of a complex automaton, that gave out the same results on the same application. Only, he will not shrink from the necessary incisions, and openings, and separation of parts, although, instead of a lifeless automaton, it should be a sentient and sorely agonized animal. So that there is not even with him any reversal of the law of sympathy. There may be the feebleness, or there may be the negation of it. Certain it is, that it has given way to other laws of superior force in his constitution. And, without imputing to him aught so monstrous as the positive love of suffering, we may even admit for him a hatred of suffering, but that the love of science had overborne it.

In the views that we have now given, and which we deem of advantage for the right practical treatment of our question, it may be conceived that we palliate the atrociousness of cruelty. It is forgotten, that a charge of foulest delinquency may be made up altogether of wants or of negatives; and, just as the human face, by the mere want of some of its features, although there should not be any inversion of them, might be an object of utter loathsomeness to beholders, so the human character, by the mere absence of certain habits, or certain sensibilities, which belong ordinarily and constitutionally to our species, may be an object of utter abomination in society. The want of natural affection forms one article of the Apostle's indictment against our world; and ertain, it is, that the total want of it were stigma enough for the designation of a monster. The mere want of religion, or rreligion, is enough to make man an outcast rom his God. Even to the most barbarous of our kind you apply, not the term of anti-humanity, but of inhumanity—not the term of antisensibility: and you hold it enough for the purpose of branding him for general execration, that you convicted him of complete and total insensibility. He is regaled, t is true, by a spectacle of agony—but not because of the agony. It is something else, herewith associated, which regales him. But still he is rightfully the subject of most emphatic denunciation, not because regaled by, but because regardless of, the agony. We do not feel ourselves to be vindicating the cruel man, when we affirm it to be not altogether certain, whether he rejoices in the extinction of life; for we count it a deep atrocity, that, unlike to the righteous man of our text, he simply does not regard the life of a beast. You may perhaps have been accustomed to look upon the negatives of character, as making up a sort of neutral or midway innocence. But this is a mistake. Unfeeling is but a negative quality; and yet, we speak of an unfeeling monster. It is thus that even the profound experimentalist, whose delight is not in the torture which he inflicts, but in the truth which he elicits thereby, may become an object of keenest reprobation: not because he was pleased with suffering, but simply because he did not pity it—not because the object of pain, if dwelt upon by him, would be followed up by any other emotion than that which is experienced by other men, but because, intent on the prosecution of another object, it was not so dwelt upon. It is found that the eclat even of brilliant discovery does not shield him from the execrations of a public, who can yet convict him of nothing more than simply of negatives—of heedlessness, of heartlessness, of looking upon the agonies of a sentient creature without regard, and therefore without sensibility. The true principle of his condemnation is, that he ought to have regarded. It is not that, in virtue of a different organic structure, he feels differently from others, when the same simple object is brought to bear upon him. But it is, that he resolutely kept that object at a distance from his attention, or rather, that he steadily kept his attention away from the object; and that, in opposition to all the weight of remonstrance which lies in the tremours, and the writhings, and the piteous outcries of agonized Nature. Had we obtained for these the regards of his mind, the relentings of his heart might have followed. His is not an anomalous heart; and the only way in which he can brace it into sternness, is by barricading the avenue which leads to it. That faculty of attention, which might have opened the door, through which suffering without finds its way to sympathy within, is otherwise engaged; and the precise charge, on which either morality can rightfully condemn, or humanity be offended, is, that he wills to have it so.

It may be illustrated by that competition of speed which is held, with busy appliance of whip and of spur, betwixt animals. A similar competition can be imagined between steam-carriages, when, either to preserve the distance which has been gained, or to recover the distance which has been lost, the respective guides would keep up an incessant appliance to the furnace, and the safety-valve. Now, the sport and the excitement are the same, whether this appliance of force be to a dead or a living mechanism; and the enormity of the latter does not lie in any direct pleasure which is felt in the exhaustion, or the soreness, or, finally, in the death of the over-driven animal. If these awake any feeling at all in the barbarous rider, it is that of pain; and it is either the want or the weakness of this latter feeling, and not the presence of its opposite, which constitutes him a barbarian. He does not rejoice in animal suffering—but it is enough to bring down upon him the charge of barbarity, that he does not regard it.

But these introductory remarks, although they lead, I do think, to some most important suggestions for the management of the evil, yet they serve not to abate its appalling magnitude. Man is the direct agent of a wide and continual distress to the lower animals, and the question is, Can any method be devised for its alleviation? On this subject that scriptural image is strikingly realized, "The whole inferior creation groaning and travailing together in pain," because of him. It signifies not to the substantive amount of the suffering, whether this be prompted by the hardness of his heart, or only permitted through the heedlessness of his mind. In either way it holds true, not only that the arch-devourer man stands pre-eminent over the fiercest children of the wilderness as an animal of prey, but that for his lordly and luxurious appetite, as well as for his service or merest curiosity and amusement, Nature must be ransacked throughout all her elements. Rather than forego the veriest gratifications of vanity, he will wring them from the anguish of wretched and ill-fated creatures; and whether for the indulgence of his barbaric sensuality, or barbaric splendour, can stalk paramount over the sufferings of that prostrate creation which has been placed beneath his feet. That beauteous domain whereof he has been constituted the terrestrial sovereign, gives out so many blissful and benignant aspects; and whether we look to its peaceful lakes, or its flowery landscapes, or its evening skies, or to all that soft attire which overspreads the hills and the valleys, lighted up by smiles of sweetest sunshine, and where animals disport themselves in all the exuberance of gaiety—this surely were a more befitting scene for the rule of clemency, than for the iron rod of a murderous and remorseless tyrant. But the present is a mysterious world wherein we dwell. It still bears much upon its materialism of the impress of Paradise. But a breath from the air of Pandemonium has gone over its living generations. And so "the fear of man, and the dread of man, is now upon every beast of the earth, and upon every fowl of the air, upon all that moveth upon the earth, and upon all the fishes of the sea; into man's hands are they delivered: every moving thing that liveth is meat for him; yea, even as the green herbs, there have been given to him all things." Such is the extent of his jurisdiction, and with most full and wanton license has he revelled among its privileges. The whole earth labours and is in violence because of his cruelties; and, from the amphitheatre of sentient Nature, there sounds in fancy's ear the bleat of one wide and universal suffering,—a dreadful homage to the power of Nature's constituted lord.

These sufferings are really felt. The beasts of the field are not so many automata without sensation, and just so constructed as to give forth all the natural signs and expressions of it. Nature has not practised this universal deception upon our species. These poor animals just look, and tremble, and give forth the very indications of suffering that we do. Theirs is the distinct cry of pain. Theirs is the unequivocal physiognomy of pain. They put on the same aspect of terror on the demonstrations of a menacing blow. They exhibit the same distortions of agony after the infliction of it. The bruise, or the burn, or the fracture, or the deep incision, or the fierce encounter with one of equal or superior strength, just affects them similarly to ourselves. Their blood circulates as ours. They have pulsations in various parts of the body like ours. They sicken, and they grow feeble with age, and, finally, they die just as we do. They possess the same feelings; and what exposes them to like suffering from another quarter, they possess the same instincts with our own species. The lioness robbed of her whelps causes the wilderness to ring aloud with the proclamation of her wrongs; or the bird whose little household has been stolen, fills and saddens all the grove with melodies of deepest pathos. All this is palpable even to the general and unlearned eye; and when the physiologist lays open the recesses of their system by means of that scalpel, under whose operation they just shrink and are convulsed as any living subject of our own species, there stands forth to view the same sentient apparatus, and furnished with the same conductors for the transmission of feeling to every minutest pore upon the surface. Theirs is unmixed and unmitigated pain—the agonies of martyrdom, without the alleviation of the hopes and the sentiments, whereof they are incapable. When they lay them down to die, their only fellowship is with suffering, for in the prison-house of their beset and bounded faculties, there can no relief be afforded by communion with other interests or other things. The attention does not lighten their distress as it does that of man, by carrying off his spirit from that existing pungency and pressure which might else be overwhelming. There is but room in their mysterious economy for one inmate; and that is, the absorbing sense of their own single and concentrated anguish. And so in that bed of torment, whereon the wounded animal lingers and expires, there is an unexplored depth and intensity of suffering which the poor dumb animal itself cannot tell, and against which it can offer no remonstrance; an untold and unknown amount of wretchedness, of which no articulate voice gives utterance. But there is an eloquence in its silence; and the very shroud which disguises it, only serves to aggravate its horrors.

We now come to the practical treatment of this question—to the right method of which, we hold the views that are now offered to be directly and obviously subservient.

First, then, upon this subject, we should hold no doubtful casuistry. We should advance no pragmatic or controversial doctrine. We should carefully abstain from all such ambiguous or questionable positions, as the unlawfulness of animal food, or the unlawfulness of animal experiments. We should not even deem it the right tactics for this moral warfare, to take up the position of the unlawfulness of field-sports, or yet the unlawfulness of those competitions, whether of strength or of speed, which at one time on the turf, and at another in the ring, are held forth to the view of assembled spectators. We are aware that some of these positions are not so questionable, yet we should refrain from the elaboration of them; for we hold, that this is not the way by which we shall most effectually make head against the existing cruelties of our land. The moral force by which our cause is to be advanced, does not lie even in the soundest categories of an ethical jurisprudence—and far less in the dogmata of any paltry sectarianism. We have almost as little inclination for the controversy which respects animal food, as we have for the controversy about the eating of blood; and this, we repeat, is not the way by which the claims of the inferior animals are practically to be carried. To obtain the regards of man's heart in behalf of the lower animals, we should strive to raw the regards of his mind towards hem. We should avail ourselves of the lose alliance that obtains between the rewards of his attention, and those of his sympathy. For this purpose, we should importunately ply him with the objects of uffering, and thus call up its respondent motion of sympathy, that among the ther objects which have hitherto engrossed his attention, and the other desires or motions which have hitherto lorded it ver the compassion of his nature and overpowered it, this last may at length be retored to its legitimate play, and reinstated n all its legitimate pre-eminence over the ther affections or appetites which belong o him. It affords a hopeful view of our ause, that so much can be done by the mere obtrusive presentation of the object to he notice of society. It is a comfort to mow, that in this benevolent warfare we ave to make head, not so much against he cruelty of the public, as against the heedlessness of the public; that to hold forth a right view, is the way to call forth a right sensibility; and, that to assail the seat of any emotion, our likeliest process is to make constant and conspicuous exhibition of the object which is fitted to awaken it. Our text, taken from the profoundest book of experimental wisdom in the world, keeps clear of every questionable or casuistical dogma; and rests the whole cause of the inferior animals on one moral element, which is, in respect of principle, and on one practical method, which is, in respect of efficacy, unquestionable: "A righteous man regardeth the life of his beast." Let a man be but righteous in the general and obvious sense of the word, and let the regard of his attention be but directed to the case of the inferior animals, and then the regard of his sympathy will be awakened to the full extent at which it is either duteous or desirable. Still it may be asked to what extent will the duty go? and our reply is, that we had rather push the duty forward than be called upon to define the extreme termination of it. Yet we do not hesitate to say, that we foresee not aught so very extreme as the abolition of animal food; but we do foresee the indefinite abridgement of all that cruelty which subserves the gratifications of a base and selfish epicurism. We think that a christian and humanized society will at length lift their prevalent voice, for the least possible expense of suffering to all the victims of a necessary slaughter—for a business of utmost horror being also a business of utmost despatch—for the blow, in short, of an instant extermination, that not one moment might elapse between a state of pleasurable existence and a state of profound unconsciousness. Again, we do not foresee, but with the perfecting of the two sciences of anatomy and physiology, the abolition of animal experiments; but we do foresee a gradual, and, at length, a complete abandonment of the experiments of illustration, which are at present a thousand-fold more numerous than the experiments of humane discovery.

As to field-sports, we for the present, abstain from all prophecy, in regard, either to their growing disuse, or to the conclusive extinction of them. We are quite sure, in the mean time, that casuistry upon this subject would be altogether powerless; and nothing could be imagined more keenly, or more energetically contemptuous, than the impatient, the impetuous disdain wherewith the enamoured votaries of this gay and glorious adventure would listen to any demonstration of its unlawfulness. We shall therefore make no attempt to dogmatise them but of that fond and favourite amusement which they prosecute with all the intensity of a passion. It is not thus that the fascination will be dissipated. And, therefore, for the present, we should be inclined to subject the lovers of the chase, and the lovers of the prize-fight, to the same treatment, even as there exists between them, we are afraid, the affinity of a certain common or kindred character. There is, we have often thought, a kind of professional cast, a family likeness, by which the devotees of game, and of all sorts of stirring or hazardous enterprise admit of being recognized; the hue of a certain assimilating quality, although of various gradations, from the noted champions of the hunt, to the noted champions of the ring or of the racing-course; a certain dash of moral outlawry, if I may use the expression, among all those children of high and heated adventure, that bespeaks them a distinct class in society,—a set of wild and wayward humourists, who have broken them loose from the dull regularities of life, and formed themselves into so many trusty and sworn brotherhoods, wholly given over to frolic, and excitement, and excess, in all their varieties. They compose a separate and outstanding public among themselves, nearly arrayed in the same picturesque habiliments—bearing most distinctly upon their countenance the same air of recklessness and hardihood—admiring the same feats of dexterity or danger—indulging the same tastes, even to their very literature—members of the same sporting society—readers of the same sporting magazine, whose strange medley of anecdotes gives impressive exhibition of that one and pervading characteristic for which we are contending; anecdotes of the chase, and anecdotes of the high-breathed or bloody contest, and anecdotes of the gaming-table, and, lastly, anecdotes of the high-way. We do not just affirm a precise identity between all the specimens or species in this very peculiar department of moral history. But, to borrow a phrase from natural history, we affirm, that there are transition processes, by which the one melts, and demoralises, and graduates insensibly into the other. What we have now to do with, is the cruelty of their respective entertainments—a cruelty, however, upon which we could not assert, even of the very worst and most worthless among them, that they rejoice in pain, but that they are regardless of pain. It is not by the force of a mere ethical *dictum*, in itself, perhaps, unquestionable, that they will be restrained from their pursuits. But when transformed by the operation of unquestionable principle, into righteous and regardful men, they will spontaneously abandon them. Meanwhile, we try to help forward our cause, by forcing upon general regard, those sufferings which are now so unheeded and unthought of. And we look forward to its final triumph, as one of those results that will historically ensue, in the train of an awakened and a moralized society.

The institution of a yearly sermon against cruelty to animals, is of itself a likely enough expedient, that might at least be of some auxiliary operation, along with other and more general causes, towards such an awakening. It is not by one, but by many successive appeals, that the cause of justice and mercy to the brute creation will at length be practically carried. On this subject I cannot, within the limits of a single address, pretend to aught like a full or a finished demonstration. This might require not one, but a whole century of sermons; and many therefore are the topics which necessarily I must bequeath to my successors, in this warfare against the listlessness and apathy of the public. And, beside the force and the impression of new topics, if there be any truth in our doctrine, there is a mighty advantage gained upon this subject of all others by the repetition of old topics. It is a subject on which the public do not require so much to be instructed, as to be reminded; to have the regard of their attention directed again and again to the sufferings of poor helpless creatures, that the regard of their sympathy might at length be effectually obtained for them. This then is a cause to which the institution of an anniversary pleading in its favour, is most precisely and peculiarly adapted. And besides, we must confess, in the general, our partiality for a scheme that has originated the Boyle, and the Bampton, and the Warburtonian lectureships of England, with all the valuable authorship which has proceeded from them. An endowment for an annual discourse upon a given theme, is, we believe, a novelty in Scotland; though it is to similar institutions that much of the best sacred and theological literature of our sister country is owing. We should rejoice if, in this our comparatively meagre and unbeneficed land, both these themes and these endowments were multiplied. We recommend this as a fit species of charity, for the munificence of wealthy individuals. Whatever their selected argument shall be, whether that of cruelty to animals, or some one evidence of our faith, or the defence and illustration of a doctrine, or any distinct method of Christian philanthropy for the moral regeneration of our species, or aught else of those innumerable topics that lie situated within the reach and ample domain of that revelation which God has made to our world—we feel assured that such a movement must be responded to with beneficial effect, both by the gifted pastors of our Church, and by the aspiring youths of greatest power or greatest promise among its candidates. Such institutions as these would help to quicken the energies of our establishment; and through means of a sustained and reiterated effort, directed to some one great lesson, whether in theology or morals, they might impress, and that more deeply every year, some specific and most salutary amelioration on the principles or the practices of general society.

Yet we are loath to quit our subject without one appeal more in behalf of those poor sufferers, who, unable to advocate their own cause, possess, on that very account, a more imperative claim on the exertions of him who now stands as their advocate before you.

And first, it may have been felt that, by the way in which we have attempted to resolve cruelty into its elements, we instead of launching rebuke against it, have only devised a palliation for its gross and shocking enormity. But it is not so. It is true, we count the enormity to lie mainly in the heedlessness of pain; but then we charge this foully and flagrantly enormous thing, not on the mere desperadoes and barbarians of our land, but on the men and the women of general, and even of cultivated and highbred society. Instead of stating cruelty to be what it is not, and then confining the imputation of it to the outcast few, we hold it better, and practically far more important, to state what cruelty really is, and then fasten the imputation of it on the commonplace and the companionable many. Those outcasts to whom you would restrict the condemnation, are not at present within the reach of our voice. But you are; and it lies with you to confer a ten-fold greater boon on the inferior creation, than if all barbarous sports, and all bloody experiments were forthwith put an end to. It is at the bidding of your collective will to save those countless myriads who are brought to the regular and the daily slaughter, all the difference between a gradual and an instant death. And there is a practice realized in every-day life, which you can put down—a practice which strongly reminds us of a ruder age that has long gone by;—when even beauteous and high-born ladies could partake in the dance, and the song, and the festive chivalry of barbaric castles, unmindful of all the piteous and the pining agony of dungeoned prisoners below. We charge a like unmindfulness on the present generation. We know not whether those wretched animals whose still sentient frameworks are under process of ingenious manufacture for the epicurism or the splendour of your coming entertainment,—we know not whether they are now dying by inches in your own subterranean keeps, or through the subdivided industry of our commercial age, are now suffering all the horrors of their protracted agony, in the prison-house of some distant street where this dreadful trade is carried on. But truly it matters nought to our argument, ye heedless sons and daughters of gaiety! We speak not of the daily thousands who have to die that man may live; but of those thousands who have to die more painfully, just that man may live more luxuriously. We speak to you of the art and the mystery of the killing trade—from which it would appear, that not alone the delicacy of the food, but even its appearance, is, among the connoisseurs of a refined epicurism, the matter of skilful and scientific computation. There is a sequence, it would appear—there is a sequence between an exquisite death, and an exquisite or a beautiful preparation of cookery; and just in the ordinary way that art avails herself of the other sequences of philosophy,—the first term is made sure, that the second term might, according to the metaphysic order of causation, follow in its train. And hence, we are given to understand, hence the cold-blooded ingenuities of that previous and preparatory torture which oft is undergone, both that man might be feasted with a finer relish, and that the eyes of man might be feasted and regaled with a finer spectacle. The atrocities of a Majendie have been blazoned before the eye of a British public; but this is worse in the fearful extent and magnitude of the evil—truly worse than a thousand Majendies. His is a cruel luxury, but it is the luxury of intellect. Yours is both a cruel and a sensual luxury: and you have positively nought to plead for it but the most worthless and ignoble appetites of our nature.

But, secondly, and if possible to secure your kindness for our cause, let me, in the act of drawing these lengthened observations to a close, offer to your notice the bright and the beautiful side of it. I would bid you think of all that fond and pleasant imagery, which is associated even with the lower animals, when they become the objects of a benevolent care, which at length ripens into a strong and cherished affection for them—as when the worn-out hunter is permitted to graze, and be still the favourite of all the domestics through the remainder of his life; or the old and shaggy house-dog, that has now ceased to be serviceable, is nevertheless sure of its regular meals, and a decent funeral; or when an adopted inmate of the household is claimed as property, or as the object of decided partiality, by some one or other of the children; or, finally, when in the warmth and comfort of the evening fire, one or more of these home animals take their part in the living groupe that is around it, and their very presence serves to complete the picture of a blissful and smiling family. Such relationships with the inferior creatures, supply many of our finest associations of tenderness, and give, even to the heart of man, some of its simplest yet sweetest enjoyments. He even can find in these some compensation for the dread and the disquietude wherewith his bosom is agitated amid the fiery conflicts of infuriated men. When he retires from the stormy element of debate, and exchanges, for the vindictive glare, and the hideous discords of that outcry which he encounters among his fellows,—when these are exchanged for the honest welcome and the guileless regards of those creatures who gambol at his feet, he feels that even in the society of the brutes, in whose hearts there is neither care nor controversy, he can surround himself with a better atmosphere far, than in that which he breathes among the companionships of his own species. Here he can rest himself from the fatigues of that moral tempest which has beat upon him so violently; and, in the play of kindliness with these poor irrationals, his spirit can forget for awhile all the injustice and ferocity of their boasted lords.

But this is only saying, that our subject is connected with the pleasures of sentiment. And therefore, in the third and last place, we have to offer it as our concluding observation, that it is also connected with the principles of deepest sacredness. It may be thought by some that we have wasted the whole of this Sabbath morn, on what may be ranked among but the lesser moralities of human conduct. But there is one aspect, in which it may be regarded as more profoundly and more peculiarly religious than any one virtue which reciprocates, or is of mutual operation among the fellows of the same species. It is a virtue which oversteps, as it were, the limits of a species, and which, in this instance, prompts a descending movement, on our part, of righteousness and mercy towards those who have an inferior place to ourselves in the scale of creation. The lesson of this day is not the circulation of benevolence within the limits of one species. It is the transmission of it from one species to another. The first is but the charity of a world. The second is the charity of a universe. Had there been no such charity, no descending current of love and of liberality from species to species, what, I ask, should have become of ourselves? Whence have we learned this attitude of lofty unconcern about the creatures who are beneath us? Not from those ministering spirits who wait upon the heirs of salvation. Not from those angels who circle the throne of heaven, and make all its arches ring with joyful harmony, when but one sinner of this prostrate world turns his footsteps towards them. Not from that mighty and mysterious visitant, who unrobed Him of all his glories, and bowed down his head unto the sacrifice, and still, from the seat of his now exalted mediatorship, pours forth his intercessions and his calls in behalf of the race he died for. Finally, not from the eternal Father of all, in the pavilion of whose residence there is the golden treasury of all those bounties and beatitudes that roll over the face of nature, and from the footstool of whose empyreal throne there reaches a golden chain of providence to the very humblest of his family. He who hath given his angels charge concerning us, means that the tide of beneficence should pass from order to order, through all the ranks of his magnificent creation; and we ask, is it with man that this goodly provision is to terminate—or shall he, with all his sensations of present blessedness, and all his visions of future glory let down upon him from above, shall he turn him selfishly and scornfully away from the rights of those creatures whom God hath placed in dependence under him? We know that the cause of poor and unfriended animals has many an obstacle to contend with in the difficulties or the delicacies of legislation. But we shall ever deny that it is a theme beneath the dignity of legislation; or that the nobles and the senators of our land stoop to a cause which is degrading, when, in the imitation of heaven's high clemency, they look benignly downward on these humble and helpless sufferers. Ere we can admit this, we must forget the whole economy of our blessed gospel. We must forget the legislations and the cares of the upper sanctuary in behalf of our fallen species. We must forget that the redemption of our world is suspended on an act of jurisprudence which angels desired to look into, and for effectuating which, the earth we tread upon was honoured by the footsteps, not of angel or of archangel, but of God manifest in the flesh. The distance upward between us and that mysterious Being, who let himself down from heaven's high concave upon our lowly platform, surpasses by infinity the distance downward between us and every thing that breathes. And He bowed himself thus far for the purpose of an example, as well as for the purpose of an expiation; that every Christian might extend his compassionate regards over the whole of sentient and suffering nature. The high court of Parliament is not degraded by its attentions and its cares in behalf of inferior creatures, else the Sanctuary of Heaven has been degraded by its counsels in behalf of the world we occupy, and in the execution of which the Lord of heaven himself relinquished the highest seat of glory in the universe, and went forth to sojourn for a time on this outcast and accursed territory.

SERMONS

PREACHED IN ST. JOHN'S CHURCH,

GLASGOW.

PREFACE.

The following Sermons are of too miscellaneous a character to be arranged according to the succession of their topics, and they are, therefore, presented to the reader as so many compositions that are almost wholly independent of each other.

Two of the Sermons treat of Predestination, and the Sin against the Holy Ghost. There are topics of a highly speculative character, in the system of Christian Doctrine, which it is exceedingly difficult to manage, without interesting the curiosity rather than the conscience of the reader. And yet, it is from their fitness of application to the conscience, that they derive their chief right to appear in a volume of Sermons; and I should not have ventured any publication upon either of these doctrines, did I not think them capable of being so treated as to subserve the great interests of practical godliness.

The Sermons all relate to topics that I hold to be strictly congregational, with the exception of the thirteenth and fourteenth in the volume, which belong rather to Christian Economies, than to Christian Theology—to the "outer things of the house of God," rather than to the things of the sanctuary, or the intimacies of the spiritual life. I, perhaps, ought therefore to apologize for the appearance of these two in a volume of Congregational Sermons, and yet I have been led by experience to feel the religious importance of their subject, and I think that much injury has been sustained by the souls of our people, from the neglect of obvious principles both in the business of education, and in the business of public charity. I have, however, more comfort in discussing this argument from the press, than from the pulpit, which ought to be kept apart for loftier themes, and which seems to suffer a sort of desecration when employed as the vehicle for any thing else than the overtures of pardon to the sinner, and the hopes and duties of the believer.

SERMON I.

The Constancy of God in His Works an Argument for the Faithfulness of God in His Word.

"For ever, O Lord, thy word is settled in heaven. Thy faithfulness is unto all generations: thou hast established the earth, and it abideth. They continue this day according to thy ordinances: for all are thy servants."—*Psalm* cxix. 89, 90, 91.

In these verses there is affirmed to be an analogy between the word of God and the works of God. It is said of his word, that it is settled in heaven, and that it sustains its faithfulness from one generation to another. It is said of his works, and more especially of those that are immediately around us, even of the earth which we inhabit, that as it was established at the first so it abideth afterwards. And then, as if to perfect the assimilation between them, it is said of both in the 91st verse, "They continue this day according to thine ordinances, for all are thy servants;" thereby identifying the sureness of that word which proceeded from his lips, with the unfailing constancy of that Nature which was formed and is upholden by his hands.

The constancy of Nature is taught by universal experience, and even strikes the popular eye as the most characteristic of those features which have been impressed upon her. It may need the aid of philosophy to learn how unvarying Nature is in all her processes—how even her seeming anomalies can be traced to a law that is inflexible—how what might appear at first to be the caprices of her waywardness, are, in fact, the evolutions of a mechanism that never changes—and that the more thoroughly she is sifted and put to the test by the interrogations of the curious, the more certainly will they find that she walks by a rule which knows no abatement, and perseveres with obedient footstep in that even course, from which the eye of strictest scrutiny, has never yet detected one hair-breadth of deviation. It is no longer doubted by men of science, that every remaining semblance of irregularity in the universe is due, not to the fickleness of Nature, but to the ignorance of man—that her most hidden movements are conducted with a uniformity as rigorous as fate—that even the fitful agitations of the weather have their law and their principle—that the intensity of every breeze, and the number of drops in every shower, and the formation of every cloud, and all the occurring alternations of storm and sunshine, and the endless shiftings of temperature, and those tremulous varieties of the air which our instruments have enabled us to discover, but have not enabled us to explain—that still, they follow each other by a method of succession, which, though greatly more intricate, is yet as absolute in itself as the order of the seasons, or the mathematical courses of astronomy. This is the impression of every philosophical mind with regard to Nature, and it is strengthened by each new accession that is made to science. The more we are acquainted with her, the more are we led to recognise her constancy; and to view her as a mighty though complicated machine, all whose results are sure, and all whose workings are invariable.

But there is enough of patent and palpable regularity in Nature, to give also to the popular mind, the same impression of her constancy. There is a gross and general experience that teaches the same lesson, and that has lodged in every bosom a kind of secure and steadfast confidence in the uniformity of her processes. The very child knows and proceeds upon it. He is aware of an abiding character and property in the elements around him—and has already learned as much of the fire, and the water, and the food that he eats, and the firm ground that he treads upon, and even of the gravitation by which he must regulate his postures and his movements, as to prove, that infant though he be, he is fully initiated in the doctrine, that Nature has her laws and her ordinances, and that she continueth therein. And the proofs of this are ever multiplying along the journey of human observation: insomuch, that when we come to manhood, we read of Nature's constancy throughout every department of the visible world. It meets us wherever we turn our eyes. Both the day and the night bear witness to it. The silent revolutions of the firmament give it their pure testimony. Even those appearances in the heavens, at which superstition stood aghast, and imagined that Nature was on the eve of giving way, are the proudest trophies of that stability which reigns throughout her processes—of that unswerving consistency wherewith she prosecutes all her movements. And the lesson that is thus held forth to us from the heavens above, is responded to by the earth below; just as the tides of ocean wait the footsteps of the moon, and, by an attendance kept up without change or intermission for thousands of years, would seem to connect the regularity of earth with the regularity of heaven. But, apart from these greater and simpler energies, we see a course and a uniformity every where. We recognise it in the mysteries of vegetation. We follow it through the successive stages of growth, and maturity, and decay, both in plants and animals. We discern it still more palpably in that beautiful circulation of the element of water, as it rolls its way by many thousand channels to the ocean—and, from the surface of this expanded reservoir, is again uplifted to the higher regions of the atmosphere—and is there dispersed in light and fleecy magazines over the four quarters of the globe—and at length accomplishes its orbit, by falling in showers on a world that waits to be refreshed by it. And all goes to impress us with the regularity of Nature, which in fact teems, throughout all its varieties, with power, and principle, and uniform laws of operation—and is viewed by us as a vast laboratory, all the progressions of which have a rigid and unfailing necessity stamped upon them.

Now, this contemplation has at times served to foster the atheism of philosophers It has led them to deify Nature, and to make her immutability stand in the place of God. They seem impressed with the imagination, that had the Supreme Cause been a being who thinks, and wills, and acts as man does, on the impulse of a felt and a present motive, there would be more the appearance of spontaneous activity, and less of mute and unconscious mechanism in the administrations of the universe. It is the very unchangeableness of Nature and the steadfastness of those great and mighty processes wherewith no living power that is superior to Nature, and is able to shift or to control her, is seen to interfere—it is this which seems to have impressed the notion of some blind and eternal fatality on certain men of loftiest but deluded genius. And, accordingly, in France, where the physical sciences have, of late, been the most cultivated, have there also been the most daring avowals of atheism. The universe has been affirmed to be an everlasting and indestructible effect; and from the abiding constancy that is seen in Nature, through all her departments, have they inferred, that thus it has always been, and that thus it will ever be.

But this atheistical impression that is derived from the constancy of Nature, is not peculiar to the disciples of philosophy. It is the familiar and the practical impression of every-day life. The world is apprehended to move on steady and unvarying principles of his own; and these secondary causes have usurped, in man's estimation, the throne of the Divinity. Nature in fact is personified into God: and as we look to the performance of a machine without thinking of its maker,—so the very exactness and certainty, wherewith the machinery of creation performs its evolutions, has thrown a disguise over the agency of the Creator. Should God interpose by miracle, or interfere by some striking and special manifestation of providence, then man is awakened to the recognition of him. But he loses sight of the Being who sits behind these visible elements, while he regards those attributes of constancy and power which appear in the elements themselves. They see no demonstration of a God, and they feel no need of him, while such unchanging, and such unfailing energy continues to operate in the visible world around them; and we need not go to the schools of ratiocination in quest of this infidelity, but may detect it in the bosoms of simple and unlettered men, who, unknown to themselves, make a god of Nature, and just because of Nature's constancy; having no faith in the unseen Spirit who originated all and upholds all, and that, because all things continue as they were from the beginning of the creation.

Such has been the perverse effect of Nature's constancy on the alienated mind of man: but let us now attend to the true interpretation of it. God has, in the first instance, put into our minds a disposition to count on the uniformity of Nature, insomuch that we universally look for a recurrence of the same event in the same circumstances. This is not merely the belief of experience, but the belief of instinct. It is antecedent to all the findings of observation, and may be exemplified in the earliest stages of childhood. The infant who makes a noise on the table with his hand, for the first time, anticipates a repetition of the noise from a repetition of the stroke, with as much confidence as he who has witnessed, for years together, the invariableness wherewith these two terms of the succession have followed each other. Or, in other words, God, by putting this faith into every human creature, and making it a necessary part of his mental constitution, has taught him at all times to expect the like result in the like circumstances. He has thus virtually told him what is to happen, and what he has to look for in every given condition—and by its so happening accordingly, he just makes good the veracity of his own declaration. The man who leads me to expect that which he fails to accomplish, I would hold to be a deceiver. God has so framed the machinery of my perceptions, as that I am led irresistibly to expect, that every where events will follow each other in the very train in which I have ever been accustomed to observe them—and when God so sustains the uniformity of Nature, that in every instance it is rigidly so, he is just manifesting the faithfulness of his character. Were it otherwise, he would be practising a mockery on the expectation which he himself had inspired. God may be said to have promised to every human being, that Nature will be constant—if not by the whisper of an inward voice to every heart, at least by the force of an uncontrollable bias which he has impressed on every constitution. So that, when we behold Nature keeping by its constancy, we behold the God of Nature keeping by his faithfulness—and the system of visible things, with its general laws, and its successions which are invariable, instead of an opaque materialism to intercept from the view of mortals the face of the Divinity, becomes the mirror which reflects upon them the truth that is unchangeable, the ordination that never fails.

Conceive that it had been otherwise—first, that man had no faith in the constancy of Nature—then how could all his experience have profited him? How could he have applied the recollections of his past, to the guidance of his future history? And, what would have been left to signalize the wisdom of mankind above that of veriest infancy? Or, suppose that he had the implicit faith in Nature's constancy, but that Nature was wanting in the fulfilment of it—that at every moment his intuitive reliance on this constancy, was met by some caprice or waywardness of Nature, which thwarted him in all his undertakings—that, instead of holding true to her announcements, she held the children of men in most distressful uncertainty, by the freaks and the falsities in which she ever indulged herself—and that every design of human foresight was thus liable to be broken up, by ever and anon the putting forth of some new fluctuation. Tell me, in this wild misrule of elements changing their properties, and events ever flitting from one method of succession to another, if man could subsist for a single day, when all the accomplishments without, were thus at war with all the hopes and calculations within. In such a chaos and conflict as this, would not the foundations of human wisdom be utterly subverted? Would not man, with his powerful and perpetual tendency to proceed on the constancy of Nature, be tempted, at all times, and by the very constitution of his being, to proceed upon a falsehood? It were the way, in fact, to turn the administration of Nature into a system of deceit. The lessons of to-day, would be falsified by the events of to-morrow. He were indeed the father of lies who could be the author of such a regimen as this—and well may we rejoice in the strict order of the goodly universe which we inhabit, and regard it as a noble attestation to the wisdom and beneficence of its great Architect.

But it is more especially as an evidence of his truth, that the constancy of Nature is adverted to in our text. It is of his faithfulness unto all generations that mention is there made—and for the growth and the discipline of your piety, we know not a better practical habit than that of recognising the unchangeable truth of God, throughout your daily and hourly experience of Nature's unchangeableness. Your faith in it is of his working—and what a condition would you have been reduced to, had the faith which is within, not been met by an entire and unexpected accordancy with the fulfilments that are without! He has not told you what to expect by the utterance of a voice—but he has taught you what to expect by the leadings and the intimations of a strong constitutional tendency—and, in virtue of this, there is not a human creature who does not believe, and almost as firmly as in his own existence, that fire will continue to burn, and water to cool, and matter to resist, and unsupported bodies to fall, and ocean to bear the adventurous vessel upon its surface, and the solid earth to uphold the tread of his footsteps; and that spring will appear again in her wonted smiles, and summer will glow into heat and brilliancy, and autumn will put on the same luxuriance as before, and winter, at its stated periods, revisit the world with her darkness and her storms. We cannot sum up those countless varieties of Nature; but the firm expectation is, that throughout them all, as she has been established, so she will abide to the day of her final dissolution. And I call upon you to recognise in Nature's constancy, the answer of Nature's God to this expectation. All these material agents are, in fact, the organs by which he expresses his faithfulness to the world; and that unveering generality which reigns and continues every where, is but the perpetual demonstration of a truth that never varies, as well as of laws that never are rescinded. It is for us that he upholds the world in all its regularity. It is for us that he sustains so inviolably the march and the movement of those innumerable progressions which are going on around us. It is in remembrance of his promises to us, that he meets all our anticipations of Nature's uniformity, with the evolutions of a law that is unalterable. It is because he is a God that cannot lie, that he will make no invasion on that wondrous correspondency which he himself hath instituted between the world that is without, and our little world of hopes, and projects, and anticipations that are within. By the constancy of Nature, he hath imprinted upon it the lesson of his own constancy—and that very characteristic wherewith some would fortify the ungodliness of their hearts, is the most impressive exhibition which can be given of God, as always faithful, and always the same.

This, then, is the real character which the constancy of Nature should lead us to assign to him who is the Author of it. In every human understanding, he hath planted a universal instinct, by which all are led to believe that Nature will persevere in her wonted courses, and that each succession of cause and effect which has been observed by us in the time that is past, will, while the world exists, be kept up invariably, and recur in the very same order through the time that is to come. This constancy, then, is as good as a promise that he has made unto all men, and all that is around us on earth or in heaven, proves how inflexibly the promise is adhered to. The chemist in his laboratory, as he questions Nature, may be almost said to put her to the torture, when tried in his hottest furnace, or probed by his searching analysis, to her innermost arcana, she, by a spark, or an explosion, or an effervescence, or an evolving substance, makes her distinct replies to his investigations. And he repeats her answer to all his fellows in philosophy, and they meet in academic state and judgment to reiterate the question, and in every quarter of the globe her answer is the same—so that, let the experiment, though a thousand times repeated, only be alike in all its circumstances, the result which cometh forth is as rigidly alike, without deficiency, and without deviation. We know how possible it is for these worshippers at the footstool of science, to make a divinity of matter; and that every new discovery of her secrets should only rivet them more devotedly to her throne. But there is a God who liveth and sitteth there, and these unvarying responses of Nature are all prompted by himself, and are but the utterances of his immutability. They are the replies of a God who never changes, and who hath adapted the whole materialism of creation to the constitution of every mind that he hath sent forth upon it. And to meet the expectation which he himself hath given of Nature's constancy, is he at each successive instant of time, vigilant and ready in every part of his vast dominions, to hold out to the eye of all observers, the perpetual and unfailing demonstration of it. The certainties of Nature and of Science are, in fact, the vocables by which God announces his truth to the world—and when told how impossible it is that Nature can fluctuate, we are only told how impossible it is that the God of Nature can deceive us.

The doctrine that Nature is constant, when thus related, as it ought to be, with the doctrine that God is true, might well strengthen our confidence in him anew with every new experience of our history. There is not an hour or a moment, in which we may not verify the one—and, therefore, not an hour or a moment in which we may not invigorate the other. Every touch, and every look, and every taste, and every act of converse between our senses and the things that are without, brings home a new demonstration of the steadfastness of Nature, and along with it a new demonstration both of his steadfastness and of his faithfulness, who is the Governor of Nature. And the same lesson may be fetched from times and from places, that are far beyond the limits of our own personal history. It can be drawn fom the retrospect of past ages, where, from the unvaried currency of those very processes which we now behold, we may learn the stability of all his ways, whose goings forth are of old, and from everlasting. It can be gathered from the most distant extremities of the earth, where Nature reigns with the same unwearied constancy, as it does around us—and where savages count as we do on a uniformity, from which she never falters. The lesson is commensurate with the whole system of things—and with an effulgence as broad as the face of creation, and as clear as the light which is poured over it, does it at once tell that Nature is unchangeably constant, and that God is unchangeably true.

And so it is, that in our text there are presented together, as if there was a tie of likeness between them—that the same God who is fixed as to the ordinances of Nature, is faithful as to the declaration of his word; and as all experience proves how firmly he may be trusted for the one, so is there an argument as strong as experience, to prove how firmly he may be trusted for the other. By his work in us, he hath awakened the expectation of a constancy in Nature, which he never disappoints. By his word to us, should he awaken the expectation of certainty in his declarations, this he will ever disappoint. It is because Nature is so fixed, that we apprehend the God of Nature to be so faithful. He who never falsifies the hope that hath arisen in every bosom, from the instinct which he himself hath communicated, will never falsify the hope that shall arise in any bosom from the express utterance of his voice. Were he a God in whose hand the processes of Nature were ever shifting, then might we conceive him a God from whose mouth the proclamations of grace had the like characters of variance and vacillation. But it is just because of our reliance on the one, that we feel so much of repose in our dependence upon the other—and the same God who is so unfailing in the ordinances of his creation, do we hold to be equally unfailing in the ordinances of his word.

And it is strikingly accordant with these views, that Nature never has been known to recede from her constancy, but for the purpose of giving place and demonstration to the authority of the word. Once, in a season of miracle, did the word take the precedency of Nature, but ever since hath Nature resumed her courses, and is now proving by her steadfastness, the authority of that, which she then proved to be authentic by her deviations. When the word was first ushered in, Nature gave way for a period, after which she moves in her wonted order, till the present system of things shall pass away, and that faith which is now upholden by Nature's constancy, shall then receive its accomplishment at Nature's dissolution. And O, how God magnifieth his word above all his name, when he tells that heaven and earth shall pass away, but that his word shall not pass away—and that while his creation shall become a wreck, not one jot or one tittle of his testimony shall fail. The world passeth away—but the word endureth for ever—and if the faithfulness of God stand forth so legibly on the face of the temporary world, how surely may we reckon on the faithfulness of that word, which has a vastly higher place in the counsels and fulfilments of eternity.

The argument may not be comprehended by all, but it will not be lost, should it lead any to feel a more emphatic certainty and meaning than before, in the declarations of the Bible—and to conclude, that he who for ages hath stood so fixed to all his plans and purposes in Nature, will stand equally fixed to all that he proclaims, and to all that he promises in Revelation. To be in the hands of such a God, might well strike a terror into the hearts of the guilty—and that unrelenting death, which, with all the sureness of an immutable law, is seen, before our eyes, to seize upon every individual of every species of our world, full well evinces how he, the uncompromising Lawgiver, will execute every utterance that he has made against the children of iniquity. And, on the other hand, how this very contemplation ought to encourage all who are looking to the announcements of the same God in the Gospel, and who perceive that there he has embarked the same truth, and the same unchangeableness on the offers of mercy. All Nature gives testimony to this, that he cannot lie—and seeing that he has stamped such enduring properties on the elements even of our perishable world, never should I falter from that confidence which he hath taught me to feel, when I think of that property wherewith the blood which was shed for me, cleanseth from all sin; and of that property wherewith the body which was broken, beareth the burden of all its penalties. He who hath so nobly met the faith that he has given unto all in the constancy of Nature, by a uniformity which knows no abatement, will meet the faith that he has given unto any in the certainty of grace, by a fulfilment unto every believer, which knows no exception.

And it is well to remark the difference that there is between the explanation given in the text, of Nature's constancy, and the impression which the mere students or disciples of Nature have of it. It is because of her constancy that they have been led to invest her, as it were, in properties of her own; that they have given a kind of independent power and stability to matter; that in the various energies which lie scattered over the field of visible contemplation, they see a native inherent virtue, which never for a single moment is slackened or suspended—and therefore imagine, that as no force from without seems necessary to sustain, so as little, perhaps, is there need for any such force from without to originate. The mechanical certainty of all Nature's processes, as it appears in their eyes to supersede the demand for any upholding agency, so does it also supersede, in the silent imaginations of many, and according to the express and bold avowals of some, the demand for any creative agency. It is thus, that Nature is raised into a divinity, and has been made to reign over all, in the state and jurisdiction of an eternal fatalism; and proud Science, which by wisdom knoweth not God, hath in her march of discovery, seized upon the invariable certainties of Nature, those highest characteristics of his authority and wisdom and truth, as the instruments by which to disprove and to dethrone him.

Now compare this interpretation of monstrous and melancholy atheism, with that which the Bible gives, why all things move so invariably. It is because that all are thy servants. It is because they are all under the bidding of a God who has purposes from which he never falters, and hath issued promises from which he never fails. It is because the arrangements of his vast and capacious household are already ordered for the best, and all the elements of Nature are the ministers by which he fulfils them. That is the master who has most honour and obedience from his domestics throughout all whose ordinations there runs a consistency from which he never deviates; and he best sustains his dignity in the midst of them, who, by mild but resistless sway, can regulate the successions of every hour, and affix his sure and appropriate service to every member of the family. It is when we see all, in any given time, at their respective places, and each distinct period of the day having its own distinct evolution of business or recreation, that we infer the wisdom of the instituted government, and how irrevocable the sanctions are by which it is upholden. The vexatious alternations of command and of countermand; the endless fancies of humour, and caprice, and waywardness, which ever and anon break forth, to the total overthrow of system; the perpetual innovations which none do foresee, and for which none, therefore, can possibly be prepared—these are not more harassing to the subject, than they are disparaging to the truth and authority of the superior. It is in the bosom of a well-conducted family, where you witness the sure dispensation of all the reward and encouragement which have been promised, and the unfailing execution of the disgrace and the dismissal that are held forth to obstinate disobedience. Now those very qualities of which this uniformity is the test and the characteristic in the government of any human society, of these also is it the test and the characteristic in the government of Nature. It bespeaks the wisdom, and the authority, and the truth of him who framed and who administers. Let there be a King eternal, immortal, and invisible, and let this universe be his empire—and in all the rounds of its complex but unerring mechanism, do I recognise him as the only wise God. In the constancy of Nature, do I read the constancy and truth of that great master Spirit, who hath imprinted his own character on all that hath emanated from his power; and when told that throughout the mighty lapse of centuries, all the courses both of earth and of heaven, have been upholden as before, I only recognise the footsteps of him who is ever the same, and whose faithfulness is unto all generations. That perpetuity, and order, and ancient law of succession, which have subsisted so long, throughout the wide diversity of things, bear witness to the Lord of hosts, as still at the head of his well-marshalled family. The present age is only re-echoing the lesson of all past ages—and that spectacle, which has misled those who by wisdom know not God, into dreary atheism, has enhanced every demonstration both of his veracity and power, to all intelligent worshippers. We know that all things continue as they were from the beginning of creation. We know that the whole of surrounding materialism stands forth, to this very hour, in all the inflexibility of her wonted characters. We know that heaven, and earth, and sea, still discharge the same functions, and subserve the very same beneficent processes. We know that astronomy plies the same rounds as before, that the cycles of the firmament move in their old and appointed order, and that the year circulates as it has ever done, in grateful variety, over the face of an expectant world—but only because all are of God, and they continue this day according to his ordinances—for all are his servants.

Now, it is just because the successions which take place in the economy of Nature, are so invariable, that we should expect the successions which take place in the economy of God's moral government to be equally invariable. That expectation which he never disappoints when it is the fruit of a universal instinct, he surely will never disappoint when it is the fruit of his own express and immediate revelation. If because God hath so established it, it cometh to pass, then of whatsoever it may be affirmed that God hath so said it, it will come equally to pass. I should certainly look for the same character in the administrations of his special grace, that I, at all times, witness in the administrations of his ordinary providence. If I see in the system of his world, that the law by which two events follow each other, gives rise to a connexion between them that never is dissolved, then should he say in his word, that there are certain invariable methods of succession, in virtue of which when the first term of it occurs, the second is sure at all times to follow, I should be very sure in my anticipations, that it will indeed be most punctually and most rigidly so. It is thus, that the constancy of Nature is in fullest harmony with the authority of Revelation—and that, when fresh from the contemplation of the one, I would listen with most implicit faith to all the announcements of the other.

When we behold all to be so sure and settled in the works of God, then may we look for all being equally sure and settled in the word of God. Philosophy hath never yet detected one iota of deviation from the ordinances of Nature—and never, therefore, may we conclude, shall the experience either of past or future ages, detect one iota of deviation from the ordinances of Revelation. He who so pointedly adheres to every plan that he hath established in creation, will as pointedly adhere to every proclamation that he hath uttered in Scripture. There is nought of the fast and loose in any of his processes—and whether in the terrible denunciations of Sinai, or those mild proffers of mercy that were sounded forth upon the world through Messiah, who upholdeth all things by the word of his power, shall we alike experience that God is not to be mocked, and that with him there is no variableness, neither shadow of turning.

With this certainty then upon our spirits, let us now look, not to the successions which he hath instituted in nature, but to the successions which he hath announced to us, in the word of his testimony—and let us, while so doing, fix and solemnize our thoughts by the consideration, that as God hath said it, so will he do it.

The first of these successions, then, on which we may count infallibly, is that which he hath proclaimed between sin and punishment. The soul that sinneth it shall die. And here there is a common ground on which the certainties of divine revelation meet and are at one with the certainties of human experience. We are told in the Bible, that all have sinned, and that, therefore, death hath passed upon all men. The connexion between these two terms is announced in Scripture to be invariable—and all observation tells us, that it is even so. Such was the sentence uttered in the hearing of our first parents; and all history can attest how God hath kept by the word of his threatening—and how this law of jurisprudence from heaven is realized before us upon earth, with all the certainty of a law of Nature. The death of man is just as stable and as essential a part of his physiology, as are his birth, or his expansion, or his maturity, or his decay. It looks as much a thing of organic necessity, as a thing of arbitrary institution—and here do we see blended into one exhibition, a certainty of the divine word that never fails, and a constancy in Nature that never is departed from. It is indeed a striking accordancy, that what in one view of it appears to be a uniform process of Nature, in another view of it, is but the unrelenting execution of a dread utterance from the God of Nature. From this contemplation may we gather, that God is as certain in all his words, as he is constant in all his ways. Men can philosophize on the diseases of the human system—and the laborious treatise can be written on the class, and the character, and the symptoms, of each of them—and in our halls of learning, the ample demonstration can be given, and disciples may be taught how to judge and to prognosticate, and in what appearances to read the fell precursors of mortality—and death has so taken up its settled place among the immutabilities of Nature, that it is as familiarly treated in the lecture-rooms of science, as any other phenomena which Nature has to offer for the exercise of the human understanding. And, O, how often are the smile and the stoutness of infidelity seen to mingle with this appalling contemplation—and how little will its hardy professors bear to be told, that what gives so dread a certainty to their speculation is, that the God of Nature and the God of the Bible, are one—that when they describe, in lofty nomenclature, the path of dying humanity, they only describe the way in which he fulfils upon it his irrevocable denunciation—tha the is but doing now to the posterity of Adam what he told to Adam himself on his expulsion from Paradise—and that, if the universality of death prove how every law in the physics of creation is sure, it just as impressively proves, how every word of God's immediate utterance to man, or how every word of prophecy, is equally sure.

And in every instance of mortality which you are called to witness, do we call upon you to read in it the intolerance of God for sin, and how unsparingly and unrelentingly it is, that God carries into effect his every utterance against it. The connection which he hath instituted between the two terms of sin and of death should lead you from every appeal that is made to your senses by the one, to feel the force of an appeal to your conscience by the other. It proves the hatefulness of sin to God, and it also proves with what unfaltering constancy God will prosecute every threat until he hath made an utter extirpation of sin from his presence. There is nought which can make more palpable the way in which God keeps every saying in his perpetual remembrance, and as surely proceeds upon it, than doth this universal plague wherewith he hath smitten every individual of our species, and carries off its successive generations from a world that sprung from his hand in all the bloom and vigour of immortality. When death makes entrance upon a family, and perhaps, seizes on that one member of it, all whose actual transgressions might be summed up in the outbreakings of an occasional waywardness, wherewith the smiles of infant gaiety were chequered—still how it demonstrates the unbending purposes of God against our present accursed nature, that in some one or other of its varieties, every specimen must die. And so it is, that from one age to another, he makes open manifestation to the world, that every utterance which hath fallen from him is sure; and that ocular proof is given to the character of him who is a Spirit, and is invisible; and that sense lends its testimony to the truth of God, and the truth of his Scripture; and that Nature, when rightly viewed, instead of placing its inquirers at atheistical variance with the being who upholds it, holds out to us the most impressive commentary that can be given on the reverence which is due to all his communications, even by demonstrating, that faith in his word is at unison with the findings of our daily observation.

But God hath further said of sin and of its consequences, what no observation of ours has yet realized. He hath told us of the judgment that cometh after death, and he hath told us of the two diverse paths which lead from the judgment-seat unto eternity. Of these we have not yet seen the verification, yet surely we have seen enough to prepare us for the unfailing accomplishment of every utterance that cometh from the lips of God. The unexcepted death which we know cometh upon all men, for that all have sinned, might well convince us of the certainty of that second death which is threatened upon all who turn not from sin unto the Saviour. There is an indissoluble succession here between our sinning and our dying—and we ought now to be so aware of God as a God of precise and peremptory execution, as to look upon the succession being equally indissoluble, between our dying in sin now, and rising to everlasting condemnation hereafter. The sinner who wraps himself in delusive security—and that, because all things continue as they have done, does not reflect of this very characteristic, that it is indeed the most awful proof of God's immutable counsels, and to himself the most tremendous presage of all the ruin and wretchedness which have been denounced upon him. The spectacle of uniformity that is before his eyes, only goes to ascertain that as God hath purposed, so, without vacillation or inconstancy, will he ever perform. He hath already given a sample, or an earnest of this, in the awful ravages of death; and we ask the sinner to behold, in the ever-recurring spectacle of moving funerals, and desolated families, the token of that still deeper perdition which awaits him. Let him not think that the God who deals his relentless inflictions here on every son and daughter of the species, will falter there from the work of vengeance that shall then descend on the heads of the impenitent. O, how deceived then are all those ungodly, who have been building to themselves a safety and an exemption on the perpetuity of Nature! All the perpetuity which they have witnessed, is the pledge of a God who is unchangeable—and who, true to his threatening as to every other utterance which passes his lips, hath said, in the hearing of men and of angels, that the soul which is in sin shall perish.

But, secondly, there is another succession announced to us in Scripture, and on the certainty of which we may place as firm a reliance as on any of the observed succesions of Nature—even that which obtains between faith and salvation. He who believeth in Christ, shall not perish, but shall have life everlasting. The same truth which God hath embarked on the declarations of his wrath against the impenitent, he hath also embarked on the declarations of his mercy to the believer. There is a law of continuity, as unfailing as any series of events in Nature, that binds with the present state of an obstinate sinner upon earth, all the horrors of his future wretchedness in hell—but there is also another law of continuity just as unfailing, that binds the present state of him who putteth faith in Christ here, with the triumphs and the transports of his coming glory hereafter. And thus it is, that what we read of God's constancy in the book of Nature, may well strengthen our every assurance in the promises of the gospel. It is not in the recurrence of winter alone, and its desolations, that God manifests his adherence to established processes. There are many periodic evolutions of the bright and the beautiful along the march of his administrations—as the dawn of morn; and the grateful access of spring, with its many hues, and odours, and melodies; and the ripened abundance of harvest; and that glorious arch of heaven, which science hath now appropriated as her own, but which nevertheless is placed there by God as the unfailing token of a sunshine already begun, and a storm now ended—all these come forth at appointed seasons, in a consecutive order, yet mark the footsteps of a beneficent Deity. And so the economy of grace has its regular successions, which carry, however, a blessing in their train. The faith in Christ, to which we are invited upon earth, has its sure result and its landing-place in heaven—and just with as unerring certainty as we behold in the courses of the firmament, will it be followed up by a life of virtue, and a death of hope, and a resurrection of joyfulness, and a voice of welcome at the judgment-seat, and a bright ascent into fields of ethereal blessedness, and an entrance upon glory, and a perpetual occupation in the city of the living God.

To all men hath he given a faith in the constancy of Nature, and he never disappoints it. To some men hath he given a faith in the promises of the gospel, and he is ready to bestow it upon all who ask, or to perfect that which is lacking in it—and the one faith will as surely meet with its corresponding fulfilment as the other. The invariableness that reigns throughout the kingdom of Nature, guarantees the like invariableness in the kingdom of grace. He who is steadfast to all his appointments, will be true to all his declarations—and those very exhibitions of a strict and undeviating order in our universe, which have ministered to the irreligion of a spurious philosophy, form a basis on which the believer can prop a firmer confidence than before, in all the spoken and all the written testimonies of God.

With a man of taste, and imagination, and science, and who is withal a disciple of the Lord Jesus, such an argument as this must shed a new interest and glory over his whole contemplation of visible things. He knows of his Saviour, that by him all things were made, and that by him too all things are upholden. The world, in fact, was created by that Being whose name is the Word, and from the features that are imprinted on the one, may he gather some of the leading characteristics of the other. More expressly will he infer from that sure and established order of Nature, in which the whole family of mankind are comprehended, that the more special family of believers are indeed encircled within the bond of a sure and a well-ordered covenant. In those beauteous regularities by which the one economy is marked, will he be led to recognise the "yea" and the "amen" which are stamped on the other economy—and when he learns that the certainties of science are unfailing, does he also learn that the sayings of Scripture are unalterable. Both he knows to emanate from the same source; and every new experience of Nature's constancy, will just rivet him more tenaciously than before to the doctrine and the declarations of his Bible. Furnished with such a method of interpretation as this, let him go abroad upon Nature, and all that he sees will heighten and establish the hopes which Revelation hath awakened. Every recurrence of the same phenomena as before, will be to him a distinct testimony to the faithfulness of God. The very hours will bear witness to it. The lengthening shades of even will repeat the lesson held out to him by the light of early day—and when night unveils to his eye the many splendours of the firmament, will every traveller on his circuit there, speak to him of that mighty and invisible King, all whose ordinations are sure. And this manifestation from the face of heaven, will be reflected to him by the panorama upon earth. Even the buds which come forth at their appointed season on the leafless branches; and the springing up of the flowers and the herbage, on the spots of ground from which they had disappeared; and that month of vocal harmony wherewith the mute atmosphere is gladdened as before, with the notes of joyous festival; and so, the regular march of the advancing year through all its footsteps of revival, and progress, and maturity, and decay—these are to him but the diversified tokens of a God whom he can trust, because of a God who changeth not. To his eyes, the world reflects upon the word the lesson of its own wondrous harmony; and his science, instead of a meteor that lures him from the greater light of revelation, serves him as a pedestal on which the stability of Scripture is more firmly upholden.

The man who is accustomed to view aright the uniformity of Nature's sequences, will be more impressed with the certainty of that sequence which is announced in the Bible between faith and salvation—and he, of all others, should re-assure his hopes of immortality, when he reads, that the end of our faith is the salvation of our souls. In this secure and wealthy place, let him take up his rest, and rejoice himself greatly with that God who has so multiplied upon him the evidences of his faithfulness. Let him henceforth feel that he is in the hands of one who never deviates, and who cannot lie—and who, as he never by one act of caprice, hath mocked the dependence that is built on the foundation of human experience, so, never by one act of treachery, will he mock the dependence that is built on the foundation of the divine testimony. And more particularly, let him think of Christ, who hath all the promises in his hand, that to him also all power has been committed in heaven and in earth—and that presiding therefore, as he does, over that visible administration, of which constancy is the unfailing attribute, he by this hath given us the best pledge of a truth that abideth the same, to-day, and yesterday, and for ever.

We are aware, that no argument can of itself work in you the faith of the Gospel—that words and reasons, and illustrations, may be multiplied without end, and yet be of no efficacy—that if the simple manifestation of the Spirit be withheld, the expounder of Scripture, and of all its analogies with creation or Providence, will lose his labour—and while it is his part to prosecute these to the uttermost, yet nought will he find more surely and experimentally true, than that without a special interposition of light from on high, he runneth in vain, and wearieth himself in vain. It is for him to ply the instrument, it is for God to give unto it the power which availeth. We are told of Christ, on his throne of mediatorship, that he hath all the energies of Nature at command, and up to this hour do we know with what a steady and unfaltering hand he hath wielded them. Look to the promise as equally steadfast, of "Lo, I am with you always, even unto the end of the world"—and come even now to his own appointed ordinance in the like confidence of a fellowship with him, as you would to any of the scenes or ordinations of Nature, and in the confidence that there the Lord of Nature will prove himself the same that He has ever been.* The blood that was announced many centuries ago to cleanse from all sin, cleanseth still. The body which hath borne in all past ages the iniquity of believers, beareth it still. That faith which appropriates Christ and all the benefits of his purchase, to the soul, still performs the same office. And that magnificent economy of Nature which was established at the first, and so abideth, is but the symbol of that higher economy of grace which continueth to this day according to all its ordinances.

"Whosoever eateth my flesh, and drinketh my blood," says the Saviour, "shall never die." When you sit down at his table, you eat the bread, and you drink the wine by which these are represented—and if this be done worthily, if there be a right correspondence between the hand and the heart in this sacramental service, then by faith do you receive the benefits of the shed blood, and the broken body; and your so doing will as surely as any succession takes place in the instituted courses of Nature, be followed up by your blessed immortality. And the brighter your hopes of glory hereafter, the holier will you be in all your acts and affections here. The character even now will receive a tinge from the prospect that is before you—and the habitual anticipation of heaven will bring down both of its charity and its sacredness upon your heart. He who hath this hope in him purifieth himself even as Christ is pure—and even from the present, if a true approach to the gate of his sanctuary, will you carry a portion of his spirit away with you. In partaking of these, his consecrated elements, you become partakers of his gentleness and devotion, and unwearied beneficence—and because like him in time, you will live with him through eternity.

---

* This Sermon was delivered on the morning of a Communion Sabbath.

SERMON II.

The expulsive Power of a new Affection.

"Love not the world, neither the things that are in the world. If any man love the world, the love of the Father is not in him."—1 John ii. 15.

THERE are two ways in which a practical moralist may attempt to displace from the human heart its love of the world—either by a demonstration of the world's vanity, so as that the heart shall be prevailed upon simply to withdraw its regards from an object that is not worthy of it; or, by setting forth another object, even God, as more worthy of its attachment, so as that the heart shall be prevailed upon not to resign an old affection, which shall have nothing to succeed it, but to exchange an old affection for a new one. My purpose is to show, that from the constitution of our nature, the former method is altogether incompetent and ineffectual—and that the latter method will alone suffice for the rescue and recovery of the heart from the wrong affection that domineers over it. After having accomplished this purpose, I shall attempt a few practical observations.

Love may be regarded in two different conditions. The first is, when its object is at a distance, and then it becomes love in a state of desire. The second is, when its object is in possession, and then it becomes love in a state of indulgence. Under the impulse of desire, man feels himself urged onward in some path or pursuit of activity for its gratification. The faculties of his mind are put into busy exercise. In the steady direction of one great and engrossing interest, his attention is recalled from the many reveries into which it might otherwise have wandered; and the powers of his body are forced away from an indolence in which it else might have languished; and that time is crowded with occupation, which but for some object of keen and devoted ambition, might have drivelled along in successive hours of weariness and distaste—and though hope does not always enliven, and success does not always crown this career of exertion, yet in the midst of this very variety, and with the alternations of occasional disappointment, is the machinery of the whole man kept in a sort of congenial play, and upholden in that tone and temper which are most agreeable to it. Insomuch, that if through the extirpation of that desire which forms the originating principle of all this movement, the machinery were to be stopped, and to receive no impulse from another desire substituted in its place, the man would be left with all his propensities to action in a state of most painful and unnatural abandonment. A sensitive being suffers, and is in violence, if, after having thoroughly rested from his fatigue, or been relieved from his pain, he continue in possession of powers without any excitement to these powers; if he possess a capacity of desire without having an object of desire; or if he have a spare energy upon his person, without a counterpart, and without a stimulus to call it into operation. The misery of such a condition is often realized by him who is retired from business, or who is retired from law, or who is even retired from the occupations of the chase, and of the gaming table. Such is the demand of our nature for an object in pursuit, that no accumulation of previous success can extinguish it—and thus it is, that the most prosperous merchant, and the most victorious general, and the most fortunate gamester, when the labour of their respective vocations has come to a close, are often found to languish in the midst of all their acquisitions, as if out of their kindred and rejoicing element. It is quite in vain with such a constitutional appetite for employment in man, to attempt cutting away from him the spring or the principle of one employment, without providing him with another. The whole heart and habit will rise in resistance against such an undertaking. The else unoccupied female, who spends the hours of every evening at some play of hazard, knows as well as you, that the pecuniary gain, or the honourable triumph of a successful contest, are altogether paltry. It is not such a demonstration of vanity as this that will force her away from her dear and delightful occupation. The habit cannot so be displaced, as to leave nothing but a negative and cheerless vacancy behind it—though it may so be supplanted as to be followed up by another habit of employment, to which the power of some new affection has constrained her. It is willingly suspended, for example, on any single evening, should the time that wont to be allotted to gaming, require to be spent on the preparations of an approaching assembly.

The ascendant power of a second affection will do, what no exposition, however forcible, of the folly and worthlessness of the first, ever could effectuate. And it is the same in the great world. You never will be able to arrest any of its leading pursuits, by a naked demonstration of their vanity. It is quite in vain to think of stopping one of these pursuits in any way else, but by stimulating to another. In attempting to bring a worldly man, intent and busied with the prosecution of his objects, to a dead stand, you have not merely to encounter the charm which he annexes to these objects—but you have to encounter the pleasure which he feels in the very prosecution of them. It is not enough, then, that you dissipate the charm, by your moral, and eloquent, and affecting exposure of its illusiveness. You must address to the eye of his mind another object, with a charm powerful enough to dispossess the first of its influence, and to engage him in some other prosecution as full of interest, and hope, and congenial activity, as the former. It is this which stamps an impotency on all moral and pathetic declamation about the insignificance of the world. A man will no more consent to the misery of being without an object, because that object is a trifle, or of being without a pursuit, because that pursuit terminates in some frivolous or fugitive acquirement, than he will voluntarily submit himself to the torture, because that torture is to be of short duration. If to be without desire and without exertion altogether, is a state of violence and discomfort, then the present desire, with its correspondent train of exertion, is not to be got rid of simply by destroying it. It must be by substituting another desire, and another line or habit of exertion in its place—and the most effectual way of withdrawing the mind from one object, is not by turning it away upon desolate and unpeopled vacancy—but by presenting to its regards another object still more alluring.

These remarks apply not merely to love considered in its state of desire for an object not yet obtained. They apply also to love considered in its state of indulgence, or placid gratification, with an object already in possession. It is seldom that any of our tastes are made to disappear by a mere process of natural extinction. At least, it is very seldom that this is done through the instrumentality of reasoning. It may be done by excessive pampering—but it is almost never done by the mere force of mental determination. But what cannot be thus destroyed, may be dispossessed—and one taste may be made to give way to another, and to lose its power entirely as the reigning affection of the mind. It is thus, that the boy ceases, at length, to be the slave of his appetite, but it is because a manlier taste has now brought it into subordination—and that the youth ceases to idolize pleasure, but it is because the idol of wealth has become the stronger and gotten the ascendency—and that even the love of money ceases to have the mastery over the heart of many a thriving citizen, but it is because drawn into the whirl of city politics, another affection has been wrought into his moral system, and he is now lorded over by the love of power. There is not one of these transformations in which the heart is left without an object. Its desire for one particular object may be conquered; but as to its desire for having some one object or other, this is unconquerable. Its adhesion to that on which it has fastened the preference of its regards, cannot willingly be overcome by the rending away of a simple separation. It can be done only by the application of something else, to which it may feel the adhesion of a still stronger and more powerful preference. Such is the grasping tendency of the human heart, that it must have a something to lay hold of—and which, if wrested away without the substitution of another something in its place, would leave a void and a vacancy as painful to the mind, as hunger is to the natural system. It may be dispossessed of one object, or of any, but it cannot be desolated of all. Let there be a breathing and a sensitive heart, but without a liking and without affinity to any of the things that are around it, and in a state of cheerless abandonment, it would be alive to nothing but the burden of its own consciousness, and feel it to be intolerable. It would make no difference to its owner, whether he dwelt in the midst of a gay and goodly world, or placed afar beyond the outskirts of creation, he dwelt a solitary unit in dark and unpeopled nothingness. The heart must have something to cling to—and never, by its own voluntary consent, will it so denude itself of all its attachments, that there shall not be one remaining object that can draw or solicit it.

The misery of a heart thus bereft of all relish for that which wont to minister enjoyment, is strikingly exemplified in those, who, satiated with indulgence, have been so belaboured, as it were, with the variety and the poignancy of the pleasurable sensations that they have experienced, that they are at length fatigued out of all capacity for sensation whatever. The disease of ennui is more frequent in the French metropolis, where amusement is more exclusively the occupation of higher classes, than it is in the British metropolis, where the longings of the heart are more diversified by the resources of business and politics. There are the votaries of fashion, who, in this way, have at length become the victims of fashionable excess—in whom the very multitude of their enjoyments, has at last extinguished their power of enjoyment—who, with the gratifications of art and nature at command, now look upon all that is around them with an eye of tastelessness—who, plied with the delights of sense and of splendour even to weariness, and incapable of higher delights, have come to the end of all their perfection, and like Solomon of old, found it to be vanity and vexation. The man whose heart has thus been turned into a desert, can vouch for the insupportable languor which must ensue, when one affection is thus plucked away from the bosom, without another to replace it. It is not necessary that a man receive pain from any thing, in order to become miserable. It is barely enough that he looks with distaste to every thing—and in that asylum which is the repository of minds out of joint, and where the organ of feeling as well as the organ of intellect, has been impaired, it is not in the cell of loud and frantic outcries where you will meet with the acme of mental suffering. But that is the individual who outpeers in wretchedness all his fellows, who throughout the whole expanse of nature and society, meets not an object that has at all the power to detain or to interest him; who neither in earth beneath, nor in heaven above, knows of a single charm to which his heart can send forth one desirous or responding movement; to whom the world, in his eye a vast and empty desolation, has left him nothing but his own consciousness to feed upon—dead to all that is without him, and alive to nothing but to the load of his own torpid and useless existence.

It will now be seen, perhaps, why it is that the heart keeps by its present affections with so much tenacity—when the attempt is, to do them away by a mere process of extirpation. It will not consent to be so desolated. The strong man, whose dwelling-place is there, may be compelled to give way to another occupier—but unless another stronger than he, has power to dispossess and to succeed him, he will keep his present lodgment inviolable. The heart would revolt against its own emptiness. It could not bear to be so left in a state of waste and cheerless insipidity. The moralist who tries such a process of dispossession as this upon the heart, is thwarted at every step by the recoil of its own mechanism. You have all heard that Nature abhors a vacuum. Such at least is the nature of the heart, that though the room which is in it may change one inmate for another, it cannot be left void without the pain of most intolerable suffering. It is not enough then to argue the folly of an existing affection. It is not enough, in the terms of a forcible or an affecting demonstration, to make good the evanescence of its object. It may not even be enough to associate the threats and terrors of some coming vengeance, with the indulgence of it. The heart may still resist the every application, by obedience to which it would finally be conducted to a state so much at war with all its appetites as that of downright inanition. So to tear away an affection from the heart, as to leave it bare of all its regards, and of all its preferences, were a hard and hopeless undertaking—and it would appear as if the alone powerful engine of dispossession, were to bring the mastery of another affection to bear upon it.

We know not a more sweeping interdict upon the affections of Nature, than that which is delivered by the Apostle in the verse before us. To bid a man into whom there is not yet entered the great and ascendant influence of the principle of regeneration, to bid him withdraw his love from all the things that are in the world, is to bid him give up all the affections that are in his heart. The world is the all of a natural man. He has not a taste, nor a desire, that points not to a something placed within the confines of its visible horizon. He loves nothing above it, and he cares for nothing beyond it; and to bid him love not the world, is to pass a sentence of expulsion on all the inmates of his bosom. To estimate the magnitude and the difficulty of such a surrender, let us only think that it were just as arduous to prevail on him not to love wealth, which is but one of the things in the world, as to prevail on him to set wilful fire to his own property. This he might do with sore and painful reluctance, if he saw that the salvation of his life hung upon it. But this he would do willingly, if he saw that a new property of tenfold value was instantly to emerge from the wreck of the old one. In this case there is something more than the mere displacement of an affection. There is the overbearing of one affection by another. But to desolate his heart of all love for the things of the world, without the substitution of any love in its place, were to him a process of as unnatural violence, as to destroy all the things he has in the world, and give him nothing in their room. So that, if to love not the world be indispensable to one's Christianity, then the crucifixion of the old man is not too strong a term to mark that transition in his history, when all old things are done away, and all things are become new.

We hope that by this time, you understand the impotency of a mere demonstration of this world's insignificance. Its sole practical effect, if it had any, would be to leave the heart in a state which to every heart is insupportable, and that is a mere state of nakedness and negation. You may remember the fond and unbroken tenacity with which your heart has often recurred to pursuits, over the utter frivolity of which it sighed and wept but yesterday. The arithmetic of your short-lived days, may on Sabbath make the clearest impression upon your understanding—and from his fancied bed of death, may the preacher cause a voice to descend in rebuke and mockery on all the pursuits of earthliness—and as he pictures before you the fleeting generations of men, with the absorbing grave, whither all the joys and interests of the world hasten to their sure and speedy oblivion, may you, touched and solemnized by his argument, feel for a moment as if on the eve of a practical and permanent emancipation from a scene of so much vanity. But the morrow comes, and the business of the world, and the objects of the world, and the moving forces of the world come along with it—and the machinery of the heart, in virtue of which it must have something to grasp, or something to adhere to, brings it under a kind of moral necessity to be actuated just as before—and in utter repulsion towards a state so unkindly as that of being frozen out both of delight and of desire, does it feel all the warmth and the urgency of its wonted solicitations—nor in the habit and history of the whole man, can we detect so much as one symptom of the new creature —so that the church, instead of being to him a school of obedience, has been a mere sauntering place for the luxury of a passing and theatrical emotion; and the preaching which is mighty to compel the attendance of multitudes, which is mighty to still and to solemnize the hearers into a kind of tragic sensibility, which is mighty in the play of variety and vigour that it can keep up around the imagination, is not mighty to the pulling down of strong-holds.

The love of the world cannot be expunged by a mere demonstration of the world's worthlessness. But may it not be supplanted by the love of that which is more worthy than itself? The heart cannot be prevailed upon to part with the world, by a simple act of resignation. But may not the heart be prevailed upon to admit into its preference another, who shall subordinate the world, and bring it down from its wonted ascendency? If the throne which is placed there, must have an occupier, and the tyrant that now reigns has occupied it wrongfully, he may not leave a bosom which would rather detain him, than be left in desolation. But may he not give way to the lawful sovereign, appearing with every charm that can secure his willing admittance, and taking unto himself his great power to subdue the moral nature of man, and to reign over it? In a word, if the way to disengage the heart from the positive love of one great and ascendent object, is to fasten it in positive love to another, then it is not by exposing the worthlessness of the former, but by addressing to the mental eye the worth and excellence of the latter, that all old things are to be done away, and all things are to become new.

To obliterate all our present affections, by simply expunging them, and so as to leave the seat of them unoccupied, would be to destroy the old character, and to substitute no new character in its place. But when they take their departure upon the ingress of other visitors; when they resign their sway to the power and the predominance of new affections; when, abandoning the heart to solitude, they merely give place to a successor who turns it into as busy a residence of desire, and interest, and expectation as before—there is nothing in all this to thwart or to overbear any of the laws of our sentient nature—and we see how, in fullest accordance with the mechanism of the heart, a great moral revolution may be made to take place upon it.

This, we trust, will explain the operation of that charm which accompanies the effectual preaching of the gospel. The love of God, and the love of the world, are two affections, not merely in a state of rivalship, but in a state of enmity—and that so irreconcilable, that they cannot dwell together in the same bosom. We have already affirmed how impossible it were for the heart, by any innate elasticity of its own, to cast the world away from it, and thus reduce itself to a wilderness. The heart is not so constituted, and the only way to dispossess it of an old affection, is by the expulsive power of a new one. Nothing can exceed the magnitude of the required change in a man's character—when bidden as he is in the New Testament, to love not the world; no, nor any of the things that are in the world—for this so comprehends all that is dear to him in existence, as to be equivalent to a command of self-annihilation. But the same revelation which dictates so mighty an obedience, places within our reach as mighty an instrument of obedience. It brings for admittance, to the very door of our heart, an affection which, once seated upon its throne, will either subordinate every previous inmate, or bid it away. Beside the world, it places before the eye of the mind, him who made the world, and with this peculiarity, which is all its own —that in the Gospel do we so behold God, as that we may love God. It is there, and there only, where God stands revealed as an object of confidence to sinners—and where our desire after him is not chilled into apathy, by that barrier of human guilt which intercepts every approach that is not made to him through the appointed Mediator. It is the bringing in of this better hope, whereby we draw nigh unto God —and to live without hope, is to live without God, and if the heart be without God, the world will then have all the ascendency. It is God apprehended by the believer as God in Christ, who alone can dispossess it from this ascendency. It is when he stands dismantled of the terrors which belong to him as an offended lawgiver, and when we are enabled by faith, which is his own gift, to see his glory in the face of Jesus Christ, and to hear his beseeching voice, as it protests good will to men, and entreats the return of all who will to a full pardon, and a gracious acceptance—it is then, that a love paramount to the love of the world, and at length expulsive of it, first arises in the regenerating bosom. It is when released from the spirit of bondage, with which love cannot dwell, and when admitted into the number of God's children, through the faith that is in Christ Jesus, the spirit of adoption is poured upon us—it is then that the heart, brought under the mastery of one great and predominant affection, is delivered from the tyranny of its former desires, and in the only way in which deliverance is possible. And that faith which is revealed to us from heaven, as indispensable to a sinner's justification in the sight of God, is also the instrument of the greatest of all moral and spiritual achievements on a nature dead to the influence, and beyond the reach of every other application.

Thus may we come to perceive what it is that makes the most effective kind of preaching. It is not enough to hold out to the world's eye the mirror of its own imperfections. It is not enough to come forth with a demonstration, however pathetic, of the evanescent character of all its enjoyments. It is not enough to travel the walk of experience along with you, and speak to your own conscience, and your own recollection of the deceitfulness of the heart, and the deceitfulness of all that the heart is set upon. There is many a bearer of the Gospel message, who has not shrewdness of natural discernment enough, and who has not power of characteristic description enough, and who has not the talent of moral delineation enough, to present you with a vivid and faithful sketch of the existing follies of society. But that very corruption which he has not the faculty of representing in its visible details, he may practically be the instrument of eradicating in its principle. Let him be but a faithful expounder of the gospel testimony.—Unable as he may be to apply a descriptive hand to the character of the present world, let him but report with accuracy the matter which revelation has brought to him from a distant world,—unskilled as he is in the work of so anatomizing the heart, as with the power of a novelist to create a graphical or impressive exhibition of the worthlessness of its many affections—let him only deal in those mysteries of peculiar doctrine, on which the best of novelists have thrown the wantonness of their derision. He may not be able, with the eye of shrewd and satirical observation, to expose to the ready recognition of his hearers the desires of worldliness—but with the tidings of the gospel in commission, he may wield the only engine that can extirpate them. He cannot do what some have done, when, as if by the hand of a magician, they have brought out to view, from the hidden recesses of our nature, the foibles and lurking appetites which belong to it.—But he has a truth in his possession, which into whatever heart it enters, will, like the rod of Aaron, swallow up them all—and unqualified as he may be, to describe the old man in all the nicer shading of his natural and constitutional varieties, with him is deposited that ascendent influence under which the leading tastes and tendencies of the old man are destroyed, and he becomes a new creature in Jesus Christ our Lord.

Let us not cease, then, to ply the only instrument of powerful and positive operation, to do away from you the love of the world. Let us try every legitimate method of finding access to your hearts for the love of him who is greater than the world. For this purpose, let us, if possible, clear away that shroud of unbelief which so hides and darkens the face of the Deity. Let us insist on his claims to your affection—and whether in the shape of gratitude, or in the shape of esteem, let us never cease to affirm, that in the whole of that wondrous economy, the purpose of which is to reclaim a sinful world unto himself—he, the God of love, so sets himself forth in characters of endearment, that nought but faith, and nought but understanding, are wanting, on your part, to call forth the love of your hearts back again.

And here let me advert to the incredulity of a worldly man; when he brings his own sound and secular experience to bear upon the high doctrines of Christianity—when he looks on regeneration as a thing impossible—when feeling as he does, the obstinacies of his own heart on the side of things present, and casting an intelligent eye, much exercised perhaps in the observation of human life, on the equal obstinacies of all who are around him, he pronounces this whole matter about the crucifixion of the old man, and the resurrection of a new man in his place, to be in downright opposition to all that is known and witnessed of the real nature of humanity. We think that we have seen such men, who, firmly trenched in their own vigorous and homebred sagacity, and shrewdly regardful of all that passes before them through the week, and upon the scenes of ordinary business, look on that transition of the heart by which it gradually dies unto time, and awakens in all the life of a new-felt and ever-growing desire towards God, as a mere Sabbath speculation; and who thus, with all their attention engrossed upon the concerns of earthliness, continue unmoved, to the end of their days, amongst the feelings, and the appetites, and the pursuits of earthliness. If the thought of death, and another state of being after it, comes across them at all, it is not with a change so radical as that of being born again, that they ever connect the idea of preparation. They have some vague conception of its being quite enough that they acquit themselves in some decent and tolerable way of their relative obligations; and that, upon the strength of some such social and domestic moralities as are often realized by him in whose heart the love of God has never entered, they will be transplanted in safety from this world, where God is the Being with whom it may almost be said, that they have had nothing to do, to that world where God is the Being with whom they will have mainly and immediately to do throughout all eternity. They admit all that is said of the utter vanity of time, when taken up with as a resting place. But they resist every application made upon the heart of man, with the view of so shifting its tendencies, that it shall not henceforth find in the interests of time, all its rest and all its refreshment. They, in fact, regard such an attempt as an enterprise that is altogether aerial—and with a tone of secular wisdom, caught from the familiarities of every-day experience, do they see a visionary character in all that is said of setting our affections on the things that are above; and of walking by faith; and of keeping our hearts in such a love of God as shall shut out from them the love of the world; and of having no confidence in the flesh; and of so renouncing earthly things as to have our conversation in heaven.

Now, it is altogether worthy of being remarked of those men who thus disrelish spiritual Christianity, and, in fact, deem it an impracticable acquirement, how much of a piece their incredulity about the demands of Christianity, and their incredulity about the doctrines of Christianity, are with one another. No wonder that they feel the work of the New Testament to be beyond their strength, so long as they hold the words of the New Testament to be beneath their attention. Neither they nor any one else can dispossess the heart of an old affection, but by the impulsive power of a new one—and, if that new affection be the love of God, neither they nor any one else can be made to entertain it, but on such a representation of the Deity, as shall draw the heart of the sinner towards him. Now it is just their unbelief which screens from the discernment of their minds this representation. They do not see the love of God in sending his Son into the world. They do not see the expression of his tenderness to men, in sparing him not, but giving him up unto the death for us all. They do not see the sufficiency of the atonement, or of the sufferings that were endured by him who bore the burden that sinners should have borne. They do not see the blended holiness and compassion of the Godhead, in that he passed by the transgressions of his creatures, yet could not pass them by without an expiation. It is a mystery to them, how a man should pass to the state of godliness from a state of nature—but had they only a believing view of God manifest in the flesh, this would resolve for them the whole mystery of godliness. As it is, they cannot get quit of their old affections, because they are out of sight from all those truths which have influence to raise a new one. They are like the children of Israel in the land of Egypt, when required to make bricks without straw —they cannot love God, while they want the only food which can aliment this affection in a sinner's bosom—and however great their errors may be both in resisting the demands of the Gospel as impracticable, and in rejecting the doctrines of the Gospel as inadmissible, yet there is not a spiritual man (and it is the prerogative of him who is spiritual to judge all men) who will not perceive that there is a consistency in these errors.

But if there be a consistency in the errors, in like manner is there a consistency in the truths which are opposite to them. The man who believes in the peculiar doctrines, will readily bow to the peculiar demands of Christianity. When he is told to love God supremely, this may startle another, but it will not startle him to whom God has been revealed in peace, and in pardon, and in all the freeness of an offered reconciliation. When told to shut out the world from his heart, this may be impossible with him who has nothing to replace it—but not impossible with him, who has found in God a sure and a satisfying portion. When told to withdraw his affections from the things that are beneath, this were laying an order of self-extinction upon the man, who knows not another quarter in the whole sphere of his contemplation, to which he could transfer them—but it were not grievous to him whose view has been opened up to the loveliness and glory of the things that are above, and can there find, for every feeling of his soul, a most ample and delighted occupation. When told to look not to the things that are seen and temporal, this were blotting out the light of all that is visible from the prospect of him in whose eye there is a wall of partition between guilty nature and the joys of eternity—but he who believes that Christ hath broken down this wall, finds a gathering radiance upon his soul, as he looks onwards in faith to the things that are unseen and eternal.

Tell a man to be holy—and how can he compass such a performance, when his alone fellowship with holiness is a fellowship of despair? It is the atonement of the cross reconciling the holiness of the lawgiver with the safety of the offender, that hath opened the way for a sanctifying influence into the sinner's heart, and he can take a kindred impression from the character of God now brought nigh, and now at peace with him. Separate the demand from the doctrine, and you have either a system of righteousness that is impracticable, or a barren orthodoxy. Bring the demand and the doctrine together—and the true disciple of Christ is able to do the one, through the other strengthening him. The motive is adequate to the movement; and the bidden obedience of the Gospel is not beyond the measure of his strength, just because the doctrine of the Gospel is not beyond the measure of his acceptance. The shield of faith, and the hope of salvation, and the Word of God, and the girdle of truth—these are the armour that he has put on; and with these the battle is won, and the eminence is reached, and the man stands on the vantage ground of a new field and a new prospect. The effect is great, but the cause is equal to it—and stupendous as this moral resurrection to the precepts of Christianity, undoubtedly is, there is an element of strength enough to give it being and continuance in the principles of Christianity.

The object of the Gospel is both to pacify the sinner's conscience, and to purify his heart; and it is of importance to observe, that what mars the one of these objects, mars the other also. The best way of casting out an impure affection is to admit a pure one; and by the love of what is good, to expel the love of what is evil. Thus it is, that the freer the Gospel, the more sanctifying is the Gospel; and the more it is received as a doctrine of grace, the more will it be felt as a doctrine according to godliness. This is one of the secrets of the Christian life, that the more a man holds of God as a pensioner, the greater is the payment of service that he renders back again. On the tenure of "Do this and live," a spirit of fearfulness is sure to enter; and the jealousies of a legal bargain chase away all confidence from the intercourse between God and man; and the creature striving to be square and even with his Creator, is, in fact, pursuing all the while his own selfishness instead of God's glory; and with all the conformities which he labours to accomplish, the soul of obedience is not there, the mind is not subject to the law of God, nor indeed under such an economy ever can be. It is only when, as in the Gospel, acceptance is bestowed as a present, without money and without price, that the security which man feels in God is placed beyond the reach of disturbance—or, that he can repose in him, as one friend reposes in another—or, that any liberal and generous understanding can be established betwixt them—the one party rejoicing over the other to do him good—the other finding that the truest gladness of his heart lies in the impulse of a gratitude, by which it is awakened to the charms of a new moral existence. Salvation by grace—salvation by free grace—salvation not of works, but according to the mercy of God—salvation on such a footing is not more indispensable to the deliverance of our persons from the hand of justice, than it is to the deliverance of our hearts from the chill and the weight of ungodliness. Retain a single shred or fragment of legality with the Gospel, and you raise a topic of distrust between man and God. You take away from the power of the Gospel to melt and to conciliate. For this purpose, the freer it is, the better it is. That very peculiarity which so many dread as the germ of Antinomianism, is, in fact, the germ of a new spirit, and a new inclination against it. Along with the light of a free Gospel, does there enter the love of the Gospel, which in proportion as you impair the freeness, you are sure to chase away. And never does the sinner find within himself so mighty a moral transformation, as when under the belief that he is saved by grace, he feels constrained thereby to offer his heart a devoted thing, and to deny ungodliness.

To do any work in the best manner, you would make use of the fittest tools for it. And we trust, that what has been said may serve in some degree, for the practical guidance of those who would like to reach the great moral achievement of our text—but feel that the tendencies and desires of Nature are too strong for them. We know of no other way by which to keep the love of the world out of our heart, than to keep in our hearts the love of God—and no other way by which to keep our hearts in the love of God, than building ourselves up on our most holy faith. That denial of the world which is not possible to him that dissents from the Gospel testimony, is possible, even as all things are possible to him that believeth. To try this without faith, is to work without the right tool or the right instrument. But faith worketh by love; and the way of expelling from the heart the love that transgresseth the law, is to admit into its receptacles the love which fulfilleth the law.

Conceive a man to be standing on the margin of this green world; and that, when he looked towards it, he saw abundance smiling upon every field, and all the blessings which earth can afford, scattered in profusion throughout every family, and the light of the sun sweetly resting upon all the pleasant habitations, and the joys of human companionship brightening many a happy circle of society—conceive this to be the general character of the scene upon one side of his contemplation; and that on the other, beyond the verge of the goodly planet on which he was situated, he could descry nothing but a dark and fathomless unknown. Think you that he would bid a voluntary adieu to all the brightness and all the beauty that were before him upon earth, and commit himself to the frightful solitude away from it. Would he leave its peopled dwelling places, and become a solitary wanderer through the fields of non-entity? If space offered him nothing but a wilderness, would he for it abandon the homebred scenes of life and of cheerfulness that lay so near, and exerted such a power of urgency to detain him? Would not he cling to the regions of sense, and of life, and of society?—and shrinking away from the desolation that was beyond it, would not he be glad to keep his firm footing on the territory of this world, and to take shelter under the silver canopy that was stretched over it?

But if, during the time of his contemplation, some happy island of the blest had floated by; and there had burst upon his senses the light of its surpassing glories, and its sounds of sweeter melody; and he clearly saw, that there, a purer beauty rested upon every field, and a more heart-felt joy spread itself among all the families; and he could discern there a peace, and a piety, and a benevolence, which put a moral gladness into every bosom, and united the whole society in one rejoicing sympathy with each other, and with the beneficent Father of them all.—Could he further see, that pain and mortality were there unknown; and above all, that signals of welcome were hung out, and an avenue of communication was made for him—perceive you not, that what was before the wilderness, would become the land of invitation; and that now the world would be the wilderness? What unpeopled space could not do, can be done by space teeming with beatific scenes, and beatific society. And let the existing tendencies of the heart be what they may to the scene that is near and visible around us, still if another stood revealed to the prospect of man, either through the channel of faith, or through the channel of his senses—then, without violence done to the constitution of his moral nature, may he die unto the present world, and live to the lovelier world that stands in the distance away from it.

SERMON IH.

The sure Warrant of a Believer's Hope.

"For if, when we were enemies we were reconciled to God by the death of his Son: much more, being reconciled, we shall be saved by his life."—*Romans* v. 10.

St. Paul, who, by the way, is by far the most argumentative of all the Apostles—and who, from being the most successful of them all, proves that argument is both a legitimate and a powerful weapon in the work of making Christians, sometimes undertakes to reason upon one set of premises, and then to demonstrate how much more valid and irresistible is the conclusion which he tries to establish, when he is in actual possession of another and more favourable set of premises. In this way a great additional strength is made to accrue to his argument—and the how much more with which he finishes, causes it to come with greater power and assurance upon his readers—and it is this which gives him the advantage of what is well known, both in law and in logic, under the phrase of *argumentum a fortiore*, or, an argument which affirms a thing to be true in adverse and unpromising circumstances, and therefore far more worthy of being held true in likelier circumstances. It is quite a familiar mode of reasoning in common discourse. If a neighbour be bound to sympathise with the distresses of an unfortunate family, how much more, when that neighbour is a relative? If I obtained an offer of friendship from a man in difficulties, how much more may I count upon it should he now be translated into a state of sufficiency and ease? If, in the very heat of our quarrel, and under the discouragement of all my provoking insolence towards him, my enemy forbear the vengeance which he had the power to inflict, how much more, should the quarrel be made up, and I have been long in terms of reconciliation with him, may I feel myself secure from the effects of his indignation? Such also is the argument of my text. There is one state of matters in which God sets forth a demonstration of friendship to the world, and this is compared with the present and actual state of matters, more favourable than the former, and from which, therefore, the friendship of God may be still more surely inferred, and still more firmly confided in. But it will be further seen, that in this short sentence of the Apostle, there lies a compound argument which admits of being separated into distinct parts. There is a reference made to a two-fold state of matters, which, by being resolved into its two particulars, brings out two accessions of strength to the conclusion of our Apostle, which are independent of each other. He, in fact, holds forth a double claim upon our understanding, and we propose to view successively the two particulars of which it is made up.

There is first, then, a comparison made between one state of matters, and another state of matters which obtain in our earth—and there is at the same time a comparison made between one state of matters, and another state of matters which obtain in heaven—and from each of these there may be educed an argument for strengthening the assurance of every Christian, in that salvation which the Gospel has made known to us.

Let us first look, then, to the two states upon earth—and this may be done either with a reference to this world's history, or it may be done with a reference to the personal history of every one man who is now a believer.

That point of time in the series of general history at which reconciliation was made, was when our Saviour said that it is finished, and gave up the ghost. God may be said to have then become reconciled to the world, in as far as he was ready to enter into agreement with all who drew nigh in the name of this great propitiation. Now think of the state of matters upon earth, previous to the time when reconciliation in this view was entered upon. Think of the strength of that moving principle in the bosom of the Deity, which so inclined him towards a world then lying in the depths of ungodliness—and from one end to another of it, lifting the cry of rebellion against him. There was no movement on the part of the world towards God—no returning sense of allegiance towards him from whom they had revolted so deeply—no abatement of that profligacy which so rioted at large over a wide scene of lawless, and thankless, and careless abandonment—no mitigation of that foul and audacious insolence by which the throne of heaven was assailed; and a spectacle so full of offence to the unfallen was held forth, of a whole province in arms against the lawful Monarch of creation. Had the world thrown down its weapons of disobedience—had a contrite and relenting spirit gone previously forth among its generations—had the light which even then glimmered in the veriest wilds of Paganism, just up to the strength and degree of its influence, told aright on the moral sensibilities of the deluded and licentious worshippers—had they, whose conscience was a law unto themselves, just acted and followed on as they might under the guidance of its compunctious visitations—had there been any thing like the forth-going of a general desire, however faint, towards that unknown Being, the sense and impression of whom were never wholly obliterated—then it might have been less decisive of God's will for reconciliation, that he gave way to these returning demonstrations on the part of his alienated creatures, and reared a pathway of communication by which sinners may draw nigh unto God. But for God to have done this very thing, when these sinners were persisting in the full spirit and determination of their unholy warfare—for him to have done so, when instead of any returning loyalty rising up to him like the incense of a sweet-smelling savour, the exhalations of idolatry and vice blackened the whole canopy of heaven, and ascended in a smoke of abomination before him—for him to have done so at the very time that all flesh had corrupted its ways, and when either with or without the law of revelation, God saw that the wickedness of man was great in the earth, and that every imagination of the thoughts of his heart was only evil continually—in these circumstances of deep and unalleviated provocation, and when God may have eased him of his adversaries, by sweeping the whole of this moral nuisance away from the face of the universe which it deformed—for such a time to have been a time of love, when majesty seemed to call for some solemn vindication, but mercy could not let us go—surely, if through such a barrier between God and the guilty, he, in the longings of his desire after them, forced a pathway of reconciliation, he never will turn himself away from any, who, cheered forward by his own intreaties, are walking upon that path. But if, when enemies, he himself found out an approach by which he might beckon them to enter into peace with him, how much more when they are so approaching, will he meet them with the light of his countenance, and bless them with the joys of his salvation.

But this argument may be looked to in another way. Instead of fixing our regards upon that point in the general history of the world, when the avenue was struck out between our species and their offended Lawgiver; and through the rent vail of a Saviour's flesh, a free and consecrated way of access was opened for the guiltiest of them all—let a believer in Christ fix his regards upon that passage in his own personal history at which he was drawn in his desires and in his confidence to this great Mediator, and entered upon the grace wherein he now stands, and gave up his evil heart of unbelief, and made his transition out of darkness to the marvellous light of the Gospel. Let him compare what he was, when an alien from God, through wicked works of his own, with what he is when a humble but confiding expectant of God's mercy through the righteousness of another. Who translated him into the condition which he now occupies? Who put into his heart the faith of the Gospel? Who awakened him from the dormancy and unconcern of nature? Who stirred up that restless but salutary alarm which at length issued in the secure feeling of reconciliation? There was a time of his past life when the whole doctrine of salvation was an offence to him, when its preaching was foolishness to his ears; when its phraseology tired and disgusted him; when, in light and lawless companionship, he put the warnings of religious counsel, and the urgency of menacing sermons away from his bosom—a time when the world was his all, and when he was wholly given over to the idolatry of its pursuits, and pleasures, and projects of aggrandizement—a time when his heart was unvisited with any permanent seriousness about God, of whom his conscience sometimes reminded him, but whom he soon dismissed from his earnest contemplation—a time when he may have occasionally heard of a judgment, but without one practical movement of his soul towards the task of preparation—a time when the overtures of peace met him on his way, but which he, in the impetuous prosecution of his own objects, utterly disregarded—a time when death plied him with its ever-recurring mementoes, but which he, overlooking the short and summary arithmetic of the few little years that lay between him and the last messenger, placed so far on the background of his anticipation, that this earth, this passing and perishable earth, formed the scene of all his solicitudes. Is there none here present who remembers such a time of his by-gone history, and with such a character of alienation from God and from his Christ, as I have now given to it? And who, I ask, recalled him from this alienation? By whose guidance was he conducted to that demonstration either of the press or of the pulpit, which awakened him? Who sent that afflictive visitation to his door, which weaned his spirit from the world, and wooed it to the deathless friendships, and the ever-during felicities of heaven? Who made known to him the extent of his guilt, with the overpassing extent of the redemption that is provided for it? It was not he himself who originated the process of his own salvation. God may have abandoned him to his own courses; and said of him as he has done of many others, "I will let him alone, since he will have it so;" and given him up to that judicial blindness, under which the vast majority of the world are now sleeping in profoundest lethargy; and withheld altogether that light of the spirit which he had done so much to extinguish. But if, instead of all this, God kept by him in the midst of his thankless provocations—and while he was yet a regardless enemy, made his designs of grace to bear upon him—and throughout all the mazes of his chequered history, conducted him to the knowledge of himself as a reconciling God—and so softened his heart with family bereavements, or so tore it from all its worldly dependencies by the disasters of business, or so shook it with frightful agitation by the terrors of the law, or so shone upon it with the light of his free Spirit, as made it glad to escape from the treachery of nature's joys and nature's promises, into a relying faith on the offers and assurances of the Gospel—why, just let him think of the time when God did so much for him—and then think of the impossibility that God will recede from him now, or that he will cease from the prosecution of that work in circumstances of earnest and desirous concurrence on the part of the believer, which he himself begun in the circumstances either of his torpid unconcern, or of his active and haughty defiance. The God who moved towards him in his days of forgetfulness, will not move away from him in his days of hourly and habitual remembrance—and he who intercepted him in his career of rebellion, will not withdraw from him in his career of new obedience—and he who first knocked at the door of his conscience, and that too in a prayerless, and thankless, and regardless season of his history, will not, now that he prays in the name of Christ, and now that his heart is set upon salvation, and now that the doctrine of grace forms all his joy and all his dependence; he who thus found him out a distant and exiled rebel, will not abandon him now that his fellowship is with the Father, and with the Son. It is thus that the believer may shield his misgiving heart from all its despondencies. It is thus that the argument of the text goes to fortify his faith, and to perfect that which is lacking in it. It is thus that the how much more of the Apostles should cause him to abound more and more in the peace and the joy of believing—and should encourage every man who has laid hold on the hope set before us, to steady and confirm his hold still more tenaciously than before, so as to keep it fast and sure even unto the end.

With a man who knows himself to be a believer, this argument is quite irresistible, and it will go to establish his faith, and to strengthen it, and to settle it, and to make it perfect. But it is possible for a man really to believe, and yet to be in ignorance for a time whether he does so or not—and it is possible for a man to be in earnest about his soul, and yet not to have received that truth which is unto salvation—and it is possible for him to be actuated by a strong general desire to be right, and yet to be walking among the elements of uncertainty—and it is possible for him to be looking to that quarter whence the truths of the Gospel are offered to his contemplation, and yet not to have attained the distinct or satisfying perception of them—thoroughly engaged in the prosecution of his peace with God, determinedly bent on this object as the highest interest he can possibly aspire after, labouring after a settlement, and, under all the agonies of a fierce internal war, seeking, and toiling, and praying for his deliverance. It is at the point of time when faith enters the heart, that reconciliation is entered upon—nor can we say of this man, that he is yet a believer, or, that he has passed from the condition of an enemy to that of a friend. And yet upon him the argument of the text should not be without its efficacy. It is such an argument as may be employed not merely to confirm the faith which already exists, but to help on to its formation that faith which is struggling for an establishment in the heart of an inquirer. It falls, no doubt, with fullest and most satisfying light upon the heart of a conscious believer—and yet may it be addressed, and with pertinency too, to men under their first and earliest visitations of seriousness. For give me an acquaintance of whom I know nothing more than that his face is towards Zion—give me one arrested by a sense of guilt and of danger, and merely groping his way to a place of enlargement—give me a soul not in peace, but in perplexity, and in the midst of all those initial difficulties which beset the awakened sinner, ere Christ shall give him light—give me a labouring and heavy laden sinner, haunted by the reflection, as if by an arrow sticking fast, that the mighty question of his eternity is yet unresolved. There are many I fear amongst you to whom this tremendous uncertainty gives no concern—but give me one who has newly taken it up, and who, in the minglings of doubt and despondency, has not found his way to any consolation— and even with him may it be found, that the same reason which strengthens the hope of an advanced Christian, may well inspire the hope of him who has still his Christianity to find, and thus cast a cheering and a comforting influence on the very infancy of his progress. For if it was in behalf of a careless world that the costly apparatus of redemption was reared—if it was in the full front and audacity of their most determined rebellion, that God laid the plan of reconciliation—if it was for the sake of men sunk in the very depths of ungodliness, that he constructed his overtures of peace, and sent forth his Son with them amongst our loathsome and polluted dwelling-places—if to get at his strayed children, he had thus to find his way through all those elements of impiety and ungodliness, which are most abhorrent to the sanctity of his nature, think you, my brethren, think you that the God who made such an advancing movement towards the men whose faces were utterly away from him—is this a God who will turn his own face away from the man who is moving towards God, and earnestly seeking after him, if haply he may find him?

This argument obtains great additional force, when we look to the state of matters in heaven at the time that we upon earth were enemies, and compare it with the state of matters in heaven, now that we are actually reconciled, or are beginning to entertain the offers of reconciliation. Before the work of our redemption, Jesus Christ was in primeval glory—and though a place of mystery to us, it was a place of secure and ineffable enjoyment—insomuch, that the fondest prayer he could utter in the depths of his humiliation, was to be taken back again to the ancient of days, and there to be restored to the glory which he had with him before the world was. It was from the heights of celestial security and blessedness that he looked with an eye of pity on our sinful habitation—it was from a scene where beings of a holy nature surrounded him, and the full homage of the Divinity was rendered to him, and in the ecstacies of his fellowship with God the Father, all was peace, and purity, and excellence—it was from this that he took his voluntary departure, and went out on his errand to seek and to save us. And it was not the parade of an unreal suffering that he had to encounter; but a deep and a dreadful endurance—it was not a triumphant promenade through this lower world, made easy over all its obstacles by the energies of his Godhead; but a conflict of toil and of strenuousness—it was not an egress from heaven on a journey brightened through all its stages by the hope of a smooth and gentle return; but it was such an exile from heaven as made his ascent and his readmittance there the fruit of a hard won victory. We have nothing but the facts of revelation to guide or to inform us, and yet from these we most assuredly gather, that the Saviour, in stepping down from the elevation of his past eternity, incurred a substantial degradation —that when he wrapped himself in the humanity of our nature, he put on the whole of its infirmities and its sorrows—that for the joy which he renounced, he became acquainted with grief, and a grief, too, commensurate to the whole burden of our world's atonement—that the hidings of his Father's countenance were terrifying to his soul—and when the offended justice of the Godhead was laid upon his person, it required the whole strength of the Godhead to sustain it. What mean the agonies of the garden? What mean the bitter cries and complainings of abandonment upon the cross? What meaneth the prayer that the cup might pass away from him, and the struggle of a lofty resolution with the agonies of a mighty and unknown distress, and the evident symptoms of a great and toilsome achievement throughout the whole progress of this undertaking, and angels looking down from their eminences, as on a field of contest where a great Captain had to put forth the travailing of his strength, and to spoil principalities and powers, and to make a show of them openly? Was there nothing in all this, do you think, but the mockery of a humiliation that was never felt—the mockery of a pain that was never suffered—the mockery of a battle that was never fought? No, my brethren, be assured that there was, on that day, a real vindication of God's insulted majesty. On that day there was the real transference of an avenging hand, from the heads of the guilty to the head of the innocent. On that day one man died for the people, and there was an actual laying on of the iniquities of us all. It was a war of strength and of suffering in highest possible aggravation because the war of elements which were infinite. The wrath which millions should have borne, was all of it discharged. Nor do we estimate aright what we owe of love and obligation to the Saviour, till we believe, that the whole of that fury, which if poured out upon the world, would have served its guilty generations through eternity—that all of it was poured into the cup of expiation.

A more adequate sense of this might not only serve to awaken the gratitude which slumbers within us, and is dead—it might also, through the aid of the argument in my text, awaken and assure our confidence. If when we were enemies, Christ ventured on an enterprise so painful—if, when loathsome outcasts from the sacred territory of heaven, he left the abode of his Father, and exchanged love, and adoration, and congenial felicity among angels, for the hatred and persecution of men—if, when the agonies of the coming vengeance were still before him, and the dark and dreary vale of suffering had yet to be entered upon, and he had to pass under the inflictions of that sword which the eternal God awakened against his Fellow, and he had still to give himself up to a death equivalent in the amount of its soreness to the devouring fire, and the everlasting burnings, which but for him believers would have borne—if, when all this had yet to be travelled through, he nevertheless, in his compassionate longing for the souls of men, went forth upon the errand of winning them to himself,—let us just look to the state of matters in heaven then, and compare it with the state of matters now.

Christ has there ascended on the wings of victory—and he is now sitting at God's right hand, amid all the purchased triumphs of his obedience—and the toil, and the conflict, and the agony, are now over—and from that throne of mediatorship to which he has been exalted, is it his present office to welcome the approaches of all who come, and to save to the uttermost all who put their trust in him. And is it possible, we would ask, my brethren, is it possible that he who died to atone, now that he lives, will not live to make intercession for us? Can the love for men which bore him through a mighty and a painful sacrifice, not be strong enough to carry him onwards in peace and in triumph to its final consummation? Will he now abandon that work which his own hands have so laboriously reared?—or leave the cause for which he has already sustained the weight of such an endurance, in the embryo and unfinished state of an abortive undertaking? Will he cast away from him the spoils of that victory for which he bled; and how can it be imagined for a moment, but by such dark and misgiving hearts as ours, that he whose love for a thankless world carried him through the heat and the severity of a contest that is now ended, will ever, with the cold and forbidding glance of an altered countenance spurn an inquiring world away from him?

The death of a crucified Saviour, when beheld under such a view, is the firm stepping stone to confidence in a risen Saviour. You may learn from it that his desire and your salvation are most thoroughly at one. Of his good-will to have you into heaven, he has given the strongest pledge and demonstration, by consecrating, with his own blood, a way of access, through which sinners may draw nigh. And now, that as our forerunner, he is already there—now that he has gone up again to the place from which he arose—now that to the very place which he left to die, and that, that the barrier to its entrance from our world may be moved away, he has ascended alive and in glory, without another death to endure, for death has no more the dominion over him—will ever he do any thing to close that entrance which it has cost him so much to open? Will he thus throw away the toil and the travail of his own soul, and reduce to impotency that apparatus of reconciliation which he himself has reared, and at an expense, too, equal to the penance of many millions through eternity? What he died to begin, will he not now live to carry forward; and will not the love which could force a way through the grave to its accomplishments—now that it has reached the summit of triumph and of elevation which he at present occupies, burst forth and around the field of that mighty enterprise, which was begun in deepest suffering, and will end in full and finished glory?

This is a good argument in all the stages of a man's Christianity. Whether he has found, or is only seeking—whether he be in a state of faith, or in a state of inquiry—whether a believer like Paul and many of the disciples that he was addressing, or an earnest and convinced sinner groping the way of deliverance, and labouring to be at rest, there may be made to emanate from the present circumstances of our Saviour, and the position that he now occupies, an argument either to perpetuate the confidence where it is, or to inspire it where it is not. If, when an enemy, I was reconciled, and that too by his death—if he laid down his life to remove an obstacle in the way of my salvation, how much more, now that he has taken it up, will he not accomplish that salvation? It is just fulfilling his own desire. It is just prospering forward the very cause that his heart is set upon. It is just following out the facilities which he himself has opened—and marching onward in glorious procession, to the consummation of those triumphs, for which he had to struggle his way through a season of difficulties that are now over. It is thus that the believer reasons himself into a steadier assurance than before—and peace may be made to flow through his heart like a mighty river—and resting on the foundation of Christ, he comes to feel himself in a sure and wealthy place—and the good-will of the Saviour rises into an undoubted axiom—so as to chase away all his distrust, and cause him to delight himself greatly in the riches of his present grace, and in the brightening certainty of his coming salvation.

And this view of the matter is not only fitted to heighten the confidence that is already formed—but also to originate the confidence that needs to be inspired. It places the herald of salvation on a secure and lofty vantage ground. It seals and authenticates the offer with which he is intrusted—and with which he may go round among the guiltiest of this world's population. It enables him to say, that for guilt even in the season of its most proud and unrepentant defiance, did Christ give himself up unto the death—and that to guilt even in this state of hardihood, Christ in prosecution of his own work has commissioned him to go with the overtures of purchased mercy—and should the guilt which has stood its ground against the threatenings of power, feel softened and arrested by pity's preventing call, may the preacher of forgiveness affirm in his Master's name, that he, who for the chief of sinners, bowed himself down unto the sacrifice, will not now, that he has arisen a Prince and a Saviour, stamp a nullity upon that contest, the triumph of which is awaiting him; but the bitterness of which has passed away. He will not turn with indifference and distaste from that very fruit which he himself has fought for. But if for guilt in its full impenitency, he dyed his garments, and waded through the arena of contest and of blood—then should the most abandoned of her children begin a contrite movement towards him, it is not he who will either break the prop for which he feels, or quench his infant aspiration. He will look to him as the travail of his own soul, and in him he will be satisfied.

We know not what the measure of the sinfulness is of any who now hear us. But we know, that however foul his depravity, and however deep the crimson dye of his manifold iniquities may be, the measure of the gospel warrant reaches even unto him. It was to make an inroad on the territory of Satan, and reclaim from it a kingdom unto himself, that Christ died—and I speak to the farthest off in guilt and alienation amongst you—take the overture of peace that is now brought to your door, and you will add to that kingdom which he came to establish, and take away from that kingdom which he came to destroy. The freeness of this Gospel has the honour of him who liveth and was dead for its guarantee. The security of the sinner and the glory of the Saviour, are at one. And with the spirit of a monarch who had to fight his way to the dominion which was rightfully his own, will he hail the returning allegiance of every rebel, as a new accession to his triumphs, as another trophy to the might and the glory of his great undertaking.

But, amid all this latitude of call and of invitation, let me press upon you that alternative character of the Gospel, to which I have often adverted. I have tried to make known to you, how its encouragements rise the one above the other to him who moves towards it. But it has its corresponding terrors and severities, which also rise the one above the other to him who moves away from it. If the transgressor will not be recalled by the invitation which I have now made known to him, he will be riveted thereby into deeper and more hopeless condemnation. If the offer of peace be not entertained by him, then, in the very proportion of its largeness and generosity, will the provocation be of his insulting treatment in having rejected it. Out of the mouth of the Son of man there cometh a two-edged sword. There is pardon free as the light of heaven to all who will. There is wrath, accumulated and irretrievable wrath, to all who will not. "Kiss the Son, therefore, lest he be angry, and ye perish from the way: when his wrath is kindled but a little, blessed only are they who put their trust in him."

It is the most delusive of all calculations to put off the acceptance of the Gospel, because of its freeness—and because it is free at all times—and because the present you think may be the time of your unconcern and liberty, and some distant future be the time of your return through that door which will still be open for you. The door of Christ's Mediatorship is ever open, till death puts its unchangeable seal upon your eternity. But the door of your own heart, if you are not receiving him, is shut at this moment, and every day is it fixing and fastening more closely—and long ere death summon you away, may it at length settle immoveably upon its hinges, and the voice of him who standeth without, and knocketh, may be unheard by the spiritual ear—and, therefore, you are not made to feel too much, though you feel as earnestly as if now or never was the alternative on which you were suspended. It is not enough, that the Word of God, compared to a hammer, be weighty and powerful. The material on which it works must be capable of an impression. It is not enough, that there be a free and forcible application. There must be a willing subject. You are unwilling now, and therefore it is that conversion does not follow. To-morrow the probability is, that you will be still more unwilling—and, therefore, though the application be the same, the conversion is still at a greater distance away from you. And thus, while the application continues the same, the subject hardens, and a good result is ever becoming more and more unlikely—and thus may it go on till you arrive upon the bed of your last sickness, at the confines of eternity—and what, I would ask, is the kind of willingness that comes upon you then? Willing to escape the pain of hell—this you are now, but yet not willing to be a Christian. Willing that the fire and your bodily sensations be kept at a distance from each other—this you are now, for who of you at present, would thrust his hand among the flames? Willing that the frame of your animal sensibilities shall meet with nothing to wound or torture it—this is willingness of which the lower animals, incapable of religion, are yet as capable as yourself. You will be as willing then for deliverance from material torments as you can be now—but there is a willingness which you want now, and which, in all likelihood, will then be still more beyond the reach of your attainment. If the free Gospel do not meet with your willingness now to accept and submit to it, neither may it then. And I know not, my brethren, what has been your experience in death-beds, but sure I am, that both among the agonies of mortal disease, and the terrors of the malefactor's cell, Christ may be offered, and the offer be sadly and sullenly put away. The free proclamation is heard without one accompanying charm—and the man who refused to lay hold of it through life, finds, that in the impotency of his expiring grasp, he cannot apprehend it. And O, if you but knew how often the word of faith may fall from the minister, and the work of faith be left undone upon the dying man, never would you so postpone the purposes of seriousness, or look forward to the last week of your abode upon earth as to the convenient season for winding up the concerns of a neglected eternity.

If you look attentively to the text, you will find that there is something more than a shade of difference between being reconciled and being saved. Reconciliation is spoken of as an event that has already happened—salvation as an event that is to come. The one event may lead to the other; but there is a real distinction between them. It is true, that the salvation instanced in the preceding verse, is salvation from wrath. But it is the wrath which is incurred by those who have sinned wilfully, after they had come to the knowledge of the truth—"when there remaineth no more sacrifice for sin, but a certain fearful looking for of judgment and fiery indignation, which shall devour the adversaries." Jesus Christ will save us from this by saving us from sin. He who hath reconciled us by his death, will, by his life, accomplish for us this salvation. Reconciliation is not salvation. It is only the portal to it. Justification is not the end of Christ's coming—it is only the means to an ultimate attainment. By his death he pacified the lawgiver. By his life he purifies the sinner. The one work is finished. The other is not so, but it is only going on unto perfection. And this is the secret of that unwillingness which I have already touched upon. There is a willingness that God would lift off from their persons the hand of an avenger. But there is not a willingness that Christ would lay upon their persons the hand of a sanctifier. The motive for him to apprehend them is to make them holy. But they care not to apprehend that for which they are apprehended. They see not that the use of the new dispensation, is for them to be restored to the image they have lost, and, for this purpose to be purged from their old sins. This is the point on which they are in darkness—"and they love the darkness rather than the light, because their deeds are evil." They are at all times willing for the reward without the service. But they are not willing for the reward and the service together. The willingness for the one they always have. But the willingness for both they never have. They have it not to-day—and it is not the operation of time that will put it in them to-morrow. Nor will disease put it in. Nor will age put it in. Nor will the tokens of death put it in. Nor will the near and terrific view of eternity put it in. It may call out into a livelier sensation than before, a willingness for the reward. But it will neither inspire a taste nor a willingness for the service. A distaste for God and godliness, as it was the reigning and paramount principle of his life, so may it be the reigning and paramount principle of his death-bed. As it envenomed every breath which he drew, so may it envenom his last—and the spirit going forth to the God who gave it, with all the enmity that it ever had, God will deal with it as with an enemy.

SERMON IV.

The Restlessness of human Ambition.

"How say ye to my soul, Flee as a bird to your mountain?—O that I had the wings of a dove, that I may fly away, and be at rest."—*Psalm* xi. 1. *and* lv. 6.

To all those who are conversant in the scenery of external nature, it is evident, that an object to be seen to the greatest advantage must be placed at a certain distance from the eye of the observer. The poor man's hut, though all within be raggedness and disorder, and all around it be full of the most nauseous and disgusting spectacles—yet, if seen at a sufficient distance, may appear a sweet and interesting cottage. That field where the thistle grows, and the face of which is deformed by the wild exuberance of a rank and pernicious vegetation, may delight the eye of a distant spectator by the loveliness of its verdure. That lake, whose waters are corrupted, and whose banks poison the air by their marshy and putrid exhalations, may charm the eye of an enthusiast, who views it from an adjoining eminence, and dwells with rapture on the quietness of its surface, and on the beauty of its outline—its sweet border fringed with the gayest colouring of Nature, and on which spring lavishes its finest ornaments. All is the effect of distance. It softens the harsh and disgusting features of every object. What is gross and ordinary, it can dress in the most romantic attractions. The country hamlet it can transform into a paradise of beauty, in spite of the abominations that are at every door, and the angry brawlings of the men and the women who occupy it. All that is loathsome and offensive, is softened down by the power of distance. You see the smoke rising in fantastic wreaths through the pure air, and the village spire peeping from among the thick verdure of the trees, which embosom it. The fancy of our sentimentalist swells with pleasure, and peace and piety supply their delightful associations to complete the harmony of the picture.

This principle may serve to explain a feeling which some of you who now hear me may have experienced. On a fine day, when the sun threw its unclouded splendours over a whole neighbourhood, did you never form a wish that your place could be transferred to some distant and more beautiful part of the landscape? Did the idea never rise in your fancy, that the people who sport on yon sunny bank are happier than yourself—that you would like to be buried in that distant grove, and forget, for a while, in silence and in solitude, the distractions of the world—that you would like to repose by yon beautiful rivulet, and soothe every anxiety of your heart by the gentleness of its murmurs—that you would like to transport yourself to the distance of miles, and there enjoy the peace which resides in some sweet and sheltered concealment? In a word, was there no secret aspiration of the soul for another place than what you actually occupied? Instead of resting in the quiet enjoyment of your present situation, did not your wishes wander abroad and around you—and were not you ready to exclaim with the Psalmist in the text, "O that I had the wings of a dove; for I would fly to yonder mountain, and be at rest?"

But what is of most importance to be observed is, that even when you have reached the mountain, rest is as far from you as ever. As you get nearer the wished-for spot, the fairy enchantments in which distance had arrayed it, gradually disappear; when you at last arrive at your object, the illusion is entirely dissipated; and you are grieved to find, that you have carried the same principle of restlessness and discontent along with you.

Now, what is true of a natural landscape, is also true of that *moral landscape*, which is presented to the eye of the mind when it contemplates human life, and casts a wide survey over the face of human society. The position which I myself occupy is seen and felt with all its disadvantages. Its vexations come home to my feelings with all the cer tainty of experience. I see it before mine eyes with a vision so near and intimate, as to admit of no colouring, and to preclude the exercise of fancy. It is only in those situations which are without me, where the principle of deception operates, and where the vacancies of an imperfect experience are filled up by the power of imagination, ever ready to summon the fairest forms of pure and unmingled enjoyment. It is all resolvable, as before, into the principle of distance. I am too far removed to see the smaller features of the object which I contemplate. I overlook the operation of those minuter causes, which expose every situation of human life to the inroads of misery and disappointment. Mine eye can only take in the broader outlines of the object before me, and it consigns to fancy the task of filling them up with its finest colouring.

Am I unlearned? I feel the disgrace of ignorance, and sigh for the name and the distinctions of philosophy. Do I stand upon a literary eminence? I feel the vexations of rivalship, and could almost renounce the splendours of my dear-bought reputation for the peace and shelter which insignificance bestows. Am I poor? I riot in fancy upon the gratifications of luxury, and think how great I would be, if invested with all the consequence of wealth and of patronage. Am I rich? I sicken at the deceitful splendour which surrounds me, and am at times tempted to think, that I would have been happier far, if, born to a humbler station, I had been trained to the peace and innocence of poverty. Am I immersed in business? I repine at the fatigues of employment, and envy the lot of those who have every hour at their disposal, and can spend all their time in the sweet relaxations of amusement and society. Am I exempted from the necessity of exertion? I feel the corroding anxieties of indolence, and attempt in vain to escape that weariness and disgust which useful and regular occupation can alone save me from. Am I single? I feel the dreariness of solitude, and my fancy warms at the conception of a dear and domestic circle. Am I embroiled in the cares of a family? I am tormented with the perverseness or ingratitude of those around me; and sigh in all the bitterness of repentance, over the rash and irrecoverable step by which I have renounced for ever the charms of independence.

This, in fact, is the grand principle of human ambition, and it serves to explain both its restlessness and its vanity. What is present is seen in all its minuteness, and we overlook not a single article in the train of little drawbacks, and difficulties and disappointments. What is distant is seen under a broad and general aspect, and the illusions of fancy are substituted in those places which we cannot fill up with the details of actual observation. What is present fills me with disgust. What is distant allures me to enterprise. I sigh for an office, the business of which is more congenial to my temper. I fix mine eye on some lofty eminence in the scale of preferment. I spurn at the condition which I now occupy, and I look around me and above me. The perpetual tendency is not to enjoy his actual position, but to get away from it—and not an individual amongst us who does not every day of his life join in the aspiration of the Psalmist, "O that I had the wings of a dove, that I may fly to yonder mountain, and be at rest."

But the truth is, that we never rest. The most regular and stationary being on the face of the earth, has something to look forward to, and something to aspire after. He must realize that sum to which he annexes the idea of a competency. He must add that piece of ground which he thinks necessary to complete the domain of which he is the proprietor. He must secure that office which confers so much honour and emolument upon the holder. Even after every effort of personal ambition is exhausted, he has friends and children to provide for. The care of those who are to come after him, lands him in a never-ending train of hopes, and wishes, and anxieties. O that I could gain the vote and the patronage of this honourable acquaintance—or, that I could secure the political influence of that great man who honours me with an occasional call, and addressed me the other day with a cordiality which was quite bewitching—or that my young friend could succeed in his competition for the lucrative vacancy to which I have been looking forward, for years, with all the eagerness which distance and uncertainty could inspire—or that we could fix the purposes of that capricious and unaccountable wanderer, who, of late indeed has been very particular in his attentions, and whose connection we acknowledge, in secret, would be an honour and an advantage to our family—or, at all events, let me heap wealth and aggrandizement on that son, who is to be the representative of my name, and is to perpetuate that dynasty which I have had the glory of establishing.

This restless ambition is not peculiar to any one class of society. A court only offers to one's notice a more exalted theatre for the play of rivalship and political enterprise. In the bosom of a cottage, you may witness the operation of the very same principle, only directed to objects of greater insignificance—and though a place for my girl, or an apprenticeship for my boy, be all that I aspire after, yet an enlightened observer of the human character will perceive in it the same eagerness of competition, the same jealousy, the same malicious attempts to undermine the success of a more likely pretender, the same busy train of passions and anxieties which animate the exertions of him who struggles for precedency in the cabinet, and lifts his ambitious eye to the management of an empire.

This is the universal property of our nature. In the whole circle of your experience, did you ever see a man sit down to the full enjoyment of the present, without a hope or a wish unsatisfied? Did he carry in his mind no reference to futurity—no longing of the soul after some remote or inaccessible object—no day-dream which played its enchantments around him, and which, even when accomplished, left him nothing more than the delirium of a momentary triumph? Did you never see him, after the bright illusions of novelty were over—when the present object had lost its charm, and the distant begun to practise its allurements—when some gay vision of futurity had hurried him on to a new enterprise, and in the fatigues of a restless ambition, he felt a bosom as oppressed with care, and a heart as anxious and dissatisfied as ever?

This is the true, though the curious, and I had almost said, the farcical picture of human life. Look into the heart which is the seat of feeling, and you there perceive a perpetual tendency to enjoyment, but not enjoyment itself—the cheerfulness of hope, but not the happiness of actual possession. The present is but an instant of time. The moment you call it your own, it abandons you. It is not the actual sensation which occupies the mind. It is what is to come next. Man lives in futurity. The pleasurable feeling of the moment forms almost no part of his happiness. It is not the reality of to-day which interests his heart. It is the vision of to-morrow. It is the distant object on which fancy has thrown its deceitful splendour. When to-morrow comes, the animating hope is transformed into the dull and insipid reality. As the distant object draws near, it becomes cold and tasteless, and uninteresting. The only way in which the mind can support itself, is by recurring to some new anticipation. This may give buoyancy for a time—but it will share the fate of all its predecessors, and be the addition of another folly to the wretched train of disappointments that have gone before it.

What a curious object of contemplation to a superior being, who casts an eye over this lower world, and surveys the busy, restless, and unceasing operations of the people who swarm upon its surface. Let him select any one individual amongst us, and confine his attention to him as a specimen of the whole. Let him pursue him through the intricate variety of his movements, for he is never stationary; see him with his eye fixed upon some distant object, and struggling to arrive at it; see him pressing forward to some eminence which perpetually recedes away from him; see the inexplicable being, as he runs in full pursuit of some glittering bauble, and on the moment he reaches it, throws it behind him, and it is forgotten; see him unmindful of his past experience, and hurrying his footsteps to some new object with the same eagerness and rapidity as ever; compare the ecstacy of hope with the lifelessness of possession, and observe the whole history of his day to be made up of one fatiguing race of vanity, and restlessness, and disappointment;

"And, like the glittering of an idiot's toy,
Doth Fancy mock his vows."

To complete the unaccountable history, let us look to its termination. Man is irregular in his movements, but this does not hinder the regularity of Nature. Time will not stand still to look at us. It moves at its own invariable pace. The winged moments fly in swift succession over us. The great luminaries which are suspended on high, perform their cycles in the heaven. The sun describes his circuit in the firmament, and the space of a few revolutions will bring every man among us to his destiny. The decree passes abroad against the poor child of infatuation. It meets him in the full career of hope and of enterprise. He sees the dark curtain of mortality falling upon the world, and upon all its interests. That busy, restless heart, so crowded with its plans, and feelings, and anticipations, forgets to play, and all its fluttering anxieties are hushed for ever.

Where, then, is that resting-place which the Psalmist aspired after? What are we to mean by that mountain, that wilderness, to which he prayed that the wings of a dove may convey him, afar from the noise and distractions of the world, and hasten his escape from the windy storm, and the tempest? Is there no object, in the whole round of human enjoyment, which can give rest to the agitated spirit of man? Will he not sit down in the fulness of contentment, after he has reached it, and bid a final adieu to the cares and fatigues of ambition? Is this longing of the mind a principle of his nature, which no gratification can extinguish? Must it condemn him to perpetual agitation, and to the wild impulses of an ambition which is never satisfied?

We allow that exercise is the health of the mind. It is better to engage in a trifling pursuit, if innocent, than to watch the melancholy progress of time, and drag out a weary existence in all the languor of a consuming indolence. But nobody will deny that it is better still, if the pursuit in which we are engaged be not a trifling one—if it conducts to some lasting gratification—if it leads to some object, the possession of which confers more happiness than the mere prospect—if the mere pleasure of the chase is not the only recompense—but where, in addition to this, we secure some reward proportioned to the fatigue of the exercise, and that justifies the eagerness with which we embarked in it. So long as the exercise is innocent, better do something than be idle: but better still, when the something we do, leads to a valuable and important termination. Any thing rather than the ignoble condition of that mind which feels the burden of itself—and which knows not how to dispose of the weary hours that hang so oppressively upon it. But there is certainly a ground of preference in the objects which invite us to exertion—and better far to fix upon that object which leaves happiness and satisfaction behind it, than dissipate your vigour in a pursuit which terminates in nothing—and where the mere pleasure of occupation is the only circumstance to recommend it. When we talk of the vanity of ambition, we do not propose to extinguish the principles of our nature, but to give them a more useful and exalted direction. A state of hope and of activity is the element of man—and all that we propose, is to withdraw his hopes from the deceitful objects of fancy, and to engage his activity in the pursuit of real and permanent enjoyments.

Man must have an object to look forward to. Without this incitement the mind languishes. It is thrown out of its element, and, in this unnatural suspension of its powers, it feels a dreariness, and a discomfort, far more unsufferable than it ever experienced from the visitations of a real or positive calamity. If such an object does not offer, he will create one for himself. The mere possession of wealth, and of all its enjoyments, will not satisfy him. Possession carries along with it the dulness of certainty, and to escape from this dulness, he will transform it into an uncertainty—he will embark it in a hazardous speculation, or he will stake it at the gaming-table; and from no other principle than that he may exchange the lifelessness of possession, for the animating sensations of hope and of enterprise. It is a paradox in the moral constitution of man; but the experience of every day confirms it—that man follows what he knows to be a delusion, with as much eagerness, as if he were assured of its reality. Put the question to him, and he will tell you, that if you were to lay before him all the profits which his fancy anticipates, he would long as much as ever for some new speculation; or, in other words, be as much dissatisfied as ever with the position which he actually occupies—and yet, with his eye perfectly open to this circumstance, will he embark every power of his mind in the chase of what he knows to be a mockery and a phantom.

Now, to find fault with man for the pleasure which he derives from the mere excitement of a distant object, would be to find fault with the constitution of his nature. It is not the general principle of his activity which I condemn. It is the direction of that activity to a useless and unprofitable object. The mere happiness of the pursuit does not supersede the choice of the object. Even though you were to keep religion out of sight altogether, and bring the conduct of man to the test of worldly principles, you still presuppose a ground of preference in the object. Why is the part of the sober and industrious tradesman preferred to that of the dissipated gambler? Both feel the delights of a mind fully occupied with something to excite and to animate. But the exertions of the one lead to the safe enjoyment of a competency. The exertions of the other lead to an object which, at best, is precarious, and often land you in the horrors of poverty and disgrace. The mere pleasure of exertion is not enough,to justify every kind of it: you must look forward to the object and the termination—and it is the judicious choice of the object which, even in the estimation of worldly wisdom, forms the great point of distinction betwixt prudence and folly. Now, all that I ask of you, is to extend the application of the same principle to a life of religion. Compare the wisdom of the children of light, with the wisdom of a blind and worldly generation; the prudence of the Christian who labours for immortality, with the prudence of him who labours for the objects of a vain and perishable ambition. Contrast the littleness of time, with the greatness of eternity—the restless and unsatisfying pleasures of the world, with the enjoyments of heaven, so pure, so substantial, so unfading—and tell me which plays the higher game—he, all whose anxiety is frittered away on the pursuits of a scene that is ever shifting, and ever transitory; or he, who contemplates the life of man in all its magnitude; who acts upon the wide and comprehensive survey of its interests, and takes into his estimate the mighty roll of innumerable ages.

There is no resting-place to be found on this side of time. It is the doctrine of the Bible, and all experience loudly proclaims it. I do not ask you to listen to the complaints of the poor, or the murmurs of the disappointed. Take your lesson from the veriest favourite of fortune. See him placed in a prouder eminence than he ever aspired after. See him arrayed in brighter colours than ever dazzled his early imagination. See him surrounded with all the homage that fame and flattery can bestow—and after you have suffered this parading exterior to practise its deceitfulness upon you, enter into his solitude—mark his busy, restless, dissatisfied eye, as it wanders uncertain on every object—enter into his mind, and tell me if repose or enjoyment be there; see him the poor victim of chagrin and disquietude—mark his heart as it nauseates the splendour which encompasses him—and tell me, if you have not learned, in the truest and most affecting characters, that even in the full tide of a triumphant ambition, "man labours for the meat which perisheth, and for the food which satisfieth not."

What meaneth this restlessness of our nature? What meaneth this unceasing activity which longs for exercise and employment, even after every object is gained, which first roused it to enterprise? What mean those unmeasurable longings, which no gratification can extinguish, and which still continue to agitate the heart of man, even in the fulness of plenty and of enjoyment. If they mean any thing at all, they mean, that all which this world can offer, is not enough to fill up his capacity for happiness—that time is too small for him, and he is born for something beyond it—that the scene of his earthly existence is too limited, and he is formed to expatiate in a wider and a grander theatre—that a nobler destiny is reserved for him—and that to accomplish the purpose of his being, he must soar above the littleness of the world, and aim at a loftier prize.

It forms the peculiar honour and excellence of religion, that it accommodates to this property of our nature—that it holds out a prize suited to our high calling—that there is a grandeur in its objects, which can fill and surpass the imagination—that it dignifies the present scene by connecting it with eternity—that it reveals to the eye of faith the glories of an unperishable world—and how, from the high eminences of heaven, a cloud of witnesses are looking down upon earth, not as a scene for the petty anxieties of time, but as a splendid theatre for the ambition of immortal spirits.

SERMON V.

The transitory Nature of visible Things.

"The things that are seen are temporal."—2 *Corinthians* iv. 18.

THE assertion that the things which are seen are temporal, holds true in the absolute and universal sense of it. They had a beginning, and they will have an end. Should we go upwards through the stream of ages that are past, we come to a time when they were not. Should we go onward through the stream of ages that are before us, we come to a time when they will be no more. It is indeed a most mysterious flight which the imagination ventures upon, when it goes back to the eternity that is behind us—when it mounts its ascending way through the millions and the millions of years that are already gone through, and stop where it may, it finds the line of its march always lengthening beyond it, and losing itself in the obscurity of as far removed a distance as ever. It soon reaches the commencement of visible things, or that point of its progress when God made the heavens and the earth. They had a beginning, but God had none; and what a wonderful field for the fancy to expatiate on, when we get above the era of created worlds, and think of that period when, in respect of all that is visible, the immensity around us was one vast and unpeopled solitude. But God was there in his dwelling-place, for it is said of him that he inhabits eternity; and the Son of God was there, for we read of the glory which he had with the Father before the world was. The mind cannot sustain itself under the burden of these lofty contemplations. It cannot lift the curtain which shrouds the past eternity of God. But it is good for the soul to be humbled under a sense of its incapacity. It is good to realize the impression which too often abandons us, that he made us, and not we ourselves. It is good to feel how all that is temporal lies in passive and prostrate subordination before the will of the uncreated God. It is good to know how little a portion it is that we see of him and of his mysterious ways. It is good to lie at the feet of his awful and unknown majesty—and while secret things belong to him, it is good to bring with us all the helplessness and docility of children to those revealed lessons which belong to us and to our children.

But this is not the sense in which the temporal nature of visible things is taken up by the Apostle. It is not that there is a time past in which they did not exist—but there is a time to come in which they will exist no more. He calls them temporal, because the time and the duration of their existence will have an end. His eye is full upon futurity. It is the passing away of visible things in the time that is to come, and the ever during nature of invisible things through the eternity that is to come, which the Apostle is contemplating. Now, on this one point we say nothing about the positive annihilation of the matter of visible things. There is reason for believing, that some of the matter of our present bodies may exist in those more glorified and transformed bodies which we are afterwards to occupy. And for any thing we know, the matter of the present world, and of the present system may exist in those new heavens and that new earth, wherein dwelleth righteousness. There may be a transfiguration of matter without a destruction of it—and, therefore it is, that when we assert with the Apostle in the text, how things seen are temporal, we shall not say more than that the substance of these things, if not consigned back again to the nothing from which they had emerged, will be employed in the formation of other things totally different—that the change will be so great, as that all old things may be said to have passed away, and all things to become new —that after the wreck of the last conflagration, the desolated scene will be re-peopled with other objects; the righteous will live in another world, and the eye of the glorified body will open on another field of contemplation from that which is now visible around us.

Now, in this sense of the word temporal, the assertion of my text may be carried round to all that is visible. Even those objects which men are most apt to count upon as unperishable, because, without any sensible decay, they have stood the lapse of many ages, will not weather the lapse of eternity. This earth will be burnt up. The light of yonder sun will be extinguished. These stars will cease from their twinkling. The heavens will pass away as a scroll—and as to those solid and enormous masses which, like the firm world we tread upon, roll in mighty circuit through the immensity around us, it seems the solemn language of revelation of one and all of them, that from the face of him who sitteth on the throne, the earth and the heavens will fly away, and there will be found no place for them.

Even apart from the Bible, the eye of observation can witness, in some of the hardest and firmest materials of the present system, the evidence of its approaching dissolution. What more striking, for example, than the natural changes which take place on the surface of the world, and which prove that the strongest of Nature's elements must, at last, yield to the operation of time and of decay—that yonder towering mountain, though propped by the rocky battlements which surround it, must at last sink under the power of corruption—that every year brings it nearer to its end—that at this moment, it is wasting silently away, and letting itself down from the lofty eminence which it now occupies—that the torrent which falls from its side never ceases to consume its substance, and to carry it off in the form of sediment to the ocean— that the frost which assails it in the winter loosens the solid rock, detaches it in pieces from the main precipice, and makes it fall in fragments to its base—that the power of the weather scales off the most flinty materials, and that the wind of heaven scatters them in dust over the surrounding country—that even though not anticipated by the sudden and awful convulsions of the day of God's wrath, nature contains within itself the rudiments of decay—that every hill must be levelled with the plains, and every plain be swept away by the constant operation of the rivers which run through it—and that, unless renewed by the hand of the Almighty, the earth on which we are now treading must disappear in the mighty roll of ages and of centuries. We cannot take our flight to other worlds, or have a near view of the changes to which they are liable. But surely if this world which, with its mighty apparatus of continents and islands, looks so healthful and so firm after the wear of many centuries, is posting visibly to its end, we may be prepared to believe that the principles of destruction are also at work in other provinces of the visible creation—and that though of old God laid the foundation of the earth, and the heavens are the work of his hands, yet they shall perish; yea, all of them shall wax old like a garment, and as a vesture shall he change them, and they shall be changed.

We should be out of place in all this style of observation, did we not follow it up with the sentiment of the Psalmist, "These shall perish, but thou shalt endure; for thou art the same, and thy years have no end." What a lofty conception does it give us of the majesty of God, when we think how he sits above, and presides in high authority over this mighty series of changes—when after sinking under our attempts to trace him through the eternity that is behind, we look on the present system of things, and are taught to believe that it is but a single step in the march of his grand administrations through the eternity that is before us —when we think of this goodly universe, summoned into being to serve some temporary evolution of his great and mysterious plan—when we think of the time when it shall be broken up, and out of its disordered fragments other scenes and other systems shall emerge—surely, when fatigued with the vastness of these contemplations, it well becomes us to do the homage of our reverence and wonder to the one Spirit which conceives and animates the whole, and to the one noble design which runs through all its fluctuations.

But there is another way in which the objects that are seen are temporal. The object may not merely be removed from us, but we may be removed from the object. The disappearance of this earth, and of these heavens from us, we look upon through the dimness of a far-placed futurity. It is an event, therefore, which may regale our imagination; which may lift our mind by its sublimity; which may disengage us in the calm hour of meditation from the littleness of life, and of its cares; and which may even throw a clearness and a solemnity over our intercourse with God. But such an event as this does not come home upon our hearts with the urgency of a personal interest. It does not carry along with it the excitement which lies in the nearness of an immediate concern. It does not fall with such vivacity upon our conceptions, as practically to tell on our pursuits, or any of our purposes. It may elevate and solemnize us, but this effect is perfectly consistent with its having as little influence on the walk of the living, and the moving and the acting man, as a dream of poetry. The preacher may think that he has done great things with his eloquence—and the hearers may think that great things have been done upon them—for they felt a fine glow of emotion, when they heard of God sitting in the majesty of his high counsels, over the progress and the destiny of created things. But the truth is, my brethren, that all this kindling of devotion which is felt upon the contemplation of his greatness, may exist in the same bosom. with an utter distaste for the holiness of his character; with an entire alienation of the heart and of the habits from the obedience of his law; and above all, with a most nauseous and invincible contempt for the spiritualities of that revelation, in which he has actually made known his will and his way to us. The devotion of mere taste is one thing—the devotion of principle is another. And as surely as a man may weep over the elegant sufferings of poetry, yet add to the real sufferings of life by peevishness in his family, and insolence among his neighbours—so surely may a man be wakened to rapture by the magnificence of God, while his life is deformed by its rebellions, and his heart rankles with all the foulness of idolatry against him.

Well, then, let us try the other way of bringing the temporal nature of visible things to bear upon your interests. It is true, that this earth and these heavens, will at length disappear; but they may outlive our posterity for many generations. However, if they disappear not from us, we most certainly shall disappear from them. They will soon cease to be any thing to you—and though the splendour and variety of all that is visible around us, should last for thousands of centuries, your eyes will soon be closed upon them. The time is coming when this goodly scene shall reach its positive consummation. But, in all likelihood, the time is coming much sooner, when you shall resign the breath of your nostrils, and bid a final adieu to every thing around you. Let this earth, and these heavens be as enduring as they may, to you they are fugitive as vanity. Time, with its mighty strides, will soon reach a future generation, and leave the present in death and in forgetfulness behind it. The grave will close upon every one of you, and that is the dark and the silent cavern where no voice is heard, and the light of the sun never enters.

But more than this. Though we live too short a time to see the great changes which are carrying on in the universe, we live long enough to see many of its changes—and such changes too as are best fitted to warn and to teach us; even the changes which take place in society, made up of human beings as frail and as fugitive as ourselves. Death moves us away from many of those objects which are seen and temporal—but we live long enough to see many of these objects moved away from us —to see acquaintances falling every year—to see families broken up by the rough and unsparing hand of death—to see houses and neighbourhoods shifting their inhabitants—to see a new race, and a new generation—and, whether in church or in market, to see unceasing changes in the faces of the people who repair to them. We know well, that there is a poetic melancholy inspired by such a picture as this, which is altogether unfruitful—and that, totally apart from religion, a man may give way to the luxury of tears, when he thinks how friends drop away from him—how every year brings along with it some sad addition to the registers of death— how the kind and hospitable mansion is left without a tenant—and how, when you knock at a neighbour's door, you find that he who welcomed you, and made you happy, is no longer there. O that we could impress by all this, a salutary direction on the fears and on the consciences of individuals—that we could give them a living impression of that coming day, when they shall severally share in the general wreck of the species—when each of you shall be one of the many whom the men of the next generation may remember to have lived in yonder street, or laboured in yonder manufactory---when they shall speak of you, just as you speak of the men of the former generation--who, when they died, had a few tears dropped over their memory, and for a few years will still continue to be talked of. O, could we succeed in giving you a real and living impression of all this; and then may we hope to carry the esson of John the Baptist with energy to your fears, "Flee from the coming wrath." But there is something so very deceiving in the progress of time. Its progress is so gradual. To-day is so like yesterday that we are not sensible of its departure. We should make head against this delusion. We should turn to personal account every example of change or of mortality. When the clock strikes, it should remind you of the dying hour. When you hear the sound of the funeral bell, you should think, that in a little time it will perform for you the same office. When you wake in the morning, you should think that there has been the addition of another day to the life that is past, and the subtraction of another day from the remainder of your journey. When the shades of the evening fall around you, you should think of the steady and invariable progress of time—how the sun moves and moves till it will see you out—and how it will continue to move after you die, and see out your children's children to the latest generations.

Every thing around us should impress the mutability of human affairs. An acquaintance dies—you will soon follow him. A family moves from the neighbourhood—learn that the works of man are given to change. New familes succeed—sit loose to the world, and withdraw your affections from its unstable and fluctuating interests. Time is rapid, though we observe not its rapidity. The days that are past appear like the twinkling of a vision. The days that are to come will soon have a period, and will appear to have performed their course with equal rapidity. We talk of our fathers and grandfathers, who figured their day in the theatre of the world. In a little time, we will be the ancestors of a future age. Posterity will talk of us as of the men that are gone, and our remembrance will soon depart from the face of the country. When we attend the burial of an acquaintance, we see the bones of the men of other times—in a few years, our bodies will be mangled by the power of corruption, and be thrown up in loose and scattered fragments among the earth of the new made grave. When we wander among the tombstones of the church-yard, we can scarcely follow the mutilated letters that compose the simple story of the inhabitant below. In a little time, and the tomb that covers us, will moulder by the power of the seasons—and the letters will be eaten away—and the story that was to perpetuate our remembrance, will elude the gaze of some future inquirer.

We know that time is short, but none of us know how short. We know that it will not go beyond a certain limit of years; but none of us know how small the number of years, or months, or days may be. For death is at work upon all ages. The fever of a few days may hurry the likeliest of us all from this land of mortality. The cold of a few weeks may settle into some lingering but irrecoverable disease. In one instant the blood of him who has the promise of many years, may cease its circulation. Accident may assail us. A slight fall may precipitate us into eternity. An exposure to rain may lay us on the bed of our last sickness, from which we are never more to rise. A little spark may kindle the midnight conflagration, which lays a house and its inhabitants in ashes. A stroke of lightning may arrest the current of life in a twinkling. A gust of wind may overturn the vessel, and lay the unwary passenger in a watery grave. A thousand dangers beset us on the slippery path of this world; and no age is exempted from them—and from the infant that hangs on its mother's bosom, to the old man who sinks under the decrepitude of years, we see death in all its woful and affecting varieties.

You may think it strange—but even still we fear, we may have done little in the way of sending a fruitful impression into your consciences. We are too well aware of the distinction between seriousness of feeling, and seriousness of principle, to think that upon the strength of any such moving representation as we are now indulging in, we shall be able to dissipate that confounded spell which chains you to the world, to reclaim your wandering affections, or to send you back to your weekday business more pure and more heavenly. But sure we are you ought to be convinced, how that all which binds you so cleavingly to the dust is infatuation and vanity; that there is something most lamentably wrong in your being carried away by the delusions of time—and this is a conviction which should make you feel restless and dissatisfied. We are well aware that it is not human eloquence, or human illustration, that can accomplish a victory over the obstinate principles of human corruption—and therefore it is that we feel as if we did not advance aright through a single step of a sermon, unless we look for the influences of that mighty Spirit, who alone is able to enlighten and arrest you—and may employ even so humble an instrument as the voice of a fellow mortal, to send into your heart the inspiration of understanding.

I now shortly insist on the truth, that the things which are not seen are eternal. No man hath seen God at any time, and he is eternal. It is said of Christ, "whom having not seen, we love, and he is the same to-day, yesterday, and for ever." It is said of the Spirit, that, like the wind of heaven he eludes the observation, and no man can tell of him whence he cometh, or whither he goeth—and he is called the Eternal Spirit, through whom the Son offered himself up without spot unto God. We are quite aware, that the idea suggested by the eternal things which are spoken of in our text, is heaven, with all its circumstances of splendour and enjoyment. This is an object which, even on the principles of taste, we take a delight in contemplating; and it is also an object set before us in the Scriptures, though with a very sparing and reserved hand. All the descriptions we have of heaven there, are general, very general. We read of the beauty of the heavenly crown, of the unfading nature of the heavenly inheritance, of the splendour of the heavenly city—and these have been seized upon by men of imagination, who, in the construction of their fancied paradise, have embellished it with every image of peace, and bliss, and loveliness; and, at all events, have thrown over it that most kindling of all conceptions, the magnificence of eternity. Now, such a picture as this has the certain effect of ministering delight to every glowing and susceptible imagination. And here lies the deep-laid delusion, which we have occasionally hinted at. A man listens, in the first instance, to a pathetic and high-wrought narrative on the vanities of time—and it touches him even to the tenderness of tears. He looks, in the second instance, to the fascinating perspective of another scene, rising in all the glories of immortality from the dark ruins of the tomb, and he feels within him all those ravishments of fancy, which any vision of united grandeur and loveliness would inspire. Take these two together, and you have a man weeping over the transient vanities of an ever-shifting world, and mixing with all this softness, an elevation of thought and of prospect, as he looks through the vista of a futurity, losing itself in the mighty range of thousands and thousands of centuries. And at this point the delusion comes in, that here is a man who is all that religion would have him to be—a man weaned from the littleness of the paltry scene that is around him—soaring high above all the evanescence of things present, and things sensible—and transferring every affection of his soul to the durabilities of a pure and immortal region. It were better if this high state of occasional impressment on the matters of time and of eternity, had only the effect of imposing the falsehood on others, that man who was so touched and so transported, had on that single account the temper of a candidate for heaven. But the falsehood takes possession of his own heart. The man is pleased with his emotions and his tears—and the interpretation he puts upon them is, that they come out of the fullness of a heart all alive to religion, and sensibly affected with its charms, and its seriousness, and its principle. Now, my brethren, I will venture to say, that there may be a world of all this kind of enthusiasm, with the very man who is not moving a single step towards that blessed eternity, over which his fancy delights to expatiate. The moving representation of the preacher may be listened to as a pleasant song—and the entertained hearer return to all the inveterate habits of one of the children of this world. It is this, my brethren, which makes me fear that a power of deceitfulness may accompany the eloquence of the pulpit—that the wisdom of words may defeat the great object of a practical work upon the conscience—that a something short of a real business change in the heart, and in the principles of acting, may satisfy the man who listens, and admires, and resigns his every feeling to the magic of an impressive description—that, strangely compounded beings as we are, broken loose from God, and proving it by the habitual voidness of our hearts to a sense of his authority, and of his will; that, blind to the realities of another world, and slaves to the wretched infatuation which makes us cleave with the full bent of our affections to the one by which we are visibly and immediately surrounded; that utterly unable, by nature, to live above the present scene, while its cares, and its interests are plying us every hour with their urgency; that the prey of evil passions which darken and distract the inner man, and throw us at a wider distance from the holy Being who forbids the indulgence of them; and yet with all this weight of corruption about us, having minds that can seize the vastness of some great conception, and can therefore rejoice in the expanding loftiness of its own thoughts, as it dwells on the wonders of eternity; and having hearts that can move to the impulse of a tender consideration, and can, therefore, sadden into melancholy at the dark picture of death, and its unrelenting cruelties; and having fancies that can brighten to the cheerful colouring of some pleasing and hopeful representation, and can, therefore, be soothed and animated when some sketch is laid before it of a pious family emerging from a common sepulchre, and on the morning of their joyful resurrection, forgetting all the sorrows and separations of the dark world that has now rolled over them—O, my brethren, we fear, we greatly fear it, that while busied with topics such as these, many a hearer may weep, or be elevated, or take pleasure in the touching imagery that is made to play around him, while the dust of this perishable earth is all that his soul cleaves to; and its cheating vanities are all that his heart cares for, or his footsteps follow after.

The thing is not merely possible—but we see in it a stamp of likelihood to all that experience tells us of the nature or the habitudes of man. Is there no such thing as his having a taste for the beauties of landscape, and, at the same time, turning with disgust from what he calls the methodism of peculiar Christianity? Might not he be an admirer of poetry, and at the same time, nauseate with his whole heart, the doctrine and the language of the New Testament? Might not he have a fancy that can be regaled by some fair and well-formed vision of immortality—and, at the same time, have no practical hardihood whatever for the exercise of labouring in the prescribed way after the meat that endureth? Surely, surely, this is all very possible—and it is just as possible, and many we believe to be the instances we have of it in real life, when an eloquent description of heaven is exquisitely felt, and wakens in the bosom the raptures of the sincerest admiration, among those who feel an utter repugnancy to the heaven of the Bible—and are not moving a single inch through the narrowness of the path which leads to it.

SERMON VI.

On the Universality of spiritual Blindness.

"Stay yourselves, and wonder; cry ye out, and cry: they are drunken, but not with wine; they stagger, but not with strong drink. For the Lord hath poured out upon you the spirit of deep sleep, and hath closed your eyes: the prophets and your rulers, the seers hath he covered. And the vision of all is become unto you as the words of a book that is sealed, which men deliver to one that is learned, saying, Read this, I pray thee: and he saith, I cannot; for it is sealed. And the book is delivered to him that is not learned, saying, Read this, I pray thee: and he saith, I am not learned."—*Isaiah* xxix. 9—12.

WHAT is affirmed in these verses of a vision and prophecy, holds so strikingly true of God's general revelation to the world, that we deem the lesson contained in them to be not of partial, but permanent application—and we therefore proceed immediately, to the task of addressing this lesson, both to the learned and unlearned of the present day.

Let me, in the first place, dwell for a little on the complaints which are uttered by these two classes respecting the hidden and impenetrable character of the book of God's communication—and, in the second place, try to explain the nature of that sleep which is upon both, and in virtue of which both are alike in a state of practical blindness to the realities of the divine word—and, in the third place, raise a short application upon the whole argument.

I. There is a complaint uttered in these verses, first by the learned—and, secondly, by the unlearned—and we shall consider each of them in order.

1st. If a book be closed down by a material seal, then, till that seal be broken, there lies a material obstacle even in the way of him who is able to read the contents of it. And we have no doubt, that the possession of the art of reading would form the most visible and prominent distinction, between the learned and the unlearned in the days of Isaiah. But it no longer, at least in our country, forms the distinction between these two classes. Many a man who can barely read in these days, will still say, and say with truth, that he is not learned. We must now therefore strike a higher mark of distinction—and, in reference to the Bible, such a mark can be specified. This book is often made the subject of a much higher exercise of scholarship than the mere reading of it. It may be read in its original languages. It may be the theme of many a laborious commentary. The light of contemporary history may be made to shine upon it, by the diligence of an exploring antiquarian. Those powers and habits of criticism, which are of so much avail towards the successful elucidation of the mind and meaning of other authors, may all be transferred to that volume of which God is the author—and what, after all this, it may be asked, is the seal or the obstacle which stands in the way of learned men of our present generation? How is it that any of them can now join in the complaint of their predecessors, in the days of Isaiah—and say, I cannot read this book because it is sealed? Or, is there any remaining hindrance still, in virtue of which, the critics, and the grammarians, and the accomplished theologians of our age, are unable to reach the real and effective understanding of the words of this prophecy?

Yes, my brethren, there is such an obstruction as you now inquire after—and it is wonderful to tell, how little the mere erudition of Scripture helps the real discernment of Scripture—how it may be said, of many of its most classical expounders, that though having eyes, they see not, and though having ears, they hear not—how doctrine, which if actually perceived and credited, would bring the realities of an eternal world to bear with effect upon their conduct, is, operatively speaking, just as weak as if they did not apprehend it even in its literal significancy—how the mere verbiage of the matter is all in which they appear to be conversant, without any actual hold of sight, or of conviction, on the substance of the matter—how dexterously they can play at logic with the terms of the communication, and how dimly and deficiently they apprehend the truths of it—how, after having exhausted the uttermost resources of scholarship on the attempt of forcing an entrance into the region of spiritual manifestation, they only find themselves labouring at a threshold of height and of difficulty, which they cannot scale—how, as if struck with blindness, like the men of Sodom, they weary themselves in vain to find the door—and after having reared their stately argumentation about the message of peace, they have no faith; about the doctrine of godliness, they have no godliness.

And it is not enough to say, that all this is not due to the want of discernment, but to the want of power—for the power lies in the truth—and the truth has only to be seen or believed, that it may have the power. The reflection may never have occurred to you—but it is not the less just on that account, how little of actual faith there is in the world. Many call it a mere want of impression. We call it a want of belief. Did we really believe, that there was a God in existence—did we really believe, that with the eye of a deeply interested judge, he was now scrutinizing all the propensities of our heart, and appreciating, with a view to future retribution, all the actions of our history—did we really believe, that sin was to him that hateful enemy with which he could keep no terms, and to which he could give no quarter; and that with every individual who had fallen into it, either in its guilt it must be expiated, and in its presence be finally done away, or the burden of a righteous vengeance would rest upon his person through eternity—did we really believe, that in these circumstances of deepest urgency, a way of redemption has been devised, and that to all whom the tidings of it had reached the offer of deliverance, both from sin in its condemnation, and from sin in its power, was made, through the atoning blood and sanctifying spirit of a complete and omnipotent Saviour—did we really believe, that such an offer was lying at the door of every individual, and that his reliance upon its honesty constituted his acceptance of the offer—did we really believe, that throughout the fugitive period of our abode in this world, which was so soon to pass away, God in Christ was beseeching every one of us to reconciliation; and even now, as if at the place of breaking forth, was ready to begin that great renewing process whereby there is made a commencement of holiness upon earth, and a consummation both of holiness and happiness in heaven—were these, which we all know to be the truths of Christianity, actually believed, the power of them upon our hearts would come, and come immediately, in the train of the perception of them by our understandings. If we remain unquickened by the utterance of them, it is because, in the true sense of the term, we remain unconvinced by them. The utterance of them may be heard as a very pleasant song—and the representation of them be viewed as a very lovely picture—but the force of a felt and present reality is wanting to the whole demonstration. And all that reason can do is to adjust the steps of the demonstration—and all that eloquence can do, is to pour forth the utterance—and all that conception can do is to furnish its forms and its colouring to the picture. And after learning has thus lavished on the task the whole copiousness of its manifold ingredients, may we behold in the person of its proudest votary, that his Christianity to him is nothing better than an aerial phantom—that it is of as little operation in disposting sense, and nature, and ungodliness from his heart, as if it were but a nonentity, or a name—that to his eye a visionary dimness hangs over the whole subject matter of the testimony of the Bible—and still untranslated into the life, and the substance, and the reality of these things, he may join in the complaint of the text, as if they lay sealed in deepest obscurity from his contemplation.

Make what you like in the way of argument, of so many simple conceptions, if the conceptions themselves do not carry the impress of vividness and reality along with them—the reasoning, of which they form the materials, may be altogether faultless—and the doctrine in which it terminates, be held forth as altogether impregnable—yet will it share in all the obscurity which attaches to the primary elements of its formation—and while nature can manage the logical process which leads from the first simple ideas, to the ultimate and made-out conclusion, she cannot rid herself of the dimness in which, to her unrenewed eye, the former stand invested; and she must, therefore, leave the latter in equal dimness.

The learned just labour as helplessly under a want of an impression of the reality of this whole matter, as the unlearned—and if this be true of those among them, who, with learning and nothing more, have actually tried to decipher the meaning of God's communication—if this be true of many a priest and many a theologian, with whom Christianity is a science, and the study of the Bible is the labour and the business of their profession—what can we expect of those among the learned, who, in the pursuits of a secular philosophy, never enter into contact with the Bible, either in its doctrine or in its language, except when it is obtruded on them? Little do they know of our men of general literature, who have not observed the utter listlessness, if not the strong and active contempt wherewith many of them hear the doctrine of the book of God's counsel uttered in the phraseology of that book—how, in truth, their secret impression of the whole matter is, that it is a piece of impenetrable mysticism—how, in their eyes, there is a cast of obscurity over all the peculiarities of the Gospel—and if asked to give their attention thereto, they promptly repel the imposition under the feeling of a hopeless and insuperable darkness, which sits in obsolete characters over the entire face of the evangelical record. There may be bright and cheering examples to the contrary, of men in the highest of our literary walks, who, under a peculiar teaching, have learned what they never learned from all the lessons of the academy. But apart from this peculiar influence, be assured that learning is of little avail. The sacred page may wear as hieroglyphical an aspect to the lettered, as to the unlettered. It lies not with any of the powers or processes of ordinary education to dissipate that blindness, wherewith the god of this world hath blinded the mind of him who believes not. To make the wisdom of the New Testament his wisdom, and its spirit his spirit, and its language his best-loved and best-understood language, there must be a higher influence upon the mind, than what lies in human art, or in human explanation. And till this is brought to pass, the doctrine of the atonement, and the doctrine of regeneration, and the doctrine of fellowship with the Father and the Son, and the doctrine of a believer's progressive holiness, under the moral and spiritual power of the truth as it is in Jesus, will, as to his own personal experience of its meaning, remain so many empty sounds, or so many deep and hidden mysteries—and just as effectually, as if the book were held together by an iron clasp, which he has not strength to unclose, may he say of the same book lying open and legible before him, that he cannot read it, because it is sealed.

2. So much for the complaint of the learned; and as for the complaint of the unlearned, it happily, in the literal sense of it, is not applicable to the great majority of our immediate countrymen, even in the very humblest walks of society. They can put together its letters, and pronounce its words, and make a daily exercise, if they choose, of one or more of its chapters. They have learning enough to carry them thus far, but not so far as to keep them from joining the unlearned of my text in the complaint that I am not learned. They cannot, for example, estimate the criticism of many an expounder. They have not time to traverse the weary extent of many a ponderous and elaborate commentary. And those who have had much of Christian intercourse with the poor, must have remarked the effect which their sense of this inferiority has upon many an imagination —how it is felt by not a few of them, that they labour under a hopeless disadvantage, because they want the opportunities of a higher and a more artificial scholarship, and that if they could only get nearer to their teachers in respect of literary attainment, they would be nearer that wisdom which is unto salvation, and that though they can read the book in the plainest sense of the term, they cannot read it with any saving or salutary effect, just because, in the language of my text, they say that they are not learned. And thus it is, that the man who has the literary accomplishments after which they sigh, meets with two distinct exhibitions to instruct and to humble him. The first is, when the poor look up to him as to one who, because he has the scholarship of Christianity, must have the saving knowledge of it also, when he intimately feels that the luminary of science may shine full upon him, while not one ray to cheer or to enlighten, may pass into his heart from the luminary of the Gospel. The second is, when he observes among the poor, those who live, and who rejoice under the power of a revelation, to which himself is a stranger, those who can discern a beauty and an evidence in the doctrine of Christ, which have never beamed with full radiance upon his own understanding—those whose feelings and whose experience move in a consonancy with the truths of the New Testament, which, in his own experience, he never felt—those whose daily path bespeaks the guidance of a wisdom which never yet shone upon his own way, and who are blest with a peace and a joy in believing, which have never found entrance into his own desolate bosom.

This gives us a new sight of the peculiarity which lies in the Bible—and by which it stands distinguished from all other compositions. There may remain a seal upon its meaning to him, who, in the ordinary sense of the term, is learned, while the seal may be removed, and the meaning lie open as the light of day to him, who in the same sense is unlearned. It may come with all the force of a felt and perceived reality upon the one, while the reality is not perceived, and therefore not felt by the other. To the man of literary accomplishment, the report of eternal things may reach no other influence than that of a sound upon his ear, or of a shadowy representation upon the eye of his fancy. To the unlettered workman, it may reach an influence as substantial and as practical, as the report of to-morrow's work, or to-morrow's wages. The latter may be led to shape his actual measures by the terms of the message of revelation. The former may lavish all the powers of science, and subtlety, and speculation upon the terms—and yet be as untouched in his personal habits by all the information which it lays before him, as if the message were untrue. It is not learning that has made the difference; for the veil may be upon the eyes of him who is rich in this acquirement, while it is taken away from him who, in respect of scholarship, is poor, and blind, and destitute. There is not a single weapon in the whole armoury of human learning, by which the proudest of its votaries can force his entrance into a region of spiritual manifestation. The wise and prudent cannot, on the strength of any of their own peculiar resources, they cannot, with all their putting forth of desire and energy, attain unto those things which are revealed unto babes. There is a barrier here against which all the machinery of the schools may be made to play without effect. And it would look as if argument might as soon remove the film from the eye of him who labours under a natural blindness, as dissipate that thick and impalpable obscurity which lies in the way of all spiritual discernment.

There are two immediate uses to which all this may be rendered subservient. The first, to rebuke the poor for an apology which they are sometimes heard to make, when convicted of blindness and ignorance in regard to the essential truths of Christianity. The second, while we do not sustain the apology, to encourage them with the assurance, that it is just as competent for them to be wise unto salvation, as for those in the higher and more cultivated walks of human society.

In pressing home the truths and overtures of Christianity on the poor, we often meet with the very answer of the text, "I am not learned." This answer is not copied by them from the text. But the text, true as the Bible strikingly and universally is, in all its descriptions of Nature, copied it from them. It is in truth a very frequent conception among them, that had they the advantages of a higher scholarship than what they actually possess, they would be nearer the wisdom which is unto salvation. This ministers a kind of false security to their hearts, under the consciousness of a lack of knowledge, and that too of vital necessity to their immortal well-being. They think that there is an ignorance which necessity attaches to their condition; and that this should alleviate the burden of their condemnation, in that they know not God. They spend the day in drudgery, and think, that on this account, they must a so spend it in a state of desolation, as to the whole light and learning of the Gospel. They are apt to look upon it, not as their fault, but as their doom, that they are strangers to the doctrine of peace and of righteousness; and often regard it to be as effectual a plea for justifying their ignorance of what is sacred, as of what is profane and secular, that they are not learned.

Now we refuse this apology altogether; and we should like to warn you in time, that it will stand you in no stead, nor be of any avail to you in the day of reckoning. The word of the Lord is in your hands, and you can at least read it. The candle of the Lord may be lighted in your hearts, and you can at least pray for it. The Gospel is preached unto you as well as unto others; and you can at least attend to it. There will no incurable darkness settle upon your minds, unless you love the darkness. There will no fixed and obstinate unbelief adhere to your understandings, unless your deeds are evil. This will be your condemnation, if you are found to be without knowledge and without faith. But be assured, that all the aids and promises of Christianity are unto you as well as unto others; and if you grieve not the spirit by your wilful resistance—if you put not at a distance from you that Holy Ghost which is given to those who obey him, by your disobedience—if you despise not the grace of God by your daily and habitual neglect of those mercies—in the use of which alone, God undertakes to meet you with its influences—then be assured, that all the comforts of the Gospel, and all its high and heavenly anticipations, will descend more richly upon you, than upon the noble and wealthy of our land; and let your work through the week be what it may, there is not an hour of it which may not be sweetened by a blessing from above, which may not be regaled and heightened into rapture by the smile of a present Deity.

It is not merely to blame you, that we thus speak. It is further to encourage you, my friends, and that, by an assurance which we cast abroad among you, and that, too, with all the confidence of one who has the warrant of inspiration. The knowledge which is life everlasting, is just as accessible to the poor, as it is to the rich, who have time to prosecute, and money to purchase education. Whatever the barrier may be, which rises as a wall of separation between Nature and the Gospel, it is just as impenetrable to the learned as it is to the unlearned—and however the opening through that barrier is made, it is made as often and oftener, for the purpose of sending a beam of spiritual light into the heart of the latter, than into the heart of the former. The Gospel may as effectually be preached unto the poor as unto the wealthy. Simply grant to the one the capacity of reading, and the opportunity of hearing, and he is, at the very least, in as fair circumstances for becoming one of the children of light as the other. In respect to human science, there is a distinction between them. In respect of the gospel, that distinction is utterly levelled and done away. Whatever the incapacity of Nature be for the lessons and the light of revelation, it is not learning, commonly so called, which resolves the incapacity; and until that peculiar instrument be actually put forth which can alone resolve it, the book of revelation may pass and repass among them; the one complaining that he cannot read it, because he is not learned; the other equally complaining that he cannot read it, because it is sealed.

II. Let us now proceed, in the second place, to explain a circumstance which stands associated in our text, with the incapacity both of learned and unlearned, to discover the meaning of God's communications; and that is the spirit of a deep sleep which had closed the eyes of the people, and buried in darkness and insensibility the prophets, and the rulers, and the seers, as well as the humblest and most ignorant of the land.

The connexion between the one circumstance and the other is quite palpable. If a peasant and a philosopher, for example, were both literally asleep before me, and that so profoundly, as that no voice of mine could awaken them; then they are just in the same circumstances, with regard to any demonstration which I address to their understandings. The powers and acquirements of the latter would be of no avail to him in such a case. They are in a state of dormancy, and that is just as firm an obstacle in the way of my reasoning, or of my information, as if they were in a state of non-existence. Neither would it at all help the conveyance of my meaning to their mind, that while dead to all perception of the argument which issued from my lips, or even of the sound which is its vehicle, the minds of both of them were most busily alive and active amongst the imagery of a dream; the one dreaming too, perhaps, in the style of some high intellectual pursuit; and the other dreaming in the style of some common and illiterate occupation. Such, indeed, may be the intoxication of their fancy, that in respect of mental delirium, they may be said to be drunken, but not with wine, and to stagger, but not with strong drink. Still, though in the language of the text, I should cry out, and cry, it may be just as difficult to awaken them to a sense of what I am saying, out of a reverie of imagination, as it is to awaken them out of a simple and unconscious slumber. Nay, the very engagement of their fancy, with its ever-floating and aerial pictures, may have the effect of more strongly detaining the mind from the call which I vainly lift, for the purpose of arousing them. And as the visionary scenes, whether of bliss, or of anxiety, or of sadness, or of eager pursuit, or of bright or of fearful anticipation, pass successively before them, the reality of my waking address may fall unheeded upon each; and though the one be learned, and the other be unlearned, it, in respect of their listening to me, and their understanding of me, totally annuls this difference between them, that their eyes are firmly closed, and a deep sleep is poured upon them both.

Such, it is possible to conceive, may be the profoundness of this lethargy, as to be unmoved by the most loud and terrifying intimations. I may lift this note of alarm, that a fire has broken out in the premises, and is on the eve of bursting into their apartment—and yet such may be the deathlike sleep of both, that both may lie motionless and unconscious on the very confines of their approaching dissolution. Or, what would be more affecting still, both, in the airy chase of their own imagination, may be fully engrossed among the pictures and the agitations of a dream, and be inwardly laughing, or crying, or striving, or pursuing, or rejoicing; and that, while the flame is at their door, which in a few minutes is to seize upon and to destroy them.

When a man is asleep and dreaming, he is alive only to his own fancies, and dead to all the realities of the visible world around him. Awaken him, and he becomes intelligent and alive to these realities, but there may still be other realities to which he is not yet awakened. There may remain a torpor upon his faculties, in virtue of which, he may have as little sense and as little feeling of certain near and impending realities, as the man who is wrapt in the insensibility of his midnight repose has of earth and of all its concerns. The report of an angry God, and a coming eternity, may as little disturb him as the report of a conflagration in the premises, disturbs the sleeping inmate before he is awakened. It is not learned argument which works out, in the one case, the escape of him who is in danger. Could we only awaken him, we would need no argument. Neither is it learned argument which works out, in the other case, the escape of him who is in danger. It is the cry of, "Awake, O sinner," lifted with power enough to arouse him out of his spiritual lethargies. It is the shaking of the soul out of those heavy slumbers, under which it is weighed down to deep and strong insensibility, about the awful urgencies of guilt, and danger, and death, by which it is encompassed. When the house which covers a sleeping peasant and a sleeping philosopher, is in flames, it is not by a demonstration of philosophy that the one is awakened, and the other is left to perish in the ruin; and when both are awakened by the same call, it is not at the bidding of philosophy that the one hastens his escape, while the other lingers in the midst of destruction. They need only to be recovered to the use of senses which were alike suspended with both, that both may flee with equal promptitude from the besetting calamity. And the same of the coming wrath—the same of the consuming fire, that is now ready to burst on the head of the guilty, from the storehouse of treasured vengeance—the same of all the surrounding realities of God, and judgment, and eternity, which lie on every side of us. It is not philosophy which awakes him who has it, to a sense of these things. Neither is it the want of philosophy which keeps him who has it not, fast asleep among the vanities and day-dreams of a passing world. All the powers of philosophy, operating upon all the materials of philosophy, will never dissolve the infatuation of him who is not yet aroused either from the slumbers, or from the visions of carnality. To effect this, there must be either the bestowment of a new sense, or the restoration of an old sense, which has been extinguished. And be he learned or be he unlearned, such an awakening as this will tell alike upon both. The simple view of certain simple realities, to which the vast majority of the world are asleep, will put each of them into motion. And when his eyes are once opened by the force of such a demonstration, will he either flee from the coming wrath, or flee for refuge to the hope set before him in the Gospel, without the bidding or the voice of philosophy to speed his way.

And that the vast majority of the world are, in truth, asleep to all those realities which constitute the great materials of religion, may be abundantly proved by experience—and we cannot proceed far in the details of such a proof, without leading many an individual hearer to carry the topic home to his own experience. For this purpose, let us just compare the kind of feeling and perception which we have about an event that may happen on this side of time, with the feeling and perception about an event, as nearly similar as possible, that will happen on the other side of time, and try how much it is that we are awake as to the former, and asleep as to the latter. Should we assuredly know, that in a few years we are to be translated into a splendid affluence, or sunk into the most abject and deplorable poverty, how keen would be our anticipation, whether of hope or of fear: and why? Because we are awake unto these things. We do assuredly know, that in a few years we pass that mysterious portal, which leads to bliss, or pain, or annihilation—and these are certainties which we do not keenly anticipate, and just because we are asleep unto these things. Should we behold a neighbour on the same path of enterprise with ourselves, suddenly arrested by the hand of bankruptcy, and be further told to our conviction, that the same fatality is sure to encounter all who are treading that path, we would retrace, or move aside, or do our utmost to evade it—because all awake to the disgrace and wretchedness of bankruptcy. We every month behold such a neighbour arrested by the hand of death—nor can we escape the conviction, that sooner or later, he will cast his unfailing weapon at ourselves; and yet no one practical movement follows the conviction, because we are asleep to a sense of the mighty ruin which awaits us from unsparing and universal mortality. Should the house in which you live, be entered with violence by the executioners of a tyrant's will, and a brother, or a child, be hurried away to a perpetual dungeon—if made to know, that it was because such a doom had been laid upon the whole family, and that sooner or later, its infliction was most surely in reserve for every successive member of it—would not you be looking out in constant terror, and live in constant insecurity, and prove how feelingly you were awake to a sense of the sufferings of an earthly imprisonment? But though death break in upon our dwelling, and lay a ruthless grasp on the dearest of its inmates, and leave the assurance behind him, that he will not cease his inroads on this devoted household, till he has swept it utterly away—all we know of the loneliness of the church-yard, and all we read of the unseen horrors of that eternity to which the impenitent and the unbeliever are carried by the ministers of the wrath of God, fail to disturb us out of the habit of living here, as if here we were to live for ever; and that, just because while awake to all the reality which lieth on this side of the grave, we are asleep to the consideration both of the grave itself, and of all the reality which lies beyond it.

Now, the question comes to be, how is this sleep dissipated? Not, we affirm, and all experience will go along with us, not by the power of natural argument—not by the demonstrations of human learning, for these are just as powerless with him who understands them, as with him who makes his want of learning the pretence for putting them away—not by putting the old materials of thought into a new arrangement—not by setting such things as the eye of Nature can see, or its ear can hear, or its heart can conceive, into a new light—not by working in the varied processes of combination, and abstraction, and reasoning, with such simple and elementary ideas as the mind of man can apprehend. The feelings and the suggestions of all our old senses put together, will not make out for us a practical impression of the matters of faith—and there must be a transition as great as that by which man awakens out of the sleep of nature, and so comes to see the realities of Nature which are around him—there must be a something equivalent to the communication of a new sense, ere a reality comes to be seen in those eternal things, where no reality was felt or seen, however much it may have been acknowledged before.

It is true, that along the course of our ordinary existence, we are awake to the concerns of our ordinary existence. But this is not a wakefulness which goes to disturb the profoundness of our insensibility, as to the concerns of a higher existence. We are in one sense awake, but in another most entirely, and, to all human appearance, most hopelessly and irrecoverably asleep. We are just in the same condition with a man who is dreaming, and so moves for the time in a pictured world of his own. He is not steeped in a more death-like indifference to the actual and the peopled world around him, than the man who is busy for the short and fleeting pilgrimage of his days upon earth, among its treacherous delusions, is shut in all his sensibilities, and all his thoughts, against the certainties of an immortal state. And the transition is not greater from the sleeping fancies of the night to the waking certainties of our daily business, than is the transition from the day-dreams of a passing world, to those substantial considerations, which wield a presiding authority over the conduct of him who walketh not by the sight of that which is around him, but by the faith of the unseen things that are above him, and before him. To be thus translated in the habit of our mind, is beyond the power of the most busy and intense of its natural exercises. It needs the power of a new and simple manifestation; and as surely as the dreamer on his bed behooves to be awakened, ere he be restored to a just sense of his earthly condition, and of his earthly circumstances, so surely must there be a distinct awakening made to pass on the dark, and torpid, and overborne faculties of us all, ere the matters of faith come to be clothed to our eye in the characters of certainty, and we be made truly to apprehend the bearing in which we stand to the God who is now looking over us, to the eternity which is now ready to absorb us.

This awakening calls for a peculiar and a preternatural application We say preternatural, for such is the obstinacy of this sleep of nature, that no power within the compass of nature can put an end to it. It withstands all the demonstrations of arithmetic. Time moves on without disturbing it. The last messenger lifts many a note of preparation, but so deep is the lethargy of our text, that he is not heard. Every year do his approaching footsteps become more distinct and more audible; yet every year rivets the affections of the votary of sense more tenaciously than before, to the scene that is around him. One would think, that the fall of so many acquaintances on every side of him, might at length have reached an awakening conviction into his heart. One would think, that standing alone, and in mournful survey amid the wreck of former associations, the spell might have been already broken, which so fastens him to a perishable world. O, why were the tears he shed over his children's grave, not followed up by the deliverance of his soul from this sore infatuation? Why, as he hung over the dying bed of her with whom he had so oft taken counsel about the plans and the interests of life, did he not catch a glimpse of this world's vanity, and did not the light of truth break in upon his heart from the solemn and apprehended realities beyond it? But no. The enchantment, it would appear, is not so easily dissolved. The deep sleep which the Bible speaks of, is not so easily broken. The conscious infirmities of age cannot do it. The frequent and touching specimens of mortality around us, cannot do it. The rude entrance of death into our own houses, and the breaking up of our own families, cannot do it. The melting of our old society away from us, and the constant succession of new faces, and new families, in their place, cannot do it. The tolling of the funeral bell, which has rung so many of our companions across the confines of eternity, and in a few little years, will perform the same office for us, cannot do it. It often happens, in the visions of the night, that some fancied spectacle of terror, or shriek of alarm, have frightened us out of our sleep, and our dream together. But the sleep of worldliness stands its ground against all this. We hear the moanings of many a death-bed—and we witness its looks of imploring anguish—and we watch the decay of life, as it glimmers onwards to its final extinction—and we hear the last breath—and we pause in the solemn stillness that follows it, till it is broken in upon by the bursting agony of the weeping attendants—and in one day more, we revisit the chamber of him, who, in white and shrouded stateliness, lies the effigy of what he was—and we lift the border that is upon the dead man's countenance, and there we gaze on that brow so cold, and those eyes so motionless—and, in two days more, we follow him to his sepulchre, and mingled with the earth, among which he is to be laid, we behold the skulls and the skeletons of those who have gone before him—and it is the distinct understanding of nature, that soon shall have every one of us to go through the same process of dying, and add our mouldering bodies to the mass of corruption that we have been contemplating. But mark the derangement of nature, and how soon again it falls to sleep among the delusions of a world, of the vanity of which it has recently got so striking a demonstration. Look onwards but one single day more, and you behold every trace of this loud and warning voice dissipated to nothing. The man seemed, as if he had been actually awakened; but it was only the start and the stupid glare of a moment, after which he has lain him down again among the visions and the slumbers of a soul that is spiritually dead. He has not lost all sensibility any more than the man that is in a midnight trance, who is busied with the imaginations of a dream. But he has gone back again to the sensibilities of a world which he is so speedily to abandon; and in these he has sunk all the sensibilities of that everlasting world, on the confines of which he was treading but yesterday. All is forgotten amid the bargains, and the adventures, and the bustle, and the expectation of the scene that is immediately around him. Eternity is again shut out; and amid the dreaming illusions of a fleeting and fantastic day, does he cradle his infatuated soul into an utter unconcern about its coming torments, or its coming triumphs.

Yes! my brethren, we have heard the man of serious religion denounced as a visionary. But if that be a vision which is a short-lived deceit—and that be a sober reality which survives the fluctuations both of time and of fancy—tell us if such a use of the term be not an utter misapplication; and whether, with all the justice, as well as with all the severity of truth, it may not be retorted upon the head of him, who, though prized for the sagacity of a firm, secular, and much exercised understanding, and honoured in the market-place for his experience on the walks and ways of this world's business, has not so much as entered upon the beginning of wisdom, but is toiling away all his skill and all his energy on the frivolities of an idiot's dream.

SERMON VII.

On the new Heavens and the new Earth.

"Nevertheless we, according to his promise, look for new heavens and a new earth, wherein dwelleth righteousness."—2 *Peter* iii. 13.

There is a limit to the revelations of the Bible about futurity, and it were a mental or spiritual trespass to go beyond it. The reserve which it maintains in its informations, we also ought to maintain in our inquiries—satisfied to know little on every subject, where it has communicated little, and feeling our way into regions which are at present unseen, no further than the light of Scripture will carry us.

But while we attempt not to be "wise above that which is written," we should attempt, and that most studiously, to be wise up to that which is written. The disclosures are very few and very partial, which are given to us of that bright and beautiful economy, which is to survive the ruins of our present one. But still there are such disclosures—and on the principle of the things that are revealed belonging unto us, we have a right to walk up and down, for the purpose of observation, over the whole actual extent of them.

What is made known of the details of immortality, is but small in the amount, nor are we furnished with the materials of any thing like a graphical or picturesque exhibition of its abodes of blessedness. But still somewhat is made known, and which, too, may be addressed to a higher principle than curiosity, being like every other Scripture, "profitable both for doctrine and for instruction in righteousness."

In the text before us, there are two leading points of information, which we should like successively to remark upon. The first is, that in the new economy which is to be reared for the accommodation of the blessed, there will be materialism, not merely new heavens, but also a new earth. The second is, that, as distinguished from the present, which is an abode of rebellion, it will be an abode of righteousness.

I. We know historically that earth, that a solid material earth, may form the dwelling of sinless creatures, in full converse and friendship with the Being who made them—that, instead of a place of exile for outcasts, it may have a broad avenue of communication with the spiritual world, for the descent of ethereal beings from on high—that, like the member of an extended family, it may share in the regard and attention of the other members, and along with them be gladdened by the presence of him who is the Father of them all. To inquire how this can be, were to attempt a wisdom beyond Scripture: but to assert that this has been, and therefore may be, is to keep most strictly and modestly within the limits of the record. For, we there read, that God framed an apparatus of materialism, which, on his own surveying, he pronounced to be all very good, and the leading features of which may still be recognised among the things and the substances that are around us—and that he created man with the bodily organs and senses which we now wear—and placed him under the very canopy that is over our heads—and spread around him a scenery, perhaps lovelier in its tints, and more smiling and serene in the whole aspect of it, but certainly made up, in the main, of the same objects that still compose the prospect of our visible contemplations—and there, working with his hands in a garden, and with trees on every side of him, and even with animals sporting at his feet, was this inhabitant of earth, in the midst of all those earthly and familiar accompaniments, in full possession of the best immunities of a citizen of heaven—sharing in the delight of angels, and while he gazed on the very beauties which we ourselves gaze upon, rejoicing in them most as the tokens of a present and presiding Deity. It were venturing on the region of conjecture to affirm, whether, if Adam had not fallen, the earth that we now tread upon, would have been the everlasting abode of him and his posterity. But certain it is, that man, at the first, had for his place this world, and, at the same time, for his privilege, an unclouded fellowship with God, and, for his prospect, an immortality, which death was neither to intercept nor put an end to. He was terrestrial in respect of condition, and yet celestial in respect both of character and enjoyment. His eye looked outwardly on a landscape of earth, while his heart breathed upwardly in the love of heaven. And though he trode the solid platform of our world, and was compassed about with its horizon—still was he within the circle of God's favoured creation, and took his place among the freemen and the denizens of the great spiritual commonwealth.

This may serve to rectify an imagination of which we think that all must be conscious—as if the grossness of materialism was only for those who had degenerated into the grossness of sin; and that, when a spiritualizing process had purged away all our corruption, then, by the stepping-stones of a death and a resurrection, we should be borne away to some ethereal region, where sense, and body, and all in the shape either of audible sound, or of tangible substance, were unknown. And hence that strangeness of impression which is felt by you, should the supposition be offered, that in the place of eternal blessedness there will be ground to walk upon; or scenes of luxuriance to delight the corporeal senses; or the kindly intercourse of friends talking familiarly, and by articulate converse together; or, in short, any thing that has the least resemblance to a local territory, filled with various accommodations, and peopled over its whole extent by creatures formed like ourselves—having bodies such as we now wear, and faculties of perception, and thought, and mutual communication, such as we now exercise. The common imagination that we have of paradise on the other side of death, is, that of a lofty aerial region, where the inmates float in ether, or are mysteriously suspended upon nothing—where all the warm and sensible accompaniments which give such an expression of strength, and life, and colouring, to our present habitation, are attenuated into a sort of spiritual element, that is meagre, and imperceptible, and utterly uninviting to the eye of mortals here below—where every vestige of materialism is done away, and nothing left but certain unearthly scenes that have no power of allurement, and certain unearthly ecstacies, with which it is felt impossible to sympathize. The holders of this imagination forget all the while, that really there is no essential connection between materialism and sin—that the world which we now inhabit, had all the amplitude and solidity of its present materialism, before sin entered into it—that God so far, on that account, from looking slightly upon it, after it had received the last touch of his creating hand, reviewed the earth, and the waters, and the firmament, and all the green herbage, with the living creatures, and the man whom he had raised in dominion over them, and he saw every thing that he had made, and behold it was all very good. They forget that on the birth of materialism, when it stood out in the freshness of those glories which the great Architect of Nature had impressed upon it, that then the "morning stars sang together, and all the sons of God shouted for joy." They forget the appeals that are made every where in the Bible to this material workmanship—and how, from the face of these visible heavens, and the garniture of this earth that we tread upon, the greatness and the goodness of God are reflected on the view of his worshippers. No, my brethren, the object of the administration we sit under, is to extirpate sin, but it is not to sweep away materialism. By the convulsions of the last day, it may be shaken, and broken down from its present arrangements, and thrown into such fitful agitations, as that the whole of its existing frame-work shall fall to pieces, and by a heat so fervent as to melt its most solid elements, may it be utterly dissolved. And thus may the earth again become without form, and void, but without one particle of its substance going into annihilation. Out of the ruins of this second chaos, may another heaven and another earth be made to arise; and a new materialism, with other aspects of magnificence and beauty, emerge from the wreck of this mighty transformation; and the world be peopled as before, with the varieties of material loveliness, and space be again lighted up into a firmament of material splendour.

Were our place of everlasting blessedness so purely spiritual as it is commonly imagined, then the soul of man, after, at death, having quitted his body, would quit it conclusively. That mass of materialism with which it is associated upon earth, and which many regard as a load and an incumbrance, would have leave to putrefy in the grave without being revisited by supernatural power, or raised again out of the inanimate dust into which it had resolved. If the body be indeed a clog and a confinement to the spirit, instead of its commodious tenement, then would the spirit feel lightened by the departure it had made, and expatiate in all the buoyancy of its emancipated powers, over a scene of enlargement. And this is, doubtless, the prevailing imagination. But why, then, after having made its escape from such a thraldom, should it ever recur to the prison-house of its old materialism, if a prison-house it really be. Why should the disengaged spirit again be fastened to the drag of that grosser and heavier substance, which many think has only the effect of weighing down its activity, and infusing into the pure element of mind an ingredient which serves to cloud and to enfeeble it. In other words, what is the use of a day of resurrection, if the union which then takes place is to deaden, or to reduce all those energies that are commonly ascribed to the living principle, in a state of separation? But, as a proof of some metaphysical delusion upon this subject, the product, perhaps, of a wrong though fashionable philosophy, it would appear, that to embody the spirit is not the stepping-stone to its degradation, but to its preferment. The last day will be a day of triumph to the righteous—because the day of the re-entrance of the spirit to its much-loved abode, where its faculties, so far from being shut up into captivity, will find their free and kindred developement in such material organs as are suited to them. The fact of the resurrection proves, that, with man at least, the state of a disembodied spirit, is a state of unnatural violence—and that the resurrection of his body is an essential step to the highest perfection of which he is susceptible. And it is indeed an homage to that materialism, which many are for expunging from the future state of the universe altogether—that ere the immaterial soul of man has reached the ultimate glory and blessedness which are designed for it, it must return and knock at that very grave where lie the mouldered remains of the body which it wore—and there inquisition must be made for the flesh, and the sinews, and the bones, which the power of corruption has perhaps for centuries before, assimilated to the earth that is around them—and there, the minute atoms must be re-assembled into a structure that bears upon it the form and the lineaments, and the general aspect of a man—and the soul passes into this material frame-work, which is hereafter to be its lodging-place for ever—and that, not as its prison, but as its pleasant and befitting habitation—not to be trammelled, as some would have it, in a hold of materialism, but to be therein equipped for the services of eternity—to walk embodied among the bowers of our second paradise—to stand embodied in the presence of our God.

There will, it is true, be a change of personal constitution between a good man before his death, and a good man after his resurrection—not, however, that he will be set free from his body, but that he will be set free from the corrupt principle that is in his body—not the materialism by which he is now surrounded will be done away, but that the taint of evil by which this materialism is now pervaded, will be done away. Could this be effected without dying, then death would be no longer an essential stepping-stone to paradise. But it would appear of the moral virus which has been transmitted downwards from Adam, and is now spread abroad over the whole human family—it would appear, that to get rid of this, the old fabric must be taken down, and reared anew; and that, not of other materials, but of its own materials, only delivered of all impurity, as if by a refining process in the sepulchre. It is thus, that what is "sown in weakness, is raised in power"—and for this purpose, it is not necessary to get quit of materialism, but to get quit of sin, and to purge materialism of its malady. It is thus that the dead shall come forth incorruptible—and those, we are told, who are alive at this great catastrophe, shall suddenly and mysteriously be changed. While we are compassed about with these vile bodies, as the Apostle emphatically terms them, evil is present, and it is well, if through the working of the Spirit of grace, evil does not prevail. To keep this besetting enemy in check, is the task and the trial of our Christianity on earth—and it is the detaching of this poisonous ingredient which constitutes that for which the believer is represented as groaning earnestly, even the redemption of the body that he now wears, and which will then be transformed into the likeness of Christ's glorified body. And this will be his heaven, that he will serve God without a struggle, and in a full gale of spiritual delight—because with the full concurrence of all the feelings and all the faculties of his regenerated nature. Before death, sin is only repressed—after the resurrection, all sin will be exterminated. Here he has to maintain the combat, with a tendency to evil still lodging in his heart, and working a perverse movement among his inclinations; but after his warfare in this world is accomplished, he will no longer be so thwarted—and he will set him down in another world, with the repose and the triumph of victory for his everlasting reward. The great constitutional plague of his nature will no longer trouble him; and there will be the charm of a genial affinity between the purity of his heart, and the purity of the element he breathes in. Still it will not be the purity of spirit escaped from materialism, but of spirit translated into a materialism that has been clarified of evil. It will not be the purity of souls unclothed as at death, but the purity of souls that have again been clothed upon at the resurrection.

But the highest homage that we know of to materialism, is that which God, manifest in the flesh, has rendered to it. That He, the Divinity, should have wrapt his unfathomable essence in one of its coverings, and expatiated amongst us in the palpable form and structure of a man; and that he should have chosen such a tenement, not as a temporary abode, but should have borne it with him to the place which he now occupies, and where he is now employed in preparing the mansions of his followers; that he should have entered within the vail, and be now seated at the right hand of the Father, with the very body which was marked by the nails upon his cross, and wherewith he ate and drank after his resurrection—that he who repelled the imagination of his disciples, as if they had seen a spirit, by bidding them handle him and see, and subjecting to their familiar touch the flesh and the bones that encompassed him; that he should now be throned in universal supremacy, and wielding the whole power of heaven and earth, have every knee to bow at his name, and every tongue to confess, and yet all to the glory of God the Father—that humanity, that substantial and embodied humanity, should thus be exalted, and a voice of adoration from every creature, be lifted up to the Lamb for ever and ever—does this look like the abolition of materialism, after the present system of it is destroyed; or does it not rather prove, that transplanted into another system, it will be preferred to celestial honours, and prolonged in immortality throughout all ages?

It has been our careful endeavour, in all that we have said, to keep within the limits of the record, and to offer no other remarks than those which may fitly be suggested by the circumstance, that a new earth is to be created, as well as a new heavens for the future accommodation of the righteous. We have no desire to push the speculation beyond what is written, but it were, at the same time, well, that in all our representations of the immortal state, there was just the same force of colouring, and the same vivacity of scenic exhibition that there is in the New Testament. The imagination of a total and diametric opposition between the region of sense and the region of spirituality, certainly tends to abate the interest with which we might otherwise look to the perspective that is on the other side of the grave; and to deaden all those sympathies that we else might have with the joys and the exercises of the blest in paradise. To rectify this, it is not necessary to enter on the particularities of heaven—a topic on which the Bible is certainly most sparing and reserved in its communications. But a great step is gained simply by dissolving the alliance that exists in the minds of many between the two ideas of sin and materialism; or proving, that when once sin is done away, it consists with all we know of God's administration, that materialism shall be perpetuated in the full bloom and vigour of immortality. It altogether holds out a warmer and more alluring picture of the elysium that awaits us, when told, that there, will be beauty to delight the eye; and music to regale the ear; and the comfort that springs from all the charities of intercourse between man and man, holding converse as they do on earth, and gladdening each other with the benignant smiles that play on the human countenance, or the accents of kindness that fall in soft and soothing melody from the human voice. There is much of the innocent, and much of the inspiring, and much to affect and elevate the heart, in the scenes and the contemplations of materialism—and we do hail the information of our text, that after the dissolution of its present frame-work, it will again be varied and decked out anew in all the graces of its unfading verdure, and of its unbounded variety—that in addition to our direct and personal view of the Deity, when he comes down to tabernacle with men, we shall also have the reflection of him in a lovely mirror of his own workmanship; and that instead of being transported to some abode of dimness and of mystery, so remote from human experience, as to be beyond all comprehension, we shall walk for ever in a land replenished with those sensible delights, and those sensible glories, which, we doubt not, will lie most profusely scattered over the "new heavens and the new earth, wherein dwelleth righteousness."

II. But though a paradise of sense, it will not be a paradise of sensuality. Though not so unlike the present world as many apprehend it, there will be one point of total dissimilarity betwixt them. It is not the entire substitution of spirit for matter, that will distinguish the future economy from the present. But it will be the entire substitution of righteousness for sin. It is this which signalizes the Christian from the Mahometan paradise—not that sense, and substance, and splendid imagery, and the glories of a visible creation seen with bodily eyes are excluded from it, but that all which is vile in principle, or voluptuous in impurity, will be utterly excluded from it. There will be a firm earth, as we have at present, and a heaven stretched over it, as we have at present; and it is not by the absence of these, but by the absence of sin, that the abodes of immortality will be characterized. There will both be heavens and earth, it would appear, in the next great administration—and with this speciality to mark it from the present one, that it will be a heavens and earth, "wherein dwelleth righteousness."

Now, though the first topic of information that we educed from the text, may be regarded as not very practical, yet the second topic on which I now insist, is most eminently so. Were it the great characteristic of that spirituality which is to obtain in a future heaven, that it was a spirituality of essence, then occupying and pervading the place from which materialism has been swept away, we could not, by any possible method, approximate the condition we are in at present to the condition we are to hold everlastingly. We cannot etherealize the matter that is around us—neither can we attenuate our own bodies, nor bring down the slightest degree of such a heaven to the earth that we now inhabit. But when we are told that materialism is to be kept up, and that the spirituality of our future state lies not in the kind of substance which is to compose its frame-work, but in the character of those who people it—this puts, if not the fulness of heaven, at least a foretaste of heaven, within our reach. We have not to strain at a thing so impracticable, as that of diluting the material economy which is without us; we have only to reform the moral economy that is within us. We are now walking on a terrestrial surface, not more compact, perhaps, than the one we shall hereafter walk upon; and are now wearing terrestrial bodies, not firmer and more solid, perhaps, than those we shall hereafter wear. It is not by working any change upon them that we could realize, to an extent, our future heaven. And this is simply done by opening the door of our heart for the influx of heaven's affections—by bringing the whole man, as made up of soul, and spirit, and body, under the presiding authority of heaven's principles.

This will make plain to you how it is that it could be said in the New Testament, that the "kingdom of heaven was at hand"—and how, in that book, its place is marked out, not by locally pointing to any quarter, and saying, Lo here, or lo there, but by the simple affirmation that the kingdom of heaven is within you—and how, in defining what it was that constituted the kingdom of heaven, there is an enumeration, not of such circumstances as make up an outward condition, but of such feelings and qualities as make up a character, even righteousness, and peace, and joy in the Holy Ghost—and how the ushering in of the new dispensation is held equivalent to the introduction of this kingdom into the world—all making it evident, that if the purity and the principles of heaven begin to take effect upon our heart, what is essentially heaven begins with us, even in this world; that instead of ascending to some upper region, for the purpose of entering it, it may descend upon us, and make an actual entrance of itself into our bosoms; and that so far, therefore, from that remote and inaccessible thing which many do regard it, it may, through the influence of the word which is nigh unto you, and of the Spirit that is given to prayer, be lighted up in the inner man of an individual upon earth, whose person may even here, exemplify its graces, and whose soul may even here realize a measure of its enjoyments.

And hence one great purpose of the incarnation of our Saviour. He came down amongst us in the full perfection of heaven's character, and has made us see, that it is a character which may be embodied. All its virtues were, in his case, infused into a corporeal frame-work, and the substance of these lower regions was taken into intimate and abiding association with the spirit of the higher. The ingredient which is heavenly, admits of being united with the ingredient which is earthly—so that we, who, by nature are of the earth, and earthly, could we catch of that pure and celestial element which made the man Christ Jesus to differ from all other men, then might we too be formed into that character by which it is that the members of the family above differ from the outcast family beneath. Now, it is expressly said of him, that he is set before us as an example; and we are required to look to that living exhibition of him, where all the graces of the upper sanctuary are beheld as in a picture; and instead of an abstract, we have in his history a familiar representation of such worth, and piety, and excellence, as could they only be stamped upon our own persons, and borne along with us to the place where he now dwelleth—instead of being shunned as aliens, we should be welcomed and recognised as seemly companions for the inmates of that place of holiness. And, in truth, the great work of Christ's disciples upon earth, is a constant and busy process of assimilation to their Master who is in heaven. And we live under a special economy, that has been set up for the express purpose of helping it forward. It is for this, in particular, that the Spirit is provided. We are changed into the image of the Lord, even by the Spirit of the Lord. Nursed out of this fulness, we grow up unto the stature of perfect men in Christ Jesus—and instead of heaven being a remote and mysterious unknown, heaven is brought near to us by the simple expedient of inspiring us where we now stand, with its love, and its purity, and its sacredness. We learn from Christ, that the heavenly graces are all of them compatible with the wear of an earthly body, and the circumstances of an earthly habitation. It is not said in how many of its features the new earth will differ from, or be like unto the present one—but we, by turning from our iniquities unto Christ, push forward the resemblance of the one to the other, in the only feature that is specified, even that "therein dwelleth righteousness."

And had we only the character of heaven, we should not be long of feeling what that is which essentially makes the comfort of heaven. "Thou lovest righteousness, and hatest iniquity; therefore, God, thy God, hath anointed thee with the oil of gladness, above thy fellows." Let us but love the righteousness which he loves, and hate the iniquity which he hateth, and this, of itself, would so soften and attune the mechanism of our moral nature, that in all the movements of it, there should be joy. It is not sufficiently adverted to, that the happiness of heaven lies simply and essentially in the well-going machinery of a well-conditioned soul—and that according to its measure, it is the same in kind with the happiness of God, who liveth for ever in bliss ineffable, because he is unchangeable in being good, and upright, and holy. There may be audible music in heaven, but its chief delight will be in the music of well-poised affections, and of principles in full and consenting harmony with the laws of eternal rectitude. There may be visions of loveliness there, but it will be the loveliness of virtue, as seen directly in God, and as reflected back again in family likeness from all his children—it will be this that shall give its purest and sweetest transports to the soul. In a word, the main reward of paradise, is spiritual joy —and that, springing at once from the love and the possession of spiritual excellence. It is such a joy as sin extinguishes on the moment of its entering the soul; and such a joy as is again restored to the soul, and that immediately on its being restored to righteousness.

It is thus that heaven may be established upon earth, and the petition of our Lord's prayer be fulfilled, "Thy kingdom come." This petition receives its best explanation from the one which follows: "Thy will be done on earth as it is done in heaven." It just requires a similarity of habit and character in the two places, to make out a similarity of enjoyment. Let us attend, then, to the way in which the services of the upper sanctuary are rendered—not in the spirit of legality, for this gendereth to bondage; but in the spirit of love, which gendereth to the beatitude of the affections rejoicing in their best and most favourite indulgence. They do not work there, for the purpose of making out the conditions of a bargain. They do not act agreeably to the pleasure of God, in order to obtain the gratification of any distinct will or distinct pleasure of their own, in return for it. Their will is, in fact, identical with the will of God. There is a perfect unison of taste and of inclination, between the creature and the Creator. They are in their element, when they are feeling righteously, and doing righteously. Obedience is not drudgery, but delight to them; and as much as there is of the congenial between animal nature, and the food that is suitable to it, so much is there of the congenial between the moral nature of heaven, and its sacred employments and services. Let the will of God, then, be done here, as it is done there, and not only will character and conduct be the same here as there, but they will also resemble each other in the style, though not in the degree of their blessedness. The happiness of heaven will be exemplified upon earth, along with the virtue of heaven—for, in truth, the main ingredient of that happiness is not given them in payment for work; but it lies in the love they bear to the work itself. A man is never happier than when employed in that which he likes best. This is all a question of taste; but should such a taste be given as to make it a man's meat and drink to do the will of his Father, then is he in perfect readiness for being carried upwards to heaven, and placed beside the pure river of water of life, that proceedeth out of the throne of God and of the Lamb. This is the way in which you may make a heaven upon earth, not by heaping your reluctant offers at the shrine of legality, but by serving God because you love him; and doing his will, because you delight to do him honour.

And here we may remark, that the only possible conveyance for this new principle into the heart, is the Gospel of Jesus Christ —that in no other way, than through the acceptance of its free pardon, sealed by the blood of an atonement, which exalts the Lawgiver, can the soul of man be both emancipated from the fear of terror, and solemnized into the fear of humble and holy reverence—that it is only in conjunction with the faith which justifies, that the love of gratitude, and the love of moral esteem, are made to arise in the bosom of regenerated man; and, therefore, to bring down the virtues of heaven, as well as the peace of heaven, into this lower world, we know not what else can be done, than to urge upon you the great propitiation of the New Testament—nor are we aware of any expedient by which all the cold and freezing sensations of legality can be done away, but by your thankful and unconditional acceptance of Jesus Christ, and him crucified.

SERMON VIII.

The Nature of the Kingdom of God.

" For the kingdom of God is not in word, but in power."—1 *Corinthians* iv. 20.

There is a most important lesson to be derived from the variety of senses in which the phrases " kingdom of God," and " kingdom of heaven," are evidently made use of in the New Testament. If it, at one time, carry our thoughts to that place where God sits in visible glory, and where, surrounded by the family of the blessed, he presides in full and spiritual authority—it, at another time, turns our thoughts inwardly upon ourselves, and instead of leading us to say, Lo, here, or lo, there, as if to some local habitation at a distance, it leads us, by the declaration, that the "kingdom of God is within us," to look for it into our own breast, and to examine whether heavenly affections have been substituted there in the place of earthly ones. Such is the tendency of our imagination upon this subject, that the kingdom of heaven is never mentioned, without our minds being impelled thereby to take an upward direction—to go aloft to that place of spaciousness, and of splendour, and of psalmody, which forms the residence of angels; and where the praises both of redeemed and unfallen creatures, rise in one anthem of gratulation to the Father, who rejoices over them all.

Now, it is evident, that in dwelling upon such an elysium as this, the mind can picture to itself a thousand delicious accompaniments, which, apart from moral and spiritual character altogether, are fitted to regale animal, and sensitive, and unrenewed man. There may be sights of beauty and brilliancy for the eye. There may be sounds of sweetest melody for the ear. There may be innumerable sensations of delight, from the adaptation which obtains between the materialism of surrounding heaven, and the materialism of our own transformed and glorified bodies. There may even be poured upon us, in richest abundance, a higher and a nobler class of enjoyments—and separate still from the possession of holiness, of that peculiar quality, by the accession of which a sinner is turned into a saint, and the man who, before, had an entire aspect of secularity and of the world, looks as if he had been cast over again in another mould, and come out breathing godly desires, and aspiring, with a newly created fervour, after godly enjoyments. And so, without any such conversion as this, heaven may still be conceived to minister a set of very refined and intellectual gratifications. One may figure it so formed, as to adapt itself to the senses of man, though he should possess not one single virtue of the temple, or of the sanctuary; and one may figure it to be so formed, as, though alike destitute of these virtues, to adapt itself even to the spirit of man, and to many of the loftier principles and capacities of his nature. His taste may find an ever-recurring delight in the panorama of its sensible glories; and his fancy wander untired among all the realities and all the possibilities of created excellence; and his understanding be feasted to ecstacy among those endless varieties of truth, which are ever pouring in a rich flood of discovery, upon his mind; and even his heart be kept in a glow of warm and kindly affection among the cordialities of that benevolence, by which he is surrounded. All this is possible to be conceived of heaven; and when we add its secure and everlasting exemption from the agonies of hell, let us not wonder, that such a heaven should be vehemently desired by those who have not advanced by the very humblest degree of spiritual preparation, for the real heaven of the New Testament—who have not the least congeniality of feeling with that which forms its most essential and characteristic blessedness—who cannot sustain on earth for a very short interval of retirement, the labour and the weariness of communion with God—who, though they could relish to the uttermost, all the sensible and all the intellectual joys of heaven, yet hold no taste of sympathy whatever, with its hallelujahs, and its songs of raptured adoration—and who, therefore, if transported at this moment, or if transported after death, with the frame and character of soul that they have at this moment, to the New Jerusalem, and the city of the living God, would positively find themselves aliens, and out of their kindred and rejoicing element, however much they may sigh after a paradise of pleasure, or a paradise of poetry.

It may go to dissipate this sentimental illusion, if we ponder well the meaning which is often assigned to the kingdom of heaven in the Bible; if we reflect, that it is often made to attach personally to a human creature upon earth, as well as to be situated locally in some distant and mysterious region away from us—that to be the subject of such a kingdom, it is not indispensible that our residence be within the limits of an assigned territory, any more, in fact, than that the subject of an earthly sovereign should not remain so, though travelling, for a time, beyond the confines of his master's jurisdiction. He may, though away from his country in person, carry about with him in mind a full principle of allegiance to his country's sovereign; and may, both in respect of legal duty, and of his own most willing and affectionate compliance with it, remain associated with him both in heart and in political relationship. He is still a member of that kingdom in the domains of which he was born; and in the very same way, may a man be travelling the journey of life in this world, and be all the while a member of the kingdom of heaven. The being who reigns in supreme authority there may, even in this land of exile and alienation, have some one devoted subject, who renders to the same authority the deference of his heart, and the subordination of his whole practice. The will of God may possess such a moral ascendency over his will, as that when the one commands, the other promptly and cheerfully obeys. The character of God may stand revealed in such charms of perfection and gracefulness to the eye of his mind, that by ever looking to him he both loves and is made like unto him. A sense of God may pervade his every hour, and every employment, even as it is the hand of God which preserves him continually, and through the actual power of God, that he lives and moves, as well as has his being. Such a man, if such a man there be on the face of our world, has the kingdom of God set up in his heart. He is already one of the children of the kingdom. He is not locally in heaven, and yet his heaven is begun. He has in his eye the glories of heaven; though, as yet, he sees them through a glass darkly. He feels in his bosom the principles of heaven; though, still at war with the propensities of nature, they do not yet reign in all the freeness of an undisputed ascendency. He carries in his heart the peace, and the joy, and the love, and the elevation of heaven; though under the incumbrance of a vile body, the spiritual repast which is thus provided, is not without its mixtures, and without its mitigation. In a word, the essential elements of heaven's reward, and of heaven's felicity, are all in his possession. He tastes the happiness of heaven in kind, though not in its full and finished degree. When he gets to heaven above, he will not meet there with a happiness differing in character from that which he now feels; but only higher in gradation. There may be crowns of material splendour. There may be trees of unfading loveliness. There may be pavements of emerald—and canopies of brightest radiance—and gardens of deep and tranquil security—and palaces of proud and stately decoration—and a city of lofty pinnacles, through which there unceasing flows a river of gladness, and where jubilee is ever rung with the concord of seraphic voices. But these are only the accessaries of heaven. They form not the materials of its substantial blessedness. Of this the man who toils in humble drudgery, an utter stranger to the delights of sensible pleasure, or the fascinations of sensible glory, has got already a foretaste in his heart. It consists not in the enjoyment of created good, nor in the survey of created magnificence. It is drawn in a direct stream, through the channels of love and of contemplation, from the fullness of the Creator. It emanates from the countenance of God, manifesting the spiritual glories of his holy and perfect character, on those whose characters are kindred to his own. And if on earth there is no tendency towards such a character—no process of restoration to the lost image of the Godhead —no delight in prayer—no relish for the sweets of intercourse with our Father, now unseen, but then to be revealed to the view of his immediate worshippers—then, let our imaginations kindle as they may, with the beatitudes of our fictitious heaven, the true heaven of the Bible is what we shall never reach, because it is a heaven that we are not fitted to enjoy.

But such a view of the matter seems not merely to dissipate a sentimental illusion which obtains upon the subject. It also serves to dissipate a theological illusion. Ere we can enter heaven, there must be granted to us a legal capacity of admission —and Christ by his atoning death, and perfect righteousness, has purchased this capacity for those who believe; and they, by the very act of believing, are held to be in possession of it, just as a man by stretching out his hand to a deed or a passport, becomes vested with all the privileges which are thereby conveyed to the holder. Now, in the zeal of controversialists, (and it is a point most assuredly about which they cannot be too zealous)—in their zeal to clear up and to demonstrate the ground on which the sinner's legal capacity must rest, there has, with many, been a sad overlooking of what is no less indispensable, even his personal capacity. And yet even on the lowest and grossest conceptions of what that is which constitutes the felicity of heaven, it would be no heaven, and no place of enjoyment at all, without a personal adaptation on the part of its occupiers, to the kind of happiness which is current there. If that happiness consisted entirely in sights of magnificence, of what use would it be to confer a title-deed of entry on a man who was blind? To make it heaven to him, his eyes must be opened. Or, if that happiness consisted in sounds of melody, of what use would a passport be to the man who was deaf? To make out a heaven for him, a change must be made on the person which he wears, as well as in the place which he occupies, and his ears must be unstopped. Or, if that happiness consisted in fresh and perpetual accessions of new and delightful truth to the understanding, what would rights and legal privileges avail to him who was sunk in helpless idiotism? To provide him with a heaven, it is not enough that he be transported to a place among the mansions of the celestial: he must be provided with a new faculty, and as before a change behooved to be made upon the senses; so now, ere heaven can be heaven to its occupier, a change must be made upon his mind. And, in like manner, my brethren, if that happiness shall consist in the love of God for his goodness, and in the love of God for the moral and spiritual excellence which belongs to him—if it shall consist in the play and exercise of affections directed to such objects as are alone worthy of their most exalted regard—if it shall consist in the movements of a heart now attracted in reverence and admiration towards all that is noble, and righteous, and holy—it is not enough to constitute a heaven for the sinner, that God is there in visible manifestation, or that heaven is lighted up to him in a blaze of spiritual glory. His heart must be made a fit recipient for the impression of that glory. Of what possible enjoyment to him is heaven, as his purchased inheritance, if heaven be not also his precious and his much-loved home? To create enjoyment for a man, there must be a suitableness between the taste that is in him, and the objects that are around him. To make a natural man happy upon earth, we may let his taste alone, and surround him with favourable circumstances—with smiling abundance, and merry companionship, and bright anticipations of fortune or of fame, and the salutations of public respect, and the gaieties of fashionable amusement, and the countless other pleasures of a world, which yields so much to delight and to diversify the short-lived period of its fleeting generations. To make the same man happy in heaven, it would suffice simply to transmit him there with the same taste, and to surround him with the same circumstances. But God has not so ordered heaven. He will not suit the circumstances of heaven to the character of man; and therefore to make it, that man can be happy there, nothing remains but to suit the character of man to the circumstances of heaven; and, therefore it is, that to bring about heaven to a sinner, it is not enough that there be the preparation of a place for him; there must be a preparation of him for the place—it is not enough that he be meet in law, he must be meet in person—it is not enough that there be a change in his forensic relation towards God, there must be a change in the actual disposition of his heart towards him; and unless delivered from his earth-born propensities—unless a clean heart be created, and a right spirit renewed—unless transformed into a holy and godlike character, it is quite in vain to have put a deed of entry into his hands—heaven will have no charm for him—all its notes of rapture will fall with tasteless insipidity upon his ear—and justification itself will cease to be a privilege.

Let us cease to wonder, then, at the frequent application, in Scripture, of this phrase to a state of personal feeling and character upon earth; and rather let us press upon our remembrance the important lessons which are to be gathered from such an application. In that passage where it is said, that the "kingdom of God is not meat and drink, but righteousness, and peace, and joy in the Holy Ghost," there can be no doubt that the reference is altogether personal, for the apostle is here contrasting the man who, in these things, serveth Christ, with the man who eateth unto the Lord, or who eateth not unto the Lord. And in the passage now before us, there can be as little doubt, that the reference is to the kingdom of God, as fixed and substantiated upon the character of the human soul. He was just before alluding to those who could talk of the things of Christ, while it remained questionable whether there was any change or any effect that could at all attest the power of these things upon their person and character. This is the point which he proposed to ascertain on his next visit to them. "I will come to you shortly, if the Lord will, and will know not the speech of them which are puffed up, but the power. For the kingdom of God is not in word, but in power." It is not enough to mark you as the children of this kingdom; or as those over whose hearts the reign of God is established; or as those in whom a preparation is going on here for a place of glory and blessedness hereafter—that you know the terms of orthodoxy, or that you can speak its language. If even an actual belief in its doctrine could reside in your mind, without fruit and without influence, this would as little avail you. But it is well to know, both from experience and from the information of him who knew what was in man, that an actual belief of the Gospel, is at all times an effectual belief—that upon the entrance of such a belief, the kingdom of God comes to us with power, being that which availeth, even faith, working by love, and purifying the heart, and overcoming the world.

One of the simplest cases of the kingdom of God in word, and not in power, is that of a child, with its memory stored in passages of Scriptures, and in all the answers to all the questions of a substantial and well-digested catechism. In such an instance, the tongue may be able to rehearse the whole expression of evangelical truth, while neither the meaning of the truth is perceived by the understanding, nor, of consequence, can the moral influence of the truth be felt in the heart. The learner has got words, but nothing more. This is the whole fruit of his acquisition; nor would it make any difference, in as far as the effect at the time is concerned, though, instead of words adapted to the expression of Christian doctrine, they had been the words of a song, or a fable, or any secular narrative and performance whatever. This is all undeniable enough—if we could only prevail on many men, and many women, not to deny its application to themselves—if we could only convince our grown-up children of the absolute futility of many of their exercises—if we could only arouse from their dormancy our listless readers of the Bible—our men, who make a mere piece-work of their Christianity; who, in making way through the Scriptures, do it by the page, and, in addressing prayers to their Maker, do it by the sentence; with whom the perusal of the sacred volume, is absolutely little better than a mere exercise of the lip, or of the eye; and a preference for orthodoxy is little better than a preference for certain familiar and well-known sounds; where the thinking principle is almost never in contact with the matter of theological truth, however conversant both their mouths and their memories may be with the language of it—so that in fact the doctrine by the knowledge of which, and the power of which it is, that we are saved, lies as effectually hidden from their minds, as if it lay wrapt in hieroglyphical obscurity; or, as if their intellectual organ was shut against all communication with any thing without them; and thus it is, that what is not perceived by the mental eye, having no possible operation upon the mental feelings, or mental purposes, the kingdom of God cometh to them in word only while not in power.

But again, what is translated word in this verse, is also capable of being rendered by the term reason. It may not only denote that which constitutes the material vehicle by which the argument conceived in the mind of one man is translated into the mind of another; it may also denote the argument itself; and when rendered in this way, it offers to our notice a very interesting case, of which there are not wanting many exemplifications. In the case just now adverted to, the mere word is in the mouth, without its corresponding idea being in the mind; but in the case immediately before us, ideas are present as well as words, and every intellectual faculty is at its post, for the purpose of entertaining them—the attention most thoroughly awake —and the curiosity on the stretch of its utmost eagerness—and the judgment most busily employed in the work of comparing one doctrine, and one declaration with another—and the reason conducting its long or its intricate processes; and, in a word, the whole machinery of the mind as powerfully stimulated by a theological, as it ever can be by a natural or scientific speculation—and yet, with this seeming advancement that it makes from the language of Christianity to the substance of Christianity, what shall we think of it, if there be no advancement whatever in the power of Christianity—no accession to the soul of any one of those three ingredients, which, taken together, make up the apostle's definition of the kingdom of God—no augmentation either of its righteousness, or its peace, or its joy in the Holy Ghost— the man, no doubt, very much engrossed and exercised with the subject of divinity, but with as little of the real spirit and character of divinity, thereby transferred into his own spirit, and his own character, as if he were equally engrossed and equally exercised with the subject of mathematics—remaining, in short, after all his doctrinal acquisitions of the truth, an utter stranger to the moral influence of the truth; and proving, in the fact of his being practically and personally the very same man as before, that if the kingdom of God is not in word, it is as little in argument, but in power.

If it be of importance to know, that a man may lay hold by his memory, of all the language of Christianity, and yet not be a Christian—it is also of importance to know that a man may lay hold by his understanding, of all the doctrine of Christianity, and yet not be a Christian. It is our opinion, that in this case the man has only an apparent belief, without having an actual belief—that all the doctrine is conceived by him, without being credited by him—that it is the object of his fancy, without being the object of his faith—and that, as on the one hand, if the conviction be real, the consequence of another heart, and another character, will be sure; so, on the other hand, and on the principle, of "by their fruits shall ye know them," if he want the fruit, it is just because he is in want of the foundation—if there be no produce, it is because there is no principle; having experienced no salvation from sin here, he shall experience no salvation from the abode of sinners hereafter. If faith were present with him, he would be kept by the powers of it unto salvation, from both; but destitute as he proves himself to be now of the faith which sanctifies, he will be found then, in the midst of all his semblances, and all his delusions, to have been equally destitute of the faith which justifies.

And it is, perhaps, not so difficult to stir up in the mind of the learned controversialist, and the deeply-exercised scholar, the suspicion, that with all his acquirements in the lore of theology, he is, in respect of its personal influence upon himself, still in a state of moral and spiritual unsoundness, it is not so difficult to raise this feeling of self-condemnation in his mind, as it is to do it in the mind of him who has selected his one favourite article, and there, resolved, if die he must, to die hard, has taken up his obstinate and immoveable position—and retiring within the intrenchment of a few verses of the Bible, will defy all the truth and all the thunder of its remaining declarations; and with an orthodoxy which carries on all its play in his head, without one moving or one softening touch upon his heart, will stand out to the eye of the world, both in avowed principle, and in its corresponding practice, a secure, sturdy, firm, impregnable Antinomian. He thinks that he will have heaven, because he has faith. But if his faith do not bring the virtues of heaven into his heart, it will never spread either the glory or the security of heaven around his person. The region to which he vainly thinks of looking forward, is a region of spirituality; and he himself must be spiritualized, ere it can prove to him a region of enjoyment. If he count on a different paradise from this, he is as widely mistaken as they who dream of the luxury that awaits them in the paradise of Mahomet. He misinterprets the whole undertaking of Jesus Christ. He degrades the salvation which He hath achieved, into a salvation from animal pain. He transforms the heaven which He has opened into a heaven of animal gratifications. He forgets, that on the great errand of man's restoration, it is not more necessary to recal our departed species to the heaven from which they had wandered, than it is to recal to the bosom of man its departed worth, and its departed excellence. The one is what faith will do on the other side of time. But the other just as certainly faith must do on this side of time. It is here that heaven begins. It is here that eternal life is entered upon. It is here that man first breathes the air of immortality. It is upon earth that he learns the rudiments of a celestial character, and first tastes of celestial enjoyments. It is here, that the well of water is struck out in the heart of renovated man, and that fruit is made to grow unto holiness, and then, in the end, there is life everlasting. The man whose threadbare orthodoxy is made up of meagre and unfruitful positions, may think that he walks in clearness, while he is only walking in the cold light of speculation. He walks in the feeble sparks of his own kindling. Were it fire from the sanctuary, it would impart, to his unregenerated bosom, of the heat, and spirit, and love of the sanctuary. This is the sure result of the faith that is unfeigned—and all that a feigned faith can possibly make out, will be a fictitious title deed, which will not stand before the light of the great day of final examination. And thus will it be found, I fear, in many cases of marked and ostentatious professorship, how possible a thing it is to have an appearance of the kingdom of God in word, and the kingdom of God in letter, and the kingdom of God in controversy—while the kingdom of God is not in power.

But once more—instead of laying a false security upon one article, it is possible to have a mind familiarized to all the articles —to admit the need of holiness, and to demonstrate the channel of influence by which it is brought down from heaven upon the hearts of believers—to cast an eye of intelligence over the whole symphony and extent of Christian doctrine—to lay bare those ligaments of connection by which a true faith in the mind is ever sure to bring a new spirit and a new practice along with it: and to hold up the lights both of Scripture and of experience, over the whole process of man's regeneration. It is possible for one to do all this—and yet to have no part in that regeneration—to declare with ability and effect the Gospel to others, and yet himself be cast away—to unravel the whole of that spiritual mechanism, by which a sinner is transformed into a saint, while he does not exemplify that mechanism upon his own person—to explain what must be done, what must be undergone in the process of becoming one of the children of the kingdom, while he remains one of the children of this world. To him the kingdom of God hath come in word, and it hath come in letter, and it hath come in natural discernment; but it hath not come in power. He may have profoundly studied the whole doctrine of the kingdom—and have conceived the various ideas of which it is composed—and have embodied them in words—and have poured them forth in utterance—and yet be as little spiritualized by these manifold operations, as the air is spiritualized by its being the avenue for the sounds of his voice to the ears of his listening auditory. The living man may, with all the force of his active intelligence, be a mere vehicle of transmission. The Holy Ghost may leave the message to take its own way through his mind—and may refuse the accession of his influence, till it make its escape from the lips of the preacher—and may trust for its conveyance to those aerial undulations by which the report is carried forward to an assembled multitude—and may only, after the entrance of hearing has been effected for the terms of the message, may only, after the unaided powers of moral and physical nature have brought the matter thus far, may then, and not till then, add his own influence to the truths of the message, and send them with this impregnation from the ear to the conscience of any whom he listeth. And thus from the workings of a cold and desolate bosom in the human expounder, may there proceed a voice which on its way to some of those who are assembled around him, shall turn out to be a voice of urgency and power. He may be the instrument of blessings to others, which have never come with kindly or effective influence upon his own heart. He may inspire an energy, which he does not feel, and pour a comfort into the wounded spirit, the taste of which, and the enjoyment of which is not permitted to his own—and nothing can serve more effectually than this experimental fact to humble him, and to demonstrate the existence of a power which cannot be wielded by all the energies of Nature—a power often refused to eloquence, often refused to the might and the glory of human wisdom—often refused to the most strenuous exertions of human might and human talent, and generally met with in richest abundance among the ministrations of the men of simplicity and prayer.

Some of you have heard of the individual, who, under an oppression of the severest melancholy, implored relief and counsel from his physician. The unhappy patient was advised to attend the performances of a comedian, who had put all the world in ecstacies. But it turned out, that the patient was the comedian himself—and that while his smile was the signal of merriment to all, his heart stood uncheered and motionless, amid the gratulations of an applauding theatre—and evening after evening, did he kindle around him a rapture in which he could not participate—a poor, helpless, dejected mourner, among the tumults of that high-sounding gaiety, which he himself had created.

Let all this touch our breasts with the persuasion of the nothingness of man. Let it lead us to withdraw our confidence from the mere instrument, and to carry it upwards to him who alone worketh all in all. Let it reconcile us to the arrangements of his providence, and assure our minds, that he can do with one arrangement, what we fondly anticipated from another. Let us cease to be violently affected by the mutabilities of a fleeting and a shifting world—and let nothing be suffered the power of dissolving for an instant, that connection of trust which should ever subsist between our minds and the will of the all-working Deity. Above all, let us carefully separate between our liking for certain accompaniments of the word, and our liking for the word itself. Let us be jealous of those human preferences which may bespeak some human and adventitious influence upon our hearts, and be altogether different from the influence of Christian truth upon Christianized and sanctified affections. Let us be tenacious only of one thing—not of holding by particular ministers—not of saying, that "I am Paul, or Cephas, or Apollos"—not of idolizing the servant, while the Master is forgotten,—but let us hold by the Head, even Christ. He is the source of all spiritual influence—and while the agents whom he employs, can do no more than bring the kingdom of God to you in word—it lies with him either to exalt one agency, or to humble and depress another—and either with or without such an agency, by the demonstration of that Spirit, which is given unto faith, to make the kingdom of God come into your hearts with power.

SERMON IX.

On the Reasonableness of Faith.

"But before faith came, we were kept under the law, shut up unto the faith which should afterwards be revealed."—*Galatians* iii. 23.

"SHUT up unto the faith." This is the expression which we fix upon as the subject of our present discourse—and to let you more effectually into the meaning of it, it may be right to state, that in the preceding clause "kept under the law," the term *kept*, is, in the original Greek, derived from a word which signifies a sentinel. The mode of conception is altogether military. The law is made to act the part of a sentry, guarding every avenue but one—and that one leads those who are compelled to take it to the faith of the Gospel. They are shut up to this faith as their only alternative—like an enemy driven by the superior tactics of an opposing general, to take up the only position in which they can maintain themselves, or fly to the only town in which they can find a refuge or a security. This seems to have been a favourite style of argument with Paul, and the way in which he often carried on an intellectual warfare with the enemies of his master's cause. It forms the basis of that masterly and decisive train of reasoning, which we have in his epistle to the Romans. By the operation of a skilful tactics, he, (if we may be allowed the expression) manœuvred them, and shut them up to the faith of the Gospel. It gave prodigious effect to his argument, when he reasoned with them, as he often does, upon their own principles, and turned them into instruments of conviction against themselves. With the Jews he reasoned as a Jew. He made a full concession to them of the leading principles of Judaism—and this gave him possession of the vantage ground upon which these principles stood. He made use of the Jewish law as a sentinel to shut them out of every other refuge, and to shut them up to the refuge laid before them in the Gospel. He led them to Christ by a school-master which they could not refuse—and the lesson of this school-master, though a very decisive, was a very short one. "Cursed be he that continueth not in all the words of this law to do them." But, in point of fact, they had not done them. To them belonged the curse of the violated law. The awful severity of its sanctions was upon them. They found the faith and the free offer of the Gospel to be the only avenue open to receive them. They were shut up unto this avenue; and the law, by concluding them all to be under sin, left them no other outlet but the free act of grace and of mercy laid before us in the New Testament.

But this is not the only example of that peculiar way in which St. Paul has managed his discussions with the enemies of the faith. He carried the principle of being all things to all men into his very reasonings. He had Gentiles as well as Jews to contend with; and he often made some sentiment or conviction of their own, the starting point of his argument. In this same epistle to the Romans, he pleaded with the Gentiles the acknowledged law of nature and of conscience. In his speech to the men of Athens, he dated his argument from a point in their own superstition. In this way he drew converts both from the ranks of Judaism, and the ranks of idolatry; and whether it was the school of Gamaliel in Jerusalem, or the school of poetry and philosophy in countries of refinement, that he had to contend with, his accomplished mind was never at a loss for principles by which he bore down the hostility of his adversaries, and shut them up unto the faith.

But there is a fashion in philosophy as well as in other things. In the course of centuries, new schools are formed, and the old, with all their doctrines, and all their plausibilities, sink into oblivion. The restless appetite of the human mind for speculation, must have novelties to feed upon—and after the countless fluctuations of two thousand years, the age in which we live has its own taste, and its own style of sentiment to characterize it. If Paul, vested with a new apostolical commission, were to make his appearance amongst us, we should like to know how he would shape his argument to the reigning taste and philosophy of the times. We should like to confront him with the literati of the day, and hear him lift his intrepid voice in our halls and colleges. In his speech to the men of Athens, he refers to certain of their own poets. We should like to hear his reference to the poetry and the publications of modern Europe—and while the science of this cultivated age stood to listen in all the pride of academic dignity, we should like to know the arguments of him who was determined to know nothing save Jesus Christ, and him crucified.

But all this is little better than the indulgence of a dream. St. Paul has already fought the good fight, and his course is finished. The battles of the faith are now in other hands—and though the wisdom, and the eloquence, and the inspiration of Paul have departed from among us, yet he has left behind him the record of his principles. With this for our guide, we may attempt to do what he himself calls upon us to do. We may attempt to be followers of him. We may imitate him in the intrepid avowal of his principles—and we may try, however humbly and imperfectly, to imitate his style of defending them. We may accommodate our argument to the reigning principles of the day. We may be all things to all men—and out of the leading varieties of taste and of sentiment which obtain in the present age, and in the present country, we may try if we can collect something, which may be turned into an instrument of conviction for reclaiming men from their delusions, and shutting them up unto the faith.

There is first, then, the school of Natural Religion—a school founded on the competency of the human mind to know God by the exercise of its own faculties—to clothe him in the attributes of its own demonstration—to serve him by a worship and a law of its own discovery—and to assign to him a mode of procedure in the administration of this vast universe, upon the strength and the plausibility of its own theories. We have not time at present, for exposing the rash and unphilosophical audacity of all these presumptions. We lay hold of one of them, and we maintain, that if steadily adhered to, and consistently carried into its consequences, it would empty the school of natural religion of all its disciples—it would shut them up unto the faith, and impress one rapid and universal movement into the school of Christ.

The principle which we allude to makes a capital figure in their self-formed speculations; and it is neither more nor less than the judicial government of God over moral and accountable creatures. They hold that there is a law. They hold the human race to be bound to obedience. They hold the authority of the law to be supported by sanctions; and that the truth, and justice, and dignity of the Supreme Being are involved in these sanctions being enforced and executed. One step more, and they are fairly shut up unto the faith. That law which they hold to be in full authority and operation over us, has been most unquestionably violated. We appeal, as Paul did before us, to the actual state of the human heart, and of human performances. We ask them to open their eyes to the world around them—to respect, like true philosophers, the evidence of observation, and not to flinch from the decisive undeniable fact which this evidence lays before them. Men are under the law, and that law they have violated. "There is not a just man on earth, that sinneth not." It is not to open, shameless, and abandoned profligacy, that we are pointing your attention. We make our confident appeal to the purest and loveliest of the species. We rest our cause with the most virtuous individual of our nature. We enter his heart, and from what passes there, we can gather enough, and more than enough to overthrow this tottering and unsupported fabric. We take a survey of its desires, its wishes, its affections; and we put the question to the consciousness of its possessor, if all these move in obedient harmony even to the law of natural religion. The external conduct viewed separately and in itself, is, in the eye of every enlightened moralist, nothing. It is mere visible display. Virtue consists in the motive which lies behind it; and the soul is the place of its essential residence. Bring the soul, then, into immediate comparison with the law of God. Think of the pure and spiritual service which it exacts from you. Amid all the busy and complicated movements of the inner man, is there no estrangement from God? Are there no tumultuous wanderings from that purity, and goodness, and truth, which even philosophers ascribe to him? Is there no shortcoming from the holiness of his law, and the magnificence of his eternity? Is there no slavish devotion to the paltry things of sense and of the world? Is there no dreary interval of hours together, when God is unfelt and unthought of? Is there no one time when the mind delivers itself up to the guidance of its own feelings, and its own vanities—when it moves at a distance from heaven; and whether in solitude or among acquaintances, carries along, without any reference to that Being whose arm is perpetually upon me; who, at this moment, is at my right hand, and measures out to me every hairbreadth of my existence—who upholds me through every point of that time which runs from the first cry of my infancy, to that dark hour when the weight of my dying agonies is upon me—whose love and whose kindness are ever present to give me every breath which I draw, and every comfort which I enjoy? We grant the disciples of natural religion the truth of their own principle, that we are under the moral government of the Almighty; and by the simple addition of one undeniable fact to their speculation, we shut them up unto the faith.

The simple fact is, that we are rebels to that government, and the punishment of these rebels is due to the vindication of its insulted authority. To say, that God will perpetually interpose with an act of oblivion, would be vastly convenient for us; but what then becomes of that moral government which figures away in the demonstrations of moralists? Does it turn out, after all, to be nothing more than an idle and unmeaning declamation, on which they love to expatiate; without any thing like real attention or belief on the part of the thinking principle? If they are not true to their own professed convictions, we can undertake to shut them up to nothing. This is slipping from under us; but it is by an actual desertion of their own principle. If you cannot get them to stand to the argument, the argument is discharged upon them in vain. If this be the result, we do not promise ourselves that all we can say shall have any weight upon their convictions; not, however, because they have gained a victory, but because they have betaken themselves to flight. At the very moment that we thought of shutting them up, and binding them in captivity to the obedience of the truth, they have turned about and got away from us—but how? By an open renunciation of their own principle. Look at the great majority of infidel and demi-infidel authors, and they concur in representing man as an accountable subject, and God as a judge and a lawgiver. Examine then the account which this subject has to render; and you will see, in characters to glaring to be resisted, that with the purest and most perfect individual amongst us, it is a wretched account of guilt and deficiency. What make you, of this? Is the subject to rebel and disobey every hour, and the King, by a perpetual act of indulgence, to efface every character of truth and dignity from his government? Do this, and you depose the legislator from his throne. You reduce the sanctions of his law to a name and a mockery. You give the lie to your own speculation, You pull the fabric of his moral government to pieces; and you give a spectacle to angels which makes them weep compassion on your vanity—poor, pigmy, perishable man, prescribing a way to the Eternal, and bringing down the high economy of Heaven to the standard of his convenience, and his wishes. This will never do. If there be any truth in the law of God over the creatures whom he has formed, and if that law we have trampled upon, we are amenable to its sentence. Ours is the dark and unsheltered state of condemnation—and if there be a single outlet or way of escaping, it cannot be such a way as will abolish the law, and degrade the Lawgiver; but it must be such a way as will vindicate and exalt the Deity—as will pour a tide of splendour over the majesty of his high attributes—and as in the sublime language of the prophet, who saw it from afar, will magnify his law, and make it honourable. To this way we are fairly shut up. It is our only alternative. It is offered to us in the Gospel of the New Testament. I am the way, says the Author of that Gospel, and by me, if any man enter in, he shall be saved. In the appointment of this Mediat r—in his death, to make propitiation for the sins of the world—in his triumph over the powers of darkness—in the voice heard from the clouds of heaven, and issuing from the mouth of God himself, "This is my beloved Son, in whom I am well pleased"—in the resistless argument of the Apostle, who declares God to be just, and the justifier of him that believeth in Jesus—in the undoubted miracles which accompanied the preaching of this illustrious personage, and his immediate followers—in the noble train of prophecy, of which he was the object and the termination—in the choir of angels from heaven, who sung his entrance into the world—and in the sublime ascension from the grave, which carried him away from it—in all this we see a warrant and a security given to the work of our redemption in the New Testament, before which philosophy and all her speculations vanish into nothing. Let us betake ourselves to this way. Let us rejoice in being shut up unto it. It is passing, in fact, from death unto life; or, from our being under the law, which speaks tribulation and wrath to every soul of man that doeth evil, to being under the grace which speaks quietness and assurance for ever to all that repair to it. The Scripture hath concluded all to be under sin, that the promise by faith of Jesus Christ might be given to them that believe.

We now pass on from the school of natural religion to another school, possessing distinct features; and of which we conceive the most expressive designation to be, the school of Classical Morality. The lessons of this school are given to the public in the form of periodical essays, elaborate dissertations on the principles of virtue, eloquent and often highly interesting pictures of its loveliness and dignity, the charm that it imparts to domestic retirement, and its happy subservience to the peace, and order, and well-being of society. It differs from the former school in one leading particular It does not carry in its speculations so distinct and positive a reference to the Supreme Being. It is true, that our duties to him are found to occupy a place in the catalogue of its virtues, but then the principle on which they are made to rest, is not the will of God, or obedience to his law. They are rather viewed as a species of moral accomplishment, the effect of which is to exalt and embellish the individual. They form a component part of what they call virtue; but if their virtue be looked upon in no other light than as the dress of the mind, we maintain, that in the act of admiring this dress, and of even attempting to put it on, you may stand at as great a distance from God, and he be as little in your thoughts, as in the tasteful choice of your apparel, for the dress and ornament of the body. The object of these writers is not to bring their readers under a sense of the dominion and authority of God. The main principle of their morality, is not to please God, but to adorn man—to throw the splendour of virtue and accomplishment around him—to bring him up to what they call the end and dignity of his being—to raise him to the perfection of his nature—and to rear a spectacle for the admiration of men and of angels, whom they figure to look down with rapture, from their high eminence, on the perseverance of a mortal in the career of worth, and integrity, and honour. This is all very fine. It makes a good picture; but what we insist upon is, that it is a fancy picture; that, without the limits of Christianity and its influence, you will not meet with a single family, or a single individual to realize it—that the whole range of human experience furnishes no resemblance to it—and that it is as unlike to what we find among the men of the world, or in the familiar walks of society, as the garden of Eden is unlike the desolation of a pestilence. The representation is beautiful; but it is still more flattering than it is fair. It is a gaudy deception, and stands at as great a distance from the truth of observation, as it does from the truth of the New Testament. There is positively nothing like it in the whole round of human experience. It is the mere glitter of imagination. It may serve to throw a tinsel colouring over the pages of an ambitious eloquence; but with business and reality for our objects, we may describe the tour of many thousand families, or take our station for years in the market-place, and in our attempts to realize the picture which has been laid before us, we will be sure to meet with nothing but vanity, fatigue, and disappointment. Now, the question we have to put to the disciples of this school is, are they really sincere in this admiration of virtue? Is it a true process of sentiment within them? We are willing to share in their admiration and to ascend the highest summit of moral excellence along with them. We join issue with them on their own principle, and coupling it with the obvious and undeniable facts of man's depravity, we shut them up unto the faith. Virtue is the idol which they profess to venerate; and this virtue, as it exists in their own conceptions, and figures in their own dissertations, they cannot find. In proportion to their regard for virtue, must be their disappointment at missing her; and when we witness the ardour of their sentiments, and survey the elegance of their high-wrought pictures, what must be the humiliation of these men, we think, when they look on the world around them, and contrast the purity of their own sketches, with the vices and the degradation of the species. Grosser beings may be satisfied with the average morality of mankind; but if their be any truth in their high standard of perfection, or any sincerity in their aspirations after it, it is impossible that they can be satisfied. By one single step do we lead them from the high tone of academic sentiment, to the sober humility of the Gospel. Give them their time to expatiate on virtue, and they cannot be too loud or eloquent in her praises. We have only a single sentence to add to their description: The picture is beautiful, but on the whole surface of the world we defy them to fasten upon one exemplification; and by every grace which they have thrown around their idol, and every addition they have made to her loveliness, they have only thrown mankind at a distance more helpless and more irrecoverable from their high standard of duty and of excellence.

The tasteful admirer of eloquent description and beautiful morality, turns with disgust from those mortifying pictures of man, which abound in the New Testament. We only ask them to combine, with all this finery and eloquence, what has been esteemed as the best attribute of a philosopher, respect for the evidence of observation. We ask them to look at man as he is, and compare him with man as they would have him to be. If they find that he falls miserably short of their ideal standard of excellence, what is this but making a principle of their own the instrument of shutting them up unto the faith of the Gospel, or, at least, shutting them up unto one of the most peculiar of its doctrines, the depravity of our nature, or the dismal ravage which the power of sin has made upon the moral constitution of the species. The doctrine of the academic moralist, so far from reaching a wound to the doctrine of the Apostle, gives an additional energy to all his sentiments. "My mind approves the things which are more excellent, but how to perform that which is good, I find not." "I delight in the law of God after the inward man." "But the good that I would, I do not, and the evil that I would not, that I do."

But the faith of the Gospel does not stop here. It does not rest, satisfied with shutting you up unto a belief of the fact of human depravity. That depravity it proposes to do away. It professes itself equal to the mighty achievement of rooting out the deeply seated corruption of our nature—of making us new creatures in Christ Jesus—of destroying the old man and his deeds, and bringing every rebellious movement within us under the dominion of a new and a better principle. If sincere in your admiration of virtue, you are shut up unto the only expedient for the re-establishment of virtue in the world. That expedient is the Spirit of God working in the heart of believers—quickening those who were dead in trespasses and sins, and bringing into action the same mighty power which raised Jesus from the grave, for raising us who believe in Jesus to newness of life and of obedience. This is the process of sanctification laid before us in the New Testament. A wonderful process it undoubtedly is; but are we who walk in a world of mystery, who have had only a few little years to look about us, and are bewildered at every step amid the variety of his works and of his counsels, are we to reject a process because it is wonderful? Must no step, no operation of the mighty God be admitted, till it is brought under the dominion of our faculties?—and shall we who strut our little hour in the humblest of his mansions, prescribe a law to him whose arm is abroad upon all worlds, and whose eye can take in, at a single glance, the unmeasurable fields of creation and providence? Be it as wonderful as it may—enough for us that it is made sure by the distinct and authentic testimony of heaven; and if, from the mouth of Jesus, who is heaven's messenger, we are told, that "unless a man be born of the Spirit, he cannot enter into the kingdom," it is our part submissively to acquiesce, and humbly to pray for it. Whatever repugnance others may feel to this part of the revealed counsels of God, those who look to a sublime standard of moral excellence, and sigh for the establishment of its authority in the world, ought to rejoice in it. It is the only remaining expedient for giving effect and reality to their own declamations, and they are fairly shut up unto it. Long have they tried to repair the disorders of a ruined world. Many an expedient has been fallen upon. Temples have been reared to science and to virtue; and from the lofty academic chair, the wisdom of this world has lifted its voice amid a crowd of listening admirers. For thousands of years, the unaided powers and principles of humanity, have done their uttermost; and tell us, ye advocates for the dignity of the species, the amount of their operation. If you refuse to answer, we shall answer for you; and do not hesitate to say, that mighty in promise, and wretched in accomplishment, you have positively done nothing—that all the wisdom of the schools, and all its vapouring demonstrations, have not had the least perceptible weight, when brought to bear upon the mass of human character, and human performance; that the corruption of the inner man has not yielded at all to your reasoning, and remains as unsubdued and as obstinate a principle as ever; that the power of depravity in the soul of man is beyond you; and that setting aside the real operation of Christianity in the hearts of individuals and the surface dressing which the hand of legislation has thrown over the face of society, the human soul, if seen in its nakedness, would still be seen in all its original deformity—as strong in selfishness, as lawless in propensity, as devoted to sense and to time, as estranged from God, as unmindful of the obedience, and as indifferent to the reward and the inheritance of his children.

The machine has gone into disorder; and there is not a single power within the compass of the machinery itself that is able to repair it. You must do as you do in other cases; you must have recourse to some external application. The inefficacy of every tried expedient shuts you up unto the only remaining one. Every human principle has been brought to bear upon it in vain, and we are shut up unto the necessity of some other principle that is beyond humanity, and above it. The Spirit of God is that mighty principle. That Spirit which moved on the face of the waters, and made light, and peace, and beauty to emerge out of the wild war of nature and her elements, is the revealed agent of heaven, for repairing the disorders of sin, and restoring the moral creation of God to health and to loveliness. It will create us anew unto good works. It will make us again after that image in which we were originally formed. It will sanctify us by the faith that is in Jesus. And by that mighty power whereby it is able to subdue all things unto itself, it will obtain the victory over that spirit which now worketh in the children of disobedience. The resurrection of Jesus from the dead is the first fruit of its operation; and to him who believes it is the satisfying pledge of its future triumphs. That body, which, left to itself, would have mouldered into fragments, is now in all the bloom of immortality, at the right hand of the everlasting throne. We have tried the operation of a thousand principles in vain. Let us repair to this, so great in promise, and so mighty in performance. It has already achieved its wonders. It has wrought those miracles of faith and fortitude which, in the first ages of Christianity, threw a gleam of triumph over the horrors of martyrdom. It has given us displays of the great and the noble which are without example in history; and from the first moment of its operation in the world, it has been working in those unseen retirements of the cottage and the family, where the eye of the historian never penetrates. The admirers of virtue are fairly shut up unto the faith; for faith is the only avenue that leads to it. "To your faith add virtue," says the Apostle; and that you may be able to make the addition, the promise of the Spirit is given to them that believe.

We should now pass on to another school,

the school of fine feeling and poetical sentiment. It differs from the former in this—that while the one, in its dissertations on virtue, carries you up to the principles of duty, the other paints and admires it as a tasteful exhibition of what is fair and lovely in human character. The one makes virtue its idol because of its rectitude; the other makes virtue its idol because of its beauty; and the process of reasoning by which they are shut up unto the faith, is the same in both. Look at the actual state of the world, and you find that both the rectitude and the beauty are a-wanting. If you admire the one, and love the other, you are shut up unto the only expedient that is able to restore them—and that expedient is sanctioned by the truth of heaven, and has all the power of omnipotence employed in giving effect to the operation—the Spirit of God subduing all things unto itself—putting the law in our hearts, and writing it in our minds—and by bringing the soul of man under the influence of "whatsoever things are pure, or honest, or lovely, or of good report," creating a finer spectacle, and rearing a fairer and more unfading flower, than ever grew in the gardens of poetry.

The processes are so entirely similar, that we would not have made it the distinct object of your attention, had it not been for the sake of an argument in behalf of the faith, which may be addressed with great advantage to the literary and cultivated orders of society. There are few people of literary cultivation, who have not read a novel. In this fictitious composition, there are often one or two perfect characters that figure in the history, and delight the imagination of the reader; and you are at last landed in some fairy scene of happiness and virtue, which it is quite charming to contemplate, and which you would like to aspire after; perhaps some interesting family in the bosom of which love, and innocence, and tranquility, have fixed themselves—where the dark and angry passions never enter—where suspicion is unknown, and every eye meets another in the full glance of cordiality and affection—where charity reigns triumphant, and smiles beneficence and joy upon the humble cottages which surround it. Now this is very soothing, and very delightful. It makes you glad to think of it. The fancy swells with rapture, and the moral principle of our nature lends its full approbation to a scene so virtuous and so exemplary. So much for the dream of fancy. Let us compare it with the waking images of truth. Walk from Dan to Beersheba, and tell us, if without and beyond the operation of Gospel motives, and Gospel principles, the reality of life ever furnished you with a picture that is at all like the elegance and perfection of this fictitious history. Go to the finest specimen of such a family. Take your secret stand, and observe them in their more retired and invisible moments. It is not enough to pay them a ceremonious visit, and observe them in the put on manners and holiday dress of general company. Look at them when all this disguise and finery are thrown aside. Yes, we have no doubt, that you will perceive some love, some tenderness, some virtue; but the rough and untutored honesty of truth compels us to say, that along with all this, there are at times mingled the bitterness of invective, the growlings of discontent, the harpings of peevishness and animosity, and all that train of angry, suspicious, and discordant feelings, which imbitter the heart of man, and make the reality of human life a very sober affair indeed, when compared with the high colouring of romance, and the sentimental extravagance of poetry.

Now, what do we make of all this? We infer, that however much we may love perfection, and aspire after it, yet there is some want, some disease in the constitution of man, which prevents his attainment of it—that there is a feebleness of principle about him—that the energy of his practice does not correspond to the fair promises of his fancy; and however much he may delight in an ideal scene of virtue and moral excellence, there is some lurking malignity in his constitution, which, without the operation of that mighty power revealed to us in the Gospel, makes it vain to wish, and hopeless to aspire after it.

SERMON X.

On the Christian Sabbath.

"And he said unto them, The Sabbath was made for man, and not man for the Sabbath."—*Mark* ii. 27.

The first recommendation of the Sabbath is the place which it occupies in the decalogue. There was much of Jewish observancy swept away with the ruin of the national institutions. There was much of it designed for a temporary purpose, and which fell into disuse among the worshippers of God after that purpose was accomplished. A Christian of the present day, looks upon many of the most solemn services of Judaism in no other light than as fragments of a perishable ritual—nor does he ever think, that upon himself they have any weight of personal obligation. But this does not hold true of all the duties and all the services of Judaism. There is a broad line of distinction between that part of it which is now broken up, and that part of it which still retains all the authority of a perpetual and immutable law. Point us out a single religious observance of the Hebrews that is now done away, and we are able to say of it, and of all the others which have experienced a similar termination, that they, every one of them, lie without the compass of the ten commandments. They have no place whatever in that great record of duty which was graven on tables of stone, and placed within the holy of holies, under the mercy-seat. Now, how does the law of the Sabbath stand as to this particular? Does it lie within or without a limit so tangible, and forming so distinct and so noticeable a line of demarcation? We see it then standing within this record, of which all the other duties are of such general and such imperishable obligation. We meet with it in the interior of that hallowed ground, of which every other part is so sacred and so inviolable. We perceive it occupying its own conspicuous place in that register of duties, all of which have the substance and the irrevocable permanency of moral principle. On reading over the other articles of this memorable code, we see all of them stamped with such enduring characters of obligation, as no time can wear away; and the law of the Sabbath taking its station in the midst of them, and enshrined on each side of it among the immutabilities of truth, and justice, and piety. It is true, that much of Judaism has now fallen into desuetude, and that many of its dearest and most distinguished solemnities are now regarded in no other light than as the obsolete and repealed observances of an antiquated ritual. But it is worthy of being well observed that the whole of this work of demolition took place around and without the line of demarcation. We see no attempt whatever to violate the sanctity of the ground which this line encloses. We no where see any express or recorded incursion upon any one of the observances of the decalogue. We perceive an Apostle in the New Testament making his allusion to the fifth of these observances, and calling it the first commandment with promise; and by the very notice he bestows on the arrangement of the duties, are we given to understand, that no attempt had been made to disturb their order, or to depose any one of them from the place which had been assigned to it. We should count it an experiment of the most fearful audacity, without the intimation of any act of repeal passed in the high legislature of heaven, to fly in the face of that Sabbath law, which stands enrolled among the items of so notable and so illustrious a document; and nothing short of a formal and absolute recallment can ever tempt us to think, that the new dispensation of the Gospel has created so much as one vacancy in that register of duties, which bears upon the aspect of its whole history the impress of a revealed standard that is unalienable and everlasting. We cannot give up one article in that series of enactments which, in every one age of the Christian world, has been revealed as a code, not of ceremonial but of moral law. We cannot consent, but on the ground of some resistless and overbearing argument, to the mutilation of the integrity of this venerable record. We see throughout the whole line of the Jewish history, that it stood separate and alone; and that free from all the marks of national or local peculiarity, it bore upon it none of the frailty of the other institutions, but has been preserved and handed down to us an unchanged standard of duty, for all generations. We see, at the very commencement of the Mosaic dispensation how God himself thought fit to signalize it; for, from the place where he stood, did he proclaim the ten commandments of the law, in the hearing of the assembled multitude; while every other enactment, whether moral or ceremonial, was conveyed to the knowledge of the people, through the medium of a human legislator. And we should feel that, in dethroning any one of the perceptive impositions of the decalogue from its authority over our practice, we were bidding defiance to the declared will of the Eternal; and resisting a voice which sounds as loudly and as impressively to our conscience, as the one that issued in thunder from the flaming top of Sinai, and scattered dismay among the thousands of Israel.

But, secondly, in the practice of the Christian world, the Sabbath has been moved forward by one day; and the remembrance to which it is now consecrated, is a different one from that of the creation of the world. For this change we can find no positive enactment; but we can quote the uncontrolled observation of it down from the period of the apostolic age. We are sure that a practice so early and so universal, could not have been introduced without the sanction of Heaven's inspired messengers. And, mark the limit of that liberty which has been taken with the fourth commandment. It amounts to nothing more than the circumstantial change of a day. Had the early Christians felt themselves warranted to take more liberty, they would have taken it; for then was the time when Christianity took its determinate movement away from the practices of the old dispensation, and established all its distinctions as a religion of principle, and a religion of spiritual character. But widely as the one religion departed from the other, there never, in any one age of the church, has been a departure from the observance of a Sabbath, appropriated to the more solemn and peculiar exercises of piety. The change in the day goes to prove that Christianity is not a religion of mere days. But while it has abandoned one particular day, you find it transferring itself to another; and in the choice of that other it is guided by the affecting remembrance of an event, the contemplation of which is fitted to strengthen the faith, and to refresh the piety, and to waken the best and most religious feelings of those who are spiritually engaged in it. It commemorates the rise of the crucified Saviour from the grave—of him who is the first fruits of them who slept—of him who by that Spirit which is committed to him, raises all those who are dead in tresspasses and sins, to newness of life—of him who is the great agent of Heaven for repairing all the disorders and all the deformities of the moral world—of him by whom, as the word of God, the universe was at first created, but who has since earned a more enduring title to the memory of Christians, by taking upon him that great scheme, in virtue of which, there are to emerge out of this ruined and rebellious province, a new heaven and a new earth, wherein dwelleth righteousness. At the first creation of the world, the Spirit moved over the turbulence of its confused and jarring elements, and awoke them all to order and to harmony. When Adam fell, we know not what precise mischief it inflicted on the material world; but we know that the moral world went back again into a wild chaos of dark and disorderly rebellion; and the heart of man lost its obedience to the attractive influences of that great principle which can alone subdue it into harmonious accordancy with the law of God; and the resurrection of Christ from the grave was a mighty and essential step in the counsels of heaven for quelling all the violence of this elementary war; "for unless I go away, the comforter cannot come; but if I go to my Father, I shall send him." And from the place which he now occupies, does the Spirit come down at the commission of the exalted Saviour, and he moves on the face of this spiritual chaos, and is ever and anon reclaiming some portion of a moral and renovated empire from the rugged domain of a world lying in wickedness. And the time is yet to come when this ever-renovating Spirit shall fulfil its conclusive triumph, by spreading an entire aspect of worth, and piety, and moral loveliness over the wide extent of a now sinful creation.

And thus it is, that while the day of Sabbath has been changed, there is a most affecting remembrance which gives to the observation of Sabbath the full import and significancy of its original purpose—the remembrance of a new creation emerging from an old one—the animating view of life and immortality rising in splendour from the corruption of the grave—the contemplation of an ascended Saviour, who pours the promise of the Father on all his believing disciples—and working in them by the Spirit the graces of the new creature, prepares them for a welcome entrance into those regions, where sin is unknown, and where death is swallowed up in victory.

But, thirdly, in addition to the slight circumstantial change which has been made upon the Sabbath, and which we are sure no honest and enlightened Christian can ever construe into an entire and absolute repeal of the whole institution—there is a general change affecting every one of the ten commandments, but which was never so well understood till the new dispensation was fully and fairly ushered into the world.

We do not mean to say, that the worthies of the Old Testament were utter strangers to that doctrine of grace on which the Spirit of God, working in larger measure on the minds of the Apostles, from the day of Pentecost, has poured so clear and so celestial a splendour. We believe that many Jews were, under the shadow of their types and their sacrifices, trained to the faith, and the humility, and the affectionate obedience of creatures who knew themselves to be incapable of perfect conformity to the law of God—and that, in the act of serving him, they stood on essentially the same footing of mercy to pardon and grace to help in the time of need, on which a spiritual Christian of the day now feels himself to be so firmly and so conclusively established. The change we are alluding to, then, did not take place at the first settlement of the new dispensation. It only came out at that time into more distinct exhibition; and it consists in this; that whereas the direct and natural way of taking up the promulgated law of God, is to take it up as a law of works, and to labour at the performance of it on the understood condition of "This do, and ye shall live"—and as this condition has not been fulfilled by a single son or daughter of the species, then, unless some new arrangement of the matter between God and man had been entered into, life was forfeited by every one of us, and we should just have been what the New Testament tells us we actually are, anterior to our reception of the Gospel, the children of wrath, and under the full operation of the sentence, that "the soul which sinneth it shall die." Now, it would lead us away from our subject into a most interminable excursion, did we say all that might be pertinently and substantially said on the precise turn which the Gospel has given to the obligation of the law. Eternal life is no longer the wages of perfect obedience. It is the gift of God through Jesus Christ our Lord. The man who has faith to perceive the reality of this gift, lays hold of it, and rejoices in all the enlargement of conscious forgiveness, and in all the cordialities of a secure and confident reconciliation, with the God whom he had offended. But this faith does not set him loose from any one of the duties of obedience. Had no other doctrine been proposed to the believer, than the single one of forgiveness through the redemption that is in the blood of Jesus, then we can conceive how the dawning of the Gospel faith might be a signal for the emancipation of the whole man from the restraints of moral obligation. But other doctrines have been proposed; and faith, which is neither more nor less than a reliance on the divine testimony, gives an equally honest and welcome admission to all the particulars of that testimony. It embraces all the particulars of God's communication; and such is the amplitude of its grasp, that though as a principle, it is single and undivided, and can be defined within the limits of a short sentence; yet grant us the existence of this principle, and then you grant us room enough, and provision enough for giving effect to every one of the lessons of revelation. When faith attaches itself to the doctine of reconciliation through Christ, it will make him who possesses it, to walk before God without fear. When faith attaches itself to the doctrine, that "without holiness no man can see God," it makes him who possesses it, to "walk before God without fear, in righteousness and in holiness." When faith attaches itself to the doctrine that unless ye do such and such commandments, ye shall not inherit the kingdom of God, it makes him who possesses it, feel as constraining an urgency of personal interest in the work of keeping these commandments, as if the old covenant of works had got up again, and he behooved to ply his assiduous task for the rewards of perfect obedience. When faith attaches itself to the doctrine of every man receiving his award at the judgment-seat, according to the deeds done in the body, it makes him who possesses it just strive with as much earnestness to multiply good deeds—as if each performance done at the bidding of the Saviour, was a distinct addition to the treasure reserved for him in heaven. But faith does attach itself to every one of these doctrines, or it is no faith at all. It gives the homage of its reliance to each particular of the law and the testimony. It clears its unfettered way from among the perplexities of human arrangement; and disowning every authority but that of the one master, it sits at his feet with the docility of a little child, and appropriates to its right influence every item of his communications. And thus it is, that the man who is in simplicity and in good faith a believer, while he rejoices all the day long in the sunshine of a countenance which he knows to be friendly to him, labours all the day long at his faithful and assiduous task of doing every thing to the glory of God. There is room enough in his enlarged heart for knowing, that while the one is his offered privilege, the other is his required duty—and free as he is, from all the embroilments of a darkening speculation, he does not wait for the adjustment of any human controversy on the subject, but taking himself to his Bible, he both lives in all the security of the offered reconciliation, and without questioning the simple announcement of the Saviour, that "if ye love me, ye will keep my commandments," he also lives in all the diligence of one who is "steadfast and unmoveable, and always abounding in the work of the Lord."

It is true, that there is a difference between being under the law, and under grace. But how does this difference affect the morality of a Christian? Let us take the deliverance of an Apostle upon the subject. "Shall we sin," says Paul, "because we are not under the law, but under grace? God forbid." Quite the contrary, for it is precisely because we are under grace, that sin hath not dominion over us. We must shorten this explanation, and bring it to bear on the observation of the Sabbath. The great interest of practical obedience is upheld under the dispensation of the Gospel, by all the securities of positive and preceptive obligation. But more than this—there is such a change wrought by grace in the heart of every believer, that he not only understands the obligation, but is made cordially to acquiesce in it. There is such a revolution in his desires, that it is now his meat and drink to do the will of that God, against whom there existed within him the most stubborn and revolting enmity. The man who by faith, now looks on God as his friend, will have no difficulty in understanding this change, for he feels it; and there is not a believer on the face of the earth who does not, from the time of his becoming so, love that law which he aforetime violated. This law was at first graven on tables of stone, and held out for the government of a helpless and guilty race, who were both unable and unwilling to yield to it the loyalty of their obedience; and it therefore served to them for a ministry of condemnation.

When the dispensation of grace was brought in, this law was not abrogated. One of the most illustrious exercises of the grace of God, consisted in his putting forth a device for securing the observance of his laws, and this device is neither more nor less than putting the law in our hearts, and writing it in our minds. On the change taking place from our being under the law, to our being under grace, the law, to use the language of the Bible, is taken down from the place it formerly occupied on tablets of stone, and from which it frowns upon us in all the wrath of its violated dignity; and it is graven on the fleshly tablets of the heart—or, in other words, the man is endowed with a liking for that which he formerly rebelled against. And grant him possessed of the genuine principle of faith; and there can be no doubt, that the spirit, true to his office, has been at work within him, and has given a new bent to his affections, and has turned them to the love of those commandments which he aforetime hated and resisted, and has established in his bosom this omnipotent security for obedience, that the taste and the inclinations of the new creature are now upon his side; and as if carried forward by the spontaneous and inborn alacrity of a constitutional impulse, does the man who is thus transformed, and thus acted upon by that Spirit, for which he never ceases to pray, run with delight in the way of all the commandments.

Now, we have already attempted to satisfy you, that there is no erasure of the fourth commandment from that lettered record of the law, which is met with in your Bibles, and where the institution of the Sabbath is graven as indelibly as any one of the unchangeable moralities among which it is situated. But by the new dispensation of the Gospel, this law is made to stand in another place. It is conveyed, as it were, from its old position, on a tablet of stone, and written in the characters of a living epistle on the tablet of a believer's heart. Now the question we have to put is, in this transference of the law from its old to its new repository, does any one of its articles fall away from it, and is lost, as it were, in the passage, by being loosened and detached from the other articles among which it was incorporated? We can specify some, at least, of the ten commandments, which have found their way safe and entire to the heart of him who has embraced the Gospel, and lives under the power of its purifying influences. We are sure that such a man will have his supreme affections fastened upon God, and renouncing every idol, whether of wealth, or of ambition, or of vanity, that can dethrone the Father of his spirit from his rightful ascendency, he will prefer no one object of regard, or of reverence before him. We are sure that such a man will be quite in earnest to have a right knowledge and conception of God—that the Being he worships may be the true God—and lest, by directing his homage to some false and distorted picture of his own fancy, he may incur all the guilt, and be carried away by all the delusion of him who falls down to a material image, in lowly and bending adoration. We are sure that such a man will do honour to the hallowed name of his Master, who is in heaven, and be sickened and appalled by that profaneness which is so current in many of our companies. We are sure that such a man will revere his earthly parents, and will stand by them in the midst of their sinking infirmities; and whether in the form of a declining father, or a widowed mother, who has thrown the whole burden of her dependence on the children who remain to her, we are sure that he will never turn a contemptuous ear to the feebleness of their entreating voice—but will bid his proud and aspiring manhood give up to their authority all its waywardness, and all its tumultuous independence. We are quite sure, that in the heart of such a man, there is an aspiration of kindliness towards everything that breathes, and that the commandment, "Thou shalt not kill," carries in his bosom the widely extended import of thou shalt not conceive one purpose, nor carry against a single human being, one rankling sentiment of malignity. We are sure that such a man, far removed from all that is licentious in practice, will recoil, even in the unseen solitude of thought, from all that is licentious in conception, and spurning away from the pure sanctuary of his heart every evil and unhallowed visitation, he will present to the approving eye of Heaven, all the adornments of a spiritual temple, all the graces and all the beauties of an unspotted offering. We are sure that such a man, with a hand unsoiled by any one of the gains of injustice, will with all the sensitiveness of high-minded and honourable principle, keep himself as nobly aloof from substantial as from literal dishonesty. He will feel superior to every one of those tolerated artifices, and those practical disguises, which, throughout the great mass of mercantile society, have so hardened and so worn down the consciences of those, who, for years, have been speeding and bustling their way amongst a variety of manifold transactions—and in the high walk of simplicity and godly sincerity, will he carry along with him the impress of one of the peculiar people, amid all the legalized fraudulency of a selfish and unprincipled generation. We are quite sure that such a man, seeing he had put on the deeds of the new creature, would never suffer the burning infamy of a lie to rest upon him. All that was within him, and about him, would be clear as the ethereal firmament. The wiles of a deceitful policy would be utterly unknown to him. The openness and the ingenuousness of truth, would sit upon his forehead, and his every utterance bear upon it as decided a stamp of authority, as if shielded by a solemn appeal to God and to the judgment-seat. And, lastly, we are quite sure that such a man could not breathe a single avaricious desire after the substance of another. His heart is set on another treasure. He has entered the service of another master than the mammon of unrighteousness. His affections have settled on a more enduring substance. With the eye of faith, he looks to heaven, and to its unfading and unperishable riches; and all the splendours of this world's vain and empty magnificence, sink into worthlessness before them. He can eye the golden career of his more prosperous neighbours, without one wistful sentiment either of covetousness or of envy; and feels not the meanness and the hardships of his humbler condition, amid the tranquillities of a heart that is cherishing a better prospect, and reposing on the sure anticipation of a happier and more enduring home.

Well, then, in the heart of this man, of whom we suppose nothing more than that he has drunk in the genius of our better dispensation, we find graven in the most legible and distinct characters, nine of the commandments. We meet with all the ten in the letter of the Old Testament, and we find nine out of these ten in a state of most vigorous and entire operation, under the spirit of the New Testament. What has become of the fourth commandment? Has it sunk and disappeared under the stormy vicissitudes of that middle passage, through which all the rest have found their way, from the tablets of a literal inscription, and have gotten their secure and inviolable lodgment within the tablet of a Christian heart? If we look into that heart, do we meet with no trace of the commandment we are in quest of? Will you tell us, that the law of the Sabbath is erased, we will not say from the remembrance, but from the affection of any one of the actual Christians by whom you are surrounded? Has it left behind it a vacancy in that spiritual tablet which is graven by the Spirit of God, when he writes the law in the believer's heart, and puts it into his mind? This is a question of observation—and speaking from our own observation, we never, in the whole round of it, met with a man, drawn by the cords of love to the doing of the other commandments, and carrying in his heart either a distaste or an indifference for the fourth of them? We may have seen men high in honour, and earning by their integrity the rewards of an unsullied reputation amongst their fellow-citizens, carrying a visible contempt for the Sabbath law throughout the whole line of their Sabbath-history—but all the truth and all the justice of these men are such constitutional virtues as may exist in a character which owns not and feels not the power of godliness; and sure we are that wanting this power, several of the other commandments can be specified, to which they are as utter strangers as to the commandment of the seventh day. We repeat it, therefore, that if you grant us a man who bears about with him in his bosom, a warm and conscientious attachment to all the articles of the decalogue but this one, before we look at him, we say with confidence, that search him, and both in his heart and in his practice, this one is to be found; and that we shall not fail to meet the Sabbath law as firmly established as any other within the secrecies of his bosom, and standing out as conspicuously on the front of his external observations. We never, in the whole course of our recollections, met with a Christian friend, who bore upon his character every other evidence of the Spirit's operation, who did not remember the Sabbath day, and keep it holy. We appeal to the memory of all the worthies who are now lying in their graves, that eminent as they were in every other grace and accomplishment of the new creature, the religiousness of their Sabbath-day shone with an equal lustre amid the fine assemblage of virtues which adorn them. In every Christian household, it will be found, that the discipline of a well-ordered Sabbath is never forgotten amongst the other lessons of a Christian education—and we appeal to every individual who now hears us, and who carries the remembrance in his bosom of a father's worth, and a father's piety, if on the coming round of the seventh day, an air of peculiar sacredness did not spread itself over that mansion where he drew his first breath, and was taught to repeat his infant hymn, and lisp his infant prayer. Rest assured, that a Christian, having the love of God written in his heart, and denying the Sabbath a place in its affections, is an anomaly that is no where to be found. Every Sabbath image, and every Sabbath circumstance, is dear to him. He loves the quietness of that hallowed morn. He loves the church-bell sound, which summons him to the house of prayer. He loves to join the chorus of devotion, and to sit and listen to that voice of persuasion which is lifted in the hearing of an assembled multitude. He loves the retirement of this day from the din of worldly business, and the inroads of worldly men. He loves the leisure it brings along with it—and sweet to his soul is the exercise of that hallowed hour, when there is no eye to witness him but the eye of heaven—and when in solemn audience with the Father, who seeth him in secret, he can, on the wings of celestial contemplation, leave all the cares, and all the vexations, and all the secularities of an alienated world behind him. O, how is it possible, that a man can be under the dominion of a principle of piety, who does not love that day which brings round to piety its most precious opportunities? How is it possible, that he can wear the character of a religious being, if the very day which offers him the freest time for the lessons and the exercises of religion, is spent in other exercises, or idly suffered to roll over his head in no exercise at all? How is it possible, that there can exist within him any honest care of his eternity, if the best season for carrying on, without disturbance, the preparations of eternity, pass away in disgust and in weariness? How is it possible, with all the tenderness of his instinctive nature for the members of his family, that there can be one particle of tenderness for their souls, if this day run on at large from all the restraints of Christian discipline, and careless parents, giving themselves up to neglect and to indolence, make no effort to reclaim the wild ignorance of children, untaught and untrained to that wisdom which is unto salvation? The thing is not to be conceived; and upon the strength of all these impossibles, do we assert, that every real Christian has the love of the Sabbath engraven on the tablet of the inner man—that if you had a window to his bosom, you would there see the fourth commandment filling up as large a space of that epistle, which is written not with ink, but with the Spirit of the living God, as it does on the decalogue of Moses—that this is not the peculiarity of some accidental Christians, meeting our observation on some random walk over the face of Christian society—that it is the constant and universal attribute of all Christians—that in every age of the church the love of the Sabbath, and an honest delight in all its pious and profitable observances, have ever stood out among the visible lineaments of the new creature in Jesus Christ our Lord—that the great Spirit, whose office it is to inscribe the law of God on the hearts of those whose sins are forgiven them, and whom he has admitted into the privileges of his new and his better covenant, has never omitted, in a single instance, to make the remembrance of the Sabbath one of the most conspicuous, and one of the most indelible articles of that inscription. And thus has it happened, that without any statutory enactment in the whole compass of the New Testament upon the subject—without any formal setting forth of Sabbath observation, or any laying down of a Sabbath ceremonial, the grave, the solemn, the regular, and with all this, the affectionate keeping of this distinguished day, has come down to us through a series of eighteen centuries, and may be recognised to this hour as the ever-present badge of every Christian individual; and as the great index and palladium of religion in every Christian land.

We shall just say one thing more upon this subject at present. What now becomes of him, who, like a special pleader, with a statute-book in his hand, thinks that the New Testament has set him at large from every other style of Sabbath observation, because he cannot find in it any laying down of Sabbath observances? He will not own the force of any obligation till it be shown to him as one of the clauses in the bond. His constant appeal is to the bond. He will not exceed, by a single inch, the literalities of the bond. He will square his every service, and his every offering by the bond; and when he is charged with any one of the misdemeanours of Sabbath-breaking, he will tell you that it is not specified in the bond. Why, my brethren, if the bond be what he stands upon, he just wakens up against himself the old ministry of condemnation. If it be on the just and even footing of the bond that he chooses to have his exactly literal dealings with God, on this footing God will enter into judgment with him; and soon, and very soon, will he convict him of his glaring deficiencies from his own favourite standard, the bond. Ah, my brethren, when a Christian serves his reconciled Father, it is the service of a liberal and spontaneous attachment. His aim is to please him and to glorify him to the uttermost; and he is never more delighted than when it is in his power to offer the God whom he loves, some of those substantial testimonies of affection which no jealousy can extort by any of its enactments, and the letter of no law is able to embody in any of its descriptions. With such a spirit, and such a cordiality within, we cannot doubt for a moment the delight which such a man will take in the Sabbath, and how dear to his bosom will the affecting remembrance be to which it is consecrated, and how diligently he will cultivate its every hour to the purpose for which it was made—and how, knowing that the Sabbath was made for man, he will earnestly and honestly give himself to the task of realizing all its usefulness to himself and to his family. And do you think, that God will not see this? Do you think, that he will stand in need of any literal specifications by which he may mark the character of this man on the day of retribution? Will he not be able to read that epistle which he himself has engraven on the fleshly tablets of his heart? Will he not know his own? Will he not recognise all the lineaments of that new creature, which has been fashioned by his own spirit—and on that day when the secrets of every heart are laid open, will not the Sabbath observations of an honest and affectionate believer, flowing, as they do, from the impulses of a love for that law which is written on his mind, be put down among those good deeds which shall be found to praise, and honour, and glory, at the solemn reckoning of the judgment seat.

SERMON XI.

On the Doctrine of Predestination.

"And now I exhort you to be of good cheer: for there shall be no loss of any man's life among you, but of the ship. Paul said to the centurion and to the soldiers, Except these abide in the ship, ye cannot be saved."—*Acts* xvii. 22, 31.

The comparison of these two verses lands us in what may appear to many to be a very dark and unprofitabe speculation. Now, our object in setting up this comparison, is not to foster in any of you a tendency to meddle with matters too high for us; but to protect you against the practical mischief of such a tendency. You have all heard of the doctrine of predestination. It has long been a settled article of our church. And there must be a sad deal of evasion and of unfair handling with particular passages, to get free of the evidence which we find for it in the Bible. And independently of Scripture altogether, the denial of this doctrine brings a number of monstrous conceptions along with it. It supposes God to make a world, and not to reserve in his own hand the management of its concerns. Though it should concede to him an absolute sovereignty over all matter, it deposes him from his sovereignty over the region of created minds, that far more dignified and interesting portion of his works. The greatest events of the history of the universe, are those which are brought about by the agency of willing and intelligent beings; and the enemies of the doctrine invest every one of these beings with some sovereign and independent principle of freedom, in virtue of which it may be asserted of this whole class of events, that they happened, not because they were ordained of God, but because the creatures of God, by their own uncontrolled power, brought them into existence. At this rate, even he to whom we give the attribute of omniscience, is not able to say at this moment, what shall be the fortune or the fate of any individual—and the whole train of future history is left to the wildness of accident. All this carries along with it so complete a dethronement of God—it is bringing his creation under the dominion of so many nameless and undeterminable contingencies—it is taking the world and the current of its history so entirely out of the hands of him who formed it—it is withal so opposite to what obtains in every other field of observation, where, instead of the lawlessness of chance, we shall find that the more we attend, the more we perceive of a certain necessary and established order—that from these and other considerations which might be stated, the doctrine in question, in addition to the testimonies which we find for it in the Bible, is at this moment receiving a very general support from the speculations of infidel as well as Christian philosophers.

Assenting, as we do, to this doctrine, we state it as our conviction, that God could point the finger of his omniscience to every one individual amongst us, and tell what shall be the fate of each, and the place of each, and the state of suffering or enjoyment of each at any one period of futurity, however distant. Well does he know those of us who are vessels of wrath fitted for destruction, and those of us whom he has predestinated to be conformed to the image of his dear Son, and to be rendered meet for the inheritance. We are not saying, that we, or that any of you could so cluster and arrange the two sets of individuals. This is one of the secret things which belong to God. It is not our duty to be altogether silent about the doctrine of predestination; for the Bible is not silent about it, and it is our duty to promulgate and to hold up our testimony for all that we find there. But certain it is, that the doctrine has been so injudiciously meddled with—it has tempted so many ingenious and speculative men to transgress the limits of Scripture—it has engendered so much presumption among some, and so much despondency among others—it has been so much abused to the mischief of practical Christianity, that it were well for us all, could we carefully draw the line between the secret things which belong to God, and the things which are revealed, and belong to us and to our children.

With this view, we shall, in the first place, lay before you the observations which are suggested by the immediate history in the passage now submitted to you. And, in the second place, we shall attempt to evince its application to us of the present day, and how far it should carry an influence over the concerns of practical godliness.

I. In the 22d verse Paul announces in absolute terms, that all the men of the ship were to be saved. He had been favoured with this intimation from the mouth of an angel. It was the absolute purpose of God, and no obstacle whatever could prevent its accomplishment. To him belongs that knowledge which sees every thing, and that power which determines every thing; and he could say to his prophet, "These men will certainly be saved." Compare this with what we have in the 31st verse. By this time the sailors had given up all hope of the safety of the vessel. They had toiled, as they thought, in vain—and in despair of doing any good, they ceased from working the ship, and resolved to abandon her. With this view they let down the boat to try the chance of deliverance for themselves, and leave the passengers to perish. Upon this Paul, though his mind had been previously assured, by an intimation from the foreknowledge and predestination of God, that there should be no loss of men's lives, put on all the appearance of earnestness and urgency—and who can doubt, that he really felt this earnestness at the moment of his speaking to the centurion, when he told him, that unless these men should abide in the ship, they would not be saved? He had before told them, in the most unrestricted terms, that they would be saved. But this does not restrain his practical urgency now—and the urgency of Paul gave an alarm and a promptitude to the mind of the centurion—and the centurion ordered his soldiers to cut the ropes which fastened the boat to the vessel, that the sailors, deprived of this mode of escape, might be forcibly detained among them—and the soldiers obeyed—and the sailors were kept on board, and rendered the full benefit of their seamanship and their exertions. They did what other passengers could not do. They lightened the ship. They took up the anchors. They loosed the rudder-bands. They hoisted up the mainsail to the wind—and the upshot of this long intermediate process, with all its steps, was, that the men escaped safe to the land, and the decree of God was accomplished.

Now, in the first instance, it was true, in the most absolute sense of the word, that these men were to be saved. And in the second instance, it was no less true, that unless the sailors abode in the ship, they could not be saved. And the terms of this apparent contradiction admit of a very obvious reconciliation on the known truth, that God worketh by instruments. He may carry every one purpose of his into immediate accomplishment by the direct energy of his own hands. But in point of fact, this is not his general way of proceeding. He chooses rather to arrive at the accomplishment of many of his objects by a succession of steps, or by the concurrence of one or more visible instruments, which require time for their operation. This is a truth to which all nature and all experience lend their testimony. It was his purpose that, at the moment I am now addressing you, there should be light over the face of the country, and this purpose he accomplishes by the instrumentality of the sun. There is a time coming, when light shall be furnished out to us in another way—when there shall be no need either of the sun or the moon to lighten the city of our habitation—but when the glory of God shall lighten it, and the Lamb shall be the light thereof. But this is not the way at present, and, therefore, it is both true, that it was God's purpose there should be light over us and around us at this moment, and that unless the sun had risen upon us this morning, there would have been no such light. It may be the purpose of God to bless the succeeding year with a plentiful harvest. He could accomplish this purpose in two ways. He could make the ripened corn start into existence by a single word of his power. But this is not the actual way in which he carries such designs into accomplishment. He does it by the co-operation of many visible instruments. It is true, he can pour abundance among us even in the midst of adverse weather and unfavourable seasons. But he actually does it by means of favourable weather and favourable seasons. It is not in spite of bad weather that we receive from his hands the blessings of plenty—but in consequence of good weather—sunshine and shower succeeding each other in fit proportion—calm to prevent the shaking of the corn, and wind in sufficient quantity to winnow it, and make a prosperous ingathering. Should it be the purpose of God to give a plentiful harvest to us next year, it will certainly happen, and yet it may be no less true, that unless such weather come, we shall have no such plentiful harvest. God who appoints the end, orders and presides over the whole series of means which lead to it. These visible causes are all in his hand. They are the instruments of his power. The elements are his, and he can either restrain their violence, or let them loose in fury upon the world.

Now, look upon human beings as the instruments of his pleasure, and you have an equally complete explanation of the passage before us. You will be made to understand how it is true, that it was God's absolute purpose that the men of the vessel should be saved, and how it is equally true, that unless the sailors abode in the ship, they could not be saved. Why, the same God who determined the end, gave certain efficacy to the means which he himself had instituted and set agoing for the accomplishment of the end. It does not at all affect the certainty of God's influence over these means, that in addition to wind, and water, and material elements, there were also human beings employed as instruments for carrying his purpose into execution. It is expressly said of God, not only that he stilleth the waves of the sea, but that he also stilleth the tumults of the people, and that he can turn the heart of man as the rivers of water, turning it whithersoever he will. He appoints the end, and it does not at all lessen the sure and absolute nature of the appointment, that he brings it about by a long succession of means, provided that it is his power which gives effect to every step in the progress and operation of these means. Now, in the case before us, there was just such a progress as we pointed out in the case of a favourable harvest. He had determined, that all the men of the vessel should be saved; but agreeably to the method of his administration in other cases, he brought it about by the operation of instruments. He did not save them against the use of instruments, but he did it by the use of instruments. The instruments he employed were men. Paul speaking to the centurion—the centurion ordering the soldiers to cut the ropes, and let the boat away from the vessel—the sailors obliged to work for their own safety—these were the instruments of God, and he had as much command over them as of any others he has created. He brought about the saving of the men by means of those instruments, as certainly as he brings about a good harvest by the instrument of favourable weather, and congenial seasons. He is as much master of the human heart, and its determinations, as he is of the elements. He reigns in the mind of man, and can turn its purposes in any way that suits his purposes. He made Paul speak. He made the centurion listen and be impressed by it. He made the soldiers obey. He made the sailors exert themselves. The conditional assertion of the 31st verse was true; but he made the assertion serve the purpose for which it was uttered. He overruled the condition, and brought about the fulfilment of the absolute prophecy in the 22d verse. The whole of this process was as completely overruled by him as any other process in nature—and in virtue too of the very same power by which he can cause the wind of heaven to fly loose upon the world, make the rain descend, the corn ripen into harvest, and all the blessings of plenty sit in profusion over a happy and a favoured land.

There is no inconsistency, then, between these verses. God says in one of them, by the mouth of Paul, that these men were certainly to be saved. And Paul says in the other of these verses, that unless the centurion and soldiers were to do so and so, they should not be saved. In one of the verses, it is made to be the certain and unfailing appointment of God. In the other, it is made to depend on the centurion. There is no difficulty in all this, if you would just consider, that God, who made the end certain, made the means certain also. It is true, that the end was certainly to happen, and it is as true that the end would not happen without the means—but God secured the happening of both, and so gives sureness and consistency to the passage before us.

Now, it is worth while to attend here both to the conduct of Paul who gave the directions, and to the conduct of the centurion who obeyed them. Paul, who gave the directions, knew, in virtue of the revelation that was made to him some time before, that the men were certainly to be saved, and yet this does not prevent him from urging them to the practical adoption of means for saving themselves. He knew that their being saved was a thing predestinated, and as sure as the decree of heaven could make it; but he must likewise have known, that while it was God's counsel they should be saved, it was also God's will that they should be saved by the exertions of the sailors—that they were the instruments he made choice of—that this was the way in which he wished it to be brought about; and Paul had too high a reverence for the will of God, to decline the use of those practical expedients, which formed the likeliest way of carrying this will into effect. It is a very striking circumstance, that the same Paul who knew absolutely and unequivocally that the men were to be saved, could also say, and say with truth, that unless the sailors were detained in the ship, they should not be saved. Both were true, and both were actually brought about. The thing was done by the appointment of God, and it was also done by a voluntary act on the part of the centurion and his soldiers. Paul knew of the appointment, but he did not feel himself exempted by this knowledge, from the work of practically influencing the will of the people who were around him; and the way in which he got them to act, was by bringing the urgency of a prevailing argument to bear upon them. He told them that their lives depended upon it. God put it into Paul's heart to make use of the argument, and he gave it that influence over the hearts of those to whom it was addressed, that by the instrumentality of men, his purpose, conceived from eternity, and revealed beforehand to the Apostle, was carried forward to its accomplishment.

And again, as the knowledge that they were to be saved, did not prevent Paul from giving directions to the centurion and soldiers for saving themselves, neither did it prevent them from a practical obedience to these directions. It does not appear whether they actually, at this time, believed Paul to be a messenger of God—though it is likely, from the previous history of the voyage, that they did. If they did not, then they acted as the great majority of men do, they acted as unconscious instruments for the execution of the divine purposes. But if they did believe Paul to be a prophet, it is highly striking to observe, that the knowledge they had gotten from his mouth of their really and absolutely escaping with their lives, did not slacken their utmost degree of activity in the business of working for the preservation of their lives, at a bidding from the mouth of the same prophet. He is a prophet from God—and whatever he says must be true. He tells us that we are to escape with our lives—let us believe this and rejoice in it. But he also tells us, that unless we do certain things, we shall not escape with our lives—let us believe this also, and do these things. A fine example, on the one hand, of their faithful dependence on his declarations, and, on the other, of their practical obedience to his requirements. If one were to judge by the prosperous result of the whole business, the way in which the centurion and soldiers were affected by the different revelations of Paul, was the very way which satisfied God—for it was rewarded with success, and issued both in the fulfilment of his decree, and the completion of their deliverance.

II. We now come to the second thing proposed, which was to evince the application of the passage to us of the present day—and how far it should carry an influence over the concerns of practical godliness.

We shall rejoice in the first instance, if the explanation we have now given, have the effect of clearing away any of those perplexities which throw a darkening cloud over the absolute and universal sovereignty of God. We are ready enough to concede to the Supreme Being the administration of the material world, and to put into his hand all the force of its mighty elements. But let us carry the commanding influence of Deity into the higher world of moral and intelligent beings. Let us not erect the will of the creature into an independent principle. Let us not conceive that the agency of man can bring about one single iota of deviation from the plans and the purposes of God; or that he can be thwarted and compelled to vary in a single case by the movement of any of those subordinate beings whom he himself has created. There may be a diversity of operations, but it is God who worketh all in all. Look at the resolute and independent man, and you there see the purposes of the human mind entered upon with decision, and followed up by vigorous and successful exertion. But these only make up one diversity of God's operations. The will of man, active, and spontaneous, and fluctuating as it appears to be, is an instrument in his hand—and he turns it at his pleasure—and he brings other instruments to act upon it—and he plies it with all its excitements—and he measures the force and proportion of each of them—and every step of every individual receives as determinate a character from the hand of God, as every mile of a planet's orbit, or every gust of wind, or every wave of the sea, or every particle of flying dust, or every rivulet of flowing water. This power of God knows no exceptions. It is absolute and unlimited, and while it embraces the vast, it carries its resistless influence to all the minute and unnoticed diversities of existence. It reigns and operates through all the secrecies of the inner man. It gives birth to every purpose. It gives impulse to every desire. It gives shape and colour to every conception. It wields an entire ascendency over every attribute of the mind; and the will, and the fancy, and the understanding, with all the countless variety of their hidden and fugitive operations, are submitted to it. It gives movement and direction through every one point in the line of our pilgrimage. At no one moment of time does it abandon us. It follows us to the hour of death, and it carries us to our place and our everlasting destiny in the region beyond it. It is true, that no one gets to heaven, but he, who by holiness, is meet for it. But the same power which carries us there, works in us the meetness. And if we are conformed to the image of the Saviour, it is by the energy of the same predestinating God, whose good pleasure it is to give unto us the kingdom prepared for us before the foundation of the world.

Thus it is that some are elected to everlasting life. This is an obvious doctrine of Scripture. The Bible brings it forward, and it is not for us, the interpreters of the Bible, to keep it back from you. God could, if it pleased him, read out, at this moment, the names of those in this congregation, who are ordained to eternal life, and are written in his book. In reference to their deliverance from shipwreck, he enabled Paul to say of the whole ship's company, that they were to be saved. In reference to your deliverance from wrath and from punishment, he could reveal to us the names of the elect among you, and enable us to say of them that they are certainly to be saved.

But again, the same God who ordains the end, ordains also the means which go before it. In virtue of the end being ordained and made known to him, Paul could say that all the men's lives were to be saved. And in virtue of the means being ordained and made known to him, he could also say, that unless the sailors abode in the ship, they should not be saved. In the same manner, if the ordained end were made known to us, we could, perhaps, say of some individual among you, that you are certainly to be saved. And if the ordained means were made known to us, we could say, that unless you are rendered meet for the inheritance of the saints in light, you shall not be saved. Now, the ordination of the end, God has not been pleased to reveal to us. He has not told us who among you are to be saved, as he told Paul of the deliverance of his ship's company. This is one of the secret things which belong to him, and we dare not meddle with it. But he has told us about the ordained means, and we know, through the medium of the Bible, that unless you do such and such things, you shall not be saved. This is one of the revealed things which belong to us, and with as great truth and practical urgency as Paul made use of, when he said to the centurion and soldiers, that unless these men abide in the ship ye shall not be saved, do we say to one and to all of you, unless ye repent ye shall not be saved—unless ye do works meet for repentance, ye shall not be saved—unless ye believe the Gospel of our Lord Jesus Christ, ye shall not be saved—unless ye are born again, ye shall not be saved—unless the deeds done in your body be good deeds, and ye bring forth those fruits of righteousness which are by Jesus Christ to the praise and glory of God, ye shall not be saved.

Mark the difference between the situation of Paul urging upon the people of the ship the immediate adoption of the only way by which their lives could be saved, and the situation of an ordinary minister urging it upon the people of his church, to take to that way of faith and repentance, by which alone they can save their souls from the wrath that is now abiding on them. Paul did know that the people were certainly to escape with their lives, and that did not prevent him from pressing upon them the measures which they ought to adopt for their preservation. Even, then, though a minister did know those of his people whose names are written in the book of life, that ought not to hinder him from pressing it upon them to lay hold of eternal life—to lay up their treasure in heaven —to labour for the meat that endureth—to follow after that holiness, without which no man shall see the Lord—to be strong in the faith, and such a faith too as availeth, even faith which worketh by love, and of which we may say, even those whom we assuredly know to be the chosen heirs of immortality, that unless this faith abideth in them, they shall not be saved. But it so happens, that we do not know who are, and who are not, the children of election. This is a secret thing belonging to God, and which is not imparted to us; still it would be our part to say to those of whose final salvation we were assured, believe the Gospel, or you shall not be saved—repent, or you shall not be saved—purify yourselves, even as God is pure, or you shall not be saved. But we are not in possession of the secret—and how much more then does it lie upon us to ply with earnestness the fears and the consciences of our hearers, by those revealed things which God hath been pleased to make known to us? What! if Paul, though assured by an angel from heaven of the final deliverance of this ship's company, still persists in telling them, that if they leave certain things undone, their deliverance will be impossible—shall we, utterly in the dark about the final state of a single hearer we are addressing, let down for a single instant the practical urgency of the New Testament?

The predestination of God respecting the final escape of Paul and his fellow-travellers from shipwreck, though made known to the Apostle, did not betray him into the indolence which is ascribed, and falsely ascribed, to the belief of this doctrine; nor did it restrain him from spiriting on the people to the most strenuous and fatiguing exertions. And shall we, who only know in general that God does predestinate, but cannot carry it home with assurance to a single individual, convert this doctrine into a plea of indolence and security? Even should we see the mark of God upon their foreheads, it would be our duty to labour them with the necessity of doing those things, which, if left undone, will exclude from the kingdom of God. But, we make no such pretensions. We see no mark upon any of your foreheads. We possess no more than the Bible, and access through the Mediator to him, who, by his Spirit, can open our understandings to understand it. The revealed things which we find there belong to us, and we press them upon you—"Unless ye repent, ye shall all likewise perish." "If ye believe not in the Son of God, the wrath of God abideth on you." "Be not deceived, neither covetous, nor thieves, nor extortioners, nor drunkards, shall inherit the kingdom of God." "He who forsaketh not all, shall not be a disciple of Christ." "The fearful, and the unbelieving, and the abominable, and all liars shall have their part in the lake which burneth with fire and brimstone." These are plain declarations, and apart from the doctrine of predestination altogether, they ought, and if they are believed and listened to, they will have a practical influence upon you. We call upon you not to resist this influence, but to cherish it. If any of you are the children of election, it is by the right influence of revealed things upon your understandings and your consciences, that this secret thing will be brought to pass. Paul said as much to the centurion and the soldiers, as that if you do the things, I call upon you to do, you will certainly be saved. They did what he bade them, and the decree of God respecting their deliverance from shipwreck, a decree which Paul had the previous knowledge of, was accomplished. We also feel ourselves warranted to say to one and to all of you, "Believe in the Lord Jesus Christ, and ye shall be saved." "Repent and be converted, and your sins shall be forgiven you." Return unto God, and he will be reconciled. If you do as we bid you, God's decree respecting your deliverance from hell, a decree which we have not the previous knowledge of, will be made known by its accomplishment.

Again, we call upon you, our hearers, to compare your situation with that of the centurion and the soldiers. They were told by a prophet that they were to be saved, and when that prophet told them what they were to do for the purpose of saving themselves, they obeyed him. They did not say, "O it is all predestinated, and we may give up our anxieties and do nothing." They were just as strenuous and active, as if there had been no predestination in the matter. Paul's previous assurance, that all was to end well, had no effect in lulling them to indolence. It did end well, not however without their exertions, but by their exertions. How much more does it lie upon you to enter with earnestness upon the business of doing. We can give you no assurance of its being the decree of God, that any of you shall be saved. But we can give you the assurance, that you will be saved, if you do such and such things. Surely, if the people whom Paul addressed, did not feel themselves exempted by their knowledge of God's decree, from practically entering upon those measures which carried forward its accomplishment, you, who have no such knowledge, must feel doubly impelled by the uncertainty which hangs over you, to the work of making your calling and your election sure. You know in general, that predestination is a doctrine of the Bible, but there is not one of you who can say of himself, that God has made known his decrees to me, and given me directly to understand, that I am the object of a blessed predestination. This is one point of which you know nothing; but there is another point of which you know something—and that is, if I believe, if I repent, if I be made like unto Christ, if I obtain the Holy Spirit to work in me a conformity to his image—and I am told, that I shall obtain it if I ask it—then by this I become an heir of life, and the decree of which I know nothing at the outset of my concern about salvation, will become more and more apparent to me as I advance in a meetness for heaven, and will, at length, become fully, and finally, and conclusively made known by its accomplishment. I may suffer my curiosity to expatiate on the question, "Am I, or am I not, of the election of God?" But my wisdom tells me that this is not the business on hand. It is not the matter which I am called on to do with at present. After Paul said to his companions, that it was quite indispensable to their safety that the sailors should be kept in the vessel, what did the centurion and his men do? Did they fall a speculating about the decrees? Did they hug themselves in the confidence, that as their safety was a point sure and determined upon, they need to take no trouble at all in the concern? O no! No sooner did Paul give the word, than they acted upon it. They gave themselves up with all the promptitude of men whose lives were at stake, to the business on hand. They cut the ropes—they let go the boat—they kept in the sailors—and from the very first moment of Paul's address to them on the subject, all was bustling, and strenuous, and unremitting activity; till, by the unwearied perseverance of those living and operative instruments, the decree of God was accomplished. Now, they were much better acquainted with the decree which respected them, than you are with the decree respecting you. They had the beforehand knowledge of it, and will you be less active, or less strenuous, than they?

Do, therefore, betake yourselves to the business on hand. Let our exhortations to embrace the free offer of the Gospel—to rely on Christ as your Saviour—to resolve against all your iniquities, and turn unto him—to ply the throne of grace for the strengthening influence of the Spirit, by which alone you are enabled to die unto all sin, and live unto all righteousness—let this have an immediate, and a stirring, and a practical influence upon you. If you put this influence away from you, you are in a direct way now of proving what we tremble to think may be rendered clear and indisputable at last, on the great day of the revelation of hidden things, that you have neither part nor lot in the matter. Whatever the employment be which takes you up, and hinders you from entering immediately on the work of faith and repentance, it is an alarming symptom of your soul, that you are so taken up—and should the employment be an idle dreaming, and amusing of yourselves with the decrees and counsels of heaven, it is not the less alarming.

Some will spend their time in inquiries about the number of the saved, when they ought to be striving for themselves, that they might obtain an entrance into the strait gate; and some will waste those precious moments in speculating about the secrets of the book of life, which they should fill up by supporting themselves, and making progress through the narrowness of the way that leads to it. The plain business we lay upon you, is to put away from you the evil of your doings—to submit yourselves to Christ as he is offered to you—to fly to his atoning sacrifice for the forgiveness of your offences—to place yourselves under the guidance of his word, and a dependence on the influences of his Spirit—to live no longer to yourselves, but to him—and to fill up your weeks and your days with those fruits of righteousness, by which God is glorified. We stand here by the decree of heaven, and it is by the same decree that you are now sitting round and listening to us. We feel the importance of the situation we occupy; and though we believe in the sovereignty of God, and the unfailingness of all his appointments, this, instead of restraining, impels us to bring the message of the Gospel, with all the practical urgency of its invitations, and its warnings, to bear upon you. We feel, with all our belief in predestination, that our business is not to forbear this urgency, but to ply you with it most anxiously, and earnestly, and unceasingly; and you should feel, with the same belief in your mind, that your business is not to resist this urgency, but to be guided by its impulse. Who knows but we may be the humble instrument, and you the undeserved subjects of some high and heavenly ordination? The cutting of the ropes was the turning point on which the deliverance of Paul's company from shipwreck was suspended. Who knows but the urgency we now ply you with, telling upon you, and carrying your purposes along with it, may be the very step in the wonderful progress of God's operations, on which your conversion hinges? We, therefore, press the Gospel with all its duties, and all its promises, and all its privileges upon you. O listen, and resolve, and, manfully forsaking all that keeps you from the Saviour, we call upon you, from this moment, to give yourselves up unto him; and be assured, it is only by acting in obedience to such calls laid before you in the Bible, and sounded in your ear from the pulpit, that your election unto life can ever be made known in this world, or reach its positive consummation in eternity.

And now you can have no difficulty in understanding how it is th . we make our calling and our election sure. It is not in the power of the elect to make their election surer in itself than it really is; for this is a sureness which is not capable of receiving any addition. It is not in the power of the elect to make it surer to God—for all futurity is submitted to his all-seeing eye, and his absolute knowledge stands in need of no confirmation. But there is such a thing as the elect being ignorant for a time of their own election, and their being made sure of it in the progress of evidence and discovery. And therefore it is that they are called to make their election sure to themselves, or to make themselves sure of their election. And how is this to be done? Not by reading it in the book of God's decrees—not by obtaining from him any direct information about his counsels—not by conferring with prophet or angel, gifted with the revelation of hidden things. But the same God who elects some unto everlasting life, and keeps back from them all direct information about it, tells them that he who believeth, and he who repenteth, and he who obeyeth the Gospel, shall obtain everlasting life. We shall never in this world have an immediate communication from him, whether we are of the elect or not—but let us believe—let us repent—let us obey the Saviour, and from the first moment of our setting ourselves to these things in good earnest, we may conceive the hope of a place among the heirs of immortality. In the progress and success of our endeavours, this hope may advance and grow brighter within us. As we grow in the exercises of faith and obedience, the light of a cheering manifestation is more sensibly felt, and our hope ripens into assurance. "Hereby do we know that we know him, by our keeping his commandments," is an evidence which every year becomes clearer and more encouraging; and thus, by a well-sustained perseverance in the exercises of the Christian life, do we labour with all diligence to make our calling and election sure. We call upon you, in the language of the Apostle, to have faith, and to this faith add virtue, and knowledge, and temperance, and patience, and godliness, and brotherly kindness, and charity. It is by the doing of these things, that you are made sure of your calling and election, "for if ye do these things," says Peter, "ye shall never fail, and an entrance shall be ministered unto you abundantly into the everlasting kingdom of our Lord and Saviour Jesus Christ."

If there be any of you who have not followed this train of observation—if it still remain one of those things of Paul which are hard to be understood—let us beseech you, at least, that you wrest it not to your own destruction, by remitting your activity, and your diligence, and your pains-taking in the service of Christ. Why, the doctrine of election leaves our duty to exhort, and your duty to obey, on the same footing on which it found them. We are commissioned to lay before you the free offer of the Gospel—to press it on the acceptance of one and all of you—to assure every individual amongst you of a hearty welcome from the Lord God merciful and gracious—to call you to the service of Christ, that great Master of the household of faith—to urge it upon you, that you must renounce every other master, and, casting all your idols, and vanities, and iniquities away from you, to close with the invitation, and be diligent in all the duties and performances of the Gospel. If you resist, or put off—if, blind to the goodness of God in Christ Jesus, you suffer it not to lead you to repentance—if the call of "awake to righteousness, and sin not," make no practical impression on you—if the true assurance of pardon for the sins of the past, do not fill your heart with the desire of sanctification for the future—if the word of Christ be not so received by you as to lead to the doing of it—then you are just leaving undone those things, of which we say in the words of the text, "Except these things be done, ye cannot be saved"—and to all the guilt of your past disobedience, you add the aggravation of putting away from you both the offered atonement and the commanded repentance of the Gospel, and "how can you escape if you neglect so great a salvation?"

SERMON XII.

On the Nature of the Sin against the Holy Ghost.

"Wherefore I say unto you, All manner of sin and blasphemy shall be forgiven unto men: but the blasphemy against the Holy Ghost shall not be forgiven unto men. And whosoever speaketh a word against the Son of man, it shall be forgiven him: but whosoever speaketh against the Holy Ghost, it shall not be forgiven him, neither in this world, neither in the world to come."—*Matthew* xii. 31, 32.

LET us never suspend the practical influence of what we do know, by idly rambling in a vain and impertinent pursuit after what we do not know. Thus much we know from the Bible, that God refuses not his Holy Spirit to them who ask it—that every right movement of principle within us is from him—that when we feel an impulse of conscience, we feel the Spirit of God knocking at the door of our hearts, and challenging from us that attention and that obedience which are due to the great Lawgiver—that if we follow not the impulse, we provoke and dissatisfy him who is the Author of it—and that there is such a thing as tempting him to abandon us altogether, and to surrender the friendly office of plying us any longer with his admonitions and his warnings. Hence, an emphatic argument for immediate repentance. By every moment of delay, we hasten upon ourselves the awful crisis of being let alone. The conscience is every day getting harder; and he who sits behind, and is the unseen Author of all its instigations, is lifting every day a feebler voice; and coming always nearer and nearer to that point in the history of every determined sinner, when, left to his own infatuation, he can hold up a stubborn and unyielding front to all that instrumentality of advice and of expostulation which is brought to bear upon him. The preacher plies him with his weekly voice, but the Spirit refuses to lend it his constraining energy; and all that is tender, and all that is terrifying in his Sabbath argument plays around his heart, without reaching it. The judgments of God go abroad against him, and as he carries his friends or his children to the grave, a few natural tears may bear witness to the tenderness he bore them—but that Spirit who gives to these judgments all their moral significancy, withholds from him the anointing which remaineth, and the man relapses as before into all the obstinate habits, and all the uncrucified affections which he has hitherto indulged in. The disease gathers upon him, and gets a more rooted inveteracy than ever; and thus it is, that there are thousands and thousands more, who, though active and astir on that living scene of population which is around us, have an iron hardness upon their souls, which makes them, in reference to the things of God, dark and sullen as the grave, and fast locks them in all the insensibility of spiritual death. Is there no old man of your acquaintance, who realizes this sad picture of one left to himself that we have now attempted so rapidly to set before you? Then know, that by every deed of wilful sin, that by every moment of wilful delay in the great matter of repentance, that by every stifled warning of conscience, that by every deafening of its authoritative voice among the temptations of the world, and the riot of lawless acquaintances, you are just moving yourself to the limits of this helpless and irrecoverable condition. We have no doubt, that you may have the intention of making a violent step, and suddenly turning round to the right path ere you die. But this you will not do but by an act of obedience to the reproaches of a conscience that is ever getting harder. This you will not do without the constraining influence of that Spirit, who is gradually dying away from you. This you will not do but in virtue of some overpowering persuasion from that monitor who is now stirring within you, but with whom you are now taking the most effectual method of drowning his voice, and disarming him of all his authority. Do not you perceive, that in these circumstances, every act of delay is madness—that you are getting by every hour of it into deeper water—that you are consolidating a barrier against your future return to the paths of righteousness, which you vainly think you will be able to surmount when the languor and infirmity of old age have got hold of you—that you are strengthening and multiplying around you the wiles of an entanglement, which all the strugglings of deathbed terror cannot break asunder—that you are insulting the Spirit of God by this daily habit of stifling and neglecting the other and the other call that he is sounding to your moral ear, through the organ of conscience. And O the desperate hazard and folly of such a calculation! Think you, think you, that this is the way of gaining his friendly presence at that awful moment, when the urgent sense of guilt and of danger forces from the sinner an imploring cry as he stands on the brink of eternity?

"How long, ye simple ones, will ye love simplicity, and the scorners delight in their scorning, and fools hate knowledge? Turn ye at my reproof. Behold I will pour out my spirit unto you; I will make known my words unto you. Because I have called, and ye refused; I have stretched out my hand, and no man regarded; but ye have set at nought all my counsel, and would none of my reproof: I also will laugh at your calamity; I will mock when your fear cometh. When your fear cometh as desolation, and your destruction cometh as a whirlwind; when distress and anguish cometh upon you: then shall they call upon me, but I will not answer; they shall seek me early, but they shall not find me."

You see, then, how a man may shut against himself all the avenues of reconciliation. There is nothing mysterious in the kind of sin by which the Holy Spirit is tempted to abandon him to that state in which there can be no forgiveness, and no return unto God. It is by a movement of conscience within him, that the man is made sensible of sin—that he is visited with the desire of reformation—that he is given to feel his need both of mercy to pardon, and of grace to help him—in a word, that he is drawn unto the Saviour, and brought into that intimate alliance with him by faith, which brings down upon him both acceptance with the Father, and all the power of a new and a constraining impulse, to the way of obedience. But this movement is a suggestion of the Spirit of God, and if it be resisted by any man, the Spirit is resisted. The God who offers to draw him unto Christ, is resisted. The man refuses to believe, because his deeds are evil; and by every day of perseverance in these deeds, the voice which tells him of their guilt, and urges him to abandon them, is resisted; and thus, the Spirit ceases to suggest, and the Father, from whom the Spirit proceedeth, ceases to draw, and the inward voice ceases to remonstrate; and all this because their authority has been so often put forth, and so often turned from. This is the deadly offence which has reared an impassable wall against the return of the obstinately impenitent. This is the blasphemy to which no forgiveness can be granted, because in its very nature, the man who has come this length, feels no movement of conscience towards that ground on which alone forgiveness can be awarded to him—and where it is never refused even to the very worst and most malignant of human iniquities. This is the sin against the Holy Ghost. It is not peculiar to any one age. It does not lie in any one unfathomable mystery. It may be seen at this day in thousands and thousands more, who, by that most familiar and most frequently exemplified of all habits, a habit of resistance to a sense of duty, have at length stifled it altogether, and driven their inward monitor away from them, and have sunk into a profound moral lethargy, and so will never obtain forgiveness—not because forgiveness is ever refused to any who repent and believe the Gospel, but because they have made their faith and their repentance impracticable. They choose not to repent; and this choice has been made so often and so perseveringly, that the Spirit has let them alone. They have obstinately clung to their love of darkness rather than of light, and the Spirit has at length turned away from them since they will have it so. They wish not to believe, because their deeds are evil, and that Spirit has ceased to strive with them, who has so often spoken to them in vain; and whose many remonstrances have never prevailed upon them to abandon the evil of their doings.

Take all this attentively along with you, and the whole mysteriousness of this sin against the Holy Ghost should be done away. Grant him the office with which he is invested in the Word of God, even the office of instigating the conscience to all its reprovals of sin, and to all its admonitions of repentance—and then, if ever you witnessed the case of a man whose conscience had fallen into a profound and irrecoverable sleep, or, at least, had lost to such a degree its power of control over him, that he stood out against every engine which was set up to bring him to the faith and the repentance of the New Testament—behold in such a man a sinner against conscience to such a woful extent, that conscience had given up its direction of him; or, in other words, a sinner against the Holy Ghost to such an extent, that he had let down the office of warning him away from that ground of danger and of guilt on which he stood so immovably posted; or, of urging him onward to that sure road of access, where if a man seek for pardon, he will never miss it, and where, if he cry for the clean heart and the right spirit, he will not cry in vain.

And as there is nothing dark or incomprehensible in the nature of this sin, so there is nothing in it to impair the freeness of the Gospel, or the universality of its calls and of its offers, or its power of salvation to all who will, or that attribute which is expressly ascribed to it, that where sin abounded, grace did much more abound. It is never said that pardon through that blood, which is distinctly stated to cleanse from all sin—it is nowhere said, that this pardon is extended to any but to those who believe. If you do not believe, you do not get pardon—and if you will not believe, because you love darkness rather than light—if you will not believe, because you will not abandon those evil deeds which the Spirit tells you through the conscience, that you must forsake in coming unto Christ—if his repeated calls have been so unheeded and so withstood by you, that he has at length ceased from striving, then the reason why your sin is unpardonable, is just because you have refused the Gospel salvation. The reason why your case is irrecoverable, is just because you have refused the method of recovery so long, and so often, that every call of repentance has now come to play upon you in vain. The reason why you lie under a guilt that can meet with no forgiveness, is not that one or all of your sins are of a die so deep and so inveterate, that the cleansing power of the Saviour's atonement cannot overmatch them. Let the invitation to the fountain that is opened in the house of Judah, circulate among you as freely as the preacher's voice; for sure we are, that there does not stand, at this moment, within the reach of hearing us, any desperado in vice, so sunk in the depths of his dark and unnatural rebellion, that he is not welcome if he will. But, if ye *will not* come that ye may have life, this is your sin.

This is the barrier in the way of your forgiveness. Grant us repentance and faith, and we know not of a single mysterious crime in the whole catalogue of human depravity, that the atoning blood of our Saviour cannot wash away. But withhold from us repentance and faith—let us see the man who stands unrebuked out of his wickedness by all that conscience has reproached him with—unmoved out of the hardness of his unbelief by all that power of tenderness which should have softened his unrelenting bosom, when told of the Saviour who had poured out his soul unto the death for him —if all this contempt and resistance of his has been so long and so grievously persisted in, that the Spirit has ceased to strive—then, it is not the power of the Gospel that is in fault, but the obstinacy of him who has rejected it. The sufficiency of the Gospel is not detracted from by so much as a jot or a tittle. To this very hour may we proclaim it as the savour of life unto life, to the very worst of sinners who receive it. But if he so turn aside from its invitations, and the habit be so fixed with him, and conscience get into a state of such immovable dormancy, that the Spirit gives him over, it is not that the Gospel does not carry a remedy along with it for one and all of his offences, but because he refuses that Gospel, that it is to him the savour of death unto death.

A king publishes a wide and unexpected amnesty to the people of a rebellious district in his empire, upon the bare act of each presenting himself within a limited period, before an authorized agent, and professing his purposes of future loyalty. Does it at all detract from the clemency of this deed of grace, that many of the rebels feel a strong reluctance to this personal exhibition of themselves; and that the reluctance strengthens and accumulates upon them by every day of their postponement; and that even before the season of mercy has expired, it has risen to such a degree of aversion on their part, as to form a moral barrier in the way of their prescribed return, that is altogether impassable? Will you say, because there is no forgiveness to them, that there is any want of amplitude in that charter of forgiveness which is proclaimed in the hearing of all; or, that pardon has not been provided for every offence, because some offenders are to be found, with such a degree of perverseness and of obstinacy in their bosom, as constrains them to a determined refusal of a'l pardon?

The blood of Christ cleanseth from all sin; and there is not a human creature, who, let him repent and believe, will ever find the crimson inveteracy of his manifold offences to be beyond the reach of its purifying and its peace-speaking power. And tell us if it detract by a single iota from the omnipotence of this great Gospel remedy, that there are many sinners in the world who refuse to lay hold of it. To the hour of death it is within the reach of all and of any who will. This is the period in the history of each individual, at which this great act of amnesty expires, and to the last minute of his life, it is competent for me and for every minister of the Gospel to urge it upon him, in all the largeness and in all the universality which belong to it—and to assure him, that there is not a single deed of wickedness with which his faithful memory now agonizes him, not one habit of disobedience that now clothes his retrospect of the past in the sad colouring of despair, all the guilt of which, and all the condemnation of which, the blood of the offered Saviour cannot do away. But, though we may offer, that is not to say that he will accept. Though we may proclaim, and urge the proclamation in his hearing, with every tone of truth and of tenderness, that is not to say, that our voice will enter with power, or make its resistless way through those avenues of his heart, where he has done so much to rear a defending barrier, that may prove to be impenetrable. Though there be truth in our every announcement, that is not to say, that the demonstration of the Spirit will accompany it—even that Spirit who long ere now may have left to himself the man, who, his whole life long, has grieved and resisted him. It is still true, that the pardon lies at his acceptance: and it may be as true, that there can be no pardon to him because he has brought such an inveterate blindness upon his soul, that he will neither receive the truth, nor love it, nor feel those genuine impulses by which it softens the heart of man to repentance. And thus it is, that while the blood of Christ cleanseth the every sin of every believer, the sin against the Holy Ghost shall not be forgiven, because with this sin, and with its consequences upon him, man wills not, and repents not, and believes not.

And now for the interesting question,— How am I to know that I have committed this sin, that is said to be beyond the reach of forgiveness? We are sure that the right solution of this question, if well understood, would go to dissipate all that melancholy which has been felt upon the subject, by many a bewildered inquirer. You cannot take a review of the years that are gone, and fetch up this mysterious sin to your remembrance out of the history of the sins that are past. There is not one of them, which, if turned away from, in the faith of that pardon that is through the blood of the atonement—there is not one of them beyond the reach of the great redemption of the Gospel. The sin against the Holy Ghost is not some awful and irrevocable deed, around which a disordered fancy has thrown its superstitious array, and which beams in deeper terror upon the eye of the mind, from the very obscurity by which it is encompassed. There ought to be no darkness and no mystery about it. The sin against the Holy Ghost is such a daring and obstinate rebellion against the prerogatives of conscience—that all its calls to penitency have been repelled—and all the urgency of its admonitions to flee to the offered Saviour, has been withstood—and all this obstinacy of resistance has been carried forward to such a point in the history of the unhappy man, that his conscience has ceased from the exercise of its functions; and the Holy Spirit has laid down his office of prompting it; and the tenderness of a beseeching God may be sounded in his ear—but unaccompanied as it is by that power which makes a willing and obedient people, it reaches not his sullen and inflexible heart. And instead, therefore, of looking for that sin among those imaginary few who mourn and are in distress, under an overwhelming sense of its enormity, I look for it to those thousands, who, trenched among the secularities of the world, or fully set on the mad career of profligacy, are posting their careless and infatuated way—and suffering Sabbaths and opportunities to pass over them— and turn with contempt from the foolishness of preaching—and hold up the iron front of insensibility against all that is appalling in the judgments of God—and cling to this perishable scene under the most touching experiences of its vanity—and walk their unfaltering path amid all the victims which mortality has strewn around them—and every year drink deeper into the spirit of the world—till the moral disease rises to such an inveteracy, that all the engines of conversion, unaided as they are, by that peculiar force and demonstration which is from on high, fall powerless as infancy upon them, and every soul amongst them, sunk in torpor immovable, will never, never be made to know the power and the life of a spiritual resurrection.

We know nothing that goes farther to nullify the Bible, than the habit of subjecting the interpretation of its passages to any other principle, than that all its parts must consist and be in harmony with each other.

There has a world of mischief been done by the modifications that have been laid on the obvious meaning of Scripture, with the purpose of rendering it more palatable to our independent views of what is right, and wise, and reasonable. This, in fact, is deposing the word of God from that primitive authority which belongs to it, as the court of highest appeal—all whose decisions are final and irreversible. Grant us that there is no contradiction between what we find in the book of God's counsel, and what we know by the evidence of our own experience, or the overbearing testimony of others—and such we hold to be the ignorance of man about the whole of that spiritual and unseen world which lies beyond the circle of his own observation, that we count it not merely his most becoming piety, but we count it also his soundest and most enlightened philosophy, to sit down with the docility of a little child to all that is intimated and made known to him by a well-attested revelation. After the deductions we have just now made, we know of no other principle on which we should ever offer to modify a verse or a clause of the written record; but the principle of that entire consistency which must reign throughout all its communications. We know of no other cross-examination which we have a right to set up on this witness to the invisible things of faith—than to try it by itself, and to condemn it, if possible, out of its own mouth, by confronting together its own depositions. We are only at freedom to sustain or to qualify the literal sense of one of its announcements, by the literal and equally authoritative sense of some other of its announcements. And such is our respect for the paramount authority of Scripture, that we know of no discovery more pleasing, than that by which the apparent inconsistency between two places, is so cleared up, that all necessity for encroaching upon the literal sense of either of them is completely done away—for it goes to establish our every impression of the unviolable sanctity of its various communications, and to heighten our belief that every semblance of opposition between the particulars of the divine testimony, exists not in the testimony itself, but in the misapprehension of our own dark and imperfect understandings.

Now, if you look to the 31st verse of the 12th chapter of Matthew, you will perceive, that all who think the sin against the Holy Ghost to lie in the commission of some rare and monstrous, but at the same time specific iniquity, cannot admit the first clause of the verse without qualifying it by some of the undeniable doctrines of the New Testament. They would say, it is not true that all manner of sin shall be forgiven unto men, with the exception of this blasphemy against the Holy Ghost, which they conceive to occur but seldom in the history of human wickedness. They would say, that there is forgiveness to no sin whatever but on the faith and the repentance of him who has incurred it—and we must, therefore, suppose this, and qualify the clause by this indispensable condition, and thus make the clause to tell us, how such is the power of the Gospel, that all the sin and blasphemy shall be forgiven of those who have embraced it—save that one sin against the Holy Ghost, for the remission of which, not even their acceptance of the Gospel of Christ could avail them.

Now, the explanation we have given of this sin renders all this work of annexing terms and modifications to this verse of the Bible unnecessary, and gives, we think, even to its literal and unrestricted meaning, a most lucid consistency with all that is leading and that is undeniable in the doctrine of the New Testament. If the sin against the Holy Ghost be just that sin, in virtue of which the calls and offers of the Gospel are so rejected, as to be finally and irreversibly put away from us, then it is true, it is absolutely and unreservedly true, that all other manner of sin shall be forgiven but this one only. All who so reject this Gospel, have sinned against the Holy Ghost—and none who accept this Gospel have incurred this sin, nor shall they want the forgiveness that is there provided for them. It is quite in vain to think, that the sin against the Holy Ghost is confined to that period of the world at which our Saviour made his personal appearance in it. The truth is, that it is since Christ withdrew from the world, that he now carries forward by the Spirit, as his agent and substitute, the business of pressing home upon men the acceptance of the Gospel, by working with their consciences. He employs the Spirit as his witness, since he himself has gone away from us; and as in the business of entertaining the calls and the offers of the New Testament, our doings are more exclusively with this Spirit, and not at all with the Saviour himself personally, we are surely as much in the way of now committing the sin in question, as in those days when the Holy Ghost was not so abundantly given, because Jesus Christ was not then glorified. All those, be assured, who refuse the Gospel now, do so because they refuse the testimony of this witness—do so because they stifle within them the urgency of his rebuke, when he tells them of faith and of repentance—do so when he offers to convince them on principles that would be clear to themselves, could they only be so far arrested by the imperious claims of God and of eternity, as to attend to them—convince them that they are indeed on a way of guilt and of alienation, which, if not turned from, through the revealed Mediator, will land them in the condemnation of a most righteous and unmitigable law. And thus, in the day of reckoning, will this verse, in its most plain and obvious literality, be so accomplished on the hosts who are assembled round the judgment-seat—that all who are free from this sin shall have their every other sin forgiven, just because they have obeyed the Gospel in embracing the overtures of forgiveness—and that all who, on that day, shall find no escape, and no forgiveness, have this doom laid upon them, just because each, without exception, has incurred the sin to which no forgiveness is awarded, by the very act of neglecting the great salvation.

The sin, then, against the Holy Ghost, so far from conferring any rare distinction of wickedness on him who is guilty of it, is, in fact, the sin of all who, living under the dispensation of the Gospel, have, by their rejection of it, made it the "savour of death unto death." It is a sin which can be charged upon every man who has put the overtures of forgiveness away from him. It is a sin which if, on the great day of examination, you are found to be free from, will argue your acceptance of the Gospel, a virtue of which its forgiveness is made sure to you. And it is a sin, which, if found in that day to adhere to you, will argue your final refusal of this same Gospel, in virtue of which your forgiveness is impossible—because you are out of the only way given under heaven whereby men can be saved. So that this sin, looked upon by many as the sin of one particular age, or, if possible to realize it in the present day, as only to be met with in a few solitary instances of enormous and unexpiable transgression, is the very sin upon which may be made to turn the condemnation and the ruin of the existing majority of our species.

Before we are done with this subject, there is one question that remains to be disposed of. Does it appear, from the historical circumstances of the case, that that conduct of the Pharisees which called forth from our Saviour the denunciation of the text, bears a resemblance to the account we have given of the sin against the Holy Ghost, as exemplified by the men of the present generation? In their rejecting of Christ, was there a determined rebellion of purpose against the light of their own conscience? Was there a wilful and resolved suppression of the force of evidence? Was there a habitual stifling within them of the movement and the impulse of moral principle? Was there a firm and deliberate posting of themselves on the ground of opposition, in the whole of their past resistance to this Jesus of Nazareth? Was there an obstinate keeping of this ground? Was there an audacious and desperate intent of holding out against all that could be offered in the shape of proofs or of remonstrances on the side of Christianity? Was there a voluntary darkening, on their part, of the light of truth when it began to dawn upon their souls, and threatened to carry their convictions away from them? Was there a habit of fetching up, at all hazards, every argument, however false and however blasphemous it may be, on which they might rest the measures of a proud and interested party, and thus might give the shape and the colour of plausibility to that systematic opposition they had entered on?

It strikes us, that the whole history of the Pharisees in the New Testament, holds them out in the very attitude of mind which we have now described to you. And think you not that in the work of maintaining this attitude against the warfare of all that moral and miraculous argument which was brought to bear upon them, they never smothered the instigations of conscience, and through it rebelled against that Spirit, who conveyed, by this organ of the inner man, the whispers of his still but impressive voice? "Which of you convinceth me of sin," says the Saviour, "and if I tell you the truth, why do you not believe me?" Did conscience never tell them how impossible it was that Jesus of Nazareth could lie? Did not the words of him who spake as never man spake, bear upon them the impress of truth as well as of dignity? Is there not such a thing as the suspicious aspect of an impostor, and is there not also such a thing as the open, the declared, the ingenuous, and altogether overbearing aspect of integrity—and is it not conceivable, how, in this way, the words of the Saviour might have carried such a moral evidence along with them, as to stamp an unquestionable character on all his attestations? Now, was there no resisting of the Holy Spirit in the act of shutting the eye of the judgment against the whole weight and authority of this character? In the person of Jesus of Nazareth, the men of that day were honoured with the singular privilege of beholding God manifest in the flesh—of seeing all the graces of the Holy Spirit substantiated, without one taint of imperfection, on the life and character of one who wore the form of the species—of witnessing, if we may so express ourselves, a sensible exhibition of the Godhead—of hearing the truth of God fall in human utterance upon their ears, with a tone of inimitable candour—of seeing the earnest longing of God after the creatures he had formed, stamped in living and undeniable traces upon a human countenance—of beholding the tenderness of God expressed in human tears, by him who wept over the sins and the sufferings of mankind—and all the goodness of Deity distinctly announcing itself in the mild and impressive sympathies of a human voice.

Think you not that there was no struggling with their own consciences, and no wilful blinding of their own hearts, on the part of those by whom such an exhibition was resisted? Surely, surely, the Spirit of God did much to subdue their acquiescence in the alone way of salvation—when all his fruits and all his accomplishments were gathered upon the person of the Redeemer into one visible assemblage—when the whole force of this moral ascendency was made so nearly and so repeatedly to bear upon them—when truth, with all its pleading energy, assailed them—and gentleness tried to win them over to the cause of their own eternity—and the soft eye of compassion beamed upon them—and the unwearied forbearance, which no weight of personal injustice could overcome, told them how, for their sakes, Jesus of Nazareth was ready to do all and to suffer all—and patience, even unto martyrdom, left a meek, but a firm testimony behind it. O! think you not, that in the perverse representations, and the spiteful malignity, and the sullen immoveable hardness, by which all this was withstood and overborne, there was such an outrage upon the authority of conscience, and such a dark and determined principle of rebellion against him who prompts it with all its instigations, as by provoking him to cast them off from all his further communications, might raise an eternal barrier against that faith, and that repentance, and that obedience to the Gospel of Christ, through which alone forgiveness is extended to a guilty world.

To aggravate still further this resistance to the moral claims of the Saviour, on the part of his inflexible enemies, let us see how these very claims told on the consciences of other men. The officers whom they sent to apprehend him, when they went, faltered from the purpose, at what they saw and heard—and when they returned with their errand unfulfilled, and the answer in their mouth, that "surely never man spake like this man," they found the masters they had to deal with were made of sterner materials—men who knew not what it was to falter—men who reproached them for their moral sensibility—and who had sternly resolved, at all hazards, and in defiance to all principle, to rid themselves of this dangerous pretender. Again, when they instigated Pilate to a capital sentence against him, the Roman governor was shaken by all that he observed of this innocent victim —but look all the while at the unrelenting constancy with which they kept by their purpose; and in the barbarous prosecution of it schooled the governor out of his difficulties; and raised the phrenzy of the populace; and surrounded the best and kindest of the species with the scowl of a brutal and reviling multitude. And, lastly, when he had sealed his testimony by his blood, mark how the man who presided over the execution, was overpowered into the acknowledgment, that "Surely this was the Son of God;" and how they, unsoftened and unsubdued, stood fast to their object— and got his body to be watched, and a story to be devised, and a falsehood of deliberate manufacture to be thrown afloat, with which they might stem the growing faith of our Saviour's resurrection. Now, in this difference between the resolved and inflexible hatred of the Jewish persecutors of Christ, and the relentings of other men, do you see no suppression of the voice of conscience— no resistance to that light of principle which sends forth an occasional gleam over the path of the determinedly reprobate, do you see no one of those ingredients which give to the sin against the Holy Ghost all the malignancy that belongs to it—or, rather, in this hard and unmovable hostility against one whose challenge to convince him of sin, they dared not to entertain; against one, of whom they could not fail to perceive, that he was the mildest, and the sincerest, and the most unoffending, and the most unwearied in well-doing of all the characters that had met their observation, do you not perceive how it was in the cause of their own offended pride, and their own threatened interest, that they made their systematic resistance to every moral argument, and hurried away their minds from every painful remonstrance—and that, too, in the very style in which the obstinately impenitent of the day do, in resistance to every demonstration of guilt, and to every warning of danger, walk in the counsel of their own hearts, and in the sight of their own eyes.

It is very true, that it was upon an outward act of speaking, on the part of the Pharisees, that our Saviour uttered this remarkable denunciation. But remember what he says himself upon this subject— how the things which come out of a man are evil, because they are the products of a heart which is evil. Remember what is said a few verses before—how our Saviour, who knew what was in man, knew the thoughts of those Pharisees; and it is upon his knowledge of their thoughts, that he ascribed such a malignity, and laid such a weight of condemnation on the words which conveyed them. Remember what is said a few verses after, where the fruit is represented as bad, just because the tree is bad—where the words have their whole character of evil imparted to them, just because it is out of the abundance of the heart that the mouth speaketh, and out of the evil humours of the heart, that the man bringeth forth evil things. And surely, when, after our Saviour had uttered such a peculiar sentence of condemnation on the sin against the Holy Ghost, he expressly connects the words of the mouth, with the disposition of the heart, ere he tells us that it was by our words we shall be justified, and by our words we shall be condemned—we ought no longer to do what we are sure is done by many in their obscure imaginations upon this subject, we ought not to liken the sin against the Holy Ghost to the spell of some magical incantation, deriving the whole of that deadly taint which belongs to it, from some infernal charm with which the utterance of mere language is darkly and unaccountably impregnated. But knowing that every denunciation of our great Spiritual Teacher, had some clear and unchangeable principle of morality to rest upon—and perceiving, as we do, that on this very occasion he refers us to the disposition of the heart, as that which gives to the utterance of the tongue all its malignity, let us, when reading of this desparate guilt of the Pharisees, look to the spirit and moral temper of the Pharisees, and if possible, gather a something that may carry to our own bosoms a salutary and convincing application.

And a single glance at the circumstances may be enough to satisfy us, that never, in any one recorded passage of their history, did they evince the bent of so inflexible a determination against the authority of conscience—never such a wilful darkening of their own hearts against the light and the power of evidence, as in the passage that is now before us. The whole weight of that moral argument on which we have already expatiated, was reinforced by a miracle so striking and so palpable in its effects, that all the people were thrown into amazement. But what constituted the peculiarity of the miracle was, that it was just such a miracle as the Pharisees themselves had been accustomed to look upon with veneration, and had viewed as an example of successful hostility against the empire of darkness. They had faith in these possessions. They counted every one of them to be the work of Beelzebub, and the casting out of any of them as a direct triumph of warfare against the prince of the devils. They themselves, it would appear, laid claim to the power of dispossessing these demons, and we have no doubt that the imagination of such a power residing with them and their children, or proselytes, would help to give them that prophetical sanctity in the eyes of the common people, which they so much aspired after.

But when the very thing on which they tried to strengthen their own claims to authority, was done by that man, the progress of whose authority, among his countrymen, they were determined, at all hazards, to arrest; they went round the whole compass of their principles, and quashed the voice of every one of them, rather than own the hand of God, or submit to the demonstration of his power in the miracle before them. It was indeed a desperate fetch that they made for an argument, when the very work in which they gloried, and on which they founded the credit of their own order, was so maligned and misrepresented by them. They had ever been in the habit of ascribing the possessions of that age to the power of Beelzebub—and now to give a colour to their hatred to Jesus and his claims, they suppose the house of Beelzebub to be divided against itself, and they ascribe to his power a miracle, the doing of which went to dispossess him of a part of his empire. They pretended that their sons or their proselytes had the power of casting out those possessions, and never failed to ascribe this power to the Spirit and the countenance of God—but now they turned round upon the matter, and by rearing the argument against the Saviour in the direct face of their own principle, did they prove how firmly they were resolved to lay hold of any thing, rather than admit the claims of one who was so offensive to them. Thus did they give, perhaps at this moment, a more conspicuous evidence than they had ever done before, how every proof and every remonstrance would all be wasted upon them. The Spirit of God had gone his uttermost length with them, and on abandoning them for ever, he left behind him their blood upon their own head, and the misery of an irrecoverable condition, that was of their own bringing on. He had long borne with them—and it will be seen in the day of reckoning, when all mysteries are cleared up, how great the patience, and the kindness, and the unwearied perseverance were which they had resisted. For though the spirit strives long, he does not strive always; and they brought on this crisis in their history, just by the very steps in which every impenitent man brings it on in the present day, by a wilful resistance to the light of their own understanding; by a resolute suppression of the voice of their own conscience.

But we must bring all these explanations to a close. The distinction between speaking against the Son of man, and speaking against the Holy Ghost, may be illustrated by what he says of the difference between bearing witness of himself, and another bearing witness of him. If he had had no other testimony than his own to offer, they had not had sin. If he had not done the works before them which none other man did, and which no mere son of man could do, they had not had sin. If he had nothing to show on which to sustain the character that signalized him above the mere children of men, their resistance could have been forgiven; but he had shown the most abundant evidence on this point—he had just performed a deed which their every habit, and their every conception, led them to ascribe to the Spirit and the power of God, and he had brought forward what to their own judgments was the testimony of the Spirit, and they resisted it. It was no longer now an opposition to man, and a railing of man, and a contemptuous negligence of man: all this is sinful; but it was not that which blocked up the way against the remission of sin; it was when they reviled him who offered to lead them on in that way, that they were ever strengthening the barrier which lay across the path of acceptance. While the last and most conclusive proof that would be given of Jesus having indeed the seal and the commission of the Spirit upon him, was not yet tried and found ineffectual; all their opposition to him still partook of opposition to one of whom the most decisive evidence that he was any thing more than the Son of man, was still in reserve. It still partook of opposition to a fellow-man. But when that decisive evidence was at length offered, and the Spirit interposed with his last and greatest attempt to vindicate his own seal, and to authenticate his own commission on the person of Jesus of Nazareth; then that which was before the speaking evil of the Son of man become the speaking evil of the Son of God; and that, aggravated to the uttermost length that it now would be permitted to go. And the Pharisees, by smothering the light of all that evidence which the Holy Spirit had brought forward, both in the miracles that were done, and in the graces of that sinless example which was set so impressively before them, had by that time raised in their hearts such an entrenchment of prejudice against the faith of the Gospel, and so discouraged the Holy Spirit from any farther attempt to scale and to surmount it, that all recovery was hopeless, and all forgiveness was impossible.

SERMON XIII.

On the Advantages of Christian Knowledge to the Lower Orders of Society.

"Better is a poor and a wise child than an old and foolish king, who will no more be admonished."—
Ecclesiastes iv. 13.

THERE is no one topic on which the Bible, throughout the variety of its separate compositions, maintains a more lucid and entire consistency of sentiment, than the superiority of moral over all physical and all external distinctions. This lesson is frequently urged in the Old Testament, and as frequently reiterated in the New. There is a predominance given in both to worth, and to wisdom, and to principle, which leads us to understand, that within the compass of human attainment, there is an object placed before us of a higher and more estimable character than all the objects of a common-place ambition—that wherever there is mind, there stands associated with it a nobler and more abiding interest than all the aggrandizements which wealth or rank can bestow—that within the limits of the moral and intellectual department of our nature, there is a commodity which money cannot purchase, and possesses a more sterling excellence than all which money can command. This preference of man viewed in his essential attributes, to man viewed according to the variable accessories by which he is surrounded—this preference of the subject to all its outward and contingent modifications—this preference of man viewed as the possessor of a heart, and of a spirit, and of capacities for truth and for righteousness, to man signalized by prosperity, and clothed in the pomp and in the circumstance of its visible glories—this is quite akin with the superiority which the Bible every where ascribes to the soul over the body, and to eternity over time, and to the Supreme Author of Being over all that is subordinate and created. It marks a discernment, unclouded by all those associations which are so current and have so fatal an ascendency in our world—the wisdom of a purer and more ethereal region than the one we occupy—the unpolluted clearness of a light shining in a dark place, which announces its own coming to be from above, and gives every spiritual reader of the Bible to perceive the beaming of a powerful and presiding intelligence in all its pages.

One very animating inference to be drawn from our text, is, how much may be made of humanity. Did a king come to take up his residence among you—did he shed a grandeur over your city by the presence of his court, and give the impulse of his expenditure to the trade of its population—it were not easy to rate the value and the magnitude which such an event would have on the estimation of a common understanding, or the degree of personal importance which would attach to him, who stood a lofty object in the eye of admiring townsmen. And yet it is possible, out of the raw and ragged materials of the obscurest lane, to rear an individual of more inherent worth, than him who thus draws the gaze of the world upon his person. By the act of training in wisdom's ways the most tattered and neglected boy who runs upon our pavements, do we present the community with that which, m wisdom's estimation, is of greater price than this gorgeous inhabitant of a palace. And when one thinks how such a process may be multiplied among the crowded families that are around us—when one thinks of the extent and the density of that mine of moral wealth, which retires, and deepens, and accumulates, behind each front of the street along which we are passing—when one tries to compute the quantity of spirit that is imbedded in the depth and the frequency of these human habitations, and reflects of this native ore, that more than the worth of a monarch may be stamped, by instruction, on each separate portion of it—a field is thus opened for the patriotism of those who want to give an augmented value to the produce of our land, which throws into insignificance all the enterprises of vulgar speculation. Commerce may flourish, or may fail—and amid the ruin of her many fluctuations, may elevate a few of the more fortunate of her sons to the affluence of princes. Thy merchants may be princes, and thy traffickers be the honourable of the earth.

But if there be truth in our text, there may, on the very basis of human society, and by a silent process of education, materials be formed, which far outweigh in cost and true dignity, all the blazing pinnacles that glitter upon its summit—and it is, indeed, a cheering thought to the heart of a philanthropist, that near him lies a territory so ample, on which he may expatiate—where for all his pains, and all his sacrifices, he is sure of a repayment more substantial, than was ever wafted by richly laden flotilla to our shores—where the return comes to him, not in that which superficially decks the man, but in a solid increment of value fixed and perpetuated on the man himself—where additions to the worth of the soul form the proceeds of his productive operation—and where, when he reckons up the profits of his enterprise, he finds them to consist of that, which, on the highest of all authorities, he is assured to be more than meat, of that which is greatly more than raiment.

Even without looking beyond the confines of our present world, the virtue of humble life will bear to be advantageously contrasted with all the pride and glory of an elevated condition. The man who, though among the poorest of them all, has a wisdom and a weight of character, which makes him the oracle of his neighbourhood—the man, who, vested with no other authority than the meek authority of worth, carries in his presence a power to shame and to overawe the profligacy that is around him—the venerable father, from whose lowly tenement the voice of psalms is heard to ascend with the offering up of every evening sacrifice—the Christian sage, who, exercised among life's severest hardships, looks calmly onward to heaven, and trains the footsteps of his children in the way that leads to it—the eldest of a well-ordered family, bearing their duteous and honourable part in the contest with its difficulties and its trials—all these offer to our notice such elements of moral respectability, as do exist among the lowest orders of human society, and elements, too, which admit of being multiplied far beyond the reach of any present calculation. And while we hold nothing to be more unscriptural than the spirit of a factious discontent with the rulers of our land—while we feel nothing to be more untasteful than the insolence of a vulgar disdain towards men of rank, or men of opulence—yet should the king upon the throne be taught to understand, that there is a dignity of an intrinsically higher order than the dignity of birth or power—a dignity which may be seen to sit with gracefulness on the meanest of his subjects—and which draws from the heart of the beholder a truer and profounder reverence.

So that, were it for nothing more than to bless and adorn our present state, there cannot be an attempt of greater promise, than that of extending education among the throng of our peasantry; there cannot be a likelier way of filling the country with beauteous and exalted spectacles—there cannot be a readier method of pouring a glory over the face of our land, than that of spreading the wisdom of life, and the wisdom of principle, throughout the people who live in it—a glory differing in kind, but greatly higher in degree, than the glories of common prosperity. It is well that the progress of knowledge is now looked to by politicians without alarm—that the ignorance of the poor is no longer regarded as more essential to the devotion of their patriotism, than it is to the devotion of their piety—that they have, at length, found that the best way of disarming the lower orders of all that is threatening and tumultuous, is not to enthral, but to enlighten them; that the progress of truth among them, instead of being viewed with dismay, is viewed with high anticipation—and an impression greatly more just, and greatly more generous, is now beginning to prevail, that the strongest rampart which can possibly be thrown around the cause of public tranquillity, consists of a people raised by information, and graced by all moral and all Christian accomplishments.

For our own part, we trust, that the mighty interval of separation between the higher and lower orders of our community, will, at length, be broken down, not by any inroad of popular violence; not by the fierce and devouring sweep of any revolutionary tempest; not even by any new adjustment, either of the limits of power, or the limits of property; not, in short, as the result of any battle, fought either on the arena of war, or on the arena of politics; but as the fruit of that gradual equalization in mind and in manners, to which even now a sensible approach is already making on the part of our artisans and our labourers. They are drawing towards an equality, and on that field, too, in which equality is greatly most honourable. And we fondly hope, that the time is coming, when, in frank and frequent intercourse, we shall behold the ready exchange of confidence on the one side, and affection on the other —when the rich and the poor shall love each other more, just because they know each other more—when each party shall recognise the other to be vastly worthier of regard and of reverence than is now apprehended—when united by the sympathies of a common hope, and a common nature, and on a perfect level with all that is essential and characteristic of humanity, they shall, at length, learn to live in love and peacefulness together, as the expectants of one common heaven—as the members of one common and rejoicing family.

But, to attain a just estimate of the superiority of the poor man who has wisdom, over the rich man who has it not, we must enter into the calculation of eternity—we must look to wisdom in its true essence, as consisting of religion, as having the fear of God for its beginning, and the rule of God for its way, and the favour of God for its full and satisfying termination—we must compute how speedily it is, that, on the wings of time, the season of every paltry distinction between them must, at length, pass away; how soon death will strip the one of his rags, and the other of his pageantry, and send them, in utter nakedness, to the dust; how soon judgment will summon them from their graves, and place them in outward equality before the great disposer of their future lot, and their future place, through ages which never end; how, in that situation, the accidental distinctions of life will be rendered void, and personal distinctions will be all that shall avail them; how, when examined by the secrets of the inner man, and the deeds done in their body, the treasure of heaven shall be adjudged only to him whose heart was set upon it in this world; and how tremendously the account between them will be turned, when it shall be found of the one, that he must perish for lack of knowledge, and of the other, that he has the wisdom which is unto salvation.

And here it is of importance to remark, that to be wise as a Christian is wise, it is not essential to have that higher scholarship which wealth alone can purchase—that such is the peculiar adaptation of the Gospel to the poor, that it may be felt in the full force of its most powerful evidence, by the simplest of its hearers—that to be convinced of its truth, all which appears necessary is, to have a perception of sin through the medium of the conscience, and a perception of the suitableness of the offered Saviour through the medium of a revelation, plain in its terms, and obviously sincere and affectionate in its calls. Philosophy does not melt the conscience. Philosophy does not make luminous that which in itself is plain. Philosophy does not bring home, with greater impression upon the heart, the symptoms of honesty and good will, which abound in the New Testament. Prayer may do it. Moral earnestness may do it. The Spirit, given to those who ask him, may shine with the light of his demonstration, on the docility of those little children, who are seeking, with their whole hearts, the way of peace, and long to have their feet established on the paths of righteousness. There is a learning, the sole fruit of which is a laborious deviation from the truth as it is in Jesus. And there is a learning which reaches no farther than to the words in which that truth is announced, and yet reaches far enough to have that truth brought home with power upon the understanding—a learning, the sole achievement of which is, to read the Bible, and yet by which the scholar is conducted to that hidden wisdom, which is his light in life, and his passport to immortality—a learning, which hath simply led the inquirer's way to that place, where the Holy Ghost hath descended upon him in rich effusion, and which, as he was reading in his own tongue, the wonderful works of God, has given them such a weight and such a clearness in his eyes, that they have become to him the words whereby he shall be saved. And thus it is, that in many a cottage of our land, there is a wisdom which is reviled, or unknown, in many of our halls of literature—there is the candle of the Lord shining in the hearts of those who fear him— there is a secret revealed unto babes, which is hidden from the wise and the prudent— there is an eye which discerns, and a mind that is well exercised on the mysteries of the sure and the well-ordered covenant— there is a sense and a feeling of the preciousness of that cross, the doctrine of which is foolishness to those who perish— there is a ready apprehension of that truth which is held at nought by many rich, and many mighty, and many noble, who will not be admonished—but which makes these poor to be rich in faith, and heirs of that kingdom which God hath prepared for those who love him.

We know not, if any who is now present, has ever felt the charm of an act of intercourse with a Christian among the poor—with one, whose chief attainment is, that he knows the Bible to be true; and that his heart, touched and visited by a consenting movement to its doctrine, feels it to be precious. We shall be disappointed, if the very exterior of such a man do not bear the impress of that worth and dignity which have been stamped upon his character—if, in the very aspect and economy of his household, the traces of his superiority are not to be found—if the promise, even of the life that now is, be not conspicuously realized on the decent sufficiency of his means, and the order of his well-conditioned family—if the eye of tasteful benevolence be not regaled by the symptoms of comfort and cheerfulness which are to be seen in his lowly habitation. And we shall be greatly disappointed, if, after having survived the scoff of companions, and run through the ordeal of nature's enmity, he do not earn, as the fruits of the good confession that he witnesses among his neighbours, the tribute of a warm and willing cordiality from them all—if, while he lives, he do not stand the first in estimation, and when he dies, the tears and acknowledgments of acquaintances, as well as of kinsfolk do not follow him to his grave—if, even in the hearts of the most unholy around him, an unconscious testimony is not borne to the worth of holiness, so as to make even this world's honour one of the ingredients in the portion of the righteous. But these are the mere tokens and visible accompaniments of Christian excellence—the passing efflorescence of a growth that is opening and maturing for eternity. To behold this excellence in all its depth, and in all its solidity, you must examine his mind, and there see the vastly higher elements, with which it is conversant, than those among which the children of this world are grovelling: there see how, in the hidden walk of the inner man, he treads a more elevated path than is trodden either by the daughters of gaiety, or the sons of ambition; there see how the whole greatness and imagery of heaven are present to his thoughts, and what a reach and nobleness of conception have gathered upon his soul, by his daily approaches to heaven's sanctuary. He lives in a cottage; and yet he is a king and priest unto God. He is fixed for life to the ignoble drudgery of a workman, and yet he is on the full march to a blissful immortality. He is a child in the mysteries of science, but familiar with greater mysteries. That preaching of the cross, which is foolishness to others, he feels to be the power of God, and the wisdom of God. That faithfulness which annexes to all the promises of the Gospel—that righteousness which is unto the believer—that fulness in Christ, out of which the supplies of light and of strength are ever made to descend on the prayers of all who put their trust in him—that wisdom of principle, and wisdom of application, by which, through his spiritual insight into his Bible, he is enabled both to keep his heart, and to guide the movements of his history,—these are his treasures—these are the elements of the moral wealth, by which he is far exalted above the monarch, who stalks his little hour of magnificence on earth, and then descends a ghost of departed greatness into the land of condemnation. He is rich, just because the word of Christ dwells in him richly in all wisdom. He is great, because the Spirit of glory and of God rests upon him.

So that, the same conclusion comes back upon us with mightier emphasis than before. If a poor child be capable of being thus transformed, how it should move the heart of a city philanthropist, when he thinks of the amazing extent of raw material, for this moral and spiritual manufacture that is on every side of him—when he thinks, that in going forth on some Christian enterprise among a population, he is, in truth, walking among the rudiments of a state that is to be everlasting—that out of the most loathsome and unseemly abodes, a glory can be extracted, which will weather all the storms, and all the vicissitudes of this world's history—that in the filth and raggedness of a hovel, that is to be found, on which all the worth of heaven, as well as all the endurance of heaven, can be imprinted—that he is, in a word, dealing in embryo with the elements of a great and future empire, which is to rise, indestructible and eternal, on the ruins of all that is earthly, and every member of which shall be a king and a priest for evermore.

And before I pass on to the application of these remarks, let me just state, that the great instrument for thus elevating the poor, is that Gospel of Jesus Christ, which may be preached unto the poor. It is the doctrine of his cross finding an easier admission into their hearts, than it does through those barriers of human pride, and human resistance, which are often reared on the basis of literature. Let the testimony of God be simply taken in, that on his own Son he has laid the iniquities of us all—and from this point does the humble scholar of Christianity pass unto light, and enlargement, and progressive holiness. On the reception of this great truth, there hinges the emancipation of his heart from a thraldom which represses all the spiritual energies of those who live without hope, and, therefore, live without God in the world. It is guilt—it is the sense of his awakened and unexpiated guilt; which keeps man at so wide a distance from the God whom he has offended. Could some method be devised, by which God, jealous of his honour, and man jealous of his safety, might be brought together on a firm ground of reconciliation—it would translate the sinner under a new moral influence, to the power of which, and the charm of which he, before, was utterly impracticable. Jesus Christ died, the just for the unjust, to bring us unto God. This is a truth, which, when all the world shall receive it, all the world will be renovated. Many do not see how a principle, so mighty in operation, should be enveloped in a proposition so simple of utterance. But let a man, by his faith in this utterance, come to know that God is his friend, and that heaven is the home of his fondest expectation; and in contact with such new elements as these, he will evince the reach, and the habit, and the desire of a new creature. It is this doctrine which is the alone instrument of God for the moral transformation of our species. When every demonstration from the chair of philosophy shall fail, this will achieve its miracles of light and virtue among the people—and however infidelity may now deride—or profaneness may now lift her appalling voice upon our streets—or licentiousness may now offer her sickening spectacles—or moral worthlessness may have now deeply tainted the families of our outcast and long-neglected population,—however unequal may appear the contest with the powers and the principles of darkness—yet let not the teachers of righteousness abandon it in despair; God will bring forth judgment unto victory, and on the triumphs of the word of his own testimony, will he usher in the glory of the latter days.

There is one kind of institution that never has been set up in a country, without deceiving and degrading its people; and another kind of institution that never has been set up in a country, without raising both the comfort and the character of its families. We leave it to the policy of our sister kingdom, by the pomp and the pretension of her charities, to disguise the wretchedness which she cannot do away. The glory of Scotland lies in her schools. Out of the abundance of her moral and literary wealth, that wealth which communication cannot dissipate—that wealth, which its possessor may spread and multiply among thousands, and yet be as affluent as ever, that wealth which grows by competition, instead of being exhausted, this is what, we trust, she will ever be ready to bestow on all her people. Silver and gold she may have none—but such as she has she will give—she will send them to school. She cannot make pensioners of them, but will, if they like, make scholars of them. She will give them of that food by which she nurses and sustains all her offspring—by which she renders wise the very poorest of her children—by which, if there be truth in our text, she puts into many a simple cottager, a glory surpassing that of the mightiest potentates in our world. To hold out any other boon, is to hold out a promise which she and no country in the universe, can ever realize—it is to decoy, and then most wretchedly to deceive—it is to put on a front of invitation, by which numbers are allured to hunger, and nakedness, and contempt. It is to spread a table, and to hang out such signals of hospitality, as draw around it a multitude expecting to be fed, and who find that they must famish over a scanty entertainment. A system replete with practical mischief can put on the semblance of charity, even as Satan, the father of all lying and deceitful promises, can put on the semblance of an angel of light. But we trust, that the country in which we live will ever be preserved from the cruelty of its tender mercies—that she will keep by her schools, and her Scriptures, and her moralizing process; and that, instead of vainly attempting so to force the exuberance of Nature, as to meet and satisfy the demands of a population whom she has led astray, she will make it her constant aim so to exalt her population, as to establish every interest that belongs to them, on the foundation of their own worth and their own capabilities—that taunted, as she has been, by her contemptuous neighbour, for the poverty of her soil, she will at least prove, by deed and by example, that it is fitted to sustain an erect, and honorable, and high-minded peasantry; and leaving England to enjoy the fatness of her own fields, and a complacency with her own institutions, that we shall make a clean escape from her error, and never again be entangled therein—that unseduced by the false lights of a mistaken philanthropy, and mistaken patriotism, we shall be enabled to hold on in the way of our ancestors; to ward off every near and threatening blight from the character of our beloved people; and so to labour with the manhood of the present, and the boyhood of the coming generation, as to enrich our land with that wisdom which is more precious than gold, and that righteousness which exalteth a kingdom.

SERMON XIV.

On the Duty and the Means of Christianizing our Home Population.

"And he said unto them, Go ye into all the world, and preach the Gospel to every creature."—*Mark* xvi. 15.

CHRISTIANITY proceeds upon the native indisposition of the human heart to its truths and its lessons—and all its attempts for the establishment of itself in the world are made upon this principle. It never expects that men will, of their own accord, originate that movement by which they are to come in contact with the faith of the Gospel; and, therefore, instead of waiting till they shall move toward the Gospel, it has been provided, from the first, that the Gospel shall move towards them. The Apostles did not set up their stationary college at Jerusalem, in the hope of embassies from a distance to inquire after the recent and wondrous revelation that had broke upon the world. But they had to go forth, and to preach among all nations, beginning at Jerusalem. And, in like manner, it never was looked for, that men, in the ardour of their curiosity, or desire after the way of salvation, were to learn the language of the Apostles, that they might come and hear of it at their mouth. But the Apostles were miraculously gifted with the power of addressing all in their own native language—and when thus furnished, they went actively and aggressively about among them. It is no where supposed that the demand for Christianity is spontaneously, and in the first instance, to arise among those who are not Christians; but it is laid upon those who are Christians, to go abroad, and, if possible, to awaken out of their spiritual lethargy, those who are fast asleep in that worldliness, which they love, and from which, without some external application, there is no rational prospect of ever arousing them. The dead mass will not quicken into sensibility of itself; and, therefore, unless some cause of fermentation be brought to it from without, will it remain in all the sluggishness of its original nature. For there is an utter diversity between the article of Christian instruction, and the articles of ordinary merchandise. For the latter there is a demand, to which men are natively and originally urged by hunger or by thirst, or by the other physical sensations and appetites of their constitution. For the former there is no natural appetite. It is just as necessary to create a spiritual hunger, as it is to afford a spiritual refreshment; and so from the very first, do we find, that for the spread of Christianity in the world, there had to be not an itinerancy on the part of inquirers, but a busy, active, and extended itinerancy on the part of its advocates and its friends.

Now, those very principles which were so obviously acted on at the beginning, are also the very principles that, in all ages of the church, have characterized its evangelizing processes. The Bible Society is now doing, by ordinary means, what was done by the miracle of tongues, in the days of the Apostles—enabling the people of all nations to read, each in their own tongue, the wonderful works of God. And the Missionary Societies are sending forth, not inspired Apostles, gifted with tongues, but the expounders of apostolical doctrine, learned in tongues, over the face of the globe. They do not presume upon such a taste for the Gospel in heathen lands, as that the people there shall traverse seas and continents, or shall set themselves down to the laborious acquisition of some Christian language, that they might either have access to Scripture, or the ability of converse with men that are skilled in the mysteries of the faith. But this taste which they do not find, they expect to create; and for this purpose, is there now an incessant application to Pagan countries, of means and instruments from without, and many are the lengthened and the hazardous journies which have been undertaken—and voyages of splendid enterprise have recently been crowned with splendid moral achievements; insomuch, that even the ferocity and licentiousness of the savage character have given way under the power of the truth; and lands, that within the remembrance of many now alive, rankled with the worst abominations of idolatry, have now exchanged them for the arts and the decencies of civilization; for village schools, and Christian Sabbaths, and venerable pastors, who first went forth as missionaries, and, as the fruits of their apostolic labour, among these outcast wanderers, can now rejoice over holy grandsires, and duteous children, and all that can gladden the philanthropic eye, in the peace, and purity, and comfort of pious families.

Now, amid the splendour and the interest of these more conspicuous operations, it is often not adverted to, how much work of a missionary character is indispensable for perpetuating, and still more for extending Christianity at home—how families, within the distance of half a mile, may lapse, without observation or sympathy on our part, into a state of practical heathenism—how, within less than an hour's walk, hundreds may be found, who morally and spiritually live at as wide a separation from the Gospel and all its ordinances, as do the barbarians of another continent—how, in many of our crowded recesses, the families, which, out of sight, and out of Christian sympathy, have accumulated there, might, at length, sink and settle down into a listless, and lethargic, and to all appearance, impracticable population—leaving the Christian teacher as much to do with them as has the first missionary when he touches on a yet unbroken shore. It is vain to expect, that by a proper and primary impulse originating with themselves, those aliens from Christianity will go forth on the inquiry after it. The messengers of Christianity must go forth upon them. Many must go to and fro amongst the streets, and the lanes, and those deep intricacies that teem with human life, to an extent far beyond the eye or imagination of the unobservant passenger, if we are to look for the increase either of a spiritual taste, or of scriptural knowledge among the families. That mass which is so dense of mind, and, therefore, so dense of immortality, must be penetrated in the length and in the breadth of it; and then many will be found, who, however small their physical distance from the sound of the Gospel, stand at as wide a moral distance therefrom, as do the children of the desert, and to overpass this barrier, to send out upon this outfield, such ministrations as might reclaim its occupiers to the habits and the observations of a Christian land, to urge and obtrude, as it were, upon the notice of thousands, what, without such an advancement, not one of them might have moved a footstep in quest of—these are so many approximations, that, to all intents and purposes, have in them the character, and might, with the blessing of God, have also the effect of a missionary enterprise.

When we are commanded to go into all the world, and preach the Gospel to every creature, our imagination stretches forth beyond the limits of Christendom; and we advert not to the millions who are within these limits, nay, within the sight of Christian temples, and the sound of Sabbath bells, yet who never heard the Gospel of Jesus Christ. They live to manhood, and to old age, deplorably ignorant of the way of salvation, and in ignorance, too, not the less deplorable than it is wilful. It is this which so fearfully aggravates their guilt, that on the very confines of light, they remain in darkness: and thereby prove, that it is a darkness which they love, and which they choose to persist in. Thus it will be found more tolerable for the heathen abroad, than for the heathen at home; and therefore it is, that for the duty of our text, the wilds of Pagan idolatry, or of Mahometan delusion, are not the only theatres—that for its full performance, it is not enough that we equip the missionary vessel, and go in quest of untaught humanity at a distance, and hold converse with the men of other climes, and of other tongues, and rear on some barbarous shore, the Christianized village, as an outpost in that spiritual warfare, by which we hope, at length, to banish depravity and guilt, even from the farthest extremities of our species. These are noble efforts, and altogether worthy of being extended and multiplied a hundred fold. But they are not the only efforts of Christian philanthropy; nor can they be sustained as a complete discharge from the obligation of preaching the Gospel to every creature under heaven. For the accomplishment of this, there must not only be a going forth on the vast and untrodden spaces that are without; there must be a filling up of the numerous and peopled vacancies that are within—a busy, internal locomotion, that might circulate, and disperse, and branch off to the right and to the left, among the many thousand families which are at hand: And thoroughly to pervade these families; to make good a lodgment in the midst of them, for the nearer or the more frequent ministrations of Christianity than before; to have gained welcome for the Gospel testimony into their houses, and, in return, to have drawn any of them forth to attendance on the place of Sabbath and of solemn services; this, also, is to act upon our text, this is to do the part, and to render one of the best achievements of a missionary.

"How can they believe," says Paul, "without a preacher,"—and "how can they preach, except they be sent?" To make sure this process, there must be a juxtaposition between him who declares the word, and them who are addressed by it; but to make good this juxtaposition, the Apostle never imagines that alienated man is, of his own accord, to move towards the preacher—and therefore, that the preacher must be sent, or must move towards him. And, perhaps, it has not been adverted to, that in the very first steps of this approximation, there is an encouragement for going onward, and for plying the families of a city population with still nearer and more besetting urgencies than before. It is not known how much the very juxtaposition of an edifice for worship, tells upon the churchgoing habit of the contiguous householders; how many there are who will not move at the sound of a distant bell, that with almost mechanical sureness, will go forth and mingle with the stream of passengers who are crowding the way to a place that is at hand—how children, lured, perhaps, at the first, by curiosity, are led so to reiterate their attendance, as to be landed in a most precious habit for youth and for manhood—how this tendency spreads by talk, and sympathy, and imitation, through each little vicinity;

and thus, in groups, or in clusters, might adjoining families be gained over to the ordinances of religion—how the leaven, when once set a-going, might spread by the fermentation of converse, and mutual sentiment, through the whole lump; till over the face of a whole city department, the Christian fabric, which stands conspicuously in the midst of it, and whither its people are rung every Sabbath, to the ministrations of the Gospel, might come to be its place of general repair; and attendance there be at length proceeded on as one of the decencies of its established observation. Some of the influences in this process may appear slight or fanciful to the superficial eye; and yet they are known and familiarly known, to be of powerful operation.

You must surely be aware, that it makes all the practical difference in the world, to the retail and custom even of an ordinary shop, should it deviate, by a very small hairbreadth, from the minutest convenience of the public—should it retire, by ever so little from the busy pavement, or have to be ascended by two or three steps, or require the slightest turn and change of direction from the beaten path which passengers do inveterately walk in. And human nature on a week-day, is human nature on the Sabbath. There is no saying on how slight or trivial a circumstance it may be made to turn; and odd as the illustration may appear, we feel confident that we have not, at present, either a profound or a pious hearer, who will undervalue one single steppingstone, by which a hearer more might be brought to the house of God—who will despise any of the means, however humble, that bring a human creature within the reach of that word, which is able to sanctify and save him—who will forget the wonted style of God's administrations, by which, on these minutest incidents of life, the greatest events of history are oft suspended—or, who will deny that the same Being, who, by the flight of a single bird, turned the pursuers of Mahomet away from him, and so spared the instrument by which a gross and grievous superstition hath found an ascendency over millions of immortal spirits, that he can enlist in the cause of his own Son, even the least and slightest familiarities of human practice; and with links, which in themselves are exceeding small, can fasten and uphold the chain, which runs through the earthly pilgrimage of man, and reaches to his eternity.

But after all, though local conveniency may allure, in the first instance, to the house of God, local conveniency will not detain the attendance of multitudes, unless there be a worth and a power in the services which are rendered there—unless there be a moral earnestness in the heart of the preacher, which may pour forth a sympathy with itself through the hearts of a listening congregation—unless, acquitting himself as an upright minister of the New Testament, he expound with faithfulness and some degree of energy, those truths which are unto salvation; and so distribute among his fellow-sinners, the alone substantial and satisfying food of the soul—unless such a demonstration be given of the awful realities in which we deal, as to awaken in many bosoms the realizing sense of death, and of the judgment-seat—and above all, unless the demands of the law, with its accompanying severities and terrors, be so urged on the conviction of guilty man, as to make it fall with welcome upon his ear, when told, that unto him a Saviour has been born. These are the alone elements of a rightful and well-earned popularity. Eloquence may dazzle—and argument may compel the homage of its intellectual admirers—and fashion may even, when these are wanting, sustain through its little hour of smile and sunshine, a complacent attendance on the reigning idol of the neighbourhood—but it is only if armed with the panoply of Scriptural truth, that there will gather and adhere to him a people who hunger for the bread of life, and who make a business of their eternity. To fill the church well, we must fill the pulpit well, and see that the articles of the peace-speaking blood, and the sanctifying Spirit, are the topics that be dearest to the audience, and on which the Christian orator who addresses them most loves to expatiate. These form the only enduring staple of good and vigorous preaching; and unless they have a breadth, and a prominency, and a fond reiteration in the sermons that shall be delivered from the place where we now stand,[*] they either will not, or ought not to be listened to.

Yet grieved and disappointed should we be, did he confine himself to Sabbath ministrations—did he not go forth, and become the friend and the Christian adviser of all who dwell within the limits of his vineyard—did he not act the part of an Apostle among you, from house to house, and vary the fatigue of his preparations for the pulpit, by a daily walk amongst the ignorant, or the sick, or the sorrowful, or the dying. It is your part to respect, as you would a sanctuary, that solitude to which, for hours together, he should commit himself, in the work of meditating the truths of salvation; and it is his part to return your delicacy by his labours of love, by the greetings of his cordial fellowship, by his visits of kindness. It is a wrong imagination on the side of a

---

[*] This Sermon was preached at the opening of a city chapel, which has a local district assigned to it, and whose rule of seat-letting is on the territorial principle.

people, when they look on the Sabbath for a vigorous exposition of duty or doctrine, from him whom they tease, and interrupt, and annoy, through the week; and it is a wrong imagination on the side of a pastor, when looking on the church as the sole arena of his usefulness, he does not relax the labour of a spirit that has been much exercised on the great topics of the Christian ministry, by frequent and familiar intercourse among those, whom, perhaps, he has touched or arrested by his Sabbath demonstrations. You ought to intrude not upon his arrangements, and his studies; but he ought, in these arrangements, to provide the opportunities of ample converse with every spiritual patient, with every honest inquirer. You should be aware of the distinction that he makes between that season of the day which is set apart for retirement, and that season of the day which lies open to the duty of holding courteous fellowship with all; and of hiding not himself from his own flesh. It is the gross insensibility which obtains to the privileges both of a sacred and literary order—it is the disturbance of a perpetual inroad on that prophet's chamber, which ought, at all times, to be a safe retreat of contemplation—it is the incessant struggle that must be made for a professional existence, with irksome application, and idle ceremony, and even the urgencies of friendship; these are sufficient to explain those pulpit imbecilities, of which many are heard to complain, while themselves they help to create them. And, therefore, if you want to foster the energies of your future clergyman; if you would co-operate with him in those mental labours, by which he provides through the week for the repast of your Sabbath festival; if it is your desire that an unction and a power shall be felt in all his pulpit ministrations; if here you would like to catch a glow of heaven's sacredness, and receive that fresh and forcible impulse upon your spirits, which might send you forth again with a redoubled ardour of holy affection and zeal on the business of life, and make you look and long for the coming Sabbath, as another delightful resting-place on your journey towards Zion—then suffer him to breathe, without molestation, in that pure and lofty region, where he might inhale a seraphic fervency, by which to kindle among his hearers his own celestial fire, his own noble enthusiasm. If it be this, and not the glee of companionship, or the drudgeries of ordinary clerkship that you want from your minister, then leave, I beseech you, his time in his own hand, and hold his asylum to be inviolable.

But, we trust, that from this asylum his excursions will be frequent; and sure we are, that nought but an affectionate forth-going is necessary on his part, that he may have a warm and a willing reception upon yours. It is utterly a mistake, that any population, whatever be their present habits, will discourage the approaches of a Christian minister to their families. It is a particularly wrong imagination, that in cities there is a hard or an insolent defiance among the labouring classes, which no assiduities of service or of good-will on the part of their clergyman can possibly overcome. Let him but try what their temperament is in this matter, and he will find it in every way as courteous and inviting, as among the most primitive of our Scottish peasantry. Let him be but alert to every call of threatening disease among his people, and the ready attendant upon every deathbed—let him ply not his fatiguing, but his easy and most practicable rounds of visitation in the midst of them—let him be zealous for their best interests, and not in the spirit of a fawning obsequiousness, but in that of a manly, intelligent, and honest friendship, let him stand forth as the guardian of the poor, the guide and the counsellor of their children; it is positively not in human nature to withstand the charm and the power which lie in such unwearied ministrations; and if visibly prompted by the affinity that there is in the man's heart for his fellows of the species, there will, by a law of the human constitution, be an affinity in theirs towards him, which they cannot stifle, though they would; and they will have no wish to stifle it.

It is to this principle, little as it has been recognised, and still less as it has been proceeded on, it is to this that we confide the gathering at length of a congregation within these walls, and that too from the vicinities by which we are immediately surrounded. That the chapel will be filled at the very outset, from the district which has been assigned to it, we have no expectation. But we do fondly hope, as the fruit of his unwearied services, that its minister will draw the kind regards of the people after him; that an impression will be made by his powerful and reiterated addresses in the bosom of their families, which may not stop there; that the man who prays at every funeral, and sits by every dying bed, and seizes every opening for Christian usefulness that is afforded to him by the visitations of Providence on the houses of the surrounding neighbourhood, and who, while a fit companion for the great in his vineyard, is a ready, and ever accessible friend to the poorest of them all; it is utterly impossible, that such a man, after his work of varied and active benevolence, will have nought to address on the Sabbath but empty walls. After being the eye-witness of what he does, there will spring up a most natural desire, and that cannot be resisted, to hear what he says. It is not yet known how much such attentions as these, kept up, and made to play in busy and constant recurrence upon one local neighbourhood; it is not yet known how much and how powerfully they tell in drawing the hearts of the people towards him who faithfully and with honest friendship, discharges them. They will make the pulpit which he fills a common centre of attraction to the whole territory over which he expatiates; and we need not, that we may see exemplified in human society the worth and importance of the pastoral relationship, we need not go alone among the sequestered vales, or the far and upland retreats of our country parishes. It is not a local phenomenon dependent on geography. It is a general one, dependent on the nature of man; on those laws of the heart, which no change of place or of circumstances can obliterate. To gain the moral ascendency of which we speak, it is enough if the upright and laborious clergyman have human feelings and human families on every side of him. It signifies not where. Give him Christian kindness, and this will pioneer a way for him amongst all the varieties of place and of population. Beside the smoke, and the din, and the dizzying wheel of crowded manufactories, will he find as ready an introduction for himself and for his office, as if his only walk had been among peaceful hamlets, and with nought but the romance and the rusticity of nature spread out before him. It is utterly a wrong imagination, and in the face both of experience and of prophecy, that in towns there is an impracticable barrier against the capabilities and the triumphs of the Gospel—that in towns the cause of human amelioration must be abandoned in despair—that in towns it is not by the architecture of chapels, but by the architecture of prisons, and of barracks, and of bridewells, we are alone to seek for the protection of society—that elsewhere a moralizing charm may go forth among the people, from village schools and Sabbath services, but that there is a hardihood and a ferocity in towns, which must be dealt with in another way, and against which all the artillery of the pulpit is feeble as infancy—that a foul and feverish depravity has settled there, which no spiritual application will ever extinguish: for amid all the devisings for the peace and order of our community, do we find it to be the shrewd and sturdy apprehension of many, that all which can be achieved in our overgrown cities, is by the strength of the secular arm; that a stern and vigorous police will do more for public morals, than a whole band of ecclesiastics; that a periodical execution will strike a more salutary terror into the hearts of the multitude, than do the dreadest fulminations of the preacher's voice; and this will explain the derision and the distrust wherewith that argument is listened to, which goes to set forth the efficacy of Christian doctrine, or to magnify the office of him who delivers it.

We can offer no computation that will satisfy such antagonists as these, of the importance of Christianity even to the civil and the temporal well-being of our species; and we shall, therefore, plead the authority of our text, for extending its lessons to every creature—for going forth with it to every haunt and every habitation where immortal beings are to be found—for not merely carrying it beyond the limits of Christendom, but for filling up with instruction the many blank, and vacant, and still unoccupied places, teeming with population, that, even within these limits have not been overtaken. What! shall we be told, that if there is a man under heaven, whom the Gospel has not yet reached, it is but obedience to a last and solemn commandment, when the missionary travels even to the farthest verge of our horizon, that he may bear it to his door—shall we be told of the thousands who are beside us, that, though their souls are perishing for lack of knowledge, we might, without one care or one effort abandon them? Are we to give up as desperate, the Christian reformation of our land, when we read of those mighty achievements, and those heavenly outpourings, by which even the veriest wilds of heathenism have been fertilized—or, with such an instrument to work by as that of the Gospel of Jesus Christ, which in the hands of the Spirit of God, hath wrought its miracles on the men of all ages, shall we forbear, as a hopeless enterprise, the evangelizing of our own homes, the eternal salvation of our own families? "Be of good cheer," says the Spirit to the apostle, "I have much people for thee in this city;" and that, a city, too, the most profligate and abandoned that ever flourished on the face of our world. And still the Lord's hand is not shortened, that it cannot save. Neither is his ear heavy, that it cannot hear. It is open as ever to the cry of your intercessions—and on these, we would devolve our cause. We entreat the fellowship of your prayers. We know, that all human exertion, and eloquence, and wisdom, are vain without them—that, lacking that influence, which is gotten down by supplications from on high, sermons are but high-sounding cymbals, and churches but naked architecture—that mere pains are of no avail, and that it only lies within the compass of pains and prayers, to do any thing.

And we, indeed, have great reason for encouragement, when we think of the subject of our message. When we are bidden in the text to preach, it is to preach the Gospel—it is to proclaim good news in the hearing of the people—it is to sound forth the glad tidings of great joy—it is to tell even the chief of sinners, that God is now willing to treat him as a sinner no longer; that he invites him to all the honours of righteousness; and that in virtue of a blood which cleanseth from all sin, and of an obedience, to the rewards of which he is freely and fully invited, there is not a guilty creature in our world, who may not draw nigh. Should he who preaches within these walls, turn out the faithful and the energetic expounder of this word of salvation—should the blessing of God be upon his ways, and that demonstration which cometh from on high, accompany his words—should he, filled with zeal in the high cause of your immortality, be instant among you in season, and out of season—and devoted to the work of his sacred ministry, he make it his single aim to gather in a harvest of unperishable spirits, that by him as an instrument of grace, have been rescued from hell, and raised to a blissful eternity—should this be indeed the high walk of his unremitting toil, and his unwearied perseverance—then, such is the power of the divine testimony, when urged out of the fulness of a believer's heart, and made to fall with the impression of his undoubted sincerity on those whom he addresses; that for ourselves we shall have no fear of a good and a glorious issue to this undertaking; and, therefore, as Paul often cast the success of his labours on the prayers of them for whom he laboured, would I again entreat that your supplications do ascend to the throne of grace for him who is to minister amongst you in word and in doctrine—that he may, indeed, be a pastor according to God's own heart, who shall feed a people here with knowledge and with spiritual understanding—that the travail of his soul may be blest to the conversion of many sons and daughters unto righteousness—that he may prove a comfort to all your hearts, and a great public benefit to all your families.

SERMON XV.

On the Distinction between Knowledge and Consideration.

"The ox knoweth his owner, and the ass his master's crib: but Israel doth not know, my people doth no consider."—*Isaiah* l. 3.

It would appear, from this verse, that the children of Israel neither knew nor considered—but still there is a distinction suggested by it between these two things. And in the book of the prophet Malachi, we have a similar distinction, when the Lord says to the priests, "If ye will not hear, and if ye will not lay it to heart." It is, in fact, possible for a man to do one of these things, and not to do the other. He may know the truth, and yet he may not consider it. He may hear, and yet not lay to heart. Nay, he may have heard of a particular doctrine so often as to have got it by heart, without ever laying it to heart. And this, we hold, to be the just and the applicable complaint that may be uttered of many professing Christians in our day.

And thus it is, that we may gather the difference which there is between knowledge and wisdom. The one is a speculative acquirement. The other is a practical faculty or habit. By the latter, we turn to its right and profitable use the former. Thus it is, that there may be great folly along with great scholarship; and, on the other hand, may an unlettered mind be illustrious in wisdom. You have, perhaps, seen when there was great wealth, and yet, from the want of judicious management, great want of comfort in a family; and what stands in fine and beautiful contrast with this, you may have witnessed the union of very humble means, with such a skill and consideration in the guidance of them, as to have yielded a respectable appearance, and a decent hospitality, and the sufficiency of a full and regular provision. And so, with the treasures of intellect, the acquisitions of the mind, whereof one may be rich, being possessed of most ample materials in all knowledge and information, and yet have an ill-conditioned mind notwithstanding; and another destitute of all but the most common and elementary truths, may yet, by a wise application of them, have attained to the true light and harmony of the soul, and be in sound preparation both for the duties of time, and for the delights of eternity.

All have so learned to number their days as to know the extreme limit of human life upon earth; yet all have not so learned to number their days as to apply their hearts unto wisdom. They are aware of their latter end, but they consider not their latter end.

I. This distinction between knowledge and wisdom, is abundantly realized even on the field of earthly and of sensible experience. The man of dissipation may have his eyes open to the ruin of character and of fortune that awaits him, yet the tyranny of his evil desires constrains him to a perseverance in the ways of wretchedness. The man of indolence may foresee the coming bankruptcy that will ensue on the slovenly management of his affairs, yet there is a lethargy within that weighs him down to fatal inactivity. The man of prone and headlong irritation, may be able to discern the accumulating mischief that he raises against himself in the hostility of those who are around him, and may even look forward to the time when, deserted by the friendship of all, he shall live a neglected outcast from all human companionship, yet continue as before to be hurried away by the onward violence that seizes him. In all these instances, there is no want of knowledge in possession. But there is a want of knowledge in use, or knowledge in application. The unhappy man has the truth of the matter in his head. But he does not lay it with the authority of a commander upon his practice. The present urgency carries it over all thought of the future consequences. He has received the truth, but he does not give heed unto the truth. He does not charge it upon his attention, or give effectual warning of it to his fears, or to his sense of prudence and of interest. It is not of his ignorance that we complain, but of his inconsideration. And thus, apart from the things of spiritual contemplation altogether, and on the mere ground of every day life, with its passions and pursuits in this world, may the distinction to which we now advert, be abundantly exemplified.

II. But what we have now affirmed, even of those events and consequences that take place along the journey of this world, is still more strikingly apparent of that great event which marks its termination. There is not a human creature of most ordinary mind, and who hath overstepped the limits of infancy, that does not know of death, and with whom it does not rank among the most undoubted of the certainties that await him. And it is not only that of which he is most thoroughly assured; but it is that of which, in the course of observation and history, he is most constantly reminded. And many are the aids and the accompaniments which might serve to deepen his impression of it. The horror of every death that he witnesses; and the pathos of every death which he deplores; and the distress, even unto the measure of tragic sensibility, which is felt when some tie of near and affecting relationship is broken; and every act of attendance on those last obsequies, when acquaintances meet to carry one of their number to his grave; and the aspect of seriousness that gathers upon every inquiring neighbourhood, when the word spreads that some one of their friends is dying; and the frequency of those funeral processions that pass along our streets, and so mingle the business of death with the moving throng of the people and the carriages, which the business of life has pressed into its service; these are the remembrances that ever and anon hold up the lesson of our mortality, and one might think, should effectually keep it from sinking for a single hour into oblivion. But how is it truly and experimentally? That death of which we all know so well, is scarcely ever in our thoughts. The momentary touch of grief, and of seriousness, wherewith we are at times visited, speedily goeth into utter dissipation. With as cheerful and assured footsteps, do we tread the face of this world, as if it were the scene of our immortality; and the latter end of life is totally unseen in the obscure and undefined distance at which we have placed it, on the field of our contemplations. It argues for the strength of that recoil with which nature shrinks from the thought of its own dissolution, that all these loud and repeated demonstrations pass so unheeded by—and that walking though we be, over the accumulated ruins of so many generations, we nevertheless will talk as merrily, and lift up our heads as securely, as though beings who were to live for ever. It seems not to work the slightest abatement in the eagerness of man after this world's interests, that a few years will sweep them utterly away; and when we look to the busy engrossment of all his faculties with the plans and the pursuits of earthliness, it is but too manifest, that it is one thing to know of death, and another to consider of it.

This heedlessness of our latter end, is of a character still more obstinate and incurable than any such heedlessness as we have already quoted, of reputation or fortune in the world. It needs no impetuous appetite to overbear the thought of death; for in the calm equanimity of many a sober and aged citizen, you will find him as profoundly asleep to the feeling of his own mortality, as he is to any of the feelings or instigations of licentiousness. It needs no overweighing indolence of temperament to be all listless and unmoved by the fears of our coming death-bed; for many are to be found, who consume every hour in the activities of business and of daring adventure, without one emotion of seriousness on the awful catastrophe that awaits them.

It needs no imprudence, or unguarded violence, to betray a man into the forgetfulness of death: for many is the cool and practised calculator, and many is the sage of tranquil philosophy, and many is the crafty politician, who can look far into consequences, and is skilled in all the expedients of his vocation; and of whom it may be said, that the mind of each is steeped in the oblivion of death. We are heedless of much that is before us, even in this world; but as to its last and closing scene, there is a peculiar inveteracy of heedlessness that we do not have as to any of the other futurities of our earthly existence. Death is the stepping-stone between the two worlds; and so it somewhat combines the palpable of matter, with the shadowy and the evanescent of spirit. It is the gateway to a land of mystery and of silence, and seems to gather upon it something of the visionary character which the things of faith have to the eye of the senses. It is not a thing unseen; but being an outlet to the region of invisibles, there settles upon it a degree of that faintness and obscurity wherewith the carnal eye regards all that is told of the matters of eternity. And so, amid all the varieties of temperament in our species, there is a universal heedlessness of death. It seems against the tendency of nature to think of it. There is an opposite bias that ever inclines us away from this dark contemplation, towards the warm and living realities of the peopled world around us. The mind refuses to dwell on that dreary abode of skulls and of sepulchres, and makes its willing escape from all this hideous imagery, to society, and to business, and to the whole interest and variety of life. Instead of some mighty impulse being required to dispossess us of the thought, it costs an effort of unnatural violence to uphold it in our bosoms. The thing is known, but it is not considered: and the giddy dance of life is carried onwards, as if there were no destroyer upon the way—the tide of human existence is borne as restlessly along, as if there were no grave to absorb it.

This might serve to convince us, how unavailing is the mere knowledge, even of important truth, if not accompanied by the feeling, or the practical remembrance of it. The knowledge, in this case, only serves to aggravate our folly, and to bring, on the utter heedlessness of our lives, a more full and emphatic condemnation. And on the subject of death, we would ask, how is it that your fatal insensibility can be justified? Has God left this matter without a witness? Has he not strewed the whole path of your existence in the world with the mementos of its affecting termination? Has he not pointed the eye of your experience to the agonies of many a death-bed, and brought it irresistibly down upon your convictions, that these are the very agonies through which you have to pass? In every death of an acquaintance does he not lift a voice of warning unto yourselves; and when that acquaintance is a relative or a friend, does he not seek to grave upon your softened heart the lesson of mortality in characters of deeper remembrance? Has he not tried to find access for the truth, through the varied avenues of feeling, and of observation, and of conscience? And living, as you do, in the land of dying men, have you not seen enough of this world's changes to make the history of your life one continued sermon upon the grave? God has not been wanting in those demonstrations of Providence, which should have riveted a seriousness upon your hearts, and transformed you out of the careless, and gay, and worldly creature that you still are. We protest, by the many sick-beds over which you have hung, and by the deaths which you have witnessed, and by the tears which you have shed over them, that you have long ago had enough to loosen your hold upon earth, and to break that accursed spell by which you are so bound to its lying vanities. You have enough to dislodge from your bosom the spirit of the god of this world; and O! therefore, that you were wise, that you understood these things, that you considered your latter end.

There is no topic on which the distinction that there is between knowledge and consideration stands more palpably before us than that of death. All are assured of its coming, yet how few so bethink, or so bestir themselves, as to be prepared for its coming. The position which this event occupies in the line of our existence, gives to it a peculiar advantage for illustrating the distinction in question. It stands on the extreme horizon of what is sensible, and beyond it lie the dimness and the mystery of an untrodden land. On this side of it are the matters of experience. On the other side of it are the matters of faith. Now, it partakes with the one in the certainty wherewith all must regard it; and it partakes with the other in the nullity of its practical influence, over the vast majority of our species. As an object of knowledge, there belongeth to it the assurance of a most unquestioned truth; as an object of consideration, there belongeth to it the airy lightness of a vain and visionary fable. It is believed, but it is not minded; and while, on the one hand, it ranks among those experimental realities which are most assuredly known, it, on the other hand, ranks among those illusions of the fancy which are practically and habitually disregarded. It stands forth to the eye in all the plainness of ocular demonstration, and yet with as little power as if it were a tale of necromancy. It is quite obvious, that in the things of faith, there is a want of ascendant power over the life of man; and, to justify man, this has been ascribed to their want of evidence. But where is the want of evidence in death? This is not a thing of faith, but a thing of observation; and makes it as clear as day, that even when the evidence is complete and irresistible, the effect may be as utterly unsubstantial, as if it were a thing of nought. This ought to alarm us. It should lead us to apprehend, that there was enough of argument, on the side even of what is spiritual and unseen, to condemn our indifference to it. If the certainty of death do not move us, it may not be the uncertainty of what is on the other side of death, that can account for the sluggishness of our obstinate and unmoved carnality. One thing is certain, that we can see an acquaintance fall into his grave, and yet continue to live here, as if this were our eternity. And does not this make it probable, that though that acquaintance were to rise again, and to tell us of the world of spirits upon which he had entered, we should be unaffected as before by the real eternity that is awaiting us? Christ says to us himself, that if we believe not Moses and the prophets, neither should we believe though one rose from the dead. This is the way in which we meet the demand of infidelity, for more of proof, and more of information. The fact is that thousands have died before us, and are still dying around us, and yet the heart of man remains unvisited by any practical sense of his mortality. And the presumption, therefore, is, that though one of these thousands were to revive, and to re-appear amongst us, fraught with the tidings of heaven's glory, and hell's unutterable despair, we should still keep our ground against him, and the heart of man be unvisited as before by any practical sense of his immortality. It is not more of evidence that we want. There is as much as ought to convince us now—and if not convinced, there is as much as will condemn us afterwards. The cause of our irreligion is not that we could not know, but that we do not, and will not consider.

This is a great practical use to which our insensibility about death is capable of being turned. It proves, that our insensibility about eternal things, may be due to something else than to the defect of that evidence by which they are accompanied. It causes us to perceive, that a truth may be surely known, and yet not be pondered, or not be proceeded upon. Surely to know it is one thing—seriously to reflect upon it is another; and thus it may be, that the irreligion of the world is due not to the want of a satisfying demonstration on God's part, for this might have excused us; but, to the want of right consideration on ours, and this is inexcusable.

III. Let us now pass onwards, then, to the invisibles of faith—to those things which do not, like death, stand upon the confines of the spiritual region, but are wholly within that region, and which man hath not seen by his eye, or heard by his ear—to the awful realities that will abide in deep and mysterious concealment from us, so long as we are in the body, and which not till the body is dissolved, will stand in direct manifestation before us. This character of unseen and spiritual, is not confined to things future. There are things present which are spiritual also. There is a present Deity, who dwelleth in light, it is true, but it is light inaccessible —who is encompassed with glory, but it is glory which we, in the body, cannot approach unto—who stands revealed to angels and adoring spirits; but whom no man hath seen, neither can see. He is the King eternal and immortal, but he is also the King invisible—who, though not far from any one of us, is remote as infinity itself, from the ken of our earthly senses—and shrouded in the obscurity of his own unfathomable nature, is he so veiled and darkened from all human contemplation, that we cannot behold him.

And yet, even of this great Spirit we may be said, in one sense, to know, however little it is that we may consider him. There are averments about God which we have long recognised, and ranked among our admitted propositions, though we seldom recur to them in thought, and are never adequately impressed by them. We know, or think we know, that God is; and that all other existence is suspended upon his will; and that, were it not for his upholding arm, the whole of Nature would go into dissolution; and that while he sits in high authority over all worlds, there is not one individual member of his vast family, that is overlooked by him; and, more particularly, that he looks with the eye of a wise and a watchful judge, into every heart, and every conscience; and that he claims a right and a property in the services of all his creatures; and that he is more absolutely the owner and the master of them all, than is man of the machine that he hath made, and to whose touch all its movements are subordinate; and that he is a God of august and inviolable sacredness, in whose presence evil cannot dwell, and between the sanctity of whose nature and sin, there is a wide and implacable enmity; and that he does not sit in lofty and remote indifference to the characters of his children, but takes deep, and perpetual, and most vigilant concern in them all—loving their righteousness, hating their iniquity, treasuring their thoughts, and their purposes, and their doing, in the book of his remembrance; and that, with a view to the manifestation of them, on that day, when time shall be no more, and each of his accountable offspring shall have their condition awarded to them through eternity—when the mystery of God shall be finished, and the glory of his attributes shall be made to shine forth at the close and the consummation of all things.

Now, most of these things you know, or profess to know. They are recognised by you as true propositions, and not to have them among the articles of your creed, would be deemed by you as monstrous and revolting infidelity. Most of you would shudder at the thought of an atheism, which could deny the existence of God, or of a blasphemy that could disown his government, or of a heresy that could profane his character by stripping it of its truth, and justice, and holiness. So dear, in fact, are your long-established notions of the Divinity, that you could not bear them to be meddled with; and would hold that man to be the enemy of your repose, who should offer to violate them. So that, there do exist in your mind certain positions which regard a Deity, the affirmative of which carries your consent, and the denial of which would painfully be offensive to you—and thus far may you be said to know God, and to believe in him.

Now, as a proof how distinct this knowledge of God is from the consideration of him, I will venture to say, that even the first and simplest of all these propositions is, by many, unthought of for days and weeks together. The truth, that God is, which all here present would shudder to deny, is out of habitual regard, and habitual remembrance. It lies like a forgotten thing in some deep and latent depository; and as to its being brought forth of its hiding-place, for hourly use and meditation, this we never meet with, but among a saintly and selected few, who are indeed a very peculiar people. When God is acknowledged, we cannot lift the charge of theoretical atheism; but when, along with this, God is unminded, surely then may we lift the charge of practical atheism. Now this is the very charge that we prefer against the vast majority of our world. They have a knowledge of God; but this, so far from extenuating their thoughtlessness, brings upon it its most fearful aggravation. It is just because they stand pre-eminent among the creatures of our world, in the faculty of understanding God, that they also stand pre-eminent in the crime of their ungodliness. It is for this, that they suffer in the comparison with "the ox that knoweth his owner, and the ass that knoweth his master's crib;" and what they have learned of God, or are capable of learning, will bring upon their heedlessness of him, and of his ways, its severest condemnation.

It is, indeed, one of the most fearful mysteries of the human spirit, that a truth which, of all others, most intimately concerns us, should yet, of all others, be the most gladly bidden away into oblivion—that, as rid of an unwelcome visitor, the mind of man is never more at ease, or in its kindred and rejoicing element, than when God is not in all his thoughts—that then it is, when, as broken loose from imprisonment, the heart revels in its own desires, and securely blesses its deliverance from the hateful presence of one who constrained and overawed it—that the creature should thus hide itself, as it were, from the Creator, and in virtue of his perpetual recoil from the Being who formed, and who upholds him, should so keep up a perpetual distance from God—that wholly given over to the idolatry of the things that are made, the Maker should, to him, be little better than a non-entity, or a name; this is the marvel of the strange and wayward nature that belongs to us, and may well lead us to apprehend the visitation upon it of some sore leprosy, the shock of some great and total derangement.

For what truth of weightier import to us all than simply that there is a God—that all the busy and unceasing movements around us are suspended on the will of a living Sovereign—that those mighty forces which constantly uphold the play and the mechanism of things, are not the random energies of Nature that is unconscious; but that one sitteth above, and wieldeth them all at his pleasure—that a powerful and a presiding intelligence hath originated all, and overrules all—and that while our only converse and concern are with the near and the visible, that are on every side of us, there is an unseen Spirit, to whom belongeth the mastery, and with whom alone it is that we have mainly and substantially to do?

Now, how is it that man practically responds to this real condition of his being? Tell me, from the intimate assurances of your own conscience, or tell me, from the broad and palpable character that sits upon the doings of your acquaintances, whether God hath the ascendency over them. Is there, all the day long, a felt solemnity on your spirits, because of God, which follows you whithersoever you go, and causes you to walk with him in the world? Or, are you familiarized with the habit of submitting your will to his will? Or, have you ever, for an hour together, looked upon yourselves in the light of being the servants of another, and have accordingly run and laboured as at the bidding of that other? Or, utter strangers to this, do you not walk in the counsel of your own heart? Do you not move as independently, as if in yourself it was that you lived, and moved, and had your being? In the work that you prosecute, and the comforts that you enjoy, and even the obligations of which you acquit yourselves to relatives, and to friends, is there any fear of God before your eyes? —and is not the fear of disgrace from men, a far more powerful check upon your licentiousness, than the fear of damnation from him who is the judge and the discerner of men? The mind is ever crowded with thoughts, and wishes, and purposes, that pass in busy succession, through its chambers of imagery, and minister the food of its unremitting contemplations. Tell me how much of God and godliness there is in them all. Turn the inward survey upon yourselves, and report to us how much of this heavenly fruit groweth and flourisheth there. O you have but spied the nakedness of the land—God is unto you a wilderness, and your heart is to him a spiritual desolation!

This emptiness of a man's heart as to the recognition of God, runs throughout the whole of his history. He is engrossed with what is visible and secondary, and he thinks no farther. The sense of a present and presiding Deity, is habitually absent from his soul; and just because he will not stir himself up to consideration, that he may lay hold of God, is he bounded, as if by an impassable limit, to earth and to earthliness. It needs a force of thought and of reflection, to bear him across this barrier, which, whether from indolence, or carnality, or a misgiving conscience, he does not choose to put into operation; and thus, does he live without God in the world. When he enjoys, it is without gratitude. When he labours, it is without the impulse of an obedient loyalty. When he admires, it is without carrying the sentiment upwardly unto heaven, whence all that is lovely on the face of our world, was strewn for its embellishment, and the delight of its beholders. And thus, may a traveller on his tour of recreation, through some goodly land, be carried forward from scene to scene, till the whole landscape of an empire shall have passed behind him like a shifting panorama—and, as he eyes the beauteous succession of verdant fields, and massy foliage, and the many pictures of comfort or elegance in human habitations, and the rapid variety wherewith, in the speed and the turning of his movements, he is, at one time, closed upon by the limits of a sweet and sequestered valley, and, at another, breaks out in full and open perspective, on the glories of half a province; why, may all the ecstacy he feels be lavished on the spectacles before him, without one thought of that master hand, which spread out the whole of this magnificence, and poured the tide of lustre over it. No piety may mingle with this contemplation; and not for the want of knowledge, but the want of thought, may there be as little of God in the eye of this raptured enthusiast, as in the brute unconscious gaze of the creature that hath no understanding.

Now, this is God's controversy with man in the text. He there complains of our heedlessness. He feels himself slighted, that we so seldom think of him, and that he should be thus neglected and set at nought by his own offspring. And this inconsideration of ours, is matter of blame, just because it is a matter of wilfulness. Man has a voluntary control over his thoughts. He can turn and transfer them from one object of mental contemplation to another. He may think of God when he chooses. He may recal his scattered imaginations, and summon all that is within him to an act of attendance upon God. He may bid his mind cease from its rambles, and its reveries, and lift itself up to the abode of the Eternal. He may lay an arrest on the processes of the inner man, and say to it, with authority, that now is the moment for an aspiration, or a solemn feeling towards God. He may repeat and multiply this effort into a habit of seriousness. It may mix itself in with his ordinary business. It may accompany him on his walk, even through the streets of the crowded city. It may season the hours of his social fellowship; and what, at first, is difficult, and irregular, and rare, may thus, by dint of perseverance, settle down into an habitual tendency. He may, at length, be familiarized to the thought of God, as his master and his owner; and, at length, putting on the attitude of a daily and hourly obedience, as the eye of a servant looketh towards his master, so may his eye be ever towards God. This is not the attitude of nature; but it may be tried and practised, and, at length, effectually learned. But you will never reach it, unless you begin; you will never succeed in it, unless you persevere. And, therefore, my plain advice to you is, that you now set to it in good earnest. Lay a mandate upon your thinking faculty, and send it heavenward to God. There is many a useless moment that may thus be turned to account—many an idle waste in our existence, that may thus be reclaimed to sacredness. This is true spiritual education—the practice of godliness, instead of the theory—the way of going about it—and by which the soul may, at length, be disciplined to the habit of setting God always before it.

It is the absence of this habit which constitutes the ungodliness of man. There cannot be a fouler provocation than that man should be satisfied to do without God; and this is the provocation inflicted by all who have other cares and other pleasures, which take up the whole of their hearts, and have no room there for God or for godliness. Each of you can best tell whether you fall under this description of habit and of character. Is it not the truth now, that God is scarcely in all your thoughts?—that you feel no encouragement in any of his promises, neither do you tremble under the fearfulness of his denunciations? that you are otherwise employed than in the prosecution of your interest with him? and are busied with plans, and objects, and anticipations of your own, wherewith his will, and his glory, have nothing to do? This is your guilt. This, in the estimation of heaven's jurisprudence, is the very essence of sinfulness. Quite consistent, we do admit, with much to soften and much most honourably to signalize you; but involving you in the direct charge, that none of you understandeth, and none of you seeketh after God.

IV. But the distinction between those who only know, and those who also consider, is never more strongly marked than in the peculiar doctrines of the Gospel. And fearful is the hazard, lest knowledge, and it alone, should satisfy the possessor; lest he should settle down into a treacherous complacency, because he has made a right adjustment of the articles of his creed; lest he count it enough, that he has acquiesced, at all points, in the orthodoxy of the question; and so come forth with a flaming Christianity, that lies more in dogmatism than in devotion, more in a sturdy intolerance of error, than in a true and tender sincerity of heart. And the very controversies of the church have served to foster this delusion. The very quantity of debate and of argument that has been expended on theology, leads to a most hurtful misconceiving of this matter. You know, that the design of argument is to carry you onward to a set of just and accurate convictions. This, in fact, is the landing place to which it brings you, and at which it leaves you; and the danger is, that having brought you there, you go no further—and this place of arrival becomes your place of rest, and stationary residence. It is the pride, and ambition, and the zeal of every intellectual combatant, to carry the understanding of his reader; and having done this, he is apt to sit down and be satisfied with the triumphs of his gotten victory; and the scholar himself, seized with the very same infection, may sit down, too, as if he had attained an ultimate good, in which he may rejoice, and where he may now securely and fearlessly repose. And yet, the whole amount of his acquisition may be a mere notional Christianity—a list of doctrines that are settled and set by—that are as much within the grasp of his knowledge as many other articles of human speculation and science—but are just as little reiterated upon as they by a habit of frequent and feeling consideration. And hence a familiar exhibition to all who live in this our scholastic land, where a people, fresh from their catechisms, are primed and charged with orthodoxy, and all whose articles stand before you in well-marshalled and metaphysical array—who have a religion in their heads, but that has there an almost exclusive occupancy—whom many a stout defender of the faith would rejoice in as his own, but in whom the Author and the Finisher of faith, finds little of that love or that obedience which to him are the alone tests of discipleship—a people whom none can challenge for ignorance, but whose still unmortified tempers, and still unabated worldliness, may prove, that though they do know, yet they do not consider.

It were well, if such people could be extricated from the strongholds of their yet impregnable Antinomianism. It were well to alarm their conscience with the saying, that no knowledge and no belief will give them justification, which does not give sanctification also. All their doctrinal acquirements are precisely of as little avail as is the knowledge of death, if they think not of dying—or, as their knowledge of a God, if they give no earnest heed to him. It is well that they know; but the blessing is turned into a condemnation and a curse, if, while they know, they do not consider.

There are no topics on which there has been so much of controversy, or that has given rise to so many an elaborate dissertation, as the person and offices of Christ. And, doubtless, the scholarship has been well employed, that rescued from the entanglements of sophistry, the precious truth of the divinity of our Saviour. And well may England rejoice in those lettered ecclesiastics, who have put down, as far as argument could do it, the infidelity that decried the truth of his high and heavenly apostleship. And worthier far than all the revenue of all her colleges, is the return of criticism and of demonstration that they have made in behalf of his great sacrifice, and of his unchangeable and everlasting priesthood. Yet, let it not be disguised, that the knowledge of all these *credentials* is one thing, and the serious, the practical consideration of them, is another—that many a commentator has mastered the difficulties of the question, who has not been solemnized by the thought of its urgent and affecting realities—that stalled orthodoxy, with her clear understanding, but untouched heart, has often launched upon heresy her mighty fulminations, and manfully asserted the truth which she never felt—that the peasant may catch direct from his Bible, what the dignitary has gathered by wading through the erudition of distant centuries; and this veriest babe in literature may outstrip the literary giant, because he not only knows the truth, but wisely and duteously considers it.

Let us, in like manner, look unto Jesus with the eye of a plain Christian, instead of looking at him with the eye of a profound critic, or commentator. For this purpose, let us lay hold of things that are palpably and unambiguously told of him, and see whether, without learning of him that which we do not know, much might not be made by considering of him that which we do know—and whether, out of such materials of thought as are within reach of all, there might not a far more solemn impression come upon the heart, and a far more powerful influence upon the character, than are to be witnessed even among the most zealous and declared professors of our day.

First, then, he is the Apostle of our profession, or we profess him to be our Apostle. Let us consider him as such. Let us bethink ourselves of all which this title implies. It means one who is sent. The twelve were called apostles, because sent to preach the Gospel unto every creature. And, in like manner, he too is an Apostle, because sent by his Father into the world. He came to us from a place of deep and unknown mystery—he traversed that domain which separates the land of spirits from the peopled and familiar land in which we dwell—he burst upon our senses from a region where all is invisible—and far more wonderful than if he had been a visitor from another planet than our own, did he light upon our world from the dwelling-place of him who is the uncreated source of all worlds, from the very abode and sanctuary of the Eternal. How it ought to move us with awe at the approach of such a messenger, when we think of the glory and the sacredness of his former habitation!—of those ineffable communions that he had with the Father before the world was —and deep insight into all those mysteries of God, that are to us unsearchable! How it ought to fasten upon it the gaze of every mortal eye, that on the shore of our world there has been an arrival from the dark and the shrouded infinity which lies beyond it —that, at length, out of realms which are afar, a traveller hath come; and that, though veiled from everlasting in the obscurity of a remote and lofty nature, he hath now stood revealed to the observation of human senses, and poured forth an utterance that can be taken up by human ears!

And what ought to fasten upon him a still more intense regard, he comes with a message to our world—he comes straight from the Divinity himself, and charged by him with a special communication—God had broken silence, and this great Apostle of our profession was the bearer of that voice which speaketh from heaven unto the children of men. It was a thing of mighty import, indeed, that there should have been an actual errand to us from the pavilion of the Almighty's residence—that one familiarly acquainted there should have come to tabernacle here, and to enter upon converse and companionship with men—that he did announce himself, and on satisfying credentials, to have been sent amongst us from the upper paradise, with tidings that he had to deliver, and on a work that had been given him to do. And it ought, at least, to make no difference, that now he has returned to the place from whence he came. For he left behind him the records of his wondrous embassy—and the authentic and the authoritative voice of heaven still speaketh to us there—and with our hands upon the Bible, we are in contact with the very materials of a communication from the Deity. In the breast of the Godhead, there was a motion and a desire towards our species, and here is the expression of it—the very transcript of that message which our Apostle brought, and which our Apostle left amongst us—the word that actually came from the secret place of the Eternal, and is fraught with those revealed things, which now belong to us and to our children. I declare not a novelty in your hearing. It is not a matter of which you are ignorant, and which you need to know. But it is a matter of which you are wofully heedless, and which you need to consider We do not need to teach you what is new. But we need to arrest you by the sense of what is old and forgotten. We charge your neglect of the Scriptures of our faith upon your neglect of that great Apostle, who is the Author and the Finisher of our faith. By your daily indifference to the word that is written, you inherit all the guilt, and will come under the very reckoning of those, who, in the days of the Saviour, treated with neglect and indifference, the word that was spoken. Our challenge against you is, that the Bible is to you a thing of insipidity—that it is not desired by you as the aliment of your souls—that though unread for days together, you miss no necessary food, you feel no vacancy, you are visited with no hunger, you can do very well without this nourishment of the spiritual life, and so give reason to fear, that within you there is no spiritual principle to sustain. And looking unto that of which this written document is the memorial, do we charge upon all who slight the perusal of it, that they trample into insignificance a formal embassy from heaven—that they treat with contumely the messenger who came thenceforth unto our world—that God by him has spoken, and they have disregarded—that the daily spectacle of the Bible before their eyes, is a daily solicitation on the part of Christ to be heard, and by their continued heedlessness to which, they, all their lives, set his character, as an Apostle, utterly to scorn.

The way to repair this treatment, is forthwith to give your diligence unto the book —and to press upon your moral sense, as you open it, that now you are about to enter into converse with God—and thus to fix and solemnize your attention, while you read those words of which Christ may be called the Apostle or the messenger. The act of reading the Bible, is the act of holding conference with the Deity—and while this is what all know, this is what few consider.

There is one topic which stands connected with the apostleship of Christ, and that stamps a most peculiar interest on the visit which he made to us from on high. He is God manifest in the flesh. In the character of a man, hath he pictured forth to us the attributes of the Divinity. He is the brightness of his Father's glory, and the express image of his person—yet, in virtue of the humanity wherewith he is invested, hath he offered, even to the eye of sense, a palpable representation of the Godhead. "He who hath seen me, hath seen the Father,"—and we, by fastening our attentive regards upon his person and history, may gather the very aspect and lineaments of the King invisible. That Being, who had been so long wrapt in profoundest secrecy from our world—that Being, whom none could apprehend, for no eye of mortal could carry him through that dark and untrodden interval, by which the two regions of sense and of spirit stand apart from each other—the Being, who ever since the entrance of sin, had laid his jealous interdict on the approaches of our species, and withdrawn himself by a remote and lofty separation away from us—he, at length, broke out from this vail of deepest mystery, and in the person of him who is at once his representative and his Apostle, does he now stand before us in visible manifestation. And we, by considering this Apostle, learn of God. By looking unto him, we look unto the likeness of our Creator, and we become acquainted with him. In the purity, and the gentleness, and the simple majesty of Christ, do we read the characteristics of the Deity. And O how it concerns us to know, from this narrative of unwearied well-doing, that there is so much of benevolence in heaven—that the Sovereign who sits in high authority there, is as good as he is great—that there is a meekness to soften the majesty of his nature, and a compassionate longing after those men whom the hand of justice was lifted up to destroy—that even in the holy of holies, there dwells a tenderness for our degraded species—and could the securities of heaven's throne only be upholden, that there were a good-will and a mercy on high, ready to burst forth upon our world and to circulate at large over all its families.

But this leads us to another topic of consideration, the priesthood of Christ. The atonement that he made for sin has a foremost place in orthodoxy. It is reiterated in all our catechisms. It forms the burden and the argument of many a ponderous dissertation. And to the popular mind, too, is it fully as familiar as to the accomplished scholar in theology. Insomuch, that scarcely an individual can be met with, even in the humblest walks of society, who does not know, and who could not tell, that Christ died for the world. But as we have often said, there is a knowledge without consideration. A truth may be acquired, and then, cast as it were into some hidden corner of the mind, may it lie forgotten, as in a dormitory. And thus it fares with many a precious doctrine of the Bible. We learn it most readily from the question-book. We give the vote to it of our most prompt and zealous affirmative. We enlist it among the articles of our creed—and espousing it as our own belief, do we become partisans, or even advocates in its favour. And yet all this may consist with an entire practical heedlessness—with a deep torpor and unconcern about that truth which may have come to us most abundantly in word, though not at all in power. The soul may be habitually inadvertent to that as a principle, which is most zealously professed, and even contended for as an opinion. And accordingly, we are told by the apostle, of this very doctrine, that Christ died for our sins according to the Scriptures, how possible it is for men to receive it, yet not to remember it—that they may have once committed it to their understanding, as an article of faith, without having charged it upon their memory as an article of hourly and habitual recurrence—that it may have been consented to by the mind, without being dwelt upon by the mind—in which case, says Paul, you have believed in vain; and just because you keep not in memory, or, rather, consider not, and call not up to memory, that which I have preached unto you.

And, therefore, would I again bid you consider him who is the High Priest of your profession. I call upon you ever and anon to think of this sacrifice—and to ward off the legality of nature from your spirits, by a constant habit of recurrence, upon your part, to the atonement that he hath made, and to the everlasting righteousness that he hath brought in. Without this, the mind is ever lapsing anon into alienation and distrust—and the habitual jealousy of guilt, when not met, at all times, by a sense of that blood which washes it away, will throw us back again to our wonted distance from God—and instead of breathing the free air of confidence in him, or rejoicing in the sunshine of his reconciled countenance, there will be a flaw of suspicion in all our intercourse, and instead of loving him as a friend, we shall still stand in dread of him as an accuser. There may be the occasional recognition of Christ, and, perhaps, along with it a gleam of light and of liberty. But the general state will be, that of a mind which is overcast. And, therefore, to keep all clear, and habitually clear, would I advise a regular forthgoing of your believing thoughts, to the great decease that was accomplished at Jerusalem. I would have you to look unto Jesus Christ, and unto him crucified, and be lightened thereby. Forget not that for guilt there has been an appropriate remedy provided in the Gospel—and the way for you to stand delivered from all your fears of its vengeance and its agony, is to think of the vengeance that has already been poured out, and of the agony that has already been endured for it. Be very sure, that when justice is satisfied, then mercy, set at large from this obstruction, is free to rejoice over you. And justice is satisfied. The sufferings of the garden and the cross, have absorbed it all—nor after Christ hath poured out his soul unto the death for you, will it seek, in the horrors of your condemned eternity, for a double redress, and a double vindication. O, come out then, from the prison-house of despondency—and, when you think of your sins, think also of the ransom which has been paid for them. On the strength of this, do make your resolute stand against the spirit of bondage—and looking, and looking hourly unto the victim who has already bled a full expiation, do uphold yourself in the confidence, that sin is made an end of, that transgression is finished, that reconciliation for iniquity is made, and that now the believer, released from captivity, may walk before God in the security and the triumph of an everlasting righteousness.

In other sacrifices, the priest is distinguishable from the victim. Here they are the same. He was the victim when dying. He is the High Priest, now that he is risen again. And thus does he still plead, in the ear of God, the offering that was once made, and the power of which endureth continually. That incense, with the savour of which God was well pleased, he is at all times well pleased to be reminded of— and only consider him who fills his mouth with this argument in behalf of all who repair to him, who can argue his sacrifice as an adequate redemption for the chief of sinners, and whose glory as a physician and a Saviour, is most illustrated, when the most desperate of offenders come unto him, and are healed. It is not enough, that you have, at one time, imported this into your understanding, and given it a place there among the articles of your belief. It is by keeping it in memory—it is by renewing upon it your mental acts of faith and dependence—it is by again and again repairing to it—and looking habitually unto him as your Intercessor and High Priest, even as the children of Israel looked daily to Jerusalem, at the times of their morning and evening sacrifice. It is thus, that peace is kept up in the heart—and it is thus, that instead of coming upon us at starts, and in the shape of a momentary visitation, it maintains the continuous flow within us, of a river that is at once mighty and inexhaustible. It is thus, that this doctrine of our faith, instead of having only once made its entrance into our creed, is used by us at all times as a cordial—and the thought of Christ, as our acceptable and all-prevailing High Priest, is often present to the mind, and always felt to be precious.

And never forget that the way to maintain peace of conscience, is also the way to maintain purity of character. This is a mystery of the Christian life which the world apprehendeth not—and yet so realized, we think, by universal experience, that never do we reckon, in the history of the church, or in any of its members, had wilful sin place at the same time along with a full exercise of faith on the testimony of God. It is peace in the conscience, in fact, that keeps up love in the heart. It is this which, by putting joy, and hope, and confidence in the bosom, furnishes the soul with the most powerful springs of obedience. It is this which awakens gratitude in the bosom, that ere now was beset with the cold distractions of legality; and under the constraining influence of the love of Christ, is it ever found, that the most joyful believer is also the most fruitful believer, living no longer to himself, but to Christ who died for him, and who rose again.

THE END.

www.ingramcontent.com/pod-product-compliance
Lightning Source LLC
Chambersburg PA
CBHW050417170426
43201CB00008B/436